Dictionary of Literary Biography

1 *The American Renaissance in New England,* edited by Joel Myerson (1978)

2 *American Novelists Since World War II,* edited by Jeffrey Helterman and Richard Layman (1978)

3 *Antebellum Writers in New York and the South,* edited by Joel Myerson (1979)

4 *American Writers in Paris, 1920-1939,* edited by Karen Lane Rood (1980)

5 *American Poets Since World War II,* 2 parts, edited by Donald J. Greiner (1980)

6 *American Novelists Since World War II, Second Series,* edited by James E. Kibler Jr. (1980)

7 *Twentieth-Century American Dramatists,* 2 parts, edited by John MacNicholas (1981)

8 *Twentieth-Century American Science-Fiction Writers,* 2 parts, edited by David Cowart and Thomas L. Wymer (1981)

9 *American Novelists, 1910-1945,* 3 parts, edited by James J. Martine (1981)

10 *Modern British Dramatists, 1900-1945,* 2 parts, edited by Stanley Weintraub (1982)

11 *American Humorists, 1800-1950,* 2 parts, edited by Stanley Trachtenberg (1982)

12 *American Realists and Naturalists,* edited by Donald Pizer and Earl N. Harbert (1982)

13 *British Dramatists Since World War II,* 2 parts, edited by Stanley Weintraub (1982)

14 *British Novelists Since 1960,* 2 parts, edited by Jay L. Halio (1983)

15 *British Novelists, 1930-1959,* 2 parts, edited by Bernard Oldsey (1983)

16 *The Beats: Literary Bohemians in Postwar America,* 2 parts, edited by Ann Charters (1983)

17 *Twentieth-Century American Historians,* edited by Clyde N. Wilson (1983)

18 *Victorian Novelists After 1885,* edited by Ira B. Nadel and William E. Fredeman (1983)

19 *British Poets, 1880-1914,* edited by Donald E. Stanford (1983)

20 *British Poets, 1914-1945,* edited by Donald E. Stanford (1983)

21 *Victorian Novelists Before 1885,* edited by Ira B. Nadel and William E. Fredeman (1983)

22 *American Writers for Children, 1900-1960,* edited by John Cech (1983)

23 *American Newspaper Journalists, 1873-1900,* edited by Perry J. Ashley (1983)

24 *American Colonial Writers, 1606-1734,* edited by Emory Elliott (1984)

25 *American Newspaper Journalists, 1901-1925,* edited by Perry J. Ashley (1984)

26 *American Screenwriters,* edited by Robert E. Morsberger, Stephen O. Lesser, and Randall Clark (1984)

27 *Poets of Great Britain and Ireland, 1945-1960,* edited by Vincent B. Sherry Jr. (1984)

28 *Twentieth-Century American-Jewish Fiction Writers,* edited by Daniel Walden (1984)

29 *American Newspaper Journalists, 1926-1950,* edited by Perry J. Ashley (1984)

30 *American Historians, 1607-1865,* edited by Clyde N. Wilson (1984)

31 *American Colonial Writers, 1735-1781,* edited by Emory Elliott (1984)

32 *Victorian Poets Before 1850,* edited by William E. Fredeman and Ira B. Nadel (1984)

33 *Afro-American Fiction Writers After 1955,* edited by Thadious M. Davis and Trudier Harris (1984)

34 *British Novelists, 1890-1929: Traditionalists,* edited by Thomas F. Staley (1985)

35 *Victorian Poets After 1850,* edited by William E. Fredeman and Ira B. Nadel (1985)

36 *British Novelists, 1890-1929: Modernists,* edited by Thomas F. Staley (1985)

37 *American Writers of the Early Republic,* edited by Emory Elliott (1985)

38 *Afro-American Writers After 1955: Dramatists and Prose Writers,* edited by Thadious M. Davis and Trudier Harris (1985)

39 *British Novelists, 1660-1800,* 2 parts, edited by Martin C. Battestin (1985)

40 *Poets of Great Britain and Ireland Since 1960,* 2 parts, edited by Vincent B. Sherry Jr. (1985)

41 *Afro-American Poets Since 1955,* edited by Trudier Harris and Thadious M. Davis (1985)

42 *American Writers for Children Before 1900,* edited by Glenn E. Estes (1985)

43 *American Newspaper Journalists, 1690-1872,* edited by Perry J. Ashley (1986)

44 *American Screenwriters, Second Series,* edited by Randall Clark, Robert E. Morsberger, and Stephen O. Lesser (1986)

45 *American Poets, 1880-1945, First Series,* edited by Peter Quartermain (1986)

46 *American Literary Publishing Houses, 1900-1980: Trade and Paperback,* edited by Peter Dzwonkoski (1986)

47 *American Historians, 1866-1912,* edited by Clyde N. Wilson (1986)

48 *American Poets, 1880-1945, Second Series,* edited by Peter Quartermain (1986)

49 *American Literary Publishing Houses, 1638-1899,* 2 parts, edited by Peter Dzwonkoski (1986)

50 *Afro-American Writers Before the Harlem Renaissance,* edited by Trudier Harris (1986)

51 *Afro-American Writers from the Harlem Renaissance to 1940,* edited by Trudier Harris (1987)

52 *American Writers for Children Since 1960: Fiction,* edited by Glenn E. Estes (1986)

53 *Canadian Writers Since 1960, First Series,* edited by W. H. New (1986)

54 *American Poets, 1880-1945, Third Series,* 2 parts, edited by Peter Quartermain (1987)

55 *Victorian Prose Writers Before 1867,* edited by William B. Thesing (1987)

56 *German Fiction Writers, 1914-1945,* edited by James Hardin (1987)

57 *Victorian Prose Writers After 1867,* edited by William B. Thesing (1987)

58 *Jacobean and Caroline Dramatists,* edited by Fredson Bowers (1987)

59 *American Literary Critics and Scholars, 1800-1850,* edited by John W. Rathbun and Monica M. Grecu (1987)

60 *Canadian Writers Since 1960, Second Series,* edited by W. H. New (1987)

61 *American Writers for Children Since 1960: Poets, Illustrators, and Nonfiction Authors,* edited by Glenn E. Estes (1987)

62 *Elizabethan Dramatists,* edited by Fredson Bowers (1987)

63 *Modern American Critics, 1920-1955,* edited by Gregory S. Jay (1988)

64 *American Literary Critics and Scholars, 1850-1880,* edited by John W. Rathbun and Monica M. Grecu (1988)

65 *French Novelists, 1900-1930,* edited by Catharine Savage Brosman (1988)

66 *German Fiction Writers, 1885-1913,* 2 parts, edited by James Hardin (1988)

67 *Modern American Critics Since 1955,* edited by Gregory S. Jay (1988)

68 *Canadian Writers, 1920-1959, First Series,* edited by W. H. New (1988)

69 *Contemporary German Fiction Writers, First Series,* edited by Wolfgang D. Elfe and James Hardin (1988)

70 *British Mystery Writers, 1860-1919,* edited by Bernard Benstock and Thomas F. Staley (1988)

71 *American Literary Critics and Scholars, 1880-1900,* edited by John W. Rathbun and Monica M. Grecu (1988)

72 *French Novelists, 1930-1960,* edited by Catharine Savage Brosman (1988)

73 *American Magazine Journalists, 1741-1850,* edited by Sam G. Riley (1988)

74 *American Short-Story Writers Before 1880,* edited by Bobby Ellen Kimbel, with the assistance of William E. Grant (1988)

75 *Contemporary German Fiction Writers, Second Series,* edited by Wolfgang D. Elfe and James Hardin (1988)

76 *Afro-American Writers, 1940-1955,* edited by Trudier Harris (1988)

77 *British Mystery Writers, 1920-1939,* edited by Bernard Benstock and Thomas F. Staley (1988)

78 *American Short-Story Writers, 1880-1910,* edited by Bobby Ellen Kimbel, with the assistance of William E. Grant (1988)

79 *American Magazine Journalists, 1850-1900,* edited by Sam G. Riley (1988)

80 *Restoration and Eighteenth-Century Dramatists, First Series,* edited by Paula R. Backscheider (1989)

81 *Austrian Fiction Writers, 1875-1913,* edited by James Hardin and Donald G. Daviau (1989)

82 *Chicano Writers, First Series,* edited by Francisco A. Lomelí and Carl R. Shirley (1989)

83 *French Novelists Since 1960,* edited by Catharine Savage Brosman (1989)

84 *Restoration and Eighteenth-Century Dramatists, Second Series,* edited by Paula R. Backscheider (1989)

85 *Austrian Fiction Writers After 1914,* edited by James Hardin and Donald G. Daviau (1989)

86 *American Short-Story Writers, 1910-1945, First Series,* edited by Bobby Ellen Kimbel (1989)

87 *British Mystery and Thriller Writers Since 1940, First Series,* edited by Bernard Benstock and Thomas F. Staley (1989)

88 *Canadian Writers, 1920-1959, Second Series,* edited by W. H. New (1989)

89 *Restoration and Eighteenth-Century Dramatists, Third Series,* edited by Paula R. Backscheider (1989)

90 *German Writers in the Age of Goethe, 1789-1832,* edited by James Hardin and Christoph E. Schweitzer (1989)

91 *American Magazine Journalists, 1900-1960, First Series,* edited by Sam G. Riley (1990)

92 *Canadian Writers, 1890-1920,* edited by W. H. New (1990)

93 *British Romantic Poets, 1789-1832, First Series,* edited by John R. Greenfield (1990)

94 *German Writers in the Age of Goethe: Sturm und Drang to Classicism,* edited by James Hardin and Christoph E. Schweitzer (1990)

95 *Eighteenth-Century British Poets, First Series,* edited by John Sitter (1990)

96 *British Romantic Poets, 1789-1832, Second Series,* edited by John R. Greenfield (1990)

97 *German Writers from the Enlightenment to Sturm und Drang, 1720-1764,* edited by James Hardin and Christoph E. Schweitzer (1990)

98 *Modern British Essayists, First Series,* edited by Robert Beum (1990)

99 *Canadian Writers Before 1890,* edited by W. H. New (1990)

100 *Modern British Essayists, Second Series,* edited by Robert Beum (1990)

101 *British Prose Writers, 1660-1800, First Series,* edited by Donald T. Siebert (1991)

102 *American Short-Story Writers, 1910-1945, Second Series,* edited by Bobby Ellen Kimbel (1991)

103 *American Literary Biographers, First Series,* edited by Steven Serafin (1991)

104 *British Prose Writers, 1660-1800, Second Series,* edited by Donald T. Siebert (1991)

105 *American Poets Since World War II, Second Series,* edited by R. S. Gwynn (1991)

106 *British Literary Publishing Houses, 1820-1880,* edited by Patricia J. Anderson and Jonathan Rose (1991)

107 *British Romantic Prose Writers, 1789-1832, First Series,* edited by John R. Greenfield (1991)

108 *Twentieth-Century Spanish Poets, First Series,* edited by Michael L. Perna (1991)

109 *Eighteenth-Century British Poets, Second Series,* edited by John Sitter (1991)

110 *British Romantic Prose Writers, 1789-1832, Second Series,* edited by John R. Greenfield (1991)

111 *American Literary Biographers, Second Series,* edited by Steven Serafin (1991)

112 *British Literary Publishing Houses, 1881-1965,* edited by Jonathan Rose and Patricia J. Anderson (1991)

113 *Modern Latin-American Fiction Writers, First Series,* edited by William Luis (1992)

114 *Twentieth-Century Italian Poets, First Series,* edited by Giovanna Wedel De Stasio, Glauco Cambon, and Antonio Illiano (1992)

115 *Medieval Philosophers,* edited by Jeremiah Hackett (1992)

116 *British Romantic Novelists, 1789-1832,* edited by Bradford K. Mudge (1992)

117 *Twentieth-Century Caribbean and Black African Writers, First Series,* edited by Bernth Lindfors and Reinhard Sander (1992)

118 *Twentieth-Century German Dramatists, 1889-1918,* edited by Wolfgang D. Elfe and James Hardin (1992)

119 *Nineteenth-Century French Fiction Writers: Romanticism and Realism, 1800-1860,* edited by Catharine Savage Brosman (1992)

120 *American Poets Since World War II, Third Series,* edited by R. S. Gwynn (1992)

121 *Seventeenth-Century British Nondramatic Poets, First Series,* edited by M. Thomas Hester (1992)

122 *Chicano Writers, Second Series,* edited by Francisco A. Lomelí and Carl R. Shirley (1992)

123 *Nineteenth-Century French Fiction Writers: Naturalism and Beyond, 1860-1900,* edited by Catharine Savage Brosman (1992)

124 *Twentieth-Century German Dramatists, 1919-1992,* edited by Wolfgang D. Elfe and James Hardin (1992)

125 *Twentieth-Century Caribbean and Black African Writers, Second Series,* edited by Bernth Lindfors and Reinhard Sander (1993)

126 *Seventeenth-Century British Nondramatic Poets, Second Series,* edited by M. Thomas Hester (1993)

127 *American Newspaper Publishers, 1950-1990,* edited by Perry J. Ashley (1993)

128 *Twentieth-Century Italian Poets, Second Series,* edited by Giovanna Wedel De Stasio, Glauco Cambon, and Antonio Illiano (1993)

129 *Nineteenth-Century German Writers, 1841-1900,* edited by James Hardin and Siegfried Mews (1993)

130 *American Short-Story Writers Since World War II,* edited by Patrick Meanor (1993)

131 *Seventeenth-Century British Nondramatic Poets, Third Series,* edited by M. Thomas Hester (1993)

132 *Sixteenth-Century British Nondramatic Writers, First Series,* edited by David A. Richardson (1993)

133 *Nineteenth-Century German Writers to 1840,* edited by James Hardin and Siegfried Mews (1993)

134 *Twentieth-Century Spanish Poets, Second Series,* edited by Jerry Phillips Winfield (1994)

135 *British Short-Fiction Writers, 1880-1914: The Realist Tradition,* edited by William B. Thesing (1994)

136 *Sixteenth-Century British Nondramatic Writers, Second Series,* edited by David A. Richardson (1994)

137 *American Magazine Journalists, 1900-1960, Second Series,* edited by Sam G. Riley (1994)

138 *German Writers and Works of the High Middle Ages: 1170-1280,* edited by James Hardin and Will Hasty (1994)

139 *British Short-Fiction Writers, 1945-1980,* edited by Dean Baldwin (1994)

140 *American Book-Collectors and Bibliographers, First Series,* edited by Joseph Rosenblum (1994)

141 *British Children's Writers, 1880-1914,* edited by Laura M. Zaidman (1994)

142 *Eighteenth-Century British Literary Biographers,* edited by Steven Serafin (1994)

143 *American Novelists Since World War II, Third Series,* edited by James R. Giles and Wanda H. Giles (1994)

144 *Nineteenth-Century British Literary Biographers,* edited by Steven Serafin (1994)

145 *Modern Latin-American Fiction Writers, Second Series,* edited by William Luis and Ann González (1994)

146 *Old and Middle English Literature,* edited by Jeffrey Helterman and Jerome Mitchell (1994)

147 *South Slavic Writers Before World War II,* edited by Vasa D. Mihailovich (1994)

148 *German Writers and Works of the Early Middle Ages: 800-1170,* edited by Will Hasty and James Hardin (1994)

149 *Late Nineteenth- and Early Twentieth-Century British Literary Biographers,* edited by Steven Serafin (1995)

150 *Early Modern Russian Writers, Late Seventeenth and Eighteenth Centuries,* edited by Marcus C. Levitt (1995)

151 *British Prose Writers of the Early Seventeenth Century,* edited by Clayton D. Lein (1995)

152 *American Novelists Since World War II, Fourth Series,* edited by James R. Giles and Wanda H. Giles (1995)

153 *Late-Victorian and Edwardian British Novelists, First Series,* edited by George M. Johnson (1995)

154 *The British Literary Book Trade, 1700-1820,* edited by James K. Bracken and Joel Silver (1995)

155 *Twentieth-Century British Literary Biographers,* edited by Steven Serafin (1995)

156 *British Short-Fiction Writers, 1880-1914: The Romantic Tradition,* edited by William F. Naufftus (1995)

157 *Twentieth-Century Caribbean and Black African Writers, Third Series,* edited by Bernth Lindfors and Reinhard Sander (1995)

158 *British Reform Writers, 1789-1832,* edited by Gary Kelly and Edd Applegate (1995)

159 *British Short-Fiction Writers, 1800-1880,* edited by John R. Greenfield (1996)

160 *British Children's Writers, 1914-1960,* edited by Donald R. Hettinga and Gary D. Schmidt (1996)

161 *British Children's Writers Since 1960, First Series,* edited by Caroline Hunt (1996)

162 *British Short-Fiction Writers, 1915-1945,* edited by John H. Rogers (1996)

163 *British Children's Writers, 1800-1880,* edited by Meena Khorana (1996)

164 *German Baroque Writers, 1580-1660,* edited by James Hardin (1996)

165 *American Poets Since World War II, Fourth Series,* edited by Joseph Conte (1996)

166 *British Travel Writers, 1837-1875,* edited by Barbara Brothers and Julia Gergits (1996)

167 *Sixteenth-Century British Nondramatic Writers, Third Series,* edited by David A. Richardson (1996)

168 *German Baroque Writers, 1661-1730,* edited by James Hardin (1996)

169 *American Poets Since World War II, Fifth Series,* edited by Joseph Conte (1996)

170 *The British Literary Book Trade, 1475-1700,* edited by James K. Bracken and Joel Silver (1996)

171 *Twentieth-Century American Sportswriters,* edited by Richard Orodenker (1996)

172 *Sixteenth-Century British Nondramatic Writers, Fourth Series,* edited by David A. Richardson (1996)

173 *American Novelists Since World War II, Fifth Series,* edited by James R. Giles and Wanda H. Giles (1996)

174 *British Travel Writers, 1876-1909,* edited by Barbara Brothers and Julia Gergits (1997)

175 *Native American Writers of the United States,* edited by Kenneth M. Roemer (1997)

176 *Ancient Greek Authors,* edited by Ward W. Briggs (1997)

177 *Italian Novelists Since World War II, 1945-1965,* edited by Augustus Pallotta (1997)

178 *British Fantasy and Science-Fiction Writers Before World War I,* edited by Darren Harris-Fain (1997)

179 *German Writers of the Renaissance and Reformation, 1280-1580,* edited by James Hardin and Max Reinhart (1997)

180 *Japanese Fiction Writers, 1868-1945,* edited by Van C. Gessel (1997)

181 *South Slavic Writers Since World War II,* edited by Vasa D. Mihailovich (1997)

182 *Japanese Fiction Writers Since World War II,* edited by Van C. Gessel (1997)

183 *American Travel Writers, 1776-1864,* edited by James J. Schramer and Donald Ross (1997)

184 *Nineteenth-Century British Book-Collectors and Bibliographers,* edited by William Baker and Kenneth Womack (1997)

185 *American Literary Journalists, 1945-1995, First Series,* edited by Arthur J. Kaul (1998)

186 *Nineteenth-Century American Western Writers,* edited by Robert L. Gale (1998)

187 *American Book Collectors and Bibliographers, Second Series,* edited by Joseph Rosenblum (1998)

188 *American Book and Magazine Illustrators to 1920,* edited by Steven E. Smith, Catherine A. Hastedt, and Donald H. Dyal (1998)

189 *American Travel Writers, 1850-1915,* edited by Donald Ross and James J. Schramer (1998)

190 *British Reform Writers, 1832-1914,* edited by Gary Kelly and Edd Applegate (1998)

191 *British Novelists Between the Wars,* edited by George M. Johnson (1998)

192 *French Dramatists, 1789-1914,* edited by Barbara T. Cooper (1998)

193 *American Poets Since World War II, Sixth Series,* edited by Joseph Conte (1998)

194 *British Novelists Since 1960, Second Series,* edited by Merritt Moseley (1998)

195 *British Travel Writers, 1910-1939,* edited by Barbara Brothers and Julia Gergits (1998)

196 *Italian Novelists Since World War II, 1965-1995,* edited by Augustus Pallotta (1999)

197 *Late-Victorian and Edwardian British Novelists, Second Series,* edited by George M. Johnson (1999)

198 *Russian Literature in the Age of Pushkin and Gogol: Prose,* edited by Christine A. Rydel (1999)

199 *Victorian Women Poets,* edited by William B. Thesing (1999)

200 *American Women Prose Writers to 1820,* edited by Carla J. Mulford, with Angela Vietto and Amy E. Winans (1999)

201 *Twentieth-Century British Book Collectors and Bibliographers,* edited by William Baker and Kenneth Womack (1999)

202 *Nineteenth-Century American Fiction Writers,* edited by Kent P. Ljungquist (1999)

203 *Medieval Japanese Writers,* edited by Steven D. Carter (1999)

204 *British Travel Writers, 1940–1997,* edited by Barbara Brothers and Julia M. Gergits (1999)

205 *Russian Literature in the Age of Pushkin and Gogol: Poetry and Drama,* edited by Christine A. Rydel (1999)

206 *Twentieth-Century American Western Writers, First Series,* edited by Richard H. Cracroft (1999)

207 *British Novelists Since 1960, Third Series,* edited by Merritt Moseley (1999)

208 *Literature of the French and Occitan Middle Ages: Eleventh to Fifteenth Centuries,* edited by Deborah Sinnreich-Levi and Ian S. Laurie (1999)

209 *Chicano Writers, Third Series,* edited by Francisco A. Lomelí and Carl R. Shirley (1999)

210 *Ernest Hemingway: A Documentary Volume,* edited by Robert W. Trogdon (1999)

211 *Ancient Roman Writers,* edited by Ward W. Briggs (1999)

212 *Twentieth-Century American Western Writers, Second Series,* edited by Richard H. Cracroft (1999)

213 *Pre-Nineteenth-Century British Book Collectors and Bibliographers,* edited by William Baker and Kenneth Womack (1999)

214 *Twentieth-Century Danish Writers,* edited by Marianne Stecher-Hansen (1999)

215 *Twentieth-Century Eastern European Writers, First Series,* edited by Steven Serafin (1999)

216 *British Poets of the Great War: Brooke, Rosenberg, Thomas. A Documentary Volume,* edited by Patrick Quinn (2000)

217 *Nineteenth-Century French Poets,* edited by Robert Beum (2000)

218 *American Short-Story Writers Since World War II, Second Series,* edited by Patrick Meanor and Gwen Crane (2000)

219 *F. Scott Fitzgerald's* The Great Gatsby: *A Documentary Volume,* edited by Matthew J. Bruccoli (2000)

220 *Twentieth-Century Eastern European Writers, Second Series,* edited by Steven Serafin (2000)

221 *American Women Prose Writers, 1870–1920,* edited by Sharon M. Harris, with the assistance of Heidi L. M. Jacobs and Jennifer Putzi (2000)

Documentary Series

1 *Sherwood Anderson, Willa Cather, John Dos Passos, Theodore Dreiser, F. Scott Fitzgerald, Ernest Hemingway, Sinclair Lewis,* edited by Margaret A. Van Antwerp (1982)

2 *James Gould Cozzens, James T. Farrell, William Faulkner, John O'Hara, John Steinbeck,* *Thomas Wolfe, Richard Wright,* edited by Margaret A. Van Antwerp (1982)

3 *Saul Bellow, Jack Kerouac, Norman Mailer, Vladimir Nabokov, John Updike, Kurt Vonnegut,* edited by Mary Bruccoli (1983)

4 *Tennessee Williams,* edited by Margaret A. Van Antwerp and Sally Johns (1984)

5 *American Transcendentalists,* edited by Joel Myerson (1988)

6 *Hardboiled Mystery Writers: Raymond Chandler, Dashiell Hammett, Ross Macdonald,*

edited by Matthew J. Bruccoli and Richard Layman (1989)

7 *Modern American Poets: James Dickey, Robert Frost, Marianne Moore,* edited by Karen L. Rood (1989)

8 *The Black Aesthetic Movement,* edited by Jeffrey Louis Decker (1991)

9 *American Writers of the Vietnam War: W. D. Ehrhart, Larry Heinemann, Tim O'Brien, Walter McDonald, John M. Del Vecchio,* edited by Ronald Baughman (1991)

10 *The Bloomsbury Group,* edited by Edward L. Bishop (1992)

11 *American Proletarian Culture: The Twenties and The Thirties,* edited by Jon Christian Suggs (1993)

12 *Southern Women Writers: Flannery O'Connor, Katherine Anne Porter, Eudora Welty,* edited by Mary Ann Wimsatt and Karen L. Rood (1994)

13 *The House of Scribner, 1846-1904,* edited by John Delaney (1996)

14 *Four Women Writers for Children, 1868-1918,* edited by Caroline C. Hunt (1996)

15 *American Expatriate Writers: Paris in the Twenties,* edited by Matthew J. Bruccoli and Robert W. Trogdon (1997)

16 *The House of Scribner, 1905-1930,* edited by John Delaney (1997)

17 *The House of Scribner, 1931-1984,* edited by John Delaney (1998)

18 *British Poets of The Great War: Sassoon, Graves, Owen,* edited by Patrick Quinn (1999)

19 *James Dickey,* edited by Judith S. Baughman (1999)

See also DLB 210, 216, 219

Yearbooks

1980 edited by Karen L. Rood, Jean W. Ross, and Richard Ziegfeld (1981)

1981 edited by Karen L. Rood, Jean W. Ross, and Richard Ziegfeld (1982)

1982 edited by Richard Ziegfeld; associate editors: Jean W. Ross and Lynne C. Zeigler (1983)

1983 edited by Mary Bruccoli and Jean W. Ross, associate editor Richard Ziegfeld (1984)

1984 edited by Jean W. Ross (1985)

1985 edited by Jean W. Ross (1986)

1986 edited by J. M. Brook (1987)

1987 edited by J. M. Brook (1988)

1988 edited by J. M. Brook (1989)

1989 edited by J. M. Brook (1990)

1990 edited by James W. Hipp (1991)

1991 edited by James W. Hipp (1992)

1992 edited by James W. Hipp (1993)

1993 edited by James W. Hipp, contributing editor George Garrett (1994)

1994 edited by James W. Hipp, contributing editor George Garrett (1995)

1995 edited by James W. Hipp, contributing editor George Garrett (1996)

1996 edited by Samuel W. Bruce and L. Kay Webster, contributing editor George Garrett (1997)

1997 edited by Matthew J. Bruccoli and George Garrett, with the assistance of L. Kay Webster (1998)

1998 edited by Matthew J. Bruccoli, contributing editor George Garrett, with the assistance of D. W. Thomas (1999)

Concise Series

Concise Dictionary of American Literary Biography, 7 volumes (1988-1999): *The New Consciousness, 1941-1968; Colonization to the American Renaissance, 1640-1865; Realism, Naturalism, and Local Color, 1865-1917; The Twenties, 1917-1929; The Age of Maturity, 1929-1941; Broadening Views, 1968-1988; Supplement: Modern Writers, 1900–1998.*

Concise Dictionary of British Literary Biography, 8 volumes (1991-1992): *Writers of the Middle Ages and Renaissance Before 1660; Writers of the Restoration and Eighteenth Century, 1660-1789; Writers of the Romantic Period, 1789-1832; Victorian Writers, 1832-1890; Late-Victorian and Edwardian Writers, 1890-1914; Modern Writers, 1914-1945; Writers After World War II, 1945-1960; Contemporary Writers, 1960 to Present.*

Concise Dictionary of World Literary Biography, 20 volumes projected (1999-   ): *Ancient Greek and Roman Writers; German Writers; African, Carribbean, and Latin-American Writers.*

IN MEMORY OF
Betty Jane Sperber Harris,
Peggy Moore Whyte, and
Raymond Putzi

American Women
Prose Writers,
1870–1920

Dictionary of Literary Biography® • Volume Two Hundred Twenty-One

American Women Prose Writers, 1870–1920

Edited by
Sharon M. Harris
University of Nebraska, Lincoln
with the assistance of
Heidi L. M. Jacobs
University of Nebraska, Lincoln
and
Jennifer Putzi
University of Nebraska, Lincoln

A Bruccoli Clark Layman Book
The Gale Group
Detroit • San Francisco • London • Boston • Woodbridge, Conn.

Printed in the United States of America

The paper used in this publication meets the minimum requirements
of American National Standard for Information Sciences–Permanence
Paper for Printed Library Materials, ANSI Z39.48-1984. ∞™

Library of Congress Cataloging-in-Publication Data

American women prose writers, 1870–1920 / edited by Sharon M. Harris, with the assistance of
Heidi L. M. Jacobs and Jennifer Putzi.
    p. cm.–(Dictionary of literary biography: v. 221)
"A Bruccoli Clark Layman book."
Includes bibliographical references and index.
ISBN 0-7876-3130-2 (alk. paper)
1. American prose literature–Women authors–Bio-bibliography–Dictionaries. 2. American prose litera-
ture–19th century–Bio-bibliography–Dictionaries. 3. American prose literature–20th century–Bio-bibli-
ography–Dictionaries. 4. Women authors, American–Biography–Dictionaries. I. Harris, Sharon M.
II. Jacobs, Heidi L. M. III. Putzi, Jennifer. IV. Series.

PS362.A83 2000
818'408099287
[B 21]

00–020604

Contents

Plan of the Series xiii
Introduction xv

Octavia Albert (1853–ca. 1889) 3
   Phoebe Jackson

Mary Antin (1881–1949) 8
   Betty Bergland

Mary Austin (1868–1934) .19
   Linda K. Karell

Amelia Edith Huddleston Barr (1831–1919) 31
   Rose Norman

Lillie Devereux Blake (1833–1913) 39
   Grace Farrell

S. Alice Callahan (1868–1894) 47
   Annette Van Dyke

Kate McPhelim Cleary (1863–1905) 52
   Susanne George Bloomfield

Anna Julia Cooper (1858–1964) 61
   Jennifer A. Kohout

Mary Abigail Dodge (Gail Hamilton)
(1833–1896). 73
   Annmarie Pinarski

Alice Morse Earle (1853–1911) 82
   Katharine Gillespie

Edith Maude Eaton (Sui Sin Far) (1865–1914) 91
   Nicole Tonkovich

Winnifred Eaton (Onoto Watanna) (1875–1954) . .103
   Maureen Honey

Sarah Barnwell Elliott (1848–1928) 113
   Susan Neal Mayberry

Annie Adams Fields (1834–1915) 120
   Deborah M. Evans

Mary Hallock Foote (1847–1938) 128
   Victoria Lamont

Mary E. Wilkins Freeman (1852–1930). 137
   Marylynne Diggs

Charlotte Perkins Gilman (1860–1935) 148
   Robin Miskolcze

Emma Goldman (1869–1940) 159
   Priscilla Wald

Anna Katharine Green (1846–1935) 168
   Marie T. Farr

Susan Hale (1833–1910) 175
   Karen Dandurand

Frances Ellen Watkins Harper (1825–1911) 182
   Maggie Montesinos Sale

Constance Cary Harrison (Mrs. Burton Harrison)
(1843–1920) 193
   Kathy Ryder

Mary Jane Holmes (1825–1907) 203
   Barbara J. McGuire

Alice James (1848–1892) 211
   Kristin Boudreau

Sarah Orne Jewett (1849–1909) 219
   Melanie Kisthardt

Mrs. A. E. Johnson (Amelia Johnson)
(ca. 1858–1922) 230
   Wendy Wagner

Emma Dunham Kelley (? – ?) 238
   Barbara McCaskill

Lucy Larcom (1824–1893) 246
   Shirley Marchalonis

Laura Jean Libbey (1862–1924) 253
   Jean Carwile Masteller

Queen Liliʻuokalani (1838–1917) 265
   Lydia Kualapai

Victoria Earle Matthews (1861–1907) 272
   Shirley Wilson Logan

María Cristina Mena (María Cristina Chambers)
(1893–1965) 280
   E. Thomson Shields Jr.

Mourning Dove (Humishuma)
(between 1882? and 1888?–1936) 284
   Alanna Kathleen Brown

Elizabeth Stuart Phelps (1844–1911) 294
   Mary Bortnyk Rigsby

Agnes Repplier (1855–1950) 305
   Paul Hansom

María Amparo Ruiz de Burton
(1832–1895) 310
   José F. Aranda Jr.

Contents

Amanda Smith (1837–1915). 317
    Venetria K. Patton

Harriet Prescott Spofford
    (1835–1921). 322
    Jennifer Putzi

Gene Stratton-Porter (1863–1924). 332
    Anne K. Phillips

Susie King Taylor (1848–1912) 339
    Joycelyn K. Moody

Ida B. Wells-Barnett (1862–1931). 347
    Stephanie Athey

Frances E. Willard (1839–1898) 357
    Mary Hurd

Martha Wolfenstein (1869–1906) 366
    Rosalind G. Benjet

Constance Fenimore Woolson (1840–1894) 370
    Sharon L. Dean

Anzia Yezierska (ca. 1880–1970) 381
    Julie Prebel

Books for Further Reading 389
Contributors 393
Cumulative Index 397

Plan of the Series

. . . Almost the most prodigious asset of a country, and perhaps its most precious possession, is its native literary product—when that product is fine and noble and enduring.

Mark Twain*

The advisory board, the editors, and the publisher of the *Dictionary of Literary Biography* are joined in endorsing Mark Twain's declaration. The literature of a nation provides an inexhaustible resource of permanent worth. We intend to make literature and its creators better understood and more accessible to students and the reading public, while satisfying the standards of teachers and scholars.

To meet these requirements, *literary biography* has been construed in terms of the author's achievement. The most important thing about a writer is his writing. Accordingly, the entries in *DLB* are career biographies, tracing the development of the author's canon and the evolution of his reputation.

The purpose of *DLB* is not only to provide reliable information in a convenient format but also to place the figures in the larger perspective of literary history and to offer appraisals of their accomplishments by qualified scholars.

The publication plan for *DLB* resulted from two years of preparation. The project was proposed to Bruccoli Clark by Frederick G. Ruffner, president of the Gale Research Company, in November 1975. After specimen entries were prepared and typeset, an advisory board was formed to refine the entry format and develop the series rationale. In meetings held during 1976, the publisher, series editors, and advisory board approved the scheme for a comprehensive biographical dictionary of persons who contributed to North American literature. Editorial work on the first volume began in January 1977, and it was published in 1978. In order to make *DLB* more than a reference tool and to compile volumes that individually have claim to status as literary history, it was decided to organize volumes by

From an unpublished section of Mark Twain's autobiography, copyright by the Mark Twain Company

topic, period, or genre. Each of these freestanding volumes provides a biographical-bibliographical guide and overview for a particular area of literature. We are convinced that this organization—as opposed to a single alphabet method—constitutes a valuable innovation in the presentation of reference material. The volume plan necessarily requires many decisions for the placement and treatment of authors who might properly be included in two or three volumes. In some instances a major figure will be included in separate volumes, but with different entries emphasizing the aspect of his career appropriate to each volume. Ernest Hemingway, for example, is represented in *American Writers in Paris, 1920–1939* by an entry focusing on his expatriate apprenticeship; he is also in *American Novelists, 1910–1945* with an entry surveying his entire career, as well as in *American Short-Story Writers, 1910–1945, Second Series* with an entry concentrating on his short stories. Each volume includes a cumulative index of the subject authors and articles. Comprehensive indexes to the entire series are planned.

Since 1981 the series has been further augmented by the *DLB Yearbooks,* which update published entries and add new entries to keep the *DLB* current with contemporary activity. There have also been *DLB Documentary Series* volumes which provide biographical and critical source materials for figures whose work is judged to have particular interest for students. One of these companion volumes is devoted entirely to Tennessee Williams.

We define literature as the *intellectual commerce of a nation:* not merely as belles lettres but as that ample and complex process by which ideas are generated, shaped, and transmitted. *DLB* entries are not limited to "creative writers" but extend to other figures who in their time and in their way influenced the mind of a people. Thus the series encompasses historians, journalists, publishers, book collectors, and screenwriters. By this means readers of *DLB* may be aided to perceive literature not as cult scripture in the keeping of intellectual high priests but firmly positioned at the center of a nation's life.

DLB includes the major writers appropriate to each volume and those standing in the ranks behind them. Scholarly and critical counsel has been sought in deciding which minor figures to include and how full their entries should be. Wherever possible, useful references are made to figures who do not warrant separate entries.

Each *DLB* volume has an expert volume editor responsible for planning the volume, selecting the figures for inclusion, and assigning the entries. Volume editors are also responsible for preparing, where appropriate, appendices surveying the major periodicals and literary and intellectual movements for their volumes, as well as lists of further readings. Work on the series as a whole is coordinated at the Bruccoli Clark Layman editorial center in Columbia, South Carolina, where the editorial staff is responsible for accuracy and utility of the published volumes.

One feature that distinguishes *DLB* is the illustration policy—its concern with the iconography of literature. Just as an author is influenced by his surroundings, so is the reader's understanding of the author enhanced by a knowledge of his environment. Therefore *DLB* volumes include not only drawings, paintings, and photographs of authors, often depicting them at various stages in their careers, but also illustrations of their families and places where they lived. Title pages are regularly reproduced in facsimile along with dust jackets for modern authors. The dust jackets are a special feature of *DLB* because they often document better than anything else the way in which an author's work was perceived in its own time. Specimens of the writers' manuscripts and letters are included when feasible.

Samuel Johnson rightly decreed that "The chief glory of every people arises from its authors." The purpose of the *Dictionary of Literary Biography* is to compile literary history in the surest way available to us—by accurate and comprehensive treatment of the lives and work of those who contributed to it.

The *DLB* Advisory Board

Introduction

In the years following the Civil War, the most significant change in the circumstances of women was their increased visibility in public life. This visibility was born out of economic necessity and a dawning acceptance of women's continuing efforts to contribute in diverse ways to the public life of the reassembled nation. In growing numbers, women moved into the professions, onto the lecture platform, into the manufactory, and to urban areas or the West. Their experiences and visions in this radically shifting social landscape were captured in their literary endeavors.

Whereas women's prose writings in the first half of the nineteenth century were typically short stories and novels, by the 1870s publishers sought a far greater range of prose writings. Fiction remained a staple of women's writings, but autobiography, biography, and the topical essay became major prose genres sought by publishers. In part this broadening of interest was due to the fact that the 1870s was a period of economic boom; the publishing industry thrived under such conditions and was willing to expand its offerings. With literacy on the rise, especially among women, publishers found their markets and their readership significantly expanded. Immigrants entering the country by the tens of thousands gave rise to new publishing outlets as well. By the end of the century nearly 1,200 foreign-language periodicals were being published in the United States. Further, people of color became a greater force in publishing. By 1900 African American magazines and newspapers numbered nearly 1,000, while Native Americans were developing a periodical press with at least 20 publications, and Chinese Americans in the Western states produced several weeklies. Both popular and literary periodicals abounded. Women founded more than 100 journals and newspapers in these years as well, ranging from Mary Seymour Foot's *Business Woman's Journal* (founded 1889) to the *Woman's Era,* a Boston newspaper founded in 1894 by African American women who were members of the New Era Club.

"Woman's fiction," defined by Nina Baym as fiction that focuses on a young woman's struggle for self-mastery in the face of conventional expectations about women's roles in society, had dominated the market until the 1860s, but thereafter waned in popularity. Other prose styles gained increased recognition: most notable were realist and/or regional novels, short stories, and sketches; journalism; and autobiographical narratives. Serializations became one of the most popular forms of literary production; many novels were serialized before appearing in book form, and writers such as Laura Jean Libbey established highly successful careers by serializing literature that was directed at immigrants and workers. Regionalism, primarily rendered through short stories and sketches, captured the diversification within publishing as well as readers' keen interest in previously little-known regions of their country. The short story was an especially popular form for many women writers, including Harriet Prescott Spofford, Sui Sin Far, Mary Wolfenstein, Constance Fenimore Woolson, and Anzia Yezierska.

While the field of publishing became a more profitable venture between 1870 and 1920, it was also often the site of difficult business negotiations that were sometimes far more profitable for publishers than writers. Early in this period, women were particularly subject to discrimination in terms of payment for their writing, as Mary Abigail Dodge exposed in her indictment of publishers, *A Battle of the Books* (1870). By the 1890s, however, that trend had diminished. Though few women were publishers, many women moved into editorial positions during this era. Such roles not only fulfilled individual women's creative and business desires, but they also afforded women greater input into and knowledge about the publishing process itself. Susan Hale, Ida B. Wells-Barnett, and many other women became magazine and newspaper editors at the turn of the century, helping to change the face of U.S. publishing.

The 1870s was a decade of extensive advancement of the literary realist movement that survived into the early twentieth century and beyond. Realism was a genre that allowed writers to respond to the unprecedented economic, social, and political changes in the reunified states. Of particular interest to realists were depictions of commonplace life, authentic speech patterns, and the ideal of reporting life "as it is" without the transcendence so popular in the Romantic movement earlier in the century. The topics dissected by realist writers were as varied as the writers themselves: mill and factory life, rural life, female sexuality, class differences, and psychology (both before and after the extensive influence of Sigmund Freud). Mary E. Wilkins Freeman and Sarah Orne Jewett have survived as the dominant women regionalists, but from the 1870s until 1920 women entered the field in significantly increasing numbers. Sarah Barnwell Elliott examined rural Tennessee life and Kate M. Cleary, midwestern life; Sarah Pratt McLean Greene, best known for *Cape Cod Folks* (1881), also wrote about her experiences in the territories of Washington and California; and in the early twentieth century Edith Wharton exposed the realities of upper-class life, while Willa Cather explored immigrant pioneers' struggles on the Nebraska plains. Naturalism, using realist techniques but influenced by the sciences and especially Darwinism, also attracted several writers, including Elliott (*Jerry,* 1891), Kate Chopin (*The Awakening,* 1899), Charlotte Perkins Gilman ("The Yellow Wallpaper," 1892), and Mary Antin (*The Promised Land,* 1901).

Many realist writers emerged from the field of journalism, where their skills in rendering life "as it is" had been honed. Some women, such as Nelly Bly (Elizabeth Cochrane) and Wells-Barnett, made journalism their primary literary endeavor. As a newspaper editor and co-owner of the *Free Speech and Headlight,* Wells-Barnett not only demonstrated her individual achievements but also acted as a model for other women of her generation. Other writers combined journalism and realist fiction writing. Frances E. Watkins Harper, for instance, was an early contributor to the *National Anti-Slavery Standard* and the *Liberator,* and her fiction, particularly *Iola Leroy: or, Shadows Uplifted* (1892), reflects these commitments to social change. Victoria Earle Matthews crafted a career for herself in freelance journalism, writing for such newspapers as *The New York Times,* the *New York Herald,* the *Boston Advocate,* and the *Washington Bee.* Gilman also combined journalism and fiction writing. She published *The Forerunner,* a monthly feminist magazine, from 1909 to 1916. Much of Gilman's own feminist writings of the period appeared in *The Forerunner.*

Other prose genres that emerged or gained renewed interest in this period included historical studies, both in fiction and nonfiction. Particularly popular were historical novels, such as Amelia Huddleston Barr's *Remember the Alamo* (1888), Mary Johnston's historical romances of colonial Virginia, and the recently recovered historical novels of María Amparo Ruiz de Burton, whose *The Squatter and The Don* (1885) critiques U.S. political policies in relation to Mexico. Several women became recognized historians as well. Susie King Taylor, author of *A Black Woman's Civil War Memoirs*

(1902), was the only African American woman to write about her participation in the Civil War. Octavia V. Rogers Albert recorded the oral narratives of former slaves in *The House of Bondage* (1890) in order to challenge the inaccuracies of traditional histories about slavery. Alice Morse Earle also began her explorations of U.S. colonial history, especially focusing on Puritan women's lives; her writings, including *Colonial Dames and Good Wives* (1895), *Margaret Winthrop* (1895), and *Colonial Days in Old New York* (1896), influenced colonial studies well into the twentieth century.

Women writers contributed to the development of several other popular genres during this period as well. Anna Katharine Green, one of the earliest American practitioners of the detective genre, popularized it with her 1878 best-seller *The Leavenworth Case.* The serialized mystery became a popular genre as well, aided in its success by the writings of Mary Roberts Rinehart, including *The Man in Lower 10* (1906) and *The Circular Staircase* (1908). Many stories also featured girl heroines, a genre popularized by the earlier success of Louisa May Alcott's *Little Women* (1869). Works such as Jean Webster's *Daddy Long-Legs* (1912) presented strong characters and positive representations of young females.

The 1920s effected many changes in the conceptualization of modernism; the early modernists emphasized craft and posited literature as the supreme art form; their work, reflecting the instability of the era in the wake of the fracturing of religious beliefs that accompanied the emphases on the sciences, often posited a skepticism about social visions. While poetry tended to dominate the early modernist movement, several modernist prose writers emerged in this period. The examination of identity was central to many modernists' writings, and the contributions of Sui Sin Far, Wharton, and Yezierska to modernism reflected its highly diverse nature.

Modern technologies increasingly influenced the modernist movement, but such advancements had an impact on earlier social and literary visions as well. The period from the 1870s through the early twentieth century constitutes one of the most vital periods of new technology in U.S. history, and women played a variety of roles—supportive and resistant—in this arena. By 1888 nearly three thousand women had applied for patents. The automobile made mobility commonplace by the early twentieth century, and technology such as the camera and motion pictures reinforced the interest in realism and helped shape modernist aesthetics. The era covered in this volume is notable for the radical changes that developed in attitudes about women and technology: from the conservative, domestic vision of Catherine Beecher to the radical notions advocated by

Gilman in *Women and Economics* (1898). In the first part of this period, the vast majority of women's lives were influenced most extensively by the domestic technology movement spearheaded by Beecher, who called for increased adoption of new technologies in the home.

While technological advancements reshaped women's domestic lives, the majority of writers in this period who addressed such issues did so from the perspective of concerns about the impact of technology on industrial laborers. By the 1870s women were moving into more kinds of paid employment. In *Contending Forces* (1900), Pauline Hopkins presents a turn-of-the-century overview of African American women's work in the laundry business, boardinghouses, stenography, and other forms of employment. The bitter labor disputes of the 1890s led to the organization of national unions, including the American Federation of Labor. Many women, however, were excluded from the unions or subjected to discrimination within the union system. The membership of the American Federation of Labor numbered four million in 1920, but only 6.6 percent were women, for whom union membership often meant not being hired. Thus many women, and especially women of color, remained in lower-paying jobs. Against the backdrop of union disputes and the emergence of industrial leaders such as John D. Rockefeller, J. P. Morgan, and Andrew Carnegie, several women became labor activists; others became writers who examined workers' conditions; others established settlement houses and wrote about their experiences in such institutions; and still others explored the consequences of industrialization on rural and urban environments. Lucy Larcom presented a firsthand account of the effects of mid-nineteenth-century industrialism on young women in *A New England Girlhood, Outlined from Memory* (1889). If cautious in its critique, Larcom's autobiography was a significant early contribution to nonfictional examinations of industrialism. Women's critiques of capitalism endured throughout the turn of the century, from Elizabeth Stuart Phelps's labor novel *The Silent Partner* (1871) to Jane Addams's *Democracy and Social Ethics* (1902), a nonfictional analysis of U.S. industrialization and its effects upon immigrants and the urban poor. Some women, including Olive Tilford Dargan, Lucy Parsons, and Emma Goldman, aligned themselves with Marxism, but the majority of women writers argued for better conditions and equality for women workers within capitalism rather than for its eradication.

If these broad cultural issues were reflected in women's writings between 1870 and 1920, issues specific to women's lives also became major themes of women's literature in that period. The predominant issues addressed in the literature are education, suffrage

and other reform movements, women's communities, female sexuality, and issues of race and ethnicity. Understanding the background of these social issues is essential to understanding the diverse new themes in women's writings at the turn of the century.

The call for increased educational opportunities for women began in the eighteenth century, but in the period from 1870 to 1920 women made the most significant advancements in obtaining advanced educations. Most notable was the growing expectation that middle- and upper-class women would receive some systematic education. Although working-class women were still unlikely to be educated, some of them began to gain at least rudimentary literacy, and higher education institutions began to grant access to some women. In the beginning, some colleges and universities restricted women to a less-rigorous curricula than offered to male students, but as more and more women succeeded in their advanced studies, such discriminations diminished. Land-grant institutions opened to women, and women's colleges were established. By 1880, 60 percent of teachers were women; while this advancement allowed women new opportunities for work outside the home that was still considered genteel (unlike millwork), it was also marked by decreased wages as teaching became aligned with the concept of "women's work." Increasingly, women of color joined the numbers of teachers, administrators, and reformers of the educational system. Fanny Jackson Cappin, like many other northern blacks, moved to the South as a missionary teacher; Victoria Earle Matthews, largely self-educated, established the White Rose Mission, a Home for Colored Girls and Women, in New York City with the goal of training females in Christian principles of self-help; Mary McLeod Bethune, a lifelong education activist, founded Bethune-Cookman College in Florida; and Anna Julia Cooper received a Master's degree from Oberlin College in 1887 and at the age of sixty-six received her doctorate from the Sorbonne. In *A Voice from the South* (1892), Cooper's collected essays and speeches demonstrated her commitment to higher education for African American women.

In increasing numbers and varying roles, women entered the ranks of higher education. Oberlin College was at the forefront of accepting women of all races and African American men as students. In 1871 Frances Willard became the first woman president of a college, Evanston College for Ladies. Women's and black colleges were instrumental in opening new opportunities for previously excluded students. Bennett College, one of the first black institutions of higher learning, was founded in 1873 in Greensboro, North Carolina. The Atlantic Baptist Female Seminary in Atlanta, Georgia, which became Spelman College, was founded in 1881, and the original student body included eleven African American women. Bryn Mawr College, the first women's college to offer graduate studies, was founded in 1885, and Radcliffe College in 1894.

For all of the advancement women made in education from 1870 to 1920, they still had to face the conflicts between increased opportunity and conventional attitudes about women's roles. Many women writers of the period examined this conflict, some in terms of resistance to social restrictions and others in terms of women's own conflicted expectations of work, marriage, and motherhood. Frances E. Watkins Harper, Gilman, Mary Austin, and other writers engaged these issues in their fiction and nonfiction. While increased educational opportunities for all women were a cause for celebration, for African Americans and Native Americans it also often meant the erasure or destruction of African and Native heritages. For African Americans, the process was subtle. While black colleges in the years following the Civil War were instrumental in the mass education of African Americans, most of the curricula of these schools were at the level of secondary education. Thus, for higher education, most African Americans attended white colleges, which were highly traditional in format. As Zitkala-Ša detailed in her autobiographical writings, for Native Americans the processes of erasure were more overt. Ancient systems of tribal education were eradicated by mission schools that practiced assimilationist agendas. The elimination of tribal sovereignty and self-determination was accompanied by a reservation system that enacted a mission-based educational system. Even the later boarding schools replicated a curricula of assimilation. Much of Native American literature in the period of 1870 to 1920 was in resistance to the loss of tribal customs and languages.

Suffrage also became an increasingly volatile political issue in the post–Civil War years, and writers of the period clearly aligned themselves with pro- or antisuffrage positions. Even those advocating suffrage were confronted with a variety of organizations supporting the vote for women. In 1872 the controversial Victoria Woodhull, who advocated "free love," ran for the presidency of the United States as a candidate of the Equal Rights Party. In the same year, Susan B. Anthony and fifteen women were arrested in New York for attempting to vote in the presidential election. While the original impetus toward woman suffrage in this era was seemingly made in the name of all women, the issue of race soon fractured the women's rights movement. While Harriet Purvis, an African American activist, was elected vice president of the National Woman's Suffrage Association (NWSA) in 1876, Anthony's and Elizabeth Cady Stanton's insistence

upon a national focus for suffrage soon developed into racist commentary that led many women, black and white, to leave the NWSA. In essays, poetry, and fiction, writers such as Harper, Sophia Alice Callahan, and Lucy Stone argued for an inclusive movement. In resistance to many racist attitudes expressed by some of the other members, Harper participated in the American Woman's Suffrage Association (AWSA). In 1913 Wells-Barnett organized the Alpha Suffrage Club to encourage African American women's commitment to suffrage. In the western states suffrage found its greatest acceptance: Wyoming granted suffrage in 1869, Utah in 1870, the Washington Territory in 1883, and Idaho in 1896. A national suffrage law that included all women was not enacted until 1920; women's writings in the period of 1870 to 1920 were highly influential in swaying the change in public opinion about women's right to vote.

Suffrage and labor were not the only reform movements in which women became active and about which they wrote with increasing fervor. The largest women's organization of the nineteenth century was the national Women's Christian Temperance Union (WCTU), founded in 1874. Its first president was Annie Turner Wittenmeyer, but Frances Willard, president from 1879 to her death in 1898, was the sustaining force of the union. Racism pervaded the WCTU just as it had the NWSA, and in the South many African American women formed the WCTU #2 or other statewide unions for black women. The issue of temperance pervaded women's literature and debates through the turn of the century. Religious organizations like the WCTU dominated women's groups at the end of the nineteenth century. In 1870 the Philadelphia Colored Women's Christian Association was founded, and in 1886 Julia Richman became the first president of the newly established Young Women's Hebrew Association. For Willard and other women of the period, involvement in social movements such as these gave them their first opportunity to write for a public audience.

Another large organizational movement in which thousands of women were involved in this era was the women's club movement. For educated Euramerican women, many of whom were still not a part of the workforce outside the home, clubs became a socially acceptable means of active participation in social movements. The club system was highly organized: in the 1890s the General Federation of Women's Clubs brought under its umbrella two hundred clubs representing twenty thousand women. As with the suffrage movement, however, most Euramerican women's clubs excluded women of color. African American women organized their own clubs; the National Association of

Colored Women, for example, was founded in 1896 by Mary Church Terrell as the umbrella organization for black women's clubs. While Native American women's organizations were not as numerous, significant associations did emerge, including the Women's National Indian Association (WNIA), founded in 1879 by Amelia S. Quinto and Mary L. Bonney. The WNIA was one of the most enduring organizations founded in this period. In 1888 the WNIA began publishing *Indian's Friend;* the periodical continued publication until 1951. Literature was an important element of clubs' activities: the study and writing of literature was a common activity, often as a means of increasing members' exposure to published literature, political essays, and scientific tracts. Some members advanced to publishing their essays and poetry in the national publications of the clubs.

Various charity organizations were developed or aided by women in this period, as reflected both in women's activities and women's writings advocating activist causes. Annie Adams Fields, best known as a literary salonist in the last half of the nineteenth century, was deeply involved in issues of public charity. In 1883 she published *How to Help the Poor,* a best-selling guide on how to centralize charity. The settlement house movement was another significant element in the politically motivated reform movements of the era. Addams and Ellen Starr instigated the settlement house movement with the establishment of Hull-House in Chicago in 1889. By 1900 approximately one hundred settlement houses had been established, mostly by women. In *Twenty Years at Hull House* (1910) Addams reflected upon the philosophy that had driven her to establish Hull House: the idea that social reform would best be implemented through social workers' settlement in the communities they sought to revive. Hull House was not only the social workers' residence; it became a center for political and civic group meetings and, at its height, recorded two thousand visitors a week.

All of these reform movements were part of the larger cultural shift that was tagged the "New Woman" movement at the end of the nineteenth century. While some women writers, including Gene Stratton-Porter, Laura Jean Libbey, and Emma Dunham Kelly, continued to advocate a conservative ideology, many women writers embraced the New Woman philosophy. In opposition to conservative ideologies of True Womanhood that had long posited women's roles as domestic and maternal, the New Woman sought to define her own sense of self rather than have it proscribed for her. The New Woman ideology encompassed various issues, but central was the reconstruction of womanhood to ensure economic and personal independence and public as well as private activism. The New

Woman philosophy was in currency approximately from 1890 to 1920 and emphasized women's physical abilities, intellectual acuity, and right to equality with men in labor and social endeavors. While writers advocating this radical philosophy exposed the varied limitations on women in turn-of-the-century U.S. culture, they also reimagined women's potential and offered a diverse spectrum of feminist perspectives on women's experiences. Thus, clearly autobiographically inspired novels, such as Mary Hunter Austin's *A Woman of Genius* (1912), appeared. So, too, did women's prose emerge that focused specifically on women's communities. In *The Country of the Pointed Firs* (1896) Sarah Orne Jewett examined older women's friendships in isolated rural regions; Gilman, on the other hand, envisioned a feminist utopia in *Herland* (1915).

The New Woman era also gave birth to political radicalism. Gilman, Emma Goldman, Alice James, and Wells-Barnett were among the more notable radicals who emerged in this era. Radicals came in varied forms. James, for instance, is a complex example of a radical: on the one hand, she was an oppressed woman existing in a family of famous men without asserting her own right to public recognition; on the other hand, she espoused political radicalism as an avid feminist, an advocate of Irish nationalism, and an advocate of the poor through her participation in the Female Humane Society. The diary was the most common form of women's prose writing in the nineteenth century. Most radicals, however, preferred a public voice. Thus, unlike James, Wells-Barnett was an outspoken and public antilynching campaigner and women's rights activist. *Southern Horrors* (1892) is an early compendium of her views. Goldman was a feminist and anarchist who wrote several books and founded *Mother Earth* in 1906 as a forum for radical essays of political, philosophical, and literary focus. Her various political actions, including advocacy of draft resistance in the pre–World War I era, led to her deportation to Russia in 1919. An advocate of free love, atheism, birth control, and free speech, Goldman's lectures (*Anarchism and Other Essays,* 1917), writings, and editorial role mark her lifelong commitment to individual freedoms and political resistance.

Freudian hypotheses, the New Woman movement, and other varied philosophical and cultural changes at the turn of the century also began to reshape attitudes about female sexuality, and the theme of sexuality became extremely popular in women's writings at the turn of the century. While Freeman suggests in stories such as "A New England Nun" (1891) and "Louisa" (1891) that a woman could live happily without marriage, Jewett began to explore the sexual nature of women's friendships in her short fiction. Gilman explicitly challenges the medical profession's oppression of women in "The Yellow Wallpaper" and explores woman-to-woman reproduction in *Herland*. Pauline Hopkins examines the issue of slavery as a rape culture and the source of the stereotypes of the African American woman as promiscuous. Like many African American women writers of the period, Hopkins posited marriage and motherhood as reconstructions of black female virtue against such stereotypes. Wells-Barnett recognized the complex sexual issues at work in the relation between the rape of slaves and the later mob lynchings of black men who were almost always accused of raping white women; while black women's virtue had been denied by custom and law during slavery, the lynchings reinforced white women's virtue and white men's marking of their sexual territory through violence. For the most part, women's literature of the period cautiously pushed the boundaries of the unsaid in relation to female sexuality, in both its positive and abused aspects. These early inroads paved the way for more-open expressions in the twentieth century.

Like female sexuality, issues of race and ethnicity were some of the most volatile themes addressed in women's prose writings of the period. Within the Caucasian population, class and language skills became markers of difference in this era of enormous immigration. From 1860 until the turn of the century, fourteen million immigrants came to the United States, significantly altering the ethnic makeup of the country. An unprecedented cultural change occurred in a relatively short period of time, and cultural conflicts emerged on many levels of social interaction. Arguments for a "melting pot" philosophy veiled assimilationist attitudes, while new immigrants were challenged by altering senses of identity and cultural dislocation. Not since the years of the Middle Passage slave trade had the ethnic composition of the nation changed so visibly. Women writers of all races struggled with these issues, but perhaps most significant to the changing face of literature was the production of writings that focused on immigrant experiences. Yezierska, for instance, was a Polish Russian Jew who immigrated to New York City in 1890. Her first book, *Hungry Hearts and Other Stories* (1920), depicts authentic experiences of the immigrant ghetto life.

This era of ethnic diversity also allowed many ethnic and religious groups that had long been inhabitants of the United States to emerge as significant public and literary voices, a circumstance especially true for Jewish Americans. Jews had settled in the New World in the eighteenth century, but the mass migration of Eastern European Jews in the late nineteenth century triggered several autobiographical narratives that variously demonstrated the sense of connection maintained

between European and U.S. Jews at that time. Mary Antin's writings capture both experiences. *From Plotzk to Boston* (1899) is the immigrant's autobiography of relocation, while her enormously successful *The Promised Land* reflects a vision of hope for the country, even in the period of cultural unrest following the Spanish-American War. Martha Wolfenstein was the first Jewish American woman writer to publish stories with Jewish characters in mainstream, secular literary magazines such as *Lippincott's* and *Outlook*. Her short stories were collected in *Idylls of the Gass* (1901) and *The Renegade and Other Stories* (1905).

For Native Americans, issues of race were addressed in their literary productions in quite different ways from that of African Americans or the many newly arrived immigrants. The westward movement in the years after the Civil War greatly affected Native American tribal and national sovereignty. The pressure to assimilate was a political as well as a cultural factor. There had long been mostly passive responses by Euramericans to Native American removal, yet the 1877 forced march of the Poncas from the Dakota Territory to Indian Territory led to increased voices of resistance. While the government continued assimilationist and eradication measures, including the General Allotment Act of 1887, which eliminated Native American rights to own tribal lands collectively, writers began to use the power of their pens to protest such actions.

Many Euramerican women, including Helen Hunt Jackson, author of *A Century of Dishonor* (1881) and *Ramona* (1884), argued on behalf of Native American rights, but the most sustained literary and political endeavors came from Native Americans themselves. In resistance to the eradication of tribal sovereignty and to educational systems of assimilation, Native writers began a revival of interest in Native cultures. Some of the earliest protest literature came from the Omaha Ponca Committee, in response to the forced march of the Poncas to Indian Territory in Oklahoma. Autobiographical narratives were especially significant in detailing both the changes encountered and the survival of cultural beliefs and practices. *Our Monthly* was established in 1870 by Presbyterian missionaries who ran the Tullahassee Manual Labor School in the Creek Nation, but the periodical became an early outlet for Creek writers. Suzette LaFlesche (Inshata Theumba), a member of the Omaha tribe, lectured on wrongs against Native Americans and in the 1880s edited the *Weekly Independent,* a Populist newspaper. Several other periodicals emerged as well, including the *Baconian,* a literary journal published from 1898 until 1907 at the Bacone Indian University near Muskogee. Myrta Eddleman Sams and Ora V. Eddleman Reed, Cherokee sisters, were instrumental in establishing the Native American press through the founding and editing of *Twin Territories: The Indian Magazine of Oklahoma* at the turn of the century.

Although short fiction, essays, and poetry dominated the Native American press, Sophia Alice Callahan emerged as the first known Native American woman to publish a novel. Of Creek and Euramerican heritage, Callahan published *Wynema: A Child of the Forest* in 1891. While many of the Native American publications were for a Native audience, Callahan's novel was intended for a diverse readership. The novel demonstrates the complex cultural negotiations necessary for a Native American woman writer and for all people of color in a white-dominated society. Written four months after the Massacre at Wounded Knee, *Wynema* is an important text in Native American responses to that event. Written from 1913 to 1916, Mourning Dove's *Cogewea* (1927) was also intended for a mixed audience, but it presents the story of "a half-blood" girl's struggle to negotiate between Native Americans and the cattle ranchers in Montana. Like her other work, *Coyote Stories* (1933), which is an edited version of her earlier *Okanogan Sweathouse* collection, *Cogewea* is rich with Okanogan folklore and is presented from the Native American point of view.

Many African Americans had used literature for both creative and political purposes prior to Reconstruction, but the postwar years constitute a national renaissance of African American literature that extended to the seminal Harlem Renaissance of the 1920s and 1930s. Rather than silencing African American writers, events such as the racial backlash after Reconstruction, the increasingly segregated nature of the country in the wake of *Plessy* v. *Ferguson* (which established the "separate but equal" doctrine in 1896), the subsequent Jim Crow laws that segregated all public and private facilities, and the revival of the Ku Klux Klan in 1915 acted as an impetus to their increased literary productivity. The pen became the sword of resistance.

The African American press flourished between 1870 and 1920. By 1891 the African American publishing industry was developed to a degree that it warranted a full-length study, *The Afro-American Press and Its Editors* (1891), which included a section titled "Our Women in Journalism." Several major black newspapers of the period (including the *Boston Advocate,* the *Washington Bee,* and the *Cleveland Gazette*) were important outlets for women journalists. The *Repository of Religion and Literature and of Science and the Arts,* founded by the African Methodist Episcopal Church in 1858, continued to be a major source for women writers, as did the *Woman's Era,* founded in 1894 by members of the National Federation of Afro-American Women. The

Woman's Era was a particularly significant publication, headed by Josephine St. Pierre Ruffin. The monthly was a central publishing force in voicing African American women's political visions.

Charlotte Spears Bass became the first African American woman newspaper editor in North America as editor of the *California Eagle.* The kinds of publications in which African American women were involved were as varied as the women themselves: the radical activist Lucy Parsons was editor and publisher of the monthly *Freedom: A Revolutionary Anarchist-Communist Monthly,* while Julia Ringwood Coston took on the same roles with *Ringwood's Afro-American Journal of Fashion.* The emergence in 1900 of the *Colored American Magazine* (1900–1909), a literary periodical founded by Boston's Colored Cooperative Publishing Company, gave writers significant new opportunities, including Pauline Hopkins's position as columnist for the women's section of the journal.

Several African American women gained notable fame in these years. Hopkins became a major force among African Americans in novel writing (*Contending Forces,* 1900), while Wells-Barnett emerged as one of the most outspoken critics of racism in U.S. society. Hopkins, Wells, and Harper, all of whom have become well-known in literary critical circles, were colleagues with other significant writers who are perhaps less well-known but who contributed to the African American reconstruction of racial representations. Victoria Earle Matthews, a journalist who was also active in women's organizational movements, published *Aunt Lindy* in 1893, the same year that Amanda Smith published *An Autobiography,* which recounted her life as an internationally renowned evangelist, while Emma Dunham Kelley's *Medga* (1891) presented the story of young Baptist women's conversion experiences.

Minority groups other than Native Americans and African Americans also presented voices of resistance and alternative social visions in this era. Although the literature of early Chicana writers has received little critical attention in U.S. studies to date, Mexican American writers explored historical and autobiographical narratives, short stories, novels, and folklore as genres appropriate to their realistic or imaginative interests. María Amparo Ruiz de Burton published two novels in the nineteenth century that reflect her acute awareness of the attitudes many Euramericans held toward the people of Mexico. *Who Would Have Thought It?* (1872) is a biting satire of Northern racism and religious hypocrisy, published during Reconstruction and in opposition to the representation of the North as the environment of freedom and equality. In 1885 Ruiz de Burton published *The Squatter and The Don,* an examination of Mexican and U.S. relations in 1870s California; it continued her indictment of political and social structures in the United States.

Of the 14 million immigrants who came to the United States between 1860 and 1900, only about 300,000 were Asian. Chinese immigrants (who constituted approximately 264,000 of the Asian immigrants) were the primary labor force for the transcontinental railroad, but the completion of the railroad had devastating economic and racist results for this particular group of immigrants. They were barred from most kinds of labor, and increasing tensions led to mob violence in 1871 when a group of Euramericans in San Francisco attacked Chinese American laborers, killing twenty-one people. Economic downswings coupled with increased racism led in 1882 to the Chinese Exclusion Act. Japanese immigrants, while certainly subject to racist attitudes, were not subject to these restrictions, largely because they did not constitute an economic threat to other workers and because it seemed to many citizens that they were more willing to assimilate. The Eaton sisters, Edith and Winnifred, were writers of Chinese and English heritage who personified the cultural conflicts surrounding Asian Americans in the late nineteenth and early twentieth centuries.

Publishing under the name of Sui Sin Far, Edith Eaton was a journalist and fiction writer (*Mrs. Spring Fragrance,* 1912) who courageously insisted upon her Chinese heritage in an era of rampant Sinophobia. She exposed Americans' racist attitudes at the same time that she delved into the complexities of Chinese Americans' lives in the United States. Winnifred Eaton, on the other hand, chose to pass as Japanese American. Publishing under the name of Onoto Watanna, she became a best-selling novelist at the turn of the century with such successful works as *Miss Numé of Japan* (1899) and *A Japanese Nightingale* (1901). In widely divergent manners, the Eaton sisters reflect the variety of responses to racism that women of color adopted in these volatile years.

Racial and ethnic issues necessarily raise the issue of U.S. imperialism in the late nineteenth and early twentieth centuries. Earlier decades had seen major westward movements, and in the last half of the nineteenth century Americans demonstrated a resurgence of interest in settling in the West. The Homestead Act of 1862 had begun the process anew, but it took on a wide range of developments after 1870: metropolises such as San Francisco boomed, and mining towns and cattle towns emerged. Single women seeking employment, married women beginning new lives with their families, suffragists seeking new opportunities for legislation, immigrants seeking better livelihoods and land ownership, women of color seeking less traditional forms of employment and opportunities for independence—all accepted the challenge of the New West.

Women writers thrived under this new endeavor, as they captured life in these previously unheralded regions in their texts. Mary Hallock Foote's *The Led-Horse Claim* (1883), for instance, is one of the first novels to depict the life of western mining towns, while Mary Hunter Austin recounts her family's move from Los Angeles to the San Joaquin Valley in *One Hundred Miles on Horseback* (1889). Austin became a regular contributor to the *Overland Monthly,* a periodical devoted to representations of the New West. A highly romanticized representation of the West, however, was perpetuated at home and abroad. Women both resisted or participated in imperialistic endeavors, and they used the increased interest in travel that accompanied imperialism to publish a massive amount of travel narratives in this period. Some travel narratives were little more than personalized diaries, but Susan Hale combined travel with historical research to produce a series of successful narratives, including *The Story of Mexico* (1889). Constance Cary Harrison, on the other hand, produced several novels, including *The Anglomaniacs* (1890) and *Good Americans* (1898), that satirized U.S. citizens traveling in Europe.

One of the early-twentieth-century reactions to the U.S. and other countries' imperialist activities was the international peace movement. Activists and writers in the movement included Addams (*Newer Ideals of Peace,* 1907) and Crystal Eastman, who founded the Woman's Peace Party of New York in 1914 and cofounded the National Woman's Peace Party in 1915. The NWPP became the Women's International League for Peace and Freedom in 1922 and has remained in existence since.

From Reconstruction to the prelude to World War I, from literary realism and regionalism to the emergence of modernism, from women's struggles for participation in all public endeavors to the right to vote, the period of 1870 to 1920 was marked by enormous cultural changes in a relatively short period of time. This volume seeks to capture some of those changes and to highlight the ways in which women responded through literature not only to such changes but also to the opportunity for written expression itself. Whether imaginative or realistic, fiction or nonfiction, women's literature became a cultural force in this period. Writers such as Cather, Wharton, and Chopin have long been recognized for their literary contributions to U.S. arts. But the breadth of aesthetic, political, and thematic visions of women writers in the period of 1870 to 1920 is represented in this volume. The inclusion of María Amparo Ruiz de Burton, Amelia Johnson, Susan Hale, and other writers who previously have been marginalized in U.S. literary studies–and who represent hundreds of other notable writers of the period–should remind readers of the diverse perspectives that are represented in American literature at the turn of the century.

–Sharon M. Harris, Heidi L. M. Jacobs, Jennifer Putzi

Acknowledgments

This book was produced by Bruccoli Clark Layman, Inc. Karen L. Rood is senior editor for the *Dictionary of Literary Biography* series. Charles Brower and Carol A. Fairman were the in-house editors.

Production manager is Philip B. Dematteis.

Administrative support was provided by Ann M. Cheschi and Dawnca T. Williams.

Accountant is Kathy Weston. Accounting assistant is Angi Pleasant.

Copyediting supervisor is Phyllis A. Avant. Senior copyeditor is Thom Harman. The copyediting staff includes Brenda Carol Blanton, James Denton, Worthy B. Evans, Melissa D. Hinton, William Tobias Mathes, and Jennifer S. Reid. Freelance copyeditor is Rebecca Mayo.

Editorial associates are Margo Dowling and Richard K. Galloway.

Layout and graphics supervisor is Janet E. Hill. Graphics staff includes Karla Corley Brown and Zoe R. Cook.

Office manager is Kathy Lawler Merlette.

Photography editors are Charles Mims, Scott Nemzek, and Paul Talbot. Digital photographic copy work was performed by Joseph M. Bruccoli and Zoe R. Cook.

SGML supervisor is Cory McNair. The SGML staff includes Tim Bedford, Linda Drake, Frank Graham, and Alex Snead.

Systems manager is Marie L. Parker.

Typesetting supervisor is Kathleen M. Flanagan. The typesetting staff includes Kimberly Kelly, Mark J. McEwan, Patricia Flanagan Salisbury, and Alison Smith. Freelance typesetter is Delores Plastow.

Walter W. Ross did library research. He was assisted by Steven Gross and the following librarians at the Thomas Cooper Library of the University of South Carolina: circulation department head Tucker Taylor; reference department head Virginia W. Weathers; Brette Barclay, Marilee Birchfield, Paul Cammarata, Gary Geer, Michael Macan, Tom Marcil, and Sharon Verba, reference librarians; interlibrary loan department head John Brunswick; and Robert Arndt, Jo Cottingham, Hayden Battle, Marna Hostetler, Nelson Rivera, Marieum McClary, and Erika Peake, interlibrary loan staff.

Jean Carwile Masteller wishes to credit the Houghton Library, Harvard University, for permission to quote from Laura Jean Libbey's letters.

Dictionary of Literary Biography® • Volume Two Hundred Twenty-One

American Women Prose Writers, 1870–1920

Dictionary of Literary Biography

Octavia Albert

(24 December 1853 – ca. 1889)

Phoebe Jackson
Michigan State University

BOOK: *The House of Bondage; or, Charlotte Brooks and Other Slaves* (New York: Hunt & Eaton / Cincinnati: Cranston & Stowe, 1890).

Because of her critical engagement with social issues that confronted African Americans at the turn of the century, Octavia Albert's *The House of Bondage; or, Charlotte Brooks and Other Slaves* (1890) remains an important historical work. Albert's concern that the history of African American enslavement be remembered led her to interview former slaves in Louisiana. These interviews vividly depict both the struggles and successes of ordinary people who lived through the years of slavery.

Albert's own life spans the crucial years of slavery and Reconstruction. Octavia Victoria Rogers was born a slave on 24 December 1853 in Oglethorpe, Georgia. The details of her early family life are unknown. After emancipation she was able to attend Atlanta University, where she trained to be a teacher. She accepted her first teaching position in Montezuma, Georgia, where she met the Reverend A. E. P. Albert, a fellow teacher and newly ordained minister. They were married on 21 October 1874 and had one daughter, Laura. Albert moved to Houma, Louisiana, with her husband, where he assumed the ministry. In Houma, Albert befriended local people, all former slaves, who became the subjects for the interviews that she conducted over the course of approximately thirteen years. Albert apparently suffered an untimely death, the circumstances of which are not known; the preface to *The House of Bondage,* authored by her husband and daughter, implies that she died in 1889.

Initially, Albert's work was published posthumously as a series of articles printed in the *South-west-*

Octavia Albert (from The House of Bondage; or, Charlotte Brooks and Other Slaves, *1890)*

ern Christian Advocate from January to December 1890. At the time, according to I. Garland Penn in his *The Afro-American Press and Its Editors* (1891), the *Advocate,* an organ of the Methodist Church, had "the largest circulation of any paper in New Orleans" and was read by both white and black audiences. In the preface to *The House of Bondage* the Reverend Albert writes that because the series received such a favorable reception, the editor was encouraged to publish it in book form. Late in 1890 *The House of Bondage* was published in both New York and Cincinnati. By reaching an even wider audience, Albert achieved a goal she set out to accomplish—to ensure that the history of African American slavery not be forgotten.

In 1878 Albert began the first of her many interviews with former slaves. At the start of her book, she explains her reason for undertaking such a project, that "the half was never told concerning this race that was in bondage nearly two hundred and fifty years." Albert asserts that the status of African Americans in her day, their illiteracy and impoverished condition, can be attributed to their former masters, who felt little obligation or responsibility toward them. Though they preached the Scriptures and attended church regularly, white plantation owners treated their slaves like brutes.

Albert's interviews begin with a woman named Charlotte Brooks, whom the narrator calls Aunt Charlotte. In the interview the narrator asks Aunt Charlotte direct questions; the questions are recorded along with her informant's responses. When asked, for example, how she is feeling at the beginning of the interview, Aunt Charlotte responds that her bones still ache from the years she spent as a slave working long hours in the sugarcane fields. Such seemingly innocuous questions offer the opportunity to review the physical abuse that many slaves sustained at the hands of their masters. Thus, the reader also learns that Aunt Charlotte was sold three times and that she had a child who died when he was two years old.

Interwoven into the narrative of Aunt Charlotte's life are the stories of other slaves whom she befriends. Aunt Charlotte describes her first meeting with Aunt Jane Lee, who, like herself, was originally from Virginia. The appearance of Aunt Jane figures prominently in Aunt Charlotte's life, as she is the person who brings the Protestant religion to the slaves in Catholic Louisiana. Aunt Jane's ability to read Scripture enables the other slaves such as Aunt Charlotte to begin practicing and ultimately maintain their Protestant religion. Aunt Charlotte's recollection of Aunt Jane segues into another story about Nellie Johnson, Sam Wilson, and Richard, all of whom had the courage to run away. Their stories offer examples of slaves refusing to give up their own humanity even though such resistance could have dire consequences for them, as they were usually beaten if they were returned to their masters.

After finishing Aunt Charlotte's story, which is the longest in the book, Albert continues to interview other slaves whom she has met in Houma. This middle section of the book includes interviews with John and his second wife, Lorendo, Sallie Smith, and Uncle Stephen Jordan. Their stories detail the experiences of being separated from one's family, of running away from one's master, and of being sold along with cattle. These are also stories of the extraordinary perseverance of people who, though treated inhumanely, managed to survive. Toward the latter part of the book Albert interviews three people who, after emancipation, have successfully risen into the black middle class.

By recording the lives of so many slaves, Albert departs from the traditional slave narrative that emphasizes the life of one individual. Instead, her text represents a community of voices, where the lives of individual slaves necessarily intersect with one another. Because their lives are intricately woven together, Aunt Charlotte cannot tell her story without including the stories of other people who formed her community. As such, unlike the traditional slave narrative, Albert's interviews underscore dramatically the collective impact of slavery.

The House of Bondage demonstrates the influence of regionalism and local color that was popular in the United States during the latter half of the nineteenth century. The people Albert interviews, for example, are ordinary individuals whose stories poignantly illustrate the day-to-day travails they had endured during slavery. In recording their dialogue Albert attempts to include aspects of their regional dialect. Given the opportunity, she also explains customs peculiar to the South, such as addressing an older person as "uncle" or "aunt" as a form of respect. More important, for her purposes, Albert seems insistent upon highlighting the different religious practices between the Protestants of Virginia and the Catholics of Louisiana, who, among other things, made their slaves work on the Sabbath. At various points during her interviews Albert's subjects request that she cite a hymn; in other instances, they recall a song from their slave days, all of which are duly recorded. Such occurrences help to bridge the gap between the interviewer and her interviewee, making their accounts more personalized.

While Albert's book bespeaks the influence of regionalism and local color, it stands clearly in opposition to the literature emerging from the plantation school. During the 1880s fiction that reconciled the differences between the North and South gained in popularity. Novelists such as Thomas Nelson Page and Joel Chandler Harris rewrote the relationship between slaves and their owners, creating the so-called plantation myth, which tended to romanticize life on the plantations. In their depictions blacks are loyal servants who get along well with their masters. By contrast, Albert's interviews with former slaves offer an alternative version of the events that took place. Aunt Charlotte's description of Ella, for example, who was tied up and left to die by her mistress, disabuses the reader of any romantic notions about plantation life. As such, Albert's text stands as an unequivocal refutation of a newly mythologized South.

Much like antebellum slave narratives, *The House of Bondage* includes prefatory "authenticating testimonials"; their inclusion serves a wholly different purpose, however: they bespeak the position and condition of women writing during the nineteenth century. After all, according to the ideology of True Womanhood prevalent at the time, women best served themselves and their families by tending to domestic affairs. Though the twentieth-century historian John W. Blassingame characterized Albert as one of the "few well-trained interviewers" of her time, her publishers nevertheless deemed it necessary to include three prefaces that speak not only to Albert's experiential and educational qualifications but also to her womanly attributes so important during the time. The first prefatory remarks begin with her family members. In the words of her husband and her daughter, Albert was a "precious and devoted mother and wife," whose moral character still influences and guides them in life. The somewhat longer introduction by the well-known minister Willard F. Mallalieu attests to the fact that Albert had experienced "the accursed system" of slavery firsthand. Finally, an unnamed "Compiler" chronicles a short biographical sketch that cites Albert's academic credentials. Like the other two entries, the Compiler also reaffirms that Albert "was an angel of mercy." Taken together, all three prefaces suggest that Albert's interviews are a manifestation of a Christian woman whose moral forthrightness influenced her to write.

Because hers is a postbellum narrative, Albert does not limit herself to a discussion of slavery and its abuses. Instead, she extends the narrative to include the achievements that blacks have attained both before and after emancipation. In the last third of the book, she interviews people such as Colonel Douglass Wilson, who tells her how "the colored troops fought nobly" during the Civil War. She also records the successes of the black middle class. For example, Albert interviews Uncle Cephas, who describes how he learned to read and write when such ventures were commonly disallowed by slave owners. Eventually Uncle Cephas earned his freedom and began a suc-

THE HOUSE OF BONDAGE

OR

CHARLOTTE BROOKS AND OTHER SLAVES

ORIGINAL AND LIFE-LIKE, AS THEY APPEARED IN THEIR
OLD PLANTATION AND CITY SLAVE LIFE; TOGETHER
WITH PEN-PICTURES OF THE PECULIAR INSTI-
TUTION, WITH SIGHTS AND INSIGHTS
INTO THEIR NEW RELATIONS
AS FREEDMEN, FREEMEN,
AND CITIZENS

BY

MRS. OCTAVIA V. ROGERS ALBERT

WITH AN INTRODUCTION

BY

REV. BISHOP WILLARD F. MALLALIEU, D.D.

NEW YORK: HUNT & EATON
CINCINNATI: CRANSTON & STOWE
1890

Title page for Albert's collection of interviews with former slaves

cessful blacksmithing business. Soon thereafter, he helped other slaves to gain their freedom, who in turn achieved their own successes in fields such as politics and medicine. By interviewing people from the black middle class, Albert seems acutely aware of the necessity of demonstrating the achievements of African Americans during Reconstruction. Since many former slaves had made little economic progress but continued to be financially indebted to their southern employers, these accounts of successful African Americans illustrate that some people were able to overcome the legacy of the abuses of slavery. As Albert remarks to Colonel Wilson, "I believe we should not only treasure these things, but should transmit them to our children's children."

While much of her book is devoted to interviewing poor, illiterate former slaves, these final chapters suggest a different vision of the African American experience after Reconstruction, one in which Albert can include herself as a subject. Albert's own middle-class position is obvious throughout her text because of the difference in language between herself and her interviewees. While her subjects use a regional dialect, her conversation bespeaks her university education. In these last interviews Albert demonstrates her own familiarity with others of the black middle class. Because of her husband's position as a minister, Albert's social circle includes many successful African Americans. For example, she interviews Wilson, "a colored man of considerable prominence not only in Louisiana but in the nation," when both of their families are vacationing at the same "popular water-place on the Mississippi Sound."

At the end of *The House of Bondage* Albert describes attending two prominent events of the nineteenth century: the Cotton Centennial Exposition in New Orleans in 1884 and the General Conference of the Methodist Episcopal Church in New York City in 1888. She reports that the representatives present at the General Conference had come from all over the world and included "fifty-three colored delegates." Albert ably demonstrates her active participation in the black middle class by citing with obvious familiarity the names of the people in attendance at a reception given by the wife of General U. S. Grant for the black delegates of the conference. Impressed with the eloquence of the Reverend Doctor Daniel Minors's talk to the assembly, Albert tries to recall for her audience the entirety of his speech. Minors's speech, which Albert describes as "a real masterpiece of polished eloquence," is yet another example of the achievements made by former slaves. By describing the events of both poor, illiterate slaves and the successful black middle class like herself, Albert illustrates the range of African American experience during the late nineteenth century. Moreover, her examples also suggest, as Frances Smith Foster has aptly remarked, that the existence of the lower class has more to do with "a situation of chance than of choice."

Throughout *The House of Bondage* the subject of religion figures prominently. For many of the slaves religion was key to their survival in bondage. As Aunt Charlotte remarks, "My heavenly Father took care of me in slave-time. He led me all the way along, and now he has set me free, and I am free both in soul and body." Religion continues to be the key to their survival after emancipation. Regardless of the poverty and hunger she still endures, Aunt Charlotte opines, "true, we can't get anything to eat sometimes, but trials make us pray more." Moreover, during slavery, religion helps the slaves to adhere to important moral values. Thus, Richard, a friend of Aunt Charlotte's and a fellow Christian, refuses to marry another

woman at his master's urging when he already has a wife on a different plantation. Because of his commitment to his wife, Richard suffers repeated beatings when he dares to "slip off" to go visit her. In another narrative God intercedes on behalf of runaway slaves Sallie and her brother, Warren, because of their enduring faith. Throughout their time in the woods, Sallie and Warren never cease praying to God. As a result, when they are eventually caught, their mistress declines to beat them but instead gives them breakfast. Such accounts not only demonstrate the importance of religious devotion but also serve to reinforce it.

Though religion is central to Albert's text, she questions the hypocrisy of white southern Christians during slavery. She wonders at the treatment that white Christians could deliver to their slaves. As she remarks to Aunt Charlotte, "when I pause and think over the hard punishments of the slaves by the whites, many of whom professed to be Christians, I am filled with amazement." Albert reminds her readers that even after emancipation white southern Christians continue to take advantage of their black workers. Aunt Charlotte explains that the planters pay low wages to their workers and then entice them to spend their money on whiskey, ensuring that they never get ahead. On an institutional level, Albert questions the vision and the willingness of the Methodist and Baptist Churches to send missionaries to other countries when there are so many poor people in their midst who might be saved. She finds it a mystery that white Christians are reluctant "to extend a helping hand to these needy souls who have served them so long and faithfully."

Albert's interviews also illustrate that the cruelty exacted by white southern Christians knew no limits. In his interview with Albert, Uncle John describes the abuses that Yankee soldiers had to endure while imprisoned in Andersonville, Georgia. As he explains, runaway white prisoners were routinely run down and set upon by bloodhounds, exactly like the slaves for whom they were fighting. Moreover, in the summer months, thousands of Yankee soldiers died from exposure to the sun. According to Brother Samson, who worked at the Andersonville stockade, "the wagons used to run night and day burying the prisoners in the warm season." These accounts lead Albert to wonder at the extent of human debasement "where religion abounds, and where the Gospel was preached Sunday after Sunday."

While Albert could critique the hypocrisy of white southern Christians toward blacks and white Yankees, she registers a palpable abhorrence on the topic of Catholicism. In that vein Albert shares a distinctly anti-Catholic attitude that was prevalent during the turn of the century when Catholics, along with Eastern European Jews and southeastern Europeans, experienced the wrath of nativist fears. In her book, the Catholics of Louisiana come under particular disparagement because they forced their slaves to work on Sunday rather than allowing them to go to church. Aunt Charlotte explains that when she tried to pray, she was whipped by "marster" for doing so. The narrator also reminds her audience that the Catholic Church was opposed to emancipation and that "the pope was the only power in the world that recognized the Confederacy."

At the end of the book Albert demonstrates an awareness of novelistic devices. Though she has conducted her interviews over a period of thirteen years, her book comes full circle with the last chapter titled "A Touching Incident." Albert describes her visit to the Cotton Centennial Exposition of 1884, where she heard the great orator Reverend Doctor Coleman Lee. When she later asks him about his past, she learns that his mother had come from Virginia and was Jane Lee, whom Charlotte Brooks had held in such high esteem. Jane Lee, also attending the convention, overhears their conversation and introduces herself as his mother; thus a family broken apart by the inhumanity of slavery is once again reunited. By reintroducing Jane Lee, the ending of the book effectively recalls the beginning and, more important, the community of people who shared and endured the history of slavery.

The House of Bondage continues to be an important postbellum account of slavery. As an historical document, Albert's book notably chronicles the recollections of seven former slaves while at the same time underscoring the collective impact of slavery. Her text, appearing years after the Civil War, provides a vivid reminder of the necessity to continue to tell stories about the enslavement of the African American people.

References:

John W. Blassingame, ed., *Slave Testimony: Two Centuries of Letters, Speeches, Interviews, and Autobiographies* (Baton Rouge: Louisiana State University Press, 1977), pp. lxi–lxii;

Frances Smith Foster, Introduction to *The House of Bondage* (New York: Oxford University Press, 1988), pp. xxvii–xliii;

Foster, *Written by Herself: Literary Production by African American Women, 1746–1892* (Bloomington: Indiana University Press, 1993), pp. 154–177;

M. A. Majors, *Noted Negro Women, Their Triumphs and Activities* (Chicago: Donohue & Henneberry, 1893), pp. 219–227;

James Olney, "'I Was Born': Slave Narratives, Their Status as Autobiography and as Literature," in *The Slave's Narrative,* edited by Charles T. Davis and Henry Louis Gates Jr. (New York: Oxford University Press, 1985), pp. 148–175;

I. Garland Penn, *The Afro-American Press and Its Editors* (Springfield, Mass.: Willey, 1891), pp. 223–227.

Mary Antin
(13 June 1881 – 15 May 1949)

Betty Bergland
University of Wisconsin–River Falls

See also the Antin entry in *Yearbook 1984.*

BOOKS: *From Plotzk to Boston* (Boston: Clarke, 1899);
The Promised Land (Boston: Houghton Mifflin, 1912);
They Who Knock at Our Gates: A Complete Gospel of Immigration (Boston & New York: Houghton Mifflin, 1914).
Edition: *The Promised Land,* foreword by Oscar Handlin (Boston: Houghton Mifflin, 1969).

SELECTED PERIODICAL PUBLICATIONS–
UNCOLLECTED:
FICTION
"Malinke's Atonement," *Atlantic Monthly,* 108 (September 1911): 300–319;
"The Amulet," *Atlantic Monthly,* 111 (January 1913): 31–41;
"The Lie," *Atlantic Monthly,* 112 (August 1913): 177–190.
NONFICTION
"First Aid to the Alien," *Outlook,* 101 (29 June 1912): 481–485;
"How I Wrote *The Promised Land,*" *New York Times Book Review,* 30 June 1912, p. 392;
"A Woman to Her Fellow Citizens," *Outlook,* 102 (2 November 1912): 482–486;
"A Confession of Faith," *Boston Jewish Advocate* (15 February 1917): 5;
"His Soul Goes Marching On," *Berkshire Courier,* 91 (14 May 1925): 1;
"The Soundless Trumpet," *Atlantic Monthly,* 159 (April 1937): 560–569;
"House of the One Father," *Common Ground,* 1 (Spring 1941): 36–42.

Mary Antin (American Jewish Historical Society)

Mary Antin occupies a central place in American prose writings on immigration and is most identified with her 1912 autobiography, *The Promised Land.* Written and published in the pre–World War I period of mass immigration and Americanization, the work came to represent for much of the twentieth century not just the story of a Russian Jewish immigrant girl but the experience of Americanization itself. In the wake of an ethnic revival, Houghton Mifflin republished the work in 1969 with an introduction by Oscar Handlin, and by 1985, when the Princeton University Press reprinted the volume, the original 1912 publication had gone through thirty-four printings and sold eighty-five thousand copies. In 1997 Penguin released an edition that reproduced for the first time since 1912 the eighteen black-and-white photographs from the original. In addition, excerpts from Antin's autobiography can be found in both primary- and secondary-school textbooks throughout the century. Scholars have described Antin's narrative in broad terms. Albert E. Stone writes that "*The Promised Land* dramatizes the historical experience of Americanization in frankly mythic terms," arguing that Antin "represents herself as the prototypical immigrant transformed into a new self." James Craig Holte concludes that "Mary Antin provides an example of Americanization at its best," and because the work has been so widely read and received, Mary V. Dearborn writes that it has become "an immigrant classic." While *The Promised Land* is often equated with Antin's life, it excludes most of her mature life with its greater complexities. In the late twentieth century, interdisciplinary scholarship focused on issues of gender, and ethnicity has led to a renewed interest in Antin and a reassessment of her life and work.

Born 13 June 1881 in Polotzk, Russia, to Esther Weltman and Israel Antin, Mary was named Maryashe and nicknamed Mashinke or Mashke. Her mother was the only child of an unusually prosperous businessman. As a young girl Esther assisted her father in his business, managing the accounting as well as Russian and Polish customers, but at age sixteen a marriage was arranged for her with Israel Antin. Though from a less prosperous family, Antin had distinguished himself in scholarship and study for the rabbinate. When Esther's father died in 1885, she inherited the family business. Antin, who had left his studies, joined his wife in the enterprise, and for some years the family thrived in Polotzk.

Mary Antin writes in her autobiography that they lived well in the early years of her life: her parents worked in the store and employed servants for the domestic chores, and tutors were hired for the oldest children, Frieda and Mary, who studied Hebrew, Russian, German, and arithmetic. During this period two more children, Joseph and Deborah, were born. However, illness struck the family: first Israel, then the children, and finally Esther, who was bedridden for two years. Rising medical bills eventually led to financial ruin. Their financial struggles, in combination with anti-Semitic policies and pogroms that prevailed in Russia at the time, ultimately compelled the Antins to emigrate, along with a mass migration of Eastern European Jews at the end of the nineteenth and early twentieth centuries.

Polotzk, located on the Dvina River, which flows into the Baltic Sea in the province of Vitebsk, existed within the Pale of Settlement, an area of land where Jews were permitted to reside. Located between the Baltic and Black Seas, the Pale was created by the Imperial Russian government after the third partition of Poland in 1795. Historically, the city of Polotzk existed under various rules (Kievan Russian, Mongolian, Lithuanian, and Polish), but it was annexed by Russia in 1772. A center of Hasidic Judaism, Polotzk had a population of more than twenty thousand in the 1897 census, of which 61 percent was Jewish. In the year Antin was born, Czar Alexander II was assassinated in St. Petersburg and was succeeded by Alexander III, whose more repressive anti-Jewish policies led to the first major wave of Jewish emigration. In 1891 Israel Antin emigrated to the United States during the second wave. For three years he labored in the United States while his family remained in Polotzk; during that time Frieda and Mary ended their studies and became apprentices in a milliner's shop. In 1894 Antin sent for his four children and their mother.

In Boston, Israel Antin enrolled three of his children (Mary, Deborah, and Joseph) in the Chelsea Public School, while Frieda went to work in a garment factory. For him, like many immigrants, education meant hope for the next generation. Thus, to extend Mary's formal education in America, Antin told school officials his daughter was eleven, not thirteen, and since Mary was small of stature, the claim was credible. Later, Antin fictionalized this event in her story "The Lie" (*Atlantic Monthly,* August 1913). The importance of school for the Antin family is conveyed throughout her writings, but especially in her description of the first day in school. In *The Promised Land* Antin writes: "I think Miss Nixon guessed what my father's best English could not convey. I think she divined that by the simple act of delivering our school certificates to her he took possession of America." Denied formal education in Russia as a Jew and as a girl, Antin thrived and excelled in school. She completed first through fourth grades in half a year. In fifth grade she found a mentor and friend in her teacher, Miss Dillingham, who submitted Antin's poem "Snow" to the journal *Primary Education.* Upon seeing her name in print, Antin was determined to become a writer. Her poetry appeared in newspapers such as the *Boston Herald* and the *Transcript.* At her grammar-school graduation ceremony in 1897 she was presented as a model of what the American system of free education could do for an immigrant.

Antin caught the attention of Jewish leaders in Boston, including Hattie L. Hecht. Hecht introduced her to Philip Cowen, editor of the weekly *American Hebrew,* through whom Antin met Josephine Lazarus, sister of the American poet and activist Emma Lazarus. Hecht persuaded Cowen to arrange for the publication of a letter Antin wrote in the summer of 1894 to her maternal uncle Moshe Hayyim Weltman in Polotzk about the six-week journey to Boston. It was translated from Yiddish into English with the help of Rabbi

Page from Antin's 1894 letter to her uncle Moshe Hayyim Weltman in Russia, which was published in 1899 as From Plotzk to Boston *(courtesy of the Trustees of the Boston Public Library)*

Solomon Schindler and published in 1899 as *From Plotzk to Boston*. The British writer Israel Zangwill, who later examined the immigrant experience in his drama *The Melting Pot* (1909), wrote the introduction for the book.

Zangwill refers to Antin as the "infant phenomenon" in his introduction, stating that she was eleven when she wrote the letters. Actually thirteen in 1894, Antin nevertheless evokes the enthusiasm of a young girl and the immediacy of a recent journey. Zangwill describes Antin's writing as the "raw stuff of art" and alludes to her "quick senses" and "keen powers of observation." The original Yiddish letter, bound and located in the Boston Public Library, includes a brief "History of This Manuscript," written by Antin in 1914 for the twentieth anniversary of the family's landing in Boston. She explains that she found the original Yiddish letter "in the possession of my uncle, Berl Weltman, in Vilna" on her way to revisit Polotzk in 1910. She learned that the letter had "circulated widely in Polotzk, had been sent around to various branches of the family in different parts of Russia, finally winding up in Vilna." She notes that it miraculously survived the revolution of 1905, "when everybody made it a point to destroy useless papers of every description, so as to have the fewer questions to answer when the police came to make domiciliary searches." She also explains the error in the title: "The name of my native town appeared in this erroneous form because the gentleman who edited my manuscript had never heard of Polotzk, but was familiar with the name Plotzk, and my corrections on the proofs were ignored."

The sixty-three-page volume traces the journey from Polotzk to Vilna and concludes with the reunion of the Antins in Boston. Zangwill argues that Antin's narrative is a "human document of considerable value" for it gives a vision of the "inner feelings of the people themselves" and the "magic vision of free America" that lures immigrants. Further, it "enables us to see almost with our own eyes how the invasion of America appears to the impecunious invader." Prophetically, Zangwill predicts spiritual suffering for this gifted Russian girl, which he associates with the "curse of reflectiveness." Antin's first book was reviewed in the *New York Times Saturday Review* (27 May 1899) and Josephine Lazarus reviewed it for the *Critic* (April 1899). Patterns emerge in this first book that are evident in later writings: like later works, *From Plotzk to Boston* was commissioned (a request from her uncle and Antin's teachers, mentors, and benefactors); like her fiction and nonfiction, it serves educational ends; and, like most of her writing, it is autobiographical. At the peak of her writing career, Antin wrote to Randolph Bourne on 11 August 1913, stating "*Everything* I write is autobiography."

The publication of Antin's first book contributed to her celebrity status, ongoing correspondence with her mentors, and friendship with Lazarus. She also entered Boston Latin Grammar School for Girls (class of 1901) with hopes of attending college at Radcliffe. Antin's high-school education in the Boston Latin Grammar School was exceptional, considering the limited possibilities of public education for all Americans at the turn of the century. Before 1898 there were no public high schools in New York City, and for most students in the Progressive Era, school ended with the sixth or eighth grade. The Antins were determined to provide their promising daughter with an education, even if the family fared less well as a result. During Mary's school years, Israel Antin operated a variety of grocery stores in the Boston area–first a refreshment stand on Revere Beach and later grocery stores in Chelsea and South Boston. Serving Boston's poor in tenement districts made it difficult to collect payment, and the combined family earnings (including Frieda's work in the garment factory and Joseph's newspaper sales) were all necessary for their survival. Two more Antin children were born in Boston–May and Celia–to compound the financial difficulties. When the business on Arlington Street failed, Israel sought a loan from the Hebrew Immigrant Aid Society to establish another business, and the family moved to a poorer district in Boston's South End–first to 11 Wheeler Street and later Dover Street. Thus, as Antin continued her studies she lived between two social classes, represented by the Boston Latin Grammar School and the tenement districts. As Sam Bass Warner writes in *Province of Reason* (1984), "the tensions of family, school and street pulled relentlessly at Mary."

During this time Antin joined the Natural History Club at Hale House, and on one of their outings met Amadeus William Grabau. Grabau came to Boston from Albany, New York, to pursue his geological studies, first at the Massachusetts Institute of Technology and later at Harvard University. Subsequently, Grabau taught geology at the Rensselaer Polytechnic Institute and at Tufts College; he also served as a guide and lecturer for the Museum of the Boston Society of Natural History. The son of a German Lutheran minister, Grabau was born in 1870 in Cedarburgh, Wisconsin, but he completed his secondary schooling in Buffalo, New York. Though they were from different cultures, Antin and Grabau, eleven years her senior, both came from immigrant families committed to religion and education. Additionally, both were intellectually gifted, sharing a faith in reason and a love of learning. On 5 October 1901 Antin and Grabau were married. That fall Grabau took a position as lecturer in paleontology at Columbia University, and the couple moved to New York City.

For Antin, the period from 1901 to the outbreak of World War I in 1914 represented change and literary productivity: Antin moved from her own family and mentors in Boston and adjusted to her role as a faculty wife and mother in New York. She became a celebrity because of her writings and joined the national lecture circuit. She attended the Teacher's College at Columbia University in 1901–1902 and Barnard College from 1902 to 1904, although she never enrolled in a degree program or completed a degree. In New York City Antin's friendship with Lazarus deepened. Though they were of different ages and backgrounds, both struggled, according to Warner, with "how to orient themselves in an environment that included modern secular Judaism, anti-Semitism, and uprooted Eastern European orthodox Jewish settlements." Grabau became a professor at Columbia in 1905, and about this time the Grabaus moved to Scarsdale. Their only child, Josephine Esther, was born on 21 November 1907 in New York City and named after Lazarus as well as Antin's mother, Esther Weltman. In 1910 Antin returned to Polotzk for a visit, though little is known about this trip. She completed her autobiography, which Lazarus had encouraged her to write, on 10 April 1910.

The Promised Land is Antin's best known and most enduring work. Serialized in the *Atlantic Monthly* in 1911–1912 and published in book form in 1912, it was dedicated to Lazarus. At about the same time she published a short essay, "How I Wrote *The Promised Land*," in the *New York Times Book Review* (30 June 1912). The autobiography was an immediate best-seller. For many readers it represented a paradigmatic immigrant memoir. For others, such as critic Alvin H. Rosenfeld, *The Promised Land* helped establish the pattern for modern Jewish autobiography. Antin's own assessment in her introduction explains its broad appeal: "I believe that its chief interest lies in the fact that it is illustrative of scores of unwritten lives." The narrative is about transformation, as the opening lines convey: "I was born, I have lived, and I have been made over."

The Promised Land consists of twenty chapters, divided roughly equally between the Antins' life in Russia and the United States. In the first half of the autobiography, she focuses on the collective experience of Jews in the Pale, imagining a non-Jewish, Anglo-American audience for whom Judaic religious observances and beliefs may be unfamiliar and historical circumstances of czarist policies abstract or remote. Thus, she includes a glossary of more than six pages of Yiddish and Hebrew terms at the back of the autobiography. Antin documents economic hardship, religious persecu-

tion, and the daily life of a community in the Pale–her family serves as a microcosm for that communal story. In the latter chapters, Antin foregrounds her life as a child and adolescent, emphasizing her transformation to American citizen and her discovery of natural history and focusing on school experiences.

The book has generally been seen in the context of Americanization, both as a specific movement in the first two decades of the twentieth century and as a general process. The historical movement of Americanization is characterized by two poles: one at which it was identified with Anglo-Saxon culture, and the other, with multiple ethnic identities linked to a national culture, described by Philip Gleason in *The Harvard Encyclopedia of American Ethnic Groups* (1980) as "cosmopolitan nationalism." During the period from 1900 to 1920, notes Gleason, "the former emphasis became more dominant, eventually giving the whole movement a repressive and nativistic tone." Given the task of educating immigrant children, schools have been central to this process of Americanization. Antin illustrates this process throughout her autobiography as she identifies with teachers and the school system–which represses, but does not erase, Jewish knowledge and practices. Antin explains her school success: "I was Jew enough to have an aptitude for language; I was Antin enough to read each lesson with my heart." Identification with the school, a process her father supported, meant the immigrant exchanged one history for another. Antin writes, "the story of the exodus was not history to me in the sense that the story of the American revolution was." Association with George Washington offered an historical narrative and an alternative sense of peoplehood: by exchanging the Hebrew prophets for Washington, Antin imagined a parallel story for the "luckless sons of Abraham." Prior national discourses for Antin signified tyranny, exclusion, and oppression: Polotzk was "not my country. It was *Goluth*–exile." By contrast, the discourse of Americanization promised peoplehood by inclusion.

Thus, for Antin, the new national discourse signaled emancipatory promise and democracy: "Over and over and over again I discover that I am a wonderful thing, being human; that I am the image of the universe, being myself; that I am the repository of all the wisdom in the world, being alive and sane at the beginning of this twentieth century. The heir of the ages am I, and all that has been is in me, and shall continue to be in my immortal self." Because of the identification with narratives of nationhood, the autobiography is often interpreted as nationalistic and patriotic. Antin's attachment to America can be understood in part because of her being denied an education in Polotzk. Warner writes, "In Russia Mary Antin had been

Page from the manuscript for Antin's introduction to her 1912 memoir, The Promised Land *(courtesy of the Trustees of the Boston Public Library)*

excluded from public education because she was Jewish, and she had been forbidden Jewish education because she was a girl." Though she grew up hearing the names of "Rebeccah, Rachel and Leah," she also learned that "woman's only work was motherhood," that "a girl was born for no other purpose," and the kitchen was "a girl's real schoolroom." Consequently, New World educational opportunities in public schools and libraries gave Antin cause to celebrate. In the chapter "The Kingdom of the Slums," Antin recalls living on Dover Street, a poor immigrant neighborhood of tenements, but she called the Boston Public Library "home." The library, she writes, remained "mine because I was a citizen; mine, though I was born an alien; mine, though I lived on Dover Street. My palace—*mine!*" Later, she adds, "I was at home here."

Generally, reviews of *The Promised Land* were favorable; Grabau collected more than two hundred of them in a scrapbook. The attention stimulated her literary career, making the years from 1911 to 1914 her most prolific ones. Living and writing during the peak period of emigration from Europe and during the Progressive Era, Antin focuses primarily on the meaning of immigration—both for the immigrant and for American society—in the period before World War I. Her works are set in both the Old World and the New.

In the same year that her autobiography began its serialization in the *Atlantic Monthly,* where all her fiction appeared, she published her first story, "Malinke's Atonement." Set in Polotzk and focusing on a poor and struggling widow, Breine Henne, and her two children, Yosele and Malinke, the story demonstrates Antin's ability to portray sympathetically and powerfully her Russian Jewish past. The story addresses poverty but eschews blame, beginning: "It was not the fault of Breine Henne, the egg-woman, if her only daughter, Malinke, had to assume the burdens of housekeeping before she cast her milk teeth." Establishing the resourcefulness of the two female characters, Antin situates the family in the larger historical and political context: "The law of circumstance was potent in Polotzk, next to the law of the Czar." Gender distinctions figure prominently in the story, as Malinke is told by the Rebbe: "You are only a girl. . . . Girls don't need to know things out of books." On one level, the story revolves around a Sabbath meal; Malinke's mother sends her to the rabbi to ask if a chicken with "a bit of crooked wire in the intestine" is kosher and can be eaten. On another level it is about Jewish religious practices and divine justice—whether a just God would condemn a poor and hungry family to discard food. Believing in divine justice, defying a *rav,* and feeling the wrath and forgiveness of God, Malinke is eventually rewarded when the *rav* offers her an education, adding,

"I pray that I have the wisdom to teach you." The story demonstrates Malinke's faith in a just divinity and a rational universe, both of which are recurring themes in Antin's writing.

Her two other fictional stories, both published in 1913, address immigration and demonstrate the growth of the writer's talent and imagination. "The Amulet," set in Polotzk, is rich in dialogue and description and reminiscent of the folktales of Eastern European Jewish tradition so powerfully captured by Isaac Bashevis Singer. In this story, Yankel and his wife, Sorele, long for a child. The narrator describes the lonely Sorele in her home with little to occupy her hands and mind. Yankel, whose first wife died barren, seeks comfort, buying an amulet for ten rubles on his business travels. His wife becomes pregnant, but he later learns that if the child is a girl, the wife will die. Distraught that he may lose even his wife, Yankel seeks refuge in the synagogue until he learns his wife bore a son and both are fine. Again, the story is about religious faith and divine justice, though the tale is embedded with misogyny.

"The Lie," Antin's last published work of fiction, evokes the lie her father told to obtain educational opportunities for her. The story is much more, however: it teaches American readers about Jewish immigrants through David Rudinsky and his parents, portraying their lives through the perspective of a sympathetic teacher, Miss Ralston. Bright and curious, David is also innocent and sensitive. When he misses school because of illness, Miss Ralston visits David at home, above the first-floor candy shop that his parents operate. There she learns the cause of his illness: David's father lied about his age to secure his place in school; when David discovered the lie, he became sick. Antin's narrator writes of the teacher: "She recognized in his story one of those ethical paradoxes which the helpless Jews of the Pale, in their search for a weapon that their oppressors could not confiscate, have evolved for their self-defense. She knew that to many honest Jewish minds a lie was not a lie when told to an official." Miss Ralston, representing American authority, sees the nobility of the immigrant in his desire to learn. In this capacity, Ralston says to David: "Talking with your parents downstairs I saw why it was that the Russian Jews are so soon at home here in our dear country. In the hearts of men like your father, dear, is the true America." Here, as in most of her writing, Antin portrays the immigrant as noble.

Her short nonfiction prose varies in content. Three essays were published in 1912, one on her autobiography and two on political issues of the historical moment. The brief essay, "First Aid to the Alien," is an ironic treatment of Americanization, revealing Antin's sense of humor. Set on a train in America, the essay focuses on a young botanist's irritation with Italian immigrant children who have tossed paper and peelings on the floor of the train. He teaches the boys to pick up the trash and in the process schools them about citizenship in America. Later, the botanist receives a letter from a friend, a teacher who rails against his foolishness in teaching his young pupil to equate the American flag and patriotism with picking up trash: the message of the botanist's lesson reduced America to mean, *"No rubbish on the floor."* The essay satirizes reformers who preach only law and order.

A more gripping essay, published the same year, is "A Woman to Her Fellow Citizens," an argument for the Progressive Party and an endorsement of its 1912 presidential candidate, Theodore Roosevelt. It reveals Antin's command of the language and her striking use of reason in the charged political climate. Generally, it also represents an argument for progressive reforms that Antin identifies with a "fight for righteousness." She takes on the label "radical"–defining it as "one who goes to the root of every question to be solved!"–yet she affirms a range of reformist progressive programs: "clean government . . . slums torn down . . . healthy mothers in place of milk stations . . . widening city streets and planting trees and insisting on air spaces." Progressivism, resting on the faith that rational knowledge could transform social ills, receives a clear formulation by Antin: "If scientists find that heredity and environment are equal factors in shaping a man, then the legislatures shall pass such laws as will insure to every future American the best possible birth and the finest possible nurture." In many ways this essay brings together all of Antin's concerns–her faith in the American system to serve its people and her ability to use reason and effective language in the service of causes about which she felt passionately, especially immigration. Although the suffrage movement was gaining momentum by 1912, Antin states in this essay, "I am not a suffragist." Nowhere in her writing, however, does Antin discuss her resistance to suffrage.

Antin's third book, *They Who Knock at Our Gates: A Complete Gospel of Immigration,* was published in 1914. The work might best be seen in context of the Dillingham Commission, established by Congress in 1907 to investigate the so-called new emigrants from eastern and southern Europe. In a report released in 1911 the commission concluded that the "new" immigrants differed from the "old" and called for emigration restriction. In opposition, *They Who Knock at Our Gates* develops the argument that immigrants provide the foundation of the nation and therefore, the immigration gates should be kept open. Organizing the book into three parts, Antin calls the Declaration of Independence the basic American law–comparable to the Law of Moses for the Israelites–and asserts

that it is violated by the exclusion of immigrants. In the second section Antin insists that Americans depend on immigrants, while the "real exploiters of our country's wealth are not the foreign laborers but the capitalists who pay their wages." It is not the immigrants who ruin the country, she argues; rather, politicians make immigrants into scapegoats "for all the sins of untrammeled capitalism." In the last section, "The Fiery Furnace," she alludes to the biblical book of Daniel, comparing the faith of the Israelites in their God to deliver them "from the fiery furnace" with the faith of the immigrants: both looked to the promised land. She cites Grace Abbott, the progressive reformer, who said of the new immigrants: "It was their faith in America . . . that touched me the most." *They Who Knock at Our Gates* appears abstract and formal, yet its logic–reflecting progressive faith in reason to guide civilization–remains a striking feature of the book. Unlike Antin's other publications, this work has not been reissued and is generally ignored in discussions of her writings.

The outbreak of war in Europe had cataclysmic effects on Antin, both in her personal and creative life, from which she never fully recovered. From 1913 to 1918 she traveled throughout the United States giving lectures on such topics as "The Responsibility of American Citizenship," "The Civic Education of the Immigrant," "Jewish Life in the Pale: A Lesson for Americans," and "The Zionist Movement." Her lecture tours were sponsored first by the Progressive Party and later by the National Americanization Committee, the National Security League, and the Committee on Public Information. Antin's only publication during this time was "A Confession of Faith," a short essay for the *Boston Jewish Advocate* (15 February 1917), in which she argues for a Jewish homeland to safeguard Jewish culture, "some place set apart where they may live their group life unmolested."

Although she is often described as promoting patriotism, her letters to her husband's friend Thomas Watson suggest other possible explanations for her decision to embark on a lecture tour. In the fall of 1915 Antin wrote Watson and arranged to repay a 1906 loan of $100 that Grabau received from Watson, with interest, planning to surprise Grabau with the receipt. She alludes to the "bothersome debt," Grabau's "meager income" of $2,500, "petty worries about household bills," and the "good fortune" that through her writing she can relieve him of some of these "harrowing things." A lecture tour earned between $6,000 and $10,000 a season, and she went "only where I was called." Later, commenting on the lecture tour to writer Mary Austin, Antin claims that the lectures began because of a "series of curious accidents," and "driven by a sense of civic duty, I kept on, although I hated the life and discounted the value of my efforts." She also

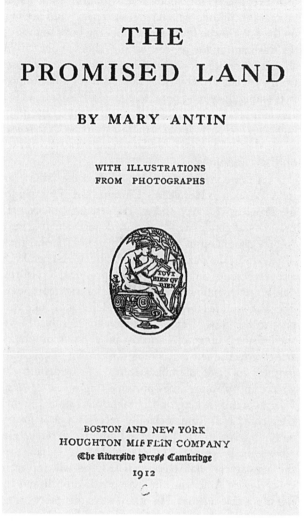

THE PROMISED LAND

BY MARY ANTIN

WITH ILLUSTRATIONS
FROM PHOTOGRAPHS

BOSTON AND NEW YORK
HOUGHTON MIFFLIN COMPANY
The Riverside Press Cambridge
1912

Frontispiece and title page for Antin's idealized account of her experiences of immigration and Americanization

added that her husband followed her public career with the "same affectionate pride . . . just as he had watched my literary beginnings."

While Antin lectured for the Allied cause, her husband supported Germany. According to Grabau's student, Hervey Shimer, the professor admired German science and could see little wrong with his ancestral homeland. In an 11 March 1925 letter to Austin, Antin remarked how her husband changed in 1914 and described its effect: "my lover-husband turned into a dreadful hostile stranger who terrorized the household and scandalized the community (no, I am not exaggerating; these are matters of history). I suffered, through my failure to adjust myself, a nervous break-down." Tensions in the Grabau household inevitably mounted and were felt by their daughter, who later claimed, "They saw what they were doing to me and finally

agreed to separate for my sake." On 12 July 1917 Antin wrote from Hartsdale, New York, to Watson, accepting the offer of a serial loan of a hundred dollars a month "until my affairs in Scarsdale are settled," implying the separation had occurred. In the following month she wrote to Watson that her father had died and she would be with her mother and sisters, adding, "I am tired, but not tired enough to fail them." The Grabaus' marriage had become a casualty of the war.

Reflecting on this period in a letter to Rabbi Abraham Cronbach in 1937, Antin assesses that toll: "The war was hard on me, too. . . . The war swept away the home in Scarsdale." The war also "swept away" her marriage and Grabau's teaching post. Grabau "expressed his German sympathies rather forcibly," according to Shimer, leading to his dismissal from Columbia University in 1919. Before Grabau's departure for China in 1920, Antin wrote to Watson on 11 September 1920, indicating she had seen Grabau in June and was shocked by his "painfully diseased appearance." Of her husband, Antin writes that he was "the man for whom I laid out clean linens as he needed it for fifteen years . . . a woman fetters herself with a sense of responsibility. . . . I do not know what I am to Amadeus at this moment. He to me is the man who brought glory into my life, and chaos. He is the one who cherished me like father and mother and lover and dearest friend in one; he is the one who wounded me and trampled on me and made sport of the sufferings he inflicted." Grabau left for China in 1920 as China Foundation Research Professor at the National University at Peking and chief paleontologist of the Chinese Geological Survey, where he had a distinguished career. According to Shimer, the estranged couple did correspond, and Grabau dedicated what he considered his most important book, *The Rhythm of the Ages* (1940), "To my wife Mary Antin, my daughter Josephine, and my granddaughters Margaret and Elizabeth Ross." He visited the United States only once at the special invitation of the Geological Society of America to attend an International Geological Congress at Washington in 1933. Antin and Grabau reputedly met during that visit. Recent research, however, suggests that Grabau sought a divorce and remarried by 1942.

After the collapse of her marriage and household, Antin suffered a nervous breakdown, a point in her life that, as, she later wrote to Mary Austin, "commenced my real education." Though she continued on the lecture circuit sporadically after 1916, she writes, "When I wasn't lecturing I was under treatment by an assortment of neurologists." She refers to her "psychoneurosis" and continuing education in the "hells of sanitariums, at the hands of doctors of various schools of psychotherapy." Evelyn Salz reasons that Antin suffered from a bipolar (manic-depressive) disorder, and for a time in the early 1920s she was a patient at the Austen Riggs Psychiatric Center in Stockbridge, Massachusetts. In 1923 she "abandoned the doctors" and moved to Gould Farm, a "service community, specializing in mental and physical rehabilitation," founded in 1913 by William Gould and set on 550 acres in Great Barrington, Massachusetts. When Gould died on 8 May 1925, Antin submitted an article to the *Berkshire Courier* celebrating his life and work. At the end of the article the editors identified Antin as a resident of Gould Farm, who after her "extraordinary recovery" decided to make Gould Farm her home and the study of the Gould methods her next work.

Efforts to regain her literary career are found throughout her correspondence in the mid 1920s. This desire is especially evident in her appeal to the nature writer and novelist Austin, whom Antin knew only through her writings. On 11 March 1925, referring to Austin as a "sister spirit," Antin wrote, "What is the matter with me? and how to remedy what's wrong?" Questioning her inability to write, she sought to understand that loss. In that process she reevaluated her earlier publications. In 1926 she contacted Houghton Mifflin about her last book, asking them to stop releasing it: "Why do you still circulate that . . . piece of rhetoric, *They Who Knock?* Who buys it? It is out of date!" She asked, "Will my kind publishers give the matter another think?" Houghton Mifflin cited the "inspirational quality of the book" and argued that it was selling about two hundred copies a year, too many to "choke it." Antin finally agreed to "not interfere any further in the matter." At the end of 1926 she appealed to Houghton Mifflin to intervene with the *Boston Herald* and its treatment of her life and autobiography. The newspaper annually used the occasion of Washington's birthday to produce what she called "patriotic hash." In a satiric self-portrait she mocked the paper's reading of *The Promised Land,* and she offered a parody of the patriotic essays on her life. The parody acknowledges her nervous breakdown, yet it states she emerged in a healthier state than before. The parody also affirms that "no one can be found sufficiently informed, or sufficiently prophetic, to read us the riddle of M---A---'s ten year silence." In 1927 Antin wrote to the Boston Public Library about donating the manuscript of *The Promised Land.* In the exchange of letters that followed she refers to the altered conditions of her life: "I have grown steadily poorer . . . and richer in personal freedom." She adds that she might prefer to be "stripped to one suit of clothes and my typewriter."

Her extensive correspondence with friends, editors, rabbis, intellectuals, and writers continued in the 1930s. What is most evident during these years is a spiritual searching. In 1931 she and Josephine Grabau met the Indian spiritual leader Meher Baba when Thomas Watson invited Baba to the United States for the first time. While Josephine remained a follower of Baba throughout her life and met her husband through him, Antin moved away from the group. In the late 1930s she became interested in mysticism. In 1936 Antin returned to Gould Farm, and in the following year she published her first article in twenty years, "The Soundless Trumpet" (*Atlantic Monthly,* April 1937). The essay reflects on mysticism and the nature of scientific knowledge; Antin insists on the existence of both. The essay also reveals that Antin, isolated from her family, husband, and past, longed for connection with the world. She concludes: "My fleeting glimpses into the heart of things, the nostalgic sweetness of my moments of absorption into the world about me, the thrill of the soundless trumpet summoning me to cross the barrier of sense—all these are only the faintest tremblings of the Veil in the inconstant breath of my too feeble aspiration. I know what to look for, but I have not seen it."

Antin's spiritual and philosophical quest is also evident in her last essay, "House of the One Father" (*Common Ground,* Spring 1941). In both these final essays Antin seeks explanatory frameworks for reconciling opposing cultures and epistemologies. In "House of the One Father" she addresses more specifically the complexity of her own identity as a Jew and as an American. She reconciles any tensions she may have felt by linking Judaism and democracy: "'What is democracy,' I declaimed, 'except the ancient Hebrew idea of the Fatherhood of God, from which follows the Brotherhood of Man.'" She insists on the "Hebrew-Christian basis of American democracy," arguing that the "two philosophical systems, the Hebrew and the American, were essentially one." Once again she affirms America, where differences shrink, where doors of opportunity and inclusion open, and where "each was a door to the House of the One Father." Aware of growing fascism in Europe and the plight of European Jews, Antin asserts her Jewish identity: "I shall claim the Jewish badge; but in my Father's house of many mansions I shall continue a free spirit." Yearning for a world without labels, Antin writes, "Let me pass in the world under any label the social vision of the time may apply." Antin affirms a bond to any persecuted group and commits to "do my part" where America or individual liberty is threatened.

During the last years of her life Antin changed residence from Winchester, Massachusetts, near her family, to Gould Farm, then to Scarsdale, Albany, and New York City. Occasionally, she requested advances on her royalties, and in 1940 she sought a bank loan against the royalties on her published works. Having battled cancer, Antin died at Pinehurst Nursing Home in Suffern, New York, on 15 May 1949. Her obituary appeared in *The New York Times* on 18 May.

Mary Antin is probably most remembered for her autobiography of immigration that captured much of the mythologized Americanization experience in her narrative of transformation. Yet, much of her life remains absent in that story. Thus, the celebrated narrative also exposes the contradictions of the mythic national discourse, not only for one Russian Jewish immigrant woman but for the many others for whom the promised land did not fully realize its promises.

Letters:

Evelyn Salz, "The Letters of Mary Antin: A Life Divided," *American Jewish History,* 84, no. 2 (1994): 71–80;

Salz, ed., *Selected Letters of Mary Antin* (Syracuse, N.Y.: Syracuse University Press, 1999).

References:

Mary V. Dearborn, *Pocahontas's Daughters: Gender and Ethnicity in American Culture* (New York: Oxford University Press, 1986), p. 10;

James Craig Holte, *The Ethnic I: A Sourcebook for Ethnic-American Autobiography* (New York: Greenwood Press, 1988), p. 31;

Pamela A. Nadell, introduction to *From Plotzk to Boston* (New York: Markus Wiener, 1986), pp. v–xxi;

Alvin H. Rosenfeld, "Inventing the Jew: Notes on Jewish Autobiography," in *The American Autobiography: A Collection of Critical Essays,* edited by Albert E. Stone (Englewood Cliffs, N.J.: Prentice-Hall, 1981), pp. 133–156;

Jonathan D. Sarna and Ellen Smith, eds., *The Jews of Boston: Essays on the Occasion of the Centenary (1895–1995) of the Combined Jewish Philanthropies of Greater Boston* (Boston: The Combined Jewish Philanthropies of Greater Boston, 1995);

Ellery Sedgwick, "Mary Antin," *American Magazine,* 77 (March 1914): 64–65;

Werner Sollors, introduction to *The Promised Land* (New York: Penguin, 1997), pp. xi–l;

Sam Bass Warner, *Province of Reason* (Cambridge, Mass.: Harvard University Press, 1984), pp. 21–33;

Israel Zangwill, foreword to *From Plotzk to Boston* (Boston: Clarke, 1899), pp. 7–9.

Papers:

Unpublished manuscripts, correspondence, and other materials related to Mary Antin can be found in the following collections: the American Jewish Archives (Horace M. Kallen Papers, Abraham Cronbach Correspondence, Max Heller Correspondence); the Boston Public Library; Brown University Library (Maud Howe Elliott Papers); College of Physicians of Philadelphia (Israel Bram Collection); Columbia University (Randolph Bourne Papers); Henry Huntington Library (Mary Austin Papers); Houghton Library, Harvard University (Houghton Mifflin Papers); Jewish Theological Seminary of America (Bernhard G. Richards Correspondence); the Library of Congress; Massachusetts Historical Society (Ellery Sedgwick Papers); Princeton University Libraries (General manuscripts); Syracuse University Library (Anita Weschler Papers); Temple University Library (John M. Stahl Papers); University of Arkansas Libraries (John Gould Fletcher Papers); University of California, Bancroft Library (Simon Lubin Papers); and the University of Pennsylvania Libraries (Van Wyck Brooks Papers).

Mary Hunter Austin

(9 September 1868 – 13 August 1934)

Linda K. Karell
Montana State University

See also the Austin entries in *DLB 9: American Novelists, 1910–1945; DLB 78: American Short-Story Writers, 1880–1910;* and *DLB 206: Twentieth-Century American Western Writers, First Series.*

BOOKS: *The Land of Little Rain* (Boston: Houghton, Mifflin, 1903); abridged edition, with photographs by Ansel Adams (Boston: Houghton Mifflin, 1950);

The Basket Woman: A Book of Fanciful Tales for Children (Boston: Houghton, Mifflin, 1904);

Isidro (Boston: Houghton, Mifflin, 1904; London: Constable, 1905);

The Flock (Boston: Houghton, Mifflin, 1906; London: Constable, 1906);

Santa Lucia: A Common Story (New York & London: Harper, 1908);

Lost Borders (New York & London: Harper, 1909);

Outland, as Gordon Stairs (London: Murray, 1910; New York: Boni & Liveright, 1919);

The Arrow-Maker: A Drama in Three Acts (New York: Duffield, 1911; revised edition, Boston: Houghton Mifflin, 1915);

Christ in Italy: Being the Adventures of a Maverick among Masterpieces (New York: Duffield, 1912);

A Woman of Genius (Garden City, N.Y.: Doubleday, Page, 1912; revised edition, Boston: Houghton Mifflin, 1917);

The Green Bough: A Tale of the Resurrection (Garden City, N.Y.: Doubleday, Page, 1913);

The Lovely Lady (Garden City, N.Y.: Doubleday, Page, 1913);

California: Land of the Sun, text by Austin, paintings by Palmer Sutton (New York: Macmillan, 1914; London: Black, 1914); revised as *Lands of the Sun* (Boston: Houghton Mifflin, 1927);

Love and the Soul Maker (New York & London: Appleton, 1914);

Suffrage and Government: The Modern Idea of Government by Consent and Woman's Place in It, with Special Ref-

Mary Hunter Austin in 1929 (Henry E. Huntington Library and Art Gallery)

erence to Nevada and Other Western States, by Austin and Ann Martin (New York: National American Woman Suffrage Association, 1914);

The Man Jesus, Being a Brief Account of the Life and Teaching of the Prophet of Nazareth (New York: Harper, 1915); revised and enlarged as *A Small Town Man* (New York & London: Harper, 1925);

The Sturdy Oak: A Composite Novel of American Politics by Fourteen American Authors, by Austin and others (New York: Holt, 1917);

The Ford (Boston: Houghton Mifflin, 1917);

The Trail Book (Boston: Houghton Mifflin, 1918);

The Young Woman Citizen (New York: Woman's Press, 1918);

No. 26 Jayne Street (Boston: Houghton Mifflin, 1920);

The American Rhythm (New York: Harcourt, Brace, 1923); revised and enlarged as *The American Rhythm: Studies and Reexpressions of Amerindian Songs* (Boston: Houghton Mifflin, 1930);

The Land of Journeys' Ending (New York: Century, 1924; London: Allen & Unwin, 1925);

Everyman's Genius (Indianapolis: Bobbs-Merrill, 1925; London: Bobbs-Merrill, 1926);

The Children Sing in the Far West (Boston: Houghton Mifflin, 1928);

Taos Pueblo, text by Austin, photographs by Adams (San Francisco: Grabhorn Press, 1930);

Amerindian Songs (Boston: Houghton Mifflin, 1930);

Experiences Facing Death (Indianapolis: Bobbs-Merrill, 1931; London: Rider, 1931);

Starry Adventure (Boston: Houghton Mifflin, 1931);

Earth Horizon: An Autobiography (Boston: Houghton Mifflin, 1932);

Can Prayer Be Answered? (New York: Farrar & Rhinehart, 1934);

Indian Pottery of the Rio Grande (Pasadena, Cal.: Esto, 1934);

One-Smoke Stories (Boston: Houghton Mifflin, 1934);

The Mother of Felipe and Other Early Stories, edited by Franklin Walker (Los Angeles: Book Club of California, 1950);

One Hundred Miles on Horseback, edited by Donald P. Ringler (Los Angeles: Dawson's Book Shop, 1963);

Western Trails: A Collection of Short Stories by Mary Austin, edited by Melody Graulich (Reno & Las Vegas: University of Nevada Press, 1987);

Cactus Thorn: A Novella by Mary Austin (Reno & Las Vegas: University of Nevada Press, 1988);

Beyond Borders: The Selected Essays of Mary Austin, edited by Reuben J. Ellis (Carbondale: Southern Illinois University Press, 1996);

A Mary Austin Reader, edited by Esther F. Lanigan (Tucson: University of Arizona Press, 1996).

Editions: *Stories from the Country of Lost Borders,* edited, with an introduction, by Marjorie Pryse (New Brunswick, N.J.: Rutgers University Press, 1987);

The Basket Woman: A Book of Indian Tales (Reno: University of Nevada Press, 1999).

PLAY PRODUCTIONS: *The Arrow-Maker,* New York, New Theatre, 27 February 1911;

Fire, Carmel, California, Forest Theatre, 1912;

The Man Who Didn't Believe in Christmas, New York, Cohan and Harris Theatre, 1916.

OTHER: "The Tremblor," in *The California Earthquake of 1906,* edited by David Starr Jordan (San Francisco: Robertson, 1907);

"My First Publication," in *My Maiden Effort: Being the Personal Confessions of Well-Known American Authors as to Their Literary Beginnings,* edited by Gelett Burgess (Garden City, N.Y. & Toronto: Doubleday, Page, 1921); republished as "How I Learned to Read and Write," in *My First Publication,* edited by James D. Hart (San Francisco: Book Club of California, 1961);

"Non-English Writings II," in *The Cambridge History of the American Novel,* volume 4, edited by William Peterfield Trent, John Erskine, Stuart P. Sherman, and Carl Van Doren (New York: Putnam, 1921; Cambridge: Cambridge University Press, 1921);

"The American Form of the Novel," in *The Novel of Tomorrow and the Scope of Fiction, by Twelve American Novelists* (Indianapolis: Bobbs-Merrill, 1922);

"Aboriginal American Literature," in *American Writers on American Litertature,* edited by John Macy (New York: Liveright, 1931);

George W. Cronyn, ed., *The Path on the Rainbow: An Anthology of Songs and Chants from the Indians of North America,* introduction by Austin (New York: Liveright, 1934).

SELECTED PERIODICAL PUBLICATIONS—
UNCOLLECTED:

FICTION

"The Wooing of the Seniorita," *Overland Monthly,* 29 (March 1897): 258–263;

Fire: A Drama in Three Acts, Play-book of the Wisconsin Dramatic Society, 2 (October–December 1914): 3–25; 11–26; 18–30;

The Man Who Didn't Believe in Christmas, St. Nicholas Magazine, 45 (December 1917): 156–162;

NONFICTION

"Greatness in Women," *North American Review,* 217 (February 1923): 197–203;

"Regionalism in American Fiction," *English Journal,* 21 (February 1932): 97–107;

"The Folk Story in America," *South Atlantic Quarterly,* 33 (January 1934): 10–19.

At her death in 1934, Mary Hunter Austin was a well-known and accomplished figure in American letters, with contributions to feminism, modernism, regionalism, and Native American studies to her credit. Her oeuvre includes more than thirty book-length works, many short stories, several plays, poetry, literary theory, cultural studies, and more than two hundred published periodical pieces. Despite her prolific output, Austin's books were frequently unavailable to the general public during her lifetime, and her reputation was secured largely by her publications in literary magazines and by the popular public lectures she gave. Following her death, Austin's writing all but disappeared from public view. Although her writing has literary links to nature writers Henry David Thoreau, Ralph Waldo Emerson, and John Muir, for years Austin was pejoratively labeled a minor female regionalist writer. This dismissive categorization had the result of excluding Austin from the canon of American literature. Subsequently, Austin has undergone a critical renaissance, and her writing proves itself timely in its continued ability to fascinate, captivate, and challenge her readers.

In 1932, just two years before her death, Austin published her autobiography, *Earth Horizon*. The detailed account of her childhood in that work highlights several of the themes that eventually dominated her writing: female abandonment and subsequent survival, spirituality and its relation to female creativity, and the high social cost to women of telling the truth about their lives. Austin was born Mary Hunter on 9 September 1868, in Carlinville, Illinois. There were four children in the Hunter family: Mary; her older brother, Jim; her sister, Jennie; and her younger brother, George. Her father, Captain George Hunter, had served in the Civil War and never regained his health following his service. When he died in 1878, ten-year-old Mary was distraught. Her relationship with her father was close, and Captain Hunter apparently gave his daughter the acceptance and emotional support she never received from her mother.

Soon after her father's death, Jennie Hunter died following an attack of diphtheria—with which Mary was also afflicted—leaving her with a second, keenly felt loss. Of Jennie, Austin wrote that "the loss of her is never cold in me. . . . She was the only one who ever unselfishly loved me. She is the only one who stays." Austin never fully recovered from the double loss of father and sister, the two members of the family with whom she felt a supportive and loving connection. Their deaths, coupled with Mary's conviction that her mother was disappointed that it was she, and not Jennie, who survived the illness, left her feeling alone and abandoned.

By Austin's account, her mother, Susanna Graham Savilla Hunter, was emotionally remote throughout Austin's life, but her physical reticence and emotional distance were particularly damaging to Mary as a child. Susanna Hunter offered her daughter little comfort for her grief and instead turned her focus to Mary's brother Jim. For Susanna, Jim became the man of the family following her husband's death. In her autobiography Austin relates that this fairly common reconstitution of family prompted her to assert her own identity. A breakfast dispute with her mother, during which Mary's request for an egg cooked differently than Jim's "became a constantly annoying snag in the perfect family gesture of subservience to the Head, which all her woman's life had gone to create," proved a feminist awakening that led Austin to decide that home "shouldn't be the place of the apotheosis of its male members."

Although hurt by her mother's repeated rejections, Mary was not immobilized by them. Her strength may derive in part from the social shifts in opportunities for women, as well as lessening constraints in the behaviors expected of them. Mary saw herself as part of a changing generation where she "wasn't by any means the only girl of that period insisting on going her own way against the traditions, and refusing to come to a bad end on account of it." Although Mary's relationship with her mother was ambivalent and remained so for the rest of her mother's life, she grew up with a conviction of her own intelligence and capability that permeated both her fiction and nonfiction writing. This sense of self is strengthened by her recognition of a strong female ancestry. In her autobiography Austin describes herself as the descendent of a line of strong, capable women who refused to capitulate entirely to male expectations.

Yet, despite its substantial pain, Mary's childhood was also filled with the opportunities her imagination and intelligence created. A literary child, Mary was an avid reader. Her father's collection of the classics included British writers William Shakespeare, John Keats, Percy Bysshe Shelley, Robert Browning, and John Ruskin, as well as American writers Herman Melville, Nathaniel Hawthorne, Edgar Allan Poe, Henry Wadsworth Longfellow, and Emerson. Besides reading these authors, Mary had a library card and voraciously read whatever came into the house. She also began to write while a young girl, composing poetry and what she called "A Play to be Sung" by the age of ten.

Austin rehearsing the cast of her play Fire *at the Forest Theatre in Carmel, California, 1913 (Henry E. Huntington Library and Art Gallery)*

Perhaps as a way to survive her traumatic experiences of abandonment and loss, to express her creativity, or both, Mary experienced herself as two distinct personalities: "I-Mary" and "Mary-by-herself." I-Mary was the confident, capable, and assured personality who needed little attention from adults, while Mary-by-herself was more vulnerable, frightened, and uncertain of her abilities. Perhaps because I-Mary came to her during a reading lesson, Mary associated her with reading and writing, so much so that the "mere sight of the printed page would often summon her." Whatever her impetus, I-Mary's value to the young girl was substantial. Feeling rejected by her mother, who seemed to Mary to withdraw from even touching her, "I-Mary suffered no need of being taken up and comforted; to be I-Mary was more solid and satisfying than to be Mary-by-herself." Perhaps anticipating dismissal, Austin insists on I-Mary's reality in her autobiography: "When you were I-Mary, you could see Mary-by-herself as part of the picture, and make her do things that, when you were she, could not be done at all; such as walking a log high over the creek, which gave Mary-by-herself cold prickles to think about." By creating a multiple self, Austin takes part in a subversive process often prac-

ticed by female autobiographers who simultaneously claim authority and deflect the claim onto an "other" self who cannot be controlled by the same constraints.

Austin's literary exploration of multiple selfhood can be seen in her later writing, in which she creates self-contained, authoritative, and independent female characters reminiscent of I-Mary. In Austin's fiction these characters exist comfortably without men. For example, Mrs. Wills in "The Return of Mr. Wills" discovers that she has more money, time, and satisfaction after she is abandoned by her husband. Seyavi in "The Basket Maker" learns "how much more easily one can do without a man than might at first be supposed" and reveals her creativity and financial capability in her artistry. In "The Walking Woman" Austin celebrates a lone female character who, willingly separated from all aspects of society, gains wisdom and freedom. Abandonment, particularly the abandonment of wives by their husbands, threads itself though much of Austin's fiction, but often that abandonment is ultimately seen as benefiting the central female character, whose personality, talent, or pleasure is unleashed only when she is relieved of the constraints of male expectations. Multiple selfhood takes a somewhat different form in Austin's novel, *A Woman of Genius* (1912), in which she investigates the split required of creative women when they are forced by cultural expectations to choose between passionate love and creative careers.

Also important in Austin's childhood–and in her later writing–are a series of spiritual experiences that began when she was a child. Although she was raised as a Methodist, Mary rejected organized religion early. She read the Bible thoroughly as a child, but less from devotion to its message than to win the money and attention her grandfather offered to his first grandchild to accomplish this formidable task. Then "God happened to Mary under the walnut tree." Austin writes of an experience she had at about age five and a half, when she felt a sense of union with "earth and sky and tree and windblown grass and the child in the midst of them." Although Austin lost her sense of this spiritual reality for part of her childhood, it returned to her when she moved to California and experienced that environment for the first time. As an adult, Austin came to feel most at home with the spiritual beliefs of the Paiute Indians she met in California, and she eventually claimed that these beliefs allowed her to write.

Other episodes in Austin's early years seem to have had an impact on her later theories of literature and writing. For example, Austin's understanding of story is essential to an appreciation of much of her writing. As a child she was punished for telling what her mother called stories. She angered her mother when she refused to discriminate between fact and fiction and persisted in relating events that happened to someone else as if she herself had been there. "Mother set her right. To say you'd seen things when you hadn't was storying, and storying was wicked." Yet, Mary's refusal was partly the result of an occasional inability to differentiate for certain between what she had seen and what she had imagined. Nonetheless, she mustered characteristic resolve and resistance: "And how did you know the difference between seeing and thinking you had seen? . . . Mother said she supposed she'd have to punish you or you'd grow up a storyteller. Well, you *did* see them. If you got punished for it, you'd simply have to stand it."

This childhood resistance can be seen in Austin's later writing, particularly *Lost Borders* (1909). In this collection of short stories she confronts the tenuous boundaries between fact and fiction as her narrator threads stories together to form a larger narrative. Throughout the narrative, the sometimes unreliable female narrator is careful to state where, or from whom, she received the stories she tells. In the opening story of the collection, "The Land," the narrator hears a macabre secondhand story about a woman who is preserved in a salt crystal, still wearing a red dress, after she dies when her wagon is trapped in a salt lake. "Afterward I came across the proof of the affair in the records of the emigrant party but I never tried telling it again." Combining the threat of "storying" with the insistence of the child who will tell her own truth, the narrator here is telling her own "story"–in this case, lying–because the story is published, preserved within "The Land" like the woman's body is preserved in the salt crystal. Yet, the story is also telling an important truth, warning of the danger in crossing boundaries without a respectful caution toward the land one travels across.

Austin's storytelling also pays homage to its oral foundation, something that links her style more closely to the Native American traditions that influenced her. Throughout *Lost Borders* her narrator is careful to cite the stories' origins, challenging the fixity of the written record as well as the notion of the author as the sole originator of a text. In Native American storytelling, particularly with its emphasis on orality, Austin found a literary form that resonated with her own understanding and influenced her literary production. As she records in *Earth Horizon*, Austin eventually came to a theory of literature that claimed "the story pattern is older than the man; that the story as communication between creature and creature is an older function of story art than the schools had taught her." The poetic, resonant, and sometimes obscure style of *Lost Borders* tries to capture that sense of the ancient and enduring power of storytelling.

Mary graduated from Blackburn College in Illinois in 1888, but not without a struggle that reveals the gender-biased expectations surrounding women's education at this time. In 1885, while at the State Normal School preparing to teach, she had a breakdown. Her doctor suspected that her breakdown "might have had something to do with the natural incapacity of the female mind for intellectual achievement," but in *Earth Horizon* Austin claimed that it was more likely caused by poor nutrition, inadequate heat, and "five months rasping insistence on a regime that violated all the natural motions of her own mind." At Blackburn College she was elected class poet and published in the college magazine, *The Blackburnian,* but she rejected a focus in English because "how do they know, these professors?– they've never written any books," and studied science instead.

After Mary received her degree in 1888, she immediately moved to California with her mother to homestead lands her brother Jim had filed on. The writing for which Austin is most famous, her writing about the California landscape, had its start with this move. The Hunters settled on 540 acres of unirrigated land in Tejon Pass, near the Mojave Desert and about thirty miles from Bakersfield. They were unprepared to become dry farmers, however, and several years of drought further plagued their efforts. After arriving in California, Mary developed malnutrition and experienced an emotional collapse. In *Earth Horizon* Austin described this illness as "a black spell of wanting to know" in which she was as "consumed with interest as with enchantment. Her trouble was that the country failed to explain itself. If it had a history, nobody would recount it." Her cure was twofold. First, wild grapes were discovered and helped her recover physically. Second, her acquaintance with General Edward Beale, owner of the Tejon Ranch, helped Mary learn enormous amounts about the land, its inhabitants, and its history. The sheer availability of information aided in her recovery, and her early impressions of this area of California became a foundational aspect of her most popular nature writing. Another consequence of her move to California was a release "from the long spiritual drought" that occurred after she reencountered "the warm pervasive sweetness of ultimate reality, the reality first encountered so long ago under the walnut tree."

In 1889 Mary's essay "One Hundred Miles on Horseback" was published in *The Blackburnian*. Besides launching a forty-five-year writing career, this travel essay has strong elements of Austin's characteristic writing style. First, it is autobiographically influenced by her trip to California; it has the energy and enthusiasm of one seeing the land for the first time. Much of Austin's writing is autobiographical in nature, and Austin seemed especially talented at transferring raw experience into fiction. Second, in her essay Austin celebrates the land she finds, describing it in caring detail meant to evoke a larger intuitive or spiritual understanding of the land. While clearly an early and undeveloped piece, "One Hundred Miles on Horseback" captures the lyric sense of the land that became emblematic of Austin's most popular writing about California.

During her first year in California, Mary refused an engagement with a divinity student in Illinois and began instead to seek out a way to make money to contribute to the family. After working for some time as a tutor and teacher, she stopped teaching when she could not pass a required certification examination. She became engaged to Wallace Stafford Austin during the summer of 1890, and they were married on 19 May 1891. Wallace Austin was a vineyardist, an engineer, a speculator, and a sometimes farmer; he repeatedly failed in whatever career endeavor he undertook, however. From the beginning the Austins' marriage was a mismatch that became increasingly more troubled as the years passed. In addition to Wallace Austin's inability to settle into a successful career that would allow him to provide for his family, the Austins did not communicate well, something for which Austin blames her husband: "After years of rasping, disappointed struggle, during which she contrived to pull their practical affairs into some sort of working shape, he never once came toward her; was most silent when there was most need of talking; absent when there was the sharpest demand for his presence. . . . Once he had given himself to me, my husband never looked at another woman; but he also never looked with me at any single thing. He never, more than he could help, afforded me a clue as to where he himself might be looking." The Austins moved repeatedly during their first years of marriage as Wallace pursued various career opportunities, including teaching. During these years Austin worked on her writing, gathering information from and about the California landscape that eventually inspired her writing.

Although still early in her career, Austin already felt that the West was to be her main literary focus. When the Austins moved to San Francisco, Austin introduced herself to poet Ina Coolbrith. Coolbrith's poetry was published in eastern magazines, a mark of success Austin admired. Because of Coolbrith's reputation and connections–she had associations with the *Overland Monthly,* a highly regarded periodical that published only quality original material–Austin went to her for advice about preparing her own work for publication. Coolbrith was helpful and supportive and advised Austin to see the current editor of the *Overland Monthly.* In this way Austin had three short stories accepted for publication by the magazine: "The Mother of Felipe," Austin's first professional publication, appeared in the November 1892 issue, followed by "The Wooing of the Seniorita" and "The Conversion of Ah Lew Sing," both published in 1897. All three stories were influenced by her observations of the California environment.

Also in 1892, the Austins' only child, Ruth, was born severely mentally retarded. The actual cause of Ruth's disabilities is unknown; Austin blamed a genetic inheritance from her husband's side of the family, but inadequate medical support at Ruth's

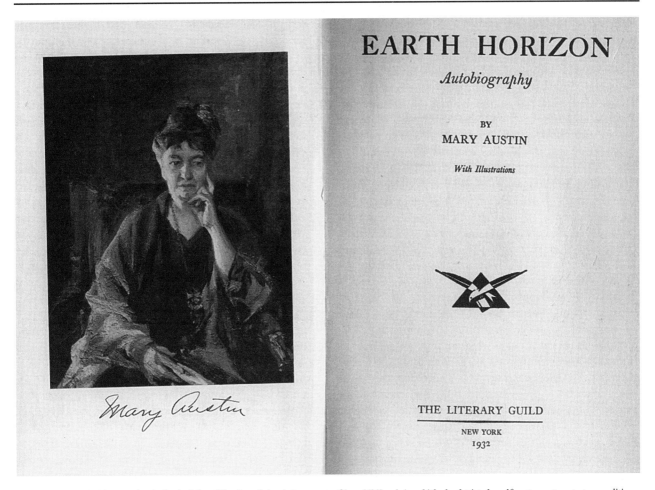

EARTH HORIZON
Autobiography

BY
MARY AUSTIN

With Illustrations

THE LITERARY GUILD
NEW YORK
1932

Frontispiece and title page for the book-club publication of Austin's account of her childhood, in which she depicts herself as two separate personalities: "I-Mary" and "Mary-by-herself"

birth may also have been the cause. Austin felt she was blamed for Ruth's disabilities by her family, and particularly by her mother. Upon discovering the truth about Ruth, Susanna said to Austin, "I don't know what you've done, daughter, to have such a judgment upon you." Austin's disappointment must have been acute; she omits all but the briefest discussions of Ruth in her autobiographical writing.

Austin continued to write, working on small stories and sketches influenced by the desert landscape she had come to love; meanwhile, the entire responsibility for Ruth's considerable care fell to her. In 1899 she experimented with life apart from her husband by moving with her daughter to Los Angeles, where she took a lecturing position with the State Normal School. She claims that her hope was to "lay hold of a means of subsistence which would warrant her husband in joining her; in making good a maintenance in a more promising *milieu*," but it is also likely that she tired of the isolation and was eager to circulate her writing. As she was so skilled at doing, Aus-

tin used the separation to establish literary contacts, and she developed a relationship with Eve and Charles Lummis. Lummis was an authority on the Southwest and editor of *Land of Sunshine*. He was also associated with a circle of western writers who met at his home. Austin became a member of the Arroyo literary circle, and she was appointed to the staff of the magazine in 1902 when it was renamed *Out West*. Austin published four stories, poems, and a novelette in Lummis's magazine. Austin eventually returned to Wallace and Owens Valley to attempt a reconciliation that ultimately failed.

In 1903 *The Land of Little Rain,* a collection of short stories celebrating the California landscape and its inhabitants, appeared. The stories in *The Land of Little Rain* were first serialized in the *Atlantic Monthly,* and the published collection, along with the popular serialized stories, helped to establish Austin's reputation as a western writer. Included in the collection is "The Basket Maker," a short story about a Paiute Indian woman named Seyavi. In this story Austin returns to several important themes, including an exploration of the independent female artist, Native American art and values, and the distances created by disparate cultures. In "The Basket Maker" Seyavi sells her baskets in a culture that does not appreciate the beauty of the artwork she creates. Despite her cultural separation from Seyavi, Austin's narrator struggles to understand Seyavi's philosophy of artistic creation, which emphasizes the utility of beauty.

The early 1900s were productive for Austin. Beginning in 1900, she published regional poetry in the children's magazine *St. Nicholas,* and in July 1900 she published a short story, "The Shepherd of the Sierras," in the *Atlantic Monthly.* In 1904 she published *The Basket Woman: A Book of Fanciful Tales for Children* and *Isidro,* her novel about Hispanic California. These were followed in 1906 by *The Flock,* Austin's meditative description of sheepherding and its history. Although Austin was professionally successful during these years, her marriage continued to suffer. Additionally, Ruth's care weighed on her and limited her ability to write. Austin says little about her relationship with her daughter in her autobiography, but she records her grief when, in 1905, she placed Ruth in an institution "for the enfeebled" in Santa Clara, California. To questions about Ruth, Austin replied, "We have lost her." Ruth lived until 1918, although Austin never saw her again. By 1906 Austin had left Wallace and moved to Carmel, where she built a home. The Austins remained formally married until 1914, when Wallace sued for divorce on the grounds of desertion.

During this time, Austin claims, her encounters with a Native American medicine man taught her to write. In California she felt herself connected to Paiute Indian life and so began an association with Native American cultures that lasted, in both positive and troubling formulations, for the duration of her life. Identifying a reality that she called "The Friend-of-the-Soul-of-Man," which she claimed was apprehended through rhythm and the patterns of writing, Austin said that she "learned what it meant; how to prevail; how to measure her strength against it. Learning that, she learned to write." By claiming an association with Native American spirituality and literary styles, Austin both appropriates aspects of another culture and gladly acknowledges that she has been influenced by it. In her lifetime Austin was well respected as an authority on native cultures, but she also received substantial criticism from contemporaries for her undocumented claims to expertise in cultures in which she had little factual knowledge. Although Austin knew no native languages and never lived among the Indians she wrote about, her

writing and lecturing gradually led to her establishment in the popular consciousness as an expert in Native American cultures and literature with her troubling combination of ethnocentric beliefs and good intentions. Austin's "translations" of Indian verse were not true translations, but partial ones to which she added words and phrases, rearranging them to create her sense of Native American life. She called these resulting poems "re-expressions" in "Amerindian" verse. In 1923 she published *The American Rhythm,* in which she puts forward a complicated and intuitively based thesis regarding poetic rhythm. Austin firmly believed that the land and its inhabitants are connected, and thus the landscape affects literary production. Austin saw poetic cadence as a function of the environment and Native American literature as the truest example of the American environment.

However appropriate charges of cultural appropriation might be, it is also important to remember that Austin resists claiming that her writing is from a native point of view or that she writes as a Native American (although she does make a dubious and unprovable claim to Native American ancestry). Although she never fully escapes the stereotypes of her day, she is consistently aware of the cultural differences that separate her, or her narrators, from the Indians she depicts. Her claims to knowledge of Native American cultures are combined with careful and respectful acknowledgment of the ways in which her association with those cultures, however brief or fractured, influences her own writing. Indeed, she urges American writers to look at indigenous forms of literature for inspiration, rather than to recall ancient Greek writings, as was the tendency among some contemporary modernists. She was also actively involved in protecting Native American arts from commercialization.

Between 1908 and 1909 Austin became an international traveler, journeying to Europe and living for a time in London. Herbert Hoover, who became president of the United States in 1929, and his wife, Lou Henry Hoover, were in London, and Austin used the occasion of her travels to reintroduce herself to her former California acquaintances. Hoover, who at this time was an internationally successful mining engineer and businessman, introduced Austin to other writers, publishers, and people of literary importance whom they felt could help advance her writing career. Although no longer living in California, Austin published *Lost Borders,* another collection of short stories set in the California desert. In *Lost Borders* Austin attributes a feminine gender and a conscious agency to the desert landscape. In a now-famous passage in "The Land," Austin creates a desert whose physical attributes are remarkably like her own:

> If the desert were a woman, I know well what like she would be: deep-breasted, broad in the hips, tawny, with tawny hair, great masses of it lying smooth along her perfect curves, full-lipped like a sphinx, but not heavy-lidded like one, eyes sane and steady as the polished jewel of her skies, such a countenance as should make men serve without desiring her, such a largeness to her mind as should make their sins of no account, passionate, but not necessitous, patient—and you could not move her, no, not if you had all the earth to give, so much as one tawny hair's-breadth beyond her own desires.

Throughout *Lost Borders* this female desert shapes, and even determines, the outcome for the characters. In "The Ploughed Lands" a Shoshone woman, Tiawa, cannot win Gavin, the white man who becomes lost and whom she guides back to "the ploughed lands," away from the desert, which Austin represents as "another mistress who might or might not loose his bonds." Beliefs that regional environment dramatically influences literary production and that environment must make itself fully present as a character are evident in this collection. Austin later published these ideas in her article "Regionalism in American Fiction" (*English Journal,* February 1932).

Also in *Lost Borders,* Austin continues her feminist critique of a patriarchal culture that refuses to grant women the respect to which their talents and power entitles them—to that culture's detriment. In "The Ploughed Lands" Gavin becomes undone by the spell cast on him by the desert. Unable to find his way alone, and equally unable to respond to Tiawa's desire for him, Gavin is restored to a sense of independent agency only after he is led back to the secure boundaries represented by the ploughed lands of white civilization. The raw, untamable power of the female desert leaves him impotent and befuddled. With bitingly astute humor, in "The Return of Mr. Wills" Austin rewrites the dime-novel Westerns she read as a young girl. Drawn away from his family for the hope of a lost mine, for Mr. Wills "the clew of a lost mine was the baldest of excuses merely to be out and away from everything that savored of definiteness and responsibility." Mr. Wills's abandoned wife, however, finds her financial and emotional situation substantially improved without her husband, and when he returns to settle "on his family like a blight," she is left with the small but palpable certainty that the desert will act as her ally and that "in time its insatiable spirit will reach out and take Mr. Wills again."

As a character, Austin's desert is willful and capable of violence, but she is mostly a danger to those white men who attempt to dominate her. Native Americans, women, and marginalized men such as Austin's ore-pocket hunter are at home in the desert and come to no harm there. In the final story of the collection, "The Walking Woman," Austin creates an unforgettable but mysterious woman whose walking releases her from the social constraints of femininity and provides for the narrator a model of strength and truth-telling. Critic Faith Jaycox argues that "The Walking Woman" is also a revision of formulaic Western narrative in its refusal to grant agency to the script of male violence encoded in the "outlaw" narrative. Reconfiguring the outlaw as the female Walking Woman, called Mrs. Walker by the locals because no one knows her name, Austin celebrates a woman who has no name, no permanent home, and walks freely across the land despite the danger of violence she faces as a lone woman. As Jaycox notes, "The Walking Woman" deserves comparison to Charlotte Perkins Gilman's "The Yellow Wallpaper" (1892) with their opposite prescriptions for a cure to female illness. Where the narrator of "The Yellow Wallpaper" faces insanity as a result of her enforced confinement, the Walking Woman embraces independence and freedom when she walks off her illness in the open landscape.

Austin's feminism, as well as her ability to take events from her own life and transform them into compelling art, is evident in her other writing as well. In 1912 Austin published two works, the short story "Frustrate" (*Century Magazine,* January 1912) and her most popular novel, *A Woman of Genius.* Both are informed by Austin's own experiences of trying to combine a traditional marriage with a woman's commitment to her artistic goals. In "Frustrate," which can be read autobiographically as a damning commentary on her failed marriage, Austin examines a woman's growing dissatisfaction with her husband, who, she realizes, will never be able to understand her. Nor, the narrative strongly suggests, will anyone else give credence to her pain: "I know that I am a disappointed woman and that nobody cares at all about it, not even Henry; and if anybody thought of it, it would only be to think it ridiculous." The narrator, not able to understand "why we shouldn't have what we like out of life," leaves her husband and joins an artists' circle, where she finds that the male artists continue to privilege beauty over talent. An older woman writer notices her and gives some sage advice for developing her own "game" rather than

Austin in 1932 (photograph by Will Connell)

credited as being; here as elsewhere in Austin's writing, values are gendered and methods of interpretation are affected by those gendered values. A woman's value is often judged by her ability to decorate a male-dominated environment and to tend to men's needs. Austin's refusal to capitulate, which she often cleverly represents as sheer inability for which she must not be judged, is typical, as is her subversive response in writing a story that reveals the gendered attitudes that undermine women's ability.

In *A Woman of Genius* Austin investigates in depth the social pressures that contrive to construct a version of womanhood, naturalize the behaviors it requires, and then punish women who do not conform to its constraints. *A Woman of Genius* has been compared to Rebecca Harding Davis's "Life in the Iron Mills" (1861), Elizabeth Stuart Phelps's *The Story of Avis* (1877), Kate Chopin's *The Awakening* (1899), Theodore Dreiser's *Sister Carrie* (1900), and Edith Wharton's *The House of Mirth* (1905). Austin's novel explores heroine Olivia Lattimore's childhood, marriage, motherhood, and the death of her child, as well as her gradually accelerating success in the theater. In Olivia, Austin creates a version of herself as the artist-hero, trying to discover how to balance marriage, motherhood, and other obligations of womanhood with the seemingly incompatible goals of a career. Olivia's marriage to Tommy Betterworth is as mismatched as Austin's to Wallace Austin; in her depiction of the marriage, Austin explores how Olivia's identity is crushed under enforced ignorance.

Olivia, like most women at the turn of the century, has no vocabulary for her questions about her developing sexuality. She realizes that "it might have all turned out very well if I had been what I seemed to him and to my family." Olivia has no path to follow in order to develop her talents as an actress, and her marriage is largely a result of impoverished options; it disintegrates under the growing distance between Tommy's expectations and Olivia's commitment to her career. At the conclusion of the novel Olivia is refused a passionate coupling when Garret, the man she loves, will not accept her artistic goals. Not coincidentally, however, Olivia forces Garret's choice; her commitment to acting, though costly, is nonetheless represented as valuable itself. Olivia enters a companionate relationship with a man who, while not sparking passion, will support her aspirations to the stage. The ending of the novel is ambiguous: Austin has Olivia's beau claim that their relationship might be better than "the vision and the dream" because "it would be company."

focusing on appearance. "Frustrate" ends on a sustained note of unhappiness as the narrator still regrets that her own appearance does not match the ideal and bemoans the ways in which society does not help those women who are unable to play its game. For the narrator, growing old promises only the hope that her pain will lessen.

Austin's own appearance caused her some anxiety; in *Earth Horizon* she writes, "I think it extremely likely that Mary had never been so homely or *gauche* in appearance as she had grown up thinking herself." Her comment reveals she felt unable to meet "the pink-and-white, ringletted wax-doll prettiness which was the American ideal at the time." Austin's concern was not misplaced; until recently, her appearance and particularly her weight have been frequently mentioned negatively in assessments of her work. "Frustrate" also reveals that artistic creation is not the transcendent enterprise it is often

A Woman of Genius was written and published when Austin was living in New York City, where she moved in 1910. Austin lived in New York for more than a decade, successfully continuing her writing career, associating herself with feminist activities, and embellishing her status as an expert on Native American literature and culture. In February 1911 Austin's play *The Arrow-Maker* was produced by the New Theatre on Broadway. Advertised as an Indian extravaganza, the play, with its all-white cast, closed early amid harsh reviews citing its unimaginative plot, pretentiousness, and a host of other problems. Despite this literary slap, the play strengthened Austin's growing reputation as a Native American authority.

During Austin's New York years, she had a tempestuous romantic relationship with muckraking journalist Lincoln Steffens, whom she met in Carmel in 1906. Their relationship apparently ended when Steffens did not reciprocate Austin's passionate feelings, but his literary ghost haunted Austin's fiction for some time. The novel *No. 26 Jayne Street* (1920), which Austin described in *Earth Horizon* as her best, reflects some of these New York experiences. Set in New York, the novel explores socialism, aiming "to uncover the sleazy quality of current radicalism, in which the personal expression of radicals contradicted and reversed the political expression." *No. 26 Jayne Street* casts Steffens as the unscrupulous Adam Frear, a man who is unwilling to revise his relationships with women by living according to the philosophy he espouses. In her letters Austin accused Steffens of leading her on and not being honest about his feelings toward her. Steffens, who was involved with another woman during the time of his association with Austin, is devastatingly portrayed. Frear is duplicitous, asking heroine Neith Schuyler to marry him while he is still involved with another woman.

In 1924 Austin published *The Land of Journeys' Ending,* in which she returns again to the style of nature writing that launched her career. Austin also returned to the West permanently, moving to Santa Fe and building Casa Querida (Beloved House). Around 1927 Austin wrote *Cactus Thorn* (1988), a novella in which she revisits her relationship with Lincoln Steffens, casting Steffens as the emotionally unscrupulous politician Grant Arliss. In this novella Austin combines the lyrical nature writing of her earlier work with the social critique and commentary of her New York years. The easterner Arliss has an affair with Dulcie Adelaid, a Western woman whose emotional honesty and physical passion fascinate him. Although he declares a commitment to Dulcie, Arliss eventually betrays her love and returns to New

York, where he makes plans to wed a woman whose wealthy and prominent family can advance his political career. Like Frear in *No. 26 Jayne Street,* Arliss is unable to live by his own rhetoric, and his behavior is represented as immoral and cowardly next to the courage Dulcie displays. Dulcie travels to New York, challenges Arliss on his behavior, and kills him. She then returns, uncaught and unpunished, to her home in the West.

With the character of Dulcie, Austin creates a woman who has an essential link to the mystic power of the desert. Upon meeting her, Arliss realizes that "for all the effect she had upon him, she might, like the horned lizard starting from under his foot, have assembled herself from the tawny earth and hot sand, or at a word resolve herself into the local element." This essential female identity allows her passionate response, but it also requires that she be respected: "The desert sort of sucks you empty and throws you away. That is, unless you are willing to take what it gives you in place of what you had." When Arliss fails to live up to his own rhetoric, he is doomed; Dulcie becomes as much an agent of Arliss's self-imposed doom as his betrayed lover. The novella was initially rejected by Houghton Mifflin and later published in 1988 after it was discovered with Austin's papers by Austin scholar Melody Graulich.

In 1932 Austin published her autobiography, *Earth Horizon,* which became a Literary Guild selection. In it she creates a novelistic narrator by referring to herself in the third person. In the introduction Austin claims that by the first third of her life an important and immanent pattern was set for her that made it "clear that I would write imaginatively, not only of people, but of the scene, the totality which is called Nature, and that I would give myself intransigently to the quality of experience called Folk, and to the frame of behavior known as Mystical." Austin's autobiography centers on the time and events she considered most important—her youth and early years as a writer. By doing so, however, Austin suppresses most of her productive New York years. *Earth Horizon* is compelling for many reasons: it is an entertaining recollection of an unusual life; it introduces the main themes of Austin's fiction; and it is an exceptionally strong feminist critique for its time and its genre.

Austin had many encounters with ill health during her life, including breakdowns and depression, a diagnosis of breast cancer in 1907, and a heart attack in 1932. She died in 1934, and her ashes are sealed in cement on Mt. Picacho near her Casa Querida.

Letters:

T. M. Pearce, *Literary America, 1903–1934: The Mary Austin Letters* (Westport, Conn.: Greenwood Press, 1979).

Bibliography:

Joseph Gaer, *Mary Austin, Bibliography and Bibliographical Data,* monograph no. 2 (Berkeley: University of California Press, 1934).

Biographies:

Helen MacKnight Doyle, *Mary Austin: A Woman of Genius* (New York: Gotham House, 1939);

Augusta Fink, *I-Mary: A Biography of Mary Austin* (Tucson: University of Arizona Press, 1983);

Esther Lanigan Stineman, *Mary Austin: Song of a Maverick* (New Haven: Yale University Press, 1989).

References:

Melody Graulich and Betsy Klimasmith, eds., *Exploring Lost Borders: Critical Essays on Mary Austin* (Reno: University of Nevada Press, 1999);

Mark T. Hoyer, *Dancing Ghosts: Native American and Christian Syncretism in Mary Austin's Work* (Reno: University of Nevada Press, 1998);

Faith Jaycox, "Regeneration through Liberation: Mary Austin's 'The Walking Woman' and Western Narrative Formula," *Legacy,* 6 (Spring 1989): 5–12;

Karen S. Langlois, "A Fresh Voice from the West: Mary Austin, California, and American Literary Magazines, 1892–1910," *California History,* 64 (Spring 1990): 22–35;

Thomas Matthew Pearce, *The Beloved House* (Caldwell, Idaho: Caxton, 1940);

Pearce, *Mary Hunter Austin* (Boston: Twayne, 1965);

Nancy Porter, afterword to *A Woman of Genius,* by Austin (Old Westbury, N.Y.: Feminist Press, 1985), pp. 295–321;

Marjorie Pryse, introduction to *Stories from the Country of Lost Borders,* by Austin (New Brunswick, N.J.: Rutgers University Press, 1987).

Papers:

Mary Hunter Austin's letters, manuscripts, and other related papers are housed in the Mary Hunter Austin Collection in the Henry E. Huntington Library, San Marino, California. Austin's letters to Lincoln Steffens are collected at the Columbia University Library, New York.

Amelia Edith Huddleston Barr

(29 March 1831 – 10 March 1919)

Rose Norman
University of Alabama in Huntsville

See also the Barr entry in *DLB 202: Nineteenth-Century American Fiction Writers.*

BOOKS: *Romances and Realities: Tales of Truth and Fancy* (New York: J. B. Ford, 1876 [i.e., 1875]);

The Young People of Shakespeare's Dramas: For Youthful Readers (New York: Appleton, 1882);

Cluny McPherson: A Tale of Brotherly Love (New York: American Tract Society, 1883);

Scottish Sketches (New York: American Tract Society, 1883);

The Hallam Succession: A Tale of Methodist Life in Two Countries (New York: Dodd, Mead, 1884);

Jan Vedder's Wife (New York: Dodd, Mead, 1885);

The Lost Silver of Briffault (New York: Phillips & Hunt / Cincinatti: Cranston & Stowe, 1885);

The Last of the MacAllisters (New York: Harper, 1886);

Between Two Loves: A Tale of the West Riding (New York: Harper, 1886; London: Warne, 1894);

The Bow of Orange Ribbon: A Romance of New York (New York: Dodd, Mead, 1886);

A Daughter of Fife (New York: Dodd, Mead, 1886);

The Harvest of the Winds, and Other Stories (London, Clarke, 1886);

The Squire of Sandal-Side: A Pastoral Romance (New York: Dodd, Mead, 1886);

A Border Shepherdess: A Romance of Eskdale (New York: Dodd, Mead, 1887; London: Clarke, 190?);

Paul and Christina (New York: Dodd, Mead, 1887);

Christopher, and Other Stories (New York: Philips & Hunt / Cincinnati: Cranston & Stowe, 1888);

Master of His Fate (New York: Dodd, Mead, 1888); republished as *In Spite of Himself: A Tale of the West Riding* (London: Clarke, 1888);

The Novels of Besant and Rice (New York: Dodd, Mead, 1888);

Remember the Alamo (New York: Dodd, Mead, 1888); republished as *Woven of Love and Glory* (London: Warne, 1890);

Feet of Clay (New York: Dodd, Mead, 1889);

Friend Olivia (New York: Dodd, Mead, 1890);

Amelia Edith Huddleston Barr (University of Texas at Austin)

The Beads of Tasmer (New York: Bonner, 1890; London: Clarke, 1893);

The Household of McNeil (New York: Bonner, 1890);

She Loved a Sailor (New York: Dodd, Mead, 1890);

Love for an Hour Is Love Forever (New York: Dodd, Mead, 1891);

Mrs. Barr's Short Stories (New York: Bonner, 1891);

A Rose of a Hundred Leaves: A Love Story (New York: Dodd, Mead, 1891);

A Sister To Esau (New York: Dodd, Mead, 1891);

Michael and Theodora: A Russian Story (Boston: Bradley & Woodruff, 1892);

The Preacher's Daughter: A Domestic Romance (Boston: Bradley & Woodruff, 1892);

A Singer from the Sea (New York: Dodd, Mead, 1893);

Girls of a Feather: A Novel (New York: Bonner, 1893);

Lone House (New York: Dodd, Mead, 1893);

The Mate of the "Easter Bell" and Other Stories (New York: Bonner, 1893);

The Flower of Gala Water (New York: Bonner, 1894);

Bernicia (New York: Dodd, Mead, 1895);

A Knight of the Nets (New York: Dodd, Mead, 1896);

Winter Evening Tales, 2 volumes (New York: Christian Herald, 1896);

The King's Highway (New York: Dodd, Mead, 1897);

Prisoners of Conscience (New York: Century, 1897);

Stories of Life and Love (New York: Christian Herald, 1897;

Maids, Wives, and Bachelors (New York: Dodd, Mead, 1898);

I, Thou, and the Other One: A Love Story (New York: Dodd, Mead, 1898);

Trinity Bells: A Tale of Old New York (New York: Christian Herald, 1899);

Was It Right to Forgive? A Domestic Romance (Chicago & New York: H. S. Stone, 1899);

The Maid of Maiden Lane: A Sequel to "The Bow of Orange Ribbon": A Love Story (New York: Dodd, Mead, 1900);

The Lion's Whelp: A Story of Cromwell's Time (New York: Dodd, Mead, 1901);

Souls of Passage (New York: Dodd, Mead, 1901);

A Song of a Single Note: A Love Story (New York: Dodd, Mead, 1902);

The Black Shilling: A Tale of Boston Towns (New York: Dodd, Mead, 1903);

Thyra Varrick: A Love Story (New York: Taylor, 1903; London: Unwin, 1904);

The Belle of Bowling Green (New York: Dodd, Mead, 1904);

Cecilia's Lovers (New York: Dodd, Mead, 1905);

The Man Between: An International Romance (New York & London: Authors & Newspapers Association, 1906); republished as *Love Will Venture In* (London: Chatto & Windus, 1907);

The Heart of Jessy Laurie (New York: Dodd, Mead, 1907);

The Strawberry Handkerchief: A Romance of the Stamp Act (New York: Dodd, Mead, 1908);

The Hands of Compulsion (New York: Dodd, Mead, 1909);

The House on Cherry Street (New York: Dodd, Mead, 1909);

A Reconstructed Marriage (New York: Dodd, Mead, 1910);

A Maid of Old New York: A Romance of Peter Stuyvesant's Time (New York: Dodd, Mead, 1911);

Sheila Vedder (New York: Dodd, Mead, 1911);

All the Days of My Life: An Autobiography, the Red Leaves of a Human Heart (New York & London: Appleton, 1913);

Three Score and Ten: A Book for the Aged (New York & London: Appleton, 1913);

Playing with Fire (New York & London: Appleton, 1914);

The Measure of a Man (New York & London: Appleton, 1915);

The Winning of Lucia: A Love Story (New York & London: Appleton, 1915);

Profit and Loss (New York & London: Appleton, 1916);

Christine, a Fife Fisher Girl (New York & London: Appleton, 1917);

Joan: A Romance of an English Mining Village (New York & London: Appleton, 1917);

An Orkney Maid (New York & London: Appleton, 1918);

The Paper Cap: A Story of Love and Labor (New York & London: Appleton, 1918);

Songs in the Commmon Chord: Songs for Everyone to Sing, Tuned to the C Major Chord of This Life (New York & London: Appleton, 1919).

Editions: *Christopher, and Other Stories* (Freeport, N.Y.: Books for Libraries Press, 1971);

Scottish Sketches, 2 volumes (Freeport, N.Y.: Books for Libraries Press, 1971);

Remember the Alamo, introduction by Raymund A. Paredes (Boston: Gregg Press, 1979);

All the Days of My Life: An Autobiography; The Red Leaves of a Human Heart (Arno, 1980).

SELECTED PERIODICAL PUBLICATIONS–
UNCOLLECTED: "Women's Views of Divorce," *North American Review,* 150 (January 1890): 117–123;

"Flirting Wives," *North American Review,* 156 (January 1893): 69–74;

"Good and Bad Mothers," *North American Review,* 156 (April 1893): 408–415;

"The Modern Novel," *North American Review,* 159 (November 1894): 592–600;

"Discontented Women," *North American Review,* 162 (February 1896): 201–209.

Amelia Edith Huddleston Barr was thirty-nine when she began a writing career that lasted nearly forty years, bringing her, as Philip Graham wrote in *Notable American Women* (1971), to "the front rank of popular American novelists." At her death she had published nearly eighty books, including sixty novels and novellas, of which the best known are *Jan Vedder's Wife* (1885) and *The Bow of Orange Ribbon* (1886). Two of her novels, *Remember the Alamo* (1888) and *The Man Between: An International Romance* (1906), are available in full text on the World Wide Web. Some of her books are still in print, but she has received little critical attention, and her work is largely unknown today. Yet, her novels remain highly readable and worthy of study for her skill in characterization and her ability to appeal to the popular imagination of her day.

Amelia Edith Huddleston was born in Ulverston, Lancashire, England, the second of six children, of whom only three daughters survived childhood. Her mother, Mary Singleton Huddleston, came from a Quaker family, and her father, William Henry Huddleston, was a Methodist minister. Owing to her father's work, the family moved every two or three years, living in various small towns in the north of England and on the Isle of Man. From early childhood, she loved books, and she wrote her first story while still a teenager. She re-creates her childhood and adolescence in rich detail in *All the Days of My Life: An Autobiography, the Red Leaves of a Human Heart* (1913): "I had become very ambitious. I longed to write books and to travel and to see the great cities and the strange peoples I had read about." When she was sixteen, her father lost most of his private income through a business reversal, and his health began to fail. Barr sought to contribute to the family income by teaching school in Norfolk, and a year later she enrolled in a Wesleyan school for teachers in Glasgow, Scotland. In Glasgow she met Robert Barr, a large mill owner whom she married in 1850. They lived in Glasgow until 1853 when they immigrated to the United States after the failure of Robert Barr's business. The first of their nine children, Mary, was born in 1852, and the second, Eliza (called Lilly or Lillie), was born while her parents were preparing to immigrate. On the ship, her husband met a wealthy politician who aided them in settling in Chicago, where a third child was born and died within the year. In her Chicago home, Barr opened a small school for girls, but in November 1854 her husband, while trying to involve himself in local politics, came into conflict with the politician who had helped him, and the family had to leave Chicago suddenly. They settled first in Memphis, Tennessee, but an epidemic of yellow fever caused them to move again, this time to Austin, Texas, where Robert worked in the state tax office. They lived in Austin from 1857 to 1866 and had five more children, two of whom died. After the Civil War they moved to Galveston, Texas. Barr's husband and two sons died in the yellow fever epidemic of 1867; another son was born with yellow fever and died.

After seventeen years of marriage and nine children, Barr was left to support herself and three daughters, including the seven-year-old Alice, who was mentally disabled. After failing to make a living running a boardinghouse in Galveston, Barr moved her family to New Jersey, where, through a Texas friend,

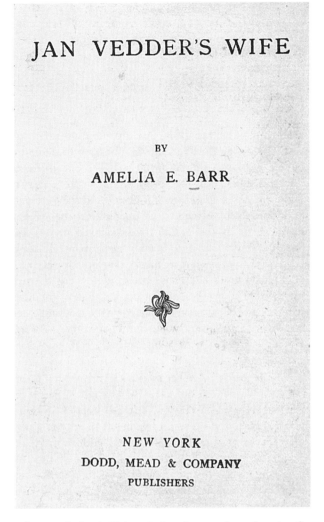

JAN VEDDER'S WIFE

BY

AMELIA E. BARR

NEW YORK
DODD, MEAD & COMPANY
PUBLISHERS

Title page for Barr's third novel, about the separation and reunion of a fisherman and his wife in the Shetland Islands

she was hired by William Libbey, a businesswoman whose three sons she tutored for nearly two years. Then, with Mr. Libbey's aid, she began to sell her short fiction and moved to New York City in 1870. At this time she also sought assistance from American minister and social reformer Henry Ward Beecher, whom she had met when she lived in England. Beecher invited her to write for his magazine, the *Christian Union*, and also helped her get work with other New York papers. Thereafter, she supported herself entirely by writing. She published her first novel, *Eunice Leslie* (ca. 1871), as a serial in *Working Church* in the early 1870s. Barr often published short novels first in periodicals and later as books, though occasionally, as with *Eunice Leslie* and later with *Femmentia's Experience* (1890) no book version appears in the record. Her first work published in book form was a collection of short stories and essays, *Romances and Realities* (1876). Success and recognition came with her third novel, *Jan Vedder's Wife*, in 1885.

Barr's novels, including *Jan Vedder's Wife,* remain of interest because of a certain simplicity of style and a gift for storytelling. Contemporary reviewers such as Oscar Fay Adams (*Andover Review,* March 1889) praise her books for their sincerity and optimism, as well as "her evident capability for projecting herself into the life of a by-gone time, and living in it as if it were the present." Her novels are character-driven, and her characters are multifaceted. Her abiding interest is in human relationships and in showing good-hearted, fair-minded people working out the problems life sends them. In Barr's fictional universe, problems arise from human failings such as ignorance and greed, and they are generally resolved through right action by a benevolent character motivated by Christian charity. Barr was also an avid student of history who spent many hours in New York libraries researching background for her novels. The settings she chose most often were the mill towns of northern England in the first half of the nineteenth century, Scottish coastal towns and islands, and New York City from pre-Revolutionary times forward. Her novels typically have one or more romantic plots, strongly influenced by the historical or social setting.

Jan Vedder's Wife began as a short story that Barr's daughter convinced her to revise as a novel. Set in the isolated Shetland Islands off the west coast of Scotland, it emphasizes the lives and livelihood of seagoing people. The story of Jan and Margaret Vedder's marriage, separation, eventual reunion and a long, happy life together, reveals Barr's perceptiveness to both the husband's and the wife's points of view. Typically for Barr, the novel centers on the strongest male character, Jan Vedder, a lighthearted, popular fisherman without family or riches. Jan attracts Margaret Fae, the only child of Peter Fae, a wealthy store owner in the little town of Lerwick, and she marries him despite her father's objections. Their marriage is strained by their different attitudes toward money—Margaret hoards, and Jan is a spendthrift. The situation worsens as Jan has a series of financial setbacks, until Margaret moves back to her father's house. Margaret's life takes a downward turn when her recently widowed father remarries a woman Margaret's age, chastening her proud spirit considerably. The low point comes when Jan gets into a fight, is found severely wounded near a cliff by the sea, and mysteriously disappears, leading to years of gossip about whether he committed suicide or Peter Fae killed him. At this point, Barr alternates two plots: what happens to Margaret and Peter in Lerwick and what happens to Jan Vedder himself.

Barr is remarkable in bringing to life characters that might readily be reduced to stereotypes in the hands of a lesser writer. Peter Fae and his young second wife, for example, are fully realized characters. Like many of Barr's novels, the book explores the education of a wife, though with narrative sympathy evenly divided between husband and wife. The strongest theme in *Jan Vedder's Wife* concerns what Barr believed was necessary to make a good marriage: mutual respect and a measure of equality, but with the wife clearly subordinated to the husband. Although the novel focuses mostly on Jan, his character does not really change; he only becomes more successful. Margaret, however, changes radically from a proud woman who hoards money to a humbled woman who seeks to help others. Barr applied the ideal of service to everyone, but the lesson of chastened pride she more often assigned to women.

After *Jan Vedder's Wife* Barr published one or more books a year for more than thirty years, while continuing to write poetry and shorter pieces for newspapers and magazines. For many years, she wrote weekly stories for publisher Robert Bonner's popular New York paper, the *Ledger,* and she contributed regularly to *Harper's Weekly, Harper's Bazar, Frank Leslie's Magazine, St. Nicholas, Century Magazine,* the *Advance,* and religious journals such as the *Christian Union,* the *Christian Herald,* and the *Illustrated Christian Weekly.* On trips to England, she also sold her work to various English papers. Her writing brought her a comfortable income that enabled her to spend summers in the Hudson River Valley, where she bought and renovated a home, Cherry Croft, in 1890. She wintered in New York City hotels and summered at Cherry Croft until a few years before her death, when she moved to Richmond Hill, Long Island.

It is not pride or selfishness, but innocence that challenges the heroine of *The Bow of Orange Ribbon* (1886). Set in pre-Revolutionary New York City, it is the first of a series of ten novels tracing New York history up to the early twentieth century. Though once again a domestic story in which a father objects to his daughter's choice of husband, *The Bow of Orange Ribbon* tells a different story from *Jan Vedder.* The main characters are a prosperous Dutch family, the Van Heemskirks; their Scottish neighbors, the Semples; and Captain Richard Hyde, the dashing English soldier who visits a guest in the Semple house. The courtship of Richard Hyde and Katherine Van Heemskirk at first seems to move in the direction of the seduction novel. Katherine, young and naive, and Richard, dashing and debt-ridden, seem bound for ruin when her father objects to their relationship and they begin to meet secretly. Richard begs a favor—the bow of orange ribbon—which leads to a duel in which her father's preferred match for Katherine, Neil Semple, gives Richard a nearly mortal wound. During Richard's recovery, Katherine is manipulated into secretly marrying him, and after he recovers, they move to England. Barr does not sensationalize the melodrama inherent in these situations; instead, she develops her characters in such a way that none is wholly villainous or doomed, and we can sympathize with all of them, particularly Katherine's doting father, Joris Van Heemskirk. While the plotline is purely romantic, Barr researched the novel for two years in order to make the historical details accurate and even studied Dutch to present authentic dialect for the Van Heemskirks.

Barr uses the Yorkshire dialect in a series of industrial novels and short stories set in mill towns in the north of England where she grew up. Her main characters in the industrial novels are usually landed gentry who prosper through a cotton or woolen mill, though sometimes she depicts a mill owner who has risen from the working class, as in the novella "Crowther and Thirsk" in *Christopher, and Other Stories* (1888) and the novels *Between Two Loves: A Tale of the West Riding* (1886) and *Master of His Fate* (1888). She repeatedly makes the point in her novels that the mill is a good thing only in benevolent hands, a point demonstrated in *The Measure of a Man* (1915). Set in the years before and during the American Civil War, *The Measure of a Man* depicts the consequences when a blockade cuts off the cotton supply from America and one mill after another closes, throwing workers into poverty. The benevolent mill owner, John Hatton, nearly bankrupts himself by keeping his mill open as long as there is cotton, rather than closing it to protect his profits.

The most political of Barr's industrial novels is *The Paper Cap: A Story of Love and Labor* (1918), which takes place in the 1830s, when the weaving industry was shifting from traditional handlooms to mechanized labor. Barr depicts the resistance of weavers and landed gentry to industrialization, including the spoiling of the countryside by factories, but generally concludes in favor of progress. The main plot of *The Paper Cap* dramatizes the passage of the Reform Bill of 1832, which extended the vote to men of the working class. Squire Annis is a model patron of the working class who initially opposes mechanization for creating "factory slaves" but comes to see that a mill will be the best way to restore prosperity to the working class in his region, and hence to his own estate. The autonomy of traditional weavers who own their own looms and often their own cottages is shown as desirable but insupportable in the face of cheap goods produced by machines. Rather than dwell on the loss, Barr represents people as capable of adapting to this social change.

By and large, Barr's novels have little ethnic diversity. The main characters are usually English or Americans of English or Dutch ancestry, with greatest pride of ancestry going to English of Yorkshire stock. She occasionally includes Jewish people as minor char-

acters, such as the moneylender Jacob Cohen in *The Bow of Orange Ribbon,* portrayed favorably, though in stereotypic roles. Writing in her autobiography about the African Americans and Native Americans she knew in Texas, she is casually racist and treats these groups largely as an unreliable servant class. Two novels that do give significant attention to ethnic characters and themes are *Remember the Alamo* (1888) and *She Loved a Sailor* (1890), both set in the 1830s. *Remember the Alamo* focuses on an upper-class Mexican American family in which the husband is a New Yorker of English ancestry and the wife a Mexican of Castilian ancestry. The conflict in this novel arises not so much from divided loyalties involved in the choice between Texan and Mexican military forces, as from the attempt of a villainous Roman Catholic priest to gain control of the family fortune by persuading the wife and daughters to go into a convent while the men in the family are away at war. Raymund A. Paredes, in his introduction to the 1979 edition, regards Barr's treatment of Mexican Americans here as unexceptional in portraying Anglo-American culture as superior to Mexican culture; for example, in the characterization of the two daughters: one is strong and smart like her father, the other emotional and gullible like her Hispanic mother.

In *She Loved a Sailor* Barr again emphasizes a mixed heritage family and the politics of the Jacksonian era, but here the family are enslaved African Americans, and the plot chiefly concerns the efforts of Anglo characters to free them. The novel follows the romances of two New Yorkers, one of whom, Jane Keteltas, marries a Southerner, Nigel Forfar, and moves to a rural area near Memphis. The situation is a familiar one in slavery literature: the Northerner, struggling to adapt to Southern ways, discovers that her husband's dead father had a second family by an enslaved woman with whom he lived as man and wife and raised four children as his own, assuring them that they were legally free and educating the children in the North. On his father's death, Nigel had destroyed their free papers and reenslaved the mother and two daughters, who were visiting their father in the South. Barr's use of this plot emphasizes Jane's successful attempts to prevent the capture of the two sons in the North and to bring the two daughters to safety. Whereas Barr's Mexican American family in *Remember the Alamo* includes fully developed main characters, the African American characters here are sketchily drawn with emphasis on the tragedy and danger of their situation. Similarly, all of the white Southerners are highly stereotypical, and Jane's husband, Nigel, comes near to being as villainously one-dimensional as the Catholic priest in *Remember the Alamo*. The novel draws on Barr's recollections of the year she lived in Memphis in the 1850s, vividly portraying a beautiful but degraded country in which even the enslaved conspire to maintain an insidious system of domination and control.

Barr is more interested in Christian themes of service and love than in political themes, but her views are not inconsistent with the conservative feminism of her day. On woman suffrage, she wrote, "Any one who lived in England during the early half of the nineteenth century would be a suffragist," but she takes a jaundiced view of women's capacity to work together for social change. In various novels she depicts the perils of women's legal and economic subordination. In *Friend Olivia* (1890), for example, she creates sympathy for the vengeful Anastasia de Burg by showing her forced to marry a man who beats her and threatens to lock her up in the attic, where an iron ring attests to the fate of a previous unruly mistress of that manor. In this novel and in an article for the *North American Review,* she comes out in favor of divorce in cases of "flagrant cruelty." Yet, Barr rarely emphasizes the wrongs of women, preferring instead to urge women to rise above adversity and rely on Christian faith. In the preface to her autobiography, she urges women to follow her own example: "I have drunk the cup of [women's] limitations to the dregs, and if my experience can help any sad or doubtful woman to outleap her own shadow, and to stand bravely out in the sunshine to meet her destiny, whatever it may be, I shall have done well."

Barr's belief, as reported in her autobiography and reflected in her books, was that God repays personal industry and integrity. Her description of her own working life as a writer documents her astonishing literary productivity and accounts, in some measure, for the moral element in her books. Barr began writing professionally to escape teaching, and for fifteen years was turning out at least one story and poem a week for the *New York Ledger.* Throughout her life she continued to rely on the periodical press, producing so much that she used two pseudonyms (her daughters' names) in order to place this volume of work. She estimated she took a week or less to write a story, and five weeks to three months to write a novel, not counting time for historical research. Not only did she learn her craft in a situation that required volume, but everything for the *Ledger* "had to be intensely moral," since this was a paper that advertised itself as "The Wholesome Educator of Millions"; yet, Barr's moralizing is well-handled, and sanctimony is absent from her work.

Barr's novels seem to have had a reliable audience in the low thousands, though her novels usually went through several editions. In writing for a popular audience, she was clearly aware that she needed to make certain appeals to what she described in a letter to an aspiring writer as "the great class of mediocre intelligence." Yet, many of her novels reveal an engagement with character and scene that ranks them a cut above the general level of popular writing. Barr's work resembles that of Sarah Orne Jewett in her use of dialect, richness of local detail, and interest in character. She had a gift for describing scenes in nature and for enlivening subordinate characters with realistic detail. Barr's novels, however, have a broader range of setting and subject matter and more plot than is usually associated with local colorists. She was especially interested in recreating historical periods: American resistance to the Stamp Act in *The Bow of Orange Ribbon,* the crisis over the English Reform bill in *The Paper Cap,* the reign of Oliver Cromwell in *Friend Olivia* and *The Lion's Whelp* (1901), and the Texas war against Mexico in *Remember the Alamo.* She gave those events a personal and domestic flavor. Scenes in Parliament, for example, are not recorded directly but are reported to family members by Squire Annis in *The Paper Cap.* Battle scenes in *The Lion's Whelp* and *Remember the Alamo* are reported to anxious families who have been waiting at home for news.

In the 1890s Barr's short stories were collected in several volumes: *Mrs. Barr's Short Stories* (1891), *The Mate of the "Easter Bell" and Other Stories* (1893), *Winter Evening Tales* (1896), and *Stories of Life and Love* (1897). Barr's short stories have the same sort of plots, characters, and settings as her novels, but they lack depth and complexity. They were, in many cases, intended as Sunday School literature and are chiefly didactic in tone. They are actually no more didactic than many of her novels, but the novel form gives her space to develop characters, and creating lively, realistic characters is what she did best. Her short-story collections do, however, provide a good cross-section of her work, since they read like condensed versions of her novels. Indeed, several of Barr's novels, such as *Lone House* (1893), *A Knight of the Nets* (1896), *Prisoners of Conscience* (1897), and *Trinity Bells* (1899), were first published as short stories.

In both essays and fiction, Barr emphasizes the importance of the traditional family and idealizes women's domestic role. Writing for the *North American Review* in 1893 on the topic "Good and Bad Mothers," she exalts motherhood and the family: "Family! Country! Humanity! these three, but the greatest of these is Family; and the heart of the family is the good mother." This essay recalls issues she had addressed in earlier works. In *The Measure of a Man,* for instance, she had depicted Jane Hatton, wife of the prosperous mill owner, as attempting to control her family size through abortions. Arguing with her husband, John, she says, "Highly civilized men don't want children," to which he replies, "The profession of motherhood is woman's great natural office; no others can be named with it. The family must be put before everything else as a principle." Since they have only one child at this point, and John Hatton is portrayed as a generous and kind husband in love with his wife, Jane is made to seem selfish and unreasonable. All the narrative sympathy is with John, who, rather than force his will on his wife, wisely thinks to himself, "She must be led to convince herself. I will trust her to God."

Trusting to God is a common solution to problems in Barr's essays and in her novels. Jane Hatton, for example, experiences a mystical spiritual transformation after which she welcomes motherhood. Barr rarely creates unregenerate villains and always arranges happy endings, writing in her autobiography that "I have always found myself unable to make evil triumph. Truly in real life it is apparently so, but if fiction does not show us a better life than reality, what is the good of it?" What draws her attention is the good in people, and she emphasizes characters who rise to their better nature. In *Jan Vedder's Wife,* for example, the banker who loans Jan Vedder all the money in Margaret Vedder's life savings without her knowledge at first seems to be a stereotypical miser, but by the end of the book he has become Margaret Vedder's best friend. Widowed and childless himself, he arranges to leave his fortune for the benefit of widows and orphans, with Margaret Vedder superintending the funds. Similarly, in *Friend Olivia,* the revengeful Anastasia de Burg, a woman who throughout the book has been wholly motivated by selfish desires, ultimately devotes herself to the care of her beloved half brother, an equally villainous pirate who has been blinded by lightning.

Barr was writing yet another novel when she died of a cerebral hemorrhage in 1919, just short of her eighty-eighth birthday. She was never a best-selling author, nor did she aspire to high art; but she was a serious writer, committed to her work, and she had a loyal following of readers. Barr spoke repeatedly of her enjoyment of writing, particularly novel writing. Writing quickly came naturally to her, and she even enjoyed rewriting her work. When she had to rewrite *Friend Olivia* to suit the demands of serial publication, she said she also worked at "trying how much richer and better I could make it." The result is one of her best novels. In a 1912 *New York Times* interview Barr reported that she wrote her novels entirely for enjoyment, that she could not actually make a living from them—a startling claim from so prolific and popular an author. Her comments may indicate that she was not able to drive a hard bargain with her publishers, and it is generally true that regular book publishing did not pay nearly as well as serialized novels or (page for page) short fiction, poetry, and articles for the popular press. In her first fifteen years as a writer, for example, she claims to have earned at least $1,000 a year from her poetry alone. Typically, Barr sold her novels outright, rather than negotiating royalties, earning at the most $1,000 for *Remember the Alamo* in 1887, and often less, according to her autobiography. In contrast, Richard Gilder's *Century Magazine* paid $3,000 for the serialization of *Friend Olivia* in 1888, and at the peak of her productivity and prosperity in 1891–1892, she earned

Barr at work

$2,500 each for four novels written as serials for the *Ledger.*

Barr's books received regular reviews in *The New York Times, Athenaeum,* and other literary journals of the day; the reviewers often praised her talent as a storyteller and the wholesomeness of her plots. Some of her novels are less successful than others (*Trinity Bells,* for example), but all share qualities summed up by reviewer Hamilton W. Mabie in *Book Buyer* (September 1891): "There is a hearty contempt for convention in her stories; a hearty zest for sound and simple people; people who do not sophisticate, who have passions and are not ashamed of them; who love frankly and unreservedly; who believe in themselves and their fellows and God." These qualities and her rich characterization earned her a steady audience of readers and generally favorable critical assessment in her day. The most serious analysis of Barr's novels in comparison to other writers of the day was done by Oscar Fay Adams in an 1889 *Andover Review* article assessing the twelve novels she had written at that time. Adams ranks *Jan Vedder's Wife* as the best work of fiction yet published by an American woman and concludes that she "may very well rank as the foremost woman novelist in America." Barr's literary reputation was never higher than in Adams's review; the quality of her books seems to have declined somewhat when she began writing for serial publication in the early 1890s. Appreciations and reminiscences written after her death in 1919, such as Hildegarde Hawthorne's in the *Bookman,* emphasize her productivity, "the strong charm of sincerity," and the fact that her books "were fresh, youthful and sweet to the last."

These qualities lighten the burden of morality that drives her novels and make them entertaining reading to this day. Barr does not probe complex human motivations nor explore difficult philosophical or ethical questions. When she addresses issues such as poverty and social injustice, there is usually a straightforward solution because her fictional world is a place of hope and possibility. In all her work, she strikes what she describes in her poetry as "the Common Chord—the C major of life." It is this capacity for striking the "Common Chord" that gives her work an enduring power worthy of greater critical attention than she has yet received.

Interview:

"Writing Fiction Not Profitable, Says Amelia Barr," *New York Times,* 21 July 1912, pt. 5, p. 5.

References:

Oscar Fay Adams, "The Novels of Mrs. Barr," *Andover Review* (March 1889): 248–268;

Robert Bogard, "Amelia Barr, Augusta Evans Wilson, and the Sentimental Novel," *Marab,* 2 (Winter 1965–1966): 13–25;

Philip Graham, "Texas Memoirs of Amelia E. Barr," *Southwestern Historical Quarterly,* 69 (1966): 473–498;

Hildegarde Hawthorne, "Amelia E. Barr—Some Reminiscences," *Bookman,* 51 (May 1920): 283–286;

Kate Dickinson Sweetser, "Amelia Barr and the Novice," *Bookman,* 58 (October 1923): 172–178.

Papers:

The letters, papers, and manuscripts of Amelia Edith Huddleston Barr are scattered among thirty libraries in sixteen states. The most significant sites are the University of Texas at Austin (two letters and a 48-page typescript of *A Knight of the Nets* (1896) with handwritten notes); the Barker Center for American History, Austin, Texas (eleven letters, eight of them photostats, and an undated glass plate of the Barr family); the State Archives Library, Austin, Texas, Lillie Barr Munro Collection and Lillie Barr Munro Correspondence (eleven typescript chapters of an unpublished novel by Barr, two photographs of Barr, a memoir by Lillie Barr Munro describing Austin in 1856–1867, and two letters from Lillie Barr Munro regarding the collection); Fales Library, New York University (twelve letters); Overbury Collection, Wollman Library of Barnard College (three letters and three brief, fragmentary manuscripts); Butler Library, Columbia University (four letters); Middlebury College Library (one letter); Houghton Library, Harvard (four letters, including one to John Greenleaf Whittier); Schlesinger Library, Radcliffe (two letters); and the University of Virginia Library, Barrett Collection (49 letters and two brief manuscripts).

Lillie Devereux Blake

(12 August 1833 – 30 December 1913)

Grace Farrell
Butler University

See also the Blake entry in *DLB 202: Nineteenth-Century American Fiction Writers.*

BOOKS: *Southwold: A Novel,* as Lillie Devereux Umsted (New York: Rudd & Carleton, 1859);

Rockford; or, Sunshine and Storm, as Umsted (New York: Carleton, 1863);

Zoe (Oswego, N.Y.: American News Company, 1866);

Forced Vows; or, A Revengeful Woman's Fate (New York: Beadle & Adams, 1870);

Fettered for Life; or, Lord and Master. A Story of To-day (New York: Sheldon, 1874);

The Fables (New York: Blaber, 1879);

Woman's Place To-day. Four Lectures, in Reply to the Lenten Lectures on "Woman" by the Rev. Morgan Dix (New York: Lovell, 1883);

A Daring Experiment and Other Stories (New York: Lovell, Coryell, 1892).

Edition: *Fettered for Life,* afterword by Grace Farrell (New York: Feminist Press, 1996).

SELECTED PERIODICAL PUBLICATIONS–
UNCOLLECTED:

POETRY

"Despair," anonymous, *Knickerbocker Magazine,* 51 (May 1858): 449;

"A Coquette's Retrospection," *Knickerbocker Magazine,* 61 (May 1863): 412;

"Reparation," *Galaxy,* 11 (April 1871): 592–593;

"Love and Death," *Galaxy,* 16 (November 1873): 661;

"The Sea People," *Galaxy,* 20 (December 1875): 789.

FICTION

"My Last Conquest," anonymous, *Harper's Weekly,* 1 (14 November 1857): 734;

"A Tragedy of the Mammoth Cave," anonymous, *Knickerbocker Magazine,* 51 (February 1858): 112–121;

"John Owen's Appeal," as Lillie D. Umsted, *Harper's New Monthly Magazine,* 22 (December 1860): 72–81;

Lillie Devereux Blake (portrait by William Oliver Stone, 1859; from Katherine Devereux Blake and Margaret Louise Wallace, Champion of Women: The Life of Lillie Devereux Blake, 1943)

"A Lonely House," anonymous, *The Atlantic Monthly,* 7 (January 1861): 40–51;

"A Wild Night Ride," as Essex, *Forney's War Press,* 1 (1 March 1862): 1;

"The Rescued Fugitives," as Essex, *Forney's War Press,* 1 (22 March 1862): 4;

"Carrying False Colors," as Essex, *Forney's War Press,* 1 (3 May 1862): 1, 8;

"A Romance of the Battle of Fair Oaks," as Essex, *Forney's War Press,* 1 (26 July 1862): 1, 8;

"A Midsummer Sail," as Essex, *Forney's War Press,* 1 (20 September 1862): 1, 8;

"Life on the Mountains," as Essex, *Forney's War Press,* 1 (24 October 1862): 1; (1 November 1862): 1; (8 November 1862): 1, 8;

"The Slave's Revenge," as Essex, *Forney's War Press,* 2 (15 November 1862): 1;

"My Cruise in the Dream," as Mrs. L. Devereux Umsted, *Home Journal* (29 November 1862): 1; (6 December 1862): 1;

"Brothers by Birth–Foes in the Field," as Mrs. L. Devereux Umsted (Essex), *Forney's War Press,* 2 (21 March 1863): 1; (28 March 1863): 1; (4 April 1863): 1; (11 April 1863): 1;

"Shot through the Heart: A Tragedy of Fredericksburgh," anonymous, *Knickerbocker Magazine,* 61 (May 1863): 413–421;

"The Tenant of the Stone House," as Mrs. Lillie Devereux Umsted, *Frank Leslie's Illustrated Newspaper,* 16 (1 August 1863): 297–298; (8 August 1863): 313–314;

"The Gloved Lady," as L. Devereux Umsted, *Frank Leslie's Illustrated Newspaper,* 16 (22 August 1863): 345–346; (29 August 1863): 361–362;

"A Visit to a Fortuneteller," as Lillie Devereux Umsted, *Frank Leslie's Illustrated Newspaper,* 18 (2 July 1864): 229–230;

"In Prison," as Essex, *New York Weekly Mercury,* 28 (27 May 1865): 6–7; (3 June 1865): 5–6;

"The Dead Letter," as Essex, *New York Weekly Mercury,* 28 (11 November 1865): 3;

"A Clap of Thunder," as Di Fairfax, *New York Ledger,* 21 (27 January 1866): 3;

"Found Drowned," *New York Weekly Mercury,* 30 (5 October 1867): 4;

"Who Won the Prize," *Saturday Evening Post* (21 October 1871): 2;

"Ten Years' Devotion," *New York Sunday Times,* 22 August 1875, p. 1;

"The Veteran's Last Parade," *Sunday Press,* 25 December 1882;

"Tessie's Merry Christmas," *Albany Sunday Press,* 23 December 1883;

"Roses and Death," *Short Stories,* 29 (January 1898): 98–101.

NONFICTION

"The Social Condition of Woman," anonymous, *Knickerbocker Magazine,* 61 (May 1863): 381–388;

"Work for Lady Orators," *New York Times,* 3 November 1871, p. 2;

"The Case of Susan B. Anthony," *New York Times,* 31 May 1873, p. 5;

"When Women Grow Old," *Home Journal* (1 July 1874): 1;

"A Speaker's Fright," *Era* (1876);

"Jailoress Jones," *Era* (March 1876);

"Kate Southern," *Evening Telegram,* 20 May 1878;

"Silver Lake," *Evening Telegram,* 27 September 1878;

"Kate Cobb's Fate," *Evening Telegram* (25 January 1879);

"Woman's Plea for Woman: Mrs. Blake on Men's Jokes at Women's Expense," *Evening Telegram,* 5 February 1879;

"The Women of Utah," *Evening Telegram,* 11 February 1879;

"Our Indian Policy," *Evening Telegram,* 18 April 1879;

"Needed Reforms: Seats for Shop Girls," *Christian Union* (19 February 1882);

"Woman's Conjugal Rights," *Christian Union* (28 March 1882);

"Police Matrons," *Christian Union* (1 April 1882);

"Dr. Hammond's Estimate of Women," *North American Review,* 137 (November 1883): 495–501;

"Ladies in the White House," *Evening Telegram,* 7 March 1885;

"Notes and Comments," *North American Review,* 142 (March 1886): 317;

"U. S. Grant," *Evening Telegram,* 17 April 1886;

"Are Women Fairly Paid?" *Forum,* 2 (October 1886): 201–211;

"Martha Washington and Other Notable Women of the Revolutionary Period," *Business Woman's Journal,* 1 (May–June 1889): 1, 74–76;

"Legislative Advice," *Woman Suffrage Leaflet,* 7 (May 1895);

"Memory of the Civil War," *New York Press,* 12 June 1898;

"Forgotten Belles," *Fashions* (May 1898): 152–153;

"Reminiscences," *New York Times,* 15 February 1899;

"Objects to Prizefighting," *New York Times,* 18 September 1899, p. 6;

"Brutality," *Evening Journal,* 21 November 1899;

"Co-Education," *New York Times,* 24 December 1899, p. 23;

"Looking Backward to Two Christmas Days of Long Ago," *New York Times,* 18 December 1904;

"The Duties of the Father," *New York Times,* 11 April 1905, p. 10.

During the spring of 1874, when Susan B. Anthony read aloud to her ailing mother, the book she chose was Lillie Devereux Blake's new novel, *Fettered for Life.* "It will stimulate every girl reader to have something beside marriage to depend on for support," Anthony recorded in her daybook for Sunday, 5 April. Blake's novel was unabashedly political, depicting, through a cross-section of social levels, the consequences of female subordination in the home and in the workplace, thus addressing some of the most pressing social questions of the late nineteenth century.

Blake, who lived from 1833 to 1913, was a fiction writer, journalist, essayist, and lecturer, a cultural critic who commented on a wide range of social conventions, especially those regarding women. Her prose is of particular interest because it spans both the Civil War and the suffrage movement and moves between sentimental, realistic, and naturalistic forms. She was a gifted writer who published in such journals as *The Atlantic Monthly, Harper's,* and the *North American Review,* but her life circumstances forced her into the mass market of popular magazines. There, attuned to the attitudes and expectations of her readership, she developed strategies for satisfying her audience while articulating radical revisions of the status quo. Hers was a prose of disguise, layered with carefully hidden agendas that undercut commonly held perceptions regarding women.

Blake was born Elizabeth Johnson Devereux in Raleigh, North Carolina, on 12 August 1833. Her parents were second cousins and childhood sweethearts, Sarah Elizabeth Johnson of Stratford, Connecticut, and George Pollok Devereux of North Carolina. Both were descendants of the Puritan poet and divine Jonathan Edwards. Blake's was a privileged background. Her mother's father was a judge, the son of the first U.S. senator from Connecticut and grandson of the rector of Trinity Church in New York City. On her mother's side, Blake descended from the founders of Columbia University; years later, beneath portraits of her ancestors, she presented a petition to admit women to Columbia, an action that led to the founding of Barnard College. Her father, descended from the first governor of North Carolina, was the child of a wealthy southern landowner and a seafaring Irish rover. When he returned from a five-year grand tour of Europe following his graduation from Yale, he married her mother.

Blake's birth was preceded by those of two sisters who died in infancy and followed by another girl, who died shortly after birth. Her mother was pregnant again in the spring of 1837 when, on their yearly journey from North Carolina to Connecticut, George Devereux became ill in Suffolk, Virginia, and died there of a stomach hemorrhage at the age of forty-two. Blake's mother continued the journey home to Stratford and gave birth in August to another girl, named Georgina after her father. Because Blake's father was a second son with no male heirs, property that seems to have been intended for him upon the death of an uncle was not forthcoming. Half of a $1.6-million estate went to Blake's paternal grandmother, who settled $100,000 upon each of her two granddaughters.

Blake was raised in New Haven, Connecticut, and educated in the Yale undergraduate curriculum by tutors. In 1855 she married Frank Umsted, a lawyer from Philadelphia, and settled briefly in St. Louis, where her first daughter was born. She felt stultified both by the confinement of pregnancy and maternity and by the limitations of a middle-class married woman's life. As she wrote in the draft of her unfinished autobiography, "the forced inaction of my life was intolerable to me. . . . my heart was often full of fierce rebellion against the fate that had imprisoned a spirit full of restless activity in a woman's form and condemned it to stagnation."

To give her life a purpose that marriage and motherhood had not automatically bestowed upon it, Blake began writing for publication. She sent her first story, "My Last Conquest," to *Harper's Weekly,* vowing that if it were rejected she would give up her dream of being a writer. It was published in the 14 November 1857 issue. Thereafter she produced a steady stream of narratives in which she stretches sentimental notions of womanhood by undermining stereotypes of feminine frailty and purity. In "My Last Conquest" Blake uses both military and stage metaphors to make the drawing room into a battleground between the sexes and implies that prescribed feminine behavior is an act. While the sentimental model held up the guileless woman as an ideal, Blake reveals guilelessness itself to be a learned role in a patriarchal script that suppresses women by emptying them of their own desires and ambition.

Blake battled to contain her own ambitious nature and to submit her life to the script decreed for a married woman, but her desires were never extinguished by her restrictive circumstances, and her personal turmoil haunted her early works. Tales such as "A Tragedy of the Mammoth Cave," published in *The Knickerbocker* (February 1858), treat two of her characteristic themes– desire that has no sanctioned outlet and frustration turned to revenge. Throughout her work, Blake insists that women share in the human capacity for desire, violence, and even murderous rage. Her furious and vengeful women serve her much as the obsessed madwomen of other nineteenth-century women authors served them: as Sandra Gilbert and Susan Gubar put it in their *No Man's Land* (1988), these authors "constructed the emblematic figure of an enraged but tormented madwoman in order simultaneously to repress and express their feelings of anger."

After moving to New York and giving birth to a second daughter, Blake began her first novel, *Southwold,* which was published in February 1859 and went into second and third editions within two weeks. In *Southwold* Blake establishes a strategy for presenting radical ideas that she uses throughout her life's work. Within the double-voiced narrative of the novel, its feminist heroine–strong, passionate, trapped in a world of hypocrisy in which she has no sanctioned place—is condemned as evil by a narrator who is imbued with conventional mores. Unlike the furious first wives of much nineteenth-century fiction, who, in a neat psychological metaphor, are safely split off from the heroines and consigned to attics, Blake's heroine is herself a madwoman. With a personality much like that of her author—ambitious, shrewd, and given to startling pronouncements on such matters as the negative effects of Christianity on the freedom of women—Medora Fielding discovers that her only patrimony is insanity. Inherited from her paternal grandmother, who died in an asylum, Medora's madness manifests itself in her stride: she "paced with restless steps up and down a short distance, turning ever at a certain point and walking fiercely back to her original starting-place, as if she were confined within barriers, instead of at liberty to wander away for miles." As Blake well knew, a woman was not at liberty to wander away; she was confined within the barriers devised by a social order that limited her actions and suppressed her desires. Insanity is indeed her patriarchal legacy: Medora's confinement is both symptom and source of her madness.

After the exuberance of her first success, "misfortunes and trials," as Blake later wrote in her autobiography, "were coming fast that would drive me into a fierce struggle for my daily bread, a struggle which would absorb all my powers and leave me small opportunities for culture." Three months after *Southwold* appeared, Frank Umsted, having lost Lillie's considerable fortune, killed himself at age twenty-six with a pistol shot to the head. Abandoned to support two small children and traumatized by memories of the suicide, Blake reveals in her journals both a refusal to define herself as a victim and a resistance to remarriage as a solution to her widowhood and the precarious financial situation that resulted from it. She resisted what she called in "The Social Condition of Woman" (*Knickerbocker Magazine,* May 1863) the "degrading necessity of . . . selling herself," and instead she began writing again.

Poet James Russell Lowell, Blake's editor at *The Atlantic Monthly,* wrote to her on 3 April 1860 about one of her early stories, "It is rather savage, perhaps, but I liked it for leaving the ordinary highway." Written shortly after the suicide of her husband and published on the eve of the Civil War, "A Lonely House" draws on the archetype of the Cain and Abel story, depicting two brothers who kill one another after their widowed mother dies. Although she never gave direct public voice to the private grief that is evident in her journals, through the figure of the widow who sequesters herself in the house after her husband's death Blake was able to convert her grief into a meditation on concealment and self-destruction. She displaces both the violent sui-

cide of her own husband and the suppressed rage of the story's widow into a reciprocal fratricide. The brothers subtly become one another's double, and, thus, each kills the self by killing the other; homicide and suicide are halves of a single act that shatters the ingrained nomenclature of genealogy and continuity.

Read alongside Abraham Lincoln's 1858 "House Divided" speech, this story provides a metaphorical resonance with the Civil War, which both shattered and made a nation. It eerily foreshadows national mourning over a divided civic house in which brother killed brother. When Lincoln declared that a house divided against itself cannot stand, he chose a biblical metaphor that employed the rhetoric of domesticity associated with women's writing of the nineteenth century. Unlike the rhetoric of rugged individualism, Lincoln's imagery linked the worldly sphere of war, designated as masculine, to home and hearth, the province of women. The Civil War hastened the unraveling of these gendered divisions, a process that Blake continues in subversive ways throughout her most radical postwar fiction. "A Lonely House" conjoins martial and domestic elements to reveal how, as in the nation itself, violence both caused division and was caused by the divisiveness within. Violence lay within the domestic envelope, within the house divided.

To earn a living, Blake had to forego publishing in prestigious journals such as *The Atlantic Monthly* and write for the mass market in popular magazines. Under her own name and a variety of pseudonyms (including Essex, Charity Floyd, Violet, Aesop, Tiger Lily, Di Fairfax, and Lulu Dashaway), she routinely sold stories to Frank Leslie's publications, as well as to *Harper's Weekly, The Saturday Evening Post,* the *New York Leader,* the *Sunday Times,* and a wide variety of other periodicals. She contracted with the *New York Evening Post, New York World,* and *Philadelphia Press* to serve as a Washington-based war correspondent during 1861–1862 and again during 1865–1866. Armed with letters of introduction from such people as Theodore Dwight Woolsey and cabinet secretaries in the Lincoln administration, Blake quickly formed a network of acquaintances that led her into some of the city's most powerful circles. Most of her newspaper pieces were anonymous, and only a few were clipped and have been saved in her archives; many of her short stories from this period survive, however.

These stories, which Blake wrote under the name Essex for *Forney's War Press,* a supplement to the *Philadelphia Press,* move from sentimental to realistic styles as she cautiously introduces violence into her fiction. The realities of war reports and battlefront engravings, printed side by side with her *Forney's War Press* fiction, seem to intrude upon the content of her stories. She weaves in realistic settings and actual events, deals with a range of social classes, and overrides sentimental evasions to deal with death and loss. Her stories bridge the gap between home and battleground. Domestic concerns push tentatively against the boundaries of war; marriage plots collide with war plots; and via disguises, women cross over from female havens to male arenas. Essex herself is disguised, cloaked under a male-sounding name that allows her safe passage between a woman's world of popular fiction and the mixed audience of *Forney's War Press.*

"A Wild Night Ride" (1 March 1862) makes explicit the war's violent invasion of the domestic sphere while safely containing it within a dream sequence. In a nightmarish chase, during which a young Yankee soldier flees Rebel forces, his fiancée inexplicably appears; the couple is captured and summarily executed just as the dreaming narrator awakens. Consumed by sheer terror, first of the chase and then of the execution, the soldier and his lover are reunited astride a galloping horse. The dreaming hero takes time to relish the unexpected intimacy of the moment: "the night was so lovely, the swaying motion was so pleasant, and I held Laura so close, that I could not realize my danger." The violence of the battle chase, manifested in the swaying motion of the galloping horse, dissolves into a sexualized moment that pierces through to complex connections between home and battleground, sex and violence.

"The Rescued Fugitives" is the first of several of her Civil War stories in which Blake deals with race and slavery. As the story sifts through racial stereotypes, one often undercutting another, it gives evidence of the culture's struggle with changing social codes and values. Throughout the story Blake subverts the prevailing views of her audience by presenting and contradicting stereotypical views of her slave protagonist, Neptune. The piling up of stereotypes suggests both the fluidity of the boundaries of racial stereotypes at a moment in history when events had thrust them into question and the confusion that is concomitant with struggles in the popular culture to re-envision the slave as freedman. Like a visual puzzle that, with a variety of predominant details, hides its most significant image, Blake's most compelling image of Neptune, one that subverts existing stereotypes, shows him as the capable leader of white men.

In 1864 Lillie Devereux Umsted fell in love with Grinfill Blake, a New York businessman several years her junior, whom she married in 1866. She continued to support herself through her writing. By the 1870s Lillie Blake, no longer anonymous, had found her voice as a lecturer for the suffrage movement. She was considered an indomitable speaker. *The New York Times*

Devereux at about fourteen

found her to be "forceful and eloquent"; the *New York Herald* declared Blake "the most brilliant lady speaker in the city"; and the *Albany Sunday Times* asserted, "there are very few speakers on the platform who have the brightness, vivacity and fluency of Lillie Devereux Blake."

From the 1870s until the first decade of the twentieth century Blake lectured and published on civil reform and suffrage as well as on a wide range of social topics, from the brutality of prizefighting to the value of coeducation. In "Kate Cobb's Fate" (*Evening Telegram,* 25 January 1879) she rallies around a woman who found herself in prison because of a man's betrayal; in "Woman's Conjugal Rights" (*Christian Union,* 28 March 1882) she exposes the systematic discrimination against female teachers who are not allowed to keep their jobs if they marry; in "Kate Southern" (*Evening Telegram,* 20 May 1878), using the case of a woman who was condemned to death after killing her husband in a jealous rage, she exposes the inequities involved in a criminal justice system that routinely acquitted men guilty of the same crime. In 1889 she wrote a series of articles on woman suffrage for the *Workman's Advocate* and was a popular speaker for the labor movement. In addition, from 1884 to 1904 Blake wrote a column for the *Woman's Journal,* the Boston-based voice of Lucy Stone's and Henry Blackwell's American Woman Suffrage Association (AWSA). The AWSA and the New York–based National Woman Suffrage Association (NWSA), to which Blake belonged, had split over the ratification of the Fourteenth Amendment, which excluded women from the vote. They merged into the National American Woman Suffrage Association (NAWSA) in 1890. Blake's columns played a conciliatory role as the two sides of the woman's movement began to come together.

Blake served as president of the New York State Woman Suffrage Association from 1881 until 1892. In 1886 she founded the Society for Political Study; in 1897 she also founded and served as president of the New York Woman Suffrage Union. She chaired the Civic and Political Equality Union of New York City in 1898, and in 1900 she founded and served as president of the National Legislative League.

Blake also initiated actions that ultimately led to the founding of Barnard College of Columbia University. Her great-great-grandfather had been Columbia's first president when it was known as Kings College, and her great-grandfather had been the first president after the American Revolution, when its name was changed to Columbia College; yet, Blake and her daughters were excluded from admission. In 1873 she delivered an application to President F. A. P. Barnard for admission of five female candidates and prepared a plea that Barnard supported before the board of trustees. The board referred the proposal to committee, effectively halting action on it. As a result of Blake's initiative, however, President Barnard renewed her plea over the course of several years until in 1883, as a first step, women were admitted to the Columbia Collegiate Course for Women. In 1889 Barnard College was formed as an annex to Columbia. Blake actually was opposed to this latter course of action, because she wanted women to be admitted to Columbia on an equal footing with men and not relegated to a separate institution.

The argument between Blake and those wishing to establish a separate institution for women reflects the argument between those nineteenth-century feminists who wanted women integrated into the public world without regard to sex and those who emphasized gender differences in their struggle for women's rights. This argument struck at the heart of Blake's feminist philosophy. Her first essay on women, published anonymously in 1863, was, as the historian of journalism

Frank Luther Mott called it, "a startling article . . . demanding for women 'entire equality on every point—politically, legally and socially.'" The radical premise of "The Social Condition of Woman" is that gender identity is secondary to human identity. Blake maintained that women as well as men have the need for self-fulfilling action in the world, and she clearly identifies marriage, in a social order that excludes women from other means of earning their livelihoods, as institutionalized prostitution. Blake was a radical in the mode of Mary Wollstonecraft, Frances Wright, and Elizabeth Cady Stanton, who based their suffragism on the principle that women and men share a common nature and thus must share common rights. For the most part, however, American suffragists, including Susan B. Anthony, followed the thinking of Catharine Beecher and others, who emphasized the distinctive nature of women, their special needs, and unique role. They sought to elevate women's role within the domestic sphere and to extend that role into the public world. Blake's premise that gender identity is secondary to human identity countered the heart of the social ideology of womanhood in nineteenth-century America, which was based on the presumption that the sexes were radically different.

This argument is the hidden subtext of Blake's best-known novel, *Fettered for Life*. Praised by Nathaniel Parker Willis's *Philadelphia Home Journal* (6 May 1874) as a "thrilling story . . . a powerful book" and by the *New York World* (13 April 1874) as "among the most readable and notable books of the year," Blake's fifth novel sold 1,300 copies on the day of its publication. It went into several editions during the spring of 1874 and was reissued again in 1885. Its importance has been recognized by some twentieth-century scholars: *The Feminist Companion to Literature in English* (1990), for example, refers to the novel as "a feminist classic," and David Reynolds, in his *Beneath the American Renaissance: The Subversive Imagination in the Age of Emerson and Melville* (1988), calls it "the most comprehensive women's rights novel of the nineteenth century." *Fettered for Life* addresses the post–Civil War status of women, interweaving women's rights issues and abolitionist and temperance concerns with the plight of urban seamstresses and problems of personal freedom. Moreover, under the cover of these social issues lies a subtle attack upon the pervasive assumption that the sexes are by nature different. Because this agenda pushed against the boundaries of some nineteenth-century ideologies of womanhood, Blake had to present her ideas covertly. Through the revelations of a cross-dresser, the novel suggests that gender, like a garment, is a surface detail and that the profound differences between the sexes, used to create a hierarchy and to justify social inequities, are themselves not preordained givens but are social constructions.

In its focus on women and work, *Fettered for Life* is one of many novels of the last third of the nineteenth century that participated in an intense social debate concerning the changing status of women, including Louisa May Alcott's *Work: A Story of Experience* (1873), William Dean Howells's *Dr. Breen's Practice* (1881), and Elizabeth Stuart Phelps's *Dr. Zay* (1882). In *Fettered for Life* Blake insists that, beyond economic necessity, work was a vital activity for women as well as for men, bringing meaning to life and definition to self. This idea countered the notion that women should only work for the good of others and not of self, undermined the primacy of marriage in the fulfillment of women's lives, and posed a threat to the dominance of husbands through whom wives were supposed to be defined. Blake's ideology was a precursor of that which enabled the next generation of writers, including Charlotte Perkins Gilman and Kate Chopin, to depict with sympathy women who awakened to their own selves and desires. In the face of a culture that acknowledged in them no needs beyond fulfilling those of others, Blake's characters sought a voice other than that which the patriarchal culture might script for them.

While Blake insisted that only meaningful work could fulfill a person, male or female, domestic novelists more often conveyed the clear cultural message that only motherhood could fulfill a woman; motherhood solved their heroines' ennui and gave purpose to their sacrifice of self. The sentimental ethos of the nineteenth century was epitomized by self-sacrificing maternal devotion. Blake recognized this veneration of motherhood as one way to contain females within a fixed domestic order. In 1883 she published *Woman's Place To-Day. Four Lectures, in Reply to the Lenten Lectures on "Woman" by the Rev. Morgan Dix,* in which she publicly ridicules the rector of Trinity Church in New York City for his pronouncement that "Maternity is the glory of womanhood, and in this she is redeemed": "If from the easy chair of his study he dimly discerns . . . a wretched mother shuddering on the brink of the river, and clasping to her breast a miserable baby that is her shame and her disgrace, to her he says, 'Maternity is your highest function!'" Dix's response to women seeking "better opportunities for their sex," Blake asserts, is to bid "them be silent; meekness, forbearance, patience are the virtues which most adorn womanhood." But, she counters, "The chariot of progress is moving on. At its front sits awakened womanhood with the glory of hope in her starry eyes, and not even the Rector of Trinity Church is strong enough to block the wheels of that triumphant car."

Aware as she was of the struggles of mothers seeking to raise children in a world that denied women financial independence, Blake never ceases to point out the hypocrisy inherent in such idealized versions of motherhood. The lectures, published as *Woman's Place To-Day,* earned public recognition for her and drew ignominy down on Dix. The book, writes Elinore Hughes Partridge, "created a sensation in the contemporary press and did much to awaken women into active workers for suffrage."

The success of *Woman's Place To-Day* marked a change in Anthony's relationship with Blake. It brought to a head Anthony's resentment of Blake's insistence that the work for civil-rights legislation for women had to be undertaken along with the fight for suffrage. During her career in New York State, Blake organized legislative action that proved instrumental in modifying many laws that discriminated against women. Through her leadership, Civil War nurses became eligible for pension benefits; women became eligible for civil-service positions; mothers were made joint guardians of their children; and for the first time women could serve on school boards and work in all public institutions where women were incarcerated. Blake worked for twenty years to have policewomen hired in New York City and then lobbied for equity in their pay, promotions, and benefits. She even headed a woman's delegation that, protest banners unfurled, sailed out to the Statue of Liberty, newly arrived from France in 1886, to point out the hypocrisy of having a female statue of liberty at the gateway of a nation in which women were not free. Anthony disapproved; she believed strongly that energies diverted from suffrage weakened the cause.

In spite of Anthony's growing hostility, Blake attained such prominence in the woman suffrage movement that, in 1900, Stanton supported her to succeed Anthony as president of the NAWSA. However, after collaborating with Stanton on *The Woman's Bible* and defending her against an 1896 NAWSA resolution denouncing the book, Blake had incurred the ill will of a younger generation of more conservative suffrage leaders. Thereafter, she was systematically marginalized from the NAWSA, and her contributions to it were minimized in its official records. For instance, in 1897, for the first time, she was not invited to speak at the annual NAWSA Convention. In 1899 Anthony summarily dismissed the Committee on Legislative Advice, which Blake had ably chaired for five years. Under the auspices of the legislative committee, Blake coached other suffragists around the country on how to lobby their legislators and congressional representatives on issues of concern to women. In response to the dismissal, Stanton wrote to Blake: "You have not been treated by our young coadjutors with less consideration than I have been. They refused to read my letters and resolutions to the conventions. They have denounced the Woman's Bible unsparingly; not one of them has ever reviewed or expressed the least appreciation of *Eighty Years and More.* . . . Because of this hostile feeling I renounced the presidency and quietly accept the situation, and publish what I have to say in the liberal papers. . . . I have outgrown the Suffrage Association."

In 1900 Ida Harper, who with Anthony was editing the fourth volume of the *History of Woman Suffrage* (1881–1922), wrote to Blake that "there is no one in the state who has kept such close watch on the legislative work and knows so much about it as yourself. It needs a chapter by itself, and this should be written by you. It will be a pleasure to me to give you a chapter in this *History,* and I think also that you deserve to have it." Blake submitted her chapter, but it did not survive Anthony's animosity: little found its way into the official *History of Woman Suffrage.*

Blake's last book, *A Daring Experiment and Other Stories* (1892), includes an allegory on gender issues. "A Divided Republic," delivered as a lecture in 1885, describes a total migration of women to uncharted western territories, a move that initially delights the men left behind: "There was much rejoicing among the writers also. Mr. Howells remarked that now he could describe New England girls just as he pleased and no one would find fault with him; and Mr. Henry James was certain that the men would all buy the 'Bostonians,' which proved so conclusively that no matter how much of a stick a man might be, it was far better for a woman to marry him than to follow even the most brilliant career." Blake, so thoroughly political a writer herself, understood that because their sexual politics reflected the temper of the times, the didacticism of Howells and James was rendered invisible. Their work invited aesthetic over political comment.

On 25 November 1889 the *Woman's Illustrated World* published a profile of Blake that concluded with high praise and a call for future generations to remember her contribution:

> Through twenty-nine states of the Union, from the Pacific to the Atlantic, Mrs. Blake has traveled, taught, pleaded and petitioned in the interest of her sister women; when the victory is won; when all laws subversive of woman's liberty are erased from the statute books, when the married mother has a right to her chil-

dren, when women can cast the ballot in the interest of peace, morality and good government, let it be remembered that this glorious consummation is in great part the result of the twenty years patient work and unflinching heroism of Mrs. Lillie Devereux Blake.

Yet, Blake herself had little hope that either her literary work or the significant role she played in the woman's movement would survive the editing of history. Throughout her long career, however, Lillie Blake remained true to a feminist agenda based upon an assumption that sexual difference should not be privileged over other differences among people. At the end of the nineteenth century this vision moved her to the margins of the woman's movement; subsequently, however, it has located her more centrally in the unfolding feminist debate on difference and provides a place for her in an expanded literary canon that no longer excludes the political. She died at age eighty, on 30 December 1913, after a fall that broke her hip.

Biography:

Katherine Devereux Blake & Margaret Louise Wallace, *Champion of Women: The Life of Lillie Devereux* (New York: Revell, 1943).

References:

Grace Farrell, afterword to *Fettered for Life* (New York: Feminist Press, 1996), pp. 381–430;

Farrell, "Legacy Profile: Lillie Devereux Blake," *Legacy,* 14 (Fall 1997): 146–153;

Frank Luther Mott, *History of American Magazines 1850–1865,* volume 2 (Cambridge, Mass.: Harvard University Press, 1930–1968), p. 49;

Elinore Hughes Partridge, ed., *American Prose and Criticism, 1820–1900* (Detroit: Gale, 1983), pp. 192–193;

David Reynolds, *Beneath the American Renaissance: The Subversive Imagination in the Age of Emerson and Melville* (New York: Knopf, 1988), p. 401.

Papers:

The major collection of Lillie Devereux Blake documents, including her diaries, autobiography, letters to her, and a variety of clippings, is housed in the Missouri Historical Society Library in St. Louis, Missouri. A smaller collection is in the Sophia Smith Collection of Smith College Library, Northampton, Massachusetts.

S. Alice Callahan

(1 January 1868 – 7 January 1894)

Annette Van Dyke
University of Illinois at Springfield

See also the Callahan entry in *DLB 175: Native American Writers of the United States.*

BOOK: *Wynema: A Child of the Forest* (Chicago: H. J. Smith, 1891).

Edition: *Wynema: A Child of the Forest,* edited, with an introduction and notes, by A. LaVonne Ruoff (Lincoln: University of Nebraska Press, 1997).

Not only is S. Alice Callahan's *Wynema: A Child of the Forest* (1891) believed to be the first novel written by a Native American woman, it is also thought to be the first novel written in Oklahoma, then Indian Territory. The book enjoyed some success after its publication, receiving notice in the newspaper of the Muskogee Indian Territory, *Our Brother in Red* (6 June 1891). The reviewer identified Callahan as a high-school teacher at Harrell's Institute and a Creek Indian and noted, "She is an intelligent, Christian lady and we look forward with pleasure to the time when our other duties will permit us to read the book. It is certainly cheap at 25 per copy."

The book was mentioned again in 1911 in an article about the death of Callahan's father, but then disappeared from circulation until 1955, when an Oklahoma historian, Carolyn Thomas Foreman, discovered a copy in the Library of Congress. She notes that even remaining members of the Callahan family had lost their copies in moves from Oklahoma to California and that earlier Oklahoma historians had failed to notice any mention of *Wynema*. The scarcity of copies of the novel has meant that it has received little attention from historians and scholars in spite of renewed interest in Native American literature.

Born in Sulphur Springs, Texas, on 1 January 1868, Sophia Alice Callahan was only twenty-three when her novel was published. She was the daughter of Samuel Benton Callahan, who was of Scotch and Irish descent through his father and Creek descent through his mother. Samuel Callahan was enrolled

S. Alice Callahan (Oklahoma Historical Society)

on the Creek Nation Rolls as one-eighth Creek Indian. Callahan's mother, Sarah Elizabeth Thornberg Callahan, was the daughter of a Methodist minister in Sulphur Springs. Alice was one of eight children and part of what the newspapers called the "Creek aristocracy"—Native Americans of the day who had amassed a fair amount of wealth and who held prominent positions in both Native American and Euramerican societies.

The Creek Nation, an amalgamation of Muskogee- and non-Muskogee-speaking groups, had originally been located in Alabama and Georgia. They had adapted to the onslaught of European immigrants by incorporating European material culture that they supported by hunting, although they had been sedentary agriculturists prior to contact. In their original Southeast territories, they were both matrilineal and matrilocal. They had survived competing European groups by their political savvy and by exploiting the European love of fur and leather. They were steadily driven inland by the U.S. military, however, in accordance with government policies to usurp native lands.

In 1833, when Alice Callahan's father was three years old, his family, along with others of the Creek Nation, was forced by Federal government troops from Alabama to Indian Territory despite their prominent positions in Alabama society. During the infamous Trail of Tears removal, many members of the Creek Nation ended up in what became Oklahoma. Callahan's grandfather died on the forced march and was buried along the way. The family settled in Sulphur Springs, where Callahan's father attended public school. He also attended McKenzie College in Clarksville, Texas, and edited the *Sulphur Springs Gazette* for two years before coming to Indian Territory in 1858.

Samuel Callahan established a large and prosperous cattle ranch and farm near Okmulgee. Before Alice's birth, he served as a representative of the Creek and Seminole Nations to the Confederate Congress during the Civil War. During his service in the war, his wife and two children were driven out by Union sympathizers, the family's home and store burned, and their cattle and horses killed or disbursed. Alice's mother found her way back to Sulphur Springs on horseback with her two children and a black nursemaid. After the war, it was some time before Captain Callahan could convince his wife to return to Okmulgee. He soon returned, however, and rebuilt the ranch. Alice was born in Sulphur Springs following the war and educated there.

Captain Callahan was prominent in Creek politics from the mid 1800s, when the tribal government was set up under the auspices of the federal government, until it was disbanded in favor of allotment of the land to individuals. He served as clerk of the Creek Nation's Senate in the Creek National Council for four years and as clerk and later justice of the Supreme Court of the Creek Nation. He was a Creek

delegate to Washington and served as executive secretary to several Creek chiefs. He also served as editor of the *Muskogee Indian Journal,* official organ of the Creek Nation, and was involved in Indian education, serving as superintendent of the Wealaka Boarding School when Alice died at age twenty-six.

Little is known of Alice Callahan's life. She attended Wesleyan Female Institute in Staunton, Virginia, in 1887–1888. She took an examination for a teacher's certificate in grammar, arithmetic, geography, history, and physics in 1892. These subjects were typical for many female-oriented institutions, which were noticeably lacking in the classical subjects considered important for the education of males of the era. In a letter of the time, however, Callahan indicated a desire to continue her studies in Staunton, to emphasize languages, literatures, and mathematics and especially to advance her Latin studies.

Callahan taught at Wealaka Mission School in 1892–1893 and Harrell Institute in Muskogee in 1893. She had planned to finish her education in Staunton that year so that she could open her own school, but she was called back to Muskogee because of the illness of several teachers at Harrell. She was stricken with acute pleurisy on 26 December 1893 and died two weeks later. A tribute in *Our Brother in Red* (11 January 1894) said that "Miss Callahan was of a literary turn of mind and was much superior to the average intellectuality. Her abilities as a teacher have never been excelled in this territory."

Wynema was published in 1891, the year before Callahan took over her duties at Wealaka Mission School. Nothing can be discovered in the records beyond the dedication to the book as to the circumstances surrounding the writing and publishing of it. The title, *Wynema,* was a popular name in Native American country at the time, and many young women bore it. Historically, Wynema was the name of a woman subchief of the Modocs, known for saving the Indian commissioner, A. B. Meacham, from being killed in a fight in 1872 . Creek poet Alexander Posey's daughter was also named Wynema. In the novel the town that is created is named Wynema, indicating its honorific or generic use.

Wynema traces the education of a young Creek girl, Wynema, from her acquaintance with a young Methodist woman teacher from the South, Genevieve Weir, to Wynema's eventual status as a teacher herself. Wynema is portrayed as an extremely able student, and at her request a school is set up in her village with her parents' support. The romantic plot has as love interest the affection between Miss Weir and Gerald Keithly, the minister from the nearby Methodist mission school, and eventually a romance involving Wynema and Miss Weir's brother, Robin. The story is told through an outside narrator, and the first few chapters focus on Genevieve Weir's reactions to her alien environment, often corrected by Keithly, who takes the part of the Creeks, since Wynema is at that point too young to be a spokesperson. Thus, the story is seldom seen from the perspective of the Native American characters, and when it is, their point of view seems somewhat disruptive. Callahan had difficulty weaving the serious factual material about the important issues of the time into her romantic plot, although such was clearly her intent. The dedication of *Wynema* reads: "TO THE INDIAN TRIBES OF NORTH AMERICA Who have felt the wrongs and oppression of their pale-faced brothers, I lovingly dedicate this work, praying that it may serve to open the eyes and heart of the world to our afflictions, and thus speedily issue into existence an era of good feeling and just dealing toward us and our more oppressed brothers."

In spite of the drawbacks of the romantic framework and the story being told primarily through the Euramerican characters, Callahan comments on the politically volatile issues affecting the Creek Nation. She addresses the Dawes General Allotment Act of 1887, which was being seriously argued in the territory at the time; how the Creeks were cheated out of their per capita payment in Indian Territory; and how they had passed a law when they still lived in the Southeast that any chief who supported the sale of their land would be killed. Like many African American and Euramerican women novelists of the period, Callahan includes a temperance argument, as well as an argument for woman suffrage. She also recounts the 1890 massacre at Wounded Knee and elements of Creek culture, including "blue dumplings," a favorite food; the busk or green-corn ceremony; and the death chant.

Callahan's sources for her story do not appear to draw significantly on the oral tradition, except perhaps on stories concerning the Creeks' struggle to hold their land in their former territory. She draws heavily on newspaper articles of the time, even quoting some in the section about land allotment and Wounded Knee. Her information about Creek culture appears to be firsthand.

Wynema was written, like other reform novels of the era such as Harriet Beecher Stowe's *Uncle Tom's Cabin* (1852), for a white audience. While it has romance woven into the plot, it does not follow the pattern of women's fiction popular in that time, which usually showed a heroine overcoming misfortune with her acumen, determination, ingenuity, and

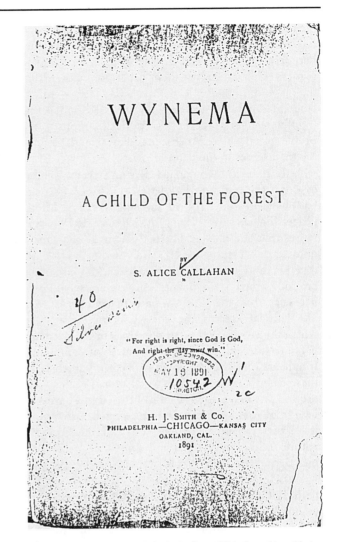

Title page for Callahan's only book, the first published novel by a Native American woman

bravery. Although the name of the novel would lead the reader to believe that the character Wynema would be the focus of the plot, she actually faces few hardships, and it is the white character, Genevieve Weir, who must confront ingrained stereotypes and misconceptions about Native Americans.

During the late 1800s much education for women was focused on providing a solid Protestant grounding. The women's institutions, including the one Callahan attended, sent missionaries to spread literacy and Christianity in Indian Territory. Writing for a white audience, Callahan not surprisingly makes her main character, Genevieve Weir, choose bringing literacy and Christianity "to the Indians in the territory" as her life's work. Genevieve is depicted as an intelligent, pretty, young Christian lady from a well-to-do Southern family. Her family feels she is physically unfit to bear the hardships of a life among the Indians, but she feels God's "call to go too strenuously, to allow any obstacles to obstruct her path." To engage the sympathy of her female readers, Callahan gives them a heroine with whom they could identify. The novel also has a subtly embedded political agenda, however: if Callahan was to influence her readers to accept her solutions to the problems of Native Americans, they would have to see themselves in the heroine.

Little is known about Callahan's reading interests, but she indicates in a letter to a friend that she had been reading British novelist William Makepeace Thackeray's *Vanity Fair* (1847–1848). She writes that she did not like his portrayal of women, quoting his comments "It's only women who get together and hiss and shriek and cackle" and "the best of women are hypocrits—A good housewife is of necessity humbug." She was particularly interested in his "satirical" treatment of the world and the way "in which the words, actions and feelings of the dramatis personae are exhibited without excuse or comment." It appears that she attempted to incorporate some of these techniques in her own work; words such as *savage* and *uncivilized* often seem to be used in a sarcastic vein. Callahan also mentions reading British novelists Edward Bulwer-Lytton and Charles Dickens, adding to her background in the novel of social commentary.

Like many other women novelists of the period, Callahan was particularly concerned with women's rights issues. In the novel Wynema says: "The idea of freedom and liberty was born in me." She notes that Creek women "have no voice in the councils; we do not speak in any public gathering, not even in our churches; but we are waiting for our more civilized white sisters to gain their liberty, and thus set us an example which we shall not be slow to follow." Since the Creeks were originally matrilocal and matrilineal, women would have had more public say and power before European contact. By Callahan's time European influence had steadily eroded the power of women among the Creeks. Callahan's argument for women's rights in *Wynema* demonstrates her awareness of her Creek heritage as well as her understanding of the larger women's movement in the United States.

Like many nineteenth-century novelists, Callahan is interested in Christian education and represents the Christian ministers and educators in the best light in her novel. Her publisher comments in the introduction that *Wynema* shows "the magnificent results accomplished by those who have gone among them to teach and to preach." Callahan herself was correspondence secretary to the Conference Officers

of Parsonages and Home Mission Society in 1893. Like her contemporaries, Callahan sets forth a domestic ethic to order life instead of the values of money and exploitation. The enemies of the Native Americans are those who do not practice the loving values of Christianity. Callahan carefully balances her Christian beliefs and her advocacy of non-Christian Native Americans in *Wynema,* although it is clear that the white values of a Christian education have primacy. When speaking of allotment, Wynema says, "There are so many idle, shiftless Indians who do nothing but hunt and fish; then there are others who are industrious and enterprising; so long as our land remains as a whole, in common, these lazy Indians will never make a move toward cultivating it; and the industrious Indians and 'squaw men' will enclose as much as they can for their own use." Genevieve Weir argues, "Were the land divided, these poor, ignorant, improvident, short-sighted Indians would be persuaded and threatened into selling their homes, piece by piece, perhaps, until finally they would be homeless outcasts, and then what would become of Poor Lo!" Even though Callahan presents her concern for traditional ways, her language implies that they are inferior.

Several chapters are unusual in the context of the novel because they focus on the stories of Native American characters rather than the white characters' perceptions of Native Americans. In chapter 20 several of the white men from the mission near Wynema's home, including Wynema's husband, Robin Weir, have gone to the South Dakota area to consult with the Native Americans who have left the reservation. Their mission is to tell them that the government agents who have squandered the supplies and goods that the Native Americans were to have received and who are responsible for their starving plight have been fired. To avoid more trouble, the white men advise the Native Americans to go back to the reservation and await the coming supplies. The Native Americans do not follow their advice, and the reader is introduced to the rebellious Native American leaders Great Eye, Wildfire, and Wildfire's wife, Miscona. The elderly Miscona, the other women, and their children return to the reservation while Wildfire and his followers prepare for conflict. Chapter 21, "Civilization or Savage Barbarity," opens as Miscona and several other women, some with their babies, return to the rebel camp against the wishes of the men. All are slaughtered in the ensuing battle. In chapter 22 Robin Weir, who has returned to Wynema in the Oklahoma area, brings with him a Sioux woman, Chikena, a survivor of the atrocities in the South Dakota area who tells her story. These chapters in particular demonstrate Callahan's bicultural authorial voice, her mixed-blood perception of being both within and outside of Native American culture. The highest calling of Callahan's Native American characters is not to convert other Native Americans but to stop the slaughter and unfair treatment so that their lives can be lived in peace side by side with the Euramericans.

The book ends with "the happy families nestling in the villages, near together. There they are, the Caucasian and American, the white and the Indian; and not the meanest, not the most ignorant, not the despised; but the intelligent, happy, beloved wife is WYNEMA, A CHILD OF THE FOREST." Like other women novelists of her time, Callahan does not hold to an ethic that women should be secluded in their homes; rather she asserts that everyone belongs in the home. The world and the home become one. This domestic ethic adds to the power of women.

The publisher's preface to the novel claims "the fact that an Indian, one of the oppressed, desires to plead her cause at a tribunal where judge and jury are chosen from among the oppressors is our warrant for publishing this little volume." The publisher feels certain that "whoever reads these pages will be convinced that this protest against the present Indian policy of our government is sincere, earnest, and timely." However, unlike Stowe's *Uncle Tom's Cabin* and other reform novels of the nineteenth century, there is no evidence that *Wynema* made an appreciable difference in government policy or entered the public's consciousness. It may take a more contemporary critical audience to acknowledge the significance of Callahan's text.

References:

Paula Gunn Allen, *The Sacred Hoop: Recovering the Feminine in American Indian Traditions* (Boston: Beacon, 1986);

Nina Baym, *Woman's Fiction: A Guide to Novels by and about Women in America, 1820–1870* (Ithaca, N.Y.: Cornell University Press, 1978);

Carolyn Thomas Foreman, "S. Alice Callahan: Author of *Wynema, A Child of the Forest*," *Chronicles of Oklahoma,* 33 (Autumn 1955): 306–315;

Catherine Hobbs, ed., *Nineteenth-Century Women Learn to Write* (Charlottesville: University Press of Virginia, 1995);

A. LaVonne Ruoff, "Justice for Indians and Women: The Protest Fiction of Alice Callahan and Pauline Johnson," *World Literature Today,* 66 (Spring 1992): 249–255;

Annette Van Dyke, "An Introduction to *Wynema, A Child of the Forest,* by Sophia Alice Callahan," *Studies in American Indian Literatures,* 4, nos. 2 & 3 (1992): 123–128;

J. Leitch Wright Jr., *Creeks and Seminoles: The Destruction and Regeneration of the Muscogulge People* (Lincoln: University of Nebraska Press, 1986).

Papers:

A few letters by S. Alice Callahan, as well as letters by others about her death, are held in the Grant Foreman Collection, Oklahoma Historical Society, Oklahoma City.

Kate McPhelim Cleary

(22 August 1863 – 16 July 1905)

Susanne George Bloomfield
University of Nebraska at Kearney

BOOKS: *The Lady of Lynhurst,* as Mrs. Kate Chrystal (Chicago: Street & Smith, 1884);

Vella Vernel: or, An Amazing Marriage, as Mrs. Sumner Hayden, Street & Smith's Select Series, no. 3 (Chicago: Street & Smith, 1887);

Like a Gallant Lady (Chicago: Way & Williams, 1897);

Poems by Margaret Kelly McPhelim and Her Children, Kate McPhelim Cleary, Edward Joseph McPhelim (Chicago: Published by her grandchildren, 1922);

The Nebraska of Kate McPhelim Cleary, edited by James M. Cleary (Lake Bluff, Ill.: United Educators, 1958);

Kate McPhelim Cleary: A Literary Biography with Selected Works, edited by Susanne K. George (Lincoln: University of Nebraska Press, 1997).

SELECTED PERIODICAL LITERATURE— UNCOLLECTED:

POETRY

"A Warning to Novelists," *Puck* (13 December 1893): 294;

"When Mother's Cookin' fer Company," *Puck* (13 July 1894): 272;

"Ma and Mag," *Puck* (27 October 1897): 14;

"Kipling," *Kipling Journal* (December 1935): 126–130.

FICTION

"Lost in a Cornfield," *St. Nicholas* (September 1891): 812–817;

"The Mildewed Pocketbook," *Puck* (13 December 1891): 323;

"Some Prairie Pictures: 'The Camper,' 'A Man Out of Work,' and 'A Race Horse to the Plow,'" *Chicago Tribune,* 28 April 1895, p. 46;

"Some Prairie Sketches: 'The Judas Tree,' 'A Western Wooing,' and 'A Dust Storm in Nebraska,'" *Chicago Tribune,* 16 June 1895, p. 41;

"'Tramp,' the True Story of a Brave Dog," *Chicago Tribune,* 5 February 1899, p. 39;

"Why We Didn't Hear Nilsson," *Chicago Tribune,* 19 March 1899, section 5, p. 2;

"The Story of Frances Dever," *Chicago Tribune,* 23 April 1899, section 6, p. 2;

Kate McPhelim Cleary in 1897

"The Jilting of Jane Ann," *Chicago Tribune,* 7 May 1899, p. 53;

"Two Decoration Days and the Time Between," *Chicago Tribune,* 28 May 1899, p. 50;

"Old Man Kennedy's Daughter: A Story of the Last Fourth of July," *Chicago Tribune,* 2 July 1899, p. 43;

"The Agent at Magnolia," *Chicago Tribune,* 6 August 1899, p. 30;

"The Boy's Mother," *Chicago Tribune,* 8 February 1900, p. 7;

"T. J. Smith," *Chicago Tribune,* 6 May 1900, p. 63;

"What the Winner's Hand Threw By," *Chicago Tribune*, 13 May 1900, p. 43;

"The Romance of a Ring," *Chicago Tribune,* 27 June 1900, p. 16;

"The Mission of Kitty Malone," *McClure's* (November 1901): 88–96;

"'And the Joy That Came at Last!': A Decoration Day Story," *Chicago Tribune,* 30 May 1902, p. 13;

"The Statelier Mansion," *Cosmopolitan* (November 1903): 106–112.

NONFICTION

"Angel Food with Variations," *Good Housekeeping* (July 1891): 26–28;

"Ten Tongues: And How To Cure Them, How To Cook Them and How To Serve Them," *Good Housekeeping* (November 1891): 223–225;

"For the Housewife: Trifles That Make Perfection: Part I & II," *Housewife* (June–July 1893);

"Dedicating a Book," *Chicago Tribune,* 11 December 1898, p. 42;

"Apropos of Story-Writing," *Writer,* 15 (January 1902): 8;

"Midnight Mass under Three Flags," *Extension* (January 1909): 13–14.

When Kate McPhelim Cleary died at age forty-one in 1905, she had been publishing poems, stories, articles, and novels for twenty-seven years. Forced to publish by economic necessity at age fourteen when she sold her first short story, Cleary's writings throughout her life helped support her loved ones. She wrote literally hundreds of works for newspapers, especially the *Chicago Tribune* and the *Chicago Daily News,* and prestigious periodicals such as *McClure's, Belford's Monthly, Cosmopolitan, Good Housekeeping, Puck, St. Nicholas,* and *Youth's Companion.* During her lifetime she was well known in the Midwest, especially in the Chicago area, as a humorist and a writer of realistic, sometimes naturalistic, stories about the settlement period of the West. Her best works appeared between 1895 and 1899, years of extreme stress, both financial and emotional, in her life.

Born 22 August 1863 in Richibucto, New Brunswick, Kate McPhelim lived her early years in comfort. After the unexpected death in 1865 of her father, James McPhelim, a pioneer in the Canadian lumber and shipping business, the family remained in New Brunswick. McPhelim received a solid education at the Sacred Heart Convent in St. John, where she studied art and the classics. In the late 1870s her mother encountered financial difficulties, and the family returned temporarily to Ireland, the homeland of Margaret McPhelim and her husband. The Irish, however, were experiencing extreme food shortages, and the McPhelims joined the immigrants flocking to America.

The family arrived in Philadelphia about 1879, and the next year moved to Chicago, where Kate McPhelim completed her education at St. Xavier's Convent School.

The 1880s were difficult years for Margaret McPhelim and her children, Edward, Frank, and Kate. The family struggled to survive on a sporadic income from their "Irish estate" and money the family earned by writing. In an autobiographical short story, "Why We Didn't Hear Nilsson" (*Chicago Tribune,* 19 March 1899), Cleary described their financial situation during this time as "absurdly poor," explaining, "When our poverty reached its lowest ebb–the stage where it ceased to continue lamentable and became ridiculous– we were prompt to see its vulnerable points and we hurled at these, between a sob and a laugh, sharp lances of wit." This ability to find humor in adversity served her well throughout her life.

By pooling their writing talents and employing humor and wit to face crises, they managed to survive hunger and despair. McPhelim, her mother, and Edward all wrote for the popular press, selling their poems for thirty-six dollars a dozen and their short stories to the family story papers and the ten-cent magazines. To supplement their income, McPhelim also hand-painted decorative tiles and sold illustrations to newspapers and periodicals.

While in Chicago, Kate met a charming and gregarious Irishman, Michael Timothy Cleary, to whom she became engaged. Interested in relocating to the West for his health, Michael traveled to Nebraska and, with the help of his brother-in-law, invested in a lumber business in the newly formed town of Hubbell, situated on the Nebraska-Kansas border. Michael returned to Chicago and married Kate on 26 February 1884. Kate had just finished her first novel for Street and Smith, *The Lady of Lynhurst* (1884), a popular work for their "Leading Novel" series. In March the young couple, accompanied by Margaret McPhelim, stepped off the Burlington and Missouri train onto the wooden sidewalks of Hubbell, a former cornfield that only four years earlier had mushroomed into a town of one hundred buildings in just ninety days.

By September the Clearys had moved into a large, two-story, beautifully furnished Victorian-style home, and Kate, under the urging of Street and Smith, began work on a second novel, *Vella Vernel: or, An Amazing Marriage* (1887). She also wrote a few local-color sketches about life in the rural western community. Since her husband's lumber and coal business was flourishing in the growing town, however, she wrote only for her own satisfaction and did not actively pursue publishing; instead, she employed her creative talents in homemaking. A little more than two years later,

Cleary's husband, Michael Cleary, in his office at the M. T. Cleary Lumber and Coal Company of Hubbell, Nebraska

on 19 January 1887, the Clearys' first son, James, was born.

The following October, Cleary finished *Vella Vernel,* and Street and Smith published the novel, a sentimental work that the publishers proclaimed was based on actual events set in a major western American city. A comedy of manners focusing on mistaken identities and several pairs of star-crossed lovers, the novel rises above pulp fiction in its local-color descriptions of Chicago and the Interstate Industrial Exposition as well as in its humor, subtle wit, and flashes of satire.

From 1887 to 1894 Cleary's writing and publishing were wide-ranging. Firmly declaring her views on the position of female writers in American literature in "The New Man" (*Puck,* 10 July 1895), she asserted that too many critics emphasized women writers' homemaking abilities above their literary talents, and too few dealt with "what women have done in literature, without any apology for their having presumed to do it." Cleary stood up for the woman writer who would "send her soul beyond the four walls of the kitchen," and she put her beliefs into practice. She wrote children's poems for *St. Nicholas,* humorous poems and satiric sketches for *Puck,* sentimental short stories for

Chicago and Detroit newspapers, and articles on cooking and homemaking for *Good Housekeeping.* Her first naturalistic tales about the West also appeared, most importantly "Feet of Clay" in *Belford's Monthly* (April 1893) and "Told of a Prairie Schooner" in the *Chicago Tribune* (ca. 1893).

During these same eight years, Cleary's children Marguerite, Gerald, Rosemarie, and Vera Valentine were born; her brother Frank, mother, and daughter Marguerite died; and Cleary herself barely survived complications from childbirth fever. As a result, through her doctor's treatment for the pain, she became addicted to morphine.

In 1895 Cleary's life seemed to be spiraling downward. Her husband left temporarily for Chicago in February due to health and business failures and remained absent from Nebraska for more than nine months. During his absence, Rosemarie, age three, died in March, and Vera Valentine came down with typhoid fever, the same illness that had taken the life of Marguerite. Cleary, who had not yet regained her health from the childbirth complications, nursed her daughter through the illness while suffering a series of what she termed in her letters as "heart attacks" and dysentery, perhaps from an effort to withdraw from her reliance on morphine for pain relief.

Throughout these traumatic events Cleary retreated to her typewriter, sometimes writing humorous social satires such as "A Call on the Bride" (*Chicago Tribune,* 11 August 1895), "The New Man," and "A Bicycle Conundrum" (*Puck,* 28 August 1895) and other times composing somber tales of hardship on the plains, such as "For the Rest of Her Life" (*Chicago Tribune,* 2 June 1895), "Some Prairie Sketches: 'The Judas Tree,' 'A Western Wooing,' and 'A Dust Storm in Nebraska'" (*Chicago Tribune,* 16 June 1895), and "An Incident of the Prairie: A Board, a Saw, a Few Nails, and a Mother's Hot Tears" (*Chicago Tribune,* ca. 1895) to relieve her financial and emotional burdens. With these writings Cleary began to find her voice, and her ambivalent attitude toward life on the plains surfaced. Cleary understood the West as a region of extremes. In her poem "To Nebraska," which prefaces her novel *Like a Gallant Lady* (1897), she explains her love/hate relationship with Nebraska, a place that had been both kind and cruel to her, a place that harbored her as a "bride, and slave and guest." She had found happiness in the natural beauty of the prairie and in her growing family; yet, she had suffered hardships and losses, too, like those of her neighbors. From her comfortable home on the main street of Hubbell, Cleary could look with pity and compassion at the visiting rural women, who had too little money to spend, too much hard physical labor to endure, and too many children to raise. At the same time she could laugh at the pretensions of her neighbors, who were trying to duplicate genteel eastern society in the dusty middle of nowhere.

In 1896 Cleary's husband stayed in Hubbell, and her life regained some emotional as well as economic balance. She and her son Jim actively participated in William McKinley's presidential campaign, with Cleary writing speeches, poems, and songs to support the Republican candidate. Another son, Edward, or "Teddy," was born in January 1897, and that fall Cleary published her third novel, *Like a Gallant Lady,* this time with Way and Williams, who also published Kate Chopin's *The Awakening* the next year. The plot of *Like a Gallant Lady* involves a young woman from Chicago who comes to Bubble, Nebraska, after learning of the death of her fiancé and becomes a mystery as she uncovers an insurance scam. Cleary introduces each chapter with an appropriate quotation from William Shakespeare, whom she revered and from whom she borrowed themes, character types, and plot devices, especially the idea of a potion that would produce a deathlike trance.

Although Cleary employed sentimental conventions for popular appeal, the novel is noteworthy for

several successes. *Like a Gallant Lady* features a strong, independent, intelligent woman as the central character. Cleary prefaced her novel with a quotation from Elizabeth Barrett Browning: "The World's male chivalry has perished out, / But Women are Knights Errant to the last." Cleary's protagonist, Ivera Lyle, embarks on a personal quest and discovers a fraud in which her fiancé had become entangled as well as the illegitimate child that he fathered. After several twists and turns of the plot, Ivera discovers that her fiancé has not really been buried at all but remains hidden away in a vegetative state. Ivera denounces him and returns to Chicago, followed by a handsome Englishman, Jack Jardine, who has come West to make his fortune and with whom she has fallen in love. Cleary does not conclude with the arbitrary marriage, however, for Ivera does not need to be rescued, and it is clear that she does not mean to return to Nebraska.

Cleary's Western setting and local-color descriptions also add realism and depth to the novel, countering the romantic plot. She includes rich details of daily life in a small frontier town throughout the work, such as her descriptions of the railroad station, the community opera house, and the local tavern, as well as the embryonic town and its inhabitants: "the staring crowd of flannel-shirted, top-booted men, of clumsy women, of gaping children; the brand new buildings, many in process of erection, straggling across riven cornfields."

When Ivera first views the plains, she is impressed by the beauty and solitude of the region, remarking, "It was an idyllic morning, the sky blue and luminous, the earth wearing a fresh-washed face, the air crisp and caressing." Ivera considers the "absolute absence of sound" as peaceful and restful. After the protagonist has stayed in Nebraska for several months and spoken with rural women, she revises her opinion of the region, comparing the silence to "gigantic coils that crushed out individuality–almost extinguished identity" and noting that the only people who write romantically about the plains are those who have had no personal experience there. As for the farm women, Cleary respected their courage but echoed Hamlin Garland in describing the drudgery and hopelessness of their lives. Alluding to Rudyard Kipling's story "The Strange Ride of Morrowbie Jukes" (1885) and Jukes's endeavor to escape from the plague pit, she could see no way out for these imprisoned pioneers.

Cleary's minor characters add strength to the novel. The most memorable is Maria McLelland, a character who recurs in her fiction and serves not only as a source of local color and comic relief but also as a confidante for the young protagonist. Another humorous character is Peter Jennings, a stereotypical Englishman, a Western version of Cyrano de Bergerac who

Cleary (seated on porch railing) and her husband (standing in yard) at their home in Hubbell, September 1884

serves as a foil to Jardine. Interestingly, Cleary added the character of a morphine-addicted country doctor, Dr. Eldridge, as one of the villains involved in the insurance fraud.

In the reviews of *Like a Gallant Lady,* many critics favorably compared Cleary to Garland, especially his stories compiled in *Main-Travelled Roads,* published in 1891. The novel typically received positive reviews, except from some Nebraska critics who flinched at Cleary's harsh depiction of the plains and its inhabitants, and in 1900 the book went into a second printing.

Due to the economic depression of the 1890s, the American economy was plummeting, and by 1898 Cleary's husband's business and his health were failing. While she stayed in Hubbell to manage the household, family, and finances, Michael Cleary traveled to find a suitable climate, ultimately deciding to relocate the family in Chicago. Meanwhile, Cleary resumed her eclectic publishing, editing her brother's poetry for the *Chicago Tribune,* writing humorous and occasional verse, stories, and articles, and producing a couple of sentimental short stories. She seemed to be cleaning up the family's business and cleaning out her desk drawers of publishable material in preparation for the move.

By July 1898 the Clearys had rented an apartment in Austin, Illinois, a strongly Irish suburb of Chicago, and Michael began work as the secretary and treasurer for Dumont and Cleary, an advertising agency. Upon her return to the city, the *Chicago Chronicle* paid tribute to Cleary as one of the three leading women humorists in Chicago, calling her a "natural humorist," citing her contributions to *Puck* and other periodicals, and noting her laughter-loving Irish temperament and bohemian unconventionality. Distance from the West gave Cleary a better perspective on the region, and she began writing her most successful stories, patterned after, and in some cases revised from, the ones she had created in 1895.

The first of the 1899 stories published in the *Chicago Tribune* were humorous, lighthearted satires of Western life, such as "Jim Peterson's Pension" (19 February 1899), "The Rebellion of Mrs. McLelland" (2 April 1899), and "An Ornament to Society" (9 April 1899). Cleary's primary object of ridicule was the constricting ideal of nineteenth-century womanhood. Life had forced Cleary to be strong and independent, for she had helped support first her mother and brothers and then her husband and four children. The image of the New Woman emerging during the 1870s and 1880s fit her perfectly.

Expanding upon a minor character that had proved successful in her earlier sketches and in *Like a Gallant Lady,* "The Rebellion of Mrs. McLelland" humorously comments upon the much-discussed "woman problem" of the 1890s. No longer content to be complaisant, self-effacing housewives, many American women were beginning to stand up to their husbands and demand their rights. Mrs. Maria McLelland, ironically stouter and taller than her frail yet domineering husband, has spent her life bending to her husband's miserly will–helping her spouse with the hard physical labor of the farm; stoically lining her dresses with used, bleached flour sacks; making neckties for her stepson out of her wedding bonnet; and patiently waiting to be allowed to visit her only child from her first marriage.

When Maria receives a telegram saying that her granddaughter, whom she has never seen, has fallen seriously ill and is perhaps dying, she knows her husband will not allow her to waste the money for train fare to Chicago. When she thinks of the three farms that they own, however, "of the fat cattle, the two hundred hogs, the six thousand bushels of cribbed corn," she straightens her back, decides to borrow the money from her neighbor's niece, packs her suitcase, hitches up the horse and buggy, and heads to town. On the way she meets her outraged husband: "Thirty years of obedience, sacrifice, submission, and now insubordination–now rebellion! A General, struck in the face by a private, could not feel more outraged–more aghast." Upon discovering that he has money stashed in the barn, she grows even more resolute and determines to take her fair share. "I can and I will," she declares; she returns to the farm, absconds with the secret money, and leaves her husband to fend for himself for two weeks.

Upon Maria's return, after untangling complications that arose from her "theft," she admits that her rebellion was "worth standin' up against pa for–though I don't know as I'll ever do it again." As her lonely and hungry spouse sits down submissively to his favorite meal of chicken potpie, the reader knows that Maria will not have to submit to his authority or resist his will again, for she has shown her ability to be both strong and self-reliant.

After humorously assaulting the submission and selflessness expected of nineteenth-century wives and mothers, Cleary directed her satiric barbs at the artificiality of Victorian society in "Jim Peterson's Pension." The Petersons have lived austerely since Jim Peterson hurt his arm fifteen years earlier and had to quit his job. The industry and competence of his wife keeps the fam-

ily clothed, well fed, and content. When the Petersons unexpectedly receive $2,160 in back pension money, Mrs. Peterson becomes "money-proud," spending it on lavishly remodeling and refurbishing the house, buying elaborate gowns, and giving an extravagant reception in "frantic attempts to enter the exclusive circle which every town, no matter how small, boasts." Satirizing the Petersons' "pretensions to social distinction," Cleary concludes the story with Mrs. Peterson's realization of the folly of her misconceived attempts to be "society people." Sunk again into poverty, Mrs. Peterson gallantly takes control of her life, denounces the ill-fitting social pretensions, and wins back the respect once afforded her by the community.

"An Ornament to Society" is perhaps Cleary's most overt satire on the concept of the Cult of True Womanhood. She attacks the superficial education of the typical Victorian woman, with her frizzy hair and her gilt-framed paintings, and reconstructs a new program that would produce a woman radiating health and independence. The conflict of the story arises when Cleopatra's mother dies, after making her father promise to raise the girl to be "an ornament to sassiety." An outdoor girl, she is forced into the parlor and taught to embroider doilies, paint china, and play the organ. When she rebels, her father sends her to a convent to make a lady of her. She becomes so homesick for the farm and the animals, however, that she convinces the hired man to take her home, and her father is so busy courting the neighboring widow that he leaves Cleopatra to herself.

On her own, Cleopatra matures naturally and gracefully. She is honest and caring about her father's wishes yet strong enough to confront the social constraints placed on women at the time. A young woman, prescribed Cleary, should have the freedom to roam where she pleases, should be self-taught from nature, and should be physically active, even in those pursuits that are typically male-dominated. Cleopatra is androgynous, able to plow fields, break wild stallions to ride, and nurse sick livestock as well as enjoy the companionship of friends at a taffy pull or the intellectual stimulation of country "literaries." Cleary offers Cleopatra as her ideal of the true Western woman, to whom "Life was such a good thing–and health–and energy–and the vast sweep of the immeasurable world around and companionship with birds, and animals, and trees, and streams, and all nature's delicious, ever-varying, never satiating sweetness!" To Cleary, such a woman, freed from societal taboos and expectations, defined a cult of new womanhood.

Cleary's Western satires give firsthand interpretations of life in the new West. In their westward movement, pioneers frequently transported cultural baggage

*Cleary vacationing with her four surviving children—Vera
Valentine, James, Edward, and Gerald—in
South Haven, Michigan, July 1901*

had been realistically recording the harshness of life on the plains.

"Nebraska," a narrative poem of eighteen stanzas, although thick with vernacular dialect and sentiment, depicts the struggle of a frontier woman attempting to raise ten children—with another one on the way—in a sod house. When the baby dies, she covers it with a blanket made from her wedding gown and continues to rock the cradle. The reader assumes that the woman has lost her sanity, at least temporarily. This poem echoes the naturalistic theme of some of Cleary's earlier works, such as "Feet of Clay," which also depicts the negative effects of the environment on women. In that story a young bride from the East is unable to endure the physical and emotional isolation of a Nebraska homestead, especially the traumatic birth of her first child, and her family has to come and take the mother and her baby back east. The sympathies of the townspeople in the story go to the husband, however, for having married such a weak woman: "There had been nothing in her life to cause insanity. It must have been heredity."

Cleary saw such women on the streets of Hubbell and peering from their dwellings in the surrounding countryside. This naturalistic attitude in her works was undoubtedly influenced by the daily life she viewed around her, her own financial disillusionment, and the subject, style, and tone of works being published by popular writers such as Garland, Jack London, Frank Norris, and Stephen Crane.

In many of Cleary's realistic/naturalistic short stories, she portrays men and women as having little opportunity for choice, bound by socioeconomic restrictions, environmental and biological forces, and gender. Women are further victimized by isolation from supportive networks of women. Many of the stories Cleary published in the *Chicago Tribune* in 1899, such as "His Onliest One," "The Road That Didn't Lead Anywhere" (14 May 1899), and "How Jimmy Ran Away" (5 November 1899), depict various people living in captivity on the sparsely populated frontier and envision no possibility for them to escape.

In "The Road That Didn't Lead Anywhere" an uneducated girl becomes a mother at fifteen. She lives in a log cabin on an isolated portion of prairie with her baby, injured during his delivery with forceps by a drunken doctor. Her husband, a farmer, blacksmith, and coarse drunk, dominates her life, and she has never been out of the county in which she was born. A stranger who comes to work for her husband takes pity on the young wife and pays for surgery to correct the child's defect. This kindness is the only bright spot in the girl's life, however, for there will be many more

that hindered social growth, such as the constricting Victorian ideals of womanhood and pretentious views of social class. The democratic spirit also accompanied them, however, and found room to expand on the vast plains. Cleary, an independent and resourceful woman in her own right, encouraged that free spirit in her writings by humorously pointing out the follies of mankind and constructing alternatives. Her humor and her ability to lighten the burdens of others through her writing not only helped her endure her own hardships but also perhaps prodded society into reexamining its unnatural expectations for women.

By the end of 1899 Michael Cleary's business venture began to fail, and the money the Clearys had received from the sale of their house and their business in Hubbell dwindled. To help support her family, Cleary published stories at an increased pace, and their tone became more somber. This trend, however, was not new in Cleary's writing, for beginning with her poem "Nebraska," recited at the opening of the Nebraska Day ceremonies at the Chicago World's Fair of 1893, and the short sketch "Told of a Prairie Schooner," published that same year in the *Chicago Tribune,* she

such deliveries, and her future will forever lie within the confines of the homestead.

In "His Onliest One" a young brother and sister from Holland homestead in Nebraska, waiting for "just a few good crops" in order to purchase the farm and build a fine, frame farmhouse. When the sister's boyfriend arrives from Holland to claim her as his bride, the brother will not allow her to leave. After the sister spends years helping her brother succeed, he surprises her by getting married and bringing home his bride and her mother, for whom the sister must also cook and clean. She runs away and reunites with her old boyfriend, and then she begins helping him succeed on his farm in Iowa.

"How Jimmy Ran Away" describes the imprisonment of an old man by social and financial forces. Jimmy, who once was "a prosperous farmer and had served a term in the legislature," divides his farms between his two children when his wife dies, and his children promise to let him live with them the rest of his life. To his overworked daughter, however, seventy-five-year-old Jimmy becomes an unwelcome burden, so he runs away to live with his son, now wealthy from his inheritance. He discovers that he is an embarrassment to his prominent son and returns reluctantly to his daughter. Although Cleary supplied a sentimental ending to appeal to her readers, this story and another, "For the Rest of Her Life," emphasize the problems of the elderly, who are often unappreciated, neglected, and discarded–trapped by their dependency upon their children.

From 1900 through 1902, in spite of the success of her writing career, Cleary's life was in chaos. Neither her health nor her husband's improved, and all of Michael Cleary's various enterprises failed, forcing the family to move from one rented flat to another. Once again, Cleary had to set aside her literary aspirations and write for her family's survival. She returned to the most lucrative market, the daily short story, where she could churn out conventional sentimental fiction that needed no creativity or revision. With the exception of two stories accepted by *McClure's*, "The Stepmother" (September 1901), a harsh story about the wife of a homesteader, and "The Mission of Kitty Malone" (November 1901), a tale about a poor Irish couple in Chicago, all of her short stories published during this period are formulaic.

Cleary's typical contribution to the "Story of the Day" column in the *Chicago Tribune* was a sentimental romance with a Cinderella theme. Her heroine usually is a beautiful young girl between ages seventeen and twenty whose major conflict is choosing the right dress or husband. The hero is a handsome older man whose life is lonely or meaningless and who needs a woman to share his elegant home. Cleary knew which fantasies would sell

and could compose them quickly. Even in these stories, however, she could not sublimate her satiric wit or her graceful style, and often autobiographical elements inform the texts. Stories such as "The Boy's Mother" (*Chicago Tribune,* 8 February 1900), "The Romance of a Ring" (*Chicago Tribune,* 27 June 1900), "The Price Paulina Paid" (ca. 1900), "The Destiny of Delores" (ca. 1901), and "A Lenten Costume" (*Chicago Tribune,* 31 March 1900) illustrate her desire to rise above accepted mediocrity. She called this writing her "good bad stuff."

Cleary most certainly would have preferred to write only "good stuff." In "The Destiny of Delores" she wrote of a young woman who goes to Chicago to become a successful writer, believing she could work hard for newspapers and become famous. Delores soon realizes that "she had exaggerated ideas of the facility with which one, imaginative, although untrained, might earn a living by literary work," however, and that "mediocrity counts for more than crude, unpolished talent."

Cleary, too, had many counts against her in the literary world. She was a mother with children to care for and raise; she was a wife with a physically and financially dependent husband; and she was a woman writer who did not belong to any of the well-defined writing groups in Chicago at the turn of the century. Although Cleary had a strong literary background in the classics, she did not have the time or money to attend the university and thus become part of the "Harvard Gang," as Chicago's academic circle was called. The literary groups formed by the social elite of the city, such as the Little Room, the Cliff Dwellers, the Chicago Club, and the Fortnightly, would not accept her because they considered newspaper writing as subliterature. And even though she had published voluminously in newspapers, her gender kept her out of the male-only clubs frequented by journalists, such as the Press Club and the White Chapel Club. Thus, Cleary remained isolated from the literary worlds of Chicago.

In order to meet the emotional, physical, and financial demands of her family, Cleary continued to rely on morphine, legally and easily obtained from any druggist. By June 1902 she admitted herself to a private sanatorium to help her withdraw from her addiction. The treatment was unsuccessful, and for another year Cleary struggled to maintain her flow of stories. She even accepted a position on the staff of *Home World,* a new woman's magazine, a short-lived periodical for which she contributed many of the articles, ranging in subject from cooking, sewing, and raising children to house decoration and plant selection.

By the time Cleary collapsed in 1903, while again moving her family because her husband had once more changed occupations, her output of stories had dwindled significantly. Her health and endurance were so depleted that even morphine and alcohol could not keep her going. She was admitted for treatment on 13 October to the Illinois Northern Hospital for the Insane in Elgin, Illinois. Thirty days later she was able to write her first letter, to her son Jim, then a student at the University of Illinois. She stated that she had lost twenty-four pounds during treatment but had gotten her weight up to ninety-six pounds. By the end of November, she wrote to Jim that her recovery was "absolute" and she was "chafing against inaction." She also declared, "I shall not soon take up housekeeping in any case–chiefly for the reason that it will pay me better to write."

In December, Cleary was transferred to the "well" ward and had gained forty-nine pounds. Recovering her typewriter and some manuscripts from the warehouse where the family's belongings were stored, she began sending out popular fiction to the newspaper syndicates. Checks began arriving in the mail for her in Elgin, which, to her chagrin, she could not cash until she was released. By February she was writing ten short stories a week and was working on a special article for a group of doctors from Chicago. That month, too, she learned that she could be released on a three-month parole. If that was successful, she would be formally "cured" and discharged.

For unknown reasons, Cleary's husband would not sign for her release or be responsible for her parole, so Elia Peattie, a writer and close friend, came for her, and she resided at the Peatties' home during those three months. With her parole successfully completed in May, Cleary found an apartment for herself in downtown Chicago, where she lived precariously on money coming in from the sale of her potboilers. She continued writing, working to complete another novel, "A Woman of Nebraska," which *McClure's* had shown interest in publishing. With magazines such as *Collier's* offering lucrative cash prizes for stories, she began entering their contests, knowing that even if she did not place, her story might still be published at a per-word rate.

Meanwhile, Cleary was helping support her children, who were in private schools or universities, and she and her husband were on friendly, but not intimate, terms. She refused to live with him, declaring, "If I had done more writing and less housekeeping I would be better off in every way today." Money trickled in regularly, and soon she could afford to begin payments on a new typewriter and lease a better room at a hotel across the street. Throughout 1904 and into 1905, Cleary's popular short stories, usually without bylines, appeared regularly in the *Chicago Daily News* and other syndicated newspapers.

Just as Cleary was consulting with Houghton Mifflin on the publication of a collection of her short stories, her husband suddenly entered a petition on 6 July 1905 in Cook County Court to have her declared insane and

again committed to the Illinois Northern Hospital. Although the jury of seven men declared her "not insane," a shaken Cleary returned to her hotel and remained in bed. Ten days later her husband brought her children to visit her; an argument ensued, and Cleary became pale. As she started up to her room with her youngest son, Teddy, to give him a poem she had written especially for him, she collapsed and died. She would have celebrated her forty-second birthday the next month.

Because she was a well-known writer in Chicago and because of the dramatic events of her life, Cleary's death made front-page headlines in most of the regional newspapers. The stories did not spare any details of her addiction or marital status, and although an autopsy performed by a coroner's jury declared the death to be due to "fatty degeneration of the heart accompanied by fatty degeneration of the liver," most people assumed her death was caused by drugs. Cleary had suffered from heart problems most of her life, even before her marriage, and the week that she died, Chicagoans endured record high temperatures, with lists of heat-related deaths published daily in the newspapers.

Cleary's last published work was the poem she had written to give to her son as a gift. It was published by the *Record Herald* along with the sensational details of her death and catalogues her overwhelming love of life and her children: "I love the world with all its brave endeavor, / I love its winds and floods, and suns and sands, / But oh, I love– most deeply and forever– / The clinging touch of timid little hands."

Despite her short and troubled life, Cleary added significantly to American literature because of the diversity of her writing. Her popular stories document the myths accepted by turn-of-the-century society, especially the sentimental cult of domesticity, and her pastoral poems echo the agrarian ideal of the frontier. Her more realistic and naturalistic works describing the hardships of the settlement period provide a contrast to the accepted myth of the West as a Garden of Eden and the pioneers as new American Adams and Eves. Perhaps Cleary's strongest contributions are her humorous stories, sketches, and poems, especially those set in Nebraska. Her lighthearted satire and her realistic descriptions of the plains combine to paint a true picture of the West at the turn of the century–and an even truer picture of humanity.

Reference:

Susanne K. George, *Kate McPhelim Cleary: A Literary Biography with Selected Works* (Lincoln: University of Nebraska Press, 1997).

Anna Julia Cooper

(10 August 1858 – 27 February 1964)

Jennifer A. Kohout
University of Toledo

BOOKS: *A Voice from the South, by a Black Woman of the South* (Xenia, Ohio: Aldine, 1892);

The Social Settlement: What It Is, and What It Does (Washington, D.C.: Murray Brothers, 1913);

L'Attitude de la France a l'égard de l'esclavage pendant la Révolution (Paris: Imprimerie de la Cour d'Appel, 1925); translated, with a foreword, by Frances Richardson Keller as *Slavery and the French Revolutionists* (Lewiston, N.Y.: Mellen, 1988);

Legislative Measures Concerning Slavery in the United States (Washington, D.C.: Privately printed, 1942);

Equality of Races and the Democratic Movement (Washington, D.C.: Privately printed, 1945);

Personal Recollections of the Grimké Family & The Life and Writings of Charlotte Forten Grimké (N.p., 1951);

The Third Step (N.p., n.d.).

Edition: *A Voice from the South, by a Black Woman of the South* (New York: Negro Universities Press, 1969).

OTHER: *Le Pèlerinage de Charlemagne: Voyage à Jérusalem et à Constantinople,* edited and translated by Cooper (Paris: Lahure, 1925);

"The Colored Woman's Office," in *Social Theory: The Multicultural and Classic Readings,* edited by Charles Lemert (Boulder, Colo.: Westview Press, 1993), pp. 193–199;

"Womanhood: A Vital Element in the Regeneration and Progress of a Race," in *I Am Because We Are: Readings in Black Philosophy,* edited by Fred Lee Hord (Amherst: University of Massachusetts Press, 1995), pp. 231–242.

One of the most intriguing and dedicated figures to emerge in the struggle for African American rights after slavery is Anna Julia Cooper. Cooper lived to be 105 years old, witnessing the Civil War, Reconstruction, the reign of the Ku Klux Klan, and the hopeful early civil-rights period. Her work as an author is only one aspect of her life of service; she was also for many years a distinguished educator and community leader.

Anna Julia Cooper

Anna Julia Haywood was born on 10 August 1858 in Raleigh, North Carolina, the daughter of a slave, Hannah Stanley Haywood, and an unnamed white father who was quite possibly her mother's master, George Washington Haywood. Cooper spent the first five years of her life as a slave. She recalls that during the Civil War she "served many an anxious slave's superstition to wake up the baby & ask directly 'Which sid is goin' to win de war? Will de Yankees beat de Rebs & will Linkum free de Niggers.'" After the defeat of the Confederacy, a movement arose to build schools for the newly freed African Americans in the South; in 1868, at age nine, Cooper was enrolled in St. Augustine's Normal School, which educated teachers who in turn provided instruction to that population. Because of her unusual academic abilities, it has been speculated that she had some schooling previous to enrolling at St. Augustine's. She entered the school as a scholarship student, receiving an annual stipend of $100 to cover board and tuition. Her responsibility, in exchange for the scholarship, was to tutor other students, a task that seemed to be most natural for her since she had been reading and teaching others to read from a young age.

At St. Augustine's, Haywood received her first lesson about the male-dominated realm of education. As she wrote later in her collection of essays, *A Voice from the South, by a Black Woman of the South* (1892):

> A boy, however meager his equipment and shallow his pretensions, had only to declare a floating intention to study theology and he could get all the support, encouragement and stimulus he needed. . . . A self-supporting girl had to struggle on by teaching in the summer and working after school hours to keep up with her board and bills, and actually fight her way against positive discouragements to the higher education. . . . And when at last that same girl announced her desire to go to college it was received with the same incredulity and dismay as if a brass button of one of those candidate's coats had propounded a new method of squaring the circle or trisecting the arc.

Haywood met with this attitude when she applied to be a candidate for the ministry at St. Augustine's. The school's principal, the Reverend Dr. Smedes, allowed her to enter the program after she lodged a complaint about its discriminatory policies. In her complaint Haywood remarked that "the only mission opening before a girl in his school was to marry one of those candidates." Haywood actually did marry one of the theology candidates at the school, George A. C. Cooper, on 21 June 1877 in the chapel at St. Augustine's. They both worked for the school while they continued their studies, and they planned to pursue paths that would allow them to give back to the communities that had sustained them as children. George Cooper died on 27 September 1879, however, leaving Cooper a widow at age twenty-one.

Widowed, but now able to teach freely, as married women were forced to resign their teaching positions, Cooper stayed at St. Augustine's until 1881, when she traveled to Ohio to attend Oberlin College, one of the few universities in the country to admit African American women. After writing to the president of the college, James Harris Fairchild, Cooper

was admitted to Oberlin and was not required to pay tuition, a condition she had requested due to her dire financial situation. She taught during the school year and summers to cover her living expenses, as she had while at St. Augustine's, and graduated from Oberlin College in 1884. Upon graduation she went to Wilberforce College to teach and was placed in charge of the department of modern languages and science. She stayed at Wilberforce one year and, in response to her mother's concerns, returned home to Raleigh and taught at St. Augustine's once again. In 1887 Cooper was awarded an M.A. degree in mathematics, due to her three years of teaching experience at the college level. In September of that year she left Raleigh for a teaching position at the Washington Colored High School in the District of Columbia.

Originally located in the Miner Building at Seventeenth and Church Streets, in 1873 the school moved to the corner of Seventeenth and M Streets, into the same building as the Charles Sumner Elementary School. It became locally known as the M Street School because the high-school classrooms faced M Street. When it moved again in 1891 to a building located between New Jersey and New York Avenues and built specifically for use as a high school, it remained the M Street School, and Cooper spent a majority of her long life either teaching or serving as principal of the school. When Cooper first arrived at the M Street School, she was assigned to teach mathematics and science. Within four years she was teaching the last-year Latin courses as well. Under the direction of three principals, Francis L. Cardozo, Robert N. Mattingly, and Robert H. Terell, Cooper and the other teachers at the M Street School were dedicated to providing their students with the best possible education, including college preparatory curricula. This method of instruction for African Americans was coming under great scrutiny at the time, due to Booker T. Washington's influence and his model of success, Tuskegee Institute.

At this time in her life Cooper met the prominent civil-rights activists Charlotte Forten Grimké and her husband, Francis J. Grimké. Cooper and Charlotte Grimké remained friends for nearly twenty-six years. Upon the death of Charlotte Grimké, her husband requested that Cooper write Grimké's biography, which was published in 1951 as *Personal Recollections of the Grimké Family & The Life and Writings of Charlotte Forten Grimké*. The Grimkés and Cooper became a cornerstone of African American intelligentsia in Washington, who spent Friday evenings at the Grimké home and Sunday evenings at Cooper's home.

Architect's drawing for the M Street School in Washington, D.C., where Cooper served as principal from 1902 to 1906 (District of Columbia Department of General Services)

In 1892 Cooper published *A Voice from the South, by a Black Woman of the South,* her defining work. Its essays touch upon the most pressing problems that the United States was facing in healing its racial and gender divisions. Like Harriet Jacobs, author of *Incidents in the Life of a Slave Girl* (1861), Cooper felt that the newly freed African American woman should relate her own experiences: "our Caucasian barristers are not to blame if they cannot *quite* put themselves in the dark man's place, neither should the dark man be wholly expected fully and adequately to reproduce the exact Voice of the Black Woman."

A Voice from the South was received well by both the reading public and the press. The *New York Independent* remarked that the text was "a piercing and clinging cry which it is impossible to hear [and] not to understand—which it is impossible to shake off." The *Boston Transcript* recognized her work as "an intimate exposition of qualities of her people which whites [were] . . . slow to appreciate." The *Detroit Plaindealer* claimed "there has been no book on the race question that has been more cogently and forcibly written by either white or black authors. The book is not only a credit to the genius of the race, but to woman whose place and sphere in life men have so long dictated."

In *A Voice from the South* Cooper examines the chronic American afflictions of racism and sexism, carefully delineating the African American woman's situation in the 1890s. In "Womanhood: A Vital Element in the Regeneration and Progress of a Race" Cooper argues that African American people will not be able to overcome the burden of slavery until black men acknowledge their connection with black women. Extending this idea to all of society, she argues that women provide a unique sensibility to social and political circles, despite being barred from those arenas. Cooper claims that the sense of duty and community felt in American society stems directly from female influence, and by not acknowledging these traits and debts men limit how far that society can progress. This influence is most important to African Americans. As Cooper notes:

> We are the heirs of a past which was not our fathers' moulding. "Every man the arbiter of his own destiny" was not true for the American Negro of the past: and it is no fault of his that he finds himself to-day the inheritor of a manhood and womanhood impoverished and debased by two centuries and more of compression and degradation.

> But weaknesses and malformations, which to-day are attributable to a vicious schoolmaster and a pernicious system, will a century hence be rightly regarded as proofs of innate corruptness and radical incurability.

Now the fundamental agency under God in the regeneration, the re-training of the race, as well as the ground work and starting point of its progress upward, must be the *black woman*.

With all the wrongs and neglects of her past, with all the weakness, the debasement, the moral thralldom of her present, the black woman of to-day stands mute and wondering at the Herculean task devolving upon her. But the cycles wait for her. No other hand can move the lever. She must be loosed from her bands and set to work.

Cooper was convinced that without the influence of black women, African American people would forever be unable to assert their rights as an integral part of U.S. American society and culture.

Cooper was an energetic advocate for women's educational opportunities. As a teacher at the M Street School, and through her association with the Grimkés and other members of the African American intelligentsia, Cooper was adamant in demanding educational opportunities not only for African American men but also for women of all races. While *A Voice from the South* at times argues that well-educated women make better wives and mothers, it would seem from her own life that this argument is a rhetorical ploy to gain educational opportunities at any cost. Having a master's degree at this point in her life, as well as being devoted to teaching—so devoted that she never considered remarrying, which would have barred her from the profession she loved—Cooper was an effective advocate for the educational opportunities she had to fight and scrimp for. Even in her argument concerning marriage and motherhood, however, she manages to make it clear that education makes it much easier for women to be independent and for women to demand much more from men:

I grant you that intellectual development, with the self-reliance and capacity for earning a livelihood which it gives, renders women less dependent upon the marriage relation for physical support (which, by the way, does not always accompany it). Neither is she compelled to look to sexual love as the one sensation capable of giving tone and relish, movement and vim to the life she leads. . . . The question is not now with the woman "How shall I so cramp, stunt, simplify and nullify myself as to make me eligible to the honor of being swallowed up into some little man?" but the problem, I trow, now rests with the man as to how he can so develop his God-given powers as to reach the ideal of a generation of women who demand the noblest, grandest and best achievements of which he is capable.

As an active participant in the feminist movement in the 1900s, Cooper took issue with the racism rampant within the movement. With both the suffrage and civil-rights movements working the same political circuits, the issue of whether the vote should be given to African American men or white women became a problem and caused a rift between the two groups that had worked together during the abolition movement. In her essay "Woman Versus the Indian" Cooper points out that feminist ideals and missions for changing the situation for women would not be complete until fundamental rights and opportunities had been extended to all women—regardless of race, religion, or creed. She was one of the first writers to argue for a more global feminist perspective.

Cooper was also one of the first to call for a distinct African American literature—thus giving her support to the burgeoning class of new writers that included Ida B. Wells-Barnett, Frances E. W. Harper, William Wells Brown, and Charles Chesnutt. Cooper felt that for too long American literature had been defined by white men whose experiences belied the diversity of the nation. In *A Voice from the South* she responded to this assumption with a challenge:

"Who are Americans?" comes rolling back from ten million throats. Who are to do the packing and delivering of goods? Who are the homefolks and who are the strangers? Who are the absolute and original tenants in fee-simple? The red men used to be owners of the soil—but they are about to be pushed over into the Pacific Ocean. They, perhaps, have the best right to call themselves "Americans" by the right of primogeniture.

The supremacy of one race,—the despotism of a class or the tyranny of an individual can not ultimately prevail on a continent held in equilibrium by such conflicting forces and by so many and such strong fibred races as there are struggling on this soil.

Cooper was an adamant advocate for the notion of U.S. citizenship as it could be, for the promise that America could fulfill. She felt that promise would never be realized unless the mixing and blending of the many races that settled upon the continent could occur without domination and oppression, and she delivered this challenge to both African American and Anglo American society.

Others have suggested that Cooper also supported a progressive religious doctrine in *A Voice from the South*. In *A "Singing Something": Womanist Reflections on Anna Julia Cooper* (1994) Karen Baker-Fletcher argues that throughout the work Cooper is advocating a theology of political action and change for the

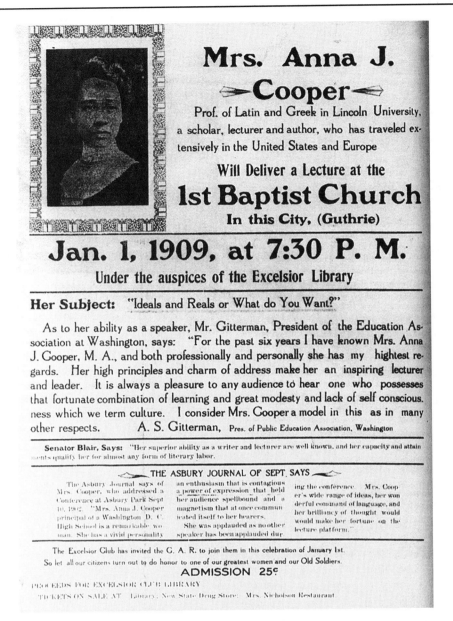

Notice for one of the many lectures Cooper delivered during her long career (Anna J. Cooper Manuscript Collection, Moorland-Spingarn Research Center, Howard University)

poor and oppressed. This approach is most apparent in the essays "What Are We Worth?" and "The Gain from a Belief," in which Cooper argues that all people have a debt to pay the world in terms of the time, money, and energy spent in raising and educating them. She thus promotes an ideology of direct action and reaction, and she argues that without some religious belief Americans, especially African Americans, cannot have a healthy, whole society and a country that strives to improve itself. Her attacks on philosophers such as David Hume, Voltaire, and Auguste Comte and their promotion of agnos-

ticism are reflective of her confidence in the notion that without God and morality humans have no ideal to emulate and hence the transition into greedy and heartless beasts is made easier and more manageable.

Cooper believed that a distinct African American literature combined with a progressive religious philosophy made for a more complete society as well as a healthy and effective response to overcoming the paralyzing effects of racism that plagued African Americans. As she remarked in the chapter of *A Voice From the South* titled "What Are We Worth?":

What have you produced, what consumed? What is your real value in the world's economy? What do you give to the world over and above what you have cost? What would be missed had you never lived? What are you worth? What of actual value would go down with you if you were sunk into the ocean or buried by an earthquake to-morrow? Show up your cash account and your balance sheet. In the final reckoning do you belong on the debit or the credit side of the account? according to a fair and square, an impartial and practical reckoning. It is by this standard that society estimates individuals; and by this standard finally and inevitably the world will measure and judge nations and races.

Cooper was convinced that production and creation were key tools African Americans needed to utilize for integrating into mainstream society. Unlike Washington, who advocated an economic path for integration, Cooper was aware that it would not simply be money that would change the image of African American peoples. Having a strong economic base would certainly play a part, but Cooper felt that Washington's plan of vocational training was not the only way to reach that goal. She was convinced that participation in arts and letters would also be necessary, as African Americans had been supporting themselves and half a nation by their labor since being brought to America in the 1600s.

Without aspirations and training toward loftier goals, African Americans would never be able to withstand or refute the barrage of racist beliefs and actions that they faced. In this light Cooper also felt that without a firm sense of a higher power, such strength to progress would never be found. While she advocated a religious base of action and thought for all of the United States, she found it a crucial point for African Americans: "The great, the fundamental need of any nation, any race, is for heroism, devotion, sacrifice; and there cannot be heroism, devotion, or sacrifice in a primarily skeptical spirit." Thus, she attempted to rally the African American intelligentsia, the so-called Talented Tenth of the African American population:

Do you *believe* that the God of history often chooses the weak things of earth to confound the mighty, and that the Negro race in America has a veritable destiny in His eternal purposes,–then don't spend your time discussing the "Negro Problem" amid the clouds of your fine havanna, ensconced in your friend's well-cushioned arm-chair and with your patent leather boot-tips elevated to the opposite mantel. Do those poor "cowards in the South" need a leader–then get up and lead them! Let go your purse-strings and begin to *live* your creed.

Cooper supported that philosophy throughout *A Voice from the South* as well as in her own life. Many of the essays in *A Voice from the South* were originally lectures that Cooper gave to a variety of audiences. In 1893 she was one of three African American women invited to speak at the World's Congress of Representative Women, and in 1900 she spoke at the Pan-African Congress Conference. As a public figure involved in African American social circles in Washington, D.C., as well as the global community, Cooper took her position as a community leader seriously. In 1901 she participated in the development of the first Colored Social Settlement in the District of Columbia and in 1906 was appointed supervisor of the house. The mission of the settlement was to better the living and working conditions of poor urban African Americans. It strove to offer opportunities for many people, including working mothers, by providing day care and school lessons for small children and young women, who had the chance to play on a basketball team and participate in sewing classes and social events. Young men also benefited from the work of the settlement: boys participated in school classes, chess teams, and social and military clubs.

Along with her settlement work, Cooper became active in forming a chapter of the Young Women's Christian Association (YWCA) in Washington in 1905. The Washington Colored YWCA provided housing for young African American women at a time when housing was not always readily available or safe. It also provided classes in culinary arts, sewing, Bible study, music, missionary work, and African American history.

During this period of her life Cooper's professional career was steadily advancing. She was appointed principal of the M Street School in 1902, replacing Robert Terell. As principal she continued to uphold the aims of the school as they had been provided by the superintendent of the Colored Schools of Washington City and Georgetown, George F. T. Cook. He was emphatic that the objective of schools for colored students should be "to present to the pupils . . . incentives to higher aim in education." During her tenure Cooper pushed for accreditation for the high school from some of the finest white colleges in the United States, fought for scholarships for her best and brightest students, and left behind a legacy of successful alumni, including Sadie Tanner Mossell, the first African American woman to earn a Ph.D. in economics from the University of Pennsylvania; Joseph H. Douglass, grandson of Frederick Douglass, a violinist who was the first black concert musician asked to record for the Victor Recording Company; and Jean Toomer, author of the novel *Cane* (1923).

Her success was also noted by international scholars and visitors. In 1903 Abbé Felix Klein from the Catholic Institute of Paris visited the M Street School, looking for an example of educational opportunities for African Americans. He was so impressed with his visit and his interview with Cooper that he mentioned the school in his book *In the Land of Strenuous Life* (1905). This kind of publicity in the midst of the political battles over methods of instruction for African American students was not what the Washington Board of Education wanted for the M Street School, and it expressed its displeasure with Cooper soon afterward.

During the 1904–1905 school year Cooper was the target of malicious slander due to her dedication to classical education for African American students. Her allegiance to the theories of W. E. B. Du Bois during a time when Washington's call for strict vocational training—a call most popular with racist whites, who knew such a program protected their interests in high-wage-earning fields—caused members of the Washington Board of Education to allege that she was unable to command discipline in her school, that students who were not academically fit for higher education had been allowed to continue in the program, and that students had exhibited shameful behavior such as drinking and smoking. Supporters of Cooper were either misrepresented in the press or unable to present their views at public board meetings held to sort through the allegations.

When these tactics failed to disarm Cooper's community and professional support, her opponents turned to an even more damaging method of defaming her. Years previously, Cooper had been called upon by the death of a close friend to care for two teenaged children, Lula and John Love. In 1905 John Love was a teacher at the M Street School, and rumors began circulating that Cooper and Love were having an affair. At the time Love was thirty-five years old and Cooper, forty-eight. Cooper never officially responded to the rumor, and circumstantial evidence suggests that it had a basis in truth. Cooper's grandniece Regia Bronson threw out letters from Love to Cooper, one of which is said to have held a proposal of marriage, but not before Bronson told Paul Cook about their existence. There is no proof that Cooper in any way responded to the overtures made by Love, and it is unclear whether she felt that the relationship was improper or simply not attractive. Remarriage would have made her unable to continue her teaching career, however, and she had been a widow for nearly thirty years. Regardless of the validity of the rumors, the trouble they caused for Cooper serves as an example of the sexual double bind women were placed in

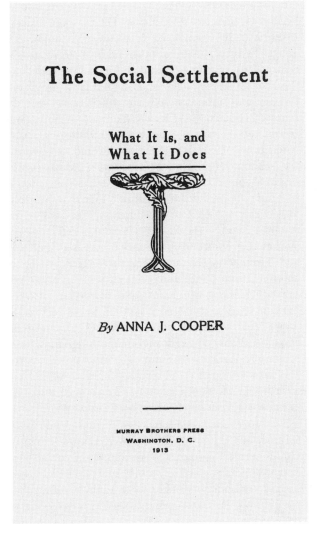

Cover for Cooper's booklet on the settlement movement

during the late 1800s and early 1900s: because of her position as both widow and teacher, Cooper was forced into an asexual role; anything hinting otherwise would have smacked of impropriety to the society in which she lived.

The controversy surrounding Cooper was based on political beliefs and the change of power from those who advocated opportunities for African Americans to those who aligned themselves with whites and the philosophy of education illustrated at the Tuskegee Institute. In fact, during the 1905 commencement ceremonies at the M Street School, Washington himself was invited to speak, and during that speech he both addressed the controversy involving Cooper and endorsed Roscoe Conkling Bruce as Cooper's replacement. On 14 September 1906 Bruce was named the new principal of the M Street School, and Cooper was left unemployed.

Immediately following this painful episode in her life, Cooper left Washington, D.C., for the Lincoln Institute in Jefferson City, Missouri. She taught languages at the Lincoln Institute until 1910, when she returned to Washington and resumed her work with the YWCA as the chairwoman of the girls' programs. During the summers between 1907 and 1910 she renewed contact with Oberlin College, giving serious consideration to pursuing a doctoral degree. After contacting the president of Oberlin and discovering the school did not offer the degree, however, she began a course of study in belles lettres based solely on academic pursuit for pleasure rather than purpose. When she returned to Washington, she took a job teaching Latin at the M Street School, a difficult decision at best considering the amount of personal pain and humiliation she had faced there. Her two foster children, John and Lula Love, were grown and self-sufficient by this point, and the home she had lived in during the earlier part of her career at M Street had been sold when she left Washington for Missouri. When she returned to Washington, Cooper took up residence with Emma Merritt, with whom she had worked on YWCA projects. This arrangement afforded her freedom to undertake projects and programs that might have earlier been impossible.

One of these projects was a trip to France in the summer of 1911, where she enrolled as a student in La Guilde Internationale in Paris. She returned the next two summers to pursue studies in French literature, history, and phonetics. The next summer, rather than returning to Paris, Cooper enrolled as a doctoral student at Columbia University in New York City and thus began pursuing one of her most important personal goals. Between the summer of 1913 and the summer of 1917, Cooper finished the required course of study and demonstrated her ability to complete the necessary research for translating a college edition of *Le Pèlerinage de Charlemagne*. The only obstacle in her path was Columbia's one-year residency requirement, which would have forced Cooper to stop teaching and thus lose her pension and any other hope of financial support after her retirement.

While she was searching for a way to satisfy this requirement without leaving her teaching job, Cooper again met with the challenge of raising children that were not her own. In 1915 Margaret Hinton Haywood died, leaving her husband, John R. Haywood, Cooper's nephew, with the care of their five children. Unable to carry this responsibility alone, Haywood sought Cooper's help in caring for and raising the children, ranging in age from twelve years to six months. To accommodate such a change, Cooper moved out of the home she shared with Merritt and bought a large home at 201 T Street in Washington's LeDroit Park, a neighborhood formerly reserved for whites. At the age of fifty-five, Cooper once again became a foster mother.

To keep her dream of a doctorate alive, Cooper began to translate *Le Pèlerinage de Charlemagne* in her free moments. When the work was completed, it was published in Paris in 1925. During this time Cooper began to consider transferring the credits and work she had done toward her doctorate at Columbia University to the University of Paris at the Sorbonne. This transfer would require her to produce, in conjunction with her translation of *Le Pèlerinage de Charlemagne,* a dissertation as well. When she was stricken with a "fortuitous bout of the flu" in 1923, she decided to ask for a year's sick leave, which would allow her to travel to Paris and finish her doctoral work. Cooper left the United States without knowing that her request for a leave of absence had not been properly processed by her supervisor, and so in the midst of preparing to defend her dissertation, "L'Attitude de la France a l'Egard de l'Egalite des Races" (The Attitude of France Regarding the Equality of the Races), she was presented with a telegram that read "Rumored dropped if not returned within 60 days." Determined not to lose her teaching position and the retirement benefits that went with it, Cooper returned to the high school "5 minutes before 9 on the morning of the 60th day of my absence."

After returning to teaching she spent all of her available time working on her dissertation in an alcove that the Library of Congress allowed her to use, since African Americans were not allowed into the main sections of the Library of Congress at this time. In 1924 her dissertation was finished, and Cooper requested an emergency excused absence so that she might return to France to defend her dissertation in a process called a *soutenance,* or oral examination. This request was refused by her supervisor, and so Cooper returned to her work until March 1925, when she returned to Paris without permission from the school. As she herself remembered, "if they drop me this time it shall be for doing as I darn please. If I perish, I perish!" Her *soutenance* was held on 23 March 1925, and at the end of the afternoon, one of the judges proclaimed "vous etes Docteur" (you are a doctor). Cooper thus became the fourth African American woman to earn a Ph.D.

During Cooper's period of study, the M Street School was going through another series of changes. Because of recent political developments in the environment surrounding African American educational opportunities, as well as the battle over the right to govern the District of Columbia, the M Street School was given a new building, and its name (the idea for which is attributed to Cooper) was changed to the Paul Laurence Dunbar High School. Cooper was responsible for writing the first draft of its alma mater, which was presented in January 1916. The school was only one part of a larger change that was occurring in Washington. The curriculum had been affected by the debates over the educational theories of Washington and DuBois, teachers had come and gone—many times because of unfair and discriminatory practices—and the school's administration had changed hands many times. In the midst of this change, the process for evaluating teachers had become one of peer review, which left qualified but unpopular teachers to fend for themselves. Cooper was one of those teachers hurt by this system.

After completing her doctorate in 1925, Cooper returned to Dunbar High School and resumed her teaching duties. In 1925 Cooper had been given a professional rating she felt was unfair and that put her retirement benefits at risk. All teachers of the Washington school system had been required to take written examinations that in Cooper's mind had been "designed rather to 'stump' the candidate than test his ability to teach the subject." Because all teachers in some way failed to pass all sections of these examinations, they were to count as only one part of the whole evaluation. Based on her test performance, Cooper had been passed over for a promotion and a raise by persons with lower ratings in other areas. Cooper took the action as another spiteful attack by the Washington Board of Education and found the circumstance infuriating and financially damaging. Her complaint concerning discriminatory practices went unheeded, and by the end of 1929 Cooper left the Washington School District, which she had given more than forty years of service.

Upon her retirement from teaching high school, Cooper accepted another challenge. Frelinghuysen University, located in Washington, was conceived in 1917 for the purpose of adult education and had been under the direction of Jesse Lawson, a man dedicated to educating those whose financial means would not allow them the time or the funds to attend formal schooling. His goal was to provide for those of Washington's African American population who needed educational, spiritual, and social programs. The university designed home schools and educational centers throughout Washington. As the university progressed, it began to aspire to higher education and offered courses in practical arts as well as high school, college, and graduate work. In 1927 Lawson died, and a new president was needed to allow the school to continue its most important work. Cooper became the next president of Frelinghuysen University in the summer of 1930.

As Cooper began her tenure as president, she learned that the school had suffered financial difficulties and was operating solely on tuition, with no emergency funds of any kind. By June 1931, however, with financial savvy and expertise Cooper had been able to set things in order and begin a fund-raising drive to provide tuition supplements and a savings fund for the school. The fund-raising drive did not go as smoothly as planned, however, and when the school lost its lease on its only building, the university had no choice but to move its operations into Cooper's private home. Annexed to the university was the Hannah Stanley Opportunity School, an institution that Cooper solely controlled in honor of her mother (the Haywood was dropped without comment). Her will protected the T Street home for both the Opportunity School and Frelinghuysen University.

Both schools continued to survive, although not without a struggle. Frelinghuysen was initially able to confer degrees, but in 1930, about the time that Cooper became president, the school lost that right under Public Law No. 949, which allowed the Washington Board of Education the authority to license all district-operated institutions of education. Each institution was responsible for providing evidence that the directors and trustees of the institution were qualified for their positions and that the degrees awarded would be for work equaling the requirements of other educational institutions that conferred the same degrees. The rescinding of the original license likely stemmed from the history of antagonism between Cooper and the board. Another setback occurred in 1931, when the law instructors pulled out from Frelinghuysen and started their own school.

By 1937 the university was still suffering financially, and Cooper, at the age of seventy-five, applied for employment with the Education Division of the Works Progress Administration in order to supplement the university with funds. She did not get the position applied for, but her dedication to the success of the university is evident in undertaking such a responsibility. In 1940, after a ten-year struggle trying to get the ability to confer degrees, Cooper and the Board of Trustees of Frelinghuysen University changed the name of the school to the Frelinghuysen Group of Schools for Colored Working People. In that same year Cooper decided it was time for her to step down as president, and she became the registrar. She fully retired in 1950 at the age of eighty-eight. In 1958 Anna Julia Cooper celebrated her one hundredth birthday. On that day, she was interviewed by a reporter from *The Washington Post*. In the interview

~~Editor of the Crisis.~~   The Humor of Teaching
                                    by Dr Anna J Cooper

I have read with interest the strictures of Professor Davis
on the Negro College Student & likewise the three or four
answers from students in a subsequent issue of Crisis.
I am impressed particularly with the true teacher-spirit
of Mr. Davis' faultfinding & the high detachment of his
aim & purpose in writing. His Criticism while severe
is not carping or slanderous neither is it the flippant
sort that seizes an opportunity to rush to print for the vain
glory of making talk thro the news papers; rather is it
the honest findings & chastening of an intelligent
father who wishes to correct an imperfect son,— con-
structive, as all criticism should be, with an eye single
to the ideal, not a relative, standard. The "Answers" too
so far are not the tiresome attack & counter-attack that
get us nowhere beyond the over brilliant sparring
exhibition of hit & thrust: they suggest causes & further
criticisms — one, the need of ripe scholarship among teachers
themselves, specifically the frivolous fledgelings just out of
college & serving an indeterminate sentence to teach on
their way to something hoped for; a second, the dry-as-
dust abstractions & mental gymnastics embalmed in
an outworn college curriculum that have no discoverable
connection with the practical life interests of the student
& never made to grip his attention & disclose where he,
the individual John Jones, can catch on, etc. etc.
        If you will allow, I should like to add one
other point of view in the same spirit of meeting our

First and last pages from the manuscript for Cooper's essay "The Humor of Teaching," written for publication in a 1930 issue of Crisis
(W. E. B. Du Bois Collection, University of Massachusetts)

sent their sons all the way to Rhodes to get the touch of Apollonius. An instructor who is himself keen about the enigma of the Universe, or even about the enigma of Mississippi & Texas, will find his flaming torch as "catching" from a chair in Greek & Latin as he would with a stereotyped or borrowed syllabus in Civics or a book "plan" on the Reconstruction period.

The trouble I suspect is that those who furnish the coin & "suggest" the promotions in Negro Education are not themselves a-wearying & a-worrying to see any Renaissance or primal naissance of real thinking in Negro Schools, & yet God knows they need it.

Anna J. Cooper,

she summed up the philosophy of her life most tellingly: "it isn't what we say about ourselves, it's what our life stands for." Cooper's life stood for the right of all people to have educational and employment opportunities. On 27 February 1964 Cooper died in her home in Washington, D.C., at the age of 105.

The majority of Cooper's life was dedicated to the service of others and the education of the African American community. Born a slave, able to receive the education that made her teaching and administrative career possible, receiving a Ph.D. from the University of Paris in her sixties, and working with students until well into her eighties, Cooper saw the worst and the best of American life and letters. A few lines from a poem, "No Flowers Please," which she wrote on her eighty-second birthday, reflects the essence of Anna Cooper's life:

No flowers please, just the smile of sweet understanding
The knowing look that sees Beyond and says gently & kindly
Somebody's Teacher on Vacation now. Resting for the Fall Opening.

References:

Elizabeth Alexander, "'We Must Be about Our Father's Business': Anna Julia Cooper and the In-Corporation of the Nineteenth-Century African-American Woman Intellectual," *Signs, 20* (Winter 1995): 336–356;

Karen Baker-Fletcher, *A "Singing Something": Womanist Reflections on Anna Julia Cooper* (New York: Crossroad, 1994);

Hazel Carby, *Reconstructing Womanhood: The Emergence of the Afro-American Woman Novelist* (New York & Oxford: Oxford University Press, 1987), pp. 3, 6, 7, 96–108, 114–117, 118, 120;

Paul Phillips Cooke, Introduction to *Anna J. Cooper: A Voice from the South,* by Louise Daniel Hutchinson (Washington: Smithsonian Institution Press, 1981), pp. xiii–xiv;

Frances Smith Foster, *Written by Herself: Literary Production by African American Women, 1746–1892* (Bloomington: Indiana University Press, 1993), pp. 5–8, 10, 21, 180, 186, 190;

Leona C. Gabel, *From Slavery to the Sorbonne and Beyond: The Life and Writings of Anna J. Cooper* (Northampton, Mass.: Department of History, Smith College, 1982);

Sharon Harley, "Anna J. Cooper: A Voice for Black Women," in *The Afro-American Woman: Struggles and Images,* edited by Harley and Rosalyn Terborg-Penn (Port Washington, N.Y.: Kennikat Press, 1978), pp. 87–96;

Louise Daniel Hutchinson, *Anna J. Cooper: A Voice from the South* (Washington: Smithsonian Institution Press, 1981);

Claudia Tate, *Domestic Allegories of Political Desire: The Black Heroine's Text at the Turn of the Century* (New York & Oxford: Oxford University Press, 1992);

Mary Helen Washington, Introduction to *A Voice from the South, by a Woman of the South* (New York: Negro Universities Press, 1969), pp. xxvii–liv.

Papers:

The Anna Julia Cooper papers are housed at the Moorland-Spingarn Research Center, Howard University, Washington, D.C.

Mary Abigail Dodge
(Gail Hamilton)
(31 March 1833 – 17 August 1896)

Annmarie Pinarski

BOOKS: *Country Living and Country Thinking* (Boston: Ticknor & Fields, 1862);

Courage! (New York: Richardson, 1862);

Gala-Days (Boston: Ticknor & Fields, 1863);

Stumbling-Blocks (Boston: Ticknor & Fields, 1864);

A New Atmosphere (Boston: Ticknor & Fields, 1865);

Skirmishes and Sketches (Boston: Ticknor & Fields, 1865);

Red-Letter Days in Applethorpe (Boston: Ticknor & Fields, 1866);

Summer Rest (Boston: Ticknor & Fields, 1866);

Wool-Gathering (Boston: Ticknor & Fields, 1867);

Woman's Wrongs: A Counter-Irritant (Boston: Ticknor & Fields, 1868);

Memorial to Mrs. Hannah Stanwood Dodge (Cambridge, Mass.: Riverside, 1869);

A Battle of the Books (Cambridge, Mass.: Riverside, 1870);

Woman's Worth and Worthlessness: The Complement to "A New Atmosphere" (New York: Harper, 1872);

Little Folk Life (New York: Harper, 1872);

Child World (Boston: Shepard & Gill, 1873);

Twelve Miles from a Lemon (New York: Harper, 1874);

Nursery Noonings (New York: Harper, 1875);

Sermons to the Clergy (New York: Harper, 1876);

First Love Is Best (Boston: Estes & Lauriat, 1877);

What Ye Think of Christ (Boston: Estes & Lauriat, 1877);

Our Common School System (Boston: Estes & Lauriat, 1880);

Divine Guidance: Memorial of Allen W. Dodge (New York: Appleton, 1881);

English Kings in a Nutshell (New York: American Book, 1885);

A Washington Bible Class (New York: Appleton, 1890);

Biography of James G. Blaine (Norwich, Conn.: Henry Bill, 1895);

X-Rays (Hamilton, Mass.: Privately printed, 1896);

Chips, Fragments, and Vestiges, edited by H. Augusta Dodge (Boston: Lee & Shepard, 1902).

Mary Abigail Dodge, 1896 (portrait from Gail Hamilton's Life in Letters, *1901)*

OTHER: "The Pursuit of Knowledge under Difficulties," in *Atlantic Tales: A Collection of Stories from the Atlantic Monthly* (Boston: Ticknor & Fields, 1866), pp. 93–146;

"Cassus Belli," in *The Insuppressible Book,* edited by Dodge (Boston: Cassino, 1885).

SELECTED PERIODICAL PUBLICATION–
UNCOLLECTED: "An Object Lesson in Woman's
Rights," *Sophia Smith Research Collection,* 1, no. 4
(1892): 1–41.

In the essay "Men and Women," first published
in a nine-part series from January to March 1859 in the
abolitionist newspaper *National Era* and then reprinted
in the collection *Country Living and Country Thinking*
(1862), Mary Abigail Dodge presents a primer for
women who desire independence, autonomy, and
self-reliance, qualities that Dodge vigorously pursued
for herself. With a pragmatic eye, Dodge, who wrote
under the name Gail Hamilton, objects to the gendered
proscriptions of her day that would inhibit women's
freedoms, both geographical and intellectual. She
writes: "There are no wild wanderings at [women's]
own sweet will, no experimental deviations from the
prescribed route, no hazardous but delightful flying off
in a tangent on the spur of the moment." With these
words Dodge cogently identifies the stultifying social
conventions that fostered the so-called Cult of True
Womanhood for white, middle-class women in nineteenth-century American society. Rather than accept
the "prescribed route" for women of her class, Dodge
lived and wrote with unceasing resistance to the stereotypical expectations for women of her race and economic standing.

"Men and Women" is one of Dodge's earliest
treatments of her trademark themes–the relations
between men and women, the meaning of womanhood,
and the limitations of a woman's sphere. Dodge's ideas
on these issues were complex and at times seemingly
paradoxical. While she often espoused essentialist
thinking on gender roles, she also believed that women
should be encouraged to cultivate self-reliance through
equal educational opportunities. On the one hand,
Dodge spoke of women's inherent moral superiority
and nurturing capacities, thus accepting certain dominant ideologies regarding domesticity and femininity
that shaped popular conceptions of white, middle-class
womanhood. On the other hand, she denounced the
cultural messages that promoted women's passivity, frivolity, and dependence on marriage and motherhood
for identity and fulfillment. The contradictions that
mark Dodge's beliefs underscore the ideological tensions and monumental changes that were occurring in
the late-nineteenth-century United States. As a result of
the campaign for woman suffrage, the Civil War, the
rise of industrial capitalism, and the growing numbers
of women working for wages, women were becoming
increasingly visible participants in the public life of the
nation. Dodge embraced the opportunities that this
"new atmosphere" provided; she lived an independent

life, unfettered by marriage and domesticity yet deeply
interested in both subjects throughout her career as an
essayist and political journalist. Neither a radical nor a
reactionary for her day, Dodge's conventional beliefs
were tempered by her insistence upon a woman's right
to foster ideals of self-reliance and intellectual independence as articulated by writers such as Ralph Waldo
Emerson.

The opportunities afforded Dodge early in her
life set the stage for her prolific literary accomplishments as well as her advocacy on behalf of education
for women. The youngest of seven children, she was
born into a comfortable middle-class family in Hamilton, Massachusetts, on 31 March 1833. Her father,
James Brown Dodge, was a well-respected farmer, and
her mother, Hannah Stanwood Dodge, taught school
before she married, all the while maintaining her love
of reading. An accident at the age of two left Dodge
blind in one eye, and, subsequently, she was acutely
self-conscious of her physical difference. She wrote in a
notebook in 1850 that she was "surpassingly ugly, ugly
in form–ugly in feature." Her lack of confidence in her
physical appearance, however, did not hinder Dodge
from excelling in school. Her parents and schoolteachers recognized her intelligence early on and encouraged
her to continue her studies with vigor. Educational possibilities were expanding for women at this time, as
female seminaries that prepared girls for their futures as
wives and mothers were gaining widespread acceptance. At the age of twelve Dodge attended boarding
school at Cambridge for one year and then the following year was sent to the Ipswich Female Seminary, from
which she graduated in 1850. Her education there
included French, Latin, history, and chemistry. Despite
these intellectual rigors, Dodge's formal education
ended here since, unlike her male peers, she was unable
to pursue a college degree.

While her education prepared her ostensibly for
domestic duties, Dodge had other plans in mind. She
opted for a career of some kind over marriage and
dreamed of becoming a writer. Expressing her desire to
remain an unmarried woman, Dodge wrote to her
brother in 1860: "I'm not married and I don't think I
shall be. I can't afford the time, and besides, the men
ought to be given to the women who can't get along
without them. I can support myself." After graduating
from Ipswich, she turned to teaching, first at Ipswich
until 1854, then at Hartford Female Seminary, and
finally, from 1855 to 1858, at Hartford High School. In
many ways Dodge was a successful teacher whose students respected her knowledge and enjoyed her companionship. She became increasingly dissatisfied with
the long hours, bureaucratic complications, and low
wages to which female teachers were subjected, how-

ever. Her letters to friends and relatives reveal a persistent concern over her personal finances during this time. She had chosen teaching as a career primarily for the steady income it offered, but she soon realized she had little time for writing. Still, by 1856 she had submitted essays and poetry to the *National Era* and the *Independent,* a well-respected and widely circulated Protestant newspaper. Dodge's writing so impressed Gamaliel Bailey, the editor of the *National Era,* that he invited her to Washington, D.C., and offered her a job as governess of his children. The move to Washington was a turning point for Dodge. She established herself as a writer, contributing social analysis and political commentary to such journals as the *Congretionalist* and the *Atlantic Monthly.* At this time she adopted the name Gail Hamilton as a way to protect her privacy and to voice her objection to the kind of personal publicity that could detract from the serious content of her writing.

After the death of Bailey in 1860, Dodge returned to Hamilton, where she began to write full time under her pseudonym. She produced hundreds of articles on political, social, and cultural issues as well as scores of poems. Her poetry was collected posthumously into a unified volume, *Chips, Fragments, and Vestiges* (1902); her essays, on the other hand, were popular and highly regarded and were frequently compiled during her lifetime. She published more than twenty-five volumes, including a novel, travel writing, and children's stories. Her first collection of essays, *Country Living and Country Thinking,* establishes many of the themes that Dodge revisits and revises throughout her career. The essay "Men and Women" is the centerpiece of this volume, but other essays likewise comment on gender relations and women's issues as well as authorship and the provocations of rural life. Furthermore, this compilation provides insight into Dodge's distinctive style and mode of argumentation and analysis. In "Men and Women," for example, Dodge seamlessly weaves together inductive and deductive logic, rhetorical questions, and elaborate scenarios to construct her arguments. Moreover, when her essays feature a first-person persona, as in the humorous "My Garden," Dodge employs discursive techniques such as exaggeration, sarcasm, and satire to challenge conventional thinking and force readers to reconsider widely accepted ideas. Dodge's elaborate rhetorical skills allowed her to express her strong and often argumentative viewpoints with clarity and conviction, thus fortifying her reputation as a keen analyst of late-nineteenth-century mores.

Published originally in 1862 in the *Atlantic Monthly,* "My Garden" typifies Dodge's use of irony, exaggeration, and understatement and situates her within a tradition of American women humorists that includes Caroline Kirkland and Phoebe Cary. The essay begins in mock seriousness with the first-person narrator "apologizing" for her gender, anticipating the "disappointment" of some readers who desire the authority of a male writer. She writes that it is "equally trying to feel your interest clustering round a narrator's manhood, all of your individuality merging in his, till, of a sudden, you catch the swell of crinoline, and there you are." By exposing the readers' stereotypical expectations for male and female writing, Dodge reveals the absurdity of categorizing style and voice based on gender alone. The essay continues its exploration of the relations between the sexes in the form of a combative dialogue on gardening between the female narrator and her rival, Halicarnassus, a character who appears in other essays as well. Their discussions are structured as a battle of wits as the narrator attempts to prove herself as Halicarnassus's equal. The humor results as Dodge plays with cultural stereotypes of femininity and masculinity, portraying Halicarnassus as the overconfident, authoritative expert gardener and the narrator as a novice who tolerates Halicarnassus's arrogance while trying to outsmart him with her own gardening plans. In the end the garden fails, but the narrator emerges as a likable character whose surprising conclusions about human nature challenge "common-sense" philosophy while emphasizing the contrasts between urban and rural life heightened by industrialization.

"My Garden" also explores the theme of separate spheres through humor. The tone is often self-deprecating, and the tension between the narrator and Halicarnassus remains unresolved, a clear comment on the state of gender relations that Dodge herself perceived. In *The Disobedient Writer: Women and Narrative Tradition* (1995), Nancy A. Walker interprets this essay on another level, arguing that Dodge employs the garden setting for an Eden story that suggests the narrator's "metaphoric exclusion from the creation of literature." Certainly Dodge acknowledged the professional and cultural barriers to literary achievement for women, most notably in a section from "Men and Women." This lengthy and argumentative piece considers, among other subjects, the relationship between women writers and their male critics. In the context of women's paradoxical situation in the marketplace, Dodge identifies the "criticism of women's books" as unjustly "half-flattering, half-contemptuous . . . condescending praise." The prejudice against women writers, according to Dodge, was clearly evident in the criticism of Elizabeth Barrett Browning's book-length poem *Aurora Leigh* (1857), which reviewers censured as obscure and awkward, a "failure" because of the gender of its author. Despite the "paternalism" of those male publishers and reviewers, Dodge calls for women to write:

as she theorizes for herself, "authorship is not a thing to be quietly chosen. It chooses you; you do not choose it." Dodge further explains her own approach to writing and her critics in a later essay, "My Book," from *Skirmishes and Sketches* (1865). Dodge presents herself here as a confident writer free of the anxieties and self-doubts that plague many others. This self-assurance enables Dodge to handle her critics with ease by dismissing their charges of irrelevance, egotism, arrogance, and illogic one by one. With tongue in cheek, Dodge finally promises never to stop writing.

The challenge Dodge issues to women to write is part of a more ambitious agenda for women's self-improvement, the underlying assumption of many of her treatises on women's rights. "Men and Women" includes strident critiques not only of the institutions aimed to prevent women's advancement but also of the everyday practices and rituals that maintained women's lesser status. For example, Dodge bemoans the differences in attire that place a woman at a disadvantage when she desires to travel. Because women are not as free as men to travel, this difference strengthens women's ties to the hearth and home and thus reinforces the ideology of separate spheres. Furthermore, Dodge recognized that the "ordinary" affairs of life, such as starching and whitening collars, occupy considerable time, thereby contributing to the limitations that are placed on women's improvements of self and soul. Throughout "Men and Women," Dodge's analysis is just as precise, replete with anecdotal and observational evidence of claims in the form of stories that run seamlessly together, thus constructing a critical vantage point for women readers.

The overarching target of the criticism in "Men and Women" and elsewhere is the ideology of separate spheres, which requires "self-sacrifice, moral heroism, silent influence, [and] might of love" from women. Dodge affirms these attributes and considers women's roles as wives and mothers essential for maintaining a civil society; however, she rejects the idea that women should be limited to the private sphere as men have defined it. Rather, even if women choose marriage and motherhood, if they "have glimmerings of something higher," such as authorship, they should pursue their desires without censure from their husband or society. With this message, Dodge extends the late-nineteenth-century ideal of self-improvement to women, inviting them to partake fully in their Christian duty to develop their character to the fullest extent: "You want a subject, field, career. Very well. Find one, or make one if you can. Exert yourself to the utmost." For Dodge, a woman who is "strong, brave, self-poised" is fulfilling her civic and Christian obligations much more

than a woman who is dependent, narcissistic, and weak.

Dodge adopts perhaps her most passionate tone in "Men and Women" when she focuses on the social and cultural imperatives insisting that marriage is a woman's natural state. Late-nineteenth-century law and custom dictated marriage as the foundation of the family and the nation, without which civilization would deteriorate and progress would cease. While Dodge did not challenge these essential ideological conventions, she took to task the unreasonable fictions that pressured women to marry for the wrong reasons. She did not believe in marrying "because, as I have frequently heard alleged, a woman's nature is such that she must love somebody"; nor did she believe women should marry out of necessity or for a home, happiness, station, or respectability. Rather, Dodge envisioned a utopian fantasy for middle-class white women, a time in which a woman would marry because love "brings her nearer to God, strengthens her to brave endurance, stimulates heroic action, and makes all greatness possible." Because Dodge understood marriage within the context of self-improvement and not as an end in itself, her axiom "womanhood is greater than wifehood" values female individualism over the marriage contract to invoke a privileged state of being in which the self is not sacrificed for another.

"Men and Women" proposes that a woman's self-worth is contingent upon unbridled access not only to education but also to a multiplicity of life choices that would necessarily expand her sphere while leaving the home intact. This theme receives a sharpened examination in Dodge's book-length essay *A New Atmosphere,* which appeared in 1865. The second chapter announces the injustice that the rest of the book serves to elucidate: "The laws and customs regarding the education of girls and the employment of women may be wrong and difficult in righting; but a more elemental wrong is the coarse, mercenary and revolting tone of sentiment in which girls are brought up and women live." Women are "steeped in the idea" that "the great business of their life is marriage," thereby undermining self-reliance and creating a nation of myopic and dependent females. Just as Emerson in "Self-Reliance" (1841) enumerated the "revolutions" that must occur for man to enjoy a "greater self-reliance," Dodge in *A New Atmosphere* sketches out simple, practical measures to "relieve" women of their indignities, thus providing a map for change that does not rely on punitive actions. Indeed, Dodge demands attitudinal and ideological shifts rather than legal reforms to ensure a contract of gender equality entered into by both sexes. One significant attitudinal change Dodge suggests is a revaluing of masculine and feminine qualities so that one sex is neither superior nor inferior to the other. Dodge writes that "manly and womanly together make the perfect being. It is woman in man. . . . it is man in woman." To this extent Dodge echoes Margaret Fuller's ideas on the complementarity of the sexes. In *Woman in the Nineteenth Century* (1844) Fuller contends that "male and female represent the two sides of the great radical dualism. But in fact they are perpetually passing into one another." Likewise Dodge considers woman and man, male and female "one flesh." In *New England: Indian Summer* (1940), literary critic Van Wyck Brooks cemented the connection between the two writers when he called Dodge "a sort of Margaret Fuller watered down, and also peppered up."

Besides this androgynous ideal, the other measures that Dodge advocates range from expanding women's experiences to allowing girls to choose an active life. Most importantly for Dodge, if a father is unable to provide for his daughters in a manner that maintains their dignity and respect, girls should pursue an occupation rather than marry out of mere economic necessity. Dodge referred to this type of social arrangement as "prostitution," thus suggesting it is both criminal and immoral. She surveys various occupations but points out that the wage gap prohibits employment outside of the domestic sphere from appearing as valuable and worthwhile. Her arguments gain force because she delineates the individual consequences of this wage difference, pointing out that women, like men, often have families to support. Her analysis precludes an indictment of institutionalized gender differences in this matter, however, and instead she blames the individual greed of men for perpetuating wage discrepancies. In this section the essay cogently names the problem, but in terms of solutions Dodge offers a mythic hope that if women "assert themselves" and "work well," this injustice will be ameliorated. To this extent Dodge offers to women the American dream of uncompromised success based on hard work.

The theme central to *A New Atmosphere* is the marriage market, a "clumsy mechanical contrivance," a "mirage" that soon turns into a series of household drudgeries. The critique begun in "Men and Women" is attenuated by specific discussions of the limitations of marriage as it is conceived and practiced by middle-class white Americans. The language and metaphors Dodge uses suggest a combative tone marked by anger toward social conventions rather than individual men. Speaking in generalities about the conditions under which men and women live, Dodge argues for a reconsideration of marriage so that it more closely mirrors its original intention to join men and women in God's love. Dodge's appeal to a Christian ethos, her often contentious demands to overturn gender stereo-

types, and her detailed descriptions of the national state of relations between men and women emphasize a reformist agenda intended to improve not only individuals but also the national character, for "the relations between men and women are the granite foundation upon which the whole world rests. Society will be elevated only just so fast and so far as these relations become what God intended them to be."

Throughout the book, Dodge relies on various types of persuasive appeals, but the strategy she employs most skillfully is to begin her arguments from the point of view of the opposition. She anticipates well the possible objections to her claims and the accusations that women's demands are frivolous and ungrounded. She faces her critics directly, mocking their tone and point of view while exaggerating their dismissive treatments of women's concerns: "Doubtless there are many men who say: To what purpose is all this? The world is getting on very well. . . . neither men nor women make any particular complaint. . . . Pray let well enough alone." She acknowledges, for example, the supposed advantages of the technological innovations of the nineteenth century that save women's labor, but immediately attacks this well-worn assumption by arguing that these new devices have not prevented women's workloads from increasing. While some suffragists cited the evolution of machine production as the advent of women's new position in the public sphere, Dodge expresses skepticism toward the liberating effects of technology for women. Furthermore, she challenges stereotypical assumptions such as women's propensity for extravagance and expense to construct an argument for women's economy in the home. As men complain of women's imprudence and therefore undermine the serious objections lodged in *A New Atmosphere,* Dodge retorts by insisting upon the judiciousness necessary to run an economic household, an objective she believed most women held.

Dodge builds her arguments in *A New Atmosphere* slowly and circuitously, but nonetheless she focuses on changing the ideology of marriage to benefit women. Of course, part of this discourse must necessarily include a discussion not only of marriage but also of women's reciprocal roles as mothers. The ideology of separate spheres, which Dodge protested, provided the foundation for the ideology of mothering that sentimentalized white middle-class motherhood, elevating the maternal figure to iconic status as the moral linchpin of family and society in the Victorian United States. According to cultural historian Sharon Hays, the ideology of appropriate mothering circulated extensively through literature on child-rearing, which instructed women to lavish affection on their children while vigilantly maintaining their own virtue and instilling virtue and hence good citizenship in their children. Catherine Beecher, one of the foremost proponents of appropriate mothering, summed up the valorization of motherhood well when she wrote: "The roots of all pure love, of piety and honor must spring from this home. . . . No honor can be higher than to know she has built such a home . . . to preside there with such skill that husband and children will rise up and call her blessed." To accomplish these objectives the mother needed to foster an intensely emotional and psychic bond with her children, a proposition that Dodge disputed on several levels.

In both *A New Atmosphere* and the short essay "A Spasm of Sense" from the collection *Gala-Days* (1863), Dodge presents her concerns about the dominant ideology of motherhood that permeated her cultural milieu. *A New Atmosphere* suggests a different paradigm for parenting, one in which the father is not a Puritan patriarch but an additional parenting agent who is actively and equally involved in child-rearing. Using sentimental language to describe the joys that children bring, Dodge admonishes fathers to exert a strong, loving influence in their children's lives, especially over boys, "to keep [them] from vicious companions and vicious habits." Rather than usurping the mother's place, the father occupies a balanced position with the mother–"honored, revered, and loved"–qualities usually reserved for the maternal figure alone. Dodge identifies the vulgar pursuit of materialism as a hindrance for fathers to fulfill their "fatherly duties" and participate in the "well-spring of care and anxiety" that child-rearing demands. Her most provocative line of argument insists that women are not inherently more capable of child-rearing than men, thereby exposing the notion of "maternal drives" as a socially constructed fiction.

"A Spasm of Sense" intervenes into the discourse of motherhood directly by debating the tenets of a popular advice book, Helen E. Brown's *The Mother and Her Work* (1862). In characteristic fashion Dodge uses exaggeration and inflammatory language to draw in readers, reporting that this "little book" contains "poison." The "strychnine" it presents counsels women to sacrifice themselves to benefit their children, advice that Dodge calls "morally" and "socially wrong." The "great fault" of American mothers is that they "swamp themselves in a slough of self-sacrifice," annihilating their own character in the process. Though she retreats slightly from her position on the fiction of "maternal duties" here and pronounces that "nature has fitted babies more closely to mothers than fathers," Dodge nonetheless exhorts women to maintain interests outside of their domestic duties, because "God never intended her to wind herself up in a cocoon." In this way Dodge's potentially extremist views are once again tempered by a Christian

ethos; a mother's "self-abnegation" and "self-renunciation" are antithetical to Dodge's vision of Christian motherhood. Her viewpoints challenge the model of "long-suffering" womanhood that still held cultural currency in favor of a vision of motherhood strongly reflexive of her own ideal of the self-reliant woman.

Although Dodge favored changes in cultural values about womanhood and motherhood, she did not align herself with the legal reform of the suffrage movement. Throughout her early treatments of women's issues, Dodge makes subtle reference to suffrage or the "women's movement" as an inevitable outcome of the inequities and injustices women have endured. She did not believe that suffrage was the solution to relieve women of economic discrimination, cultural stereotypes, or educational disparities, however. Indeed, she expressed more ambivalence about woman suffrage than either support or condemnation and confesses that "towards female suffrage, in itself considered, I have never been able to feel otherwise indifferent." In *Woman's Wrongs: A Counter-Irritant* (1868), a discursive response to an 1867 tract, *Women's Rights,* by the Reverend John Todd, Dodge provides her first lengthy discussion of suffrage, which she eventually expands upon and amends in *Woman's Worth and Worthlessness: The Complement to "A New Atmosphere"* (1872). Dodge begins *Woman's Wrongs* by excoriating Todd's viewpoints, logic, and argument on the necessity of limiting woman's sphere, calling his discourse "impotent," "ridiculous," "ill-directed," and "fatuous." These words mark the start of one of Dodge's most vituperative attacks, rivaled only by a later work, *A Battle of the Books* (1870), in which she charges her publisher of cheating her out of her rightful percentages. As Susan Coultrap-McQuinn reports, best-selling nineteenth-century writer Harriet Beecher Stowe highly recommended *Woman's Wrongs,* calling it "decidedly the brightest, cleverest, healthiest, noblest kind of a book."

At times in *Woman's Wrongs* it seems as if Dodge supports suffrage. Indeed, many of her arguments, especially those in favor of women's strength and independence, correspond directly with suffragist theory. Stating that there exists a "scarcity of reasons brought against female suffrage," Dodge proceeds to dismantle the main arguments brought by antisuffragists, namely, that the vote will change woman's nature and woman's sphere, making women "bold, pushing, and masculine," in essence "unwomanly." Dodge responds to these fears first by addressing the assumption that women do not hold political opinions, which provided the basis for antisuffragists to argue that suffrage will change women's character by forcing them to move outside of their sphere. In her trademark argumentative style, Dodge uses pages of questions to push the arguments against suffrage to their logical limits. She asks: "is there anything in the nature of woman which would lead us to suppose that her devotion to politics would be greater than that her husband? On the contrary, would not the change from the narrow circle of her domestic home to the great circle of her national home be a benefit to her?" With these questions Dodge weds national and domestic arrangements, insinuating the possibility of a better citizenry if woman suffrage prevailed.

According to Aileen S. Kraditor, author of *The Ideas of the Woman Suffrage Movement 1890–1920* (1971), the assumption driving most antisuffrage arguments was the separate-but-equal doctrine of respective spheres, which insisted that social harmony depended upon women's staying at home, having children, and remaining outside of the public sphere. Even if Dodge did not embrace suffrage wholeheartedly, she could not tolerate this viewpoint: thus, at the core of *Woman's Wrongs* is the speculation "certainly we shall never know what woman's natural sphere is till she has the absolutely unrestricted power of choice." These words nicely summarize the thesis of Dodge's body of writing but do not extend to an endorsement of suffrage. While Dodge deconstructs the idea that women's exclusion from politics is unnatural and thus wrong, she is dubious of the "definite benefits" that would accrue for women at an everyday, material level if suffrage was won. In this way Dodge reflects a powerful if tangential argument made by antisuffragists. Kraditor reports that those who were not convinced that the extension of suffrage would cause serious problems might be persuaded that the vote was not worth fighting for. Like those campaigning against suffrage, Dodge wondered how the vote could improve the wages of working women, open up occupations or educational possibilities otherwise closed to women, or elevate them socially or morally to a higher ground within the U.S. citizenry.

The most provocative aspect of *Woman's Wrongs* is the skillful use of suffrage and antisuffrage rhetoric and theory to build an argument that refuses categorization. In fact, the closest that Dodge comes to taking a position on suffrage occurs in a speculative framework. Dodge writes that if given the choice to extend suffrage to women or to restrict it further among men, she would choose the latter in order to ensure only intelligence and virtue flourish at the ballot box. Because the vote should signify "sagacity, ability, and worth," Dodge tentatively suggests the ownership of property as the criterion for suffrage. These elitist restrictions would qualify some women while also barring some men. The limitation proposed here anticipates the arguments of suffragists near the turn of the century who were willing to place exclusions on voting privileges to

prohibit "new immigrants" from participating in government. Although Dodge realized woman suffrage "appears to be a foregone conclusion" at some point in history, she uses the issue throughout *Woman's Wrongs* as a platform for articulating her message of self-reliance and economic and intellectual independence for women. A later tract, *Woman's Worth and Worthlessness,* once again addresses suffrage, yet with another modification of her views. Here Dodge moves toward disapproving of suffrage because it would place an undue burden on women whose responsibilities toward home and nation are already manifold. This retreat from her more ambivalent position expressed a few years earlier was probably a result of her increasing misgivings about the "extreme" rhetoric of the suffragists.

Dodge commented on the issues of women's rights and suffrage most extensively in the early part of her career, thereby establishing her reputation as a controversial yet popular writer who by the 1880s could dictate the economic terms of her writing. She wrote to one editor, as recorded in *Gail Hamilton's Life in Letters* (1901), asking for and receiving "two hundred dollars an article, without limit to length. Free range as to themes over this world and the next." Her themes spanned both national and international affairs, ranging in topics from the Civil War to civil-service reform to religion. A staunch supporter of abolition, Dodge presents her views on the "righteousness of the cause" in "Our Civil War" from *Country Living and Country Thinking*. Her series of articles opposing civil-service reform are notable for their clear recommendations, and her commentary on Christianity offers specific responses to religious debates of the day. For example, the essay "Christ as a Preacher" from *Skirmishes and Sketches* explicates the Gospels to show that Christ was received enthusiastically by the masses. Her other collections of essays on Christianity include *Sermons to the Clergy* (1876), *What Ye Think of Christ* (1877), and *A Washington Bible Class* (1890), all of which present liberal views on Christianity, validating the positive consequences of Christian love.

While much of her writing addresses serious matters, a different persona emerges in works such as the essay collections *Summer Rest* (1866) and *Twelve Miles from a Lemon* (1874), which reproduce the tongue-in-cheek tone of "My Garden." These works explore life in rural New England, focusing specifically on women's experiences. The title essay from *Twelve Miles from a Lemon,* for instance, presents the struggles of a woman who must prepare the family meals while relying on inconsistent deliveries of staple products. The lemon here functions as a metaphor for the conveniences of urban life as compared with the difficulties of the rural setting. The folksy persona appears again in Dodge's

TWELVE MILES FROM A LEMON.

By GAIL HAMILTON,

AUTHOR OF

"WOMAN'S WORTH AND WORTHLESSNESS," "LITTLE FOLK LIFE," ETC.

NEW YORK:
HARPER & BROTHERS, PUBLISHERS,
FRANKLIN SQUARE
1874.

Title page for Dodge's collection of essays about the inconveniences of rural life

travel writing, such as the title essay from *Gala-Days* and *Wool-Gathering* (1867). This latter work chronicles the narrator's trip through the Midwest to the final destination of Minnesota, back to New England via the southern states. A lighthearted tone introduces the book, as the narrator admits that "there is no moral to this story. I told it because it is so pretty a picture in my memory that I like to unfold it." This remark is slightly misleading, however, as Dodge situates serious critiques on Manifest Destiny and U.S. imperialism among her observations.

Typical of nineteenth-century travel writing at the height of U.S. westward expansion, *Wool-Gathering* attempts to capture the beauty, simplicity, and charm of the unspoiled land and its occupants. "A lifetime would fail us," writes Dodge, "before we could see all the wonders of this great country of ours." At times the lavish description verges on the effusive, as when Dodge concludes that "this great Western country is so wonderful, so alluring to the eye, so rich in the promise of every good, so strange and vast and uncomprehended." Figu-

rative language dominates her discourse, as Dodge describes dams "as broad as a road" and rivers tripping through deep, shadowy gorges. Rarely is the language banal, for Dodge's intent is to appreciate the vestiges of the untamed wilderness. Occasionally, a cautionary tone emerges that anticipates the loss of the wilderness under the burdens of industrialization. For instance, on leaving Saint Paul the narrator confesses she "is glad the city has dissolved away. Under the leveling influence of trade, I fear the wild bright tangle of these precipitous shores would have been tamed down into prosy landings." A somber point of view surfaces again when the narrator reminds readers of the "atrocities" committed by the U.S. government against Native Americans. Finally, as Dodge travels through the South, she witnesses extreme poverty, all the while tempering her criticisms of the government and U.S. institutions with an admiration of the land itself.

Dodge launched her most vociferous public criticism not against the government, the clergy, or suffragists but against the system of gentlemen publishers, who she believed preyed on unsuspecting authors, defrauding them of their rightful pay. According to Coultrap-McQuinn, Dodge discovered while reading an article on pay for authors that she was not receiving the 10 percent royalties on her books that was the customary rate. Dodge wrote her publisher, James T. Fields, to seek a remedy to the problem but remained unsatisfied. The dispute finally went to arbitration, but not before a public battle ensued with both parties soliciting support for their positions. Though she was awarded monetary compensation and a court order to receive 10 percent royalties, Dodge did not feel vindicated. In 1870 she published *A Battle of the Books,* which told the story of the dispute in a fictional setting one hundred years in the past. This essay contains copies of the actual news stories and correspondence relating to her conflict with Fields, a narrative of the events, advice to authors regarding their business dealings, and insights into Dodge's feelings about compensation. As a woman, Dodge was always acutely aware of pay inequity; this case personalized her concerns, for, as she said, "there is no such thing as independence" "without money." In *A Battle of the Books* Dodge weaves these two themes together by proposing an analogy between authorship and womanhood, stressing the ways in which naive authors are victimized by ruthless male publishers accustomed to the operations of the public sphere. In the end Dodge sold approximately 1,500 copies of the book, losing money because of the poor sales.

The battle with Fields ended their business relationship, and Dodge found another publisher for her books. Moreover, Howard Ticknor, Fields's associate, fired Dodge from her position as a contributing editor of the children's magazine *Our Young Folks*. By then, however, Dodge had established a reputation also as a children's author, writing books such as *Red-Letter Days in Applethorpe* (1866), *Child World* (1873), and *Nursery Noonings* (1875). She attempted one novel, which failed commercially: *First Love Is Best* (1877) is a sentimental look at the courtship of her female protagonist. By 1871 Dodge was spending the winters in Washington, D.C., at the household of James G. Blaine, a Republican leader and speaker of the House of Representatives, and his wife, Dodge's first cousin. According to Margaret Lyman Langworthy, their association sparked rumors that Dodge wrote Blaine's speeches; certainly she helped him write his two-volume memoir, *Twenty Years in Congress* (1884–1886). In company with the Blaines, Dodge mixed with Washington dignitaries, exerted her influence through political commentary, and finally traveled through Europe in 1878. After Blaine's death, Dodge wrote *Biography of James G. Blaine* (1895), a voluminous, eulogizing account that reproduces scores of letters between Blaine and other Washington leaders.

Besides her association with the Blaines, her petition on behalf of Florence Chandler Maybrick, an American woman accused and convicted of murdering her English husband, marked the latter part of Dodge's life. From 1889 to her death on 17 August 1896 from a cerebral hemorrhage, Dodge championed Maybrick's cause, writing letters to lawyer, poet, and fiction writer Oliver Wendell Holmes, for example, requesting his assistance with the case and self-publishing an argumentative treatment of the case titled "An Object Lesson in Woman's Rights" (1892). The essay begins by excoriating Frances Willard, a prominent leader of the suffrage and temperance movements, for failing to take an active role in Maybrick's case. Dodge then reexamines the evidence that convicted Maybrick and finds fault with the civil procedure, proposing that gender bias affected the court's treatment of Maybrick. Whereas

Dodge tentatively suggests in *A Battle of the Books* that male publishers discriminated against women, in "An Object Lesson in Woman's Rights" she boldly draws a clear connection between Maybrick's gender and the court's handling of the case. The "object lesson" presented here underscores Dodge's penchant for controversy and fortifies her reputation as a defender of women's rights whose unpredictable views on issues ranging from suffrage to equal pay prompted Harriet Prescott Spofford (in a biographical sketch introducing *Gail Hamilton's Life in Letters*) to designate Dodge "the most brilliant woman of her generation."

Letters:

Gail Hamilton's Life in Letters, edited by H. Augusta Dodge (Boston: Lee & Shepard, 1901).

References:

Susan Coultrap-McQuinn, *Doing Literary Business: American Women Writers in the Nineteenth Century* (Chapel Hill: University of North Carolina Press, 1990), pp. 105–136;

Aileen S. Kraditor, *The Ideas of the Woman Suffrage Movement 1890–1920* (New York: Anchor, 1971);

Margaret Lyman Langworthy, "Mary Abigail Dodge," in *Notable American Women 1607–1950: A Biographical Dictionary,* edited by Edward James (Cambridge, Mass.: Harvard University Press, 1971), pp. 493–495;

Nancy A. Walker, *The Disobedient Writer: Women and Narrative Tradition* (Austin: University of Texas Press, 1995), pp. 28–31.

Papers:

A substantial collection of Mary Abigail Dodge's letters, uncorrected and final drafts, and notebooks is housed at the Essex Institute, Salem, Massachusetts. A less voluminous collection of essays from their original sources is located at the Sophia Smith Research Collection, Smith College, Northampton, Masssachusetts.

Alice Morse Earle

(27 April 1853 – 16 February 1911)

Katharine Gillespie
Sam Houston State University

BOOKS: *The Sabbath in Puritan New England* (New York: Scribners, 1891; London: Hodder & Stoughton, 1892);

China Collecting in America (New York: Scribners, 1892);

Customs and Fashions in Old New England (New York: Scribners, 1893; London: Nutt, 1893);

Costume of Colonial Times (New York: Scribners, 1894);

Colonial Dames and Good Wives (Boston & New York: Houghton, Mifflin, 1895);

A Monument to Prison Ship Martyrs (New York: American Historical Register, 1895);

Margaret Winthrop (New York: Scribners, 1895);

Colonial Days in Old New York (New York: Scribners, 1896);

Curious Punishments of Bygone Days (Chicago: Stone, 1896);

The Stadt Huys of New York (New York: Little, 1896);

In Old Narragansett: Romances and Realities (New York: Scribners, 1898);

Home Life in Colonial Days (New York & London: Macmillan, 1898);

Stage-Coach and Tavern Days (New York: Macmillan, 1900);

Child Life in Colonial Days (New York & London: Macmillan, 1900);

Old-Time Gardens, Newly Set Forth (New York & London: Macmillan, 1901);

Sun Dials and Roses of Yesterday (New York & London: Macmillan, 1902);

Two Centuries of Costume in America, 1620–1820 (New York & London: Macmillan, 1903).

OTHER: *Early Prose and Verse,* edited by Earle and Emily Ellsworth Ford (New York: Harper, 1893);

Diary of Anna Green Winslow, a Boston School Girl of 1771, edited by Earle (Boston & New York: Houghton, Mifflin, 1894).

SELECTED PERIODICAL PUBLICATIONS–
UNCOLLECTED: "Narragansett Pacers," *New England Magazine,* new series 2 (March 1890): 39;

Alice Morse Earle

"Ghost, Poet, and Spinet," *New England Magazine,* new series 3 (February 1891): 778–784;

"The New England Meeting-House," *Atlantic Monthly,* 67 (February 1891): 191–204;

"Top Drawer in the High Chest," *New England Magazine,* new series 4 (July 1891): 649–655.

"The Queen's Closet Opened," *Atlantic Monthly,* 68 (August 1891): 215–227;

"China Hunter in New England," *Scribner's Magazine,* 10 (September 1891): 345–358;

"A New England Kismet," *Scribner's Magazine,* 11 (March 1892): 295–302;

"The Oldest Episcopal Church in New England," *New England Magazine,* new series 7 (January 1893): 577–593;

"Old-Time Marriage Customs in New England," *Journal of American Folk-lore,* 6 (April–June 1893): 97–102;

"A Boston School Girl in 1771," *Atlantic Monthly,* 72 (August 1893): 218–224;

"Old-Time Church Music in New England," *Outlook,* 48 (November 1893): 933–934;

"St. Valentine's Day in Olden Times," *Outlook,* 49 (February 1894);

Review of *The Pottery and Porcelain of the United States,* by Edwin Atlee Barber, *Dial,* 16 (1 April 1894): 212–213;

"Pinkster Day," *Outlook,* 49 (April 1894): 743–744;

Review of *Discovery by Count Teleki of Lakes Rudolph and Stephani,* by Ludwig von Hohnell, *Dial,* 16 (1 May 1894): 269–272;

"Church Communion Tokens," *Atlantic Monthly,* 74 (August 1894): 210–214;

Review of *The Mountains of California,* by John Muir, *Dial,* 18 (1 February 1895): 75–77;

"Flower-lore of New England Children," *Atlantic Monthly,* 75 (April 1895): 459–466;

"Fashions of the Nineteenth Century," *Chautauquan,* 21 (May–June 1895);

"A Baptist Preacher and Soldier of the Last Century," *New England Magazine,* new series 12 (June 1895): 407–414;

"Rhoda's Legacy," *Outlook,* 51 (June 1895): 1095–1096;

Review of *The Fast and Thanksgiving Days of New England,* by W. DeLoss Love, *Dial,* 19 (16 July 1895): 41–43;

"Old-Time Flower Gardens," *Scribner's Magazine,* 20 (April 1896): 161–178;

"The Bilboes," *Chap Book,* 5 (August 1896): 289–295;

"Punishments of Authors and Books," *Chap Book,* 5 (September 1896): 512–520;

"The Ducking Stool," *Chap Book,* 5 (September 1896): 353–363;

"The Pillory," *Chap Book,* 5 (October 1896): 443–450;

"The Whipping Post," *Chap Book,* 5 (November 1896): 561–568;

"The Scarlet Letter," *Chap Book,* 6 (November 1896): 31–37;

"Schools and Education in American Colonies," *Chautauquan,* 26 (January 1898): 362–366;

"Colonial Household Industries," *Chautauquan,* 26 (February 1898): 475–549;

"Indian Corn in Colonial Times," *Chautauquan,* 26 (March 1898): 586–590;

"Black Jacks," *Chap Book,* 9 (May 1898): 21–22;

"Mead or Metheglin," *Chap Book,* 9 (May 1898): 482–483;

"Huff-cup and Nippitatum," *Chap Book,* 9 (June 1898): 83;

"Among Friends," *New England Magazine,* new series 19 (August 1898): 18–23;

"Sunday in New Netherland and New York," *Atlantic Monthly,* 78 (October 1898): 543;

"A Gallant Silken Trade," *New England Magazine,* new series 22 (July 1900): 557–563;

"Coral Cactus and Rosy Cake," *New England Magazine,* new series 23 (December 1900): 470–474;

Review of *The Writings of "Colonel William Byrd, of Westover in Virginia, esqr.,"* edited by John Spencer Bassett, *Dial,* 32 (1 May 1902): 308–310;

"Dancing Flowers and Flower Dances," *New England Magazine,* new series 26 (July 1902): 556–560;

"Sun-dials Old and New," *New England Magazine,* new series 29 (January 1904): 563–577;

"Samplers," *Century Magazine,* 83 (March 1912): 676–685.

In the late nineteenth and early twentieth centuries, Alice Morse Earle wrote eighteen books and more than thirty articles on the cultural life of the early English settlements in the New World. These works played a key role in the turn-of-the-century colonial revival movement and contributed to the establishment of the study of colonial American history as a discrete historical period. Using original manuscripts, diaries, letters, legal documents, and court records culled from the Long Island Historical Society and the American Antiquarian Society, Earle produced such studies of early U.S. daily life as *Colonial Dames and Good Wives* (1895), *Colonial Days in Old New York* (1896), *Home Life in Colonial Days* (1898), *In Old Narragansett: Romances and Realities* (1898), *Child Life in Colonial Days* (1900), and *Stage-Coach and Tavern Days* (1900). In 1894 she also edited the *Diary of Anna Green Winslow, a Boston School Girl of 1771,* and in 1895 she wrote a biography of Margaret Winthrop, the wife of the first governor of the Massachusetts Bay Colony, John Winthrop.

Despite this prodigious body of work, Earle is typically overlooked as an authority by such twentieth-century authors of colonial American studies as Vernon Parrington, Yvor Winters, Thomas Johnson, Perry Miller, Edmund S. Morgan, and Daniel Boorstein. To remedy this oversight, Laurel Thatcher Ulrich writes in the preface to her *Good Wives: Image and Reality in the Lives of Women in Northern New England 1650–1750* (1980), her title "consciously echoes Alice Morse Earle's *Colonial Dames and Good Wives*" and is meant to honor "an early generation of women's historians who

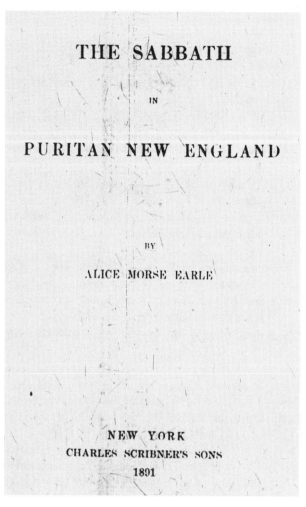

Title page for Earle's first book

through familial relations. Colonial society was best understood through examinations of its domestic arrangements and the household objects of everyday life. By "reading" everything from kitchen arrangements to clothing, Earle sought to identify and preserve a whole range of colonial English social practices for postcolonial generations. Pointing to a wealth of historical data, Earle suggested that colonial Americans socialized their children through education; hence, she wrote books for those interested in recovering the daily lives of their "great grand mothers." Earle, like twentieth-century feminists, did not believe that such a perspective was less central to the recovery of the past than the historical discipline's conventional approach of focusing on the achievements of so-called great men.

Earle was the contemporary of such Progressive figures as Charlotte Perkins Gilman, Herbert Croly, John Dewey, Thorstein Veblen, and Jane Addams. Yet, her works stand in a relationship of what might be termed productive tension with Progressive values. In keeping with the Progressivist belief in the intellectual capacity of women, Earle's works reveal the degree to which women were actively involved in the discipline of history writing prior to the twentieth century, and they contribute to ongoing discussions over what a female-centered historical perspective might look like as compared to a more conventional one. Like the Progressives, she viewed education as a social good and the domestic sphere as the source of training and, by extension, of national stability and character. She incorporated Friedreich Froebel's educational principle of "mother's play" into her own child-rearing practices and into her works on gardening and costuming. Earle's relationship to the Progressive belief in the ability of the technocratic state to solve all social ills is more complicated, however. Her surveys of colonial political practices lead her to denounce the Puritan magistrate's totalizing control at some points and to approve of it at others. Perhaps more important, she implicitly undercuts a Progressive pretense to omniscience. In her narrative technique she continually contextualizes her knowledge as contingent and subject to reflection and revision by succeeding generations.

Earle's works also raise questions regarding the larger social motivations of the Colonial Revival. In keeping with arguments that suggest the Colonial Revival movement was a reactionary response to the large numbers of non-English immigrants then entering the United States, Earle assumed (one might say established) a reading audience of Americans interested in recovering the world of their "grand mothers," those who stemmed from English roots, in order to establish New England history as a synecdoche for American history in general. On the other hand, her work just as

skillfully practiced what later scholars dismissed as pots-and-pans history."

As the reference to "pots-and-pans history" suggests, Earle's books are commonly packaged as history for juveniles and placed in the children's sections of libraries. It is interesting, however, to consider the degree to which this circumstance may be a logical outcome of her own goals as a cultural historian. She specifically referred to her works as "Domestic and Social Histories of Olden Times," and, as she writes in her foreword to *Child Life in Colonial Days,* it is her "hope that children as well as grown folk will find in these pages much to interest them in the accounts of the life of children of olden times." Earle made the transmission of cultural values by the family a primary focus of her work in the colonial period and thereby helped to found such methodological approaches to the past as family history, women's history, and cultural studies. Colonial social bonds, she argued, had been forged

often situates the Puritan past, even as it relates to the family, as a time from which America has "progressed."

In keeping with her Progressive generational affiliation, Earle's public interests as a writer proceeded from her personal experience. She was born in Worcester, Massachusetts, on 27 April 1853, at a time when large numbers of Americans were leaving their homes in rural areas and small towns and moving to cities in search of work. Her father, Edwin Morse, left his childhood home in rural Andover, Massachussets, in 1834 to seek greater opportunities as a machinist. He settled in the rapidly growing textiles town of Worcester, married, and became a widower when his wife died giving birth to their son, Edwin Augustus. Six years later he married his cousin, Abby Clary Goodhue, who had also been eager to leave her drab life as a widow in Maine for greater possibilities in Worcester. Edwin Morse moved from machinist to partner in a tool company and later became a First National Bank director. Abby gave birth first to a stillborn son and then to two daughters, Mary Alice (later Alice) and Frances Clary Morse. The Morse family had gravitated toward Worcester as an urban center; they lived in an industrial neighborhood, although they had a large home and a yard encompassing a well-tended garden. The family moved into a larger house in a nicer Worcester neighborhood sometime after 1855, where they remained until the last surviving member, Frances, died in 1933.

Alice Morse was educated at Worcester High School and Gannet's boarding school in Boston. Her marriage in 1874 to Henry Earle, a descendent of an established Rhode Island family, precipitated even further her family's generational shift from country to city, working class to middle class. A rubber broker, Earle moved his family to Brooklyn, New York, in 1877. In 1880 they moved to a larger, more formal house, where Alice Earle bore her children–Henry, Alexander Morse, Alice (who later became a popular botanical artist), and Mary–and began to educate them in accordance with values that she reconstructed from her perceived cultural heritage. Throughout the 1880s Earle had her children photographed in Puritan period garb and engaged them in what she believed were such beneficial and rural colonial activities as gardening. As she intimates in *Costume of Colonial Times* (1894) and *Two Centuries of Costume in America, 1620–1820* (1903), one could literally fashion one's self after the past as a way of establishing a cultural identity for the present and future. At the age of thirty-six, she began to write.

Like her contemporary Gilman, Earle may not have been fully comfortable with the idea of stepping outside of prescribed female roles and taking up the pen. Significantly, Earle, unlike Gilman, aligned herself much more with practitioners of the Republican "Cult of True Womanhood" than she did with radical suffragists. She belonged to many groups that were oriented less toward the vote and more toward women's contributions to an English colonial history and to the education of children. She belonged to the Brooklyn Woman's Club, a group that established free kindergartens in Brooklyn; Mrs. Field's Literary Club, a women's reading group; the National Society of New England Women; the Daughters of the American Revolution; and the Society of Colonial Dames. Thus, in an interview that she gave in 1900, long after her career as a writer was established, she discussed her impetus for authorship in such a way that revealed a typically female anxiety about appearing to have sought out a public career as a writer. She claimed that her first work did not appear until "The New England Meeting-House" was published in the February 1891 *Atlantic Monthly*, when in fact her first article, "Narragansett Pacers," was published in *New England Magazine* in March 1890. Even Earle's narrative about her motivations for writing "The New England Meeting-House" locates her well within the private sphere of the family. According to Earle, she based this study upon materials collected by her father out of interest in his family's home church in Chester, Vermont, where he had spent part of his boyhood before moving to Andover.

Despite, or perhaps because of, her concern with the private rather than the public woman, Earle tapped into a receptive, largely female, audience. In 1891 Charles Scribner's Sons published her first book, *The Sabbath in Puritan New England*, which was so popular that it went through twelve editions. In 1892 she published *China Collecting in America*, a work credited with influencing the pioneer collector and curator Charles Presby Wilcomb in his reproductions of colonial kitchens for the Golden Gate Park Museum in San Francisco. This antiquarian study was followed by others: *Costume of Colonial Times; Old-Time Gardens, Newly Set Forth* (1901); *Sun Dials and Roses of Yesterday* (1902); and *Two Centuries of Costume in America, 1620–1820*.

Such works as *China Collecting in America* connect Earle with the colonial revival movement. The beginning of this movement is often set at the 1879 Philadelphia International Centennial Exhibition, where displays of colonial artifacts helped to launch a national mania for collecting relics of "the olden time" and even for designing whole houses in a nativist "American colonial" style of architecture. In 1891 the World's Columbian Exposition helped to extend the revival by including exhibitions of colonial period rooms, and in 1893 Anne Hollingsworth Wharton wrote in *Through Colonial Doors* that "The Revival of interest in Colonial and Revolutionary times has become a marked feature of the life of to-day." Collecting was an integral aspect

CUSTOMS AND FASHIONS

IN

OLD NEW ENGLAND

BY

ALICE MORSE EARLE

" Let us thank God for having given us such ancestors; and
let each successive generation thank him not less fervently,
for being one step further from them in the march of ages."

NEW YORK
CHARLES SCRIBNER'S SONS
1893

Title page for Earle's study of Puritan mores

of the colonial revival, with revivalists investing social significance in English antiques and cultural artifacts. Believing that they embodied a time of greater craftsmanship and, hence, of morality, everything from furniture to farm implements were collected, restored, and displayed. Morse's older half brother, Edwin A. Morse, and his wife were also collectors of "antique" furniture and ceramics; and her sister, Frances Clary Morse, published an antiquarian study in 1902, *Furniture of the Olden Time*.

Collecting implies a social philosophy that views the home as a nursery for nurturing national character, in this case a New England–based one. Earle's perspectives on antiquarianism also reflected a Darwinian-based belief in the home as the biological basis for a group's survival. This philosophy is evident in Earle's methodology as a cultural historian. Published in 1893, her third book, *Customs and Fashions in Old New England*,

opens literally from a baby's-eye view of the world and argues that child-rearing was at the heart of New England society's success in the Darwinian New World. She writes that "the Spartan struggle for life" that the infant faced in the "ill-heated houses of the colonists" in New England was the "initial step in the rigid system of selection enforced by every detail of the manner of life in early New England." Because, as she reports, "the mortality among infants was appallingly large," she concludes that "the natural result—the survival of the fittest—may account for the present tough endurance of the New England people." She argues that the Puritans were a model for child-rearing, claiming that "Of the demeanor of children to their parents naught can be said but praise." Puritan children were "respectful in word and deed," and "every letter, every record shows that the young Puritans truly honored their fathers and mothers." While lauding Puritan child-rearing practices for their rigor, she also celebrates the degree to which they departed from a stereotypical and Hawthorne-inflected "grimness." She writes that "It were well" for children "to thus obey the law of God, for by the law of the land high-handed disobedience of parents was punishable by death." She writes, however, "I do not find this penalty ever was paid, as it was under the sway of grim Calvin, a fact which redounds to the credit of both justice and youth in colonial days."

The apparent nationalism in such characterizations lends itself well to those who argue that the colonial revival among Progressives was a reaction against modernity and against a perceived breakdown of English cultural hegemony during a period of large-scale immigration. The preface that Earle wrote to her 1894 edition of *The Diary of Anna Green Winslow,* a "young miss" of "New England parentage" whom she holds up as a model for girls of her own day, restages a party scene that bespeaks ethnic purity: "the rows of demure little Boston maids, all of New England Brahmin blood, in high rolls, with nodding plumes and sparkling combs, with ruffles and mitts, little miniatures of their elegant mammas, soberly walking and curtseying through the stately minuet." At the same time, Earle's works often reveal an interest in re-creating American colonial history as a more complex era against which the merits of modern society could be evaluated and debated. As much as they represent her attraction to the past, such studies as *Customs and Fashions in Old New England* also reveal Earle's Progressive ambivalence toward this "primitive colony with primitive manners." She marvels at a diet typically fed to young Puritan children, found in an "old almanac of the eighteenth-century." "Fancy," she exclaims, "a young child nowadays making a meal of brown bread and cheese with warm beer!" Yet, she sighs, "In such ways were reared our

Revolutionary heroes." She uses her histories to inter-ject Toqueville-like opinions into Progressive debates over what skill levels should be demanded of immi-grants when she argues that New England was an "an exceptional plantation" populated "by men of special intelligence, and almost universally of good education" and concludes that "it was inevitable that early and pro-found attention should be paid to the establishment of schools." She also reflects upon the pedagogical means by which Puritans educated their children, however, and concludes, "I often fancy I should have enjoyed liv-ing in the good old times, but I am glad I never was a child in colonial New England." Such a childhood would have included, she notes, being baptized with ice water, eating brown bread and warm beer, memorizing lengthy catechisms, being "constantly threatened with fear of death and terror of God," having to commit Michael Wigglesworth's long "Day of Doom" to mem-ory, and being whipped with a tattling stick.

In keeping with her apparent support of the tem-perance laws of her own time, she notes that "rigid" prohibition laws "had their effect, and New Englanders throughout the seventeenth century were sober and law-abiding." Yet, at another point she criticizes "the omnipotent Puritan law-giver, who meddled and inter-fered in every detail, small and great, of the public and private life of the citizen." She also decries what she views as the premodern Puritan practice of marrying for money rather than love. While correspondence between "sweethearts" and "married lovers, such as Governor Winthrop and his wife Margaret," survived to prove the existence of romantic love, the "numberless letters and records throughout New England prove the unvarying spirit of calculation that pervaded fashion-able courtship."

On the issue of slavery she notes a contradiction in English society much commented upon by subse-quent historians: that "early planters came to New England to obtain and maintain liberty," and that sla-very and "other feudal servitudes" were prohibited under the ninety-first article of the Body of Liberties adopted by the colony. Nonetheless, she criticizes that they required little persuasion "to adopt quickly what was then the universal and unquestioned practice of all Christian nations—slavery," and she records the fact that "Josselyn found slaves on Noddle's Island in Bos-ton Harbor at his first visit, though they were not held in a Puritan family." She avoids the conventional chau-vinism of the northern New Englander against the southerner when she writes that she had "never seen in any Southern newspapers advertisements of negro sales that surpass in heartlessness and viciousness the adver-tisements of our New England newspapers of the eigh-teenth century."

Through such observations, Earle constructs colonial society as something more than a simple model the basic principles of which could be preserved and restored as one would a china cup. Through infusing cultural history with Darwinian principles, she also establishes it as a complex subject for debate over which traits "survived" the colonial era to become American culture and which ones had to be selectively eradicated. Earle's methodology and larger historical perspective can be seen at work in her readings of antique objects and such obsolete practices as stagecoach driving. In one scene from *Customs and Fashions in Old New England,* she ambivalently measures the distance between herself and colonial life, waxing nostalgic when she reflects upon a hearth-and-home vision of the past: "Around the great glowing fireplaces in an old New England kitchen centered all of homeliness and comfort that could be found in a New England home." She also notes, however, that around this hearth "every homely utensil and piece of furniture, every domestic conve-nience and inconvenience, every home-made makeshift, every cumbrous and clumsy contrivance of the old-time kitchen here may be found, and they show to us, as in a living photograph, the home life of these olden days." By the standards of the modern Progressive emphasis upon "simplicity," the Puritan kitchen is one of model convenience but also of a backwards inconvenience. Its "cumbrous and clumsy contrivances" suggest the tedious hardships of women's lives as much as they do the picturesque quality of the hearth. From such a model, Earle implies, "Progressive" American society has evolved into even greater models of simplicity and convenience.

Similarly, in *Stage-Coach and Tavern Days* she uses the actual words of contemporary travelers to describe both "the virtues and vicissitudes of the travel of early days by Stage-coach in America." She tells us that she does not "believe that travellers in coaching days found much pleasure in long journeys by stage-coach," though she does claim that safety in America was much greater than in Great Britain. By focusing on both the positive and negative aspects of the colonial period, Earle consti-tutes early America as a culture that is not easily assimi-lated to the desire for a usable past. If it is usable, it is usable to the degree that it challenges modern Ameri-cans to feel attraction for those days at the same time they feel a kind of relief in having escaped its physical discomforts, as well as its unenlightened excesses.

Nowhere is this approach more evident than in Earle's 1896 study *Curious Punishments of Bygone Days.* Her account of such Puritan disciplinary devices as bil-boes, ducking stools, stocks, pillories, and scarlet letters is "endurable," as she argues in the foreword, "because it has a past only and no future." She imagines that her

COLONIAL DAMES
AND
GOOD WIVES
WRITTEN BY
ALICE MORSE EARLE

bienfou rien
The Riverside Press

BOSTON AND NEW YORK
HOUGHTON, MIFFLIN & COMPANY
THE RIVERSIDE PRESS CAMBRIDGE
M DCCC XCV

Title page for the work in which Earle argues that the Virginia colony did not thrive because of its early lack of women

Progressive era readers' "hot indignation" "dies down into a dull ember of curiosity when we reflect that they will never be pilloried or ducked again." At the same time, she anticipates the response of even more evolved, twentieth-century readers who will look back and, she hopes, "be not too harsh in judgement" on her own "Progressive" era, an era which she characterizes in neo-Puritanical terms as "an age that had to form powerful societies and associations to prevent cruelty—not to hardened and vicious criminals—but to faithful animals and innocent children." If her Darwinism allows her to establish New England society as the original point from which a true American species has descended, it also provides her with a model of history as a contingent science, one whose models, including her own, are continually and inevitably subject to revision, selection, and correction.

Earle is connected with popular historical novelists of the time (including S. Weir Mitchell, Paul Leicester Ford, Mary Johnson, and Maurice Thompson) who, in keeping with Progressivist—and scientific—suspicion of religion, revived the colonial era as a period of general interest while screening out the Puritan reliance upon Calvinist theology. She assures her audience that she "will not give any of the accounts on full, for the expression of religious thought shown therein is so contrary to the sentiments of today that it would not be pleasing to modern readers." Given the fact that Earle's "modern readers" were predominantly women whose sentiments she both shared and sought to influence, her desire to please them is notable, and her focus upon the domestic sphere as a social sphere of historical and biological significance is particularly evident in her studies of women. In her 1895 works *Colonial Dames and Good Wives* and *Margaret Winthrop* she seeks to make what she constitutes as the invisible—women in history—more visible and viable as subjects for inquiry into a culture's social and biological composition. In *Colonial Dames and Good Wives* she argues that the colony of Virginia "did not thrive" because of its early lack of women. She starts out the chapter "Consorts and Relicts" by focusing on the landing of "ninety possible wives—ninety homesick, seasick but timidly inquisitive English girls—on Jamestown beach." This tableau, she argues, is one of those "scenes in colonial life which stand out of the past with much clearness of outline." Because "no details survive, to present to us a vivid picture," however, she as a cultural historian of women's roles has to step in to flesh out the scene and to offer a decidedly feminine perspective upon the matrilineal dimension of Virginia's survival.

The methodology underlying *Margaret Winthrop* is equally representative of Earle's attempt to make women's lives into a central feature of historical evaluation. Earle notes that "no portrait or description of her exists; nor are there any save scanty references to her personal appearance." To reconstruct Winthrop's life she reverses the conventions of traditional historiography by placing the chapter on Margaret Winthrop's husband, the celebrated Governor John Winthrop, at the end in a section titled "Public Events and Closing Days." As she writes, "On many of the details of Winthrop's public life I shall dwell but shortly in this biography of his wife. They have all been told in graphic language in his journal, and with corroborative evidence from other sources in many histories of New England." Even this brief consideration of John Winthrop's public political career, however, is not Earle's last word; she also includes a Winthrop family genealogy. Genealogies were a significant part of the colonial revival and, like Earle's interest in the biological determinants of English cultural survival, were influenced by Darwinism. She writes that "this biography of Margaret Winthrop must not be concluded without briefly telling of her children and her descendants," which she then proceeds to do in matrilineal terms.

The bulk of the book reconstructs Margaret Winthrop's quiet, private life through her letters and other literatures detailing domesticity during Winthrop's historical period. It paints a portrait of Winthrop in terms of the Cult of True Womanhood: as a private woman heroically concerned with the exhausting demands and minutiae of premodern housework. Earle's description of the most tedious task of them all, the "evolution of the household linen," takes up pages, describing the hours it took to complete this task in what seems to be real time.

Earle even makes the argument that John Winthrop's identity as a governor was heavily influenced by his family life. As evidence, she focuses upon an entry that Winthrop made in his journal just after Margaret arrived in Massachusetts. Earle notes that Winthrop interrupts his record of political and theological events to recount a dream he had when upon "coming into his chamber he found his wife (she was a very gracious woman) in bed, and three or four of their children lying by her, with most sweet and smiling countenances with crowns upon their heads, and blue ribbons about their leaves." Winthrop interprets the dream for his wife to mean that "God would take of her children to make them fellow heirs with Christ in his kingdom." Earle relates the dream for "the evidence it gives of the pure and elevated influences of the Winthrop's home life" upon his career as a public official, and for the "characterization" it provides of the woman behind the man: "a very gracious woman" with a "sweet face" and "lovely countenance."

Earle's focus upon Margaret Winthrop as a private woman leads her to look with skepticism upon Anne Hutchinson, an historical personage much studied by modern feminists for her success at—and banishment for—using her home for women's meetings, which became the basis for her own public ministry in Massachusetts Bay. Earle calls Hutchinson the "woman parishioner . . . who well-nigh ended the Commonwealth" and argues that she could find no basis for Hutchinson's claim that such meetings were common. She praises Hutchinson's skills as a midwife's assistant and a counselor but also faults her for her inability, as Earle sees it, to effectively communicate her "mystical" teachings to posterity.

Earle betrays an ambivalence toward Hutchinson, whose "confused" voice entered the public record through such ostensibly domestic activities as midwifery and women's gatherings. She is similarly ambiv-

Title page for Earle's account of domestic life in prerevolutionary America

alent toward her own "public" reconstructions of the "private" past. A majority of her works center around women as historical subjects, suggesting a decidedly feminist sensibility. Nonetheless, on 18 April 1895, while in the process of writing *Colonial Dames and Good Wives,* she sent a letter to William C. Brownell, her editor at Scribner's, which ended with her distancing herself as a private reader from the brand of public writing for which she had become known: "I am not so over fond of the woman aspect of everything that I should ever, of my own choice, care for any book specially on any woman." Such a statement suggests that on some level Earle was aware of the implicit contradiction of publicly extolling the virtues of private womanhood. For Earle and her readers the tension between acting as one type of woman in order to champion her opposite was both problematic and productive; one might say that entering into the public sphere of print linked Earle with the outspoken and dangerously public Hutchinson–a villainess of her cultural history–as much as it did her heroine, the private and near invisible Margaret Winthrop.

Through her meditations on the past, Earle constituted the modern present as both "progressive" from and nostalgic for the colonial past. This complex relationship to Puritan history also links her with a long line of New England writers–Washington Irving, Charles Brockden Brown, Catharine Maria Sedgwick, Lydia Maria Child, and Hawthorne–who drew the Puritans into the present by measuring the distance that set them apart. Throughout her writings Earle continually invokes Hawthorne's name, a practice that mitigates to some degree any notion that she merely incorporated Puritan values into turn-of-the-century America in a simplistic way. Now that Earle's contributions to the field of colonial American studies have become more of a focus, her complex representation–or rather historiographic and imaginative reconstruction–of that period will be much debated. Such a debate is a measure of her success because what is difficult to contest is the degree to which she desired to constitute the colonial past as "the past." Modern historians who look to that past are discovering a far richer–a far more multiethnic and trans-Atlantic–set of influences than the single source that Earle delineated. Nonetheless, her historical position as one of the first to ask subsequent generations to look in the first place is becoming more secure.

Throughout her later years, Earle traveled a great deal throughout the world and in 1908 was even shipwrecked with her sister, Frances, during a trip from Boston to Egypt. Their steamer, the *Republic,* was hit by another ship off Nantucket Lightship and was cut in half. Both Earle and her sister were saved in lifeboats, but Earle fell back into the water and almost drowned. Her health was permanently weakened, leading to her death from chronic nephritis on 16 February 1911 at age fifty-

seven. She was buried in the Rural Cemetery in her birthplace of Worcester.

References:
Esther C. Averill, "Alice Morse Earle, A Writer Who Popularized Old New England," *Old-Time New England,* 37 (January 1947): 73–78;

Melinda Young Frye, "The Beginnings of the Period Room in American Museums: Charles P. Wilcomb's Colonial Kitchens, 1896, 1906, 1901," in *The Colonial Revival in America,* edited by Alan Axelrod (New York: Norton, 1985), pp. 217–240;

"General Gossip of Authors and Writers," *Current Literature,* 29 (September 1900): 286–287;

Michael Kammen, *Mystic Chords of Memory: The Transformation of Tradition in American Culture* (New York: Knopf, 1991);

Bridget May, "Progressivism and the Colonial Revival," *Winterthur Portfolio,* 26, no. 2/3 (1991): 107–122;

William B. Rhodes, "The Colonial Revival and the Americanization of Immigrants," in *The Colonial Revival in America,* pp. 341–361;

Beverly Seaton, "A Pedigree for a New Century: The Colonial Experience in Popular Historical Novels," in *The Colonial Revival in America,* pp. 278–293;

Laurel Thatcher Ulrich, *Good Wives: Image and Reality in the Lives of Women in Northern New England 1650–1750* (New York: Vintage, 1980);

Susan Reynolds Williams, "In the Garden of New England: Alice Morse Earle and the History of Domestic Life," dissertation, University of Delaware, 1992.

Papers:
The American Antiquarian Society in Worcester, Massachusetts, contains Alice Morse Earle's Biographical Materials and Photographs. Letters by Earle can be found in the Rare Book Department in the Boston Public Library, the Sophia Smith Collection at Smith College, and the Special Collections Department at Northwestern University. The Worcester Room in the Worcester Public Library contains the Morse Family Vertical File.

Edith Maude Eaton
(Sui Sin Far)
(15 March 1865 – 7 April 1914)

Nicole Tonkovich
University of California, San Diego

BOOKS: *Mrs. Spring Fragrance* (Chicago: A. C. McClurg, 1912);

Mrs. Spring Fragrance and Other Writings, edited by Amy Ling and Annette White-Parks (Urbana: University of Illinois Press, 1995).

SELECTED PERIODICAL PUBLICATIONS–UNCOLLECTED:

FICTION

"A Trip in a Horse Car," *Dominion Illustrated,* 1 (13 October 1888): 235;

"Misunderstood: The Story of a Young Man," *Dominion Illustrated,* 1 (17 November 1888): 314;

"A Fatal Tug of War," *Dominion Illustrated,* 1 (8 December 1888): 362–363;

"The Origin of a Broken Nose," *Dominion Illustrated,* 2 (11 May 1889): 302;

"Robin," *Dominion Illustrated,* 2 (22 June 1889): 394;

"Albemarle's Secret," *Dominion Illustrated,* 3 (19 October 1889): 254;

"In Fairyland," *Dominion Illustrated,* 5 (18 October 1890): 270;

"The Gamblers," *Fly Leaf,* 1 (February 1896): 14–18;

"Ku Yum," *Land of Sunshine,* 5 (June 1896): 29–31;

"The Story of Iso," *Lotus,* 2 (August 1896): 117–119;

"A Love Story of the Orient," *Lotus,* 2 (October 1896): 203–207;

"Sweet Sin, A Chinese-American Story," *Land of Sunshine,* 8 (April 1898): 223–226;

"A Chinese Ishmael," *Overland Monthly,* 34 (July 1899): 43–49;

"The Story of Tin-A," *Land of Sunshine,* 12 (January 1900): 100–103;

"Ku Yum's Little Sister," *Chicago Evening Post,* 13 October 1900;

"A Chinese Tom-Boy," *Montreal Daily Witness,* 16 October 1900;

"O Yam–A Sketch," *Land of Sunshine,* 13 (November 1900): 341–343;

Edith Maude Eaton (Sui Sin Far), 1903

"The Coat of Many Colors," *Youth's Companion,* 76 (April 1902): n.p.;

"The Horoscope," *Out West,* 19 (November 1903): 521–524;

"Ku Yum and the Butterflies," *Good Housekeeping,* 48 (March 1909): 299;

"The Half Moon Cakes," *Good Housekeeping,* 48 (May 1909): 584–585;

"The Kitten-Headed Shoes," *Delineator,* 75 (February 1910): 165.

NONFICTION

"A Chinese Feud," *Land of Sunshine,* 5 (November 1896): 236–237;

"The Chinese Woman in America," *Land of Sunshine,* 6 (January 1897): 59–64;

"Engaged Girl in China," *Ladies Home Journal,* 19 (January 1902): 14;

"Wing Sing of Los Angeles on His Travels," (attributed to Sui Sin Far) *Los Angeles Express,* 3–6, 10, 24 February 1904;

"Wing Sing in Montreal," (attributed to Sui Sin Far), *Los Angeles Express,* 27 February, 9 March 1904.

Although the classification is difficult and imprecise, the first Chinese American writer to publish fiction and journalism is conventionally understood to be Sui Sin Far (Edith Maude Eaton). At a time when few other writers of Asian ancestry were publishing—and these in a limited range of nonfiction genres such as polemic, travel writing, and anthropological studies—Sui Sin Far, a woman whose father was British and whose mother was half Chinese, wrote nearly forty insightful short stories based on the lives of Chinese immigrants in Canada and the United States. She also published several dozen factual accounts of the issues that confronted immigrants and peoples of mixed races in both countries. Near the end of her life she published two autobiographical sketches and collected her stories and sketches into a single volume, *Mrs. Spring Fragrance* (1912). Her primary interest to literary scholars has been as a writer of short fiction; her journalism has been largely overlooked.

Locating a first writer in whom to ground an ethnic literary tradition has important political ramifications. Yet, being so precisely labeled would have discomfited Sui Sin Far, whose writing was intended to effect a reconciliation among the racially divided communities to which she was loyal. At the end of her autobiographical sketch "Leaves from the Mental Portfolio of an Eurasian" (1909) she declares, "After all I have no nationality and am not anxious to claim any. Individuality is more than nationality. . . . I give my right hand to the Occidentals and my left to the

Orientals, hoping that between them they will not utterly destroy the insignificant 'connecting link.'" Understanding Sui Sin Far's commitment to the possibility of such a reconciliation offers insight into the choices she made regarding her life, her career, and her writing. A woman who could easily "pass" for white, who dressed in western clothing, and who spoke only English, Sui Sin Far chose, nonetheless, to emphasize her Asian heritage. She refused to marry, implying in her autobiographical writings that to marry a white man would have entailed denying her Chinese lineage, while to marry a Chinese man would have exposed her to a similar prejudice because she was not of "pure" blood. Moreover, she did not want to subject her offspring to the discrimination facing children of mixed racial heritage.

The name "Sui Sin Far," under which Edith Eaton published most of her later works, takes the variants Sui Seen Far and Sui Sin Fah. According to Annette White-Parks in her *Sui Sin Far/Edith Maude Eaton: A Literary Biography* (1995), "the syllables cannot be separated. . . . Meaning depends on the sequence . . . and does not work if the sequence is broken." The name, according to Xiao-Huang Yin, translates as "water fragrant flower," or narcissus, and signifies "dignity and indestructible love for family and homeland." It is apparently a pseudonym that Eaton chose for herself as a means of emphasizing her Asian heritage and is perhaps related to a childhood name used by her family. Consistent with her biracial identifications, she used both Sui Sin Far and Edith Eaton in her writing and her daily life, telling a Dartmouth College student with whom she corresponded that "I have both an English and a Chinese name."

Edith Maude Eaton was born in Macclesfield, England, on 15 March 1865. Her father, Edward Eaton, was the son of a British merchant who met his wife, Grace A. (Lotus Blossom) Trefusis, in Shanghai, where he had been established in business by his father. She was a half-Chinese woman who had been adopted early in life by British parents and educated in Britain. Recently she had returned to China as a missionary. Married in 1860, the couple lived in China, where their first son was born; then in Britain; and then briefly in the United States. The family finally settled in Montreal. There Edward Eaton put aside his mercantile interests to become a painter. Brilliant but improvident, he barely managed to support his family—which eventually included fourteen children. In Canada and later in the United States, the Eaton children faced legal and social discrimination because of their mixed racial heritage. In both countries political parties had endorsed anti-Chinese platforms; supported exclusion laws that attempted to ban the immigration of a people who, only decades before, had been welcomed as a source of cheap labor; and enacted zoning laws to confine resident Chinese to restricted urban neighborhoods. In both nations, Anglo-Americans were assumed to be socially superior, while Chinese were understood to be quaint, exotic, unassimilable, heathen, and inferior to all other races.

Although they had been raised and socialized as "white," spoke English—not Chinese—at home, and had been educated in British and Canadian schools, the Eaton children were accepted neither by the dominant white culture in which they lived nor by the Chinese community. Thus, in order to work and to educate themselves, several of them assumed racial identifications that shielded them from the negative consequences of such discrimination. Edward, the eldest brother, passed for white and married an Anglo woman; a sister, May Darling, who lived in California, claimed to be Spanish. Another sister, Lillie Winnifred, who also wrote fiction, assumed the Japanese pseudonym Onoto Watanna and constructed an autobiography to match, asserting that she had been born to a Japanese noblewoman in Nagasaki in 1879, when, in fact, she had been born in Montreal in 1875. She, too, married a white man. While Winnifred Eaton apparently chose to assume a Japanese identity as a means of marketing books, Edith, by contrast, chose to identify with her Chinese ancestry as a means of exposing, discussing, and attempting to mitigate issues of racism in Canada and the United States.

Sui Sin Far was passionately devoted to her family, particularly to her mother. As the eldest daughter of a large family, she functioned as a second mother to her siblings, a role that included helping to support the family financially. While still a child, she peddled lace and flowers; to the end of her adult life, she continued to send part of her earnings to various family members. For most of her life, Sui Sin Far was peripatetic, living in eastern and western Canada, Jamaica, California, the Pacific Northwest, the northeastern United States, and, finally, Montreal. In each case she settled in urban centers with large populations of Chinese immigrants. A self-taught stenographer, she opened her own office in Montreal in 1894. At other times in her life, she worked as a secretary, a freelance newspaper reporter, and a publicist for the Canadian Pacific Railway. She suffered ill health for most of her adult life, beginning with a bout with rheumatic fever at age fourteen, which weakened her heart. Later, in Jamaica, she contracted malaria. Despite her physical

Eaton in the 1890s

infirmities, she worked feverishly to support herself and saved enough money to transport her sisters from Montreal to the west coast, where she taught them stenography and helped them to become self-supporting. Yet, in the second autobiographical sketch, published in the *Boston Globe* (5 May 1912) two years before her death, she identified herself primarily as a writer.

Many letters written during Sui Sin Far's adult life document how difficult it was for her to find the solitude necessary to undertake sustained writing projects. It is not inaccurate to speculate that the quality and quantity of her writing is inversely proportional to the amount of time she had to spend working to support herself. In 1900, however, she wrote editor Charles F. Lummis that she had decided "to try hard to do more writing. In fact," she asserted, "I want to earn my living that way." Yet, a series of rejections from major magazines soon convinced her to "[give] up story writing entirely." Over the following eight years, Sui Sin Far moved seven times and—based on the evidence of texts currently located and attributed to her—published only infrequently. In 1907, "through a wreck on the Great

Northern Railway in North Dakota . . . I lost everything, save life, my trunk containing my manuscripts, scrapbooks, etc. having been destroyed in the fire caused by the accident."

Despite these doubts and setbacks, Sui Sin Far emerged as a successful professional writer. Only two years after the railway accident, she published her autobiographical essay "Leaves from the Mental Portfolio of an Eurasian" in the *Independent,* a major eastern periodical. This essay marks the beginning of a four-year period of productivity and confidence. During these years, Sui Sin Far's writings reached a most appreciative readership, who recognized both the artistry and political significance of her work. Relocating to Boston, she completed her first book, *Mrs. Spring Fragrance,* a collection of new and previously published material. After publishing three more sketches, she apparently ceased writing.

In both her fiction and her journalism, Sui Sin Far sought to make the lives of Chinese immigrants in the United States and Canada understandable to white readers. Taking advantage of the dominant cultural fascination with things oriental, she described the quaintness of Chinese life in the West, limning such customs as arranged marriages, fortune telling, and holiday celebrations. In this regard her writing resembles other journalism and fiction of the period, particularly the sketches and stories that appeared in western regional magazines, such as *Land of Sunshine* and *Overland Monthly,* whose purpose was to exoticize the culturally diverse populations of the west coast as a way of promoting regional tourism. Although in her choice of subjects Sui Sin Far follows the tradition of regional journalism, she did not indulge in the "outsider" stance that characterized many such essays. She refused to simplify, trivialize, or stereotype her subjects. Rather, she shows her readers the significance of these "colorful" customs and rituals, both to the immigrant cultures that celebrate them and to the larger Anglo communities whose lives are enriched by them. Sui Sin Far balanced these essays, documenting customs and practices that differentiated Chinese immigrants from their white neighbors, with sketches that demonstrated how immigrant families accommodated themselves to western culture. These sketches and stories reveal a complex and ironic understanding—on the part of the immigrants as well as of the journalist herself—of what the dominant culture considered to be successful or genuine acculturation. In them she emphasizes devotion to family, giving particular attention to the domesticity and tidiness of Chinese wives. In an effort to overturn discriminatory legislation that had segregated Chinese children from white schools in California, she advocates integrating classrooms so that immigrant children will more quickly become assimilated. She published documentary features about Chinese laundries and restaurants, as well as profiles of scholars, workers, and businessmen that demonstrate the creativity, artistry, and devotion to a western work ethic that characterized this community.

Sui Sin Far's writing provides an important corrective to the sensational and inaccurate representations of Asian populations that flooded the popular press at the turn of the twentieth century. For example, Sui Sin Far's journalism about west coast Chinatowns appeared at approximately the same time as a number of novels written by women missionaries. The purpose of these books was to establish the uniquely enlightened position enjoyed by white American women, as well as to raise money to support foreign proselytizing. These overwrought and often inaccurate novels emphasized the "heathen" practices of polygamy and footbinding, portraying China and its inhabitants as ignorant savages. Other sinophobic fiction of the period looked closer to home. The virulently anti-Chinese or "yellow peril" fiction written by Jack London and Frank Norris, among others, portrays Chinese immigrants as stereotypically inscrutable, evil, unassimilable, and ultimately a dangerous source of contamination to the pure white population that surrounds them.

In a more conventionally literary sense, Sui Sin Far's prose may be seen as a part of the local-color tradition. Writers such as Bret Harte and Willa Cather embraced the realist movement, emphasizing in their writings the peculiarities of specific regions of the United States. Many of Sui Sin Far's sketches and essays seem to fall within this classification, especially because of their physical presentation. *Mrs. Spring Fragrance,* for example, was bound in a scarlet cover embellished with gold calligraphy. Each page is decorated with Chinese characters and "oriental" ink-wash designs. This oriental motif is repeated in the magazines in which she published, where her stories are illustrated with photographs and engravings that perpetuated the most dominant cultural stereotypes. Paradoxically, when photographs of Sui Sin Far herself accompanied these writings, as they often did, they showed a woman dressed in conventional western attire, whose physical features did not suggest her Asian identifications. As the disjunction of these images suggests, the narrator of local-color fiction assumes a position separate from and often superior to the subjects whose peculiarities are being represented. Thus local-color writing often obscures the power relations encoded in race, gender, social

Eaton's parents, Edward and Grace Eaton, circa 1910

class, and location that are foundational to its emphasis on peculiarity.

It should be emphasized that the illustration of her pieces, whether with orientalist sketches or photographs of the author, was largely out of Sui Sin Far's control. Moreover, her prose suggests her excruciating awareness of the relations of power entailed in writing and publishing, particularly if the subject of that writing is already coded as racially alien. Therefore, she scrupulously avoids the more egregious exoticism associated with local color, insisting that Chinese immigrant families were not just a momentary phenomenon that added an exotic dimension to west coast culture. Because these people were a permanent part of that culture, not just a peculiarity, she argued ferociously for an acknowledgment of their humanity: for the rights of Chinese immigrants to work for equal wages, to establish businesses that would be patronized by whites as well as by Asians, and to claim the rights of citizenship as "native sons and daughters of the Golden West." Moreover, she attempts to prove that without the contributions of Asian immigrants, the United States could not have achieved its present political, economic, and social dominance in world affairs.

Another explanation of the apparent disjunction between the orientalist form and the activist content of Sui Sin Far's writings is that she often assumed a trickster stance. White-Parks suggests that she embraced "the role of author as trickster" and asserts that such a stance is a way of upsetting "her readers' monologic view of reality by opening multiple perspectives." In support of this contention, White-Parks notes such examples as Sui Sin Far's habits of publishing anonymously or pseudonymously, as well as her characteristic fictional technique of hiding her meaning, producing a text whose surface reads as a culturally acceptable narrative but whose subtext may encode more radical and/or threatening agendas. Such a classification also suggests a productive way of comparing Sui Sin Far's prose with that produced in other ethnic traditions wherein the trickster figure appears. At the same time, it should be stressed that the uniquely identifying characteristics of Sui Sin Far's writing derive from her precise location in space and time. Her prose addresses specific legal, social, and political exigencies facing Chinese immigrants in turn-of-the-century North America.

It might be argued that while the physical presentation of Sui Sin Far's stories, with its illustrations and embellishments, is orientalist, her nonfiction prose is, by contrast, quite straightforward. Typically, her journalism is not illustrated, either with her portrait or with engravings of exotically dressed Chinese women, adorable Chinese babies, or calligraphic decorations. For the most part, its titles avoid the exotic, childlike, and romantic flavor of the fictional (such as "Ku Yum and the Butterflies," March 1909), favoring a straightforward announcement of topic, such as "Chinatown Needs a School" (first published in the *Los Angeles Express,* 1903). Moreover, the agenda of her journalism is clear. Based in fact, it is always advocacy journalism. The earliest example of such a text is Sui Sun Far's "A Plea for the Chinaman: A Correspondent's Argument in His Favor," an impassioned letter to the editor of the *Montreal Daily Star* (1896), arguing for the rights of Chinese immigrants. Eschewing ambiguity about her own racial identifications, "E. E." argues that "It needs a Chinaman to stand up for a Chinese cause." She systematically counters erroneously stereotypical Anglo perceptions of the Chinese in Montreal and in the United States. As her central example she narrates a visit she has recently made to New York's Chinatown, located "in the slum portion of the city," about which she had been told "dreadful tales." Despite the warning that "if I went in there alone I would never come out alive or sound in mind or body," she asserts, "I went there and returned the better for my visit." Like the other, more subtle essays that follow, this letter insists that the dominant white culture must not, only understand but also accept Asian immigrants, according them the basic legal rights that accompany citizenship. "A Plea for the Chinaman" marks the end of this first period of Sui Sin Far's writing. Written specifically to protest the passage of a proposed $500 per person "head tax" on Chinese immigrants to Canada, Sui Sun Far's letter maintains an acute awareness of the limits of freedom for those living "in the land of the free." It directly addresses the real consequences of discriminatory legislation, advocates legal reform, and, perhaps most centrally, locates the basis for those claims and arguments in the ethnic identifications of its writer.

This is not to argue for the accuracy, objectivity, and perfection of Sui Sin Far's entire oeuvre. Because she did not speak Chinese, she often was not welcome in Chinese homes. Having been raised by British parents, she shared many of the prejudices of the dominant culture. As a teacher in Protestant-sponsored Chinese mission schools, she was committed to assimilation as the solution to "the Chinese problem." She remained unaware of the complexities of class structures in urban Chinatowns, nor did she investigate the grinding poverty and vice that plagued most Chinese ghettoes. The pattern of such fissures and omissions in her fiction, letters, and essays yields a fascinating map of the possibilities—as

well as of the limits—of multicultural understanding in turn-of-the-century United States and Canada.

Several scholars have been engaged in identifying and collecting Sui Sin Far's published work. The task is not yet complete and has been complicated by the fact that many of her early pieces were unsigned and appeared in ephemeral venues such as railroad brochures and magazines. Those that have been located may be divided into four periods, the first three being an initial period of journalism produced and published in Canada and narrated from an Anglo-Canadian point of view, a period of "outreach" that sees the publication of her first Chinese fictions and an increasingly strong identification with issues of concern to Chinese immigrants, and a period of facticity, in which, realizing the power of addressing a broad audience, Sui Sin Far undertakes explicitly social and political concerns. Following a four-year hiatus, the final period of her prose writing includes a preponderance of short fiction of high literary quality that was recognized by the eastern literary establishment as having promise above and beyond simple local-color sketches.

The impetus to Sui Sin Far's writing seems to have been her early newspaper work. As a young woman she picked and set type for the *Montreal Daily Star* to supplement her earnings from secretarial work. From 1888 to 1895, she submitted freelance sketches to *Dominion Illustrated,* the *Montreal Daily Witness,* and the *Montreal Daily Star.* Most of these pieces are unsigned or identified simply with the initials "E. E." They have been attributed to Sui Sin Far on the basis of their thematic and stylistic similarity to her later work. Among these early writings are short stories that critique the conventions of romantic love. An early feature story, "A Trip in a Horse Car" (1888), sketches the inhabitants of a downtown cab who are brought together momentarily by the exigencies of moving about the city but whose origins, lives, and destinations are strikingly different. The horse car thus becomes a microcosm for the city of Montreal.

Most of the pieces written in this period are brief anecdotes, sometimes as short as a single paragraph. Focusing on the experience of Chinese immigrants in Montreal, the articles stem from Sui Sin Far's already sharp awareness of racism and its effects on the lives of immigrant peoples. Like conventional journalism, these sketches concentrate on details of persons and places. In their tone they also undertake a more polemic agenda, demonstrating how ordinary people are affected by impersonal and often discriminatory legislation—laws that touch not only those who are subject to them but also those who must enforce them and those whose lives are invisibly altered by the rule of law. For example, "A Chinese Party," first published in the *Montreal Daily Witness* (7 November 1890), tells of nineteen successful Chinese businessmen who, despite their evident command of the English language and their financial success are forced by law to "travel in bond, like a Saratoga trunk." After making a civilized picnic, they successfully bribe a Customs officer to allow them to "go downtown to see some friends." In an ironic aside, the narrator remarks that although the bribe prompts the official to remember "that he was a man. . . . He took that $1,000 all the same." This essay humanizes immigrant figures who were more frequently characterized as parasites on capitalistic society and shows their awareness that the supposedly disinterested enforcement of law is subject to its enforcer's baser instincts. The overall effect of the essay is to demonstrate to readers who believe they are unaffected by irrational laws that they are no different in tastes, insight, and talents than those whose race subjects them to such "mortifying" legislation.

Two other sketches in the tradition of the journalistic human interest story introduce Canadian readers to the lives of immigrants and their children. "Half-Chinese Children" (first published in the *Montreal Daily Star,* 20 April 1895), based on an interview with "an American lady, the wife of a Chinese merchant," demonstrates the dual burden borne by children of mixed races. Rejected as impure by both parental cultures, such children become centrally important to Sui Sin Far's writing and find their voice in the plaintive question of the children limned in "Leaves from the Mental Portfolio of an Eurasian" who ask, "Why did papa and mamma born us?" "Girl Slave in Montreal" (first published in the *Montreal Daily Witness,* 4 May 1894) introduces the life and circumstances of the "only two women from the flowery land" who live in Montreal. (Sui Sin Far, writing as the anonymous "lady reporter of the '*Witness,*'" does not count herself among that population.)

Between 1895 and 1900, Sui Sin Far's identification with the Chinese residents of Montreal and New York strengthened. Rather than stemming from ideological identifications or abstract curiosity, these "outreach" essays and stories are based on her firsthand encounters with Chinese immigrants. Of this period, she later recalls, "I meet many Chinese persons, and when they get into trouble am often called upon to fight their battles in the papers. This I enjoy." In 1896 Sui Sin Far published the first of her Chinese short stories in *Fly Leaf* and *Lotus,* magazines published or edited by her brother-in-law, Walter Blackburn Harte. She traveled in the northeastern

Title page for Eaton's first book, a collection of stories that confront popular stereotypes concerning Chinese Americans

United States and then to Jamaica, where she joined her sister Winnifred and worked as a stenographer and journalist. She soon returned to Montreal to recuperate from malaria. By 1898 she had begun to travel extensively in the United States and southwest Canada, visiting San Francisco, Los Angeles, Seattle, and Vancouver, all cities with large Chinese populations. In June of that year she joined her sister May in San Francisco, where May worked as a photo finisher. In the summer of the following year she journeyed to Southern California where she met Lummis, who had already published several of her short stories in *Land of Sunshine.* Because Lummis insisted that all the fiction published in his magazine have identifiably western regional settings, "Ku Yum" (June 1896), "A Chinese Feud" (November 1896), and "The Chinese Woman in America" (January 1897) are located in California, although their author had not yet visited the state. "The Chinese Woman in America," an essay with a more general focus than California, is tied to the West by an accompanying photo captioned "Chinese Mothers in California." Later stories, published in *Land of Sunshine* after Sui Sin Far had visited southern California, have slightly more developed settings. "O Yam–A Sketch" (1900), for example, opens with a paragraph that locates the tale in a "Southern California village" where "searchers for health basked in sunshine and tourists wandered amongst its flower-buried cottages and crumbling ruins; for there, in times gone by, a Spanish Mission had stood."

Lummis, who fancied himself a mentor of several important regional women writers, introduced Sui Sin Far to *Land of Sunshine* readers in a one-page biographical sketch illustrated with her portrait in November 1900. His editorial column, "In Western Letters," profiled "the delicate little Sui Sin Fah, a 'discovery' of this magazine three or four years ago." According to Lummis, "our little 'Chinese Contributor'" was possessed of a "breeding that is a step beyond our strenuous Saxon blood, and a native perception as characteristic . . . a Chinawoman transplanted and graduated." The gap between this dismissive and inaccurate sketch and what Lummis knew of Sui Sin Far based on his personal acquaintance and their correspondence is an accurate measure of how the fiction of this period was necessarily framed to appear in mainstream white venues. It recalls Sui Sin Far's observation in "Leaves from the Mental Portfolio of an Eurasian" that "some funny people . . . advise me to 'trade' upon my nationality. They tell me that if I wish to succeed in literature in America I should dress in Chinese costume, carry a fan in my hand, wear a pair of scarlet beaded slippers . . . and come of high birth."

Other fiction followed, retaining the local-color emphasis as Sui Sin Far's travels brought her into contact with the multicultural populations of several urban areas. These writings expose the contingency of the realism associated with local-color writing. They often take as their theme the psychological effects on women of being separated from their families. Their realism addresses a readership that values family closeness during the children's adult years; moreover, it signals the concerns of a culture newly concerned with the psychological effect of women's increasingly independent lifestyles. The purported ethnic realism of these tales is equally contingent. The fact that Sui Sin Far could produce sketches set in California Chinatowns before she had entered the state suggests that the effect of realism lies with the reader, who is prepared to assume that all Chinatowns are more or less similar, regardless of their location.

During this second period, Sui Sin Far's writings become lengthier. They imagine and address a wider readership, often blurring the boundaries between fiction and journalism. Her short stories frequently contain surprise denouements whose effect is to demonstrate how racial difference modifies the structures of literary genres. "A Chinese Feud," for example, introduces Sui Sin Far's first identifiable Chinese American characters. The happy resolution of its central love story is foreclosed by a quarrel between the bride's Americanized family and the groom's recently arrived parents, who still value their Chinese identities. Thus the "Romeo and Juliet" romance plot is expanded to include family tensions caused by race and nationalism. It is in this period that Sui Sin Far begins to explore the possibilities of passing. The first signification of the term, of course, is that peoples of mixed races may pass as white. Sui Sin Far's autobiographical "Leaves from the Mental Portfolio of an Eurasian" narrates several short episodes that suggest her own experiences with being mistaken for a white woman. Portraits taken of the author at this period show a woman whose facial features are ambiguous and who affected a style of dress that predisposed observers to think of her as "white." Her stories explore other variations of the theme of "passing" as well. "Ku Yum," for example, takes as its theme the exchange of identities between a plain-featured woman and her more beautiful maid.

While in Los Angeles, Sui Sin Far again became interested in journalism, exploring how documentary writing might present the cases of immigrants living under discriminatory conditions. Between 1902 and 1905 she researched and published a number of factual essays that attempted to show the residents of the West Coast how their Chinese neighbors lived. No longer are her Chinese subjects merely picturesque, quaint, or amusing. As she wrote to Robert Underwood Johnson, editor of *Century Magazine,* she wished to distinguish her writing from those who wrote "clever and interesting Chinese stories" that "seem to . . . stand afar off from the Chinaman–in most cases treating him as a joke." In the journalism of this third period, then, she relates the lives of her Chinese subjects to the broadest conception of American values. As the United States endorsed another, more punitive, and permanent version of the Chinese Exclusion Act, Sui Sin Far demonstrated to her readers how loyally Chinese citizens embraced western lifestyles.

Sui Sin Far explores the widest possibilities of her dual ethnic identification in this period's journalism. An insider in Chinatown because she identified herself as Chinese, yet an outsider because of her connections with the world of Anglo journalism, she conducted sympathetic first-person interviews with informants whom she represents as articulate, thoughtful, and complex. Rather than report on life in Chinatown as an outsider and seemingly objective observer, as did her contemporaries Arnold Genthe and Jacob Riis, Sui Sin Far visited Chinatown laundries and businesses; she was invited into the private spaces of Chinese homes. Rather than assume an omniscient and objective journalistic stance, she allowed her informants to represent themselves, to correct what she had previously written about them, and to articulate their own understandings of their positions in American culture.

As a journalist, Sui Sin Far was fully aware of the consequences involved in representing cultural and "racial" others; moreover she was personally aware of the potential damage of such erroneous reports, as well as of reportage that presented only partial representations of complex cultural phenomena. Therefore, she sought publication of her documentary essays in venues that rejected sensationalism. Her first series of columns appeared in the *Los Angeles Express,* a newspaper that promoted itself as "A Clean, Up-to-Date, Home Newspaper Printed and Edited for the Family Circle." Here, as elsewhere, she writes of Chinese women who are not exotically dressed prostitutes but "Christian and Americanized" mothers. Although they still dress in traditional Chinese costume, they have the same worries, concerns, joys, and sorrows as their white counterparts. They want good schools for their children; they want their daughters to marry responsible young men who share their cultural values. In these essays Chinese laundrymen are transfigured from the cartoonish stereotypes into intrepid, responsible, and creative businessmen. Sui Sin Far reminds her readers that the laundryman has other dimensions to his life, that he may be an artist or a poet as well, and that he is likely a native-born citizen of the United States. Countering the most unreflective and ignorant stereotypes of Chinese as rat-eaters, she details the cleanliness and healthfulness of Chinese cuisine, remarking, "There is nothing on a Chinaman's table to remind one of living animals and birds—no legs, heads, limbs, wings or loins. . . . The Chinaman comes to the table to eat—not to work" (20 October 1903). The contrast with more-barbaric Anglo culinary procedures is clearly but subtly established. She emphasizes that Chinese immigrants are not "sojourners" who have come to the United States only long enough to amass a fortune to take back to China, but involved citizens, interested in the local

Eaton's gravestone in Mount Royal Cemetery, Montreal

politics of Los Angeles, the national issues confronting Canada and the United States, and the politics of China as well. Their political knowledge thus may even exceed that of their white counterparts, for they recognize the central importance of Asia to contemporary American business interests. In these closely observed factual accounts, Sui Sin Far succeeded in presenting a more balanced and accurate account of immigrant life. Even Lummis was constrained to admit that "To others the alien Celestial is at best mere 'literary material'; in [Sui Sin Far's] stories he (or she) is a human being."

A second series of essays published in the *Los Angeles Express* under the pseudonym Wing Sing has been attributed to Sui Sin Far as well. Unlike the earlier series, these columns are written in dialect. Yet, in emphasis and phrasing, as well as in their evident familiarity with railroad travel, and set in the the Chinese communities of San Francisco and Montreal, these columns suggest Sui Sin Far's authorship. In "Wing Sing of Los Angeles on his Travels," which appeared in February and March 1904, she again embraces the trope of "passing." This time, rather than passing as white, she crosses genders, adopting the persona of a "foreign born" Angeleno. "Wing Sing," according to the *Express* byline, is "the pen name of a well-known Americanized Chinese merchant" of the city who has left to visit China, traveling by way of Montreal. Over the course of the eight columns, Wing Sing encounters an Irishman, with whom he discusses the Chinese contributions to building the railroad on which they travel, and undertakes a seriocomic exploration of the consequences of the Exclusion Act for Chinese men who have come to the United States without their wives. Wing Sing observes wryly that the exclusion laws have been a boon to his marriage: since his wife must remain in China, he need not worry that she will become Americanized and thus too independent to obey his absolute rule. The life of one such independent and Americanized Chinese woman is explored in "Aluteh" (first published in the *Chautauquan,* December 1905), the final story published before Sui Sin Far's four-year silence. The title character, a woman "gifted with quick perceptions" and possessed of determination and resolve, saves her father and a local magistrate from disgrace (from *Mrs. Spring Fragrance and Other Writings,* 1995). Her character anticipates the stronger women Sui Sin Far created in the final and most successful period of her writing.

Financial pressures, coupled with a period of difficulty in getting stories published, may have been the reason Sui Sin Far ceased writing between 1905 and 1909. The resurgence and strength of the work of her final period, however, is accurately forecast by a series of articles titled "The Chinese in America," written in 1909 for the *Westerner* magazine of Seattle. Although the themes of these essays are similar to those of the earlier *Los Angeles Express* series, they evidence a finely honed sense of a readership beyond the immediately local. She introduces these essays by arguing for the importance of the Asian population in West Coast cities, linking the emergent power of the United States in world politics to the way the nation has treated its Chinese American citizens. In her words, "what [these citizens] think and what they write about Americans will surely influence to a great extent, the conduct of their countrymen towards the people of the United States." Having projected the potential influence of the Chinese on American-Chinese political relations of the future, she reminds readers of the considerable part Chinese have played in U.S. history as well, asserting that "every true Westerner will admit that the enlarged life in which

he is participating today could not have been possible without the Chinese." Here Sui Sin Far abandons the objective journalistic reportorial stance for that of a first-person narrator whose identification with her countrymen is overt. In this series she begins to recount the personal experiences that have led her to this more aggressive stance.

This attitude characterizes the widely reproduced "Leaves from the Mental Portfolio of an Eurasian," as well. In this brief autobiographical essay, the first-person narrator presents an impressionistic collection of sketches that follow one another in quick chronological succession. Each scene is a self-contained anecdote narrating a moment that has contributed to Sui Sin Far's awareness of herself as a racial subject. Cumulatively, they explain her choice to identify herself as Eurasian. Signed "Sui Sin Far," the essay is accompanied by a half-page oval photograph of its author. Although the framing and pose of this portrait signify "white authorship," the essay does not vaunt the potential superiority afforded a self-identified racial subject who has been accepted by the white literary establishment. On the contrary, this essay, which marks Sui Sin Far's wide acceptance as an author, seems to take an uncompromising stance against the common nineteenth-century pattern of binary racial thinking. Both portrait and essay demonstrate the limits of such a pattern. Occidental cannot be assumed to be superior to Oriental. Nor can "white" men justifiably claim dominance over men or women of color. The experimental portfolio of the essay form challenges conventional literary evaluations based on genre, as well, by demonstrating the complexity of interpretation that may result from a simple, disjoined, potentially incomplete, but infinitely expandable form.

In 1910 Sui Sin Far moved to Boston, where, with the financial support of several mentors, she was able finally to devote most of her time to writing. Over the next several years, she wrote several new stories, which she combined with previously published materials in a collection, *Mrs. Spring Fragrance.* This volume continues the themes of her earlier journalism and fiction by portraying the Chinese as complex and interesting people who exceed the stereotypes attributed to them, both as new immigrants and as fully assimilated citizens. In these stories the reader encounters Chinese subjects who have so fully mastered English that they can eloquently represent themselves; moreover, the title character is writing a book—in English—about American women. *Mrs. Spring Fragrance* is divided into two sections. The first, "Mrs. Spring Fragrance," features stories in which Chinese or Eurasian narrators daintily deconstruct the behaviors and prejudices of American men and women. The second section, "Tales of Chinese Children," comprises short tales ostensibly written for children, and that have children at their center. Their simplicity is belied, however, by the seriousness and even violence of their content and theme.

"Mrs. Spring Fragrance" includes Sui Sin Far's most powerful fiction. "The Wisdom of the New" and "Pat and Pan" both demonstrate the potentially disastrous consequences of the dominant culture's well-meaning charitable interventions into the lives of ethnic others. "Her Chinese Husband" (first published in the *Independent,* 18 August 1910) and "A White Woman Who Married a Chinese Man" (first published as "A White Woman Who Married a Chinaman" in the *Independent,* 10 March 1910) explore the issues of assimilation and intermarriage. These titles openly counter a cultural stereotype that was largely left unspoken in turn-of-the-century United States. Received wisdom held that while Asian women might find their overall status improved by marrying white men, white women would always reject the social degradation entailed in marrying Asian men. These stories challenge that perception, exposing the conditions of abuse that may prevail in a marriage where the male partner enjoys the privileges of law, race, and patriarchal custom. The white woman who is their narrator has left her abusive and unfaithful American husband. She and her children are rescued from starvation and homelessness by a gentle and loving Chinese man. Her white children play contentedly with their half-Chinese siblings and playmates. She herself enacts a reverse passing—as a Chinese wife. Miscegenation is thus transformed into a positive and productive amalgamation.

In other stories from *Mrs. Spring Fragrance*—"The Smuggling of Tie Co," "Tian Shan's Kindred Spirit," and "A Chinese Boy-Girl"—the "passing" narrator of "Her Chinese Husband" is transformed into a cross-dressed woman who slips across borders to confound discriminatory national laws. A prized son is dressed as a girl by his parents to confound the evil spirits who have caused the death of his older brothers. Although his simple story asks to be read as a demonstration of the quaint beliefs of the Chinese, it also encodes a tale of survival, suggesting that in order to preserve precious cultural beliefs, Chinese generally may disguise themselves by assuming traits that are not valued by the evil dominant culture. Finally, in an ironic refusal of the straightforward crossings of heterosexuality, stories such as "The Chinese Lily" and "The Sing-Song Woman" explore the strength of affectional relations between women.

Mrs. Spring Fragrance received positive reviews in the eastern press. Not surprisingly, reviewers' evaluation of the book is framed by the their preconceptions about the author's race. Yet, these reviewers do acknowledge that the book offers valuable new perspectives on Anglo-Chinese relationships. They see Sui Sin Far as the representative of a new kind of immigrant—one who has become Americanized and who has entered the realm of cultural production. Shortly after the appearance of *Mrs. Spring Fragrance,* her autobiographical feature story published in the *Boston Globe* bears out this theme. Introduced with another photographic portrait that presents Sui Sin Far as ambiguously raced, the article presents her as a fully realized author. In the fashion of a typical immigrant success story, its narration is teleological, showing how her difficult experiences in life have culminated in the inevitable appearance of her book.

Only a few essays followed the publication of *Mrs. Spring Fragrance.* Although documentary evidence suggests that Sui Sin Far had begun to work on a novel, the manuscript has not been located. A series of family tragedies brought her back to Canada, where she died in April 1914. She was buried in Mount Royal cemetery in Montreal, where the Chinese community erected a memorial gravestone that praised her pioneering efforts on their behalf.

Sui Sin Far's importance as a prose writer is enhanced by her penetrating insights into the social and political problems encountered by children of mixed racial backgrounds. Her work, long overlooked because of literary preferences for longer prose characterized by complexity and ambiguity, demonstrates a different and important kind of literary value. Her short sketches capture the humanity of her subjects without reducing them to stereotypes, without denigrating their cultural backgrounds, and without insisting that they be understood in terms of dominant cultural values. Seen in the context of a larger corpus of American literary history, her work demonstrates that the local-color tradition is less limited and stereotypically compromised than the work of white writers has suggested. Sui Sin Far, however, would have identified her most significant accomplishment as having earned the praise of her own people. As she asserted in "Leaves from the Mental Portfolio of an Eurasian," "My heart leaps for joy when I read one day an article by a New York Chinese in which he declares, 'The Chinese in America owe an everlasting debt of gratitude to Sui Sin Far for the bold stand she has taken in their defense.'"

References:

Elizabeth Ammons, "Audacious Words: Sui Sin Far's *Mrs. Spring Fragrance*," in her *Conflicting Stories: American Women Writers at the Turn into the Twentieth Century* (New York: Oxford University Press, 1991), pp. 105–120;

Winnifred Eaton [Babcock], *Me, a Book of Remembrance* (New York: Century, 1915);

Amy Ling, "Creating One's Self: The Eaton Sisters," in *Reading the Literatures of Asian America,* edited by Ling and Shirley Goek-lin Lim (Philadelphia: Temple University Press, 1992), pp. 305–318;

Ling, "Edith Eaton: Pioneer Chinamerican Writer and Feminist," *American Literary Realism,* 16 (Autumn 1983): 287–298;

Ling, "Pioneers and Paradigms: The Eaton Sisters," in *Between Worlds: Women Writers of Chinese Ancestry,* edited by Ling (New York: Pergamon, 1990), pp. 21–55;

Ling, "Revelation and Mask: Autobiographies of the Eaton Sisters," *a/b: Auto-Biography Studies,* 3 (Summer 1987): 49;

Ling, "Writers with a Cause: Sui Sin Far and Han Suyin," *Women's Studies International Forum,* 9 (1986): 411–419;

C. F. L. [Charles F. Lummis], "In Western Letters," *Land of Sunshine,* 13 (November 1900): 336;

S. E. Solberg, "Sui Sin Far/Edith Eaton: First Chinese American Fictionist," *MELUS,* 8 (Spring 1981): 27–39;

Nicole Tonkovich, "Genealogy, Genre, Gender: Sui Sin Far's 'Leaves from the Mental Portfolio of an Eurasian,'" in *Beyond the Binary: Reconstructing Cultural Identity in a Multicultural Context,* edited by Timothy B. Powell (New Brunswick, N.J.: Rutgers University Press, 1999), pp. 236–260;

Annette White-Parks, "Journey to the Golden Mountain: Chinese Immigrant Women," in *Women and the Journey: The Female Travel Experience,* edited by Bonnie Frederick and Susan McLeod (Pullman: Washinton State University Press, 1993), pp. 101–117;

White-Parks, "A Reversal of American Concepts of 'Other-ness' in the Fiction of Sui Sin Far," *MELUS,* 20 (1995): 17–34;

White-Parks, *Sui Sin Far/Edith Maude Eaton: A Literary Biography* (Urbana: University of Illinois Press, 1995);

Xiao-Huang Yin, "Between the East and West: Sui Sin Far–the First Chinese-American Woman Writer," *Arizona Quarterly,* 47 (Winter 1991): 49–83.

Papers:

Most of Sui Sin Far's papers were destroyed in the 1907 Great Northern Railway accident in North Dakota. Some of her letters are housed at Dartmouth College Library, Special Collections; Huntington Library, Charles F. Lummis Collection, San Marino, Cal.; and the Southwest Museum, Charles F. Lummis Collection, Los Angeles, Cal.

Winnifred Eaton
(Onoto Watanna)
(21 August 1875 – 8 April 1954)

Maureen Honey
University of Nebraska at Lincoln

BOOKS: *Miss Numè of Japan: A Japanese-American Romance* (Chicago: Rand McNally, 1899);

A Japanese Nightingale (New York & London: Harper, 1901);

The Wooing of Wistaria (New York & London: Harper, 1902);

The Heart of Hyacinth (New York & London: Harper, 1903);

The Love of Azalea (New York: Dodd, Mead, 1904);

Daughters of Nijo: A Romance of Japan (New York & London: Macmillan, 1904);

A Japanese Blossom (New York & London: Harper, 1906);

The Diary of Delia, Being a Veracious Chronicle of the Kitchen with Some Side-lights on the Parlour (New York: Doubleday, Page, 1907);

Tama (New York & London: Harper, 1910);

The Honorable Miss Moonlight (New York & London: Harper, 1912);

Me: A Book of Remembrance, anonymous (New York: Century, 1915);

Marion: The Story of an Artist's Model, as "Herself and the author of 'Me'" (New York: Watts, 1916);

Sunny-San (New York: Doran, 1922);

Cattle (London: Hutchinson, 1923); as Winnifred Eaton (New York: Watt, 1924);

His Royal Nibs, as Winifred Eaton Reeve (New York: Watt, 1925).

PRODUCED SCRIPTS: *False Kisses,* adaptation by Eaton (as Winifred Reeve), Universal, 1921;

Mississippi Gambler, dialogue by Eaton (as Reeve) and H. H. Van Loan, Universal, 1929;

Shanghai Lady, screenplay by Eaton (as Reeve), Houston Branch, and John Colton, Universal, 1929;

East Is West, screenplay by Eaton (as Reeve) and Tom Reed, Universal, 1930;

Undertow, adaptation and screenplay by Eaton (as Reeve) and Edward T. Lowe, Universal, 1930;

Winnifred Eaton during the 1920s

Young Desire, adaptation and dialogue by Eaton (as Reeve) and Matt Taylor, Universal, 1930;

SELECTED PERIODICAL PUBLICATIONS—UNCOLLECTED:

FICTION

"Two Converts," *Harper's Monthly,* 103 (September 1901): 585–589;

"Eyes that Saw Not," by Eaton and Bertrand Babcock, *Harper's Monthly,* 105 (June 1902): 30–38;

"The Loves of Sakura Jiro and the Three-Headed Maid," *Century,* 65 (March 1903): 755–760;

"Miss Lily and Miss Chrysanthemum, The Love Story of Two Japanese Girls in Chicago," *Ladies Home Journal,* 20 (August 1903): 11–12;

"The Wrench of Chance," *Harper's Weekly,* 50 (20–27 October 1906): 1494–1496, 1505, 1531–1533;

"An Unexpected Grandchild," *Lippincott's,* 84 (December 1909): 684–700.

NONFICTION

"The Japanese Drama and the Actor," *Critic,* 41 (September 1902): 230–237;

"Every-day Life in Japan," *Harper's Weekly,* 48 (2 April 1904): 500–503, 527–528;

"The Marvelous Miniature Trees of Japan," *Woman's Home Companion,* 31 (June 1904): 16;

"The Japanese in America," *Eclectic,* 148 (February 1907): 100–104.

Winnifred Eaton was a Chinese Canadian writer at the turn of the century who published fifteen books and constructed a public identity as Onoto Watanna, author of several best-selling romances set in Japan featuring American, English, Japanese, and Eurasian characters. She wrote the first novel authored by an Asian American, *Miss Numè of Japan: A Japanese-American Romance* (1899), while her sister Edith Eaton, who wrote under the name Sui Sin Far, is credited with being the first Asian American to publish fiction. The Eaton sisters pioneered a creative path for Asian American writers, particularly women, in the twentieth century as they inserted a new voice into Canadian American literature, that of the Chinese, Japanese, or Eurasian subject, and attempted to counter the dominant cultural stereotypes of Asians as the inhuman, orientalized other.

Eaton has been overshadowed by her sister, whose work has been reprinted and whose life was the subject of a biography published in 1995; Edith Eaton's life and her Chinese tales have attracted considerable critical attention. In their own lifetimes, however, Winnifred was the sister who gained critical acclaim, wide readership, and commercial success, while Edith struggled to publish until her death at age forty-nine in 1914. This reversal in positions has much to do with Winnifred's problematic adoption of not only a Japanese pseudonym but also a fabricated Japanese personal history in which she claimed to have been born in Nagasaki to a noble Japanese family, occasionally varying the tale to say that her father was English.

Eaton was actually the daughter of an English silk merchant turned artist, Edward Eaton, who in the early 1860s in Shanghai met and married Grace A. Trefusis, a Cantonese woman who had been adopted by missionaries in China and educated in England. Their oldest son was born in China in 1864; shortly thereafter the family left for England. During the next ten years they immigrated to the United States, returned to England, and then immigrated to North America again, settling in Montreal in the early 1870s. Lillie Winnifred Eaton was born on 21 August 1875, the eighth of the family's fourteen surviving children.

Contemporary critics have faulted Eaton for denying her Chinese heritage at a time when Chinese North Americans were under attack as subhuman invaders who threatened dominant Eurocentric values and whose economic situations were perilous in many cases. The Chinese Exclusion Act of 1882 barred Chinese entry into the United States, an indication of the depth of nativist resistance to Chinese immigrants, leaving thousands of Chinese men stranded without families. Edith, writing as Sui Sin Far, fought against this prejudice through her positive portrayal of the Chinatown communities in Seattle and San Francisco in her sketches, short stories, and essays. Winnifred, in contrast, presented herself as a more acceptable Asian when she masqueraded as Onoto Watanna at a time when the Japanese were being courted as trading partners by the West during the Meiji Restoration, and the few people of Japanese descent living in North America were generally students, diplomats, and businessmen. Anti-Japanese sentiment surfaced with the Gentlemen's Agreement of 1908, the Alien Land Law passed in California in 1913, and the 1924 Immigration Act, which severely restricted the numbers of immigrants from Japan and prevented them from owning land in California. As Eaton began her writing career, she saw this bias as a window of opportunity to market herself as a "good Asian." Although currently under revision, Eaton's false identity as a Japanese noblewoman has been theorized by many contemporary scholars as a betrayal of her own people in general and her Chinese mother and activist sister in particular. In addition, her fiction has not aged as well as that of her sister, since she wrote formulaic romances with seemingly little substance and her Japanese heroines often seem caricatured and subservient to Anglo men.

Even Eaton's critics acknowledge the feminist themes that run through her novels and life, however, and her immense popularity in the early twentieth century presents interesting material for scholars formulating new critical approaches to a female literary tradition that is specifically formulaic and laced with genre conventions particular to the romance. The complex issues behind Eaton's multifaceted identity, moreover, have stimulated critical investigations of survival strategies for those women marginalized by race as well as gender or class when they search for appropriate artistic expression.

The Eaton family lived in a French working-class suburb of Montreal when Winnifred was born, and Edward's income as a clerk—he either rejected or was asked to leave the family silk business—was barely enough to support them. In her biography of Sui Sin Far, *Sui Sin Far/Edith Maude Eaton: A Literary Biography* (1995), Annette White-Parks provides graphic evidence of the hardships the family endured when Eaton was growing up, relating that typhus, tuberculosis, and smallpox were dangers in their overcrowded district, which had a high infant mortality rate. The Eatons moved several times within this poor district between 1873 and 1891, and a child was born almost every year while Edward shifted to painting as a full-time career in 1883. In 1876, the year after Eaton was born, the older Eaton children were removed from public school and educated at home, which exacerbated the difficulties of living in a household of more than a dozen people dependent on the earnings of an artist and whatever the older children could bring home. Eaton alludes to her crowded and noisy home in her autobiography, *Me: A Book of Remembrance* (1915); she complains about having to care for the younger children while still a little girl, and chronicles the effects of going hungry much of the time. Despite the family's impoverished circumstances, the children enjoyed a stimulating cultural atmosphere at home under the tutelage of their mother.

Eaton's novel *Marion: The Story of an Artist's Model* (1916) also describes much of the hardship undergone by the family at this time. It begins around 1884, the year before the smallpox epidemic that swept through the Eaton neighborhood, and suggests an awareness of class, gender, and race oppression on the author's part that enriches readers' understanding of her decision to write popular novels as Onoto Watanna. *Marion* is a portrait of Sara Eaton, who was seven years older than Eaton and who wanted to be an actress or a painter. Sara was obviously as much an inspiration to Eaton as was her eldest sister, Edith, portrayed as Ada in the novel. Marion's artistic aspirations are hampered by the desperate need of the family for money. Marion endeavors to support herself as an artist's apprentice, model, and actress while she prepares for a painting career in Boston and New York; Ada continually reminds her that she must contribute to the family as much of her earnings as possible. Marion's career choice is discouraged by their father, who is bitter about his own painting career, and by Ada, who sees in it a dangerous unsavoriness that threatens her younger sister's sexual reputation.

These admonitions are borne out by the prejudices and importunities of men Marion encounters as a young art student dependent on male artists for jobs and on male suitors for financial help. She is stereo-typed as exotic, propositioned, assaulted, insulted, and driven to modeling nude in the course of the narrative, while throughout protesting her right to live an independent life of artistic integrity and personal freedom. She is typecast as a model for orientalist paintings by her dark and foreign looks. Fearing the poverty that drains her family's creativity and battling the gender prejudice that causes men to objectify her and marginalize her art, Marion articulates the difficulties encountered by an economically challenged woman of color struggling to support herself as an artist. The novel provides a glimpse of Eaton's keen awareness of the dangers she had faced as a young woman in a harsh urban environment and the enormity of the obstacles she faced as a writer.

Me and *Marion* were published after Eaton's success as Onoto Watanna, author of nine best-selling Japanese romances between 1899 and 1912, one of which, *A Japanese Nightingale* (1901), was adapted to the Broadway stage (1903), and later to the screen (1917). Her novels were published by Rand McNally; Harper; Macmillan,; Dodd, Mead; and Doubleday during this period, and they received positive reviews while being translated into several languages. Having published *Miss Numè of Japan* with Rand McNally in 1899, which she wrote while supporting herself as a stenographer in Chicago, Eaton built on this success by moving to New York City with little money and finding work as a reporter for a Brooklyn newspaper, where she met her first husband, Bertrand Babcock, another journalist, whom she married in 1901. *A Japanese Nightingale,* her second book, became an overnight best-seller and was tranlated into four languages. On her royalties alone, Eaton was able to support herself, her husband, and her four children in New York during the decade that followed.

The early fame only intensified Eaton's dilemma around her exotic existence as Onoto Watanna. She had found her literary voice and the commercial validation she had sought, but at the cost of a false public identity—a circumstance further complicated by her status as a married woman and the mother of young children. In 1901, for example, *Harper's Weekly* published a feature on Onoto Watanna complete with a photo of her in kimono, describing her as an "Anglo-Japanese" born and raised in Japan with "vivid memories of her girlhood" and "a natural aptitude for writing choice English." Further falsifying the real author is a citation of her age as twenty-three, when she was actually twenty-six. Similarly, *Current Literature* ran a note on Onoto Watanna in 1902 that acknowledged she was "Mrs. B. W. Babcock" in private but also gave the inaccurate age while further embellishing the earlier story of her Japanese origin, saying her father was in the consu-

Binding for Eaton's 1901 novel, about the love affair between a Eurasian geisha and a young American

lar service and she was educated in the United States and England. Positive reviews of Eaton's writing underscore the centrality of this fictionalized biography to perception of the fiction itself: *A Japanese Nightingale,* as a reviewer wrote in *Harper's Weekly,* "was really an achievement for one so young, and a vague analogy between it and her life . . . gives it additional interest." Another issue of *Harper's Weekly* published a glowing review of *The Heart of Hyacinth* (1903) that again subtracts years from Eaton's age. Three photos accompany the piece showing "Onoto Watanna" in Western dress, further complicating her identity.

For a woman who prided herself on being modern, independent, and urban, yet who tied herself to an old-world persona from Japan rather than China, the dislocation that must have accompanied this charade created as many problems of voice as it solved, and these are alluded to in her anonymous autobiography, *Me,* written after Edith died in 1914 and Eaton was recuperating from surgery. In this backward glance at her life during the years she lived in Jamaica, working as a stenographer, then in Chicago, where she wrote her first stories and novels, the narrator discloses her anguish over questions of identity and their inextricable connection to her writing. The narrative reveals what Amy Ling and others have noted as a degree of self-hatred, Eaton's preference for Anglo beauty standards: "People stared at me . . . as if I interested them or they were puzzled to know my nationality. I would have given anything to look less foreign. My darkness marked and crushed me." Racism toward black people in Jamaica is displayed in the narrative as well. At the same time the narrator feels inadequate in the midst of the fame she has earned and guilty about its tenuous connection to her heritage, which is left vague but surfaces repeatedly in the memoir. Referring to Edith, who is unnamed, as "a girl with more real talent than I" and the monument that marks Edith's grave in commemoration of the work she did "for my mother's country," the narrator laments her own poor contribution to that same project: "my dreams of the fame and fortune that not alone should lift me up, but all my people, were built upon a substance as shifting as sand and as shadowy as mist." Elsewhere she states: "My success was founded upon a cheap and popular device, and that jumble of sentimental moonshine that they called my play seemed to me the pathetic stamp of my insufficiency. Oh, I had sold my birthright for a mess of potage! . . . I can truly say of my novels that they are strangely like myself, unfulfilled promises."

The anonymous authorship of *Me* and *Marion,* both published by new presses for her, underscores the constraints placed on Eaton by her success as Onoto Watanna. She could not "come out" as a Chinese Canadian woman with little formal education from a poor Montreal family without risking the loss of her publishing outlets, not to mention her income, having duped the public into thinking she was a Japanese aristocrat. At the same time she yearned to define herself as an artist and as a woman of a real time, place, and heritage while wincing, perhaps, at the betrayal of Edith and her mother in the obituary she wrote for her sister, which maintained the fiction that a Japanese noblewoman mothered the Eaton sisters.

The haunting self-doubt displayed in her anonymous memoir came after a decade and a half of nonstop publishing success, from 1899 to 1912, when Eaton is known to have published ten novels, several essays, and short stories. All this work was published under the name Onoto Watanna, as was one later Japanese novel, *Sunny-San,* published in 1922. Altogether the record shows that Eaton published fifteen books between 1899 and 1925, thirteen novels and two fictionalized memoirs.

The best known of these publications are the ten Japanese novels. These were lavishly illustrated by Japanese artists and printed on decorative paper featuring pictures of women in kimono, birds, flowers, and other symbols of Japan. They were marketed as gift books, suitable for a parlor table or Christmas stocking, and were designed to be read at one sitting. Most reviews were positive. *The New York Times* (19 August 1899) described *Miss Numè of Japan* as "a well-done piece of writing," while William Dean Howells, writing in the *North American Review* (21 December 1901), said of *A Japanese Nightingale:* "There is a quite indescribable freshness in the art of this pretty novelette. . . . such a lesson in the art of imitating nature has not come under my hand for a long while." *Harper's Weekly* (21 December 1901) said of the latter: "it is a gem from the Orient of permanent value," while *Current Literature* (Fall 1902) wrote of it: "*A Japanese Nightingale* . . . suggested something of the strength and power and poetry which she possesses." Japanese writers are also on record as crediting Onoto Watanna's novels with accuracy in depicting Japanese customs.

Contemporary critics have not been as kind to this fiction as were reviewers of Eaton's day, in part because the dialect she uses to present women's speech, for example reversing *r*'s and *l*'s, has historically marked Asian characters as alien and childlike, and in part because the melodramatic literary conventions she employs, common to prewar popular fiction, are hopelessly dated. There are, nevertheless, progressive themes running through the Japanese novels that are of interest to modern readers and important ways in which they challenge race and class prejudice while protesting mistreatment of women. The first novel in this series, *Miss Numè of Japan,* lays out the themes and techniques Eaton exploited so successfully. It features two biracial couples whose love is condemned by their respective families and cultures. Numè is betrothed at age three to a childhood friend, Orito, by their fathers, who are close friends desiring a family connection. While fond of Orito, Numè does not want to marry him when she becomes a young woman; nor does Orito love her in that sense. Both fall in love with Americans from prominent backgrounds who are themselves engaged to each other and whose families are equally determined to see them marry.

While each love story is important to the theme of the narrative–that people should not be forced to marry by families bent on their own selfish ends–the affair between Orito and the debutante with whom he is enchanted is especially significant because his character is drawn in sharp contrast to Asian stereotypes ubiquitous at the time. He is a highly educated Harvard graduate, of wealthy background, handsome, brilliant, and ardently romantic, all qualities that attract the most beautiful American woman on board the ship on which the lovers meet. Although engaged to an American diplomat in Japan, she clearly prefers Orito but rejects him in the end because of pressure from her mother and her own inherited prejudice. Orito's subsequent despair leads to a series of catastrophic events, including his death, while Numè's determination to marry the man of her choice produces happiness when they ultimately wed.

All of the Japanese novels revolve around love stories of this kind, in which couples persist in loving each other when divided by class, racial or other prejudice, forced separations, or family prohibition. Frequently the heroine is an outcast who must resort to cunning for her survival as well. *A Japanese Nightingale* features a Eurasian geisha who charms an American university graduate and causes him ethical difficulties when he is able to buy her hand in marriage. Occupying in many ways the position of concubine although presented as a virgin, this character is the sole support of a brother's education in America and gives all her money to her widowed mother. *The Wooing of Wistaria* (1902), which features a cast made up entirely of Japanese characters, concerns the daughter of a banished samurai in the Tokugawa era. Her mother was murdered the day after her birth, and she was raised by the class of outcasts known as *eta* or *burakumin* (leather workers and menial laborers). Aware of her half-caste status, this character's paternal aunt drives a wedge between her niece and the noble prince she loves.

In *The Heart of Hyacinth,* which is set shortly after the Matthew Perry expedition opened Japan to commerce with the West in 1854, the son of an English sailor and widowed Japanese mother grows up with the orphaned child of a white woman brought to his mother's home and then raised as a Japanese girl. Betrothed to the son of a wealthy Japanese businessman despite his contempt for her background, the heroine finds herself drawn more to her Eurasian adopted brother, who has been educated in the West. She not only breaks her engagement to marry the Eurasian but rejects the courtship of an English lawyer hired by her biological father to find her.

The Love of Azalea (1904) centers on another orphan, one of Japanese descent who marries a white minister. The couple is forced apart by a Japanese tradesman who covets Azalea and actually buys her. Having borne her husband's child, Azalea is economically dependent on her wealthy oppressor but abandons him to live by her wits in the countryside. In *Daughters of Nijo: A Romance of Japan* (1904), another novel with only Japanese characters, the daughter of a royal family breaks her engagement to a crown prince to marry a court sculptor who comes from a farming family. *A Japanese Blossom* (1906) features a Japanese widower who marries an American, and they blend their children by other marriages. *Tama* (1910) focuses on the blind orphaned daughter of a Buddhist nun and English sailor who were murdered by villagers when the child was ten and who has since lived by her cunning in the woods. She falls in love with a white doctor afflicted with smallpox scars who protects her from the villagers, restores her sight, and marries her.

The Honorable Miss Moonlight (1912) and *Sunny-San* (1922) also feature orphans, both geishas who are owned by cruel teahouse owners and rescued by men who love them. In the former, the characters are once again all Japanese. The rescuer is a prince, but the couple is forced apart by his family, and the heroine nearly dies after the divorce, becoming a beggar while pregnant with her lover's child. *Sunny-San* takes place largely in the United States, where the Eurasian heroine has been brought by four young American men who want to Americanize her. Marred by racist allusions, the narrative nevertheless excoriates an American senator, the heroine's father, who bought her Japanese mother in a loveless match that was ruptured when she ran away with her baby rather than give her to him.

Abuse of women is common in these novels. Some heroines are beaten or sold into servitude as virtual concubines. Others are banished from households to fend for themselves as orphans. Most are in vulnerable economic circumstances with no means of support except as geishas in a feudal landscape that is undergoing rapid capitalist development in the late nineteenth century. Japanese women at this time were trapped in a patriarchal world where they had little say in their destiny, and it is significant that this is the setting to which Eaton returned time after time. It allowed her to protest subjugation of women by family and economic structures not so far removed from Victorian America but safely displaced to a foreign land. She constructed fairy tales of benevolent rescue by Japanese or Caucasian Prince Charmings, to be sure, but her heroines also take fate into their own hands in seemingly powerless situations, finding ways to survive the dislocations that propel them into outcast positions. They parallel similar narratives of rescue by American writers who featured orphaned girls reduced to prostitution or servitude in late-nineteenth-century urban America. Despite their reliance on rescue, however, the women of Eaton's Japanese novels actively choose their lovers without regard to class, status, or race, despite their economic vulnerability, and reject the men to whom they are pledged or sold.

It is true there are troubling stereotypes in these novels of Asian men as cruel tyrants who make women their slaves, and too often white men intervene as rescuers, reinforcing a supremacist master narrative of Western patriarchal colonialism. At the same time, while white men often attract these abused women, so too do Japanese or Eurasian men, and Caucasians frequently abandon their Japanese wives in irresponsible affairs. Similarly, Western values are upheld in many instances, but Japanese traditions are valorized as equally important, and disregard of them is explicitly condemned. The novels move in contradictory directions: they are laced with Asian stereotypes of brutal tradesmen, manipulative evil matriarchs, and childlike female servility, but they also offer Asian characters who are heroic, ethical, romantic, and handsome. Women in particular are featured in positive roles as supportive of one another and as strong, willful survivors capable of self-sufficiency.

Similarly, Japan is portrayed in traditional exotic terms complete with samurai, teahouses, and jinrickshas, but it is also a place where department stores are

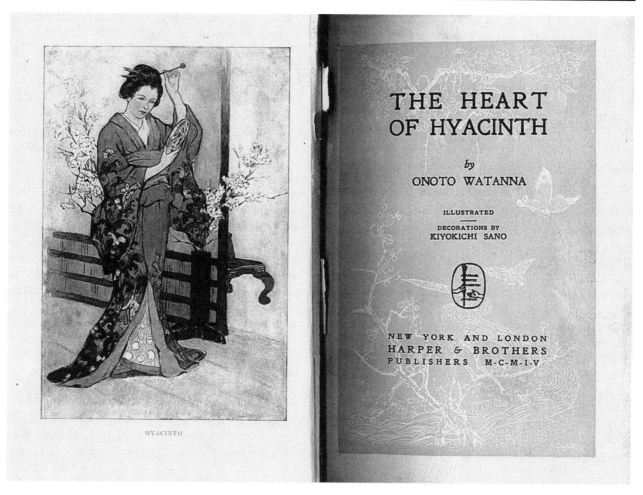

HYACINTH

Frontispiece and title page for Eaton's fourth novel, set in Japan shortly after the arrival of Commodore Matthew Perry in 1854

rapidly being built; Western sailors, lawyers, and doctors abound; and "meek" women rebel against the traditions that bind them. While white male ministers and other representatives of Western culture are uncomfortably presented as superior to Japanese men steeped in male privilege, there are enough examples of Eurasian or Japanese heroes who treat women well to contest the stereotypes that run through the narratives. Likewise, the explicit valorization of Japanese culture in all of the novels helps subvert the often parallel privileging of Western ways. The three works that feature only Japanese characters, in particular, reinforce a clear theme in Eaton's Japanese fiction of the essential validity standing behind Asian difference, the existence of an ancient, rich civilization superior in many ways to the West.

Finally, the overriding theme of these novels is that love surfaces spontaneously in young people regardless of class, caste, or race divisions and is a force that needs to be nurtured if the world is ever to eliminate violence, cruelty, hatred, and even war. Although

the love is often self-abnegating, being that of a young Japanese girl for an older white man, other pairings abound that interrogate class privilege, racism, caste bias, and patriarchal domination. At a time when miscegenation laws were unquestioned in America, with few biracial couples daring to transgress them, Eaton's Japanese novels stand as a flawed but consistent counternarrative that foregrounds lovers who risk everything to be together. Ultimately, the novels posit young unprejudiced love as a force stronger than the power of money, family, racial bias, or patriarchal authority.

These themes run through the magazine publications from this period as well. The heroine of "Two Converts" (*Harper's Monthly,* September 1901) leaves her loveless marriage to a Japanese man to marry a white missionary, while the reverse occurs in "The Wrench of Chance" (*Harper's Weekly,* 20–27 October 1906) when the battered Japanese wife of an Irish sailor falls in love with a Japanese doctor. "Miss Lily and Miss Chrysanthemum, The Love Story of Two Japanese Girls in Chicago" (*Ladies Home Journal,* August 1903) features a Eurasian teacher in Chicago who breaks her engagement to a wealthy Japanese chemist to marry an American lawyer, and a Japanese illusionist successfully woos a white woman working in his group of New York carnival performers in "The Loves of Sakura Jiro and the Three-Headed Maid" (*Century,* March 1903).

Eaton buttressed her attacks on prejudice against biracial romance implicit in these tales with nonfiction articles in which she explicates and defends Japanese customs: "The Japanese Drama and the Actor" (*The Critic,* September 1902), "The Marvelous Miniature Trees of Japan" (*Woman's Home Companion,* June 1904), "Every-day Life in Japan" (*Harper's Weekly,* 2 April 1904), and "The Japanese in America" (*The Eclectic,* February 1907). "The Japanese in America" is an impassioned criticism of a *New York Times* article that made derogatory remarks about Japanese who insisted they were superior to whites and reported that American correspondents to the Russo-Japanese War returned with "eternal condemnation for everything Japanese." Rising in spirited defense of the right of Japanese immigrants to be ambitious and to have pride in their culture, she turned the essay into a broadside against anti-Asian prejudice: "To speak of the Oriental nations as inferior is to make an ignorant and stupid statement. . . . Are we no better than in the time when the white-skinned Spaniards came all conquering to exterminate the darker-hued man of the New World? Do the Western nations, indeed, cherish the childish delusion that a race as proud and intelligent as the Japanese or Chinese could be likewise subjected?"

This full-throated assault on the bigotry that Eaton and her siblings experienced all their lives suggests that her writings were designed to do more than entertain, that a theme of tolerance for Asian peoples and culture was consciously woven through her Japanese romances. Reinforcing this interpretation are the final lines of her 1907 essay, in which she says she is Irish as well as English, Chinese as well as Japanese: "Both my fatherland and my motherland have been the victims of injustice and oppression. Sometimes I dream of the day when all of us will be world citizens—not citizens merely of petty portions of the earth, showing our teeth at each other, snarling, sneering, biting, and with the ambition of the murderer at our heart's core—every man with the savage instinct of the wild beast to get the better of his brother—to prove his greater strength—his mightier mind—the superiority of his color."

Whether because the anti-Japanese sentiment Eaton attacks in "The Japanese in America" increased after the 1906 Russo-Japanese War or because the charade of Onoto Watanna became increasingly problem-atic, there is a clear break in her publication record after *A Japanese Blossom* was published in 1906. In 1907 Eaton tried to publish a different narrative, that of an Irish domestic servant, under the name Winnifred Mooney. It was titled *The Diary of Delia, Being a Veracious Chronicle of the Kitchen with Some Side-lights on the Parlour* and initially serialized in *The Saturday Evening Post.* The name change was vetoed by her publishers, but the novel can be viewed as an attempt to move closer to her true identity as an Irish English/Chinese Canadian woman of a complex class background. It is a comic account of a domestic worker written in Irish dialect and quite different in tone from the romantic melodramas for which she was famous. Although she published two more Japanese novels in 1910 and 1912, *The Diary of Delia* signaled Eaton's desire to break free of her own mold and venture into other narrative structures. Significantly, she wrote her two anguished memoirs after a three-year publication void, both published anonymously in 1915 and 1916 by presses other than her editorial home of Harper Brothers. This period was one of significant changes in Eaton's personal life: her sister Edith died in 1914; her father died in 1915; her mother moved to New York shortly after her husband's death; and she divorced the alcoholic Babcock in 1916 to marry an American tugboat entrepreneur and rancher, Francis Fournier Reeve, the next year. Moving to his Alberta cattle ranch after the marriage, Winnifred Eaton Babcock Reeve did not publish another novel for six years.

This hiatus in Eaton's literary production was followed by one last Japanese novel published under her pen name in 1922 and two final novels with no Japanese characters at all, set on an Alberta cattle ranch and both credited to her real name. *Cattle* (1923) and *His Royal Nibs* (1925) follow similar thematic paths, highlighting the author's characteristic concerns with abuse of women, the struggle of lovers to overcome barriers set between them by society, and her efforts to integrate the disparate pieces of her identity. *Cattle* is Eaton's bleakest, most violent novel. It features a brutal Canadian cattle rancher who ruthlessly poaches from the Indian reserve that borders his property in his desire to build up the biggest cattle operation in Alberta. He is so abusive to his gentle wife that she is childless after eight miscarriages over the course of their long, unhappy marriage. Furthermore, he has raped an Indian woman whose subsequent child was forced to live in his home and was brain damaged by blows from his father.

The violence of this evil man is visited upon the heroine, Nettie Day, a motherless girl of fifteen who looks after her poor farmer father and nine siblings; when her father dies and the farm is sold, she is bought by the tyrannical cattle baron. Although treated well by his kind wife, Nettie is raped by her employer and bears his child, a son who dies in infancy by his father's hand. Counterbalancing this grim tale is the love for Nettie Day of an ambitious ranch hand, a benevolent doctor, and a staunchly feminist woman farmer who takes her in when she is pregnant. Together they grow a valuable field of corn while forming an intense personal bond. The brutality of the wealthy baron is juxtaposed with the maternal space created by the two women who care for the Native American teenager fathered by their enemy and who do all the work on a successful farm where no animals are hurt or slaughtered.

His Royal Nibs similarly features Hilda, the oldest motherless girl of a family with ten children; but the patriarch of the cattle ranch on which she lives, although unavoidably cruel to the branded and dehorned cattle, is a mirror image of the villain in *Cattle*. His ranch also adjoins an Indian reserve, but he employs the inhabitants routinely, treating them fairly, while the heroine is the apple of his eye, his favorite child. She follows in her father's footsteps, becoming an accomplished horsewoman and cattle rancher while delivering food daily to the Indian reserve, where she is loved, particularly by an unhappy young woman with a mixed-race baby. In both novels adolescent girls make their way in a macho frontier environment, a bleak and motherless landscape that ultimately furnishes gentle caretakers who enable them to inhabit a cultured, literate, more humane world. They are rescued by husbands, however, only after they have proven themselves capable of succeeding at men's work. Ethnic themes exist in both works, as there are Native Americans and two Chinese cooks, but they are muted; the love stories and major dramas involve white characters. Marginality continues to surface, however, via gender and class issues, and Eaton's consistent protest against violence is arguably more apparent in these last two novels than it was in the preceding thirteen books.

With the publication of her ranching novels, Eaton's fiction-writing career came to an end, but there remained one last professional venture: from 1925 to 1931 she worked in Hollywood as a scriptwriter and scenarist for Universal and MGM studios. There she wrote for *Shanghai Lady* (1929) and other films and her own adapted novels. Not much is known about this period of her life, but it is clear that by the time she settled in Canada with her second husband, Eaton had distanced herself from her Japanese persona and reclaimed her English Canadian side. James Doyle reports that in her later years, after she returned to Canada from Los Angeles, Eaton told a Canadian reporter soon after Canada entered World War II that she was ashamed of her Japanese novels and proud of the fact that she had a Chinese mother. Such a refutation of her claim to fame undoubtedly emerged from the political climate surrounding her, but as well there is a kind of closure on her former inability to come to terms with the ethnic fault lines that plagued her as the first Asian American novelist.

The source of Eaton's pen name is as elusive as the woman wielding the pen. Amy Ling reports several versions of what might have inspired the pseudonym Onoto Watanna. "Onoto" was the name of a pen made in England and imported by Japan from 1907 until 1955. According to another, the Western-made Onoto pen was used by most Japanese writers in the Meiji era. A third version is that Eaton took the name from a character in turn-of-the-century Eurasian writer Lafcadio Hearn's work. Finally, it is possible that the pen's manufacturer got permission from Winnifred Eaton to use her name. Certainly she chose the name because it sounded Japanese, although it is not in fact an authentic Japanese name. There is, in addition, characteristic wit in her adopting a pen name that is actually the name of a pen. Similarly, embedded in *Watanna* is a clue to the author's real identity: she employs a double *n*, a non-Japanese spelling that evokes her preferred spelling of *Winnifred,* even though her birth certificate identifies her as "Lillie Winifred." Ultimately, the origin of "Onoto Watanna" reflects the mysteries of Eaton's life, obscured by denial, nativist bigotry, gender and class oppression, camouflage, and market restrictions.

Winnifred Eaton died on 8 April 1954 at age seventy-eight in Butte, Montana, en route to her Calgary home after a western vacation in the country where she achieved professional success. It is fitting that she died in the United States, where she lived for eighteen years and created Onoto Watanna. Eaton was buried in Calgary, however, in the country of her birth and the place she chose to live out her remaining twenty-three years. Her papers are there as well.

Except for Edith, who remained single and claimed a Chinese identity, all of Winnifred's upwardly mobile, impressively successful siblings married Caucasians and passed for Mexican or Caucasian themselves. As Amy Ling observes, they all chose to accommodate the racism from which they suffered in the manner of ethnic chameleons who survive by blending into their environment. Eaton's own act of camouflage took place on a much more public level and thus leaves troubling questions about the authenticity of her work and its lasting value to literary scholars engaged in the recovery of lost writers. To what degree is the fiction of Onoto Watanna riddled with demeaning Asian stereotypes adopted out of self-hatred and opportunism? To what use can such fiction be put when those same stereotypes animate the contemporary cultural scene?

Even if a strong counternarrative that subverts cultural stereotypes can be identified in Eaton's work, does reviving that work contribute to her betrayal of her Chinese identity?

These are questions that will likely vex Eaton scholars for some time to come, yet they are worth wrestling with: her groundbreaking literary venture cannot be discounted given the paucity of nonwhite voices in print at the dawn of the twentieth century. Perhaps it is sufficient to acknowledge the enormity of Eaton's accomplishment without praising unduly the literary content and to hear her voice with its many discordant notes without judging too harshly her failures. Above all, this first Asian American novelist tells much about the pitfalls awaiting women of color as they have attempted to find their voice in modern America.

References:

Diana Birchal, *Her* (Urbana: University of Illinois Press, forthcoming 2000);

James Doyle, "Sui Sin Far and Onoto Watanna: Two Early Chinese-Canadian Authors," *Canadian Literature,* 140 (Spring 1994): 50–58;

Amy Ling, *Between Worlds: Women Writers of Chinese Ancestry* (New York: Pergamon, 1990): 21–55;

Ling, "Chinese American Women Writers: The Tradition behind Maxine Hong Kingston," in *Redefining American Literary History,* edited by A. LaVonne Brown Ruoff and Jerry W. Ward Jr. (New York: Modern Language Association, 1990): 219–230;

Ling, "Creating One's Self: The Eaton Sisters," in *Reading the Literatures of Asian America,* edited by Ling and Shirley Geok-lin Lim (Philadelphia: Temple University Press, 1992): 305–318;

Ling, "Gender Issues in Early Chinese American Autobiography," in *A Gathering of Voices on the Asian American Experience,* edited by Annette White-Parks (Ft. Atkinson, Wis.: Highsmith, 1994): 101–111;

Ling, "Winnifred Eaton: Ethnic Chameleon and Popular Success," *MELUS,* 2 (Fall 1984): 5–15;

White-Parks, *Sui Sin Far/Edith Maude Eaton: A Literary Biography* (Urbana: University of Illinois Press, 1995).

Papers:

Winnifred Eaton's papers are housed at the University of Calgary.

Sarah Barnwell Elliott

(29 November 1848 – 30 August 1928)

Susan Neal Mayberry
Alfred University

BOOKS: *The Felmeres* (New York: Appleton, 1879);
A Simple Heart (New York: Ireland, 1887);
Jerry (New York: Holt, 1891);
John Paget (New York: Holt, 1893);
The Durket Sperret (New York: Holt, 1898);
An Incident and Other Happenings (New York: Harper, 1899);
Sam Houston, Beacon Biographies of Eminent Americans, edited by M. A. De Wolfe Howe (Boston: Small, Maynard, 1900);
The Making of Jane (New York: Holt, 1901);
Sewanee: Past and Present (Sewanee, Tenn.: Sewanee University Press, 1909).

OTHER: "Some Data," in *From Dixie,* edited by Mrs. K. P. Minor (Richmond, Va.: West, Johnson, 1893);
"Augustine Birrel," "E. B. Browning," and "Sir Richard Burton," in *Library of the World's Best Literature,* 30 volumes, edited by Charles Dudley Warner (New York: Peale & Hill, 1896–1897).

PLAY PRODUCTION: *His Majesty's Servant,* London, Imperial Theater, 6 October 1904.

SELECTED PERIODICAL PUBLICATIONS–
UNCOLLECTED: "Jack Watson–A Character Study," *Current,* 6 (11 September 1886): 164–167;
"Loitering in Paris," *Louisville Courier-Journal,* 9 January 1887, p. 16;
"From Paris to Pisa," *Louisville Courier-Journal,* 23 January 1887, p. 14;
"Rome," *Louisville Courier-Journal,* 13 February 1887, p. 9;
"Across the Way," *Louisville Courier-Journal,* 20 March 1887, p. 14;
"The Land of Ham," *Louisville Courier-Journal,* 21 March 1887, p. 4;
"Miss Eliza," *Independent,* 39 (24 March 1887): 26–27;
"Sights in Egypt," *Louisville Courier-Journal,* 20 April 1887, p. 2;

Yours very truly,
Sarah Barnwell Elliott

"Jerusalem," *Louisville Courier-Journal,* 29 April 1887, p. 2;
"Jerusalem the Holy," *Louisville Courier-Journal,* 8 May 1887, p. 19;
"The City of Flowers," *Louisville Courier-Journal,* 12 May 1887, p. 3;
"Florence," *Louisville Courier-Journal,* 5 June 1887, p. 16;

"An Idle Man," *Independent,* 39 (9 June 1887): 26–28;

"Etruscan Gods," *Louisville Courier-Journal,* 18 June 1887, p. 4;

"Siena, Italy," *Louisville Courier-Journal,* 3 July 1887, p. 14;

"In the Tyrol," *Louisville Courier-Journal,* 19 July 1887, p. 4;

"Merry England," *Louisville Courier-Journal,* 14 August 1887, p. 14;

"Oxford, England," *Louisville Courier-Journal,* 16 August 1887, p. 2.

"Old England," *Louisville Courier-Journal,* 28 August 1887, p. 16;

"As a Little Child," *Independent,* 39 (8 December 1887): 226–228;

"A Florentine Idyl," *Independent,* 40 (2 February 1888): 26–29;

"Stephen's Margaret," *Independent,* 40 (5 July 1888): 26–28;

"Some Recent Fiction," *Sewanee Review,* 3 (November 1894): 90–104;

"Father Tabb's Poems," *Sewanee Review,* 3 (May 1895): 431–436;

"Jim's Victory," *Book News,* 16 (October 1897): 47–53;

"Miss Ann's Victory," *Harper's Bazar,* 31 (9 April 1898): 317–318;

"A Race That Lives in Mountain Coves," *Ladies Home Journal,* 15 (September 1898): 11–12;

"Hands All Round," *Book News,* 17 (September 1898): 1–6;

"Fortune's Vassals," *Lippincott's Magazine,* 64 (August 1899): 163–253;

"Progress," *McClure's Magazine,* 14 (November 1899): 40–47;

"Rest Remaineth," *Pilgrim,* 1 (1900): n.p.;

"Beside Still Waters," *Youth's Companion,* 72 (9 August 1900): 385–386;

"Alone," *Harper's Bazar,* 30 (15 September 1900): 1238;

"The Spirit of the Nineteenth Century in Fiction," *Outlook,* 67 (19 January 1901): 153–158;

"Some Remnants," *Youth's Companion,* 75 (18 April 1901): 198–199;

"Study of Song in Florence," *Harper's Bazar,* 36 (March 1902): 215–222;

"A Little Child Shall Lead Them," *Youth's Companion,* 76 (18 December 1902): 649–650;

"What Polly Knew," *Smart Set,* 9 (February 1903): 121–123;

"After Long Years," *Youth's Companion,* 77 (23 April 1903): 197–198;

"Old Mrs. Dally's Lesson," *Youth's Companion,* 78 (29 December 1904): 660–661;

"Hybrid Roses," *Harper's,* 113 (August 1906): 434–449;

"Ibsen," *Sewanee Review,* 15 (January 1907): 75–99;

"The Opening of the Southwestern Door," *Youth's Companion,* 81 (28 February 1907): 100–101;

"The Wreck," *Youth's Companion,* 81 (19 December 1907): 637–639;

"Two Collections of Verse," *Sewanee Review,* 16 (October 1908): 506–507;

Review of *Little Brown Brother,* by Stanley P. Hyatt, *Sewanee Review,* 16 (October 1908): 507–509;

"A Study of Women and Civilization," *Forensic Quarterly Review,* 1 (February 1910): 90–101;

"Readjustments," *Harper's Magazine,* 120 (May 1910): 824–832;

"An Epoch-Making Settlement Between Labor and Capital," *Forensic Quarterly Review,* 1 (June 1910): 129–144;

"Manifesto," *Nashville Banner,* 17 August 1912, sec. 2, p. 7;

"The Last Flash," *Scribner's Magazine,* 57 (June 1915): 692–695;

"The Sewanee Spirit," *Bulletin of the University of the South,* 13 (August 1918);

Review of *The Life and Letters of James Monroe Taylor,* by Elizabeth Hazelton Haight, *Sewanee Review,* 28 (July 1920): 467–472;

Review of *Old and New: Sundry Papers,* by Charles H. Grandgent, *Sewanee Review,* 29 (January 1921): 122–123;

Review of *La Dame de Sainte Hermine,* by Grace King, *Sewanee Review,* 32 (July 1924): 373–374;

Review of *The Avalanche,* by Ernest Poole, *Sewanee Review,* 32 (October 1924): 503–505;

Review of *The Southern Plantation,* by Francis P. Gaines, *Sewanee Review,* 33 (July 1925): 353–357;

Review of *Southern Pioneers,* edited by Howard W. Odum, *Sewanee Review,* 34 (April 1926): 238–239.

Novelist, short-story writer, playwright, essayist, and suffragist Sarah Bull Barnwell Elliott enjoyed a fair measure of personal and professional success in her day. She is important as a precursor of the Southern literary renaissance and as an early feminist. Elliott's varied body of writing reveals a woman of keenness and wit, a risk-taker and perceptive observer who held to strong opinions and was not afraid to state them. Her biography reveals a wealthy and prestigious family background, an enlightened education, and an unmarried freedom that opened doors to her that were closed to the majority of nineteenth-century American women, especially Southern women. Sharing traits with the turn-of-the-century "New Woman" that she delineated in her fiction, Elliott wrote to her brother in 1871, "When a woman gives up all idea of matrimony, she either turns saint or woman's rights." Though she threatened the former, by 1895 she was supporting herself by writing in New York City, where she also took up the suffragist cause. Her journal entry for 1 January 1896, reads: "Yesterday I took possession of my own time, of myself." Early biographical sketches of Elliott's long and fruitful life generally describe her in relation to the men of her family, citing her as the daughter and sister of distinguished Episcopal bishops as opposed to a professional in her own right. Her remarkable contributions must be viewed in the context of a period of national crisis, economic adversity, and conservative anti-intellectualism as well as the prevailing Southern skepticism toward women, spinsters, and ardent feminists. In addition, the nineteenth-century South's admiration and support for oratory over literary effort, an attitude that hardened into almost a regional indifference toward native writers, provided another obstacle to Elliott's professional career. Surrounded by a family of prominent men of letters, Elliott was, however, the only member of her family to earn a national—even international—reputation as a writer, but her achievements were virtually ignored in the South until 1913, when she was awarded an honorary doctorate of civil law from the University of the South.

Elliott's intense regional loyalty, comparatively liberal stance, religious faith in moral betterment for all, and her writing skills were shaped by a family legacy of intellectual ability and leadership. Born on 29 November 1848 in Montpelier, Georgia, into the intimate circle that was the tidewater South's planter aristocracy, Sarah Bull Barnwell Elliott was the fifth child and second daughter of the Right Reverend Stephen Elliott Jr., first Episcopal bishop of Georgia, and his second wife, Charlotte Bull Barnwell. Sarah was named for her maternal grandmother, and her forbears on that side of the family were among the earliest settlers in South Carolina and Georgia and included no fewer than four colonial governors. Her father's ancestors were English Quakers who settled in Charleston before 1690. Sarah's grandfather, Stephen Elliott, was cofounder and editor of the distinguished but short-lived *Southern Review* and a founder of what later became the University of South Carolina and the Medical College of Charleston, earning for himself the title "Father of Free Public Education" in South Carolina. The grandfather's emphasis on enlightenment over wealth influenced both his son and his grandchildren. Another writer in the family, Elliott's uncle William Elliott, became a model for his niece's literary realism. The local-color vein of her work, her rejection of the romantic mythmaking of many postbellum Southern writers, and her moral impulse were influenced by her uncle's realistic depictions of the world of the Carolina country squire. His collected newspaper sketches, *Carolina Sports by Land and Water* (1846), became a minor sports classic. Her father's lib-

eralism and missionary spirit, which drove him in 1841 from a career in South Carolina politics to Savannah, Georgia, and the ministry, undoubtedly influenced the daughter's stories outlining the gradual elevation of slaves through religious instruction and education. This conviction of the rightness of full citizenship both for African Americans and for women translated into her fiction and a 1910 essay, "Women and Civilization."

Significantly, Sarah Elliott's birthplace was the site of a seminary for young women, the Georgia Episcopal Institute, founded by Bishop Elliott in 1842. In 1845 the bishop moved his family from Savannah to Montpelier, where he could personally direct the school's operation while continuing to oversee his diocese. Sarah's natural aptitude was encouraged by a scholarly atmosphere in a pleasant rural setting and by parents of unusual intelligence and social distinction who had the courage and vision to promote the education of women at a time when there were few institutions of higher education even for men. While profits from a working farm, endowments, and tuition were intended to render the school self-supporting, Bishop Elliott was forced to pledge his own estate to pay the salaries of an exceptionally fine faculty from the North and Europe. His belief in the ultimate eradication of slavery and discomfort with his own position as slaveholder were resolved when all of his property, including his slaves, was sold to pay the school's debts, and the family returned to Savannah in 1852 to a life of genteel poverty.

Elliott's later stories picture a childhood reflecting the traditions, hospitality, grace, and tolerance that even critic H. L. Mencken, who decried the New South's dearth of culture in his 1917 essay "The Sahara of the Bozart," conceded to be the old South's "art of living." However, the Elliott family recognized that this "exhilarating experience," this "vague thing that we call culture," was maintained upon the backs of slaves. Relatives had for years transgressed the slave laws that forbade the teaching of reading or keeping of accounts by slaves. Elliott not only endorsed her family's approbation of abolition; she also developed through her early and close association with black people an affection and understanding of them as individuals. In her stories African Americans are treated for the most part sympathetically, but sentimental stereotypes are eschewed for the distinctiveness of a character such as Kizzy in "Faith and Faithfulness" (1896) with her sensitivity and devotion to her former mistress.

Promoting the highest tenets of eighteenth-century enlightenment culminating in social responsibility, generations of Elliotts had consciously cultivated skill in oral and written expression along with a belief in regular intellectual discipline aimed at a knowledge of history, literature, and the natural sciences as well as a love

Elliott at her house in Sewanee, Tennessee, where she lived for most of her life

of music and poetry. The writings of the Elliott children, including Sarah, reveal two major influences on their early development: the impact of religion on their daily lives and the need to earn a living by their wits rather than by the agricultural labor of others. As such, though frugality was the norm, early life was secure and cheerful despite the lack of material possessions. While an extended family network supplemented gifts of foodstuffs and social entertainment, there were no funds to provide higher education for the girls, though each of the brothers was prepared for one of the professions.

Elliott's education was completed at home during the turbulent Civil War years, when the Elliotts attempted to maintain some semblance of family life in Savannah despite the hardships of the Union occupation of the city. She saw little of her father, who was preoccupied during this time with political and church issues and with his last great accomplishment, the founding of a church-supported university in the South. By the time classes opened at the University of the South in Sewanee, Tennessee, in 1867, Bishop Elliott

had died suddenly, dealing Sarah the severest blow of her childhood. Her recovery from this loss and her entry into the adult world were symbolized by her decision to take a new name; she called herself Sada for the rest of her life.

Sewanee and the 1870s proved to be significant for Elliott's career. Shuffled among relatives after Bishop Elliott's death, the Elliott women accompanied newly married brother John, who took a position at the University of the South in Sewanee. Initially accommodated in one of the dormitories, they all moved into a house designed and built by John and referred to as "Saint's Rest," with an adjoining dwelling called "Sinner's Hope" housing a dozen university students. In an unpublished novel, "Madeline," Elliott describes an aristocratic Southern matron who felt humiliated by being forced to keep a boardinghouse, one of the few respectable ways for a nineteenth-century woman to augment her family income. Southern hospitality was maintained even under such circumstances, however, and Elliott continued the tidewater practice of keeping "open house" every Sunday afternoon long after her mother's death. Elliott described herself in letters as "obstinate, rather selfish and supercilious, quite a tease, not very intimate with anything but her own shadow"; and while she promised not to disgrace the family with a "vocation in the Forum," she also asserted that she was not "made for a Saint." At twenty-two she was evolving for herself an alternative way of life–that of detached recorder of experience. Despite increased responsibility for and the small, daily frustrations of living in a large family, including "that everlasting baby, howling in the next room," she devoted a few hours each day to her writing, developing a terse, public voice and a style that sold her books.

In 1878 Elliott attempted to publish some of her manuscripts. Her writing career was launched in her thirty-first year when D. Appleton Company of Chicago published her first novel, *The Felmeres,* in the spring of 1879. Having chosen to "quite sneer matrimony down" as she divided her time among work, community and family responsibilities, and looking after the boarding house as well as her mother and younger sister, Elliott continued to vacillate between the polarities of "sainthood or woman's rights." A similar conflict confronts heroine Helen Felmere, who, in the midst of a tract on religious speculation, appears less woman than vehicle for a discussion of the legal and moral position of nineteenth-century women. Like Dorothea of George Eliot's 1871–1872 novel, *Middlemarch,* Helen marries out of duty; she is refused, because of her atheism, the right to rear her child as she would and possesses, as her only defense, her property, which her Christian in-laws try to take from her. Though couched in religious arguments, the feminist issues of marriage, property, and personal destiny are rendered more effectively in this darkly gothic tale than its martyr/heroine.

Elliott developed the complexity as well as the breadth of her characterization over the next decade as opportunities for travel and study suggested a greater variety of themes, settings, and vehicles for writing. Accompanying her brother, Bishop Robert Elliott, back to Texas for a visit after a family wedding, she took over the reportorial duties of the diocesan newsletter, the *Church Record,* for which Bishop Elliott was a principal contributor. For four months, "S.B.E." enlivened the generally dull format of the newsletter with her unmistakably vivacious style, publishing a description of a journey through northern Mexico, a mildly satiric column discussing decorum in the frontier churches, and even funeral accounts. Back in Sewanee, Elliott attempted to shape her frontier experiences into stories, and the Texas territory was the setting for three short pieces, a character sketch, and two lengthy short stories. Unlike *The Felmeres,* which was modeled after the mid-century British novel, this fiction emphasized American

local color, introducing regional dialect, frontier justice and scenery, and a moralistic tone.

Elliott's work was further enriched in 1886 when she became the first woman to attend summer classes at Johns Hopkins University, where women were not formally admitted as students until 1890. Largely self-educated, Elliott continued the family tradition of advocating higher education for women as well as men by helping to formulate in 1910 a plan for an extension school at the University of the South. The opportunity in 1886–1887 to accompany her ailing brother Robert to Europe and the Holy Land led to a contract with the *Louisville Courier-Journal* to publish several of her pieces as well as a series of travel sketches she proposed to write from various cities along the way. Partially funded by the sale of her story "A Simple Heart" to *The Independent,* a large national weekly magazine, the trip placed Elliott in the company of other nineteenth-century American writers who had made similar journeys. Though aware of Mark Twain's *Innocents Abroad* (1869), Elliott strove for originality in writing that was didactic but not without satiric humor founded on incongruity. Robert Elliott's condition having deteriorated in Egypt enough to require his return home, she continued her observations alone. Her last letter was printed on 28 August, two days after her brother's death at Sewanee. Elliott's sixteen sketches were never collected, although seven short stories–also none of which were collected– and the European scenes in her last novel were inspired by her experiences abroad.

Experiments with frontier or European settings and a variety of subjects and themes had taught Elliott the fundamentals of her craft but had not produced what would be her most important contributions to the literature of local color and realism. Following the advice of expatriate writer Constance Fenimore Woolson, in whose emphasis on realistic Southern characters Elliott recognized her own strength, she began upon her return home to depict the prewar and postwar South she knew best for the national audience she aspired to reach. Elliott found readers receptive in the 1880s to her realistic rendering of mountain cove people, blacks, returned veterans, and impoverished gentlewomen, and, having acquired the service of Woolson's New York literary agent, she began to place stories with *Harper's, Scribner's,* and *Lippincott's.* She also transformed her grief over brother Robert's death into a novel, *John Paget* (1893), which contained numerous parallels with the bishop's life and ideas about the decline of orthodoxy, the growth of wealth, and the problems of industrialization.

Simultaneously, Elliott embarked on a more ambitious project, a local-color novel delineating characters from the Cumberland Mountains. Combining her knowledge of mountain habits and speech with research on railroads, mining operations, and current economic theories, she produced *Jerry* (1891), her most popular novel and greatest financial success. It is the story of a mountain boy who, fleeing his brutal father, is adopted by a backcountry gold miner. Jerry is educated by the town doctor, becoming a teacher and community labor leader, and inherits the miner's secret fortune but, corrupted by wealth, falls to a tragic end. An overnight success, the book led to the publication of *John Paget* and a reissuing of *The Felmeres*. Elliott's professional success was insured with the publication of a series of spare, well-written, realistic stories based on her family experiences and providing a kind of loose social history of the Deep South from 1850.

Elliott used the freedom provided by her new-found financial security and the death of her mother to move to New York City and, for the first time in her forty-seven years, devote her time entirely to herself. She remained in New York "in the thick of things" from 1896 to 1901, writing two more novels, a novella, a biography of General Sam Houston, seventeen short articles and stories, and a short-story collection, as well as entertaining and being entertained by a wide circle of friends that included some of the great names in American letters of her day. Elliott was commissioned by the magazine *Outlook* to write an essay titled "The Spirit of the Nineteenth Century in Fiction" and also ventured into writing for the theater. *His Majesty's Servant*, a romantic play about the English Cavaliers, opened at the Imperial Theater, London, on 6 October 1904, and ran successfully for one hundred performances.

Discouraged by the shift in popular taste away from local-color material and responding to family crises, Elliott returned to Sewanee in 1902 to become adoptive parent, at the age of fifty-four, to the three adolescent sons of her dead sister, Charlotte. In the nine years that followed she succeeded in helping "her boys," Stephen, Charles, and John Puckette, finish college at the University of the South and enter the professional world. She wrote little except children's fiction during this time, but after another brief visit to Europe in 1907–1908, she became engrossed in the conflicts of the economically recovering New South. She contributed to and helped edit the *Forensic Quarterly Review*, a magazine created to address the growing concerns of the Southern middle class about labor, race, and women's rights. The subject of her last major publication, *The Making of Jane* (1901), as well as the novella "Fortune's Vassals" (*Lippincott's Magazine*, August 1899), indicate, however, where her heart really lay. These portraits of New Women struggling for independence from both the restrictions of family obligations and the shallow life of a socialite and prize in the marriage game

rendered Elliott the unanimous choice in 1912 to head and write a "Manifesto" for the Tennessee Equal Suffrage Association; she was reelected as president in 1913.

Elliott's activism, begun with her membership in the Woman's Political Union of New York, recalled her to New York in 1911 to deliver a lecture called "A Sketch of the History of the Woman Suffrage Movement in the United States," the title of which suggests the extent of her knowledge of the movement and her skill at public speaking. She served as vice president for the Southern States Woman Suffrage Conference and, together with fellow activists Laura Clay of Kentucky and Mary Johnston of Virginia, became one of the first women to address the Tennessee legislature. Resigning from the Tennessee Association as a result of overwork and the strain of a split in the organization, Elliott's efforts eventually contributed to Tennessee becoming the thirty-sixth and crucial state to ratify the Nineteenth Amendment which, in 1920, granted women the right to vote.

Desiring to lend her name and influence to presidential politics, she chaired the state Democratic women's committee and saw her candidate, Woodrow Wilson, victorious in 1912. In the 1920s, her interest in politics dwindling with the return to power of the Republicans, Elliott lived quietly at Sewanee, was active in community and university affairs, and wrote a few pieces about Sewanee life and several book reviews for the *Sewanee Review*, that indicate the scope of her reading.

Since 1870 Elliott had been a beloved fixture at Sewanee: a writer in residence and something of an official hostess, she retained a clear mind, a healthy skepticism, and a sense of irony. She had devoted a lifetime to writing stories in the vein of writer and editor William Dean Howells's modified realism, sober and devoid of folk humor. She attempted to counter Southern myth with truth, romance with reality, describing complex social problems in the midst of which liberalism had struggled to survive. Her accurate portraits of prewar life show a high-minded older generation whose children opt for the professions over the plantation, but her fiction is more occupied with the harsher effects of the postwar years on the various social groups. While her writing is limited by an occasional preachiness, excessive sentimentality, and an inability to lift her vision to a universal plane, it points to the direction that Southern literature would go for the next thirty years: concerned with individualism and the search for identity, preoccupied with themes of guilt, frustration, violence, and death.

Elliott's best work reveals that, despite her personal humor, she viewed life as essentially tragic and held the artist responsible for examining the disparity between what is and what could be. Though the gulf between her ideals and their realization remained wide, her vision included hope. She had lived to see successes in realms that were important to her: in relations between North and South, in rights for blacks and women, in the maturation of her adopted sons and her adopted university, and in her own writing. The world had rewarded her external accomplishments with an honorary degree and a listing in *Who's Who in America* (1910). She had lived up to her long-held belief that, for the writer, life was a study. When she met death from cancer at age seventy-nine, Elliott was awaiting publication of a story titled "The Infinite Wrong," which had been tentatively accepted by *The Manchester Guardian*.

References:

Stephen B. Barnwell, *The Story of an American Family* (Marquette, Mich.: Privately printed, 1969);

Alexander Cowie, *The Rise of the American Novel* (New York: American Book, 1948);

Allison R. Ensor, "A Tennessee Woman Abroad: The Travel Letters of Sarah Elliott Barnwell, 1886–1887," *Tennessee Historical Quarterly,* 52 (Fall 1993): 185–191;

Clara Childs Mackenzie, *Sarah Barnwell Elliott* (Boston: Twayne, 1980);

Helen Waite Papashvily, *All the Happy Endings: A Study of the Domestic Novel in America, the Women Who Wrote It, the Women Who Read It in the Nineteenth Century* (New York: Harper, 1956);

Louis D. Rubin Jr., *William Elliott Shoots a Bear: Essays on the Southern Literary Imagination* (Baton Rouge: Louisiana State University Press, 1975);

Anne Firor Scott, *The Southern Lady: From Pedestal to Politics 1830–1930* (Chicago: University of Chicago Press, 1970);

Elizabeth A. Taylor, *The Woman Suffrage Movement in Tennessee* (New York: Bookman, 1957);

C. Vann Woodward, *The Burden of Southern History* (Baton Rouge: Louisiana State University Press, 1960);

Nathalia Wright, "Sarah Barnwell Elliott," *Notable American Women 1607–1950,* volume 1, edited by Edward T. James (Cambridge, Mass.: Belknap Press of Harvard University Press, 1971), pp. 578–579.

Papers:

The Sarah Barnwell Elliott Papers, including unpublished manuscripts, photographs, clippings, and miscellaneous correspondence, are housed in the Jessie Ball duPont Library, the University of the South, Sewanee, Tennessee.

Annie Adams Fields

(6 June 1834 – 5 January 1915)

Deborah M. Evans
Middlebury College

BOOKS: *Ode. Recited by Miss Charlotte Cushman, at the Inauguration of the Great Organ in Boston, Nov. 2, 1863,* anonymous (Cambridge, Mass.: Felch, Bigelow, 1863);

Asphodel (Boston: Ticknor & Fields, 1866);

The Children of Lebanon (Boston: Privately printed, 1872);

The Return of Persephone: A Dramatic Sketch (Cambridge, Mass.: Privately printed, 1877);

James T. Fields: Biographical Notes and Personal Sketches, anonymous (Boston: Houghton, Mifflin, 1881);

Under the Olive (Boston: Houghton, Mifflin, 1881);

Extract of a Paper upon District Conferences (New York: Charity Organization Society, 1882);

How to Help the Poor (Boston: Houghton, Mifflin, 1883);

Whittier: Notes of His Life and Friendships (New York: Harper, 1893);

A Shelf of Old Books (New York: Scribners, 1894; London: Osgood, McIlvaine, 1894);

The Singing Shepherd, and Other Poems (Boston: Houghton, Mifflin, 1895);

Authors and Friends (Boston & New York: Houghton, Mifflin, 1896; London: Unwin, 1896);

Nathaniel Hawthorne (Boston: Small, Maynard, 1899; London: Kegan Paul, Trench, Trübner, 1899);

Orpheus: A Masque (Boston: Houghton, Mifflin, 1900);

Charles Dudley Warner (New York: McClure Phillips, 1904);

A Letter from Mrs. Fields to the Arbella Club, "A Friendly Circle of Girls" (Boston: Atheneum, 1912).

OTHER: "Upon the Constitution and Duties of a District Conference," in *Proceedings of the Eighth Annual [National] Conference of Charities and Correction, Held at Boston, July 25–30, 1881,* edited by F. B. Sanborn (Boston: Williams, 1881);

Letters of Celia Thaxter, edited by Fields and Rose Lamb (Boston: Houghton, Mifflin, 1895);

Annie Adams Fields in the late 1850s (daguerreotype by Southworth and Hawes)

Life and Letters of Harriet Beecher Stowe, edited by Fields (Boston: Houghton, Mifflin, 1897; London: Sampson Low, Marston, 1897);

"Which Are the New England Classics? A Ten Minute Talk," in *Six New England Classics: Talks and Lectures. Course V. Booklovers Reading Club,* edited by Fred Lewis Pattee (Philadelphia: Booklovers Library, 1901), pp. 65–71;

Letters of Sarah Orne Jewett, edited by Fields (Boston: Houghton Mifflin, 1911; London: Constable, 1911).

SELECTED PERIODICAL PUBLICATIONS–
UNCOLLECTED: "The Holly-Tree Coffee Rooms,"
The Christian Union (February 1872): 175;

"A Beautiful Charity," *Harper's*, 55 (July 1877): 200–205;

"Problems of Poor Relief," *Sunday Afternoon*, 1 (February 1878): 136–143;

"A Glimpse at Some of Our Charities. Part I," *Harper's*, 56 (February 1878): 441–450;

"A Glimpse at Some of Our Charities. Part II. The Employment, Education, and Protection of Women," *Harper's*, 56 (March 1878): 596–608;

"Three Typical Workingmen," *Atlantic Monthly*, 42 (December 1878): 717–727;

"Saint Cecilia," *Harper's*, 61 (November 1880): 809–819;

"Mr. Emerson in the Lecture Room," *Atlantic Monthly*, 51 (June 1883): 818–832;

"Glimpses of Emerson," *Harper's*, 68 (February 1884): 457–467;

"Acquaintance with Charles Reade," *Century*, 7 (November 1884): 67–79;

"Monster Asylums," *Nation* (December 1884): 544;

"Work for Paupers and Convicts," *Nation* (September 1886): 194;

"Lend a Hand, for 'Pain Is Not the Fruit of Pain,'" *Lend a Hand*, 1 (January 1886): 7–8;

"The Contributors and the Children: The Poet Who Told the Truth," *Wide Awake*, 23 (December 1886): 87–88;

"Glimpses of Longfellow in Social Life," *Century*, 9 (April 1886): 884–893;

"The Contributors and the Children: [Noble Born]," *Wide Awake*, 24 (April 1887): 342;

"Three Real Cases," *Lend a Hand*, 3 (August 1888): 455–456;

"A Shelf of Old Books: Leigh Hunt," *Scribner's*, 3 (March 1888): 285–305;

"The Contributors and the Children: About Clothes," *Wide Awake*, 26 (January 1888): 85–87;

"A Helping Hand," *Wide Awake*, 27 (August 1888): 143–149;

"The Aged Poor," *Chautauquan*, 9 (1889): 517–519;

"A Second Shelf of Old Books: Edinburgh," *Scribner's*, 5 (April 1889): 453–476;

"Special Work of Associated Charities," *Lend a Hand*, 4 (April 1889): 285–288;

"Guerin's 'Centaur,'" *Scribner's*, 12 (August 1892): 224–232;

"Tennyson," *Harper's*, 86 (January 1893): 309–312;

"Whittier: Notes of His Life and of His Friendship," *Harper's*, 86 (February 1893): 38–59;

"Third Shelf of Old Books," *Scribner's*, 16 (September 1894): 338–359;

"Celia Thaxter," *Atlantic Monthly*, 75 (February 1895): 254–266;

"Oliver Wendell Holmes: Personal Recollections and Unpublished Letters," *Century*, 27 (February 1895): 505–515;

"Days with Mrs. Stowe," *Atlantic Monthly*, 78 (August 1896): 145–156;

"Reminiscences of Harriet Beecher Stowe," *Living Age*, 216 (January 1898): 145–147;

"The Inner Life of John Greenleaf Whittier," *Chautauquan*, 30 (1899): 194–198;

"Two Lovers of Literature: Charles and Mary Cowden Clarke," *Century*, 36 (May 1899): 122–131;

"Notes on Glass Decoration," *Atlantic Monthly*, 83 (June 1899): 807–811;

"George Eliot," *Century*, 36 (July 1899): 442–446;

"Dr. Southwood Smith: Pioneer of English Sanitary Reform," *Charities Review*, 10 (March 1900): 28–34;

"Mary Russell Mitford," *Critic*, 37 (December 1900): 512;

"Saint Theresa," *Atlantic Monthly*, 91 (March 1903): 353–363;

"Notable Women: Mme. Blanc ('Th. Bentzon')," *Century*, 44 (May 1903): 134–139.

Annie Adams Fields, best known as the consummate literary hostess, wife to publisher and editor James T. Fields, and, in later years, companion to Sarah Orne Jewett, regionalist author of *The Country of the Pointed Firs* (1896), has remained something of an enigma to literary critics until recently. Commonly regarded as the center around which other, more luminous literary lights shone, she must also be considered from other perspectives: that of poet, diarist, editorial voice, social worker, and author of literary memoirs.

She was born Ann West Adams on 6 June 1834, the daughter of prominent Boston physician Zabdiel Boylston Adams and Sarah May Holland Adams. Related through her father to two presidents, John Adams and John Quincey Adams, and through her mother to Louisa May Alcott, Fields was second youngest of the couple's seven children, two of whom died in infancy. Annie Adams was particularly close to her two older sisters, who shared her interest in art, travel, and intellectual pursuits as well as her creativity. Sarah Holland Adams, eleven years her senior, produced the first English translation of the German author Herman Grimm; Elizabeth ("Lissie") Adams, nine years older and Annie's closest sibling, became an artist whose best work was portrait painting.

Zabdiel Adams paved the way for his daughters' successes by advocating a strong secondary education for the girls; he sent them to the rigorous and progressive George B. Emerson School for Young Ladies. Emerson, formerly the principal of Boston's Classical School for

148 Charles Street in Boston, Fields's home and the site of the literary salon she hosted with her husband, James T. Fields

Chapel by the Reverend Gannett—the man who performed Fields's first marriage—on 15 November 1854.

Marriage brought Annie Fields into the literary circles around which Fields's business revolved, and she quickly became a favorite. After living briefly with the Adams family, the couple moved to 148 Charles Street, an address soon recognized by the literary elite as an inviting retreat. Noted for her grace, her tact, her keen sense of humor, and her ability to draw on quotations or references readily, Fields was well suited to the role of editor's wife. She nurtured the Ticknor and Fields writers, making them feel valued, welcomed, and at home. Among their frequent visitors were Oliver Wendell Holmes, who lived next door, and Thomas Bailey Aldrich, who lived across the street. Henry Wadsworth Longfellow, James Russell Lowell, and William Dean Howells came often from Cambridge, and Ralph Waldo Emerson and Nathaniel Hawthorne traveled in from Concord. John Greenleaf Whittier and Celia Thaxter, who became two of Annie's close friends as well, were guests at the Fieldses' home, as were Harriet Beecher Stowe, Charles Dudley Warner, Louis Agassiz, Henry James Sr., and Cyrus Bartol.

During Fields's lifetime the house overlooked the street at one end and her extensive gardens and the Charles River on the other. Fields lived in this home for at least part of the year for sixty years. On the second floor, the library ran the length of the house—this "waterside museum," as Henry James later described it in *The American Scene* (1907), was a pastoral retreat, decorated with green sofas, curtains, and rugs, and home to the couple's growing book collection, which eventually included two hundred volumes from the English writer Leigh Hunt's library; many first editions and autographed books; sketches; paintings by William Morris Hunt and Sir Joshua Reynolds, as well as a famous portrait of the young Charles Dickens that later hung in the Boston Museum of Art; statues and busts, including some Greek and Roman replicas; and a grand piano. Both Fields and her husband wrote separate essays on their library; the title of James's piece, "My Friend's Library," suggests how much he viewed it as a space they shared in their literary endeavors.

In addition to their circle of American literary friends, the Fieldses cultivated international relationships as well. They traveled to Europe twice, in June 1859 and in April 1869, to visit friends and literary acquaintances such as Alfred Tennyson, Dinah Mulock Craik, Charles Reade, the Brownings, Walter Savage Landor, Wilkie Collins, and Dickens. Occasionally European authors paid the Fieldses return visits: in a veritable social coup, Dickens, who made a practice of avoiding staying in private homes, lodged with them for four days during his second American tour in 1867–1868.

Boys, ran a women's school similar in many respects to a female seminary. He did not, however, limit his curriculum to classes in domestic skills or etiquette. His students learned Latin, French, Italian, mathematics, natural history, geography, history, literature, and even the importance of "good health"; as a result, Adams received a singularly excellent education for a young woman of her time, which resulted in her love of classics and literature. Emerson also believed that young women should be imbued with a lifelong commitment to charitable works; this idea greatly influenced Adams's life and is reflected in her many literary works on the theme of charity.

At the age of twenty, Adams married Fields, a partner in the firm Ticknor and Fields, which published many of Boston's best-known writers. Fields had been engaged to Adams's cousin Mary Willard, who died of tuberculosis before the marriage could take place. James later married Mary's sister Eliza, who also died of tuberculosis before their second anniversary. Despite these tragedies, his romantic attentions remained focused in the family, and he and Adams were married at King's

Though Fields's diplomacy and grace as a hostess were unparalleled, that was not the limit of her talents. She was also a careful reader and critic who had a great influence on the careers of many writers. For years Fields was, in effect, an unacknowledged coeditor of the *Atlantic Monthly,* of which James Fields had become editor in 1861. In keeping with the image of a helpful wife, her contributions were not formally recognized–nor did she expect them to be; she worked as a silent partner to her husband. Fields clearly respected his wife's opinions, however, as did many of the writers he worked with: Rebecca Harding Davis once began a letter to the Fieldses with no direct address, only the explanation: "I don't know which to write to–I cannot separate you!" Elizabeth Peabody recognized Fields's influence on her husband's editorial judgments and wrote to her concerning a contribution to "get Mr. Fields to read it before the March number is made up–& I want you to take care that it is not mislaid."

While fledgling writers such as Abby Morton Diaz somewhat understandably deferred to the Fieldses, even more prominent writers, including Whittier and Stowe, wrote requesting Fields's intervention and editorial services. Whittier, for example, might send a poem to Fields and ask her to pass it on to her husband if she thought it good enough; Stowe, on one occasion, sent James Fields an essay encouraging U.S. citizens to "buy American" and enclosed the following note: "Please let Annie look it over & if she & you think I have said too much of the Waltham watches make it right." Going beyond asking for Fields's editorial assistance, Stowe encouraged her to add her own thoughts to the essay if appropriate: "If Annie thinks of any other thing that ought to be mentioned & will put it in for me she will serve both the cause & me." The trust these authors placed in Fields's judgment is clear, as is the understanding that she had some measure of influence in what was published in the *Atlantic.*

Indeed, Fields intervened for some authors she thought worthy of publication. One such writer to benefit was her cousin Alcott. Fields read Alcott's poem "Thoreau's Flute" at Hawthorne's suggestion and, after making several editorial comments, sent it back to Alcott; the poem was published three months later. She was instrumental in getting Elizabeth Stuart Phelps's first novel, *The Gates Ajar* (1868), into print as well; the novel proved to be an astonishing success, and Phelps continued to count on Fields's advice and friendship throughout her life. Henry James's essay "Compagnons de Voyage" might not have been published had Fields not enthusiastically recommended it to her husband, nor would Hawthorne's notebooks. Although in later years a falling out between Sophia Hawthorne and Fields over royalties damaged the friendship that had developed between the families, for years theirs was a powerful bond. Soon after Hawthorne died, Fields urged Sophia to prepare his manuscripts for publication. Eventually, the Hawthorne family's precarious financial situation and Sophia's trust in "darling Annie" resulted in the publication of *Passages from the American Notebooks* (1868).

In addition to this record of influence, Fields's legacy includes a chronicle that casts significant light on American literary history. During these years she recognized the importance of the events that were occurring around her, and she began to keep a regular diary, which she self-consciously titled in July 1863 "Journal of Literary Events and glimpses of interesting people." In these sixty-one unpublished volumes, Fields expresses her desire to "record something of the interesting events in literature which are constantly passing under my knowledge." She was so successful, in fact, that when James Fields published his essays on Hawthorne and Dickens in the *Atlantic,* he drew passages directly from Fields's diaries for the articles; her work is not attributed, but she in fact co-authored these pieces.

The diaries record events Fields herself witnessed as well as those related to her secondhand by her husband; for instance, she transcribes conversations of Longfellow, Emerson, Holmes, and Hawthorne at meetings of the Saturday Club her husband attended. In addition to providing personal glimpses of Dickens, Hawthorne, Tennyson, and Mark Twain, the diaries give the modern reader some new insight into the interconnectedness of women writers' lives: Fields came into contact, personally or by letter, with a variety of literary women, including Catharine Sedgwick, Lydia Maria Child, Julia Ward Howe, Elizabeth Peabody, Rose Terry Cooke, Mary Wilkins Freeman, Elizabeth Stuart Phelps, Rebecca Harding Davis, Helen Hunt Jackson, Willa Cather, and Sarah Orne Jewett.

One of the most appealing features of the diaries, besides their value as a literary resource, is Fields's ability to tell witty and insightful personal anecdotes about the literary figures who visited Charles Street. For example, she recounts Henry James spending an afternoon in Hastings, England, trying to find a muzzle for his dog; she describes Harriet Beecher Stowe strewing crumbs on the tablecloth and spilling food on her dress–"Her oblivion to all cares of this sort are terrible and wonderful," Fields writes; and she shows Emerson at a lecture by French historian Ernest Renan, not comprehending the language and looking to Lowell for a cue as to how to react. While these diaries were personal and private, the information Fields records suggests that she was aware that they might serve a more public use at some time in the future.

Fields's diaries also indicate that she thought of herself first and foremost as a poet, one whose talents were thwarted by the energies devoted to entertaining and housekeeping. Though she did not devalue these activities, and in fact saw her role as hostess as vitally important—so much so that she continued the activity after her husband's death—she nevertheless envied those who could spend more uninterrupted hours at the pen. As Cather perceptively observed in her essay "148 Charles Street," "sixty years of hospitality, so smooth and unruffled for the recipients, cost the hostess something—cost her a great deal." Fields's diaries reflect her constant battle between the demands on her time as hostess and her drive to write well: "I know there is the heart of a singer hidden in me and I long sometimes to break loose—but on the whole I sincerely prefer to make others comfortable and happy as I can now do and say fie! to my genius if he does not sing to me from the sauce-pans all the same." Unlike a writer such as Emily Dickinson, who made a point to shut herself away from many domestic and social obligations, Fields was torn between her value as a social facilitator and a private artist.

A review of her publications reveals that poetry was a lifelong endeavor for Fields. She considered poetry her genius, and her verse was well received, if not enthusiastically lauded. Initially, her husband published her poems anonymously in the *Atlantic,* often apparently to fill empty space at the end of a story or article, and she later published in other prestigious periodicals such as *Harper's* and *Scribner's.* Her first major work, the privately printed *Ode at the Inauguration of the Great Organ* (1863), was published anonymously, but was read at a public benefit in Boston on 2 November 1868 by the celebrated actress and Fieldses' family friend Charlotte Cushman.

Fields also wrote a long work on the Shakers, *The Children of Lebanon* (1872); *The Return of Persephone: A Dramatic Sketch* (1877), a reexamination of the myth with a focus on the mother-daughter relationship; and her first volume of poetry, *Under the Olive* (1881). This text includes works such as "Helena," in which the "voiceless" Helen of Troy tells her story and which might be read as a reflection of Fields's desire to speak herself through verse, rather than simply be spoken of by others. In a precursor to feminist thought, she lets Helen's voice be heard rather than consign her to a fate of objectification, as implied in an epigraph from the *Iliad* with which Fields begins the poem: "Zeus gives us a doom that is dreadful / Ever to live in the songs and to be a theme for the minstrels." Fields's Helen makes a claim to her identity: "I am Helen of Argos, / I am Helen of Sparta, / I, the daughter of Egypt, / I, the inflamer of Troy." In "To the Poetess" and "Not By Will, and Not By Striving" she continues to reflect on the difficulties and triumphant beauties of the poet. For most of her life, Fields continued her striving, hoping to produce a great work of poetry. *Asphodel* (1866), a melodramatic novel in

the form of a Greek tragedy and Fields's only foray into long fiction, remains of interest primarily because of the biographical connections to the family life of James Russell Lowell. Though she never achieved the greatness she sought, Fields continuously worked on her poetry in the coming years.

At the same time she turned her energies even more toward public service, perhaps at the inspiration of Dickens and his interest in social reform. She started a series of coffeehouses that offered the poor laborer an alternative for the barroom as a place to socialize after working hours. Her success here drew her into other ventures, such as a home for working women and workrooms to employ seamstresses put out of work by the Boston fire of 1872. Recognizing a need for improvement in the administration of various social programs, Fields began to work toward the centralization of social services. She and Mabel Lodge began the Cooperative Society of Visitors, later part of Boston Associated Charities, which visited homes of the poor to assess need and recommend allocation of various resources.

Fields's book *How to Help the Poor* (1883) was an unofficial statement of the philosophies and organizational structure of Boston Associated Charities, advocating that the donors give time as well as money to aid the poor. The book sold well and was reprinted twice. Fields argued that the poor needed immediate relief, as well as work and education; only through direct contact with the poor could other classes begin to understand the underlying causes of poverty and take real measures toward change. She believed that environment was an important factor contributing to the "moral disease" of many and that moral education in school would be a large part of the remedy, especially for children. For the elderly who were ready and able to work to change their situations, she advocated significant assistance; for the "unworthy" poor, as she termed them, those unwilling to work or unable to stop drinking, she prescribed the almshouse. On the whole, the book and her other articles on charitable works—including "Problems of Poor Relief" (*Sunday Afternoon,* February 1878), "Work for Paupers and Convicts" (*The Nation,* September 1886), and "The Aged Poor" (*Chautauquan,* 1889)—demonstrate a long-term concern for the poor and an interest in remedying an increasingly distressing social ill.

In addition to her activism for the poor, Fields advocated women's rights. She supported such causes as woman suffrage and women's secondary education. In 1871 she joined a group working to promote a women's college in Boston, and she worked with her husband that same year to organize a series of free lectures in English literature to be delivered by the most notable names in the Fields circle—Holmes, Emerson, Phillips Brooks, and James Fields himself—as a means of assessing how many

Fields and Sarah Orne Jewett in the drawing room at 148 Charles Street

women would be interested in enrolling in college courses. They wanted women admitted to Harvard University, and though they fell short of that goal, when the Harvard "Annex"–later known as Radcliffe College–opened in 1879, Fields was on its advisory board; she later served in the same capacity for the coeducational Boston University as well. In addition, Fields started a club of women writers in 1877 that gathered at Charles Street weekly to read their work. The club, informally termed "the Pandora" in tribute to Fields's translation of Johann Wolfgang von Goethe's *Pandora* (1810), included notable women such as Lucy Larcom, Louisa Dresel, Phelps, and Howe.

During the last years of the Fieldses' marriage, they underwent a change in lifestyle. James suffered a variety of illnesses and retired from the demands of publishing and editing in 1870–1871. He traded one set of demands for another, however, and became a popular figure on the lecture circuit, which led to frequent absences from home. Neither Fields nor her husband enjoyed the separation, and they built a seaside home in the North Shore town of Manchester in 1874, in part hoping for a respite from the social obligations of Boston; their social schedule remained active, however, and they entertained frequently.

When James Fields died in April 1881, Fields went into mourning for a few months, during which she saw

few people. One means she chose for her emotional recuperation was to write *James T. Fields: Biographical Notes and Personal Sketches* (1881). This book was important for her in several ways: it eased her pain at the death of her beloved husband, it brought her back to work, and it was the first of the literary memoirs in which her most important literary contributions were made. For the first time she began to make public the chronicling process begun in her private diaries. Essays on Emerson appeared in the *Atlantic Monthly* and *Harper's,* while "Acquaintance with Charles Reade" and "Glimpses of Longfellow in Social Life" were published by *Century* magazine in 1886.

At the same time she renewed her acquaintance with Jewett, a young writer the Fieldses had met occasionally in Boston. Jewett offered Fields the companionship and solace she needed at an isolated point in her life. The two women quickly developed an intense friendship and settled into a pattern of life that allowed Fields to continue her work–entertaining, writing, and social work–with an even greater emphasis on her own literary output. She spent winters in Boston and summers in Manchester, accompanied by Jewett, who made trips to her home in South Berwick, Maine, in the early fall and late spring. Fields accompanied Jewett only for short visits, fearing to leave her other responsibilities untended for long.

Although Jewett's fame eventually surpassed that of Fields, such was not the situation when they met in

1881. Jewett, then thirty-two years old, was the novice, just seeing her writing career take shape; Fields, at forty-seven, was a much more established figure in Boston literary circles. Nonetheless, Jewett quickly found a place in the Charles Street household as "our dear Sarah," and the women shared an interest in writing, publishing, and the arts and theater; they entertained together, offering "Saturday afternoons," among the most popular, prestigious literary gatherings of the day, and traveled somewhat extensively, twice to the West Indies and five times to Europe. In addition to maintaining friendships with authors such as Whittier, Phelps, Thaxter, and James, they were a particularly supportive presence for young female artists, and their growing circle of friends included writers Alice Brown, Laura Howe Richards, Mary Noailles Murfree, and Octave Thanet; poets Louise Imogen Guiney, Louise Chandler Moulton, and Edith Thomas; and artists and sculptors Louisa Dresel, Anne Whitney, and Sarah Wyman Whitman.

The Fields-Jewett relationship seems to defy conventional definition; as partners in what has been labeled a typical "Boston marriage," common among women of their circle, their primary emotional bond was to each other for the remainder of their lives together. Fields's biographer Judith Roman comes closest to defining it when she notes that theirs was an intimate, nonconfining relationship, one in which an "easy exchange of roles . . . fostered both freedom and security for the two women." They served different needs for each other, at times taking on the roles of mother and daughter, or patient and doctor; they were supportive of each other's literary work; and as the remaining correspondence suggests, they had a childish playfulness between them (Fields referred to Jewett as "Pinny" and Jewett referred to Fields as "Fuff" or "Mouse," and their letters often take on an affected, childish diction).

During the 1880s and 1890s Fields was more productive in literary terms than she had been at any point previously; her energies now focused on developing her own literary talents. She continued to write poetry, producing a second volume of verse, *The Singing Shepherd, and Other Poems* (1895). Less classically inspired than the previous volume, these lyric poems address subjects such as the Civil War, nature, religion, and poetry, as well as offer dedications to personal friends. On the whole the volume is more interesting and challenging than her first, but one still has the sense that the poetic muse evades Fields. During her lifetime Fields achieved only limited success as a poet; she was published frequently, but her work was never, for example, anthologized with that of other female writers of her day. Only *Orpheus: A Masque* (1900) followed this second book. Though poetry remained her avocation, her more successful contributions to letters were in other areas.

Her real fame as a writer rests on her literary memoirs and reminiscences, such as "Mr. Emerson in the Lecture Room" (*Atlantic Monthly,* June 1883), *Whittier: Notes of His Life and Friendships* (1893), *A Shelf of Old Books* (1894), *Letters of Celia Thaxter* (1895), *Life and Letters of Harriet Beecher Stowe* (1897), and *Nathaniel Hawthorne* (1899). One of Fields's most successful books, *A Shelf of Old Books* is a series of short memoirs suggested by a perusal of the shelves of her extensive library. The volume is divided into three sections: "Leigh Hunt"; "Edinburgh," including reminiscences of John Brown, David Douglas, John Wilson ("Christopher North"), Thomas DeQuincey, Robert Burns, Allan Ramsay, and Sir Walter Scott; and "From Milton to Thackeray," which includes facsimiles of letters from William Thackeray, Adelaide Proctor, and Charles Lamb. The book appeals to the bibliophile—Fields helps the reader to feel the excitement her husband felt when, upon purchasing a used copy of Samuel Johnson's romance, *Rasselas* (1759), he found a letter "in the well known handwriting of Dr. Johnson himself."

Perhaps the clearest statement of her reason for writing these volumes is found in her thoughts as she peruses the volumes of Hunt's collection: "there is a sacredness about the belongings of good & great men which is quite apart from the value and significance of the things themselves. Their books became especially endeared to us; as we turn the pages they have loved, we can see another hand pointing along the lines, another head bending over the open volume. A writer's books make his workshop and his pleasure house in one, and in turning over his possessions we discover the field in which he worked and the key to his garden of hesperides." She clearly recognizes the worth of these reminiscences to new readers and places a value on the preservation of literary memory. Books themselves become a vehicle for bridging the gap between generations of writers.

The year 1896 marked a pinnacle for both Jewett and Fields: Jewett's *The Country of the Pointed Firs* was published, as was Fields's *Authors and Friends,* her best-selling work and most interesting literary legacy. This volume, too, comprises personal reminiscences, and the list of subjects includes the closest members of the Fields literary circle: Longfellow, Emerson, Holmes, Stowe, Thaxter, Whittier, and two concluding essays on the much-admired Lord and Lady Tennyson. In her comments on Stowe, Fields notes: "on the whole we may rather wonder at the high average value of the literary work by which she lived, especially when we follow the hints given in her letters of her interrupted and crowded existence." Clearly she admires and respects a woman who, despite overwhelming domestic challenges, was able to write "one of the greatest stories the world has yet produced," *Uncle Tom's Cabin* (1852). Yet, she remarks that for

Stowe, books were a "medium of the ideas of the age" and the "promulgators of morals and religions" and that Stowe was not a "student of literature." Fields herself never underestimated the value of an education in the classics of literature, while still keeping her eyes open to new work. Of her close friend Thaxter's life she writes, "Her eyesight was keener, her speech more distinct, the lines of her thoughts more clearly defined, her verse more strongly marked in its form, and the accuracy of her memory more to be relied upon than was the case with almost anyone of her contemporaries." Notably, the essays are primarily elegiac, covering the previous generation of writers, due to Victorian convention that disallowed writing on living figures.

In September 1902 Fields's life underwent another substantive change when Jewett suffered injuries to her head and spine after being thrown from a horse. Jewett suffered from headaches for the remainder of her life and was virtually unable to resume writing; she wrote only letters and an occasional piece after that date. Fields, meanwhile, kept up her work, publishing a short biography of Charles Dudley Warner in 1904, and made a trip abroad to Sicily, this time without Jewett. Fields kept busy during these years, holding weekly sessions of the Boston Authors Club, a group of elderly men and women writers, at her home in 1905. In 1908 Fields's strength began to wane; Jewett, in fact, feared that her friend's life was near its end. Fields outlived her, however: Jewett suffered a stroke on 4 February and died on 24 June of that year. Fields's last publication was the heavily edited *Letters of Sarah Orne Jewett* (1911). She died on 5 January 1915 after a brief illness.

A nineteenth-century woman in most senses, one of increasingly few representatives of Boston's literary heyday, Fields lived to see the advent of modernism. For many she came to represent a past that no longer existed except for her presence; yet, Fields would not be relegated to that past. She kept current, and as Cather wryly noted, "She had the genius of survival. She was not, as she once laughingly told me, 'to escape anything, not even free verse or the Cubists!'" In her reminiscences of Fields, Cather also notes that "besides being distinctly young on one hand, on the other Mrs. Fields seemed to me to reach back to Waterloo. . . . she had talked to Leigh Hunt about Shelley and the starlike beauty of his face–and it is now more than a century since Shelley was drowned." For Cather and many of her contemporaries, Annie Adams Fields was a bridge between the two ages. She was in many senses a facilitator–between authors as

a hostess, and, as a writer, between generations who could become acquainted with one another.

Biography:

Judith A. Roman, *Annie Adams Fields: The Spirit of Charles Street* (Bloomington: Indiana University Press, 1990).

References:

James C. Austin, *Fields of the Atlantic Monthly* (San Marino, Cal.: Huntington Library, 1953);

Paula Blanchard, *Sarah Orne Jewett: Her World and Her Work* (Reading, Mass.: Addison-Wesley, 1994);

Willa Cather, "148 Charles Street," in her *Not under Forty* (New York: Knopf, 1936);

Josephine Donovan, "Annie Adams Fields and Her Network of Influence," in her *New England Local Color Literature: A Women's Tradition* (New York: Ungar, 1983), pp. 38–49;

Rita K. Gollin, "Annie Adams Fields, 1834–1915," *Legacy,* 4 (Spring 1987): 27–33;

Gollin, "Subordinated Power: Mr. and Mrs. James T. Fields," in *Patrons and Protégées: Gender, Friendship and Writing in Nineteenth-Century America,* edited by Shirley Marchalonis (New Brunswick: Rutgers University Press, 1988), pp. 141–161;

M. A. DeWolfe Howe, *Memories of a Hostess: A Chronicle of Eminent Friendships Drawn Chiefly from the Diaries of Mrs. James T. Fields* (Boston: Atlantic Monthly Press, 1922);

Henry James, *The American Scene* (New York: Harper, 1907);

James, "Mr. and Mrs. James T. Fields," *Atlantic Monthly,* 116 (July 1915): 21–31;

Elizabeth Stuart Phelps, *Chapters from a Life* (Boston: Houghton, Mifflin, 1896);

Harriet Prescott Spofford, *A Little Book of Friends* (Boston: Little, Brown, 1916);

Warren S. Tryon, *Parnassus Corner: A Life of James T. Fields* (Boston: Houghton Mifflin, 1963).

Papers:

The Massachusetts Historical Society holds the Annie Adams Fields diaries covering the years 1859–1860 and 1863 to 1877, with later entries for 1896, 1898, 1905, and from 1907 to 1912. Substantial collections of Fields's letters and manuscripts are located at the Huntington Library, the Houghton Library at Harvard, the New York Public Library, the Boston Public Library, and the Massachusetts Historical Society.

Mary Hallock Foote

(19 November 1847 – 25 June 1938)

Victoria Lamont
University of Waterloo

See also the Foote entries in *DLB 186: Nineteenth-Century American Western Writers; DLB 188: American Book and Magazine Illustrators to 1920;* and *DLB 202: Nineteenth-Century American Fiction Writers.*

BOOKS: *The Led-Horse Claim: A Romance of a Mining Camp* (Boston: Osgood, 1883);

John Bodewin's Testimony (Boston: Ticknor, 1886);

The Last Assembly Ball: and, The Fate of a Voice (Boston & New York: Houghton, Mifflin, 1889);

The Chosen Valley (Boston & New York: Houghton, Mifflin, 1892);

Coeur d'Alene (Boston & New York: Houghton, Mifflin, 1894);

In Exile, and Other Stories (Boston & New York: Houghton, Mifflin, 1894)—includes "The Rapture of Hetty";

The Cup of Trembling, and Other Stories (Boston & New York: Houghton, Mifflin, 1895);

The Little Fig-Tree Stories (Boston & New York: Houghton, Mifflin, 1899);

The Prodigal (Boston & New York: Houghton, Mifflin, 1900);

The Desert and the Sown (Boston & New York: Houghton, Mifflin, 1902);

A Touch of Sun and Other Stories (Boston & New York: Houghton, Mifflin, 1903);

The Royal Americans (Boston & New York: Houghton Mifflin, 1910);

A Picked Company (Boston & New York: Houghton Mifflin, 1912);

The Valley Road (Boston & New York: Houghton Mifflin, 1915);

Edith Bonham (Boston & New York: Houghton Mifflin, 1917);

The Ground-Swell (Boston & New York: Houghton Mifflin, 1919);

A Victorian Gentlewoman in the Far West: The Reminiscences of Mary Hallock Foote, edited by Rodman W. Paul (San Marino, Cal.: Huntington Library, 1972);

Mary Hallock Foote

The Idaho Stories and Far West Illustrations of Mary Hallock Foote, edited by Barbara Cragg, Dennis M. Walsh, and Mary Ellen Walsh (Boise: Idaho State University Press, 1988).

SELECTED PERIODICAL PUBLICATIONS–UNCOLLECTED: "The Picture in the Fire-place Bedroom," *St. Nicholas,* 2 (February 1875): 248–250;

"A California Mining Camp," *Scribner's Monthly,* 15 (February 1878): 480–493;

"How Mandy Went Rowing with the 'Cap'n,'" *St. Nicholas,* 5 (May 1878): 449–453;

"A Sea-port on the Pacific," *Scribner's Monthly,* 16 (August 1878): 449–460;

"A 'Muchacho' of the Mexican Camp," *St. Nicholas,* 6 (December 1878): 79–81;

"The Cascarone Ball," *Scribner's Monthly,* 18 (August 1879): 614–617;

"A Story of the Dry Season," *Scribner's Monthly,* 18 (September 1879): 766–781;

"The Children's 'Claim,'" *St. Nicholas,* 7 (January 1880): 238–245;

"Cousin Charley's Story," *St. Nicholas,* 8 (February 1881): 171–176;

"A Diligence Journey in Mexico," *Century Illustrated Magazine,* 23 (November 1881): 1–14;

"A Provincial Capital of Mexico," *Century Illustrated Magazine,* 23 (January 1882): 321–333;

"From Morelia to Mexico City on Horseback," *Century Illustrated Magazine,* 23 (March 1882): 643–655;

"Menhaden Sketches: Summer at Christmas-Time," *St. Nicholas,* 12 (December 1884): 116–124;

"A Four-Leaved Clover in the Desert," *St. Nicholas,* 21 (May–June 1894): 644–650; 694–699;

"The Borrowed Shift," *Land of Sunshine,* 10 (December 1898): 13–24;

"How the Pump Stopped at the Morning Watch," *Century Illustrated Magazine,* 58 (July 1899): 469–472;

"The Eleventh Hour," *Century Illustrated Magazine,* 71 (January 1906): 485–493.

OTHER: "Gideon's Knock," in *The Spinners' Book of Fiction* (San Francisco: Paul Elder, 1907), pp. 77–91.

One of the foremost Western writers of her age, Mary Hallock Foote is today regarded primarily as a local-color writer whose writing does not merit scrutiny, except from literary historians interested in her work as an archive of a bygone age. Yet, in her own day she was hailed, along with American writers and artists such as Owen Wister, Frederic Remington, and Bret Harte, as one of the finest chroniclers of the frontier experience. Writing in 1922, the renowned Western illustrator William Allen Rogers marveled that "somehow she and Wister, two products of the most refined culture of the East, got closer to the rough frontier character than any writers I know." Wister himself wrote in 1911 that Foote was the first writer "to honor the cattle country and not to libel it." Also among Foote's admirers were author and *Atlantic Monthly* editor William Dean Howells, Western author Helen Hunt Jackson, and Rudyard Kipling, who was Foote's friend and correspondent.

Foote's additional talents as an illustrator gained her prestigious commissions as well as an appointment as juror for an art competition at the Chicago World's Fair in 1893.

These hallmarks of literary and artistic achievement, however, were not enough to secure Foote a place in more recent American literary criticism. Following her death in 1938, her work received little attention until 1971, when Wallace Stegner's Pulitzer Prize–winning novel *Angle of Repose,* based upon Foote's then-unpublished memoir, *A Victorian Gentlewoman in the Far West* (1972), generated renewed interest in the forgotten author. Foote scholar Mary Ellen Williams Walsh has recently documented the extent to which Stegner relied on the memoirs for his own plots, characters, and descriptions; many passages in his novel are indeed lifted directly from the memoirs. That Stegner was able to borrow so much original material from Foote in order to secure his own literary reputation is suggestive of the extent to which her skill as a writer has not been adequately recognized.

The youngest of four children, Mary Anna Hallock was born on 19 November 1847 to Quaker parents, Nathaniel and Ann Burling Hallock, on a farm near Milton, New York. Although she was to spend a relatively brief period of her life here before immigrating West, her literature bears the indelible stamp of the pastoral seclusion and intellectual atmosphere in which the Hallock family preferred to live. Alienated from the broader community because of their dissenting religion, the Hallocks—in Foote's words, "the Quaker branch that went too far"—had also fallen out with their fellow Quakers after Foote's uncle, preacher Nicholas Hallock, offended the southern members with his vocal abolitionism. The Hallocks' doubly marginalized social status made close family ties and solitary intellectual pursuits all the more important to the family's daily life.

In 1864 Foote attended the Cooper Institute School of Design for Women in New York City. For three years she studied illustration and cultivated what was to become her lifelong friendship with Helena de Kay, daughter of an established New York family. If her childhood on a Milton farm had developed in Foote an appreciation for the pastoral and the intellectual, her experience at the Cooper Institute, especially her friendship with Helena, broadened Foote's social connections considerably. Through Helena, who later married editor Richard Watson Gilder, editor of *Scribner's Monthly* and its successor, *Century Illustrated Magazine,* Foote secured illustration commissions as well as her first prose publication and developed a broad circle of friends

Foote's husband, Arthur De Wint Foote

and acquaintances in New York society. Among these was mining engineer Arthur De Wint Foote.

In 1876, after a three-year courtship, Mary and Arthur were married in the Hallocks' home in Milton. Arthur had originally proposed that they be married in California, near the mine he managed in New Almaden. "But I should have needed far more nerve than I possessed for the adventure itself to have entered another family in that way," Foote wrote in her memoirs, "moreover I had a very good little job of my own that winter." By this time Foote was enjoying a successful career as an illustrator, and she refused to leave everything she had for Arthur unless he was prepared to demonstrate the depth of his own commitment. Arthur agreed to return to Milton for the ceremony, which had to be a small and rushed affair so that he could return with Foote to the mine in New Almaden. "No girl ever wanted less to 'go West' with any man," Foote wrote, "or paid a man a greater compliment by doing so."

Foote sustained an ambivalent attitude toward both marriage and western migration—mutually implicating processes in her own experience—throughout much of her fiction. Certainly, her earliest western experiences did little to assuage the anxi-

ety she felt as a young bride. Within a year of the Footes' attempt to set up housekeeping in New Almaden and the birth of their first child, Arthur Burling, Arthur uprooted his new family and brought them to Santa Cruz, where he had been reassigned. In 1878 Arthur took on fieldwork in Deadwood, South Dakota, sending Foote and the baby to stay with Foote's parents in Milton. In 1880 a second attempt to settle, this time at a mining camp in Leadville, Colorado, was thwarted when labor and boundary disputes forced a shutdown of the mine Arthur had been hired to manage. Foote's childhood home in Milton again supplied refuge when the homeless family moved there until Arthur could secure another post.

During this period, characterized by temporary settlement, frequent domestic upheaval, and long separations from Arthur, Foote turned more seriously to writing fiction. Although she had become a highly sought-after illustrator, receiving prestigious commissions for gift-book editions of Nathaniel Hawthorne's *The Scarlet Letter* and Henry Wadsworth Longfellow's *The Skeleton in Armor* (both published in 1877), illustrating proved impractical in the remote mining camps where she was compelled to live. The inhabitants and scenery were not suitably pastoral for the romantic subjects her publishers preferred; woodblocks and other supplies proved cumbersome; and publishers' deadlines were inflexible and difficult to meet. Because of frequent domestic disruptions, Foote soon discovered that writing was a far more flexible means of occupying her time and mind, not to mention augmenting Arthur's often meager and unpredictable income.

Foote became a Western writer almost by default: whereas men such as Wister and Remington were, for the most part, paid by publishers to travel West in order to produce fiction and illustrations, Foote's choices were narrowly circumscribed by those of her husband, in whose adventurous spirit she did not wholeheartedly share. Nevertheless, her western experience proved to be her most marketable literary capital, with eastern audiences eager to consume firsthand accounts of the mythic wild West. Foote, however, did not subscribe to idealistic versions of the West. Although she was keenly aware of its mythic status as an individualist proving ground, much of her fiction contrasts the different circumstances under which men and women travel to and live in the West.

Among Foote's earliest short stories, "In Exile," first published in the *Atlantic* (1881) and still regarded as one of her finest works of fiction, introduces the theme of what literary critic Lee Ann Johnson has called "marriage by default," where a woman's choices in marriage are predicated upon sacrifice and loss rather than desire and its fulfillment. "In Exile," as well as some of Foote's later works, situates this theme in a western context in order to highlight the paradox of the West as a confining rather than a liberating space for women. Its heroine, Frances Newell, a schoolmistress in a California mining town, falls in love with an engineer and must silently suffer with the knowledge that he is already engaged to a well-to-do woman in Boston. In a particularly illuminating passage, Frances ponders the contrast between her own circumstances and those of her beloved, Arnold: "What can he, what can any man, know of loneliness? He may go out and walk about on the hills; he may go away altogether, and take the risks of life somewhere else. A woman must take no risks. There is not a house in the camp where he might not enter to-night, if he chose." In the end, Frances and Arnold marry, but largely because circumstances compel the union: Arnold's fiancée rejects him while Frances's friend in the East, with whom she had planned to live, dies. Foote had originally planned a less hopeful resolution to the affair, but editor William Dean Howells complained that the original ending was "too wantonly sad." As a compromise Foote ended the story with marriage but insisted upon preserving the melancholy key of the original.

Foote's first novel, *The Led-Horse Claim: A Romance of a Mining Camp,* further develops the theme of women's exile in the West. Serialized in *Century Magazine* in 1882, it is closely based on events that took place in 1880 during Arthur's short-lived stint as mine manager in Leadville. A rivalry between two mines laying claim to the same vein of silver figures as the context of a love affair between Cecil Conrath, sister to the manager of the Shoshone mine, and George Hilgard, manager of the rival Led-Horse mine. The claim dispute eventually erupts into a violent confrontation between members of the two rival mines, and Cecil's brother is fatally wounded. Cecil at first blames and rejects Hilgard for her brother's death.

Again, editorial intervention prevented Foote from ending the novel on this tragic note. To please Gilder, her editor, she added to the original manuscript a coincidental reunion between the two lovers, but again would not completely compromise her original plan. Thus, the wedding that closes the novel is depicted in funerary terms, with Cecil's family dressed in "their dull, black mourning robes." A final reminder of the deadly circumstances leading to Cecil's marriage is supplied in the novel's closing lines, describing Conrath's burial next to his long-dead mother: "One might fancy the mother, in her sleep, reaching out unconsciously and covering her child."

As in much of Foote's fiction, the tragic circumstances of westering women in *The Led-Horse Claim* are engendered through the choices of their male relations. Contrary to the observations of historian Richard Slotkin, who has exhaustively studied the tendency of western American mythology to naturalize the historical conditions of western development—that is, to depict historical events as the consequence of natural law rather than human choice—Foote underlines her western romance with realistic depictions of the frontier mining economy. As Johnson observes, Foote problematizes the relationship between East and West through her attention to detail. She reminds her readers that both mines are closely controlled by eastern interests; she depicts the uneasy relationships between well-educated, privileged mine managers and their rugged western lifestyle; and she emphasizes the unstable status of the institution of property in the West and the ugly competition between otherwise worthy men. Similarly, in several other novels, the West is depicted, not as the land of unlimited opportunity and refuge from social and economic ills, but as the very site of their production. The frontier is the setting for a fraught court battle in *John Bodewin's Testimony* (1886), land-claim fraud in *The Chosen Valley* (1892), and a violent miners' strike in *Coeur d'Alene* (1894).

For Foote, western entrepreneurialism particularly undermines the traditional culture of middle-class women like herself, who are not necessarily willing westerners. In *The Led-Horse Claim,* the unpredictable economic behavior of men at the mining camp hinders the production of a stable domestic life for their families:

> Cecil's life at the mine was a lonely one. Even the ladies who lived in the populous parts of the camp struggled vainly to fulfill duly that important feminine rite, the exchange of calls. There were difficulties of roads and of weather, and of finding the missing houses of acquaintances, which in the progressive state of the city topography, had been unexpectedly shunted off into other streets. A new street had barely time to be named and numbered, before it was moved backward or forward, or obliterated altogether, in the intermittent attempts of the city government to reconcile United States patents with "jumpers" claims.

For Foote, the West was no exception to the general pattern of boom-and-bust economics that prevailed in America for much of the late nineteenth century.

With Arthur continuously moving from one assignment to another, the Footes relied increasingly on her writing to augment their unpredictable income. The extra money was especially needed in the years following Arthur's involvement in a massive irrigation project in Boise, Idaho, begun in 1882. That same year, their second child, Elizabeth, was born; a third child, Agnes, was born in 1886. The eventual failure of the project in 1891 all but bankrupted the family. To cope with his mounting failures, Arthur turned increasingly to alcohol, placing further strains upon the marriage. Faced with an alcoholic husband, financial worries, a series of family illnesses, and small children to look after, Foote had become significantly less productive by the late 1880s.

Perhaps fueled by the intense stress under which Foote was living during this difficult period, the tragic impulses underlining her earlier fiction are more fully developed in "A Cloud on the Mountain" first published in *Century Magazine* (November 1885). The daughter of a humble cattle rancher, Ruth Mary Tully is on the verge of womanhood when a party of engineers spends the night at the family ranch. There is a brief flirtation between Ruth Mary and Kirkwood, one of the younger engineers, but it means considerably less to him than it does to Ruth Mary. Meanwhile, Ruth Mary's parents assume that she will marry her father's business partner, who was recently maimed in an accident and for whom she feels pity and compassion, but not love.

If "In Exile" develops the theme of women's confinement in the West, "A Cloud on the Mountain" represents the silencing aspects of the western terrain: the story reaches its climax when an impending flood threatens to wipe out Kirkwood's mining camp. In an attempt to warn Kirkwood, Ruth Mary embarks on a reckless raft trip downriver. Just as the camp comes into view, she is swept up in the flood. The "cry of her despair went up and was lost, as boat and message and messenger were lost—gone utterly, gorged at one leap by the senseless loss." Ruth Mary's death by drowning, forever keeping hidden her desire for Kirkwood, figures the malevolent, silencing power of the western landscape. Kirkwood, meanwhile, is oblivious to her experience: "the pity of it, when he thinks of it sometimes, seems to him more than he can bear . . . yet if Ruth Mary had still been there at the ranch on the hills, she would have been, to him, only 'that nice little girl of Tully's who married the one-eyed packer.'"

The Footes' life continued to worsen after the failure of the Idaho irrigation project in 1891; Arthur embarked upon another, smaller irrigation scheme, only to be cheated out of his claim to land he had intended to develop. Foote processed both of these traumatic experiences in her 1892 novel, *The Chosen Valley*. It is the story of an engineer not unlike Arthur Foote, who invests all he has in an irrigation project only to see his dream destroyed by a combination of economic uncertainty and unscrupulous business associates. Foote concludes her novel with a scathing critique of western entrepreneurialism:

> The ideal scheme is ever beckoning from the West; but the scheme with an ideal record is yet to find—the scheme that shall breed no murmerers, and see no recreants; that shall avoid envy, hatred, malice, and all uncharitableness; that shall fulfill its promises, and pay its debts, and remember its friends, and keep itself unspotted from the world. Over the graves of the dead, and over the hearts of the living, presses the cruel expansion of our country's material progress: the prophets are confounded, the promise withdrawn, the people imagine a vain thing.

The failed irrigation schemes marked Foote's writing pragmatically as well as thematically. In her memoirs, she termed her work of this period "pot-boiling"—short stories hastily written for quick and badly needed cash. Perhaps to capitalize on the predictable financial success of 'wild West' formula stories, Foote wrote one herself: "The Rapture of Hetty," first published in *Century Magazine* in 1891. In this brief and erotically charged tale, a forbidden romance emerges between Hetty Rhodes, "prettiest of all the bunch-grass belles," and Basset, youngest son of "a pastoral and nomadic house." Basset is "socially under a cloud" after a rival for Hetty's affection accuses him of altering brands on neighboring livestock—a common form of cattle rustling on the unfenced ranges of the midwestern frontier. Because she refuses to comment upon these events, Hetty herself appears to abide by popular opinion regarding Basset. Foote invites us, however, to question this reading of Hetty's silence by suggesting that "a girl may not testify" of matters concerning her sexuality. Hetty's own desire is more clearly, if still indirectly, articulated when Basset arrives an "unbidden guest" at a Christmas dance, demands a dance with Hetty, and "plunge[s], with his breathless, smiling dancer in his arms . . . into the dim outer place to the door where his horse stood saddled, and they were gone." As if to emphasize the unspeakable status of female desire, Foote marks its fulfillment with her heroine's disappearance into the wilderness.

Although recent criticism of Foote's writing has not held this story in high regard, it is of interest because of the way the author takes up certain formulaic components of the popular West in order to depict the fulfillment of female desire. This is a startling departure from her earlier female characters, whose marriages are achieved on the basis of circumstance rather than desire ("In Exile"), or are marked by death and tragedy (*The Led-Horse Claim*). Another "potboiler," "The Watchman" (*Century Magazine*, November 1893) represents the confining position more typical of Foote's other female characters. In this short story, the heroine, Nancy Lark, is caught in the middle of an ugly dispute between her father, a poor homesteader, and her suitor, Travis, the manager of a local irrigation project. Travis is fired when Nancy's father sabotages the irrigation ditch, deliberately flooding his own property in order to collect damages from the irrigation company. Although her allegiance is at first torn between the two feuding men, Nancy eventually marries Travis, signaling her tacit repudiation of her father's rebelliousness. The story's ambivalent closure identifies the married Nancy with a tamed landscape, both controlled by male agency: "Flowers bloom upon its banks, heaven is reflected in its waters, fair and broad are the fertile pastures that lie beyond; but the best-trained ditch can never be a river, nor the gentlest wife a girl again."

In 1895, after almost twenty years of perpetual financial and domestic instability, the Footes settled in Grass Valley, California, where Arthur had been engaged by the North Star Mining Company. The engagement proved longer and more prosperous than expected, enabling Foote to return from "potboiling" to serious novel-writing. In 1902 she published *The Desert and the Sown,* still considered one of her finest novels. That same year, Owen Wister, whom many critics considered Foote's male counterpart in Western writing, published his paradigmatic Western novel, *The Virginian.* Although the two authors admired and were influenced by each other's work, Foote did not share in Wister's uncompromising celebration of the "old West," nor did she mourn its imminent passing. Two adventurous males—Paul Bogardus and his estranged father, Adam—are represented in Foote's 1902 novel of the West; neither of them is accorded the heroic status of Wister's Virginian, after whom most subsequent male heroes of the popular western—from Zane Grey's Lassiter in *Riders of the Purple Sage* (1912) to the title character in Jack Schaefer's *Shane* (1949)—are modeled. Foote's novel begins with Paul's departure on a risky hunting expedition, leaving behind his mother, Emily, and his fiancée, Moya. On this journey in the wilderness, Paul is coincidentally reunited with his estranged father, Adam Bogardus, whom Emily has long since

Frontispiece for Foote's first book, The Led-Horse Claim *(1883), about a rivalry between two mining camps*

given up for dead. Hoping to reunite his parents, Paul returns home with his father, now known as Packer John, only to find that Emily, now wealthy and status-conscious, will not acknowledge the old man. Thus rejected, Adam returns to his ignominious life in the wilderness. By the end of the novel, Emily reverses her position and accepts Adam as her husband; however, his death conveniently delivers her from the social compromises that such a gesture might otherwise involve.

Paul is deeply critical of his mother's bigotry, but the novel tacitly justifies Emily's reluctance to reunite with her husband. In this respect, Foote's position on gender relations in the West opposes that of Wister and the many popular writers who followed his example by depicting female heroines prepared to sacrifice their status and reputation for the sake of their frontier heroes. Foote herself had left family, friends, and career for the sake of her adventurous husband, a choice she later regretted. "I had not reckoned on the schemes," she writes in her memoir,

Foote with family members and a friend in Boise, Idaho, circa 1894–1895: (back row) Foote, Bessie Hallock Sherman, and Nelly Linton; (front row) Foote's niece Mary Birney Sherman and Foote's three children, Agnes, Betty, and Arthur

[Arthur] had risen, poor wretch, in obedience to his own inheritance, from the ashes of all the jobs that gave out, the cement dream that failed, the men you couldn't work for and be a man yourself, the climates we could not live in; he had resigned . . . with not a tangible thing in sight: I couldn't count this appalling undertaking as anything more than the stuff of wakeful nights for mothers of young babies.

Emily Bogardus makes a similarly reckless choice, repudiating her family to marry a Western adventurer, but is delivered from its consequences by the early separation from her husband. She is not prepared to make the same mistake twice. Her future daughter-in-law functions in the novel as the primary spokesperson on Emily's behalf: "I think most women have a tendency towards the state of being unmarried," Moya tells Paul, "and if one had–children, it would increase upon one very fast. A widow and a mother–for twenty years. How could she be a wife again?"

In addition to *The Desert and the Sown,* Foote published one other novel during her Grass Valley years, *The Prodigal* (1900), and two short-story collections. This burst of productivity ended suddenly, however, with the unexpected death of her youngest

daughter, Agnes, in 1904. Agnes's death so devastated her that for several years following the tragedy Foote wrote little, turning down requests for submissions and interviews and setting aside the novel she had been working on at the time of Agnes's death. Not until late in the decade did she recover sufficiently to resume her writing, publishing *The Royal Americans* in 1910, the first of five novels completed during the most stable and prosperous period of her life. The children were grown, the mine in Grass Valley continued to operate smoothly, and Arthur's adventurous spirit had been curbed by age: Foote now had the resources to write on her own terms.

Although the novels of this period of relative repose revisit themes familiar from Foote's earlier works, they register the very different vantage point from which she was writing now that she was no longer faced with chronic crisis and anxiety. In *The Royal Americans* and *A Picked Company* (1912), she shifts from the highly localized settings characterizing her earlier novels, often closely based upon her own immediate circumstances, to the more sweeping chronological and geographic terrain of the historical romance. Several other of these later novels are deeply introspective: *Edith Bonham* (1917), the story of an intense, even erotic, friendship between two women, is a tribute to Foote's lifelong friend Helena de Kay Gilder, who died in 1916; *The Ground-Swell* (1919), a mother's first-person narration of her relationship with her daughter, commemorates her late daughter, Agnes. In her memoirs, Foote described the perspective that generated this turn to the panoramic and the introspective:

> Everyone knows the magic perspectives of memory—it keeps what we loved and alters the relative size and value of many things that we did not love enough—that we hated and resisted and made mountains of at the time. It turns the dust of our valleys of humiliation, now that the sun of our working hours has set, into a sad and dreamy splendor which will fade into depths beyond depths of unknown worlds of stars.

Now that Foote was distanced from the many experiences that had taught her to question popular myths of the West, she became something of a mythologizer herself. *A Picked Company,* the story of an overland trek during the 1840s, covers expansive thematic as well as geographic terrain, weaving together themes and issues that Foote had treated more disparately in her earlier, less panoramic, novels. Its overarching plot involves Reverend Yardley's dream of establishing a Congregational colony in Oregon, handpicked by himself and founded upon strict religious principles. Along with his son, Jimmy, the Reverend includes in his party Silence and Alvin Hannington; their daughter, Barbie; and their niece, Stella Mutrie. Ill-equipped to supply anything but moral guidance for the trek, the Reverend also engages the services of Bradburn, who lacks moral principles but is expert in negotiating the rugged wilderness.

Although this scenario situates the novel within a highly romanticized discourse of the West, Foote maintains the critical distance from popular Western myths cultivated in her earlier works. If the Reverend's project is to take a select group of righteous individuals into the wilderness "to exercise and preserve their goodness, alone with the worship and the works of God," Foote's project is to challenge his idealism. The Reverend's plan, indeed, is "mutilated in the very inception" by the fact that he must engage Bradburn as a "temporal guide" for his party. A more sinister version of the wilderness guide-hero, made famous by James Fenimore Cooper and the scores of dime novelists who emulated him, Bradburn does not share the innate moral principles characterizing Western heroes such as Cooper's Natty Bumppo, Wister's Virginian, and Zane Grey's Las-

siter. The morally vulnerable Stella Mutrie, whose secular and flirtatious nature her aunt and uncle hope to reform through the westering experience, is soon seduced by Bradburn and leaves the party shortly after her pregnancy is discovered. Whereas Bradburn endures no immediate repercussions for his actions, the Reverend orders that Stella be cast out of the party in order to save his project from the moral contamination her pregnancy represents. Jimmy takes pity on Stella and offers to escort her to the nearest fort, even though by doing so he jeopardizes his budding romance with Barbie Hannington. Jimmy risks his own prospects in the group again when he kills Bradburn in a duel fought for Stella's sake.

In the figure of Bradburn, whose affair with Stella embroils the novel's principle characters in these inescapable moral dilemmas, Foote further develops her critique of western male heroism in a way that anticipates the emergence of what has recently become known as the anti-Western. In novels such as Walter Van Tilburg Clark's *The Oxbow Incident* (1940) and movies such as Clint Eastwood's *Unforgiven* (1992), moral conflict is neither clearly defined nor simplistically resolved. In a similar vein, Foote refuses the tendency toward nostalgia for an idealized western past, familiar in the Western writings of many of her contemporaries including Wister, Theodore Roosevelt, and historian Frederic Jackson Turner, all of whom believed that the ideal American was produced through the pioneering experience. In *A Picked Company,* Foote's critique of this thesis is particularly strident. Far from redeemed by her western trek, the unfortunate Stella becomes a prostitute in a dissipated mining town, becomes pregnant and marries, and is killed by her new husband, who then takes his own life. Foote closes her tale of the Reverend's mission on a less tragic but similarly ambivalent note: with the exception of Silence Hannington, who does not survive the journey, the Reverend's party arrives at their destination and begins the construction of their new community, but "after so noble a beginning their work showed rather small in its immediate results. . . . Here and there a life was altered, a sincere convert made, but far many more acquired a cynicism as to the Christian's Road to Heaven that was very sad for the Christian hope of bringing light to souls in darkness."

The anticlimactic closure to the journey of the "picked company" was in many ways similar to the way in which the Footes' western adventures ended. They did not live out their lives on the western homestead they had established but returned to the East, living with their daughter in Hingham, Massachusetts. On 25 June 1938, shortly before her ninety-first birthday, Mary Hallock Foote died, having survived Arthur by five years. She left behind a written legacy of stories, sketches, and novels that comprises one of the nineteenth century's most important literary voices of the American West. The popularity of this reluctant westerner suggests that she was far from alone in seeking an alternative to the rugged individualism celebrated by many of her male counterparts. With the recent emergence of the New Western criticism, which examines the history and literature of those excluded from traditional western historiography as epitomized by Turner, alternative western voices are becoming increasingly important. Mary Hallock Foote deserves a more prominent place in the project of recovering these forgotten voices of the American West, especially given her unparalleled literary achievements.

Biography:

Doris Bickford-Swarthout, *Mary Hallock Foote: Pioneer Woman Illustrator* (Deansboro, N.Y.: Berry Hill Press, 1996).

References:

Shelley Armitage, "The Illustrator as Writer: Mary Hallock Foote and the Myth of the West," in *Under the Sun: Myth and Realism in Western American Literature,* edited by Barbara Howard Meldrum (Troy, N.Y.: Whitston, 1985), pp. 150–175;

Regina Armstrong, "Representative American Women Illustrators," *Critic,* 37 (August 1900): 131–141;

Mary Lou Benn, "Mary Hallock Foote: Early Leadville Writer," *Colorado Magazine,* 33 (April 1956): 93–108;

Benn, "Mary Hallock Foote in Idaho," *University of Wyoming Publications,* 20 (15 July 1956): 157–178;

Richard W. Etulain, "Mary Hallock Foote: A Checklist," *Western American Literature,* 10 (May 1975): 59–65;

Etulain, "Mary Hallock Foote (1847–1938)," *American Literary Realism, 1870–1910,* 5 (Spring 1972): 145–150;

Helena de Kay Gilder, "Author Illustrators, II: Mary Hallock Foote," *Book Buyer,* 11 (August 1894): 338–342;

Melody Graulich, "Legacy Profile: Mary Hallock Foote (1847–1938)," *Legacy,* 3 (Fall 1986): 43–52;

Lee Ann Johnson, *Mary Hallock Foote* (Boston: Twayne, 1980);

James H. Maguire, *Mary Hallock Foote* (Boise, Idaho: Boise State College, 1972);

Rodman W. Paul, "When Culture Came to Boise: Mary Hallock in Idaho," *Idaho Yesterdays,* 20 (Summer 1976): 2–12;

William Allen Rogers, *A World Worth While: A Record of 'Auld Acquaintance'* (New York: Harper, 1922), pp. 183–188;

Richard Slotkin, *The Fatal Environment: the Myth of the Frontier in the Age of Industrialization* (Middletown, Conn: Wesleyan University Press, 1985);

Robert Taft, *Artists and Illustrators of the Old West: 1850–1900* (New York: Scribner's, 1953);

Mary Ellen Williams Walsh, "*Angle of Repose* and the Writings of Mary Hallock Foote: A Source Study," *Critical Essays on Wallace Stegner,* edited by Anthony Arthur (Boston: G. K. Hall, 1982): pp. 184–209;

Owen Wister, *Members of the Family* (New York: Macmillan, 1911), p. 15.

Papers:

Substantial collections of Mary Hallock Foote's papers are housed at the Stanford University Library; Henry E. Huntington Library, San Marino, California; the Bancroft Library, University of California, Berkeley; and the Houghton Library, Harvard University.

Mary E. Wilkins Freeman

(31 October 1852 – 13 March 1930)

Marylynne Diggs
Clark College

See also the Freeman entries in *DLB 12: American Realists and Naturalists* and *DLB 78: American Short-Story Writers, 1880–1910.*

BOOKS: *Decorative Plaques: Designs by George F. Barnes, Poems by Mary E. Wilkins* (Boston: Lothrop, 1883);

Goody Two-Shoes and Other Famous Nursery Tales, by Clara Doty Bates and Mary E. Wilkins (Boston: Lothrop, 1883);

The Cow with the Golden Horns and Other Stories (Boston: Lothrop, 1884);

The Adventures of Anne: Stories of Colonial Times (Boston: Lothrop, 1886);

A Humble Romance and Other Stories (New York: Harper, 1887); republished in two volumes as *A Humble Romance and Other Stories* and *A Far-Away Melody and Other Stories* (Edinburgh: Douglas, 1890);

A New England Nun and Other Stories (New York: Harper, 1891; London: Osgood, McIlvane, 1891);

The Pot of Gold and Other Stories (Boston: Lothrop, 1892; London: Ward, Lock, Bowden, 1892);

Young Lucretia and Other Stories (New York: Harper, 1892; London: Osgood, McIlvane, 1892);

Jane Field: A Novel (London: Osgood, McIlvane, 1892; New York: Harper, 1893);

Giles Corey, Yeoman: A Play (New York: Harper, 1893);

Pembroke: A Novel (New York: Harper, 1894; London: Osgood, McIlvane, 1894);

Comfort Pease and Her Gold Ring (New York, Chicago & Toronto: Revell, 1895);

Madelon: A Novel (New York: Harper, 1896; London: Osgood, 1896);

Jerome, A Poor Man: A Novel (New York & London: Harper, 1897);

Once Upon a Time and Other Child-Verses (Boston: Lothrop, 1897; London: Harper, 1898);

Silence, and Other Stories (New York & London: Harper, 1898);

The People of Our Neighborhood (Philadelphia: Curtis / New York: Doubleday, McClure, 1898); repub-

Mary E. Wilkins Freeman

lished as *Some of Our Neighbors* (London: Dent, 1898);

The Jamesons (New York: Doubleday & McClure, 1899);

The Heart's Highway, A Romance of Virginia in the Seventeenth Century (New York: Doubleday, Page, 1900; London: Murray, 1900);

The Love of Parson Lord and Other Stories (New York & London: Harper, 1900);

The Portion of Labor (New York & London: Harper, 1901);

Understudies: Short Stories (New York & London: Harper, 1901);

Six Trees: Short Stories (New York & London: Harper, 1903);

The Wind in the Rose-Bush and Other Stories of the Supernatural (New York: Doubleday, Page, 1903; London: Murray, 1903);

The Givers: Short Stories (New York & London: Harper, 1904);

The Debtor: A Novel (New York & London: Harper, 1905);

"Doc" Gordon (New York: Authors and Newspapers Association, 1906);

By the Light of the Soul (New York & London: Harper, 1906);

The Fair Lavinia and Others (New York & London: Harper, 1907);

The Shoulders of Atlas (New York & London: Harper, 1908);

The Whole Family, A Novel by Twelve Authors, by Freeman and others(New York: Harper, 1908);

The Winning Lady and Others (New York & London: Harper, 1909);

The Green Door (New York: Moffat, Yard, 1910);

The Butterfly House (New York: Dodd, Mead, 1912);

The Yates Pride: A Romance (New York & London: Harper, 1912);

The Copy-Cat & Other Stories (New York & London: Harper, 1914);

An Alabaster Box, by Freeman and Florence Morse Kingsley (New York: Appleton, 1917);

Edgewater People (New York & London: Harper, 1918);

The Best Stories of Mary E. Wilkins, selected by Henry Wysham Lanier (New York & London: Harper, 1927);

Collected Ghost Stories, introduction by Edward Wagenknecht (Sauk City, Wis.: Arkham House, 1974);

The Uncollected Short Stories of Mary Wilkins Freeman, compiled by Mary R. Reichardt (Jackson: University Press of Mississippi, 1992).

SELECTED PERIODICAL PUBLICATIONS–UNCOLLECTED:

FICTION

"Pastels in Prose: In the Marshland, Camilla's Snuff Box, Shadows, Death," *Harper's* (December 1892): 147;

"The Long Arm," *Pocket Magazine* (1 December 1895): 1–76;

Eglantina: A Romantic Parlor Play, Ladies' Home Journal (July 1910): 13, 14, 38.

NONFICTION

"If They Had a Million Dollars: What Nine Famous Women Would Do If a Fortune Were Theirs," *Ladies' Home Journal* (September 1903): 10;

"He Does Not Want a Fool," *Delineator* (July 1908): 80, 135;

"How I Write My Novels: Twelve of America's Most Popular Authors Reveal the Secrets of Their Art," *New York Times,* 25 October 1908, magazine section, pp. 3–4;

"A Woman's Tribute to Mr. Howells," *Literary Digest,* 44 (9 March 1912): 485;

"New England, 'Mother of America,'" *Country Life in America,* 22 (July 1912): 27–32, 64–67;

"The Girl Who Wants to Write: Things to Do and to Avoid," *Harper's Bazar,* 47 (June 1913): 272;

"Mary E. Wilkins Freeman: An Autobiography," *Saturday Evening Post,* 190 (8 December 1917): 25, 75.

PLAY PRODUCTION: *Giles Corey, Yeoman,* Boston, Theater of Arts and Letters, 27 March 1893.

PRODUCED SCRIPTS: *The Pilgrim's Progress,* motion picture, by Freeman and William Dinwiddie, 1915;

False Evidence, motion picture (based on the novel *Madelon*), Metro Pictures, 1919.

The life of Mary E. Wilkins Freeman has too often been compared to that of the spinsters who populate much of her fiction. Although she lived most of her life in small New England villages and did not marry until she was forty-nine years of age, Freeman's life was far less isolated and her work far more diverse than many readers realize. Freeman was born in a cultural moment in which Puritanism, Transcendentalism, and Abolitionism and the health and purity movements were influential trends. She lived out the last decade of her life during the Jazz Age of the 1920s, an era in which indulgence in spiritual and political fulfillment took a backseat to commercial gratification in the last gasp of economic growth prior to the stock market crash of 1929, an event that preceded Freeman's death by a year.

Between these decades, Freeman saw vast changes occurring in the New England villages like those in which she spent most of her life. The effects of a declining cottage industry in shoe manufacturing, a decreasing male population, and emerging cultures and economies unfamiliar to small-town inhabitants all find a place in Freeman's fiction. What emerges from a study of her life and her work, however, is not an isolated woman composing photographic representations of an era and judging its barren landscape and obstinate people, as critics and biographers have suggested; rather, one sees a woman with a complex life whose corpus of work–comprising fourteen novels, more than two hundred short stories, three plays, three volumes of poetry, stories for children, several nonfiction pieces, and two screenplays—resists simplification and generalization. Freeman experienced poverty and wealth, rural and city living, "spinsterhood" and marriage. Although much of her work focuses on the lives of women and the poor, it also treats a broader array of issues and contributes to the literary and social debates of her time, which have remained relevant: debates about regionalism and realism, sexual identity, class and labor relations, and race.

Freeman was born Mary Ella Wilkins on 31 October 1852 in the small shoe manufacturing town of Randolph, Massachusetts. She was the first surviving child of Warren Wilkins and Eleanor Lothrop Wilkins, both of whom came from longstanding New England families. Though a shy and socially awkward child, her isolation was lessened in 1859 by the birth of her sister, Anna (or "Nan"), and the beginning of her lifelong friendship with schoolmate Mary John Wales. In 1867, just after the Civil War, her father, a house builder and carpenter, moved the family from the increasingly depressed Randolph to Brattleboro, Vermont, a town renowned as the birthplace of America's first playwright, Royall Tyler, and the location of Robert Wesselhoeft's Water Cure spa, which had attracted intellectuals, artists, and public figures before the war. In Brattleboro, Warren Wilkins entered the dry-goods business with his friend Orrin Slate. Expecting this move to improve their financial security, the family purchased land in a fashionable section of Brattleboro and moved into a small cottage until their new house could be built. In Brattleboro, Freeman developed a friendship with Evelyn "Evie" Sawyer, with whom she shared intellectual pursuits as well as a lack of interest in the young men of the village. The two became inseparable and remained friends for life. In 1870 Freeman attended Mt. Holyoke Female Seminary, but she left after only one year when she found the school's rigidity unpleasant. The school's book of rules included both major infractions, such as tardiness and absence from church, and minor infractions, such as "walking over wet floors" or talking "above a whisper" in the halls. The students were to report these infractions, and those who broke the rules were required to "make public confession of their misdeeds." Years later she wrote to a friend, "I was very young . . . and went home at the end of the year a nervous wreck. . . . As I remember, I did not behave at all well at Mt. Holyoke, and I am inclined to attribute it to monotony of diet and too strenuous goadings of conscience." After returning to Brattleboro, she attended classes at a seminary in West Brattleboro and tried teaching, but not with any success or enjoyment.

Freeman's lack of success at school, her difficulty finding profitable labor, and her disinterest in marriage did not help the family's already disappointing economic circumstances. During the lean years of the 1870s, a period of general depression throughout the country, Warren Wilkins sold his stock in the dry-goods business and returned to carpentry, a decision that worsened the family's financial situation. In 1876 Mary's sister, Nan, died, and in 1877 the family moved into the Reverend Thomas Pickman Tyler's house, where Eleanor Wilkins entered employment as the Tylers' housekeeper. This move was a difficult one for the family, especially for Eleanor Wilkins, who had come from a prominent family and considered herself a social equal to the Tylers, and for Mary, who had a lingering affection for the Tylers' son, Hanson, a naval ensign who was rarely home. When Eleanor Wilkins died unexpectedly of a heart attack in 1880, Freeman and her father moved from the Tyler house to a small cottage. It was there that Freeman first began writing in an attempt to earn money. In the fall of 1882 Warren Wilkins moved to Florida, where he hoped to find year-round construction opportunities and a better climate for his own failing health. By the spring of 1883, however, his condition had deteriorated, and he died, leaving his thirty-one-year-old daughter without a family. During the following winter, Freeman made extended visits to the homes of Mary John Wales in Randolph and Evie, who then lived with her husband, Charles Severance, in Shelburne Falls, Massachusetts. Later in 1884 she moved in with the Wales family in Randolph, where she remained until her marriage to Charles Manning Freeman in 1902.

By the time of her father's death, Freeman's writing had begun to earn her some money and recognition. The income from her early writings, in addition to payments from commercial property she inherited when her father died, enabled her to pursue writing as a profession. In 1881 the children's publication *Wide Awake* printed two of Freeman's ballads for children, "The Beggar King" and "The Tithing Man," earning her ten dollars and an invitation to contribute more pieces to the magazine. In January 1882 "The Shadow Family," her first story for an adult audience, was published in the *Boston Sunday Budget* and won a fifty-dollar prize. She contributed poems and stories for periodical publication during these years, but one of her best breaks came in 1883 when *Harper's Bazar,* at the time the most popular magazine for a female audience, published "Two Old Lovers." The story brought in twenty-five dollars and marked the beginning of a continuing literary relationship with Harper and Brothers. In June 1884 *Harper's New Monthly Magazine,* a prestigious periodical publishing such notable American writers as William Dean Howells, Sarah Orne Jewett, Elizabeth Stuart Phelps, and George Washington Cable, printed "A

A HUMBLE ROMANCE

AND OTHER STORIES

BY

MARY E. WILKINS

NEW YORK

HARPER & BROTHERS, FRANKLIN SQUARE

LONDON: 30 FLEET STREET

1887

Title page for Freeman's first collection of local-color stories

tures. While regionalism flourished as a popular form, however, the trend toward standardization and homogenization in general encouraged the creation of works more "realist" than regionalist, more mainstream and less particular to a place and a people. Writers such as Freeman were popular for their attention to peculiarities of place and people; yet, they were still considered "minor" or "narrow" by the literary elite. Betraying condescension toward regionalism and local-color fiction, *The Literary World* complimented Freeman's *A Humble Romance and Other Stories,* saying that while the volume was a work of "minor fiction," the "simplicity, purity, and quaintness of her stories set them apart from the outpouring of current fiction in a niche of distinction where they have no rivals." Similarly ambivalent, Howells proclaimed the stories "peculiarly American, and they are peculiarly 'narrow' in a way, and yet they are like the best modern work everywhere in their directness and simplicity," thus subtly belittling the stories while simultaneously lending his respected praise and enhancing sales of the collection. Statements such as these reveal the bias against the specificity of regionalist themes, but the popularity of such work also reveals the public's curiosity about lives once deemed common but rapidly becoming exotic in their anachronism. Freeman was aware of the "historical" appeal of her work about New England's present. In a letter to fellow regionalist writer Hamlin Garland, she wrote, "I am writing about the New England of the present day, and the dialect is that which is daily in my ears. I have however a fancy that my characters belong to a present that is rapidly becoming *past,* and that a few generations will cause them to disappear." Thus, Freeman's New England characters represent both a nostalgia for preindustrial America and the development of a distinctive American folk identity.

Regionalism, often focusing on the nonmid-Atlantic, nonmale, nonmiddle class, or nonwhite, was an ideal forum for exploring the lives of the late nineteenth century's "others." Freeman's own brand of regionalism explores regions that are more social than geographical, for she focuses not so much on the people of New England in general as on its poor and its women, on those whose lives are thwarted by poverty, lack of opportunity, inertia, or an oddly principled obstinacy. In "Old Lady Pingree" (*Harper's Bazar,* 2 May 1885) the title character is nearly destitute and lives in her family's foreclosed mansion only by the charity of its new owners. Her one source of pride is that she has saved enough money for her own burial and will not have to be "buried by the town." Freeman skillfully addresses the complex dynamics of giving and receiving when she depicts the method by which baskets of food, on which Nancy depends for sustenance, are tac-

Humble Romance," which was received favorably by reviewers. Mary E. Wilkins, as she was then known, felt she had "arrived." Her most critically acclaimed and popular work was written shortly after these early successes while she lived at the Wales homestead in Randolph. There she had her own suite of rooms, including a parlor, kitchen, and bedrooms, and Mary John Wales managed much of the household matters, freeing her to concentrate on her work.

In 1887 Harper and Brothers published a collection of twenty-eight of Freeman's stories that had previously appeared in its magazines. This first collection, *A Humble Romance and Other Stories,* allowed Freeman to make her mark in the popular post–Civil War literature of regionalist and local-color fiction. Emphasizing geographical settings and the peculiarities of the speech and manners of a region's inhabitants, regionalist fiction flourished in a newly reunited country long separated by political, religious, and racial differences and eager for insight into the particulars of America's many cul-

itly left by a charitable woman from whom Nancy would never accept overt assistance. This tension between the proud resistance of the poor to gifts and the joy of the affluent in giving is employed in "A Mistaken Charity" (*Harper's Bazar,* 26 May 1883) as well. In this story Harriet and Charlotte Shattuck enjoy their hovel of a home and the coarse sustenance they are able to glean from the wild, overgrown property. Though they receive gifts of apples, butter, and milk from neighbors, they insist that their own wild varieties of food are better. After they are persuaded to move into a "home for old ladies," Charlotte and Harriet become so dissatisfied they run away from the institution, returning to their ramshackle house and enjoying its many "chinks," which they experience not as cracks in the walls but as the wellsprings of streams of light, which give them great pleasure.

Stories such as these made the author well known for her proud, struggling spinsters, but her work does not focus only on solitary, poor women. "Two Old Lovers" (*Harper's Bazar,* 24 March 1883), set in the slow-moving town of Leyden, narrates the romance between David Emmons, literally the slowest moving of the town's laid-back residents, and Maria Brewster. Although the couple engage in a joyous routine of visiting each other, Emmons's inertia prevents a marriage proposal. Finally, on his deathbed, Emmons summons Maria and tells her, "Maria, I'm–dying, an'–I allers meant to–have asked you–to–marry me." While such ennui-induced spinsterhood or bachelorhood is in keeping with other stories in which offers of marriage come too late or are declined, Freeman also challenged and stretched conventional marriage plots by allowing female protagonists to excel in an episode of economic independence. Such episodes, however, are usually found in more traditional, domestic narrative conclusions. "A Humble Romance" (*Harper's New Monthly Magazine,* June 1884) initially seems to be a classic tale of seduction. When the orphaned and work-weary Sally elopes with Jake Russell, a forty-year-old, widowed, traveling tin salesman, conventions of the eighteenth- and nineteenth-century seduction and betrayal narrative would have us expect the worst. Although they begin their life together in happiness, he soon abandons her when he discovers that his first wife is still alive. Rather than selling her husband's business and living on their savings as his parting letter recommends, Sally takes over the business and makes it more profitable by being a better purveyor of women's household needs. When Jake returns and explains the circumstances, they renew their vows. A diversion from the conventional marriage plot similarly permits a young woman to gain some economic independence in "Robins and Hammers" (*Harper's Bazar,* 19 September

1885). Lois breaks off her engagement to John and begins to teach, making enough money to contribute to her marriage, which is eagerly anticipated at the close of the story. In all of these stories, the variations from conventional scripts allow women characters to experience economic independence before being relegated to a more confining marital space.

It is likely that Freeman's focus on economic issues, even more than the often noted depiction of spinsterhood, has an autobiographical basis given her family's economic struggles during her childhood, her mother's work as a housekeeper, and her own dependence upon the Wales family early in her writing career. Freeman's economic success increased as she entered her most productive period of writing, which ultimately became of great assistance to the Wales family, to whom she lent her financial support for the remainder of her life. Just three years after the publication of *A Humble Romance,* a readers' poll listed her, along with Harriet Beecher Stowe and Sarah Orne Jewett, as one of the best women writers. A few years later, "The Revolt of 'Mother,'" a story included in her second collection, *A New England Nun and Other Stories* (1891), was voted one of the twelve best American short stories, placing her work on a list that included Washington Irving's "The Legend of Sleepy Hollow" and Edgar Allan Poe's "The Murders in the Rue Morgue."

"The Revolt of 'Mother'" and the title story of her second collection, continue Freeman's interest in the conflicts of dependency and power presented by married life; they also explore how far women will go to gain and maintain control over the domestic sphere. In "The Revolt of 'Mother'" (*Harper's New Monthly Magazine,* September 1890), Sarah Penn moves the family and the contents of their house into the immense new barn that her nearly nonverbal husband Adoniram has decided to build instead of replacing their humble dwelling. While Sarah Penn's decision to appropriate her husband's workspace as her own domestic space represents an exhilarating act of rebellion, and Adoniram's contrite words suggest that the power dynamic in the Penn family is forever changed, the resumption of domestic business as usual (represented in Adoniram's fully prepared favorite meal) suggests also the limitations of such an act. While a woman may take control of her domestic sphere, in Freeman's work that sphere is small, and its purpose remains service to her husband and children.

However revolutionary or limited contemporary readers find this act to be, Freeman regretted that it was unrealistically bold and later, in her autobiographical essay, accounted for the frustration that occasioned its creation: "In the first place all fiction ought to be true, and 'The Revolt of Mother' is not in the least true. . . . Sometimes incessant truth gets on one's nerves. It did on mine." She also sought in her autobiography to correct any myths the story might have evoked: "There never was in New England a woman like Mother. If there had been she most certainly would not have moved into the palatial barn. . . . New England women of that period coincided with their husbands in thinking that sources of wealth should be better housed than consumers. . . . Moving into the new barn would have been a cataclysm. New England women seldom bring cataclysms about their shoulders."

Perhaps Freeman's belief in the unrealistic though wonderfully suggestive nature of such a cataclysmic revolt accounts for her focus in other stories on a different kind of resistance, one enacted by not entering marriage at all rather than by trying to alter its power structure. In "A New England Nun" (*Harper's Bazar,* 7 May 1887) the unmarried Louisa Ellis takes great delight in her home and the domestic employments she engages in there, enjoying a self-sufficiency and harmony with her domestic space that is disrupted by the intrusion of Joe Dagget, a suitor who, after fourteen years, returns from wealth-seeking travels to make good on an earlier offer of marriage. Ultimately Louisa releases Joe from his commitment, allowing him to marry someone else and preserving the integrity of her religiously cared-for home. Although scholars have been ambivalent about whether this decision represents self-sacrifice or self-determination, Louisa weeps briefly but wakes up to a new day feeling "like a queen." Louisa embraces the "serenity and placid narrowness" of her life and looks forward to her future with "thankfulness." Hardly the self-sacrificing spinster often projected onto Freeman's work by early scholars, Louisa Ellis more closely resembles the heroes of American Renaissance fiction who, like Washington Irving's Rip Van Winkle or James Fenimore Cooper's Natty Bumppo, preserve their autonomy by refusing to be coupled. While these heroes liberate themselves by escaping the domestic sphere for the great outdoors, Louisa finds her refuge within the home. Surprising alternatives to domestic servitude would resurface later in Freeman's fiction, taking a more ominous tone in "Old Woman Magoun" (*Harper's New Monthly Magazine,* October 1905). In this story a woman allows her grandchild to eat poisonous berries and die rather than permitting her to become a commodity of exchange in marriage through which her estranged natural father would have paid off his gambling debt to an unscrupulous and apparently lecherous man. As with many narratives written by women authors at the turn of the century—Kate Chopin's *The Awakening* (1899) being the most notable example—Freeman's fiction presents death or

spinsterhood as a transcendance of the seemingly unchangeable conditions of married life.

Because of the plethora of unhappily married women and happily unmarried women in her work, Freeman has been of interest not only to feminist scholars, who see deviations from the marriage plot and acts of revolt and resistance as promising representations of a feminist spirit in rural nineteenth-century America, but also to scholars of lesbian studies, who have found intriguing Freeman's long cohabitation with Mary Wales, her marriage rather late in life, and her fiction about women who choose other women over men. There is no biographical evidence that Freeman's relationship with Wales was anything but platonic, and her relationship with Evie (Sawyer) Severance, who was married by the time Wilkins left Brattleboro, was perhaps more passionate and exclusive during their teenage years than was her relationship with Wales, which many believe resembled a practical and businesslike living arrangement. Her writing is nonetheless a promising ground for considering the emerging discourse of lesbian identity and resistance as well as writers' difficult negotiations with liberating and pathologizing rhetoric. From the mid nineteenth century to the early twentieth century, exclusive and erotic relationships between women were undergoing a redefinition. While there was a tendency in late-eighteenth- and early-nineteenth-century culture to interpret such relationships as "romantic friendships" largely devoid of sexual implications and hardly central to one's identity, by the last half of the nineteenth century, advice writers, sexologists, and scientific discourses of heredity and evolution were redefining intimacy and exclusivity between women as completely sexual in nature, representing pathological, monstrous aberrations suggestive of moral and biological degeneracy.

Freeman's work shows the effects of this trend. Her earliest story on this theme, "Two Friends" (*Harper's Bazar,* 25 June 1887), focuses on the relief two women feel when one woman proves as unfounded her companion's fear that she will marry a man and leave the house they have kept together for many years. "The Long Arm" (Pocket Magazine, 1 December 1895), a detective story cowritten with Boston columnist J. Edgar Chamberlin (*Pocket Magazine,* 1 December 1895; collected in *American Detective Fiction,* 1927), tells the story of Phoebe Dole, who murders the male love interest of her longtime companion, Maria Woods. In this story the murder, the differential power relations of the two women, and the abnormally long arm of the homicidal lesbian Phoebe all suggest that Freeman and her cowriter Chamberlin were influenced by the increasingly dominant scientific discourse about lesbian pathology. Significantly, however, Freeman gives

The Heart's Highway

A Romance of Virginia in the
Seventeenth Century

By

Mary E. Wilkins

NEW YORK
DOUBLEDAY, PAGE & CO.
1900

"SHE HELD IN MERRY ROGER UNTIL I WAS FORCED TO COME UP
AND . . . A MOCK-BIRD WAS SINGING SOMEWHERE OVER ON
THE BANK OF THE RIVER."

Frontispiece and title page for Freeman's novel inspired by Bacon's Rebellion of 1676

Phoebe narrative space to defend herself. Phoebe claims that her bond with Maria was just as "strong" as the marriage tie between men and women and "just as sacred." In fact, she claims that her companion's suitor was trying to break up their home.

Over the next fifteen years, Freeman's writing about women with feelings for and attachments to other women would be inscribed with this language of pathology as well as with a spirit of liberating transgression. In an unfinished, unpublished story, perhaps ironically titled "The Shrew," the main character calls herself a "hybrid" and a "monster," but also "a power" who "takes pleasure" in her difference from mainstream womanhood. In the novel *By the Light of the Soul* (1906), Maria Edgham is told that

she is "outside the pale" by Rosa Blair, who claims that she can always identify other people like herself by some "affinity" and that "it is not so very bad outside when one becomes accustomed to it." In *The Shoulders of Atlas* (1908), what the narrator describes as "erotic friendships, which are really diseased love-affairs with another girl," create much of the tension and conflict in the novel. Sylvia Whitman has deep feelings of longing for her young cousin Rose Fletcher. Other characters in the novel—Lucy Ayres, Eliza Farrel, and Sidney Meeks—also have ambiguous sexual identities. These characters of East Westland, as the name of the town suggests, reside on the borders of gender and sexuality, as do other, less pathologized characters in "Christmas Jenny"

(*Harper's Bazar*, 22 December 1888) and *The Portion of Labor* (1901).

While Freeman clearly participated in an emerging discourse about lesbian identity and lesbian rights, sometimes reinscribing its pathologizing rhetoric and sometimes appropriating it for subversive ends, it would be inaccurate to draw a closely autobiographical connection here, as elsewhere in her work. This tendency to draw connections between Freeman's characters and her own life has been rampant, despite the many differences between the writer and her characters. By the 1890s Freeman was hardly the isolated, provincial woman of her stories. She participated in social circles of northeastern notables, traveling often to such metropolitan centers as Boston, New York, Washington, D.C., Chicago, and Paris and enjoying the society of friends up and down the eastern seaboard. She continued to write and to expand her literary horizons, despite being overburdened with social commitments. She once complained in a letter, "Just now I am engaged in dodging lunches and dinners, and writing a novel between whiles." Such a busy social calendar was foreign to her characters.

Although Freeman had received praise for her stories, she felt she needed to write longer works and in the 1890s began writing novels and plays, which she saw as "grand operas" in contrast to the "simple little melody" of her stories. The novels opened a new vein, but critical reception of them has always been guarded. Several of these novels were romantic, often bearing traces of Nathaniel Hawthorne's work. In *Jane Field* (1892) she explored the workings of a guilty conscience that is ultimately compelled to public confession. In *Pembroke* (1894) she embellished a piece of family lore in which her maternal grandfather lived in an unfinished house after a political dispute with the father of his future bride. The literary version of this family story is notable for its different conclusion: whereas Barnabas Lothrop and Mary Thayer never married, their literary counterparts, Barnabas Thayer and Charlotte Barnard, are reunited at the end of the novel, but only after the men in the story adopt a less patriarchal worldview. The most acclaimed of her novels, *Pembroke* reflects her interest in obstinate pride and the physical manifestation of spiritual or moral states, a theme also common in the work of Hawthorne, to whose work her play *Giles Corey, Yeoman* (1893) might be compared because of its thematic focus on the Salem witchcraft trials.

Another novel, *Jerome, A Poor Man* (1897), resumed her interest in the function of pride in poverty, leading one reviewer to praise her for her "photographic realism," a term that later served to belittle the work of those thought to be mere "recorders of their times" who lacked any real artistic talent. Freeman

renewed her attention to economic issues and developed an interest in the more overtly political literature of social protest. *The Portion of Labor* is Freeman's effort at exposing the inequities of industrial capitalism, a culture from which she had retreated in earlier stories that focused more on the rural residue of the Industrial Revolution. The novel compares the working and living conditions of shoe factory laborers to the lifestyles of the factory owners, narrating a class conflict that is keenly felt by the main character, Ellen Brewster. Ellen comes from a working-class family that spoils her despite their lean circumstances. Although the opportunity arises for her to attend Vassar and marry the nephew and heir of a wealthy factory owner, Ellen declines both opportunities; instead, she goes to work at a shoe factory in order to help her family financially. When her wealthy admirer cuts wages at the factory, she organizes a strike but ultimately calls it off, arguing that there is no sense in starving to death in order to take a stand on a principle. When the factory owner later returns the wages to their original level, the conflict between the two is resolved, and they seem destined to marry. Marginalized by all classes, Ellen Brewster, though a passionate orator, has been an unsatisfying heroine for the Left, who wish she were more directly and consistently radical. Indeed, her radical valedictory address early in the novel is undercut by her later consideration of whether "this inequality of possessions is not a part of the system of creation . . . if the one who tries to right them forcibly is not meddling, and usurping the part of the Creator." At the end of the novel, when depressed stock owned by poor and gullible workers begins to rise in value, the reader begins to wonder whether the novel promotes either a notion of economic predestination or a romantic idealization of labor and inequality as fostering "growth in character of the laborer."

At the turn of the century, however, labor unrest was a controversial focus for a woman author. Like mid-nineteenth-century writers Harriet Beecher Stowe and Rebecca Harding Davis, Freeman had to balance her social protest with a "womanly sympathy," making her work read more as an expression of feeling than as a discursive assertion of politics. Thus Freeman's work in this area appears to fall short of the muckraking of Upton Sinclair, author of *The Jungle* (1906), or the proletarianism of depression-era writer Josephine Herbst, but it is perhaps better read in the context of those who wrote sentimental novels of social protest before her. Freeman was mindful of the need to please and not offend her audience, on whose appreciation she depended for her living. Although she wrote in "The Girl Who Wants to Write" that writers "must not write to please an editor or a public," she was aware of the delicate balance women writers faced in representing the unconventional while not upsetting their readers. Her collected letters reveal her concern over the practical matter of making a living by writing; indeed, she became an astute businesswoman who always negotiated to get as much as she could for her short stories and capitalized on the double profits of serial rights and book royalties for her novels.

In the 1890s and 1900s, Freeman's desire to stay marketable and earn a profit led her to explore new subjects to avoid tiring her audience with her "old women." Unfortunately, these excursions into the new were rarely met with great applause. Both *Madelon* (1896) and *The Heart's Highway, A Romance of Virginia in the Seventeenth Century* (1900) are "romances," a genre considered by the end of the nineteenth century to be both more appropriate for a woman and less aspiring for an author; as a result, we see a difference in response from the popular literary critics, who found the novels engaging, and the literary elite, who found them disappointing, if not vulgar. One critic complained about "unrefined references" to "promiscuous kissing" in *Madelon*. Another, more complimentary critic liked the novel but claimed it dealt with "the domain of the pathologist." Frank Norris, a turn-of-the-century American advocate of naturalism, called *The Heart's Highway* a descent into "colonial romance," a genre that he felt was a "discrowning" to Freeman, whom he felt had betrayed her fellow realist writers and her country by writing this novel.

Both of these novels are worthy of more attention than they have received because they stand alone in their treatment of racial issues in the work of a writer who rarely entered this discourse. *Madelon* has an exceedingly complicated plot immersed in the taboo of interracial love, mistaken identity, murderous passion, and self-sacrifice, but Leah Blatt Glasser, one of the few scholars to discuss the novel in her 1996 work *In a Closet Hidden: The Life and Work of Mary E. Wilkins Freeman*, has suggested that the contortions of plot serve to "disguise the forbidden subject matter": sexual assertiveness and violence in a woman. Burr Gordon, an Anglo-American, and Madelon Hautville, a mixed-race French Canadian and Iroquois, love each other. When Burr decides to follow convention rather than his heart, he chooses Dorothy Fair, a woman of breeding similar to his own. Madelon's jealousy drives her to attempt to murder Burr, but she stabs his cousin Lot in a case of mistaken identity. In order to protect Madelon, Burr claims responsibility for the crime, and Lot, also in love with Madelon, claims that his wounds are self-inflicted, an attempted suicide. Ultimately, Madelon must confess in order to exonerate Burr; however, there is more at work in her confes-

sion than guilt or selflessness. In claiming responsibility for the attempted murder, Madelon is asserting that women are capable of great passion and violence, something her townspeople are not willing to admit. Undercutting the effect of stretching gender expectations is Madelon's mixed-race heritage, which—in keeping with nineteenth-century discourse about race and race mixing—is represented as having a confusing and pathological influence on her mental state. Madelon's mixed-race heritage thus becomes a symbol of her "pathology," both explaining her passionate violence and making it less a comment on women's passions than on the passions of a savage "injun."

The doubleness of Madelon's racial identity is emphasized throughout the novel. She represents vulnerability and aggression, femininity and savagery. By the end of the novel she has become so focused on Burr's happiness that she tries to reunite him with Dorothy Fair. When this fails, she seems to succumb to (rather than strive to effect) a marriage to Burr. This resolution of the novel's many twists, turns, and complexities is dependent on the gradual development of self-sacrifice—rather than selfish passion—in Madelon, a development that is given the signification of colonization and assimilation to Anglo-American culture: "Civilization bowed cruelly this girl, who felt in greater measure than the gently staid female descendants of the Puritan stock around her the fire of savage or primitive passions; but she now submitted to it with the taciturnity of one of her ancestresses to the torture." Thus, while Madelon becomes more acceptable (in the eyes of both her townspeople and most of Freeman's contemporaries), she also becomes more English, more Puritan, more passive, and more feminine. As in so much of Freeman's fiction, passion and selfhood, freedom and love cannot be reconciled; one must be compromised. In *Madelon* this dynamic, so common in Freeman's work, is unique because of the racial implications of Madelon's compromise and assimilation. Race was not an issue about which Freeman wrote at length, but here she seemed to recognize the degree of strength and freedom from social norms associated with people of color while also acknowledging the cultural stereotypes of passionate sexuality and rage that contain and threaten that freedom.

Freeman's other departure, *The Heart's Highway,* is told from the first-person perspective of Harry Wingfield, a young man sent to America as a servant-tutor to young Mary Cavendish, with whom he falls in love. Their love frames this story, which, aside from the intrigue of romance, is about rebellion and dignity. In response to one of the many Navigation Acts of the late seventeenth century, Wingfield and Mary Cavendish, among other Jamestown residents of all classes, destroy

Freeman, circa 1898

hoped only to provide historical authenticity through the use of a first-person narrator entrenched in the attitudes of his time. When Wingfield is placed in the stocks after being convicted of shooting an officer in the process of the rebellion, his "ignominy" is ultimately shared by several notable townspeople, including Margery Key, who voluntarily stand with him in a gesture of pride in their rebellion against tyranny. Thus, despite its stereotypical treatment of African slaves, the novel seems to make a case for the principled defense of difference and revolt.

Freeman's productivity and popularity as a writer declined shortly after her marriage in 1902 to Charles Freeman. She moved into his house in Metuchen, New Jersey, where they lived until 1907, when they moved into a newly built house they designed themselves. Biographers disagree about whether the early years of the union were happy. The Freemans seemed to take great joy in the details of setting up a house together, but by the end of the next decade, Charles Freeman had returned to his premarital habit of heavy drinking, and Mary Wilkins Freeman had him committed to a state hospital for the insane. By 1922 she had obtained a legal separation from him. He died shortly thereafter, and Freeman had to contest his will, which left most of his estate to a servant.

According to biographer Edward Foster, Freeman once told a friend in Metuchen that she could write only in Randolph, Massachusetts; despite this perception, Freeman was still actively engaged in writing in the first years after her marriage. She published several novels, including *The Debtor* (1905), *"Doc" Gordon* (1906), and *By the Light of the Soul* (1906), none of which brought acclaim. Two highly publicized novels followed: *The Whole Family, A Novel by Twelve Authors* (1908), written collaboratively with Howells, Henry James, Elizabeth Stuart Phelps, and others, created quite a stir among the literati. Freeman wrote the second chapter of the novel with Howells's first chapter as the only prompt and took everyone by surprise by transforming his old-maid character Lily into a "new woman." Howells's outrage and the confusion of other contributors reflect the tension and controversy that remained in the early twentieth century concerning single women. *The Shoulders of Atlas* appeared at about the same time as *The Whole Family*. She wrote this highly sensational page-turner in a competition against British writer Max Pemberton sponsored by the *New York Herald*. Freeman's victory earned her a total of $20,000 in contest prize money, serial rights, and book rights.

During this time, Freeman continued to write short fiction for magazines; many of these stories were published later in collections. These collections include a volume of ghost stories titled *The Wind in the Rose-Bush*

the tobacco crops in protest against the crown's control over American exports. The novel presents these proud acts of fictitious colonists as inspired by the actual rebellion of Nathaniel Bacon, a colonial Virginia planter best known for burning Jamestown to the ground in 1676. Bacon, who hoped to destroy the local indigenous population, disregarded treaties reserving land for the Doeg and Susquehannock Indians in order to increase possession of land valued for tobacco farming. Set amid such acts of colonial rebellion and racial genocide, Freeman's novel, especially its first-person narrator Harry Wingfield, embodies many of the prejudices of the colonial period. Wingfield describes the "swarming" African slaves of the plantations as superstitious and buffoonish. Like his townspeople, Wingfield subscribes to the notion that Margery Key is a witch, though he later wonders if superstition has given her that label. The fact that Wingfield's initial judgment of Margery Key is at odds with Freeman's many stories about old unmarried women may lend support to the idea that Freeman

and Other Stories of the Supernatural (1903) and the highly mystical and symbolic collection *Six Trees* (1903). Following these collections came the Christmas-themed *The Givers* (1904) and the acclaimed *The Winning Lady and Others* (1909) as well as *The Copy-Cat & Other Stories* (1914) and *Edgewater People* (1918).

By the first decades of the twentieth century, literary tastes had changed greatly from the late nineteenth century. A literary world that had been interested in both romantic and realist fiction, in local color and regionalism was by then embracing the naturalism of Frank Norris and Theodore Dreiser and the modernism of Ezra Pound, T. S. Eliot, and Gertrude Stein. The unusual and exotic were no longer embodied in the quaint, homey, and occasionally "pathological" lives of New Englanders, but rather in Italy, France, and the "primitive" cultures described by anthropologists. In addition, American culture seemed to be striving for a more masculine iconography, as the hyper-masculine presidency of Theodore Roosevelt indicates. Things sentimental, domestic, and local or regional had become passé. Freeman was aware of this change in literary tastes and wrote in a letter, "Everything is different since the war and since even the pre-war days for I think the change antedated the war. As nearly as I can understand the situation, there is in arts and letters a sort of frantic impulse for something erratic and out of the common. . . . I am none too sure of a market for my own wares."

Despite the loss of an eager readership, her work, especially her early work, continued to win praise, and Freeman received several awards and honors. In 1925 she received the first William Dean Howells Gold Medal for Fiction, which was followed one year later by her election into the membership of the National Institute of Arts and Letters. In 1927 she saw the publication of a new collection of her short stories, *The Best Stories of Mary E. Wilkins,* a title that would seem to close the book on her career. Despite such retrospective gestures regarding her career, Freeman was planning a sequel to *Pembroke* before her death on 13 March 1930. After her death she was honored again when the American Academy of Arts and Letters dedicated its bronze doors "to Mary E. Wilkins Freeman and the Women Writers of America." Although most of her work was out of print by 1950, and the New Critics had effected a shift of focus that placed Hawthorne, Herman Melville, and Walt Whitman at the center of American literary scholarship, feminist criticism of the 1970s introduced Freeman to a new generation of American literary scholars whose interests in sexuality, class, and race have continued to expand our notions about the place of Freeman's work in relation to the literary movements of her time and its relevance to literary scholars today.

Letters:

The Infant Sphinx: Collected Letters of Mary E. Wilkins Freeman, edited by Brent L. Kendrick (Metuchen, N.J.: Scarecrow Press, 1985).

Biography:

Edward Foster, *Mary E. Wilkins Freeman* (New York: Hendricks House, 1956).

References:

Virginia Blum, "Mary Wilkins Freeman and the Taste of Necessity," *American Literature,* 65 (1993): 69–94;

Marylynne Diggs, "Romantic Friends or 'A Different Race of Creatures': The Representation of Lesbian Pathology in Nineteenth-Century America," *Feminist Studies,* 21 (1995): 317–340;

Lorne Fienberg, "Mary E. Wilkins Freeman's 'Soft Diurnal Commotion': Women's Work and Strategies of Containment," *New England Quarterly,* 62 (1989): 483–504;

Leah Blatt Glasser, *In a Closet Hidden: The Life and Work of Mary E. Wilkins Freeman* (Amherst: University of Massachusetts Press, 1996);

Linda Grasso, "'Thwarted Life, Mighty Hunger, Unfinished Work': The Legacy of Nineteenth-Century Women Writing in America," *ATQ,* 8 (June 1994): 97–118;

Shirley Marchalonis, ed., *Critical Essays on Mary Wilkins Freeman* (Boston: G. K. Hall, 1991);

George Preston, "Concerning Good English," *Bookman* (1896): 361–362;

Mary R. Reichardt, *A Web of Relationship: Women in the Short Stories of Mary Wilkins Freeman* (Jackson: University Press of Mississippi, 1992);

Horace Scudder, "Madelon," *Atlantic Monthly,* 78 (August 1896): 269–270;

Carolyn Wells, ed., *American Detective Fiction* (New York: Oxford University Press, 1927);

Perry D. Westbrook, *Mary Wilkins Freeman* (New York: Twayne, 1967).

Papers:

Mary E. Wilkins Freeman's papers are collected in the Library of the American Academy of Arts and Letters, the New York Public Library, and in the libraries of Columbia University, Princeton University, the University of Virginia, and the University of Southern California.

Charlotte Perkins Gilman

(3 July 1860 – 17 August 1935)

Robin Miskolcze
University of Nebraska at Lincoln

BOOKS: *The Labor Movement* (Oakland: Alameda County Federation of Trades, 1893);

In This Our World and Other Poems (Oakland: McCombs & Vaughn, 1893);

Women and Economics: A Study of the Economic Relation between Men and Women as a Factor in Social Evolution (Boston: Small, Maynard, 1898);

The Yellow Wallpaper, A Novella (Boston: Small, Maynard, 1899);

Concerning Children (Boston: Small, Maynard, 1900; London: Putnam, 1900);

The Home: Its Work and Influence (New York: McClure, Phillips, 1903);

Human Work (New York: McClure, Phillips, 1904);

What Diantha Did (New York: Charlton, 1910);

The Crux: A Novel (New York: Charlton, 1911);

The Man-Made World; or, Our Androcentric Culture (New York: Charlton, 1911; London: Unwin, 1911);

Moving the Mountain (New York: Charlton, 1911);

His Religion and Hers: A Study of the Faith of Our Fathers and the Work of Our Mothers (New York & London: Century, 1923);

The Living of Charlotte Perkins Gilman: An Autobiography (New York & London: Appleton-Century, 1935);

Herland, introduction by Ann J. Lane (New York: Pantheon, 1979);

Benigna Machiavelli (Santa Barbara: Bandanna Books, 1994);

With Her in Ourland: Sequel to Herland, edited by Mary Jo Deegan and Michael R. Hill (Westport, Conn.: Greenwood Press, 1997);

Unpunished, edited by Catherine J. Golden and Denise D. Knight (New York: Feminist Press, 1997).

OTHER: *The Forerunner,* 1–7, written and edited by Gilman (January 1909–December 1916).

Charlotte Anna Perkins was born on 3 July 1860 in Hartford, Connecticut, to Frederick Beecher Perkins and his distant cousin Mary Fitch Wescott Perkins. She was the youngest of three children born to

Charlotte Perkins Stetson (later Gilman), circa 1884

the couple in their first three years of marriage: the others were Thomas Henry, born on 15 March 1858, who lived only a few weeks, and Thomas Adie, born on 9 May 1859. Gilman was born into a gifted family rooted in social activism: Her father, Frederick, was the grandson of Lyman Beecher, a noted Calvinist clergyman, who, according to Ann J. Lane, "married three times and fathered twelve surviving children, which made him, according to Unitarian clergyman

Theodore Parker, 'the father of more brains than any other man in America.'" Her great-aunts include Harriet Beecher Stowe, author of *Uncle Tom's Cabin* (1852) and arguably largely responsible for changing the nation's consciousness about the issue of slavery. Born at a time of national and familial conflict and to a heritage that embodied social change, Perkins grew up to be a key social activist, and so prolific a writer that she approximated her publications to be the equivalent of twenty-five volumes of writing, an estimate closely substantiated by Gary Scharnhorst's 1985 bibliography of her work.

All of Lyman Beecher's offspring except one made their mark as activists, suffragists, educators, writers, ministers, or lawyers. "The only purely private Beecher," Lyman Beecher Stowe wrote in his *Saints, Sinners, and Beechers* (1934), "was Charlotte's grandmother Mary, Lyman and [first wife] Roxanna's fourth child." Mary stayed out of the public eye, confining herself to the traditional domestic role. She married Thomas Perkins, and they had four children: Charlotte's father, Frederick; Emily; Charles; and Katherine. Their daughters married well—Emily to the eminent writer and Unitarian clergyman, Edward Everett Hale, best known for his short story "The Man without a Country," first published in the *Atlantic Monthly* (December 1863). Katherine married William C. Gilman, a prominent attorney. One of their children, George Houghton Gilman, Perkins's first cousin, later became her second husband.

Of Mary Beecher Perkins's four children, the eldest, Frederick, had the most difficult time making his way in life. Lane describes Frederick as "A man of some literary and intellectual gifts, inspired with bursts of passion for justice and reform, a man of courage and substantial physical prowess, he was ultimately unable to put his strengths together into a well-ordered and satisfying life. He was talented but undisciplined, erratic, and unfocused. He had good impulses but not much staying power." Trying to measure up to his Beecher forebears put additional strain on Frederick. Lane goes on to say that "Frederick never quite found himself, and in the process of looking he caused a good deal of unhappiness to many close to him. He grew up in Hartford; he attended but did not graduate from Yale University, because he lost his temper, which he did often, and assaulted one of his professors." He trained for two or three professions: he attended a normal school to become a teacher, taught for a while, but soon became dissatisfied with that occupation; he studied law but did not practice it, unlike his younger brother, Charles, who joined their father in his Hartford law practice. According to Lane, "Frederick ultimately found his

vocation in the world of literature and letters. His passion for books led him to read them, write them, edit them, and, as a librarian, classify them." Gilman later wrote that her father was familiar with nine languages. He became assistant director of the Boston Public Library and in 1880 was appointed director of the San Francisco Public Library. He ultimately returned to the East, where he died in 1899.

Perkins's early life lacked the stability of a permanent home. Soon after she was born, her father left his wife and children, although he continued to provide meager support for them for the next thirteen years. As a result of Frederick's inconsistent financial contributions, Mary Perkins and their children—Charlotte and her older brother, Thomas—were forced to move at least once a year for eighteen years. Even though Frederick made brief appearances in his family's life, Mary finally decided to divorce her husband in 1873. Both mother and daughter were profoundly affected by his neglect. As Gilman explains in her autobiography, her mother, who collected her husband's fingernail clippings and locks of hair as mementoes from his infrequent visits, believed she should "deny the child all expression of affection as far as possible, so that she should not be used to it or long for it." In this way, the children would not be hurt when they were inevitably deserted, as she had been by her husband. Because of her mother's philosophy, Mary and her daughter never shared a particularly close relationship.

When Perkins inherited property in 1874, her mother enrolled the fourteen-year-old in a private school, where she excelled in the subject of elocution and gained an appreciation of physical activity that she maintained the rest of her life. At age sixteen Perkins painted advertising cards and was teaching art, and, at nineteen, she entered the Rhode Island School of Design to study art. When she was twenty-one she met the artist Walter Stetson at a lecture, and two years later, on 2 May 1884, they were married. Their daughter, Katherine Beecher, was born on 23 March 1885. Immediately after Katherine was born, Stetson began suffering from episodes of depression. Mary Perkins moved in with the Stetsons to help care for the infant. On the advice of her doctor, Stetson took a trip to Pasadena, California, to visit her longtime friend, Grace Channing, throughout the winter of 1885. She returned home feeling well enough to accept an offer from Alice Stone Blackwell to contribute to *People,* a Providence weekly newspaper sponsored by the Knights of Labor of Rhode Island, and to contribute poems to the *Woman's Journal,* published by the American Woman Suffrage Association. By the winter of 1887 Stetson had already had several articles

Stetson at about age thirty

and poems accepted by the papers. These early works often reflect Stetson's strong and enduring belief in the necessity of work, particularly for women.

Eventually, however, she was overpowered by the debilitating effects of her depression. Encouraged by her mother and husband, Stetson sought help from Dr. S. Weir Mitchell, the famous "nerve doctor," at his sanatorium in Philadelphia. Mitchell diagnosed Stetson with neurasthenia, or nerve exhaustion, a disease whose symptoms bear extensive similarities to clinical depression. He treated her with his "Rest Cure," a regimen that insisted on complete bed rest in an isolated environment. During the first stage of the treatment the patient was not allowed to read, write, sew, feed herself, or talk to others. After one month of treatment, Mitchell sent Stetson home with directions to "live as domestic a life as possible. Have your child with you all the time. . . . have but two hours' intellectual life a day. And never touch pen, brush or pencil as long as you live."

These directions were not conducive to Stetson's way of living, of course, and as she relates in her autobiography, they caused her to come "perilously close to losing my mind." In the fall of 1887, after a recogni-

tion that both were miserable in their marriage, Charlotte and Walter agreed to separate, and in September 1888 Charlotte and Katherine moved to Pasadena to be close to Channing. Although Walter sought a reconciliation the following year, the couple filed for divorce, which was granted in 1894. During 1890, however, Walter and Grace had developed a romantic relationship, and they later married, with full approval from Charlotte.

During this time of great change in her personal life, Stetson published a story that established her reputation among her contemporaries and within the modern feminist movement. Stetson first gained recognition in April 1890, when she published her poem "Similar Cases" in the *Nationalist* and received attention from reformers and a letter of praise from William Dean Howells, a respected writer and editor of the *Atlantic Monthly*. Perhaps the theme of the poem, the necessity of change in an evolving society, prompted her to write her famous story, "The Yellow Wallpaper," a story not truly recognized for its polemical nature until nearly eighty-five years later. While subsequent readers have tended to view the story as a fictional account of the author's encounter with S. Weir Mitchell, contemporary readers were more frightened by the narrative than inspired to change the treatment of depression. In fact, the story, originally published in the January 1892 edition of the *New England Magazine,* was reprinted as a horror story in William Dean Howell's *The Great Modern American Stories* in 1920. Not until 1973 did "The Yellow Wallpaper" receive a feminist reading, when the Feminist Press published an edition introduced by Elaine R. Hedges.

"The Yellow Wallpaper" is narrated in the form of a diary by an unnamed woman who undergoes a kind of rest cure as prescribed by her physician husband, John. All of the action and suspense of the story arises within the four walls of the narrator's bedroom, a former nursery and playroom with bars on its window. The narrator, who must write in secrecy since her husband wants her to stay in bed and away from pen and paper, tells her diary about the room's wallpaper, which, as weeks pass, seems to come to life. She begins to see distorted shapes and figures in the wallpaper's design, eventually recognizing a woman trying to "shake the pattern" of the discolored wallpaper "as if she wanted to get out." By the end of the story, much to her husband's horror, the narrator has locked herself in the room and has taken to peeling off the yellow wallpaper in order to free the imprisoned woman. When John finally enters her room, she is creeping along the walls, and when he faints, she merely steps over him and continues her strange task.

The rest cure apparently worsens the narrator's condition, although it is questionable whether the narrator is more sane in the beginning of the story, when she holds absolute trust in her husband's power to cure her, or at the end of the story, when she subconsciously records the parallel between the women imprisoned behind bars and herself, imprisoned and infantilized in the yellow walls of a barred playroom. Perhaps contemporary readers were horrified not by the figures in the wallpaper but by a woman's proclivity to go insane when confined within the home. The story reflects changing ideas about women's roles in society, from the True Womanhood patriarchal ideology in which the home was a sanctuary for the saintly woman to the New Woman feminist ideology that demanded new opportunities outside the restrictions of the home.

In 1891 Stetson moved to Oakland with her daughter. Oakland and San Francisco were active sites of reform, and she became increasingly involved in reform movements such as the Nationalist Party, which advocated socialism. The party was founded to promote the ideas presented by Edward Bellamy, in his utopian novel *Looking Backward: 2000–1887,* which by 1900 was the most successful novel in American publishing history, with the exception of *Uncle Tom's Cabin.* Stetson's first lecture, which launched a long career of lecturing tours, was held in front of a Nationalist club. Stetson retained many Nationalist tenets throughout the rest of her career, such as collective action, cooperative living arrangements, and revolution through the improvement of social conditions that determine the degree of evolutionary progress. Along with these ideals, however, Stetson also preserved the Nationalists' problematic tendencies toward nativism and xenophobia in a country increasingly reliant upon immigrant labor.

Stetson remained active in public speaking, giving a series of lectures through the winter of 1892, the subject of which–the relationship between economics and women–was expanded on in her later works. Approximately sixty of her lectures remain extant, yet many more were given; early in her career, she became confident enough to deliver lectures with few or no notes. In September 1892 the Trades and Labor Union of Alameda County awarded her a gold medal for her essay *The Labor Movement,* which was published as a pamphlet by the union in 1893. Stetson then became a member of the Oakland Federal Labor Union Number 5761 of the American Federation of Labor. She was also on the executive board of the Woman's Congress Association of the Pacific Coast. At the association's second annual convention in 1895, she contributed to a panel with Robert Jordan,

president of Stanford University, and Susan B. Anthony, a leader in the women's suffrage movement. In 1894 Stetson was appointed co-editor of the *Impress* by the Pacific Coast Women's Press Association and often contributed articles, stories, and editorials to this weekly paper. Stetson's reputation grew with the publication of her first book of poetry in 1893, *In This Our World and Other Poems.*

In the course of this flurry of political and literary activity Stetson's personal life became more and more complicated. In 1891 she met and developed a relationship with Adeline E. Knapp, whom she called Delle, and later, in her autobiography, Dora. Delle was a reporter, and although she traveled a great deal, Stetson and Delle moved into a boarding house together, along with Stetson's mother, who had come to Oakland in the fall of 1891. Stetson had always been a passionate friend to other women, the most notable being Grace, but her relationship with Delle seems to have been more intimate than any preceding friendship. In fact, it is likely that Stetson and Delle were lovers, as is evident in Stetson's letters, journal, and poems such as "To the Conquered." Many years later she wrote a letter to her future husband that warned him about what the newspapers might make of her relationship with Delle: "Mrs. Stetson's Love Affair with a Woman. Is this Friendship!"

Delle and Stetson's relationship became strained, however, when Mary Perkins developed cancer in 1892 and died the following year. Under the stress caused by her mother's death, as well as the ongoing divorce proceeding with Walter, Stetson permanently severed her relationship with Delle in 1893. In 1894 Walter and Charlotte's divorce was granted; yet, from the time the press heard about the unusually friendly triangle of Grace, Walter, and Charlotte, newspapers such as the *Boston Globe,* the *San Francisco Chronicle,* and the *San Francisco Examiner* ran stories capitalizing on the unorthodox relationship. The attention intensified when Stetson, burdened by financial difficulties and recurring depression, sent nine-year-old Katherine to live with Walter and Grace on the east coast.

Feeling oppressed by the public scrutiny, Stetson accepted Jane Addams's invitation to stay at her settlement house, Hull House, in Chicago, where she lived for several months and was surrounded by various reform activities. From 1895 to 1900 she was continuously traveling and lecturing around the country, while frequently contributing to the *American Fabian,* a journal advocating the development of an American form of Fabian Socialism. In 1898 she wrote her most influential book, which brought her to the highest point of fame in her career–*Women and Economics: A*

Stetson, circa 1898, the year her most influential book, Women and Economics, *was published*

Study of the Economic Relation between Men and Women as a Factor in Social Evolution.

Women and Economics is an amalgam of the variety of ideologies she had ingested thus far, along with a radical thesis: women's position in society is directly related to economic factors, factors most often dominated by men. Stetson's main objective in *Women and Economics* is to make clear that the male determines the economic status of all humans, and because of this factor, women are dependent on men for their existence. She terms this economic dependence or independence based on one's sex, the "sexuo-economic relationship." She maintains that economic independence comes from getting something in return for what you give. Women have relied on men for food, while not contributing an economic product in exchange for what they consume. Stetson agrees that women do participate in "house service" but argues that those activities are still distinct from economic activity since women are not paid for their services.

Stetson outlines several consequences of the restriction of women to domestic service. First, men have gone on to do the important work in the world—they have been the innovators in industry, art, commerce, science, manufacture, government, and reli-

gion. Second, since women's environment has been restricted to the home, "her ideas, her information, her thought-processes and power of judgment" are all limited, and especially troublesome is "the denial of freedom to act." Furthermore, since women have become excessively identified with the home, they have become "over-sexed," a term invented by Stetson to mean "to manifest in excess any of the distinctions of sex." Finally, the dominance of men in the public sphere has forced our language to associate human activities with being male, not human. Thus ". . . we have grown to consider most human attributes as masculine attributes, for the same reason that they were allowed to men and forbidden to women." Stetson points to women writers of the past such as Harriet Martineau, who had to hide her writing under her sewing when visitors came, "because 'to sew' was a feminine verb, and 'to write' a masculine one." Even with children, Stetson contends, sex distinctions are perpetuated by language. To say about a girl "she is a perfect little mother already," is to impose a maternal instinct on her. If a boy does not have paternal instincts, Stetson asks, why must a girl have maternal instincts? She believes that the women's movement has provided more equality for women, especially since more women are being educated. The crux of the entire issue, however, is the economic relation between men and women, and until more women enter the public workforce and/or are paid for their domestic services, that relation will remain unbalanced and women will suffer.

Women and Economics reflected many of the ideas of the time, particularly the English philosopher John Stuart Mill's well-known work, *On the Subjection of Women,* published in 1869. Mill claimed that the nature of women was an eminently artificial thing—"the result of forced repression in some directions, unnatural stimulation in others." Additionally, the nature of woman cannot be defined as long as women are denied access to social institutions. Stetson's position is similar. In the preface to *Women and Economics,* she states one of her purposes for writing the book: "To show how some of the worst evils under which we suffer, evils long supposed to be inherent and ineradicable in our natures, are but the result of certain arbitrary conditions of our own adoption." Yet, she takes Mill's position a step further by locating economic dependence as the root of the subjection of women. Even though she would agree with Mill that the nature of woman as it was defined then was artificial, she nevertheless believed there existed essential male and female gender traits, like strength and ferocity in males and "the facility in union, the power to make and to save" in females.

Women and Economics earned Stetson a considerable reputation, for it was reviewed favorably by a variety of influential journals and magazines, including the *Nation*, the *Woman's Journal*, *The New York Times Saturday Review of Books*, the *Boston Advertiser*, the *Denver Post*, and the *Political Science Quarterly*. The book went through many printings, and for the 1920 edition Stetson wrote a new introduction. The topics she raised in the book made repeated appearances thereafter in many of her future books, essays, poems, and short stories. After 1920, *Women and Economics* all but disappeared until the historian Carl Degler introduced a reprint in 1966.

In 1900, the year Stetson married George Houghton Gilman, she published *Concerning Children*. She dedicated the book to her daughter, Katherine, who, as Gilman writes in the dedication, "has taught me much of what is written here." For the most part, Gilman concerns herself with the discipline and education of children. She is against corporal punishment, arguing that it has no educational value for the child. If you hit a child for doing a forbidden act, the child will later commit that act in secret, thereby learning that the forbidden is acceptable as long as it is not undetected. More important, perhaps, for its nearly revolutionary implications, Gilman questions the wisdom of keeping babies in the home with their mother at all times. She claims that babies need to be socialized with other babies and that mothers are not trained to provide the necessary social education. As a solution, she proposes public nurseries, or "babygardens," as a counterpart to the kindergarten that was growing in popularity at the time. Thus, Gilman was considering the child's welfare as well as the mother's; with the child at a babygarden, the mother was free to go out into the public sphere and work, a goal she stressed in *Women and Economics*. The only other option is educating mothers to be educators, rather than assuming they have the natural ability to educate their children simply because they are mothers. Thus Gilman sought to challenge the stereotype that women are inherently maternal.

Concerning Children was not as popular as *Women and Economics* but was positively reviewed in the *Saturday Review of Books* and excerpted in *Ladies' Home Journal*. Her next book, however, *The Home: Its Work and Influence* (1903), was most derivative of *Women and Economics*, and perhaps for that reason, was more popular than *Concerning Children*. Doubtless, its popularity rested also on its witty commentary on the incongruities between the myths and realities of domestic life.

The Home: Its Work and Influence approaches a variety of myths about domestic life, and one by one, deconstructs them. For example, Gilman questions the

George Houghton Gilman, Gilman's first cousin, who became her second husband in 1900

logic behind associating the sanctity of the home with maternity. Maternity has nothing to do with the improvement of the race, only the reproduction. She questions the tendency to worship the mother of great men while conveniently forgetting the mothers of people such as John Wilkes Booth or Benedict Arnold. Unlike the popular myth of the home as a place of comfort and pleasure, homes are actually poorly ventilated, a burden on the woman who is subservient to her husband, who, in turn, is burdened by the financial responsibilities of maintaining a household. The child grows up to learn that being a woman means domestic servitude, and if that child is a girl and must stay at home, she will be "cut off from life." Part of the solution relies on better technology within the home, and part lies in giving women the option to gain employment outside of the home. If society would simply recognize the myths they have built around and within the home, the home could become a place of advancement instead of regression. The book was widely reviewed, even in major newspapers such as the *Boston Herald*, the *Chicago Tribune*, the *Detroit Free Press*, the *New York Tribune*, and the *San Francisco Examiner*. Aside from some conventional opinions in the book, such as Gilman's belief in the desirability of marriage for women and her disparaging opinion of women's aesthetic tastes, Gilman's book is an unconventional and almost heretical rendition of a sacred social institution.

Gilman's next book was four years in the making, an uncharacteristically long time for her to work on a single piece of writing. Gilman believed *Human Work* (1904) to be her most important book. It is built on the idea that human work is not and should not be perceived as the means to an individual's ends. Instead, work "is an expenditure of energy by Society in the fulfillment of its organic functions. It is performed by highly specialised individuals under press of social energy, and it is to them an end in itself, a condition of their existence and their highest joy and duty." She theorizes that social instinct or "race-preservation" is more developed than self-preservation, and so the labor of others serves communal rather than individual needs. Work is not something from which to acquire individual wealth, but fulfills a larger purpose. Gilman argues that human work is a social and civic function, not an individual one, and that the social machine is fed by workers and their machines. She wants workers to have a social consciousness that recognizes the higher purpose of work.

Whether or not Gilman's solution is viable, what is central to this book is her passionate belief in one's individual social responsibilities. Gilman's entire body of writings, from her poems to her fiction and essays, are all built on a hope for change, for progress, and for integrating private responsibilities, such as domestic service, with public life. Although Gilman was proud of *Human Work*, it was never reprinted and was less widely reviewed than either *Women and Economics* or *The Home: Its Work and Influence*.

In 1909 Gilman started *The Forerunner*, a monthly magazine that dealt with social issues. She was the editor and sole contributor, writing the entirety of the thirty-two-page magazine for seven years, from November 1909 to December 1916. Her format for the magazine was consistent. Each issue begins with an epigraph, such as "It is good to do what is right. It is bad to do what is wrong. It is worse to do nothing." The sketch on the cover of the magazine conveyed her concern not just for women but also for men and children around the world. At the end of each issue, she tells her readers that the magazine is not a woman's magazine, because it deals with human existence and is designed to stimulate thought and to offer practical solutions for that existence. The magazine consisted of short stories, poems, essays, sketches, short plays, and fiction and nonfiction works that were often serialized throughout the year. For about a year Gilman wrote a column called "Personal Problems," in which anonymous women (perhaps created by Gilman) ask what

Gilman considers to be relevant and practial questions. Most often, the questions raise a political issue, such as when "College Girl" asks how she can get her date to allow her to pay for half when they go out to dinner or the theater, since they have nearly equal incomes.

Gilman also included a "Comment and Review" section, which she used as a forum to comment on traditional notions and to review books or articles. For example, in December 1909, Gilman mocks the myth of Santa Claus, calling him "a bulbous benevolent goblin, red-nosed and gross, doing impossible tricks with reindeers and chimneys." Children should not be worrying about what they get from this imaginary man; instead, they should be giving something to their community. Children, especially young girls, should not be listening to other fairy tales as well, such as *Sleeping Beauty*. Gilman wants to know what the purpose is of a story in which the girl "is to remain starkly unconscious, using absolutely no discretion; and cheerfully marry the first man that kisses her."

The Man-Made World or, Our Androcentric Culture, serialized in *The Forerunner* in 1909, was published in book form in 1911. In the preface, Gilman dedicates her book to Lester F. Ward, who provided her with the premise of her book in the fourteenth chapter of his *Pure Sociology* (1903). In Ward's book, his Androcentric Theory and Gynaecocentric Theory is outlined, and Ward's Gynaecocentric Theory prompted the writing of *The Man-Made World*. Gilman explains that the theory is based upon the belief "that the female is the race type, and the male, originally but a sex type, reaching a later equality with the female, and, in the human race, becoming her master for a considerable historic period." Her book proposes to study the theory's effect on human development.

Because men and women live in an Androcentric culture, she begins, a culture where men have come to dominate, our culture's history has been written by men. It has become nearly impossible to differentiate between human accomplishment and male accomplishment, a point repeated from *Women and Economics*. Masculine values have overtaken such areas as literature, religion, and education. Gilman claims that most literature, particularly adventure stories and love stories, is geared specifically toward a male ideology. Adventure stories contain "predatory excitement . . . the sole province of men," and all love stories appeal to the male because the stories end when the women get married. The stories end at that point because the important part of a man's life, the pursuit, has already been told, while a woman's story is just beginning with her marriage. Religious precepts are masculine as well, since they highlight what she calls "the great devil theory." This theory asserts that learned truths and social customs as well as individual traits are rendered in terms of combat. Finally, although the origin of education is defined as maternal, Gilman contends that since the Androcentric culture never allowed girls the same education as boys; educated women are considered "unsexed"; and if the woman is a teacher, she "effeminizes her pupils; if the pupil, she effeminizes her teachers."

Gilman's second book-length piece, "Our Brains and What Ails Them," was serialized in *The Forerunner* in 1912. Its premise is that the human brain is like any other organ and therefore needs stimulation and exercise, or "mental mechanics." Mental mechanics are necessary so the brain can learn how to see things on a collective rather than an individual level. She stresses that women do not have different or inferior brains than those of men, it only seems that way since they have not been permitted to exercise them as men have.

Gilman repeats and expands on her past work in several other serialized pieces, such as "Humanness"(1913), "Social Ethics" (1914), "The Dress of Women" (1915), and "Growth and Combat" (1916). "Humanness" once again emphasizes the need to recognize the social value of work, while "Social Ethics" stresses an ethical system that maintains a collective existence. "Growth and Combat" repeats Gilman's belief that struggle and combat are masculine traits, and as long as these traits dominate, society cannot grow or progress. "The Dress of Women" reintroduces and expands on an issue she had touched on several times in earlier works. Gilman had always been indignant about uncomfortable women's clothing; she herself refused to wear corsets or tight-fitting clothing. In "The Dress of Women," Gilman highlights both the danger and absurdity of some forms of dress and the tendency of clothing to overemphasize a woman's gender. In chapter 2, for example, Gilman explains how impractical long, cotton house dresses are for the average, hardworking housewife, and proposes trousers in their place.

Some articles of clothing are particularly absurd and improper. Gilman calls the skirts of bathing suits a "hoary Emblem of the Sex," which serve no practical purpose other than for "Sex-Attraction and Display of Purchasing Power." A woman's sexuality and economic status are displayed by her dress. Furthermore, women's clothing causes others to see "the woman labeling herself with a huge 'W'; crying aloud to all 'I am female and I wish to please.'" Gilman urges her readers to recognize that clothing is part of social life and is therefore subject to evolutionary laws. As long as women continue to wear impractical and overtly

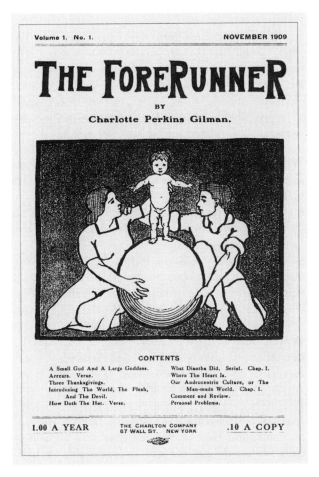

Cover for the first issue of Gilman's magazine

female clothing, their progression toward equality will be retarded.

Each issue of *The Forerunner* usually began with a short story. The themes of the stories hark back to Gilman's complaint in *The Man-Made World* that fiction does not give a true picture of woman's life, and focuses disproportionately on man's life. Thus, Gilman called for more fiction to be written about young women who prefer a career to marriage, or middle-aged women who came to recognize their discontent as social starvation, or the interrelation of women. Topics such as these are precisely the themes Gilman addresses in many of her short stories. In "According to Solomon" a woman learns to weave and maintains her own income from the sales of her products, much to the surprise and pleasure of her husband. In "What Diantha Did" Gilman provides a positive scenario for the woman about to be married. Instead of waiting until her fiancé earns enough money to marry her, Diantha opens up a multipurpose business that succeeds as a boarding house and catering service. In "The Cottagette" Malda and her older friend, Lois, stay in a cottage until Malda meets Ford Matthews and falls in love. Lois insists that Malda cook for him, while Ford insists she give all her attention to her artistic talent of needlework. Yet, a woman can make an admirable living as a housewife, as Gilman suggests in "My Astonishing Dodo," in which Dodo's life is portrayed positively because she is doing something she has always wanted to do, and because she has trained herself through formal home economic courses. "The Widow's Might" tells of a widow who was economically self-sufficient at her husband's death and has plans to sustain herself for the remainder of her life, much to the surprise of her children who were gloomily looking ahead to their filial duty to house and care for their mother.

Additionally, Gilman approached in her fiction three rather taboo scenarios: male physical assault, venereal disease, and extramarital affairs that produce illegitimate children. In "Benigna Machiavelli" Gilman offers explicit advice for effective self-defense from the abuse of men in the workplace. Benigna Machiavelli is a woman in the workforce who samples various careers to find the one best suited to her abilities and needs. In going into a variety of jobs, however, she runs into men who attempt to harass her. Benigna states clearly what a girl should do in that situation: "if he comes too close—kick, kick hard and accurately. This is 'unladylike,' but not so regrettable as being mishandled."

In "The Crux," which originally appeared in the second issue in 1910 but was published separately in 1911, Dr. Jane Bellair returns to New England after having gone to Colorado to practice medicine. She convinces a group of women to start a new life with her in the West. One of the women, Vivien Lane, goes along because her lover had gone west, and they are reunited there. Dr. Bellair discovers, however, that Vivien's lover has a venereal disease—the crux of the story. She advises Vivien not to marry her lover, since the doctor herself is incapable of having children because her former husband gave her gonorrhea.

Gilman approaches a third taboo topic in "Turned," a story that opens with two women in separate rooms crying miserably. It is eventually revealed that one is a servant, Gerta, who has become pregnant by a married man, Mr. Marroner. Mrs. Marroner is the other hurt woman. She decides that her husband is the one at fault and leaves him, taking Gerta and her baby with her. Mrs. Marroner, who has a Ph.D., makes her own way by returning to teaching and taking in boarders.

Gilman's stories never address a lower class or ethnic audience. Gerta, the servant girl, is docile, confiding, and helpless, and the rest of the women in the stories are rarely burdened with stigmas of class or race in the start of their new lives. As a former Nationalist, Gilman often positioned those of the lower classes, especially immigrants, on a low rung of the evolutionary ladder. Gilman concentrated on providing options for those women she knew best, often middle-class, Anglo-American women who were caught within embarrassing circumstances that were rarely publicly acknowledged. Gilman wanted to make venereal disease and abusive and unfaithful husbands and lovers subjects for public discussion, dissolving a secrecy that for too long maintained a status quo that mostly benefited men. In the process, however, she excluded the experiences of classes and ethnicities she found to be different from her own.

Besides "The Yellow Wallpaper," Gilman's other well-known story among American feminists today is "Herland," first serialized in *The Forerunner* from January 1915 through December 1915, and published separately for the first time by Pantheon Books in 1979. *Herland* is a utopian novel constructed around the impressions of three males who enter a land uninhabited by men, and peopled with women. Van, the narrator, Terry, and Jeff come across Herland while on an expedition and are eventually captured by the Herlanders. The three men are taught the Herlander language and teach their own to their curious tutors. Through conversations with their tutors Somel, Zava, and Moadine, the men learn that the Herlander society is one where men are not necessary to procreate, a scenario reminiscent of Ward's Gynaecocentric Theory. A woman becomes pregnant by allowing her impulse to mother to overtake her body. "Mother-love" is the Herlanders religion, a kind of reverence and respect for mothering all children, not just one's own, and women allow others to take care of their children, while they work each day as gardeners, inventors, engineers, and weavers, for example. Herland is a clean and nicely landscaped country whose citizens lead a contented existence in simple clothing and simple ways of living. Throughout *Herland,* Gilman returns time and again to many of her ideas about women and society, using Herlanders as models and Van as the inquiring observer/reader of the text of the landscape/novel. Gilman creates a dialogue between the two cultures that exposes the frivolity of most Victorian women's existence as well as the Androcentric influences that made them so. Gilman serialized a sequel to this utopian novel in the last volume of *The Forerunner* in 1916 titled *With Her in Ourland* (1997). At the end of *Herland,* Van and the Herlander Ellador marry; in the sequel both travel throughout Van's world. Ellador sees and comments on the destruction of war and the low position of women in

Charlotte and George Gilman, and their grandchildren, Dorothy and Walter Chamberlain

American society. Many of the same themes are repeated from *Herland,* and, as in the previous novel, the incongruities of modern society are revealed through persistent dialogue between Ellador and Van.

In addition to the stories, Gilman's essays in *The Forerunner* often echoed earlier themes. Women's dress, religion, ethics and morality, women's suffrage, and motherhood were all recurring topics. In the later issues of the journal, Gilman focused many of her essays on women's roles in World War I. In "War-Maids and War-Widows" for instance, Gilman urges unmarried women and widows to gain a "sense of collectivity" by taking advantage of their large numbers to demand political and economic power.

Burdened with the financial responsibility of a journal with only 1,200 subscribers, Gilman discontinued *The Forerunner* in December 1916. During her seven years as editor and writer of the magazine, she published an immense amount of writing. Her last book besides her autobiography was *His Religion and Hers: A Study of the Faith of Our Fathers and the Work of Our Mothers,* published in 1923. It echoes the theme of

Man-Made World in that religion has been limited by relying solely on men's ideas. Again, she ridiculed people's preoccupation with the reward of heaven. She calls this impulse selfish, arguing that people should care about the world they leave to their children rather than the world they enter after death. She contends that Christianity teaches its followers to be obedient, which leads to the sense of helplessness that is responsible for the exaggerated anticipation of heaven and the apathy toward what occurs here on earth. Christianity overemphasizes "a most injurious doctrine" by insisting on the essential unworthiness of individuals. Religion, says Gilman, should never be closed to intelligent inquiry. Gilman's own inquiry brings her to a proposal for a "birth-based religion" that will promote growth during life instead of hope for an afterlife. A birth-based religion emphasizes a new motherhood whose guiding principle is to maintain and improve the human race. Although *His Religion and Hers* was not popular, Gilman was proposing a reformed ethical and religious paradigm, one that looked forward to a less masculinized culture where the cultivation and growth of living supersedes the desire for rewards beyond life in death.

In *His Religion and Hers,* Gilman wrote: "Life is action. We should not say 'life' as a noun but 'living' as an active verb. The process of living is a continuously active one." Perhaps her faith in this axiom was her reasoning behind the title of her autobiography, *The Living of Charlotte Perkins Gilman.* Begun in 1929, the memoir was not published until 1935. In January 1932 she was diagnosed with breast cancer. She was dealt another blow when her husband died in May 1934. Shortly before her own death, Gilman was approached by an editor unknown to her who asked if she would write an essay stating her position on the issue of euthanasia. The article it was published in the November 1935 issue of *Forum,* a monthly magazine dedicated to social issues. Concerning suicide, Gilman wrote that there are times when "surrender is justifiable. If persons are beyond usefulness, of no service or comfort to anyone, they have a right to leave." On 17 August 1935, wracked with pain and knowing the end was near, Gilman committed suicide by inhaling a large dose of chloroform.

Charlotte Perkins Gilman is a key figure in the feminist movement. Surely she fulfills many of the definitions of modern feminism; Gilman herself stated that she wrote and spoke for men, women, and children, and that a reconceptualized role of women was essential to altering patriarchal paradigms that oppressed all people, regardless of age or gender. Although her vision of humankind was most often limited to Anglo-American, middle-class women and men, Gilman nevertheless insisted her voice—a female voice—be heard even where it was not welcome, and in the process she contributed to a social revolution that continues to this day.

Bibliography:
Gary Scharnhorst, *Charlotte Perkins Gilman: A Bibliography* (Metuchen, N.J.: Scarecrow Press, 1985).

Reference:
Ann J. Lane, *To Herland and Beyond: The Life and Work of Charlotte Perkins Gilman* (New York: Meridian, 1991).

Papers:
Charlotte Perkins Gilman's papers are housed at the Schlesinger Library at Radcliffe College.

Emma Goldman

(27 June 1869 – 14 May 1940)

Priscilla Wald
Duke University

BOOKS: *A Beautiful Ideal* (Chicago: J. C. Hart, 1908);

Patriotism: A Menace of Liberty (New York: Mother Earth, 1908);

What I Believe (New York: Mother Earth, 1908);

The White Slave Traffic (New York: Mother Earth, 1909);

Anarchism and Other Essays (New York: Mother Earth, 1910; revised, 1911);

The Tragedy of Women's Emancipation (New York: Mother Earth, 1910);

Anarchism: What It Really Stands For (New York: Mother Earth, 1911);

Marriage and Love (New York: Mother Earth, 1911);

The Psychology of Political Violence (New York: Mother Earth, 1911);

Syndicalism: The Modern Menace to Capitalism (New York: Mother Earth, 1913);

Victims of Morality and the Failure of Christianity (New York: Mother Earth, 1913);

The Social Significance of the Modern Drama (Boston: Badger, 1914);

Preparedness: The Road to Universal Slaughter (New York: Mother Earth, 1915);

Philosophy of Atheism and the Failure of Christianity (New York: Mother Earth, 1916);

Anarchism on Trial: Speeches of Alexander Berkman and Emma Goldman in the United States District Court, in the City of New York, July, 1917, by Goldman and Alexander Berkman (New York: Mother Earth, 1917);

The Truth about the Boylsheviki (New York: Mother Earth, 1918);

Deportation: Its Meaning and Menace, by Goldman and Berkman (New York: Fitzgerald, 1919);

The Crushing of the Russian Revolution (London: Freedom, 1922);

My Disillusionment in Russia (Garden City, N.Y.: Doubleday, Page, 1923);

My Further Disillusionment in Russia (Garden City, N.Y.: Doubleday, Page, 1924);

Living My Life (New York: Knopf, 1931);

Voltairine De Cleyre (Berkeley Heights, N.J.: Oriole, 1932);

Emma Goldman

Trotsky Protests Too Much (Glasgow: Anarchist-Communist Federation, 1938);

The Traffic in Women and Other Essays on Feminism, edited by Alix Kates Shulman (New York: Times Change Press, 1970);

Red Emma Speaks: Selected Writings and Speeches by Emma Goldman, edited by Shulman (New York: Random House, 1972);

Vision on Fire: Emma Goldman on the Spanish Revolution, edited by David Porter (New Paltz, N.Y.: Commonground, 1983).

"My great faith in the wonder worker, the spoken word, is no more," laments the anarchist Emma Goldman in her preface to her first collection of writings, *Anarchism and Other Essays* (1910). It is an odd admission from one who continued grand lecture tours until her incarceration in 1917 and her subsequent deportation two years later and of whom her friend and associate,

Alexander (Sasha) Berkman, wrote to a mutual friend, "EG's forte is the platform, not the pen, as she herself knows very well." Her point, however, was perhaps to substitute for the electricity that she knew she generated from the platform the "intimate" relationship that she professed to share with the reader and to honor the latter as belonging to an elite group, "the few who really want to learn, rather than the many who come to be amused." The notoriety that she achieved and the fear that she inspired attest to the truth of Berkman's words. At her best Goldman writes with an impassioned elegance that witnesses the depth of her beliefs and hints at the power that she apparently wielded from the podium. Her ideas often lack the richness and complexity of the great philosophers and theorists of anarchy; the strength of her prose inheres more in the conviction behind the expression of those ideas and the forceful clarity of their presentation. Her written work is of interest more because it registers the struggles of a remarkable and powerful woman than because it presents or analyzes the principles of anarchy in a new way. In her written work Goldman has left a record of the insights of an astute observer who was at the center of radical politics when the world was undergoing considerable change.

Goldman was fifty years old when she was deported, in December 1919, from the United States to the newly created Soviet Union. She was full of hope, as she had been thirty-four years earlier when she had made the reverse journey; and she was to be just as disappointed by what she encountered. Neither elation nor disappointment was an alien experience for her. Ever the idealist, she continually registers in her written work great hope and equally great disappointment and discouragement. The goal of human liberation through the precepts of anarchy remained her motivating beacon, however, and she died working to exhaustion to put the anarchist credo before a public that was interested, as she complained, more in novelty and performance than in ideas.

While she both lectured and wrote on a variety of the most pressing social and political issues of her day—from free speech to free love, abortion rights to the modern school—her most powerful essays were typically inspired by particular events, such as the execution of the pioneer educator Francisco Ferrer by the Spanish government or the assassination of President William McKinley and the trial of his assassin, Leon Czolgosz. Such acts of violence structured her public life, and her writings chronicle her development in response to them.

Emma Goldman was born on 27 June 1869 in Kovno, Lithuania, to Abraham Goldman, a Jewish theater manager, and his wife, Taube. Emma had two older half sisters, from her mother's previous marriage, and two younger brothers. When she was eight years old she was sent to live with her maternal grandmother in Königsberg, Prussia, where she received the extent of her formal education, three years of schooling. In 1882 she moved with her family to St. Petersburg, where she worked as a corset maker and later in a glove factory, and where she was first introduced to revolutionary politics by the students she met there. Goldman immigrated to the United States with her half sister Helena in December 1885 and went to work in a clothing factory in Rochester, New York. She attended meetings of a local German socialist group and entered into an unhappy marriage with another worker, Jacob Kershner, in February 1887.

Goldman's nascent political sympathies were stimulated by a series of incidents of labor violence in Chicago that came to be known as the Haymarket Riots. Chicago in the mid 1880s was an important center of radical labor movements in the United States, and 1886 was an eventful year for labor, with the American Federation of Labor declaring that the eight-hour workday would commence on 1 May. A well-publicized dispute at the McCormick Harvester Company resulted in a lockout and subsequent strike in February; tensions were fueled by the 1 May deadline, and violence erupted among strikers, scab workers, and police on 3 May. A protest meeting held the following evening in Haymarket Square, disrupted by the unexplained appearance of a phalanx of police, resulted in more violence when a bomb exploded and the police fired on the crowd. The response of the city was to round up and persecute labor activists and other radicals, especially among its large immigrant population. Of the eight men who were tried for the bombing, only two had actually been at the meeting; many perceived the trial as farcical, arguing that the defendants were on trial for their socialist and anarchist ideas rather than their actions or any involvement in the bombing of Haymarket Square. In her autobiography *Living My Life* (1931), Goldman calls it "the worst frame-up in the history of the United States." None of the defendants was acquitted. Three received lengthy prison sentences (two of them life), one committed suicide in prison, and the other four were hanged on 11 November 1887, an event that became a rallying point for radical America, including Goldman and many of her subsequent friends and associates.

Already moved by the events, Goldman was further inspired by hearing the celebrated socialist Johanna Greie's account of the Haymarket Riots shortly before the end of the trial. According to Goldman, the dynamic speaker summoned her to the stage after the talk ended and remarked on the "tumult of emotions" registered on Goldman's face. Learning, in response to her query, that Goldman was not acquainted with the Haymarket defendants, Greie prophesied, "I have a feeling that you will know them better as you learn their ideal, and that you will make their cause your own." Whether or not from a distance of more than four decades Goldman accurately recalled Greie's words, the experience moved her to divorce Kershner and leave Rochester, New York, to move to New Haven, Connecticut, and a life of more concentrated radical activism. She returned once to Rochester—and to Kershner, whom she remarried—before leaving permanently, this time for New York. Haymarket remained the precipitating event of her conversion to anarchism and activism, however, and a touchstone for her most important relationships, including that with Berkman, whom she met in New York in 1889.

In 1892 Goldman, Berkman, and Berkman's cousin Modest (Fedya) Stein were living and working together in Worcester, Massachusetts, and avidly following the progress of the lockout-turned-strike of the steelworkers at Andrew Carnegie's plant in Homestead, Pennsylvania. When plant manager Henry Clay Frick turned strikers' families out of company-owned homes, the three young anarchists sold their profitable ice cream parlor and prepared to move to Pittsburgh to assist the strikers. When Frick sent in three hundred armed Pinkerton guards, however, the strike turned bloody, and, as Goldman reports in her autobiography, the three decided that "words had lost their meaning in the face of the innocent blood spilled on the banks of the Monongahela." Goldman reports Berkman's veritable growth in stature as he declared Frick "the responsible factor in this crime" who "must be made to stand the consequences." Thus, he decided on an *attentat*—not a murder, Goldman is quick to explain, but a political statement.

Berkman's plan was to make a bomb, kill Frick, and live long enough to explain his action in court before killing himself. The deed would call attention to "the real cause" of the Homestead struggle, and it "would also strike terror in the enemy's ranks and make them realize that the proletariat of America had its avengers." Berkman did not count on the difficulties of bomb-making, however, and the gun and dagger he took instead to Homestead did not quite serve him as he had intended. Although badly wounded, Frick survived, Berkman having been "overpowered by working-men," as the newspapers reported, in whose name he had designed and committed his *attentat*. The detectives then divested Berkman of the dynamite cartridge he was holding in his mouth.

Worst of all for Goldman was not the response of the general public, but of many of their comrades,

Goldman in Rochester, New York, in 1886, shortly after her immigration to the United States (International Institute of Social History)

including Johann Most, a charismatic anarchist who had launched Goldman both intellectually and professionally in her anarchist work. Far from awakening social conscience, the *attentat* proved extremely unpopular and, for Most, silly. Finally, Berkman received a sentence of twenty-two years, rather than the expected maximum of seven, in prison for his deed. During Berkman's years in prison, the sexual relationship between him and Goldman was replaced by a much stronger political bond. As she reports in her autobiography, Goldman was motivated continually in her actions and her writings by thoughts of Berkman, with whom she was not allowed to communicate during much of that time.

Berkman's attempt on Frick's life and the consequences of that act were so important to Goldman's understanding of her life and work that she was willing to risk permanent exile from the United States rather than exclude an account of her involvement in it from her autobiography, as attorney Arthur Leonard Ross suggested to her in 1928. Readers of *Living My Life* have speculated that Goldman's desire to be allowed to reenter the United States at times influenced her account of her life. While preparing to write that work, she consulted many friends and associates; in that light, her response to Ross's suggestion is especially striking: "I appreciate deeply your interest in my autobiography and in my chances of a possible return to the States," she wrote to him. "But it will be out of the question to consider your suggestion of eliminating the story. . . . my connection with Berkman's act and our relationship is the leitmotif of my forty years of life" since. Calling it "the pivot" around which she wrote her story, she concluded, "I would rather never again have the opportunity of returning than to eliminate what represents the very essence of my book." Berkman's action and Goldman's relationship to it is indeed a leitmotif, picking up on the Haymarket Square protests and foreshadowing the many *attentats* and massacres around which her intellectual development, life decisions, and the narrative of the autobiography turn.

Goldman's international notoriety began with the assassination of McKinley in 1901 and her outspoken defense of Czolgosz. The assassin allegedly "confessed," as the headlines shouted, that Goldman had "incited" his action. The McKinley assassination–or *attentat*, as the anarchists preferred to call it–was not the first violent action with which the government or the press had tried to connect her, but in its coverage of the event the mainstream press invoked Goldman as an inspiration and monstrous embodiment of national terror. Following a brief prison stay allegedly in connection with the event, she was unable to find anyone who would rent her an apartment in Manhattan or employ her despite her excellent qualifications as a nurse. For a time the notorious Emma Goldman was forced to become the innocuous "Miss E. G. Smith."

Goldman had known Czolgosz, slightly, under the name of Nieman. In May 1901 she had recommended material for him to read, and, upon his request, she had presented him to some of her anarchist colleagues as a potential comrade. She herself had only met him twice, and it was not until she saw a picture of McKinley's assassin in the newspapers that she had any reason to connect him either with Czolgosz or with his deed. Her defense of the *attentat,* however, earned her the opprobrium of the general public and even of many of her professedly anarchist friends. Unable to rent a hall in which to lecture, Goldman resorted to the printed word. In "The Tragedy of Buffalo," which appeared in the October 1901 issue of *Free Society,* a journal edited by her friend Abe Isaak, she argues that "Leon Czolgosz and other men of his type, far from being depraved creatures of low instincts are in reality supersensitive beings unable to bear up under too great social stress." She contended that such men become violent "because they cannot supinely witness the misery and suffering of their fellows. The blame for such acts must be laid at the door of those who are responsible for the injustice and inhumanity which dominate the world."

Writing from prison, even Berkman, although supportive of his beloved companion, questioned the propagandistic and educational value of Czolgosz's deed "because the social necessity for its performance was not manifest." Czolgosz, argued Berkman, had struck against a political rather than economic oppressor and "in modern capitalism economic exploitation rather than political oppression is the real enemy of the people. Politics is but its handmaid." Goldman felt especially betrayed by Berkman's analysis not only because he was her closest friend and comrade but also because he of all people, she believed, should understand the import of the young man's actions, being himself in the midst of a prison term for his own attempted *attentat;* Berkman's act of violence, in fact, served as a point of reference in Goldman's work for other such acts, including Czolgosz's. Explaining and giving meaning to Berkman's *attentat* motivated much of her writing, from her earliest essays to her autobiography.

After her politicization in the wake of the Haymarket Riots, the other major political transformation of Goldman's life was her disillusionment with the outcome of the Bolshevik Revolution. In June 1917 she and Berkman were arrested and charged with conspiracy to obstruct the military draft, for which Goldman was sentenced to two years in the Missouri state prison. Released in 1919, she found that her American citizenship, which she had acquired through her marriage to Kershner, had been revoked, and she was deported to the Soviet Union, arriving in January 1920. Goldman soon became suspicious of the Bolsheviks' justification of their suppression of political opposition, which they explained as a military necessity stemming from "the blockade, the intervention, the counterrevolutionary plotters." Goldman, and later Berkman, who shared her exile, watched in growing dismay as anarchists who had fought for and with the Bolsheviks were jailed, banished, and executed for expressing their beliefs and hierarchies were set in place that resembled nothing so much as the inequities that had inspired the revolution. Heroes of the revolution, such as Nestor Makhno, an anarchist leader of a peasant rebel army who had fought important battles for the Bolsheviks, were alternately condemned and hunted and celebrated as history was written and rewritten visibly in accordance with political expediency.

From her jail cell in Jefferson City, Missouri, in the two years prior to her deportation, Goldman had looked to Russia for hope and sustenance. She had been devastated by the criticisms leveled against the Bolshevik government by her beloved heroine, the Russian radical Catherine Breshkovskaya. From her cell she had written to Breshkovskaya, begging "her to bethink herself, not to go back on her glorious past and the high hopes of Russia's present generation." Marveling at Breshkovskaya's apparent collusion with "the worst enemies of Russia" in the United States "the wretched gang that was conniving to undo the achievements of the Revolution," Goldman "scorned her suggestion," she recalls in her autobiography, that she "would some day be on her side and work with her against the Bolsheviki, who were defying the entire reactionary world." Within weeks of her deportation, Goldman recalled Breshkovskaya's prediction, and the events in the port city of Kronshtadt in 1921 led to her resolve to leave the Soviet Union and fulfill her old heroine's prophecy.

The government-ordered massacre of the sailors and other residents of Kronshtadt followed upon the mass meeting called by the Kronshtadt sailors, "the advance guard in the October Revolution," as Goldman explains in *My Further Disillusionment in Russia* (1924), in support of striking workers in Petrograd. In response to the meeting, at which the sailors and citizens of Kronshtadt expressed their support of the revolution but "voiced the popular demand for Soviets elected by the free choice of the people," the participants in the Kronshtadt meeting were declared counter-revolutionists, and within a week their city was bombarded and their population decimated. "Thus," laments Goldman, "Kronstadt was 'liquidated' and the 'counter-revolutionary plot' quenched in blood." Shortly after Kronshtadt, Goldman and Berkman fled to Europe, where their criticism of the Bolsheviks dismayed many of their former comrades, leading to a severe reduction in their speaking engagements.

The years between Haymarket and Kronshtadt had been productive ones for Goldman. She had lectured often throughout the United States and the West. From March 1906 through August 1917, she had published, edited, and written for the widely circulated anarchist journal *Mother Earth,* and from October 1917 through May 1918, for its short-lived successor, the *Mother Earth Bulletin.* The personages that appear in *Living My Life* embody radical politics in the United States from the 1890s through the 1920s. She had shared the platform, her life, and, later, her exile with such figures as Most, Voltairine de Cleyre, Eugene V. Debs, Margaret Sanger, and John Reed. She had known writers, editors, and publishers from Margaret Anderson to Abraham Cahan, Hutchins Hapgood to Helen Keller. She had heard Sigmund Freud lecture in Vienna in the 1890s, where she had also seen Eleonora Duse play the

Modern ideas on War, Labor and the Sex Question are revolutionizing thought. If you believe in learning things yourself, it will pay you to hear

Emma Goldman

Who will deliver a Series of Lectures in Portland on Vital Subjects at

Portland, Subject and Dates:

Sunday, August 1st, 3 P. M.
THE PHILOSOPHY OF ANARCHISM
Sunday, August 1st, 8 P. M.
THE "POWER" OF BILLY SUNDAY
Monday, August 2nd, 8 P. M.
MISCONCEPTIONS OF FREE LOVE
Tuesday, August 3rd, 8 P. M.
FRIEDRICH NIETZSCHE—The Intellectual Storm Center of Europe
Wednesday, August 4th, 8 P. M.
JEALOUSY—Its Cause and Possible Cure
Thursday, August 5th, 8 P. M,
ANARCHISM AND LITERATURE
Friday, August 6th, 8 P. M.
THE BIRTH CONTROL (Why and How Small Families Are Desirable)
Saturday, August 7th, 8 P. M.
THE INTERMEDIATE SEX (A Discussion of Homosexuality)
Sunday, August 8th, 3 P. M.
WAR AND THE SACRED RIGHT OF PROPERTY
Sunday, August 8th, 8 P. M.
VARIETY OR MONOGAMY—WHICH?
ADMISSION 25 CENTS
8 Lectures With MOTHER EARTH, Subscription $2.50
OVER
Scandinavian Socialist Hall, 4th and Yamhill

Handbill for a series of lectures Goldman gave in 1909 (Special Collections, Library of the University of California, Santa Barbara)

valiant Magda in Hermann Sudermann's *Heimat* (1893). She had seen Sarah Bernhardt perform in Victorien Sardou's 1882 play *Fédora* in New Haven but thought Duse "attained a higher zenith."

Goldman's 993-page *Living My Life* and her earlier accounts of her two years in the Soviet Union, *My Disillusionment in Russia* (1923) and *My Further Disillusionment in Russia*—both of which she incorporated into the autobiography—register the rhetorical talents for which she was celebrated as a speaker more nearly than her earlier journalism; yet, even the work written before and during the *Mother Earth* years bears witness to the contagious passion with which she infected her audience.

Goldman and Alexander Berkman in New York City in 1917, awaiting trial on charges of conspiracy to obstruct the military draft, a crime for which Goldman served two years in prison

Two collections of essays and various articles and pamphlets attest to the breadth of her interests and concerns. The power of the work in *Anarchism and Other Essays* derives more from Goldman's ability to convey ideas than her capacity to forge new ones. The essays represent her reflections on her lived experience. She is hardly the first would-be reformer, for example, to enjoin her readers to "rise above . . . foolish notions of 'better than thou,' and learn to recognize in the prostitute a product of social conditions," as she does in "The Traffic in Women," first published in 1910 in Goldman's *Anarchism and Other Essays*. Yet, when she insists that "the girl feels herself a complete outcast, with the doors of home and society closed in her face" and that "her entire training and tradition is such that the girl herself feels depraved and fallen, and therefore has no ground to stand upon, or any hold that will lift her up, instead of dragging her down," she derives her analysis from experience. Desperate for money at the time of Berkman's *attentat*, the twenty-three-year-old anarchist determined to sell all that she felt she had—her body. "I wanted to take flight," she recalls in *Living My Life*, "run back to my room, tear off my cheap finery, and scrub myself clean. . . . I continued my tramp, but something stronger than my reason would compel me to increase my pace the moment a man came near me." Goldman's flirtation with streetwalking ends when the man she finally solicits recognizes her as "a novice in the business," having noticed, he explains, her "haunted expression and . . . increased pace the moment a man came near" her. He gives her ten dollars and sends her home. Yet, Goldman on several occasions was compelled to take up residence among prostitutes, with no one else willing to house her, and if her own experience ended comically, she knew many others who had not been so fortunate. That knowledge lends the essay its force, turning it into more than a predictable indictment of the sex market under capitalism.

The Psychology of Political Violence (1911) offers a similar example of how directly Goldman's analysis grew out of her personal experiences. Surely, Goldman had her own involvement in such events as the McKinley assassination in mind when she introduced her subject with the observation that "to analyze the psychology of political violence is not only extremely difficult, but also very dangerous. If such acts are treated with understanding, one is immediately accused of eulogizing them. If, on the other hand, human sympathy is expressed with the *Attentäter*, one risks being considered a possible accomplice. Yet it is only intelligence and sympathy that can bring us closer to the source of human suffering and teach us the ultimate way out of it." Personal conviction rather than systematic analysis generates the assertion that "those who have studied the character and personality of these men, or who have come in close contact with them, are agreed that it is their supersensitiveness to the wrong and injustice surrounding them which compels them to pay the toll of our social crimes."

Writing at a time when the nascent fields of sociology and social psychology were inventing a new vocabulary of social observation and new categories of investigation (such as criminology), Goldman speaks more in the language of the novelist than in that of the social scientist. "And what happens to a man with his brain working actively with a ferment of new ideas," she asks in the same essay, "with a vision before his eyes of a new hope dawning for toiling and agonizing men, with the knowledge that his suffering and that of his fellows in misery is caused not by the cruelty of fate, but by the injustice of other human beings—what happens to such a man when he sees those dear to him starving, when he himself is starved?" Goldman understands why they "feel that their violence is social and not anti-social, that in striking when and how they can, they are striking, not for themselves, but for human nature, outraged and despoiled in their persons and in those of their fellow sufferers." It is not hard to imagine the impact of such words on an audience, especially if they are delivered by a speaker as magnetic as Goldman allegedly was, and perhaps listeners would be more prepared to exonerate those "piteous victims of the Furies and the Fates" than readers, who have more time for sober reflection.

The other collection of essays published prior to Goldman's exile represents a different facet of her work but nonetheless grows out of her political commitments and similarly is of more interest for the insights it offers into Goldman than for its analysis of its subject matter. In *The Social Significance of the Modern Drama* (1914), Goldman collects essays on Scandinavian, German, French, English, Irish, and Russian drama, having found "very little worthy to be considered in a social light" among the products of U.S. dramatists. Like many works of literary criticism, *The Social Significance of the Modern Drama* offers readings of literature that reflect the author's understanding of the function and purpose of art and that are designed to define what constitutes important—even great—works. Yet, Goldman's readings are especially and explicitly polemical, illustrating her conviction that the playwrights she considers "know that society has gone beyond the stage of patching up, and that man must throw off the dead weight of the past, with all its ghosts and spooks, if he is to go foot free to meet the future." This revolutionary theme defines as it characterizes modern drama, and playwrights whose work does not fit under this rubric are, by her definition, not "modern"; it constitutes "the social significance which differentiates modern dramatic art from art for art's sake. It is the dynamite which undermines superstition, shakes the social pillars, and prepares men and women for the reconstruction."

Many among her cohort found Goldman's interest in art troubling and questioned its relevance to her political activity. Yet, she argues in this volume, great artists not only "mirror in their work as much of the spiritual and social revolt as is expressed by the most fiery speech of the propagandist"; more importantly, they also "compel far greater attention." Her readings consist mainly of plot summaries that explain the revolutionary messages of the plays—the oppressive nature and deforming impact of social institutions and the ways in which they make fetishes of the values of bourgeois culture. Against many of the propagandists among her acquaintances, Goldman believed "that only those who go to the remote are capable of understanding the obvious" and that belief accounts for her occasional attention to more aesthetic concerns. Although suspicious of what constituted beauty in modern culture, Goldman nonetheless found an important place for literature and even for the category of "literariness" in her political aesthetic. Still, the essays collected in this volume hold more interest as examples of political literary criticism than as detailed readings of the work of individual dramatists that, for Goldman, constituted bourgeois criticism.

Goldman is celebrated by contemporary feminist scholars; yet, her feminism was complicated, and at times compromised, even as it was frequently motivated by her understanding of anarchism. Certainly not the first to view marriage as primarily an economic relationship, she advocated free love—the deregulation of passion—and pointed to the liberation that often followed for women "whom economic necessity has forced to become self-supporting." Although contemptuous of the prevalence of what she understood as women's sexual possessiveness and jealousy, she nonetheless understood how the economic position especially of middle-class women underwrote those emotions. With "physical attraction" as "her only stock in trade," she argues in "Jealousy: Causes and a Possible Cure," it is no wonder that women become "envious of the charm and value of other women as threatening her hold upon her precious property." Jealousy, then, grows not out of love but out of the institutional structures of capitalism that warp the finest of emotions.

Universal suffrage was, to Goldman, "our modern fetich," and "woman, even more than man" was "a fetich worshipper." More than suffrage, she argues in "Woman Suffrage," women needed to refuse their positions as sex commodities. A strong supporter of birth control, Goldman argued for the importance of women's choice of sexual partner, sexual relationship, and reproduction. Her own decision not to have children was a difficult one, but she could not accommodate children to her vision of the life of political activism to which she felt called. Repeatedly, her long-term romantic relationships foundered on her partners' wishes—despite their professed convictions to the contrary—to make her a conventional wife and mother. The cause of universal suffrage, for Goldman, distracted women, who would make bolder advances toward equality by opposing fetishized institutions such as marriage and conventional motherhood. "The tragedy of woman's emancipation," she argues in a 1910 essay by that title, lies in the illusion of liberation; emancipation follows only when "woman has learned . . . to stand firmly on her own ground and to insist upon her own unrestricted freedom, to listen to the voice of her nature, whether it call for life's greatest treasure, love for a man, or her most glorious privilege, the right to give birth to a child." Free love included, for Goldman, the freedom to choose same-sex partners; yet, unless the special topic of her lecture or article was homosexuality, desire, in her work, was nearly always heterosexual. Similarly, she spoke passionately against racism,

My Further Disillusionment in Russia

By
Emma Goldman

*Being a Continuation of Miss Goldman's
Experiences in Russia as given in "My
Disillusionment in Russia"*

Garden City   New York
Doubleday, Page & Company
1924

*Title page for Goldman's account of the brutality of the Soviet
Bolshevik regime*

but unless it was the explicit topic of the address, her political analysis rarely included race and racism as social problems intrinsic to capitalist oppression and thereby worthy of address.

Although Goldman continued to write articles and pamphlets and to deliver lectures after leaving the Soviet Union, the main corpus of her work took a notable turn. Whereas she drew implicitly—for the most part—from her experiences in her earlier work, she culled her later analyses more overtly from her adventures. The Bolsheviks' stringent regulation amplified the censorship that Goldman associated with any media, and the celebration of the October Revolution by the Western radicals underscored the urgency of her corrective. Nothing could better tell the story, she knew, than her own eyewitness account of what she had seen and experienced while living under the Bolshevik government. *My Disillusionment in Russia* and *My Further Disil-*

lusionment in Russia read as memoirs of the anarchist's gradual discovery of the abuses of the Bolshevik government, and she drew heavily on both books in her subsequent autobiography. The afterword to the second volume, however, constitutes one of her most important analyses.

Indeed, that analysis motivated both volumes, which, as Goldman explains in *Living My Life,* were written as one long study intended to explain not only the failure of the revolution, but also its causes, mainly the organization and centralization of political power in the state. In this work Goldman sought to warn "the workers of Europe and America of the destructive effects of Statism." So important to the project was this afterword that Goldman tried to stop the sales of the work when she discovered that her original manuscript, titled "My Two Years in Russia," had been published as *My Disillusionment in Russia,* with the last twelve chapters, including the afterword, omitted. The mistitled and partial work, she believed, conveyed disillusionment with the Russian Revolution rather than with "the pseudo-revolutionary methods of the Communist State." Ultimately, Goldman prevailed upon her publisher, Doubleday, Page and Company, to publish the missing chapters as a separate volume, but the title remained that chosen by the publisher. In her subsequent autobiography Goldman expresses exasperation at the dullness of the reviewers of the first volume of the Russia book, who, with the exception of a Buffalo librarian, had failed to notice the evident truncation of the work.

While the Russia books herald a new direction in Goldman's writing, *Living My Life* marks its successful culmination. Taking her experiences as the explicit subject, Goldman is free to unfold her story in the personal style with which she seems most comfortable. *Living My Life* is as engaging as it is informative, an account of a changing world from the perspective of a committed political activist, the kind of person who would call her autobiography *Living My Life,* a title that suggests activity and ongoing process rather than coherence.

"Fifty years—thirty of them in the firing line—had they borne fruit or had I merely been repeating Don Quixote's idle chase?" asks Goldman roughly two-thirds of the way through *Living My Life* and from the perspective of the Jefferson City jail. "Had my efforts served only to fill my inner void, to find an outlet for the turbulence of my being? Or was it really the ideal that had dictated my conscious course?" The bold honesty of these questions starkly motivates *Living My Life* as it characterizes the tone of the work. At all moments the reader feels the presence of an almost paradoxical reflective activism. Deeply committed to her cause, the author of *Living My Life* never rests in its seductive absolutism. She acknowledges the temptation that she had experienced, during her time in the Soviet Union, to take the hand of an unquestioning Bolshevik and say, "I am with you. I see with your eyes and will serve with the same blind faith as you and your sincere comrades." Yet, "alas," she remarks, "there was no such short and easy way out of the mental anguish for those who seek for life beyond dogma and creed." Mental anguish, in the hands of this skillful narrator, turns to a motivating quest and provides Goldman the mandate to explore her own conscience as she investigates the structures of her own and her cultures' beliefs. There are times when the temptation to rest—in her beliefs, in a particular place or moment—seems overwhelming, even destined to overtake the narration, as when she recalls once sitting on a "terrace, the *samovar* before us, the sky streaked with blue and amethyst, the sun a ball of fire slowly sinking into the Black Sea. The city with all its terror and suffering seemed far off, and the green bowered nook an idyll. If it would last awhile longer, I mused . . . but one lived in seconds only."

In all respects Goldman's oeuvre represents the work of one who "lived in seconds only." Her sensibility is clearly that of one who "did not believe that a Cause which stood for a beautiful ideal, for anarchism, for release and freedom from conventions and prejudice, should demand the denial of life and joy." She gave her life to that cause, wholly and freely, and the cause gave it back to her to live. Toward the end of her life she fought despair, her own and Berkman's. She survived his suicide in June 1936, fought with the anarchists in Spain during the Civil War, and continued to write and to lecture throughout the West. In response to a question, she wrote the essay "Was My Life Worth Living?" (*Harper's Magazine,* December 1934), in which she explains that the widespread governmental opposition to anarchists testified to the tacitly acknowledged power of the belief. "Considered from this angle," she writes, "I think my life and my work have been successful. . . . I have always striven to remain in a state of flux and continued growth, and not to petrify in a niche of self-satisfaction. If I had my life to live over again, like anyone else, I should wish to alter minor details. But in any of my more important actions and attitudes I would repeat my life as I have

lived it. Certainly I should work for Anarchism with the same devotion and confidence in its ultimate triumph."

Goldman died on 14 May 1940 in Canada. Three months earlier she had suffered a stroke while raising money to support the anarchists in their fight against Francisco Franco's fascists in Spain. To the end of her life she had refused to believe in lost causes, and she is buried, appropriately, in Chicago's Waldheim Cemetery, with the Haymarket martyrs whose fates had become so enmeshed with her own.

Letters:

Nowhere at Home: Letters from Exile of Emma Goldman and Alexander Berkman, edited by Richard Drinnon and Anna Marie Drinnon (New York: Schocken, 1975).

Biographies:

Richard Drinnon, *Rebel in Paradise: A Biography of Emma Goldman* (Chicago: University of Chicago Press, 1961);

B. N. Ganguli, *Emma Goldman: A Portrait of a Rebel Woman* (New Delhi: Allied, 1979);

Candace Falk, *Love, Anarchy, and Emma Goldman* (New York: Holt, Rinehart & Winston, 1984);

Alice Wexler, *Emma Goldman: An Intimate Life* (New York: Pantheon, 1984).

References:

Bonnie Haaland, *Emma Goldman: Sexuality and the Impurity of the State* (Montreal: Black Rose, 1993);

Joseph Ishill, *Emma Goldman: A Challenging Rebel,* translated by Herman Frank (Berkeley Heights, N.J.: Oriole, 1957);

Alix Kates Shulman, *To the Barricades: The Anarchist Life of Emma Goldman* (New York: Crowell, 1971);

Martha Solomon, *Emma Goldman* (Boston: Twayne, 1987).

Papers:

The major achival sources and collections of Emma Goldman's papers can be found in the Emma Goldman Papers Project, University of California at Berkeley, and the International Institute of Social History, Amsterdam.

Anna Katharine Green

(11 November 1846 – 11 April 1935)

Marie T. Farr
East Carolina University

BOOKS: *The Leavenworth Case: A Lawyer's Story* (New York: Putnam, 1878); republished as *The Great Detective Story: The Leavenworth Case* (London: Nicholson, 1878);

A Strange Disappearance (New York: Putnam, 1879; London: Routledge, 1884);

The Sword of Damocles: A Story of New York Life (New York: Putnam, 1881; London: Ward, Lock, 1884);

The Defense of the Bride and Other Poems (New York: Putnam, 1882);

XYZ: A Detective Story (New York: Putnam, 1883; London: Ward, Lock, 1883);

Hand and Ring (New York: Putnam, 1883);

The Mill Mystery (New York & London: Putnam, 1886);

Risifi's Daughter: A Drama (New York & London: Putnam, 1887);

7 to 12: A Detective Story (New York & London: Putnam, 1887);

Behind Closed Doors (New York & London: Putnam, 1888);

The Forsaken Inn (New York: Bonner, 1890; London: Routledge, 1890);

A Matter of Millions (New York: Bonner, 1891; London: Routledge, 1891);

The Old Stone House and Other Stories (New York & London: Putnam, 1891);

Cynthia Wakeham's Money (New York & London: Putnam, 1892);

Marked "Personal," as Mrs. Charles Rohlfs (New York & London: Putnam, 1893);

Miss Hurd: An Enigma (New York & London: Putnam, 1894);

Dr. Izard (New York & London: Putnam, 1895);

The Doctor, His Wife, and the Clock (New York & London: Putnam, 1895);

That Affair Next Door (New York & London: Putnam, 1897);

Lost Man's Lane: A Second Episode in the Life of Amelia Butterworth (New York & London: Putnam, 1898);

Anna Katharine Green

Agatha Webb (New York & London: Putnam, 1899);

The Circular Study (New York & London: McClure, Phillips, 1900);

A Difficult Problem: The Staircase at the Heart's Delight, and Other Stories (New York: Lupton, 1900; London: Ward, Lock, 1903);

One of My Sons (New York & London: Putnam, 1901);

Two Men and a Question (New York: Lupton Leisure Hour Library, 1901);

Three Women and a Mystery (New York: Lovell, 1902);

The Filigree Ball: Being a Full and True Account of the Solution of the Mystery Concerning the Jeffrey-Moore Affair (Indianapolis: Bobbs-Merrill, 1903; London: Unwin, 1904);

The Millionaire Baby (Indianapolis: Bobbs-Merrill, 1905; London: Chatto & Windus, 1905);

The House in the Mist (Indianapolis: Bobbs-Merrill, 1905; London: Nash, 1910);

The Amethyst Box (Indianapolis: Bobbs-Merrill, 1905); republished as *The Amethyst Box and Other Stories* (London: Chatto & Windus, 1905);

The Woman in the Alcove (Indianapolis: Bobbs-Merrill, 1906; London: Chatto & Windus, 1906);

The Chief Legatee (New York & London: Authors and Newspapers Association, 1906); republished as *A Woman of Mystery* (London: Collier, 1909);

The Mayor's Wife (Indianapolis: Bobbs-Merrill, 1907);

Three Thousand Dollars (Boston: Badger, 1910);

The House of the Whispering Pines (New York & London: Putnam, 1910);

Initials Only (New York: Dodd, Mead, 1911; London: Nash, 1912);

Masterpieces of Mystery (New York: Dodd, Mead, 1913); republished as *Room Number 3 and Other Detective Stories* (New York: Burt, 1913);

Dark Hollow (New York: Dodd, Mead, 1914; London: Nash, 1914);

The Golden Slipper and Other Problems for Violet Strange, as Mrs. Charles Rohlfs (New York & London: Putnam, 1915);

To the Minute, Scarlet and Black: Two Tales of Life's Perplexities (New York & London: Putnam, 1916);

The Mystery of the Hasty Arrow (New York: Dodd, Mead, 1917);

The Step on the Stair (New York: Dodd, Mead, 1923; London: John Lane, 1923).

SELECTED PERIODICAL PUBLICATION–
UNCOLLECTED: "Why Human Beings Are Interested in Crime," *American Magazine*, 87 (February 1919): 38–39, 82–86.

During the nineteenth century Anna Katharine Green Rohlfs was an internationally known writer of detective fiction whose works were translated into at least five languages and who was admired by literary critics such as Walter Besant and politicians such as Theodore Roosevelt, Woodrow Wilson, and future prime minister of England Stanley Baldwin. Between the two world wars, however, her books were unread and forgotten. Feminist critics have subsequently revived her reputation as they have rediscovered how her originality, intriguing plots, and invention of the first series detectives—including two stereotype-defying women investigators—won respectability for mystery fiction among the middle class and helped shape future development of the genre. Her commentaries on class and ethnic differences, particularly in the New York area with which she was intimately familiar, provide a strong moral and social vision that Patricia D. Maida identifies as stemming from Green's Calvinist antecedents. Like many of her contemporaries, she negotiated between femininity and feminism—though Green, who refused to support woman suffrage, would have repudiated the latter label.

Green's ambition was to be a poet and dramatist, but her literary and financial success was achieved through her mystery fiction. Although *The Leavenworth Case: A Lawyer's Story* (1878), was not the first single-volume American detective novel by a woman, it was the first best-selling one and earned Green the title "Mother of Detective Fiction." However, critics in the 1920s and 1930s found her style elaborately formal, euphemistic, and romantic, if not melodramatic. In a career that began nine years before Sir Arthur Conan Doyle introduced Sherlock Holmes in *A Study in Scarlet* (1888) and ended three years after Agatha Christie published *The Mysterious Affair at Styles* (1920), Green wrote thirty-three novels, several collections of short fiction, a volume of poetry—*The Defense of the Bride and Other Poems* (1882)—and a Renaissance verse drama, *Risifi's Daughter* (1887). Perhaps it is not surprising that over a forty-five-year writing career her technique should go out of style. Yet some of the best-known mystery writers, such as Mary Roberts Rinehart, John Dickson Carr, and Christie, pay tribute in their works to Green's significant influence. Christie, who recalled hearing *The Leavenworth Case* read aloud when she was a child, utilizes plot devices and characters descended from Green's creations.

Born in Brooklyn on 11 November 1846 to middle-class parents of New England lineage, Anna Catherine Green (she later changed the spelling of her middle name) grew up in a family dominated by her father, James Green, an important defense attorney. The Greens moved frequently around the Manhattan-Brooklyn area but in 1857 settled in Buffalo, the city to which Anna returned after her marriage. Her mother, Katherine Ann Whitney Green, died in childbirth when Anna was only three years old, and her sister, Sarah, thirteen years older than Anna, became her "mother-sister." When their father later remarried, Anna found encouragement from her stepmother, Grace Green, in her early writing attempts.

THE

LEAVENWORTH CASE:

A LAWYER'S STORY.

BY

ANNA KATHARINE GREEN.

NEW YORK:
G. P. PUTNAM'S SONS,
182 FIFTH AVENUE.
1878.

Title page for Green's first novel, which earned her the title "Mother of Detective Fiction"

One of the few women in the nineteenth century who had access to higher education, Green attended Ripley Female College, where she developed both her goal of becoming a poet and, as the president of the Washington Irving Society, her interest in the New York region's folklore. Her tales, like Irving's "The Legend of Sleepy Hollow" (1819–1820), retain a mysterious atmosphere but eventually dispel the supernatural aura through rational explanation. After graduation she sent her poems to Ralph Waldo Emerson, who praised their "power of expression" but discouraged her from pursuing a career as a poet. In order to see her poems published, she first turned to fiction, hiding these efforts from her father, who found fiction inappropriate for women but whose approval she gained after reading him the finished manuscript of her first mystery.

Publication of *The Leavenworth Case* made Green, at age thirty-two, an instant success both in America and Europe; dramatized, filmed twice, and republished regularly, the novel eventually sold more than a million copies. Six years and three novels later Green had an established reputation and, like the English poet Elizabeth Barrett, found herself in love with a younger man–the son of German immigrants and an actor whose future seemed none too secure. In 1884, after he had promised her father to give up acting, Green married Charles Rohlfs. Rohlfs, who after Green's death acted in the stage version of her first novel, wryly admitted on his fiftieth wedding anniversary that after a while he became tired of being known as "the husband of The Leavenworth Case." After first designing iron stoves, he turned to furniture design, creating the Mission style, which eventually earned him an international reputation. During the first decades of the marriage, however, the family, which included their three children and Green's sister, Sarah, was dependent largely on Green's literary earnings.

The Leavenworth Case–which became a subject of debate by the Pennsylvania legislature as to whether it could actually have been authored by a woman– developed Edgar Allan Poe's implausible locked-room mystery into a believable plot device. Indeed, praised for its realism, the novel was used by Yale College to illustrate how circumstantial evidence may be deceptive. As the daughter of a well-known criminal lawyer, Green knew and provided her readers specifics of police procedure, such as the elaborately detailed coroner's inquest in the opening chapters.

The novel introduces Green's series detective, Ebenezer Gryce, whom she made quite different from Poe's Dupin; acknowledging the French crime writer Emile Gaboriau's influence, she made her primary character not an amateur but a policeman, like Gaboriau's creation, M. Lecoq, who was one of the first police detectives and known for his use of scientific analysis in solving crimes. According to Maida, both James Green and the New York metropolitan police chief served as models. As Green later recounts in the story "The Staircase at the Heart's Delight," Gryce made his reputation as a young policeman by solving a series of drowning deaths among wealthy men of New York. Gryce is also humanly imperfect, however. In the thirteen works in which he appears, he suffers from arthritis, gradually ages, condescends to his assistant, Amelia Butterworth, and occasionally makes mistakes. Described in this first novel as "a portly, comfortable personage with an eye that never pounced, that did not even rest–on you. If it rested anywhere, it was always on some insignificant object in your vicinity, some vase, inkstand, book or button," Gryce's wandering eye is misleading, for his sharp observations and consequent deductions exonerate the innocent and condemn the guilty.

Lauded by the English novelist Wilkie Collins for her "powers of invention" and "imagination," Green introduced some elements of detective fiction in *The Leavenworth Case* that have since become staples, even clichés, of the genre. As Alma Murch observes in *The Development of the Detective Novel* (1958), these include not only the first series detective but also "the rich old man, killed when on the point of signing a new will; the body in the library; the dignified butler with his well-trained staff; detailed medical evidence as to the cause and estimated time of death; the coroner's inquest and the testimony of expert witnesses; the authority on ballistics who can identify the gun that fired the shot . . . even . . . a sketchmap of the scene of the crime and a reproduction of the torn-off fragment of a letter, not unlike the one that later occupied Sherlock Holmes's attention in *The Reigate Squire*." Green also provides a gathering of the suspects in a confrontation scene at the conclusion.

Believing that "the essentials of a good mystery story are first of all an interesting plot with a new twist–a queer turn that has never before been attempted," Green began *The Leavenworth Case* with but two central ideas: that the murderer should be first to announce the crime, and that a conversation overheard by the narrator be attributed to the wrong woman. Thus the story begins with the discovery of the murdered millionaire Horatio Leavenworth in a locked room just as he was about to change his will to disinherit his favored niece, Mary. Leavenworth had a past grudge against the English, and Mary has had the temerity to marry an Englishman. Because she has "been taught to worship money," however, she has sent her husband away and attempted to keep the marriage secret.

A major thread of *The Leavenworth Case* is the gap between the American middle class (to which Gryce belongs) and the upper class (to which the Leavenworth family belongs). Social class, as Green reiterates, depends on breeding as well as wealth. In her 1887 work *7 to 12,* for example, a discreet police detective is called for–"by birth and education what is called a gentleman." Gryce, who in later novels appears in several guises, has, however, one major drawback: "I cannot pass myself off for a gentleman"; evidently he lacks the appropriate haughty stare. Gryce, in fact, is so conscious of class difference between himself and the Leavenworths as to feel the need to call upon a member of the New York aristocracy, an attorney, to play amateur detective and gain information to which Gryce does not have access. Like the later creations of Sherlock Holmes's associates, Watson and Hastings, the attorney in Green's mystery narrates the novel and serves as the detective's confidante; he even provides a love interest as he seeks to exonerate Mary's sister, Eleanore, from suspicion.

In this novel, as in others such as *A Strange Disappearance* (1879), Green sees membership in the upper class as carrying with it certain obligations. Characters such as Mary Leavenworth, or Holman Blake in the later novel, whose proud haughtiness and concern for money lead them to reject the people who love them, are humbled by the unselfish and unquestioning belief of those they have scorned. When Mary's guilt seems inescapable, her husband's belief in her innocence restores her to a proper sense of priorities, and she dramatically rejects the inheritance the murderer of her uncle attempts to bestow upon her by throwing her diamond earrings at his feet. Similarly, Blake, who has rejected his wife because of her lower-class origins and criminal father and brother, recognizes his love for her only after she has disappeared. At the end he discovers he cannot even offer her his wealth, since she, not he, is his father's heir. In both novels Gryce manipulates the discovery and confession, bringing the true murderer to justice and leading to reconciliation of the lovers.

This confluence of social and moral judgments in Green's work is based on her belief that "evil qualities are inevitably those which center in Self. . . . Wipe out Self, and you will wipe out crime." While she is interested in the criminal's psychology, she identifies people's emotions, "especially their hidden emotions," as of utmost importance. As she observes in "Why Human Beings Are Interested in Crime" (*The American Magazine,* February 1919), readers are more interested in the motive than the crime, because "These people are like us; or . . . they are what we perhaps only dream of being–rich, cultivated, powerful." Coming from the middle class, she indulges the middle-class reader's interest in the lives of the wealthy, sometimes getting her plot ideas from newspaper clippings her readers sent her. Green disliked calling her work detective novels, preferring that they be called "criminal romances"; she considered both the mystery and the love interest essential, even if the latter had to be subordinated to the central element of detection.

Thus, in contrast to proud, selfish characters, Green presents characters who sacrifice themselves: in *Agatha Webb* (1899), a mother kills herself to prevent her son from unknowingly murdering her; in *A Strange Disappearance,* a wife leaves her husband's house rather than bring scandal upon him; in *XYZ: A Detective Story* (1883), a young man accepts the blame for a theft committed by his brother; in *The House in the Mist*

First page of Green's publishing contract with G. P. Putnam's Sons (Harry Ransom Humanities Research Center, University of Texas at Austin)

(1905), a young woman gives up an inheritance because she has had a child out of wedlock. Even in her blank-verse tragedy, *Risifi's Daughter,* Green depicts a Renaissance nobleman who kills himself to allow his brother to inherit the title and thus win the woman they both love.

If Green's villains are drawn largely, though not entirely, from the lower and middle classes, her detectives are drawn from all spheres of life. The clever Miss Saunders, narrator–companion in *The Mayor's Wife,* is of good but impoverished background. Caleb Sweetwater, a poor musician supporting a widowed mother, solves the murder of Agatha Webb and thus solidifies his ambitions to become a detective. He appears again in several novels as Gryce's assistant in the New York Police Department. The widower Gryce is middle-class, as is the young detective–narrator of *The Filigree Ball.* Horace Byrd, a young detective who may originally have been intended to replace Gryce, is a gentleman. The two women who most interest modern readers, Amelia Butterworth, a shrewd, wealthy, middle-aged spinster with whom Gryce forms an ambiguously described attachment, and Green's "New Woman" detective, the debutante Violet Strange, belong to the elite society of New York.

The three novels featuring Amelia Butterworth—*That Affair Next Door* (1897), *The Problem of Lost Man's Lane: A Second Episode in the Life of Amelia Butterworth* (1898), and *The Circular Study* (1900)—and *The Golden Slipper and Other Problems for Violet Strange* (1915) best reflect Green's paradoxical response to Victorian ideals of femininity. In reality, she was the breadwinner in her family for many years, laboring steadily and professionally at her craft. Publicly, however, she drew attention to her role as traditional housewife, telling an interviewer in *Literary Digest* (13 July 1918) that, besides her children and grandchildren, "I have a husband, my garden, my house, and my friends. Writing is only a part of my life." In her novels neither Amelia nor Violet is married—though the latter meets her husband-to-be in the course of her detecting—and in *That Affair Next Door* Amelia both declares a husband a "doubtful blessing" and competes with Gryce to solve the crime. Two recent articles by Joan Warthling Roberts and Cheri L. Ross argue that Butterworth was an early, if not the first, feminist detective.

Amelia is probably based on a real-life woman Green describes in "Why Human Beings Are Interested in Crime" as "a member of the best society in one of our large cities, who helped in the investigation of a mysterious crime and was largely responsible for solving the case," someone who "did it simply because she has the kind of mind which enjoys unraveling a mystery." Amelia's interest in the murdered woman

next door dates "from the moment I found that this affair, at first glance so simple, and at the next so complicated, had aroused in me a fever of investigation which no reasoning could allay." Working with both intuition and logic–supposedly distinctly masculine and feminine spheres–she arrives at the solution.

In this novel Green depicts Butterworth's attempt to win Gryce's respect for her acumen not only as a humorous battle of the sexes, but also as a serious comment on society's undervaluing of women's abilities. In the next novel, *Lost Man's Lane,* the focus is on Amelia, whose help Gryce solicits by arousing her curiosity and competitive spirit. Yet, while she solves one mystery, he is the one who discovers the solution to the mysterious disappearances of people who enter the lane. Believing she has failed in the competition, Amelia is surprised by Gryce's proffer of an enigmatic, possibly romantic, tribute.

The third novel, *The Circular Study,* examines men's attitudes toward rape, as a dying father extracts a promise from his sons to seek vengeance on John Poindexter, the man entrusted with his daughter but who violated her. It is not the violation itself but the rejection by her lover, who kills himself upon hearing of the rape, that causes Evelyn's death. Her brother Thomas–who is to carry out the vengeance by marrying Poindexter's daughter, Eva, and then abandoning her–falls in love with her and refuses, at which point another brother threatens both Eva and him. Faced with the choice of dishonor or death, Eva is transformed: "a flaming angel stood where but a moment before the most delicate of women weakly faltered." In this novel Amelia's collaboration with Gryce in solving the death of Thomas's brother makes up for what she sees as her failure in *Lost Man's Lane.* Having found the body, identified the people at the scene, and delivered Eva safely to New York to face the consequences of her act, Miss Butterworth "sank back on the carriage cushions with an inexorable look, which, nevertheless, did not quite conceal a quiet complacency which argued that she was not altogether dissatisfied with herself or the result of her interference in matters usually considered at variance with a refined woman's natural instincts." The final lines of the novel seem to suggest a future collaboration between Butterworth and Gryce, but it never took place.

By the time *The Golden Slipper and Other Problems for Violet Strange* was published fifteen years later, American women's roles—as well as the stylistic conventions of detective fiction—had changed drastically, and Green's description of her protagonist seems to reflect the author's confusion. Violet is described as "vivacity incarnate," childlike, with disarming dimples, but with "a woman's lofty soul." She is also intelligent and keenly observant. Because of her social position and her ability to solve problems of the upper classes discreetly, without scandal, Violet is employed by a private detective agency. Her employer is dismayed to find that only the money she earns moves her to take cases, but Green indicates that she is working for a particular reason: her sister has been disowned by their father for having married against his will and is consequently living in poverty; Violet wants to give her a year's study abroad to begin a singing career.

At the end of the final story she reveals her motivation to Roger Upchurch, whom she is to marry, explaining that her sister has made her successful debut and that someday she hopes to reveal her sister's success to her father. Critics have pointed out the recurrence of Green's authoritarian fathers, and it is clear that in this series of stories, as in other works, a strong resentment of unjust treatment vies with an equally strong desire for reconciliation. Violet's father, after all, looks at the wall where her sister's picture once hung with "a tear in his hard eye."

Green's last book is *The Step on the Stair* (1923). Although she was not an activist in her later years, she nevertheless supported the international copyright law and cabled the British statesman William Gladstone when she read he opposed it (he replied he was misquoted and strongly supported it). She suffered a series of painful losses around this time: her elder son, Sterling, in a flying accident in 1928, and her daughter, Rosamund, in 1930. Green died in Buffalo, New York, on 11 April 1935.

Although Green's style of mystery was eclipsed to some extent by the hard-boiled crime novels of the 1920s and 1930s, her reputation has aged well. Feminist readings of her works reveal interesting ambivalences toward both class and gender, and modern readers have begun to recognize her as a precursor of their favorite mystery fiction. As Audrey Peterson concludes in her *Victorian Masters of Mystery: From Wilkie Collins to Conan Doyle* (1984), Green's "originality, the tightness of her plots, the attractiveness of her characters, and her astonishing consistency over a forty-five year span make her an author well worth a second look, while the old-fashioned qualities which banished her to obscurity have now, in an age of Victorian revival, taken on a patina of charm."

Interview:

"Anna Katharine Green Tells How She Manufactures Her Plots," *Literary Digest*, 58 (13 July 1918): 48.

References:

J. R. Broadus, "Anna Katharine Green," in *Critical Survey of Mystery and Detective Fiction,* edited by Frank Magill (Pasadena: Salem, 1988) pp. 780–788;

Rose DeShaw, "The Mother of the Modern Mystery: Anna Katherine [sic] Green (1846–1935)," *Mystery Review* (Ontario, Canada), 2 (Summer 1994): 35–38;

Gillian Gill, *Agatha Christie: The Woman and Her Mysteries* (New York & Toronto: Free Press, 1990) pp. 32, 35–36, 46, 157, 202, 217n., 226n.;

Barrie Hayne, "Anna Katharine Green," in *10 Women of Mystery,* edited by Earl F. Bargainnier (Bowling Green, Ohio: Bowling Green State University Popular Press, 1981), pp. 152–178;

Patricia D. Maida, *Mother of Detective Fiction: The Life and Works of Anna Katharine Green* (Bowling Green, Ohio: Bowling Green State University Popular Press, 1989);

Alma Murch, *The Development of the Detective Novel* (London: Peter Owen, 1958);

Audrey Peterson, *Victorian Masters of Mystery: From Wilkie Collins to Conan Doyle* (New York: Ungar, 1984);

George Haven Putnam, "Wilkie Collins on 'The Leavenworth Case,'" *The Critic,* 19 (28 January 1893): 52;

Joan Warthling Roberts, "Amelia Butterworth: The Spinster Detective," in *Feminism in Women's Detective Fiction,* edited by Glenwood Irons (Toronto: University of Toronto Press, 1995), pp. 3–11;

Cheri L. Ross, "The First Feminist Detective: Anna Katharine Green's Amelia Butterworth," *Journal of Popular Culture,* 25 (Fall 1991): 77–86.

Papers:

Anna Katharine Green's manuscripts are located in the Harry Ransom Humanities Research Center at the University of Texas. A collection of her papers may also be found at the Buffalo and Erie County Public Library.

Susan Hale

(5 December 1833 – 17 September 1910)

Karen Dandurand
Indiana University of Pennsylvania

BOOKS: *A Family Flight through France, Germany, Norway, and Switzerland,* by Hale and Edward Everett Hale (Boston: Lothrop, 1881);

A Family Flight over Egypt and Syria, by Hale and Edward Everett Hale (Boston: Lothrop, 1882);

A Family Flight through Spain (Boston: Lothrop, 1883); revised as *Young Americans in Spain* (Boston: Lothrop, 1899);

A Family Flight around Home, by Hale and Edward Everett Hale (Boston: Lothrop, 1884);

Life and Letters of Thomas Gold Appleton (New York: Appleton, 1885);

Self-Instructive Lessons in Painting with Oil and Water-Colors on Silk, Satin, Velvet and Other Fabrics, Including Lustra Paint and the Use of Other Mediums (Boston: Tilton, 1885);

A Family Flight through Mexico, by Hale and Edward Everett Hale (Boston: Lothrop, 1886);

The Story of Spain, by Hale and Edward Everett Hale (Boston: Lothrop, 1886); republished as *Spain* (New York: Putnam, 1899);

The Story of Mexico (New York: Putnam, 1889); republished as *Mexico* (London: Unwin, 1891; New York: Putnam, 1891);

Men and Manners of the Eighteenth Century (Meadville, Pa.: Flood & Vincent, 1898);

Inklings for Thinklings (Boston: Marshall Jones, 1919).

OTHER: *Balloon Post,* nos. 1–6, edited by Hale (11–17 April 1871);

Sheets for the Cradle, edited by Hale (6–11 December 1875);

The Dial of the Old South Clock, nos. 1–10, edited by Hale (5–15 December 1877);

Nonsense Book: A Collection of Limericks, illustrated by Hale (Boston: Marshall Jones, 1919).

SELECTED PERIODICAL PUBLICATION–UNCOLLECTED: "Straw into Gold," *Old and New,* 1 (1870): 754–755.

Susan Hale

Susan Hale was well known in her time not only as a writer but also as a painter and amateur actress with a flair for comedy. Her travel books for children and adults (most co-authored with her brother Edward Everett Hale), newspaper letters, and magazine sketches are characterized by humor and a colloquial style; even potentially dry factual information is lightened by a good-natured voice that refuses to take things too seriously. Hale gained some recognition as a painter in watercolors in the 1870s and 1880s, with works chosen for important exhibitions in Boston and New York. Her public readings of neglected eighteenth-century writers, many of them women, made a unique contribution to late-nineteenth-century American literary culture. She was also well known in the Boston area for her participation in amateur theatricals, not only as a comic actress but behind the scenes as well, writing scripts and originating stage business. Most notable were the one-woman plays she created and performed in major cities nationwide in the 1870s and 1880s.

Hale was "a hundred years ahead of her day," according to Caroline P. Atkinson, reminiscing about her friend more than twenty years after Hale's death. In a time when most unmarried women stayed in the family home or lived with married siblings, Hale chose instead to live by herself in rented rooms. Despite the convention holding that a woman needed an escort to travel, Hale from her teens routinely traveled alone by train to visit relatives and friends and became a competent and confident foreign traveler, readily going on her own when suitable companions were not available. Quite contrary to the stereotype of the Victorian lady confined to the parlor and by her hampering clothing, Hale engaged in vigorous outdoor exercise throughout her life: six-mile walks and a daily swim were part of her regimen, and she rode horseback from girlhood until she was well into her fifties.

Yet, the story of Hale's long life and unusual career has been told only in a few brief accounts by family and friends in the decades following her death. There has been almost no scholarly or critical work on her; she is mentioned only in passing in biographies of Edward Everett Hale, though they do provide useful background on her family. Her own letters—more than two hundred published posthumously and about two thousand more extant in manuscript—are the best source of detailed information about her life. They provide insight not only into the thoughts and daily life of one woman but into the situations of unmarried middle-class women in her time and place, and into nineteenth-century American popular culture generally. Moreover, Hale's letters are worth reading not only for the information they provide but also as literary works in their own right, engrossing examples of a genre being increasingly recognized as a legitimate literary form. Her letters are often funny, sometimes poignant, always interesting; they feature some of her best writing.

Susan Hale was born on 5 December 1833 into a Boston family that provided a richly stimulating intellectual atmosphere. Her father, Nathan Hale (nephew of the Revolutionary War hero), a lawyer by training, was owner and editor of the *Boston Daily Advertiser;* her mother, Sarah P. Everett Hale (sister of writer and orator Edward Everett), exceptionally well educated for her time, was a writer and translator and assisted in editorial work on the paper. Susan was the youngest of the seven Hale children who survived to maturity; her oldest siblings were already young adults when she was a girl. Her education took place primarily at home (as had her mother's), with instruction from her mother and older brothers and sisters as well as from tutors. She did attend school sporadically—beginning in the fall of 1849 she went for two years to a Boston school run by George B. Emerson, and she refers to attending an academy earlier. Like her older brother Edward, however, she disliked formal education and much preferred following her own course of reading and study, which in 1844, when she was ten, had included such subjects as "Ancient Geography." Under her mother's guidance she became proficient in French and studied other languages as well.

Reading and writing were staples of Hale household entertainment. They were decidedly a "literary" family, as the term was used then. Hale satirizes this quality of their childhood in "Straw into Gold," an 1870 sketch that is clearly fictionalized autobiography: "This family was so literary that the children were fed entirely with alphabets and multiplication-tables. They sat upon dictionaries when the chairs were not high enough for the table and they had newspaper aprons to protect them from the soup." Susan's early letters often comment on new books: for example, for her thirteenth birthday her mother gave her Lydia Maria Child's *Fact and Fiction* (1846); when she was seventeen she read a current best-seller, Susan Warner's *The Wide, Wide World* (1850), and was "bewitched and delighted," telling her brother she found it "not half as melancholy as I 'pected." While she was growing up, her brothers with a few of their friends established the "Franklin Circulating Library," named for the street where they lived. The stock of the library consisted of books authored by the members and other invited contributors. Most of the little volumes, written or printed by hand, range in size from about three-by-four inches to four-by-six inches and are bound with string in covers of colored, sometimes brightly marbled, paper, apparently printer's remnants. Hale's name does not appear in the list of "proprietors" in the library's report (they are all boys), but there are several volumes under feminine pseudonyms in the mid 1840s, when she was between ten and thirteen years old. Volumes by "Mrs. Windemere" in handwriting that looks like hers and with illustrations similar to those in her letters about this time are likely Susan Hale's first "books." Like the rest of the Hale family, she also wrote letters regularly; the earliest among her papers were written when she was eight years old.

Hale took up her share of the work of producing the *Boston Daily Advertiser* when she was in her teens. At seventeen she was not only reviewing books for the paper but also seems to have taken charge of the book-review operation: reporting to Edward that she and sister Lucretia (twelve years her senior) the day before had "puffed a batch of new books," she assures him she will send on anything she thinks he would be interested in reviewing. From the late 1840s through the 1850s the Hales faced financial difficulties, in large part resulting from Nathan Hale's railroad investments, that put their ability to run the *Advertiser* in jeopardy. Hale's brothers sold the paper in 1864, after their father's death the year before.

After their mother's death in late 1866, Hale and Lucretia remained in the family home until October 1867, when they broke up housekeeping and went for an extended visit with their brother Charles, who had recently become U.S. consul in Egypt. The journey was Susan's first trip abroad. After their return in early summer 1868 she chose to set up independent living arrangements and rented rooms in Boston, where she lived alone. (There was no estrangement from her sister; they sometimes vacationed together and wrote to each other at least weekly until late in the century, when Lucretia was incapacitated by blindness and mental illness.)

For many years, with the exception of 1872–1873, when she was in Europe studying art, Hale lived in a Boston apartment, spending the summers on the northern coast and in the mountains of New England, swimming, walking, and, with increasing seriousness, sketching and painting. Beginning in the mid 1880s, she made what became a permanent change in her pattern of living arrangements when she took over running Edward's summer home in Matunuck, Rhode Island. Until this time she had been only an occasional visitor there during the decade he had owned the house, but from 1885 through the rest of her life she spent summers there (a season that over the years was lengthened to begin in early spring and stretch into late fall), keeping open house for her niece and nephews and their friends as well as her own, and sometimes having Edward as a visitor. (His wife, Emily Perkins Hale, had never been enthusiastic about going there, and her relationship with Susan had been strained for several years.)

Although Edward paid the major expenses of owning and maintaining the Matunuck house, which became virtually hers in exchange for her services as housekeeper, Susan Hale placed great importance on individual self-sufficiency. She had begun when she was eighteen to contribute to the family's income—"to help dig down the mountain between the family and day-

Hale and her brother, Edward Everett Hale, circa 1855

light"—by teaching, at first running a school for young boys in the Hale home with Lucretia and giving private lessons in the classics and French to older girls. For more than twenty years, from the early 1850s to the early 1870s, she made her living primarily by organizing and instructing a class, at home or in a rented schoolroom. Hale's own dislike of formal education when she was a student seems to carry over into sardonic sympathy for her young pupils, to whom she refers in letters as "the victims" and "the little wretches"—though she also calls them "the fiends" on one occasion when she is snatching time during their recess to write to her sister. As a teacher she looks forward eagerly to the end of the school year and announces the arrival of summer vacation with glee. She tries various innovations to make her methods of instruction less oppressive and her schools less confining. For example, a prospectus among her papers, evidently from the early 1860s, announces her intention to set up "a class of a few Young Ladies for the purpose of directing their studies in History, in English, French, and other Literature." The class was to meet with her for two hours every other day, reading suggested works on their own flexible schedules; "once a week, or when it may seem desirable," they would go to an art gallery, museum, or library in place of their usual meeting. Her explicit purpose was to provide an alternative to the "confinement" of the conventional schoolroom that would "give them opportunity for ample exercise in the open air." The benefits of this arrangement–for a teacher who was herself a devotee of outdoor exercise as well as for her students–are obvious. She found teaching, even in this fairly independent, entrepreneurial way, too confining, however, and sought other ways to make her living.

One solution was to shift her teaching exclusively to painting lessons, and to this end, beginning in October 1872, she spent more than a year in Paris and Weimar studying painting, to enhance her own artistic skill and to better fit her for teaching. On her return to Boston in late 1873 she rented living space and a studio in the Boston Art Club building and supported herself by giving painting lessons to children and adults and occasionally selling a painting. She even gave lessons in the summer when, gone to some scenic place to paint, she found a pupil or two and thus earned enough to cover her expenses. Her book *Self-Instructive Lessons in Painting with Oil and Water-Colors on Silk, Satin, Velvet and Other Fabrics, Including Lustra Paint and the Use of Other Mediums* (1885) also developed from this part of her career.

Hale saw writing as a way to make a living and quite unabashedly wrote for money; she often referred to payments she received as "lucre," playing on the biblical injunction against being "greedy of filthy lucre." In 1886, when, along with Edward and his children, she was engaged in writing brief biographies for a reference book, she commented, "We have all been writing Lives of Great Men, which all of course remind us we can make our lives sublime, but also give us a good sum of money." For many years, money received for magazine and newspaper articles helped supplement her income from teaching and other sources. She also did editorial work beginning in the 1870s, although her first stint in the editorial chair was an unpaid volunteer position as editor of the *Balloon Post*. This newspaper was published in April 1871 in conjunction with the Boston "French Fair," an effort to assist war-ravaged France, where there had been great suffering among the people as a result of a months-long German siege and civil warfare that followed. For two months before the first of six daily issues was published, Hale was occupied with taking care of business and logistical details and, most important, securing contributors–among them William Dean Howells, Ralph Waldo Emerson, and Bret Harte–and choosing what was to be published (all in addition to her regular teaching duties). The *Balloon Post* was successful, and as a result she received her first contract to write regularly for a newspaper, the *Boston Transcript,* at $1,000 a year; although the arrangement was terminated after an initial six-month trial period,

she continued to write as an occasional correspondent for newspapers, among them the *Boston Advertiser* and *Boston Globe,* throughout much of her life. Other editorial work–both as volunteer and for pay–followed as well. She regularly did editorial work for Edward on *Old and New* and *Lend a Hand,* magazines he edited, though comments she makes to their brother Charles suggest payment for her services was not always forthcoming.

Travel became, in a sense, one of her occupations. She was an enthusiastic and competent traveler; always well prepared to understand the language and culture of the place she was going to visit, she had little patience with tourists who expected their hosts to speak their language and understand their customs. Sometimes she served as companion, guide, and translator for less-experienced acquaintances (she was fluent in several languages) in exchange for payment of her expenses. At other times she subsidized trips by writing travel letters for newspapers or articles for magazines, and sometimes she painted watercolors she might exhibit and possibly sell (though this practice was more often an aspect of summer vacations on the northeast coast than of her foreign travel). She also gathered material that she used in books.

Her major publications were books about places she had visited, the "Family Flight" series for young readers and two volumes for Putnam's "The Story of the Nations," a series of more than sixty volumes (including one by Sarah Orne Jewett). Hale co-authored most of her travel books with Edward; however, *A Family Flight through Spain* (1883), *The Story of Mexico* (1889), and *Young Americans in Spain* (1899) were by Hale alone.

A travel book for children was first proposed by the publisher to Edward who suggested to Hale that she undertake it herself. She expresses concern that her name would not carry sufficient weight with "the man," though, she says in a 24 January 1881 letter to her brother, she could easily write the books based on travel she had done. As it turned out, the book became a series of five published in the 1880s and co-authored except for the third–though her letters give reason to suspect Hale did the major portion of the writing for all of them. The books present the history, geography, contemporary events, and daily life of the places visited, set in the context of the adventures of the Horner family. The Horners are patterned on Edward and his family, while Miss Augusta Lejeune, or "Aunt Dut," is the fictional representation of Hale. Miss Lejeune's "favorite philosophy" echoes attitudes Hale expresses in letters when she is traveling: a visitor should "like things as they are," she writes in *A Family Flight around Home* (1884), "and not think ill of them, because they

Hale in Matunuck, Rhode Island, 1908

are different" from what he or she is used to. Consistent with this view, the narrator sometimes comments critically on American customs in contrast to foreign ones—though views expressed in many rhetorical passages are sometimes quite conventional.

The Story of Mexico, by Hale alone, might be seen as the culmination of her newspaper and magazine travel writing and of the juvenile series; it went through several printings during more than twenty years. The book reflects not only Hale's visits to Mexico but also extensive research on its history, archeology, anthropology, and geography; on the other hand, it is not a dry scholarly treatise. The series is intended for a general audience, and Hale appeals to this audience by developing through narrative what is in mythic or historical accounts; when details such as what a person looked like are unknown, she explicitly takes poetic license and supplies them. The general description of the series (included in a notice at the back of the book) says that "myths of early history will be considered though distinguished from actual history." Hale rationalizes this methodology in her own way, suggesting that pending the discovery of new information through the "researches of scientific explorers," readers may "indulge our imagination, and play with legend." Even when there is new evidence that undermines an earlier

myth, she is not willing to discard it: "in a book like this, which is permitted to gather up legend as well as fact, in order to present the attractive, even romantic, side of its subject, it would be a pity to wholly set aside the accounts of the Aztecs."

Hale takes the reader from place to place by present-day transportation—though since it is an imaginary journey readers need not delay before going to the highest altitudes nor worry about checking their baggage the evening before. At various spots she recalls what happened there long ago, collapsing the centuries by suggesting, for instance, that readers are looking at the same scene that Hernán Cortés saw three hundred years earlier. Cortés and the Spanish conquistadors become the objects of some scornful criticism. For example, she describes the Spaniards' destruction of early manuscripts, "folded . . . and enclosed in wooden covers, not unlike our books," and other cultural artifacts by the following analogy: "as if barbarians, ignorant of types and bindings, should descend upon the British Museum or Biblioteque Nationale." In a similar way she is critical of the U.S. role in its war with Mexico, quoting "General Grant's memoirs on the Mexican War," in which he calls it "one of the most unjust ever waged by a stronger against a weaker nation." Various Mexican rulers over the course of time also come in for criticism, but injustices they committed are placed in the context of similar wrongs committed by their European contemporaries. Yet, the tone of the book does not become too dark. The prevailing note is one of lively interest in the country and its people, and there is even occasional humor.

From the early 1880s through the mid 1890s, a major portion of Hale's time was devoted to and a significant part of her income was derived from readings she gave in cities throughout the United States with the sponsorship of local fund-raising organizations or women's clubs. She received expenses and a fee, with the sponsor keeping the balance of proceeds from ticket sales. Before her annual winter tour, she spent several weeks in preparation, reading or rereading the novels she had selected and choosing passages, composing introductions to the authors, and timing everything to make sure she could perform in the allotted time–usually two hours. In addition to older novels she sometimes varied the program by adding recent works. She even read from French novels in the original language and felt she could have managed the same "in German, Spanish, and Italian, if the audience were up to it." Her most frequently repeated series of readings contributed to the rediscovery and popularization of women writers who by then had been almost forgotten; of the six writers listed in an announcement for her "Readings from the Early English Novelists," four are women: Ann Radcliffe, Charlotte Lennox, Anna Maria Roche, and Frances Burney.

Often she concluded a series of readings by performing one of the one-woman plays she had created. For most of her life she had been involved in amateur theatricals, both the private variety for the amusement of the participants and their friends and the more public sort performed to entertain members of an organization or to raise money for a charity. For example, in the early 1860s she tried to secure a script and permission to perform *Our American Cousins,* perhaps to raise money for the Sanitary Commission. In early 1872 she refers to "being drawn in again to jinks at the Women's Club with Mrs. Howe!" She was also noted for comic monologues she did as part of various Boston fund-raisers and other events. The most popular of her one-woman performances was "The Elixir of Youth," a comic production in which she began as an elderly woman and was transformed by the end into an infant, with appropriate costumes for each stage of life. The play had evolved from a monologue she called the "Transformation Scene," first presented as the entertainment for a dinner (of which Annie Adams Fields was an organizer) for the North End Mission. When she performed "The Elixir of Youth" or "The Female Fool" as part of her tour, business arrangements were similar to those for her readings. Both plays and readings were quite successful for many years, and she gained some national celebrity as a result.

Hale has attracted reexamination not so much for the performances that gave her a measure of fame nor the books, articles, and newspaper letters through which she earned money and gained popularity but for her personal letters. They feature some of her best writing, perhaps because in the letters she is not writing for money nor to please the taste of an editor and meet demands of the market. More than two hundred letters she wrote to family and friends during a period of more than sixty years are collected as *Letters of Susan Hale* (1918). In addition, the Hale Family Papers in the Sophia Smith Collection at Smith College include about two thousand of her letters, most to members of her family, ranging from 1842 to 1910. Her letters, both published and unpublished, are marked from the first by a lively style and distinct voice; beginning in her teens, she frequently illustrated them with sketches. Especially in the mature letters, she portrays herself as a somewhat humorous character, always hurried and sometimes a bit flustered but always essentially competent to meet any situation. One always senses in the letters the writer's awareness of her audience, recognizing her obligation to inform, entertain, and amuse, and never to bore. The letters are often satiric, taking snobbery and sham as favorite targets but also taking aim at human behavior that is simply foolish or ill-advised. She does not hesitate to turn the satire on herself when occasion calls for it. Often there is humor of a lighter sort, with no satiric edge–amusing descriptions, often drawing on exaggeration, and clever turns of phrase. A letter dated 13 April 1866, to her sister Lucretia, for example, tells of having "splendid maple-sugar, fresh from the cow." She is intensely interested in language, often reproducing dialects (usually for humorous effect) and taking pleasure in new words. For example, in another letter to Lucretia she says she must "skeedaddle" and then adds "You have that word, don't you?" She uses slang and idiom (usually that of New England) to give the letters a colloquial tone. For the same reason, occurrences of *don't,* where *doesn't* would be correct, and of *ain't* are frequent. She often concludes a descriptive passage by asking, "Ain't it nice?" or "Ain't it splendid?"

Hale enjoyed exceptionally good health throughout most of her life and maintained a high level of physical fitness and activity unusual for a woman of her time. At seventy, she quotes with amusement the comment of Robert Browning, a Matunuck neighbor who often "chored" for her: "Mister Browning says I'm remarkable. He don't know as he ever see a gyirl of twenty ser spry as I be,–and he hopes I'll continner so."

Although she was occasionally critical of them, Hale was intensely interested in current events and cultural trends, and she embraced the wonders of new technology—for example, the automobile in which she sits smiling for the camera in a 1908 photograph. Her letters from the last decades of her life—like earlier ones—are filled with references to recent books and to performances she has attended during visits to cities.

In the last decade of her life she suffered increasing hearing loss, but she writes about it philosophically, sometimes even comically; self-pity is never allowed into her letters. Though her lifestyle changed somewhat—she no longer gave readings nor performed, and she avoided some social situations that she found uncomfortable—she continued to enjoy the natural world, to travel, and to write letters. She spent the last winter of her life in France. She returned in May 1910, having suffered a stroke that paralyzed her left arm—"not so very bad," she writes, since she was right-handed. Subsequent strokes took her mobility and limited her ability to write but did not take her desire to do so, as notes to her niece Ellen Day Hale, scrawled in pencil during the last weeks, attest. She died on 17 September 1910 and was buried in the country cemetery at Matunuck in what had become her favorite season there, when the summer visitors were gone and the natural world took on what she called a note of "tristesse."

On her seventy-sixth birthday the year before, she had written to her niece, "Well, you see I must look now at everything in the spirit of seventy-six. Would it not be funny if I should live another seventy-five years, and become one hundred and fifty; they are inventing things to prolong life." She was forward-looking but also viewed the advances of knowledge with some ambivalence: in 1909, when she learned that Robert Peary had reached the North Pole, she wrote to a contemporary, "Isn't this a dreadful business about the North Pole being found, all the mystery, all the charm, gone out of the Geography? It's now just like any other old place. . . . I am hoping you will sympathise with me in this new aggression of the twentieth century." Yet, during the nearly seventy-seven years she did live, she saw enormous changes in the world around her—and she left an invaluable record of her sometimes skeptical but more often joyous experience of them.

Letters:

Letters of Susan Hale, edited by Caroline P. Atkinson, introduction by Edward E. Hale Jr. (Boston: Marshall Jones, 1918).

References:

Jean Holloway, *Edward Everett Hale: A Biography* (Austin: University of Texas Press, 1956).

Papers:

The papers of Susan Hale (Letters and Miscellaneous Papers of Susan Hale, 1842–1910, Hale Family Papers, Sophia Smith Collection) are at Smith College, Northampton, Massachusetts.

Frances Ellen Watkins Harper

(24 September 1825 – 22 February 1911)

Maggie Montesinos Sale
Columbia University

BOOKS: *Forest Leaves* (N.p., ca. 1845);

Poems on Miscellaneous Subjects (Boston: Yerrinton & Sons, 1854; enlarged, Philadelphia: Merrihew & Thompson, 1855; enlarged again, Philadelphia: Merrihew & Son, 1871);

Moses, A Story of the Nile (Philadelphia: Merrihew & Son, 1869; enlarged, Philadelphia: Privately printed, 1889); enlarged again as *Idylls of the Bible* (Philadelphia: Privately printed, 1901);

Poems (Philadelphia: Merrihew & Son, 1871);

Sketches of Southern Life (Philadelphia: Merrihew & Son, 1872; enlarged, 1887);

Enlightened Motherhood: An Address by Mrs. Frances E. W. Harper Before the Brooklyn Literary Society, November 15, 1892 (N.p., n.d.);

Iola Leroy; or, Shadows Uplifted (Philadelphia: Garrigues Brother, 1892);

The Sparrow's Fall and Other Poems (N.p., ca. 1894);

The Martyr of Alabama and Other Poems (N.p., ca. 1895);

Atlanta Offering, Poems (Philadelphia: Ferguson, 1895);

Poems (Philadelphia: Ferguson, 1895; enlarged, 1898; enlarged again, 1900);

Light beyond the Darkness (Chicago: Donohue & Henneberry, n.d.);

The Complete Poems of Frances E. W. Harper, edited by Maryemma Graham (New York: Oxford University Press, 1988);

A Brighter Coming Day: A Frances Ellen Watkins Harper Reader, edited, with an introduction, by Frances Smith Foster (New York: Feminist, 1990);

Minnie's Sacrifice, Sowing and Reaping, Trial and Triumph: Three Rediscovered Novels by Frances E. W. Harper, edited by Foster (Boston: Beacon, 1994).

Edition: *Iola Leroy; or, Shadows Uplifted,* edited, with an introduction, by Frances Smith Foster (New York: Oxford University Press, 1988).

OTHER: *The Proceedings of the Eleventh National Woman's Rights Convention, New York, May 10, 1866* (Philadelphia: Historical Society of Pennsylvania, 1866);

Frances Ellen Watkins Harper

"Duty to Dependent Races," in *National Council of Women of the United States: Transactions* (Philadelphia: Lippincott, 1891);

"Woman's Political Future," in *World's Congress of Representative Women,* edited by May Wright Sewell (Chicago: Rand McNally, 1894), pp. 433–447.

SELECTED PERIODICAL PUBLICATIONS–
UNCOLLECTED: "Address to the Fourth Anniversary of the New York City Anti-Slavery Society: Delivered May 13, 1857," *National Anti-Slavery Standard* (23 May 1857);

"The Two Offers," *Anglo-African Magazine,* 1 (September–October 1859): 288–292, 311–313;

"Triumph: A Dream," *Anglo-African Magazine,* 2 (1860): 21–23;

"The Coloured Women of America," *Englishwoman's Review,* 15 (January 1878);

"We Are Rising," *Christian Recorder* (9 November 1879).

In the last decade, scholarship has shown Frances Ellen Watkins Harper to be one of the most significant U.S. writers of the nineteenth century. The author of several books of poetry, four novels, many essays and speeches, at least two short stories, and many additional poems, Harper not only produced an impressive canon of literary works, she also was tremendously popular, as the regular reprintings of her works demonstrate. She wrote to instruct and inspire, to chastise and move to action; hers was a literature dedicated not just to uplifting the race, but to making evident through her indignation and outrage the unjust and immoral conditions under which African Americans were forced to struggle under slavery and within the racist society that was its legacy. Her significance resides in her experimentation with and creation of new literary forms; her merging of political, social, religious, cultural, and ethical concerns; and her work for more than half a century giving voice to thousands who otherwise had little access to print and other forms of public discourse.

Long relegated to obscurity, as Melba Joyce Boyd has shown, Harper and her work for years were evaluated through critical lenses that privileged both modernist aesthetics and male-oriented topics. Thanks to the efforts of scholars such as Boyd, Hazel Carby, Frances Smith Foster, Deborah E. McDowell, Barbara Christian, and Mary Helen Washington, Harper's canon has been reprinted and is therefore accessible to late-twentieth-century audiences. Her life and work have also begun to be reevaluated by those who appreciate her emphases on black women and ethics; who recognize the importance of the historical, literary, and political contexts in which she lived, spoke, and wrote; and who value on their own terms the stated purposes and intentions of her work.

According to her longtime friend and fellow activist William Still, Frances Ellen Watkins was born on 24 September 1825 to free parents in Baltimore, Maryland, then a slave state. Within three years she was orphaned and living with relatives, most likely in the home of her uncle, William Watkins. A dedicated abolitionist and defender of civil rights, Watkins ran a school for free black youths that was well known for its classical academic orientation and strict standards of behavior. Frances Watkins attended the school until she was thirteen years old, the age at which she, like her cousins, was expected to begin earning a living. She excelled in her uncle's unusually sophisticated course of study. In particular, she learned both literary and oratorical skills and a sense of responsibility to moral, political, and religious concerns. She took her first job working in the home of the Armstrong family, where her responsibilities included caring for the children, sewing, and keeping house. Noticing young Frances's propensity for literature, her employers allowed her access to the wealth of their family-run bookstore during her spare time.

She apparently made good use of this privilege, and at the age of twenty she published her first book of poems, *Forest Leaves* (ca. 1845), of which no known copies exist. The publication of this volume ushered Watkins into a small group of African American writers fortunate enough to gain access to printed literature. Around 1850 she left Baltimore, moving to Ohio to become the first female teacher at Union Seminary, a school founded by the African Methodist Episcopal Church. William Watkins had left for Canada, after being forced to sell his house and his school in the hostile environment following the passage of the Compromise of 1850 and its new provisions for remanding fugitives from slavery. Why Watkins chose to go to Ohio rather than accompany her uncle is not known. After working for some time, she discovered she was not suited to teaching, though she had great respect for that profession. In her later fiction she always pays homage to those who choose teaching as a profession, often giving her heroes, regardless of gender, the task of educating the newly emancipated population.

During the early 1850s Maryland passed a new law that made it illegal for free blacks to enter the state on punishment of enslavement. This law made Watkins a further outcast in a country that already discriminated against anyone identified as of African heritage. Punctuating her exile was the fate of a young man who had entered Maryland only to be captured and returned to slavery. He managed to escape but was soon recaptured and died from exposure. Though Harper was reared in an environment in which agitation against slavery was the norm, her empathy with this martyred young man made the struggle more clearly her own. From this horrific story, so real a possibility for her had she attempted to return home, was born her ardent commitment to antislavery. She wrote, "Upon that grave I pledged myself to the Anti-Slavery cause."

SKETCHES

OF

SOUTHERN LIFE.

BY

FRANCES E. WATKINS HARPER.

PHILADELPHIA:
MERRIHEW & SON, PRINTERS,
No. 135 North Third Street.
1872.

Title page for Harper's collection of poems based on her travels

Harper then moved briefly to Philadelphia. She began publishing her poems in various abolitionist papers, including the *Liberator, Frederick Douglass' Paper,* and the *Provincial Freeman.* After delivering her first lectures in Boston, she was invited to a position as lecturer for the Maine Anti-Slavery Society, becoming the only black person and one of few women on the circuit. She maintained a grueling schedule, sometimes speaking two or three times a day. The already difficult conditions of nineteenth-century travel were exacerbated by her isolation from any black community and by the typical prejudices she encountered. In fact, her eloquence was so unexpected by her audiences that they sometimes claimed she must be a white woman, or even a white man, in disguise.

In 1854 her first extant volume, *Poems on Miscellaneous Subjects,* was published in Philadelphia. The great popularity of this work brought Harper to the attention of a wider audience and facilitated her way into abolitionist circles. The most popular of her books, *Poems on Miscellaneous Subjects* was reprinted several times, selling more than twelve thousand copies within five years.

Harper's long career as a fiction writer began in 1859 with the publication of "The Two Offers," the earliest extant short story by an African American writer. The story appeared in the *Anglo-African Magazine,* one of the first literary journals entirely devoted to the written efforts of African Americans. Although the characters are racially indistinct, the publication of the story in this journal indicates that it was intended for a primarily, if not exclusively, black audience. The story is significant both in its own right, and also for what it reveals about many of the issues that concerned Harper throughout her life.

In all of her fiction Harper makes women the principal judges of ethical issues; she grants them the responsibility and power of decision making. Harper builds upon sentimental fiction, which provided young women with opportunities to imagine themselves as participants in the marriage market, making decisions about whom and when to marry that would greatly influence the rest of their lives. In contrast to the protagonists of a seduction novel, in "The Two Offers" Laura Lagrange succeeds in marrying, but her life is no happier for that success. Faced with two proposals, Laura feels she must choose one. Choosing a stylish young man, with "raven hair, flashing eyes, a voice of thrilling sweetness," yet who was also "vain and superficial in his character," she lives a few happy years before her husband takes to liquor: "The laxity of his principles had rendered him unworthy of the deep and undying devotion of a pure-hearted woman." Laura becomes a victim of his weakness, eventually dying of a broken heart. Harper challenges the notion that marriage is a positive outcome in and of itself by revealing the weakness of social norms that make women entirely dependent on men, not only financially and socially, but also emotionally. Laura dies because she invests her entire being in her husband, and when he proves to be weak in character, she does not have the strength to sustain herself.

Harper contrasts Laura's fate with that of her cousin Janette, who chooses a life of celibacy, having lost her first chance at love. The title of the story, then, refers also to the two life paths offered the protagonists: the typical marriage track that assumes woman's dependency and requires man's strong character for success, and a life unmarried but not alone or lonely. Harper embellishes the spinster figure of the same period by making Janette not a maiden aunt, retired in a sister's or brother's home, but rather an activist dedicated to "a high and holy mission on the battlefield of existence," challenging slavery, enabling its fugitives, and supporting the poor, who "called her blessed, as she broke her bread to the pale lips of hunger." Harper argues that Janette's choice enables her more fully to develop her whole nature than would be possible in many marriages. Janette's path, then, is not merely a viable, if consolatory, option, but an opportunity to succeed in a different way and within a larger realm.

Watkins herself chose not to marry until she was thirty-five years old, at which age she would have been considered an old maid. Only the sketchiest facts are known about her marriage. In 1860 she married a widower, Fenton Harper, and moved to a farm in Ohio purchased largely with her own savings. A few years later, she gave birth to a daughter, Mary, who joined Fenton's three children from a previous marriage. Although Harper contributed to the household economy by making and selling butter, she continued to be active in public life. According to Still, "Notwithstanding her family cares, consequent upon married life, she only ceased from her literary and Anti-slavery labors, when compelled to do so by other duties." That she was able to pursue both family and public life suggests that her marriage was indeed built upon the kind of understanding she called for in her fiction.

Disaster struck Harper when Fenton Harper died on 23 May 1864, leaving her with four small children to feed, and his creditors descended to claim everything they had jointly owned to pay debts she did not know he had. Though she had always been sensitive to women's concerns, this experience brought Harper new appreciation for women's powerlessness under the law. "Had I died instead of my husband, how different might have been the result," she asserted at the Eleventh Woman's Rights Convention in May 1866. "By this time he would have another wife, it is likely; and no administrator would have gone into his house, broken up his home, sold his bed, and taken away his means of support." This experience reconfirmed Harper's stated belief that women should not be solely dependent on men. She rededicated herself to the causes of abolition and equal rights for all. Within months of her husband's death, Harper had moved to New England with her daughter, and she was again giving public lectures.

After the Civil War, Harper devoted her energies to the newly freed black population and the work of Reconstruction. She went to the South for the first time, coming into contact with people from all classes and walks of life, often braving dangerous situations. "I am just working," she wrote in a letter, "up to or past my strength. Traveling, conversing, addressing day and Sunday-schools." She concluded her first tour in 1867 and returned to Philadelphia but was there less than a year before she went back to the South, traveling to all but two southern states between 1868 and 1871. Empa-

thetic to the particularly difficult situation for women and especially interested in working with them, Harper always refused payment or a collection when addressing them. In all of her engagements she counseled reconciliation among all parties, urging the recognition of their common humanity in the eyes of God.

During this busy time, Harper also published a serialized novel and three additional books of poetry. *Poems* (1871) collected poems that mostly had previously been published separately. Some critics consider *Moses, A Story of the Nile* (1869), a book-length poem in blank verse on the Old Testament patriarch, to be the height of Harper's poetic endeavors. Recently, *Sketches of Southern Life* (1872), a series of poems based on Harper's travels, has received critical acclaim for its experimentation with black dialect and its focus on folk characters. Harper also experimented with dialect in *Minnie's Sacrifice,* her first novel, which was serialized in the *Christian Recorder* from 20 March to 25 September 1869. She went even further in her exploration of dialect and folk wisdom in *Iola Leroy; or, Shadows Uplifted* (1892), her last and most famous novel. Both of these novels focus on the Civil War and Reconstruction. Unlike many of her contemporaries' renditions, especially but not exclusively those by Euro-American writers, Harper's versions of dialect could be easily read aloud and understood. In addition, her folk are not caricatures, but rather articulate characters who, though uneducated, easily manipulate language to their own advantage.

Less is known about the later period of Harper's life. William Still's biographical chapter on her in his *The Underground Railroad* (1872), the major source of information about Harper's early life, ends in 1871. Harper did not write an autobiography, and she did not preserve her personal papers. Thus, most of what is known about her has to be gleaned from public documents such as newspapers that covered her activities and the records of organizations with which she was involved. For example, Harper was one of the first black women associated with three almost exclusively white women's organizations, the Women's Christian Temperance Union, the American Woman Suffrage Association, and the National Council of Women. She was the only black person to serve on the executive committee of the segregated Women's Christian Temperance Union. Between 1875 and 1883 she was superintendent of the Philadelphia and Pennsylvania chapters of the National Women's Christian Temperance Union, Colored Branch, and continued to be active with the organization as head of the Northern United States WCTU from 1883 to 1893. Even so, Harper's major fiction—*Minnie's Sacrifice, Sowing and Reaping: A Temperance Story (Christian Recorder,* 10 August

1876 – 8 February 1877), *Trial and Triumph* (*Christian Recorder,* 4 October 1888 – 14 February 1889), and *Iola Leroy*–provide the greatest clues as to Harper's concerns during her later years.

Minnie's Sacrifice traces the lives of two mulatto characters, Minnie and Louis, who, as the children of enslaved women and white masters, are reared as white and as adults have their African and slave heritage revealed to them. In the context of the Civil War, they each choose to identify with their mother's race, and, finding one another and marrying, dedicate themselves to racial uplift. *Sowing and Reaping* centers on a community struggling with the effects of the liquor trade and the money to be made in it. Two cousins, Belle and Jeanette, present in their behavior and marriage choices more and less satisfactory responses to this environment. *Trial and Triumph* has two parallel themes, concerning a community dealing with racial prejudice and a young black woman, artistically talented and spiritually inspired but deeply restless and unsatisfied, who struggles to find her vocation. *Iola Leroy,* in many ways a revision and extension of *Minnie's Sacrifice,* also focuses on light-skinned, mixed-race characters dealing with their racial and slave heritages in the context of the Civil War and Reconstruction.

Harper consistently supported woman suffrage in her writings. In *Minnie's Sacrifice, Sketches of Southern Life,* and *Sowing and Reaping,* for example, she includes debates about the appropriateness of women voting. The discussion in *Minnie's Sacrifice* entered into the suffrage debate just after the Fifteenth Amendment to the U.S. Constitution was adopted by Congress and was being ratified by the states. The debate over the wording of the amendment, which excluded race but retained gender as criteria for suffrage, was still fresh in the memories of activists who, earlier allied in their opposition to slavery, had divided themselves into camps supporting black male or white female suffrage. Harper supported suffrage for all women, not just white women, as was sometimes proposed. While she found the separation of race and gender unacceptable, she was willing to "let the lesser question of sex go." "I do not believe that giving woman the ballot is immediately going to cure all the ills of life," she asserted during the Eleventh National Woman's Rights Convention. "I do not believe that white women are dew-drops just exhaled from the skies." Harper challenged the notion of white women's innate moral superiority, arguing that "like men they may be divided into three classes, the good, the bad and the indifferent."

Yet, this critical view should not obscure Harper's consistent support of woman suffrage even at moments when the African American community was divided over the issue, and when that support might have been understood as less than full advocation for black male suffrage. In *Minnie's Sacrifice* Harper has the title character assert on the issue of suffrage: "is it not the negro woman's hour also? . . . I cannot recognize that the negro man is the only one who has pressing claims at this hour. To-day our government needs woman's conscience as well as man's judgment." Harper understood women–regardless of color or status–as having the special responsibility of being the moral guides of both men and society in general. Much of her writing explores and asserts this understanding, and in this case she presents it as the basis for women's right to suffrage.

A decade later, Harper linked the question of woman suffrage to temperance. In *Sowing and Reaping,* Mrs. Gladstone asserts, "I want women to possess power as well as influence, I want every Christian woman as she passes by a grogshop or liquor saloon, to feel that she has on her heart a burden of responsibility for its existence, I hold my dear that a nation as well as an individual should have a conscience, and on this liquor question there is room for woman's conscience not merely as a persuasive influence but as an enlightened and aggressive power." Support for woman suffrage at this point in Harper's life was linked to her involvement with the Women's Christian Temperance Union.

By 1893, after the failure of Reconstruction, the development of segregation, and the accompanying exclusion of most African American men from the polls in the South, Harper developed a new stand on suffrage. No longer supporting universal suffrage on "the broader basis of our common humanity," Harper called for moral and educational tests for voting rights. Speaking at the World Congress of Representative Women at the Columbian Exposition in Chicago, Harper was one of only a handful of black women to address the assembly and the only one to address a topic not characterized as exclusively about African American women. She voiced her indignation at the travesty of justice promulgated by Jim Crow laws, calling for a change in suffrage requirements in order to usher in the possibility of a more equitable future. Despite the title of her address, "Women's Political Future," Harper refuses to single out gender as the primary category for consideration, instead refocusing the discussion on character as the most essential quality for both female and male voters. Harper thereby emphasizes a trait open to development instead of supposedly natural characteristics such as race and gender upon which suffrage had been based. Some scholars have characterized this shift in Harper's thinking as conservative. Yet, Harper's call for moral and educational tests for suffrage sought to recast the entire value system of the nation, "laying the whole foundation anew," as she earlier had Minnie declare in *Minnie's Sacrifice.* What was needed was not the mere inclusion of all, she implicitly asserts, but new methods of attaining citizenship. This new position developed out of her recognition that "the unsteady hands of a drunkard can not cast the ballot of a freeman. The hands of lynchers are too red with blood to determine the political character of the government for even four short years." Harper complicates the claims for universal suffrage by challenging the basic tenets of liberal democracy, instead seeking to build a polity solely out of people who are dedicated to equality.

Three of Harper's four novels were published serially in the *Christian Recorder,* the official organ of the African Methodist Episcopal Church. Although Harper was a lifelong member of the Unitarian Church, she always supported the A.M.E. Church, the most significant black church denomination of the nineteenth century. In addition, A.M.E. Church publications accepted works by African American writers and had wide circulations, thereby providing her and others like her with the most immediate and broadest access to a reading audience. Her fourth novel, *Iola Leroy,* published separately by a commercial press, was the most widely distributed novel by an African American woman in the nineteenth century (and until the recent rediscovery of Harriet Wilson's 1859 *Our Nig,* it was thought to be the earliest such work as well). The other three novels have only recently been rediscovered and republished. Not all chapters of the novels have been recovered, however, an absence that points to the lack of adequate preservation of African American historical materials. Frances Smith Foster, who edited *Minnie's Sacrifice, Sowing and Reaping, Trial and Triumph: Three Rediscovered Novels by Frances E. W. Harper* (1994), decided to publish the novels despite the missing installments. As she states in her introduction, she hopes that publishing them will inspire others to search for the missing chapters and perhaps bring about their recovery. Although Harper produced fewer books than some of her white female contemporaries, who on the whole typically had far greater access to publishing networks than did she and other African Americans, Harper's four novels and eight books of poetry constitute perhaps the most sustained literary output by an African American writer during the postbellum period.

All of Harper's novels were written in the context of increasing Ku Klux Klan violence, the development of Jim Crow laws, and social practices that created segregation in lieu of slavery. *Minnie's Sacrifice* was published while Union troops still occupied Southern territory; the subsequent three novels were published after Union troops had withdrawn and efforts at Reconstruction had failed. Racial violence and other forms of racial oppression were facts of everyday life in the South. Harper decided not to devote her energies to depicting this violence, but instead to focus on strategies for building black communities from within. Her scenarios are idealized rather than realistic, demonstrating, as Claudia Tate suggests in *Domestic Allegories of Political Desire* (1992), the desire for political effectiveness through the achievement of domestic and communal well-being. Long deprived of both under slavery, late-nineteenth-century African Americans understood in political terms Harper's depictions of reunited families and successful and moral marriages and employment options; they may well have appreciated her imagining the possibilities rather than depicting the much harsher realities.

Harper centrally organized her novels through choices regarding marriage and her characters' life's work, thereby picking up and extending the issues raised in her earlier fiction. Four of her six principal female characters marry, three of them happily. Like Janette in "The Two Offers," Annette in *Trial and Triumph* loses her first love and decides to pursue a career as a teacher and moral guide for young people; and like Laura Lagrange, Jeanette Roland of *Sowing and Reaping* marries a dashing young man, only to be heartbroken as he is consumed by drink. The heroines Minnie and Iola do marry happily, as does Belle Gordon of *Sowing and Reaping.* Interestingly, in each case the heroine declines her first marriage offer, thus suggesting that it is better to wait for the right opportunity than to choose a less than acceptable offer (as do Laura and Jeanette). Belle declines the offer of the man Jeanette eventually marries, because she fears for him the fate to which he eventually succumbs, that of drunken wastrel. Iola, a beautiful mulatta light enough to pass as white, refuses the offer of a successful white doctor, who asks "only" that she hide her African heritage and slave past. Though she otherwise admires him, as a white man he does not understand and therefore cannot fully support her decision to identify herself with people of African descent. Iola later marries Dr. Latimer instead, another light-skinned mulatto, with whom she dedicates herself to uplifting the race. Belle also marries a man who shares her activist concerns, in their case the movement for temperance. Both women continue their social and political efforts after marriage, exemplifying Harper's belief that women should not become solely dependent on men and domestic life but continue to contribute their skills in a wider sphere.

Minnie also turns down her first proposal of marriage, but she later accepts another from the same man. Both chapters in which Minnie refuses and then accepts Louis Le Croix's proposals are among those still missing, however. It is possible to speculate that Minnie's

IOLA LEROY,

OR

SHADOWS UPLIFTED.

BY

FRANCES E. W. HARPER.

SECOND EDITION.

GARRIGUES BROTHERS,
PUBLISHERS' AND BOOKSELLERS,
608 ARCH STREET, PHILADELPHIA, PA.
1893.

Title page for the second edition of Harper's best-known novel, first published the previous year, about light-skinned, mixed-race characters dealing with their racial heritage during the Civil War and Reconstruction

refusal stems from Louis's support for the Confederacy and that her later acceptance depends upon his conversion to antislavery, their mutual acknowledgment of their African and slave heritages, and their decision to dedicate themselves to helping the newly emancipated population. Through these variations, Harper presents her readers with scenarios regarding options that would most shape their futures, always encouraging the path toward ethical living, and in the most successful situations connecting romantic and life's work partnerships.

Harper's novels share with other sentimental fiction of the nineteenth century this focus on marriage and women's appropriate roles. The large canon of sentimental literature produced by Euro-American women provided Harper with models for her own fictional developments. In addition, this borrowing from mainstream literary culture would have provided her readers, regardless of their background, with some familiar themes as she took them through material that often also dealt with race relations. Harper always intended her work to instruct and inspire; to do so she chose writing methods that were readily recognizable to her contemporaries, even as she combined them with other expressive traditions, such as slave narratives and sermons, to expand and refocus their meaning. So Harper often focused on marriage possibilities, but in her fiction they took on different meanings than those expressed in much of the fiction by Euro-American women, both because marriage signified something different for black women in the nineteenth century and because her perspective on marriage supported far greater autonomy for women than was typical of other fictions. Women of African descent had, for generations under slavery, been denied access to legally and socially sanctioned marriage. Being able to marry legally, as Claudia Tate has shown, and having the responsibility and right of choosing whom and when to marry demonstrated African American women's new citizenship after emancipation. Harper extends this even further by linking women's choice in marriage to the chosen work of her husband, dramatizing in her fiction what she called for in her speeches: women's conscience and character to lead the nation to a higher moral plane.

While her use of sentimentality and moral exhortation are well recognized, rarely do critics grant Harper a sense of irony and sarcasm. Critics, particularly male critics, have tended to read Harper's work superficially, as if her relation to sentimentality were simply to replicate its conventions, for example, or as if her appeal to a white audience, typically assumed to be her primary audience, dictated an appeasing if plaintive tone and message. This perspective therefore judges her work to be imitative and of minor importance, especially when compared with the more raw and violent portraits of urban ghettos created by African American male writers in later years.

Minnie's Sacrifice, however, illustrates the kind of ironic twist Harper lent to what otherwise might be construed as a simplistic sentimental scene. The novel opens with an enslaved woman, Miriam, mourning the loss of her daughter, who has just died giving birth to a light-skinned child. Miriam is interrupted by Camilla, the young mistress of the plantation. Camilla proclaims that she had hastened to "Mammy's" side as soon as she had "heard that Agnes was dead. . . . I would not even wait for my supper." When Camilla gets a glimpse of the baby, she is astonished at his whiteness. Mammy then reminds her that still "he is only a slave." Camilla declares, "I can't bear the thought of his being a slave." She then hatches a plan by which she and her father will adopt the baby as the orphan of a friend, assuring Mammy, "I know if I set my heart upon it, he won't refuse me, because he always said he hates to see me fret. Why Mammy, he bought me two thousand dollars worth of jewelry when we were in New York, just because I took a fancy to a diamond set which I saw at Tiffany's." The baby becomes Louis Le Croix, who eventually marries Minnie.

Through this portrait, Harper illustrates the unthinking character of Camilla's race and class privilege. Her exclamation that she did not even wait for her dinner before coming to Mammy, which she evidently perceives as a rather large sacrifice, contrasts sharply with the sacrifice both the old mother and the dead daughter have been forced to make under slavery. This contrast in turn foreshadows the martyrdom of Minnie, who dies, presumably from Klan violence, near the end of the novel. Though she acts kindly to save the baby from bondage, Camilla does so only because his whiteness is so close to her own that she cannot justify to herself the radically different situation into which he is born. She underscores the immense separation between herself and her father's human property by telling Miriam of her father's gift. She does not even consider that her father is also the baby's father, though she later points out their likenesses. The juxtaposition of comments demonstrates the equivalent economic value—given slavery—of Camilla's whim and Agnes's life. Thus, even though Miriam's perspective is not overtly represented, the irony of this juxtaposition encourages readers to identify with her rather than with Camilla. Harper's subtle use of irony no doubt was obvious to the primarily black audience of the *Christian Recorder.*

Through Camilla's insistence, Louis eventually becomes the joint heir of his father's estate along with Camilla, his half sister. Apparently unconcerned about his parentage, Louis grows up a true son of the South, proclaiming the South to be his mother as sectional conflicts heighten. Mammy and Camilla reveal his parentage to him as he prepares to join the Confederate army. His subsequent flight to the Union army relies upon, yet revises, the plot of the slave-narrative tradition. Instantly alienated from the identity he had created and plunged into a new sense of reality, Louis comes to understand what it is to be unfree and hunted. Although he reveals only that he is searching for the Union army, not his African heritage, every black person he meets aids his escape. In one extreme case, a "colored man" hides Louis while the Confederates are actively hunting him, and though "his master beat him severely. . . . he would let neither threats nor torture wring the secret from his lips." Louis thus is thrown into an experience that mirrors that of individuals escaping slavery. When he reaches the "borders of the confederacy, and stood once more upon free soil, [he appreciated] that section as he had never done before."

Though well-educated and middle-class, Louis and Minnie become much more refined in their sensibilities after they discover and accept their African heritage and decide to embrace the newly freed population. From them they learn as much if not more than they teach. This relationship is underscored by the novel's final chapter, in which the women with whom Minnie worked mourn her death, looking to God for solace and comforting themselves with the faith that Minnie is now in a better place. Louis, grief stricken, listens in on their prayerful conversation, feeling comforted by their faith. Harper's representation of the newly emancipated population as having a stronger faith than the octoroon characters who are the ostensible heroes of the novel does not simply replicate the racialist notion that Africans are naturally more spiritual because they are closer to nature. Rather, Harper suggests that the long history of suffering creates the conditions in which faith is forged, and under which it is tried. The common association between the Israelites in Egypt and Africans in America in Harper's writing acts as an organizing and authorizing feature. Elsewhere she develops this connection more fully, most especially in her book-length poem, *Moses, A Story of the Nile.* In *Minnie's Sacrifice* Minnie is a Christ figure who gives her life and thereby inspires those around her to dedicate themselves more deeply to the cause of uplift and regeneration in which they are already engaged.

Not all of Harper's fiction deals with racial issues. Characters in her second novel, *Sowing and Reaping,* are racially indistinct, though the novel's publication in the *Christian Recorder* suggests its lessons were still intended for a black audience. Although the subtitle of *Sowing and Reaping* is "A Temperance Tale," the novel is as much an investigation of appropriate gender roles and class relations as it is a statement about the perils of liquor. Harper connects the two issues together from the outset. The novel opens with two voices discussing why another character, John Andrews, gave up his saloon. One comments, "They say that his wife was bitterly opposed to the business. . . . She has never seemed happy since John has kept saloon." His companion replies, "Well, I would never let any woman lead me by the nose. I would let her know that as the living comes by me, the way of getting it is my affair, not hers, as long as she is well provided for." Harper represents women as the moral guides who should lead men away from both personal consumption of drink and participation in business that is connected with the liquor trade. She also shows the resistance to her position common in beliefs about men's and women's appropriate roles, implicitly in the separation of public and private spheres. Harper's fiction typically characterizes men as more focused on breadwinning and women on mar-

Idylls of the Bible

...BY...

MRS. F. E. W. HARPER

PHILADELPHIA
1006 BAINBRIDGE STREET
1901

Frontispiece and title page for Harper's book-length poem, an enlarged version of her Moses, A Story of the Nile *(1869)*

riage and moral guidance, though Paul Clifford in this novel and Iola in *Iola Leroy* are exceptions to this pattern. Harper thereby reproduces a gendered split regarding appropriate concerns for men and women; but she also complicates this split by asserting a vital connection between these concerns rather than accepting them as wholly separate.

Indeed, Harper critiques the role of placating wife in her portrait of Jeanette, thereby showing the danger of relegating women to a secondary and entirely domestic existence. Having been rejected by Belle, the temperance advocate, Charles Romaine turns to her more socially oriented cousin, Jeanette. In the scene in which he declares his affection and his intentions, Charles describes what he wants in a wife: "My best friend is a dear, sweet girl who sits by my side, who always welcomes me with a smile, and beguiles me so with her conversation, that I take no note of the hours until the striking of the clock warns me it is time to leave." Charles outlines the character of a pliant, supportive, engaging woman who, though she speaks often, speaks of little and certainly has few thoughts of her own. Harper subtly mocks this character type, who was often presented by cultural discourses of her own time as the perfect woman and appropriate companion for a man.

As the plot unfolds, Harper reveals this kind of gender relation to be extremely weak. At first Jeanette's influence keeps Charles at home, "but soon the novelty wore off, and Jeanette found out to her great grief that her power to bind him to the simple attractions of home were as futile as a role of cobwebs to moor a ship to the shore, when it has drifted out and is dashing among the breakers." Little more than a novelty, Jeanette's marriage cannot withstand the harsher but stronger attraction her husband feels for liquor. Jeanette is partially to blame, Harper implies, not only by her earlier lack of concern about Charles's drinking, but by the weak character she chose to adopt in her life and in her marriage.

In *Trial and Triumph* Harper returns to racial issues, exploring the difficulties facing dark-skinned and light-skinned characters of African heritage as they seek employment and education. In addition, she extends the novel of seduction by exploring the repercussions of seduction, abandonment, and orphanage upon the development of an innocent child. Harper explicitly points to the prenatal history of the protagonist, Annette, whose unwed mother died when she was quite young, as cause of her restlessness and unruliness. She presents the faults and weaknesses of the parents as visited upon the child in Annette's difficulty fitting in and behaving according to the standards of her community. She also makes Annette unusually gifted, however, thereby balancing her character. Difficult to handle, Annette is characterized by the grandmother who rears her as the black sheep of the family. Harper criticizes this moment as undermining the child's self-respect, that which most needed bolstering. Annette's grandmother notices and punishes her ill behavior, but she fails to recognize her aspirations—either spiritual or literary. The damage done by seduction and abandonment does not end with the death of the betrayed woman, Harper suggests, but rather continues on in the next generation. Annette does eventually triumph, however, by developing into a capable teacher beloved by her students and her community alike.

Harper's best-known novel, *Iola Leroy* has received considerable critical attention. Like *Minnie's Sacrifice,* the novel explores the dilemmas of characters light enough to pass as they make places for themselves as self-identified African Americans. In refusing to hide their racial and slave backgrounds, characters in both novels challenge other fictions of the nineteenth century, such as Lydia Maria Child's *Romance of the Republic* (1867), that dramatized the assimilation of mixed-race people into the white population. Both Child's and Harper's novels contest those fictions that demarcate absolutely between black and white—and enslaved and free—communities by showing the arbitrary, if nevertheless powerful, character of racial definitions and by blurring the meaning of class distinctions. *Minnie's Sacrifice* and *Iola Leroy* both challenge Child's narrative as well by presenting characters who, though light enough and well-educated enough to pass as wholly white, choose instead to identify themselves as of African heritage and to recognize their mothers' personal history of slavery.

In addition to her fiction, Harper published several books of poetry in her later years, including *The Sparrow's Fall and Other Poems* (ca. 1894), *Atlanta Offering, Poems* (1895), *Poems* (1895; enlarged, 1898 and 1900), *The Martyr of Alabama and Other Poems* (ca. 1895), *Light beyond the Darkness,* and *Idylls of the Bible* (1901), a reworking of the earlier *Moses, A Story of the Nile.* These collections often included poems that had previously been published either separately or in other collections as well as new works. The number of reprinted editions of these and other works testify to Harper's continued popularity with readers.

Harper continued to be active in organizations for progressive political and social change until the end of her life. In 1896 she helped to found the National Association of Colored Women, becoming its vice president the following year. This organization brought together such notable women activists as Harriet Tubman, Mary Church Terrel, and Ida Wells-Barnett in addressing on a national scale the struggle for civil rights for blacks and women. Its founding marked the emergence of a national movement by black women, who had previously been organizing in various clubs on the local level.

Harper also was active in the Universal Peace Union from at least 1893 until her death in 1911. This organization was dedicated to immigrant rights, economic justice, woman suffrage, and universal human rights as well as the abolition of war. *The Peacemaker,* the official organ of the organization, often carried notices of Harper's speeches to the assembly and copies of her poems, one published as late as 1909. Upon her passing, Alfred H. Love, the president of the union, remembered "the effect of her presence and her neat, eloquent and conclusive remarks at our meetings, for she made every effort to make them all, regardless of distance, and always paid her own way, this being a trait of her character evinced even at the close of her life." He summarized the power of her contributions, throughout her life as well as in her work with the union, as "voicing the inspiration of the hour and the reciprocal feeling of her nature, just at the right time and in the most graceful and magnetic manner."

Harper's health declined after 1901. Though offered assistance by several convalescent homes, some of which she had helped establish, she refused, citing her desire for independence and love of liberty. Her daughter, Mary, who apparently lived with her throughout her life, died a short time before she did. Harper died on 22 February 1911. The First Unitarian Church of Philadelphia, of which she had been one of the oldest and most devoted members, published a tribute to her in the *New York Age,* one of the nation's leading black newspapers. Her passing "brings to a close a life of self-sacrifice and public usefulness covering a period of more than seventy years. . . . her consecrated espousal of every cause for human betterment made her the leader and inspirer of thousands of men and women who came within the ever-widening circle of her influence." Harper's activist and writing career was truly remarkable for its length and consistency, as well as for its depth and breadth. She has finally begun to be recognized as, in the words of Frances Smith Foster, not only "the most popular African-American writer of the nineteenth century but also one of the most important women in United States history."

References:

Elizabeth Ammons, "Legacy Profile: Frances Ellen Watkins Harper (1825–1911)," *LEGACY,* 2 (Fall 1985): 61–66;

Margaret Hope Bacon, "'One Great Bundle of Humanity': Frances Ellen Watkins Harper (1825–1911)," *Pennsylvania Magazine of History and Biography,* 113 (January 1989): 21–43;

Melba Joyce Boyd, *Discarded Legacy: Politics and Poetics in the Life of Frances E. W. Harper* (Detroit: Wayne State University Press, 1994);

Hazel Carby, *Reconstructing Womanhood: The Emergence of the Afro-American Woman Novelist* (New York: Oxford University Press, 1987);

Barbara Christian, *Black Women Novelists: The Development of a Tradition, 1892–1976* (Westport, Conn.: Greenwood Press, 1980);

Theodora Williams Daniel, "The Poems of Frances E. W. Harper. Edited with a Biographical and Critical Introduction, and Bibliography." M.A. thesis, Howard University, 1937;

John Ernest, "From Mysteries to Histories: Cultural Pedagogy in Frances E. W. Harper's *Iola Leroy,*" *American Literature,* 64 (September 1992): 497–518;

Frances Smith Foster, introduction to *A Brighter Coming Day: A Frances Ellen Watkins Reader,* edited by Foster (New York: Feminist Press, 1990), pp. 3–40;

Foster, *Written by Herself: Literary Production by African American Women, 1746–1892* (Bloomington: Indiana University Press, 1993);

Leroy Graham, "William Watkins, The Teacher," in *Baltimore: The Nineteenth Century Black Capital* (Washington, D.C.: University Press of America, 1982);

Maryemma Graham, "The Threefold Cord: Blackness, Womanness, and Art: A Study of the Life and Work of Frances Ellen Watkins Harper," M.A. thesis, Cornell University, 1973;

Paul Lauter, "Is Frances Ellen Watkins Harper Good Enough to Teach?" *LEGACY,* 5 (Spring 1988): 27–32;

Alfred H. Love, "Memorial Tribute to Mrs. Frances E. W. Harper," *The Peacemaker,* 30 (1911): 118–119;

Deborah E. McDowell, "'The Changing Same': Generational Connections and Black Women Novelists," *New Literary History,* 18 (Winter 1987): 281–302;

Carla Peterson, *Doers of the Word: African American Women Speakers and Writers in the North (1830–1880)* (New York: Oxford University Press, 1995);

J. Rosenthal, "Deracialized Discourse: Temperance and Racial Ambiguity in Harper's 'The Two Offers' and *Sowing and Reaping,*" in *The Serpent in the Cup: Temperance in American Literature,* edited by Rosenthal and David S. Reynolds (Amherst: University of Massachusetts Press, 1997);

Dorothy Sterling, *We Are Your Sisters: Black Women in the Nineteenth Century* (New York: Norton, 1984);

William Still, *The Underground Railroad* (Chicago: Johnson, 1970);

Claudia Tate, *Domestic Allegories of Political Desire: The Black Heroine's Text at the Turn of the Century* (New York: Oxford University Press, 1992);

Mary Helen Washington, *Invented Lives: Narratives of Black Women, 1860–1960* (New York: Doubleday/Anchor, 1988);

Elizabeth Young, "Warring Fictions: *Iola Leroy* and the Color of Gender," *American Literature,* 64 (June 1992).

Constance Cary Harrison
(Mrs. Burton Harrison)
(25 April 1843 – 21 November 1920)

Kathy Ryder
University of South Florida

BOOKS: *In Memory of Monimia Fairfax Cary* (New York, 1875);

Golden-Rod, an Idyll of Mount Desert (New York: Harper, 1879);

The Story of Helen of Troy (New York: Harper, 1881);

Woman's Handiwork in Modern Homes, 2 volumes (New York: Scribners, 1881);

The Old-Fashioned Fairy Book (New York: Scribners, 1884);

Bric-a-Brac Stories (New York: Scribners, 1885);

Bar Harbor Days (New York: Harper, 1887);

The Home and Haunts of Washington (New York: Century, 1887);

Short Comedies for Amateur Players, As Given at the Madison Square and Lyceum Theaters, New York, by Amateurs (New York: DeWitt, 1889; London: Griffin Farran, 1892);

Alice in Wonderland: A Play for Children in Three Acts (New York: DeWitt, 1890);

The Anglomaniacs (New York: Cassell, 1890);

Flower de Hundred: The Story of a Virginia Plantation (New York: Cassell, 1890);

Behind a Curtain, a Monologue in One Act (New York: DeWitt, 1892);

The Mouse-Trap: A Comedietta, in One Act, as Played at the Madison Square Theatre, New York City, January 13, 1887 (New York: DeWitt, 1892);

Tea at Four O'Clock: A Drawing-Room Comedy in One Act (New York: DeWitt, 1892);

Two Strings to Her Bow: A Comedy in Two Acts (New York: DeWitt, 1892);

A Daughter of the South and Shorter Stories (New York: Cassell, 1892);

An Edelweiss of the Sierras, Golden-Rod, and Other Tales (New York: Harper, 1892);

Belhaven Tales: Crow's Nest; Una and King David (New York: Century, 1892);

Some Work of the Associated Artists, edited by Candace Wheeler (New York: Harper, 1893);

Frontispiece to Harrison's A Virginia Cousin and Bar Harbor Tales, *1895*

Sweet Bells Out of Tune (New York: Century, 1893);

A Bachelor Maid (New York: Century, 1894);

A Virginia Cousin and Bar Harbor Tales (Boston & New York: Lamson, Wolffe, 1895);

A Visit to Mrs. Anne Thackeray Ritchie (Boston: Dodd, Mead, 1895);

An Errant Wooing (New York: Century, 1895);

History of the City of New York: Externals of Modern New York (New York: A. S. Barnes, 1896);

The Merry Maid of Arcady, His Lordship, and Other Stories (Boston, New York & London: Lamson, Wolffe, 1897);

A Son of the Old Dominion (Boston: Lamson, Wolffe, 1897);

The Well-Bred Girl in Society (Philadelphia: Curtis, 1898);

Good Americans (New York: Century, 1898);

A Triple Entanglement (Philadelphia: Lippincott, 1899);

The Carcellini Emerald, with Other Tales (Chicago: H. S. Stone, 1899);

The Circle of a Century (New York: Century, 1899);

The Fairy Godmother's Story. A House Party: An Account of Stories Told at a Gathering of Famous American Authors (Boston: Small, Maynard, 1900);

A Princess of the Hills: An Italian Romance (Boston: Lothrop, 1901);

The Unwelcome Mrs. Hatch: A Drama of Everyday (New York: C. G. Burgoyne, 1901);

Sylvia's Husband (New York: Appleton, 1904);

The Carlyles: A Story of the Fall of the Confederacy (New York: Appleton, 1905);

Latter-Day Sweethearts (New York & London: Authors and Newspapers Association, 1906);

The Count and the Congressman (New York: Cupples & Leon, 1908);

Transplanted Daughters (London: Unwin, 1909);

Recollections Grave and Gay (New York: Scribners, 1911; London: Smith, Elder, 1912).

PLAY PRODUCTIONS: *The Mouse-Trap: A Comedietta, in One Act,* New York, Madison Square Theatre, 13 January 1887;

Behind a Curtain: A Monologue in One Act, New York, Madison Square Theater, 14 January 1887.

OTHER: "Richmond Scenes in '62," in *Battles and Leaders of the Civil War, Being for the Most Part Contributions by Union and Confederate Officers, Based Upon the Century War Series,* 4 volumes, edited by R. U. Johnson and C. C. Buel (New York: Century, 1887–1888);

Augustin Eugène Scribe, *A Russian Honeymoon: A Comedy in Three Acts,* adapted and arranged by Harrison (New York: Dewitt, 1890);

Weeping Wives: A Comedietta in One Act from the French of Siraudin and Lambert Thibout, translated and adapted by Harrison (Chicago: Dramatic Publishing, 1892);

"Society and Social Usages," in *The Woman's Book: Dealing Practically with the Modern Conditions of Home-Life, Self-Support, Education, Opportunities, and Every-Day Problems,* 2 volumes, by Harrison and others (New York: Scribners, 1894).

SELECTED PERIODICAL PUBLICATIONS– UNCOLLECTED:

FICTION

"Penelope's Swains," *Century Illustrated Magazine,* 41 (February 1891): 509–517;

"Gay's Romance," *Century Illustrated Magazine,* 43 (1891–March 1892): 728–736;

"When the Century Came In: A Story," *Scribner's Magazine,* 12 (August 1892): 170–180;

"Monsieur le Comte: A Story," *Blackwood's Magazine,* 157 (1894): 764;

"Miss Selina's Settlement: A Story," *Century Illustrated Magazine,* 53 (February 1897): 586–592;

"Author's Reading, and its Consequences: Story," *Harper's Magazine,* 97 (October 1898): 729–737;

"Peggy's 'Possum Hunt,'" *St. Nicholas,* 39 (January 1912): 244–248.

NONFICTION

"Sarah Fairfax of Virginia," *Scribner's Magazine,* 12 (1875): 301;

"A Little Centennial Lady," *Scribner's Magazine,* 13 (July 1876): 301–311;

"Lord Thomas Fairfax," *Scribner's Magazine,* 18 (1878): 715–728;

"My Lord Fairfax, of Virginia," *Scribner's Magazine,* 18 (September 1879): 715–728;

"A Virginia Girl in the First Year of the War," *Century Illustrated Magazine,* 30 (August 1885): 606–614;

"Washington at Mount Vernon after the Revolution," *Century Illustrated Magazine,* 37 (April 1889): 834–850;

"Washington in New York in 1789," *Century Illustrated Magazine,* 37 (April 1889): 850–859;

"Cherubina de Willoughby, the Last of the Heroines," *Critic,* 17 (27 December 1890): 337–338;

"Colonel William Byrd of Westover, Virginia," *Century Illustrated Magazine,* 42 (June 1891): 163–178;

"Some Sins of Society," *Outlook,* 50 (22 December 1894): 1090;

"Thackerayana," *Critic,* 26 (1894): 447; 27 (1895): 80;

"American Rural Festivals," *Century Illustrated Magazine,* 50 (July 1895): 323–333;

"Myth of the Four Hundred," *Cosmopolitan,* 19 (1895): 329;

"A Hunt-Supper in Old Virginia," *Littell's Living Age,* 214 (1896): 485;

"Study in Husbands," *North American Review,* 162 (January 1896): 108–113;

"My Favorite Novelist and Novel," *Munsey's Magazine,* 17 (1897): 538;

"The Woman of Fashion," *Munsey's Magazine,* 17 (1897): 699;

"The Millenary of King Alfred in 1901," *New York Times,* 5 February 1898, Saturday Supplement, II: 96;

"With Washington in the Minuet," *Ladies Home Journal,* 15 (February 1898): 1–2;

"When Fashion Graced the Bowery," *Ladies Home Journal,* 15 (March 1898): 11–12;

"Daughter of the House and her Duties," *Harper's Bazar,* 33 (3 March 1900): 174;

"Henley Week," *Cosmopolitan,* 29 (1900): 241–252;

"Home Life as a Profession," *Harper's Bazar,* 33 (19 May 1900): 148–150;

"Kemble, Frances Anne," *Critic,* 37 (1900): 520;

"Wives of the Presidents of the U.S.," *Cosmopolitan,* 30 (1900): 406;

"First Lady of the Land," *Cosmopolitan,* 30 (February 1901): 406–414;

"Newport Lawn Fete," *New York Times,* 24 August 1901, IV: 7;

"Belasco Suit," *New York Times,* 14 November 1901, I: 9;

"Pension Opposed," *New York Times,* 26 November 1901, III: 513;

"Winwood's Luck," *Lippincott's Magazine,* 68 (1901): 336;

"A Driving Trip," *Outing,* 43 (1903): 185;

"Bar Harbor," *Independent,* 55 (June 1903): 1308–1313;

"Eastern U.S., and its Leaders," *Everybody's Magazine,* 10 (1903): 490;

"Story of My New York Drawing-Room," *Woman's Home Companion,* 37 (September 1910): 11–12;

"Mrs. Harrison Remembers," *Bookman,* 34 (December 1911): 343–346.

Taking material from the conventions of the sentimental romance, her Civil War years, and her acquaintance with aristocratic, politically important Southern families, Constance Cary Harrison wrote about fashionable society's genealogies, morals, customs, and matrimonial maneuvers of the last half of the nineteenth century. Her Virginia kinship relations, detailed in her autobiography *Recollections Grave and Gay* (1911), furnished the social credentials and elite class affiliation that sustained Harrison throughout her life. Her work belongs to a body of narratives different from the illustrated stories produced by newspaper, dime novel, and nickel and dime pamphlets between the 1840s and 1890s. Harrison's "silver fork" novels were reviewed and serialized in the major periodicals—*Century, Scribner's, Harper's Bazar,* and *The Atlantic Monthly*—and then published as books. By the 1880s realism and then naturalism supplanted the sentimental and romantic fictions that had domi-

nated the literary scene, and by 1900 the public taste for best-selling pulp fiction had permanently divided literary art into two camps—serious fiction and popular. Harrison's writing, aimed at the genteel Victorian middle class, hovered on the margin between the two. Her work is a valuable register of American social custom and history because it is marked by the ideological rifts produced by her stake in the turbulent social and political contexts in which she lived.

Constance Cary was born in Lexington, Kentucky, on 25 April 1843 to Archibald Cary and Monimia Fairfax Cary, the middle child and only daughter of the Cary children. Constance had two brothers—Falkland Fairfax, the eldest, who died in 1855 at age sixteen, and Clarence, three years her junior. Harrison wryly comments in *Recollections Grave and Gay* that Southerners "too often" married their cousins. Her father, Archibald Cary of Carysbrooke, Virginia, was the son of Wilson Jefferson Cary, a nephew of Thomas Jefferson, who married Virginia Randolph. An earlier Archibald Cary, of Ampthill, Virginia, also married a Randolph. In the fifth marriage between the two families, Constance's father wed his cousin Monimia Fairfax. Thus her grandparents as well as her parents were cousins. Constance's husband, Burton Norvell Harrison, was distantly related to her through the Randolph family.

Archibald Cary's family established itself in the Virginia colony in the 1640s. He grew up on a slave-holding plantation near Charlottesville in Fluvanna County, Virginia; studied law at the University of Virginia; and opened his first practice in Port Gibson, Mississippi. He moved to Lexington, Kentucky, in 1843 to continue legal study at Transylvania University. After the birth of his daughter, the family returned to Virginia to live at Vaucluse, Monimia's family estate. His wealthy father-in-law, Thomas, ninth Lord of Fairfax, was a devout Swedenborgian, a member of a society that followed the theology of Emanuel Swedenborg, an eighteenth-century Swedish philosopher, scientist, and Christian mystic. Thomas insisted that his four sons and two daughters be baptized in the faith. Acting on his religious scruples, he was the first Virginia gentleman to materially respond to the South's slavery-reformation impulse, which gave rise between 1789 and 1831 to more than one hundred emancipation organizations, including the American Colonization Society in Virginia. Thomas manumitted his slaves, taught each a trade, and, at his expense, sent the efficient ones to Liberia, an African colony of black emigrants.

His humanitarian efforts notwithstanding, Thomas was disagreeable and made life difficult for Archibald and his young family. Harrison remembers

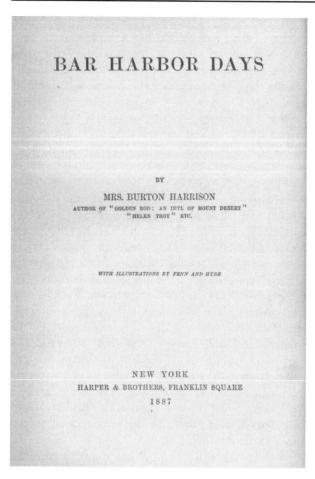

BAR HARBOR DAYS

BY

MRS. BURTON HARRISON

AUTHOR OF "GOLDEN ROD; AN IDYL OF MOUNT DESERT"
"HELEN TROY" ETC.

WITH ILLUSTRATIONS BY FENN AND HYDE

NEW YORK

HARPER & BROTHERS, FRANKLIN SQUARE

1887

Title page for Harrison's novel for adolescent readers,
narrated by two beagles

her grandfather with distaste. She once glimpsed him lying in bed—"the picture of that stern ivory profile against the pillow, and the long locks like spun glass beside it, haunted me for years with shuddering." According to her younger brother, Clarence, their grandfather not only saw the ghost of a female servant reflected in a mirror but also had places set at the table for dead family members.

Archibald evidently wished to distance himself from his father-in-law's reach. He moved to Martinsville, Virginia, 160 miles south of Alexandria on the North Carolina border, a four-day trip on horseback. Here Archibald taught school. He later settled 132 miles from the elderly patriarch in Cumberland, Maryland, a quiet town situated on the northern branch of the Potomac River in the Cumberland Valley. Archibald practiced law and edited the *Cumberland Civilian,* a weekly newspaper with a liberal bias. In Port Gibson, Mississippi, he edited an anti–Andrew Jackson weekly. Keenly interested in local and state government and politics, he was, according

to Harrison, an ardent Whig politician whose printed pamphlets, speeches, and editorials breathed "the fiery spirit of his creed."

An attentive father, Archhibald delighted his children with family gossip and endless stories, encouraging the development of good reading, writing, and intellectual habits. He and Monimia fostered in their daughter an interest in politics, a belief in the potential of America and its institutions, and an aggressive, upper-class social instinct. From her earliest years Harrison was committed to preserving kinship and class affiliations and consolidating her social position. She clearly understood to what extent these might be relied upon to serve her. As an heir to and purveyor of the superior virtues and customs of "older civilizations," Harrison believed that Southerners of her class comprised "the cornerstone of the commonwealth." As she wrote in *Recollections Grave and Gay,* her refugee acquaintances in the Confederate capital of Richmond were "the direct outgrowth of the best Colonial stock," imminently "equipped to conduct the functions of good society."

The Cary family's experiences during the Civil War years shaped Harrison's social identity as well as her writings. After her father—not yet forty—died in 1854 of typhoid fever, eleven-year-old Constance and eight-year-old Clarence returned with their mother to Vaucluse, the Fairfax family estate near Alexandria. Monimia's father, Thomas Fairfax, had also died, leaving Vaucluse to his widow, who opened her home to her two widowed daughters, their six children, and various aunts and cousins who stayed for varying periods of time. Harrison read what books she found in the library, continuing the education she received in Cumberland that began with home tutoring in Latin, followed by instruction at Miss Jane Keenah's day school. Her mother thought she spent too much time roaming, riding, and shooting with Clarence and her male cousins, so she hired a French governess to tutor her daughter. Although Harrison "writhed" under Mademoiselle Adami's "mincing conventionalities of social doctrine," she liked reading in French and continued it "unremittingly" all of her life. At age fourteen she was enrolled in Hubert Pierre Lefebvre's boarding school in Richmond. Here she met upper-class Southern girls whose families owned slaves. Her acquaintance with them convinced her that slavery created a smug, indolent white population that could not care for itself. She abhorred her schoolmates's treatment of slaves.

When the Civil War erupted in the spring of 1861, Harrison and Clarence went to live with a relative in Clarke County, Virginia, while Monimia and her sister Mrs. Hyde traveled to Manassas Junction, Virginia, to volunteer as nurses. In their absence Vaucluse was burned to its foundations, and the grounds were used as a Union camp. Harrison joined her mother several months later, while fifteen-year-old Clarence enlisted in an Alexandria regiment as a marker, a soldier who forms the pivot of a wheeling column or marks the direction of an alignment. Clarence later served as a midshipman on a Confederate gunboat. The harsh immediacy of war forced the pampered eighteen-year-old to mature quickly. She gradually stopped complaining about the muddy, lukewarm drinking water and rationed food; the heat; and forced association with people not of her class. Following her mother's lead, she carded lint from cotton to make bandages, tended the wounded soldiers on the trains that stopped in Manassas nearly every night, fretted over Clarence's safety, and grieved over the war dead. Before Richmond fell in 1865, she and Monimia lived at the hospital at Camp Winder, nursing the dying and wounded. Monimia was to become the model for the selfless, tender, untiring female character who appears in many of Harrison's novels: "Sleeping on a soldier's bunk, rising at dawn, laboring till midnight, my mother faced death and suffering with the stout spirit that was a rock of refuge to all around her. Her record, in short, was that of a thousand other saintly women during that terrible strife."

Harrison's depiction of her mother exemplifies her culture's notion of the true Southern lady. However, its emphasis on hard work departs from the outwardly delicate, gracious, deferential stereotype to include the nineteenth century's evangelical ideal of devotion to work, faith, patience, inner strength, and avoidance of frivolity. This blended model of womanhood had circulated in her family since the time of her paternal grandmother, Virginia Randolph Cary, who wrote two books on proper child-rearing. In her *Letters on Female Character* (1831), Cary noted that female trials and women's "allotted duties" demand "the strength of Christian principle to ensure their correct and dignified performance," while "the nature of female trials requires all the meliorating power of faith, to induce a requisite measure of patience and fortitude."

Harrison's cousins Hetty and Jennie Cary joined her at Manassas in 1861. Threatened with arrest and jail, Hetty had been expelled from Baltimore for shaking a contraband Confederate banner from a window of her father's home while Union troops marched past. Carrying smuggled drugs for hospitals and uniforms for friends, Hetty, Jennie, and their brother ran a Union blockade. Harrison emulated Hetty's feistiness in February 1863. Monimia

and her sister had inherited money from the estate of their late brother. Documents verifying the inheritance had to be deposited in Rigg's Bank in Washington, D.C., by one of the sisters. Some six weeks after President Lincoln signed the Emancipation Proclamation that freed more than three million men, women, and children from slavery, Harrison and her aunt crossed Union lines with the papers that would assure a comfortable future for the two families. Although the pair was captured and briefly held, they returned safely to Richmond with not only money but also fashionable new clothes and hats.

The young Cary women made two distinctive contributions to the Confederate cause: Jennie set James Ryder Randall's poem "Maryland" to the tune of "Lauriger Horatius," adding the word "My" to create "Maryland, My Maryland," one of the Confederacy's best-known battle songs. In September 1861 Harrison and Jennie sang it to a regiment from Maryland at the camp in Manassas. A month later Harrison, Hetty, and Jennie were asked by a Confederate Congressional Committee to make the first Confederate battle flags. Hetty sent hers to General Joseph E. Johnston; Jennie's went to General P. G. T. Beauregard. This flag later draped the coffins of Beauregard and Confederate president Jefferson Davis. Harrison's flag, her name embroidered in gold letters at a corner, went to General Earl Van Dorn. It now hangs between glass in the Maryland Room at Richmond's Museum of the Confederacy.

When Harrison and her mother moved to Richmond from Manassas in 1862, she contributed stories, verses, and sketches to various Richmond newspapers, collecting her first payments in 1864 from *The Southern Illustrated News* and *The Magnolia Weekly*. The "greatest feather in [her] literary cap" was a poem published in *The Examiner,* "the wail of a mother for a son shot in battle before Richmond. Probably I imitated Mrs. [Elizabeth Barrett] Browning, but without knowing it, for I always tried to write what I knew or could feel myself." She wrote "Blockade Correspondence" between "Secessia"—a fictional character emblematic of the Confederate position from the point of view of a young woman in Baltimore—and "Refugitta," the name under which she wrote her articles in Richmond. "Skirmishing," Harrison's first novel, was destroyed in April 1865 when her publisher's office burned in the siege of Richmond.

Like her friend, the diarist Mary Boykin Chesnut, whom she often visited in Richmond before its fall, Harrison was caught between the romantic illusions of Southern mythology and the war's reality. Chesnut questioned the war's causes, women's roles, and a social system requiring so bloody a sacrifice to uphold it. Although she hated the war's devastation, Harrison uncritically supported the Southern cause, glorifying its military leaders and soldiers and "the stout spirit of the South." Descriptive passages in *Recollections Grave and Gay,* some drawn from her war diaries, others written nearly fifty years later, while marked by a sympathy for suffering, give the impression of a voyeur wedded to romantic stereotypes and enthralled by dramatic spectacle: "Presently, emerging from the golden mist, we saw, first, horsemen, pacing leisurely; then caissons and guns; and after them, rank upon rank of marching men in gray! And above the dust, banners of scarlet crossed with blue."

A week after the First Battle of Bull Run, Constance rode on horseback over the field. Her brief account shows the blend of impressionism and reportorial detail that was to distinguish her later narrative style: "Hillsides were marked with hecatombs of dead horses and scattered with hasty graves. The trees and undergrowth were broken and bullet-riddled. The grass between the scars of upturned earth was green as if it had known no baptism of fire and blood. . . . I saw a ghastly semblance of a hand protruding at one spot." Two years later, returning south with her aunt from their journey to Washington, D.C., Harrison remains a pensive tourist: "We crept wearily over deep-rutted clay roads . . . through melancholy wastes of landscape strewn with felled trees and burned houses. We recognized Camp Pickens, the seat of former gay visits to the troops, only by the junction of the Manassas and Orange railroads. At another old camping ground the earth was inlaid with hundreds of shoes cast away by Union troopers, newly shod. Handsome homesteads crowning the hills looked at us through empty eye-sockets."

Harrison's romance with Burton Norvell Harrison, whom she married on 26 November 1867 in New York at her great-aunt Nancy Cary Randolph Morris's estate, Morrisanna, began in Manassas, Virginia, early in the Civil War. "A man of tact, vivid intelligence, and high courtesy," the Yale graduate was Jefferson Davis's private secretary. Burton was captured with President Davis and imprisoned in Fort Monroe, Virginia, and later in Fort Delaware, the U.S. arsenal in Washington, D.C. While he smuggled letters from prison concealed in hollowed-out carrots and cucumbers by a vegetable seller, Harrison and Monimia tried to gain his release through political influence. He was freed in January 1866. In the following year he traveled to Canada and Europe, studied for and passed the New York State bar exam, and joined the law firm of a former judge.

Meanwhile, Harrison and her mother sailed to Paris in October 1866 for a year—"It was thought best for us ex-Confederates of both sexes to keep quietly out of public observation while still the wave of feeling (enormously increased by the assassination of Lincoln) dashed high." There she studied voice training at the Paris Conservatory and bought her wedding trousseau. After her marriage she and Burton slipped into the echelons of old New York society. Over the next forty years Harrison wrote magazine articles, novels, plays, and short fiction, sang with choral societies and directed amateur theatricals, volunteered at Bellevue Hospital, chaired the board of the Child's Hospital and Nursery, raised funds for the Statue of Liberty's pedestal, and donated $32,150—the proceeds from ticket sales to her plays—to charities.

The Harrisons had three sons, Fairfax (born 1869), Francis Burton (born 1873), and Archibald Cary (born 1876). Fairfax, named after Constance's deceased brother, became president of the Southern Railway system. He eventually reestablished the Fairfax family estate in Fauquier County, Virginia, on property once owned by the original Lord Fairfax of Yorkshire. Francis Burton served as a New York congressman, and later governor general of the Philippines. Harrison's beloved brother, Clarence, who spent his war years in the Confederate navy, studied law in Charleston, South Carolina, then joined his brother-in-law's New York firm Harrison & Wesson.

Burton Harrison's legal career included service as a public prosecutor in the Tweed Ring trials; he also represented New York City's first Rapid Transit Commission, and the Western Union Telegraph and New York Telephone companies. Shortly before Burton's death in 1904, he was offered an ambassadorship to Italy, which he declined because of poor health. After her husband died, Harrison moved to Washington to live near her sons.

Harrison's first published book, *In Memory of Monimia Fairfax Cary* (1875), was followed by thirty-four others. Not all were novels: *Woman's Handiwork in Modern Homes* (1881) is written in the same vein as *An American Girl's Book* (1831) and *The Lady's Receipt Book* (1846), Eliza Leslie's popular works on domestic science. *The Well-Bred Girl in Society* (1898), a guide for mothers hoping to navigate young daughters through the treacherous shoals of fashionable society, also aims at the genteel middle-class market. Its subtext, that a man exchanges the social prestige and protection of marriage for female beauty, fertility, and servitude, is repeated in virtually all of her work. With the exception of her fairy tales and *Bar Harbor Days* (1887), a novel for adolescents narrated by two beagles, Harrison's fiction focuses on marriage, romantic and redemptive love, sexual and social jealousy, the virtues of domesticity, and preserving elite class and gender distinctions. *Flower de Hundred* (1890) and *A Bachelor Maid* (1894) address the two great political movements of the nineteenth century, the abolition of slavery and women's rights. *The Anglomaniacs* (1890) wittily examines the commodification of fashionable young women and New York society's marriage market. *The Circle of a Century* (1899), which shows the influences of Sigmund Freud, Charles Darwin, and Gregor Mendel on Harrison's notion of genetic legacy, contends that negative psychological and physical traits pass through generations of families whose cousins intermarry. *The Unwelcome Mrs. Hatch* (1901) expands on the social outcast theme developed as a subplot in *A Bachelor Maid*, Harrison's most complex, thoughtful novel. *The Unwelcome Mrs. Hatch* suggests that a passionate woman whose behavior violates the convention of female rectitude remains morally superior to men if unjust circumstances induced her fall from grace, and if she sincerely strives for redemption through love and self-sacrifice.

A Bachelor Maid and *The Unwelcome Mrs. Hatch* alter the sentimental formula to address social issues but retain the didactic thrust that characterizes sentimental fiction's evangelical prescription for living. Realism struggles with sentimental romance to produce an ambivalence that is not resolved, despite Harrison's insistence on happy endings. The novels are noteworthy from several perspectives. The anger, discontent, and misery of the central characters subvert the domestic ideal both novels promote. Harrison's strong, spiritually pure, nurturing woman who sustains the domestic sanctuary, supports and redeems her husband, teaches her children good conduct, and works to reform the degenerate society outside her home also protests her restricted freedom, her role as a dependent, her lack of personhood, and the double standard that permits men to behave inappropriately, even licentiously, without losing their honor.

The novels incorporate into the genteel domestic narrative elements of the working-girl novel, a popular genre flourishing from the 1870s through the first decade of the twentieth century. Chaste working women are juxtaposed with "unworthy" women who promote themselves in society through sexually assertive, crafty behavior. Conniving, destitute Sarah Stauffer of *A Bachelor Maid* makes money through teaching and championing suffragette causes but abandons her ideals when she finds a marriageable, wealthy man. Virtuous, impoverished Marian Lorimer Hatch of *The Unwelcome Mrs. Hatch*, once wealthy and privileged, earns her living by fashioning party favors. While Harrison depicts a woman's

honest labor as good, labor is never privileged above inheriting or marrying wealth. In contrast, novels such as Laura Jean Libbey's widely read *Little Rosebud's Lovers; or, The Cruel Revenge* (1886) glorify women's labor, infusing borrowed middle-class respectability into the working-girl idiom. Libbey transforms the working girl into a lady without erasing her identity as a working girl, a metamorphosis Harrison could not conceive.

Harrison's central female characters conform to her culture's assumptions about appropriate gender roles and relations and thus defer to fantasies of male control. Virtuous motherhood is the primary value. The heroines achieve some independence and new social identities through arduous trials and self-negation but choose at the end to be subsumed in domesticity. In *A Bachelor Maid* budding feminist Marion Irving realizes she cannot live without a man and the social distinction marriage brings; Marian Lorimer Hatch, condemned by society for running away with another man to escape her abusive, unfaithful husband in *The Unwelcome Mrs. Hatch*, chooses to die rather than burden her newly married daughter. To be recuperated as "good," she must accommodate others by removing herself as a source of potential embarrassment or trouble. Her death is reminiscent of Lillie's in Harriet Beecher Stowe's *Pink and White Tyranny, a Society Novel* (1871). Lillie realizes her selfishness and, repenting, dies. In death Marian and Lillie achieve what they could not in life–they become saintly mothers as well as objects of erotic desire. Indeed, rectitude marks each of Harrison's heroines. She reiterates the exhortation to female goodness in her guide to female decorum *The Well-Bred Girl in Society*. What men respect in women of their own social class, she says, is "first the possession of that fine moral fibre, purely womanly, and yet stout as tempered steel, that makes them realize in her presence the gulf that divides her from the unworthy of her sex."

She depicts women who challenge the patriarchal ideal of sexual purity and marital subservience as predators fated to live as outcasts. In *A Bachelor Maid* Sarah, Marion's genteel companion, once lived with a man who left her. Afterward, she presents herself as a widow, surviving socially through manipulation and deception. Well-educated, intellectually progressive, and ambitious, Sarah's misfortune is poverty, which drives her to conceal her past. Promoting the Higher Woman cause, her mission is to "overcome the isolation of the married woman . . . to show her there are other things to absorb her" than subserviency to a husband and childbirth. Although Sarah criticizes a woman's dependence on "man's

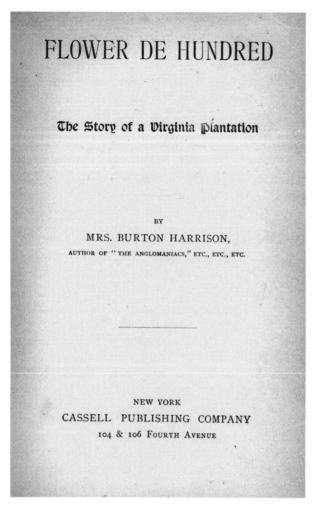

FLOWER DE HUNDRED

The Story of a Virginia Plantation

BY

MRS. BURTON HARRISON,

AUTHOR OF " THE ANGLOMANIACS," ETC., ETC., ETC.

NEW YORK

CASSELL PUBLISHING COMPANY

104 & 106 FOURTH AVENUE

Title page for Harrison's romanticized depiction of the South from the antebellum period through Reconstruction

love for her earthly happiness" and her willingness to become "an abject echo" of male opinion, she recants her feminist ideals in favor of marrying into wealth and social status. When Sarah's ploy to seduce and marry Marion's admirer fails, she flatters Marion's widowed father, Judge Irving, into marriage. An unhappy Marion nobly decides to forgive her deceptions and acknowledge Sarah as her father's wife. Ironically, the new Mrs. Justice Irving, now assured of social acceptance, leaves her husband for a prolonged lecture tour advocating women's rights.

In *The Unwelcome Mrs. Hatch,* Harrison again explores the gender bias informing social relations. Although Marian Lorimer Hatch has the "fine moral fibre" that distinguishes her from less worthy women, she is unjustly condemned and divorced by her bigoted, deceitful husband Dick Lorimer, a wealthy New York financier. Early in their marriage Lorimer flaunts his mistress Madge in the home he shares with Marian. Painfully angered, Marian rebels and plans to run away with an admirer. She writes a goodbye letter, leaves, then returns, deciding to forgive Lorimer for the sake of their child, Gladys. He has read her letter, however, and accuses her of infidelity. Marian is cast out. Lorimer refuses to let her see her young daughter; her friends reject and humiliate her; and thus the once wealthy, privileged Marian changes her surname to Hatch to disguise her past and ekes out a living as a seamstress. Lorimer's second wife, his former mistress Madge, is a coarser version of the conniving Sarah in *A Bachelor Maid.* At Madge's instigation, Lorimer continues to hound and castigate Marian years after her youthful indiscretion. In the tradition of the sentimental novel's victimized heroines, Marian transcends her circumstance through self-sacrifice, choosing to suffer silently and to forgive Lorimer's cruelties rather than reveal her identity to Gladys.

Because of the double standard based on the patriarchal ideal of a woman's spotless virtue in the South's elite plantation culture, even a flawless reputation could be tainted by malicious gossip and innuendo. Thus a sexually assertive woman unlucky enough to be exposed was condemned, ostracized, and often persecuted. Harrison likely drew the social outcast themes from her family's connection to the notorious "Bizarre scandal" of 1792–1793, which shocked and titillated generations of Virginia's aristocrats. Elements of the scandal, which centered on young Ann (Nancy) Cary Randolph, Harrison's great-aunt, are reinscribed in *The Unwelcome Mrs. Hatch* and *A Bachelor Maid.* While living with her married sister Judith and her husband Richard at Bizarre, the Randolph plantation, sixteen-year-old Nancy allegedly became involved with Richard's brother Theodorick, who died on 14 February 1792 at the age twenty-two before they could marry. By some accounts, Richard was also her partner in a conspiracy. In October, when Richard, Judith, and Nancy visited their cousin Randolph Harrison, Nancy became ill. Only her brother-in-law attended her. Two days later slaves found the remains of a newborn white child or fetus on a woodpile. It was rumored that Nancy had either miscarried or induced an abortion, or that Richard had killed the infant.

Public speculation reached so feverish a pitch that Richard and the Randolph clan felt slandered and demanded legal intervention. At a subsequent court hearing, Judith Randolph denied wrongdoing by either Richard or Nancy. The charges were dismissed, but the scandal pursued them. Richard died three years later under clouded circumstances, reportedly by poisoning; for years after, Judith was the subject of cruel gossip; and Nancy was forced to flee Virginia by John Randolph, Richard's brother, who accused her of sleeping with a slave and later, when she lived in Richmond, of prostitution. Nancy moved to Connecticut, where she became reacquainted with Gouvernor Morris, an old family friend who hired her to serve as housekeeper at Morrisanna, his New York estate. She wed Morris on Christmas Day in 1809. Although married and the mother of a son, Nancy remained the target of John Randolph's hostility. He blamed her for the misery he believed she had brought upon his family. Thus, twenty years after the scandal, he stirred up its memories, circulating letters that charged her with immorality and fornication. When Constance Cary married Burton Harrison at Morrisanna in 1867 in a wedding hosted by Nancy Cary Randolph Morris, echoes of the scandal and its consequences still lingered. The "Bizarre scandal" is detailed in Catherine Clinton's meticulously researched *The Plantation Mistress: Woman's World in the Old South* (1982). Something offensive evidently occurred that involved Nancy Cary Randolph, her sister, and her brother-in-law, but it is not clear whether the teenager was pregnant, or if so, by which Randolph brother. Clinton points out that scholars do not agree on the facts because historical accounts differ.

Harrison's fiction set in the South weaves together the romantic militarism of mock-chivalry and the moral precepts of Christianity. From the cavalier tradition came the worship of ladies, military discipline, noblesse oblige, and a celebration of glory; from Christian teachings came the concepts of determinism, inherited guilt, devotion to duty, self-examination, and a conviction of individual moral responsibility. These conventions, typical of Southern writing of the period, produce an ideological uneasiness in Harrison's writing that she tries to resolve by subsuming it in the moral glories of domesticity. *Flower de Hundred* romanticizes the Lost Cause as it follows generations of Throckmortons, a slaveholding family, through the turmoils of the Civil War and Reconstruction. Like Mark Twain's *Pudd'nhead Wilson* (1894), Harrison's plot revolves around the issues of patrilineage and patrimony. The novel focuses on the tribulations of Miles and Dick, who are misidentified as infants when found after a shipwreck. Twain uses the device of identical infants switched at birth to explore miscegenation, the racial dynamics of sexuality, and America's turn-of-the-century confusion over individual moral identity. Morality in *Pudd'nhead Wilson* is relative, a social acquisition, expedient, not absolute. Harrison's approach to social and psychological division is sentimental and romantic; moral values and identities are clear. Her heroes know who they are. Harrison repeats the themes in *Flower de Hundred* of love lost, love found, and redemption through sacrifice in *The Carlyles: A Story of the Fall of the Confederacy* (1905). She links the cavalier ideal to the development of sound moral character through adversity. Refined and strengthened by their war experiences, the patriotic heroes of these works plan to rebuild the South afresh through prayer, labor, patience, and hope. *The Carlyles* and *Flower de Hundred* are novels of nostalgia; both argue that the future, not the idyllic past, is corrupted.

Although Harrison disavowed slavery, she treats African Americans negatively in her fiction and autobiography. They are reduced to sentimental stereotypes—the loyal retainer or nurturing mammy—given grotesque characteristics, patronized, or mocked. She describes blacks as threats in her autobiography: "Some Negroes of the lowest grade, their heads turned by the prospect of wealth and equality, together with a mob of miserable poor whites, drank themselves mad with liquor scooped from the gutters." Looting from the burned districts after the fall of Richmond, they were "reinforced . . . by convicts escaped from the penitentiary." *Flower de Hundred,* the most interesting and well written of her Confederate romances, both rationalizes and denounces slavery. In it she argues that most slaveholders were "a race of conscientious men full of a high sense of personal honor and responsibility to God" whose job is to "watch" over "undeveloped souls." Their lives were especially difficult because they were isolated on plantations, surrounded by "masses of ignorant peasants" who were always ready to relapse into barbarous habits. Blacks were "so characterized by sensuality, so habituated to the vices of the untruthful, so steeped in the cunning with which the servile class everywhere contends against its rulers, so shut off from the sense of accountability and duty" that they needed the moral guidance and protection of firm, kind masters. At the same time, she contends that the "altogether wretched" system hampered the South's development, wrapping it "in an anaconda's folds." Progress and enlightenment occur only where there is equality and the possibility of "actual equal attainment." Despite this claim, she notes resentfully that self-assertive, free blacks "jostle white people out of place, wear pince-nez in the cornfields, and travel with 'grip sacks' and high hats, demanding for themselves in our Southern States far more of social consideration than the peasant classes of any other nation upon earth either receive or expect." Harrison, a racist and elitist, did not speak for, but certainly spoke to, a large audience of genteel middle-class Americans whose conservatism was affirmed by her work. Protective of her social status, Harrison observed the dictates of decorum and avoided ruffling genteel feathers.

Harrison lived through nineteen presidencies, several wars, and an era of revolutionary change. In 1920, as American modernism shaped the direction of art and literature throughout the Western world and Woodrow Wilson served his last year as president, Constance Cary Harrison died on 21 November at age seventy-seven in Washington, D.C. She is buried next to Burton at Ivy Hill Cemetery in Alexandria, Virginia.

References:

Catherine Clinton, *The Plantation Mistress: Woman's World in the Old South* (N.Y.: Random House, 1982), pp. 114–117;

Michael Denning, *Mechanic Accents: Dime Novels and Working-Class Culture in America* (London & New York: Verso, 1987), p. 12;

Elizabeth Fox-Genovese, *Within the Plantation Household: Black and White Women of the Old South* (Chapel Hill, N.C.: University of North Carolina Press, 1988);

Mary Kelley, "The Sentimentalists: Promise and Betrayal in the Home," *Signs,* 4 (Spring 1979): 434–446;

Elaine Showalter, *Sister's Choice: Tradition and Change in American Women's Writing,* Clarendon Lectures (Oxford: Clarendon Press, 1991);

Jane P. Tompkins, "The Other American Renaissance," in *American Renaissance Reconsidered,* edited by Walter Benn Michaels and Donald E. Pease (Baltimore: Johns Hopkins University Press, 1989), pp. 34–57;

C. Vann Woodward, ed., *Mary Chesnut's Civil War* (New Haven & London: Yale University Press, 1981).

Papers:

Constance Cary Harrison's papers are housed in the Special Collections Department of the University of Virginia Library in Charlottesville and in various Family Papers Collections at the Virginia Historical Society in Richmond.

Mary Jane Holmes

(5 April 1825 – 6 October 1907)

Barbara J. McGuire
University of Washington

See also the Holmes entry in *DLB 202: Nineteenth-Century American Fiction Writers*.

BOOKS: *Tempest and Sunshine; or, Life in Kentucky* (New York: Appleton, 1854; London, 1854);

The English Orphans; or, A Home in the New World (New York: Appleton, 1855);

The Homestead on the Hillside, and Other Tales (New York: Miller, Orton & Mulligan, 1856);

'Lena Rivers (New York: Miller, Orton & Mulligan, 1856);

Meadow Brook (New York: Miller, Orton, 1857);

Dora Deane; or, The East India Uncle; and Maggie Miller; or, Old Hagar's Secret (New York: Saxton, 1859);

Cousin Maude, and Rosamond (New York: Saxton, Barker, 1860);

Marian Grey; or, The Heiress of Redstone Hall (New York: Carleton, 1863; London, 1863);

Darkness and Daylight (New York: Carleton, 1864);

Hugh Worthington (New York: Carleton, 1865);

The Cameron Pride; or, Purified by Suffering (New York: Carleton / London: Low, 1867);

The Christmas Font: A Story for Young Folks (New York: Carleton / London: Low, 1868);

Rose Mather: A Tale of the War (New York: Carleton / London: Low, 1868);

Ethelyn's Mistake; or, The Home in the West (New York: Carleton / London: Low, 1869);

Millbank; or, Roger Irving's Ward (New York: Carleton / London: Low, 1871);

Edna Browning; or, The Leighton Homestead (New York: Carleton / London: Low, 1872);

West Lawn, and the Rector of St. Mark's (New York: Carleton / London: Low, 1874);

Edith Lyle (New York: Carleton / London: Low, 1876);

Mildred (New York: Carleton / London: Low, 1877);

Daisy Thornton and Jessie Graham (New York: Carleton / London: Low, 1878);

Forrest House (New York: Carleton, 1879);

Chateau d'Or; Norah; and Kitty Craig (New York & London: Carleton, 1880);

Mary Jane Holmes

Red-Bird: A Brown Cottage Story (New York: Carleton / London: Low, 1880); republished as *Red-Bird's Christmas Story* (New York: Dillingham, 1892);

Madeline (New York: Carleton / London: Low, 1881);

Queenie Hetherton (New York: Carleton / London: Low, 1883);

Christmas Stories (New York: Carleton / London: Low, 1885);

Bessie's Fortune (New York: Dillingham, 1885);

Gretchen (New York: Dillingham / London: Low, 1887);

Marguerite (New York: Dillingham, 1891);

Dr. Hathern's Daughters: A Story of Virginia, in Four Parts (New York: Dillingham, 1895);

Mrs. Hallam's Companion, and The Spring Farm and Other Tales (New York: Dillingham, 1896);

Paul Ralston (New York: Dillingham, 1897);

The Tracy Diamonds (New York: Dillingham, 1899);

The Cromptons (New York: Dillingham, 1902; London: Unwin, 1902);

The Merivale Banks (New York: Dillingham, 1903);

Rena's Experiment (New York: Dillingham, 1904);

The Abandoned Farm, and Connie's Mistake (New York: Dillingham, 1905);

Lucy Harding: A Romance of Russia (New York: American News, 1905).

Mary Jane Holmes's first article appeared in print when she was fifteen years old. By the time of her death at the age of eighty-two, her canon included more than forty novels and novellas, several collections of tales and stories, and many magazine publications. This extensive authorial production, combined with book sales in excess of two million copies, establishes Holmes as one of the most prolific and widely read writers of nineteenth-century America. She is also notable as one of the few women of her era to achieve financial independence with her pen. Long-term, relatively lucrative contracts with thriving publishing houses, an ever-increasing base of devoted readers, and frequent reprints of her novels afforded Holmes the leisure to pursue over the course of several decades the activity she loved best: composing what she described as "natural" stories of "domestic life as I know it to exist."

For Holmes, natural stories were tales that dramatized fundamental moral principles shaping the everyday lives of men and, in particular, women. Her fiction, while not overtly didactic, makes explicit distinctions between good and bad, noble and base, sensitive and callous; she designed her narratives not only for entertainment but also for edification. Her commitment to write stories "such as mothers are willing their daughters should read, and such as will do good instead of harm," contributed to her popularity with the general public. Offering intimate glimpses into the private worlds of both rural communities and middle-class households, Holmes magnified, with a slightly theatrical spin, the common ethical choices many of her readers faced daily: decisions regarding the sanctity of marriage and family, the balance between sacrifice and ambition, and the conflict between spiritual and secular interests.

The moral sensibilities, humanitarian themes, and democratic ideals that pervade the work of Mary Jane Hawes Holmes had their genesis in her family history.

The Hawes family established early roots in the New England community, mostly in Massachusetts and New York. Her grandfather, Joel Hawes, was a soldier in the Revolutionary War, and one of her uncles, Colonel Lyman Hawes, served a brief stint as an elected representative to the New York State Assembly. Another uncle, the Reverend Joel Hawes, was an eminent Episcopalian minister who wrote, in addition to many sermons, several essays designed to instill moral probity in his readers, such as "Lectures to Young Men" and "A Looking-Glass for Ladies."

Despite the local prominence of some of her ancestors, little is known about Holmes's parents, Preston Hawes and Fanny (Olds) Hawes. According to one early biographer, Preston Hawes was an "intellectual," Fanny Hawes was "a lover of poetry and romance," and both parents were strong supporters of their daughter's literary aspirations. If Preston and Fanny Hawes had a taste for the cerebral, they nonetheless were of plain country stock: Holmes's birth in 1825 marked her entry not into the polished, elite circles of Boston or New York City but into the simple farming community of Brookfield, Massachusetts. The fifth of nine children in a family of modest means, Holmes by necessity learned to shoulder a large measure of responsibility at an early age. By the time she was thirteen she had secured a position as a teacher in a local school, a job that proved to be the first step in a career as an educator that spanned nearly fifteen years. Writing, however, was always paramount to Holmes; throughout her youth she dabbled in fanciful storytelling, reportedly assuring her friends, "some day I will write a book that you all will read."

In 1849 she married Daniel Holmes, a newly minted Yale graduate. Soon after, the couple moved to Versailles, Kentucky, where both Holmes and her new husband taught school until 1852. The following year the couple moved back north, to Brockport, New York, where Daniel Holmes began a law career. Except for their many travels abroad, the Holmeses spent the remainder of their lives in Brockport, in a small home they dubbed "Brown Cottage." At Brown Cottage Holmes renewed her childhood passion for writing: zealously channeling her creative energies, she began and rapidly completed her first novel, *Tempest and Sunshine; or, Life in Kentucky,* which was published in 1854. Thereafter she averaged almost a novel per year until her death in 1907. Childless, financially secure, and comfortably established in Brockport, she was able to devote much of her life to, as she put it, writing "what people want."

Given the extent of her popularity, Holmes clearly understood what nineteenth-century readers wanted, and she supplied it in abundance. Twentieth-century critics have accused Holmes of catering to the public's tastes for predictable, complacent fiction; the standard argument of her detractors is that her stories had broad appeal because they affirmed, in a dully complicitous sort of way, the conservative middle-class values and sensibilities of her audience. Further, Holmes has been dismissed as a mere sentimentalist, a purveyor of overwrought emotion, and a manufacturer of verbose, superficial prose. Fred Lewis Pattee's evaluation of Holmes in *The Feminine Fifties* (1940) is typical of the general critical response: "Her style was rococo to the extreme, over-florid, fantastic, feebly pretentious." Holmes certainly is not the only popular writer to receive negative reviews; most women authors of her era have been targets of similar charges, especially those who, like Holmes, wrote in the sentimental vein. Recent feminist scholarship, however, has done much to counteract the obviously biased and hasty generalizations leveled against women's popular fiction. As Jane Tompkins and others have shown, sentimental novels produced by nineteenth-century American women must not be judged by rigid twentieth-century notions of what constitutes literary value. To better understand the work of Holmes in its historical context, students of the sentimental genre can turn to one of her contemporaries: in 1855 a critic for the *North American Review* praised her for her "exquisite" characterizations and "gracefully constructed" prose, adding that her "pictures of rural and village life . . . deserve to be hung up in perpetual memory as types of humanity fast becoming extinct."

Still, it is true that, taken as a whole, her narratives border on the formulaic, and it is also true that her stories are neither radical in perspective nor experimental in structure. Driven more by plot than characterization, the typical Holmes story traces the journey of a heroine from awkward pubescence to blooming womanhood; after the heroine proves her worthiness through tests of moral courage, she is rewarded with the inevitable happy marriage. Despite the adherence to certain familiar protocols and patterns, however, Holmes's stories are by no means blandly conventional. Indeed, as Nina Baym rightly points out in *Women's Fiction* (1993), her novels are "freer from middle-class conventions in general than the works of any of the women authors" of her ilk. While Holmes makes no revolutionary departures from prevailing ideologies, she nevertheless maintains a steady pressure against boundaries that impose limitations on women. For instance, during an era when a well-educated woman was considered somewhat superfluous, perhaps even a contradiction in terms, Holmes used her novels to promote one of her favorite platforms, the benefits of higher learning for women. Her heroines exhibit a hunger for knowledge

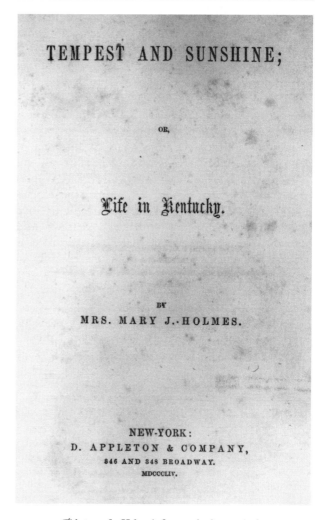

TEMPEST AND SUNSHINE;

OR,

Life in Kentucky.

BY

MRS. MARY J. HOLMES.

NEW-YORK:
D. APPLETON & COMPANY,
346 AND 348 BROADWAY.
MDCCCLIV.

Title page for Holmes's first novel, about a rivalry between two sisters

unsurpassed by their desire for marriage; they spend their adolescence in pursuit not of a mate but of an education.

Nor is it accurate to define her prose style as "rococo" or "over-florid," as Pattee has done; closer to the mark is a passage from a brief entry on Holmes in an 1893 collection of biographical sketches called *A Woman of the Century:* "Her success as an author is said by some to be the result of her powers of description; others assert that it is her naturalness, her clear, concise English and her faculty to hold the reader's sympathy from the beginning to the end." By shunning convoluted prose or gratuitous morbidity, Holmes was able to capture and retain the attention of a large audience of nineteenth-century readers.

Perhaps most surprising to those unfamiliar with her work, Holmes is the leading comic writer among all the sentimental novelists (with the possible exception of E. D. E. N. Southworth). Her humor, which ranges from burlesque-style caricature to ironic commentary, imparts a slightly tongue-in-cheek quality to her prose, leavening the moral sobriety with a lighter tone. In *Tempest and Sunshine,* for example, Holmes dryly notes a characteristic difference between Southerners and Northerners: "The Kentuckians are as famous as the Yankees for inquisitiveness, but if they inquire into *your* history, they are equally ready to give *theirs* to you, and you cannot feel as much annoyed by the kind, confiding manner, with which a Kentuckian will draw you out, as by the cool, quizzing way with which a Yankee will '*guess*' out your affairs." In this passage Holmes mocks Yankee reserve, but later in the same novel Southern informality fares no better. When Mr. Middleton, a rich but unrefined Kentucky farmer, receives unexpected visitors from New York, the ensuing dialogue is anything but serious:

> "You must excuse my rig, gentlemen, or rather, you must excuse what ain't rigged, mebby if I'd known all you city buggers was comin', I'd a kivered my bar feet."

> "You go barefoot for comfort, I suppose," said Mr. Miller.

> "Why, yes, mainly for that, I suppose," answered Mr. Middleton, "for I've got such fetched big corns on my feet, that I ain't goin' to be cramped with none of your toggery. My feet happen to be clean, for I washed 'em in the watering trough this mornin'."

Underlying the comic moments in *Tempest and Sunshine,* however, is a grave moral message. The novel centers on two young sisters, the daughters of Mr. Middleton. One daughter, Fanny, is the "sunshine" of the family, while the other daughter, Julia, is the "tempest." Whereas Fanny is loving, innocent, and flaxen-haired, her sister is spiteful and duplicitous, with a "dark and variable" complexion to match her disposition. The viperous Julia concocts a scheme, complete with staged performances and forged letters, to steal the affections of Fanny's fiancé; the scheme backfires, and Julia is disgraced. Ostensibly, the novel serves as a cautionary tale designed to warn female readers of the dangers of unseemly behavior: the good girl lives happily ever after, while her evil sister suffers horribly for her indiscretions. Yet, the real but less obvious thrust of the novel concerns the sins of the father, not the daughter. Holmes hints throughout the story that Middleton is to blame for Julia's distempers, for he clearly favors his sunshine over his tempest and treats them accordingly. His culpability is made explicit near the end of the novel, when he learns that Julia has run away: "If she could only come back, and I could do it over, I'd love

her more, and maybe she'd be better. But I treated her mean. I gin her only harsh words and cross looks."

Moreover, Holmes suggests that the father perceives both daughters more as personal property than as human beings; at one point in the story, Middleton jokingly wagers his daughters in a bet, prompting Fanny to ask, "Pa, what makes you always bet sister and me, just as though you could sell us like horses? It's bad enough to bet, and sell the blacks, I think." Holmes implies that thoughtless paternalism reduces women to little more than animals or items of mercantile exchange; she also manages to insert a dig at slaveholders such as Middleton, who "sell the blacks" with no regard for their welfare or humanity. Blacks, horses, and daughters all seem more or less on the same par for Middleton. In many of her subsequent novels, Holmes continues to expose the type of negligent authority represented by this well-meaning but heedless Kentucky farmer.

Heartened by the favorable reception of *Tempest and Sunshine,* Holmes published *The English Orphans; or, A Home in the New World* the next year, 1855. The orphans of the title are two young sisters, Ella and Mary Howard, who immigrate with their parents to America from England. Left destitute soon after by the death of both parents, Ella is adopted by a wealthy family while Mary ends up in a county poorhouse, where the horrendous conditions are made bearable only by her friendship with another inmate, "raving crazy" Sal Furbush.

The English Orphans is notable for its unflinching descriptions of the horrors of the poorhouse, but it is also a striking model of a particular brand of sentimental novel popular at midcentury, the orphan tale. The orphan tale, in which the death of a parent transforms a young female protagonist into a social outcast bereft of hearth and home, had its vogue when sentimental culture was at its height in the 1850s and 1860s. At a time when most Americans touted the family as the foundation of national prosperity, the orphan tale presented a disturbing antithesis, for it depicts the splintering of families, the alienation of daughters, and the consequent loss of innocence and stability.

The orphan tale almost invariably concludes with the construction of a new family similar to the old: the heroine eventually marries and settles down to a comfortable, middle-class domesticity, usually renouncing worldly ambitions in favor of wifehood and motherhood. Integral to the structured blueprint of the plot, however, is imaginative license. Between the playroom of the child and the parlor of the matron exists a space of liberating independence; during the long interim between the tragic moment of dispossession and the foregone conclusion of matrimony years later, the heroine embarks on a quest for identity, a bildungs-roman-style journey marked by switchback and encounter, dramatic ambiguity, and rich possibility. In this realm of autonomy and experiment, the heroine demonstrates her fortitude, drive, and moral assertiveness. In *The English Orphans,* for instance, Mary's experience in the poorhouse toughens her resolve to acquire an education; by the age of sixteen she is an accomplished student at Mount Holyoke, easily surpassing her privileged classmates' halfhearted efforts at scholarship. Throughout the novel Holmes repeatedly stresses Mary's overriding desire for enlightenment; at one point she likens Mary's yearning to a kind of insatiable craving: "She had tasted of knowledge and now thirsted for more."

Holmes followed *The English Orphans* with other, similar tales featuring young girls with ambition and spirit, such as *Dora Deane; or, The East India Uncle* (1859) and *Marian Grey; or, The Heiress of Redstone Hall* (1863). *'Lena Rivers* (1856), by all accounts her greatest commercial success, is another orphan narrative that, like *The English Orphans,* begins with family alienation and ends with family renovation. The orphan theme aside, *'Lena Rivers* is significant as one of the best examples of Holmes's attention to regional custom, dialect, and setting. Though Holmes is more of a sentimental novelist than local colorist or literary realist, she flavors her tales with details culled from her youth, effectively infusing her fiction with a distinct authenticity. In her preface to *'Lena Rivers* Holmes states that she deliberately draws on her own background in order to create a genuine atmosphere for her fiction:

> Reared among the rugged hills of the Bay State, and for a time constantly associated with a class of people known the wide world over as *Yankees,* it is no more than natural that I should often write of the places and scenes with which I have been the most familiar. In my delineations of New England character I have aimed to copy from memory, and in no one instance, I believe, have I overdrawn the picture. . . . Nearly the same remarks will also apply to my portraitures of Kentucky life and character, for it has been my good fortune to spend a year and a half in that state; and in my descriptions of country scenes and country life, I have with a few exceptions copied from what I saw.

In *'Lena Rivers,* as in much of her fiction, she elevates "country scenes and country life" far above city scenes and city life. For Holmes the country represents sincerity and pastoral simplicity, while the city represents hypocrisy and vanity. If she sometimes pokes fun at country folk and their lack of gentility, her affinity for them and for their forthright ways is manifest in her stories.

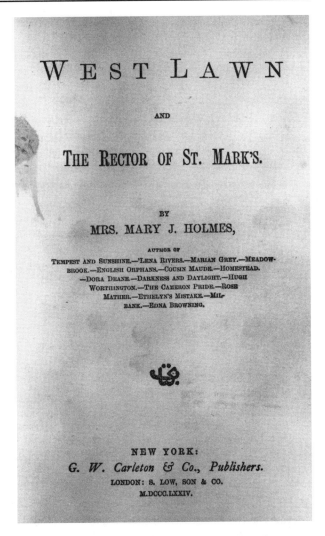

Title page for two of Holmes's melodramatic novels

By the close of the 1850s Holmes had a high profile in publishing circles, and her services as an author were sought by some of the industry's premier houses. In 1860 she granted serialization rights of her novels to Street and Smith, publishers of the *New York Weekly,* and lore has it that this contract saved Street and Smith from impending bankruptcy. Their first serialization of a Holmes story, *Marian Grey,* skyrocketed their subscription rates; other serializations proved equally profitable for both publisher and author. At the peak of her career Holmes reportedly made as much as $15,000 a year, a significant sum for any nineteenth-century writer, female or male. As another indication of her overwhelming success, three of her novels—*Tempest and Sunshine, 'Lena Rivers,* and *Dora Deane*—were adapted for the stage.

A later novel, *Rose Mather: A Tale of the War* (1868), stands out as one of Holmes's most complex and serious works. Set during the Civil War, the story follows the fortunes of the residents of Rockford, a quiet village in New York. Holmes focuses on the human cost of the war, depicting the suffering of the Rockford families as the war escalates and sons, husbands, and brothers begin to die. A composite of deftly crafted miniatures, *Rose Mather* depicts the bereavement and the terrors that stir around the firesides of the community; Holmes asks the reader to consider carefully, and with compassion, the personal tragedies of the Civil War rather than its historical import, its political implications, or its grand sweep of armies.

In a way, Holmes participates in a kind of literary photojournalism not so far removed from the gritty immediacy of a Matthew Brady pictorial. The well-known remark by a New York reporter on the work of Brady—"Mr. Brady has brought home the terrible earnestness of war. If he has not brought bodies and laid them in our dooryards, he has done something very like it"—applies equally well to Holmes. Like Brady, Holmes brings the terrible earnestness of war home and places the bodies, if not in the dooryards, then in the darkened parlors where mourners gather. In an especially powerful scene illustrating the impact of war on families, a soldier at the front cuts a lock of his hair with a bowie knife and sends it to his mother; the scene effectively captures the tension between violence and the better angels of human nature. Possibly her most fully realized work, *Rose Mather* maintains a sentimental tone while probing issues of real import, including questions of loyalty, class, the role of women in war, and morality in the context of affirmation and forgiveness.

Rose Mather was followed by a string of other stories, most of which deal with more commonplace themes, such as *Ethelyn's Mistake; or, The Home in the West* (1869), a tale of miscommunication between husband and wife that results in temporary separation, and *Christmas Stories* (1885), a collection intended for young readers. Another story from this period in Holmes's career, *West Lawn* (1874), explores the nature of love and its transforming force. The central characters in *West Lawn* are tested in the crucible of suffering and exalted by the power of love; by the end of the story each has been cast in a stronger, more resilient form. Dora, the novel's heroine, seeks the love of the good Dr. West, and through a series of moral trials she finally becomes worthy of him. Jessie, a young, hoydenish flirt, is sobered by her exposure to the tragedies in other people's lives, and when she responds with empathy, she becomes, in Holmesian terms, a complete woman.

West Lawn also has the requisite "great sin" that sparks so much of the action in a typical Holmes narrative. Robert West, the brother of Dora's bride-groom-elect, embezzles funds and then flees to California; his desertion of his family precipitates the insanity and eventual death of his wife. In a coincidence at which modern readers might scoff, Robert slips into a dangerous fever only to be saved at the last moment by the attending physician, who happens to be Dr. West, Robert's long-estranged brother. Dr. West heals Robert's soul as well as his body, for his forgiveness and affection, freely given, restores his wayward brother. To Holmes, love is not difficult to quantify because its manifestations are unmistakable and its ability to ennoble humankind is never in doubt.

Holmes made a few other departures from her standard plots. In 1880 she tried her hand at the Gothic narrative, producing *Chateau d'Or,* a dark tale of imprisonment, betrayal, and madness. In part Holmes uses this story, which is set in an appropriately gloomy castle located in an isolated region of the French countryside, to contrast American egalitarianism with European decadence. Like many of her generation, Holmes was intrigued by Continental culture but nevertheless regarded foreign customs and values with some suspicion. Accordingly, in *Chateau d'Or* she places an innocent New England girl in the clutches of an aristocratic, villainous Englishman with a history of dissipation; in this way she highlights Yankee democratic virtue against a backdrop of European ruin. As her heroine, Anna Strong, resolutely proclaims to a Frenchwoman with a less-than-virtuous past, "We are *all* nobility in America, or can be. We are all sovereigns by right." Anna's escape back to the United States and the sanctuary of her sleepy New England village drives home the idealistic point that, notwithstanding the attractions of foreign land, U.S. soil (and by extension, U.S. republicanism) is far superior.

Despite her voluminous outpouring of stories, Holmes found time to pursue other interests, leading a busy and varied life. She held leadership positions in several charitable and reform-minded organizations, including the Women's Christian Temperance Union, the Union Benevolent Society, and the Daughters of the American Revolution, and she helped establish and fund a parish house, a reading room, and a soup kitchen in Brockport. Known by her neighbors for her generosity, she supported several needy families in town and regularly tithed a sizeable portion of her income to her local church.

Moreover, despite the fact that her fiction has a homespun, almost provincial quality, Holmes was an accomplished traveler. She and her husband spent a part of every year, sometimes even two or three years at a time, traveling to such far-flung locales as Russia, Asia, Africa, Europe, and the American West; consequently, Brown Cottage became more and more filled with curios gathered from those extended jaunts around the world. The types of souvenirs she collected indicate just how extensive those travels were: according to Helen Waite Papashvily in *All the Happy Endings* (1956), Holmes decorated Brown Cottage with such curiosities as "a stone from Mars Hill, Egyptian candlesticks, a mosaic table, a Swiss music box, a piano cover embroidered by nuns, Savonarola's chair for the study and a totem pole for the front lawn."

In between writing novels and seeing the world, Holmes diligently responded to the voluminous fan mail received from devoted readers. Little of her correspondence survives, but the following note is representative of the kind of personal attention she regularly bestowed on her fans. Holmes dashed off the letter, dated 1889, from her room at the Hotel Bellevue in Paris:

> Your letter was a long time in finding me—as I have been abroad more than a year and have recently been moving rapidly from place to place—this will account for my delay in answering your request for some thought or sentiment with which to adorn your galley—alas I have neither the one nor the other—and if I even had them they would be quite blotted out by the excitement of Paris—the Exposition—the Eiffel Tower . . . ! My autograph . . . I send you with pleasure.

While the letter makes evident Holmes's reluctance to supply her admirer with a canned "sentiment" with which to "adorn" his "galley," it also reveals the easy, familiar tone she adopted with her fans and her willingness to grant them an autograph. Indeed, according to those who knew her well, her benevolence and amiability were salient characteristics of her personality; for example, after her death, her longtime housekeeper described Holmes as "slender, tall, with a little stoop to hide it, curly hair and a false fringe she ordered by mail from Chicago, violet eyes, a sweet mouth . . . she loved everybody and everybody loved her."

Clearly, the fact that Holmes had an established, loyal constituency of readers is a large part of the reason why her novels continued to sell even into the last decades of the century, when the vogue of the sentimental novel had been usurped by the ascendancy of literary realism. To some extent the stories she published during the latter half of the century represent the last gasp of a dying genre; her particular brand of fiction provided a nostalgic, if moribund, refuge for readers who clung to an outdated romantic idealism. Even so, it would be a mistake to dismiss the stories Holmes wrote between 1870 and 1905 as mere leftovers from a bygone era. For instance, throughout her career Holmes consistently frames her version of the sentimental in terms of female ambition, and her recognition that women had a public as well as a private side con-

verged with the philosophy of the burgeoning women's rights movement, which achieved national prominence during the last years of the century. In this respect her stories were as socially relevant near the turn of the century as they were during the 1850s and 1860s.

Female self-actualization is the dominant theme in the semi-autobiographical tale "The Spring Farm" (collected in *Mrs. Hallam's Companion,* 1896), a short story featuring a girl whose primary goal in life is publication: "you . . . will be proud to say you knew me once," she confides to a friend, "when the people praise the book I am going to write." Maude Graham does indeed write the book, and her marriage soon after to the man of her dreams only enhances what already is a gratifyingly creative and productive life. Nor does marriage put an end to Maude's career as a writer. In contrast to most nineteenth-century sentimental novels, in which wifehood supercedes vocation, the final line in "The Spring Farm" hints at future publications for Maude: "Whether she will ever write another book we do not know, probably she will, for where the brain seeds have taken root it is hard to dislodge them." Holmes was not a visible, vocal proponent of women's rights in political arenas, yet "The Spring Farm," like her other stories, promotes a wider sphere for women than merely the domestic.

Another factor that contributed to Holmes's longevity as a writer was her awareness of, and sensitivity to, the changing climate of the American scene. For example, in one of her last novels, *The Merivale Banks* (1903), Holmes explores the foibles and moral contradictions of the Gilded Age, an era furnished with "city-made toilets" and decorated with the livery of servants to the newly rich. She establishes the theme of the story—the detrimental effects of unchecked capitalism—with her opening sentence: "There were two of them: the First National, familiarly known as the White Bank, and a private bank, known as the Grey Bank, and they stood side by side in the same imposing block, with marble front and massive doors of oak, and broad granite steps." The story follows the rise and fall of the fortunes of the two families who own the banks, the Whites and the Greys. The Whites are the "first family" of Merivale, and in keeping with their aristocratic pretensions they are haughty, elitist, and self-fascinated. In contrast, the Greys are upstarts with humble origins. Former tenement dwellers, they have parlayed a modest, initial success into a thriving banking business; even so, they remain immune to the false lure of "new money" ostentation.

The central character is Louise Grey, the young daughter of Mr. Grey, the banker. Louise is a standard Holmesian heroine: the moral exemplar of the tale, she dresses simply, acts prudently, and, in the end, loves wisely. Louise is nature personified, in all its beauty and pleasing proportions; she even learns to sing directly from the birds that visit her garden. Holmes is guilty of belaboring the nature analogy, but she does not want readers to miss the point: Louise is the only harmonious voice in the cacophony of pretense and duplicity wrought by the communal lust for wealth.

The disclosure of her father's dubious past as a professional gambler, and his eventual bankruptcy, sullies her not at all; she rises above her father's sins on the strength of her character. At the close of the story Louise is orphaned, subject to a broken engagement, and removed to Europe; however, all these displacements are offset by the attentions of a lover who anonymously purchases her former home in her name. This act of charity, untainted by the desire for personal gain, identifies Fred Lansing as the perfect mate for Louise. Their marriage not only represents a union of like-minded souls, it also highlights the theme of the novel: real prosperity consists of a shared moral health and mutual respect uncontaminated by "the disease of speculation." What abides for Holmes in the world of fleeting acquisition is the timelessness and truth of moral rectitude.

Holmes published her last works, the novel *Lucy Harding: A Romance of Russia* and a dual volume combining two novellas, *The Abandoned Farm* and *Connie's Mistake,* in 1905, just two years before her death on 6 October 1907 at the age of eighty-two. Although modern critics have disparaged Holmes for the provincialism of her moral view, her stories are best remembered as visionary imagings of female potential; she attempted through her stories to carve out stronger positions for women, albeit within traditionally subordinate roles. Moreover, she served as a spokesperson for her generation and espoused a philosophy, based on an ethic of steadfastness tempered with empathy, that many nineteenth-century Americans embraced. Putting questions of literary value aside, one fact remains indisputable: Mary Jane Holmes was an instrumental figure in the production of nineteenth-century American sentimental literature and culture.

References:

Nina Baym, *Women's Fiction: A Guide to Novels by and about Women in America, 1820–1870,* second edition (Chicago: University of Illinois Press, 1993), pp. 188–197;

Lucy Brashear, "The Novels of Mary Jane Holmes: Education for Wifehood," in *Nineteenth-Century Women Writers of the English-Speaking World,* edited by Rhoda B. Nathan (New York: Greenwood Press, 1986), pp. 19–25;

Barbara J. McGuire, "The Orphan's Grief: Transformational Tears and the Maternal Fetish in Mary Jane Holmes's *Dora Deane; or, the East-India Uncle,*" *Legacy,* 15, no. 2 (1998): 171–187;

Arch Merrill, *Gaslights and Gingerbread* (New York: American Book-Stratford, 1959), pp. 36–45;

Helen Waite Papashvily, *All the Happy Endings: A Study of the Domestic Novel, the Women Who Wrote It, the Women Who Read It, in the Nineteenth Century* (New York: Harper, 1956), pp. 148–152;

Fred Lewis Pattee, *The Feminine Fifties* (New York: Appleton-Century, 1940), pp. 124–125.

Papers:

No collection of Mary Jane Holmes's papers exists; what papers remain are scattered throughout the holdings of various libraries, including the American Antiquarian Society library, the University of Virginia, and the Bienecke Rare Book and Manuscript Library at Yale.

Alice James
(7 August 1848 – 6 March 1892)

Kristin Boudreau
University of Georgia

BOOK: *The Diary of Alice James* (Private printing, Cambridge, Mass.: John Wilson & Son, 1894); republished as *Alice James: Her Brothers—Her Journal,* edited by Anna Robeson Burr (New York: Dodd, Mead, 1934); first unexpurgated edition, *The Diary of Alice James,* edited, with an introduction, by Leon Edel (New York: Dodd, Mead, 1964; London: Hart-Davis, 1965).

In 1894 novelist Henry James and psychologist William James exchanged letters concerning four privately published copies of a diary written by their sister, Alice, who had died two years earlier at the age of forty-three. Although a brilliant conversationalist and an avid reader with a sharply satirical mind, Alice James would have been remembered, if at all, only as the tragically ill younger sister in a famous American family had her diary not been rescued from obscurity. Though he admired the wit and intelligence of his sister's observations, however, Henry feared that the diary might find its way into print without first being carefully edited. Many of his own remarks about other people emerged in his sister's diary, and the novelist, by then famous, shuddered to think that his words had not been kept private. As he wrote to William, "I was terribly scared and disconcerted—I mean alarmed—by the sight of so many private names & allusions in print. I am still terrified by this—as I partly feel responsible as it were—being myself the source of so many of the things told, commented on &c." Recognizing the literary value of the diary, the novelist preferred "to *edit* the volume with a few eliminations of text & dissimulations of names, give it to the world & then carefully burn with fire our own 4 copies."

Though Henry's plan was not fully executed—all but his own copy survived—the road to eventual publication was circuitous. Katherine Loring, Alice's longtime companion and the only other person besides her nurse to know about the volume during her lifetime, understood that her friend had wanted the diary to be published someday, and she began by printing copies

Alice James

for herself and James's three remaining siblings. In 1934, using the original volume, Anna Robeson Burr published *Alice James: Her Brothers—Her Journal,* which included a heavily edited version of the diary. In 1964 Leon Edel restored the original names, punctuation, and newspaper clippings to the diary and republished it in its entirety. This volume established Alice James as an important figure in American letters.

Begun in May 1889 to help James deal with her oppressive solitude, the diary spans only the last years of her life, coming to a halt in March 1892, when she died of breast cancer. To learn more about her life, one must consult the copious and detailed family letters and Jean Strouse's 1980 biography. Because of the inveterate wanderlust that Henry James Sr. passed on to his children, the Jameses were often on the move. They corresponded faithfully with friends and family during their separations, however, and many of these letters still survive.

Alice James was born on 7 August 1848 in New York City, the youngest child and only daughter of Henry James Sr. and Mary Walsh James. Besides William and Henry, her older brothers included Garth Wilkinson (Wilky) and Robertson, who might also have been forgotten by history had they not served as officers in the first black regiments of the Civil War. (In 1863 Wilky was wounded in the attack on Fort Wagner led by Colonel Robert Gould Shaw.) Between 1855, when the six-year-old Alice accompanied her family to Europe for a three-year tour, and 1866, when the Jameses finally settled permanently in Cambridge, Massachusetts, the family had lived a year in Geneva; two years in Newport, Rhode Island; several months in Boston; and two years in Cambridge, where the older boys enrolled at Harvard. James later recalled her youth as "our rootless & accidental childhood."

James's education was also haphazard. The three-year visit to Europe, intended as an educational experiment for the four boys, turned out, the father confessed, to be a "chief disappointment . . . in regard to Alice, who intellectually, socially, and physically has been at a great disadvantage compared with home." Upon the family's return to Newport, Alice was enrolled in a girls' school, only to have her studies interrupted a year later when the Jameses set sail again for Europe. Returning to New England in 1860, Henry and William attended college while Wilky and Robertson enrolled at an experimental coeducational school in Concord. Although New England was the center of educational innovation in the United States, Henry James Sr. kept his daughter at home rather than taking advantage of the intellectual offerings nearby.

James never occupied the traditional role of wife and mother. Unlike many New England women of her time—such as the reformer Elizabeth Peabody, whom James knew during the 1860s; Louisa May Alcott, a family friend who earned her living as a teacher, governess, and writer; and Loring, who eventually crusaded to open Harvard University to women—James was ill-equipped to live the less traditional life of an unmarried woman. As she wrote to a friend in 1876, "Matrimony seems the only successful occupation that a woman can undertake."

Many historians and critics have ascribed James's lifelong invalidism to her need to find an "occupation" of some kind. Though her brother Henry never married, he made a rich intellectual and social life for himself in Europe, with his social life often finding its way into his novels. William James acquired both a family and a career. Alice, the story goes, made a career out of being ill. The origin of this account can be found in the claims of the Jameses themselves. Repeatedly in her diary and letters, James refers to her invalidism as if it were her profession. In 1891, facing her impending death, she writes of Henry's and William's accomplishments for the year: "Within the last year he has published *The Tragic Muse,* brought out *The American,* and written a play, *Mrs. Vibert* . . . and his admirable comedy; combined with William's *Psychology,* not a bad show for one family! especially if I get myself dead, the hardest job of all." As Henry wrote years after his sister's death, "in our family group girls seemed scarcely to have had a chance." James's "tragic health was, in a manner, the only solution for her of the practical problem of life."

James can be considered a career invalid in the sense that she was subject to nervous attacks throughout her life and was almost completely bedridden during the years covered by her diary, from 1889 to 1892. Judging by family letters, her earliest illnesses seem to have begun sometime in 1861. Those letters tell the story of a series of breakdowns throughout her life, particularly in response to emotional traumas. Though James seems to have suffered episodes of minor nervousness frequently throughout her life, her first major collapse occurred in 1868, when she was nineteen years old. Another serious breakdown, following the news of William's engagement, took place in 1878. James was too ill to attend the wedding, and years later (a month before her death) she recalled the episode as the beginning of her lifelong renunciation of a more active life: "The fact is, I have been dead so long and it has been simply such a grim shoving of the hours behind me as I faced a ceaseless possible horror, since that hideous summer of '78, when I went down to the deep sea, its dark waters closed over me and I knew neither hope nor peace; that now it's only the shrivelling of an empty pea pod that has to be completed." In these reflections James often indicated that her life was largely defined by her invalidism.

In this regard James was typical of many women of her time. The institutions that sprang up during the nineteenth century in response to hysteria, neurasthenia, and other psychosomatic disorders suggest what social historians have since confirmed: that nervous illnesses tormented many people, most of them middle- and upper-class white women such as James, and demanded large sums of money and stretches of time in treatment. In 1866 James traveled to New York City to receive motorpathic treatments. In the following years she was also treated with massage, electrotherapy, and sulfuric ether. In 1879 and 1880 Loring accompanied James on a series of convalescent trips to the Adirondack Mountains and the New England countryside. In 1883, finding herself alone after the death of her parents, James suffered steady decline and spent several months in two separate institutions, experimenting with a rest cure, an exercise cure, and electrical currents intended to stimulate the muscles.

In 1884, frustrated with her attempts at recovery, James sailed for London, where she made her home for the rest of her life. Now in her late thirties, she still suffered from the nervousness that had haunted her since adolescence. She also experienced more readily diagnosed disorders, including rheumatism, gout, a bad back, and weak knees. A serious breakdown in 1890 prompted the return of Loring, who stayed with James until her death. By this time James understood that her life consisted primarily of pain and dependence, and she wished fervently to die. The possibility of death, she wrote, "is most cheering to all parties—the only drawback being that it will probably be in my sleep so that I shall not be one of the audience, dreadful fraud! a creature who has been denied all dramatic episodes might be allowed, I think, to assist at her extinction." After a lifetime of suffering, James rejoiced at the discovery of breast cancer in 1891. She died in her Kensington house on 6 March 1892. Her body was cremated and her ashes returned to the United States, where a monument was erected in the family plot of the Cambridge cemetery. William James chose an inscription from Dante:

ed essa da martiro
e da essilo venne a questa pace

(From martyrdom and exile
she came to this peace.)

Though it may be tempting to see in this career invalid a life that consisted only of exile and martyrdom, James herself often rejected such an account. As she wrote to William in the months preceding her death, she did not wish to be regarded merely as one who had failed to achieve a fuller life. "When I am gone," she wrote, "pray don't think of me simply as a creature who might have been something else, had neurotic science been born." Toward the end of her life she issued this reflection in her diary: "the only thing which survives is the resistance we bring to life and not the strain life brings to us."

James in 1862

Looking back on her life, one can see evidence of such resistance, not merely to her fatally ill constitution but to the social problems around her. James's youthful social activities later developed into a profound political consciousness. As a girl she joined the Newport Women's Aid Society, which employed women to sew shirts and cut bandages for Union soldiers. Later, in Cambridge, she joined a sewing bee that was originally established as part of the war effort but later turned its energies toward the relief of the poor. James served as president of that society in the 1870s. In 1868 she and her mother joined the Female Humane Society for the relief of sick and poor women. During the late 1870s she was a member of the Society to Encourage Studies at Home, an organization dedicated to female education. Though her own education had been odd and random, James had read widely (often on the recommendations of her learned brothers), had attended lectures, and had indulged her political interests by reading *The Nation*. In 1875 she was invited to teach history for the Society to Encourage Studies at Home, and in doing so she began a lifelong friendship with Loring, then head of history for the society. In all of these experiences, James was awakening to a political consciousness that set her apart from her brothers.

James's other form of resistance was the diary itself. She had begun keeping a commonplace book in 1886, which she eventually abandoned for a record of her own reflections. In the spring of 1889, finding herself alone at Leamington Spa, she filled a page with this announcement: "I think that if I get into the habit of writing a bit about what happens, or rather doesn't happen, I may lose a little of the sense of loneliness and desolation which abides with me. . . . I shall at least have it all my own way and it may bring relief as an outlet to that geyser of emotions, sensations, speculations and reflections which ferments perpetually within my poor old carcass for its sins; so here goes, my first Journal!" The diary continued even when her loneliness must have abated, after the return of Loring and during the frequent visits of Henry. James's other reasons for writing are clear in the context of her life during those London years: confined to her room and to only brief visits, she felt existence limited by her invalidism and sought to enrich it with private reflections. "If I can get on to my sofa and occupy myself for four hours, at intervals, thro' the day," she wrote, "scribbling my notes and able to read the books that belong to me, in that they clarify the density and shape the formless mass within, Life seems inconceivably rich." At the same time, she was susceptible to extreme nervousness and therefore forced to contain the "geyser of emotions" within her. As she wrote after the moving experience of rereading the letters of her parents, who had been dead for eight years, "I think if I try a little and give it form its vague intensity will take limits to itself, and the 'divine anguish' of the myriad memories stirred grow less." For James, the definite shaping of otherwise formless impressions meant that even a bedridden and nervous invalid could look life in the face and not be shattered by her powerful responses. The diary records her repeated concessions to nervousness but never at the expense of a rich intellectual life.

"How grateful I am," she wrote on one occasion, "that I actually do *see*, to my own consciousness, the quarter of an inch that my eyes fall upon; truly, the subject is all that counts!" The diary reveals a woman who, though never far from the struggles of illness, enjoyed a rich inner life. She noted that her impressions were worthy of a James: "H., by the way, has embedded in his pages many pearls fallen from my lips, which he steals in the most unblushing way, saying, simply, that he knew they had been said by the family, so it did not matter." For his part, Henry later wrote that his sister's "talk, her company, her association and admirable acute mind and large spirit were so much the best thing I have, of late years, known here."

James's interest in "the resistance we bring to life" prompted her to look feelingly upon the struggles of all victims in a measure never approached by her siblings. Though both William and Henry demonstrated an aversion to human and political tyranny, James wrote movingly about the struggles of women, paupers, the working class, and, most persistently, the Irish, whose fight for Home Rule occupied her attention until her death. Her sympathy may well have been motivated by her affinity and admiration for suffering beings. "What *is* living in this deadness called life," she wrote, "is the struggle of the creature in the grip of its inheritance and against the consequences of its acts." Though she may have found suffering tragically noble, she applauded resistance and was impatient with complacency.

Her reflections on the English class system vary between anger at an unyielding hierarchy, concern for the suffering masses, and occasional irritation at their inability to rise up against their oppression. She returns frequently to the theme of family life among the poor and working classes, responding to the addition of an infant to an already large family as "one more tiny voice to swell the vast human wail rising perpetually to the skies!" and wincing over the practice of the rich to make their servants sleep in the scullery. Some of her most vehement tirades are directed against what she considered a peculiarly English breed of upper-class barbarism and the submissiveness of the poor in response: "It's this vast class in England, the only nation where it exists, which like the crying dog is ready to lick the hand that chastises, that gives you in time what you expect so little at first, a sense of unmanliness." James's contempt at such moments is matched only by her swelling pride when her favored class stood up to the wealthy, as during the London workers' strikes of 1890: "Could anything," she rhapsodized, "exhibit more beautifully the solidarity of the race than that by simply combining to walk thro' the streets on the same day, these starvelings should make Emperors, Kings, Presidents and millionaires tremble the world over!"

James also followed international events in *The Nation*. In the summer of 1889, an armed force of dervishes (nomadic Mohammedan friars), advancing toward Egypt, were killed when the British army cut off their water supply in the desert and then fired upon

James and Katherine Loring at Leamington Spa, England, in 1889 or 1890

them. The attacks continued through August, at which point James offered a brief, ironic protest in her diary: "*We* have just, with 'great valour and skill,' annihilated 1,500 more Dervishes, a 'brilliant victory.' After seven hours of fighting the starved naked wretches were cut to pieces." Several years before her brother William began writing and speaking against imperialism, James recoiled from demonstrations of political power.

The "view of the vanquished" became more painful to James as she watched the unfolding drama of Irish Home Rule. As Henry exclaimed after reading her diary, "she was really an Irishwoman!" Her lineage as the granddaughter of an Irish immigrant probably influenced her political stance less than her instinctive loathing of all imperialist enterprises, her sympathy for victims, and her aversion to English society. "But the absolute want of humour in the Briton at large is the secret of the Irish question," she remarked. In spite of such attacks, her Irishness was not mere Anglophobia, nor was it entirely uncritical. She responded exuberantly to the successful defense of Charles Stewart Parnell against charges that he had written letters condoning the Phoenix Park murders in 1882, and when she acquired Sir Charles Russell's speech on the case, she pasted the most moving excerpts in her diary. When Parnell, named correspondent in an adultery

divorce suit, refused to resign his seat, however, James "wept over" the "portent of the possible death and burial of Home Rule." She mournfully prepared to turn her back on the Irish question: "if tomorrow the Irish pronounce for him one's ear must turn itself, one's heart close itself against the woes of that tragic land."

The fate of Ireland tormented the susceptible James, who in 1890 recognized her physical vulnerability to Irish politics. As her cancer progressed and her bodily pains encroached upon her mind, however, she found herself less swayed by the political concerns that had once so moved her. She was not unconcerned with the Irish, but after May 1891, when her breast cancer was discovered, James's diary turned more frequently to the other drama that occupied her, that of her deteriorating body.

Like the political turmoil around her, James's invalidism provided her with rich material for reflection, and her habitual irony prevented her from seeing her own demise in terms of self-pity. The sympathy generated for suffering races and classes is only rarely directed inward, and then ironically, as one episode demonstrates. Comparing her rich intellectual life to the mundane tasks of the nurse who was slipping a petticoat over her head, she remarked, "'Oh! Nurse, don't you wish you were inside of *me!*'—her look of dismay and vehement disclaimer—'Inside of you, Miss, when you have just had a sick head-ache for five days!'—gave a greater blow to my vanity, than that much battered article has ever received." While William was exploring his philosophy of mind, James was discovering what her invalidism revealed about relations between individuals. The many visitors to her sick chamber taught her to reflect upon the inescapable transformation from subject to object in the presence of an audience. James discovered, likewise, that she was just as susceptible to the same imaginative rewriting of her associates. How surprising, she noted, when "reason shows you that you have endowed the creature out of your own consciousness, with all sorts of qualities and decencies which she never pretended to have, and that, just as the ignorant perceive and observe nothing, because there are no germs within, inherited or acquired, we, with our exotic perceptions, fancy we discover in the coarsest weeds possibilities of the fairest bloom and feel wronged when we are pricked by the thorns and stung by the nettles."

One of James's most important contributions in her diary concerns this reevaluation of human relations, particularly in the confrontation between weak and strong. Repeatedly, she praises the conduct of Henry, whose sympathy is both genuine and understated. "But he has always been the same since I can remember and has almost as strongly as Father that personal susceptibility—what can one call it, it seems as if it were a matter of the scarfskin, as if they perceived thro' that your mood and were saved thereby from rubbing you raw with their theory of it, or blindness to it." James's inclusion of the "theory" of suffering alongside "blindness to it" may seem curious at first. People sufficiently observant of the pains of others to compose a theory might, one would think, offer some balm for the pain. A lifetime of invalidism, however, had taught James that these theories of suffering—what she ironically called "our exotic perceptions"—tell more about the observer than the object. Though she wrote often against blindness to the pains of others, James was also wary of the sympathy that can transform an object into something more palatable for the observer. In remarking on her own illness and demise, James was well aware that the normal consolations of sympathetic visitors offered no relief for her: "all longing for fulfillment, all passion to achieve has died down within me and whether the great Mystery resolves itself into eternal Death or Glorious Life, I contemplate either with equal serenity. It is that the long ceaseless strain and tension have worn out all aspiration save the one for Rest!"

James's absolute refusal to see herself in the terms provided by her sympathetic spectators makes for a curious reversal in her diary. After her breakdown of 1890 she longed earnestly to die, and the most tragic notes in the diary are sounded in the moments when her "mortuary moment" was postponed. "Ah, woe, woe is me!" she writes, acknowledging her partial recovery, which she called a "dreary snail-like climb up a little way so as to be able to run down again!" Yet, she was also capable of presenting the discovery of her cancer in a jubilant tone: "To him who waits, all things come! . . . I have been going downhill at a steady trot; so they sent for Sir Andrew Clark four days ago, and the blessed being has endowed me not only with cardiac complications, but says that a lump that I have had in one of my breasts for three months, which has given me a great deal of pain, is a tumour, that nothing can be done for me but to alleviate pain, that it is only a question of time, etc." In the comic tradition, a resolution occurs when the heroine overcomes a longstanding obstacle and is reunited with the longed-for object. Here, James presents death as a substitution for marital union, exclaiming that her "aspirations . . . have . . . been brilliantly fulfilled." Nor are her words entirely ironic, for cancer presents her with a passage out of the void between death and recovery. In case her readers refuse to relinquish their sentimental notions about the pathos of this discovery, James explains patiently, and without a trace of irony, that she will gladly conclude this lifelong struggle: "To any one who has not been there, it will be hard to understand the enormous relief of Sir A. C.'s uncompromising verdict, lifting us out the formless vague and setting us within the very heart of the sustaining concrete."

If readers have difficulty with the tone of the diary, it may be because James breaks many familiar conventions. The biting political observations issued by a dying woman may seem out of place since the narratives of James's time reinvented the invalid as a being too good for this world, a representative of Christian martyrdom. The nearly uninterrupted ironic voice may unsettle readers accustomed to the more popular perspective of sentimental nineteenth-century accounts of illness and death. The caustic remarks about sympathy all but destroy any impulse on the part of the reader to regard the author sentimentally, and consequently one may be at a loss as to how to regard her at all. One clue to James's tone may be found in a letter written by William to his wife, in which he describes his impressions of his sister after a five-year separation. For William, his only contact with James had been through letters, which shared with the diary her characteristically satiric voice, a voice that William had considered shrill and unyielding. Briefly reunited with James in 1889, however, William discovered that her irony was "uttered in the softest most laughing way in the world" and gave "an entirely different impression."

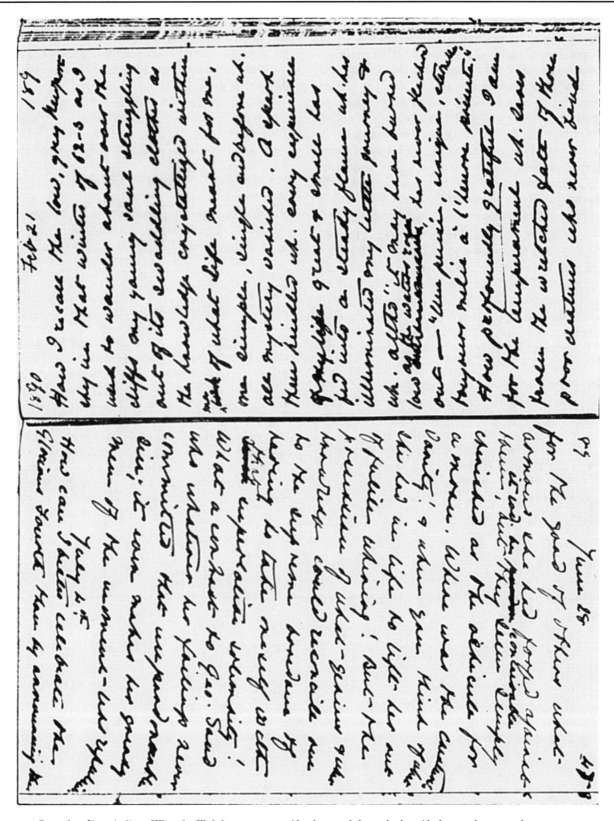

Pages from James's diary. When she filled the pages on one side, she turned the notebook upside down and wrote on the verso pages
(Collection of Alice James Vaux).

There are occasional moments in the diary where James lays aside her irony to write with more-apparent softness. Though her "little Nurse," Emily Bradfield, is the subject of many satirical episodes, she also features in a brief but touching passage. In the past, James asserts, she feared what would become of her when her parents died, "and here was the answer to my doubting heart, a little girl then toddling about a Gloucester village, was, in a foreign land, to hold out her hand to my necessity, perform all kind offices, and give me an ever deeper sense of the exquisite truth that human good outweighs all human evil, and that only from amidst the clouds shines out the true illumination."

James registers a slight misgiving toward the end of both life and work: "I am sorry for you all, for I feel as if I hadn't even yet given my message. I would there were more bursts of enthusiasm, less of the carping tone, through this, but I fear it comes by nature, and after all, the excellent Islander will ne'er be crushed by the knowledge of the eye that was upon him, through the long length of years, and the monotone of the enthusiast is more wearisome to sustain than the dyspeptic note."

Alice James was neither enthusiastic nor dyspeptic. Her long years of invalidism left her with a distaste for the sentimentalism so common among nineteenth-century reformers and novelists. She retained a profound compassion for suffering creatures, however, and, in spite of her own suffering, a vigorous sense of humor to the last.

Letters:

The Death and Letters of Alice James, edited by Ruth Bernard Yeazell (Berkeley & Los Angeles: University of California Press, 1981);

Her Life in Letters, edited by Linda Anderson (Bristol, U.K.: Thoemmes, 1996).

Biography:

Jean Strouse, *Alice James: A Biography* (Boston: Houghton Mifflin, 1980).

References:

R. W. B. Lewis, *The Jameses: A Family Narrative* (New York: Farrar, Straus & Giroux, 1991);

F. O. Matthiessen, *The James Family* (New York: Knopf, 1947).

Papers:

Most of Alice James's letters are housed in the Houghton Library, Harvard University. James's correspondence with her friend Annie Ashburner Richards is in the National Library of Scotland, Edinburgh. Several other letters are owned by the Schlesinger Library, Radcliffe College; the Pierpont Morgan Library; and the Colby College Library. Several letters to James's relatives are owned by Mr. and Mrs. Henry James Vaux of Berkeley, California. The original handwritten volumes of James's diary, along with her commonplace book, have been passed down through Robertson James's descendants and now belong to his great-granddaughter, Alice James Vaux of Portland, Oregon.

Sarah Orne Jewett

(3 September 1849 – 24 June 1909)

Melanie Kisthardt
West Chester University

See also the Jewett entries in *DLB 12: American Realists and Naturalists* and *DLB 74: American Short-Story Writers Before 1880.*

BOOKS: *Deephaven* (Boston: Osgood, 1877; London: Osgood, McIlvane, 1893);

Playdays: A Book of Stories for Children (Boston: Houghton, Osgood, 1878);

Old Friends and New (Boston: Houghton, Osgood, 1879);

Country By-Ways (Boston: Houghton, Mifflin, 1881; London: Trübner, 1882);

The Mate of the Daylight, and Friends Ashore (Boston & New York: Houghton, Mifflin, 1884);

A Country Doctor (Boston & New York: Houghton, Mifflin, 1884);

A Marsh Island (Boston & New York: Houghton, Mifflin, 1885);

A White Heron and Other Stories (Boston & New York: Houghton, Mifflin, 1886);

The Story of the Normans, Told Chiefly in Relation to Their Conquest of England (New York & London: Putnam, 1887);

The King of Folly Island and Other People (Boston & New York: Houghton, Mifflin, 1888; London: Duckworth, 1903);

Betty Leicester: A Story for Girls (Boston & New York: Houghton, Mifflin, 1890);

Strangers and Wayfarers (Boston & New York: Houghton, Mifflin, 1890; London: Osgood, McIlvane, 1891);

A Native of Winby and Other Tales (Boston & New York: Houghton, Mifflin, 1893);

Betty Leicester's English Xmas: A New Chapter of An Old Story (Baltimore: Privately printed, 1894; revised as *Betty Leicester's Christmas* (Boston & New York: Houghton, Mifflin, 1899);

The Life of Nancy (Boston & New York: Houghton, Mifflin, 1895; London: Longmans, Green, 1895);

The Country of the Pointed Firs (Boston & New York: Houghton, Mifflin, 1896; London: Unwin, 1896);

The Queen's Twin and Other Stories (Boston & New York: Houghton, Mifflin, 1899; London: Smith, Elder, 1900);

The Tory Lover (Boston & New York: Houghton, Mifflin, 1901; London: Smith, Elder, 1901);

An Empty Purse: A Christmas Story (Boston: Privately printed, 1905);

Verses, edited by M. A. DeWolfe Howe (Boston: Privately printed, 1916);

The Country of the Pointed Firs, and Other Stories, selected and arranged, with a preface by Willa Cather (Garden City, N.Y.: Doubleday, 1927; London: Cape, 1927);

The Uncollected Short Stories of Sarah Orne Jewett, edited by Richard Cary (Waterville, Maine: Colby College Press, 1971);

The Irish Tales of Sarah Orne Jewett, edited by Jack Morgan and Louis A. Renza (Carbondale: Southern Illinois University Press, 1996).

Collections: *Tales of New England* (Boston & New York: Houghton, Mifflin, 1890; London: Osgood, McIlvane, 1893);

Stories and Tales, 7 volumes (Boston & New York: Houghton, Mifflin, 1910);

The Best Stories of Sarah Orne Jewett, 2 volumes, edited by Willa Cather (Boston: Houghton Mifflin, 1925);

The World of Dunnet Landing: A Sarah Orne Jewett Collection, edited by David Bonnell Green (Lincoln: University of Nebraska Press, 1962);

Novels and Stories (New York: Literary Classics, 1996).

"Don't try to write *about* people and things, tell them just as they are." Sarah Orne Jewett quoted this advice from her father in one of her few nonfiction articles, "Looking Back on Girlhood," first published in the 7 January 1892 issue of *Youth's Companion* and later included in *The Uncollected Short Stories of Sarah Orne Jewett* (1971). Jewett often repeated this suggestion to novice writers, and it lies at the core of her aesthetic, "imaginative realism." She attributed her capacity for keen observation, joy in simple things, and impatience with affectation and insincerity to her father's influence. Knowledge of human nature and attention to detail served Jewett well throughout her career, but her sketches of country life reveal more than chronicling a waning culture. Her themes transcend "local color" and speak to generations of readers about the value of community and the nurturing wisdom of women, more than one hundred years after *The Country of the Pointed Firs* (1896).

The second of three daughters, Theodora Sarah Orne Jewett was born on 3 September 1849 in South Berwick, Maine, to Caroline F. Perry and Dr. Theodore H. Jewett. She grew up with extended family in her paternal grandfather's home, where she developed the habit of reading writers as diverse as Laurence Sterne, Henry Fielding, Tobias Smollett, Jane Austen, and Harriet Beecher Stowe. The family's circumstances were comfortable. Her paternal grandfather was a prosperous retired sea captain, and her maternal grandfather was a physician (with whom her father interned).

Jewett's formal education was erratic because she suffered from rheumatism, for which her physician father recommended being outdoors. She was allowed much freedom to romp and explore her surroundings; being still as a "good" girl might was anathema to her. She also accompanied her father on his rounds. While her illness was serious—and continued to plague her throughout her life—another factor in her inconsistent schooling is revealed in her admission that she succumbed to "instant drooping" when "shut up in school." Jewett did, however, attend the Berwick Academy from 1861 to 1865, graduating three years before publishing "Jenny Garrow's Lovers" in *The Flag of Our Union* under the pseudonym A. C. Eliot. In later years Jewett never acknowledged this conventionally melodramatic and romantic story, which was eventually republished in *The Uncollected Short Stories of Sarah Orne Jewett.* Her next endeavor, "Mr. Bruce," while also about a courtship, shows signs of the new writer's talent for re-creating the tone and tempo of oral storytelling, and she eventually collected "Mr. Bruce" in *Old Friends and New* (1879). After the story was published in the December 1869 issue of *The Atlantic Monthly,* Jewett immediately regretted acting on her sister Mary's advice to acknowledge to her family that she was the author. She recorded in her diary that once her family knew of her ambitions, the story "no longer belonged all to me."

Initially reticent about going public, by 1873 Jewett had begun to seek professional advice about her writing, even as she articulated her own views about the shape of her fiction. An 1873 letter to the editor Horace Scudder combines deference to literary authority and determination about the direction her fiction should take. Jewett referred to her sketches as experiments written with little thought and care and coyly asked, "What's to be done with such a girl?" Despite such coyness, Jewett also told Scudder in a straightforward manner that she could not write a long story, as the renowned editor and author William Dean Howells had suggested. Rather than the usual magazine stories, she preferred to write "the sketchy kind" as long as editors would accept them and people would read them. Twenty-three years later, Jewett wrote to her friend Rose Lamb, "story-writing is always experimental," emphasizing "one's own method" rather than trying to meet the expectations of editors. In 1908 Jewett gave similar advice to the struggling Willa Cather: "Don't try to write the kind of short story that this or that magazine wants—write the truth, and let them take it or leave it. . . . Make a way of your own. If that way happens to be new, don't let that frighten you." In her insistence on the experimental, Jewett anticipates modernist foregrounding of character and psychological reality over linear plot.

Jewett admired the talent of Mary Murfree, another "local-color" writer, for creating a "good big Harper's story." Contrasting her style to Murfree's, Jewett observed that her own stories were getting progressively shorter over the years, joking that they might soon be "the size of old-fashioned peppermints, and have neither beginning or end, but shape and flavor may still be left them." Her style subordinates linear plot to detail, characterization, and episode, focusing on humanity, especially on the external "trivialities and commonplaces" that reveal characters' inner lives. Jewett's preference for writing "sketchy" stories may result from the "flash" of inspiration she attributed to her observations of people, a skill she developed early in life when she followed her father on his rounds and sat quietly as he worked. Whether an idea for a story came to her while she was bored in church or waiting for a train, stories "bewitched" her, and Jewett's letters include frequent references to her "seasons of writing," and the impulsive nature of her writing. Allusions to the creative process became recurrent motifs in her fiction. From her self-proclaimed vantage point between "high" and "low" literature she asserted that her stories were often inspired by actual people and/or events and that she revised little. Yet, before putting pen to paper, Jewett often mulled over the seed for a story, sometimes for years. In a Jewett story nothing may happen in the traditional sense, while the depth of characterization sheds light on the creativity and emotions of the characters. Establishing a middle ground for her fiction may actually have allowed Jewett more freedom to experiment with form, and her deliberate and frequent articulation of her aesthetic choices reinforces her sense of herself as an artist in her chosen milieu.

Unlike many women who turned to writing to make a living, Jewett was not dependent on the income from her stories, but, as early as 1873, she thought of writing as her work, her business, not amusement, and she asked Horace Scudder for advice on securing the copyright for her stories. She was also determined to be true to her vision of her craft. When she felt strongly about the merits of a story, she vowed to publish it despite editors' objections. Although William Dean Howells rejected "Lady Ferry" and "A White Heron," and Thomas Bailey Aldrich, his successor as editor of *The Atlantic Monthly,* rejected "The Gray Man," Jewett included the first story in *Old Friends and New* and the other two in *A White Heron and Other Stories* (1886). Howells most likely rejected the first two because of their supernatural and romance elements, for as Jewett commented about her friend, "Mr. Howells thinks that this age frowns upon the romantic, that it is no use to write romance any more." Jewett did admit that "A White Heron" was not full of the smiling aspects of

Howellsian realism, but she loved it and refused to compromise her work. Near the end of her life, Jewett continued to defend "Lady Ferry" (written when she was twenty): "I still think that [Howells] made a mistake (I can hear his laugh!), but it was my whole childish heart written in." Commenting on "The Gray Man," she wrote that it would be published if she herself had to "make the type." When Henry Mills Alden rejected "An October Ride" for *Harper's Magazine,* Jewett insisted that the story of a girl's roughriding should not be considered more outrageous than "Miss Daniel Gunn," whose protagonist believes he is his sister. Mills accepted this story after she agreed to change the title to "An Autumn Holiday."

By the time Jewett came of age as a writer, the tradition of writing about rural subjects was well established by authors such as George Eliot and Harriet Beecher Stowe, both of whom Jewett read. Jewett's fiction is imbued with characteristics of sentimentalism and realism. Rereading Stowe's *The Pearl of Orr's Island* (1896) as an adult, Jewett praised the simplicity and harmony of the novel but regretted that Stowe could not "bring herself to that cold selfishness of the moment" necessary to make the second half of the book of the same quality as the first. This statement reveals a difference between Stowe's generation of women writers and Jewett's. Unlike her predecessors, Jewett set aside domestic concerns and saw herself first and foremost as a writer. Unlike Stowe's fiction, Jewett's work does not take a political stance imbedded in theological discourse. Despite these differences, however, Stowe may be considered one of Jewett's literary mothers. Describing Stowe as "standing ready like a switchman at the division by the rails" offering suggestions, Jewett once noted that she tried to imitate Stowe's talent for characterization. Jewett also frequently expressed a literary debt to Howells, but their friendship may have been based more on their mutual position as newcomers to Boston than on a shared aesthetic. Another influence was the French realist Gustave Flaubert. Jewett so admired his use of the commonplace in his fiction that she pinned two quotations from Flaubert to her desk: "Write ordinary life as if writing history," and "The writer's job is to make one dream."

These quotes suggest that in her fiction Jewett strove for a hybrid between the transcendent and the real. Yet, much of her contemporaries' critical praise for her fiction was devoted to its fidelity to real life, its local-color aspects. Local-color fiction, however, eventually fell out of favor. In 1895 Rebecca Harding Davis, whose reputation had been established in the 1860s with her realistic fiction, pondered why the rural character in fiction was frequently depicted as either petty or tragic. She called for a literature that would capture

Jewett's bedroom in her home in South Berwick, Maine

the "tender, heroic spirit" and admitted growing "impatient of human souls who make a life-drama out of their hair pictures or muddied kitchen floors." In *A Backward Glance* (1934) Edith Wharton declared that her intention in *Ethan Frome* (1927) had been "to draw life as it really was in the derelict mountain villages," not to depict it heroically or sympathetically as she said Jewett and Mary Wilkins Freeman had. By the second half of the 1890s, Stephen Crane and Frank Norris were gaining popularity with realistic fiction that exposed grave social ills. Jewett's fiction may be seen as an antidote to their views of the dark sides of life. In response to writer Hamlin Garland's query about the absence of injustice and grim realities in her fiction, Jewett contrasted her vision to that of Connecticut writer Rose Terry Cooke. She attributed the difference to regional influences, explaining that the Connecticut people about whom Cooke wrote had a greater struggle with nature and a more rigid theological heritage than had Jewett's Maine folks. While not overtly political, however, Jewett's work does indict a society that values materialism over community and personal growth and despoils the land without thought for future consequences. Conflicting views of Jewett's "realism" highlight the problem of trying to judge her fiction according to the tenets of a particular movement and point to the experimental and transitional quality of her work.

Some of Jewett's fiction does reveal the harsh realities of New England village life: feuding, abandonment, theft, poverty, and even pollution. However, characters' inner resources and possibilities for growth

offer visions of full, rather than limited, lives. "By the Morning Boat" (first published in *The Atlantic Monthly*, October 1890) describes a family abandoned by a son who goes to seek his livelihood in Boston. As he departs, the family remains "at the bars"–the "worn out" grandfather, the "anxious" mother inured to a life of being "beaten and buffeted by the waves of poverty and sorrow," and a little sister "with her dreaming heart" who watches "hungrily." The child may be the most tragic family member because her gender limits her possibilities for realizing her potential (a common theme in Jewett's fiction). Often Jewett's older characters are saved by their free will from being viewed as petty or tragic, and Jewett's narrators frequently warn the reader not to take a simplistic view of the characters. Integral to the richness of the stories is Jewett's conviction of "the possibilities of rural life," which are realized in helping others, connecting with community in small but meaningful ways. A frequently anthologized story, "The Town Poor" (*The Atlantic Monthly*, July 1890) illustrates this point. Reduced to poverty, the elderly Bray sisters become reluctant and unwelcome tenants in the farmhouse to which the selectmen have sent them. Their visitors, Miss Wright and Mrs. Trimble, are so outraged by the town's treatment of the sisters that one determines to "preach" and "make sparks fly," while the other insists on approaching the selectmen to demand that more be done for the sisters. Though Jewett was not as involved in social issues as her friend Annie Fields, stories such as "The Town Poor" and "The Flight of Betsey Lane" (*Scribner's Magazine*, August 1893) reveal Jewett's concern for the poor as well as suggesting was to ease their burdens.

The needs to know oneself, to grow, and to connect with community are all themes that run throughout all Jewett's fiction. They are already evident in her first book, *Deephaven* (1877), which not only challenges stereotypical views of villagers but also establishes the transfiguring power in female friendships. *Deephaven* is episodic and rich in character detail, emphasizing the voices of the people and the natural rhythm of their oral tradition. The main characters learn about the people not by prodding and probing, but rather in a natural way, from townspeople who relate histories and anecdotes as occasions arise. Many of Jewett's stories are structured by the nature and rhythms of oral storytelling. Wanting to write for country people as well as from their standpoint, Jewett respected the occasion of storytelling, often using a nature metaphor of nature for it. The connection between the flow of narrative and that of the the natural world is evident throughout Jewett's career. For example, in "The Courting of Sister Wisby" (*The Atlantic Monthly*, May 1887), the narrator asks the reader to "share in the winter provision" she harvested that day, and Ezra Allen in "The Mate of the Daylight" (*The Atlantic Monthly,* July 1882) is "in full flood tide of successful narration." Jewett wrote that in *Deephaven* she wanted to capture a "more true and sympathetic rendering" of the "caricatured Yankee," than had the increasing numbers of urban visitors to Maine. To make rural and urban people better acquainted would eliminate some of their suspicions of each other. Through their stories the villagers reveal the ways of a dying culture to the young outsiders Kate Lancaster and Helen Denis. Yet, *Deephaven* is more than a story about a town in which both the clocks and the people stopped years ago. It is also a story about friendship and the proper approach to a society that may seem dull to readers or visitors used to urban life. Being receptive to the villagers, Kate and Helen amass memories that preserve a vivid picture of a passing culture and its people.

When Helen ponders "how close this familiar, every-day world might be to the other," she voices Jewett's interest in the spiritual. Through her friendship with Harvard law professor Theophilus Parsons in the 1870s, Jewett became familiar with theologian Emanuel Swedenborg's ideas of consciousness and associations, and in her letters Jewett recorded how Swedenborgianism influenced her work. In *Deephaven* Captain Lant tells the girls about Mr. Down's vision of his nephew's death at sea, and Captain Sands tells of his grandmother's dream about her son's return from the sea, of a mother's sense that her child is in danger, and of a wife's premonition of her husband's death. These stories suggest Jewett's ongoing epistemological concerns and her belief in the power of communication unfettered by the limits of language.

This understanding also influenced Jewett's relationships. Dedicating *The Mate of the Daylight, and Friends Ashore* (1884) to Annie Fields, Jewett wrote that despite physical distance she felt an intense connection to her dear friend, a heartfelt "understanding" that was "like a flame on the altar to friendship." In "The Foreigner" (*The Atlantic Monthly,* August 1900) Almira Todd advises the narrator of "something beyond this world" to which she can have access if she will be receptive to the unseen rather than reoccupied with the seen. This pervasive element in Jewett's fiction again suggests that it is more than just "local color." Jewett was "heartened" that her friend Sarah Wyman Whitman, an artist, appreciated "Martha's Lady" (*The Atlantic Monthly,* October 1897), a story about the power of friendship despite separation over a lifetime. Jewett had thought people might focus only on the "scaffoldings" and miss the rich allusions. It is just such "unwritable things," Jewett asserted, that make the "heart" of the story, and she took Whitman's reading "joyfully between the lines" of Martha's "plain

story" as "one more unbreakable bond that holds fast between me and you." In 1885 Jewett reassured Laura Bellamy, a poet who worried that her writing was not well received, "the people will listen to whom the message is sent." These comments suggest not only a spirit of community that Jewett valued in her life, but also a sense of writing for two audiences: one that admired the local-color elements of her fiction and another that perceived the intangible, yet real, "unwritable things." The "golden chain of love and dependence" that she mentions in *The Country of the Pointed Firs* nourishes female communities that are dependent on each other in their relative isolation. Housebound Mercy Crane in "The Passing of Sister Barsett" (*Cosmopolitan,* May 1892) invents a series of signals to alert others when she wants or needs society, and Joanna in *The Country of the Pointed Firs* promises Mrs. Blackett to "make some sign" if she needs help in her island exile.

Jewett's spiritualism connects living beings through shared experiences and stored memories. Like Ralph Waldo Emerson, Jewett valued friendship. For her it did not require physical proximity. When one had to descend from "the mountain" where friends are together to the solitary "fret of everyday life," one could remain "strong in remembrance." Though she attended a séance in 1884 at the request of her friend Celia Thaxter, Jewett was not impressed with this form of spiritualism. Yet, she often contemplated and integrated into her stories the mystery between life and death. After Thaxter's death in 1894, Jewett wrote to Annie Fields that she had "seen" Celia, a phenomenon that prompted her to wonder "where imagination stops and consciousness of the unseen begins." Life for Jewett was a journey of self-discovery and growth, which meant not ignoring impulses often attributed only to youth. Just as she could not stand being still in school, Jewett frequently complained of growing sluggish when inactive. In her life and her fiction Jewett connects impulsive physical activity with spiritual growth. She reported one such epiphany to her young acquaintance Louisa Dresel. Approaching forty, Jewett marveled at a sudden consciousness of "unexplored territory" in herself. While she had material comforts, opportunities for travel, and stimulating company, her stories reveal that such things are not necessary for inner growth and self-realization.

By 1881 Jewett had established a network of friends with whom she corresponded regularly, sharing ideas about life and literature. This circle expanded after the death of her publisher James Fields in that same year. Jewett's relationship with his widow, Annie Fields, intensified, beginning with their first trip to Europe together in 1882. For the next eighteen years they were constant traveling companions, from Europe to Florida and the Caribbean. With few exceptions the two women established a seasonal pattern in which they spent summers together in Manchester, Massachusetts, and winters at Fields's Boston home at 148 Charles Street, where they wrote, read, and entertained a range of literary people. Henry James referred to Jewett as Fields's "adopted" daughter, which suggests that one woman was subordinate to the other. Yet, the relationship between the two women is best characterized as what was then known as a "Boston marriage," a relationship of mutual caring and nurturing, as they nursed one another through sicknesses and hosted gatherings together. Jewett was no mere visitor to the Fields home, where she was given James Fields's study. She and Annie Fields were almost inseparable, and while she met many literary people through her companion, Jewett developed a reputation independent of Annie's influence. As her social circle widened and her literary reputation grew, Jewett met and corresponded with writers such as James Russell Lowell, John Greenleaf Whittier, Henry James, Violet Paget (Vernon Lee), and Marie Thérèse Blanc-Bentzon. Jewett, however, always returned to her roots; during the spring and summer she went often to South Berwick to stay with her mother and sisters Mary and Caroline, the younger of whom married Edwin Eastman and had a son, Theodore.

Jewett once wrote to Willa Cather that the writer "needs the widest outlook upon the world," but one must write "to the human heart" through the "backgrounds" of one's native soil. While the outsider may see her characters' lives as stunted and narrow because of limited circumstances, Jewett explored their inner being, which was replete with drama and potential for growth. Though the Jewetts lived comfortably, she observed much-less affluent people when she joined her father on visits to his patients. While the country people might not possess the means for the "widest outlook" through travel, Jewett frequently examined in her fiction how such an outlook might come from within. The title story in *A White Heron and Other Stories* (1886), a story Jewett loved, illustrates how a girl may be true to herself despite limited circumstances and societal opprobrium. The story elicited praise from Louisa Dresel and from writer Mary Wilkins Freeman (whose work Jewett admired). Howells, however, never mentioned the title story in his review of *A White Heron and Other Stories,* a fact not surprising since the emphasis on the symbolic in the tale diverges from Howellsian realism.

In "A White Heron," her least realistic story, Jewett lodged a strong protest against the limitations women faced in society and literature. She reworked the conventional female bildungsroman, which typi-

cally ends in marriage or capitulation to a patriarchal and capitalist society. As in a fairy tale, the heroine, Sylvia, is removed from her mother, but the separation turns out to be an advantage because she leaves a crowded manufacturing town and a house full of children, to live with her grandmother in the country. Conflict arises when a hunter's acquisitive approach to nature challenges Sylvia's peaceful one. Since the hunter seems to like herons, Sylvia is confused by his desire to kill them and profit by their deaths. While the male in traditional tales awakens and arouses the heroine, the male in "A White Heron" threatens her peace. Confronted with this dominant figure, Sylvia is silent, terrified of the "sound of her own unquestioned voice." Ultimately, however, she does not acquiesce to what the hunter and even her grandmother expect of her. Climbing a tree, an action that suggests her raised consciousness, Sylvia views the "vast and awesome world" from her new vantage point and feels as though she "could go flying among the clouds." But she does not fly away. She returns to the ground with a renewed sense of self, silent not out of fear but out of determination not to betray what is dear to her.

In a modern sense, Jewett was not a feminist; yet, in her fiction—as in her life—she questioned the efficacy of women realizing their potential through marriage. When Whittier asked her why she had never married, Jewett reportedly responded that she had "more need of a wife" than of a husband. In this response Jewett implied that the wife as nurturing helpmate, subordinating her needs to another's, was not a role for which she was suited. She apparently found what she needed in egalitarian relationships with lasting friends Celia Thaxter, Sarah Wyman Whitman, and especially with life partner Annie Fields. Since her reality was woman centered, Jewett's stories about female relationships have an emotional intensity that her others lack. Her stories about male-female courtship often seemed contrived, not as emotionally vibrant as those about the "golden chain" of empathy among women. In the "'blooming' love story" of *A Marsh Island* (1885), the passion between Doris Owen and Dan Lester lacks passion. Unlike Sylvia, whose heart soars with the birds, Doris remains earthbound in body and spirit. Doris is not enlivened or elevated as she considers Dan's marriage proposal; rather, she feels "dumb before her inevitable fate." The marriage resolution occurs suddenly with no sense of why it is supposedly inevitable or what, if any, happiness lies in their future together. Jewett recognized that the story was not one of her best, acknowledging that she could have written a "better story without a lover in it." In fact, she later wrote a better story with a lover whose devotion to another woman lasts a lifetime ("Martha's Lady"). Jewett's effort to revise the traditional limitations on female characters in conventional literature represents one of her most significant experiments. Near the end of her life Jewett cautioned Willa Cather that writing in "the man's character" was always "something of a masquerade." Commenting on the romance in Cather's "On the Gull's Road" (1908), Jewett wrote that "a woman could love [the heroine] in that same protecting way—a woman could even care enough to wish to take her away from such a life," as did Jewett's female narrator in "The Landscape Chamber" (*The Atlantic Monthly*, November 1887), who tries to rescue a woman whose embittered old father keeps her isolated on his decaying farm. Jewett's advice suggests that Cather, like Jewett, was struggling to dramatize same-sex love. Same-sex relationships were, however, less tolerated in Cather's generation than in Jewett's. Jewett wrote unself-consciously about emotional longings for women in her diaries and letters, but in 1911 Annie Fields's editor urged her to expunge such passages from her edition of Jewett's letters lest they be misconstrued by the public. Cather, who like Jewett shared an affinity for female companions, felt the need to keep the mask, at least in her fiction. In Jewett's writing, the most realistic heterosexual courtships involve older people. Stories such as "A Winter Courtship" (*The Atlantic Monthly*, February 1889) and "William's Wedding" (*The Atlantic Monthly*, July 1910) focus on characters beyond the passion of youth. Perhaps, because of their age, the emphasis in their relationships is on mutual respect and emotional support, a theme with which Jewett was familiar in her life and adept exploring in her fiction.

In "Tom's Husband" (*The Atlantic Monthly*, February 1882) Jewett attempted to dramatize the possibility of a woman in the nineteenth century marrying and living up to her natural potential, often contradictory goals in nineteenth-century fiction. The wife, Mary, possesses business talent while Tom, her husband, prefers home life to the business world. What begins for Tom as a "fun" experiment—his wife running the business—becomes an outlet for Mary's natural talents, one which she turns to significant profit. As the experiment progresses, Tom begins to feel that domestic life has made him "rusty and behind the times" and realizes that women may consider keeping house as "disappointing and ignominious" as he does. Yet, his realization does not help to assuage the discomfort he feels when people wonder about his choice, implicitly questioning his manhood. Through this story Jewett raises possibilities that are not completely explored. While Mary leaves the business to travel with Tom in Europe, she is not wrenched away but takes time to make arrangements that leave open the possiblity for her return. Such open-ended conclusions in Jewett's fiction

emphasize the evolving quality of life, especially for women, who often were depicted in fiction as static or broken by unsuccessful forays into the world.

Two years after "Tom's Husband" Jewett again examined women following their natural tendencies and concluded that a woman needed to choose between marriage and career. Of all her work, Jewett liked *A Country Doctor* (1884) best, perhaps because she was interested in medicine when young and perhaps because it was her father's vocation. This novel offers an extended debate over gender roles and the quality of education for women. Nan Prince finds little encouragement from society for her determination to become a doctor and quite naturally resents having to adhere to instruction that she knows to be inferior after years in her childhood of following her adoptive father, Dr. Leslie, on his rounds and reading the books in his library (as Jewett did with her father). In the 1880s medical careers for women were not widely accepted, but a small number of women—notably Elizabeth Blackwell and Harriot Hunt—had managed to become doctors. Jewett implies that women's "natural" sympathies lent themselves to healing.

A Country Doctor follows the theme of Howells's *Dr. Breen's Practice* (1881) and Elizabeth Stuart Phelps's *Dr. Zay* (1882). Yet, while Howells's heroine abandons her practice when she marries and Phelps's doctor is left with the question of how to balance work and possible child rearing, Nan Prince resolves that career cannot be combined with marriage. Stressing that most women will "instinctively and gladly accept the high duties . . . of married life," Jewett pointed out that for those whose inclinations lie elsewhere, society must recognize the "unfitness of marriage." Dr. Leslie articulates the Darwinian and theological arguments in favor of Nan's following her dream: "the preservation of the race is no longer the only important question," and as " a result of natural progression and variation," some women are suited "not for better work, but for different work." Such statements anticipate Gilman's rhetoric in *Women and Economics* (1898). Dr. Leslie observed Nan's natural curiosity about medicine when she was just a child. It would be treason to God, he argues, to deny her natural gifts. It is imperative that Nan "work with the great laws of nature and not against them." Such discourse recalls Margaret Fuller's arguments in *Woman in the Nineteenth Century* (1845) and places Jewett firmly in the debate about women's destiny that was begun before her birth and continues into the present. Jewett clearly articulates in *A Country Doctor* that women must grow "as naturally as a plant grows, without being clipped or forced in any direction."

Such botanical allusions, which recur in Jewett's fiction, can be read as a metaphor for both transcendence and a more problematic ethnic theory. Jewett dedicated *Country By-Ways* (1881) to her father, who died in 1878. The collection recalls the youthful rides she shared with him, for in each story a country ride is the occasion for meditative discourse. The only "action" in this collection is the narrator's epiphanies about herself and her relationship to nature. In the Transcendentalist tradition, Jewett contemplates the "life residing in nature," as she calls it in the previously unpublished "A Winter Drive." The first-person narrator of "An Autumn Holiday" explains the preference for "walking between the roads": only the byways offer "a tour of exploration and discovery." The geographic journey beyond the main roads parallels the narrator's voyage into her own consciousness as she ponders nature's vicissitudes and her part in the natural order. Contemplating the "relationship of untamed nature to what is tamed and cultivated," the narrator says in "An October Ride," is an occasion to "grow spiritually, until we grasp some new great truth of God; but it was always true, and waited for us until we came." Her epiphanies recall the thoughts of Henry David Thoreau in their revelations about the intimate bond between people and nature. Closing out the world, the narrator of "An October Ride" begins to "wonder what I am; there is a strange self-consciousness, but I am only part of one great existence which is called nature." Such connections Jewett extends beyond enlightenment to empathy when she notes in "A Winter Drive" a "curious linking of the two lives, which makes a tree fade and die when the man or woman dies with whom it has been associated."

Just as analogies between nature and people suggest growth and potential, they also reveal Jewett's belief in the weight of heredity in determining a person's character. Some of her writing reflects the racial theories and social Darwinism of her time. In *The Country of the Pointed Firs,* however, the narrator comments that Almira grows "sluggish for lack of proper surroundings," suggesting the influence of environment on character. Just as Nan Prince needed an environment conducive to her realizing her gifts, so the "hidden fire of enthusiasm in the New England nature" needs a proper "outlet" if it is to shine, says the narrator of *The Country of the Pointed Firs.*

Class issues are also evident in some of the stories in *Country By-Ways.* Like the emphasis on nature, her writings on class suggest hierarchal notions of "race," a word which in the nineteenth century referred to ethnic difference. "From A Mournful Villager" reveals Jewett's nostalgia for a more homogeneous community in a passage on how New England towns have changed over twenty years as manufacturing "brought together large numbers either of foreigners or of a different class of people," forcing a "certain class of families rapidly" to become "extinct." She regrets also the disappearance of front yards and warns that Americans should build more fences. In these comments can be read a call for preserving "the special domain of women," the front garden. One may also read in them, however, a xenophobia prevalent in the late nineteenth century. Jewett's plea for preserving privacy in the form of front yards and fences contains allusions to a siege, a fear of some unnamed outside threat. To do away with them, for Jewett, is tantamount to "writing down the family secrets for any one to read" or "having everybody call you by your first name," an invasion Jewett finds distasteful. Her rhetoric suggests a threat not only to personal boundaries, but also to class distinctions as democracy in practice seems less palatable than it is in theory.

Through Fields, Jewett met Matthew Arnold during his October 1883–March 1884 lecture tour in the United States, and she admired his ideas about the "natural" inclinations that privilege some over others. She agreed with him that their contemporaries were mistaken to be "governed by the ignorant mass of opinion, instead of by thinkers and men who know something." Her belief in innate traits that set Anglo-Normans above other "races" is evident in *The Story of the Normans* (1887), a children's book that George Putnam asked her to write in 1881 and that took her almost six years to complete. Throughout this book current theories about race and war as evolutionary abound. Seen as an anomaly in Jewett's oeuvre, both in content and in structure, *The Story of the Normans* has been given only cursory attention by Jewett critics. Modern criticism that focuses on cultural politics and historical assumptions includes Sandra Zagarell's 1988 essay on community and exclusion, which points to a new direction for critical attention to constructs of community in Jewett and other late-nineteenth-century writers. In this vein, Jack Morgan and Louis A. Renza edited a collection of Jewett's Irish tales (1996), which reveal community anxiety about foreigners balanced with what they call Jewett's "ethnographic sensitivity." Compared to the more rancorous assertions of Nathaniel Hawthorne, Thoreau, and Emerson, Jewett's treatment of the Irish is tempered with an ambiguity that suggests a negotiation between Irish and American cultures.

Beginning with *Country By-Ways,* Jewett refined and reworked many of the themes evident in *Deephaven.* One can read into her use of nature myriad possibilities—as a metaphor for inner growth, for the spiritual immanence in nature, for positive and negative natural inclinations, for inclusion and exclusion. Even as her writing reflects some of the less enlightened ideas of her day, it also anticipates more forward-thinking issues.

While modern readers may find some of her writing ethnographically problematic, in the same collection published at the beginning of the 1880s one encounters some progressive ideas about ecological issues. In "A Winter Drive" Jewett criticizes the "short-sighted" people who look at "the wholesale slaughter of the American forests without dismay," predicts that the clearing of woodlands will be regulated by law "at some not far distant period," and calls for "tree laws as well as game laws." Industry was not only stripping the forests but also polluting the waters, and Jewett felt a great need for "preaching against this." Jewett regretted the general population's blind acceptance of the destruction of the environment. Her desire to preserve natural resources may have derived from the same impulse as her wish to preserve homes and memories of people from the past. But in these passages a sense of duty to future generations is apparent. In her writing Jewett could preserve the memory of older generations; in South Berwick she could work to preserve homes. Just so, in "The White Rose Road" (published in *The Atlantic Monthly,* September 1889) one is left with a sense of hope for the natural world. While "man has done his best to ruin the world he lives in," Jewett believes "that with a little more time we should grow wiser about our fish and other things beside." Nature possesses a wonderful capacity to reclaim its own, despite "men's footsteps," which "have worn it down" ("An October Ride"); but nature may need humanity's help to correct humanity's abuses. Jewett returned to these issues later, but not in such an overtly didactic manner.

Jewett's mother died in 1891, followed the next year by her brother-in-law. One of her closest friends, Celia Thaxter, died in 1894, and Jewett and Fields attended Harriet Beecher Stowe's funeral in 1896. Caroline, Jewett's younger sister, died after surgery in 1897, leaving her orphaned son in Mary's care. Often after a painful loss Jewett would throw herself into work, and by mid decade she had completed the book for which she is best known: *The Country of the Pointed Firs.*

The Country of the Pointed Firs offers a vision of a world in which community and empathetic imagination flourish beyond the larger, more hectic world. Into this "centre of civilization" comes the narrator, a harried writer whose stay in Dunnet Landing proves an education in the importance of recognizing one's roots. Like Kate and Helen in *Deephaven,* this narrator is seduced by the spell of the place and its inhabitants, especially Almira Todd, herbalist, homeopathic healer, mentor, and eventually, dear friend. Almira is "mateless and appealing," "strangely self-possessed and mysterious," "like the renewal of some historic soul." Following a pace of "daily life busied with rustic simplicities and the scents of primeval herbs," the narrator is renewed, ulti-

Jewett at work in her South Berwick home (Houghton Library, Harvard University)

mately abandoning the writing she hoped to complete, and in its stead discovering the values of tacit connection to a matrifocal world. As she departs, the inevitability of her return is embedded in the symbol of Joanna's coral pin, a talisman from woman to woman, a reminder of the transfiguring power of friendship. This story of women realizing their potential by being true to their natures offers a celebratory and expansive alternative to the vision of women trapped by circumstances, as are the heroines in Gilman's *The Yellow Wallpaper* (1892) and Kate Chopin's *The Awakening* (1899).

The Country of the Pointed Firs garnered much critical praise from both sides of the Atlantic, although none quite as enthusiastic as Rudyard Kipling's comment, "It's immense—it is the very life." Assessing Jewett's achievement, most reviewers, though positive, followed in the vein of the *Academy* (13 March 1897): "Miss Jewett's book is a little epic of contentment." This emphasis on smallness continued into the twentieth century. In 1904 Charles Miner Thompson referred to Jewett's "own modest and delightful art," and Henry James declared her "mistress of an art of fiction all her own, even though of a minor compass," a "beautiful little quantum of achievement." In the preface to a 1927 edition of *The Country of the Pointed Firs* and some of Jewett's other stories Willa Cather places Jewett's "masterpiece" in the company of Hawthorne's *The Scarlet Letter* (1850) and Mark Twain's *Huckleberry Finn* (1884). Such praise solidified Jewett's position in American literature. Whether or not in the company of Hawthorne and Twain, *The Country of the Pointed Firs* is an American original, grounded in the "Maine dust" and transcending it, and popular enough with twentieth-century readers to warrant its republication many times.

Jewett self-consciously assumed her position as a writer of literature belonging to what she called the "middle-ground," a position from which she felt one could best see the commonplace aspects of life that "bring out the best sort of writing." From this vantage point, perhaps, Jewett could express her "unwritable things" encoded into a fiction that seems merely picturesque. Renza argues that by assuming a "minor" position Jewett may, in fact, have been freer to challenge the main currents of literature, as well as a culture in which women could not participate fully. The separateness of such literature enabled Jewett to communicate to other women under the veil of benign little stories. Recent criticism explores exactly these issues, noting the fluidity and mythic quality of Jewett's fiction, which imagines female space and possibility. Elizabeth Ammons, Marilyn Mobley, and Sarah Sherman are among those who examine this space and reveal a characteristic of Jewett's fiction that transcends time and place.

Jewett returned to Dunnet Landing and Almira Todd in "The Queen's Twin" (*The Atlantic Monthly*, February 1899), "A Dunnet Shepherdess" (*The Atlantic Monthly*, December 1899), and "William's Wedding," published posthumously (*The Atlantic Monthly*, July 1910). "The Queen's Twin" and "A Dunnet Shepherdess" appeared in the collection *"The Queen's Twin" and Other Stories* (1899). Throughout her fiction, as in her life, Jewett seems to search for ways to preserve the past even as she looks forward. She wrote in "From A Mournful Village" (*The Atlantic Monthly*, November 1881), "There is so much to be said in favor of our own day," these "later years of ease and comfort." She allows that the "old days" were in many ways a "restricted and narrowly limited life," yet she felt the necessity of duly honoring them. Without connection to the past and community, Jewett believed, people are rootless. While she enjoyed the progress of her time, Jewett also lamented the lack of cohesiveness she perceived. Perhaps for this reason she agreed to write *The Tory Lover* (1901), an historical novel set in South Berwick during the American Revolution, which reveals her Anglophile tendencies. Hers is not a nostalgia to return to the past; rather, her writing emphasizes the need to acknowledge the past in the midst of progress.

When the editor Charles Dudley Warner asked Jewett to write an historical novel, she was initially reluctant to undertake the venture. While she seemed unable to approach this new genre with the same assuredness as she had her stories, and she was well aware of the danger of trying "to write something entirely different," Jewett apparently had long had an interest in attempting such a work. *The Tory Lover* was serialized in *The Atlantic Monthly* from November 1900 through August 1901, and it is framed by two stories that continue the themes of community and spiritual connections among women: "The Foreigner"(*The Atlantic Monthly*, August 1900) and "The Green Bowl" (*New York Herald,* 1901). Even as she exorcized her dream of writing the past, she continued to explore the themes with which she began her career and those for which she is remembered.

Jewett received an honorary Litt. D. degree from Bowdoin College, her father's alma mater, in 1901. A year later, on her fifty-third birthday, Jewett was thrown from a carriage and suffered a spinal concussion from which she never fully recovered. Dizziness and headaches plagued her and made writing more and more difficult, but she continued, when able, to visit Fields in Boston. During this time Jewett read Cather's *The Troll Garden* (1905), which Cather's colleague at *McClure's*, Witter Bynner, had sent to her. She told Bynner that she especially liked "The Sculptor's Funeral" and imagined that she and Cather "should have much to say if we could talk together." In 1908 work for *McClure's* magazine brought Cather to Boston, where she met Jewett at Fields's home. The bond between the two seems to have been immediate. After this initial meeting, they corresponded often; at one point, when Cather wrote Jewett that she was frustrated because her demanding work at *McClure's* left her little time for writing, Jewett advised Cather to find her own quiet place, to get the widest outlook on the world, and to remember her background. If she could find her "own quiet centre of life," Jewett wrote, she could—as did the narrator in *The Country of the Pointed Firs*—write to all of society. Jewett's advice to Cather indicates a generosity of spirit and an attempt to nurture, to extend the "golden chain" as had her fictional characters, bringing scattered lives together through sympathy.

While visiting Fields in March 1909 Jewett suffered a stroke that left her partially paralyzed. Returning to South Berwick at the end of April, she died after a second stroke on 24 June. In 1910 her friends established the Sarah Orne Jewett Scholarship Fund at Simmons College. As Mrs. Patton "used her plain country words" to reveal Kate and Frances to themselves and to each other in "The Green Bowl," so Jewett's fiction brings to generations revelations about themselves and their ties to one other. The bowl from a set of two that Mrs. Patton entrusts to Kate can serve as a metaphor for Jewett's life and work. These special "sister" bowls allow the owner to see into the future even as they remind one of the past. Handed down from woman to woman without regard to family relationship, the bowls signify a connection that must not be broken, for "if there were not two of us companions the life of the bowls would soon be gone." Jewett's legacy is her body of work, which speaks to future generations of the value of simple things and the necessity for staying connected to their foremothers.

Letters:

Letters of Sarah Orne Jewett, edited by Annie Fields (Boston & New York: Houghton Mifflin, 1911);

Sarah Orne Jewett Letters, edited by Richard Cary, revised and enlarged edition (Waterville, Me.: Colby College Press, 1967);

"Jewett to Dresel: 33 Letters," edited by Cary, *Colby Library Quarterly,* 11 (1975): 13–49.

References:

Elizabeth Ammons, "Going in Circles: The Female Geography of Jewett's Country of the Pointed Firs," *Studies in the Literary Imagination,* 16 (1983): 83–92;

Paula Blanchard, *Sarah Orne Jewett: Her World and Her Work* (Reading, Mass.: Addison-Wesley, 1994);

Richard Cary, *Sarah Orne Jewett* (New York: Twayne, 1962);

Josephine Donovan, *Sarah Orne Jewett* (New York: Ungar, 1980);

June Howard, ed., *New Essays on The Country of the Pointed Firs* (New York: Cambridge University Press, 1994);

Marilyn E. Mobley, "Rituals of Flight and Return: The Ironic Journeys of Sarah Orne Jewett's Female Characters," *Colby Library Quarterly,* 22 (1986): 36–42;

Gwen Nagel, ed., *Critical Essays on Sarah Orne Jewett* (Boston: G. K. Hall, 1984);

Louis A. Renza, *"A White Heron" and the Question of Minor Literature* (Madison: University of Wisconsin Press, 1984);

Sarah Way Sherman, *Sarah Orne Jewett: An American Persephone* (Hanover, N.H.: University Press of New England, 1989);

Sandra Zagarell, *"'Country's'* Portrayal of Community and the Exclusion of Difference," in *New Essays on The Country of the Pointed Firs,* edited by June Howard (New York: Cambridge University Press, 1994), pp. 39–60;

Zagarell, "Narrative of Community: The Identification of Genre," *Signs,* 13 (1988): 498–527.

Papers:

Major collections of Sarah Orne Jewett's letters and diaries are at the Houghton Library, Harvard University; the Society for the Preservation of New England Antiquities; and Colby College.

Mrs. A. E. Johnson
(Amelia Johnson)
(ca. 1858 – 29 March 1922)

Wendy Wagner
Pace University

BOOKS: *Clarence and Corinne; Or, God's Way* (Philadelphia: American Baptist Publication Society, 1890);

The Hazeley Family (Philadelphia: American Baptist Publication Society, 1894);

Martina Meriden; Or, What Is My Motive? (Philadelphia: American Baptist Publication Society, 1901).

OTHER: Harvey Johnson, *The Nations from a New Point of View,* introduction by Amelia Johnson (Nashville: National Baptist Publishing Board, 1903).

SELECTED PERIODICAL PUBLICATIONS–
UNCOLLECTED: "Nettie Ray's Thanksgiving Day," *National Baptist,* 23 (24 November 1887): 750;

"Afro-American Literature," *New York Age,* 30 January 1892;

"What Is Originality," *National Baptist Magazine,* 2 (April 1895): 85–89;

"The History of a Story: How I Wrote a Story for the *Youth's Companion* and Why It Has Not Appeared," *Richmond Planet* (22, 29 February 1896);

"Some Parallels of History," *National Baptist Magazine,* 7 (July 1899): 4.

Amelia Johnson (from Irvine Garland Penn, The Afro-American Press and Its Editors, *1892)*

"We always kept our mother busy in telling us stories, fairy tales, etc. She was so interesting to us for she was a writer, you know." So reminisced the son of Amelia Johnson, who published essays, stories, and novels as Mrs. A. E. Johnson during the late nineteenth century. For almost a century, Amelia Johnson disappeared from literary history, but the recent burst of interest in nineteenth-century African American women's writing has led to her reemergence. Johnson deserves to be studied not only because of her contribution to the tradition of the domestic novel popular in the nineteenth century but also because her writings embody the values and goals of the black Baptist women's movement of the late nineteenth century.

Biographical information about Johnson is sketchy. According to her obituary in the *Afro-American* (7 April 1922), Amelia Etta Hall Johnson was born in 1858, probably in Toronto, and raised in Montreal. Her parents, Levi and Ellen Hall, were natives of Maryland; it is possible that her parents moved to Canada to escape slavery. After her father died in 1874, Johnson and her mother moved back to Maryland, where Johnson worked as a teacher in Baltimore.

In 1877 Amelia Hall married the Reverend Harvey Johnson, a minister in the burgeoning black Baptist church, an institution on the verge of dynamic growth during the postbellum period. Johnson was born a slave near Richmond, Virginia, in 1843, and he maintained property in the area until his death in 1923. He graduated from Wayland Seminary in 1872 and became pastor of the Union Baptist Church in Baltimore that same year. Under Johnson's leadership, the membership of this church expanded almost tenfold within twenty years. In an 1888 article on African American Baptist churches, the *National Baptist* noted that "The Union Church has the largest membership of any Baptist church in Maryland. . . . Dr. Harvey Johnson, the pastor, is strong, conservative, and popular."

Harvey Johnson actively worked for civil-rights causes, and his support was influential in helping a member of his congregation become the first African American to be admitted to the Maryland bar. He also spearheaded the formation of the Brotherhood of Liberty, an organization created to oppose lynching and other forms of racial violence, which increased dramatically during the 1890s. Another cause that proved successful for Johnson was his advocacy of better schools and better teaching opportunities for African Americans in Baltimore. Reverend Johnson was also active in the national Civil Rights movement, and he attended the Niagara Convention, the precursor to the National Association for the Advancement of Colored People (NAACP), in 1901.

Harvey Johnson was also a well-respected writer and orator, and he published several of his sermons as pamphlets. These writings in particular foregrounded his belief in the separation of black Baptist denominations from the mainstream white denomination. One widely read pamphlet, *The Hamite,* proposes an Afrocentric view of history designed to foster race pride and criticizes the use of the word *Negro* as inaccurate. In 1903 several of his pamphlets and essays were collected into a book, *The Nations from a New Point of View,* and published by the newly formed National Baptist Publication Board, an organ of the black-run National Baptist Convention, which Johnson helped to establish. The introduction to this book was written by Amelia Johnson. In this introduction Johnson describes her husband's purpose in writing the book, provides a sketch of his background and his work, and liberally peppers her lengthy introduction with several accolades of Johnson and his writings from various publications and personal letters.

In a 1957 biography of his father, Harvey Johnson Jr. described his mother as his father's "best friend, and his chief comfort, his guide in all his business matters. Looking back over fifty years, I still consider this union a perfect one." That Johnson probably shared her husband's political beliefs is supported by her nonfiction essays written for various race periodicals, such as the *New York Age* and the *Richmond Planet,* but her fiction lacks any specific references to her political views.

Few of Johnson's writings other than her novels are extant. Contemporaneous sources indicate that she began writing for the black periodical press in the 1880s. In 1887 and 1888 she edited a monthly, *The Joy,* and, according to other sources, she edited and published a monthly children's magazine, *The Ivy.* No issues of either magazine survive today, but like the popular children's magazines of the day, they probably included poetry, short stories, and sketches of historical events and figures. She also served as the editor of the Children's Corner for *Sower and Reaper,* a Baltimore Baptist magazine, and published stories in both *Sower and Reaper* and *Our Women and Children,* a Baptist periodical published in Louisville, Kentucky.

Johnson's short story, "Nettie Ray's Thanksgiving Day" was reprinted in the Thanksgiving issue of the white-run *National Baptist* (24 November 1887). Originally published in *The Ivy,* "Nettie Ray's Thanksgiving Day" is typical of the didactic children's literature of the time, telling the simple tale of a girl who learns to count her blessings by being confronted with the trials of others. As the story opens, the title character is feeling distinctly ungrateful the day before Thanksgiving because her parents have been called away to see a sick relative during her short holiday from boarding school. Her sister, Nannie, and her aunt, Mattie, try unsuccessfully to coax her out of her bad mood, so Aunt Mattie takes Nettie to visit two neighbors, a blind woman named Madge and her companion, a child named Libby. Nettie is unable to understand why Madge is looking forward to Thanksgiving Day because all Nettie can see is the deprivation of Madge's and Libby's lives. Yet, Madge recounts her blessings (including the companionship of Libby and the charity she is receiving from people at her church), closing with "Oh, the Lord is good, isn't he, Miss Ray?" Miss Ray responds, "He truly is, Madge; and you are a good girl, to bear your trials so patiently." This moment provides a lesson for Nettie, and she returns home with her aunt, after they arrange to send Madge and Libby a Thanksgiving dinner, feeling more accepting of her situation, "for every time she tried to feel discontented, Blind Madge would rise up before her, with the happy contented look on her face, and she would contrast her own surrounds to those of the blind girl."

"Nettie Ray's Thanksgiving Day" was clearly intended to teach Johnson's readers the importance of bearing one's burdens without complaint and with faith. Johnson, however, seems not always to have followed that lesson in her own life. Johnson's attempt

Johnson's husband, the Reverend Harvey Johnson (Schomburg Center for Research in Black Culture, New York Public Library)

(and ultimate failure) to publish in the *Youth's Companion,* a well-known Boston children's magazine, was documented in an article she wrote for the *Richmond Planet* in 1896. In this article, which appeared in two parts over two weeks, Johnson details her correspondence with the editors of the *Youth's Companion,* a correspondence that indicates her unwillingness to accept without complaint or resistance any injustices she perceived. Claiming a desire to expand her portfolio and reputation by publishing a story with the nationally known magazine, Johnson submitted a story to the *Youth's Companion* along with a letter appealing to an editor she knew to be a Baptist. In the letter she identified herself as "a colored woman, and proud of it." When her story was rejected, she took the editors to task for rejecting her work while publishing other stories featuring racist depictions. After a series of letters back and forth, in which the editors of the *Youth's Companion* denied her charges of racism, one of her stories, "Dr. Hayes' Wire Fence," was accepted, and she received a check for twenty dollars. Several years passed, however, and the story never appeared, leading Johnson to renew her correspondence with the *Youth's Companion* and discover that her story would never be published.

Johnson's response to this rejection sheds light on her perception of herself as an African American writer. When she began her quest to publish in the *Youth's Companion,* she denied any interest in speaking to a white audience and wrote only of expanding her résumé: "It was not my desire to get before the white public, for I have but small dealings with them, and they with me." After her initial rejection, however, her letters indicate her commitment to writing stories to counter negative representations of African Americans in the white-authored literature characterizing the *Youth's Companion.* In one letter she writes, "I thought that if you would permit me to write as other people write, while you allow others to write as they wish it to appear, that my people look and act, it would help me bear it better." Later, when she is informed that her story will not be published after all, she writes that "while the *Companion* with its half million subscribers must be bigger than the desires of any one of its contributors, I was a representative of eight million people in whose interest I was making the effort." Johnson thus saw herself as a spokesperson for her race, as an author by whose works the entire race would be judged.

In 1892 Johnson wrote an essay titled "Afro-American Literature" that appeared in the black newspaper, the *New York Age.* In this essay she challenges critics who claim that African American literature is not "original." Conceding (wrongly) the point that there is no indigenous African literature, Johnson nevertheless refutes this criticism by pointing out that many writers considered "original"—even William Shakespeare—drew on previously written works. In addition, she argues that in order for African American writers to achieve the recognition they deserve, they will have to establish and support black publishing houses and other venues for African American writers. Johnson was prescient: within the following three decades, black publishing concerns would flourish, culminating in the rise and cultural power of periodicals such as *The Crisis* and *Opportunity* during the Harlem Renaissance.

Despite her call for separate, black-run publishing houses, Johnson was not unwilling to seek an audience with white publishers. Johnson was best known during her lifetime for her three novels, all of which were published by the American Baptist Publication Society, an arm of the mainstream white Baptist denomination. In fact, Johnson was the first African American to have a book published by the American Baptist Publication Society, a circumstance that proved politically useful when the organization had to defend itself against charges of racism after dropping several African American authors from the *Baptist Teacher.*

In writing for primarily white audiences, as Johnson did when she wrote her novels, she did not engage the discourse of race. Johnson's novels were ignored for many years by scholars of African American literature because her characters do not have any obvious racial characteristics and the illustrations in the books depicted white characters; thus, her novels did not appear to belong to an identifiably African American literary tradition.

As recent scholarship has shown, however, Johnson's novels belong to a tradition of black women's domestic fiction written during the post-Reconstruction period, such as Emma Dunham Kelley-Hawkins's *Megda* (1891) and *Four Girls at Cottage City* (1898). In these novels characters affirm Christian faith and love as means of addressing and rectifying social injustice. The absence of the discourse of race in Johnson's novels may thus be read as an indicator of racial affirmation, not racial denial. By foregrounding the similarities of beliefs and Christian values held by Johnson and her primarily white readership, Johnson was asserting her equal standing as a member of American society and appealing to the shared humanity of her audience.

Johnson's novels also belong to the genre of Sunday-school literature, an offshoot of the domestic evangelical literary tradition prevalent in the nineteenth century. These texts took a primarily didactic approach and were written with the intention of teaching a Sunday-school lesson about Christian values. To appeal to their younger audience, these works often focused on the experiences of young people growing up in a Christian environment. Claudia Tate describes Johnson's novels as female Christian bildungsromans; in other words, they all tell the story of the journey of a young woman toward spiritual maturity and self-knowledge. The protagonists in Johnson's novels must navigate many obstacles as they approach adulthood and develop their understanding of their Christian faith.

Because these protagonists are women, however, they must also understand their relationship to the world and to their religion in terms of their gender. The values these novels promote to their mainly young female audience are those of submission, domesticity, and self-sacrifice—values characteristic of the domestic literary tradition. These novels instruct young women not only in how to be good Christians but specifically in how to be good Christian women. They instruct women that the home is the cornerstone of society and that it is the Christian woman's role to keep the home happy and in order. They teach women to accept without complaint the responsibilities of home and the family. They encourage women to put aside their own interests to act for the good of others—their families, their communities, and implicitly their race. These nov-

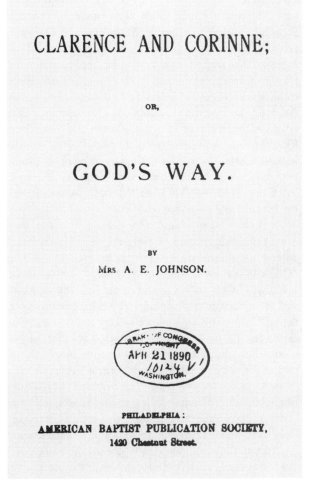

CLARENCE AND CORINNE;

OR,

GOD'S WAY.

BY

MRS. A. E. JOHNSON.

PHILADELPHIA :
AMERICAN BAPTIST PUBLICATION SOCIETY,
1420 Chestnut Street.

Title page of the Library of Congress deposit copy for Johnson's first novel, about the separation, adversities, and reunion of a brother and sister

els also acknowledge the difficulties involved in attaining these goals. The hardships that Johnson's characters face provide readers with an opportunity to see how admirable characters overcome seemingly desperate situations while still maintaining their faith.

Johnson's first novel, *Clarence and Corinne; Or, God's Way* (1890), follows the parallel lives of Clarence and Corinne Burton, who are brother and sister, as they transcend their economically and spiritually impoverished background. Hardship and deprivation characterize the siblings' lives from the beginning. The opening lines of the novel describe the Burton home as "a blot upon a beautiful picture," and the run-down, unkempt condition of the home is evident. Basically orphaned when their mother dies and their father abandons them, Clarence is placed with the local doctor, who gives him a job as an errand boy, and Corinne is placed with a local spinster, Rachel Penrose, who uses her as a household servant and overworks Corinne until she becomes severely ill. Corinne is then taken in by two kindly sisters, Mary and Helen Gray, who nurse her back to physical and spiritual health. Mary takes on Corinne's religious education, introducing her to such biblical passages as "Casting all your care upon him; for he careth for you." From this passage and others, Corinne learns to have faith in Jesus Christ and to take on her burdens willingly and without complaint. Meanwhile, Clarence's ambition takes him out of town and away from Corinne, but the intervention of a kind older woman, Mother Carter, leads to his religious conversion and his realization that he has been selfish in running away from his problems. Through a series of coincidences, the brother and sister are reunited.

Both Clarence and Corinne learn from their adversities that they must suppress their free will and submit their individual needs to the will of God, to "God's Way." As Corinne's friend Mary Gray describes it, "God's Way" involves abdicating free will and individual agency and accepting whatever circumstances bring: "Isn't it strange how we will try to make ways for ourselves, no matter how often our ways fail; and no matter how many times his ways prove best?" By the end of the novel, Clarence and Corinne's acceptance of "God's Way" is rewarded by personal satisfaction, financial and professional success, and marriage, as the brother and sister marry another brother-sister pair, Bebe and Charley Reade, and set up housekeeping together in the same house in which they grew up.

The Hazeley Family (1894), Johnson's second novel, similarly deals with the theme of salvation through love of God and devotion to duty and family. Flora Hazeley, the central character, is uprooted from the happy home she has known with the two aunts who have raised her in order to return to the home of her parents and two brothers. Her mother is an indifferent, unchristian homemaker, and Flora despairs of being happy in her new home until she meets a neighbor, Ruth Rudd, who serves as her mentor both spiritually and domestically. Ruth urges Flora not to despair of her mother and her home and encourages her to try to make her home a happy and comfortable place in which to live: "[You] might try and see if you could make it so pleasant at home [Flora's father and brothers] would not care to be away so much."

Ruth brings Flora to church, where the words of the minister make a strong impression on Flora: "Whatsoever thy hand findeth to do, do it with thy might." Flora interprets this biblical passage as a call to action, and she devotes her energies to making her home a pleasant place to live, with much success and personal satisfaction: "Her cherished dream of being instrumental in leading others into a higher and better life was now, she began to realize, leading her into the lines of

duty in her own home, and among her own people. She could not wish for more." Flora Hazeley thus serves as a model for Christian women who seek to bring about social change; however, her activities are directed toward the home, the private sphere, instead of the public sphere.

The Hazeley Family features an extensive cast of secondary characters who, like Flora, undergo spiritual awakenings, but the novel traces these conversions back to Flora's benevolent and loving influence. For example, Flora's mentor, Ruth, is rewarded for her efforts in helping Flora by being reunited with her family. Flora's influence on her family leads her kindhearted brother to come to the aid of Major Joe, a farmer who sells his goods at the local market. Major Joe is soon introduced to the rest of the Hazeley family, and Flora discovers that he and his wife are the long-lost grandparents of her dear friend Ruth. Flora reunites Ruth and her grandparents, who take in Ruth and her sister Jem after Ruth's father dies. Flora's role in this reunion is, of course, viewed as an instrument of God's will: "Think what a blessing it is that poor little Jem and I have not been left alone together in the world. Had God not led you to find our dear grandparents, how very wretched we should be now," Ruth says.

Flora's positive attitude also influences her family members, particularly her mother. "I used to be very unhappy, . . . and it was because I expected life to form itself for me—either for pleasure or happiness," Mrs. Hazeley confesses. With Flora's arrival, however, she realizes her daughter "determined to make this house a home, and a delightful one. No untoward circumstances seemed to discourage, but she was ever cheery and sprightly." Flora resists her mother's attempts, however, to ascribe these changes to Flora's individual initiative, asserting that "it's not my will, mother . . . it is God's will." *The Hazeley Family* thus reinforces the primary theme of *Clarence and Corinne:* that the individual's will must be subsumed to that of God.

The spiritual journey of Flora's brother Harry is more troubled. After the death of Mr. Hazeley, the family patriarch, Harry leaves town much as Clarence Burton did, to make his fortune. Unlike Clarence, Harry is unsuccessful and turns to alcohol and gambling. Only after a near-death experience does Harry experience his own religious conversion, with the help of similarly reformed Joel Piper. As a result, he and Joel are reunited with their families.

Another character who benefits from Flora's spiritual guidance is her longtime friend Lottie Piper, coincidentally the estranged sister of Harry's friend Joel. After the death of her mother, Lottie is sent to live with an aunt whose crotchets and demands make Lottie's

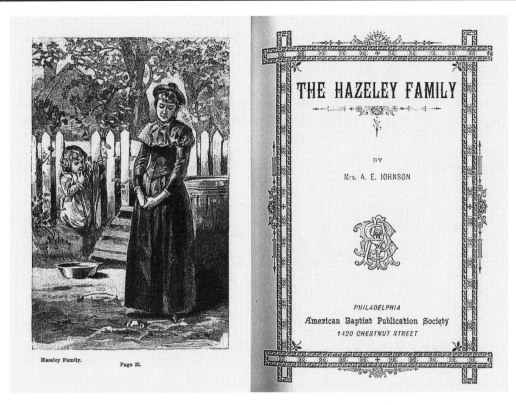

Frontispiece and title page for Johnson's 1894 novel, in which a girl leads her family to salvation

living situation unbearable. After she is struck by her aunt, Lottie runs away but is counseled by Flora to return to her aunt and to try to become an example of kindness and love that her aunt might follow. Lottie returns to her aunt and succeeds in reforming her. Thus, Lottie is rewarded for her patience and faith with marriage to Flora's brother Alec.

Martina Meriden; Or, What Is My Motive? is Johnson's final novel, published in 1901. As in Johnson's earlier novels, the protagonist and title character is a child, and the narrative recounts her journey toward self-knowledge and acceptance of a Christian worldview involving self-denial and love for Christ. At the beginning of the novel, Martina is twelve years old, and one can speculate that Johnson based the character on her own daughter, Jessie, who would have been twelve at the time of the novel's publication and who, like Martina, had two older brothers.

The plot of the novel surrounds the title character's journey toward spiritual self-awareness. *Martina Meriden* is reminiscent of Louisa May Alcott's *Little Women* (1868–1869) in its episodic narrative depicting incidents typical of children's lives and in its allusions to John Bunyan's *Pilgrim's Progress* (1678), a novel that is influential in Martina's spiritual development. Like the characters in Alcott's novel, Martina must learn the les-

son prescribed by Victorian-era evangelism: she cannot gain spiritual salvation through good works but must instead strive for salvation through her faith in and love for God, learning self-denial and self-sacrifice.

The early chapters of the novel establish Martina's solitary, introspective nature and her desire to be good and to gain entrance to heaven, a desire fortified by her experience with a playmate who dies of scarlet fever (perhaps another allusion to *Little Women*). Another recurring theme of the novel is that selfishness may be punished by negative consequences, often involving physical discomfort or injury. For example, Martina's disobedience of her mother's instructions to return home once it begins to snow leads to a miserable reoccurrence of the croup. A few chapters later, Martina's ill-conceived plan to cause a rival schoolmate worry results in a sprained ankle for Martina.

As Martina grows older, her experiences teach her that it is futile to try to gain entrance to heaven by performing good deeds. She is thus forced to question her motives. Her reading of *Pilgrim's Progress* helps her crystallize some of the important issues in her spiritual quest:

> there was something more than good resolutions needed in order to get any real satisfaction out of life;

MARTINA MERIDEN

OR

WHAT IS MY MOTIVE?

BY

MRS. A. E. JOHNSON
AUTHOR OF
"Clarence and Corinne," and "The Hazeley Family"

✳ ✳ ✳

PHILADELPHIA
American Baptist Publication Society
1420 Chestnut Street

*Title page for Johnson's final novel, about a girl's
spiritual awakening*

and if they brought no lasting contentment in this life, of what possible benefit could they be for the life to come? Martina found herself echoing mentally poor Christian's cry, 'Life! Life! Eternal life!' and she determined to follow his example and seek until she found it.

As she negotiates this crisis, she encounters two mentor figures, Mrs. Archer, her Sunday-school teacher, and Marian Watson, a family friend, whose examples help Martina learn that she should act not out of self-interest but out of love for God. The novel gives Martina one more chance to test her newfound awareness; although she is afraid, she agrees to stay with her mother's friend, Mrs. Morse, in an empty factory building in a disreputable neighborhood while Mrs. Morse's husband and son are out of town. Martina comes to realize that "God can take care of us just as well here as at home, and he will be pleased if I do this, because it is

right," and so she completes her stay with Mrs. Morse and passes her test of faith. The novel ends here, when Martina has succeeded in defining her motivations and acting accordingly.

These three novels dramatize the pitfalls that await women on these spiritual journeys, pitfalls that would have seemed all too real and dangerous to contemporary readers. In both *Clarence and Corinne* and *The Hazeley Family,* for example, alcoholism is portrayed as a destructive force. In *Clarence and Corinne,* Johnson implies that the father's alcoholism causes their mother's death of "a broken heart" and their father's abandonment of them. In *The Hazeley Family,* alcoholism is a specter that haunts the Hazeley home. Flora Hazeley is motivated to devote her energies to keeping house because she fears that her brothers and fathers will be lured away by the dissipations and pleasures of alcohol and gambling. By making the home a pleasant place for them, she hopes to distract her male relatives from the temptations of the streets. That she ultimately fails with her brother Harry is not to be read as a repudiation of the values Flora represents. Harry's fall into alcoholism is part of his own spiritual journey that will result in his call to the ministry.

The peril that alcohol represents to these characters is indicative of the concerns felt by Baptist women such as Amelia Johnson. Temperance was a nationwide movement led mainly by women responding to the power alcoholism had to destroy women's lives. Black Baptist women in particular feared that alcohol use among African Americans played into racist stereotypes and caused blacks to be looked down upon as low-class. As Evelyn Brooks Higgenbotham points out, black Baptist women also spoke out against alcohol and other dissipations and advocated redirecting funds spent on alcohol into education and other positive social and cultural programs.

Another aspect of the black Baptist women's movement's mission was to educate young women to play their proper domestic roles. Baptist women's organizations established "mother's schools" that taught housekeeping and parenting skills and wrote articles for women's magazines providing instruction in how to keep house properly. Flora Hazeley is an example of a character who has undergone the sort of education in domestic skills prescribed by these organizations. Flora's aunt Sarah, who helped raise her, instructs her thoroughly in the details of housekeeping, an education for which Flora is grateful when she grows older and must keep her mother's house. Even younger children understood the importance of keeping house. In *Martina Meriden,* Martina and her friend Charlotte set up housekeeping in an abandoned old house. Johnson holds that "the instinct of housekeeping is in most little girls, and they are never so content when playing at it."

The emphasis on housekeeping had a social as well as an individual dimension. The example of Flora Hazeley shows that the effects of one young woman's devotion to family and household duties can spill over to the lives of those around her. Flora's influence extends not only to her family but to her friends, and, Johnson implies, to society as a whole. If only every household had a Flora Hazeley, many of society's problems would be eliminated. As W. E. B. Du Bois was to say some years later, "To interpret life and the world to the little group about you, until they in turn can give back to the world a soul and a purpose—this is the function of the homemaker and nothing less."

Another recurring motif of the novels is nature. In all three novels, significant moments of religious revelation occur when the characters are in the country or otherwise enjoying nature. Martina Meriden's moment of spiritual epiphany comes when she is sitting in a park with her friend and spiritual guide, Marian Watson. Corinne Burton finds that while observing the natural beauties of Sweetbrier Farm, she is able to contemplate her feelings for and gratitude to God: "Truly, on such a morning, and amid such surroundings, it is fitting and natural that the holiest and best thoughts should be brought into play."

Johnson most explicitly uses natural imagery in *The Hazeley Family*. Major Joe is a farmer, or as he calls himself, "a gardener on a small scale." Also, Flora's name signifies her closeness to nature, as does her careful tending of a sweet potato given to her by her friend Lottie Piper. Warned by Lottie not to eat the sweet potato, Flora instead encourages it to grow, and the sweet potato's growth parallels the development of Flora into the ideal Christian woman and homemaker. As Flora's faith and love surround and embrace her family, the tendrils of the sweet potato flourish until they encompass the windowsill on which it sits.

After *Martina Meriden* appeared in 1901, Johnson never published another novel and possibly did not write any more for publication. Amelia Etta Hall Johnson died in Baltimore on 29 March 1922, on the cusp of the Harlem Renaissance. She died before she could see the gains made by African Americans during the Harlem Renaissance. A fervent advocate of African American publishing, she would have been gratified to see the expanded opportunities for black writers and the interest of white publishers in works by and about African Americans.

References:

Barbara Christian, Introduction to *The Hazeley Family* (New York: Oxford University Press, 1988);

Martin E. Dann, *The Black Press 1827–1890: The Quest for National Identity* (New York: Putnam, 1971);

Evelyn Brooks Higgenbotham, *Righteous Discontent: The Women's Movement in the Black Baptist Church, 1880–1920* (Cambridge, Mass.: Harvard University Press, 1993);

Azzie Briscoe Kozer, *Dr. Harvey Johnson: Pioneer Civic Leader* (Baltimore, 1957);

Monroe Alphus Majors, *Noted Negro Women, Their Triumphs and Activities* (Chicago: Donohue & Henneberry, 1893);

A. W. Pegues, *Our Baptist Ministers and Schools* (Springfield, Mass.: Wiley, 1892), pp. 288–293;

Irvine Garland Penn, *The Afro-American Press and Its Editors* (Springfield, Mass.: Wiley, 1892; revised edition, Washington, D.C.: New York Publishers, 1969);

Lawson A. Scruggs, *Women of Distinction: Remarkable Works and Invincible Characters* (Raleigh, N.C.: L. A. Scruggs, 1893), pp. 116–119;

Ann Allen Shockley, *Afro-American Women Writers 1746–1933: An Anthology and Critical Guide* (New York: Penguin, 1988), pp. 162–165;

Hortense J. Spillers, Introduction to *Clarence and Corinne; Or, God's Way* (New York: Oxford University Press, 1988);

Claudia Tate, *Domestic Allegories of Political Desire: The Black Heroine's Text at the Turn of the Century* (New York: Oxford University Press, 1992);

James Melvin Washington, *Frustrated Fellowship: The Black Baptist Quest for Social Power* (Macon, Ga.: Mercer, 1986).

Emma Dunham Kelley

(fl. 1890s)

Barbara McCaskill
University of Georgia

BOOKS: *Megda,* as "Forget-Me-Not" (Boston: James H. Earle, 1891);

Four Girls at Cottage City, as Emma D. Kelley-Hawkins (Providence, R.I.: Continental Printing, 1895).

Editions: *Megda,* as "Forget-Me-Not," introduction by Molly Hite (New York: Oxford University Press, 1988);

Four Girls at Cottage City, introduction by Deborah E. McDowell (New York: Oxford University Press, 1988).

Since the eighteenth-century sermons of Maria W. Stewart and the nineteenth-century preaching of Sojourner Truth, African American women have connected social activism with Christianity. The novelist Emma Dunham Kelley is both an heir to and an innovator of this lineage. She introduces dominant themes of conversion, piety, and faith to an African American woman's novel tradition that had been largely characterized by post-Reconstruction themes of sociopolitical progress and race. Her characters combine both middle-class and nationalist-feminist roles and aspirations, in a style that anticipates the early-twentieth-century fictions of manners by African American authors such as Charles Waddell Chesnutt, Alice Dunbar-Nelson, Jessie Redmon Fauset, and Nella Larsen.

Details of Kelley's life are sketchy. The dedicatory page of *Megda* (1891) indicates that her mother had been widowed. Beyond that fact, little is known. The important collective biographies of late-nineteenth-century African American women, such as Hallie Q. Brown's *Homespun Heroines and Other Women of Distinction* (1926) and Gertrude Bustill Mossell's *The Work of the Afro-American Woman* (1894), fail to mention Kelley. Nor, for example, is she prominent among the African American club women who were primarily associated with the African Methodist Episcopal Church and the National Association of Club Women. These were women whose names and writings regularly appeared in such literary and cultural magazines as *The Voice of the*

Negro, Alexander's Magazine, Colored American, A.M.E. Church Review, Woman's Era, and *Christian Recorder.*

The obscurity and enigma that surrounds Kelley's first novel, *Megda,* perhaps results from its partial eclipse by the tremendously popular *Iola Leroy; or Shadows Uplifted* (1891) by Frances Ellen Watkins Harper. *Megda,* which Kelley published under the pseudonym "Forget-Me-Not," was reprinted only one year after it first appeared. According to Claudia Tate, *Iola Leroy* similarly was reprinted twice (in 1892 and 1893) in the consecutive years after its initial publication. Yet, writes

238

Tate in her *Domestic Allegories of Political Desire* (1992), "while the literary production of black women was impressive, until the recent publication of *The Schomburg Library of Nineteenth-Century Black Women Writers,* edited by Henry Louis Gates, Jr., all that productivity with the exception of Harper's 1892 novel *Iola Leroy* had slipped through the cracks of African-American literary scholarship and fallen into oblivion, leaving *Iola Leroy* to stand alone as if it were unique."

Well into the twentieth century, scholars have written about *Iola Leroy* as if it were the first novel published in the United States by an African American woman. In fact, not only did *Megda* predate *Iola Leroy,* but there are at least three other African American women's novels that preceded it: Harriet E. Wilson's *Our Nig* (1859), Frances F. W. Harper's *Minnie's Sacrifice* (1869), and Amelia E. Johnson's *Clarence and Corinne; Or, God's Way* (1890).

Any conclusions about Kelley's life and marriage to be gathered from her novels are speculative. She eliminates detailed descriptions of landscape, architecture, dialect, dress, and other material, temporal markers of place in order to focus upon her characters' spiritual growth and to intensify their struggles to be saved. What can be proposed, however, is that Kelley may have been an educator: somehow, if not in the classroom then perhaps in the parlor of some literary club or reading society, she must have benefited from a broad immersion in the literature of Great Britain and the United States. Her novels are peppered with detailed, generous references to scenes from the popular works of these canons. *Megda,* for example, assumes a familiarity with British and American titles that Kelley and her middle-class African American contemporaries would have read including Charles Dickens's *David Copperfield* (1849–1850) and William Shakespeare's *Macbeth* (1606).

Kelley probably lived in the New England region, the setting of both of her novels. The spring season there, as in *Megda,* is cool. Megda and her schoolmates stoically cover themselves in furs and muffs and sleigh blankets against the blustery, gray rainstorms of spring and bitter, cold snowstorms of winter that characterize the riverside towns and harbor villages of Massachusetts, New York, Rhode Island, and Connecticut.

Molly Hite and Henry Louis Gates Jr. cite the resort town of Cottage City in order to locate Kelley in Massachusetts. Cottage City is the setting of her second novel, a holiday spot that travelers must access by boat from New Bedford, Massachusetts, a town in the southern part of the state. Cottage City is also mentioned in *Megda,* when three of the young women characters travel there by boat from New Bedford in order to take a respite among vacationers from Cambridge and other Massachusetts communities. Since many vacationers visited Cottage City from Providence, Rhode Island, and since *Four Girls at Cottage City* (1895) was originally published in Rhode Island, Kelly may have resided in that state for a time. Cape Cod stood second in popularity only to Newport, Rhode Island, as a posh location to see and be seen, as well as to rest and recuperate. Kelley herself acknowledges in the preface to *Four Girls at Cottage City,* in a tone reminiscent of the nineteenth-century slave narratives, that the action of her story "on the shores of bleak Cape Cod" actually did happen.

Finally, the novels may narrow Kelley's movements to Boston and its surrounding towns. In this case the anonymity and omissions that nineteenth-century writers inserted in order to lend truth—and to protect the identities of innocents—may hinder more than help. A "Dr. L– of B–," where "B–" perhaps alludes to Boston, attends to Maude of *Megda* when she is mortally ill. "L–," where Maude's burial in *Megda* transpires, may be Lowell, a factory and mill town adjacent to Boston. In *Four Girls at Cottage City* a group of young women friends raises money to place a mother and her sick child under the care of "Dr. C.–," one of Boston's leading physicians.

Boston is the city where Kelley's publisher James H. Earle and Company (founded 1869) kept offices. Earle's specialization in religious literature may explain why Kelley selected him to publish her books on young female students who struggled to convert and the young male ministers and social companions who converted them. Kelley may have been a member of the Baptist denomination, as Earle's firm had produced publications for those churches. Supporting this assumption is that, in each novel, certain non-Baptist denominations are criticized. The Presbyterians are reproached in *Megda,* for example, as are the "stiff-necked" Methodists, Episcopalians, and Universalists in *Four Girls at Cottage City.* The Presbyterians are disparaged for their doctrine, and the Methodists, Episcopalians, and Universalists for, respectively, shouting in an excessive and undignified manner during religious services, substituting philanthropy for sincere religious devotion, and having too much of a good time at theaters and dances. These judgments do not mean that Kelley, to use her own words, was among those who held to the opinion that "No denomination on earth was right except her own; all others were in danger of hell's fire." With the tone of an insider, a long monologue in *Four Girls at Cottage City,* for example, chastises an "earnest" and "zealous" Baptist woman named Laura Barton for being too eager to save souls, too judgmental about her neighbors' sins and vanities, and so ambitious to lead "a true Christian life" that she places her own plans first and God's purposes for her second.

One character in *Four Girls at Cottage City,* Erfort Richards, is unabashedly partisan toward the Baptist faith. He comments: "Now, the Baptists do not think that he who has professed himself ready to try to live a Christian life, ought to find pleasure in the enjoyments that the world offers him. You know the Bible tells us that we cannot serve both God and mammon. Either we must hate the one and love the other, or vice versa. I do not think that it really means that we are to hate in the ordinary sense of the word; but I think it means that we ought to find so much pleasure in serving God and keeping our hearts so full of love for Him, that there will be no room in them for anything else." The most orthodox of Baptists forswear, among other vices, card playing, acting, smoking, novel reading, palmistry, mesmerism, fortune-telling, dressing seductively, and dancing—everything associated with what Kelley calls "a life of endless excitement and sinful pleasure." So, too, do Kelley's pious, bourgeois women characters avoid (but not without backsliding) these activities that promote "thinking too much of the world and not enough of God." Thus Hite has identified what she calls the "specifically Baptist aspect of the conversion experience" in Kelley's fictions. Additional aspects that connect Kelley to the Baptist church are her descriptions of sermons, Holy Communion, baptisms, weddings, and other religious rituals.

Kelley's fiction may be understood in relation to other traditions of popular fiction as well. Mid-nineteenth-century heroines of sentimental fiction, such as E.D.E.N. Southworth's "madcap," cross-dressing Capitola of *The Hidden Hand* (1859), tested their independence from patriarchy. As Nina Baym writes in *Woman's Fiction* (1978), these gutsy heroines challenged the traditional qualities associated with femininity—passivity, intuition, helplessness—by being assertive and initiatory, rational, and financially and emotionally self-reliant. Rebelling against traditional expectations of gender roles, they became women who succeeded or failed as a consequence of their own efforts and characters.

The sentimental heroines may have married poorly. They may have been chased from or cheated out of an inheritance or condemned to suffer imprisonment, abuse, ridicule, impoverishment, or rape at the hands of tyrannical males. They may have been socialized to believe that their status in society depends upon the bank accounts, class affiliations, and business reputations of their husbands or other male guardians. They may have been raised with the expectation that, like so many coins and stock certificates, they were just currency to be exchanged, desired, consumed, collected,

and, ultimately, discarded when their usefulness expired. Yet, these heroines persevered to define themselves and their sex in a society where, all too often, their roles as women merely involved producing heirs, being beautiful, or bolstering the egos and mirroring the minds of whatever men chose to marry them.

Late-nineteenth-century protagonists of girls' fiction, however, rewrote this sentimental genre and reined in these sentimentalized heroines. They returned American readers to definitions of womanhood that had seemed oppressive and stifling but were now viewed as liberating and progressive. At the end of these texts, for example, the heroines emerge as wives and mothers who depend on—and willingly so—masculine prerogative. If they supported college education or independence from marriage for women, if they vetoed the existence of God and the necessity of religious faith, if they slandered middle-class American values, or if they ventured feminist notions that women were the social and intellectual equals to men, the heroines were not usually approved of. This, to quote Hite, was, then, a "limit-enforcing instrument" or genre in comparison to the liberating project of sentimental fiction.

"Girlie" is an oft-repeated term of endearment in *Megda* that invites the comparison of the novel to girls' fiction. The twenty-five chapters of Kelley's book focus on the coming-of-age of a circle of nine young women in their senior year of studies. They are the main character, Megda, or Meg Randal, and her chums (or, sometimes, rivals) Laurie Ray, Dell Manton, May Bromley, Lulu Martin, Lillian Norton, Ethel Lawton, Ruth Dean, and Maude Leonard. The names "Laurie" and "Meg" are evocative of lead male and female characters in Louisa May Alcott's best-selling *Little Women* (1869) and further demonstrate Kelley's familiarity with the sentimental genre.

As she says through the words of her heroine, Meg, Kelley is not concerned with "any of the love-sick maidens who sentimental authors write about in their trashy, five-penny novels." Rather than an erotic love of the flesh, Kelley's novels valorize a selfless love of the spirit. The successful transition of Meg and her community of schoolmates from girlhood to wifehood depends on how they develop supportive female friendships with each other and how they discover a deep, spiritual connection to their God. The girls must manifest these relationships daily through good works, courage, humility, self-sacrifice, prayer, and cheerful devotion to the duties of wifehood and motherhood.

Kelley conflates coming-of-age with Christianity near the turning point of the novel, in the sixteenth chapter, "Easter." She says: to "me there is nothing as beautiful and altogether pleasing, as a sweet, fair, pure life at the time when 'girl-hood is about to pass through the window, and womanhood stands knocking at the door'. . . . Happy they who 'remember their Creator in the days of their youth,' and early look to Him as their Guide and Protector through all the dark journey of life."

The action of *Megda* revolves around the eponymously named heroine's struggles to convert to Christianity, to acknowledge her dependence on a power greater than herself, and to accept the gift of "the deep, blessed feeling of rest and peace, joy and happiness" that salvation brings. Like her antebellum antecedent, Frado, of Harriet Wilson's Massachusetts-set *Our Nig* (1859), Meg is a hard case. One by one, her friends devote themselves to serious Bible study, receive baptism and Holy Communion, publicly witness to their faith, court, marry, and settle into family life. Yet, like Frado before her, she remains "wilful." Proud, stubborn, resisting the piety of her friends, she laughs all the time, is easily distracted by sensual and material pleasures, and allows herself to be carried away by petty jealousies, gossip, and sniping.

Gradually, the encouraging sermons and talks of her minister, the Reverend Arthur Stanley, woo Meg to God, as well as a deathbed promise to her pious friend Ethel. Meg then literally takes Ethel's place in the status quo by marrying her deceased friend's husband (the same Reverend Arthur Stanley), by becoming a mother (Meg adopts Maude's little girl when she dies an untimely death), and by dedicating her life to unselfishly serving the needs of her family and community.

As much as *Megda* epitomizes girls' fiction, it also deviates from it. Meg, as Tate notes, may end up in the socially sanctioned role of wife, but she "is not a selfless object to whom her husband dictates his desire." Tate finds that Meg, like many genteel heroines of the genre, subverts gender expectations by establishing a marriage that is more like an egalitarian, "sibling-model" or "companionate" relationship than the traditional standard of silenced wife and dominating husband.

Meg also sticks to the sentimental heroine's assertion of female independence. An "independent spirit" at the beginning of the novel, she "had always found herself to be sufficient for her own comfort and happiness; she had never found it necessary, as the other girls had done, to depend on others—to look to others for help; she had always been proudly independent of everybody; it had made her impatient with others less self-confident." At the end of the novel, Meg's personality still manifests "the natural wilfulness of her disposition."

If Kelley's fictional project is both to conform to and to revise the requirements of sentimental fiction, then her approach to the racial identities of the characters in her novels also satisfies and startles readers'

expectations. According to Elizabeth Ammons, the "preeminence of race as the issue for black women—the idea that although sex discrimination in general may be bad, it is finally the peculiar brand of sex discrimination experienced by black women *because they are black* that must be named and dealt with—appears repeatedly in turn-of-the-century fiction by black women." However, like Amelia E. Johnson's fictions, *Megda* and *Four Girls at Cottage City* deviate from this theme because of the ambiguous racial origins of the men and women characters who populate them.

Many literary critics have identified Kelley's characters as white. Even those characters described as dark-faced, such as Ruth and Maude of *Megda,* could be white, perhaps olive-complexioned or dusky. In support of this conclusion, the girls of Kelley's fictions do not discuss such concerns as segregation, discrimination in employment and educational opportunities, bigotry, lynching, rape, relationships to white women, and other issues that dominate the conversations of African American women in the uplift productions published by authors such as Harper and Pauline Elizabeth Hopkins.

About as close as Kelley draws in either of her novels to using conversation to establish her heroines' race is in *Four Girls at Cottage City,* when two friends recoil at the prospect of sitting in a theater's "nigger heaven," the balcony seats reserved for black audiences and, like the "nigger pews" in Northern Protestant churches, designed since the eighteenth century to discourage social contact between whites and blacks. Even then, it is unclear whether or not the girls, as blacks, are expressing outrage at this discriminatory exclusion or, as whites, are poking ridicule at the idea that this might be the only place for them to sit in a crowded theater.

On one level, Kelley uses the darkness and lightness of her characters conventionally. She associates darkness with devils, wickedness, and evildoers such as Maude and whiteness with angels, enlightenment, and do-gooders such as Ethel. It is appropriate, then, that Meg, who resists conversion, flashes dark eyes and dark looks and even wears a dark-colored gown when she finally does receive Christ, or that Ethel, the first to convert, possesses "skin as white as the driven snow" and eyes that are "blue and shining." Writing in her introduction to the 1988 reprint of *Four Girls at Cottage City,* Deborah E. McDowell describes such equations that draw "blackness as synonymous with evil and equated whiteness with grace" as perhaps Kelley's "capitulation to the era's race-prejudiced theology."

At the same time, by combining lightness and darkness in the descriptions of her girls, Kelley, however subtly, defies the assumptions of such a racist theology and distances herself from the derivative

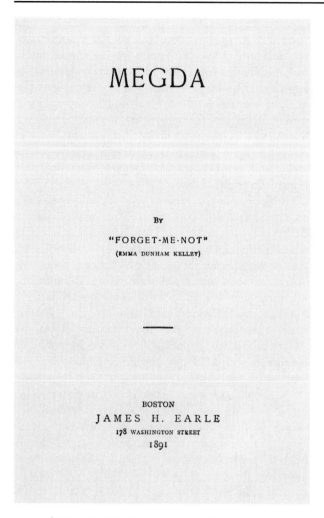

MEGDA

By

"FORGET-ME-NOT"

(EMMA DUNHAM KELLEY)

BOSTON

JAMES H. EARLE

178 WASHINGTON STREET

1891

Title page for Kelley's novel about the spiritual maturation of a group of schoolgirls

dichotomies. Throughout both of her novels, for example, her beautiful, delicate adolescent heroines possess "dark eyes" to contrast with "white hands," "dark hair" to contrast with "bright" or "shiny" eyes, or "pink cheeks" to contrast with "dark eyes." Similarly, in Kelley's first novel, when Meg first encounters her future husband, the Reverend Stanley, she realizes that she has mistaken his blue eyes for black ones. As a penultimate marker of this indistinctiveness surrounding color, when Meg and Arthur have two children of their own, their daughter is a "bright-haired, dark-eyed darling" and their son is "a dark-haired, blue-eyed child." Maude's toddler daughter, too, is a "rich, dark beauty, except her eyes, which were large and bright, but a deep blue."

This confusion calls to mind the spiritual entanglements of "our girls." Our inability as readers to see them as one race or another emblematizes their own confusion over which spiritual path to take and, by

extension, which is the right path to take toward womanhood. According to many critics, the combination of lightness and darkness within the features of one character, or among the members of one family, can be Kelley's attempt to show the generations of racial intermixture that have characterized the African American experience.

Black bourgeois anxieties about class are also inherent in the way Kelley associates color with her heroines. Whiteness may be a metaphor for the wealth, consumption, and acquisition that so many striving members of post-Reconstruction African American society aspired to, while darkness represents its antithesis: insolvency, poverty, material deprivation. The binary oppositions between blackness and whiteness manifested by the physical traits of Kelley's characters stand for what Dolan Hubbard, writing in *The Sermon and the African American Literary Imagination* (1994), calls the "latent discomfort index" of some Reconstruction and post-Reconstruction blacks, who endeavored toward the middle class by separating themselves from some of the expressive and folk traditions generated during enslavement.

Yet, Ruth, the poor, dark-skinned character of *Megda,* possesses a richness of spirit that contrasts with the narcissism and selfishness occasioned by some of her wealthier schoolmates. Many middle-class heroines of white women's sentimental fiction–such as Mariah Rocke in Southworth's *The Hidden Hand*–modeled good taste and fine manners to those who were supposed to be their social superiors. So, too, does Ruth often demonstrate more breeding, good nature, sensitivity, and compassion than her schoolmates and headmistress who may scoff at her and exclude her from their amusements. Kelley uses the Reverend Stanley, in a conversation with Meg, to expose the point of this inversion. He says: "When a person is rich, we expect more from him, where money is concerned, than we do with a poor person. It is just so with God. He does not bestow His gifts upon all His children alike. To one He gives one talent; to another two; to another three; to those He gives the most, He expects the most from." It is as if the lily-whiteness-qua-material obsession of Kelley's spiritually deficient girls is intended to rebuke those real African American women who made the society pages and threw fancy balls but neglected to assist their poorer brothers and sisters.

Reminiscent of the white mistresses and employers of the former slave Elizabeth Keckley's postbellum narrative titled *Behind the Scenes* (1868), these bourgeois black society women who Kelley shames were too caught up in the world of appearances. They erred on three counts. They stood at variance with their age's central theme of race uplift; they substituted an exclusionary affiliation with the middle class for the "woman's era's" collective identification with other women as women; and they squandered an opportunity to enrich and sanctify their souls. They would have benefited from the insight that Kelley offers in *Four Girls at Cottage City:* "Those who look as if they were born to rule are generally the ones who *are* ruled."

Kelley's subtleties surrounding race may have been responsible for the initial disinterest in or outright rejection of her work by reviewers and audiences. When the highest appellation for an African American activist or writer was to be extolled as a "race woman," some may have regarded Kelley as having reneged upon an obligation to write straightforwardly about race and skin color and the associated themes of lynching, passing, and miscegenation. Others, committed to the motto of the National Association of Colored Women (founded 1896), "Lifting as We Climb," demanded that African American women of means recognize their fates as intertwined with those of their underprivileged sisters. The white characters of *Megda* and *Four Girls at Cottage City* may have been perceived as one African American woman writer's depoliticized—or bohemian—rebuff to the urgent "uplift" project of modeling gentility, domesticity, and cultural and spiritual values to the collective masses of black American women.

Nearly a decade passed after the appearance of *Megda* before Kelley published her second novel, *Four Girls at Cottage City.* With twenty-six chapters and another evangelical theme, this novel bookends *Megda.* Kelley literally writes *Megda* into *Four Girls at Cottage City,* when its protagonists discuss the former novel and discover that they occupy the same vacationers' cottage that some of the heroines of *Megda* had visited.

Kelley must have married by 1895, since she published her book using the hyphenated surname of Kelley-Hawkins. Since the setting is also Massachusetts and the publisher is also James H. Earle, Kelley may still have been residing in New England. Her widowed mother may have passed away, since she dedicated the book to a "Second Mother" named Aunt Lottie.

This dedication to a "second mother" certainly underscores the novel's prominent treatment of what Joyce Ladner in *Tomorrow's Tomorrow* (1972) and Patricia Hill Collins in *Black Feminist Thought: Knowledge, Consciousness, and the Politics of Empowerment* (1990) call "other mothers." "Other mothers" are women who act as mentors, advisers, and friends to younger women who are not biologically related to them. Differences in class, educational attainment, marital status, or sexual orientation do not hinder the ability of "other mothers" to share intimacies among the communities of women that they encounter. In Kelley's *Four Girls at Cottage City* it is an "other mother" named Charlotte Hood, a widowed islander who functions as a confidante and spiritual guide, who manuevers four lively, late-adolescent girls toward professing a Christian faith and embracing the adult responsibilities of their gender. The foursome—the sisters Garnet and Jessie Dare, Allie Hunt, and Vera Earle—are ushered from frivolous, carefree youth to a maturity of selfless devotion by Charlotte's stories of sacrifice and suffering, forgiveness and faith. Their names may pay tribute to actual "other mothers" in African American women's social and religious organizations who modelled respectable womanhood: Vera Earle, for example, may be derived from the writer Victoria Earle Matthews.

In *Four Girls at Cottage City* eating functions in the dual manner that physicality does in *Megda.* On the one hand, the girls consume nonnutricious sweets and light meals—chocolates, cocoa, crackers, candies, suppers of sandwiches or baked beans and breakfasts of egg omelettes. It is a resort town that they are visiting, so they typically eat whatever is available to buy, and they eat whenever or wherever they feel like buying it. They often complain of voracious appetites, but the foods they consume hardly seem satiating. They resemble the ghost-daughter Beloved from Toni Morrison's novel of the same name, whose appetite for more and more sweets cannot satisfy the emotional emptiness she feels for having been murdered by her mother.

While their culinary fare may not be substantial and is procured in the marketplace, the spiritual nourishment the four girls at Cottage City receive is a different story. In addition to the religious stories that Charlotte tells them and what they hear in sermons or in readings from the Bible, the four girls glean wisdom and models for righteous conduct from passionate discussions of the literature of such British and American authors as Dickens, Henry Wadsworth Longfellow, Shakespeare, and Alfred Tennyson. They borrow or bring these books, rather than purchase them, as if to underscore that spiritual wealth cannot be measured, bartered, or bought.

If Kelley articulates a subtle nationalism in *Four Girls at Cottage City,* it is most strongly apparent in her position that "arts and sciences must go hand in hand with religion and morality." "Dickens' works," she writes, "are eternal arguments against injustice, and in writing novels he was as well employed as in preaching the gospel. Mendelsshon [*sic*], by his sublime compositions, did better serve the world than going out as a missionary to China; and Shakespeare served the world and his Maker better as a dramatist than as a bishop, preaching sermons that nobody wanted to hear."

Kelley's rhetoric echoes the statements espoused by such race leaders as Booker T. Washington, Anna Julia Cooper, and W. E. B. Du Bois, that African Americans should not neglect to appreciate the arts—and to bequeath this enthusiasm to their children—as they strove to open savings accounts, acquire land, seek admission into the best schools, and otherwise advance materially. To read, write, paint, sculpt, learn a romantic or classical language, play an instrument, or compose music meant a great deal to African Americans only one or two generations removed from a time when whites considered them to be incapable of such activities or only able to accomplish them in an imitative or derivative fashion. These activities, much the same as their religions, nourished the soul. Kelley's attitude toward art as a kind of secular religion, which collides somewhat with her Baptist leanings against theater and dance, also owes to a general climate in the United States that made culture—a piano in the parlor, a shelf of books in the bedroom, a stack of literary magazines or lavishly embossed gift books in the entranceway—a sign of middle-class attainment.

Compared to its attention to and enthusiasm about contemporaries of hers such as Frances Ellen Watkins Harper, Pauline Elizabeth Hopkins, Victoria Earle Matthews, Ida B. Wells-Barnett, Josephine St. Pierre Ruffin, Alice Dunbar-Nelson, Nannie Burroughs, Gertrude Bustill Mossell, and Anna Julia Cooper, the secular 1880s and 1890s African American press certainly seems restrained in its reception of Kelley and her novels. Yet, much more critical notice of *Megda* and *Four Girls at Cottage City* has accumulated, albeit slowly, since the 1980s and 1990s. The relationship of Kelley's novels to girls' fiction and to sentimental fiction, as well as to other genres important to women writers such as the bildungsroman, the sermon, and the spiritual autobiography, continues to fascinate critics. Most prevalent are discussions situating her novels in the ideological and literary conventions of African American women's literature that emerged between 1877 and 1915, which, in his book *The Betrayal of the Negro* (1965), historian Rayford W. Logan characterizes as the "nadir" of African Americans' experiences in this country.

Renewed scholarship on Kelley can be attributed to the academy's reevaluation of nineteenth-century African American texts, which gained momentum in the late 1960s and early 1970s as a consequence of the Civil Rights Movement, the Black Arts Movement, and integration. Also, a catalyst for this resurgence of interest in Kelley's novels has been feminists' recovery of women's literary productions, films, and visual arts that

once were dismissed as minor or else subordinated to what Tate calls "markers on a historical time line between great male master texts." In addition, perhaps readers have found Kelley's novels compelling because of an increased consciousness of the intertextuality of African American women's fiction. Articulated by such important studies as Deborah E. McDowell's "The Changing Same" (1995) and Michael Awkward's *Inspiriting Influences* (1991) is the idea that African American women's fictions of one generation resonate with thematic, aesthetic, structural, and stylistic affinities to those of a prior one, whether or not such influences have been overtly acknowledged and varied or else subconsciously enacted by the women writers themselves.

The conservatism and formalism of Kelley's novels belies their prescience. The ambiguity of race that characterizes her novels particularly anticipates the debates of the Harlem Renaissance, vocalized by Langston Hughes in his *The Nation* essay titled "The Negro Artist and the Racial Mountain" (1926). When Hughes stated that "We younger Negro artists who create now intend to express our individual dark skinned selves without fear or shame," he meant that he and his New Negro Movement peers, including James Weldon Johnson and Zora Neale Hurston, questioned the assumptions that American audiences possessed about what African American writers should write, how they should write, whom they should write to, and what characteristics identify a black aesthetic and distinguish it from a white one.

One Harlem Renaissance woman writer around whom this debate focused was Anne Spencer, of Virginia. A Southerner rather than a Harlemite, she wrote poetry that did not consistently vocalize themes of race and class and did not always conform in language and structure to such black lyrical prototypes as the dialect poem or blues. Yet, her home in Lynchburg was a wonderful salon for the Harlem Renaissance literati, and they frequently sought her out to edit or comment upon draft versions of their writings. She was not easily inserted into predetermined categories that defined African American writers, women writers, or their styles and themes. Kelley's novels similarly force readers and critics to face the omissions and misreadings that have resulted from arbitrarily assigning African American women's fiction to one category or the other. They are memorable for elegant, complex portrayals of young African American women who struggle with their spirituality against a backdrop of late-nineteenth-century, Protestant, middle-class aspirations. In *Four Girls at Cottage City* Kelley indicated that a sequel to *Megda* was planned. While there is no evidence that she actually wrote the sequel, her two extant novels provide important insights into a period of African American literary productivity.

References:

Elizabeth Ammons, *Conflicting Stories: American Women Writers at the Turn into the Twentieth Century* (New York: Oxford University Press, 1991), pp. 20–24;

Nina Baym, "Form and Ideology of Woman's Fiction," in her *Woman's Fiction: A Guide to Novels by and about Women in America, 1820–1870* (Ithaca: Cornell University Press, 1978), pp. 22–50;

Dickson D. Bruce Jr., *Black American Writing from the Nadir: The Evolution of a Literary Tradition, 1877–1915* (Baton Rouge: Louisiana State University Press,1989), pp. 11–55;

Hazel V. Carby, *Reconstructing Womanhood: The Emergence of the Afro-American Woman Novelist* (New York: Oxford University Press, 1987), pp. 95–120;

Barbara Christian, *Black Women Novelists: The Development of a Tradition, 1892–1976* (Westport, Conn.: Greenwood Press, 1980);

Anne DuCille, *The Coupling Convention: Sex, Text, and Tradition in Black Women's Fiction* (New York: Oxford University Press, 1993);

Arlene A. Elder, *The "Hindered Hand": Cultural Implications of Early African-American Fiction* (Westport, Conn.: Greenwood Press, 1978), pp. 34, 204;

Evelyn Brooks Higginbothom, *Righteous Discontent: The Women's Movement in the Black Baptist Church, 1880–1920* (Cambridge, Mass.: Harvard University Press, 1993), p. 61;

Blyden Jackson, *A History of Afro-American Literature, Volume One: The Long Beginning, 1746–1895* (Baton Rouge: Louisiana State University Press, 1989), pp. 391–393;

Ann Allen Shockley, "Emma Dunham Kelley-Hawkins: Forget-me-Not," in her *Afro-American Women Writers, 1746–1933: An Anthology and Critical Guide* (New York: New American Library, 1989), pp. 176–180;

Claudia Tate, "Allegories of Black Female Desire; or, Rereading Nineteenth-Century Sentimental Narratives of Black Female Authority," in *Changing Our Own Words: Essays on Criticism, Theory, and Writing by Black Women,* edited by Cheryl Wall (New Brunswick, N.J.: Rutgers University Press, 1989), pp. 98–126;

Tate, *Domestic Allegories of Political Desire: The Black Heroine's Text at the Turn of the Century* (New York: Oxford University Press, 1992), pp. 124–179;

Caroline McAlpine Watson, *Prologue: The Novels of Black American Women, 1891–1965* (Westport, Conn.: Greenwood Press, 1985), pp. 9–31, 142–143.

Lucy Larcom
(5 March 1824 – 17 April 1893)

Shirley Marchalonis
Pennsylvania State University, Berks Campus

BOOKS: *Similitudes, from the Ocean and Prairie* (Boston: Jewett, 1853);

Lottie's Thought-Book (Philadelphia: American Sunday-School Union, 1858);

Ships in the Mist, and Other Stories (Boston: Hoyt, 1860);

Leila among the Mountains (Boston: Hoyt, 1861);

Breathings of a Better Life (Boston: Fields, Osgood, 1866; London: Virtue, 1872);

Poems (Boston: Fields, Osgood, 1869);

Childhood Songs (Boston: Houghton, Mifflin, 1874);

An Idyl of Work (Boston: Osgood, 1875);

Landscape in American Poetry (New York: Appleton, 1879);

Wild Roses of Cape Ann and Other Poems (Boston: Houghton Osgood, 1880);

The Poetical Works of Lucy Larcom (Boston: Houghton, Mifflin, 1884);

Wheaton Seminary: A Semi-Centennial Sketch (Cambridge, Mass.: Riverside, 1885);

Beckonings for Every Day: A Calendar of Thought (Boston: Houghton, Mifflin, 1886; London: Ward, Lock, 1886);

Easter Messengers: A New Poem of the Flowers (New York: White, Stokes & Allen, 1886);

The Crystal Hills, by Larcom and John Greenleaf Whittier (Boston: Prang, 1889);

A New England Girlhood, Outlined from Memory (Boston & New York: Houghton, Mifflin, 1889);

Easter Gleams (Boston & New York: Houghton, Mifflin, 1890);

As It Is in Heaven (Boston & New York: Houghton, Mifflin, 1891);

At the Beautiful Gate, and Other Songs of Faith (Boston: Houghton, Mifflin, 1892);

The Unseen Friend (Boston: Houghton, Mifflin, 1892).

Edition: *A New England Girlhood, Outlined from Memory* (Boston: Northeastern University Press, 1986).

OTHER: *Child-Life,* edited by Larcom and John Greenleaf Whittier (Boston: Osgood, 1871);

Child-Life in Prose, edited by Larcom and Whittier (Boston: Osgood, 1873);

Lucy Larcom

Songs of Three Centuries, edited by Larcom and Whittier (Boston: Osgood, 1876);

Roadside Poems for Summer Travellers, edited by Larcom (Boston: Osgood, 1876);

Hillside and Seaside in Poetry: A Companion to "Roadside Poems," edited by Larcom (Boston: Osgood, 1877).

SELECTED PERIODICAL PUBLICATIONS–
UNCOLLECTED: "Among Lowell Mill Girls," *Atlantic Monthly,* 48 (1881): 593–612;

"American Factory Life–Past, Present, and Future," *Journal of Social Science,* 16 (1882): 141–146;

"In the Ossipee Glens," *New England Magazine* (October 1892): 192–207.

In her own time Lucy Larcom was a well-known and honored poet, but she is remembered and read for one of her few works of prose, her autobiographical *A New England Girlhood, Outlined from Memory* (1889). There are other contradictions between the reality of Larcom's life and her later reputation: literary history written in the early years of this century has been neither kind nor accurate in its presentation of her life and career. She is mentioned as a kind of appendage to John Greenleaf Whittier, who receives credit for any success she had; her role in their literary relationship and long friendship has been reduced to that of a lovesick follower. Another view, one that ignores her personal popularity, host of friends, and prosperous, supportive family, presents her as a pauper, alone and pitiful. Daniel Dulany Addison's biography of Larcom, published in 1894, a year after her death, shows her as a pious lady who spent most of her days in meditation and prayer and extends the stereotype of women poets as mindless sweet singers. She has seldom been recognized as a hardworking, well-educated, nationally known poet whose fame led to the invitation to write the autobiography for which she is remembered.

Contrary to Addison's thesis, Lucy Larcom's life was active and eventful. Born in Beverly, Massachusetts, 5 March 1824, she was the ninth of her father's ten children by two marriages. Benjamin Larcom had been a sea captain until the Embargo Act of 1807 drove him ashore, where he kept a shop selling East India goods. Though the need to provide for ten children made economy important, the family was comfortably situated; they practiced New England "plain living and high thinking" in a household of domestic activity, books, and plenty of love and freedom for the children. The family was proud of precocious Lucy's ability to read early, to memorize hymns, and to write verses.

Lucy was seven years old when Captain Larcom died and the family circumstances changed. After three years of trying to manage on her own, without depending on her relatives, Lois Barrett Larcom moved to Lowell, Massachusetts, with her younger children. In the 1830s the Lowell Experiment, an attempt to prove that America could have factories without slums and crime, was still attractive; the cotton mills of this planned industrial community drew respectable young women from New England farms and villages as well as European visitors such as Charles Dickens and Harriet Martineau who came to observe the phenomenon. To Lois Larcom, Lowell offered the chance to be self-supporting, and she became a mill boardinghouse supervisor.

At age ten Lucy began to work in the mills, doing one of the easier jobs designed for children, and in one capacity or another she remained in the mills for eleven years. She went to school, which she loved; when finances forced her to give up the chance of high school, a formal education became her dream. Like the other mill girls, she took advantage of what Lowell had to offer: she attended lectures, went to classes (she learned French and German well enough to read literary texts in the original languages and translate poetry), and used the public library to read everything she could. The Lowell years left a complex impression on Larcom: on the one hand, she developed a respect for work, self-reliance, and independence, as well as admiration for the young mountain girls who came to the mills; on the other hand, she developed respiratory ailments and a pathological hatred of noise and confined spaces that affected her for the rest of her life.

The gradual importation of foreign labor changed the Lowell Experiment, making it less appealing to the farm and mountain girls who had made it famous. Larcom's beloved older sister Emmeline had married George Spaulding, a Lowell schoolmaster. Larcom spent much time at their home, where she met George's brother, Frank, a Harvard medical student, with whom she developed an "understanding" that eventually they would marry. For these young people and their contemporaries, the future of the country seemed to lie in the West, and when the Spauldings decided to move to Illinois to help settle what was then the frontier, Larcom decided to go with them.

They arrived in Illinois in 1846, settled on the prairie farm George had bought unseen, and attempted to make themselves into pioneers. Larcom taught in a district school; her letters home offer ruefully humorous accounts of the conditions under which she taught and lived. After a few unsatisfying years, she met Philena Fobes, headmistress of Monticello Academy in Alton, Illinois. Fobes changed her life. The headmistress was interested in the bright young woman and arranged for her to become a pupil-teacher at Monticello, allowing her at last to achieve the formal education that had been her dream. When Frank Spaulding went to California in 1849, lured by gold and adventure, the plan was for Larcom to join him there when she finished her education; she had, however, seen what life in the West did to women, including her sister, and though she never stated it, she clearly had grown weary of prairie and pioneer life. In 1852, declaring that she wanted to see her family before moving to California, she returned to Beverly.

During her years in Lowell she had been a contributor to the *Lowell Offering,* and at one of their meetings she had been introduced to Whittier, then better

PROSPECTUS AND ANNOUNCEMENT
OF THE
NEW ILLUSTRATED MAGAZINE
FOR
YOUNG FOLKS.

MESSRS. TICKNOR & FIELDS, BOSTON, commenced on the first of December the publication of a new Juvenile Magazine, entitled

Our Young Folks:
AN ILLUSTRATED MONTHLY MAGAZINE
FOR
BOYS AND GIRLS.
EDITED BY
J. T. Trowbridge,
Gail Hamilton,
Lucy Larcom.

The staff of Contributors will include many of the most popular writers of Juvenile Works in America and in England.

CAPTAIN MAYNE REID will write regularly for it Stories of Adventure, similar in captivating interest to those absorbing narratives, "The Desert Home," "The Plant Hunters," "The Forest Exiles," etc.

J. T. TROWBRIDGE, the Editor, who is well known as the author of "Father Brighthopes," and other charming and popular Juveniles, will contribute to every number. He will begin in the first number a story for boys, entitled "Andy's Adventures."

GAIL HAMILTON and **LUCY LARCOM,** the Associate Editors, will preside over that portion of the magazine especially designed for girls, and in addition to their editorial supervision, will write regularly each month.

MR. and MRS. AGASSIZ will supply for every number of the first volume a paper on Natural History, with illustrations.

MRS. HARRIET BEECHER STOWE will contribute to each number, commencing with a charming sketch, entitled "Hum, the Son of Buz."

MRS. L. MARIA CHILD, Editor of the "Juvenile Miscellany," and author of "Flowers for Children," will send occasional contributions.

"CARLETON," author of "My Days and Nights on the Battle-Field," will begin in the first number a tale of battle adventure, with the title, "Winning his Way," in which he will trace the career of a young soldier, and show how promotion is earned by valor and energy.

DR. DIO LEWIS, author of "The New Gymnastics," will furnish entertaining and valuable chapters on Out-Door and In-Door Gymnastics and Sports.

EDMUND MORRIS, author of "Ten Acres Enough," will write several articles on Farming for Boys.

EDMUND KIRKE will write regularly, contributing to the first number a most interesting reminiscence of Southern experience, entitled "The Little Prisoner."

"AUNT FANNY," that eminently successful writer of Juvenile books, will also be a contributor.

MISS HARRIET E. PRESCOTT and **MISS ROSE TERRY** will furnish Stories and Sketches for its pages. Miss Terry has sent a story which will appear in the second number.

(10)

Advertisement in The Atlantic Monthly *in 1865, announcing the children's magazine that Larcom edited for the next six years*

known as an antislavery activist than a poet. From the West she sent poems back to the *Lowell Offering,* to Salem newspapers, and to Whittier, then an editor of an antislavery paper, the *National Era.* He published her poems, and she was included in the 1852 edition of Rufus W. Griswold's *Female Poets of America.* On her return to Beverly, Whittier and his sister, Elizabeth, renewed the acquaintance; Larcom became one of the women writers whom the poet loved to encourage, and his approval gave her confidence in her talent. This mentor relationship lasted for years; not until Larcom was herself a famous poet and an editor did she break away from it, although the friendship lasted all their lives.

Refusing to be dependent on her family, in 1855 Larcom took a teaching position at Wheaton Academy, in Norton, Massachusetts, where she remained for the next nine years. She continued to write poems when she could find time, and she built up her library by reviewing books for several newspapers. Always a compulsive reader, she preferred subjects such as history and theology to fiction. She was a good teacher, and former students remembered her with love, but these were years of internal conflict. She always disliked the confinement and rules of life in a school that sometimes seemed to echo the confinement of the mills; she resented the demands on her time that kept her from writing. Yet, teaching in a good school was a suitable job for a woman, and she felt guilt at her own dissatisfactions.

Adding to the conflict between the security of her job and her desire to write was her questioning of her own heavily Puritan religious belief. Larcom, as did others reared in a strong religious tradition, felt a need to find God's purpose for her life and talents. Never doubting the core of Christian belief, she did reexamine, often painfully, the ingrained precepts of her childhood. She was heavily influenced by Ralph Waldo Emerson's writings; though she could never accept the lack of a personal deity, Emerson seemed to give her permission to think beyond rigid boundaries, and his ideas shaped the individual belief she eventually developed for herself. As a minor but troubling fact, she was still engaged to Frank Spaulding, now settled permanently in California, and there, too, obligation and duty warred with her desire for a different kind of life. The result of all these conflicts was that she suffered a series of debilitating illnesses, many of which seem to have been psychosomatic, that were nonetheless strong enough to turn this friendly woman into a near-recluse and make her question her own sanity.

At the same time she was slowly building a reputation with her poems, now being published in national magazines. In 1858 she almost literally awoke to find herself famous with the publication of a poem, "Hannah Binding Shoes," which appeared in the short-lived but highly regarded art magazine *Crayon* (December, 1857). After publication she was accused of plagiarism by the *New York Knickerbocker* magazine; she was able to prove her authorship, and the controversy brought the poem to public attention. A narrative of fidelity, "Hannah Binding Shoes" has not aged well; the faithful wife never losing hope that her sailor husband will return from his last voyage, humbly binding her shoes at her window that faces the sea, resembles nineteenth-century "story" painting. "Hannah Binding Shoes" was reprinted, inspired paintings, and was twice set to music; it followed Larcom all her life. William Dean Howells, in *Literary Friends and Acquaintance* (1900), declared that it gave Larcom immortality. She never understood its fame, since she considered it second-rate, but the public loved it. The practical result was that her poems now could command a good reception everywhere, as well as more money, and in 1861 she broke into the prestigious *Atlantic Monthly* with "The Rose Enthroned," a poem that merged Darwinism and Christianity with an attempt to make sense out of the terrible war that engulfed the country. Her new fame also gave her entry into the literary world of Boston and brought her the attention and friendship of Annie Adams Fields, the author and salon patroness, and her husband, James T. Fields, publisher and editor of *The Atlantic Monthly*.

The Civil War inspired Larcom to write much patriotic poetry—of varying quality—and also resolved one conflict, her engagement. Frank Spaulding had settled in a part of California dominated by South Carolinians and had adopted their views on the war and slavery. An ardent patriot, Larcom was repelled by his attitude, and spoke her mind in the December 1863 issue of *The Atlantic Monthly*. "A Loyal Woman's No" is a poem that illustrates her characteristic ability, in both prose and poetry, to transform her personal response into a public statement.

Larcom finally broke away from Wheaton in 1864 and a year later became an editor of Fields's newest production, *Our Young Folks,* a magazine for older children. At first she shared the editorship with Gail Hamilton and John Townsend Trowbridge; later she was the sole editor. Her acquaintance widened to include other women writers, and she became more confident of herself and her abilities and less dependent on Whittier's judgments of her work, gently easing away from the mentor-pupil relationship. During these busy years her health was good, and she developed the kind of life she wanted: her own home in Beverly, with winters in Boston and autumn in the White Mountains. Fields published her first poetry collection, *Poems* (1869), and others followed: *Childhood Songs* (1874), *Wild Roses of Cape Ann and Other Poems* (1880), and *The Poetical Works of Lucy Larcom* (1884), the latter in Houghton, Mifflin's "Household Edition" format.

Not long after Fields retired in 1871, his junior partner, James R. Osgood, attempting to save the publishing house that he could not manage, sold *Our Young Folks.* For one disastrous year Larcom returned to teaching, but all the anxieties that had plagued her at Wheaton returned, and by the end of the year she had determined to support herself by her writing. She had no expectation that this bold decision would make her rich, but eventually she established herself so successfully that later she described these years as the happiest of her life. She kept her winters in the city, with friends, galleries, concerts, lectures; spring and early summer in Beverly with her family; and autumn in her beloved and inspirational White Mountains. She lived that way contentedly, if not lavishly, for the rest of her life.

Larcom's poetry is characterized by vivid use of detail that makes it richly textured and creates strong visual images. A good amateur painter, in both her poems and her paintings she showed her love for and observation of the natural world. She liked to experiment with verse form, and her poetic subjects range widely. Many of her early poems are narratives, local legends of her native Essex county or tales of the prairie; more of them are topical in the sense that whatever was going on in the world provided her with subjects—thus there were antislavery and Civil War poems—and her own reactions and responses shaped the work. Like so many of her contemporaries, and like her favorite poet and model, who was not Whittier but William Cullen Bryant, she saw the natural world as part of and leading to God; her love of mountains, also a major topic, was based on the idea that on top of a mountain one was closer to God. As she grew older, and after the famous preacher Phillips Brooks became a friend, she wrote many poems affirming her strong and comforting religious belief, an eclectic belief that had evolved through a sometimes agonizing interior journey from the rigid Calvinism of her childhood through years of questioning to a kind of joyous Christian transcendentalism. She shared the belief that the message, not the form, made a poem, and the positive letters she received from readers indicate that she voiced the thoughts and feelings of a wide audience. As personal as her work was, she was able to present her ideas in a public way.

Always aware that she needed public support to maintain the life she prized, Larcom avoided controversial subjects. As a young woman she had written antislavery poems, but as an adult she stayed away from difficult, and perhaps unwomanly, topics; her refusal to be associated with the women's movement offended Harriet Hanson Robinson, briefly endangering their nearly lifelong friendship. The few poems she wrote about women tend to stress fidelity and domesticity, and the even smaller number that attack stereotyped women's roles hide their message within narrative. Her outward stance disguises the real contradiction of her life: the fact that while she upheld conventional values, especially as they dealt with women, marriage, and children, she chose to live differently, remaining unmarried and supporting herself entirely by her writing.

There are close connections between Larcom's poetry and her prose, but success in the latter came late. Her earliest prose ventures are the lively, interesting descriptions of life on the prairie sent back to the *Lowell Offering*. She tried a few short stories; they are rich in detail that creates the western scene and atmosphere successfully and their characterization is good, but they are plotless and formless. The same strengths and weaknesses show in her only other attempt at fiction, *An Idyl of Work* (1875), a novel in blank verse about Lowell. Scenes in which the mill girls talk to each other, work, or have a holiday are excellent, but the plot is contrived and fails dismally.

When Larcom had returned from the prairie in 1852 and had come under Whittier's influence, they talked about the need for a novel of the West; to her horror, Whittier announced in the *Era* that Miss Larcom would write one. Existing drafts held by the Beverly Historical Society suggest that she planned to use her six sisters as characters, but to set the novel on the prairie. She labored, or at least worried, about the novel for several years, making false starts and constantly changing her plans for it, and finally it was tacitly abandoned.

What she did bring home from the West were short moral essays that she called "similitudes," brief tales, usually with a child as the central figure, that introduced the theme of so many of her poems: that appreciation of the beauty of nature leads human beings to understanding God. Whittier, calling her a "prose-poet," urged John P. Jewett to publish them, and they made up Larcom's first book, *Similitudes, from the Ocean and Prairie* (1853). Three similar works followed, published as small gift books with moral messages for children. For years she confined her prose writing to her journal and to long, richly detailed letters to close friends, which are a source of information about both her life and her times.

When her editorship of *Our Young Folks* ended, and she decided that no matter what happened she would never return to teaching, Larcom organized her life so that she had commissions a year in advance. James Fields suggested that she work up and present lectures, and although her shyness made her dislike public appearances, she followed his suggestion. She loved writing the essays; in fact, she had found her form and would have been happy to do nothing else. Her facility with rhyme and verse did not transfer to prose, however; essays, she noted, took her much longer than poems, because she worked harder at them, revising and carefully crafting her work. Yet, the lectures expanded her opportunities. Samuel T. Pickard, married to Whittier's niece, Elizabeth, and editor of the *Portland Transcript,* asked her to shape some of her essays into what they called "newsletters," and these became a predictable source of income, especially when several Boston papers also published them. Everything around her gave her topics: places she visited, particularly in the mountains; events in Boston; and books and authors she read and liked. She wrote a solicited piece for *The Atlantic Monthly* that looked back on life in the mills, covering the same material as her fictional *An Idyl of Work* but presenting it in much more readable fashion. A commissioned series of essays on the relationship between scenery and poetry led to *Landscape in American Poetry* (1879), illustrated by Boston artist J. Appleton Brown.

In 1888 Henry O. Houghton, the eventual victor in the struggle for control of the publishing house that had once been Ticknor and Fields, decided to initiate a series of autobiographies by famous people and asked Larcom to write one of the first. She was initially hesitant; for her professional life she had consistently refused requests from editors and anthologists for personal details. For her, the conflict between private woman and public poet was real and threatening. A few years earlier, on 17 September 1884, she had written Houghton, resisting inclusion in a publicity promotion: "If you please, I don't want to be biographied and put into the 'Thirty Portraits.'" She explained that she did not want birthdays and other personal happenings to be public knowledge. The letter goes on:

> I do not in the least object to having it understood that I have entered upon what Victor Hugo called "the youth of old age," and am cheerfully looking westward toward a new sunrise. But I prefer to see it all through that slight veil of mist which makes life, as well as nature, so much more picturesque. I should not enjoy the mountains upon which I am looking today half as well, if I could see the milestones and the telegraph-poles and the railway-stations which I suppose cover their slopes. So please let the dear public have its illusions about me, until I am dead,—or leave it to me to write my own autobiography—when I am too tired and too old to do anything else!"

Houghton was persuasive, however, and as she thought about the book, her attitude changed: "I find it will be somewhat locally historical," she wrote her editor, Horace Scudder, on 5 August 1889. "I begin to think that everybody's private history takes in the whole world." In the preface to *A New England Girlhood* she wrote: "Whatever special interest this little narrative of mine may have is due to the social influences under which I was reared, and particularly to the prominent place held by both work and religion in New England half a century ago."

The sense that she was writing history rather than autobiography shapes *A New England Girlhood*. Rich in detail and displaying again her ability to appeal to the senses, it is a study of the way people lived that subordinates personal exploration. The first seven chapters present a glowing look at her childhood in an extended family, living in a community in which everyone, even children, shared values and had their place and their work; her own process of learning that world structures the work. While she stresses her discovery of the beauty of the natural world and explains her early love of language, she turns the personal into the public by making herself one player in a larger scene, hiding behind the "slight veil of mist" she mentioned in her letter to Houghton. The great trauma of her childhood was the death of her strong, adored father, but she goes past the event almost lightly, as a family loss that

Drawing of Larcom that appeared as the frontispiece for The Poetical Works of Lucy Larcom *(1884)*

changed all the children's lives. Only in intimate letters written as an adult does she admit what the loss meant to her.

Chapters 8 to 11 deal with the years in Lowell, and again the emphasis is on the place itself and on the importance of work. Conscious of the significance of the Lowell Experiment, she presents and comments on mill culture, the work, the mountain girls, the opportunities for reading and study, and the founding of the Improvement Circle that led to the *Lowell Offering*. Like her earlier *Atlantic Monthly* article, this section is filled with information useful to historians of the period. Her own story remains a thread through the larger picture, connecting her to the time and place but minimizing her own joys and, especially, pain. Though she admits problems, the whole Lowell Experiment is presented positively; it takes comparison with some of the letters she wrote years later, or with Harriet Hanson Robinson's more realistic *Loom and Spindle* (1898), to see that there were strong negative elements, both personal and public, during those years. For Larcom and others of her time, autobiography and biography were justified by their ability to inspire and to provide examples for others, and therefore a writer needed to select carefully what went into the work.

Her departure for the West is dealt with briefly in the last chapter, though she does take time to praise her principal at Monticello and describe the education she received there. She sums up her teaching and writing "career" (a word she rejects in the final paragraph) in three pages and ends with some advice to young girls.

A New England Girlhood remains a book well worth reading, both for its presentation of a time and place and for the quality of its writing. Although Larcom assumed a modest audience of young girls, the book was widely read and favorably reviewed. She wanted to follow it with a story of life on the prairie and her sister Emmeline, but Houghton was not encouraging, and the project was put off for the future. There were many commissions for poems and articles, and even though times were changing and her poetry, like Whittier's, was less in style, she kept a wide audience for her poems, which increasingly reflected her religious thought. In the last years of her life she compiled or wrote three small devotional books, *As It Is in Heaven* (1891), *At the Beautiful Gate, and Other Songs of Faith* (1892), and *The Unseen Friend* (1892).

In the summer of 1892 Emmeline, Larcom's closest sister, died; two months later came news of Whittier's death. Larcom had not been well, and in the autumn she was diagnosed with heart trouble. She recovered and moved to Boston for her usual winter in the city, but almost at once her illness returned. The sudden death of her friend and second mentor, Phillips Brooks, in January 1893 was another blow, and Boston papers announced her serious condition. She could not be moved home to Beverly, and she was cared for by her niece, Lucy Larcom Spaulding, and by former students from Wheaton until she died on 17 April.

After her death the newspapers called her "the best of our minor poets," and she was honored by a memorial service in Trinity Church, Boston. Writing one hundred years after her birth, Justin Henry Shaw, in the *Boston Evening Transcript* (8 March 1924), hailed her as a "remarkable woman," not only a poet and a teacher, but an "editor, writer, lecturer and religionist." Her work continued to be anthologized. Like Whittier

and others of that generation, however, her fame did not last, partly, perhaps, because she spoke so much for her own time. Larcom was never a great poet, but by contemporary standards she was a good one whose work appealingly voiced beliefs and values she shared with her contemporaries. In *A New England Girlhood* she provides a vivid and attractive account of a time, a place, and a way of life.

References:

Daniel Dulany Addison, *Lucy Larcom: Life, Letters, and Diary* (Boston: Houghton, Mifflin, 1894);

Benita Eisler, *The Lowell Offering* (New York: Lippincott, 1977);

William Dean Howells, *Literary Friends and Acquaintance* (New York: Harper, 1900), p. 123;

Shirley Marchalonis, "A Model for Mentors: Lucy Larcom and John Greenleaf Whittier," in *Patrons and Protegees: Gender, Friendship and Writing in Nineteenth-Century America,* edited by Marchalonis (New Brunswick, N.J.: Rutgers University Press, 1988), pp. 94–121;

Marchalonis, *The Worlds of Lucy Larcom, 1824–1893* (Athens: University of Georgia Press, 1989);

Harriet Hanson Robinson, *Loom and Spindle* (New York: Crowell, 1898), pp. xii, 4, 28, 61, 65, 71, 89, 91–100;

Susan Hayes Ward, ed., *The Rushlight: Special Number in Memory of Lucy Larcom* (Boston: Ellis, 1894);

Adeline Dutton Train Whitney, "Lucy Larcom," in *Our Famous Women* (Hartford, Conn.: Worthington, 1883), pp. 415–436.

Papers:

Major collections of Lucy Larcom's papers are in the Beverly Historical Society and the Beverly Public Library, Beverly, Massachusetts; the Essex Institute, Salem, Massachusetts; the Houghton Library, Harvard University; the Boston Public Library and the Massachusetts Historical Society, Boston; Wheaton College Library, Norton, Massachusetts; and the University of Virginia Library.

Laura Jean Libbey

(22 March 1862 – 25 October 1924)

Jean Carwile Masteller
Whitman College

BOOKS: *A Fatal Wooing* (New York: N. L. Munro, 1883);

Madolin Rivers; or, The Little Beauty of Red Oak Seminary: A Love Story (New York: G. Munro, 1885);

A Forbidden Marriage; or, In Love with a Handsome Spendthrift (New York: American News Co., 1888; London: Milner, 1900?);

Miss Middleton's Lover; or, Parted on Their Bridal Tour (New York: American News Co., 1888; London: Milner, 1900?);

Little Rosebud's Lovers; or, A Cruel Revenge (New York: G. Munro, 1888; London: Milner, 1899?);

All for Love of a Fair Face; or, A Broken Betrothal (New York: G. Munro, 1889); republished as *A Broken Betrothal; or, All for Love of a Fair Face* (London: Milner, 1899?);

Daisy Brooks; or, A Perilous Love (New York: G. Munro, 1889; London: Milner, 1900?); revised as *A Bride for a Day; or, Fairer than a Flower* (Cleveland: Westbrook, 1890?);

The Heiress of Cameron Hall (New York: G. Munro, 1889);

Junie's Love-Test (New York: G. Munro, 1889; London: Milner, 1900?);

Leonie Locke; or, The Romance of a Beautiful New York Working Girl (New York: G. Munro, 1889; London: Milner, n.d.);

Pretty Freda's Lovers; or, Married by Mistake (New York: N. L. Munro, 1889);

A Struggle for a Heart; or, Crystabel's Fatal Love (New York: G. Munro, 1889);

That Pretty Young Girl (New York: American News Co., 1889; London: Milner, 1902);

Gilberta, the Beauty (New York: J. S. Ogilvie, 189-?);

The Flirtations of a Beauty; or, A Summer's Romance at Newport (New York: N. L. Munro, 1890);

Ione, a Broken Love Dream (New York: Bonner, 1890; London: Milner, 1900?);

Lovers Once but Strangers Now; or, The Strange Romance of Miss Beatrice Reamer (New York: American News Co., 1890);

Laura Jean Libbey (Rutgers University Library)

A Mad Betrothal; or, Nadine's Vow (New York: Bonner, 1890; London: Milner, n.d.);

Parted by Fate (New York: Bonner, 1890; London: Milner, 1899?);

Willful Gaynell; or, The Little Beauty of the Passaic Cotton Mills (New York: N. L. Munro, 1890);

The Crime of Hallow-e'en; or, The Heiress of Graystone Hall (New York: N. L. Munro, 1891);

He Loved, but Was Lured Away (New York: American News Co., 1891);

Little Leafy, the Cloakmaker's Beautiful Daughter: A Romantic Story of a Lovely Working Girl in the City of New York (New York: N. L. Munro, 1891);

The Alphabet of Love: A Thrilling Romance, Portraying the Strange Adventures of a Beautiful Young Girl (New York: N. L. Munro, 1892);

The Beautiful Coquette; or, The Love That Won Her (New York: N. L. Munro, 1892);

Beautiful Ione's Lover (New York: G. Munro, 1892; London: Milner, 1899?); republished as *Divorced by Law* (Cleveland: Westbrook, n.d.);

Daisy Gordon's Folly; or, The World Lost for Love's Sake (New York: N. L. Munro, 1892);

Dora Miller; or, A Young Girl's Love and Pride (New York: N. L. Munro, 1892);

Florabel's Lover; or, Rival Belles (New York: Bonner, 1892; London: Milner, n.d.);

Little Ruby's Rival Lovers; or, a Cruel Revenge (New York: N. L. Munro, 1892);

Lyndall's Temptation; or, Blinded by Love: A Story of Fashionable Life in Lenox (New York: N. L. Munro, 1892);

A Master Workman's Oath; or, Coralie, the Unfortunate: A Love Story Portraying the Life, Romance, and Strange Fate of a Beautiful New York Working-Girl (New York: N. L. Munro, 1892);

Olive's Courtship (New York: American News Co., 1892; London: Milner, 1900?);

Only a Mechanic's Daughter. A Charming Story of Love and Passion (New York: N. L. Munro, 1892);

We Parted at the Altar (New York: Bonner, 1892; London: W. Nicholson, 190-?); republished as *Parted at the Altar* (New York: Bonner, 1893);

When His Love Grew Cold (New York: J. S. Ogilvie, 1895);

When Lovely Maiden Stoops to Folly; or, When Lovely Woman Stoops to Folly (New York: American News Co., 1896);

Garnetta, the Silver King's Daughter; or, The Startling Secret of the Old Mine (Cleveland: Westbrook, 190-?);

Aleta's Terrible Secret; or, The Strange Mystery of a Wedding Eve (Cleveland: Westbrook, 190-?);

The Angel of the Helpless (Cleveland: Westbrook, 190-?);

Cora, the Pet of the Regiment (Cleveland: Westbrook, 190-?);

A Dangerous Flirtation; or, Did Ida May Sin? (Cleveland: Westbrook, 190-?);

Della's Handsome Lover; or, A Hasty Ballroom Betrothal (Cleveland: Westbrook, 190-?);

A Fatal Elopement; or, A Too Hasty Love Match (Cleveland: Westbrook, 190-?);

Flora Garland's Courtship; or, The Race for a Young Girl's Heart (Cleveland: Westbrook, 190-?);

Flora Temple; or, All for Love's Sake (Cleveland: Westbrook, 190-?);

The Girl He Forsook; or, The Young Doctor's Secret (Cleveland: Westbrook, 190-?);

Gladiola's Two Lovers (Cleveland: Westbrook, 190-?);

A Handsome Engineer's Flirtation (Cleveland: Westbrook, 190-?);

Jolly Sally Pendleton; or, The Wife Who Was Not a Wife (Cleveland: Westbrook, 190-?);

Kidnapped at the Altar (Cleveland: Westbrook, 190-?);

The Loan of a Lover; or, Vera's Flirtation (Cleveland: Westbrook, 190-?; London: Milner, 1900?);

My Sweetheart Idabel; or, The Romance of a Pretty Coquette (Cleveland: Westbrook, 190-?);

Pretty Madcap Dorothy; or, How She Won a Lover (Cleveland: Westbrook, 190-?);

Pretty Rose Hall; or, The Power of Love (Cleveland: Westbrook, 190-?);

The Romance of Enola (Cleveland: Westbrook, 190-?);

Was She Sweetheart or Wife? or, Pretty Guelda's Love (Cleveland: Westbrook, 190-?);

Which Loved Him Best? (Cleveland: Westbrook, 190-?);

The Lovely Maid of Darby Town; or, Constance, the Cloakmaker's Granddaughter, Laura Series, no. 1 (New York: Street & Smith, 1903); republished as *The Lovely Constance,* New Surprise Series, no. 2 (Street & Smith, 1910);

Betrothed for a Day; or, Queene Trevelyn's Love Test, Laura Series, no. 2 (New York: Street & Smith, 1903);

What Is Life Without Love? or, Why Lyda Lost Her Lover, Laura Series, no. 3 (New York: Street & Smith, 1903); republished as *A Lost Lover,* New Surprise Series, no. 8 (New York: Street & Smith, 1910);

Sweet Dolly Grey; or, The Pride of My Heart, Laura Series, no. 4 (New York: Street & Smith, 1903); republished as *The Pride of My Heart,* Eagle Series, no. 820 (New York: Street & Smith, 1913);

Sweetheart, Will You Be True? or, Love Corine, the Queen of the Golf Links, Laura Series, no. 5 (New York: Street & Smith, 1903); republished as *Will You Be True?* New Surprise Series, no. 6 (New York: Street & Smith, 1910);

Gladys, the Music Teacher's Daughter; or, For Which Lover Did Fate Intend Her? Laura Series, no. 6 (New York: Street & Smith, 1903); republished as *In Love's Springtime,* Eagle Series, no. 566 (New York: Street & Smith, 1908);

Madcap Laddy, the Flirt; or, The Favorite of the Beaux, Laura Series, no. 7 (New York: Street & Smith, 1903;

The Price of Pretty Odette's Kiss and What Came of it; or, The Girl Who Wouldn't Take a Dare, Laura Series, no. 8 (New York: Street & Smith, 1903); republished as *The Price of a Kiss,* Eagle Series, no. 720 (New York: Street & Smith, 1911);

Sweet Kitty Clover, the Heroine of Manila and the Pride of the Philippines, Laura Series, no. 9 (New York: Street & Smith, 1903);

Ought We to Invite Her?, or, Was Little Dot's Sin Beyond Forgiveness? Laura Series, no. 10 (New York: Street & Smith, 1903); republished as *Do We Want Her?* New Surprise Series, no. 6 (New York: Street & Smith, 1910);

Mischievous Maid Faynie; or, The Strange Result of a Chance Acquaintance, Laura Series, no. 11 (New York: Street & Smith, 1903); republished as *Mischievous Faynie,* New Surprise Series, no. 4 (New York: Street & Smith, 1910);

Had She Loved Him Less; or, the Story of Beautiful Violet Arleigh's Sin, Laura Series, no. 12 (New York: Street & Smith, 1903); republished as *Had She Loved Him Less; or, Betrothed by Fate,* Eagle Series, no. 704 (New York: Street & Smith, 1910);

The Beautiful Mysterious Veiled Young Girl; or, The Belle of Narragansett Pier, Laura Series, no. 13 (New York: Street & Smith, 1903);

They Say You are False, but I'll Still Believe You True, Laura Series, no. 14 (New York: Street & Smith, 1903); republished as *Pity–Not Love* (New York: Street & Smith, 1907);

India, Laura Series, no. 15 (New York: Street & Smith, 1903);

Lotta, the Beautiful Cloak Model; or, Light and Shadows of Life in a Big Department Store, Laura Series, no. 16 (New York: Street & Smith, 1903); republished as *Lotta, the Cloak Model,* Eagle Series, no. 534 (New York: Street & Smith, 1907);

The Bride of Mont Pelee; or, The Beautiful Mysterious Veiled Lady, Laura Series, no. 17 (New York: Street & Smith, 1903); republished as *Love's Young Dream,* New Surprise Series, no. 7 (New York: Street & Smith, 1910);

Happy-Go-Luck Lotty (New York: J. S. Ogilvie, 1910?);

Little Romp Edda (New York: J. S. Ogilvie, 1910);

The Clutch of the Marriage Tie; or, Jilbett, a Story of the Second Glass (Brooklyn: Brooklyn Eagle Press, 1920);

Laura Jean Libbey's . . . Latest and Greatest Romance, Wooden Wives: Is it a Story for Philandering Husbands? (New York: Publishers Printing Co., 1923).

SELECTED PERIODICAL PUBLICATIONS– UNCOLLECTED: "Which Love Proved True? or, The Strange Romance of a Beautiful Young Girl," *New York Ledger,* 26 December 1886;

"Beautiful Victorine's Folly; or, Can False Love Break a Young Girl's Heart," *Fireside Companion* (17 August 1895 – 22 February 1896).

Laura Jean Libbey is better known for a type of literature than for any single title. When she died in 1924, *The New York Times* marveled that her novels, published over a four-decade career, would fill five feet on a bookshelf. To the *Times* she seemed a quaint reminder of the past, "an era of woodcuts," when popular literature appeared weekly as serials in the family story papers with circulations as high as 350,000 per week. By 1924 the decline of Libbey's popularity highlighted the shift in fashion as specialized magazines moved away from the melodramatic stories once printed in the inexpensive story papers and reprinted in "libraries" and series produced by multiple publishers for readers who paid 5¢ for the latest installment in a weekly story paper, or 10¢ to 25¢ for the entire novel. Hardcover copies for 50¢ to $1.00 were also published both in the United States and in England. Seventy-three of her eighty-two novels survive in the story papers where they were first published. In addition, most of her novels survive in hardcover copies as well as paperbacks in the various "series" and "libraries" of publishers who frequently printed Libbey's fiction.

Having once sold between ten and fifteen million volumes, Libbey's romantic stories of virtuous young women beset by the trials of finding love in a dangerous world seemed outdated in the world of photographs and moving pictures of the 1920s. The *Times* suggested that literature of Libbey's school had, nonetheless, served as a force for Americanization for legions of loyal readers and acknowledged that even in 1924 at least twenty of Libbey's novels were still in print, especially in eastern and midwestern urban neighborhoods housing largely foreign-born populations anxious for images of American success. Some of her titles remained in print well into the 1930s, fifty years after initial publication.

News articles occasioned by her death delineate major elements of Libbey's long and financially successful career. Given Libbey's earlier success, the *Times* seemed bemused by the shifts in fashion that reduced the once popular writer to a relic of the past. Yet, in the late nineteenth and early twentieth centuries, Libbey took advantage of trends in publishing to appeal to a large audience eager for melodramatic romances about young women set in contemporary locales. During her career she published more than 80 novels and copyrighted more than 120 plays. In the 1890s she edited the *New York Fashion Bazar.* From 1898 to 1901 she wrote for the *New York Evening World,* and

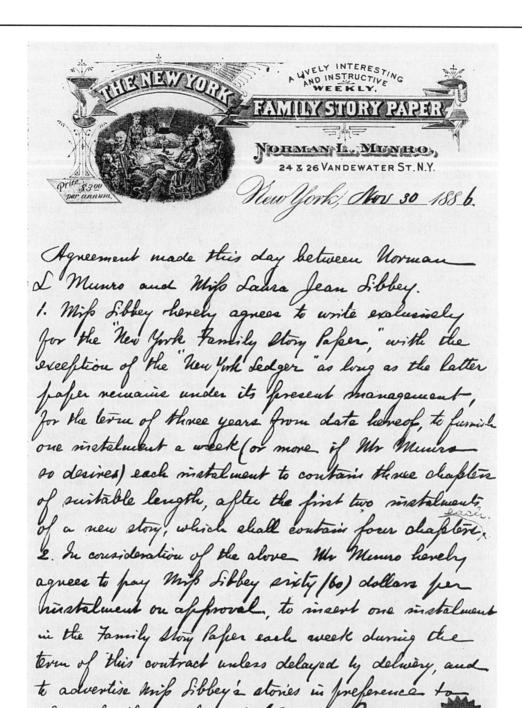

THE NEW YORK FAMILY STORY PAPER

A LIVELY INTERESTING AND INSTRUCTIVE WEEKLY.

NORMAN L. MUNRO,
24 & 26 VANDEWATER ST. N.Y.

Price $3.00 per annum.

New York, Nov 30 1886.

Agreement made this day between Norman
L Munro and Miss Laura Jean Libbey.
1. Miss Libbey hereby agrees to write exclusively
for the "New York Family Story Paper," with the
exception of the "New York Ledger" as long as the latter
paper remains under its present management,
for the term of three years from date hereof, to furnish
one instalment a week (or more if Mr Munro
so desires) each instalment to contain three chapters
of suitable length, after the first two instalments,
of a new story, which shall contain four chapters each.
2. In consideration of the above Mr Munro hereby
agrees to pay Miss Libbey sixty (60) dollars per
instalment on approval, to insert one instalment
in the Family Story Paper each week during the
term of this contract unless delayed by delivery, and
to advertise Miss Libbey's stories in preference to
those of other authors. Norman L Munro
signed: Laura J. Libbey.

Contract between Libbey and her publisher Norman L. Munro (Rutgers University Library)

in the 1910s syndicated "Laura Jean Libbey's Daily Talks on Heart Topics," a column of advice for the lovelorn. In her heyday in the 1880s and 1890s she claimed an income of $60,000 a year. Though this figure may be exaggerated, she was a successful businesswoman who negotiated contracts that garnered her substantial income even by nineteenth-century standards.

Libbey's stories retain value not only as examples of the publishing history of popular literature in the nineteenth century, but also as an earlier era's representation of gender and class. From stories of working girls caught in the dangers of the city to stories of young heiresses lured by suitors who promise adventure and excitement, her young heroines seek love and dream of a better life. In the process the stories reveal notions of manhood and womanhood, class conflict, and dreams of success that seek a fairy-tale ending without the complications of class and gender that operate at the core of the stories.

Few accounts remain of Libbey's private life. Though records of her financial affairs and travel journals detailing her grand tour of Europe and Egypt are extant, few other personal records are available. Despite occasional interviews and publicity tours to promote her work, Libbey revealed little about her life and instead created the persona of the ever-youthful writer of advice to lovers. After learning of her appearance in 1910 on the vaudeville stage, the *Bookman* expressed amazement that Libbey really existed and that her name did not merely represent "a certain kind of novel of a rather low intellectual order." Although she was sixty-two at the time of her death, both the Newark, New Jersey, and Brooklyn newspapers noted that they were forced to use youthful photographs because Libbey had made only those available. Based on information garnered from interviews with Libbey, biographical accounts often convey a mix of fact and fiction and even repeat incorrect dates of significant events in her life.

Libbey was born on 22 March 1862 to Thomas H. and Elizabeth (Nelson) Libbey. By most accounts, she was born in Brooklyn, where she spent her life, but her marriage certificate identifies her place of birth as Milwaukee, Wisconsin. She claimed to have received a private education. Although the *National Cyclopaedia of American Biography* noted in 1926 that she attended public schools in Brooklyn and studied at Vassar College for three years, Vassar has no record of her attendance. Her father was a surgeon from Maine who wrote articles for medical journals. Her mother was a more prominent presence, even a domineering one, in her life. According to Louis Gold, who served briefly as her secretary, Libbey was fond of her

mother, who died in 1896, but resented her mother's demands that she remain single. He reported that she declined several proposals during her youth. Not until two years after her mother's death did Libbey, at the age of thirty-six, marry Van Mater Stilwell, a Brooklyn lawyer. Contrary to at least one recent suggestion that she gave up her writing career after her marriage, Libbey continued writing for the story papers for several years. She not only fulfilled the terms of a contract she had negotiated with N. L. Munro's *Family Story Paper* but renewed the contract for a total of five years and recorded on the contract that she received $39,000 between 1897 and 1902. Thus, unlike many writers of the period, Libbey supported herself through her literary endeavors.

Libbey enjoyed her fame and in a curious fashion wished to witness her own immortality. According to receipts in her private papers, she purchased two cemetery lots in 1895 in the Greenwood Cemetery in Brooklyn, and after her mother's death in 1896 she purchased an imported granite monument and later a foundation, which she had engraved "Laura Jean Libbey." She then would sit in the cemetery and overhear visitors mourning her death. As the *Times* reported, Libbey claimed that "It's all right for your heirs to put it up, but then you don't see it." Her explicit directions in her will for her burial provoked extensive discussion in the newspapers: she was to be buried next to her mother; only two others—her sister and her nephew—were to be buried in the plot; and the monument in the plot and her headstone should be carved with only her name and her date of death (not her date of birth). These directions, combined with her will's directive that her husband was to receive only $5.00 plus her share of a Long Island property they owned jointly, led to speculation that the writer of romances had marital problems herself. Her friends and her husband assured the papers that he had his own fortune and that he did not expect her money; moreover, although he had his own cemetery plot, he preferred cremation. Whatever the implications of the will that left her other property, her family home, and the copyright to her works to her sister, niece, and nephew, her will captured the attention of the curious precisely because Libbey devoted her life to writing love stories and presenting herself as offering, as the title of a column in 1911 suggests, "Aid to Wounded Hearts."

Her directions in her will emphasized her insistence that she be remembered by the name that had made her famous. Perhaps recognizing the significance of the phrase "a Laura Jean Libbey" in identifying a type of writing, in 1920 she copyrighted the phrase "Laura Jean Libbey's" as a trademark for "Newspaper

1892 advertisement showing the wide availability of Libbey's novels

Articles, Film scenarios, Photo Plays and Dramatic Compositions, Works of Fiction, Sketches and Plays . . . , Novels and Periodicals." According to a letter in her papers at Rutgers University her patent lawyer proposed that she extend the trademark to cover "Candies, Printing and Writing papers, Toilet Preparations, etc." since she could "make a nice little income without any effort and without reflecting on your fame and name." He concluded that "'Laura Jean Libbey' Chocolates' might not only taste good but

would look better and this might be true of face creams, perfumery, etc." She does not appear to have acted on his proposal for Laura Jean Libbey chocolates or perfumes, but she frequently wrote publishers to confirm who held copyrights on which of her writings and pushed for additional reprintings to protect her financial interests.

Conflicting stories, most based on interviews with Libbey, recount her first publication in her teens. In one version, when she was fourteen, a teacher took an essay to Robert Bonner of the *New York Ledger,* who paid Libbey $5.00 and told her not to return until she was eighteen. According to another version, Bonner paid her $140.00, an unlikely sum for a fourteen-year-old writer, and asked her not to return but to get the experience of working for other publishers first. By yet another account, her first short story was sold for $25.00 to George Munro at the *Fireside Companion* when she was seventeen. She then spent the money on five pounds of marshmallows, which she and a friend ate on their return to Brooklyn.

Her career began in earnest in 1882 when the twenty-year-old Libbey published "Divorced by Law; or, Beautiful Ione's Sin" as a serial in the *Fireside Companion.* In May 1883 she had serials beginning the same week in both the *Fireside Companion* and the *Family Story Paper.* She published regularly in the *Fireside Companion* until late 1886, when she signed contracts to write exclusively for the *Family Story Paper* for $60 a week and for Bonner's *New York Ledger* for $100 an installment. Each contract granted her permission to publish only in the other paper. The contract with the *Family Story Paper* was renewed for three years, at the end of which she signed a three-year contract in 1889 to write for the *Fireside Companion* for $150 per installment. She renewed this contract for five more years through 1897. In 1897 she signed a five-year contract with the *Family Story Paper* for $150 per installment. She kept the receipts for each payment for an installment from 1892 to 1902 and tied the packets of receipts with red string. In addition, she wrote on several of the contracts how much she realized from the deal. She noted that from the last contract with the *Family Story Paper* she had earned $39,000.

In the early 1890s, at the same time she had serials appearing consecutively–and sometimes even two at once–in the *Fireside Companion,* she was also under contract with George Munro to edit his *New York Fashion Bazar* for $200 a week, a contract to be renewed for two years if circulation reached thirty thousand. The contract was renewed, and Libbey recorded that she realized $30,000 from that deal. As late as the end of the century, when she was under contract with the *Family Story Paper,* she was also under contract with the *Brooklyn Evening World,* "by permission of the Family Story Paper," to write four articles a week for $25 an article. Ever conscious of her finances, she noted that from this contract she earned $7,800. These records of her financial success support the conclusion of *The New York Times* in 1924 that Libbey was "one of the pioneers of the economically independent woman." However much her heroines gained wealth by inheritance or from marriage, Libbey earned her fortune by her work.

When Libbey was under contract with a paper, the editors noted in bold type that she wrote new stories for that paper only and that other papers offered only old stories, not the latest, by this popular writer. In the hyperbole of the day, the editors proclaimed her the greatest living writer and promised that "This will be followed by other works of her pen as fast as she can write." When she was under contract, her stories often still appeared in competitors' papers but as reprints of previously published stories. In addition, her novels were always in print from several publishers. Stories from N. L. Munro's *Family Story Paper,* George Munro's *Fireside Companion,* and Robert Bonner's *New York Ledger* appeared as novels in their *Choice, Ledger,* or *Popular* series; the *Seaside Library;* and *The Library of American Authors.* Both John Lovell and J. S. Ogilvie at various times held rights for reprinting as did Arthur Westbrook of Cleveland.

When Libbey published her first serials in the family story papers in the early 1880s, she supplied a type of story required by all of the sixteen-page story papers, which published serial fiction for the entire family, including westerns and detective stories for men and boys, and romances for women and girls. For a decade the story papers had also been seeking the young working woman as an audience by making the working girl a subject in stories and encouraging working-girl readers to tell their friends about the stories of seamstresses, bank-note cutters, telegraph operators, and cloak models. Thus, the working girl was promoted as both a subject and an audience for a particular brand of story. In 1884 she published "Leonie Locke; or, the Romance of a Beautiful New York Working Girl," the first of the stories that now identify her as a prototypical writer of working-girl fiction. As late as 1900, with "Lotta, the Beautiful Cloak Model; or, Light and Shadows of Life in a Big Department Store," Libbey capitalized in her subtitle–"Cordially Dedicated to the Young Ladies Employed at all the Big Department Stores Throughout the Country by their Friend and Well Wisher, Miss Laura Jean Libbey"–on the particular working environment then receiving attention from reformers and used that environment as the setting for her romance, just as earlier working-girl stories had responded to concern about the plight of seamstresses. In stories of mill workers, book-bindery workers, and store clerks, Libbey used the setting of the workplace as the stage for stories of young women adrift in the world. Frequently orphaned and without the protection of family, her virtuous young working girls defend their status as "only a working girl." Her enemies may use the phrase to suggest her lack of worth, but the heroine uses the phrase to designate her value. She may be

I, LAURA JEAN LIBBEY STILWELL, of Brooklyn, Kings
County, New York, being of sound and disposing mind, do make
publish and declare this to be my last will and Testament hereby revoking all Wills or Testamentary dispositions heretofore
made by me.

FIRST: I direct that all my just debts and funeral expenses be paid as soon after my death as may be practic-
able.

SECOND: I give, devise and bequeath unto THE
GREEN-WOOD CEMETERY of Brooklyn, New York, my burial plot con-
sisting of lots numbers 29258 and 29259 in Section 196, and
the monuments, enclosures or other property thereon, perpetually, the same not to be transferred or sold or other graves
to be permitted therein other than those of my mother, already
buried there, my sister MARY E. TAYLOR, of Brooklyn, New York,
my nephew ULMONT PAIGE, of Paterson, New Jersey, and my own.
It is my wish that I be buried on the left of my mother's
grave with similar headstone and footstone to that of my
mother. It is my further wish that on the monument now standing on said plot, and on the headstone to be erected over my
grave, the name "Laura Jean Libbey" and the date of my death
only, be carved. It is my further wish that two other graves
only, after mine, are to be made in said plot, namely that of
my sister, MARY E. TAYLOR at the right of my mother, and that
of my nephew, ULMONT PAIGE, at the left of my grave and facing
Celestras Path.

THIRD: I give and bequeath unto said THE GREEN-
WOOD CEMETERY the sum of Two Thousand Dollars ($2,000.) the
income to be used for the perpetual upkeep and care of said
plot, and for the preservation of any enclosure, monument or
other structures thereon, and if the income therefrom is sufficient, also to place cut flowers upon the graves whenever
the surplus of income warrants.

FOURTH: I give, devise and bequeath unto my hus-

First two pages of Libbey's will, in which she gives instructions for her epitaph and leaves $5.00 to her husband (Rutgers University Library)

band, VAN MATER STILWELL, the sum of Five Dollars ($5.) and
whatever interest I may have at the time of my death in property situated in Floral Park, New York. I do not make any
other provision for my said husband for good and sufficient
reasons well known to him and to me.

FIFTH: I give and bequeath unto my said nephew
ULMONT PAIGE and my niece, LAURA E. WHITE of Ridgewood, New
Jersey, jointly, all my right, title and interest in and to
the copy rights on my books and my trade marks. In the event
that either should predecease me then I give and bequeath
said right, title and interest to the survivor. If both said
ULMONT PAIGE and said LAURA E. WHITE should predecease me then
I direct that said right, title and interest shall become a
part of my residuary estate to be disposed of as hereinafter
provided.

SIXTH: I give, and devise unto THE CHASE NATIONAL
BANK OF THE CITY OF NEW YORK, having a branch known as
HAMILTON TRUST BRANCH, at No. 191 Montague Street, Borough of
Brooklyn, City of New York, or its successors, the premises
in which I now reside, known as No. 916 President Street,
Brooklyn, New York, to have and to hold the same, IN TRUST
NEVERTHELESS, subject to the following conditions:

My said sister, MARY E. TAYLOR, is to have the
use of said premises during her life or so long as she may
desire, but so long as she occupies said premises it shall
be incumbent upon her to pay all taxes and charges against
said premises, including the upkeep.

If my said sister does not desire to use or occupy said premises, then the Trustee shall let or lease the
same, defraying the taxes and charges out of the rents and
income therefrom, and pay the net income to my said sister.

It is my desire that the premises shall not be
sold until the expiration of two years from the date of my

-2-

"only a working girl," but that designation does not give anyone the right to treat her unjustly. Whether the young working-girl heroine marries the boss's son or the young laborer who makes a fortune himself and rises to the top, she leaves the workplace and represents to the rest of the working girls the rise of one of their own. Along the way, she is actually revealed to have been either the long-lost daughter of wealth herself or is adopted by a wealthy old man who bestows his wealth on her. Thus, she lives the fairy-tale ending and is an example of at least one working girl who is able to escape the hardships of labor. Michael Denning argues that these stories ultimately serve as "tales of heroic working class resistance." When the rich marry the poor and both live happily ever, the ending functions, Denning suggests, "as both a simple wish fulfillment for her readers and as a utopian vision of reorganized society." Thus, he considers Libbey's stories tales of class more than gender.

Though her romances about young working girls constitute only slightly more than 10 percent of her serials, all of Libbey's stories employ many of the same elements. Given her formulaic approach to her novels, the pattern is more important than any single work. Whether her heroine is an orphaned working girl forced to earn her own living, as noted above, or a young heiress from the countryside tossed into the harsh world because she foolishly falls in love with a treacherous character who lures her to the city (for example, *Little Rosebud's Lovers; or, A Cruel Revenge* (serialized, 1886–1887; published in book form, 1888), Libbey's romances typically subject her sixteen- or seventeen-year-old heroine to a series of injustices. Using melodramatic conventions from stage plots, the young girl endures a series of trials: multiple abductions, druggings, attempted suicides, attempted murder, fires, thefts, duels, mistaken identities, train derailments, runaway horses, carriage chases, and caustic chemicals, all in a single novel. In spite of all of these ordeals, the young heroine survives. She may swoon repeatedly at moments of crisis, but she resists assaults on her innocence and surmounts the trials she faces. Even a former heiress, once alone and homeless in the world, finds herself subject to the same assaults as the poor working girl who had faced the hardships of the workplace. Her marriage at the end reestablishes order and hierarchy in the chaotic world of the novel.

One threat to the happiness of these characters is false love. Often the young innocent girls are misled by wily suitors, who lure them into a betrothal or lead them to think they have been married. Subtitles such as "A Fatal Wooing," "A Mad Betrothal," "Married by Mistake," "A Perilous Love," "A Broken Betrothal,"

"Parted on their Bridal Tour," "A Hasty Ballroom Betrothal," "Kidnapped at the Altar," "Can False Love Break a Young Girl's Heart?" and "Did She Elope With Him?" all suggest this theme of a mistaken love or a forced or false marriage. Never consummated, these marriages turn out to have been false arrangements and thus not legal. As Denning suggests, using the title of a Bertha Clay novel, this "wife in name only" plot allows for "both a romance and a masked divorce story." Over time, Libbey seems to tell the same story again and again. The names of the heroines vary–Daisy, Rosebud, Lotta, Rose, Cora, Ruby, Viola, Dorothy, Kitty, Gladys–but the characters remain sixteen or seventeen, naive and pretty, but always innocent and above all virtuous. The word "willful" is often used to describe their character. They willfully seek their own fortunes; they willfully aim to marry the men they single out; and they willfully maintain their sense of dignity if they feel spurned by others. In other words, for all their fainting and swooning in stereotypical fashion at crucial moments, they often seem spunky, feisty characters. Yet, their redundancy is inescapable. When Bonner objected in 1887 that two stories she submitted to him were too similar (*We Parted at the Altar,* 1892, and *Daisy Gordon's Folly; or, The World Lost for Love's Sake,* 1892), Libbey retorted by distinguishing between the plots of her two stories, but the variations seem minor.

By the mid 1890s, Libbey's plots were becoming simpler and her characters more frivolous. Perhaps Libbey tired of churning out stories of her sixteen-year-old characters and tired of the series of conventional scenes. But the stories became simpler in another important way. Increasingly, the theme of finding what one of her male characters called the "true mate" replaced the formulaic conflicts of class and gender in her earlier novels. Melodramatic attempts to keep lovers apart still exist, but they serve primarily to lead lovers to discover their true feelings despite the obstacles caused by adults who make well-meaning but unfortunate attempts to arrange marriages for the young.

In 1902 the end of Libbey's last contract with the *Family Story Paper* coincided with the decline of the story papers themselves. They either went out of business or continued with declining circulations by reprinting old stories before being replaced by more specialized magazines addressed to audiences who wanted more exciting fare than the story papers supplied. Thus, Libbey's earlier stories continued to be reprinted in the story papers for another two decades until the end of the *Family Story Paper* in 1921. Additionally, in the early 1900s Street and Smith, who had never published Libbey in *Street and Smith's New*

York Weekly, acquired rights to Libbey and several other romance writers and began multiple reprintings of Libbey's work in the Laura Series, the New Surprise Series, the New Eagle Library, and the Love Story Library.

Libbey continued to write. By 1909 she had dramatized 80 to 120 plays. Writing of his brief experience, her secretary, Gold, recorded that she dictated two or three plays a week, most based on her novels. Though she obtained copyrights for these plays and worked to obtain dramatic rights for all of her novels, probably only one of her plays was produced. In 1907, as melodramas made a last appearance before the shift to moving pictures, *Parted on Their Bridal Tour,* her dramatization of *Miss Middleton's Lover; or, Parted on Their Bridal Tour* (1888), was produced by Charles E. Blaney in his Brooklyn theatre. She also performed once on the vaudeville stage in 1910 at the American Theatre in New York. This performance led *The Bookman* to exclaim with surprise, "Miss Libbey a Fact." According to Gold, her performance was not a success, and she did not appear again.

In the 1910s Libbey began to produce syndicated advice columns. Ever the businesswoman, she later also tried to negotiate movie rights to her stories and copyrighted her name as a trademark to protect her interests. Late in July of 1924 she agreed with Joseph Menchen to pose for $100 a day for exterior moving pictures. Given the changes in the publishing industry and the decline of some of her earlier publishers by the 1920s, she arranged publication of her own works and recorded receiving 50 percent of the proceeds from syndication of her stories. Even at the time of her death, several of her stories were being serialized in California. When Libbey died on 25 October 1924 of complications from cancer, she may have represented the end of an era, but she still was involved in promoting her work.

In an interview in 1909 with Victor Rousseau, Libbey had defined what she thought a novel should do: "I think a novel should do good and should lift people out of themselves, absorb them, as it were, and take them away from the dull world." She also claimed that she did not like "improbable novels that deal with things which couldn't happen in every-day life." Her fictional world, with its many abductions and close escapes from danger, certainly is not a dull world, but events tend to be highly improbable. Yet, with these improbable events and happy endings, Libbey's plots function as metaphors for the dangers awaiting young women who face a world where wealth and poverty define the extremes for characters left to struggle with the hardship of the workplace or the dangers of homelessness if they remain without

the security of home and family. As a passage from one of Libbey's advice columns, reprinted in Joyce Shaw Peterson's "Working Girls and Millionaires" (1983), reveals, Libbey recognized that life is more complicated than her formulas suggested. As she warned, "the handsome, smiling, affable, elegantly attired man who smiles . . . and whispers flattering little nothings that set your heart all in a flutter, is, nine times out of ten, of unbearable temper and manner to his family; and the plain, diffident, sincere man . . . who is plain of face and in his dress . . . is, in truth, nature's true nobleman." But in Libbey's fictional world, the character's true mate is handsome, sincere, and wealthy. In her romances the finding of a true mate dissolves the hardships her characters face throughout the novel. Ultimately, her fiction offers a dream of freedom from a harsh and dangerous world. Not surprisingly, her stories were widely read in the late nineteenth and early twentieth centuries by loyal fans such as those described in 1905 in Dorothy Richardson's *The Long Day: The Study of a New York Working Girl.* Though Richardson scorned their reading habits, the working women who discussed Libbey's novels over their lunch break did not want stories of "everyday happenings." In Libbey, they found not the everyday, but a world where dreams of wealth, beautiful homes, and a handsome lover vanquished the threats of lecherous villains and jealous villainesses. In Libbey's stories many Cinderellas found their happily-ever-after lives. Her work, like that of Lucy Larcom and other working women who contributed to the *Lowell Magazine* in the early nineteenth century, is significant in the long history of popular literature that drew a large working-class and immigrant readership into fiction reading.

Interview:

Victor Rousseau, "Celebrities at Home: Laura Jean Libbey," *Harper's Weekly,* 23 January 1909: 12–13.

References:

"Chronicle and Comment," *Bookman,* 32 (September 1910): 18–19;

Cathy N. Davidson, "Laura Jean Libbey," in *American Women Writers: A Critical Reference Guide from Colonial Times to the Present,* 5 volumes, edited by Lina Mainiero (New York: Ungar, 1982), III: 3–5;

Michael Denning, *Mechanic Accents: Dime Novels and Working-Class Culture in America* (New York: Verso, 1987);

Louis Gold, "Laura Jean Libbey," *American Mercury,* 24 (September 1931): 47–52;

"Laura Jean Libbey," *New York Times,* 28 October 1924, p. 22;

"Laura Jean Libbey Hoped to Achieve Immortality," *New York Times,* 2 November 1924, VII: p. 11;

"Laura Jean Libbey Leaves $5 to Husband," *New York Times,* 7 November 1924, p. 21;

"Laura Jean Libbey, Novelist, Dies at 62," *New York Times,* 26 October 1924, sec. II, p. 7;

Edward T. LeBlanc, *Bibliography of Fireside Companion* (Fall River, Mass.: LeBlanc, 1990);

Jean Carwile Masteller, "Romancing the Reader: From Laura Jean Libbey to Harlequin Romance and Beyond," in *Pioneers, Passionate Ladies, and Private Eyes: Dime Novels, Series Books, and Paperbacks,* edited by Larry E. Sullivan and Lydia Cushman Schurman (New York: Haworth, 1996), pp. 263–284;

Mary Noel, *Villains Galore: The Hey-day of the Popular Story Weekly* (New York: Macmillan, 1954), pp. 124, 151–152, 290–291, 295, 300;

Russel B. Nye, "The Novel as Dream and Weapon: Women's Popular Novels in the 19th Century," *Chronicle: Historical Society of Michigan* (Fourth Quarter 1975): 2–16;

Nye, *The Unembarrassed Muse: The Popular Arts in America* (New York: Dial, 1970), pp. 28–29, 36, 40, 45;

Helen W. Papashvily, *All the Happy Endings: A Study of the Domestic Novel in America* (New York: Harper, 1956), pp. 199–207;

Joyce Shaw Peterson, "Working Girls and Millionaires: The Melodramatic Romances of Laura Jean Libbey," *American Studies,* 24 (Spring 1983): 19–35;

Quentin Reynolds, *The Fiction Factory: Or, From Pulp Row to Quality Street, the Story of 100 Years of Publishing at Street & Smith* (New York: Random House, 1955), pp. 118, 157–159, 215;

Dorothy Richardson, *The Long Day: The Story of a New York Working Girl* (New York: Century, 1905), pp. 72–86;

Albert Terhune, *To the Best of My Memory* (New York: Harper, 1930), pp. 208–212;

Sue G. Walcutt, "Laura Jean Libbey," in *Notable American Women 1607–1950,* 3 volumes, edited by Edward T. James (Cambridge, Mass.: Belknap Press of Harvard University Press, 1971), II: 402–403.

Papers:

Laura Jean Libbey's personal papers, including financial records, are held in the Laura Jean Libbey Stilwell Papers, Special Collections and Archives, Rutgers University Libraries. Libbey's six volumes of travel journals of tours through Europe, Egypt, the West Indies, and Bermuda are held at the New York Public Library. Correspondence between Libbey and Robert Bonner in 1887 is also housed in the Robert Bonner Papers at the New York Public Library. The Street and Smith company records housed at the George Arents Research Library at Syracuse University detail the process of one publisher's reprinting of Libbey's fiction in the early twentieth century.

Queen Lili'uokalani

(2 September 1838 – 11 November 1917)

Lydia Kualapai
University of Nebraska at Lincoln

BOOKS: *Hawaii's Story by Hawaii's Queen* (Boston: Lee & Shepard, 1898);

The Queen's Songbook, edited by Dorothy Kahananui Gillett and Barbara Baruard Smith (Honolulu: Hui Hānai, 1999).

OTHER: *An Account of the Creation of the World according to Hawaiian Tradition,* translated by Lili'uokalani (Boston: Lee & Shepard, 1897); republished as *The Kumulipo: An Hawaiian Creation Myth* (Kentfield, Cal.: Pueo Press, 1997).

Had it not been for the fact that Queen Lili'uokalani was Hawaii's last monarch prior to the kingdom's annexation by the United States, her historical reputation would rest secure in her musical accomplishments. A gifted lyricist and musician, and a prolific composer, she attracted a large international following even by nineteenth-century standards. The luxury of unfettered musical study eluded her, however. Lydia Kamaka'eha Pākī, as she was known in the early years of her life, was destined to become one of the Hawaiian kingdom's most remarkable literary figures and, at the same time, its most enigmatic political leader. Her role as a national leader and author made her one of the most notable women in late-nineteenth-century U.S. culture.

Lydia's natural mother was Anale'a Keohokālole, an *ali'i nui* (high chief) daughter of 'Aikanaka and Kamae, both of Hawaii island; her natural father was Kaisara Kaluaiku Kamaka'ehukai Kahana Keola Kapa'akea, a *kaukau ali'i* (lesser chief) son of Kamoku'iki and Kamanawa. At her birth, she was given to her *hānai* parents, Laura Kanaholo Konia, a granddaughter of Kamehameha I and thus an *ali'i nui;* and Abenera Ka'ehu Kūho'oheiheipahu Pākī, a *kaukau ali'i.* Deeply ingrained in Hawaiian family structure and values, the tradition of *hānai,* a practice of permanent adoption, extended family ties and strengthened community relationships. Lili'uokalani knew her birth parents but emotionally bonded with her *hānai* parents, Konia and Pākī, as her mother and father. The future queen's formal education

Queen Lili'uokalani

began at age four when she was sent to the High Chiefs' Children's School, a private boarding school conducted by U.S. missionaries. There she excelled in English grammar, history, mathematics, and the arts. Though her early training at the missionary school fostered a lifelong faith in Christianity, she never permanently settled into a par-

265

ticular orthodoxy; at various times in her life she was associated with Honolulu's Kawaiahaʻo Church (Congregational), St. Andrew's Cathedral (Episcopal), and the Mormon church. On 16 September 1862, following a two-year engagement, she married John Owen Dominis, the son of a prosperous Boston sea captain. Though their marriage was childless, Lydia eventually cared for three *hānai* children, Lydia Aholo, Joseph Kaipo ʻĀeʻa, and John Dominis ʻAimoku.

When Lydia's brother, David Kalākaua, was legislatively elected to the throne in 1874, he chose his younger brother, Leleiōhoku, as the heir apparent. But with the prince's untimely death in 1877, King Kalākaua named his sister, Lydia Dominis, heir apparent; through this appointment her official name became Princess Liliʻuokalani. For her, this was no mere titular position, but a commitment to serve and protect the kingdom, and she readily assumed the private and public responsibilities of the office. During the next seventeen years she became deeply involved in the affairs of state and diplomacy. She acted as regent in Kalākaua's absence, accompanied Queen Kapiʻolani to Queen Victoria's Golden Jubilee, agitated for Native Hawaiian health care and education, served as liaison to international dignitaries visiting the islands, and earned the love and respect of the Native Hawaiian community. When Kalākaua died in 1891, Liliʻuokalani, an experienced administrator and politician, was well aware that the sovereignty of the kingdom was under serious threat. During Kalākaua's reign, his cabinet ministers—a small select group of primarily U.S. entrepreneurs, sugar investors, and descendants of missionaries—forced the king to accept a new constitution diverting power from the crown to the cabinet. This 1887 "Bayonet Constitution" was still in place when Liliʻuokalani came to the throne. In January 1893, just as she was ready to promulgate a new constitution that would restore power to the crown, the monarchy was overthrown. For many years historians pointed to the new constitution as the flash point of the overthrow; Liliʻuokalani, they argued, was "too stubborn," "too resolute," and "too determined to rule." She was cast as "the woman who brought down the Monarchy." With the recovery of the queen's diaries and other pertinent documents (in 1971), however, a more accurate picture of her life and times has been revealed. Regardless of what the queen attempted to do in promulgating a new constitution, the minority merchant and professional class was already planning to overthrow the monarchy. Surrounded by her political enemies, Liliʻuokalani's only weapon of resistance was her pen.

The chronology of the overthrow bears directly on the queen's literary production. On 14 January 1893 the U.S. minister to Hawaii, John L. Stevens, conspired with Honolulu's businessmen to depose the queen and overthrow the nation. Two days later, Minister Stevens, over-

reaching his office and acting without approval of Congress, authorized Captain G. C. Wiltse, commander of the battleship USS *Boston,* to invade the Kingdom of Hawaiʻi and support the usurpation of the government. The following day, 17 January, the anarchists deposed the queen and decreed the establishment of the Provisional Government, an interim administration whose immediate goal was U.S. annexation. The insurgents underestimated Queen Liliʻuokalani's resolve, however. Convinced that a military engagement against the cannonade of the *Boston* would be a futile sacrifice of Native Hawaiian life, and proceeding judiciously so as not to legitimize the assault against the kingdom's sovereignty, the queen yielded her authority not to the outlaw Provisional Government but to the "Government of the United States." She felt confident that the United States, a nation that had recognized the independence of the kingdom and extended diplomatic recognition to it since 1826, would justly reinstate her as the constitutional sovereign. In fact, her speedy protests to both President Benjamin Harrison and President-elect Grover Cleveland severely undermined the standing of the Provisional Government and stalled the momentum of the so-called Hawaiian Revolution.

Shortly after his inauguration President Cleveland appointed former Georgia congressman John Blount to investigate the overthrow and determine to what extent U.S. intervention had facilitated the insurrection. Blount's July 1893 report concluded that "United States diplomatic and military representatives had abused their authority and were responsible for the change in government." In his 18 December message to Congress, President Cleveland described the coup as an "act of war, committed with the participation of a diplomatic representative of the United States and without authority of Congress." Declaring that "by such act the government of a peaceful and friendly people was overthrown," the president ordered the Provisional Government to restore the monarchy. The anarchists denounced the president's edict and lobbied the U.S. Senate Committee of Foreign Relations to open a second investigation under the direction of Senator John Morgan, an annexation advocate. At the same time, the queen's emissaries in Washington worked diligently to maintain U.S. support for restoration. Their efforts proved momentarily successful. Although the Morgan Committee supported the Provisional Government, the Senate refused to ratify a treaty of annexation. In Honolulu, Queen Liliʻuokalani continued to undermine the interim administration's vulnerable position. Despite ongoing threats of assassination and rumors of deportation, the queen used her diminishing assets to underwrite the royalist press and to subsidize Native Hawaiian resistance groups. On 4 July 1894 the Provisional Government, having failed at annexation, proclaimed a new constitution and declared itself the Republic of Hawaii.

The new constitutional system created an oligarchy designed solely to maintain an economically and politically dominant minority while the republic's administration worked toward annexation. At the same time, the oligarchy precluded Native Hawaiian participation in the political process.

By late summer 1894 the Cleveland administration had informed the queen's emissaries that despite the president's earlier support the U.S. Congress was electing a "hands-off" position. There would be no assistance for either restoration or annexation; the monarchists were on their own. The close of 1894 brought increased tension to the inner circles of the republic's administration as rumors of royalist plots swept Honolulu. The queen's supporters had for some time been smuggling guns from San Francisco and stockpiling an arsenal. On 6 January, the day before the counterrevolution was to be launched, republic marshals stumbled on a group of armed royalists who dispersed after a brief exchange of gunfire; during the melee, Charles L. Carter, a central figure in the overthrow and the subsequent formation of the republic, was fatally wounded. Republic administrators declared martial law, and within days the jails overflowed with suspected conspirators. By 14 January the leaders had surrendered and more than 190 royalists had been arrested either for treason, a capital offense, or misprision of treason, that is, withholding knowledge of treasonable acts. Two days later marshals arrested the queen. That afternoon, a search of her private residence revealed a cache of weapons and evidence that she had framed a new constitution and was prepared to install a new cabinet should the revolt prove successful. The oligarches wasted no time in bringing the royalists to trial. Fearing the unpredictability of public jury trials, the administration hastily organized a military tribunal of ardent antiroyalists. In a span of thirty-six days, the court prosecuted 191 cases, of which only five were acquitted. On 24 January, in an attempt to avert the execution of the leaders, Queen Lili'uokalani abdicated her throne. Still, the assorted sentences pronounced on 12 February included death by hanging, deportation, imprisonment at hard labor, and substantial fines. International pressure, particularly from the U.S., forced the republic to reduce or nullify the most severe sentences. The queen's public hearing lasted four days. To what extent she actively participated in the restoration plot remains unclear. In a statement prepared for her defense, she testified that she "received no information from any one in regard to arms which were procured . . . nor of any men who were induced . . . to join in any such uprising." But, she adds, had she known of the counterrevolutionary plan, she would have "inviolately preserved" the secret. The queen pled "not guilty": to her mind, any action on her part to reclaim the nation was not treasonable but heroic. Found guilty of misprision of treason, Lili'uokalani

John Owen Dominis, whom Lili'uokalani married in 1862

received the maximum sentence of five years imprisonment at hard labor and a $5,000 fine; two weeks later her sentence was commuted to simply "five years imprisonment." When martial law was lifted on 19 March, the counterrevolution and any hope of restoring the monarchy were over.

'Iolani Palace, the stunning landmark of the Kalākaua dynasty and the queen's former center of administration, became her prison. Held under guard in a sparsely furnished corner apartment on the second floor, Lili'uokalani constructed a productive daily routine and immediately went to work on several creative projects. She records in her autobiography that her great consolation during the imprisonment was her music and her writing. In fact, her music, some of it surreptitiously published during her confinement, carried her voice beyond her prison walls. Of the three published compositions associated with this period—*Ku'u Pua I Paoakalani* (My Flower at Paoakalani), *Ke Aloha O Ka Haku* (The Lord's Mercy), and *Aloha 'Oe* (Farewell to Thee)—the last has grown especially significant. Lili'uokalani composed this best known of all

Hawaiian love songs while in confinement. She gave the manuscript to her friend and supporter Johnny Wilson, who oversaw its publication in Chicago in 1895. Oddly, the lyrics of the familiar chorus suggested to the censors of the republic that the queen had conceded the demise of the kingdom: "Farewell to you, farewell to you, / O fragrance in the blue depths / One fond embrace and I leave / To meet again." However, considering the context of the transcription and publication, the last phrase more likely suggests the queen's vision of a restored Hawaiian Nation.

Using the long, quiet days of imprisonment to her advantage, Liliʻuokalani began translating the Kumulipo, the two-thousand-line chant of Hawaiian cosmogonic genealogy, into English. Her strategy underlying the project was complex. She, like her brother, the late King Kalākaua, was sensitive to the genealogical debate surrounding the monarchy. Prior to Kalākaua's reign, accession followed the Kamehameha line of descent, but the premature deaths of this first dynasty's successors transformed monarchial assent to a legislative, rather than a genealogical, process. When Kalākaua won the 1874 legislative election, many Hawaiians felt that dowager Queen Emma, a great-grand niece of Kamehameha and consort to Alexander Liholiho, Kamehameha IV, should inherit the throne. Kalākaua used the Kumulipo, a chant that had hitherto remained solely in the oral tradition, to trace his genealogy to ancient Hawaiian chiefs. His Hawaiian transcription, published in 1889, proclaimed publicly his and Liliʻuokalani's aliʻi (noble) heritage. In creating an English translation—the first of its kind—Liliʻuokalani helped to protect the chant's complex cultural allusions from time's inevitable corruption. "In some cases," she notes in her introduction, "true signification has been lost." The importance of this project to Her Majesty cannot be overstated. The fact that she produced a translated edition reflects her keen understanding of the colonizing process: if the islands were not restored to Native Hawaiian control, the Hawaiian language would inevitably be supplanted by English, and Hawaiians would one day access their history through the colonizers' language. In 1898, Liliʻuokalani, at her own expense, arranged for fifty-two copies of her translation to be printed by Lee and Shepard of Boston. These, she notes in her autobiography, were not for "general circulation" but to be preserved by friends and various libraries. The strategy proved effective. A textual artifact that has survived time's assault, Liliʻuokalani's English translation of the Kumulipo continues to safeguard a vital element of Native Hawaiian tradition and culture.

On 6 September 1895, the queen was removed to Washington Place, her private residence, where she remained under house arrest until 6 February 1896, at which time she was granted restricted movement within the island of Oahu. On 6 October after twenty-one

months of confinement and restrictions, she received word that the republic's executive council had commuted the remainder of her sentence. In the meantime, the annexation debate had cooled considerably; pro-annexation lobbies in Washington and Honolulu generally agreed that their efforts and monies were misspent on President Cleveland's administration. On 16 November, however, when word of William McKinley's presidential victory reached Honolulu, the annexationists were jubilant. Unlike his predecessor, President-elect McKinley was a fervent expansionist. Once freed, Liliʻuokalani immediately requested permission to travel to the U.S. under the pretense of a family visit to Boston. Assuming that the former queen presented no political threat, republic authorities allowed her to leave the islands. Once again her enemies had underestimated her. No one was more surprised than the republic's commissioners when she moved into the Shoreham Hotel in Washington, D.C., on 22 January 1897 and launched a serious anti-annexation campaign. Her strategy was twofold. Publicly, she lobbied against annexation, attended the presidential inauguration, and closely monitored the change in administration. Privately, she authored *Hawaii's Story by Hawaii's Queen* (1898), an autobiographical landmark both in the literature of Hawaii and in late-nineteenth-century U.S. literature.

In writing and publishing her autobiography, the queen was motivated by personal and political necessity. From the time of the overthrow until the eve of annexation, Her Majesty had been largely vilified in the U.S. press as "an adroit dissembler," "a study in superstition," and "a portly, chocolate-colored lady." The most acrimonious articles were written by Hawaii's "missionary sons." These descendants of U.S. Calvinist missionaries maligned the queen's morality and denounced the Hawaiian people as "a weak aboriginal race" incapable of self-government. Particularly vitriolic were Reverend Sereno E. Bishop's articles. Writing for the *New York Independent,* Bishop described the deceased Kalākaua and the former queen Liliʻuokalani as morally debauched and racially corrupt. In an article published on 6 July 1893, he claimed that neither Kalākaua nor Liliʻuokalani had any "real hereditary royalty," but were instead the illegitimate children of Keohokālole and a "mulatto paramour." As such, he declared, "white Hawaii loathes them, and native Hawaii has no respect for them." Although transparently self-serving, annexationist propaganda succeeded in denigrating not only the monarchy but Hawaiians in general; annexation, the argument went, would protect these "child-like" and "savage" people from their own racial deficiencies. The anti-annexationist press, focusing almost entirely on the legalities and political implications of expansion, did little to counteract this depiction of the queen and her people. A rare exception is an article by the novelist and short-story writer Harriet Prescott Spofford published in the 15 May 1897 *Harper's Bazar*. "The person entering Liliuokalani's presence with any preconceived idea of a swarthy and savage island queen," writes Spofford, "finds himself tremendously mistaken." Although Spofford's avid defense of the queen's heritage, character, and politics no doubt defused the more malignant antiroyalist rhetoric, the most powerful and convincing vindication would come from the queen herself.

Published in February 1898, on the eve of U.S. annexation, *Hawaii's Story by Hawaii's Queen* stands as the only Native Hawaiian account of the overthrow written during the period, and one of the few histories of Hawaii written from a Native Hawaiian perspective. The sumptuous, four-hundred-page volume was well received, despite the partisan tone of most reviewers. The reviewer for *Public Opinion* dismissed the queen's biographical sections as "not of considerable importance" but praised her account of the overthrow as "a valuable contribution" to an issue much "befogged" and manipulated in public opinion. In San Francisco, the *Overland Monthly* described *Hawaii's Story* as "undoubtedly the most important contribution to the history of the Hawaiian Revolution and the causes leading up to it, which has been presented to the American people." On the other hand, the pro-annexationist *Independent* described the work as "one of the most pitiful stories that was ever set down by a weak sufferer in protest against the aggression of the stronger"; still, begrudges this anonymous reviewer, "the volume is handsomely gotten up, and illustrated with a full series of heliotype prints." Charles Kofoid, writing for the *Dial*, provided the most comprehensive analysis but concluded that *Hawaii's Story*, "owing to its warped and partial statements," has little value as reliable history. Kofoid defers instead to an earlier history of the overthrow written by William DeWitt Alexander, a second-generation missionary son, the Provisional Government's official historian, and an annexation Commissioner. The review with the most far-reaching and damaging implications appeared in Boston's *Literary World*: "If Queen Liliuokalani were really the author of her *Hawaii's Story*," began the anonymous writer, "she would deserve a high mark of literary credit." Instead, the reviewer hinted, "the name of some dexterous secretary and man of letters" can be read between the lines. This charge that *Hawaii's Story* was ghostwritten by Boston's Julius A. Palmer Jr., the queen's staunch supporter and personal secretary during her Washington sojourn, was subsequently cultivated by Lorrin A. Thurston, a second-generation missionary's son and annexation commissioner for the Provisional Government. Based on his reading of the queen's cryptic diaries and fueled by his deep prejudice against Native Hawaiians, Thurston declared that "Liliuokalani personally was incapable of using such clear-cut English" as employed in *Hawaii's Story*. The oligarch's charge became widely accepted as fact.

Frontispiece to Lili'uokalani's Hawaii's Story by Hawaii's Queen *(1898)*

Only recently has Thurston's assertion been investigated and disputed. A close study of the queen's extant diaries—some of them surreptitiously written in a numerical code that was not deciphered until 1971—has convinced Miriam Fuchs that Lili'uokalani "not only wrote her own book but also was someone for whom writing was imperative."

The greatest challenge Lili'uokalani faced in authoring *Hawaii's Story* was her personal and political need to appeal persuasively to a generally uninformed U.S. audience; to present herself as a well-educated, well-traveled, international politician; and, most importantly, to do so without compromising her Hawaiian identity. Notably, she embraces the latter in the opening paragraph of the volume. Observing the Hawaiian imperative to begin with the beginning, she records her genealogical relationship

Lili'uokalani toward the end of her life

with the world. First, she marks her physical connection to the *'Āina* (Earth): "The extinct crater or mountain which forms the background to the city of Honolulu is known as the Punch-Bowl. . . . Very near to its site . . . I was born." She then provides a brief description of her genealogy and refers her readers to the volume's appendices where she includes several genealogies of prominent Hawaiian families. Her family ties firmly established, Lili'uokalani provides brief, but important, glimpses of her childhood years. Here, she writes bitterly of her early experiences at the High Chiefs' Children's School. Open only to *ali'i* children with acknowledged claims to the throne, the school attempted to Anglicize Hawaii's future leaders. She painfully recalls the deprivations she felt in the Calvinist environment, including emotional coldness, physical hunger, and long separations from her family; yet, she also acknowledges that her gift for musical composition was recognized and encouraged by the school's mistress, Juliette Cooke. In their emotional and social isolation, the *ali'i* children established uncommon bonds that would later

fortify their resolve to hold the nation together. Lili'uokalani's schoolmates at this time included, for example, Alexander Liholiho (future Kamehameha IV), Emma Rooke (future queen to Kamehameha IV), Lota Kapuāiwa (future Kamehameha V), William Charles Lunalilo (elected monarch, 1873–1874), and, of course, her brother, the future King Kalākaua. In 1846 the missionary school, by then under government control, was renamed the "Royal School," and enrollment was opened to day students. One of these new students was John Owen Dominis (1832–1891), Lili'uokalani's future husband.

In her memoir, the queen gives conspicuously scant details about her thirty-year marriage. It was, no doubt, an unhappy union. From the few details provided, it appears that for much of their married life John lived with his mother at Washington Place, a spacious mansion built by his late father, while Lili'uokalani lived in various residences owned privately by her family. In describing the bond between her husband and his mother, Mary Dominis, Lili'uokalani is extraordinarily deferential: "As she felt that no one should step between her and her child, naturally I, as her son's wife, was considered an intruder; and I was forced to realize this from the beginning." John apparently made his allegiance known early in the marriage: "My husband was extremely kind and considerate to me, yet he would not swerve to the one side or to the other in any matter where there was danger of hurting his mother's feelings." What Lili'uokalani does not say is that Mary Dominis, adamantly opposed to mixed-race marriages, did not attend her son's wedding. Nor does Lili'uokalani hint at her husband's infidelities. According to Helena G. Allen in her book on Lili'uokalani, when interviewed by Congressman Blount, Dr. G. Trousseau, the Queen's family physician, described John Dominis as an "irregular husband" who had affairs but "never a regular mistress." In writing her memoirs, Lili'uokalani could thus graciously omit her husband's indiscretions: the Blount Report was already public record. Her more judicious readers could no doubt read between the lines.

Recognizing the popularity of autobiographies and "life and letters" series of famous leaders and authors at the turn of the century, Lili'uokalani used the genre not only to detail her genealogy and, briefly, her early life, but she also understood that the autobiographical format allowed her to provide a detailed account of the turmoil leading up to and surrounding the 1893 overthrow. The first half of the autobiography thus covers her genealogy, family life, her travels in England, and her return to confront the events of the "Bayonet Constitution." The remainder of *Hawaii's Story* focuses on the queen's appeals to the U.S. Congress to consider annexation not only as a legal question but a moral one. Imposing a foreign social order, she argues, particularly one perplexed by deep racial prejudices, would be a crushing blow to Native Hawaiians and Hawaiian culture. In effect, she twists late-nineteenth-century Darwinian discourse into a defense against annexation paternalism: "Will it . . . be thought strange," she asks, "that education and knowledge of the world have enabled us to perceive that as a race we have some special mental and physical requirements not shared by the other races which have come among us? That certain habits and modes of living are better for our health and happiness than others?" Affirming the physical and spiritual need to maintain a distinct nationality, government, and code of law, she reminds her readers that these marks of Hawaiian independence were appropriated not by the republic alone, but with the aid of U.S. military intervention. Her powerful closing remarks are ominous: "As [the American people and Congress] deal with me and my people, kindly, generously, and justly, so may the Great Ruler of all nations deal with the grand and glorious nation of the United States of America." On 7 July 1898, five months after the publication of *Hawaii's Story,* President McKinley signed the Newlands Joint Resolution providing for the annexation of Hawaii. The Spanish-American War, more specifically the location of the Spanish Philippines in the Pacific, brought the annexation debate to a close. Lili'uokalani returned to Honolulu on 2 August 1898. Ten days later the Hawaiian flag above 'Iolani Palace was lowered; in its place, the American flag was raised. Her Majesty did not attend the ceremony.

Lili'uokalani was no doubt pained by the defeat, but her efforts had in fact held off annexation for seven years—long enough to lay the foundation for future investigations into the events of 1893. The queen's defense of her nation did not end on 12 August 1898 with the transfer of sovereignty to the United States. Despite the numerous articles, pamphlets, and books authored by the queen's old enemies to refute her account of the overthrow and to malign her reputation, it is her version of Hawaii's story that has since been exonerated. On 23 November 1993, by a joint resolution of Congress, U.S. President William Jefferson Clinton signed into public law a formal apology "to Native Hawaiians on behalf of the people of the United States for the overthrow of the Kingdom of Hawaii." The events of the overthrow, as outlined in the apology, mirror the queen's account. Notably, nearly one hundred years after Lili'uokalani first made the argument, the Congressional apology acknowledges that "Native Hawaiian people are determined to preserve, develop and transmit to future generations their ancestral territory, and their cultural identity in accordance with their own spiritual and tradi-

tional beliefs, customs, practices, language, and social institutions." Lili'uokalani's historical autobiography now stands as the definitive account of her life and of the U.S. annexation of Hawaii at the end of the nineteenth century.

References:

Helena G. Allen, *The Betrayal of Liliuokalani, Last Queen of Hawaii, 1838–1917* (Glendale, Cal.: Arthur H. Clark, 1982);

Sereno E. Bishop, "A Royal Palace Democratized," *Independent,* 45 (6 July 1893): 905;

Miriam Fuchs, "The Diaries of Queen Lili'uokalani," *Profession,* 95 (New York: MLA, 1995): 38–40;

"Hawaii's Story," *Independent,* 50 (24 March 1898): 387;

"Hawaii's Story," *Public Opinion,* 24 (17 February 1898): 216;

"Hawaii's Story by Hawaii's Queen," *Overland Monthly,* 31 (March 1898): 285;

Lilikalā Kame'eleihiwa, *Native Land and Foreign Desires* (Honolulu: Bishop Museum Press, 1992);

George S. Kanahele, "Aloha 'Oe" and "Lili'uokalani," in *Hawaiian Music and Musicians: An Illustrated History,* edited by Kanahele (Honolulu: University of Hawai'i Press, 1979), pp. 11–13, 227–232;

Charles Kofoid, "The Story of Hawaii's Queen," *Dial,* 24 (1 April 1898): 228–231;

Alfons L. Korn and Barbara Peterson, "Lili'uokalani," in *Notable Women of Hawaii* (Honolulu: University of Hawai'i Press, 1984), pp. 240–244;

"Queen Liliuokalani's Story," *Literary World,* 29 (2 April 1898): 103;

William Russ Jr., *The Hawaiian Republic (1894–1898)* (London & Toronto: Associated University Presses, 1992);

Russ, *The Hawaiian Revolution (1893–94)* (London & Toronto: Associated University Presses, 1992);

Harriet Prescott Spofford, "The Ex-Queen of Hawaii," *Harper's Bazar,* 30 (15 May 1897): 401;

Lorrin A. Thurston, *Memoirs of the Hawaiian Revolution* (Honolulu: Advertiser Publishing, 1936), pp. 175–200.

Papers:

Queen Lili'uokalani's diaries, letters, and documents are held in the Lili'uokalani Collection at the Hawaii State Archives and in the Lili'uokalani Manuscripts at the Bernice Pauahi Bishop Museum, Honolulu. Additional letters are in the A. S. Cleghorn Collection at the Hawaii State Archives.

Victoria Earle Matthews

(27 May 1861 – 10 March 1907)

Shirley Wilson Logan
University of Maryland, College Park

BOOK: *Aunt Lindy: A Story Founded on Real Life,* as Victoria Earle (New York: Little, 1893).

OTHER: *Black-Belt Diamonds: Gems from the Speeches, Addresses and Talks to Students of Booker T. Washington,* edited by Matthews (New York: Fortune & Scott, 1898);

"The Value of Race Literature: An Address Delivered at the First Congress of Colored Women, Boston, Massachusetts, 1895" and "The Awakening of the Afro-American Woman," in *With Pen and Voice: A Critical Anthology of Nineteenth-Century African-American Women,* edited by Shirley Wilson Logan (Carbondale: Southern Illinois University Press, 1995), pp. 126–148, 149–155.

SELECTED PERIODICAL PUBLICATIONS–
UNCOLLECTED:

FICTION

"Eugenie's Mistake: A Story," *A.M.E. Church Review,* 8 (1891–1892): 256–268;

"Zelika: A Story," *A.M.E. Church Review,* 9 (July 1892): 72–78.

NONFICTION

"Letter," *Woman's Era,* 1 (1 June 1894): 13;

"Cedar Hill and Its Master: A Sketch of Frederick Douglass in His Home," *Woman's Era,* 1 (November 1894): 2–4;

"Memoranda of 'The Conference Committee' of the National Federation, the National League, and the Atlanta Congress," *Woman's Era,* 2 (February 1896): 3–4;

"Note on the Atlanta Lynch Law Resolution," *Woman's Era,* 2 (February 1896): 9;

"An Explanation," *Woman's Era,* 2 (May 1896): 7–8;

"Open Letter from Chairman of Executive Committee of N.F.A.-A.W," *Woman's Era,* 3 (June 1896): 7;

"Harriet Tubman," *Woman's Era,* 3 (June 1896): 8; (July 1896): 3;

Victoria Earle Matthews

"Thomas Clarkson's Seal," *Woman's Era,* 3 (August 1896): 4;

"An Open Appeal to Our Women for Organization," *Woman's Era,* 3 (January 1897): 2–3;

"Some of the Dangers Confronting Southern Girls in the North," *Hampton Negro Conference. Number II* (July 1898): 62–69.

Victoria Earle Matthews was one of the most vocal and active African American clubwomen and social reformers of the last decade of the nineteenth century. She was one of the chief organizers of the 250 women who sponsored the 1892 testimonial for journalist Ida B. Wells. She was cofounder of the Woman's Loyal Union and its first president. Matthews served as chair of the executive board of the National Federation of Afro-American Women (NFA-AW), chair of the Committee on Union for the Federation leading to its merger with the League of Colored Women, and national organizer of the newly formed National Association of Colored Women (NACW). The pages of the *Woman's Era,* which became the official organ of the NACW, are filled with contributions from and tributes to Matthews. She established the White Rose Home and Industrial Association for young working women and, later, the White Rose Traveler's Aid Society. Matthews was one of only a few women to deliver a formal address at the 1895 Boston Conference of the Colored Women of America. Matthews contributed articles to the major New York newspapers and leading black publications. Along with her journalistic writings and speeches, she authored several pieces of short fiction and edited *Black-Belt Diamonds: Gems from the Speeches, Addresses and Talks to Students of Booker T. Washington* (1898), a collection of excerpts from Washington's speeches. Yet, Matthews registers little if any contemporary recognition, even among scholars of the nineteenth-century women's movement. Her death at age forty-five could well account for this subsequent obscurity. Although, like Matthews, other prominent nineteenth-century African American women intellectuals began their public careers in their thirties, they lived much longer and thus had more time to establish their reputations. Further, the sparse details surrounding some aspects of Matthews's life contribute to this obscurity.

In the early 1860s the slave population of Georgia was more than four hundred thousand. Victoria Smith was born 27 May 1861 in Fort Valley, Houston County, at the time among the top five cotton-producing counties in the state. According to Matthews's marriage record, her parents were William and Caroline Smith. Fleeing to New York, Victoria's mother returned to Georgia after emancipation and obtained custody of four of her nine children, including Victoria, her youngest, and Victoria's sister Anna. Like other freed people throughout the South, Caroline Smith acted to affirm her fundamental rights, including her right to parenthood. She first moved her family to Richmond, then Norfolk, Virginia, where they remained for four years before settling in New York City in 1873, when Victoria was twelve years old. In New York, Victoria attended Grammar School 48 until the illness of a family member made it necessary for her to end her formal education. Driven by a passion for learning, she continued to take advantage of every opportunity to educate herself.

On 22 October 1879 Victoria Smith married William E. Matthews, a coachman from Petersburg,

Virginia. They had one son, Lamartine, who died at age sixteen. The silence surrounding Matthews's marriage and the circumstances of her son's death remains. Sources suggest that the marriage was unhappy, leading Matthews to focus on journalism. No other mention is made of William Matthews, even in Frances Reynolds Keyser's 14 March 1907 *New York Age* obituary of Victoria Matthews.

Shortly after her marriage Matthews began writing for various newspapers, first substituting for reporters of the large New York daily papers, including *The Times, Herald, Mail and Express, Sunday Mercury, The Earth,* and *The Phonographic World.* She was New York correspondent to the *National Leader, Detroit Plaindealer,* and the *Southern Christian Recorder,* and she also wrote for other black publications, including the *Boston Advocate, Washington Bee, Richmond Planet, Catholic Tribune, Cleveland Gazette, New York Globe, New York Age, New York Enterprise, Ringwood's Journal of Fashion, A.M.E. Church Review,* and *Woman's Era.* Matthews was also a member of the Women's National Press Association. In 1891 Garland Penn declared her the most popular woman journalist among her peers, pointing out that contributions from her were eagerly solicited by the best of black and white papers. Matthews adopted the pen name Victoria Earle and subsequently used the name Victoria Earle Matthews on most of her correspondence and publications.

In a later journalistic project Matthews assisted T. Thomas Fortune, publisher of the *New York Age,* in editing the short-lived *Atlanta Southern Age* (formerly the *Reporter*). This editorial partnership was formed during her 1895–1896 tour of the South for the NFA-AW. Fortune soon abandoned this project and returned to New York, as did Matthews.

Most of her extant journalistic contributions can be found in the pages of *Woman's Era.* They were of three kinds—columns as the New York correspondent to *Women's Era,* personal letters to the editors, and tributes to African American historical figures. Assuming a position as an associate editor of *Women's Era* in November 1894, Matthews reported as the New York correspondent on the political and social-reform activities of the Woman's Loyal Union and the black community. For example, in her July 1895 column she calls for continued public outcry against a letter from John Jacks of the Press Club of Missouri questioning African American women's morality. In another she defends the criticisms of Fortune that African American people had not done all they could to improve themselves, declaring them to be "truths—unsavory, but truths, nevertheless." In her letters she urged a national women's organization, supported the proposed Boston conference of African American women, and explained the apparent refusal of the National Federation of Afro-American Women to meet with the National League of Colored Women. Her determination to pass on the history of the race to the younger generation is evident in the tributes to Frederick Douglass, the English abolitionist Thomas Clarkson, and Harriet Tubman. In the article on Tubman, Matthews writes, "we owe it to our children to uncover from partial oblivion and unconscious indifference the great characters within our ranks."

In a May 1894 *Woman's Era* tribute to Matthews, S. Elizabeth Frazier predicted that once Matthews had completed her many works in progress, her name would become a "household word." Biographer Lawson Scruggs lists among Matthews's stories the titles "Little Things," "Well," "Under the Elm," "The Underground Way," "Steadfast and True," "Nettie Mills," "Aunt Lindy: A Story Founded on Real Life," "Eugenie's Mistake: A Story," and "Zelika: A Story." Of these, only the last three are extant. They were all originally published in the *A.M.E. Church Review,* the leading black journal of the post–Civil War era. The journal, with a circulation of 2,800 in 1889 when "Aunt Lindy" appeared in the January issue, carried articles on every phase of African American life. In that same issue "Aunt Lindy," which was republished in 1893 as a sixteen-page book, follows an essay by Frances Ellen Watkins Harper, "The National Woman's Christian Temperance Union." In volume 8 (1891–1892) "Eugenie's Mistake" precedes an essay on the value of a classical education. The July 1892 issue of the *A.M.E. Church Review,* which carried "Zelika: A Story," also included an essay by Ida B. Wells on Afro-Americans and Africa.

Set in Fort Valley, Georgia, Matthews's birthplace, *Aunt Lindy* is a postbellum story of forgiveness and restraint. A fire in the Cotton Exchange spreads throughout the town, destroying homes and lives. One victim of the blaze, an older man, lies unconscious on a cot until the local doctor carries him to a cabin at the edge of town, the home of Aunt Lindy and her husband, Joel. Aunt Lindy consents to take in the dying man. Soon after the patient is settled in Aunt Lindy's home, she recognizes him as her former owner, "Marse Jeems," who had sold her children away. After experiencing several minutes of overpowering anger and thoughts of revenge, Aunt Lindy, restrained by her religious faith, resists the temptation to kill him. She instead nurses him back to health. Her reward for this act of mercy is a financially secure old age and the homecoming of her firstborn son. Matthews's descriptions of the African American characters reinforce stereotypical images of a highly religious and emotional race. Contrasting their reactions to the fire with the reactions of the white townspeople, she writes of "shuddering groups of mute, frightened white faces" and "shrieking, prayerful, terror-stricken negroes, whose religion, being of a highly emotional character was easily

rendered devotional by any unusual excitement: their agonized 'Mi'ty Gawd! he'p us pore sinners,' chanted in doleful tones, as only the emotional Southern negro can chant or moan." Later, Aunt Lindy, described as a "tall, ancient-looking negro dame," converses with Joel regarding certain scriptural injunctions to "heal de sick an' lead the blind" as he departs to attend a "pra'r meetin'." Hearing in the distance the "olden-time melody" being sung at the meeting deters Aunt Lindy from taking her former master's life.

Stereotypical depictions aside, *Aunt Lindy* represents one of the first attempts to feature a dialect-speaking folk character as the central figure in a narrative rather than the stock caricature portrayed in some earlier literature. Additionally, with so many familial separations having occurred because of slavery, reunion with lost family members was a theme understandably appealing to postbellum black writers, including Pauline Hopkins in *Contending Forces* (1900) and Harper in *Iola Leroy* (1892). The lesson of *Aunt Lindy* is one of faith and forgiveness rewarded. In a headnote for the story, which he included in his *Early Black American Prose* (1971), William H. Robinson Jr. comments that Matthews "wrote with obvious deferentiality to white standards and values," suggesting that the title character's decision to forgive the atrocities of her former slaveholder reaffirmed "white values." Reviews during Matthews's own time generally supported her characterizations, however. In the "Literature Department" of the August 1894 *Woman's Era,* Medora W. Gould described Aunt Lindy as a "typical woman of the negro race, well advanced in years, whose heart is warm, whose hand is skillful and whose life is devoted to the service of her Maker." Gertrude Mossell declared *Aunt Lindy* a "beautiful little story . . . deserving of careful study, emanating as it does from the pen of a representative of the race, and giving a vivid and truthful aspect of one phase of Negro character." Mossell added that the story shows "how the loving forgiveness of the race, as it has always done, came out more than conqueror."

In "Eugenie's Mistake" the main character, Adele Van Arsden, returns home to Louisiana and her father's deathbed, having been reared in France by a Mme Charmet. Sole heir to the Van Arsden estate, she remains and eventually marries Royal Clifford, the owner of a neighboring property. Eugenie St. Noir, with whom she has become friends, also loves Royal and plots to destroy the happy couple. Eugenie discovers and reveals to Adele that her mother was a mulatto slave whom her father had married in violation of Louisiana law. Not wanting to see the hurt in Clifford's eyes when he learns that he has married a Negro, Adele returns to France without explanation. Clifford mourns her departure for five years, thinking that she left because she learned that his mother was not white. Ultimately, he travels to France, where they are reunited, to live happily as a black couple. "Oh, what a country America is!" remarks Adele at the close of the story. This story presents an unusual denouement to the typical tragic mulatto story, in which the heroine, discovering her "tainted" blood, must give up her "white" life and devote herself to racial uplift, as in the case of Harper's title character, Iola Leroy. In "Eugenie's Choice" the issue of choice is skirted since both central figures turn out to be of mixed blood. According to Dickson D. Bruce Jr. one might interpret this ending as "acquiescence to racism," but within the context of its production it might be better understood as a story showing happiness in racial identity and solidarity.

The title character in "Zelika" is a slave girl who is given to Valerie Claiborne, the granddaughter of a Georgia cotton-plantation slaveholder, Robert Claiborne, as a companion. The two girls grow up together, sharing all experiences except that of freedom. Zelika learns to read and write and later teaches King George, another slave, whose literacy makes him impatient for freedom. With the coming of the Civil War, King George leaves the plantation to fight for the Union army. Claiborne, old and feeble, refuses to leave the estate and in anger orders his granddaughter from his house. These events leave Zelika and Claiborne the only occupants, until the owner himself dies and the war ends. On his deathbed, the owner gives Zelika a letter telling her where to find buried money. When King George returns from the war, they recover the treasure and use it to live out their lives in peace, settling in California.

"Zelika" repeats the structure and content of *Aunt Lindy*. Both are set in Georgia in the period immediately after the Civil War, and in both, the steadfastness of a faithful servant is rewarded. While both convey a message of forgiveness and perseverance, "Zelika" is less stereotypical in its portrayals of the black characters. Neither King George nor Zelika speaks in the stylized Southern dialect ascribed to Aunt Lindy and Joel. They also seem more defiant, with King George leaving to join the army and Zelika staying, but—as she tells Claiborne—only because she has limited options outside Claiborne estates as a "fair-faced slave." The choices of Zelika and King George are influenced by the literacy they acquire; their apparent devotion to Claiborne emerges at the end as calculated patience.

By 1894 Matthews was firmly established as a member of the literary elite. A March 1894 issue of the *Indianapolis Freeman* heralded the publication of a new race monthly, *Brock's Magazine* out of New York, with contributions from H. Cordelia Ray, Ida B. Wells, and Victoria Earle, who was described as "the literateur."

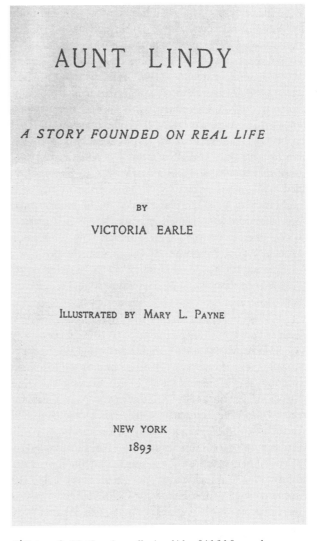

Title page for Matthews's novella, in which a faithful former slave nurses her old master after he is injured in a fire

While *Aunt Lindy,* written when Matthews was twenty-eight, is her best-known and most frequently anthologized text, her most significant contribution to literary history is her work and writing for black women's clubs and various social causes. When Matthews delivered her address "The Value of Race Literature" at the National Conference of Colored Women, held in Boston from 29 to 31 July 1895, she was helping to launch a national organization of black women. The minutes of this conference and the 1896 Washington meeting of the National Federation of Afro-American Women provide written evidence of Matthews's engaged participation in African American club women's work. She could be counted on to make or second a motion or to offer a resolution. She was always among those appointed to draft proposals and establish convention platforms and did not hesitate to express frequently dissenting opinions. For example, as chair of the Committee on Union for the NFA-AW, Matthews, after reporting on the decision to name the newly merged organization the National Association of Colored Women, voiced her personal objection to the choice, explaining that "her preference would always be for Afro-American as the name meant so much to the Negro in America." According to the conference proceedings, she added that "she had African blood in her veins and was of African Descent, which entitled her to the name Afro. While this was true, having been born in America, she was an American citizen and entitled to all the privileges as such, although many rights are constantly denied, she was entitled to the name American, therefore she claimed that the Negro in American was entitled to the name Afro-American, as much as the French, Franco-American, or the English, Anglo-American; as for the name 'colored,' it meant nothing to the Negro race. She was not a colored American, but an Afro-American."

In spite of her objection to the name, Matthews maintained a prominent role in NACW activities, serving as NACW National Organizer from 1897 to 1899. Locally, her club work revolved around the affiliate organization, the Woman's Loyal Union of New York and Brooklyn, established by Matthews and New York educator Marichita Remond Lyons on 5 December 1892. Birth of the organization followed on the heels of the October 1892 testimony to Ida Wells and marshaled the efforts of many of the same women. The union provided information and financial support to black self-help organizations such as the Home for Colored Aged Persons, managed by Matthews's sister Anna Rich. As first president of the Loyal Union, Matthews planned to form chapters of the WLU in all of the large churches of New York and Brooklyn. She also sent circulars to the leading black Southern newspapers asking about living conditions, financial prospects, and racial relations and about the possibility of forming chapters of the Loyal Union among the women.

"The Value of Race Literature" was first printed in the summer 1986 *Massachusetts Review* and later anthologized with annotations in *With Pen and Voice: A Critical Anthology of Nineteenth-Century African-American Women* (1995); the lecture helped to stimulate the climate for black intellectual literary production, as critic Claudia Tate discusses in *Domestic Allegories of Political Desire: The Black Heroine's Text at the Turn of the Century* (1992). Matthews, speaking at the night session on the second day of the Boston Conference of Colored Women shared the podium with Margaret Murray Washington, who was elected president of the newly formed organization; abolitionist William Lloyd Garrison; woman's rights activist Henry B. Blackwell; and T. Thomas Fortune. Matthews's speech resumes the theme of passing race history

on to the young, introduced in her journalistic writing, and stresses the need to produce one's own literature and tell one's own story.

"The Value of Race Literature" gives voice to the belief among nineteenth-century black intellectuals that their literature offered tangible proof of racial progress, rebutting the false characterizations of African Americans found in the writings of white authors. She argues that "any people without a literature is valued lightly the world round." Matthews offers a series of examples of these stereotypical portrayals: depiction in the pages of *Harper's* of typical "Darkies"; John Ridpath's degrading representation of blacks in his historical accounts of the great races of mankind; the story of the romance between Dr. Olney and Rhoda in William Dean Howells's *An Imperative Duty* (1891), in which Howells agonizes over how a white man comes to love a girl with a remote tinge of Negro blood; and the writings of Sir Arthur Conan Doyle, who, she says, portrays educated Negroes as bloodthirsty, treacherous, and savage. Matthews counters these characterizations with proud examples of African American literature, including works by the black women writers Phillis Wheatley, Frances Harper, Charlotte Forten Grimké, Gertrude Mossell, Ida Wells, and Josephine Ruffin. She collapses the distinction between belletristic writings and utilitarian, political, and historical writings produced by blacks, defining race literature as "all the writings emanating from a distinct class— not necessarily race matter; but a general collection of what has been written by the men and women of that Race: History, Biographies, Scientific Treatises, Sermons, Addresses, Novels, Poems, Books of Travel, miscellaneous essays and the contributions to magazines and newspapers." Defined in this broad fashion, race literature rightly encompassed all of the materials Matthews produced, but she modestly does not include herself in any of the lists. Nevertheless, Matthews clearly felt that one of the best weapons against racism was the pen.

On 11 July 1897 Matthews spoke at the San Francisco convention of the Society of Christian Endeavor. The society, organized in Maine in 1881, evolved into an international, interdenominational youth movement with a membership of more than 1.5 million by 1893. In celebration of what was apparently considered to be a prestigious speaking invitation, a special program was held prior to Matthews's departure; it was attended by prominent race leaders, including Booker T. Washington, and letters of congratulations were read.

Matthews's speech, "The Awakening of the Afro-American Woman," is, in many respects, typical of black women's postwar speeches to audiences predominated by white women. As Tate observes, discussing the prose of Matthews's contemporaries Anna Cooper and Gertrude Mossell, they evoked domestic rather than public or civil images. Matthews first reminds her listeners of the past horrors of slavery with oblique allusions to the sexual exploitation of slave women: "They had no past to which they could appeal for anything. It had destroyed, more than in the men, all that a woman holds sacred, all that ennobles womanhood. She had but the future." She marvels that, given their low beginnings, these women have accomplished as much as they have, in large part with little help from those being addressed: "She has done it almost without any assistance from her white sister; who, in too large a sense, has left her to work out her own destiny in fear and trembling." She excepts from this judgment those white women who traveled South after the war to help educate the masses: "I am not unmindful, however, of the Northern women who went into the South after the war as the missionary goes into the dark places of the world." Matthews closes with a final admonition that much more remained to be done and a closing appeal to the common Christianity of the audience: "I feel moved to speak here in this wise for a whole race of women whose rise or fall, whose happiness or sorrow, whose degradation or exaltation are the concern of Christian men and women everywhere."

Matthews appeals in the speech for changes in the laws forbidding interracial marriages and interracial railcar seating. Drawing on her own social-reform work and information gathered during her travels in the South, she also requests support for proper care of old and incapacitated persons and for improved conditions in Southern penal institutions. Less factual and more metaphorical than "The Value of Race Literature," this speech reveals the accommodations made in the shift from an audience of prominent black women to an audience composed mainly of white men and women.

On 11 February 1897, some five months before her trip to the convention in San Francisco, Matthews founded the White Rose Mission and Industrial Association. By 1897 she had shifted her interest from club work in the public arena to social work and advocacy for self-help, in large part a response to the death of her son, which, according to some sources, occurred that same year. After attending the December 1895 Congress of Colored Women of the United States at the Atlanta Exposition, Matthews toured the South for the NFA-AW. During that trip she observed the child abuse fostered by the chain-gang convict lease system referred to in "The Awakening of the Afro-American Woman." While in New Orleans, Matthews investigated the red-light districts and employment agencies.

Many prominent African Americans supported the White Rose Mission. Fortune persuaded Washington to speak at a mission fund-raiser and was said to have remarked to Matthews upon noticing the surrounding neighborhood, "My friend, I wouldn't change fields with you." Poet Paul Laurence Dunbar lectured at the home. In 1897, a year before marrying Dunbar, Alice Ruth Moore conducted classes at the mission. Often using her own money to purchase supplies, Moore described her charges as the "toughest, most God-forsaken hoodlums you ever saw." Matthews, however, seemed to have a way with even the most incorrigible students, often placing them in positions of responsibility. Perhaps as important as her own literary contributions was the exposure she provided to other African American literary works. She conducted classes in black literature and history before it was fashionable, building a library at the White Rose Mission filled with books by and about African Americans. The Loyal Union contributed to this extensive collection. The location of the mission changed several times until 1918, when permanent quarters were established on West 136th Street in Harlem. As separate housing facilities for African American women declined, the home became a meeting place and community center.

A year after establishing the mission, Matthews delivered a speech at the second Hampton Negro Summer Conference of 1898 on the exploitation of Southern girls traveling to the city for work. Toward the end of the century, conferences were organized to discuss "the Negro problem" or "the Negro question" in America. Among these were the conferences held at Hampton and Tuskegee Institutes in the 1890s, which focused on rural issues such as farming and the needs of the one-room schoolhouse. The Hampton, Virginia, conferences were presided over by Hollis Burke Frissell, principal of the Hampton Normal and Agricultural Institute from 1893 to 1917. Matthews's speech "Some of the Dangers Confronting Southern Girls in the North" was delivered at the Woman's Conference along with such presentations as "Some Observations of Farms and Farming in the South," "The Importance of Sewing in the Public Schools," and "How to Hold Young People in the Church," indicating an emphasis on rural and domestic issues. In Matthews's speech, however, she follows the young women out of their homes in the South and into the big cities of the North. Although nineteenth-century decorum precluded use of the word *prostitution*, Matthews paints a bleak picture of young women's sexual exploitation, describing in religious terms "sin-stained years of city life" during which they are used for "immoral purposes." She details Southern recruitment tactics, the high wages offered the women initially in the North, and their ensuing indebtedness. In melodramatic tones, she warns: "The common standard of life must be elevated. The 'tenderloins' must be purified. Corrective influences must be established in the infested centres. Torches must be lighted in dark places. The sending of untrained youth into the jaws of moral death must be checked. Any girl

BLACK-BELT DIAMONDS

Gems from the Speeches, Addresses,
and Talks to Students

OF

BOOKER T. WASHINGTON

Principal of Tuskegee Institute, Tuskegee, Ala.

Selected and Arranged by

VICTORIA EARLE MATTHEWS

AUTHOR OF "AUNT LINDY," ETC.

INTRODUCTION

BY T. THOMAS FORTUNE

NEW YORK

FORTUNE AND SCOTT, PUBLISHERS

4 CEDAR STREET

1898

Title page for an anthology of quotations from the African American educator, edited by Matthews

taking her chances in the cities in this stage of our history must expect in some way to be affected by the public repute of the misguided lives led by those preceding her." She makes the point that these atrocities occurred not only in New York but also in other cities, including Boston, San Francisco, and Chicago. She concludes that Virginia is an appropriate site for reform: "As Virginia seems to have been the starting point of the system, . . . it is meet that appeal should be made at this conference not only in behalf of Virginia's absent daughters, but the long-suffering cruelly wronged, sadly unprotected daughters of the entire South."

One conference recorder, reporting in the *Southern Workman and Hampton School Record* (September 1898), indicated the impact of Matthews's bleak message: "In pleasant contrast to the dark picture presented by Mrs. Matthews, was the bright one given by Mrs. Titus, of the work done in Norfolk and other cities. . . . classes in cooking and sewing have been in operation for some time." Matthews's speech and the discussion that followed it reveal a discourse still directed toward restrain-

ing, confining, and limiting the work options of women rather than preparing them to take advantage of a range of job options. Matthews does stress as one solution informed decisions about jobs in the North: "Let women and girls become enlightened, let them begin to think, and stop placing themselves voluntarily in the power of strangers. Let them search into the workings of every institution under whose auspices they contemplate traveling North." Essentially, however, the discussions defined racial uplift as working to make home more appealing, and black women's work remained confined to those activities that kept them in the community.

In 1898 Matthews published *Black-Belt Diamonds*, one of the first of many books by and about Booker T. Washington. A close friend of Washington's wife, Matthews had the idea to publish excerpts from Washington's speeches, a project that Fortune coordinated. Although Matthews, who had written articles on the Tuskegee Institute for the *New York Age,* selected and edited the excerpts, Fortune mentions her only at the end of a lengthy introduction to the collection. In the closing sentence he acknowledges that the "gems" had been "culled, with so much of industry and discrimination and devotion to the life-work of the man, by Mrs. Matthews." Fortune's essay, part of a general project to promote Washington, compares him to Henry W. Grady, former editor of the *Atlanta Constitution.* Matthews was concerned that such a comparison would ruffle Southern sensibilities, but Washington did not object.

Black-Belt Diamonds comprises seven parts, with quotes taken from such sources as Sunday evening talks at Tuskegee Institute, a Harvard University alumni dinner speech, the A.M.E. Zion Church centennial address, a Carnegie Hall speech, open letters to Fortune, and a speech delivered at Matthews's own White Rose Mission and Industrial Association. Matthews apparently selected statements summarizing the main themes of Washington's public discourse–training for the hand as well as the head, the value of patience, forgiveness and forbearance, advantages to remaining in the South, the need for a strong work ethic, and the interdependence of the "races." The absence of an editorial statement from Matthews makes it difficult to determine what criteria were applied in making the selections. Some may have invoked a shock of recognition in Matthews. Others may have been some of Washington's better-known proclamations, for example, the "Cast down your bucket" quote from his address at the 1895 Cotton States Exposition in Atlanta. There is no obvious chronological or thematic logic to the grouping of quotes, although a summarizing caption–often a line of poetry–heads each quote.

In 1905, as part of her activities on behalf of young women leaving the rural South for urban centers, Matthews established the White Rose Traveler's Aid Society, with agents posted in Norfolk, Virginia, near Hampton, and in New York, to watch for the arrival of potential victims. Matthews recognized that it was not worth the time and money to ferret out the exploiters. It was better, she claimed, to enlighten the women to the dangers that awaited them and to teach them how to search for jobs intelligently. Most, she pleaded, should stay at home.

Matthews died of tuberculosis on 10 March 1907 (although Keyser's obituary gives 10 February as the date of death). According to the register of interments, she was buried in Maple Grove Cemetery in New York City's Kew Gardens on 13 March.

By all accounts, Matthews, the consummate scholar, was a forceful if impatient leader. Keyser, one of her closest associates, characterized her as follows: "Urged on by her eager, restless spirit and that foresight which enabled her to see the end, she could not always wait for others to see, but seemed impelled to carry out her plans immediately, as if there might not be time enough to do all that had to be done." Commenting on her intensity in the August 1895 issue of *Woman's Era,* a reporter wrote, "so devoted was she to the interests of the Conference that Boston saw comparatively little in a social way of this gifted woman." In that same issue, Matthews is compared to Anna Julia Cooper and Helen Cook, both Washington club women: "Mrs. Cook, intelligent and practical, and although versed in parliamentary tactics–always a cultured lady; Mrs. Matthews, full of fire and intensity, with natural gifts as a speaker and writer; Mrs. Cooper, calm, thoughtful, and analytical–a woman to mould opinion, rather than a leader of men. Mrs. Cooper, the student; Mrs. Matthews, a born leader; Mrs. Cook, the trained leader." In her biographical sketch in *Notable American Women 1607–1950* (1971), Jean Blackwell Hutson suggests that Matthews's "high-strung temperament and impatience with those less quick in mind and less farsighted in vision sometimes hampered her dealings with others." Matthews may be one of the best examples among nineteenth-century black women of a public intellectual. She operated within the public sphere primarily through the application of her sharp wit and organizational ability. Her life was devoted to social change, and that devotion, fueled by an active mind, led her to produce the kinds of "race lit-

erature" she called for at the Boston conference. Moreover, through her own activism she also modeled the life she wanted others to live.

References:

Hallie Q. Brown, *Homespun Heroines and Other Women of Distinction* (Xenia, Ohio: Aldine, 1926), pp. 208–216;

Dickson D. Bruce Jr., *Black American Writing from the Nadir: The Evolution of a Literary Tradition, 1877–1915* (Baton Rouge: Louisiana State University Press, 1989), pp. 51–55;

Medora W. Gould, "Literature Department," *Woman's Era,* 1 (August 1894): 14;

A History of the Club Movement among the Colored Women of the United States of America (Washington, D.C.: National Association of Colored Women's Clubs, 1978);

Rayford W. Logan, *The Negro in American Life and Thought: The Nadir, 1877–1901* (New York: Dial, 1954), p. 322;

Mrs. N. F. Mossell, *The Work of the Afro-American Woman* (New York: Oxford, 1988), pp. 61–63;

Gilbert Osofsky, *Harlem, the Making of a Ghetto: Negro New York, 1890–1930* (New York: Harper & Row, 1963), pp. 56–57;

I. Garland Penn, *The Afro-American Press and Its Editors* (New York: Arno, 1969), pp. 375–377;

William H. Robinson Jr., ed., *Early Black American Prose* (Dubuque, Iowa: Brown, 1971), p. 159;

Lawson Scruggs, *Women of Distinction: Remarkable in Works and Invincible in Character* (Raleigh, N.C.: Scruggs, 1893), pp. 30–32;

Claudia Tate, *Domestic Allegories of Political Desire: The Black Heroine's Text at the Turn of the Century* (New York: Oxford University Press, 1992), pp. 134–138;

Emma Lou Thornbrough, *T. Thomas Fortune: Militant Journalist* (Chicago: University of Chicago Press, 1972), pp. 153, 165–167.

Papers:

The largest collections of material by or about Victoria Earle Matthews are in the Schomburg Center for Research in Black Culture, the New York Public Library, and the Moorland-Spingarn Research Center, Howard University, Washington, D.C.

María Cristina Mena
(María Cristina Chambers)
(3 April 1893 – 3 August 1965)

E. Thomson Shields Jr.
East Carolina University

See also the Mena entry in *DLB 209: Chicano Writers, Third Series.*

BOOKS: *The Water-Carrier's Secrets* (New York: Oxford University Press, 1942);

The Two Eagles (New York: Oxford University Press, 1943);

The Bullfighter's Son (New York: Oxford University Press, 1944);

The Three Kings (New York: Oxford University Press, 1946);

Boy Heroes of Chapultepec, A Story of the Mexican War (Philadelphia: Winston, 1953);

The Collected Stories of María Cristina Mena, edited by Amy Doherty (Houston: Arte Público, 1997).

SELECTED PERIODICAL PUBLICATIONS–
UNCOLLECTED: "Julian Carrillo: The Herald of a Musical Monroe Doctrine," *Century Magazine,* 89 (March 1915): 753–759;

"Afternoons in Italy with D. H. Lawrence," *Texas Quarterly,* 7 (1964): 114–120.

María Cristina Mena

María Cristina Mena was not a prolific writer. She published in a concentrated manner during only two periods of her seventy-two-year life: from 1913 to 1916, when ten short stories and one nonfiction article appeared, mainly in *Century Magazine,* and from 1942 to 1953 when her five children's books came out. Still, her output is an important part of Mexican American literary history. As a local-color writer, she was recognized during her life as one of the first Mexican American writers in English. As such, she was seen as an important interpreter of life in late-nineteenth- and early-twentieth-century Mexico for audiences in the United States. Yet, by the time criticism about Mexican American literature began to take form during the 1970s and 1980s, she had been relegated to a secondary position, seen as portraying strong female characters at best and as acquiescing to U.S. colonialism of Mexico at worst. With the recovery and republication of her magazine fiction, how-

ever, Mena's position in the history and politics of Mexican American literature is undergoing reconsideration.

The politics found in Mena's writing reflect her life. She was born in Mexico City on 3 April 1893, during the height of Porfirio Díaz's dictatorial reign as president of Mexico. Díaz ruled from 1877 to 1911, and most of Mena's writing portrays Mexico during this period. Though only bits and pieces have been gathered about Mena's biography, especially her childhood in Mexico, it is known that her parents were part of the ruling class during Díaz's reign. Mena's mother was of Spanish descent (or was a Spanish immigrant) and her father came from the Yucatán region of Mexico and was of European descent. Her father worked as a partner with several Americans in business ventures during the early years of her life. The money made in these ventures allowed Mena to be educated at the Hijas de María convent school in Mexico City and afterward at an English boarding school. In these schools Mena gained fluency in Spanish, English, French, and Italian.

The same influx of foreign capital and management of Mexican industry and infrastructure that allowed Mena's parents to privately educate her, however, also created social unrest among the working classes, especially the Native Americans. In 1907, as discontent over the Díaz dictatorship grew, Mena's parents sent her to New York City. From her arrival in the United States at the age of fourteen until the end of her life, Mena lived in New York, particularly Brooklyn. What happened to her parents after this time is unknown.

In New York Mena lived with family friends and continued her education. Even before coming to the United States, Mena enjoyed writing. Beginning at the age of ten, she would hide in corners and write verses she never showed to anyone else. Sometime in the first six years of her life in the United States, Mena switched to short stories about Mexico as her main genre. Her writing came from her own studies and not from any specific training. In an article in volume one of Matthew Hoehn's *Catholic Authors: Contemporary Biographical Sketches, 1930–1947* (1948) Mena is quoted as not believing in schools of writing. "I have never read, much less studied, the so-called 'methods' for learning how to write," she says. "I do not believe an aspirant for authorship needs any more than to learn from observation and much reading of good authors; that writing is something born and grows naturally through much working at it and particularly from one's own original and very personal feeling and thinking." Despite not attaching herself to any particular method of writing, Mena's work is in the local-color tradition of the early twentieth century. Her stories depend for their plot and themes on their setting in Mexico and on the social structure of the region on the eve of the Díaz regime's fall.

Mena's first stories were published in November 1913; "The Gold Vanity Set" appeared in *American Magazine* and "John of God, the Water-Carrier" in *Century Magazine*. Ten local-color stories appeared over the next two years. In 1914 Douglas Zabriske Doty, the editor of *Century Magazine*—where most of Mena's short stories were published—suggested that she write about a Mexican immigrant character in the United States. Mena replied by describing a novel-length story idea for a character perhaps much like herself: "I have in outline the personalities of a family of wealthy refugees from Mexico, with possibilities of rich comedy in their contact with American life, especially in relation to the gradual emancipation of their daughter, who in spite of the efforts of her parents to keep her in pious subjection in accordance with Mexican tradition, takes to American freedom like a duck to water and blossoms into an ardently independent young woman, with, of course, a suitable romance to crown her adventures—the whole story to be unfolded in a succession of amusing letters from the different personages to their friends at home." Mena saw herself as a writer with a great store of rich material, all coming from her Mexican American background, with the potential to be crafted in a variety of different directions. Mena never published such a novel.

It is her stories of life in Mexico for which Mena is best known. One of her first short works, "John of God, the Water-Carrier," tells the story of Juan de Dios, a boy who rescues an infant girl, Delores, whose mother has died in the aftermath of an earthquake. Juan feels responsible for the girl and decides to marry her when he has made enough money carrying water from the local well. Ultimately, Juan goes to the city in order to do even better, leaving Delores in the care of his family. By the end of the story, Delores has fallen in love with and married Juan's brother, Juan's brother has had a losing battle with the technology of water pumps, and Juan himself has had a religious experience. In this story can be found many of the elements that appear throughout Mena's fiction. Questions of city versus country, poor working for rich, gender and romance, even the value of work as an end unto itself are all part of the thematic repertoire of Mena's stories. In this manner, Mena responds to the issues raised during the Díaz regime.

Her other stories treat people across the social spectrum and at times show the interaction of Mexican and U.S. cultures. In the other work published in November 1913, "The Gold Vanity Set," a well-to-do American tourist loses her gold makeup kit; a young Native American woman turns the gold vanity set into an offering to the Virgin of Guadalupe, asking the saint to protect her from the beatings she has been receiving. The portrait of privilege and wealth in relationship with poverty and powerlessness is juxtaposed with the understanding that arises between the two women—the Native American woman and the wealthy American tourist—on the basis of the problems shared by their sex. Other stories tell of young women from upper-class families going through difficulties. In "Marriage by Miracle" (1916) an upper-class family has fallen on hard times because of the death of the patriarch. They are still a family "of carriage," but they no longer have money for horses to pull the coach. Meanwhile, the younger of two daughters has a suitor of a well-off but slightly lower-class family whom she cannot marry until her older sister is married. Several of Mena's stories, then, are about class and gender and the ways in which these elements of society interact and affect people's lives.

Two other elements of Mena's writing are worth noting for their place in Mexican American literary history. First, Mena incorporates a good portion of Mexican folklore into some of her works, whether that is the use of Roman Catholic religious icons, such as the Virgin of Guadalupe (which appears in both "John of God, the Water-Carrier" and "The Gold Vanity Set") or in the telling of an entire pre-Columbian Aztec myth as she has a grandmother tell her grandchild in "The Birth of the God of War" (1914). Second, Mena uses the language of Mexico–both Spanish and Native American terms–as a tool to bring across the special nature of Mexican culture. For example, in "Marriage by Miracle," the central family is described as being "in the station not only 'of *señoras*,' but also 'of carriage.'" The term *señoras*, or ladies, indicates social stature, for they are referred to by this appellation of respect throughout town, never by their first names. By noting that they are "of carriage," Mena has introduced a literal translation of a Spanish term to indicate that the family is (or at least was) well off. In "Doña Rita's Rivals," the title character is noted as being "of shawl–*de tápolo*," or of the respectable middle class. For, as Mena writes in this story about how women of the shawl look at the covering of lower-class women, "No maid or matron of shawl would demean her respectable shoulders with the *rebozo*–it is woven long and narrow, and is capable of being draped in a variety of graceful and significant ways–but contrariwise, young ladies of hat, authentic *señoritas* to whom the mere contact of a shawl would impart 'flesh of chicken,' delight to dignify the national investment by wearing it coquettishly at country feasts. Persons of *rebozos*–one never speaks of 'families' so far down the social scale–are the women of petty tradespeople, servants, artisans." Mena's use of the Mexican language helps portray the society into which she was born, but at the same time allows her to emphasize its beauty and its troubles.

Century Magazine, along with a few select others such as *Harper's* and *Scribner's,* was one of the predominant general magazines of its day, featuring political commentary, history, and literature. By publishing in *Century* Mena reached a wide readership of influential Americans. Amy Doherty, in her introduction to the only complete collection of Mena's short stories (1997), notes that the articles in *Century Magazine* had an overt bias against immigrants, specifically Mexican immigrants, not unusual for the United States in the early twentieth century. By having her stories published in such a periodical, Mena was able to subtly counter the anti-Mexican feelings other authors espoused.

What kept Mena from going further in her writing career after 1916 is uncertain. One possible explanation is that *Century Magazine* and others like it faced increased economic restraints during World War I and bought fewer works. However, another possibility is that when she married in 1916 at the age of twenty-three, her life took on a dif-

ferent focus. Mena married Henry Kellett Chambers, an Australian immigrant playwright and journalist who was twenty-six years older than she. Whether her new role as wife seemed to preclude writing for her or if she kept writing but was unable or unwilling to publish her work at this time is unknown. The two stories she did publish between 1916 and 1943 (one a reprint of an earlier work), as well as all her children's books published between 1942 and 1953, were done under her married name of María Cristina Chambers.

Mena did have a small resurgence in publishing during the late 1920s and early 1930s. First, "John of God, the Water-Carrier" was reprinted by T. S. Eliot in the October 1927 issue of the London literary journal *The Monthly Criterion.* The following year the story was reprinted again in the collection *The Best Short Stories of 1928 and the Yearbook of the American Short Story.* About this time she began a correspondence with British writer D. H. Lawrence, who had traveled quite a bit in Mexico and in the desert in the southwestern United States. Their correspondence continued until Lawrence's death in 1930. Following the publication of Lawrence's controversial *Lady Chatterley's Lover* (1928), Mena offered to champion the book in New York against censorship. "Am not afraid of *la cárcel*," she wrote to Lawrence on 9 August 1928. "And am free to do as I like. Let *me* sell the books and let [the booksellers] all come to me and pay for them, if they want them." The friendship between Mena and Lawrence grew to the point that she spent two weeks in the summer of 1929 with Lawrence and his wife, Frieda, in Forte de Marmi, Italy. Also visiting Lawrence while Mena was there were the British writer Aldous Huxley and his wife, María. Mena felt that her relationship with Lawrence was so important to her that in 1964, near the end of her own life, she published an article in the *Texas Quarterly* about her visit with him in Italy.

Mena's last published short story, "A Son of the Tropics," which appeared in *Household Magazine* in January 1931, was the only time she dealt directly with revolutionary politics in fiction. In particular, this story deals with the kidnapping of a rich landowner's daughter by revolutionary forces, the need for the rich landowner to face the consequences of his absentee rule over his lands, and the revolutionary leader's need to come to grips with the fact that his parentage is not pure Native American but that he is the landowner's bastard son. In the introduction to the story the editors call Mena "the foremost interpreter of Mexican life." Though there is probably much hyperbole in such a statement, the fact that Mena was one of the first Mexican Americans to publish in English and that there was little or no Mexican American literature in English, at least in the popular press, until the 1930s means that there is some truth to the description.

After her husband died of a paralytic stroke in September 1935, Mena rarely ventured from her home in

Brooklyn. She did go out, however, to attend meetings of the Catholic Library Association and the Authors Guild of New York. At these meetings she maintained her connection with the literary circle in which she and her husband had traveled. Beginning in 1942 she published five children's books, all concerned with portraying Mexico to young American readers. In fact, most of her children's books are reworkings of her short stories. There are indications, however, that she hoped to write much more. In the article from Hoehn's *Catholic Authors,* Mena is noted as wishing to "write a series of articles on the churches of Mexico and some essays portraying the soul-experiences of the Mexican people in their struggle to remain good Catholics." Again, as with her plans to write works beyond the short stories of the 1910s, it is not clear whether she did write more than the children's books but did not publish, or whether she was never able to accomplish her intended goals.

Mena died on 3 August 1965. She was remembered well enough to have an obituary titled "Mrs. Henry Chambers, 72, Short-Story Writer, is Dead" in *The New York Times.* Yet her reputation as a part of Mexican American literary history has not been all good. The earliest mention of her work in critical materials appears to be in Raymund A. Parades's important 1982 essay "The Evolution of Chicano Literature." Parades recognizes the importance of Mena's publishing in mainstream U.S. periodicals such as *Century Magazine* as well as her sympathy for the people the Díaz regime had suppressed, but in a line often quoted by other critics (either to agree or to disagree), Parades writes that "Occasionally, she struck a blow at the pretensions of Mexico's ruling class, but to little effect; Mena's genteelness simply was incapable of warming the reader's blood."

Feminist critics have revived Mena's reputation to some extent. For example, Elizabeth Ammons recognizes in her 1991 book *Conflicting Stories: American Women Writers at the Turn into the Twentieth Century* that Mena is part of a movement around the beginning of the twentieth century that allowed many women writers from a wide variety of racial backgrounds, including Sui Sin Far, Zitkala-Ša, and Mary Antin, to express themselves in widely circulated publications. These feminist critics recognize Mena for concerning herself with gender issues such as the silencing of women in society, violence against women, and the general problem of patriarchal domination over women. In these works, Mena is treated well but receives only passing notice.

Only with the recent republication of Mena's stories is she being more fully reconsidered for her role in Mexican American literature. In his 1992 anthology *North of the Rio Grande: The Mexican-American Experience in Short Fiction,* Edward Simmen published three of Mena's stories—"John of God, the Water-Carrier," "The Gold Vanity Set," and "The Education of Popo"—alongside the work of more-recent Mexican American writers. Doherty's *The Collected Stories of María Cristina Mena* is the only collection of all Mena's stories and the only lengthy analysis of her work to date. With the recovery of Mena's stories, a fuller reconsideration of her importance to Mexican American literature can take place. Her politics reflect her attachment to the social class she was born into, but they also show a willingness to question the abuse of the class structure, even a willingness to break down class barriers at times. It is on her early twentieth-century contributions to fictional representations of Mexico that Mena's growing reputation is based.

References:

Elizabeth Ammons, *Conflicting Stories: American Women Writers at the Turn into the Twentieth Century* (New York: Oxford University Press, 1991), pp. 145–147;

James T. Boulton and Margaret H. Boulton, eds., *The Letters of D. H. Lawrence,* 7 volumes (Cambridge: Cambridge University Press, 1991), VI: pp. 296–297, 377–378, 521–522;

Matthew Hoehn, "María Christina Chambers," in *Catholic Authors: Contemporary Biographical Sketches, 1930–1947,* edited by Hoehn, volume 1 (Newark, N.J.: St. Mary's Abbey, 1948), pp. 118–119;

Raymund A. Parades, "The Evolution of Chicano Literature," *Three American Literatures: Essays in Chicano, Native American, and Asian American Literature for Teachers of American Literature,* edited by Houston A. Baker Jr. (New York: Modern Language Association, 1982), pp. 33–79;

Edward Simmen, ed., *North of the Rio Grande: The Mexican-American Experience in Short Fiction* (New York: Mentor-Penguin, 1992), pp. 5–6, 39–84;

Michael Squires, "Two Newly Discovered Letters to D. H. Lawrence," *D. H. Lawrence Review,* 23 (1991): 31–35.

Papers:

There is no known collection of María Cristina Mena's papers, except for Mena's correspondence with *Century Magazine,* which is located in the Century Company Records, Rare Books and Manuscript Division, New York Public Library.

Mourning Dove
(Humishuma)
(between April 1882? and 1888? – 8 August 1936)

Alanna Kathleen Brown
Montana State University

See also the Mourning Dove entry in *DLB 175: Native American Writers of the United States.*

BOOKS: *Cogewea, the Half-Blood: A Depiction of the Great Montana Cattle Range,* by Hum-ishu-ma, *"Mourning Dove"* . . . *Given through Sho-pow-tan, with Notes and Biographical Sketch by Lucullus Virgil McWhorter* (Boston: Four Seas, 1927);

Coyote Stories, edited by Heister Dean Guie (Idaho: Caxton Printers, 1933);

Tales of the Okanogans, edited by Donald M. Hines (Fairfax, Wash.: Ye Galleon, 1976);

Mourning Dove: A Salishan Autobiography, edited by Jay Miller (Lincoln: University of Nebraska Press, 1990);

Mourning Dove's Stories, edited Clifford E. Trafzer and Richard D. Scheuerman (San Diego: San Diego State University Press, 1991).

Editions: *Cogewea, the Half-Blood: A Depiction of the Great Montana Cattle Range,* edited by Dexter Fisher (Lincoln: University of Nebraska Press, 1981);

Coyote Stories, edited by Jay Miller (Lincoln: University of Nebraska Press, 1990).

SELECTED PERIODICAL PUBLICATIONS—
UNCOLLECTED: "Learning Love Medicine," edited by Clifford E. Trafzer and Richard D. Scheuerman, *Fiction International,* 20 (Fall 1991): 142–156;

"Mourning Dove's 'The House of Little Men,'" *Canadian Literature,* edited by Alanna Kathleen Brown, 144 (Spring 1995): 49–60.

OTHER: "The Story of Green-Blanket Feet," in *Spider Woman's Granddaughters,* edited by Paula Gunn Allen (Boston: Beacon, 1989), pp. 117–125;

"Coyote Juggles His Eyes," in *Voice of the Turtle: American Indian Literature, 1900–1970,* edited by Allen (New York: One World/Ballantine, 1994), pp. 72–77;

Mourning Dove (Historical Photographs Collections, Washington State University Libraries)

"Owlwoman and Coyote," transcribed by Alanna Kathleen Brown, in *The Norton Anthology of American Literature,* 2 volumes, fifth edition, edited by Nina Baym (New York & London: Norton, 1998), I: 137–140.

The life and works of Mourning Dove (Humishuma) point to an extraordinary, although almost unremarked, period in the history of European American settlement, the end of open military conflict with indigenous peoples. The massacre of Sioux people who had gathered for a Ghost Dance at Wounded Knee on 29 December 1890 ended open hostilities. But the need to eradicate Native American peoples remained strong, and extensive federal policies were put into place to ensure "assimilation" of Indians into the dominant culture during the twentieth century. It was assumed by common folk as well as local, state, and federal officials that no Indian tribes would survive into the twenty-first century.

Mourning Dove was born and grew up during that assimilation period–from the 1880s to the 1930s. Both her life story and her literary works reveal the pressures on an individual and a Native culture to deconstruct their lives. Her life and work also reveal the ability to mitigate those pressures by using the language of the conquerors to preserve Indian culture and to comment on the swirl of events that appeared to be swallowing up their lives. Her novel, *Cogewea, the Half-Blood: A Depiction of the Great Montana Cattle Range* (1927), explores the pressures to assimilate rather than preserve traditional values for her Indian generation. She also assumes an America faced with the problematic situation of mixed-blood children. In *Mourning Dove: A Salishan Autobiography,* published in 1990, readers are provided the most thorough revelation of assimilation pressures on a collapsing Northwest Indian culture in print. In the face of that potential annihilation, *Coyote Stories* (1933) demonstrates the choice to keep the Salish oral heritage alive by utilizing the literary forms of the conquering culture.

Three issues surrounding the birth of Mourning Dove already indicate the cultural ambivalence of the time in which she was born. First, record keeping was sporadic, as white officials did not know the languages or cultures of the people they recorded and the Native peoples did not mark events by day, month, and year. Not surprisingly, Mourning Dove's birth date is in question. A 1908 marriage license states April 1882, a family anecdote suggests 1884, various tribal enrollment and allotment records list both 1886 and 1887, and Mourning Dove always asserted that her birth date was April 1888. Whatever the actual year, she was born in the decade when federal policies turned toward assimilation. The second issue is that because Euramericans did not want to learn Indian languages, Indians were given English names. A local priest named Mourning Dove "Christine" at her birth. The third and most problematic issue deals with Mourning Dove's parentage and the sexual exploitation of Indian women.

Her mother, Lucy Stuikin, was either a full-blooded Colville or of Colville and Arrow Lakes descent; her father, Joseph Quintasket, was of Nicola and Okanogan descent on his mother's side and possibly Arrow Lakes on his father's side. However, in the introduction to *Coyote Stories,* Mourning Dove asserts that her father's father was an Irishman named Haines or Haynes who worked for the Hudson Bay Company. To complicate the issue further, as a young woman Mourning Dove chose to sign her name as Christine Haines while a matron at Fort Shaw, Montana, a Bureau of Indian Affairs (BIA) schools; Mourning Dove claimed also she was one-half white in a patent in fee on her allotment in 1910, in contrast to her claim she was one-quarter white in a patent in fee request in 1921. Whatever the correct lineage, Mourning Dove (Christine Quintasket) grew up in the Kelly Hill community near Kettle Falls, Washington, on the west side of the Columbia River on the Colville Reservation.

The first phase of her life is indicative of the hardships many Northwest Native children faced in their childhood and teenage years. She was part of the first generation to be removed from the home and taught in a Catholic mission and then BIA schools. As the oldest child (her two sisters and lifelong friends, Julia and Mary Margaret, were born in 1891 and 1892, respectively), Mourning Dove was placed in the Goodwin Mission School of the Sacred Heart Convent at Ward, Washington, in 1895. Punished for speaking Salish and locked into a stairwell closet for misbehaving, Mourning Dove returned home ill within months. Sometime in 1895–1896 the family took in Jimmy Ryan, a thirteen-year-old orphaned Irish boy, and he introduced her to dime-store novels, a major turning point in her life. In that environment she discovered that she loved to read and that she took genuine pleasure in learning English. She returned to the mission school and remained until federal funding for religious instruction for Native students was cut in 1899. Mourning Dove begged her parents to let her continue her education at the newly formed, BIA-sponsored Fort Spokane School for Indians. The school was composed of converted military barracks at the confluence of the Columbia and Spokane Rivers. Soon after she left for the school in 1899–1900, tragedy struck the family and Mourning Dove returned home. Her baby sister, Marie, had fallen ill and died on 29 April 1900. Then her mother died on 8 May 1901 at thirty years of age, and Mourning Dove's baby brother, Johnny, who was four or five, died on 8 July 1902. Amid that period of grief, Mourning Dove became the female head of the household and took on the responsibility of the chores her mother had done before her.

The second stage of her life began in 1904 when Joseph Quintasket remarried, taking as his bride a twenty-five-year-old woman, Cecelia Williams. Mourning Dove decided it was time she left her childhood home. She traveled by horseback with her younger sisters, thirteen-year-old Julia and twelve-year-old Mary Margaret, to Jennings, Montana, to visit their maternal grandmother, Marie. In what reflects obvious parallels to the names and situations of the three sisters in her novel *Cogewea,* the children were separated. Julia stayed with her grandmother and eventually married a rancher called Frenchy; Margaret was sent to a traditional aunt who lived in Curlew, Washington; a brother, Louis, remained with his father; and Mourning Dove arranged to work as a matron in exchange for room and board and the privilege of attending classes at the Fort Shaw Indian School outside of Great Falls, Montana, from 1904 to 1908. While at Fort Shaw, she signed her name as Christine Haines; she spent four years not only assimilating herself but also helping other Indian children to assimilate.

On 31 July 1908 in Kalispell, Montana, Mourning Dove, now going by the name Christal, married Hector McLeod, a handsome Flathead Reservation mixed-blood, and the newlywed couple established a livery stable business in Polson, Montana. Mourning Dove, as Christal McLeod, was as close to an assimilated white identity as she ever came. Her marriage was not easy, however. A patent in fee on her allotment in 1910 speaks to Hector's addiction to alcohol, and family anecdotes reveal that McLeod was not only an alcoholic, he was abusive. Christine, who was pregnant, was hospitalized after a violent attack, and whether through damage inflicted by her husband or sterilization by a doctor, Christine was unable to have any more children.

This third period in her life led to a crucial change of direction. Mourning Dove left Montana for Portland, Oregon, in 1912 to escape her marriage, and there she wrote her first draft of *Cogewea.* To maintain her commitment to writing, she then traveled to Calgary, Alberta, probably in late 1912, to attend two years of business school in order to learn typing, shorthand, and more composition skills. By 1914 Mourning Dove had a typed draft of a novel in hand and twenty-two Okanogan legends in transcription. At that critical juncture, Mourning Dove and Lucullus Virgil McWhorter met at the Walla Walla Frontier Days Celebration. She was between the ages of twenty-six and thirty-two, and McWhorter was fifty-four. The letters from their nineteen years of collaboration and a twenty-two-year friendship from 1914 to 1936 provide extensive information about the tensions she experienced in finding her voice as a person and as a writer and a great deal about the process of working with collaborators.

In the earliest years of their correspondence, through 1920, the radical difference in expectations of Mourning Dove's family and friends versus those of McWhorter and his elder mentor, J. P. MacLean, is stark. They reveal the pull on Mourning Dove to fulfill the constant expectations others had for her. For her family, Mourning Dove was an unattached, experienced worker, needed by everyone. They considered her writing to be a hobby, and no one believed that her desire to write was more important than their needs for her. For McWhorter there was no question that Mourning Dove's writing should be of primary importance. MacLean had even larger expectations of Mourning Dove's abilities. He urged both McWhorter and Mourning Dove to write their Yakima and Okanogan legends in English and the appropriate Indian dialect, although no such lexicons existed at the time. Moreover, MacLean wanted to set up a speaking tour for Mourning Dove on the East Coast, beginning with a visit to him in Ohio, and then leading to speaking engagements from Philadelphia to Boston. Both McWhorter and MacLean wanted Mourning Dove to be an ally who could address the wrongs done to the Indian. Mourning Dove's response was to try to meet the needs of everyone. Alone, in 1915–1916, she went to the Inkameep Reserve in British Columbia to help her sister, Mary Margaret; to Napoleon, Washington, to help her father, Joseph; then she stayed with the McWhorters in the winter months to create a publishable manuscript of *Cogewea;* after that she took care of Julia's family in Jennings, Montana, while her sister recovered from an operation and the children struggled through measles; then she contracted to take care of a widower's six children in order to earn sixty-five dollars for her share of the costs in what appears to be the first contract to publish *Cogewea.* Not surprisingly, exhaustion overwhelmed her. By the winter of 1916–1917, Mourning Dove was seriously ill from a combined attack of inflammatory rheumatism and pneumonia. Letters reveal that she nearly died that January.

The severity of her illness and her slow recovery shook Mourning Dove. To heal, she chose to live with Mary Margaret and her family in British Columbia, a place where Salishan culture, language, and rituals were more intact. That choice set the pattern for the rest of her adult years. Whenever she felt like she was losing focus on her work or was experiencing high emotional distress, she would return to Canada to live in more traditional ways, practice Salish healing rituals, and then return home to the United States. That first visit after cataclysmic crisis lasted from 1916 to 1919. During those years, she taught young Indian pupils for a year on the Inkameep Reserve and struggled with continuing poor health that manifested itself in a severe toothache in 1917 and an inflamed eye problem as well as the killer flu of 1918. On 14 August 1919 she married Fred Galler, a half-blooded Wenatchee, in Okanogan County, Washington, and she returned to the United States and took up residence in Omak, Washington.

Clearly feeling more secure in her own life, Mourning Dove's letters demonstrate that from 1921 to 1928 her collaboration with McWhorter reignited. While Mourning Dove managed a house with fourteen boarders and joined her husband as a picker and packer during the orchard season, she returned to the work of transcribing Salish legends as well as editing the ones she had already recorded by 1914. Late in 1921 she sent McWhorter the thirty-eight tales that composed a manuscript titled "The Okanogan Sweat House." The title page reads "By HUM-IS HU-MA: 'MOURNING DOVE.'" In those last two months of 1921 and then throughout the following year, McWhorter concentrated his efforts on preparing Mourning Dove's Okanogan tales for publication, and an intense collaboration was carried out by mail. During 1922, however, McWhorter's frustration over the difficulties in publishing *Cogewea* overwhelmed his better judgment. He took upon himself the reworking of *Cogewea* and did not share his editing and additions with Mourning Dove. Ethnographic annotations, notes, and the insertion of poetic epigraphs for the chapters had been his initial contribution to the novel. He also had helped make sentences grammatically correct and participated in discussions about plot development. In 1922, however, McWhorter added the diatribes against Christian hypocrisy and government corruption. He also chose to elevate the language of the heroine to such a rarified air that her words ceased to be believable speech. *Cogewea* became a mouthpiece for McWhorter's rage against white hypocrisy and injustices.

After twelve years of submitting material to publishers, *Cogewea* was the first Mourning Dove manuscript to come into print. She received a copy in 1928 and immediately wrote to McWhorter on 4 June: "I have just got through going over the book Cogeawea, and am surprised at the changes that you made. . . . I felt like it was some one elses book and not mine at all. In fact the finishing touches are put there by you, and I have never seen it. . . . Oh my Big Foot, you surely roasted the Shoapees strong. I think a little too strong to get their sympathy." Her criticism of McWhorter's additions were insightful and are at the core of the ongoing interpretive debate about the novel. Other issues also plagued the publication both in its inception and consequences. Although the Four Seas Company

Lucullus Virgil McWhorter, who edited, revised, and added to Mourning Dove's novel Cogewea

of Boston had agreed to publish the manuscript in 1925, McWhorter had to threaten to report them for fraudulent use of the U.S. Postal Service to get them to publish the work. Then, after the book was out, McWhorter discovered that he had inadvertently signed away the copyright to the novel when Harl J. Cook approached Mourning Dove and McWhorter about writing a script for a movie of *Cogewea* in November 1928. A lucrative opportunity had been lost that also might have opened doors to other opportunities. Moreover, because the publishers did not promote the novel in any way, Mourning Dove made less than $25 for the publication, and the final settlement between the authors and the publisher gained her only scores of copies of the unsold novel.

Regardless of the above problems, the publication of *Cogewea* was an empowering event for Mourning Dove. Her social and political activism marked a new direction in the last eight years of her life. That activism began with Mourning Dove's efforts in 1928 to found the Eagle Feather Club, a women's organization meant to mentor, educate, and tend to the social needs of

Indian women in Omak. Moreover, with her as spokeswoman, the club addressed government commissions on the corruption of business practices and government ineptness on the reservation. In 1930 she also became a spokeswoman for the Colville Indian Association. In 1934 she offered to help Commissioner John Collier secure adoption of the new Indian Reorganization Act, and although reorganization was voted down in 1935 by the Colville Indians, Mourning Dove was elected to the Tribal Council in that same year–the first Colville woman ever to win such an office. Her life experiences, from the intense assimilation pressures of mission and BIA schools, to a first marriage mirroring Euramerican values, to her articulation of her place in the world as a mixed-blood during a period of cultural crisis, enabled her to become a strong leader for her tribe when President Franklin D. Roosevelt came into office, and the Bureau of Indian Affairs was directed to turn its energies away from assimilation to self-determination for Indian peoples.

Mourning Dove and McWhorter had achieved the close friendship of equals when they entered into their third and final period of intense collaboration, as indicated in their letters from 1929 to 1935. This time they were joined by Heister Dean Guie, a young newspaperman in his twenties who wanted to expand into freelance writing and editorial work. In 1929 McWhorter was sixty-nine years old and Mourning Dove was in her forties. They had just begun to discuss and edit McWhorter's 1921–1922 work on Mourning Dove's collection of Salish creation stories, "The Okanogan Sweat House," when McWhorter's wife died in August. McWhorter lost all heart for any of his projects, and Mourning Dove diligently applied herself to his increasingly complex linguistic and cultural questions about the tales, partly to call him back to himself. Guie now had more energy to bring to the project than either of them, and they gratefully let him take the reins. Guie viewed Indians as culturally inferior and presumed that the traditional stories had only ethnographic interest and childlike appeal. He decided to reformulate the legends to meet the standards for the juvenile literature of the day, which meant burying the more salacious Coyote stories, modifying many of the other tales, and speeding up the action by avoiding repetition, and using simpler words. Mourning Dove agreed to the modifications and changes because she had become more conscious of white behavioral norms and because, in the last years of her life, she became involved first with the Seventh Day Adventists and then the Jehovah's Witnesses.

Mourning Dove's involvement with Christian sects is representative of the Native American tendency toward inclusiveness with regard to spirituality. While growing stronger in her Indian identity, she also explored the charismatic religions coming into her community. It was a time of paradoxes, and Native peoples had to survive in a ruptured world. Mourning Dove's growing consciousness of those paradoxes, as well as her realization that younger Indians did not know what life had been like for her generation, led her to work on three final manuscripts: a novel, "Son of the Squaw," and two nonfiction collections, "Tepee Life" and "Educating the Indian." She also wanted those of the dominant culture to understand the vortex of disruptions her people had struggled to survive; she wanted them to see the settlement period through Indian eyes. She worked on these last manuscripts even while involved with Guie and McWhorter in transforming "The Okanogan Sweat House" into *Coyote Stories* from 1929 to 1931, as well as in following years. That writing commitment was maintained in the face of poor health, difficult physical work, tight finances, family deaths, and an eroding marriage. Her husband's alcoholism had grown so severe by the early 1930s that he would waste a month's pay on drinking or gamble away essential resources such as a car, and consequently the Gallers were always in debt. They patched together their marriage, crisis after crisis, and she was still willing to move with him in 1934 to a tent existence while he worked on the Grand Coulee Dam project, but trust was gone. At times, they even had physical fights.

Mourning Dove was disappointed with "Son of the Squaw," and though she wrote of recasting it in 1930, no surviving draft has ever been found. "Tepee Life" and "Educating the Indian" were never finished. On 30 July 1936, according to medical records, Christine Galler was admitted into the hospital at Medical Lake, Washington, in extreme mental distress, with abrasion marks and bruises on her chest, shins, and buttocks. Ten days later, on 8 August, the family was told that Mourning Dove had died of a brain hemorrhage. The death certificate, however, states that Christine Galler died of "exhaustion from manic depressive psychosis," a damning diminishment of her life. A pauper's cinder block engraved "Mrs. F. Galler" marked her grave site in Omak, Washington, until 1991 when, at the request of Charlie Quintasket, her half brother, Mourning Dove scholar Jay Miller paid for a more appropriate gravestone.

In all of Mourning Dove's published materials–a novel, transcriptions of Salish traditional tales, and the memoirs of her times–readers confront the dilemmas created by extensive collaboration and editing. These dilemmas result because Mourning Dove wrote in the Indian dialect of her community, which editors have always felt the need to correct, and because she was an Indian woman and the white men who served as editors assumed the patronizing authority patriarchy assures them. But these points alone do not explain the complex interactions of the people involved, their motives, their presumptions about cultures, or what it is to try to communicate cultural difference. The following discussion of her literary works examine not only the issues significant to her, but where her editors stood in relation to her work.

The fundamental problem for readers of *Cogewea* is how to read a novel that is a collaborative work in some sections, a highly edited piece in others, and the product of the editor/author in other segments. As already discussed, Mourning Dove was McWhorter's guest in Yakima while they worked together on the revision and completion of the original 1912 manuscript in the winter of 1915–1916. After Mourning Dove left, McWhorter continued to work on the notes, the dedication, and the addition of poetry headings to chapters. He shared all these with Mourning Dove, but the process was no longer collaborative, per se. The problem came in 1922 when McWhorter decided to add several sections of social/political commentary to *Cogewea* and elevate the language of its heroine, without sending the revisions to Mourning Dove for her review. Clearly, he knew that she would not approve of his changes, but he believed that the inclusion of polemic material would add substance to the novel, and thus make it more attractive to publishers. In reality, his additions, substitutions, and dialogue changes created serious disjunctures in the text. The only way to read *Cogewea* successfully is to listen for both voices.

Mourning Dove's story is semi-autobiographical. She creates a heroine struggling with a mixed-blood identity. Cogewea has been given a white education, but she also retains the knowledge of her own Indian traditions and language. She experiences herself at times in the no-man's land of interpreter or mediator. She does move easily between cultures but cannot find a home in either world. She values actions based on community needs (the Indian way) and actions guided by individual wants (the white way). She believes, and does not believe, in Native rituals. The paradigm of her situation is illustrated through the distinct choices of the three sisters: Mary, the traditionalist, who lives with their grandmother Stemteema; Julia, who has married the white rancher and has moved well along the way to assimilation; and Cogewea, the sister in-between. Mourning Dove also does not shy away from exploring the poignant aspect of being a mixed-blood, the sexual exploitation of indigenous peoples concomitant with conquest and colonization. Stemteema brings that ultimate cost into clearest focus. In the telling of the Green-Blanket Feet story, she suggests that the Great Spirit is displeased by racial intermarriage. In "The Second Coming of the Shoyahpee" she expresses her shock at having mixed-blood grandchildren, and her distrust of white men is clear: "His words are poison! his touch is death." Yet, if she wishes the knowledge of her people to pass on, she must speak about the disastrous coming of the whites with grandchildren who may only be offended by the telling since their mixed-blood is a clear indication of the loss to the physical and cultural integrity of the tribe.

Two other aspects of this Western romance are important to note. Mourning Dove's narrative describes a place and time she knew well, the Flathead Reservation of Montana in the early 1900s. Although set in Polson, a town of about five hundred settlers who wanted to fence and farm the open range, the novel is also informed by powwows, give-aways, sweat lodges, and allotment divisions. The inclusion of Salish oral traditions also forges that Western romance into the first bicultural Indian/White novel. Family tales, tribal accounts, and creation stories imbue the novel with their own moral power. The tribal stories of Green-Blanket Feet, the chief's grief over the coming of Lewis and Clark, the medicine man's vision of a catastrophic future for his people, the references to Thunderbird, or Frog Woman, reinforce Indian values. They enable Cogewea to come to an understanding of her experiences in the context of an unfolding Indian history.

McWhorter was an enthusiastic editor from his first reading of Mourning Dove's original manuscript. He immediately recognized the significance of using a novel to portray "the social status of the Indian," and was delighted by the inclusion of oral narratives. Yet, from the start McWhorter's premises differed from Mourning Dove's in two critical ways. First, McWhorter assumed, as did the majority of Euramericans, that Indian cultures would die out by the end of the twentieth century. McWhorter's poetic headings for each chapter were meant to evoke sympathy and understanding for the vanishing Indian. He did not agree, however, with the predominant assumption that such a massive genocide was a byproduct of manifest destiny. Rather, McWhorter understood that the genocide was a product of callousness and greed sanctified by notions of racial and religious superiority. Second, McWhorter distrusted his readers. He created monologue rather than dialogue in order to instruct or to reprimand. In sharp contrast, Mourning Dove trusted her readers. She unquestioningly functioned out of the belief that the storyteller's craft is to stimulate the imaginative comprehension of the listener/reader, and that such a process creates a dialogue from which meaning emerges.

There is no question that *Cogewea* is a splintered text, but the splintering is a revelation in itself, if understood. Mourning Dove's presentation of Indian spiritual and cultural values, as well as the crisis of being a halfbreed on the settlement frontier, brought new and substantive subject matter to what was already cliched, formulaic Western romance. Her adaptation of the novel to incorporate indigenous oral forms makes it a forerunner of contemporary Native American writing. On the other hand, McWhorter's impassioned defense of Native peoples gives us one of the few firsthand accounts by a white man of the degree of white corruption and Indian degradation that Euramerican settlement brought to Indian country.

The editorial issues surrounding Mourning Dove's translation of Salish oral legends is more complex because four versions are still extant. The first, and most important, is Mourning Dove's own 1921–1922 typed transcriptions, including her own handwritten corrections and some of McWhorter's, which are preserved in the Manuscripts, Archives and Special Collections Divisions of the Washington State University Libraries, Pullman, Washington. These give the richest sense of the oral context in which Mourning Dove heard the Salish tales recounted. The 1933 published version, *Coyote Stories,* which was reprinted in 1934 and 1990, is, by contrast, the most heavily edited version of the tales. Guie selected twenty-four of the original thirty-seven stories, adapted them to the juvenile literature standards of the 1930s, and added animal drawings, which draw the stories closer to something like *Aesop's Fables,* and Christian maxims for children to some of the endings. The continuing appeal of this version suggests, in part, the dominant culture's pleasure in reading what appears to be different from them, but is not really because the editing has so distorted the original material.

A more careful presentation of Mourning Dove's original transcription is the 1976 *Tales of the Okanogans,* edited by Donald M. Hines, which includes all thirty-seven of the original stories. He does make changes in the wording and format that make the textual presentation more readable. What is eroded is the sense of dramatic presentation, the liveliness of which Mourning Dove wanted to convey. The last collection is of scholarly and historical interest. The 1991 *Mourning Dove's Stories,* edited by Clifford E. Trafzer and Richard D. Scheuerman, combine eleven tales from Guie's extensive revisions to the risqué subject matter in "Okanogan Sweat House" with five stories Mourning Dove transcribed late in life. The latter include more explanatory history and Christian references than Mourning Dove's earlier work because she is a practicing Christian by this time. A study of all four versions in relation

to one another indicates the staggering effect editors can have on a writer's work, and in this case, how gender and race impact notions of personal authority and the power to rescript "primitive" literature.

The narratives themselves are closest to what might be called genesis stories, tales of creation and parables, which speak to a previous time, before humans had come, when monsters inhabited the earth and animals could talk. Later tales speak to a time when an animal being could take on a human shape, or vice-versa. In the traditionalists' spiritual view, human beings do not take precedence over other beings, and the Euramerican distinction between living and dead things, plants and stones, is not made. Moreover, in no known Indian language is there a word for "sin." People are foolish and arrogant, but not inherently evil. The character who best illustrates foolishness and the capacity to do great good is the trickster. For the Salish, that is Coyote.

Coyote is certainly a hero who provokes ambivalence. He is irresponsible, subject to swift mood swings, self-important, self-indulgent, lazy, and vain. When Coyote thoughtlessly violates taboos like eating his own children, or disguising himself to satisfy his lust for his daughter, he becomes a ridiculous figure. Not only the characters within the stories, but the hearers of the tales, know that such behaviors are demeaning and destructive. Nonetheless, there is an energy in doing and creating that makes Coyote fearless, tenacious, and innovative. When these qualities are combined with a sense of heroism and adventure, even a perverse sense of slapstick humor, Coyote can change the world. He can humble the monstrous, within and without. But the stories are more than trickster tales. They explain physical phenomena, the temperament of animals, the relationships between animal groups, as well as the behaviors appropriate or inappropriate to community survival. Such stories teach children to observe the physical world around them closely and reinforce right relations among people. To tell and retell the tales also reinforces those same values among the adult tellers and listeners.

It should be noted that while Guie altered Mourning Dove's transcriptions to an alarming extent, he had read the American readership well. *Coyote Stories,* published in 1933 at the heart of the Great Depression, was so successful it was in a second printing by 1934, and its publication drew attention to something very dear to Mourning Dove's heart. Even in a truncated form, the collection not only introduced the general reading public to stories new to them, it made them pause to consider the devastating effects of the assimilation going on around them. The reviewer for the *Daily Oklahoman* in Oklahoma City realized the importance of *Coyote Stories* when he stated that no such collection of tales existed for a number of the tribes in his own state. He then cautioned that to neglect collecting such stories meant "the loss of a spiritual heritage which [could] never be replaced."

It would not be until the 1970s, four decades after the initial publication of *Coyote Stories* and Mourning Dove's death, that the unfinished manuscripts, "Tepee Life" and "Educating the Indian," which Mourning Dove had asked her husband to edit in the 1930s were uncovered. Erna Gunther, an anthropologist who had studied with Franz Boas, and later, Jay Miller, revised and edited the materials. *Mourning Dove: A Salishan Autobiography* was published in 1990. But caution is necessary in reading the text. Readers must understand that the organization of the subject matter is Gunther's and Miller's, not Mourning Dove's, and that Miller chose to correct Mourning Dove's Indian English, thus obscuring her tone, humor, and dramatic emphasis. He also chose to extensively annotate her work in a manner that undermines her purpose and her authority as the writer of her texts.

Miller uses three sources against which to test Mourning Dove's accounts of tribal experience and her own life: the ethnographic record, the Euramerican historical record, and contemporary informants, primarily male. Contrast, for instance, the Indian story of generosity to the first white explorers to come to Kettle Falls with Miller's use of David Thompson's journals to refute the tribal recollection. Also, Miller uses Mourning Dove's half brother, Charlie Quintasket, born in 1909, to ridicule Mourning Dove's memory of her mother struggling to protect her children from near-starvation in the severe winter of 1892–1893. Such editing is at the heart of the gender and race issues informing a revision of literary and ethnohistorical scholarship. Given such problems, *Mourning Dove: A Salishan Autobiography* must be read contrapuntally. Readers should be alert to both the editor's extensive impact on the primary texts and Mourning Dove's rich observations on late nineteenth-century assimilation pressures.

It is clear from these manuscripts that the world Mourning Dove was born into already accommodated change. Tepee covers were no longer woven tule mats or worked buffalo hides, but sewn muslin or canvas. Fish hooks were made of iron, not bone and sinew, and missionaries strove to direct the spiritual lives and daily actions of the people. Mourning Dove's parents had been married in a chapel and she would be sent off to mission school. But it was also still a world where one could adopt a grandmother to bring one up in traditional ways; Mourning Dove's adopted grandmother first heard of white people when Mourning Dove was twelve years old. Mourning Dove was born into the last

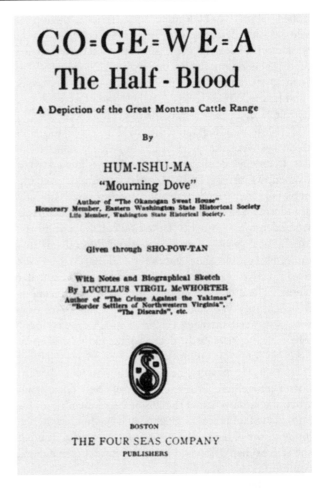

Title page for Mourning Dove's semi-autobiographical novel, set on the Flathead Reservation in Montana in the early 1900s

generation of young girls who would be guided toward traditional female powers. Her manuscripts are filled with memories about the training to become a woman shaman, the potency of love charms, even the physical training to make women strong for childbearing. Ritual taboos around menstruation, hunting and fishing, and childbearing are all discussed. So are marriage, polygamy, abandonment, adultery, divorce, remarriage, and widowhood from a Salish woman's perspective. She even chose to describe some of the more sacred rituals that unified and healed her community.

But there was a harder story to tell. That story would involve dissolution and conflict, synthesis and accommodation. Confined to reservations, Indians found that not even those treaty boundaries would be respected by whites. Before 1901, Mourning Dove would witness a mineral-rights run and a homesteading run on the Colville Reservation. Within a few decades of those events, commercial fishing projects, pollution, and ultimately the building of dams, the last with much

Indian labor, would lead to the serious depletion of salmon runs. Hunting with high-powered rifles would wipe out the plentiful game animals. When the Indians of her generation finally understood the necessity to farm, they realized that their immediate predecessors "had let the Whites have the richest and most fertile . . . bottomland, and it was too late to get it back."

More rending than the swift loss of land and resources were the survival issues splitting apart families. In an episode that reveals the diminishing status of women, Mourning Dove records the various preparations she experienced as her mother and adopted grandmother guided her toward receiving medicine-woman powers. But her father ridiculed such efforts: "If she were a boy, her future would depend on such undertakings, but she is a girl and will marry soon. She does not need a power to cook and tan hides. Let her alone." The mother's response to the father's objections is insightful: "Women are known to make good doctors. We need them every bit as much as warriors." Their conflict reveals the degree of the father's assimilation. Not only did he no longer see women as having special healing powers, he mocked the notion of Spirit power altogether. That breach is reflected once again when the father wanted to register every member of his immediate family for allotments, and the mother, agreeing with the elders, did not want to participate in what she saw as disruption and impoverishment of the tribal community.

At the end of that same "Spiritual Training" chapter, Mourning Dove recounts finally receiving an animal-power vision: a menacing dog approached her, growing larger with "a swirl of fire around him. He began to sing." But Mourning Dove grew afraid; she prayed to the Christian God, and the dog disappeared. In later years she came to believe that, in her panic, she had lost the gift of healing. As "Tepee Life" and "Educating the Indian" reveal, Mourning Dove grew up at a time when the powers of her people were still available to her. But her faith was gone. Her final manuscripts are filled with haunted reminiscences of what she experienced, but understood too late, and could not consciously recover.

Were it not for the Women's Movement of the 1970s and the explosion of a stunning series of major American Indian texts beginning with N. Scott Momaday's *House Made of Dawn* (1968), Mourning Dove's life and works may have been forgotten. Instead, the social activism of the 1960s led to a substantive challenge of the American literature canon as it was then conceived, and precursors of contemporary women writers were sought to recover an historical and literary past. Issues of coming to voice as a Native American woman writer at the turn of the last century, of understanding the set-

tlement of the West from an Indian perspective, and of learning how to read collaborative texts, have drawn considerable attention to Mourning Dove's works. At last, she is gaining the readership she so richly deserves.

Interviews:

"Colville Indian Girl Blazes Trail to New Conception of Redmen in Her Novel, 'Cogewea,' Soon to Be Published," *Spokane Review* (19 April 1916);

"Indians Do Not Fish for Sport, Says Learned Leader," *Wenatchee Daily World* (11 April 1930), p. 19.

References:

Paula Gunn Allen, *The Sacred Hoop: Recovering the Feminine in American Indian Traditions* (Boston: Beacon, 1986), pp. 81–84, 151;

Elizabeth Ammons and Annette White-Parks, *Tricksterism in Turn-of-the-Century American Literature* (New York & Oxford: Oxford University Press, 1991), pp. 121–122, 136–138, 197–199;

Susan Bernardin, "Mixed Messages: Authority and Authorship in Mourning Dove's *Cogewea, the Half-Blood: A Depiction of the Great Montana Cattle Range*," *American Literature*, 67 (September 1995): 487–509;

Peter Biedler, "Literary Criticism in *Cogewea:* Mourning Dove's Protagonist Reads *The Brand*," *American Indian Culture and Research Journal*, 19, no. 2 (1995): 45–65;

Alanna Kathleen Brown, "The Choice to Write: Mourning Dove's Search for Survival," in *Old West-New West: Centennial Essays,* edited by Barbara H. Meldrum (Moscow: University of Idaho Press, 1993), pp. 261–271;

Brown, "The Evolution of Mourning Dove's *Coyote Stories*," *Studies in American Indian Literatures*, 4 (Summer/Fall 1992): 161–180;

Brown, "Looking through the Glass Darkly: The Editorialized Mourning Dove," in *New Voices in Native American Literary Criticism,* edited by Arnold Krupat (Washington & London: Smithsonian Institution Press, 1993), pp. 274–290;

Brown, "Mourning Dove, an Indian Novelist," *Plainswoman*, 11, no. 5 (January 1988): 3–4;

Brown, "Mourning Dove, Trickster Energy, and Assimilation Period Native American Texts," in *Tricksterism in Turn-of-the-Century American Literature: A Multicultural Perspective,* edited by Ammons and White-Parks (Hanover & London: University Press of New England, 1994), pp. 126–136;

Brown, "Mourning Dove's Canadian Recovery Years, 1917–1919," *Canadian Literature,* 124 (Spring–Summer 1990): 113–122;

Brown, "Mourning Dove's Voice in *Cogewea*," *Wicazo Sa Review,* 4 (Fall 1988): 2–15;

Brown, "Profile: Mourning Dove (Humishuma) 1888–1936," *Legacy: A Journal of Nineteenth-Century American Women Writers,* 6 (Spring 1989): 51–58;

Brown, "Pulling Silko's Threads through Time: An Exploration of Storytelling," *American Indian Quarterly,* 19 (Spring 1995): 1–9;

Mary Dearborn, *Pocahontas's Daughters: Gender and Ethnicity in American Culture* (New York and Oxford: Oxford University Press, 1986), pp. 12–30;

Alice Poindexter Fisher, "The Transformation of Tradition: A Study of Zitkala Sa and Mourning Dove, Two Transitional American Indian Writers," in her *Critical Essays on Native American Literature* (Boston: G. K. Hall, 1985), pp. 202–211;

Fisher, *The Transformation of Tradition: A Study of Zitkala-Sa (Bonnin) and Mourning Dove, Two Transitional Indian Writers,* dissertation, City University of New York, 1979;

Linda Karell, "'The Story I Am Telling You Is True': Collaboration and Literary Authority in Mourning Dove's *Cogewea,*" *American Indian Quarterly,* 19 (Fall 1995): 451–465;

Charles R. Larson, *American Indian Fiction* (Albuquerque: University of New Mexico Press, 1978), pp. 173–180;

Jay Miller, "Mourning Dove: The Author as Cultural Mediator," *On Being and Becoming Indian: Biographical Studies of North American Frontiers* (Chicago: Dorsey, 1989), pp. 160–182;

Louis Owens, "Origin Mists: John Rollin Ridge's Masquerade and Mourning Dove's Mixedbloods," *Other Destinies: Understanding the American Indian Novel* (Norman & London: University of Oklahoma Press, 1992), pp. 32–48;

Martha Viehmann, "*Cogewea, The Half-Blood,* A Narrative of Mixed Descent," in *Early Native American Writing: New Critical Essays,* edited by Helen Jaskoski (New York & Oxford: Oxford University Press, 1996), pp. 204–222.

Papers:

The "Okanogan Sweat House" manuscripts and the photographs of Mourning Dove taken by McWhorter (the source of all current photographs of her) are in the Lucullus Virgil McWhorter Collection, Holland Library, Manuscripts, Archives and Special Collections Division, Washington State University, Pullman, Washington. Some of the manuscript material for "Tepee Life" and "Educating the Indian" are in the Erna Gunther Collection, Manuscripts, Archives and Special Collections Division, University of Washington, Seattle. Clifford Trafzer, Richard Scheuerman, and Jay Miller have personal copies of the final two manuscripts found by Gerry Guie. Permission to review the sealed medical records relating to Mourning Dove's death at Medical Lake, Washington, must be granted through the Superior Court of the State of Washington, Spokane County, Mental Health Department.

Elizabeth Stuart Phelps

(31 August 1844 – 28 January 1911)

Mary Bortnyk Rigsby
Mary Washington College

See also the Phelps entry in *DLB 74: American Short-Story Writers Before 1880*.

BOOKS: *Ellen's Idol* (Boston: Massachusetts Sabbath Day School Society, 1864; London: Ward, Lock & Tyler, 1872);

Up Hill; or, Life in the Factory (Boston: Henry Hoyt, 1865);

Mercy Gliddon's Work (Boston: Henry Hoyt, 1865; London: Ward, Lock & Tyler, 1873);

Tiny (Boston: Massachusetts Sabbath Day School Society, 1866; London: Ward, Lock & Tyler, 1874);

Gypsy Breynton (Boston: Graves & Young, 1866; London: Ward, Lock & Tyler, 1872);

Gypsy's Cousin Joy (Boston: Graves & Young, 1866; London: Strahan, 1873);

Gypsy's Sowing and Reaping (Boston: Graves & Young, 1866; London: Strahan, 1873);

Tiny's Sunday Nights (Boston: Massachusetts Sabbath Day School Society, 1866; London: Ward, Lock & Tyler, 1874);

Gypsy's Year at the Golden Crescent (Boston: Graves & Young, 1867; London: Strahan, 1873);

I Don't Know How (Boston: Massachusetts Sabbath Day School Society, 1868; London: Ward, Lock & Tyler, 1873);

The Gates Ajar (Boston: Fields, Osgood, 1869 [i.e., 1868]; London: Sampson Low, Son & Marston, 1869);

Men, Women, and Ghosts (Boston: Fields, Osgood, 1869; London: Sampson Low, Son & Marston, 1869);

The Trotty Book (Boston: Fields, Osgood, 1870; London: Ward, Lock & Tyler, 1872);

Hedged In (Boston: Fields, Osgood, 1870; London: Sampson Low, Son & Marston, 1870);

The Silent Partner (Boston: Osgood, 1871; London: Sampson Low, 1871);

What to Wear? (Boston: Osgood, 1873; London: Sampson Low, 1873);

Elizabeth Stuart Phelps

Trotty's Wedding Tour, and Story-book (London: Sampson Low, Marston, Low & Searle, 1873; Boston: Osgood, 1874 [i.e., 1873]);

Poetic Studies (Boston: Osgood, 1875);

The Story of Avis (Boston: Osgood, 1877; London: Routledge, 1877);

My Cousin and I (London: Sunday School Union, 1879);

Old Maids' Paradise (London: Clarke, 1879); republished as *An Old Maid's Paradise* (Boston: Houghton, Mifflin, 1885; London: Chatto & Windus, 1885);

Sealed Orders (Boston: Houghton, Osgood, 1879);

Friends: A Duet (Boston: Houghton, Mifflin, 1881; London: Sampson Low, 1881);

Doctor Zay (Boston & New York: Houghton, Mifflin, 1882);

Beyond the Gates (London: Chatto & Windus, 1883; Boston & New York: Houghton, Mifflin, 1883);

Songs of the Silent World and Other Poems (Boston & New York: Houghton, Mifflin, 1885 [i.e., 1884]);

Burglars in Paradise (Boston & New York: Houghton, Mifflin, 1886; London: Chatto & Windus, 1886);

The Madonna of the Tubs (Boston & New York: Houghton, Mifflin, 1886; London: Sampson Low, 1887);

The Gates Between (London: Ward, Lock, 1887; Boston & New York: Houghton, Mifflin, 1887);

Jack, the Fisherman (Boston & New York: Houghton, Mifflin, 1887; London: Chatto & Windus, 1887);

The Struggle for Immortality (Boston & New York: Houghton, Mifflin, 1889; London: Sampson Low, 1889);

The Master of the Magicians, by Phelps and Herbert Dickinson Ward (Boston & New York: Houghton, Mifflin, 1890; London: Heinemann, 1890);

Come Forth, by Phelps and Ward (London: Heinemann, 1890; Boston & New York: Houghton, Mifflin, 1891);

Fourteen to One (Boston & New York: Houghton, Mifflin, 1891; London: Cassell, 1891);

Austin Phelps: A Memoir (New York: Scribners, 1891; London: Nisbet, 1891);

A Lost Hero, by Phelps and Ward (Boston: Roberts, 1891);

Donald Marcy (Boston & New York: Houghton, Mifflin, 1893; London: Heinemann, 1893);

A Singular Life (Boston & New York: Houghton, Mifflin, 1895; London: Clarke, 1895);

Chapters from a Life (Boston & New York: Houghton, Mifflin, 1896; London: Clarke, 1897);

The Story of Jesus Christ: An Interpretation (Boston & New York: Houghton, Mifflin, 1897; London: Sampson Low, 1897);

Loveliness; A Story (Boston & New York: Houghton, Mifflin, 1899; London: Clarke, 1899);

The Successors of Mary the First (Boston & New York: Houghton, Mifflin, 1901);

Within the Gates (Boston & New York: Houghton, Mifflin, 1901);

Avery (Boston & New York: Houghton, Mifflin, 1902; London: Gay & Bird, 1903);

Confessions of a Wife, as Mary Adams (New York: Century, 1902; London: Richards, 1902);

Trixy (Boston & New York: Houghton, Mifflin, 1904; London: Hodder & Stoughton, 1905);

The Man in the Case (Boston & New York: Houghton, Mifflin, 1906; London: Constable, 1906);

Walled In: A Novel (New York & London: Harper, 1907);

Though Life Us Do Part (Boston & New York: Houghton Mifflin, 1908);

The Whole Family: A Novel By Twelve Authors, by Phelps and others (New York & London: Harper, 1908);

Jonathan and David (New York & London: Harper, 1909);

The Oath of Allegiance and Other Stories (Boston & New York: Houghton Mifflin, 1909; London: Constable, 1909);

The Empty House and Other Stories (Boston & New York: Houghton Mifflin, 1910); republished as *A Deserted House and Other Stories* (London: Constable, 1911);

Comrades (New York & London: Harper, 1911).

Editions: *The Gates Ajar,* introduction by Helen Sootin Smith (Cambridge, Mass.: Harvard University Press, 1964);

The Story of Avis, introduction by Carol Farley Kessler (New Brunswick, N.J.: Rutgers University Press, 1985).

OTHER: Chapter 7 of *Sex and Education: A Reply to Dr. E. H. Clarke's "Sex in Education,"* edited by Julia Ward Howe (Boston: Roberts, 1874), pp. 126–138.

SELECTED PERIODICAL PUBLICATIONS–UNCOLLECTED: "A Sacrifice Consumed," *Harper's New Monthly,* 28 (January 1864): 235–240;

"Margaret Bronson," *Harper's New Monthly,* 31 (September 1865): 498–504;

"What Shall They Do?" *Harper's New Monthly,* 35 (September 1867): 519–523;

"Why Shall They Do It?" *Harper's New Monthly,* 36 (January 1868): 218–223;

"The Gist of the Matter," *Independent,* 23 (13 July 1871): 1;

"Where It Goes," *Independent,* 23 (20 July 1871): 1;

"Unhappy Girls," *Independent,* 23 (27 July 1871): 1;

"Too Much Conscience," *Independent,* 23 (3 August 1871): 3;

"Song of the Shirt," *Independent,* 23 (10 August 1871): 1;

"What Are They Doing," *Independent,* 23 (17 August 1871): 1;

"Women and Money," *Independent,* 23 (24 August 1871): 1;

"Men and Muscle," *Independent,* 23 (31 August 1871): 1;

"The United Head," *Independent,* 23 (14 September 1871): 1;

"The New Earth," *Independent,* 23 (28 September 1871): 1;

"The Higher Claim," *Independent,* 23 (5 October 1871): 1;

"The True Woman," *Independent,* 23 (19 October 1871): 1;

"A Talk to Girls," *Independent,* 24 (4 January 1872): 1;

"A Few Words to the Girls," *Woman's Journal,* 3 (24 February 1872): 62;

"The Female Education of Women," *Independent,* 25 (13 November 1873): 1409–1410;

"A Dream within a Dream," *Independent,* 26 (19 February 1874): 1;

"The Experiment Tried," *Independent,* 26 (5 March 1874): 1–2;

"An Hour with Gwendolyn," *Sunday Afternoon,* 3 (March 1879): 230–234;

"Zerviah Hope," *Scribner's Magazine,* 21 (November 1880): 78–88;

"Last Words from George Eliot," *Harper's New Monthly,* 64 (March 1882): 568–571;

"A Brave Girl," *Wide Awake* (December 1883 – August 1884);

"Supporting Herself," *St. Nicholas,* 11 (May 1884): 517–519;

"The Empty Column," *Independent,* 36 (4 September 1884): 1121–1122;

"George Eliot," *Harper's Weekly,* 29 (14 February 1885): 102–103;

"George Eliot's Short Stories," *Independent,* 37 (30 April 1885): 545–546;

"The Décolleté in Modern Life," *Forum,* 9 (August 1890): 670–684;

"The Secretary's Murderer," by Phelps and Herbert Dickinson Ward, *Harper's Bazar,* 24 (31 January 1891): 83;

"Heaven: The Gates Ajar—25 Years After," *North American Review,* 156 (May 1893): 567–576;

"The Supply at St. Agatha's," *Century,* 25 (April 1894): 868–876;

"The World Invisible," parts 1–3, *Harper's Bazar,* 52 (April 1908): 354–356; (May 1908): 419–422; (July 1908): 619–623;

"Stories That Stay," *Century,* 58 (November 1910): 118–123.

The central metaphor for understanding the life and work of Elizabeth Stuart Phelps may be that she was born twice. The first time was in Boston, Massachusetts, on 31 August 1844. She was baptized Mary Gray and called Lily by her mother, Elizabeth Wooster Stuart Phelps, a writer of popular didactic tales, and her father, Austin Phelps, a professor of sacred rhetoric and homiletics and author of several influential religious books. The second "birth" occurred after the death of her mother in Andover, Massachusetts, eight years later, when Mary Gray took her mother's name as her own. Some accounts say this name change happened immediately after her mother's death. Others suggest that the change occurred at age twelve, when Mary Gray Phelps joined the church. Phelps wrote nothing to explain her motivation for this name change. With only a few exceptions in her forty-seven years as a writer, Phelps's work appeared under the name Elizabeth Stuart Phelps. Even after her marriage to Herbert Dickinson Ward in 1888, Phelps continued to use her adopted name, using her married name solely in private correspondence. Early bibliographers have tended to list her works under the name *Ward,* but the facts of her publishing history indicate her preference not to follow this convention of matrimony.

In many ways Phelps's successful career as a writer of more than fifty books and hundreds of magazine stories, essays, and poems was motivated by the early death of her talented mother. Phelps's self-naming was both an act of self-construction and an act of self-denial, embodying the conflicting desires to honor her inheritance while resisting its limitations, as she explored the relationships between mother and child, husband and wife, private desires and public expectations, death and life, and silence and expression. On her death at age sixty-six she left behind a record of the unavoidable internal struggles of a nineteenth-century intellectual woman.

Much of what is known about Phelps's life comes from her autobiography, *Chapters from a Life* (1896). Phelps was careful to protect the privacy of friends who were still living, however, so she left her reader with a highly selective memoir. Furthermore, the voice of her autobiography is often that of the self-deprecating nineteenth-century woman. Despite these limitations, the book is central to any study of Phelps's life because there is so little other primary material available. There are two twentieth-century biographies, by Mary Angela Bennett (1939) and Lori Duin Kelly (1983), as well as Carol Farley Kessler's *Elizabeth Stuart Phelps* (1982) in the Twayne American Authors Series.

By her own account Phelps felt pressed by the influence of family talent to seek a public forum in which to speak not only for herself but also for her family. Phelps wrote that "whatever measure of what is called success has fallen to my lot, I can ask no credit. I find myself in the chastened position of one whose literary abilities all belong to one's ancestors." First among these ancestors was her mother, about whom Phelps specifically said, "it was impossible to be her daughter and not to write." Then, thinking of her father as well, she quickly added: "Rather, I should say, impossible to be *their* daughter and not to have something to say, and a pen to say it." In her mind, the "dead men and women whose blood bounds in our being" exert a great deal of influence on "our destinies."

Austin Phelps had been a student of Andover Theological Seminary when he met Elizabeth Stuart. In 1842 he accepted the pastorate of the Pine Street Church in Boston, and that same year he married Stuart. Mary Gray Phelps was born in Boston two years later. Austin Phelps was not entirely comfortable with his pastorate in Boston, so when he was offered a position on the Andover Theological Seminary faculty in 1848, he moved his wife and daughter back to Andover. Because Phelps was not quite four at the time, she had few memories of their life in Boston. Before her mother's death in 1852, Phelps's parents had two more children, both sons: Moses Stuart, born in 1849, and Amos Lawrence, born in 1852.

Phelps's grandfathers, both ministers, were important figures in her childhood and created strong impressions on her young mind. Her maternal grandfather, Moses Stuart, was professor of sacred literature at Andover and a distinguished Protestant theologian. Phelps's direct memories of her maternal grandfather were few, but she grew up hearing stories about him and was well aware of his stature as scholar and writer. Family stories about his strict household routines provided her with other insights into his accomplishments and the sacrifices made by her maternal grandmother, Abigail Clark Stuart, to support his career.

Phelps knew her paternal grandfather much more intimately. Eliakim Phelps was a revivalist preacher, giving Phelps an alternative to the regimented and intellectualized religion of her maternal grandfather. Though Phelps described her father's father as an undistinguished "orthodox minister," he was apparently more compelling to her than her other grandfather. While working as a pastor in Geneva, New York, from 1830 to 1836, Eliakim Phelps was reported to have converted two thousand people to the Christian faith and worked with the Underground Railroad helping slaves to escape north. Phelps credited him with telling "thrilling stories" of "throbbing humanity." She also remembered Eliakim Phelps for his seven-month experience with "house-possession"—which Phelps called an "authentic and fantastic family tale." Candlesticks moving in midair, hopping chairs, leaping dishes, mysteriously bent silver forks, cold turnips falling from the ceiling, ghastly images formed from underclothing known to be kept in locked drawers, and unexplainable raps on bed heads and tables were part of what became known as "the phenomena" at the Stratford, Connecticut, parsonage in 1850. Eliakim Phelps kept a journal of the unexplained events and published a popular reli-

gious tract about them, which reached a circulation of two hundred thousand copies—an extraordinary number for the day. Phelps made note of the fact that the journal was destroyed after her grandfather's death, according to family wishes, an act echoed by her destruction of the bulk of her private correspondence shortly before her death. Whether there was indeed some kind of supernatural visitation at the parsonage or just some clever prestidigitation by Austin Phelps is less significant than the effect the story had on Phelps. She claimed that her "talks with this very interesting grandfather" provided her "first vivid sensation of the possibilities of life."

Her grandmothers were important for Phelps as well. As ministers' wives, they were highly visible women in their communities, expected to fulfill idealized social and familial expectations: to be supportive and self-sacrificing, to be devoted to Christian duty, and to provide perfect love for others. Both women had the heavy responsibilities of managing their households and of putting their husband's desires and comforts above their own. Phelps's maternal grandmother, Abigail Clark Stuart, apparently internalized the prescribed role of the ideal woman and suffered ill health as a consequence. She complied with her husband's demands for a strict daily routine and consistently communicated to her children that their father was "chosen and set apart from the rest of the world to do a great and important work." An invalid, she was feared to be near death for many years before she actually died. Harriet Beecher Stowe memorialized Abigail Clark Stuart in an 1867 poem, describing her life as a "patient mother's hourly martyrdom." Phelps's paternal grandmother was also expected to fulfill this ideal. Sarah Adams Phelps was highly regarded by her husband and her son, Austin Phelps, and her success at conforming to the role was reflected in the credit the two men gave her for her husband's success. Their praise, however, did little to relieve her of the burdens that came with being the conventional minister's wife.

Her grandmothers' generation of women and their unexpressed needs and desires created the backdrop and material for much of the granddaughter's later writing. Abigail Clark Stuart and Sarah Adams Phelps are much like the title character in Phelps's novel *The Story of Avis* (1877), who "had been bred to the reticence not uncharacteristic of the New-England religion among its more cultivated, or at least, among its more studious possessors. . . . She was expected to be a Christian woman precisely as she was expected to be a cultivated lady; in a matter of course, abundant speech was a superfluous weakness."

Phelps's mother was the first woman in the family to leave an unambiguous record of her desire to do

THE GATES AJAR.

BY

ELIZABETH STUART PHELPS.

"Splendor! Immensity! Eternity! Grand words! Great things!
A little definite happiness would be more to the purpose."
MADAME DE GASPARIN.

BOSTON:
FIELDS, OSGOOD, & CO.,
SUCCESSORS TO TICKNOR AND FIELDS.
1869.

Title page for the novel in which Phelps describes heaven

more than subordinate all her energy to husband and family, providing a compelling role model for her daughter by embodying the possibility that a woman could have a life beyond the home. She resembled her father physically and intellectually and at an early age exhibited creative talents. As a child Phelps's mother entertained family domestics, their friends, and her younger sisters with her extemporaneous stories, and she had a marked interest in painting, sculpture, and music. At sixteen, with her father's approval, she wrote, under the name H. Trusta, a few brief religious articles that were published in a magazine edited by the Reverend Jacob Abbott. Phelps remarked that her earliest memories were of her mother in the nursery reading stories that her mother had composed and illustrated herself. These illustrations, Phelps wrote, were "of an original quality, and had she not been a writer she must have achieved something as an artist." It was not until age thirty, however, that Phelps's mother could be said to have had an actual career as a writer. Her first book, *The Sunny Side; or, a Country Minister's Wife* (1851), was immediately well received, selling one hundred thousand copies in its first year. She went on to publish *A Peep at "Number Five": or, A Chapter in the Life of a City Pastor* (1852) and, in the same year, *Angel over the Right Shoulder*. She also wrote the "Kitty Brown" series for the American Sunday School Union, two collections of adult magazine fiction, and the posthumously published *Little Mary; or Talks and Tales for Children* (1854).

Phelps's mother's desire for a writing career is evident in her family journal, where she confessed that *The Sunny Side* succeeded "beyond my most sanguine dreams. It appears to me that the way is now opening for me to write,–a way which I have sighed for, long." In 1852, however, she was pregnant with her third child, writing and revising *A Peep at "Number Five,"* and managing her household. Her second son was born in August; she died in November. Her daughter remarked, "Her last book and her last baby came together, and killed her. She lived one of those rich and piteous lives such as only gifted women know; torn by the civil war of the dual nature which can be given to women only."

Phelps was careful in her autobiography to assure readers that her mother was both "a woman of intellectual power" and "the most successful of mothers." She said that her mother had been able to reconcile "genius and domestic life," but she also insisted that her mother had a nature "drawn against the grain of her times and of her circumstances . . . where our feet find easy walking, hers were hedged." This tension between women's desires and the demands of domesticity became one of the defining themes in Phelps's fiction.

Phelps's early years were dominated by grief. Moses Stuart and her mother died in the same year. Two years after the death of her mother, when Phelps was ten years old, her father married her aunt, Mary Stuart, who was already suffering from tuberculosis and died two years later. When Phelps was fourteen, Austin Phelps married Mary Ann Johnson. Their marriage produced two more sons: Francis Johnson, born in 1860, and Edward Johnson, nicknamed Trotty, born in 1863.

Despite the painful loss of her mother and other family members, Phelps's childhood had identifiable advantages. Phelps saw herself as a tomboy who liked to be an outdoor girl. She climbed trees, walked the length of the seminary fence, and enjoyed playing in her father's garden. Her autobiography includes instances of her willful disregard for proper behavior and examples of acting on impulses contrary to expectations for girls and young women. One anecdote describes the "shocked expression on the face of a not very eminent minister" with whom she engaged in dinner conversation. Phelps went so far as to characterize herself as having the "cordial defiance of a born rebel."

Growing up in Andover, a conservative university town dominated by the seminary and its adherence to the old Calvinism, was a mixed blessing. There was a pervasive acceptance of the tenets of predestination, the infallibility of the Bible, the limited atonement of Christ, the natural depravity of man, and the promise of damnation for the nonelect. Yet, Andover did not stifle intellectual exploration and development—at least not for men. Women, on the other hand, were restricted by the patriarchal religious perspective that dominated the community and were not encouraged to pursue the academic life of the seminary. They were expected to focus their attentions in the home and were generally assumed to be incapable of achievement outside the domestic realm. Phelps's father shared this low opinion of women's potential. Only because his daughter suffered from poor health did he indulge her tomboy antics and allow her free range with her studies.

Phelps was educated at Abbot Academy in Andover and then Mrs. Edwards' School for Young Ladies—conducted by an Andover faculty wife—whose curriculum, except for Greek and trigonometry, was equivalent to that usually offered only to males. Because she had unusual opportunities in this respect, Phelps found Andover a rich environment for her intellectual growth: "the life of a professor's daughter in a university town is always a little different from the lives of other girls; but the difference seems to me—unless she be by nature entirely alien to it—in favor of the girl." For Phelps, growing up in a university town meant:

> As soon as we began to think, we saw a community engaged in studying thought. As soon as we began to feel, we were aware of a neighborhood that did not feel superficially; at least, in certain higher directions. When we began to ask the "questions of life," which all intelligent young people ask sooner or later, we found ourselves in a village of three institutions and their dependencies committed to the pursuit of an ideal of education for which no amount of later, or what we call broader, training ever gives us any better word than Christian.

Yet, as is suggested by this last remark, Andover's intellectual commitments were always framed by the pervading orthodox orientation of the seminary—for which the town was well known. Phelps reported having been asked often about the Andover orthodoxy:

> Curious impressions used to be afloat about us among people of easier faiths; often, I think, we were supposed to spend our youth paddling about in a lake of blue fire, or in committing the genealogies to memory, or in gasping beneath the agonies of religious revivals.

> To be quite honest, I should say that I have not retained *all* the beliefs which I was taught—who does? But I have retained the profoundest respect for the way in which I was taught them; . . . An excess of religious education may have its unfortunate aspects. But a deficiency of it has worse.

Phelps was particularly influenced by the theology of Professor Edwards E. Park, who taught Bible lessons to the girls at Mrs. Edwards' School. The girls apparently received the same exposure to Professor Park's stern Calvinism as his male students at the seminary, and Phelps credits the instruction with teaching her to appreciate the "nature and value of exact thought." She commented: "I may not always believe all I was taught, but what I was taught has helped me to what I believe. I certainly think of those theological lectures with unqualified gratitude."

In addition to her praise for Andover, Phelps gave a great deal of credit for her intellectual development to her father, in spite of what she characterized as his "feudal views of women." She wrote: "He was my climate. As soon as I began to think, I began to reverence thought and study and the hard work of a man devoted to the high ends of a scholar's life." She described him as teaching mostly without textbooks or formal lessons, but specifically identified the beginnings of her intellectual life with his reading to her from the works of British writers Thomas De Quincey—best-known for his *Confessions of an English Opium-Eater* (1822), though Phelps does not specify what her father read—and William Wordsworth.

Phelps was an enthusiastic reader on her own as well. When she was sixteen, the year her father was reading De Quincey and Wordsworth, Phelps also discovered British poet Elizabeth Barrett Browning's blank-verse novel *Aurora Leigh* (1856) and was deeply impressed. She memorized large portions and defended it vigorously when acquaintances, particularly male friends, criticized it. She gave it high praise, indeed, identifying it as the origin of her own literary aspirations. Phelps's strong attraction to *Aurora Leigh* may have come from the fact that the character Aurora, a young woman artist, could easily be read as a romanticized version of Phelps's mother. *Aurora Leigh* influenced Phelps's imagination, as is most evident in *The Story of Avis*—which also focuses on a woman who desires a serious career as an artist—but the emphasis on women's desire for life beyond the domestic realm recurs throughout Phelps's creative work.

The year of Phelps's intellectual awakening, 1860, is also the date of the Pemberton Mill tragedy. Lawrence, Massachusetts, a manufacturing town just three and a half miles from Andover, supplied Andover residents with such things as dry goods and restaurant ice cream, and though Phelps had often traveled there for shopping and amusement, she was not particularly aware of the millworkers until the evening the roof, walls, and machinery of Pemberton Mill collapsed on 750 workers—both men and women. During the rescue process a lantern was overturned and the cotton, wool, and oil in the ruins quickly caught on fire, burning eighty-eight mill girls in a conflagration that was one of the worst factory disasters in New England history. Phelps was troubled and affected by the event and eventually turned it into a subject for her writing.

The following year, 1861, was a troubling time for Phelps. Already in poor health, her father, who had become president of the Andover Seminary in 1860, became an invalid. With the outbreak of the Civil War, the quiet life in Andover was profoundly disrupted, and the life of seventeen-year-old Phelps was deeply touched by the war as well. She and Samuel Hopkins Thompson, a Phillips Academy student in the class of 1861, had become close friends in the years prior to the outbreak of war—though Phelps does not discuss the exact nature of the relationship in *Chapters from a Life*. Thompson enlisted in the spring of 1861, was fatally wounded in the Battle of Antietam, and died on 22 October 1862.

Around this time Phelps began writing in earnest and immediately encountered the obstacles that were nearly unavoidable for women writers of her generation. With the births of her two half brothers within a period of three years, the Phelps family quickly became a family of four boys and one girl. As the only girl in the family, Phelps shared in the unending housework that a young and growing family generated. Like her protagonist Avis, Phelps never enjoyed sewing or other housekeeping tasks. These duties were doubly disagreeable—in and of themselves and for their interference in her writing activities. She acknowledged her failing to be the properly compliant young woman, admitting that she "could not have been an easy girl to 'bring up.'" Her resistance to women's work is unambiguously expressed in her memory of cutting out underclothes during March school vacations: "To this day I cannot hear the thick chu-chunk! of heavy wheels on March mud without a sudden mechanical echo of that wild, young outcry: 'Must I cut out underclothes forever? Must I go on tucking the broken end of the thread into the nick in the spool? Is *this* LIFE?'" She felt affection for her brothers but disliked the noisy household of rambunctious boys and crying babies with no better

place to write than the dining room table or the little upstairs room, which "it was not expected would be warmed in winter." The examples of her mother and the fictional Aurora Leigh inspired her to write, but she did not have family support for her work. Worse yet, it was beyond her own imagination to ask for it: "I therefore made the best of my conditions, though I do remember sorely longing for quiet."

Though Phelps wrote during her school days, her early writing does not survive, nor did she submit any of it for possible publication. She later wrote that her early work served as her apprenticeship. Her first published story was "A Sacrifice Consumed," a war story about a seamstress who loses her fiancé at Antietam, published in the January 1864 issue of *Harper's New Monthly*, when Phelps was not yet twenty years old. She did not tell anyone she had submitted the story until after *Harper's* accepted it for publication. She earned twenty-five dollars and the "awed elation" of knowing her father genuinely approved of the story. This initial success encouraged her to write "with a distinct purpose, and . . . quite steadily."

Phelps's confidence in her abilities, however, was tenuous and dependent on the approval of others. Without this early confirmation from both *Harper's* and her father, she claimed, she would not have continued her efforts. She describes her self-identification as a writer as greatly determined by "the opinion of important editors . . . and the sacredness of market value in literary ware." She revealed in her autobiography that "if nobody had cared for my stories enough to print them, I should have been the last person to differ from the ruling opinion, and should have bought at Warren Draper's old Andover book-store no more cheap printer's paper on which to inscribe the girlish handwriting (with the pointed letters and the big capitals). . . . But the editor of 'Harper's' took everything I sent him; so the pointed letters and the large capitals continued to flow towards his desk." Yet, despite her professed need for the approval of others, Phelps's career is surprisingly free of any evidence that she adjusted her writing to the standards of her publishers. When a magazine returned a story because the editor claimed it was "too tragic, or too something," she sent it elsewhere, and it was published "forthwith." Only one of her manuscripts was ever significantly rewritten as a consequence of a publisher's criticism—a Sunday-school book returned with a request for substantial revisions. Her humiliation at receiving such a rejection prompted her to rewrite the book immediately, working through the night, beginning at tea time and continuing until three o'clock in the morning. At six o'clock—after three hours of sleep—she sent the revised manuscript back to the publisher and "had his letter of unconditional acceptance . . . before another tea time." The relative ease with which she was able to publish her work suggests that Phelps's literary sensibilities were in keeping with the literary values of her day. Furthermore, her early success must have encouraged her to have confidence in the literary market, and because the literary market confirmed her style and subject matter, her early success likely encouraged her to trust her instincts and rely on her experiences and concerns. In short, nothing discouraged her from silencing the "cordial defiance of the born rebel" within her.

The publication of "A Sacrifice Consumed" marked the beginning of Phelps's financial independence. Though she was careful to acknowledge that writing for a living was hardly an easy way to make money, she also emphasized "how good a thing it is" to stand on one's "own feet, and . . . own pluck." Though she had success in publishing her work without much pressure to conform to editorial strictures, she also knew that to support herself as a writer she had to do "hack work." As were her mother's before hers, Phelps's Sunday-school books were successful. Though they were written for money and on demand, she claimed to have worked harder on the series than anything else. Sunday-school books were ordered in sets. Phelps wrote two sets of four volumes each. The "Tiny" series–*Ellen's Idol* (1864), *Tiny* (1866), *Tiny's Sunday Nights* (1866), and *I Don't Know How* (1868)–focuses on five-year-old Tiny's efforts to be good and eleven-year-old Ellen's attempts to become Christian. The "Gypsie" series (1866–1867) is about Gypsy Breynton, a twelve-year-old tomboy, who goes from trying to be good to trying to be a lady. These volumes are conventional and undistinguished, but Phelps's other books for girls, when read with these early volumes, indicate her emerging interest in critiquing social expectations of how women lived their lives. These early volumes are a form of apprenticeship that eventually led to Phelps's highly acclaimed fiction.

The next significant point in Phelps's writing career occurred in 1866 with a story that earned her serious recognition from the literary community. Likely inspired by the American author Rebecca Harding Davis–for whom Phelps had a great respect–and Davis's short story "Life in the Iron Mills," which had been published in the April 1861 issue of *The Atlantic Monthly,* Phelps responded to the horrific deaths of the eighty-eight Pemberton Mill girls by fictionalizing the event in "The Tenth of January," published in *The Atlantic Monthly* in March 1868 and collected in her *Men, Women, and Ghosts* (1869). With American literary realism still in its infancy, Phelps approached the subject of the 1860 Pemberton Mill fire with the conviction of a literary realist. She purposefully set out to gather accurate information about the tragedy and spent the best part of a month investigating every detail. Because she was a woman, she had not been allowed to visit the scene at the time of the disaster, though her brother did. In preparation for writing her story, she visited the rebuilt mills, studied the machinery, and consulted with engineers, mill officials, physicians, newspaper reporters, and eyewitnesses to the catastrophe. Only after she believed she had learned all she could did she write the story. Phelps received letters of praise and encouragement from poet John Greenleaf Whittier and author-activist Thomas Wentworth Higginson.

Phelps's other success of 1868 was *The Gates Ajar*–a novel whose title comes from a hymn that includes the lines, "And when my angel guide went up, / He left the pearly gates ajar." The novel is primarily a depiction of heaven that emerges through a series of conversations between the protagonist, Mary Cabot, and her widowed aunt, Winifred Forceythe. Set at the end of the Civil War and written as Mary Cabot's diary entries, the story focuses on twenty-four-year-old Mary's grief for her brother Royal, who has died in the war. Aunt Winifred comes from Kansas with her daughter, Faith, and has greater success than the local deacon, Doctor Bland, at comforting Mary. Heaven, according to Aunt Winifred, promises all that is best on earth–beautiful cultivated gardens and splendid natural landscapes, comfortable mansions shared by loved ones, and all that one's heart would find most fulfilling. In her introduction to a 1964 edition of the novel, Helen Sootin Smith has pointed out that *The Gates Ajar* makes use of a variety of literary forms: the sermon, with its biblical quotations, hymns, and theology; literary realism in its depiction of New England village life; the sentimental novel, with its orphaned heroines, beautiful deaths, and attention to Christian values; and sacred allegory in its outlining steps in the drama of Christian redemption.

Phelps dated her beginning of *The Gates Ajar* as near the end of 1864–when she was twenty years old–and described a process of study, writing, and rewriting that lasted approximately two years. Phelps began the novel, she said, when "our country was dark with sorrowing women." The Civil War had traumatized American women as well as men; yet, existing forms of comfort "had nothing to say to an afflicted woman. . . . Creeds and commentaries and sermons were made by men." As was her practice, she did not share any early drafts of the novel with her family or friends. Though her subject was a vision of a utopian afterlife, she did not consult her father on the theology that informs the story. When Phelps finally sent the manuscript to publisher James T. Fields for consideration, she had no idea that it would become an immensely popular book. She did, however, understand that she had "set forth upon a venture totally dissimilar to the safe and respectable careers of [her] dozen Sunday-school books." The manuscript was in the hands of Fields for two years before his wife, Annie Adams Fields, urged its publication.

The Gates Ajar was a best-seller in the United States and England, appealing to an international reading public for nearly thirty years. By 1897 the book had reached a circulation of eighty-one thousand copies in the United States and more than one hundred thousand in England. It was translated into French, German, Dutch, and Italian. Phelps received little benefit from the international sales because the international copyright law was inadequately enforced. The success of the novel in the United States can be attributed to the emotional needs of a readership suffering from the pain of the Civil War, but this explanation cannot be so easily applied to the international sales. Smith suggests that the novel successfully addressed "the spiritual disquiet created by the advance of science and the erosion of traditional Christianity. . . . *The Gates Ajar,* in familiar but simple and undemanding Christian terms, reassured those who had come to doubt the immortality of the soul and who found cold comfort in their ministers' vague assertions that life after death was a reality."

In the United States, Phelps's novel was more than a literary phenomenon. It was given out as an advertisement for patent medicine. There were Gates Ajar tippets, Gates Ajar collars, and possibly Gates Ajar cigars. Popular music was composed under the title, including a Gates Ajar funeral piece. Florists apparently sold Gates Ajar flower arrangements. Yet, the novel stirred great debate within the religious community. Phelps characterized the controversy at some length in her autobiography: "Heresy was her crime, and atrocity her name. She had outraged the church. She had blasphemed its sanctities. She had taken live coals from the altar in her impious hand. The sacrilege was too serious to be dismissed with cold contempt. Opinion battled about that poor little tale, as if it had held the power to overthrow church and state and family." She eventually stopped reading the reviews. But she did read and respond to the "storm" of personal letters that she received in response to the novel. Some of these letters included sharp criticism, but most were appreciative of the author for having written what was for many readers a tremendously comforting book.

The success of the novel brought two significant benefits to Phelps. First, it convinced her father that she needed a quiet place for writing, and she was allowed to rebuild the summer house that had been her mother's study. The second benefit was that her literary career was secure. For the next forty years she had ready publishers and readers for her books, magazine stories, pamphlets, essays, and poems.

Phelps went on to write two more books on the themes introduced by *The Gates Ajar–Beyond the Gates* (1883) and *The Gates Between* (1887). All three novels emphasize the theme of women's heavenly self-fulfillment. Though they elaborately depict an afterlife that compensates for earthly disappointments and suffering, they also offer pointed social criticism by identifying existing problems that justify divine compensation. Many critics have read these novels as consolation literature but also as utopian fiction that predates most American utopian writing by twenty years. Phelps rewrote the third novel as a play, *Within the Gates,* which was published in 1901 but never produced.

From 1868 until her marriage in 1888 Phelps's writing focused on women and women's issues. In this twenty-year period, Phelps honed her understanding of American patriarchal culture, writing in support of women's political rights, educational and occupational opportunities, dress reform, health concerns, and financial independence. She also delivered a series of lectures at Boston University in 1876, titled "Representative Modern Fiction," primarily on the work of George Eliot. Phelps's social-reform activities eventually included temperance work, and in the last years of her life she supported antivivisection legislation.

Given her commitment to social reform, it is no surprise that her novels *Hedged In* (1870), *The Silent Partner* (1871), *The Story of Avis, Friends: A Duet* (1881), and *Doctor Zay* (1882) all focus on the painful realities of women's lives. These novels, probably the best work she produced during the 1870s and 1880s, explore the sexual double standards that unjustly punish "fallen" women, the occupational restrictions that keep women out of the business world, the unfair pressure that men exert on women to meet men's needs over women's self-interest, and the difficulties that women face when they commit themselves to serious professional careers.

Many critics perceive *The Story of Avis* as the most successful of these novels. It is an unrelenting investigation of the effects of marriage on a woman's creativity and potential for fulfillment. Essentially beginning where *Aurora Leigh* stopped–with marriage between the artist and a man with the best of intentions–*The Story of Avis* was the first American novel to focus exclusively on the subject of a failed marriage. Through Avis Dobell, Phelps's "favorite heroine" and the first married woman featured in Phelps's fiction, the story attempts to give voice to the silenced aspects of women's lives. In the novel the fictional Philip Ostrander persuades Avis to marry him by making ambitious promises to support Avis's artistic career and insisting that she will not need to keep house or be the typical wife. In spite of all his good intentions, he fails to be the ideal new man. Phelps presents moments in their married life when Philip proves oblivious to Avis's viewpoints and needs. The novel makes painfully clear that wives were trapped by their husbands' moral failings and character flaws. At his strongest, Philip overwhelms Avis with his attractive presence and pulls her away from her art. At his weakest, he is the equivalent of a grown child dependent on his wife's management and patience, again pulling her away from her art. The only hope in *The Story of Avis* lies in the generation represented by Avis's daughter, appropriately named Wait.

Motherhood for Avis is not the natural fulfillment of her life, nor can she rely on instincts to know just how to be a good mother. Phelps insists that much has been left unspoken and unrecognized in women's lives:

> The robin at your door on a June morning seems to be expressing himself with lavish confidence; but, to a patient listener, his song has something of the exuberant frankness which is the most impenetrable disguise in the world. The sparrow on her nest under your terrace broods meekly; but the centuries have not wrung from one such pretty prisoner a breath of longing for the freedom of the summer-day. Do her delicate, cramped muscles ache for flight? her fleet, unused wings tremble against the long roots of the overhanging grass? She turns her soft eye upon you with a fine, far sarcasm. You may find out if you can.

The pain of a woman's confinement within a limited number of life options has a further tragic consequence. To know that one is capable of success beyond the domestic arena and to be denied the opportunity to act is another theme of the novel:

> Women understand—only women altogether—what a dreary will-o-the-wisp this old, common, I had almost said common-place, experience, "When the fall sewing is done," "When the baby can walk," "When house-cleaning is over," "When the company is gone," "When we have got through with the whooping-cough," "When I am a little stronger," then I will write the poem, or learn the language, or study the great charity, or master the symphony; then I will act, dare, dream, become. Merciful is the fate that hides from any soul the prophecy of its still-born aspirations.

During this most productive period of her career Phelps also produced two humorous novels. As early as the summer of 1869, Phelps had begun spending her summers near Gloucester, Massachusetts, where she traded the Andover heat for cooling sea breezes, and in 1876 she built a cottage at Eastern Point, near Wonson's Cove. Her experiences during these May-to-November periods in the Gloucester area provided the material for *Old Maid's Paradise* (published in London in 1879 and in Boston as *An Old Maid's Paradise* in 1885) and *Burglars in Paradise* (1886). *Old Maid's Paradise* is a series of humorous sketches about single women living on their own in a seaside community much like Gloucester. *Burglars in Paradise* features these earlier characters in a spoof on detective fiction, suggesting that the real potential burglar about whom single women should worry is a man offering friendship. While her "Gates" books depict an ideal heavenly home, these novels suggest ideal woman-centered living arrangements in the material world, constituting two more contributions to American utopian fiction, as well as humorous contributions to New England regionalist writing.

Phelps was actively and successfully engaged with social reform throughout the first decades of her literary career, but the pleasure she had in her success must have been undercut by her father's public opposition to woman suffrage. In 1878 and again in 1881, Austin Phelps published two antisuffrage articles vigorously arguing that women should not be given the vote. He was not opposed to expanding educational opportunities for women, but he insisted that women and men naturally belonged in separate spheres. In his view woman suffrage was not just against the Bible but also would dangerously disturb family life and offend the dignity of motherhood. This period was also punctuated by the sudden death of her brother Stuart in 1883 and then the death of her closest personal friend, Dr. Mary Briggs Harris, in 1886. She also suffered from increasing poor health, especially insomnia.

On 20 October 1888 Phelps married Herbert Dickinson Ward, who was twenty-seven years old—seventeen years her junior. Ward was the son of a longtime acquaintance, William H. Ward, managing editor of *The Independent,* to which Phelps often contributed. After graduating from Phillips Academy in 1880 and graduating from Amherst in 1884, Herbert Ward studied theology at Union Theological Seminary in 1885–1887 and spent one academic year at Andover in 1887–1888. Ward was also a writer, though not too successful. Together they wrote several books, but none was especially well received. The early years of their marriage were relatively happy, but the happiness did not last. As time went on, they spent more and more time apart, perhaps because Phelps's health problems kept her close to home. Information about Phelps's married life is minimal. Her willingness to try marriage late in life may be explained as an attempt to fill the void left by the deaths of her brother and dear friend.

During the last period of her career Phelps became more conservative in her attitudes toward reform and the possibilities for women's advancement. *A Singular Life* (1895)—which she claimed was her favorite book, with her favorite hero, a minister devoted to temperance work in a fishing town based on Gloucester—advocates the reform of alcoholic men as a means of improving the lives of women rather than forcefully drawing attention to the cause of women's rights.

Phelps died on 28 January 1911 of a heart condition that had been diagnosed in 1903. Her body was cremated, and her ashes were buried beneath a headstone carved with the name "Elizabeth Stuart Phelps Ward" and a design of lilies, an echo of her childhood nickname. As this inscription suggests, she was her mother's daughter and was defined by a culture that frames a woman's identity with the name of her husband.

Phelps was well known in her lifetime, and she had long-time relationships with many of the important literary figures of her day, including James T. Fields and Annie Adams Fields, Harriet Beecher Stowe, Lydia Maria Child, Celia Thaxter, Lucy Larcom, Henry Wadsworth Longfellow, Whittier, and Harriet Prescott Spofford. Nonetheless, her literary reputation did not fare well in the twentieth century. During the early years of the century Fred Lewis Pattee gave her high praise for her handling of social issues as well as her aesthetic accomplishments, but other critics paid minimal attention to her fiction and offered mixed evaluations. From the perspectives of these male critics her fiction, like the work of many nineteenth-century American women writers, suffers from the "terrible too's": too sentimental, too moral, too woman-centered, too didactic, too outspoken, and too conventional. Through much of the twentieth century Phelps was remembered as at best a minor writer. Toward the end of the century, however, feminist challenges to the literary canon and efforts to retrieve neglected works from oblivion have sparked new interest in Phelps. A reassessment of her contributions to American literature and American culture is under way.

Once started on her literary career, Phelps never entirely abandoned her concern for the lives of women. Her literary production consistently addresses ethics as well as aesthetics. In her autobiography Phelps commented on her literary philosophy:

> In a word, the province of the artist is to portray life as it is; and life *is* moral responsibility. Life is several other things, we do not deny. It is beauty, it is joy, it is tragedy, it is comedy, it is psychical and physical pleasure, it is the interplay of a thousand rude or delicate motions and emotions, it is the grimmest and the merriest motley of phantasmagoria that could appeal to the gravest or the maddest brush ever put to palette; but it is steadily and sturdily and always moral responsibility. An artist can no more fling off the moral sense from his work than he can oust it from his private life. A great artist (let me repeat) is too great to try to do so.

This attention to moral responsibility is a consistent force in her fiction, poetry, and essays.

Elizabeth Stuart Phelps was caught between a conservative Christian world that demanded conformity and self-sacrifice from women and the emerging world of the new woman, then mostly unconstructed and untested. Her family and the intellectual climate of Andover, Massachusetts, made her conscious from an early age that she was poised on the edge of debate, uncertainty, and unfinished work and, thus, opportunely positioned in nineteenth-century American culture to probe the significance of women's experiences.

Biographies:

Mary Angela Bennett, *Elizabeth Stuart Phelps* (Philadelphia: University of Pennsylvania Press, 1939);

Lori Duin Kelly, *The Life and Works of Elizabeth Stuart Phelps, Victorian Feminist Writer* (Troy, N.Y.: Whitston, 1983).

References:

Carol Farley Kessler, *Elizabeth Stuart Phelps* (Boston: Twayne, 1982);

Fred Lewis Pattee, *The Development of the American Short Story* (New York: Harper, 1923).

Papers:

Collections of Elizabeth Stuart Phelps's manuscripts are at the Andover Historical Society; the Boston Public Library; the James Duncan Phillips Library, Essex Institute; the Houghton Library, Harvard University; the Mary and William Claflin Papers, Rutherford B. Hayes Library; the Huntington Library; the Century Collection and the Elizabeth Garver Jordan Papers in the Manuscripts and Archives Division of the New York Public Library, Astor, Lenox, and Tilden Foundations; the Arthur and Elizabeth Schlesinger Library on the History of Women in America, Radcliffe College; Friends Historical Library, Swarthmore College; the Clifton Waller Barrett Library in the Alderman Library, University of Virginia; and the Beinecke Rare Book and Manuscript Library, Yale University.

Agnes Repplier

(1 April 1855 – 16 December 1950)

Paul Hansom
University of Southern California

BOOKS: *Books and Men* (Boston & New York: Houghton, Mifflin, 1888; London: Gay & Bird, 1893);

Points of View (Boston & New York: Houghton, Mifflin, 1891; London: Gay & Bird, 1891);

Essays in Miniature (New York: Webster, 1892; London: Gay & Bird, 1893);

Essays in Idleness (Boston & New York: Houghton, Mifflin, 1893; London: Gay & Bird, 1893);

In the Dozy Hours and Other Papers (Boston & New York: Houghton, Mifflin, 1894);

Varia (Boston & New York: Houghton, Mifflin, 1897; London: Gay & Bird, 1898);

Philadelphia: The Place and the People (New York & London: Macmillan, 1898);

The Fireside Sphinx (Boston & New York: Houghton, Mifflin, 1901; London: Gay & Bird, 1901);

Compromises (Boston & New York: Houghton, Mifflin, 1904; London: Gay & Bird, 1904);

In Our Convent Days (Boston & New York: Houghton, Mifflin, 1905; London: Constable, 1905);

A Happy Half Century and Other Essays (Boston & New York: Houghton Mifflin, 1908; London: Gay & Hancock, 1908);

Americans and Others (Boston & New York: Houghton Mifflin, 1912);

Germany and Democracy: The Real Issue, by Repplier and J. William White (Philadelphia: Winston, 1914; London: Darling, 1915);

Counter-Currents (Boston & New York: Houghton Mifflin, 1916; London: Constable, 1916);

J. William White, M.D.: A Biography (Boston & New York: Houghton Mifflin, 1919);

Points of Friction (Boston & New York: Houghton Mifflin, 1920);

Under Dispute (Boston & New York: Houghton Mifflin, 1924);

Père Marquette (Garden City, N.Y.: Doubleday, Doran, 1929);

Mère Marie of the Ursulines: A Study in Adventure (Garden City, N.Y.: Doubleday, Doran, 1931; London: Burns, Oates, 1931);

Agnes Repplier

Times and Tendencies (Boston & New York: Houghton Mifflin, 1931);

To Think of Tea (Boston & New York: Houghton Mifflin, 1932; London: Constable, 1933);

Junipero Serra, Pioneer Colonist of California (Garden City, N.Y.: Doubleday, Doran, 1933);

Agnes Irwin (Garden City, N.Y.: Doubleday, Doran, 1934);

In Pursuit of Laughter (New York: Houghton Mifflin, 1936);

Eight Decades: Essays and Episodes (New York: Houghton Mifflin, 1937).

OTHER: *A Book of Famous Verse,* edited by Repplier (Boston & New York: Houghton, Mifflin, 1892);
The Cat: Being a Record of the Endearments and Invectives Lavished by Many Writers upon an Animal Much Loved and Much Abhorred, edited, with translations, by Repplier (New York: Sturgis & Walton, 1912).

During her lifetime Agnes Repplier, a thin, angular, chain-smoking writer of genteel essays, was considered one of the "Big Four" American women writers–along with Edith Wharton, Amy Lowell, and Willa Cather. She consorted with poets such as Walt Whitman and Robert Lowell and with President Theodore Roosevelt. One of the most honored Roman Catholics in American letters, she was awarded honorary degrees from the University of Pennsylvania (1902), Yale University (1925), Columbia University (1927), Marquette University (1928), and Princeton University (1935). She received the Laetare Medal from the University of Notre Dame (1911) and a gold medal from the National Institute of Arts and Letters (1935) for a lifetime of literary achievement. Yet, Repplier lived and wrote during the tumultuous period in which the United States was transformed from an insular state to a world power, a time in which the values and literary tastes of the nation underwent a parallel change. By the end of her career her essays, and the East Coast conservative values they represented, were no longer in fashion.

Born in Philadelphia on 1 April 1855, Agnes Repplier was named after her mother, Agnes Mathias Repplier, and brought up in a luxurious home bought by her wealthy father. John George Repplier was a prosperous coal merchant and maintained a high profile in local social and religious groups. Repplier's mother was largely dissatisfied with her shy, retiring daughter's looks and social abilities, and some critics have speculated that this disapproval was responsible for Repplier's cultivation of an ironic, distanced style. Repplier still could not read at the age of seven, but she slowly became aware of the power of words and the centrality of "confession" as a form of literary expression.

Her formal schooling began in 1867, when she entered the Convent of the Sacred Heart, also known as Eden Hall, in Torresdale, Pennsylvania. During her two years at the school, where she was taught by French nuns, Repplier became a devout Catholic and learned to treasure religious fundamentals. Yet, she was uncomfortable with the authoritarian dictates of the church and refused to submit to blind piety. As she said in later life, "There is nothing so abhorrent–or so perilous to the soul of man–as to be ruled in temporal things by

clerical authority." This split between the material and spiritual realms recurs throughout her work. Repplier's early independent thinking and rebellious spirit led to a clash with the nuns, and she was summarily expelled. Shocked and socially embarrassed, the Reppliers sent their willful daughter to Agnes Irwin's private school in Philadelphia.

Repplier's schooling was permanently terminated in 1871, after her father lost his money in a dubious speculation. Her mother called on her to help support the family. As she had no visible skills except a certain facility with words, she turned to writing to augment the family income. Slowly, she polished her writing skills, earning a tolerable income by placing small sketches and stories in the *Philadelphia Sunday Times* and *The Young Catholic.* It was a formative period, as she dryly recognized: "Naturally, I have nothing to say, but I have spent ten years learning to say nothing tolerably well," she is quoted as saying in Emma Repplier's *Agnes Repplier: A Memoir* (1957). In January 1881 Repplier's romantic short story "In Arcady" was published in *The Catholic World.* Her writing soon came to the attention of the founder of the magazine, Father Isaac Hecker, who had been a close friend of Henry David Thoreau. Hecker was largely unimpressed with her fictional fancies and read her personality rather accurately, claiming "you are a bookish person, and you must travel along your appointed path if you are to get anywhere." Hecker told Repplier that she lacked the experience and imagination to write sentimental romance and suggested that she redirect her burgeoning talent to the essay form. Following his advice, Repplier wrote "Ruskin as a Teacher," which appeared in *The Catholic World* in 1884, launching her literary career and beginning a period of intellectual apprenticeship.

Two years later, her acceptance into the literary establishment was signaled by the acceptance of her first serious essay, "Children Past and Present," by *The Atlantic Monthly.* The publication of this essay in the April 1886 issue began a relationship that lasted until 1940, and more than forty of her essays appeared in this journal. "Children Past and Present" established a style and format that went largely unchanged for fifty years. Repplier's personal essays have a vibrancy and intelligence generally lacking in the genre. Deliberately eschewing the "broad beaten roads of history," she set about exploring the "bridle paths of biography and memoir," forging a vision that reflects both her provincial background and her broad reading. At the same time she deliberately turned her back on the contemporary scene, retreating into the realm of the genteel and personal, defending traditional manners and morals against the degrading, tasteless, and unseemly. While she maintained a strong traditionalist belief in the teachings of Catholicism, which was manifested in her general skepticism of legislated progress, her work was never didactic in the extreme. Her mind-set was tempered by a sense of proportion borrowed from the Protestant traditions surrounding her.

In 1888 Repplier published "On the Benefits of Superstition," "Curiosities of Criticism," and "The Decay of Sentiment" in *The Atlantic Monthly*. In these widely acclaimed essays Repplier defended a conservative social tradition against what she believed to be the excesses of her peers. A dogged individualist, she was a great believer in the power of personal effort and intelligence and turned away from the growing concerns of the American middle class about socialism, increasing immigration, and reformism. Repplier also refused to turn her literary expression into a political platform. In writing against the "democratic theory of art" espoused by American writer and editor William Dean Howells, a major proponent of literary realism, she turned to the literary past as a model of good sense and impeccable taste, most probably as an antidote to the fixation on the present that was shaping mainstream literature. Her witty and intelligent defense of tradition won her acclaim among the Boston literati, who invited her into their circle. Their acceptance of her was crucial for Repplier, as it allowed her to break free from the tepid atmosphere of puritanical Philadelphia and head for the vibrant literary centers of Boston and New York, then the intellectual capitals of America. Published in 1888, Repplier's first collection of essays, *Books and Men*, received strong reviews. These essays draw on a specifically British and European literary tradition, indicating the direction of Repplier's self-education. Her tendency to favor the European scene over the homegrown essentially marked her abandonment of the American social landscape for a quieter, more peaceful time.

Repplier's second collection of essays, *Points of View* (1891), continues her typically bourgeois, urbane stance. In the year the book was published she met Whitman, whose distinctly American vision was the antithesis of her own. While initially horrified by his "farmer's garb," she found the poet pleasant but a poseur. For his part Whitman thought her a "nice, young critter," though he detected an emotional distance and ironic armor in her. Whitman recognized that, as a writer, Repplier functioned largely through intellect, using the essay as a means to display erudition rather than passion or formal experimentation. Despite this tendency, Repplier's work is not sterile by any means. It mocks the vagaries of critical taste and canonization and displays a strong awareness of the nonsense in literature. In "Books That Have Hindered Me," published in the July 1889 issue of *The Atlantic* and collected in *Points of View*, she succeeded in pricking the conceited bubbles of the literary world (though not her own), exercising an aristocratic spirit in the arbitration of worth.

Repplier began to consider specifically American issues toward the end of the century, and, while she was constitutionally unable to vote, her work certainly became politically oriented. There is little doubt she occupied an uncomfortable place in American letters, and her conservative position was often at odds with the dynamism of prevailing social currents. As an intelligent woman, she was well aware of the vagaries of political direction and suspected politics was largely folly. Having an abiding faith in the rightness of consistency, Repplier had no use for or belief in the prevailing reform movements toward the end of the century. As an avowed opponent of activist and writer Jane Addams and her advocacy for the poor and immigrant communities, Repplier feared Addams's democratizing tendencies. Convinced that Addams was influenced by the "vertigo of praise," she worried about the leveling effects of reform and the removal of class privilege. For Repplier, Addams represented the "intolerable sting of that modern gadfly, the professional agitator and socialistic champion of the poor," and she chafed against such a flagrant attempt to alter prevailing social hierarchies. Rather than raising everyone up, Repplier suspected reformist ideology would lead to the inevitable worship of mediocrity.

Repplier's views on the woman suffrage movement were similarly conservative and suspicious. While she was never ashamed of her gender, she believed women could function quite well in society without voting rights. She thought that to agitate for the vote was both unseemly and unbecoming of women. As she astutely recognized, "The right to be judged as men are judged is perhaps the only form of equality which feminists fail to demand." Simply, she did not want to be judged as a man, but as a woman of considerable accomplishment. In her essay "Our Over-rated Great Grandmothers," included in her *A Happy Half Century and Other Essays* (1908), she wrote: "the economical independence of woman, her solvency in the industrial world, and her strengthening grasp upon the world of the intellect, had and has the supreme rightness of the inevitable." Already convinced of her own equality with men, agitation for the vote was largely an irrelevant issue. Repplier believed that women could live without romance and marriage, offering her own example as the perfect case in point. Never married, she was a model of the industrious woman living a productive life. She saw herself as an independent woman who maintained standards and did not create a public nuisance.

Repplier (right) with the book-collector A. Edward Newton, the literary historian Charles G. Osgood,
and Babette Newton at a tea party in Newton's library celebrating the publication of Repplier's
To Think of Tea *in November 1932 (photograph by James L. Dillon & Co.)*

If Repplier disliked suffragists and reformers with equal zeal, it was largely because of her patrician background and her general distrust of the workings of democratic participation. For her, change could not be brought about by legislation, it was a slow, moral process that worked from the spiritual to the social realm. She thought that reformers had "unswervingly and unpityingly decreased the world's content, that they might better the world's condition." Afraid of class dynamics and the potential of class-based violence, she was largely unable to understand the problems associated with poverty. Gentility was essentially a privileged experience, and for the millions of immigrants who swarmed into New York and Boston toward the end of the nineteenth century, it was a luxury beyond their ken. In her essay "Consolations of the Conservative,"

published in her *Points of Friction* (1920) she commented on her hatred of legislated change, and her firm belief that all people had their places in the great chain of being. Similarly, in "Women Enthroned" and "The Strayed Prohibitionist" her replacement of a politics of direct action and participation with moral restraint clearly illustrates the gulf between Repplier and the material facts of American social life. Yet, in the face of bewildering changes for the American middle classes, her genteel and sensible style was a comfort to conservatives everywhere. Repplier was a popular voice at the turn of the nineteenth century and undertook several lecture tours, both locally and cross-country. At the same time, she produced some of her most important books. *Essays in Miniature* (1892), *Essays in Idleness* (1893), *In the Dozy Hours and Other Papers* (1894), and her semi-autobiographical *A Happy Half Century and Other Essays* all reveal her contemplative relationship to the world.

The outbreak of World War I in 1914 led to Repplier's involvement in the political arena. Conditioned by her love of literary history, she viewed the war in precisely the sentimental and romantic terms she mocked in others. Seeing the German invasion of Belgium as a barbaric act and the sinking of the *Lusitania* in 1915 as a moral outrage, Repplier became an ardent interventionist and called for the total destruction of Germany. She launched attacks on pacifists and isolationists, championing the Allied cause as a crusade against the barbarian invader, and developing close ties to other prominent conservatives such as Roosevelt. *Germany and Democracy: The Real Issue* (1914), a propaganda pamphlet she wrote with J. William White, employs biting sarcasm to ridicule the enemies of American intervention. The relentlessly pro-Allies essays collected in her *Counter-Currents* (1916) continue this tone of moral approbation. Abandoning her usual ironic distance, she produced simplistic patriotic propaganda.

The entrance of the United States into the war in 1917 came too late to satisfy Repplier, and in the renewal of political isolationism following the Versailles treaty her mood seemed to reflect the social malaise that descended on the country. She wrote that "there are many of us who failed to regain the lightness of heart which seemed a normal condition before the horror came." It took her the better part of a decade to regain her old spirit and return to her familiar style. While collections such as *Points of Friction* (1920), *Under Dispute* (1924), and *To Think of Tea* (1932) included some of her best writing to date, she also wrote historical biographies of American Catholics that border on hagiography. Corresponding with Repplier's renewed pursuit of Catholic principles in daily life, *Père Marquette* (1929), *Mère Marie of the Ursulines* (1931), and *Junipero Serra, Pioneer Colonist of California* (1933) explore the saintly lives of Catholics in seventeenth-century North America and their struggles with their faith. In the same decade Repplier also produced *Eight Decades* (1937), a work that examines the political and spiritual direction of U.S. history during her own lifetime.

Agnes Repplier died of heart failure on 16 December 1950. As a writer of the "familiar essay," she has few equals, and she has been compared to Henry James as a "critic of flashes." Embodying the continuation of the European tradition in America, her essays are part of the American belletristic tradition so highly regarded on the East Coast, which that looked to the Old World for models. Her urbane and unaffected style has many qualities of British neoclassical prose. The steady disintegration of Repplier's social class and its literary values sounded the death knell for this genteel form. Yet, Repplier deserves recognition for her leisurely sense of humor, her long view of social direction, and her discreet focus on the details of daily life.

Biographies:

George Stewart Stokes, *Agnes Repplier: Lady of Letters* (Philadelphia: University of Pennsylvania Press, 1949);

Emma Repplier, *Agnes Repplier: A Memoir* (Philadelphia: Dorrance, 1957).

References:

Mildred Adams, "Our Miss Repplier," *American Bookman* (June 1927): 410–412;

Edythe Brown, "The Abiding Art," *Thought* (December 1930): 396–410;

Mary Ellen Chase, "The Dean of American Essayists," *Commonweal* (18 August 1933): 384–386;

Joseph Collins, *Taking the Literary Pulse: Psychological Studies of Life and Letters* (New York: Doran, 1924), pp. 55–60;

George Stratton, "Crooked Thinking in Regard to War," *Nation* (8 April 1915): 385;

Mason Wade, "Agnes Repplier at Eighty," *New Republic* (8 December 1937): 133.

Papers:

Some of Agnes Repplier's letters are in the Adelaide Neall Collection, Historical Society of Pennsylvania, and a small collection is in Special Collections at the Northwestern University Library. The largest collection of Repplier's papers is in the Owen Wister Collection at the Library of Congress.

María Amparo Ruiz de Burton

(3 July 1832 – 12 August 1895)

José F. Aranda Jr.
Rice University

See also the Ruiz de Burton entry in *DLB 209: Chicano Writers, Third Series.*

BOOKS: *Who Would Have Thought It?* anonymous (Philadelphia: Lippincott, 1872);

Don Quixote de la Mancha: A Comedy, in Five Acts, Taken from Cervantes' Novel of That Name (San Franscisco: Carmany, 1876);

The Squatter and the Don: A Novel Descriptive of Contemporary Occurrences in California, as C. Loyal (San Francisco: Carson, 1885).

Editions: *The Squatter and the Don,* edited by Rosaura Sánchez and Beatrice Pita (Houston: Arte Público, 1992);

Who Would Have Thought It? edited by Sánchez and Pita (Houston: Arte Público, 1995).

With the recovery of her novels and research into her biography, María Amparo Ruiz de Burton is assured the recognition of her talents that she, her family, and her many influential friends understood to be her due. Her slippage into obscurity can only be understood in light of the plight of most women in history: their subjugation to a male-centered universe. Like most female intellectuals of her time, Mexican and American, she understood quite clearly the limitations set on her as woman, and she contrived, however imperfectly, to set the record straight about women. Ruiz de Burton's life and works are exceptions to the rule that women do not make history. Ruiz de Burton did make history, as marginalized members of society so often do, with great courage.

Given what her life has to offer scholars and students, Rosaura Sánchez and Beatrice Pita should be acknowledged for their scholarly editions of Ruiz de Burton's novels. Their literary recovery of Ruiz de Burton was made possible by the nationwide project known as Recovering the U.S. Hispanic Literary Heritage. As a result, a whole new audience is able to read the works of the nineteenth-century Mexican American author who was, in all probability, the first such writer

to publish novels in English. Sánchez and Pita have firmly established a place for Mexican American authors within studies of nineteenth-century American literature. Other scholars will join them in redrawing the racial map of U.S. literary history by calling attention to the writings of Hispanics who were the contemporaries of authors such as Nathaniel Hawthorne, Harriet Beecher Stowe, Harriet Jacobs, and W. E. B. Du Bois.

To understand Ruiz de Burton's life, one must appreciate for the dramatically changing world into which she was born. By 1832 Mexico had barely survived a series of wars that began when Miguel Hidalgo, a Catholic priest who galvanized the nation with his call for political freedom from Spain in 1810. Independence came in 1821 under the military and political leadership of Agustín de Iturbide. Estimates of the casualties suffered during the conflicts range from two hundred thousand to five hundred thousand, out of a population of nearly six million. The peace that the 1821 Treaty of Córdoba had secured with Spain was short lived, as was Iturbide's vision for a constitutional monarchy. In 1822 the Mexican Congress elected Iturbide emperor of Mexico, a proclamation that lasted ten months. From then on, the people of Mexico revisited the chaos and insecurity of military and political upheavals that would not subside until the 1870s under the presidency of Porfirio Díaz.

Another significant development was the rapid growth of the former English colonies on the Atlantic seaboard. The War of 1812 had settled the viability of the United States. Despite widely held ambivalences, the U.S. repulsion of the British fueled an optimism in the future of the country on the North American continent. Thomas Jefferson, both as author of the Declaration of Independence and third president of the republic, shaped significantly the country's early relationship to Mexico. Jefferson's Louisiana Purchase in 1803 fused his pastoral vision of a nation of yeoman farmers with the economic necessity of territorial expansion into the continental West. Into that West lay

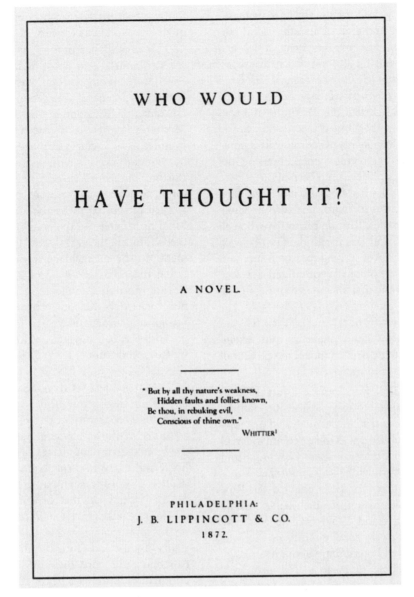

WHO WOULD

HAVE THOUGHT IT?

A NOVEL

" But by all thy nature's weakness,
    Hidden faults and follies known,
Be thou, in rebuking evil,
    Conscious of thine own."
                                WHITTIER[1]

PHILADELPHIA:
J. B. LIPPINCOTT & CO.
1872.

Title page for María Ruiz de Burton's satire on New England society, with characters based on her husband's family

Mexico, with its own colonial history of expansion, displacement and genocide of Native Americans, a de facto practice of servitude for people of color, and a caste system based on race and aristocratic lineage. Jefferson's purchase deeply troubled Spanish authorities, not least because they maintained that Napoleon Bonaparte had illegally sold a territory belonging to Spain. U.S. expansion into the Southwest and West in the early nineteenth century eventually led to armed conflict with Mexico, the only country in North America that could reasonably compete for domination of the continent.

Ruiz de Burton endured the consequences of four wars: the Texas War of Independence (1836), the Mexican-American War (1846–1848), the American Civil War (1861–1865), and the French occupation of Mexico (1864–1867). Ruiz de Burton understood military and political conflicts as providing women with opportunities to enter the history of a nation. She evidences this philosophy in her novels and in her many letters to friends on both the Atlantic and Pacific coasts.

No less significant to a biography of Ruiz de Burton are the conflicts important to women, minorities, and the lower classes: these issues and struggles arose from a history of slavery and racism, the U.S. women's movement for suffrage and civil rights, the rise of corporate monopolies and the estrangement of women from the workplace, and finally, the illegal dispossession of former Mexican citizens of their lands from Texas to California. After the Treaty of Guadalupe Hidalgo in 1848, which settled the Mexican-American War, racist practices in the United States soon found their way into laws that openly discriminated against people of Mexican descent in employment, housing, the purchase of property, and legal representation. These laws joined racist attitudes in Mexican culture to exaggerate the privileged status of "whiteness" within Mexican American communities. Ruiz de Burton saw herself as a "white" Mexican, and this racial identity played a significant role in her novel writing, personal life, and business dealings. At one point she considered developing some mining interests that she owned in Baja California with Chinese coolie labor. The fact that she entertained this idea, which never materialized beyond her employment of two Chinese male servants, exemplifies the kind of complex negotiations that scholars of Ruiz de Burton will have to traverse.

María Amparo Ruiz was born on 3 July 1832 in Loreto, Baja California, to an aristocratic family. According to Sánchez and Pita, her maternal grandfather, Don José Manuel Ruiz, was once "commander of the Mexican northern frontier in Baja California and later (1822–1825) Governor of Baja California." Their military and aristocratic connections enabled the Ruiz family to come into possession of ranch lands in Baja California. Yet, Sánchez and Pita write, "in a largely barren peninsula with a very small population, the Ruiz family undoubtedly could boast more about its prestige and political recognition than about its economic power." This discrepancy between economic status and noble lineage haunted Ruiz all her life.

Having manufactured a military confrontation with Mexico, President James K. Polk asked for a declaration of war from the U.S. Congress on 11 May 1846. Congress declared war on Mexico by the end of the day. Far from the more devastating theaters of war, Baja California was nevertheless invaded and occupied by U.S. military forces. Among the officers occupying Loreto was Captain Henry S. Burton of Norwich, Vermont. Burton and María Amparo Ruiz apparently met during the occupation.

At the signing of the Treaty of Guadalupe Hidalgo on 2 February 1848 Baja California was left in the possession of Mexico. Before the signing of the treaty, U.S. officials had promised Baja residents transport to Alta California; about 480 residents took advantage of this offer. Mexican citizens who remained or took up residency in newly conquered territories would be deemed to have elected U.S. citizenship.

Ruiz and her mother, Isabel; brother, Federico; sister, Manuela; and Pablo de la Toba, her sister's husband, were among the 480 who left for Alta California. Eventually, some of this group returned to Baja. Others, including Ruiz and her family, took up residence in Monterey as new U.S. citizens. Whether or not the promise of U.S. citizenship played a part in motivating her emigration, it is clear that Ruiz left Baja to marry Burton. The courtship and marriage of Ruiz and Burton is, Sánchez and Pita note, of folkloric quality; Ruiz is even purported to be the subject of a ballad, "The Maid of Monterey," that was sung by U.S. veterans of the California theater of war. Following the announcement of their engagement, a jealous suitor of Ruiz protested that marriage was out of the question because Burton was not Catholic. In response, California governor Richard B. Mason forbade state authorities from recognizing any marriage of a Catholic to a non-Catholic. In the end, Ruiz and Burton were married quietly by Reverend Samuel H. Willey at the home of Captain E. R. S. Canby on 9 July 1849.

Married just six days after her seventeenth birthday, Ruiz de Burton began a new life in a rapidly changing U.S. territory. The discovery of gold in 1849 at Sutter's Mill accelerated not only emigration from the United States but also California's petition for statehood and entry into the Union. The California Convention of 1849 was a mixture of excitement and dread for Californios. As the convention drew to a close, it was apparent that race would become a defining feature of the laws that protected property and insured civil rights. By the end of the century the Californios would experience the consequences of racial and ethnic discrimination in the U.S. through the loss of their lands, social standing, and political representation.

Ruiz de Burton gave birth to their first child, Nellie, on 4 July 1850. Two years later Burton was posted in San Diego. Their second child, Henry Halleck Burton, named after Burton's friend and comrade in arms Henry Wager Halleck, was born on 24 November 1852. In 1853 the Burtons purchased land from Pío Pico's Jamul land grant—a transaction that was no doubt facilitated by Ruiz de Burton's kinship ties to the Pico family. In 1855 Ruiz de Burton seems to have written some of the more popular productions for the Mission Theatre in San Diego. Her social standing as a Californio and her marriage to Burton surely made her literary debut a grand affair. Ruiz de Burton was well connected among other Californios and a great letter-writer in Spanish as well as English, keeping up extended correspondence with relatives and friends throughout her life. Burton was a war hero and a favor-

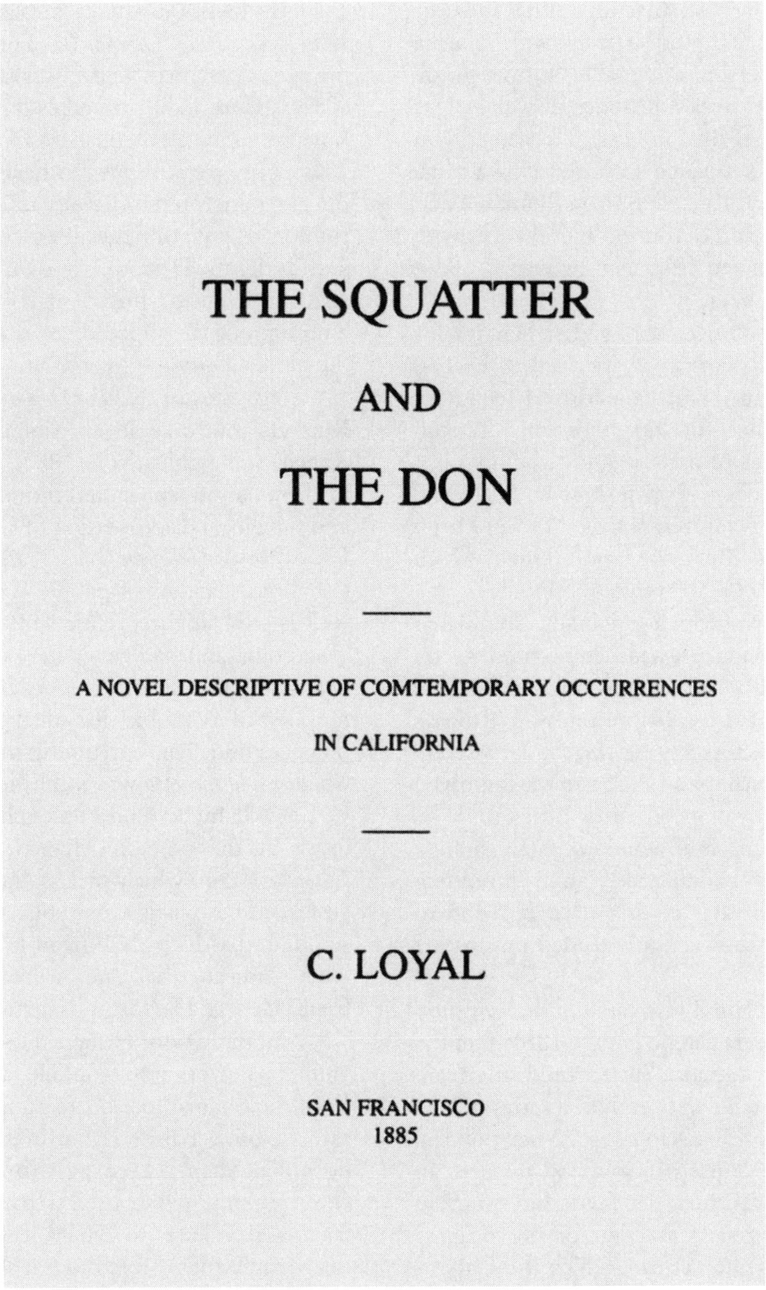

THE SQUATTER

AND

THE DON

————

A NOVEL DESCRIPTIVE OF COMTEMPORARY OCCURRENCES

IN CALIFORNIA

————

C. LOYAL

SAN FRANCISCO
1885

Title page for Ruiz de Burton's second novel, a satire on capitalistic land-grabbing during the early days of California statehood

ite son of the new state. He was well known for his avid hunting of quail. The only shadow that plagued the family was Burton's penchant for extravagant spending and a tendency not to pay his bills.

In 1859 the family was uprooted when Burton was ordered to return East. Ruiz de Burton's stay on the Atlantic coast turned out to be a ten-year period of following her husband through various assignments.

She made a home in Rhode Island; New York; Washington, D.C.; Delaware; and Virginia. As in California, Ruiz de Burton circulated among the most prominent social and political circles. She and her husband attended Abraham Lincoln's inaugural ball, meeting the president and first lady. She had an audience with President Lincoln during the Civil War, wherein she made the case that her husband should be promoted; he was promoted to major after that meeting. After the war Ruiz de Burton became good friends with Varina Davis, the wife of Jefferson Davis. The former president of the Confederacy was a prisoner of war at Fort Monroe in Virginia, and Burton became commandant of the fort and Davis's warden in late 1865. Varina Davis wrote that she and Ruiz de Burton drank tea and criticized the Yankees. Ruiz de Burton's grievances with the United States stemmed from her bitterness about the Mexican-American War.

Burton had been breveted brigadier general for his efforts to capture Petersburg, Virginia, but he had contracted malaria in the campaign. Moved to lighter duties whenever possible for health reasons, Burton died from complications of malaria and hepatitis on 4 April 1869 at Fort Adams, Newport, Rhode Island. Ruiz de Burton and her children returned to San Diego in 1870 to take up residence at the Jamul Ranch, which she had left in the care of her brother and mother.

The Jamul Ranch, which originally comprised more than half a million acres, had deteriorated. Complicating matters were auctions held in the family's absence to pay off debts from before the war. Ruiz de Burton devoted herself to securing the family's livelihood. According to Sánchez and Pita, she was involved in "the large scale cultivation of castor beans and the building of a water reservoir at Jamul . . . establishing a Cement Company to exploit the Jamul limestone deposits that her husband had first used in 1856 to make lime." Most of these ventures ended up costing her money.

Ruiz de Burton's Jamul title came under question when Anglo homesteaders claimed in the 1870s that the land was in the public domain. She secured title from the state in 1870, only to have to fend off a series of lawsuits by illegal squatters. In October 1872 her political friends persuaded the Supreme Court to dismiss an appeal that sought to overturn her favorable ruling in 1870. Afterwards, to save a fraction of the original ranch, she applied for a homestead, which the California Supreme Court granted in 1889. By then, however, Ruiz de Burton had incurred heavy legal costs and had mortgaged parcels of land to finance her family's livelihood, as well as her lawsuits and business ventures. In 1893 Ruiz de Burton's son, Harry, was forced to sell the remaining portion of the ranch to pay off family debts.

Despite her financial woes and court battles, Ruiz de Burton found time to begin her literary career in the 1870s. Instrumental in helping to secure publication for her first novel was a well-known New York lawyer, Samuel L. M. Barlow. Barlow put Ruiz de Burton in contact with her first publisher, J. B. Lippincott of Philadelphia.

In 1872 Lippincott published Ruiz de Burton's *Who Would Have Thought It?* The novel is a satire based on her experiences and observations of New England society. Ruiz de Burton takes on what she considers the sanctimonious righteousness of New England culture. The clergy, republican motherhood, abolitionism, and the gap between the rhetoric of democracy and the corruption of government all come under severe scrutiny and criticism. Despite her own positive dealings with Lincoln, even the president is ridiculed and censured. Throughout the satire there is nevertheless a belief in the perfectibility of government.

The Squatter and the Don—a novel partly based on Ruiz de Burton's legal tribulations with the Jamul Ranch—was published in 1885. The novel criticizes the ill effects of transportation monopolies on the economy and the illegal dispossession of Californios of their land. Like *Who Would Have Thought It?* this novel includes fictionalized versions of people Ruiz de Burton knew, as well as public figures. Ruiz de Burton holds California's "Big Four" railroad magnates—Leland Stanford, Collis P. Huntington, Charles Crocker, and Mark Hopkins—morally accountable for their questionable business practices and their corrupting influence on society. *The Squatter and the Don* was published under the pen name C. Loyal. Sánchez and Pita explain that it was common usage at the time in Mexico to close a letter with *Ciudadano Leal,* which means "loyal citizen." They suggest that C. Loyal is a symbolic attempt to claim a social standing that Ruiz de Burton found lacking in real life. They indicate that she borrowed money from her friend George Davidson to finance the publication.

In the 1870s Hubert Howe Bancroft began an ambitious project to compile a history of California from the Spanish period to statehood. Ruiz de Burton saw the project as an opportunity for the Californios to document their presence in the country. She solicited contributions to the project from her own Californio friends. In a letter to Bancroft, however, she lamented that many of her peers did not share her enthusiasm.

Ruiz de Burton's novels are best understood as family romances. But the designation has to do with family as it is understood in Mexican culture. In Spanish, *familia* conveys the understanding not only of an extended family but also of a network of in-laws, godparents, friends, neighbors, business associates, and even, at highly charged rhetorical moments, the nation. Both novels end in cross-ethnic marriages, symbolically aiming for a resolution of all social and political conflicts by forcing opposing parties to become a family.

Families are central to such novels as Emily Brontë's *Wuthering Heights* (1847), William Makepeace Thackeray's *Vanity Fair* (1848), Charles Dickens's *Bleak House* (1852–1853), George Eliot's *Middlemarch* (1871–

1872), and Thomas Hardy's *Tess of the D'Urbervilles* (1891). But Ruiz de Burton's deployment of the family trope has its closest double in *Anna Karenina* (1877), where Leo Tolstoy writes: "All happy families are like one another; each unhappy family is unhappy in its own way." Even though Ruiz de Burton's marriage plots would have the reader believe that a happy ending is forthcoming, as critic Anne E. Goldman observes, the marriages often carry a tinge of sadness, if not tragedy. In this context, the closest American analogue is Herman Melville's *Pierre* (1852).

While *Who Would Have Thought It?* presents much tragedy–the death of Lola Medina's mother, Lola's orphanhood, the Civil War, the forced exile of Dr. Norval–no single tragic moment sustains the level of melancholy found in *The Squatter and the Don*. In *Who Would Have Thought It?* one expects the satire to unmask the rakish and scandalous behavior of Reverend Hackwell, who seduces Mrs. Norval into a life of sensual pleasure and greed. Mrs. Norval's gullibility is a comment on the tenuous foundation of the supposed moral superiority of New England. The novel also creates and satisfies the expectation that Dr. Norval will return in time to witness his rival's fall and to bless the marriage of his son, Julian, to his ward, Lola Medina. Lola is finally reunited with her Mexican father.

The family into which Ruiz de Burton married is the probable source of the satiric anger of the novel. Henry S. Burton was the son of Oliver G. Burton, a West Point officer, and Almira Partridge of Norwich, Vermont. The Burton family likely produced models for the corrupt clergy in the novel. Henry Burton was probably related to Asa Burton, an eminent Congregational minister. On the Partridge side, Henry's mother was probably related to Alden Partridge, an educator, military theorist, and historian whose specialty was artillery science. He established a military academy from which evolved Norwich University, the oldest private military college in the United States.

Rounding out Ruiz de Burton's family in Vermont were the Willistons. After Oliver Burton's death in 1821 Almira Burton married Ebenezer Bancroft Williston, who taught Greek and Latin in Alden Partridge's academy and might have been a model for Dr. Norval. Although Williston died in 1837, family stories must have circulated about the only father Henry Burton ever really knew. In addition, Henry Burton had three stepsiblings from his mother's second marriage. The most famous was E. B. Williston, who, like his older brother, became an artillery officer and was also a breveted brigadier general during the Civil War. Henry's stepfather's cousin, George Bancroft, wrote *The History of the United States: From the Discovery of the Continent* (1834–1874). Bancroft was also the secretary of the navy in the Polk

Ruiz de Burton's son, Henry Halleck Burton, circa 1903 (The San Diego Historical Society Photograph Collection)

administration who gave the official order to seize California "in the event of war with Mexico."

For her first novel Ruiz de Burton reconceives her New England family history as Lola Medina's struggle to make a life for herself in an alien culture and environment. Lola's displacement from Mexican culture, Roman Catholicism, and aristocratic lineage symbolically unites author with character. Through Lola, Ruiz de Burton conveys her cultural shock on meeting Henry Burton's extended family. She no doubt experienced what Lola suffers in the novel: the pain of discrimination, even though she was "white"; attacks on her Catholicism; attacks on Mexican culture and society as backward and animalistic; and the insults of a regional chauvinism that led New Englanders to believe in Manifest Destiny as a moral project. Curiously, Lola is absent for most of the novel. The narrator speaks on Lola's behalf and takes revenge on her attackers. It is easy to understand Lola's marriage to Julian at the end of the novel as Ruiz de Burton's desire to revisit the romance she once imagined possible with Henry Burton, a romance that would also help resolve her nationalist anger. This ending is evidence of her longing for a cultural reckoning that remained suspended with the death of her husband.

The repressed family history of her first novel blooms more fully in *The Squatter and the Don,* which recreates the grandeur of Californio life before 1846. The loss of connection to this past reaches a climax when the traditional lands of the central Californio family in the novel, los Alamares, are occupied by Anglo squatters. The family's recourse to the law proves ineffectual against corruption and influence peddling. Goldman argues: "Where other writers defuse political violence by relocating it in a domestic space defined in opposition to the social domain, Ruiz de Burton politicizes the familial circle, so that home becomes the locus to articulate a sustained description of conflict on a national scale." Mercedes Alamar's marriage to Clarence Darrell, the son of the most prominent squatter in the novel, signals, as Goldman writes, that "the world of the Californio at the close of this book is all but extinguished." Instead of resolving social conflict through a cross-ethnic marriage, the narrator advocates a vigilante effort to rid California of its unscrupulous monopolists. Eight years after the novel was published, Ruiz de Burton was forced to sell her beloved Jamul Ranch.

María Amparo Ruiz de Burton died in 1895 in Chicago after returning from Mexico City, where she was unsuccessful in regaining possession of Rancho Ensenada de Todos Santos in Baja California. Having won title to Rancho Ensenada in 1871 in the Mexican courts, Ruiz de Burton had her claim nullified in part by Mexico's 1883 Law of Colonization, which enabled an international land company to claim Rancho Ensenada. She won the title back, only to have it reversed by the Supreme Court of Mexico in 1889. (In her later years, short on funds, Ruiz de Burton often acted as her own counsel and prepared her own court briefs.) She was unaware that her grandfather, José Manuel Ruiz, had sold the property to his son-in-law, Francisco Xavier Gastelum, in 1824; Gastelum had in turn sold it to Pedro Gastelum, a cousin, who later sold it as well.

Like many of her Californio peers, Ruiz de Burton died in poverty. Frederick Bryant Oden's research shows that Ruiz de Burton "died of gastric fever at the Sherman House on 12 August 1895." She was in Chicago soliciting political support to continue her litigation over Rancho Ensenada. She was buried in Calvary Catholic Cemetery in San Diego; her funeral was apparently well attended, and, as Oden notes, her casket was "showered with floral offerings."

Although it took almost a hundred years after her death, María Amparo Ruiz de Burton's writing has found meaning among Mexican American readers. A bilingual edition of Ruiz de Burton's letters, translated and edited by Amelia María de la Luz Montes, is forthcoming and will be a valuable resource for scholars of her work.

References:
Timothy E. Anna, *The Mexican Empire of Iturbide* (Lincoln: University of Nebraska Press, 1990);

Kathleen Crawford, "María Amparo Ruiz Burton: The General's Lady," *Journal of San Diego History,* 30 (1984): 207–208;

Richard M. Garten, "The Political Activities of S. L. M. Barlow, 1856–1864," M.A. thesis, Columbia University, 1947;

Anne E. Goldman, "*The Squatter and the Don* by María Amparo Ruiz de Burton," *MELUS,* 19 (1994): 129–131;

Goldman, "'Who ever heard of a blue-eyed Mexican?': Satire and Sentimentality in María Amparo Ruiz de Burton's *Who Would Have Thought It?*" in *Recovering the U.S. Hispanic Literary Heritage,* volume 2, edited by Erlinda Gonzales-Berry and Chuck Tatum (Houston: Arte Público, 1996);

John M. Gonzalez, "Romancing Hegemony: Constructing Racialized Citizenship in María Amparo Ruiz de Burton's *The Squatter and the Don,*" in *Recovering the U.S. Hispanic Literary Heritage,* volume 2, edited by Gonzales-Berry and Tatum (Houston: Arte Público, 1996);

Frederick Bryant Oden, "The Maid of Monterey, The Life of María Amparo Ruiz de Burton, 1832–1895," M.A. thesis, University of California, San Diego, 1992;

Raymund A. Paredes, "The Image of the Mexican in American Literature," dissertation, University of Texas at Austin, 1973;

Arthur Marvin Shaw, "Varina Davis's Letter," *The Journal of Southern History,* 16 (1950): 75–76.

Papers:
María Amparo Ruiz de Burton's letters and documents are in the Bancroft Collection at the Berkeley Library of the University of California at Berkeley; Mission Santa Barbara in Santa Barbara, California; the Huntington Library in San Marino, California; and the San Diego Historical Society.

Amanda Smith

(23 January 1837 – 6 March 1915)

Venetria K. Patton
University of Nebraska at Lincoln

BOOK: *An Autobiography: The Story of the Lord's Dealings with Mrs. Amanda Smith the Colored Evangelist* (Chicago: Meyer, 1893).

According to Jualynne E. Dodson's introduction to the 1988 edition of Amanda Smith's *An Autobiography: The Story of the Lord's Dealings with Mrs. Amanda Smith the Colored Evangelist* (1893), "Amanda Berry Smith personified the nineteenth-century black preaching woman." Smith's life is best understood within the context of black women's involvement in the African Methodist Episcopal (AME) Church, which from its inception prohibited the licensing and ordination of women preachers. Despite her lack of any official position, Smith attained prominence by preaching to AME congregations and other religious groups. Although there were other such women evangelists, Smith, Jarena Lee, Rebecca Stewart, and Zilpha Elaw were the only ones to leave autobiographical accounts of their religious endeavors. These women refused to be silent, addressing through their preaching racial uplift ideologies as well as issues of gender.

Amanda Berry was born 23 January 1837 in Long Green, Maryland, to Samuel Berry, slave of Darby Insor, and Mariam Matthews, slave of Shadrach Green. Berry was allowed to earn extra money by making brooms and husk mats, which he then sold at market. He eventually bought himself, his wife, and their five children out of slavery. Amanda was one of the five children born in slavery, although her seven younger siblings were born free. She had a limited education: entering school at eight years of age, she was first instructed by Isabella Dill in an abandoned house, then later by Dr. Joseph Hendricks at Rule's School House, and finally by Walter Murray. In all, her schooling totaled no more than ninety days. Smith left school to help support the family by serving as a maid and washerwoman.

Smith married and was widowed twice. She married her first husband, Calvin M. Devine of Columbia, Pennsylvania, in September 1854. During the

Civil War, Devine enlisted, went South with the Union army, and was killed in battle. Her second husband was Reverend James H. Smith of Philadelphia, a local deacon of the AME Church; he died in November 1869. Smith had five children from the two marriages, but only a daughter from the first marriage, Mazie, survived to adulthood.

Smith's autobiography chronicles a hard life filled with slavery, poverty, illness, and death but focuses upon her spiritual growth. In March 1856 she converted to Christianity after much soul searching. Smith notes that "though I have passed through many sorrows, many trials, Satan has buffeted me, but never from that day have I had a question in regard to my conversion." Smith did not fully experience a feeling of enduring grace or sanctification until September 1868, however, while listening to a sermon by John Inskip at Green Street Methodist Episcopal Church in New York. Shortly after her sanctification, Smith began preaching at churches in various cities. At this time she went primarily to black churches, but also to some white Methodist churches, class meetings, and prayer meetings. Smith observes: "There were then but few of our ministers that were favorable to women's preaching or taking any part, I mean in a public way; but, thank God, there always were a few men that dared to stand by woman's liberty in this, if God called her." In November 1870, Smith felt God's calling to go out and preach to the Mount Pisgah AME Church in Salem, New Jersey. In a matter of months, she was responsible for 156 conversions and 112 "accessions" to the congregation. Smith's success as an evangelist was by then well established in the northeastern United States. Like Jarena Lee and Sojourner Truth before her, Smith earned her living by preaching in camp meetings and selling her life story.

Although Smith's success was celebrated by many, it was also seen as a threat by some members of the church who were against women's ordination. This resistance was particularly apparent when she mentioned her plans to attend the general conference of the AME Church in Nashville, Tennessee, held in May 1872. Despite attempts to dissuade her from attending, Smith went, and while at the conference she was viewed with suspicion by those who supposed she was there to agitate for women's ordination. In her autobiography Smith reflects on these experiences: "even with my own people, in this country, I have not always met with the pleasantest things. But still I have not backslidden, nor felt led to leave the church." Smith consistently challenged gender expectations by preaching without the ordination received by male preachers; she was not concerned that her activities were not sanctioned by the church, however, because she had been sanctioned by God. Thus, her Christian faith led her to go against gender norms. According to the tenets of evangelicalism, the individual merges with other congregants and God, and thereby, the hierarchies of race, gender, and class are eradicated. Smith, like Lee and Truth, used the spirit of evangelicalism to transgress these boundaries.

Along with her success with local AME congregations, Smith also attracted attention from white audiences at "holiness" camp meetings, which were quite popular in the 1870s. This popularity among whites, however, was a double-edged sword. Smith notes in her autobiography that within the black community she was often referred to as a "white folks' nigger." Dodson notes the lack of support from black denominations, including Smith's own AME Church, and suggests that this disfavor in the black community in part stimulated Smith's desire to go abroad. Smith, however, does not mention this alienation as part of her motivation. In fact, she appears to dismiss the insults leveled against her by asserting that her desire is to keep in favor with God, again indicating the way in which Smith used evangelicalism to break through race and gender boundaries.

In 1878, Smith sailed to England, becoming the first black woman to work as an international evangelist. She landed in Liverpool, but her evangelism did not end there; she held services in many English cities during her twenty months in residence. Her meetings were advertised with placards proclaiming that "Mrs. Amanda Smith, the Converted Slave from America, will give Gospel Addresses and Sing." Smith reflects that she was "quite a novelty, being a woman, and a black woman at that." She proceeded to Scotland, where it was unusual for a woman to address mixed audiences. Smith acknowledges that she was at first a curiosity and that people questioned her ability to lead a gospel service, but by the third meeting, "one could not have told from their manner, and the hearty Scotch co-operation and sympathy with which they stood by me, but what they had been accustomed, not only to women preaching, but to black women, all their days." Smith states that no one treated her like a black woman, an observation that alludes to the difference in atmosphere between post–Reconstruction America and Scotland. Even at camp meetings, accommodations in the United States were usually segregated, and certain activities or services were dominated by one race. At various places in her autobiography, Smith indicates her hesitation to attend certain services because her presence might not be welcome. She seemed to feel that she was always treated with respect in Scotland, although some found her activities unusual for a woman.

Although other African American women preachers traveled throughout the United States, Smith is the first to have preached internationally. Her travels carried her overland to India by way of Paris, Florence, Rome, Naples, and Egypt. On 12 November 1879 she arrived in Bombay. While in India, Smith was appalled by what she termed "heathen idol worship": "How sad to see the different idols they worship displayed on their flags and in every possible shape and way. My heart ached, and I prayed to the Lord to send help and light to these poor heathen."

She was amazed by how tenaciously the natives held on to their "superstitions." Smith viewed her trip to India and her experience with "heathenism" there as preparation for her later trip to Africa.

On 31 December 1881 Smith sailed from Liverpool to Liberia, arriving in Monrovia on 18 January 1882. Liberia, at the time, was still seen as a promised land for African Americans who no longer believed in the possibility of enjoying the rights and privileges of American citizenship. Between 1820 and the Civil War, as many as ten thousand free blacks and emancipated slaves sailed for Liberia as part of various movements to return to their ancestral homeland. Differences in the cultural habits of the émigrés and the natives led to inevitable conflict, however.

Smith finally realized her dream of performing missionary work in Africa. This goal first came to her during the Sea Cliff camp meeting in July 1872. She had been concerned that the discussion of mission work did not include Africa. Smith recalls that she prayed, "Lord, Africa's need is great, and I cannot go, though I would like to. But Thou knowest I have no education, and do not understand the geography, so I would not know how to travel." Thinking that she was too ignorant, Smith decided to educate her daughter, Mazie, to go instead. Mazie eventually married and gave up her plans to travel abroad, however. Since Smith could not fulfill her dream through her daughter, she was forced to face her uncertainties. At various points in her text, Smith mentions her hesitation and even resistance to traveling; her statements regarding her ignorance about travel might also have been a means of masking her fear of doing something so unusual, and possibly dangerous, for a black woman.

Smith's trip to Africa was not confined to Monrovia; she traveled throughout the continent. As with many nineteenth-century women activists, temperance was a significant issue for her, and during her travels she gave many talks about the evils of alcohol. She persuaded many people to sign the Gospel Temperance pledge, but she also met resistance from class leaders and local preachers. Smith was critical of ministers who did not take up the temperance movement, which she deemed a vital element of her evangelicalism.

While in Monrovia she met William Taylor, the AME bishop of Africa, who persuaded her to travel with him to Grand Canary Island. They sailed on 16 February 1885 and arrived eight days later. Roman Catholicism was the only Christian religion practiced in this French-speaking country, and Smith was astonished by what she saw as the ignorance of the people and the arrogance of the priests. This passage offers

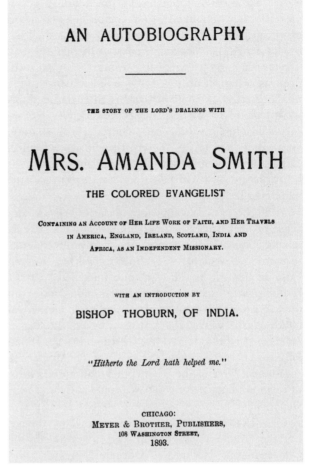

AN AUTOBIOGRAPHY

THE STORY OF THE LORD'S DEALINGS WITH

MRS. AMANDA SMITH

THE COLORED EVANGELIST

CONTAINING AN ACCOUNT OF HER LIFE WORK OF FAITH, AND HER TRAVELS IN AMERICA, ENGLAND, IRELAND, SCOTLAND, INDIA AND AFRICA, AS AN INDEPENDENT MISSIONARY.

WITH AN INTRODUCTION BY

BISHOP THOBURN, OF INDIA.

"Hitherto the Lord hath helped me."

CHICAGO:
MEYER & BROTHER, PUBLISHERS,
108 WASHINGTON STREET,
1893.

Title page for Smith's account of her conversion to Christianity and her mission work in the United States, the United Kingdom, India, and various African nations

one of her characteristically anti-Catholic statements; earlier in her autobiography she comments that, ignorant of the "subtlety of Rome," she made a serious mistake in sending Mazie to a Catholic school.

Smith and Taylor returned to Monrovia on 30 March 1885. On 22 April, Smith began traveling again. She took short trips to Mt. Olive, Marshall, and Sheflenville before returning to Monrovia. Smith had commented on her health several times before these travels, and she seemed to be in particularly poor health during these trips. Although one of the reasons she had given for initially leaving the United States was to rest, Smith was continually in motion. Her evangelism appears to have been physically draining.

Smith's travels eventually brought her to Duketown, Old Calabar, West Africa, in 1887. She clearly viewed the people she encountered as heathens in need of redemption. She described in horror the skulls lying about the town: "At the third yard, buried at the threshold, there was a human skull, over which one must walk to get in. Oh, what horror! a human grave-yard. But what about all you have not seen and heard of, of horrors? I said, 'Oh, Lord, how long shall the dreadful night of heathenism last? Oh that the day may break, and that right early. Amen.'" Human sacrifice was no longer practiced due to the influence of the missionaries, but Smith was shocked that the skulls were still tolerated. She was confounded to see so-called heathenism practiced alongside Christianity. Smith described one of the chiefs, who wore English clothes and attended the Presbyterian Church, as being "as full of superstition and heathenism as if he had never heard the Gospel."

Smith seems completely distanced from any sense of her African heritage. She recalls her parents talking about Africa, but she only knew it through pictures in a newspaper, *The Brother Jonathan Almanac.* Prior to her trip to Africa, Smith imagined "a great heathen town" with boa constrictors, lions, and panthers. Rather than changing her mind upon her arrival in Africa, she viewed the Africans through the lens of American civilization and her Christian beliefs. When Smith was asked about the religion of Africa, she responded: "Well, where I was they had no real form of religion. They were what we would call devil worshippers."

In 1888 Smith spent some time in Clay-Ashland, Liberia. While there, she helped to establish the Clay-Ashland Holiness Association, which was devoted to the discussion of personal holiness. She also made a brief visit to Cape Mount before returning to Monrovia. She spent a total of eight years in Africa. Besides observing what she viewed as heathenism, Smith also reflected on the subservient position of women. In Duketown she was particularly disturbed that the wives of kings and chiefs could not go to church. In fact, they could not go out at all without permission. She also notes that, like the women of India, African women did all of the hard work: "No matter how tired she is, her lord would not think of bringing her a jar of water, to cook his supper with, or of beating the rice; no, she must do that." Smith's concern, however, was not just that women were over-worked, but that they were owned. She describes the dowry system by which girl children were betrothed at birth. The girls had no say in the exchange, and no one could interfere in a husband's treatment of his wife.

Although Smith seemed more concerned with gender issues than race, she does comment on relations between whites and blacks. At a meeting between Liberians and a group of black immigrants, Smith was disappointed by "all the raking of white people." While she acknowledges the wrong of the whites that caused the grievances, Smith did not think it right "to forever keep looking at the wrongs, and never see any of the good, which has always gone along side by side with the wrong." She believed that the immigrants would be more likely to receive aid from whites than from the Liberians.

Some of the good to which Smith refers is the work of white missionaries. Although she acknowledged that there were some disreputable missionaries, on the whole she thought it better for white missionaries to go to Africa rather than blacks. She stated that "white missionaries as a rule, give better satisfaction, both to the natives and to the church or society which sends them out." This assertion seems surprising coming from a black missionary, but she tempers this statement with two observations. First, she notes that the most efficient black man never received a salary equal to the most inefficient white man or woman, and the black man is expected to do more work. This subtle critique of missionary leadership demonstrates that, in muted ways, Smith addresses race as well as gender matters. She also praises the work of Reverend Joseph Gomer, of the Shanghai Mission, whom she describes as "the grandest black missionary." These two observations imply that the lack of great black missionaries is not necessarily due to a lack of talent, but a lack of support.

Smith returned to the United States in 1890. By this time she was much worse physically than when she left for England in 1878. Her poor health limited the type of work she could do, and she was no longer as popular in the United States as she had been. On her initial return, Smith preached in eastern churches, but she lacked financial support from either black or white denominations. She moved to Chicago and began working in the Women's Christian Temperance Union movement in 1892. She also began writing her autobiography, which was published the next year. Smith used the profits from her book sales, as well as the proceeds from *The Helper,* a monthly newspaper she published, and personal savings and donations, to finance a black orphanage. Located in Harvey, Illinois, the orphanage was the only significant institution created for black children in the nineteenth century. It also housed a school, later named the Amanda Smith School, which struggled financially from its inception and eventually closed in 1918 after it was destroyed by fire.

Smith retired in 1912. She had received an offer from George Sebring, a friend and realtor, to move into a home provided for her in Sebring, Florida. Smith died in Sebring on 6 March 1915. Her funeral was held in Chicago at the Quinn Chapel AME Church. Children from the orphanage sang at the funeral, and addresses were made by the chairman of the orphanage committee, F. L. Barnett, and the school principal, Mrs. E. J. Austin. Reverend John Anderson presided over the service.

Smith lived a full life, which is only partly documented in her autobiography. Even with a biography that exceeds five hundred pages, the reader is left with many gaps in Smith's life. The passages that mention her second marriage hint that it was not a happy one: Smith alludes to her husband's absence at their child's funeral, for example, but does not describe her feelings in relation to these events. Similarly, she is more forthright in her discussions of the resistance she encounters because of her gender, even when there are implications that her race is just as, if not more, significant—as, for example, in the case of the placards for her appearances in England, which promote her as if she were an exotic carnival attraction. Smith ignores this implication, however, as well as the fact that she was advertised against her wishes. She seems to downplay her racial difference in favor of gender difference in order to stress her common humanity.

Smith, like other black autobiographers, is not merely concerned with presenting an objective account of her life, but also seeks to prove, in the cultural context of increased and often violent racist actions, the humanity of African Americans. She establishes this humanity through her concern for the spiritual welfare of herself and others. The genre of the autobiography is particularly suitable for her mission of evangelism, giving her the opportunity not only to record her missionary work, but also to proselytize more directly. Through her text Smith envisions the immortality of her mission, continuing to save souls even after her death. She closes her autobiography with an explanation of its purpose: "my whole object and wish is that God will make it a blessing to all who may read it."

References:

Jualynne E. Dodson, introduction to *An Autobiography: The Story of the Lord's Dealings with Mrs. Amanda Smith the Colored Evangelist,* by Smith (New York: Oxford University Press, 1988), pp. xxvii–xxxiv;

Marshall W. Taylor, *The Life, Travels, Labors, and Helpers of Mrs. Amanda Smith, the Famous Negro Missionary Evangelist* (Cincinnati: Cranston & Stowe, 1887).

Harriet Prescott Spofford

(3 April 1835 – 14 August 1921)

Jennifer Putzi
University of Nebraska at Lincoln

See also the Spofford entry in *DLB 74: American Short-Story Writers Before 1880.*

BOOKS: *Sir Rohan's Ghost: A Romance* (Boston: Tilton, 1860);

The Amber Gods and Other Stories (Boston: Ticknor & Fields, 1863);

Azarian: An Episode (Boston: Ticknor & Fields, 1864);

New-England Legends (Boston: Osgood, 1871);

The Thief in the Night (Boston: Roberts, 1872; London: Sampson Low, 1872);

Art Decoration Applied to Furniture (New York: Harper, 1878);

The Servant Girl Question (Boston: Houghton, Mifflin, 1881);

Poems (Boston: Houghton, Mifflin, 1882);

The Marquis of Carabas (Boston: Roberts, 1882);

Hester Stanley at St. Marks (Boston: Roberts, 1882);

Ballads about Authors (Boston: Lothrop, 1887);

A Lost Jewel (Boston: Lee & Shepard, 1891);

House and Hearth (New York: Dodd, Mead, 1891);

A Scarlet Poppy and Other Stories (New York: Harper, 1894);

A Master Spirit (New York: Scribners, 1896);

An Inheritance (New York: Scribners, 1897);

In Titian's Garden and Other Poems (Boston: Copeland & Day, 1897);

Stepping-Stones to Happiness (New York: Christian Herald, 1897);

Priscilla's Love-Story (Chicago & New York: Stone, 1898);

Hester Stanley's Friends (Boston: Little, Brown, 1898);

The Maid He Married (Chicago & New York: Stone, 1899);

Old Madame and Other Tragedies (Boston: Badger, 1900);

The Children of the Valley (New York: Crowell, 1901);

The Great Procession and Other Verses for and about Children (Boston: Badger, 1902);

That Betty (New York, Chicago, Toronto, London & Edinburgh: Revell, 1903);

Four Days of God (Boston: Badger, 1905);

Old Washington (Boston: Little, Brown, 1906);

Harriet Prescott Spofford

The Fairy Changeling. A Flower and Fairy Play (Boston: Badger, 1911);

The Making of a Fortune. A Romance (New York & London: Harper, 1911);

The King's Easter (Boston: World Peace Foundation, 1912);

A Little Book of Friends (Boston: Little, Brown, 1916);

The Elder's People (Boston & New York: Houghton Mifflin, 1920).

322

OTHER: "Mary Louise Booth," "Rose Terry Cooke," "Clara Louise Kellog," "Louise Chandler Moulton," in *Our Famous Women* (Hartford, Conn.: A. D. Worthington / Chicago: A. D. Nettleton, 1884), pp. 117–133, 174–206, 359–385, 498–520;

"Priscilla," in *Three Heroines of New England Romance* (Boston: Little, Brown, 1894), pp. 15–60;

Charlotte Brontë, *Jane Eyre*, introduction by Spofford (New York, 1898);

"Our Very Wishes" and "Tom's Money," in *The Wit and Humor of America*, 10 volumes, edited by Marshall P. Wilder (New York & London: Funk & Wagnalls, 1911), IX: 1637–1653 and X: 1955–1964.

SELECTED PERIODICAL PUBLICATIONS– UNCOLLECTED:

FICTION

"Yet's Christmas Box," *Harper's New Monthly Magazine,* 20 (April 1860): 644–659;

"How Charlie Came Home," *Harper's New Monthly Magazine,* 22 (January 1861): 186–198;

"The Tale of the Trefetheness," *Harper's New Monthly Magazine,* 22 (March 1861): 489–512;

"Madeleine Schaeffer," *Harper's New Monthly Magazine,* 25 (June 1862): 37–52; (October 1862): 651–660; (November 1862): 753–764;

"The Strathsays," *Atlantic Monthly,* 11 (January 1863): 99–118;

"Dark Ways," *Atlantic Monthly,* 11 (May 1863): 545–565;

"Fiery Colliery of Fiennes," *Harper's New Monthly Magazine,* 27 (October 1863): 613–627;

"Ray," *Atlantic Monthly,* 13 (January 1864): 19–39;

"Our Bridget," *Harper's New Monthly Magazine,* 28 (February 1864): 388–395;

"Sold for a Song," *Harper's New Monthly Magazine,* 28 (May 1864): 745–752;

"The Rim," *Atlantic Monthly,* 13 (May 1864): 605–615; (June 1864): 701–713; 14 (July 1864): 63–73;

"Mrs. Gisborne's Way," *Harper's New Monthly Magazine,* 29 (October 1864): 585–594;

"The True Story of Luigi," *Atlantic Monthly,* 14 (October 1864): 411–423;

"Mrs. Buswell's Christmas," *Harper's Weekly,* 8 (31 December 1864): 842–843;

"Poor Isabel," *Harper's New Monthly Magazine,* 30 (March 1865): 459–475;

"Mr. Furbush," *Harper's New Monthly Magazine,* 30 (April 1865): 623–626;

"Down the River," *Atlantic Monthly,* 16 (October 1865): 468–490;

"A Mad Night," *Beadle's Monthly,* 1 (February 1866): 160–167; (March 1866): 235–242;

"An Hour at Sea," *Harper's New Monthly Magazine,* 33 (July 1866): 250–254;

"D'Outre Mort," *Galaxy,* 2 (15 November 1866): 516–529;

"The Marshes," *Harper's New Monthly Magazine,* 35 (June 1867): 94–107;

"The Hungry Heart," *Harper's New Monthly Magazine,* 35 (November 1867): 740–748;

"Elisabetta's Christmas," *Galaxy,* 5 (January 1868): 60–77;

"Flotsam and Jetsam," *Atlantic Monthly,* 21 (January 1868): 7–16; (February 1868): 186–198; (March 1868): 313–325;

"The Black Bess," *Galaxy,* 5 (May 1868): 517–528;

"The Strange Passengers," *Lippincott's Magazine,* 1 (June 1868): 647–657;

"In the Maguerriwock," *Harper's New Monthly Magazine,* 37 (August 1868): 348–355;

"Lost and Found," *Atlantic Monthly,* 22 (August 1868): 243–251;

"The Moonstone Mass," *Harper's New Monthly Magazine,* 37 (October 1868): 655–661;

"The Unknown Guest," *Lady's Friend,* 6 (February 1869): 116–121;

"Rougegorge," *Lippincott's Magazine,* 3 (May 1869): 501–516;

"Two Hearts," *Harper's New Monthly Magazine,* 41 (August 1870): 374–383;

"Little Ben," *Atlantic Monthly,* 26 (September 1870): 309–321;

"A Pilot's Wife," *Harper's New Monthly Magazine,* 41 (November 1870): 860–868;

"Louie," *Lippincott's Magazine,* 6 (December 1870): 589–604;

"Miss Moggaridge's Provider," *Atlantic Monthly,* 27 (January 1871): 17–27;

"Footpads," *Atlantic Monthly,* 27 (April 1871): 401–413;

"Wedding Presents," *Harper's New Monthly Magazine,* 44 (February 1872): 441–447;

"Aunt Pen's Funeral," *Harper's New Monthly Magazine,* 45 (June 1872): 60–64;

"The Beautiful Miss Vavasour," *Harper's New Monthly Magazine,* 46 (May 1873): 852–858;

"Jo and I," *Harper's New Monthly Magazine,* 48 (March 1874): 562–572;

"At Last," *Scribner's Monthly,* 8 (May 1874): 90–99;

"Miss Susan's Love Affair," *Harper's New Monthly Magazine,* 53 (June 1876): 26–32;

"Romance of a Barn-Yard," *Harper's New Monthly Magazine,* 54 (February 1877): 446–448;

"The Drift-Wood Fire," *Harper's New Monthly Magazine,* 61 (November 1880): 888–893;

"The Mount of Sorrow," *Harper's New Monthly Magazine,* 67 (June 1883): 128–136;

"At the Princess Ida's," *Lippincott's Magazine,* 34 (July 1884): 50–58;

"Three Quiet Ladies of the Name of Luce," *Harper's New Monthly Magazine*, 69 (November 1884): 887–892;

"Mrs. Hetty's Husband," *Cosmopolitan*, 1 (May 1886): 135–142;

"A Watch in the Night," *Harper's New Monthly Magazine*, 88 (December 1893): 147–152;

"The Godmothers," *Cosmopolitan*, 20 (March 1896): 461–471;

"A Case of Nerves," *Harper's New Monthly Magazine*, 104 (December 1901): 61–65;

"A Sacrifice," *Atlantic Monthly*, 91 (May 1903): 616–626;

"An Angel in the House," *Harper's New Monthly Magazine*, 107 (June 1903): 78–82;

"The Ray of Displacement," *Metropolitan*, 19 (October 1903): 37–47;

"The Story of the Queen," *Atlantic Monthly*, 92 (November 1903): 586–594; (December 1903): 775–786;

"Jolly's Father," *Harper's New Monthly Magazine*, 115 (October 1907): 761–770;

"The Rose," *Harper's New Monthly Magazine*, 105 (October 1912): 739–744;

"A Homely Sacrifice," *Harper's New Monthly Magazine*, 129 (November 1914): 853–860;

"The Mad Lady," *Scribner's Monthly*, 59 (February 1916): 238–245.

NONFICTION

"Lucy Larcom's Poems," *Galaxy*, 7 (February 1869): 298–299;

"Newburyport and Its Neighborhood," *Harper's New Monthly Magazine*, 51 (July 1875): 161–180;

"Louisa May Alcott," *Chautauquan*, 9 (December 1888): 160–162;

"Mrs. Deland's Short Stories," *Book-Buyer*, 17 (December 1898): 412–414.

In a career that spanned more than sixty years Harriet Prescott Spofford produced thirty-two books, hundreds of short stories and poems, and dozens of nonfiction articles on subjects ranging from her literary acquaintances to the decoration of furniture. Spofford's stories and articles were published in the most prestigious literary periodicals of the late nineteenth and early twentieth centuries, including *The Atlantic Monthly, Harper's New Monthly Magazine*, and *Scribner's Monthly*. She also contributed frequently to some of the most popular women's magazines of the period, such as *Harper's Bazar* and *Cosmopolitan*. She was an important figure in the development of American Romanticism and of American realism. She also wrote works in popular genres such as detective fiction and the supernatural tale. Throughout her lifetime she received praise and admiration from readers and critics. Yet, her contributions to American literature have been underestimated by scholars in the late twentieth century. Her immense body of work is rarely considered as a whole. While her many short stories represent her best work, she is still known for only a few early stories. Her life and work are representative of the struggles and accomplishments of many women writers of her period, who attempted to balance domesticity and a career, financial success and art, popular appeal and critical approval.

Born in the frontier town of Calais, Maine, on 3 April 1835, Harriet Elizabeth Prescott was the first child of Joseph Newmarch Prescott and Sarah Jane Bridges Prescott. The Prescott family had settled in New England in 1640 and had apparently prospered until Prescott's grandfather, William Pepperell Prescott, a shipowner and merchant, was financially ruined during the War of 1812. Joseph Prescott struggled throughout his life to return the Prescott family to prosperity. During Harriet's childhood in Calais, her father is said to have been a lumber merchant, a lawyer, the postmaster, and the director of a Democratic newspaper called the *Down Easter*. Ill health and bad luck marked his efforts to make his fortune, and in 1850 he decided to go west, where he settled in Oregon City, Oregon. He left behind his wife and four children: Harriet, Mary Newmarch (born 2 August 1838), Katherine Montague (born 5 May 1844), and Otis Livingstone (born 5 October 1846). The last child, Edith Josephine, was born on 14 October 1850. (Two other Prescott children had died in infancy.) Joseph's move fractured the family: Sarah Prescott and the younger children remained in Calais, while Harriet went to live with an aunt, Elizabeth Prescott Betton, in Newburyport, Massachusetts. Newburyport became an important site in Spofford's life and writing. She lived there off and on until her death in 1921 and set many of her stories in Newburyport or coastal towns similar to it.

Throughout her schooling, Harriet Prescott was praised for her writing skills. In Newburyport she attended the Putnam Free School, an innovative institution that offered students an ambitious course of study. She wrote for the school newspaper *The Experiment*, and composed dramatic dialogues for the anniversary exercises. When she was sixteen, her essay on William Shakespeare's *Hamlet* won a first prize in a contest sponsored by Thomas Wentworth Higginson. At the time Higginson had been living in Newburyport for a few years, having arrived there in 1847 as pastor of the Unitarian Church. He was forced to resign his position in 1849 because of his Abolitionist beliefs, but he remained in Newburyport until 1852. He later served in the Civil War and became a frequent contributor to *The Atlantic Monthly*, but he is perhaps best known for his "Letter to a Young Contributor," to which Emily Dickinson responded in 1862. Harriet Prescott's association with Higginson was furthered by her position as a teacher of working-class students in a program that he directed in Newburyport.

After graduating from the Putnam Free School, Harriet joined Sarah Prescott and the younger children, who had settled in Derry, New Hampshire. There she attended the Pinkerton Academy from 1853 to 1855, continuing to write poetry and prose. This apprenticeship served Spofford well when she turned to her writing for financial support.

Finally, in 1856, the entire family, Joseph Prescott included, was reunited in Newburyport. However, he had not made his fortune in Oregon City, where he had served as mayor from 1852 to 1855. He returned home in ill health, and lived the next twenty years of his life as an invalid. With her mother's health also impaired, the responsibility for supporting the family fell to Prescott. For the rest of her life she supported her family financially and emotionally.

In the 1850s Prescott began publishing her work in the Boston story papers; these writings have never been identified or collected. A *Harper's Bazar* "Personal" (9 March 1872) recalled "how she toiled over her first stories, and the small prices she received for them, though the sums looked large to her inexperienced eyes." Prescott remembered, "how she once wrote all night to finish a story to be submitted in competition for a prize, and how her hand and arm were swollen and inflamed from incessant use when she laid down the completed work, and how, after all, she did not receive the prize." After the publication of her story "In a Cellar" in the February 1859 issue of *The Atlantic Monthly,* however, she found more profitable and more fulfilling work.

The international setting and intrigue of "In a cellar" caused some doubt as to whether a young woman with Prescott's limited experience could have imagined it. James Russell Lowell, the editor of the magazine, suspected that "In a Cellar" was a translation of a French story. With the support of Higginson, however, the story was published, and Prescott received $105 for it, a payment far greater than any she had received from the story papers. "In a Cellar" demonstrates many of the strengths of the author's best work: creative first-person narration, elaborate description, and complex characterization, particularly of female characters. The narrator of "In a Cellar" is a diplomat/detective whose search for a stolen diamond takes him from London to Paris. The detective plot is complicated by the appearance of Madame de St. Cyr, who has social connections but is quickly running out of money. She wants her beautiful daughter, Delphine, to make an advantageous marriage, but Delphine resists her mother's matchmaking—not because she has an idealized notion of romantic love, but rather because she desires wealth, passion, and, above all, power. In the process of finding the diamond, the nar-

Harriet Prescott as a young woman (from Elizabeth K. Halbeisen, Harriet Prescott Spofford: A Romantic Survival, *1935)*

rator provides Delphine an opportunity to fulfill her ambition, but only through marriage. The story is an incisive critique of the avenues available for ambitious women. The publication of "In a Cellar" and the enthusiastic attention that it received ensured Prescott a place on the list of contributors to the prestigious *Atlantic Monthly.* In July 1859 she attended an *Atlantic Monthly* dinner in honor of Harriet Beecher Stowe, where she met Lowell, John Greenleaf Whittier, and Henry Wadsworth Longfellow. This early success with *The Atlantic Monthly* helped Prescott to sell stories to other periodicals as well, and in 1863 Ticknor and Fields, publishers of *The Atlantic Monthly,* published her first collection of stories.

Except for the previously unpublished "Desert Sand," all the stories in *The Amber Gods and Other Stories* (1863) appeared in *The Atlantic Monthly* between 1859 and 1862: "In a Cellar" (February 1859), "The Amber Gods" (January and February 1860), "Circumstance" (May 1860), "Midsummer and May" (November and December 1860), "Knitting Sale-Socks" (February 1861), and "The South Breaker" (May and June 1862). With the exception of "Midsummer and May," these stories are among the finest of Spofford's career. The book was a critical success, and several of the stories in it were republished throughout Spofford's career. The title story expands on the theme of female ambition and power found in "In a Cellar." Arrogant, assertive, and passionate, Yone Willoughby, the antithesis of the traditional nineteenth-century heroine, is disdainful of the moral dictates of religion and society. She claims, "I'm not good, of course; I wouldn't give a fig to be good." Yone is juxtaposed with her more-traditional cousin, Louise, and their differences in character are suggested by their jewelry, clothing, and behavior toward Vaughan Rose, the man they both love. As an artist, Rose cannot resist Yone's vibrant beauty; he is drawn away from Louise and marries Yone, who recognizes that she has become his artistic inspiration: "shades and combinations that he had hardly touched or known, before, he had to lavish now; he learned more than some years might have taught him; he, who worshipped beauty, saw how thoroughly I possessed it; he has told me that through me he learned the sacredness of color."

Rose, however, soon tires of Yone, after having drained her emotionally and physically in his pursuit of beauty. At the end of the story, Yone lies dying of a hereditary disease, aware that her husband is still in love with Louise and has already begun to court her in anticipation of Yone's death. Yone's only regret is that she was not able to keep Rose's love once she won it away from her cousin. Refusing to condemn Yone's pride and apparent amorality, Prescott creates sympathy for her, and for all ambitious women, whose only access to power, influence, and art is through their physical beauty.

"The South Breaker" is an early example of the regional fiction that Spofford wrote throughout her career. Set in a coastal fishing village, this story dramatizes the awareness of storms and ships at sea that is integral to such communities. The narrator is another strong female character. Georgie is in love with Dan, who has married his young ward, Faith, in response to the pressures of the community. But Georgie believes that she and Dan are truly meant for one another: "There we were, both of us thoroughly conscious, yet neither of us expressing it by a word, and trying not to by a look,—both of us content to wait for the next life, when we could belong to one another." The superficial Faith, who is unaware of Dan's superiority to other men, falls in love with the wealthy and frivolous Gabriel des Violets and runs away with him. After they are killed in an accident on the South Breaker, Georgie and Dan are left to pursue a relationship. Strong women such as Georgie, who must adapt to the dangers inherent in coastal life, appear in other Spofford stories, such as "The Marshes" (1867), "A Pilot's Wife (1870), and "At Last" (1874).

A third story in *The Amber Gods and Other Stories* is perhaps Spofford's best-known work. "Circumstance" blends romantic and realistic techniques in a powerful story about the struggles of a woman to define herself as an artist in the midst of conflicting responsibilities and

desires. This theme apparently caught the attention of Emily Dickinson, who, after reading the story in *The Atlantic Monthly,* wrote to her sister-in-law Susan Gilbert Dickinson, "This is the only thing I ever saw in my life I did not think I could have written myself."

In "Circumstance," an unnamed frontier woman, returning home through the woods from the bedside of a sick friend, is captured by a "wild beast—the most savage and serpentine and subtle and fearless of our latitudes—known by hunters as the Indian Devil." Held captive in a tree by the beast, the woman discovers that her singing will keep it from devouring her, and she sings throughout the night until her husband finds and kill the beast. She gradually gains control over her voice and varies her songs according to the responses of the beast: "she had learned the secret of sound at last." The woman's singing holds the Indian Devil at bay; yet, his caprice forces her continually to alter her songs, to go from lullabies, to hornpipes, to an Irish jig, to "mournful ballads," and, finally, to the hymns that turn her mind to God. As the night progresses, she begins to fear that her voice might fail her. Realizing the limitations of her singing and of herself as an artist, the woman learns to take pleasure in her song, not for its life-saving potential, but for its own sake. The woman artist's struggle to create despite distractions and conflicting needs was one that Spofford had already experienced by the time the story was published in 1860, and she continued to experience it for the rest of her life.

For twentieth-century readers "Circumstance" is complicated by Spofford's treatment of the Native American presence. At the end of the story, when the woman, her husband, and their infant child emerge from the forest, they find their home and the surrounding farms destroyed: "Desolation and death were indeed there, and beneficence and life in the forest. Tomahawk and scalping-knife, descending during that night, had left behind them only this work of their accomplished hatred and one subtle foot-print in the snow." The Native Americans are labelled "savages," and their supposedly animalistic nature is reflected in the naming of the "Indian Devil," who had previously captured the woman in the forest. Spofford's conception of race and racism is quite typical of her period, but it should be examined further by modern scholars of her work. After the publication of "Circumstance," Spofford's attitude toward race is revealed primarily through stories that feature African American characters. In stories such as "The True Story of Luigi" (1864) and "Down the River" (1865), her depictions of African American characters are often sympathetic and complex but also marked by the racist stereotypes commonly used by many nineteenth-century American writers.

Other successful publications contributed to Spofford's growing reputation in the 1860s. Two romantic novels, *Sir Rohan's Ghost* (1860) and *Azarian* (1864), received warm praise and acknowledgment of their young author's potential. *Azarian,* however, received one rather lengthy negative review in the *North American Review* (January 1865) from Henry James, who objected to the author's adherence to romanticism. Despite the success of *The Amber Gods and Other Stories,* Spofford did not publish another collection of short stories until 1894. Nonetheless, she wrote many impressive stories for *The Atlantic Monthly* and other journals.

Perhaps reflecting her own experiences, many of Spofford's best stories of the 1860s address issues of women and economics. In one uncollected story, "Yet's Christmas Box" (1860), a young governess struggles to support herself through work and marriage. "The Strathsays" (1863) returns to the issue of the importance of marriage to a young woman's economic future. In this story an ambitious mother is determined to arrange marriages for her four daughters, without concern for their plans or desires. After the face of one daughter, Alice, is burned and scarred, she, her family, and her lover are forced to reassess her economic and marital potential. Despite her mother's assertion that no man would have such "a fright," Alice's lover returns, and the two are reconciled after he assures her that her physical appearance is insignificant. Throughout her career, Spofford continued to write about women's precarious economic position and their lack of opportunities outside marriage.

During the 1860s Spofford also experimented with developing popular genres. "In a Cellar" established Spofford as one of the first women to contribute to the genre of detective fiction, said to have begun in 1841 with the publication of Edgar Allan Poe's "The Murders in the Rue Morgue." She created her own detective, Mr. Furbush, for two later stories, both published in *Harper's New Monthly Magazine:* "Mr. Furbush" (1865) and "In the Maguerriwock" (1868). In contrast to "In a Cellar," which is set in fashionable Paris society, "In the Maguerriwock" is set in "an almost uncivilized region of the frontier forest" in Maine. Mr. Furbush suspects that the aptly named Mr. Craven has been involved in the murder Furbush has been hired to investigate. The sheriff tells him that he is wrong, while also underlining the precarious legal position of married women: "I couldn't say of myself that he abused any body but his wife; and a judge in Illinois decided lately that that was nothing—the wife must adopt more conciliating conduct." Craven's wife, who has been driven insane by her husband's abuse and her knowledge of the crime he has indeed committed, provides the key to the mystery with her repeated exclamation, "Three men went down cellar, and only two came up!"

Like other nineteenth-century American women writers, such as Elizabeth Stuart Phelps and Louisa May Alcott, Spofford also wrote supernatural tales, including

"The Black Bess," published in the May 1868 issue of *Galaxy.* The male narrator is an engineer who begins to imagine that he sees his fiancée, Margaret, on the tracks ahead of his train. He must decide whether to obey his urges and stop the engine, or to run the vision down, as his doctor says he should, in order to dispel his "pursuing phantom." "The Black Bess" addresses issues of sexuality and carefully analyzes men's fear of and attraction to the nineteenth-century domestic woman, as represented by Margaret. Spofford's work is remarkable for the way in which she uses the developing conventions of popular fictional genres to address women's issues.

Spofford's success as a writer corresponded with developments in her personal life that brought their own joys and sorrows. In 1860, at the age of twenty-five, Prescott became engaged to Richard S. Spofford Jr., a lawyer with a practice in Newburyport. In a 17 March 1863 letter, written during their engagement, Gail Hamilton (Mary Abigail Dodge) observed that Prescott "is as good as gold, but believes in nothing, past or future, man or woman, but is desperately in love with Dick Spofford." They were married on 19 December 1865. By all accounts the marriage was a success; the Spoffords were deeply in love and supportive of one another's careers. They eventually divided their time between Washington, D.C., and Newburyport because of Richard's flourishing legal and political career. On 30 January 1867, a son was born to the couple, only to die less than a year later. Spofford never had another child and lamented the loss of her infant in several published poems. Spofford's success and that of her husband helped to alleviate the financial burdens of her parents and siblings. Yet, as Spofford's biographer Elizabeth K. Halbeisen points out, "Although the economic pressure of the early period had indubitably lightened, there are indications in Harriet Spofford's letters of the seventies and eighties that the generosity with which she and her husband treated the Prescott-Spofford families required continual exercise of the now too facile pen."

In 1868 Spofford began to publish frequently in *Harper's Bazar,* edited by Mary Louise Booth, continuing to sell stories to this magazine into the late 1890s. Spofford's *Harper's Bazar* stories are much more conventional than those published in other periodicals. Spofford's relationship with Booth and *Harper's Bazar* is interesting, however, because it highlights the negotiations that nineteenth-century women writers had to make between domesticity and professional authorship. In an essay on Booth published in the 1884 collection *Our Famous Women,* Spofford defined *Harper's Bazar* as "a weekly journal devoted to the pleasure and improvement of the domestic circle." She went on to claim both literary merit and a moral purpose for the magazine: "There is scarcely a poet, or a story-writer, or novelist of any rank in America or England who is not a contributor to its pages, and its purity, its self-respect, its

Spofford's husband, Richard S. Spofford Jr.

high standard, and its literary excellence, are unrivalled among periodical publications. The influence of such a paper within American homes is something hardly to be computed." This emphasis on virtue and the family indicates a shift in Spofford's sense of audience since the publication of "The Amber Gods," at least for her contributions to *Harper's Bazar*. The amoral Yone Willoughby and the power-hungry Delphine St. Cyr could not have appeared in the pages of *Harper's Bazar* unless accompanied by a complete condemnation of their "unfeminine" behavior.

This glorification of the domestic intensified in writings by and about Spofford, to the point that she became virtually identified in the public mind with her house on Deer Island, Massachusetts, which she and Richard Spofford purchased in 1874. Many mentions of Spofford in newspapers and magazines include a description of her home and her domestic habits. Spofford's brother and sisters were frequently at Deer Island with their families, and both of her parents lived with her until their deaths in the early 1880s. She also had many guests at her home on the island, including writers such as Whittier and Rose Terry Cooke. Spofford was often publicly commended for being the ideal woman writer,

unwilling to sacrifice her domestic happiness for her writing. A *Harper's Bazar* "Personal" (27 April 1872) even claimed that Spofford did not enjoy writing, "but pursues it with most delicate conscience, since she has made it her work, and finishes it with the utmost care." She was said to enjoy writing poetry, a more "ladylike" genre, much more than prose. Etta R. Goodwin observed in the *Chautauquan* (September 1898), "Home life means so much to her that even when she is writing she does not demand seclusion. No more domestic woman ever existed, and no woman ever existed who believed more thoroughly in what are called the rights of women." Her authority as a hostess and housekeeper extended to her writing; she published articles and a few books on domestic subjects. Many of her articles on furniture and interior decorating, initially published in *Harper's New Monthly Magazine* and *Harper's Bazar,* were collected in *Art Decoration Applied to Furniture* (1878) and *House and Hearth* (1891).

Spofford's domestic bliss was disrupted by the death of her husband on 1 August 1888, when she was fifty-three years old. His death, as well as those of her sister Mary and her mother-in-law in the late 1880s, affected Spofford deeply, and she turned to her friends and her writing for fulfillment. She became increasingly involved with a Boston circle of women writers, which included Cooke, Alice Brown, Annie Adams Fields, Louise Imogen Guiney, Gail Hamilton, Sarah Orne Jewett, Louise Chandler Moulton, Celia Thaxter, and Anne Whitney. The extent to which these women influenced each other's work has yet to be examined. Spofford commemorated several of these relationships in *A Little Book of Friends* (1916), for which she wrote brief biographies of each woman and detailed the history of their friendship. Throughout her career Spofford published articles in various magazines on these and other women writers and their work, including Lucy Larcom (*Galaxy,* February 1869), Louisa May Alcott (*Chautauquan,* December 1888), and Margaret Deland (*Book-Buyer,* December 1898). Other important relationships of the period included her friendships with her niece Katherine Mosely and with Marion Pierce, whose father died in 1885 when she was twelve years old, leaving Marion and her brother to Spofford's care, "well knowing," as Spofford wrote in *Harper's Bazar* (21 November 1889), "the value which her considerable care and affection may be to them, and how much advantage their education may derive from her oversight and advice."

In 1894 Spofford published her second collection of adult fiction, *A Scarlet Poppy and Other Stories.* The stories in this collection are different from those in her early collection. Here Spofford turns a satirical eye on courtship and marriage in humorous stories such as "An Ideal," (*The Continent,* 24 October 1883), in which an elderly husband laments the loss of his first love, Alicia. He is taken aback when his wife points out that Alicia has grown into an old, distasteful woman and is indeed the unpleasant guest who has been staying in their house for weeks. In "Mrs. Claxton's Skeleton" a wife forces her husband to recognize her worth when she saves him and their neighbors from a flood. "A Composite Wife" (previously unpublished) is a satirical attack on men to whom all women are the same as long as they are quiet, domestic, and, above all, attentive to their mates. About to marry for the fourth time, Mr. Chipperley happily feels "that he had never been a widower," because his May, Marion, Maria, and Mary have been so completely alike. "The Tragic Story of Binns" (1886) features a romance between a cook and a butcher's boy, examining the conventions of romantic fiction.

Other humorous stories by Spofford remain uncollected. In "Lost and Found" (1868) the narrator, a shy woman who has lost her husband in New York City, fears being thought of as a prostitute or a vagrant. In "Wedding Presents" (1872), "Three Quiet Ladies of the Name of Luce" (1884), and "Mrs. Hetty's Husband" (1886), Spofford explores the economic and social situations of "old maids," creating characters that are sometimes good, sometimes pathetic, but always humorous.

Published six years after *A Scarlet Poppy and Other Stories, Old Madame and Other Tragedies* (1900) is a strong collection that experiments once again with the boundaries between romantic and realistic fiction. Several particularly good stories appear in the collection, such as "Old Madame," "Her Story," "The Wages of Sin," and "Ordronnaux."

In "Old Madame" Elizabeth Champernoune, "a stately old woman" whose aristocratic family has lost its wealth and power, attempts to cling to social superiority throughout hardships that she believes have been caused by a curse put on the family by the fisherman Ben Bevoises. Forced to watch helplessly as her family dies one by one and her last remaining granddaughter falls in love with Bevoises's grandson, Old Madame remains strong and dignified throughout her trials, and ultimately allows her granddaughter to marry young Bevoises, knowing that their wedding will mean the end of the Champernoune legacy and the aristocracy of the island. The sympathetic portrayal of this complex character reveals Spofford's respect for the struggles of independent women.

"A Lost Identity" and "Her Story" address the issue of women in insane asylums. In "Her Story," the narrator tells a visitor the story of her imprisonment in an insane asylum. She describes her relationship with her husband, Spencer, and his affair with a vivacious young woman, a distant relative of his who had come to live with them. As she passively watched her husband fall in love with the woman, the narrator began to hear voices and considered killing herself and/or her husband. The narrator's last memory before waking up in the asylum is

seeing her husband and the young woman in a passionate embrace. Committed to the asylum by her husband, she waits for the day when he will come to take her back to her home and her children: "I shall hear his voice, I shall rest in his arms, I shall be blest again." "Her Story" is a powerful contribution to a tradition of women's writings about women and insanity, including works by E. D. E. N. Southworth, Fanny Fern, Rebecca Harding Davis, and Charlotte Perkins Gilman's "The Yellow Wallpaper" (1892). Spofford returned to this topic in later stories, including "The Rose" (1912) and "The Mad Lady" (1916).

"The Wages of Sin" is one of the strongest stories from the latter half of Spofford's career. Judith Dauntry, a "fallen woman," lives with Ellis Goff, who has abandoned his wife and child for her. The couple endures harsh criticism and physical attack from the townspeople and Judith, the stronger of the two, must support Ellis and their relationship throughout this crisis. While Ellis offers to divorce his wife and marry Judith, she insists that they are "a law to ourselves" and asks: "I have no voice in making the law, why should I obey it?" When townspeople burn down Judith and Ellis's barn, Ellis is caught in the flames and becomes an invalid, completely dependent on Judith. Her strength and perseverance begin to impress others, and, after a meeting in which Judith stands up to the minister and defends her way of life, the minister preaches a sermon on "the rights of the individual sinner." The couple is gradually left alone; yet, Ellis is not strong enough to resist the intrusive morality of the community or share Judith's righteousness. He lives the rest of his life "as if he felt himself to be the thing his torturers had made him." As in so many of Spofford's stories that feature strong, irreverent women, Judith is not censured for her sins: "She had ceased to think of herself as an abandoned woman; so far as she thought of it at all she had a dim sense of being virtuous." "The Wages of Sin" is a remarkable analysis of village life and the impact that gossip and social ostracism can have on an individual and a relationship. It is also one of the most complex and sympathetic nineteenth-century portraits of a "fallen woman."

Spofford used her experiences in Washington, D.C., as the inspiration for *Old Washington* (1906), a series of interconnected stories in which she describes the upheaval of post–Civil War Washington, in which her characters struggle to find personal and professional happiness. Spofford focuses on female characters, who frequently attempt to make their voices heard in a political system that officially excludes them. The stories in the collection include "A Thanksgiving Breakfast," "A Guardian Angel," "In A Conspiracy," "A Little Old Woman," and "The Colonel's Christmas." Some of the stories are occasionally marred by simplicity and excessive conventionality. "A Guardian Angel," for example, is particularly disturbing

Deer Island-in-the-Merrimack, Spofford's home from 1874 until her death in 1915

in its portrait of Tolly, a competent black woman who tells her former owner, Mrs. Gilroy, that despite what the government says, she still belongs to the Gilroys.

"A Thanksgiving Breakfast" is notable for its portrayal of young working women: Jinny, an actress, and Celeste, a journalist. Celeste asserts the social importance of her occupation, claiming, "it isn't disgraceful. . . . You need a great deal of enlightenment. . . . I tell the social happenings; and I don't know that they are not as much to the purpose really as the political happenings." "In A Conspiracy" is a dramatic story whose heroine uses her beauty and intelligence in the service of Cuban independence. Gloria Campeador contrives to make Congressman Harry Bentinck fall in love with her so that she can persuade him to support the Cuban cause. Her work is presented as essential to the cause; another revolutionary tells her, "The work you are doing in making these friends, in silencing these enemies and these possible enemies, is equal to guns." Gloria actually falls in love with and marries Harry. With his support she becomes a powerful influence in Cuban affairs. There are several other women in *Old Washington* who attempt to influence politicians, but none are as revolutionary as Gloria. In "A Thanksgiving Breakfast" the usually retiring and demure Miss Veronica successfully lobbies to get a bill through Congress. Mrs. Spence, the main character of "A Little Old Woman," fails miserably in her attempt to make a claim for damages to her late husband's southern plantation. While visiting the Senate chambers, she has a mental breakdown, announcing that the president must surrender and that the United States belongs to her husband. All the characters in *Old Washington,* however, are ultimately supported and

strengthened by a community of people who have been displaced by the Civil War and are reconstructing their lives in the capital city.

Spofford's final collection of short stories, *The Elder's People* (1920), is the culmination of her lifelong interest in regionalism. The book is a series of fourteen interconnected stories set in a rural New England community known only as "the settlement." The people of this small town depend of the guidance of two figures: Elder Perry, a traditional male religious leader, and Miss Mahala Brooks, a wise "old maid" who "often played the part of colleague in plain clothes" to Elder Perry. The people recognize that Miss Mahala "had been not only his curate, but his conscience. He learned to know his people and love them every one, but Miss Mahala knew their fathers and their grandfathers, had seen most of them the day they were born, and could tell to a nicety what strains of inheritance they carried and what might be expected of them." While they are "Elder's People," most of the characters rely on Miss Mahala, the community, and their sense of a shared history for strength. Even Elder Perry needs advice at times and turns to his mother for wisdom and comfort in "A Blessing Called Peace" (previously published as "An Easter Blessing" in the 15 April 1911 issue of *Outlook*).

Several of the stories in this collection, including "The Deacon's Whistle" and "A Change of Heart," focus on the positive and negative roles of gossip in small communities such as the settlement. In "A Rural Telephone" old Mrs. Dacie has taken to her bed in protest of her daughter Nancy's love affair with Saul Manners. Bedridden, Mrs. Dacie listens in on other people's telephone conversations for entertainment. She tells her daughter, "Fact

is, Nancy, it's like a continnered story in the papers."
When the neighbors become frustrated with Mrs.
Dacie's habit, they repeat false gossip and fool Mrs.
Dacie into leaping out of bed and allowing Nancy and
Saul to get married. The plots of the stories revolve
around young lovers who, for one reason or another,
have been prevented from marrying. Usually through
the assistance of Miss Mahala or Elder Perry, conflicts
are resolved, couples marry, and the perpetuation of the
settlement is guaranteed.

The Elder's People was received favorably by critics,
who praised its accurate portrayal of New England life and
characters. It is an important book in Spofford's body of
work because of its realistic portrayals of characters and
their dialect, as well as the settlement itself. It deserves to
be studied alongside the regional writing of women such
as Cooke, Margaret Deland, Mary Wilkins Freeman, and
Sarah Orne Jewett. Spofford recognized the changing
tastes of readers and the literary establishment, but she
could never quite resign herself to being a strict realist. In a
19 October 1914 letter to Fred Lewis Pattee, in which she
discussed the stories later collected in *The Elder's People,* she
wrote, "But although I like to write realistic stories like
these last, yet I cannot say that I am entirely in sympathy
with any realism that excludes the poetic and romantic."

Spofford spent the last years of her life traveling in
her beloved New England and abroad for the first time in
her life. In the first decade of the twentieth century she
went to France and Spain. She died on 14 August 1921 at
her home on Deer Island and was buried in Newburyport.
She was eighty-six years old. In a career that spanned
more than sixty years, she had persisted and indeed flourished, adapting to rapid changes in literary fashion and
contributing to sentimentalism, Romanticism, realism, and
regionalism. Critics have attempted to categorize her writing, usually labeling her a romantic whose other work is
not worth serious study. Spofford's best work, however, is
not limited to romance, and her career as a whole defies
categorization. Spofford should be studied as a writer who
challenged boundaries and labels throughout her career,
as did many American women writers of the late nineteenth century.

Biography:

Elizabeth K. Halbeisen, *Harriet Prescott Spofford: A Romantic
     Survival* (Philadelphia: University of Pennsylvania
     Press, 1935).

References:

Alfred Bendixen, Introduction to *The Amber Gods and Other
     Stories* (New Brunswick: Rutgers University Press,
     1989);

Rose Terry Cooke, "Harriet Prescott Spofford," in *Our
     Famous Women* (Hartford: A. D. Worthington / Chi-
     cago: A. D. Nettleton, 1884), pp. 521–538;

Anne Dalke, "'Circumstance' and the Creative Woman:
     Harriet Prescott Spofford," *Arizona Quarterly,* 41
     (Spring 1985): 71–85;

Robin Riley Fast, "Killing the Angel in Spofford's 'Desert
     Sands' and 'The South Breaker,'" *Legacy,* 11, no. 1
     (1994): 37–54;

Judith Fetterley, ed., *Provisions: A Reader from 19th-Century
     American Women* (Bloomington: Indiana University
     Press, 1985);

Maryanne M. Garbowsky, "A Maternal Muse for Emily
     Dickinson," *Dickinson Studies,* 41 (December 1981):
     12–17;

Etta R. Goodwin, "The Literary Women of Washington,"
     Chautauquan, 27 (September 1898): 585–586;

Harper's Bazar "Personals," 4 (25 February 1871): 115; 5 (9
     March 1872): 171; 5 (27 April 1872): 283; 15 (12
     August 1882): 499; 18 (21 November 1885): 747;
     22 (6 July 1889): 491; 22 (23 November 1889): 835;
     23 (6 September 1890): 687; 25 (5 November
     1892): 891; 27 (24 February 1894): 147; 29 (28
     March 1896): 275;

Mary Gray Morrison, "Memories of Harriet Prescott
     Spofford," *Bookman,* 2 (November 1925): 315–318;

Elizabeth Stuart Phelps, "Stories That Stay," *Century Maga-
     zine,* new series, 59 (November 1910): 119;

Wilder D. Quint, "Harriet Prescott Spofford at Deer
     Island," *New York Times Saturday Review of Books and
     Art,* 26 November 1898, p. 793;

Barton Levi St. Armand, "'I Must Have Died at Ten Min-
     utes Past One': Posthumous Reverie in Harriet Pres-
     cott Spofford's 'The Amber Gods,'" in *The Haunted
     Dusk: American Supernatural Fiction, 1820–1920,* edited
     by Howard Kerr, John W. Crowley, and Charles L.
     Crow (Athens: University of Georgia Press, 1983),
     pp. 99–119;

Thelma J. Shinn, "Harriet Prescott Spofford: A Reconsid-
     eration," *Turn-of-the-Century Women,* 1 (Summer
     1984): 36–54.

Papers:

Most of the Prescott family papers are held at the Essex
Institute in Salem, Massachusetts. Other letters by Harriet
Prescott Spofford can be found in the Simon Gratz Autograph Collection at the Historical Society of Pennsylvania,
the Overbury Collection at the Barnard College Library,
the William Conant Church Papers at the New York Public Library, the Fred Lewis Pattee Papers at the Pennsylvania State University Libraries, and the Howe Library at
the University of Florida.

Gene Stratton-Porter

(17 August 1863 – 6 December 1924)

Anne K. Phillips
Kansas State University

See also the Stratton-Porter entry in *DLB Documentary Series 14: Four Women Writers for Children, 1868–1918.*

BOOKS: *The Strike at Shane's: A Prize Story of Indiana,* attributed to Stratton-Porter (Boston: American Humane Education Society, 1893);

The Song of the Cardinal: A Love Story (Indianapolis: Bobbs-Merrill, 1903; London: Hodder & Stoughton, 1913);

Freckles (New York: Doubleday, Page, 1904; London: Doubleday, Page, 1904);

At the Foot of the Rainbow (New York: Outing, 1907; London: Hodder & Stoughton, 1913);

What I Have Done with Birds: Character Studies of Native American Birds (Indianapolis: Bobbs-Merrill, 1907); revised and enlarged as *Friends in Feathers* (Garden City, N.Y.: Doubleday, Page, 1917; London: Curtis Brown, 1917);

A Girl of the Limberlost (New York: Doubleday, Page, 1909; London: Doubleday, Page, 1909);

Birds of the Bible (Cincinnati: Jennings & Graham / New York: Eaton & Mains, 1909; London: Hodder & Stoughton, 1910);

Music of the Wild: With Reproductions of the Performers, Their Instruments and Festival Halls (Cincinnati: Jennings & Graham / New York: Eaton & Mains, 1910; London: Hodder & Stoughton, 1910);

The Harvester (Garden City, N.Y.: Doubleday, Page, 1911; London: Hodder & Stoughton, 1911);

After the Flood (Indianapolis: Bobbs-Merrill, 1911);

Moths of the Limberlost (Garden City, N.Y.: Doubleday, Page, 1912; London: Hodder & Stoughton, 1912);

Laddie: A True Blue Story (Garden City, N.Y.: Doubleday, Page, 1913; London: Murray, 1913);

Birds of the Limberlost (Garden City, N.Y.: Doubleday, Page, 1914);

Michael O'Halloran (Garden City, N.Y.: Doubleday, Page, 1915; London: Murray, 1915);

Morning Face (Garden City, N.Y.: Doubleday, Page, 1916; London: Murray, 1916);

Gene Stratton-Porter (photograph by Robert M. Taylor Jr.)

A Daughter of the Land (Garden City, N.Y.: Doubleday, Page, 1918; London: Murray, 1918);

Homing with the Birds: The History of a Lifetime of Personal Experience with the Birds (Garden City, N.Y.: Doubleday, Page, 1919; London: Murray, 1919);

Her Father's Daughter (Garden City, N.Y. & Toronto: Doubleday, Page, 1921; London: Murray, 1919);

The Fire Bird (Garden City, N.Y. & Toronto: Double-day, Page, 1922; London: Murray, 1922);

The White Flag (Garden City, N.Y.: Doubleday, Page, 1923; London: Murray, 1923);

Wings (Garden City, N.Y.: Doubleday, Page, 1923);

Jesus of the Emerald (Garden City, N.Y.: Doubleday, Page, 1923; London: Murray, 1923);

The Keeper of the Bees (Garden City, N.Y.: Doubleday, Page, 1925; London: Hutchinson, 1925);

Tales You Won't Believe (Garden City, N.Y.: Doubleday, Page, 1925; London: Heinemann, 1925);

The Magic Garden (Garden City, N.Y.: Doubleday, Page, 1927; London: Hutchinson, 1927);

Let Us Highly Resolve (Garden City, N.Y.: Doubleday, Page, 1927; London: Heinemann, 1927);

Euphorbia (Berne, Ind.: Light and Life Press, 1986);

Coming through the Swamp: The Nature Writings of Gene Stratton-Porter, edited by Sydney Landon Plum (Salt Lake City: University of Utah Press, 1996).

OTHER: "The Camera in Ornithology," in *The American Annual of Photography and Photographic Times-Bulletin Almanac for 1904,* edited by W. I. Lincoln Adams (New York: Scoville Manufacturing, 1903), pp. 51–68.

SELECTED PERIODICAL PUBLICATIONS—
UNCOLLECTED: "A New Experience in Millinery," *Recreation* (February 1900): 115;

"Laddie, the Princess, and the Pie," *Metropolitan* (September 1901): 416, 421;

"How Laddie and the Princess Spelled Down at the Christmas Bee," *Metropolitan* (December 1901): 739–753;

"The Real Babes in the Woods," *Metropolitan* (August 1902): 201–213;

"Why I Wrote 'A Girl of the Limberlost,'" *Recreation* (February 1910): 145–147;

"The Gift of the Birds," *Youth's Companion* (19 March 1914): 147–148; (26 March 1914): 159–160;

"My Work and My Critics," *Bookman* (London), 49 (February 1916): 147–155;

"My Life and My Books," *Ladies' Home Journal,* 33 (September 1916): 13, 80–81;

"Why I Always Wear My Rose Colored Glasses," *American Magazine,* 88 (August 1919): 36–37, 112, 114–115, 118, 121;

"My Ideal Home," *Country Life in America,* 60 (October 1921): 40–43;

"Books for Busy People," *McCall's* (January 1924): 2, 28, 74;

"What My Father Meant to Me," *American Magazine,* 99 (February 1925): 23, 70, 72, 76;

"Shall Girls Pay Their Way?" *McCall's,* 52 (August 1925): 2, 48;

"Making Your Vote Count for Something," *McCall's* (November 1925): 2, 67;

"A Message to the Working Woman," *McCall's* (July 1926): 2, 68.

As William Lyon Phelps wrote in the *Bookman* (December 1921), during her lifetime Gene Stratton-Porter was "a public institution, like Yellowstone Park." By 1915 Americans had purchased more than eight million copies of her books, establishing her as one of the five most prominent American authors of the early twentieth century. She produced twelve novels, nine nature studies, two children's books, three volumes of poetry, and a collection of essays. According to Russel Nye, Stratton-Porter's "formula was a good one—sentimentality, faith and optimism, innocence and trust, nostalgia for country life, the curative and educational powers of Nature (with a capital N)." As Stratton-Porter explained in "My Work and My Critics" (1916), "the task I set myself was to lead every human being I could influence afield; but with such reverence instilled into their touch that devastation would not be ultimately complete." She certainly encouraged her readers—female and male—to venture "afield," and throughout her career she advocated a policy of conservation that was decades ahead of her time.

The youngest of twelve children, Geneva Grace Stratton was born on 17 August 1863 in Wabash County, Indiana. Her parents, Mark Stratton and Mary Schallenberger Stratton, had been married for almost thirty years, and the infant's eldest sister was twenty-three at the time of her birth. Throughout her childhood the future novelist was allowed to run wild, demonstrating an uncommon affinity for nature. As a result, her father, a practicing Methodist minister, ceremonially bestowed on her all the birds that made their homes on his property. Stratton selected sixty-four nests and surveyed them daily, participating in the process of feeding, raising, and protecting the young birds. As a result, many of them were remarkably content to be held, to eat from her hands, and to follow her about the farm. She trained a blue jay, a special pet that she named Hezekiah, to roll cherries across the floor, and her pet rooster, Bobby, had the run of the house. When the Strattons sold the farm and moved into Wabash, Indiana, in 1874, after the death of her elder brother Leander, Stratton took several birds with her.

Stratton's adolescence was not a happy period. Her mother died in 1875, four months after the family moved to Wabash. School presented another trial, and she never graduated. Her first success as a writer, however, came through the Wabash High School practice of

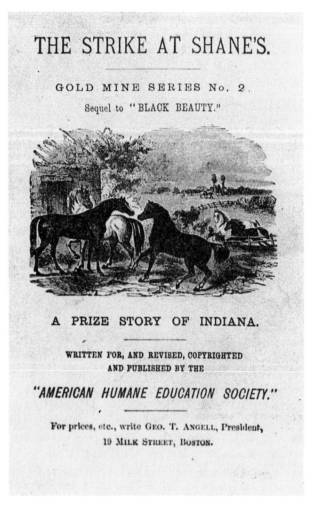

THE STRIKE AT SHANE'S.

GOLD MINE SERIES No. 2.

Sequel to "BLACK BEAUTY."

A PRIZE STORY OF INDIANA.

WRITTEN FOR, AND REVISED, COPYRIGHTED
AND PUBLISHED BY THE

"AMERICAN HUMANE EDUCATION SOCIETY."

For prices, etc., write GEO. T. ANGELL, President,
19 MILK STREET, BOSTON.

*Title page for Stratton-Porter's autobiographical first novel, which
depicts her father in a negative light*

mandatory participation in Friday afternoon school
"Rhetoricals." Assigned to compose an essay on "Math-
ematical Law," which she loathed, Stratton substituted
instead an essay on her favorite novel of the moment,
Xavier Boniface Saintine's *Picciola* (1846), a novel about
a prisoner who finds spiritual solace in a small plant
growing in a crevice of the prison wall. Despite her substitution of topic, her work was deemed a success. After
she had read the first page of her composition, the
teacher brought the superintendent of schools to hear
her presentation. Her performance was personally satisfying. As she later explained, "One instant the room
was in laughter; the next the boys turned their heads,
and the girls who had forgotten their handkerchiefs
cried into their aprons and were unashamed."

The cultural and social opportunities for young
people in northern Indiana at the time reinforced Stratton's interest in nature. In 1881, she went north with
her sisters Ada and Florence to Rome City on Sylvan

Lake for her first Chautauqua meeting, a cultural event
that was a part of a movement of summer "tent programs," at which lecturers and entertainers addressed a
variety of subjects, including religion, natural history,
and literature. In addition to temperance lectures and
church services, the participants at Sylvan Lake enjoyed
concerts and speeches. Stratton attended the Chautau-
quas at Sylvan Lake during several summers in the
1880s, and she remained enthusiastic about the Chautauqua project throughout her life, eventually becoming
a lecturer at a Chautauqua held in Coldwater, Michigan, during the Chicago World's Fair.

At one Sylvan Lake Chautauqua meeting Charles
Dorwin Porter noticed Stratton for the first time. Porter
wrote to her in September 1884, and over a period of a
year and a half they corresponded and courted. They
were married in Wabash on Wednesday, 21 April 1886.
After her marriage, she was known socially as "Mrs.
Porter," but her published work bore the name "Gene
Stratton-Porter." Initially the Porters lived at the old
Porter homestead in Decatur, Indiana, while Charles
Porter commuted between Decatur and his pharmacy
in Geneva, Indiana, and Stratton-Porter busied herself
with painting lessons, music, and writing. Her only
child, Jeannette, was born on 27 August 1887. Although
she found motherhood satisfying and fulfilling, she was
tired of her husband's absences on business. By the
spring of 1888 she had convinced Charles Porter that
they should establish a home in Geneva. At first they
lived in a small farmhouse, but after Charles became
the town banker, he and Gene designed a new home,
built out of red-cedar logs from Wisconsin, in the style
of the Forestry Building they had seen at the Chicago
World's Fair. Completed in 1895, Limberlost Cabin
was the most elaborate home in Geneva, and its fourteen rooms provided Gene with the space to pursue her
writing, her photography, and her interest in nature.
The surrounding Limberlost Swamp was a vast tract of
wilderness, home not only to diverse species of plant
and animal life but also to the criminal element, as
Stratton-Porter depicted in *A Girl of the Limberlost* (1909).

Following her experience with her essay on *Picciola*, Stratton-Porter wrote poetry and stories in private
for many years. It has been assumed that her first published work, circa 1900, consisted of a few articles for
the magazines *Outing* and *Recreation*. As Judith Reick
Long argues, however, Stratton-Porter's professional
writing career actually began in 1893, when she entered
a writing contest sponsored by the American Humane
Education Society of Boston, an organization previously known for publishing Anna Sewell's novel *Black
Beauty* (1877). According to Long, *The Strike at Shane's* is
"transparently autobiographical"; it is set on a farm in
Indiana, and the main character closely resembles Mark

Stratton. Long suggests that Stratton-Porter never acknowledged this work publicly because it presents a negative image of her father. In the story, the farmer is described as a "hard man to deal with . . . Avarice held full sway over his mind, and there was no room in his nature for kindness." The farmer habitually harasses animals, both wild and domestic, on his farm, and eventually the creatures refuse to cooperate with him. When the farm appears to be heading for disaster, Farmer Shane experiences a change of heart. His youngest daughter, Edith (modeled closely on Stratton-Porter), plays a prominent role in persuading her father to change his ways. Stratton-Porter never acknowledged *The Strike at Shane's* as her own work, and the president of the American Humane Education Society died in 1909 without revealing the author's name.

After 1892 Stratton-Porter appeared more confident of her authority in the field of literature. Long explains that "a lively literary column that carried no byline suddenly appeared in the *Geneva Herald,* the local newspaper. . . . One of the books that found favor with the anonymous reviewer was, of course, *The Strike at Shane's.*" In addition, despite her avowed contempt for club women, Stratton-Porter organized a literary society, the Wednesday Club, for the women of Geneva. When it was her turn to speak, she prepared an extensive review of Walt Whitman's *Leaves of Grass* (originally published in 1855). At the end of her presentation she rhapsodized, "If you believe in God; if you love the green grass, flowers, and trees; if you know what the leaves whisper and the waters murmur and the birds sing; if you love God's creation above man's manufacturing—read the book. If in your heart there is the throb of universal love and pity; if your hand has lain on the bare body of man and it has not frightened you, read the book. You will be better for it." Whitman evidently spoke to Stratton-Porter's theology and to her strong interest in nature studies. Throughout her career she referred to Whitman, as well as the other prominent American Transcendentalists, Ralph Waldo Emerson and Henry David Thoreau, in her work. Their belief that humans can develop a closer relation with their creator through a study of nature is central to her novels and nature studies.

Stratton-Porter emphasized that nature and a spiritual awakening achieved through an awareness of nature were the focus of her professional work. Her novels included, she claimed in *Tales You Won't Believe* (1925), only "a slight amount of fiction as a bait for those who would not take their natural history unless it were sugar-coated." Indeed, her fiction seems designed to lead readers to her nature studies, which she produced between novels. She wrote her first novel, *The*

Stratton-Porter's husband, Charles Dorwin Porter, in 1923

Song of the Cardinal (1903), after finding a bleeding cardinal that had been shot for sport. Her studies of the cardinal, which appear in volumes such as *Friends in Feathers* (1917), are designed to persuade her readers that cardinals should be protected. As she noted in

Stratton-Porter in California in 1924, the year of her death

"My Life and My Books," (1916) "I came to the realization that, if I could not reach people faster, so far as my work was concerned, the cardinals might all go as had the [passenger] pigeons."

Perhaps her best-known novel, *Freckles* (1904), is an effective combination of fiction and natural history. The story of Freckles, an orphan from Chicago who finds work in the Limberlost as a timber guard, ostensibly concerns the efforts of the villains, Black Jack and Wessner, to defeat Freckles and steal valuable timber from the swamp. Freckles is aided primarily by a young woman from the nearby town, the Swamp Angel, and her companion, the Bird Woman, a local naturalist who comes to the swamp to photograph the birds and collect specimens for her books. The essential plot, however, involves Freckles's dawning realization of the natural world and his place in it: "He gradually learned that, to the shy wood-creatures that darted across his path or peeped inquiringly from leafy ambush, he was brother." Freckles's spirit awakens in the Limberlost, where he

builds what he terms his "cathedral" and worships: "What veriest work of God was in these mighty living pillars and the arched dome of green! How like stained cathedral windows were the long openings between the trees, filled with rifts of blue, rays of gold, and the shifting emeralds of leaves!" Stratton-Porter originally intended the novel to end with Freckles being killed by a falling tree as the lumbermen move in. Having been "so long alone that he loved the solitude, his chickens, and flowers," Freckles could not survive the desecration of the Limberlost. However, after several book companies refused to publish the novel without an upbeat ending, Stratton-Porter wrote a more conventional conclusion, in which the Swamp Angel finds Freckles's long-lost relatives and consents to marry him.

Freckles tames the bird life of the swamp during his first few months there, and his friends refer to the wild birds as "Freckles' chickens" throughout the novel. He first meets the Swamp Angel when she and the Bird Woman come to the Limberlost to photograph "Little Chicken," a rare baby vulture that he has discovered. The real-life model for the vulture so prominently featured in *Freckles* appears in *What I Have Done with Birds* (1907), along with the story of how Stratton-Porter (the real-life Bird Woman) and her husband found his nest, photographed him, and studied him over a period of several weeks. Other birds characterized in the novel, such as the goldfinch, are also described in Stratton-Porter's nature studies.

A Girl of the Limberlost (1909), a sequel in which Freckles and the Swamp Angel appear near the end of the novel, concerns Elnora Comstock, the young woman who has taken possession of Freckles's books and specimens after he leaves the swamp. Where Freckles was especially interested in the Limberlost's bird life, Elnora's forte is collecting its moths. By selling her specimens to the Bird Woman, she is able to fund a high-school education for herself despite the fact that her embittered, widowed mother refuses to provide her daughter with anything more than the basic necessities. *A Girl of the Limberlost* is a gripping psychological drama about mother and daughter, but it is also another fascinating fictional depiction of the Limberlost. In the course of the novel Stratton-Porter also describes in detail the destruction of the Limberlost. Ultimately, Elnora finds it impossible to secure many species of moths. In 1912 Stratton-Porter followed up this novel with a natural history, *Moths of the Limberlost*. Her photographs and watercolor illustrations for the book are impressive. In *Moths of the Limberlost* readers may see and learn more about the species that are so lovingly described throughout *A Girl of the Limberlost*.

By the time *The Harvester* (1911), a novel dedicated to Thoreau, had achieved best-seller status, the

Lobby card for the screen adaptation of Stratton-Porter's best-known novel, released four years after her death

Limberlost was on the verge of destruction. The swamp and the forest had been converted into farms. In addition, visitors who wanted to meet the famous author were constantly interrupting her work. Thus, Stratton-Porter determined to move north to Sylvan Lake and establish a permanent, private home that would be conducive to her interests. Her husband remained in Geneva to pursue his business interests, taking the train to the new house on weekends. Stratton-Porter planned to maintain Wildflower Woods, eventually a 150-acre tract of land near Rome City, as a wildlife habitat and a preserve for as many species of Indiana flora as possible. She eventually acquired more than fourteen thousand different plants, 90 percent of which she planted herself. Stratton-Porter designed her house, the second Limberlost Cabin, out of the same cedar she had used in Geneva; she also added a darkroom and plenty of workshop space. She assisted in the building of the house, taking special interest in the construction of the stone fireplaces and gates. By the time of World War I, however, even Sylvan Lake was being converted from forest into farmland. Stratton-Porter wrote in consternation that the farmers "were madly and recklessly doing an insane thing without really understanding what they were doing."

In part because her refuge was compromised and in part because her health had suffered during the harsh winter and influenza epidemic of 1918, Stratton-Porter began to consider the possibilities of moving to California. The warm weather and the rich possibilities for nature study were not the only enticements. She was also attracted by the possibility of forming her own movie company. She had been unhappy with the motion-picture versions of her novels. In 1917, when Paramount had produced *Freckles,* the studio had asked Stratton-Porter to provide directions; during production, however, they had disregarded all of her suggestions. Ultimately, she offered Wildflower Woods to the State of Indiana and established a permanent residence in California, buying property on Catalina Island and in the Bel Air region of Los Angeles. She found great satisfaction in the company of artists she met in Hollywood, and at this time she began to write poetry. She was also highly sought after as a columnist. At the time of her death on 6 December 1924, in a collision between her limousine and a streetcar, she was writing regularly for *Good Housekeeping* and *McCall's,* two of the most popular women's magazines.

As her success with these magazines indicates, Stratton-Porter fostered a special connection with her female readers. Although she never ignored the male audience and many men did read her work, Stratton-Porter wrote directly of women's experiences and women's expertise. A female counterpart to the American politician Theodore Roosevelt, who had inspired a cult of masculinity and introduced many American men to the benefits of nature, Stratton-Porter saw herself in her article "My Work and My Critics" as the women's prophet: "For many reasons I came in time to believe that there might be a lifework for one woman in leading these other women back to the forest, and on account of my inclinations, education and rearing I felt in a degree equipped to be their Moses." She encouraged her audience in *Moths of the Limberlost* to rely on personal observation rather than textbooks and, with respect to nature, to "find out for yourself, and use all the common sense the Almighty has bestowed upon you, in arriving at your conclusions." She also felt that women were more suited to study nature, arguing in *Friends in Feathers* that "in the matter of finesse in approaching the birds, in limitless patience in awaiting the exact moment for the best exposure, in the tedious and delicate processes of the dark room, in the art of winning bird babies and parents, it is not a man's work. No man ever has had the patience to remain with a bird until he secured a real character study of it." She deplored the methods of naturalist John James Audubon, who clubbed his subjects to death before studying them. In the article "The Camera in Ornithology" (1903), she noted that Audubon's drawings looked "as if they had been cut out with a scroll saw." She argued further that most of the male-authored studies of moths were artificial and often erroneous, but in *Moths of the Limberlost* she praised especially "the women of Massachusetts, who wrote 'Caterpillars and Their Moths'" for their lifelike and accurate work.

Stratton-Porter's work as a naturalist and novelist is thus twofold. First, she encouraged personal awareness of nature for its spiritual benefits. In "Religion as a Stimulus to Success" she explained, "I am not perfectly sure in my own mind exactly what I mean when I say 'God'; that is, I do not know whether I mean a particular person, or a particular power; but I do know that the further I advance in the study of the evolution of Nature, the more I see a guid-

ing hand, a controlling power, and a marvellous brain at the back of everything." Second, she continued to explain the significance of all aspects of the natural world—the interdependence of the ecosystem—and the necessity of conserving natural resources. In *Tales You Won't Believe,* she wrote, "the deeper I delve into natural science the easier it is to see that every created thing has its use, has its purpose to accomplish in the world, and that upon Nature keeping her own balance depends the security of the whole." She claimed that her awareness of conservation stemmed from her father's discoveries on his farm: when the pigeons and other birds were exterminated, his crops suffered. "From that time on," she explained, "our whole family began to practise and to preach conservation along every line." Stratton-Porter's nature studies and novels continue to "preach conservation" to an impressively large congregation. Her message continues to be recognized for its wisdom and relevance.

Bibliography:

David G. MacLean, *Gene Stratton-Porter: A Book Collector's Guide,* revised edition (Decatur, Ind.: Americana Books, 1996).

Biographies:

Jeannette Porter Meehan, *The Lady of the Limberlost: The Life and Letters of Gene Stratton-Porter* (Garden City, N.Y.: Doubleday, Doran, 1928);

Judith Reick Long, *Gene Stratton-Porter: Novelist and Naturalist* (Indianapolis: Indiana Historical Society, 1990).

References:

Russel Nye, *The Unembarrassed Muse: The Popular Arts in America* (New York: Dial, 1970), pp. 37–38;

Bertrand F. Richards, *Gene Stratton-Porter* (Boston: Twayne, 1980).

Papers:

Nearly all of Gene Stratton-Porter's papers remain in private hands. The Indiana State University Library and The Lilly Library at Indiana University each have a few letters as well as substantial collections of her printed works.

Susie King Taylor

(8 August 1848 – 1912)

Joycelyn K. Moody
University of Washington

BOOK: *Reminiscences of My Life in Camp with the 33d United States Colored Troops Late 1st S. C. Volunteers* (Boston, 1902).

Edition: *Reminiscences of My Life in Camp with the 33d United States Colored Troops Late 1st S.C. Volunteers,* edited by Anthony Barthelemy (New York: Oxford University Press, 1988).

Virtually all that is known about Susie King Taylor is drawn from her 1902 autobiography, *Reminiscences of My Life in Camp with the 33d United States Colored Troops Late 1st S. C. Volunteers,* an extraordinarily complex, if also deceptively simple, memoir. It conforms so precisely to the rhetorical conventions of other former slaves' autobiographies of the post-Reconstruction era that it stands indisputably as a compelling representative of its tradition and times. While unequaled in the particular life story that it tells, it nonetheless features many rhetorical and stylistic similarities to other postbellum slave narratives. Yet, but for fleeting mention of her alongside Clara Barton and Thomas Higginson in a handful of Civil War chronicles, there are no records of the life of this patriotic African American former slave who served the Union as nurse, teacher, seamstress, launderer, cook, and scribe. Though modest and self-effacing, she possessed an unwavering sense of her own significance. Had she not ultimately esteemed her experiences as worthy of publication, there would be no record of the fascinating and heroic life that she led.

Reminiscences of My Life in Camp narrates less the life than the times of its author. Its compound subject is composed of those persons whom the author knew and the national events she witnessed and remarked on during her four years of military service. Yet, as autobiographer and slave narrator, Taylor also recounts specific selected incidents of her personal experience. Thus, *Reminiscences of My Life in Camp* has a complex and multifaceted rhetorical purpose: it is Taylor's own history, beginning with her maternal lineage from the American Revolution era, and it is also the

Susie King Taylor.

story of the men who made up the First South Carolina Volunteers, later designated the Thirty-third United States Colored Infantry. It is also a revised, more inclusive version of that particular military history, for Taylor deliberately chronicles the roles of women who served the Union army by serving the men who formed its troops.

Reminiscences of My Life in Camp actually begins with reminiscences of the natural longevity and national loyalty of its author's foremothers. Taylor proudly reports that her great-great-grandmother lived 120 years. Five of her seven children were sons who served in the Revolutionary War. Her daughter Susanna lived 100 years, and with her husband, Peter Simons, bore twenty-three daughters and one son. Susanna's sister Dolly, enslaved on the plantation of Valentine Grest, bore only two children, Fortune Lambert Reed-James, who died at age twelve, and Hagar Ann, born in 1824. When she was twenty-three, Hagar Ann married Raymond Baker, and the following year she delivered the first of their eight children: Susie Baker, named for her aunt, was born on 8 August 1848 on the Grest Farm in Liberty County, Georgia, some thirty miles from Savannah.

In 1855 Dolly Reed took Susie and two other Baker siblings to live with her in Savannah. Dolly apparently had been manumitted by Grest, and though her grandchildren were yet his slaves, Taylor does not report any particular hardship she suffered as a slave. Grandmother and granddaughter developed an especially close intimacy, and Taylor in narrating her evidences the same ambition, self-respect, and vitality that rendered Dolly personally and financially independent despite her location in secessionist Georgia. Moreover, Dolly's friends seem to have shared her determination and fortitude, for several of them strove surreptitiously to teach Susie and other slave children to read and write, in defiance of laws prohibiting the education of slaves. Besides Dolly's network of African American women friends, Susie's white playmate, Katie O'Connor, and later a young white neighbor, James Blouis, also helped her become literate between 1855 and 1860.

Young Susie put her new skills to immediate use by writing counterfeit passes for slave travelers in her grandmother's community. When she reveals this illicit application of her literacy, the mature narrator, much more worldly than the precocious girl who wrote the passes, defies readers to charge her with immorality. Writing her story decades after slavery had been abolished, Taylor's point is not that slaves committed illegal acts with impunity, but rather that literacy gave slaves essential skills that they applied with care, discretion, and intelligence. Rather than mock slaveholders who were unaware of the ways that slaves hoodwinked them, Taylor celebrates black intellect and ingenuity and shows herself acting in the interest of other blacks as prelude to her military endeavors. She also illustrates, however, that for every triumph over the slaveholders, there was a corresponding defeat: one night when she was eight years old, Dolly and other black Christians were arrested at worship for singing lyrics that allegedly denounced secession and slavery. The inclusion of this anecdote in *Reminiscences of My Life in Camp* allows Taylor to document the pride, subversion, and self-motivation of free and enslaved African Americans, contrary to various stereotypes of antebellum blacks.

Taylor's postemancipation depiction of her childhood as blissfully ignorant of her slave status also provides an interesting contrast to that of Harriet Jacobs's in *Incidents in the Life of a Slave Girl, Written by Herself* (1861), the only extant self-authored antebellum slave woman's autobiography. There, too, the narrator describes herself as initially oblivious to the reality of her enslavement. As an abolitionist, however, Jacobs stresses the bitterness and rage she experienced as an astute young girl gradually understanding the extent of her bondage. Happily ensconced within a slaveholding family, she asserts, she experiences no great suffering as a slave child. As she begins to perceive that their "ownership" of her proscribes her every action, however, she detests and resists slavery. Her awareness of what it means to be owned by other human beings comes at the same time that she loses many important people in her life: mother, father, friend, and benevolent mistress all die within a few months of each other. Jacobs's sentimental reconstruction of her comprehension of her slave status is designed to arouse her readers' sympathy for the dire plight of slave women.

Taylor's oblivion to her bondage, recast after the war, differently affects readers of *Reminiscences of My Life in Camp*. Taylor desires no sympathy over her childhood experiences, so she dispenses with any recollection of her experience of learning herself enslaved. Whereas in antebellum America Jacobs depends on Northern women readers' fear and abhorrence of the Southern decree that "the child shall follow the condition of the mother," Taylor instead emphasizes the extended family she enjoyed throughout her childhood. Jacobs solicits readers' sympathy; Taylor, their emulation: for her maternal relatives' interdependence, for her ancestors' patriotism and valor, for her family's persistence in acquiring literacy and property, whatever the legislation. Taylor draws attention to a specific negrophobic legislation of her day—as Jacobs does to the mother-child status rule—that the law prohibits slaves from acquiring literacy. Indirectly, then, *Reminiscences of My Life in Camp* ideally proves literary critic Robert Stepto's contention that the paramount and inextricable themes of literacy and freedom lie at the root of all African American literature.

Taylor's account of her girlhood among self-reliant African American women in the slaveholding South serves as a fitting backdrop for the story of her military service and subsequent civic leadership. She was not yet fourteen years old when the Civil War began for her on 1 April 1862, with the arrival of Union soldiers at Fort Pulaski. Within two days she had moved with her Savannah relatives to St. Catherine's, one of South Carolina's sea islands. Two weeks later, their relocation to St. Simon's Island, where they positioned themselves literally behind Union lines, effected their freedom. The author of another slave woman's postbellum narrative, Mattie J. Jackson (born circa 1846), describes her similar interaction with the Federal Army in 1861 when she sought refuge among Union soldiers at St. Louis, Missouri. Both Jackson and Taylor imply that their first experiences with the soldiers were typically romantic: each adolescent readily adored the Yankee troops. For her part Taylor paid particular attention to one black volunteer–Edward King, a literate and urbane sergeant from Savannah whom she married in July 1862. That spring, a few months shy of her fourteenth birthday, another Union officer asked her to teach former slave children at Gaston Bluff on the island. So began her career in the Union Army as schoolteacher, laundress, nurse–in whatever capacity she was needed from moment to moment. Her skills ranged from shooting and cleaning muskets to conducting classes for soldiers and civilians across St. Simon's Island. Thus, as a representative postbellum slave narrative, *Reminiscences of My Life in Camp* enumerates the diverse skills a black woman had attained in what Booker T. Washington called "the school of slavery."

As the title of her autobiography indicates, most of Taylor's text is devoted to the years she spent with the Thirty-third Infantry. The major themes of this lengthy middle section, however, are the same as those that permeate the whole work: African American heroism, intelligence, and ingenuity. Just as the chapters describing her early life demonstrate that antebellum blacks supported and sustained each other and that they frequently maneuvered around the obstacles erected by slavery and oppression, the chapters on the military chronicle the ways that Union forces–composed of blacks and whites, women and men–worked together to conquer the Confederacy. *Reminiscences of My Life in Camp* asserts Taylor's belief in the possibility of harmonious race and gender relations, particularly when cultural difference is overcome by a common goal as great as ending the Civil War.

Taylor draws on the African American rhetoric of racial uplift popular at the end of the nineteenth century to narrate her life experiences. Her chief auto-

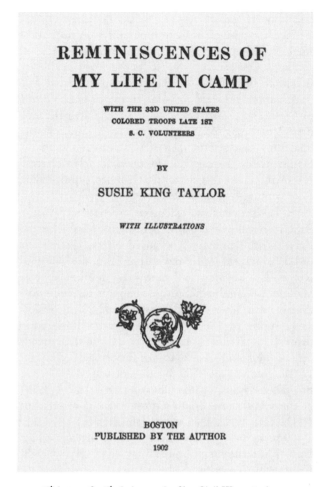

REMINISCENCES OF MY LIFE IN CAMP

WITH THE 33D UNITED STATES
COLORED TROOPS LATE 1ST
S. C. VOLUNTEERS

BY

SUSIE KING TAYLOR

WITH ILLUSTRATIONS

BOSTON
PUBLISHED BY THE AUTHOR
1902

Title page for Taylor's memoir of her Civil War experiences

biographical project is to situate all of her experiences under the one rubric of black women and men's contributions to the reconsolidation of the split Union. But because of her clearly ambivalent feelings about national progress, *Reminiscences of My Life in Camp* is marked by a tension between its author's effort to document the valiant military achievements of the racially integrated Thirty-third troops, on the one hand, and, on the other hand, her thinly veiled anger and disappointment at unremitting injustices perpetrated against blacks and women throughout the nineteenth century. A current of conflicting emotions and concerns runs beneath the whole of *Reminiscences of My Life in Camp*.

One aim of the autobiography is to establish black men's intrepidity. Taylor challenges the myth that Africans are more bestial than human, and in turn she vanquishes the stereotype of black men as Sambos or Uncle Toms; that is, men who are weak-willed and innately fearful, and therefore unable to develop and maintain loyalty to other persons. In addition to the entire regiment with which she served, whose collective stalwart, gallant acts of national defense comprise the greater part of her autobiography, Taylor offers single (and singular) examples of bravery in individual soldiers. One such example is her cousin Henry Batchloff, one of the two black corpsmen whose professional portraits are included in the original edition of *Reminiscences of My Life in Camp*. Shortly after the Colored Volunteer troops were formed in South Carolina, they engaged in their first skirmishes with the Confederates. During one of these, Batchloff risked his own life to rescue another soldier, John Baker, from capture by the Confederacy.

Taylor cites an extensive example of African American valor and patriotism in the Massachusetts Fifty-fourth Regiment, composed almost exclusively of black soldiers under the administration of Colonel Robert Gould Shaw, a young veteran from an elite abolitionist family in Boston. Though formed more than a year after South Carolina's black troops, in early spring of 1863, the Massachusetts Fifty-fourth proved so exemplary that Taylor's comrades named one of their southern campsites for Shaw. Led by the young colonel, the Fifty-fourth had waged an heroic but failed assault on the Confederacy's Fort Wagner at the Charleston, South Carolina, coast on 18 July 1863. The attack had resulted in the loss of almost 1,700 men, mostly black soldiers. Later that same July, Taylor and the men of the Thirty-third traversed the Charleston coastline, where they discovered the skulls and other remains of the Fifty-fourth Regiment. In the narrative's most grievous moment, Taylor briefly meditates on the futility and devastation of war. The loss of life at Fort Wagner is so profound, the battle so glorious, it is even singled out for remembrance and bereavement three years later when the troops are discharged.

Taylor consistently identifies her husband as "Sergeant King," and never points to any racial inequity in the black soldiers' promotions or advancements. She cites no instances of insubordination or other race or class trouble among the members of the Thirty-third, but seems chiefly interested in demonstrating that black men and white men were equally committed to restoring the Union, their commitment prevailing over personal prejudices—as, for example, when all-white troops came to the aid of the predominantly black Thirty-third. As an advocate of racial integration, Taylor uses the Union troops' mutual respect as evidence of its potential effectiveness. Moreover, she never complains that white officers primarily led the troops, but praises as imperial and virtuous the highest ranking among them, Colonel Thomas Wentworth Higginson and Lieutenant Colonel C. T. Trowbridge. Portraits of both men illustrate the text,

and more importantly, each wrote a prefatory statement to Taylor's memoir. Furthermore, Taylor dedicated *Reminiscences of My Life in Camp* to Higginson, who was universally renowned as an abolitionist, minister, litterateur, and historian. Wounded in battle in May 1864, at age forty-one he retired from military service, and three years later he published one of the most remarkable texts to emerge from the Civil War era. His memoir *Army Life in a Negro Regiment* (1870) narrates not only his extraordinary military experiences among African American soldiers, it also transcribes black folk songs and slave spirituals, rendering it among the first documentations and scholarly assessments of American slave ritual and culture.

Not surprisingly, the most significant impact of race on black soldiers' military experience, Taylor contends, is economic. In the winter of 1863, following President Abraham Lincoln's Emancipation Proclamation, African American Union soldiers were offered only half-pay for their military labor; they refused to accept it. In 1864, after more than two years of service without remuneration, they were awarded full wages and full back pay. During this period, former masters of soldiers who had been slaves were being compensated for the "loss" of their slave labor. Not until March 1865 did the Reconstruction-era federal government establish the Freedmen's Bureau, in part to ensure that African American soldiers received complete pay for military duty.

Perhaps this racism and delayed recompense stirs Taylor's ambivalence when she reports the intercultural experiences of Southern white soldiers and the integrated Unionists. She observes a tacit code of conduct to which soldiers across camps adhered, noting it most when it is breached, as when Confederate soldiers destroy southern cities to prevent Unionist plunder, or raise ambushes against marching adversaries, or pilfer Union mail. One poignant instance of the latter offense Taylor describes in considerable detail. In October 1864 mail for the Union Army at Port Royal Ferry, South Carolina, by either theft or error was sent to its Confederate counterpart. Under what Taylor calls a "flag of truce," Union Captain L. W. Metcalf crossed the Edisto River to exchange letters with Confederate officers Major Jones and Lieutenant Scott. While Scott looked on "in sullen silence," Jones told Metcalf, "We have no one to fight for. Should I meet you again, I shall not forget that we have met before." Interestingly, Taylor echoes this same sentiment when she observes that many Rebels who defected to the Union Army alleged that they did so because they "had no negroes to fight for." The episode about the interposed mail suggests the two Confederate officers' divergent attitudes toward African

Americans (especially former or fugitive slaves who served as soldiers), toward secession and civil war, and toward blacks and whites serving on the same side of the Civil War. Although the reconstruction of this episode is as understated as virtually all other anecdotes in *Reminiscences of My Life in Camp,* it is nonetheless impressive because, in relating the two Rebels' dramatic difference one from another, Taylor simultaneously throws into clear relief her own ambivalence toward integration and the futility of the war, decades after it has ended.

Taylor's pessimism about race relations is further illustrated in her depiction of both blacks and whites who behave in unpatriotic and dishonorable ways during the war. She tells the story of Henry Capers, an elderly former slave whom the Unionists banish from the Sea Islands after he aids and abets Confederate troops. Her noble kinsman Batchloff pleads with the other Volunteers to spare Capers's life, but Taylor herself condemns blacks who contribute to the Confederate cause. Her reproach is textually accentuated by a lapsed use of collective pronouns and inclusive plural subjectivity as she distances herself from traitorous and treasonous former slaves. In a subsequent chapter she recalls a skirmish at Jacksonville, Florida, in March 1863, in which white Confederate soldiers donned blackface to trick the 33d. Their disguise cost some blacks their lives, for, mistaking the Confederates for other blacks, they hesitated long enough to lose their advantage to their opponents. Thus, Taylor contrasts white ignominy with black nobility, implying that Southern whites were extraordinarily diabolical in their military pursuits.

Indeed, one dominant theme of *Reminiscences of My Life in Camp* is the violence that human beings perpetrate against each other, often in the name of justice. For example, Taylor reports that when the Union Army convicts a deserter of espionage, she and the Thirty-third Infantry witness his execution at Camp Shaw. She says that the scene will forever haunt her, the image perhaps especially horrendous because the young white neighbor who taught her to read, James Blouis, had joined the Confederacy only later to defect to the Union Army. Taylor's autobiography is full of accounts of human violence—all poignantly understated, as is her style, but detailing not only the barbarism of the war, which she continually faced as a nurse, but also a brutality associated with civic destruction: fires set to sites where she and other former slaves once lived, deserters in stocks and jails, civilians taken hostage and tortured. In the memoir's final section about her postbellum experience, Taylor enumerates diverse additional hate crimes that she

Colonel Thomas Wentworth Higginson of the Thirty-third U.S. Colored Troops, to whom Taylor dedicated Reminiscences of My Life in Camp *(Schomburg Center for Research in Black Culture, New York Public Library)*

witnessed, not the least among them rampant and random lynchings of African Americans.

Taylor's narrativized reactions to war crimes and violence indicate her tremendous patriotism and courage. While she confesses to feeling frightened on numerous occasions, it is clear that, though afraid, Taylor nevertheless exhibited great valor in the face of grave danger. She was obviously a daring adventurer, yet she took no unnecessary risks. By the time she published her autobiography she had been "cast away" at sea on three different occasions; her equanimity and prudence saved her in each instance. The first of these occurred one tempestuous December night in 1864, as she traveled from Hilton Head with three other women, a toddler, and an officer's assistant. Their boat capsized and the passenger survived by clinging to the overturned sides. At the end of the ordeal, which lasted three and a half hours, the toddler was still gripped in her mother's teeth, and the soldier had drowned; the survivors were apparently rescued by Taylor's persistent efforts to attract attention from nearby Ladys Island.

Documenting women's courage forms a central purpose of Taylor's memoir. She carefully records the contributions of women, especially African American women, who served in the war and who, more importantly, were never adequately recognized or rewarded. In all likelihood, female gender is the "technicality" to which Trowbridge refers, writing in his prefatory letter to *Reminiscences of My Life in Camp* that he regrets "that through a technicality" [Taylor was] "debarred from having her name" on the role of pensioners, as an Army Nurse." Using *Reminiscences of My Life in Camp* to acknowledge that the "comrades" were thankful for her labors, Taylor writes, "I was very happy to know my efforts were successful in camp, and also felt grateful for the appreciation of my services. I gave my services willingly for four years and three months without receiving a dollar." She also implies that the notion of "military service" should be amplified so that the assistance women provided will be acknowledged no less than that of the men who fought. She further designates as service the contributions of those persons who stole food for the soldiers and who risked imprisonment themselves by feeding and nurturing the imprisoned. This expanded definition of military service is consistent with the rhetorical strategy of her autobiography: just as she frequently uses a collective first-person pronoun to affirm that her story has a collective subject, she further implies that their military success depended on the decisive actions of many persons.

Moreover, Taylor demonstrates that she and the other women traveling with the military unit did not depend on the soldiers for their survival; in fact, she implies that the men's military success depends in part on the service of women who function as nurses, cooks, seamstresses, launderers, and scribes, and who also perform less traditional female duties, such as cleaning and caring for weapons. When Taylor reports that on 10 March 1863 Confederate troops fled their camps in Jacksonville, Florida, deserting women and children there, she both criticizes the Confederacy for its ironic lack of chivalry and highlights the contrast between the abandoned helpless women of Florida and the army women who have repeatedly proven themselves independent and self-reliant.

Reminiscences of My Life in Camp seems purposefully designed to argue for black and white women's capacity to perform and experience many aspects of life that "true women" were thought unable to endure. Taylor challenges the same false images of women as frail, sentimental, and ineffectual that earlier nineteenth-century African American women, including Harriet Jacobs and Sojourner Truth, had already contested. These poor black women untangled the intricate knot of racism, sexism, and class elitism to expose the hypocrisy of social norms for women. Their writings demonstrate that these norms had been codified by men to restrict women's development into vibrant, productive, and respected members of society. Furthermore, they argued that men had constructed the code of decorum to subjugate all women, keeping them in competition with each other to meet the standards required of "true women." According to this patriarchal code, a hardy woman on the battlefield, up to her elbows in blood or soapsuds, hardly counted as a "true woman."

Taylor contradicts the ideology of "true womanhood" even as she, like many of her turn-of-the-century contemporaries, argues simultaneously for the innate chastity and respectability of African American women, whom whites generally believed to be more beastly than human. If she sets out in *Reminiscences of My Life in Camp* to establish that black men were heroic, Taylor also uses her memoir to promote the idea that black women are genteel. However, she also urges the rejection of social codes that imply that blacks are bestial and ignorant, that women should disdain gainful employment as either too difficult or too worldly, and that poor, black, and female persons should submit to the alleged superiority of white men of property. She tacitly asserts that adherence to such codes would yield a collective citizenry with an underdeveloped social, economic, and intellectual aptitude, not only leaving one group with excessive power, but further depriving the whole of society of the potential contributions of all its members.

Thus Taylor implies that gender is a social construction rather than a biological reality. Specifically, she reconstructs a series of incidents on a train to suggest that one's gender is ultimately of less import than one's personal conduct. Fourteen years after the renowned black journalist Ida B. Wells sued the Chesapeake and Ohio Railroad for race discrimination, Taylor traveled southward by rail from Boston. She had been called to the bedside of her only son, who lay dying in Mississippi. When the train arrived in Cleveland, Ohio, on 8 February 1898, she and the other black passengers were forced by law to transfer to the train's smoking car. Just as Wells had lost her suit in appellate court, and as the Supreme Court had upheld the constitutionality of separate but equal railroad cars in the 1896 case of *Plessy* v. *Ferguson*, Taylor had no recourse but to move to the smoking car. Recalling the incident, Taylor maintains that she suffered on the train not because she was a "lady" with a particularly delicate sensibility, but rather because she was a person physically and morally intolerant of filth. On the train the following day, she is harassed by constables in search of an outlaw. In yet a third incident of her southbound journey, she notices an interim coach that separates first-class passengers from smokers; here, white "laborers" are segregated from white aristocrats. This perception inspires her petition for a comparable intraracial breakdown among African Americans, based on class status and individual deportment.

Taylor's appeal for separation along class and conduct lines appears in other post-Reconstruction African American texts. The main character in Charles Chesnutt's *The Marrow of Tradition* (1901), for example, also makes a train journey, and reaches the same conclusion favoring separate cars for elite blacks and poor ones. In another novel, *Contending Forces* (1900), Pauline Hopkins creates a vivid structural hierarchy in a turn-of-the-century Northern boardinghouse to argue sentimentally for material and moral separation within the race. This polemic in *Reminiscences of My Life in Camp* evidences Taylor's tension between representations of herself as robust and vigorous, on the one hand, and as genteel and respectable on the other. Whereas no apparent contradiction exists in these adjectives for herself, Taylor seems anxious that her readers will find them incompatible and apparently wants them to understand that, although she has withstood brutality and atrocity on the battlefield, when riding as a passenger in the train cars, she wishes to indulge her civil right to a more civilized refinement.

In the latter chapters of her book, Taylor recalls the decades following the Confederate surrender at Appomattox, Virginia, on 9 April 1865. It was not until 9 February of the next year that the Thirty-third troops were mustered out, with more than 140,000 black troops having served the Union during the war years. On 16 September 1866 her husband, Edward King, died, leaving the eighteen-year-old civilian nurse pregnant with their only child. Taylor spent the next few years putting her literacy to work for her by opening one school after another in rural Georgia. Having taught voluntarily while with the army, now she adapted her lifelong commitment to educating African Americans to her need to sustain herself and her son. Operating her own school became a practical, lucrative, postwar application of her extraordinary skills, and, just as important, provided her an opportunity to equip other blacks with skills that enabled them to participate in the vital work of reconstructing the severed nation.

Yet, for Taylor the Reconstruction period apparently did not bring the jubilation one might expect a Unionist nurse to feel in the aftermath of the war. Instead of experiencing elation and optimism,

Building in Savannah that housed one of the many schools for African Americans that Taylor established in Georgia during the Reconstruction era (Schomburg Center for Research in Black Culture, New York Public Library)

the elder narrator reveals that most African Americans who had served the Union Army felt disillusioned and embittered. They perceived that such gestures as the formation of the Freedmen's Bureau and the ratification of the Thirteenth and Fourteenth Amendments were grossly impotent in the dismantling of centuries of Southern negrophobia and race hatred. *Reminiscences of My Life in Camp* details a litany of incidents of white racist deception and exploitation of the struggling freedpeople. For Taylor, white male supremacy seems one—predictable—thing, but white women's racism was more egregious yet. For example, when the Confederate Daughters organized a boycott of postbellum theater productions of Harriet Beecher Stowe's *Uncle Tom's Cabin* (1852), contending that the antislavery shows distort Southern attitudes and mores, Taylor declares the protest both ludicrous and impertinent and expresses her offense that the women focus on so trivial a matter as entertainment but fail to object to far more serious displays of immorality and inhumanity.

By 1870 as her pupils transferred to the new public schools for freedpeople, Taylor was forced to leave her three-year-old son with her mother and to begin domestic work in Savannah. In spring 1873 she made her first trip north, when she traveled as her employers' cook to Rye Beach, New Hampshire (near Boston). She so preferred her life in New England that she joined the throngs of African Americans migrating north during Reconstruction: in 1874 she returned to Boston as a servant for a wealthy and prominent Georgia couple who moved north. With the Reverend Russell L. Taylor, whom she married in 1879, she resided in Boston for the rest of her life.

Taylor spent the last years of her life actively engaged in social and political reform. Her racial uplift work coincided with that of other African American women of the era, including other leading educators who were also authors, Anna Julia Cooper and Mary Church Terrell. Like another of these political activists, Ida B. Wells, Taylor would use her autobiography in part to condemn America's tolerance of lynching despite the indisputable evidence that it was a hate crime targeted directly at blacks. These women's collective struggle for civil and human rights in the 1880s and 1890s coalesced in the Black Women's Club Movement and the National Association of Colored Women. In 1886, the same year that Caroline Taylor (no relation) founded the Home for Friendless Girls in Washington, D. C., Taylor organized the G. A. R.'s Women's Relief Corps. During her membership, she served the organization as secretary, guard, and treasurer for three years, and in 1893 was elected president. In 1896 Taylor expanded her service to the Union Army by working with Lizzie J. Johnson, a woman who had also lived and traveled among the "colored troops" during the war; together they canvassed and located Union veterans throughout Massachusetts. Taylor proudly appended to her autobiography a roster of their reunions with these soldiers and the discoveries of other Women's Corps members.

In 1901 Russell Taylor died, leaving his widow to celebrate alone the publication of her *Reminiscences of My Life in Camp with the 33d United States Colored Troops* the following year. When she died in 1912 at age sixty-four, Susie Baker King Taylor had devoted fifty years of her exemplary life to preserving, analyzing, brooding over, and honoring the nation that she loved.

References:

Thomas Wentworth Higginson, *Army Life in a Negro Regiment, and Other Writings* (Boston: Fields, Osgood, 1870);

Robert Stepto, *From Behind the Veil: A Study of Afro-American Narrative* (Urbana: University of Illinois Press, 1979).

Ida B. Wells-Barnett

(16 July 1862 – 25 March 1931)

Stephanie Athey
Stetson University

See also the Wells-Barnett entry in *DLB 23: American Newspaper Journalists, 1873–1900*.

BOOKS: *Southern Horrors: Lynch Law in all its Phases* (New York: New York Age, 1892);

The Reason Why the Colored American Is Not in the World's Columbian Exposition–the Afro-American's Contribution to Columbian Literature, by Wells-Barnett, Frederick Douglass, I. Garland Penn, and Ferdinand L. Barnett (Chicago: Ida B. Wells, 1893);

A Red Record: Tabulated Statistics and Alleged Causes of Lynchings in the United States, 1892–1893–1894 (Chicago: Ida B. Wells, 1895);

Mob Rule in New Orleans (Chicago: Ida B. Wells, 1900);

Crusade for Justice: The Autobiography of Ida B. Wells, edited by Alfreda M. Duster (Chicago: University of Chicago Press, 1970);

Selected Works of Ida B. Wells-Barnett, edited by Trudier Harris (New York: Oxford University Press, 1991);

The Memphis Diary of Ida B. Wells: An Intimate Portrait of the Activist as a Young Woman, edited by Miriam Decosta-Willis (Boston: Beacon, 1995).

Editions: *Southern Horrors and Other Writings: The Anti-Lynching Campaign of Ida B. Wells, 1892–1900,* edited by Jacqueline Jones Royster (Boston: Bedford Books, 1997);

The Reason Why the Colored American Is Not in the World's Columbian Exposition–the Afro-American's Contribution to Columbian Literature, by Wells-Barnett, Frederick Douglass, I. Garland Penn, and Ferdinand L. Barnett, edited by Robert W. Rydell (Urbana: University of Illinois Press, 1999).

During her early twenties in Memphis, Tennessee, Ida B. Wells emerged as "the brilliant Iola," a pen name she often used as a journalist, whose forthright style and incisive political critique gained the attention and respect of a broad readership in what was then an almost exclusively male circle of black press professionals. Wells was to mature into a forceful journalist and

Ida B. Wells (later Wells-Barnett), ca. 1893

editor, one who made her living by writing. She also emerged as a major, though always controversial, figure among those who crafted the African American political agenda for the twentieth century.

Throughout her public career, Ida B. Wells-Barnett consistently broke new political and professional ground. One of but a few black women in journalism, Wells became editor of her local black weekly, the *Memphis Free Speech,* in 1889. When that paper was destroyed in the aftermath of a lynching and her own life was threatened, Wells became contributing editor and part-owner of the *New York Age* and, later, editor of Chicago's *Conservator.* Her investigative reporting led her to the scenes of recent lynchings. Through diligent fact-gathering, Wells established an unprecedented analysis of the economic and institutional nature of racial violence and its dependence on racist and sexist ideologies and gender subordination. Traveling alone, she launched a vigorous international crusade against lynching terror in the United States, speaking during the period from 1892 to 1895 to groups of men and women, white and black, in the United States, England, and Scotland.

Wells's activity had a measurable impact on the national action against racial violence and for civil rights. Always an outspoken advocate for black political independence, physical self-defense, and economic retaliation, she combined a doctrine of economic self-sufficiency with an understanding of the economic leverage African Americans must bring to bear in demanding their due. She believed national organizations must demand influence and accountability from state and federal governments. Consequently Wells was active in the National Colored Press Association and the Afro-American League. The antilynching cause, and the attacks against her character that her lectures aroused, helped galvanize the black women's club movement at a national level. She participated in the founding of organizations such as the National Association of Colored Women and the National Association for the Advancement of Colored People (NAACP). Eventually settling in Chicago, she worked there with the service club named in her honor and went on to establish the Negro Fellowship League and the Alpha Suffrage Club, the first black woman suffrage organization. She also established a kindergarten, a settlement house, and other organizations to provide essential services to Chicago's urban working-class black community as that population grew by tens of thousands between the years 1895 and 1915.

At the turn of the century, Wells-Barnett was an outspoken critic of Booker T. Washington's accomodationist politics and growing influence. By her own account, this fact cost her the good favor and support of black organizers and white philanthropists who, in this political climate, grew increasingly conservative or sought more compromising positions in order to extend their political functionality. Though she was active on the committee that inaugurated the NAACP, she could not back the course it chose to secure the support of influential white members and philanthropists. She faulted the elitism of "exclusives" among her own race, like W. E. B. Du Bois, who she felt wanted to keep the national organization and its Chicago branch "in the hands of the exclusive academic few." In a letter she declared that this academic few "credit for representing the race that they ignore and withdraw themselves from on every occasion of real need." Not least among her extraordinary accomplishments, Wells supported her

four siblings when in her teens and twenties and raised her own four children in her thirties and forties.

Ida Baker Wells was born into slavery on 16 July 1862, the first of eight children born to Jim and Elizabeth Warrenton Wells. The family lived in Holly Springs, Mississippi, where Shaw University, later known as Rust, was founded by the Freedman's Aid Society in 1866. Jim Wells was a trustee of the college, and daughter Ida attended classes there until she was fifteen years old. Her education was interrupted by a yellow-fever epidemic that struck the town in 1877–1878. While Wells was staying with her grandmother outside of Holly Springs, the epidemic claimed the lives of both parents and her infant brother. Two other siblings died shortly after. Returning to nurse the family and electing to keep the children together in spite of the advice of family friends, sixteen-year-old Ida took up full-time teaching at the school six miles from home. Eventually she sought the higher pay offered in the public schools of Memphis, forty miles to the north. She arranged work in Holly Springs for the two oldest boys, and keeping the two youngest sisters in her charge, she moved to the city and was selected as one of twenty black instructors in the public school system. Paid irregularly, Wells received a salary of approximately sixty dollars per month and took charge of seventy pupils in an overcrowded building. She became a determined and outspoken critic of the limited resources and second- and third-rate conditions that increasingly characterized education for black children.

During this period, Wells, already a mature independent woman and hardworking guardian, began to illustrate forcibly the qualities and concerns that she shared with other women of the emerging and tenuous black middle class. Raised in the communal and institutional-service framework of the black church by a deeply religious mother and reading the newspaper to a politically active father, Wells could not escape the grounding in Christian duty, Victorian respectability, and race responsibility that molded the ideological and practical commitments of many black women of her generation. Gender roles within the post-emancipation African American community were distinct from those historically held by white communities. Black women were expected to share as leaders and participants in the public work and in all aspects of theological and practical education within the black community. Yet, this active public role was fused with domestic expectations adapted from the Victorian ideal of True Womanhood. Proscriptions on courtship and sexual proprieties registered with particular force among the middle class, as black women sought to prove the error of centuries of racist sexual propaganda about their character.

Strictly circumspect about her personal reputation, yet dissatisfied with teaching, disinterested in marriage, and averse to housework, Wells felt limited by the professional options confronting black women and the domestic expectations attending black womanhood. In this early period, years before she began to edit her own paper or became internationally known as a skillful orator and relentless crusader against lynching, Wells kept a diary to take account of her writing, thought, and action in intimate terms. Declaring herself "an anomaly to my self as well as to others," she used her diary to ponder, "what kind of creature will I become?" When her aunt sought better opportunities for herself and Wells's siblings in California, she insisted Wells join them and teach in the Visalia school system. Wells felt keenly the contradiction between the woman she wished to become and what she had learned was her Christian and womanly duty. She was pained at the call to forsake the cultural stimulus and support of the African American community in dynamic Memphis in order to see to the domestic needs of her family. After tortured deliberations and reversals, Wells eventually borrowed money to return to Memphis with her youngest sister and pursue her teaching and budding writing career in that setting.

In Memphis, Wells began to demonstrate and consciously develop the personality, ambitions, and skills that distinguished her as editor and activist. Feeling sharply the lack in her own educational background, she continued her intellectual development, taking private lessons in dramatic recitation and joining the teachers' Friday evening "lyceum," a salon for recitation, literary exchange, and cultured conversation. The weekly salon ended with the reading of a new "edition" of the *Evening Star,* which Wells terms a "spicy journal" of reviews, community news, and commentary prepared and recited exclusively for this company. Wells was eventually elected editor of the salon journal and learned she liked the task well. Mailing occasional public letters to the various white and black newspapers and writing streams of private letters to friends and a shifting cast of male mentors and romantic interests–sometimes seven letters a day–Wells increasingly defined herself as a writer and political commentator in an era when her professional options as a black woman, as she perceived them, were limited to that of menial or teacher.

In 1884, when approached by a Baptist publication and asked to become a regular contributor, Wells began submitting commentaries on current matters under the pen name "Iola." These were soon reprinted in other black press publications, and "Iola" gained a larger following. It is clear even in this early journalism that any historical consideration of Wells's writing must

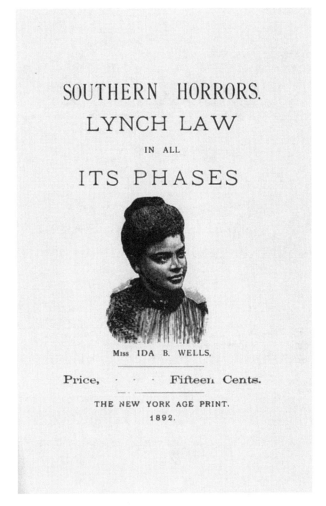

SOUTHERN HORRORS.
LYNCH LAW
IN ALL
ITS PHASES

Miss IDA B. WELLS.

Price, · · · Fifteen Cents.

THE NEW YORK AGE PRINT.
1892.

Title page for Wells's pamphlet on mob violence in the South, in which she recommends that Southern blacks arm themselves for purposes of self-defense

attend to the social concerns that drove her. Wells's first published piece in the *Living Way* discusses a lawsuit she herself had brought against the Chesapeake, Ohio and Southwestern Railroad, one of the first of its kind. Wells was frustrated that more African Americans did not seem to see the relevance of the complaint "as a race matter." She sought and won damages of $500 for the railroad's insistence that she move from the first-class coach to a separate smoking car. The year before she brought this case, the U.S. Supreme Court had declared the Civil Rights Act of 1875 unconstitutional, and the South had grown bolder in its disenfranchisement of black citizens. While the lower court outcome was therefore a great victory against the encroachment of Jim Crow legislation in her region, Wells's faith in the legal system and her "hopes for her people" were soon crushed when the Tennessee Supreme Court reversed the ruling in 1887.

A RED RECORD.

Tabulated Statistics and Alleged Causes of

Lynchings in the United States,

1892-1893-1894.

Respectfully submitted to the Nineteenth Century
civilization in "the Land of the Free and
the Home of the Brave."

BY
MISS IDA B. WELLS,
128 Clark Street,
CHICAGO.

Title page for Wells's continuation of Southern Horrors, *in which she
chronicles the hostile response to her lecture tours*

It is useful to read Wells's diary of the same period in juxtaposition with her early news writing. The diary not only provides clues to the development of Wells's style and identity as a writer, but it also shows her grappling in a personal way with the civil concerns she often took up in her columns. The diary demonstrates that her life as a writer is deeply invested in two of these thematically interrelated concerns, which form the basis of the writing and activism of her later years: first, her interest in black leadership that could forge unified action in the face of specific political challenges, and second, her concern with the role of black womanhood in advancing the race.

Wells started her diary at the close of 1885. At the age of twenty-three she began to think intensely in writing about the options before her as a determinedly single black woman, a writer and a resistant witness to the repeal of Reconstruction gains. Her diary entries are not usually personally or emotionally intense. Many open and close with prayer as a formulaic structuring device; just as frequently, others open or close with a budget record, items needed or purchased and their cost, loan payments, or bills due. In the diary's pages Wells keeps accounts of her daily expenditures, letters received and sent, reactions to news, and notes for essays.

In the diary Wells logs incidents to include in her novel. While she never wrote this novel, and her notes are too vague to reveal her concept of the novel's themes or plot, her notations are provocative. She records three interracial incidents pursued in court—the case against a black girl's fight in self-defense against a white girl and attempts to legalize two interracial sexual unions.

The diary therefore reveals literary aspirations that Wells fails to confess in her autobiography, *Crusade for Justice,* which was unpublished until 1970. In the autobiography Wells describes herself in girlhood as "a voracious reader": "I had formed my ideals on the best of Dickens's stories, Louisa May Alcott's, Mrs. A. D. T. Whitney's and Charlotte Bronte's books, and Oliver Optic's stories for boys. I had read the Bible and Shakespeare through, but I had never read a Negro book or anything about Negroes." Yet, the mature and accomplished autobiographer presents herself as a young woman without real training, merely an instinctive insight into her audience: "So in weekly letters to the *Living Way,* I wrote in a plain, common-sense way on the things which concerned our people. Knowing that their education was limited, I never used a word of two syllables where one would serve the purpose. I signed these articles 'Iola.'" This is one account of Wells's stylistic development; her early diary suggests another. In her diary she reviews novels she has finished and evaluates the characters. While on the one hand these entries suggest Wells is using the diary to study rhetorical technique and narrative prose, on the other she seems to be appraising possible models of manly and womanly behavior as well. For instance, she discusses her disappointment in the "sunshine and flowers" heroine of Victor Hugo's *Les Miserables* (1862) in much the same way she records her judgments concerning the character of her acquaintances, ministers, and neighbors. In the diary Wells practices with a sentimental style and with other more plain and direct forms of argument. It is interesting therefore to see her journalism apply each according to her estimate of what is appropriate to a given subject or audience.

Significantly, her first diary entry, for 29 December 1885, coincides with the publication of her essay "Woman's Mission," a piece that offers Yuletide reflections on woman's place in "all histories, biblical and political, ancient and modern." Women, the essay notes, have "ascended the scale of human progress" in proportion to men's increasing enlightenment. Stating that women's influence is "boundless," Wells chooses archetypal examples of their spiritual and moral impact; for instance, Eve's influential error was eventually made right by the Virgin's holy deeds. She speaks as well to women's educational mission, including their contributions through writing, and here her example is closer to her historical moment. Harriet Beecher Stowe's *Uncle Tom's Cabin* (1985), Wells points out, "was indirectly one of the causes of the abolition of slavery. " She calls upon the "masses of the women of our race" to embody purity, piety, and nobility and, as she was to repeat on many occasions, encourages thought and action in the form of charitable works.

In stark stylistic contrast, a newspaper column printed one month earlier, "Freedom of Political Action," dispenses with the heightened prose, mythic scope, and sweeping ideals in which "Woman's Mission" is steeped. Though female and thus barred from the vote, Wells designates herself a political independent and forthrightly claims the prerogative of politicking and party affiliation. She faults black voters (implicitly men)—and T. Thomas Fortune, the editor of the *Plaindealer,* in particular—for their narrow-minded, "slavish," ahistorical political analysis:

> I am not a Democrat, because the Democrats considered me a chattel and possibly might have always so considered me, because their record from the beginning has been inimical to my interests; because they had become notorious in their hatred of the Negro as a man, have refused him the ballot, have murdered, beaten and outraged him and refused him his rights. I am not a Republican, because, after they—as a party measure and an inevitable result of the war—had "given the Negro his freedom" and the ballot box following, all through their reign—while advocating the doctrine of the Federal Government's right of protecting her citizens—they suffered the crimes against the Negro, that have made the South notorious.

While all her essays on women show the impact of sentimental fiction on Wells's style, she clearly has two stylistic standards at work: the heightened style with which she exhorts the category Woman and the type of sharp-edged historical litany with which she, as a woman of political action, calls both political parties and their supporters to accountability. In the latter, Wells's prose is practical, demonstrating force and wit.

In the published essays that follow "Woman's Mission," Wells evolves a concept of women's leadership as well as their influence. Both are exercised prima-

rily in the act of safeguarding their own virtue and in instructing men in the responsibilities of noble manhood and race advancement. Wells wrote "Our Women" (1887) and "The Model Woman: A Pen Picture of the Typical Southern Girl" (1888) in order to refute the "wholesale contemptuous defamation of women." She portrays "the typical girl" of African descent as the embodiment of the Victorian ideal. In "A Story of 1900" (1886) Wells tells a "future" history of a teacher who learns that examples from life instill "manly independence." Wells's only short fiction, "Two Christmas Days: A Holiday Story" (1894), shows a competitive woman of high standards who turns her efforts to cultivating proper, sober, male achievement on behalf of the race.

In her diary from 1885 to 1887—rather than in her journalism—Wells tests the boundaries of the Victorian ideal of woman's mission with reference to herself and her political role. Indeed, as her model requires, she robustly instructed her acquaintances, even employers, in a vital and active manhood, often pushing men to the point of vexation. In keeping with this aspect of the mission, she also established a Sunday school for the special training of young men. Events and Wells's own disposition, however, caused her to modify this model and reach for forms of influence traditionally wielded by men. Her diary also foreshadows the censure she received as a result of her efforts to originate action and to organize African American men and women for political participation and social service.

For this reason, perhaps, this early diary often seems less a confessional space or a dramatic address to an ideal self and more an experiment with the perception and projection of her own image. In the diary Wells speaks of "cabinets" or photographed portraits that she frequently made and then sent to various correspondents. This series of self-portraits, calculated in their composition of subject and stance, offers an inviting metaphor for the various writing personae and literary styles Wells constructed in the diary and circulated in other forms. In its pages she strategized about the tone and position she should strike in personal letters, wondering how her "motherly" posture or commanding tone would be received. She scrutinized her own behavior, accomplishments, and dissatisfactions in light of the model of womanhood offered by her predominantly male circle of mentors, even when she strained against that model.

The photographs were also an apt figure for the control she sought over her public image. Wells was the frequent subject of gossip, which pained her. As an outspoken and active public school teacher, Wells did not threaten prevailing expectations of women's activity. However, as a woman in her mid to late twenties, still

Title page for Wells-Barnett's 1900 account of the lynching of a New Orleans man

single despite male attentions, and increasingly active in a male-dominated profession, Wells at times was seen as a novelty and at other times a threat. Her "improper" womanliness was censured by the local gossip circuit that insulted her propriety, rumoring that she had been dismissed from her post due to immorality and speculating that she was "taking money" from white men or that her young sister Lily was in fact her daughter. Though she rarely recorded these slanders in specific detail, she objected to accusations against her virtue with indignant passion.

In her professional networks outside her social circle, it was her manliness that became the issue. Continuous comparison to men was often meant to be flattering, as in T. Thomas Fortune's appraisal in 1888 that "she has become famous as one of the few of our women who handles a goose quill with diamond point as handily as any of us men in newspaper work. . . . If Iola was a man she would be a humming Independent

in politics. She has plenty of nerve; she is as smart as a steel trap, and she has no sympathy with humbug."

By 1889, when Wells became co-owner, editor, and sales manager of the *Memphis Free Speech and Headlight,* her "novelty" seemed less charming. An editorialist for the *Indianapolis Freeman* wrote, "The unwritten laws of human conduct, and of journalistic ethics shield many audacious feminine writers from castigations which they richly merit. For this almost inviolable statute the Memphis 'Free Speech and Headlight' has many reasons to be thankful." This statement ran on the same page that featured a two-part editorial cartoon lampooning Wells's journalism as mere barking nuisance, and a derivative nuisance at that. One small panel depicts Wells with her hair styled in her trademark bun, but, uncharacteristically, cross-dressed in a suit with a top hat by her side. The caption reads "I would I were a Man." Beside this panel is a cartoon of two small dogs with human heads (one with trademark bun, one in the likeness of Fortune). "Fortune and his 'Echo'" are known "for their propensity to bark" and yelp "at unseemly hours." The *Indianapolis Freeman,* depicted as a larger, more stately newshound, "is thus forced to grin and bear it."

Just as the diary gives clues to her transformative struggle with the concept of "Black womanhood" and leadership, it also indicates that her political strategy underwent a decided shift as she observed that educational and professional "advancements" were not lessening the force of prejudice against black citizens; indeed, advancement was met with increasingly repressive tactics—both legal and illegal. Her diary records comments on lynchings: she notes the shooting of thirteen black men who were attending a trial in Carrollton County, Mississippi, exclaiming "O, God when will these massacres cease." Recording the death of a black woman "taken from the county jail and stripped naked and hung up in the courthouse yard and her body riddled with bullets and left exposed to view," Wells writes on 4 September 1886, "Can such things be and no justice for it? . . . It may be unwise to express myself so strongly but I cannot help it and I know not if capital may not be made of it against me but I trust in God." Her experience with the railroad was a case in point, and one week after she writes that she is "sorely bitterly disappointed" in the failure of this case, she attended a local Negro Mutual Protective Association organized to fight white violence and the politics of accommodation. Calling the group "the best thing out," she writes on 18 April 1887: "The Negro is beginning to think for himself and find out that strength for his people and consequently for him is to be found only in unity." From this point toward the close of this first diary, her public writing moves increasingly toward radical protest.

As editor of the *Memphis Free Speech,* she had sparred with the influential editors of Northern papers and crafted a high standard of social responsibility for opinion leaders such as editors of the press. An editorial she wrote on the state of black educational resources cost her the teaching appointment that supported her. Wells took the lesson that "free speech" required economic independence and proved herself a canny businesswoman. She resolved to make a living off the newspaper, something few if any managers of a black weekly had done. Wells built a regional subscriber base for the *Free Speech* that paid within ten dollars of her annual teaching salary.

With her own press, Wells sharpened her brand of critique on national issues as well as local. Though copies of the paper no longer exist, her editorials were occasionally reprinted by white newspapers. Her incisive delivery forced examination of the presumptions underlying customary rhetoric or practice. Noting that blacks were sent to prison for stealing 5¢ while whites were honored for absconding with thousands of dollars, the paper offered this advice to the black perpetrator: "Let him steal big." Reports of a Kentucky lynching to which blacks responded with retaliatory violence received editorial endorsement: "Not until the Negro rises in his might and takes a hand in resenting such cold-blooded murders, if he has to burn up whole towns, will a halt be called in wholesale lynching." Wells's editorials used a penchant for ironic inversion and shocking statement to jar recognition of a racial or sexual double standard.

Wells's shift in political tactics was sealed on a second instance of gross injustice supported by the legal system: the 1892 lynching of friends, the razing of black businesses, the hasty arrest of many of Memphis's black citizens, and the destruction of the *Free Speech*. From March to May 1892, black Memphis refused to settle. Wells's personal proximity to these events gave her insight into the deliberate, economic motives that supported lynching terror. A prosperous black grocery and its owners had been targeted for death and destruction with the full knowledge of the leading white dailies, the legal system, and the city's "ruling men." She later told audiences that in light of this "rude awakening," she, and black Memphis with her, could no longer believe "that the maintenance of character, money-getting and education would finally solve our problem and that it depended on us to say how soon this would be brought about." Nor could she any longer accept the rape charge used to justify lynching, though she admitted that she—along with many prominent black leaders—once had.

The *Free Speech* endorsed what amounted to an economic pullout from Memphis. Wells urged black cit-

izens of Memphis to boycott the streetcar lines and to "save our money and leave a town which . . . takes us out and murders us in cold blood when accused by whites." Wells herself traveled West to send word via the *Free Speech* as to the opportunities available in that territory. By one account, as many as two thousand, and Wells writes six thousand, left Memphis, and at least two ministers packed up their entire congregations to move to Oklahoma. Six weeks after the lynching, the streetcar company superintendent and treasurer visited Wells's office to ask her to encourage black citizens to use the electric rails again.

Wells was traveling when her final editorial was printed. Attacking the "threadbare lie that Negro men rape white women," Wells implied what her own investigations had begun to uncover: that white women who willingly entered relations with black men often misrepresented the liaison as "rape" to save themselves from castigation. Threats against her life prevented her from returning to Memphis. By the time the *Free Speech* was destroyed, Wells had already begun another response to lynching, compiling the statistics and analysis that she would circulate as widely as possible at home and abroad. She purchased one quarter interest in the *New York Age* and on 5 June published a front-page, seven-column account of the Memphis terrors. The paper sold ten thousand copies and launched her anti-lynching crusade. Wells published her first pamphlet, *On Lynchings: Southern Horrors* (1892), based on this *New York Age* account. Of the information she here compiled, the African American orator Frederick Douglass said, "I have spoken, but my voice is feeble in comparison." Wells was invited to speak in New York before a joint gathering of black women's clubs, and her lecture career began.

Wells was to publish several pamphlet-length analyses of lynching. Each offered documentation and subsequently developed lengthy analysis, the first of its kind. She used press accounts and statistics gathered by the white *Chicago Tribune* and featured testimony published in other white papers to expose mob violence as a calculated attack on black economic and political power. In light of her evidence, lynching, often carried out in conjunction with mass arrests and the looting and destruction of black-owned businesses or homes, was an obvious attempt to buy or squelch the black vote, restrict black business, and ensure black consumers for white goods and services.

Yet, in spite of these facts, lynching had long been justified as an understandable outburst of rage and vengeance in response to the "outrage" of white women at the hands of brutish black rapists. In reviewing the evidence as the white press itself recorded it, Wells found that in only a third of these cases were accusations of rape made either before or after the murder. In no cases, of course, was the alleged perpetrator given a trial, and in many cases it was later shown that the charges were deliberately false. In refuting the trumped- up rape narrative that protected lynchers, Wells also addressed the violence to which black women were subject without any effective form of legal protection or redress.

Wells's writing coupled her attack on the sexual propaganda that excused lynching with an attack on the institutional mechanisms that supported it. The lynchers were supported by local authorities and by public sentiment as molded by "press and pulpit." Wells's pamphlets emphasize the collaboration of local institutions in a lynching event. In one of her most striking accounts of lynching in these terms, Wells notes that in anticipation of the hanging of Harry Smith in March 1892, the railways to Paris, Texas, offered free fares; public schools cancelled classes; whiskey shops closed; and newspapers assigned their best reporters so the event could be reported in graphic detail, reproduced, and disseminated. Smith, mounted on a float and paraded through town before he was tortured and burned, drew a crowd of ten thousand.

Faced with such realities, Wells insisted that African Americans must be prepared to act in their own defense. She herself bought a pistol after the Memphis lynchings, and in her famous declaration in *Southern Horrors* advised, "A Winchester rifle should have a place of honor in every Black home, and it should be used for that protection which the law refuses to give."

Wells's pamphlets are carefully crafted rhetorical tools. Returning from her first lecture tour abroad, she offered a statement on "Lynch Law" in the pamphlet she initiated and circulated at the World's Fair held in Chicago in 1893: *The Reason Why the Colored American Is Not in the World's Columbian Exposition* (1893). After her second tour, Wells published *A Red Record* (1895), which expanded on *Southern Horrors* and included accounts of conflicts that arose on the tour abroad. She printed *Mob Rule in New Orleans* in 1900, and her autobiography mentions one last pamphlet printed in 1922, *The Arkansas Race Riot*. Her writing routinely avoids sentiment, using facts and scenarios drawn from white press news reports. She frequently invokes patriotic rhetoric in an ironic and biting deflation of terms such as "Christian civilization," "home of the free and land of the brave." The pamphlets speak initially from personal authority, offering the story of the Memphis lynching. She demonstrates for the reader how she, and implicitly the reader, was forced to reject her long-standing belief that gradual education and elevation of her race would end violence. Her personal account is then supported by accounts of similar lynching scenarios

drawn from reports in a number of states. She offers several years of lynching statistics broken down to show the type of accusation that justified the murders.

The pamphlets propose the following public course of action: collect accurate information and make the facts known; call for loud denunciations from all who present themselves as a force for Christian morality; apply economic leverage to retaliate; work for resolutions and federal and state legislation against lynching; and call legislators and law enforcement to account when the law is violated.

In her two extended lecture tours through Scotland and England, Wells set this program in motion. She asked British business opinion to do the work black economic power could not do alone. On her second lecture tour, Wells served as a correspondent to the white Chicago *Inter-Ocean*. Her articles differ from the pamphlets in rhetorical strategy and demonstrate a publicist's eye. These reports are partly travelogue and partly a document of the proceedings of her meetings with various groups. Understanding the dependence of U.S. exporters on British industry, she began her reports with a discussion of the manufacturing interest of Liverpool or Manchester before detailing the success of her anti-lynching lectures in that vicinity. As with her pamphlets, these "Ida B. Wells Abroad" columns developed a mode of indirect self-presentation she would use at length in her autobiography. Quoting British papers, she presented her own lectures, reception, and success as seen by an impartial observer.

Traveling abroad and giving public descriptions of lynchings, Wells not only made herself a news event, she also altered the focus of the lynching spectacle. Wells trained British eyes on the white lynchers and the festive ritual that surrounds the black victim. When assessing the results of the tours, Wells noted that now U.S. governors, papers, legislators, and bishops have all been compelled to "take cognizance" and to "speak in one way or another" concerning these crimes: "This has not been because there was any latent spirit of justice voluntarily asserting itself, especially in those who do the lynching, but because the entire American people now feel, both North and South, that they are objects in the gaze of the civilized world."

On her return to the United States, Wells devoted one additional year to lectures on lynching across the nation. She then settled in Chicago and accepted the marriage proposal of Ferdinand L. Barnett, an attorney and editor of the Chicago's black *Conservator*. Married in June 1895, Wells hyphenated her name in an early example of that practice. She immediately took over editorship of the paper, until her first child, Charles, was born. At that point she retired from public affairs to attend to the job of raising an infant, though this retirement proved to be brief. She recounts criticism she received from various quarters upon marrying and therefore "deserting" the lynching cause. At two points in her autobiography she notes the irony of such remarks since she had married in part due to a lack of financial and moral support for her one-woman anti-lynching crusade.

Wells-Barnett began an autobiography, *Crusade for Justice,* in 1928. In addition to this text she left two other diaries, a fragment of her 1893 travel diary and a 1930 diary. Both are brief and feature short two- to three-line entries with some occasional, provocative paragraph-length commentaries on her activites. The autobiography is the best soure for insight into her mature years and work, however. Presented in clear, spare journalistic style, the autobiography is of interest for the details it offers on Reconstruction and post-Reconstruction persons and politics. As author, Wells-Barnett maintained a focus on her public life and offered only small glimpses into her personal life. Moving from her early years as a teacher, editor, and anti-lynching lecturer to her mature years of Chicago politicking and national activism, the autobiography extended to four hundred pages before she left it uncompleted. It is organized around specific campaigns and organizational efforts rather than a strictly chronological view of her life. In it she recounts the activism of her Chicago years in detail, making careful record of the number and type of organizations that she established or aided in Chicago at the turn of the century. She continued efforts to organize groups capable of addressing "anti-Negro" legislation in Illinois and the lynchings that continued in her state and across the nation. Wells felt the need to fight segregation and to provide simultaneously services for the the black community where white organizations and civic authorities refused to serve African Americans.

The preface opens with the exchange between the sixty-year-old author and a twenty-five-year-old woman who confesses she has often heard Wells-Barnett referred to as a modern Joan of Arc, yet she has no idea why. "Won't you please tell me what it was you did, so the next time I am asked such a question I can give an intelligent answer?" It is to this woman and other youth that Wells-Barnett dedicates the book, attesting to the facts that no record existed to which the student could turn and that few documents had recorded the "authentic race history of Reconstruction times" from the view of the participants.

Throughout the autobiography one feels Wells-Barnett's own conviction that she was called to fight lynching, a Christian duty she must undertake with or without support of her peers. One reads as well her frustration at that lack of support, which she at times

Wells-Barnett and her children, Charles, Herman, Ida, and Alfreda, in 1909

felt bordered on obstruction. The personal history offers recurring examples of Wells-Barnett's frustration with the lack of African American concern and resistance in the face of continued lynchings, riots, and forms of legislative aggression against black rights. She records criticism she had received from "some of our men for jumping in ahead of them and doing work without giving them a chance." Yet, she felt it her duty to act even when others would not. "Eternal vigilance is the price of liberty," she concludes.

Throughout the autobiography, the fragile understanding and cooperation between black and white women activists recurs with almost thematic insistence. She also devotes pages to disagreements with prominent African American leaders Booker T. Washington and W. E. B. Du Bois. She recounts her exchanges with other important personages of the era such as Douglass, Josephine St. Pierre Ruffin, Mary Church Terrell, William Monroe Trotter, Marcus Garvey, Susan B. Anthony, and Jane Addams.

With regard to her later work as an organization woman, she decries the "personal element" and misguided interests that betrayed many of the efforts she led. The text witnesses to conflicts of interest and personality that hampered work of various organizations. In her detailed procedural accounts of meetings, she seems determined to correct misperceptions and to present her own role in the many involved conflicts internal to these organizations. These accounts demonstrate Wells-Barnett's considerable savvy as to political networks, alliances, and procedural know-how. Yet, they also demonstrate her ability to alienate supporters quickly with actions she proclaimed to be matters of principle or common sense and that others perceived to be matters of self-interest on the part of a determined and practiced political strategist.

Wells-Barnett's autobiography, uncompleted as it was, does not mention her run for the Illinois Senate in 1930. Though she lost that race decisively, biographer Mildred I. Thompson suggests Wells-Barnett may have undertaken the campaign not to win but rather to demonstrate the voting strength of Illinois's black women and men. At the end of her life, Wells-Barnett noted with disappointment that even her anti-lynching contribution had been omitted from the study of black history completed by Carter Woodson in 1930. She remained active to her death, which, according to her daughter and editor Alfreda Duster, overtook her suddenly. Returning home one Saturday in March 1931, Wells-Barnett went to bed not feeling well; she died four days later of uremia.

Wells-Barnett's writing offers rare insight into the life of a late-nineteenth-century black woman who witnessed the gains of Reconstruction and their betrayal from a Southern vantage point. She was part of the political and intellectual ferment that gave rise to the African American artistic, cultural, and organizational "Renaissance" of the early twentieth century. Her work represents an aggressive black feminism emerging with the black women's club movement, and, as a militant publicist and agitator committed to urban working-class needs, she unsettles the opposition between Washington and DuBois with which historians traditionally have framed study of political debate at the turn of the century.

With the posthumous publication of her autobiography, diaries, and the continuing work of scholars who cull papers and magazines in order to reprint her essays, pamphlets, and journalism, another generation of educators, activists, and writers have the opportunity to assess the woman and her tremendous legacy anew.

Biographies:
Mildred I. Thompson, *Ida B. Wells-Barnett: An Exploratory Study of an American Black Woman, 1893–1930* (Brooklyn: Carlson Publishing, 1990);
Linda O. McMurry, *To Keep the Waters Troubled: The Life of Ida B. Wells* (New York: Oxford University Press, 1999).

References:
T. Thomas Fortune, "Mr. Fortune on the West, Glances at Indianapolis and Chicago," *New York Age* (11 August 1888): 1;
"Scintillations," *Indianapolis Freeman* (19 April 1890): 4;
David M. Tucker, "Miss Ida B. Wells and Memphis Lynching," *Phylon,* 32 (Summer 1971): 112–122;
Roland Wolseley, "Ida B. Wells-Barnett: Princess of the Black Press," *Encore,* 5 (April 1976): 2.

Papers:
Ida B. Wells-Barnett's papers are held in the Department of Special Collections, University of Chicago Library; the Frederick Douglass papers in the Library of Congress; the Claude A. Barnett papers, Chicago Historical Society; the Charles S. Deneen Newspaper Scrapbooks, Illinois State Historical Library, Springfield; the Margaret Murray Washington Papers, Tuskegee Institute Archives, Tuskegee, Alabama; Howard University, Washington, D.C.; and the Chautauqua County Historical Society. The Edith T. Ross Collection in the University of Illinois at Chicago Circle Library Manuscript Collection contains the first issue of "The Alpha Suffrage Record," a newsletter for a club founded by Wells-Barnett.

Frances E. Willard

(28 September 1839 – 17 February 1898)

Mary Hurd
East Tennessee State University

BOOKS: *Nineteen Beautiful Years, or Sketches of a Girl's Life* (New York: Harper, 1864);

Hints and Helps (New York: National Temperance Society, 1875);

History of the Woman's National Christian Temperance Union (New York: National Temperance Society, 1876);

Home Protection Manual: Containing an Argument for the Temperance Ballot for a Woman, and How to Obtain it as a Means of Home Protection (New York: "The Independent" Office, 1879);

Woman and Temperance: Or, The Work and Workers of the Woman's Christian Temperance Union (Hartford, Conn: Park / Chicago: J. S. Goodman, 1883);

How to Win: A Book for Girls (New York & London: Funk & Wagnalls, 1886);

Woman in the Pulpit (Boston & New York: Lothrop, 1888);

Glimpses of Fifty Years: The Autobiography of an American Woman (Chicago, Philadelphia, Kansas City & Oakland: Woman's Temperance Publication Association, 1889);

A Classic Town: The Story of Evanston by "an Old Timer" (Chicago: WCTU Publishing Association, 1891);

Brilliants Selected from the Writings of Frances E. Willard, compiled by Alice L. Williams (New York & Boston: H. M. Caldwell, 1893);

A Great Mother: Sketches of Madam Willard, by her Daughter Frances E. Willard and her Kinswoman Brace Norton (Chicago: WCTU Publishing Association, 1894);

My Happy Half-Century: The Autobiography of An American Woman, edited by Frances E. Cook (London: Ward, Locke & Bowden, 1894);

Do Everything: A Handbook for the World's White Ribboners (Chicago & London: Woman's Temperance Publication Association, 1895);

A Wheel within a Wheel: How I Learned to Ride the Bicycle, with Some Reflections by the Way (New York: F. H. Revell / London: Hutchinson, 1895); revised as *How I Learned to Ride the Bicycle: Reflections of an Influential 19th Century Woman,* edited by Carol O'Hare (Sunnyvale, Cal.: Fair Oaks, 1991);

Occupations for Women: A Book of Practical Suggestions, for the Material Advancement, the Mental and Physical Development, and the Moral and Spiritual Uplift of Women, by Willard, Helen Winslow, and Sallie White (Cooper Union, N.Y.: Success, 1897).

OTHER: *A Woman of the Century,* edited by Willard and Mary A. Livermore (Buffalo: C. W. Moulton, 1893); enlarged and revised as *American Women,* 2 volumes (New York & Chicago: Crowell & Kirkpatrick, 1897); republished as *Portraits and Biogra-*

phies of Prominent American Women (New York & Chicago: Crowell & Kirkpatrick, 1901).

SELECTED PERIODICAL PUBLICATION–
UNCOLLECTED: "Woman and the Temperance Question," *Journal of Social Science*, 22–23 (1887): 79–80.

When Frances E. Willard died in 1898, the Woman's Christian Temperance Union (WCTU), of which she was founder and leader, was plunged into discord, and members of the union, once held together by the force of her personality and the loyalty she commanded, foundered. To bind the contentious factions that threatened the entire organization, a propaganda campaign was launched by her staunchest followers to deify Willard, shrouding her in the mystical aura of sainthood. The Frances Willard legend reoriented the union chiefly along the narrow lines of temperance and repudiated the broader policies that Willard embraced. Many, if not most, of her reform programs proved to be of a highly ephemeral nature, essentially dying with her. Her subsequent recognition, based largely on a misrepresentation of Willard and her enormous accomplishments, demands reassessment.

The scope of Willard's efforts to change the world is reflected in her writings. Her publications include biographies of noteworthy women, ranging from portraits of family members to sketches of women who were active in social reform; her own autobiography, which was a best-seller; books explaining the history and purpose of the WCTU; and accounts of significant experiences in her life. She wrote many pamphlets offering advice to women concerning the pursuit of useful, independent lives or clarifying the intent of some of her more progressive policies. A relentless traveler and lecturer, she somehow found time to write short pieces for church periodicals or WCTU publications and letters to women nationwide that provided the base for her enormous network of personal influence.

The woman who was to lead the greatest women's organization of the nineteenth century was impelled toward reform in her childhood. Frances Elizabeth Caroline Willard was born of staunch Puritan stock on 28 September 1839 in Churchville, N.Y., fifteen miles from Rochester, to Josiah Flint Willard and Mary Thompson Hill Willard. When she was two, the family moved to Oberlin, Ohio, and then on to Janesville, Wisconsin, where her father sought open air for his health. The desolate prairie enforced painful isolation upon Willard, which was made worse by the rigid discipline and flinty religious views of her father. In the absence of friends or school, "Frank," as she insisted on being called, donned pants, wore her hair short, and imitated her brother's activities. Her brother, Oliver, went away to school, however, and "Frank" was denied education in favor of the domestic arts her father deemed appropriate for young ladies.

Willard's resentment of her father's narrowly conservative views spurred her toward overcoming them. With a meager background in education, she enrolled in Milwaukee Female College in 1857 and struggled to keep up with the class. Because her father preferred a school with a Methodist affiliation, Willard was moved to a school for women recently established at Evanston, Illinois. Though inferior to the school at Milwaukee, the North Western Female College pleased Josiah Willard with its religious atmosphere, and Willard graduated one and a half years later with what she perceived as an "imitation" of a college degree.

Determined to be financially independent, Willard took a teaching position at a one-room country school in Harlem, Illinois, ten miles west of Chicago. Within the next twelve years, Willard held ten teaching positions, capped by her rise to president of Evanston College for Ladies and her subsequent appointment as dean of the Woman's College of Northwestern University. In a bitter dispute over girls' supervision, however, Willard, who favored self-government, was stripped of her powers by Charles Fowler, the president of Northwestern, to whom she had once been engaged. Fowler, a brilliant divinity student and friend of her brother, had proposed to Willard in July 1861, and she had accepted. In February of the following year, however, Willard, unprepared to renounce her independence, terminated the engagement.

On a trip to Europe in 1868, Willard resolved to take a stand about the conventions that limited women's achievements. Believing that opposition to women was the result of unenlightened public opinion, Willard, on her return to the United States, summoned the courage to speak to missionary and church groups around Chicago. Willard's first speech, "The New Chivalry," which publicly committed her to the woman's movement, was delivered at the Centenary Church in Chicago in 1871. The enthusiastically received talk was essentially made up of her observations of women in Europe, whose "sorrowful estate" provided her with the courage to speak out. Six weeks later Willard spoke to eight hundred people in Evanston's Congregational Church on the topic "People Out of Whom More Might Have Been Made." Primarily a plea for the education of women, her address echoed American critic and reformer Margaret Fuller, who insisted that the only real object for women should be to lead a useful life.

In this speech Willard introduced the idea of Womanliness, which was to become the foundation of her program. Avoiding the pitfalls of other activists who had asserted their natural rights—and in doing so had incurred public disapproval—Willard focused on "True Womanhood" as a rationale for reform. The ideal woman of the time espoused purity, piety, and devotion to her home and family—virtues that indicated the superior nature of women to men yet conflicted with the public role of the women reformers. Willard skillfully appealed to the conservative sensibilities of her deeply religious, middle-class audience in creating a role for women that threatened neither the concept of "True Womanhood" nor traditional males.

In June 1874, following a year filled with tension, misunderstanding, and power struggle, Willard submitted her resignation to Fowler and exited the field of education. By that time the women's crusade had reached impressive size and strength, and she went East that summer to meet its leaders. The spontaneous protest against the sale of alcohol that began months before in Ohio had by this time swept through the Midwest, the West, and some areas in the East as thousands of women marched into the streets and invaded saloons in an attempt to close down the retail liquor trade. The exertions of the women were successful, signifying to them the effectiveness of direct assault upon social evil and drawing even larger numbers from their homes into public life and participation in what had become a mass movement. In September 1874 Willard was elected president of the Temperance League of Chicago. In November two hundred women meeting in Cleveland, Ohio, christened themselves the Women's Christian Temperance Union, and Willard, newly elected secretary of the Illinois Temperance Organization, was elected corresponding secretary of the national union. In 1879 she was elected national president of the Woman's Christian Temperance Union, a post she held until her death.

From the time Willard assumed the office of secretary of the union, she worked to influence its objectives. Understanding that it provided the opportunity for the work she had envisaged for the women's movement, she committed herself to the temperance cause. The problem of alcohol abuse had emerged after the American Revolution, with the Methodist Church imposing limitations on the use of distilled liquor in 1790 and urging total abstinence in 1832. Temperance agitation saw the formation of a national temperance union in 1853 and, in the early 1850s, the adoption of legislative prohibition in several states. Liquor consumption dropped but, during the Civil War, rose again rapidly and by 1874 had reached levels of heavy use and abuse. Moreover, the liquor business was connected with politics and associated with crime, corruption, and the control of public offices. Perceiving

Frontispiece for Willard's first book, a biography of her late sister, Mary

America to be a drunken society and themselves the greatest sufferers within it, women had joined the temperance movement in huge numbers. Also, as protectors of the home and nurturers of children, they saw it as their duty to guard against external threat. In the early days of the temperance movement, women had seen their role as gentle persuaders, exerting an influence at home to prevent male family members from drinking. When moral suasion proved ineffective and was abandoned in favor of legislation, however, women were inevitably moved into the public realm to defend their domestic sphere. As a result many women saw no conflict between the two spheres, believing that their responsibility to their home demanded such action. Through church networks Willard corresponded with temperance-minded women in every state and established a base at the local level that increased union membership and ensured effective action.

The position of union secretary allowed Willard to fulfill a longstanding literary aim and also exercise the talent she had displayed as a child. After returning

Willard in 1879, the year she became national president of the Women's Christian Temperance Union

home from her European trip, she had written for church publications, and in 1874 she developed a tireless habit of writing letters, speeches, short pieces, and pamphlets—all written easily but hastily and intended to clarify and promote the union's cause. One of her more impressive organizational weapons was *Our Union,* a newspaper that later merged with the *Signal* to become the *Union Signal,* the official WCTU organ. In 1875 she wrote *Hints and Helps,* a WCTU handbook, and also a story, "Margaret's Victory," which was judged a blatant vehicle for women's rights. Willard thought of herself as a propagandist whose efforts increased the power and influence of the union.

As union secretary, however, Willard discovered she could no longer follow the union's official position against suffrage, and therefore she made her public commitment to the women's ballot—quite possibly her primary goal in the women's movement. Willard's growing national reputation as a forceful orator and bold suffrage leader placed her in great demand for speaking engagements. In her speech "Home Protection Address," which was first delivered in October 1876 in Philadelphia, Willard argued that temperance could be most effectively achieved by giving women the ballot.

Later that month Willard made her plea for suffrage at the national convention of the union in Newark, New Jersey, connecting the conviction that the home was women's special province with the idea that women need the ballot to protect their homes. Although most women of the union were opposed to the idea of suffrage, Willard worked steadily and shrewdly for three years to gain support for her unpopular cause, finally gaining in 1880 the national convention's endorsement of "the ballot for women as a weapon for the protection of her home."

Willard devised the slogan "For God and Home and Native Land," which became the official motto of the union in 1876, and to this effective and emotional appeal she added white ribbon badges, signifying the purity of the home, to be worn by her followers. Willard's presentation of suffrage in terms of "home protection" was the central element in her success in promoting the ballot for women. Avoiding phrases such as "women's rights" or "woman suffrage," which to conservative Americans were terms that threatened traditional values, Willard emphasized women not as militant creatures demanding equality but as maternal ones, whose nurturing influence and moral superiority threatened only that which posed a threat to their homes. Willard promoted women as the "necessary and tender guardians of the home, of tempted manhood and untaught little children," and perceived their gaining the ballot as an essential extension of their protective instinct into the harsh, ruthless world.

Early in "Home Protection Address" Willard drew battle lines between vice, seen as an aggressive liquor industry, and virtue, characterized as a passive and unskilled woman. The liquor industry, not drunkenness, became Willard's greatest enemy. Willard strategically did not blame men for their weakness, drunkenness, or brutality but depicted them as tempted victims of a greedy home-destroyer. Endowing her opponent with human form as the metaphorical "King Alcohol," Willard suggested the battle for the ballot was a "great spiritual war" against the personification of evil. The great army was composed of women, who, as strongholds of piety, were natural participants in a holy war, and as God's weapon against evil, participated with His sanction.

Willard's manipulation of the "True Womanhood" ideal made the involvement of women necessary and reconciled her own more liberal ideals with those of her conservative audiences. A major factor in this appeal was her own representation of this ideal on the speaker's platform. A charismatic speaker, Willard delivered radical, shocking speeches that were belied by her charm and grace. Simply but elegantly attired and utterly feminine, she impressed male and female audiences alike with leadership that affirmed "True Womanhood." While reliance on the special nature of women and the sacredness of their sphere rendered palatable Willard's call for suffrage reform, it possibly restricted even wider programs of reform, which, to have been successful, would have required women to reconsider their traditional roles. Despite the astronomical leap in union membership–from 27,000 to 200,000 during the years Willard campaigned for woman suffrage–and the fact that womanhood arguments were significant in the passage of the nineteenth amendment, Willard's impact was largely personal. At her death, the union's startling reversal to narrowmindedness suggests its failure to accept Willard's broad range of reform.

In her first presidential address in 1880, Willard announced the "Do-Everything Policy," which provided other spheres of activity for women who did not desire to do temperance work. Within ten years Willard organized thirty-nine departments responsible for a wide range of activities. One of the most controversial was the "Department of Social Purity," which was formed to protect young girls. In addition to sex education, it advocated raising the age of consent, holding men equally guilty with women charged in prostitution offenses, and prosecuting fiercely in cases of rape. Willard informed the public that in twenty states the age of consent was ten years old and in one state it was seven. She organized the "Petition of the WCTU for the Further Protection of Women and Children," going to Terence Powderly, chief of the Knights of Labor, who recommended it to his followers and sent a petition to every local assembly of the knights. Presented to Congress in 1887, it, along with other petitions, awakened public opinion to these conditions. Willard called for the abolition of the double standard and for reformers to pledge themselves to a single standard. At the International Council of Women held in Washington, D.C., in 1888 to discuss social purity work, Willard said, "Out of the aggregation of men by themselves always comes harm, but, out of men and women side by side, always comes good." In "A White Life for Two," part of the "Gospel Purity Series" and published in 1890, Willard reverences the home and predicates marriage on the total equality of husband and wife. Reflecting her broad program of reform, this speech calls for woman suffrage, a coalition with labor, coeducation, strengthening laws against rape, and increasing women's control over procreation–all appearing to reaffirm traditional values. Characterizing the men in her audience as chaste and committed to marriage, she appealed to them to create conditions in which women might play their roles more fully. Men did not need to alter their traditional role as protectors of women, Willard contended, but those for whom the family was cen-

tral would have better wives, more loving marriages, and happier homes. Refusing to challenge or blame men, even for the rape of children, she in effect reinforced existing beliefs that were in conflict with the reforms she advocated.

The earliest books Willard produced were biographies of her mother and sister, the two most important women in her life. The first, a biography of her sister, Mary, *Nineteen Beautiful Years, or Sketches of a Girl's Life* (1864), was written a year after her death. Josiah Willard disapproved of the venture, but his daughter, who could not accept the fact that Mary "should live and die and make no sign," completed it while on summer vacation and without her father's support arranged for its publication in New York in early fall. Marked by sentimentality, the book moves with Willard's rhythmical phrases and is interspersed with excerpts from Mary's journal. Mary, the beautiful, sweet, feminine daughter who was four years younger than Willard, died of tuberculosis. She was thought to be recovering until a few weeks before her death on 8 June 1862. The book includes a harrowing account of Mary's death, attended by the religious zeal of her parents, who questioned her anxiously about the experience of dying until the very end. The small volume is an outpouring of love and a catharsis for the grief that threatened not to subside. Willard's biography of her mother, an effusive tribute to "Saint Courageous," was titled *A Great Mother: Sketches of Madam Willard* and was published following her mother's death in 1894.

A Woman of the Century (1893), edited by Willard and Mary A. Livermore, is a significant biographical dictionary including photographs and sketches of 1,400 prominent nineteenth-century women. Willard's most important book, her autobiography, *Glimpses of Fifty Years: The Autobiography of an American Woman* (1889), was published to commemorate her fiftieth birthday. A loosely organized, somewhat repetitive chronicle of reminiscences, the book was produced in six weeks. Organized into seven sections achieved by arranging seven tables in her study and tossing material on the table that pertained to its period, the seven-hundred-page volume includes letters, some entire speeches, lengthy excerpts from her journal, copies of petitions, official reports, and procedures for WCTU meetings. Considerable space is devoted to particularly painful experiences, such as the death of Mary, and her early teaching experiences in rural communities–notably Kankakee, Illinois, the "most irreligious community" she had ever lived in, where her loneliness and homesickness were matched only by her determination for independence. Her engagement to Charles Fowler and its subsequent breakdown following her term at Kankakee is pointedly absent. Of singular significance

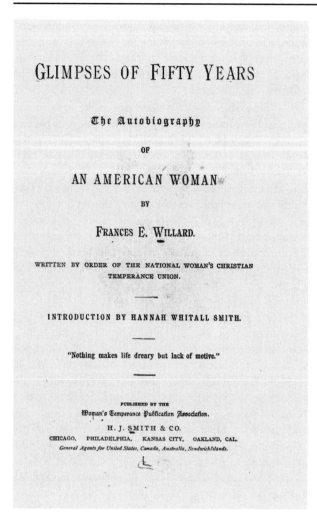

GLIMPSES OF FIFTY YEARS

The Autobiography

OF

AN AMERICAN WOMAN

BY

FRANCES E. WILLARD.

WRITTEN BY ORDER OF THE NATIONAL WOMAN'S CHRISTIAN
TEMPERANCE UNION.

INTRODUCTION BY HANNAH WHITALL SMITH.

"Nothing makes life dreary but lack of motive."

PUBLISHED BY THE
Woman's Temperance Publication Association.

H. J. SMITH & CO.
CHICAGO, PHILADELPHIA, KANSAS CITY, OAKLAND, CAL.
General Agents for United States, Canada, Australia, Sandwich Islands.

Title page for Willard's 1889 memoir, published to coincide with her fiftieth birthday

is the year at Pittsburgh Female Institute following Mary's death, where grief and despair brought her close to collapse.

Willard writes of her early efforts to reorganize the WCTU and the extraordinary amount of traveling (fifteen thousand miles annually for more than ten years) in her methodical state-by-state campaign to adopt the Home Protection Plan and then to advance the WCTU reform to all areas of the country. Her efforts to extend her own political influence were equally impressive. The organization of Home Protection Clubs developed support within the union for Prohibition, as well as a strong constituency Willard could use to associate the union with the Prohibition Party in 1884. Willard's attempts to ally the union with the Knights of Labor served to widen her influence and broaden her power base in a bid to tie economic reform with temperance.

While sketches and testimony of the influential fill pages in her autobiography, the "Silhouettes" are the more interesting features, offering glimpses into her own ideas. Her ruminations on fresh air, dress reform, exercise, and the friendships of women and her opinions of men, vegetarianism, Christian Science, and socialism are far-thinking; her views on other religions, mysticism, phrenology, spiritualism, and psychical research testify to her own broad-mindedness. Her comments on journalism, however, are perhaps the most noteworthy. In "What I Have Done and Suffered as a Pen-Holder" Willard idiosyncratically describes the development of her writing habits, which included childhood journals, the family newspaper called the *Tribune* ("its columns nicely ruled off by mother"), her early submissions to local papers, and family composition contests. She narrates how, with her sister-in-law, she assumed editorship of the *Chicago Evening Post* when her brother, Oliver, the editor, died suddenly in 1878; she eventually abandoned that position in the face of certain bankruptcy. Willard ends the section with advice to women to pursue journalism with patience because "Newspapers need women more than women need newspapers" and gifted women will raise the overall level of the journalistic temperament.

Women and Temperance: Or, The Work and Workers of the Woman's Christian Temperance Union (1883) is a compilation of sketches of temperance leaders and descriptions of their activities. Much of the material in the volume was written by Willard, with editorial help from Mary Lathbury, who was also responsible for the sketch of Willard. Sketches of early crusaders emphasize their ancestry, their zeal, and their specific participation in the crusades. Minute attention is given to the organization of the Woman's National Temperance Convention in Cleveland, Ohio, and the organization, the following year, of the WCTU, with Annie Wittenmeyer its first elected president and Frances Willard its corresponding secretary. Also included in *Women and Temperance* is detailed progress of the Home Protection Movement throughout individual states, which testifies to the impressive organizational propensities of the WCTU. Since the petition was an essential part of her drive for public support, Willard gave special coverage to the "Home Protection Petition," intended for presentation to the Illinois legislature. She details the networking of churches, all sympathetic organizations, and the outstanding religious newspapers in the state to accomplish the signing of 110,000 names and the presenting of a fifty-five pound petition to the General Assembly.

Willard's slender volume *How To Win: A Book for Girls* (1886) offers its target audience advice on opportunities for success. The book encourages the useful life and offers advice to girls on how to "get on." Willard

Willard learning to ride a bicycle in Britain in 1893

laments the "gentle women who have lived and died, and made no sign of their best gifts," and insists that wherever there is a gift, there is a "silent command of God to use it." Calling girls forth to resolution, to put far behind the "aimless reverie" and passivity their role has conditioned them to indulge in, Willard urges them to set a fixed purpose, a definite object in life, toward which they may gaze steadily and earnestly. Cultivating one's specialty, believes Willard, endows an independence that lifts the individual to the world's respect. To the inventory of possible occupations for women, namely journalism, teaching, or positions in the arts, Willard adds the "field of practical philanthropy"–or specifically the WCTU. Arguing that "women are fortunate in belonging to the less tainted half of the race," Willard insists that they require a higher standard of character and purer habits than males in order to fulfill the new ideal of coequal partnership between men and women. Willard then delves into other areas of interest to young girls–the cultivation of grace, diet and exercise, hygiene, proper clothing, avoidance of swearing and other evil habits, compassion for the less fortunate, abstinence from reading novels, and the proper age for girls to marry.

Willard loved the Methodist Church, having grown up with its teachings and having received its support in her earliest endeavors. Still, she was devastated by the Methodist hierarchy's restriction of women's roles in church governance. She incited a storm of controversy when, as newly elected president of the WCTU and delegate to the Methodist General Conference, she asked to address the conference. Following a bitter debate, Willard was grudgingly allowed ten minutes. She declined the offer, later sending a letter of regret for the furor she had inadvertently caused. *Woman in the Pulpit* (1888), a small, well-researched volume that examines the position of women in the Protestant church, is Willard's most ambitious work. Exhibiting considerable knowledge of church history and biblical text, it calls for the ordination of women, their performance of pastoral duties, and acceptance into church governance. Willard provides many examples of biblical strictures that were conveniently ignored. Paul's commandment of women to silence, however, was taken literally by the same clerics to justify restricting women from church governance. Willard examines passages that restricted women from active roles in comparison with those that allowed or encour-

Willard at work in the den of Rest Cottage, her home in Evanston, Illinois

aged them to participate, and in some cases, suggests corruption of the texts.

In *Woman in the Pulpit* Willard denounces the need of the "white male dynasty" to enjoy undisputed reign over the earth, "lording it over every heritage, and constituting the only unquestioned 'apostolic succession.'" She then contends that since "It is *men* who have given us the dead letter rather than the living Gospel, women are needed to restore life-giving spirit." Men, responsible for creeds, dogma, formula, and hierarchy, sorely need the balance of refinement, sympathy, and sweetness of the womanly nature. Willard sees wives and mothers as those most fitted to the duties of ministerial office and cites the testimony of various male and female ministers to defend her views. She reminds readers that women comprise two-thirds of the public school graduates, two-thirds of the teachers in those schools, and three quarters of church membership and that women in the Sunday school system are already theological leaders in the church.

Continuing to publish in the 1890s, Willard turned her attention in 1891 to Evanston, the town of about five hundred inhabitants where her family had moved in 1858. *A Classic Town: The Story of Evanston by "an Old Timer"* is an informal account of the "origin, history and present condition" of the suburb of Chicago. In 1895 Willard published *A Wheel within a Wheel*, which

chronicles her process of learning to ride a bicycle at the age of fifty-three. A best-seller, the book grew out of efforts to restore her health that included a regimen of calisthenics, health diets, and walking as much as her strength permitted. Her bicycle, which she named "Gladys," was a gift from her friend, Lady Somerset, and it posed a challenge to Willard that was equaled by her determination to overcome it. Willard confesses that she learned the location of "every screw and spring, spoke and tire, and every beam and bearing that went to make up Gladys." The "wooing and winning" of her bicycle inspired in Willard a whole philosophy of life. With the catchy phrase, "all failure is from a wobbling will rather than a wobbling wheel," Willard delineates the arduous process. Interspersed with pictures of her at various stages and locations in her efforts, the little book is a treatise on the hardihood of spirit, persistence of will, and patience. She treats her teachers with humor and seizes this opportunity to speculate on the "woman question": necessity for dress reform and promotion of mutual understanding between men and women who take the road together. After two months at ten or twenty minutes' practice off and on daily, Willard mastered Gladys. For Willard, learning to ride amounted to "an act of grace, if not of actual religion," and a means to exercise that meets all the requirements for vigorous activity. She lists her reasons for doing this as her love of adventure, the acquisition of power under her feet, and the fact that a great many people thought she could not do it. Willard's enormous influence probably encouraged many sedentary women to take up exercising.

Occupations for Women (1897) suggests vocations for women other than teaching. Overseen by Willard, who also wrote the introduction, this expansive project took shape with the collaboration of Helen Winslow and Sallie White. An extension of Willard's earliest conviction that women should lead useful, independent lives, the book provides information to interest women in professions such as dressmaking, farming, pet care, business, stenography, sales, advertising, real estate, insurance, medicine, politics, preaching, music, photography, interior decorating, lecturing and journalism.

At her death on 17 February 1898, dissension within the WCTU had already begun, indicating the shifts in the evaluation of her accomplishments that were about to take place. Although the temperance cause with which she is historically linked led to Prohibition with the passage of the Eighteenth Amendment to the Constitution of the United States, it was also responsible for her decline. The repeal of Prohibition in 1933 seemed to repudiate not only her contributions to Temperance but also many of her other reform causes. Her most lasting contributions–the vote for women, public kindergartens, separate correctional institutions for women–have become commonplace in American life. As records of her struggles and achievements, her writings are invaluable. Certainly they reveal the conservative attitudes and family values on which her reform programs were based. But the voice heard is restless, eloquent, and insistent with a womanly need to realize ambition, independence, and equality and, through them, improve society.

Biography:
Ruth Bordin, *Frances Willard: A Biography* (Chapel Hill: University of North Carolina Press, 1986).

References:
Ruth Bordin, *Woman and Temperance: The Quest For Power and Liberty, 1873–1900* (Philadelphia: Temple University Press, 1981);

Karlyn Kohrs Campbell, *Man Cannot Speak for Her: A Critical Study of Early Feministic Rhetoric,* volume 1 (New York: Greenwood Press, 1989);

Mary Earhart Dillon, *Frances Willard: From Prayers to Politics* (Chicago: University of Chicago Press, 1944);

Bonnie J. Dow, "The 'Womanhood' Rationale in the Woman Suffrage Rhetoric of Frances E. Willard," *Southern Communication Journal* (Summer 1991): 298–307;

Jeffrey Furst, *The Return of Frances Willard: Her Case for Reincarnation* (New York: Coward, McCann & Geoghegan, 1971);

Anna Adams Gordon, *The Beautiful Life of Frances E. Willard, A Memorial Volume* (Chicago: WCTU Publishing Association, 1898); revised and abridged as *The Life of Frances E. Willard* (Evanston: National Woman's Christian Temperance Union, 1912);

Joseph Gusfield, *Symbolic Crusade* (Urbana: University of Illinois Press, 1963);

Clara Ingram Judson, *Pioneer Girl: The Early Life of Frances Willard* (Chicago & New York: Rand McNally, 1930);

Richard W. Leeman, *"Do Everythng" Reform: The Oratory of Frances E. Willard* (New York: Greenwood Press, 1992);

Lydia Jones Trowbridge, *Frances Willard of Evanston* (Chicago: Willett, Clark, 1938).

Papers:
A substantial collection of Frances E. Willard's letters, work sheets, and manuscripts is housed at Schlesinger Library, Radcliffe College, Cambridge, Massachusetts. Willard's diaries are in the Willard Memorial Library, Evanston, Illinois.

Martha Wolfenstein

(1869 – 16 March 1906)

Rosalind G. Benjet
University of Texas at Dallas

BOOKS: *Idylls of the Gass* (Philadelphia: Jewish Publication Society of America, 1901);

A Renegade and Other Tales (Philadelphia: Jewish Publication Society of America, 1905).

MARTHA WOLFENSTEIN

Martha Wolfenstein (courtesy of the American Jewish Archives)

She may not have been the first Jewish American woman to publish fiction in the secular press, but it seems likely that Martha Wolfenstein was the first to use Jewish characters in her stories. At a time when Jewish immigrants, mostly poor and uneducated, surged into American cities from eastern Europe, Wolfenstein, an immigrant herself, chose to write stories about Jews who lived in Europe, presumably in the town where she had been born. As a child Wolfenstein immigrated with her parents, Bertha Briger Wolfenstein and Samuel Wolfenstein, from Insterburg, Prussia, to St. Louis, Missouri, where her father, the first ordained Reform rabbi in Europe, served as spiritual leader of Congregation B'nai El. Several years later, Rabbi Wolfenstein moved his family of eight to Cleveland, Ohio, when he took on the position of superintendent of the Cleveland Jewish Orphan Asylum.

Wolfenstein attended Cleveland public schools but was forced to give up formal education when her mother became ill with tuberculosis. After her mother's death the sixteen-year-old assumed the housekeeping duties for her father and four younger siblings. For a time she also served as matron of the orphanage. Her first literary experience involved translating German poetry and stories. According to her sister, Minnie Kornhauser, Wolfenstein began writing fiction when during a "long siege of illness she turned to writing as a diversion." Kornhauser's biography of her sister, which she read before the Cleveland Council Book Club, was printed in the *Jewish Review and Observer* on 26 March 1906, ten days after Wolfenstein's death, but no mention is made of Wolfenstein's death in the article.

Although Wolfenstein had once prepared an autobiographical sketch in response to a request from a London journal, she was reluctant to divulge much of her personal life, considering only the bare essentials to be of public interest. She was far more willing to discuss her literary career. Although several of Wolfenstein's stories had been published previously in the *Jewish Review and Observer* and in *Jewish Orphan Asylum Magazine,* Kornhauser relates that her sister's "first published story" was sent to *Lippincott's Magazine* by a friend without the author's knowledge. The story was an immediate success, and both *Lippincott's* and other magazine editors asked for more contributions. These requests were so numerous that Wolfenstein is said to have remarked, "Did I comply with them all I should have to write nonsense." Publication of her first book, *Idylls of the Gass,* occurred after the Jewish Publication Society asked her to submit some of her work. The stories she sent were immediately accepted, and the book was published in 1901. The Macmillan Company secured the copyright for publication in England and published an American edition in 1903.

Critical reception of the book was generally favorable. *Idylls of the Gass* was reviewed in *The New York Times* on 7 December 1901 and again on 18 July 1903 with the publication of the Macmillan edition, in which the reviewer confirms the merits of the book, observing "so sympathetically and with such surety has she drawn her figures that the reader unconsciously fills in the details and straightway marvels at the author's lucidity." Jewish journals in both England and America praised it, and Kornhauser states that "even non-Jewish reviews of it are unusually kind and sympathetic." Among those who reviewed *Idylls of the Gass* are two Jewish writers, Emma Wolf, who praised the book in the *Baltimore Comment,* and Israel Zangwill, who reviewed the book in the *Jewish Chronicle* of London. Zangwill, who had also written tales of Jews in European ghettos, emphasizes the fact that Wolfenstein's work does not seem in any way American. In fact, he finds "the only blots upon the book" to be several American phrases such as "I guess" and "I'll bet."

Wolfenstein's tales about European Jews continued to appear in *Lippincott's* and *Outlook,* and in 1905 the Jewish Publication Society of America published a second volume of her stories, *A Renegade and Other Tales.* This book, too, received mostly favorable reviews, with the *New York Times* reviewer observing that many of the stories "show a considerable dramatic power" and *Outlook* judging the book as "sound literary work." The reviewer for *The Nation,* however, found the stories uninteresting: "They are of the disappointing kind that begins with spirit and ends tamely, often concluding with a piece of forced pathos that produces actual irritation." The last two stories, although they do not directly address immigrant life, take place at least partly in America.

At a time when most Jewish American writers were concerned with adjustment to life in America, Wolfenstein's stories focus on the European experiences that motivated so many Jews to leave their homes and immigrate. Jewish American writer Mary Antin, who considered living conditions in her native Russian town to be "medieval," emphasizes the miraculous transformation to a modern, enlightened age that living in Boston meant for her in *From Plotzk to Boston,* published in 1899. Abraham Cahan's characters in *Yekl and the Imported Bridegroom* (1896, 1898) struggle with the conflicts that immigration raises between traditional

Jewish culture and the desire to become an American. Zangwill, who had reviewed Wolfenstein's first book, later moved to America and wrote a play, "The Melting Pot," in which he celebrated assimilation and predicted that immigrants would assimilate and form a new kind of American. Certainly Wolfenstein's experiences at the Jewish Orphan Asylum in Cleveland made her familiar with the plight of Jewish immigrants, but she chose to write about a world that she knew only through stories that her father had told her.

The fifteen stories of *Idylls of the Gass* trace the lives of the precocious Schimmele and his grandmother Maryam, who live in the *Judengasse* (Jews' street) in the village of Maritz. Schimmele, who has been identified as a prodigy because he was able to chant the long grace after meals at the age of four, has been sent from his family farm to live with his grandmother so that he may be educated in the village. The devout Maryam earns her living by baking cakes and pastries, but her knowledge of *kashrut* (kosher laws) is such that she is often called on to answer questions when the rabbi is unavailable. She attempts to extend her unswerving faith in God to her young grandson, teaching him prayers and urging him to study to become a rabbi. Schimmele questions the traditions and practices that his grandmother accepts unconditionally. He agrees to study to become a rabbi because there are few alternatives open to bright young Jews. Other stories enlighten the reader about Jewish practices in aiding the poor, about marriage customs, and about anti-Semitic neighbors, including some who believe that Jews engage in blood rituals. Indeed, the climax of the book is reached as the rabbi must testify in vain at a murder trial that Jews do not use Christian blood in "Passover bread."

At this point Wolfenstein's narrator comments on the absurdity of such a charge: "And in the age of Steam and Electricity, in the age of Liberty and Equality, there was witnessed an incredible, unthinkable sight; a high court of Justice in the midst of civilized Europe conducted a trial against a member of an ancient, God-fearing community for the horrible charge of Ritual Murder." After the accused are acquitted because of insufficient evidence, the villagers are brought to a frenzy and run through the town with clubs and axes, looting homes and beating Jewish people. Schimmele's blind uncle, Yossef, tries to keep the mob out, but he and Maryam are both killed in the melee as Schimmele crouches behind a stove. The boy, who has been skeptical about prayer, finds his grandmother's prayer book and prays and cries at the same time. The mob is assessed as "victims of bigotry and corruption, of ignorance and envy and hate."

Wolfenstein's second book, *A Renegade and Other Tales,* collects thirteen otherwise unrelated stories about

Jews from Maritz. This book explores the relationships between Jews and Christians, especially in "A Renegade" and "A Monk from the Ghetto." In "A Renegade" Peretz, a Jewish boy of fifteen, is sent to school in Vienna by the area's richest man, the Count, who considers him a "rare diamond." Later Peretz sends his mother a letter saying that he plans to be baptized so that he can stay in Vienna under the Count's protection. She travels to Vienna, where she learns that the kaiser will be her son's godfather at his baptism. She tries to stop the ceremony but in so doing collapses and dies; Peretz brings her home for the burial but then returns to Vienna. He eventually marries well and becomes the respected Professor Doctor Franz Josef Neuer, one of the finest Greek scholars in Europe. But after he engages in a duel with his brother-in-law, because the latter called him a "damned Jew," his wife and two daughters leave him. When he returns to Maritz to visit his old benefactor, the Count, rumors circulate that he has tuberculosis, the "wasting disease." During Passover, when Neuer's childhood friend Yaikew opens the door for Elijah, he sees Neuer standing there in evening dress. Yaikew informs him that this is not a holiday for gentiles, and Neuer leaves. Later they find him dead, stretched across the grave of his mother with a prayer book open to the kaddish. Neuer is buried at St. Benedict's, but his friend says kaddish and lights a memorial candle for him each year. Earlier in the story, the Count's daughter had complained that she did not understand her father's friendship with Dr. Neuer: "A Jew is a Jew, and remains a Jew. 'Tis in the blood." Wolfenstein's narrator suggests, then, that Jews should not assimilate completely and that hatred and prejudice will return to haunt those who try.

Whether or not the reverse–may a Gentile become a Jew?–can happen is the theme of another story, "A Monk in the Ghetto," the tragic story of a Catholic man raised by a Jewish family. The priest Ferdinand comes to his boyhood friend Reb Nathan with an infant, the child of a union between Ferdinand and his housekeeper. Nathan vows to raise the child, Rudolph, as his own, but as a Catholic, and so Rudolph grows up Catholic in Nathan's Jewish home. When the boy is twelve, his "uncle" Ferdinand calls for him to go to the gymnasium in Prague, where Ferdinand now lives. He does, but Ferdinand dies six years later. Soon afterward Nathan travels to Prague to hear a famous rabbi speak and encounters a young man wrapped in a tallith mourning. When Nathan recognizes Rudolph, he can finally tell him the details of his birth and parentage. Rudolph understands but insists that after growing up in Nathan's family he feels that he is a Jew. Nathan says he was born a Catholic and should remain one. Desolate, Rudolph becomes a monk. After many years,

Rudolph returns to Ferdinand's grave on All Saints' Day to pray; the story ends as Wolfenstein depicts him kneeling silently at the graves of Nathan and his wife, Rachel. The author concludes that religion is determined by birth and parentage and should not change according to individual choice.

Wolfenstein's subject matter seems to center on the question of audience. Although her books were well received by Jewish audiences, as reviews in Jewish publications indicate, she was surely aware that most of her audience would be made up of "old stock" Americans. The contemporary press often portrayed immigrant Jews as a group whose appearance, language, and lifestyle was strange and often repellant. Wolfenstein may have determined that stories about Jews in a far-off European setting would be more palatable reading matter for a mainstream audience than tales about Jews in American slums. The *New York Times* reviewer of *A Renegade and Other Tales* revealed how exotic Wolfenstein's characters must have seemed to Christian Americans: "These stories . . . dealing with strange men and women dwelling in strange places, bearing strange names, stirred by strange feelings–yet very plainly human–are not without fascination." With public opinion often viewing immigrants as undesirables, the reviewer's response may not have been the same if the characters had inhabited a Cleveland ghetto.

That Martha Wolfenstein was conscious of her audience is evident in "The Gass," the first story in *Idylls of the Gass.* After describing the village of Maritz, in an unnamed province of a German-speaking but also unnamed country, she addresses the reader directly, stating that the sophisticated reader might "scorn the homely Sabbath dishes" or "scoff at the simple merriment which is got there out of a clown and fiddler." She continues her journey down the street, noting that it is home only to poor Jews, but she will enter because she wants to discover "who is singing that lovely *Lecho Dodi* (a Sabbath hymn), and on a common week-day, too," as "the beautiful old melody comes riding on the air, as if the Sabbath stood waiting at the gate." Clearly, she implies that the "sophisticated reader" is one who knows little or nothing about Jewish custom and culture, and Wolfenstein feels obligated to describe and explain the travails of her forebears. The world of Wolfenstein's *Idylls of the Gass,* however, is not the "medieval" shtetl described by Mary Antin, but one of a social order governed by religious law, a world that recognizes the fact that assimilation is tempting but concludes that it is not in their best interests for Jews to leave the fold.

Perhaps the strongest of Martha Wolfenstein's beliefs revolves around the Jewish idea of *tzedakah,* or charity, not necessarily surprising since Wolfenstein lived and worked at an institution that dispensed aid to Jewish orphans. According to Jewish tradition, the highest form of charity occurs when the recipient knows nothing of the donor. For example, the Burial Society in *Idylls of the Gass* sends two money boxes to a home where there has been a death. Funds can be taken or added or the boxes can be left as they are; no one knows who donates to the Society or who takes from it for funeral expenses. Wolfenstein's interest in the distribution of funds to the poor did not go unnoticed. The *New York Times* reviewer of *Idylls of the Gass* commented on how care is taken not to offend the sensibilities of the recipients of charity: "Those ignorant of Jewish almsgiving will read with surprise how delicate are their methods."

These "delicate methods," however, were not always transferred by Jews to the New World. In a story titled "The Backstub" Wolfenstein steps out of the narrative to comment on unsavory practices in Jewish America: "I would that our modern charity organizations might have had a lesson of the Burial Society in the Gass. I would that our tender-hearted committees who line up the poor like cattle and brand them before the face of man—I would that they might have studied the methods of the Burial Society in the Gass. And our teachers, those honored makers of the nation, who cry without a tremor, 'All children who are too poor to buy books, please rise!'—the little ones pale and tremble, and often the pain draws such bitter tears—would that they might have learnt the tenderness of the Burial Society in the Gass!" These sentiments would be reinforced and reemphasized by Jewish American writer Anzia Yezierska almost twenty years later when her fictional Jewish characters find fault with the way charity is administered in America.

Martha Wolfenstein seems convinced that loyalty to Jewish principles is paramount for American Jews, recognizing assimilation as inevitable without Jewish identification. She believed that the Jewish education dispensed at the asylum was one sure way of retaining young people in the Jewish community:

> The disintegrating influence of our country is surely operating on our race; as it is upon the other races which inhabit it. The second, or at most the third generation of American-born Jews, have already lost their religion, one of the strongest strands in the bond which holds us together. Therefore must he who wishes for the defeat of this disintegrating power—as it operates upon our people—witness with hope [the asylum's] Seder service. Therefore must he witness it with high hope, since those who participate in it, though mostly, are not all of them children. A goodly number of them are young men and women, former pupils of our institution and they never lose an opportunity of celebrating with us. This is a hopeful sign.

Indeed, the Passover Seder celebration at the Cleveland Jewish Orphan Asylum was recalled as special by writer Edward Dahlberg, who spent five years there, 1912–1917. "And everybody sang *chad gadyo, chad gadyo* [a Passover song], p'sah [Passover] services were being held in the chapel, the kids were in tiptop form, they were getting two hardboiled eggs every night, who wouldn't be."

Martha Wolfenstein's concern about assimilation of Jews in America never appeared in her fiction, although it is the central theme for most among other Jewish American writers. But her final stories move her characters toward America, perhaps indicating that she had exhausted the tales of European Jews. Future work, if she had lived, might have explored American Jewish life through the eyes of one who was committed to her religion. Whether or not Martha Wolfenstein would have changed the format of her writing remains unknown. She was said to be working on a play when she died of tuberculosis on 16 March 1906, but the play was never performed or published. One year after her death, the National Council of Jewish Women of Cleveland named their home for working women Martha House in honor of Wolfenstein.

References:

Minnie Kornhauser, "Martha Wolfenstein. Her Biography as Read Before the Cleveland Council Book Club by her Sister, Mrs. Minnie Kornhauser," *Jewish Review and Observer* (26 March 1906): 8;

Marian J. Morton, ed., *Women in Cleveland: An Illustrated History* (Bloomington: Indiana University Press, 1995), p. 163.

Constance Fenimore Woolson

(5 March 1840 – 24 January 1894)

Sharon L. Dean
Rivier College

See also the Woolson entries in *DLB 12: American Realists and Naturalists; DLB 74: American Short-Story Writers Before 1880;* and *DLB 189: American Travel Writers, 1850–1915.*

BOOKS: *The Old Stone House,* as Anne March (Boston: Lothrop, 1873);

Castle Nowhere: Lake-Country Sketches (Boston: Osgood, 1875);

Two Women: 1862 (New York: Appleton, 1877);

Rodman the Keeper: Southern Sketches (New York: Appleton, 1880);

Anne (New York: Harper, 1882; London: Sampson Low, 1883);

For the Major (New York: Harper, 1883; London: Sampson Low, 1883);

East Angels (New York: Harper, 1886; London: Sampson Low, 1886);

Jupiter Lights (New York: Harper, 1889; London: Sampson Low, 1889);

Horace Chase (New York: Harper, 1894; London: Osgood, McIlvane, 1894);

The Front Yard and Other Italian Stories (New York: Harper, 1895);

Mentone, Cairo, and Corfu (New York: Harper, 1896);

Dorothy and Other Italian Stories (New York: Harper, 1896).

OTHER: "Mackinac," "Lake Superior," "The South Shore of Lake Erie," and "On the Ohio," in *Picturesque America,* 2 volumes, edited by William Cullen Bryant (New York: Appleton, 1876), I: 279–291, 393–411, 510–549; II: 146–167;

"A Brief Sketch of the Life of Charles Jarvis Woolson," essays, poems, and excerpts from notebooks and letters, in *Five Generations,* 3 volumes, by Clare Benedict (London: Ellis, 1930–1932; revised and enlarged, 1932);

Robert Gingras, ed., "'Hepzibah's Story': An Unpublished Work by Constance Fenimore Woolson," *Resources for American Literary Studies,* 10 (1980): 33–46.

Constance Fenimore Woolson

SELECTED PERIODICAL PUBLICATIONS–
UNCOLLECTED: "An October Idyl," *Harper's New Monthly Magazine,* 41 (November 1870): 907–912;

"The Happy Valley," *Harper's New Monthly Magazine,* 41 (July 1870): 282–285;

"Fairy Island," *Putnam's Magazine,* new series 6 (July 1870): 62–69;

"Charles Dickens Christmas, 1870," *Harper's Bazar,* 3 (31 December 1870): 842;

"Spots," *Lippincott's Magazine,* 7 (May 1871): 539–545;

"A Day of Mystery," *Appletons' Journal,* 6 (9 September 1871);

"The Haunted Lake," *Harper's New Monthly Magazine,* 44 (December 1871): 20–30;

"Cicely's Christmas," *Appletons' Journal,* 6 (30 December 1871): 753–758;

"A Merry Christmas," *Harper's New Monthly Magazine,* 44 (January 1872): 231–236;

"Margaret Morris," *Appletons' Journal,* 7 (13 April 1872): 394–399;

"Weighed in the Balance," *Appletons' Journal,* 7 (1 June 1872): 589–594;

"In Search of the Picturesque," *Harper's New Monthly Magazine,* 45 (July 1872): 161–168;

"American Cities–Detroit," *Appletons' Journal,* 8 (27 July 1872): 85–92;

"One *Versus* Two," *Lippincott's Magazine,* 10 (August 1872): 213–221;

"Round by Propeller," *Harper's New Monthly Magazine,* 45 (September 1872): 518–533;

"Lily and Diamond," *Appletons' Journal,* 8 (2 November 1872): 477–483;

"King Log," *Appletons' Journal,* 9 (18 January 1873): 97–101;

"On the Iron Mountain," *Appletons' Journal,* 9 (15 February 1873): 225–230;

"Mackinac Island," *Appletons' Journal,* 9 (8 March 1873): 321–322;

"The Wine Islands of Lake Erie," *Harper's New Monthly Magazine,* 47 (June 1873): 27–36;

"Ballast Island," *Appletons' Journal,* 9 (28 June 1873): 833–839;

"The Bones of Our Ancestors," *Harper's New Monthly Magazine,* 47 (September 1873): 535–543;

"The Flower of the Snow," *Galaxy,* 27 (January 1874): 76–85;

"The Story of Huron Grand Harbor," *Appletons' Journal,* 11 (18 April 1874): 484–490;

"The Waldenburg Road," *Appletons' Journal,* 12 (4 July 1874): 5–11;

"Duets," *Harper's New Monthly Magazine,* 49 (September 1874): 579–585;

"Euterpe in America," *Lippincott's Magazine,* 14 (November 1874): 627–633;

"The Ancient City," *Harper's New Monthly Magazine,* 50 (December 1874): 1–25; (January 1875): 165–185;

"The French Broad," *Harper's New Monthly Magazine,* 50 (April 1875): 617–636;

"Up the Ashley and Cooper," *Harper's New Monthly Magazine,* 52 (December 1875): 1–24;

"The Oklawaha," *Harper's New Monthly Magazine,* 52 (January 1876): 161–179;

"Crowder's Cove: A Story of the War," *Appletons' Journal,* 15 (18 March 1876): 357–362;

"Mission Endeavor," *Harper's New Monthly Magazine,* 53 (November 1876): 886–893;

"The Old Five," *Appletons' Journal,* new series 1 (November 1876): 438–446;

"Keller Hill," *Appletons' Journal,* new series 2 (May 1877): 414–421;

"Barnaby Pass," *Harper's New Monthly Magazine,* 55 (July 1877): 261–271;

"Raspberry Island. Told to me by Dora," *Harper's New Monthly Magazine,* 55 (October 1877): 737–745;

"Matches Morganatic," *Harper's New Monthly Magazine,* 56 (March 1878): 517–531;

"Miss Vedder," *Harper's New Monthly Magazine,* 58 (March 1879): 590–601;

"Black Point," *Harper's New Monthly Magazine,* 59 (June 1879): 84–97;

"'Miss Grief,'" *Lippincott's Magazine,* 25 (May 1880): 574–585;

"The Old Palace Keeper," *Christian Union,* 22 (10 November 1880): 394–396;

"The Roman May, and a Walk," *Christian Union,* 24 (27 July 1881): 76–77;

"In Sloane Street," *Harper's Bazar,* 25 (11 June 1892): 473–478.

Any attempt to reconstruct the life and literary career of Constance Fenimore Woolson must contend with a paucity of information about her. Her original manuscripts and notebooks have been lost, and most of her personal letters were also lost or burned by her friend Henry James. The few letters that survive–including letters to family and friends such as James, John Hay, Paul Hamilton Hayne, Edmund Clarence Stedman, William Dean Howells, an assortment of other acquaintances, and her personal physician–are scattered throughout the United States in various public and private collections from Massachusetts to Michigan to Virginia. A few letters have been published, but they are not readily available in a single volume. When Woolson's niece Clare Benedict, who inherited the writer's estate, collected bits and pieces of Woolson's previously published and unpublished writings, including excerpts from her letters and journals, in *Five Generations* (1930–1932) she did not date them and clearly misinterpreted some of them.

From the rubble of inadequate records, scholars have pieced together some basic facts about the life of Constance Fenimore Woolson. She was born on 5 March 1840 in Claremont, New Hampshire, the sixth daughter of Charles Jarvis Woolson, who traced his origins to colonial New England. Raised in Claremont, he had left to try a career as a journalist in New York City

Woolson at about age fifteen

nary. There she was taught by the founder, Samuel St. John, a specialist in biology, chemistry, geology, and natural history, and by Linda Guilford, a beloved teacher who had attended Mt. Holyoke Female Seminary, which also boasted a rich science curriculum. Woolson maintained contact with Guilford after graduating and going on to finishing school, and she always credited the development of her writing abilities to Guilford, not to the fashionable Madame Chegaray's School in New York City, from which Woolson graduated first in her class in 1858.

There are few extant records of life in the Woolson household. It must, however, have been a busy one. In addition to her two surviving older sisters, Georgiana and Emma, there were two younger sisters—Clara, who outlived Woolson, and Aleta, who died in the first year of her life—and a younger brother, Charlie. The family kept dogs and invited neighborhood dogs to dog funerals, suggesting that the Woolsons did not lead reclusive lives despite their grief over the deaths of several family members and the tendency toward depression that Woolson ascribed to her father and herself.

As she grew into an adolescent and young woman, Woolson watched two of her sisters die. Georgiana married Samuel Mather, a descendent of the New England Mather family, and died at age twenty-two, shortly after the birth of her second child. Emma and her husband, the Reverend Jarvis Carter, both died soon after their wedding. Clara married George Benedict and had a child, Clare, before George was killed in a train accident in 1871. Woolson's father died in 1869, and Charlie, whom Woolson saw as a privileged male child, seemed to be little help to the family. He died mysteriously in California when Woolson was an adult living in Europe. An unpublished letter at the Western Reserve Historical Society voices Woolson's deep sorrow at his death, but other family records omit him from the family tree.

Despite the many losses she experienced, Woolson emerged from her formative years in Cleveland and from the Civil War years, when she worked with volunteer associations for the Union cause, as a woman ready to embrace the life of a writer. This profession offered a means of financial support and the possibility of travel.

After her father's death she lived briefly in New York and sent poems and travel sketches to the *Daily Cleveland Herald* and to literary magazines. After the death of George Benedict, who edited the *Herald,* she returned to Cleveland. Continuing to produce poetry and travel sketches, she also had her first short stories accepted by national magazines and published a children's book, *The Old Stone House* (1873), under the pseudonym Anne March. Economics and her mother's increasing rheumatism convinced the household of four females—Woolson, her mother, Clara, and Clare—to move south. Using St.

and Boston and had returned to his hometown in 1830 to join his father's stove-manufacturing business and raise a family. Constance's mother, Hannah Cooper Pomeroy Woolson, was the daughter of James Fenimore Cooper's sister and, like others in the Cooper family, enjoyed writing.

Within a month of Woolson's birth, three of the Woolson daughters—aged two, four, and five—died of scarlet fever and were buried in a cemetery behind the Universalist church. Because Jarvis Woolson's father had died three years earlier, the Woolsons had few ties to Claremont, and they decided to join friends who had relocated to Cleveland, Ohio. A city of about six thousand when they arrived, Cleveland rapidly became industrialized. By the 1870s, when Woolson left, her mother was mourning the loss of its rural landscape to the pollution spewing from its factories.

Through her daily life during her childhood in Cleveland and through vacations and travel among the Great Lakes, Woolson grew to love the outdoors. She learned to observe the science of the landscape, having received a more thorough scientific education than most young women of her time at the Cleveland Female Semi-

Augustine, Florida, as a base, Woolson traveled to Virginia, the Carolinas, Tennessee, and Georgia, all of which she used as settings for stories.

In the South, Woolson became connected to other writers for the first time: to John Hay, through his relationship to the Mather family, and to Edmund Clarence Stedman and Paul Hamilton Hayne. She turned to them for advice about her finances and her work. Stedman, in particular, helped in her early negotiations with publishers. During the decade she lived in the South, Woolson wrote poems, travel sketches, and stories. At first she set her stories in the Great Lakes region that she knew so well from childhood, and later she used southern settings as she became familiar with the landscape and culture she observed there. She must also have begun her novel *Anne* (1882), which began to be serialized in *Harper's Magazine* in December 1880, the year she left for Europe, and continued to appear there until May 1882.

The impetus behind Woolson's departure for Europe was the death of her mother in 1879. Woolson never returned to the United States. By this time she had nearly stopped writing poetry and had established herself in the more lucrative travel-writing and fiction markets. With her increasing success, she was astute enough to use her connections to gain an introduction to novelist Henry James, whose 1878 novel *The Europeans* she had just reviewed for *The Atlantic Monthly*. From 1880 to 1883 Woolson spent time in Florence, Venice, and Rome, with some of the summer months spent in Switzerland and Germany. She then lived for three years in England, mostly in London and Warwickshire. From 1886 to 1889 she was in Italy, living mostly at the Villa Brichieri in Florence, which she shared for a brief time in 1887 with James. After a trip in 1890 through Egypt and North Africa, she spent another three years in England, in Cheltenham and Oxford, and for the final year of her life she lived in Venice.

The letters she wrote while living in Europe portray a woman who worked and lived under difficult conditions. She became increasingly hard of hearing and suffered from earaches that accompanied her hearing loss; she often had pains in one arm brought on by the physical act of writing; she felt plagued by deadlines and a sense of responsibility to her publisher; she worried about money; and she often felt lonely and rootless. These letters also indicate periods of joy and energy, however, and reveal a woman who turned a witty and observant eye toward her fellow expatriates. Her habits of observation are reflected in the three novels, the novella, the fourteen long stories, and the four travel sketches she wrote in Europe.

Four letters written to Henry James in 1882 and 1883 have given rise to much speculation, including the possibility that Woolson was in love with James, though not enough evidence survives to confirm such suggestions. James is well known for having burned the letters he received, but these four letters from Woolson seem to have escaped because they came to him while he was visiting the United States. After Woolson's death in 1894, James may have destroyed his letters to Woolson when he helped her sister and niece clean out her apartment. Speculation also continues about the circumstances surrounding Woolson's death. On 24 January 1894, during an illness, she fell or—more likely—jumped from a third-floor window in her Venice apartment.

The scarcity of documents and the temptation to speculate have resulted in differing biographies of Woolson, forcing scholars to examine how these different versions of her life advance or retard her reputation and the understanding of her work. For James's biographer Leon Edel, Woolson was a deaf spinster, a pitiful woman who committed suicide because of unrequited love for James. In this view of her life she and her work are interesting only because James felt complicity in her death and because he worked through these feelings in his late fiction. Only in the 1980s did scholars begin to question Edel's view of Woolson and to look more closely at Woolson's body of work and her other surviving papers. Because there is so little material beyond the published work, different pictures of Woolson have emerged: a woman who felt romantic love for James and a woman who felt only a literary kinship with him; a woman who would not have loved any man because her orientation was lesbian; a lonely woman whose life was fraught with sadness and a tough-minded woman who faced difficult circumstances with courage and humor. Woolson could not have been all these women, but she undoubtedly had many of their traits, with various ones becoming stronger at different periods in her life.

In her writings Woolson left a remarkable record of changing national and international perceptions of the United States. Because her work is set in three distinct regions—the Midwest, the South, and Europe—it offers diverse perspectives on a country struggling to define itself as one nation after the Civil War. Viewing the United States as an outsider—a New Englander by heritage who was transplanted to the Midwest, then to the South, and finally to Europe—Woolson asked questions about home and nationhood that resemble those asked by postcolonial literary critics of the late twentieth century: What is home? For whom is it home? How do people impose their concepts of home on others? How does literature mythologize the concept of home? Woolson's consciousness about these questions make her work a valuable resource for those interested in studying the late nineteenth century.

When Woolson set her first published prose in the Great Lakes region of the United States, she was just

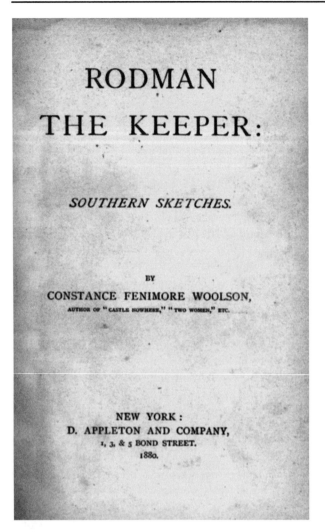

RODMAN
THE KEEPER:

SOUTHERN SKETCHES.

BY
CONSTANCE FENIMORE WOOLSON,
AUTHOR OF "CASTLE NOWHERE," "TWO WOMEN," ETC.

NEW YORK:
D. APPLETON AND COMPANY,
1, 3, & 5 BOND STREET.
1880.

Title page for Woolson's collection of stories that undermine the romantic myth of the antebellum South

such deadly 'real' stories, that I did branch out, in that one, into the realm of the imagination." This comment suggests that from the beginning of her career Woolson felt the demands of the marketplace, in this case the expectation that midwestern fiction by women should center on domestication of the wilderness. By looking to Cooper, Woolson could texture her fiction in a way that her audience would understand but also in a way that turned literary or mythical allusions to her own purpose of questioning concepts relating to home and place.

"Castle Nowhere" provides one of the clearest examples of Woolson's habit of reenvisioning cultural attitudes. Its plot involves an ark isolated on Lake Michigan and inhabited by a father figure with a shady past, by a sheltered daughter figure whom the man has saved from a threatening society, and, temporarily, by a man who is escaping society to immerse himself in the wilderness experience. Like Cooper's Thomas Hutter, Woolson's father figure depends on the society he is escaping. In pirate fashion he lures ships with a false light and then plunders the wrecks he has caused. Through the false-light image Woolson undercuts the myth that earned her granduncle such popularity. To escape into the wilderness is not to engage in the adventure of war with a clear and evenly matched enemy but to survive by taking booty from innocent victims. To escape is not to join a faithful Indian companion who represents the last and best of his race. In fact, the far-from-extinct Indians of Woolson's day were more likely to greet boats full of tourists who had come to glimpse them as local-color attractions than they were to live isolated in forests, which were fast being clear-cut by lumber barons.

The falsest myth that Woolson exposes in "Castle Nowhere" is Cooper's insistence on the compartmentalization of women into the pure but simple-minded girl too good for this evil earth or the feisty woman too tainted for marriage, woman's only legitimate role in life. Woolson makes the ark a kind of Noah's Ark in which the father figure seeks to re-create Eden for the helpless female who, he believes, should know nothing of evil and nothing of what she needs to survive, whether within or outside society. When Woolson demolished Cooper's notion of sexual purity as a spiritually superior position, she also drew on Hawthorne. Instead of rescuing a woman from society only to marry her to a monomaniacal husband, as Hawthorne does in *The Blithedale Romance* (1852), Woolson marries her character to someone who may actually help her to mature. In addition to *The Blithedale Romance,* she drew on Hawthorne's "Rappaccini's Daughter" (1844) and shows that women's freedom in the innocent, western garden can be just as threatened as it had been in the oldest societies of Europe, which are represented in Rappaccini's cultivated Italian garden.

beginning to move away from the romantic style of writers such as Nathaniel Hawthorne and her granduncle James Fenimore Cooper, both of whom she clearly echoed in some of her early work. She was keenly aware of her kinship to Cooper and exploited this relationship every time she published work under her full name, Constance Fenimore Woolson. She had published more than twenty short stories under this name before she collected seven of them, along with two previously unpublished stories, in *Castle Nowhere: Lake-Country Sketches* (1875) The title story—one of the new stories and the longest one in the collection—capitalizes on the Cooper connection through the resemblance of its plot to that of Cooper's *The Deerslayer* (1841), but it also reveals Woolson's differences from Cooper's romantic view of the wilderness and his depictions of nonconforming women as tainted. After she published the story, she wrote to Hayne that it was "something of an ideal, instead of a real tale. . . . But then I had been abused so for writing

Although Woolson "saves" her female character in "Castle Nowhere" from the insularity of the wilderness, she uses the wilderness in other stories as a way of offering women personal freedom. She did not share Cooper's view of the female isolato as an impossible construct. In fact, she felt drawn to this sort of character even as she chose a more social environment for herself. Tracing the settings for many of Woolson's Great Lakes stories, Victoria Brehm has noted in an essay included in *Critical Essays on Constance Fenimore Woolson* (1992), edited by Cheryl B. Torsney, that the women in them draw further and further into the landscape and that within the cliffs and labyrinths of Great Lakes islands they are more likely to find freedom, safety, and the power to create than do Woolson's female characters in the rough mining towns or Zoarite communities that dotted the western landscape in the nineteenth century. Woolson also knew, however, that society offered women the only real avenue for growth. She knew that people who lived in the wilderness would never, for example, develop as artists and that people who came from a high culture were unlikely to survive in even a domesticated rural environment for long. In her travel sketches Woolson was particularly good at satirizing this tendency of cultured nineteenth-century readers to want a quick experience of the local color they saw in rural America. Woolson used her travel writings to describe geographical places, to profile regional characters, and, at the same time, to satirize the tourist. Carolyn VanBergen (Rylander) has shown how Woolson used her travel writings to imagine a context-free society through which she could transform landscape and history. Whether writing sketches of the Great Lakes and St. Augustine or of Mentone, Cairo, and Corfu, Woolson observed the landscape, romanticized it, and at the same time demolished the romantic notions of her traveler-reader.

Not only did Woolson fictionalize her travel writing, but in her fiction she used the observational impulse inherent in travel writing to create an intersection of the social with the natural and the mythical. For example, in "Jeannette" (*Scribner's Monthly,* December 1874), she uses the well-known Arch Rock on Mackinac Island as the setting for a proper Bostonian suitor to try to rescue the title character, a French-Indian woman who needs no rescuing. Woolson combines this plotline with a legend about Robertson's Folly, one of the cliff formations on the island. This legend tells of an English officer who fell to his death when he followed a vision of an imaginary woman. While the legend punishes the officer for loving outside his class, Woolson's story suggests that no punishment is called for. The issue for her was not, as some have argued, marriage outside one's race and class, for she allowed this kind of marriage twice in her novel *Anne.* Rather, in "Jeannette," Woolson resisted the

marriage impulse because she refused to accept the notion that life off the island was better. She allowed Jeannette to reject the suitor because she, too, felt drawn to social isolation, even as she knew that she could not grow in such an environment.

After *Castle Nowhere* Woolson published only three more stories set in the Lake Country, perhaps because she knew that this landscape existed only in her imagination. Its rural isolation was fast disappearing as boats brought not only tourists but also lumber barons, railroad barons, and industrialists. Having begun by embracing the imagined, whose idyllic quality she could never quite believe in, she started to write about the southern landscape and culture that she had been observing. She still wrote many stories focusing on the landscape, signaling this emphasis by titling them with place names, but she also began to write fiction and travel pieces centered on the complexity of race and ethnicity. Florida provided a model of a multi-ethnic society that accommodated Anglo, Spanish, Minorcan, and black populations. Woolson's heightened awareness of race and ethnicity may explain why one of the Great Lakes stories written after those in *Castle Nowhere,* "Raspberry Island" (*Harper's New Monthly Magazine,* October 1877), includes Jewish and Indian characters and another, "Mission Endeavor" (*Harper's New Monthly Magazine,* November 1876), is one of the few stories that suggests her awareness of Indian issues. Later passages in her novels undercut the stereotype of the drunk Indian or the wild savage turned into a kind of tourist attraction. For example, in *Horace Chase* (1894), Woolson transformed an episode she had written about to her sister Georgiana twenty years earlier, turning it into a satire on whites who enjoy the sight of Indians' "half-naked bodies, their whoops and yells," and the picture they make for "whites who looked on from the ramparts above, for it needed but little imagination to fancy a bona fide attack." In this novel Woolson turned the fear she felt earlier into a respect for Indians who re-create themselves as tourist attractions while making fun of the tourists who watch them. Were they imprisoned for crimes? Did they kill white men? Woolson asks these questions in *Horace Chase* and answers, "Of course they did. Haven't the white men stolen all their land?"

Woolson did not directly promote reform in Indian policies, nor was she an outspoken advocate for the rights of African Americans. Her writings about freed slaves reveal the racist attitudes of even the most liberal whites during the nineteenth century. Yet, even as she seems racist when she uses, for example, animal images in describing her black characters, she also exposes the racism that lies beneath the actions of even the most well-meaning white characters. "King David" (*Scribner's Monthly,* April 1878), one of the stories she collected in

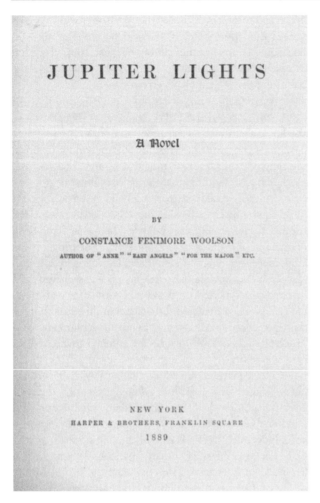

JUPITER LIGHTS

A Novel

BY

CONSTANCE FENIMORE WOOLSON
AUTHOR OF "ANNE" "EAST ANGELS" "FOR THE MAJOR" ETC.

NEW YORK
HARPER & BROTHERS, FRANKLIN SQUARE
1889

Title page for Woolson's novel about two sisters-in-law who flee after one shoots the other's abusive husband

also moves the image to the national and even the archetypal level when she destroys the house by a fire, making possible the union of North and South, represented by the woman's marriage to a Northerner.

In addition to using her southern stories and sketches as a way of commenting on regional and ethnic tensions, Woolson used the South to continue exploring women's sexuality and their integration into insulated communities. She gave a sexual quality to the Minorcan women of Florida that resembles the sexuality of some of her French-Indian characters. In doing so, she repeated a racial stereotype that depicts dark women as more passionate than fair women, but she never punished these women as writers such as Hawthorne and Cooper did. In fact, she seemed attracted to cultures such as the Minorcan in ways that are similar to her attraction toward the asexual culture of Catholic convents, which she developed in "Sister St. Luke" (*Galaxy,* April 1877), a story about a nun who gives up her convent for a brief period only to return to it by the end of the story. Woolson suggests that these cultures are simple and, therefore, can shelter women from the gender roles imposed by less-insulated social systems, but she also exposes them as limiting and patriarchal. The celibate Sister St. Luke leaves the complexity of society to return to the simplicity of convent life, where her fate is controlled by the priests who oversee it. The Minorcan child Felipa in the story of that title (*Lippincott's Magazine,* June 1876) is androgynous because she has been isolated from other women. Once she glimpses the gender-delineated world of adult sexuality, she no longer retains her freedom or her naiveté. While the adult Sister St. Luke retreats to a childlike state, the child Felipa shows the potential for growth.

As much as Woolson saw the impossibility of maintaining isolation from the race, gender, and class codes that intrude whenever even a few people come together to form a community, she also felt attracted to the creative possibilities of the isolated landscape. This landscape is often sexually charged, thus suggesting the procreative passion that Woolson saw embedded in the artistic process. The southern story that best exemplifies the integration of creativity and landscape is "The South Devil" (*The Atlantic Monthly,* February 1880), a story that uses the image of a labyrinthine landscape as a metaphor for the creative process. In this story a musician composes successfully only after he removes himself to a Florida swamp that cleanses him and reveals its music to him. He succeeds in creating a perfect musical score; yet, the music, his great work of art, remains only in his head, because he dies in the swamp. In this story Woolson raises the same theoretical question she raised in a *Castle Nowhere* story, "St. Clair Flats" (*Appletons' Journal,* 4 October 1873), set in the labyrinthine waterways of the St.

Rodman the Keeper: Southern Sketches (1880), is so heavily ironic that it deconstructs the racist attitudes inherent in its northern protagonist's intentions of educating blacks so that they can return to Africa and "wake out of sloth and slumber the thousands of souls there." Named for the biblical king, David King enslaves rather than liberates, and his experiment is doomed to failure.

Woolson's southern sketches never support the nostalgic myth of the South's glorious past because, as an outsider, Woolson was not drawn to the romance of the pre–Civil War plantation. Rather, her southern stories are grounded in observations of people who subscribed to this myth. The best exposure of this nostalgic impulse occurs in another story in *Rodman the Keeper,* "Old Gardiston" (*Harper's New Monthly Magazine,* April 1876), in which the female protagonist clings to the ruins of an ancestral home as a way of refusing to reunite with the North. Woolson uses the realism of local color as she describes the devastated South through images of the Old Gardiston house and the woman who guards its honor. Yet, she

Clair River in Michigan. In both works she asks what constitutes great art and whether or not the artwork exists if no one hears it, sees it, or reads it.

When she moved the theoretical question about the maker and the consumer of art from the isolated landscape, Woolson united it with one of her strongest themes: the role of the female artist in a male-dominated culture and publishing industry. In the course of her career, Woolson became increasingly aware of the problems facing the female artist, particularly the female writer. "The South Devil" appeared in *The Atlantic Monthly* just three months after Woolson had sailed for Europe, suggesting that it was written before she sailed, perhaps after the death of her mother in February 1879, which would explain the sense of loneliness that pervades the story. The uncollected "'Miss Grief,'" published in the May 1880 issue of *Lippincott's Magazine,* just after her arrival in Europe and before her meeting with James, is one of Woolson's finest stories and her best known. In this story Woolson took the issue of artistic creation away from setting entirely and placed it squarely in the context of the publishing industry. Alone among her stories, "'Miss Grief'" has almost no physical landscape, for Woolson had not been in Europe long enough to internalize that landscape. She had, however, been working with publishers long enough to know what kind of pressures they imposed on women writers and, as Torsney has shown in *Constance Fenimore Woolson: The Grief of Artistry* (1989), had been embroiled in her own battles with publishers. In "'Miss Grief'" Woolson explored issues that have since been well rehearsed by twentieth-century feminists, raising questions about how women create, how they publish, how they get read, and how they relate to more-famous and more-valued male writers.

It is not surprising that Woolson intensified her examination of the artist figure in her European stories. While in the South she had developed friendships with other writers, in Europe she found in James a friend who could help her understand the visual arts, to which she had had little exposure. As her surviving letters to him indicate, the two also talked about writing. Two of Woolson's best European stories—"The Street of the Hyacinth" (*Century,* May 1882), collected in *The Front Yard and Other Italian Stories* (1895), and "At the Château of Corrine" (*Harper's New Monthly Magazine,* October 1887), collected in *Dorothy and Other Italian Stories* (1896)—complicate the artist question with the marriage question and, like "'Miss Grief,'" suggest that women who would be artists face poverty and disdain. Although the artists in "The Street of the Hyacinth" and "At the Château of Corrine" both marry rather than endure the poverty of the artist, Woolson ends these stories with hints that, even in capitulation to marriage, these women exact

revenge on or triumph over a system that needs to be changed. Woolson saw the problem of balancing the integrity of the art work with the need for financial stability more often in connection with female characters, but she did not see it as only a female issue. Her undervalued story "In Sloane Street" (*Harper's Bazar,* 11 June 1892), uncollected because its English setting made it thematically unsuited for inclusion in the two posthumously published collections of Italian stories, addresses the issue in the tale of a male writer. Like Louisa May Alcott, whose biography she had read with sympathy, Woolson's male protagonist chooses to write for children, a genre associated with women, and to write for money.

Woolson knew that the children's market could have afforded her some measure of financial security, and, in fact, she had been approached by publishers to write for children. Except for her first, pseudonymous novel, *The Old Stone House,* however, she never accepted these offers, nor did she portray many young children in her books. Those she did include tend to lead lives so filled with pain that they would hardly qualify as protagonists for children's books. Woolson's "children" tend to be grown children, and their relationships with parent figures are fraught with problems. If they are male, they are often prodigal sons who exploit indulgent mothers. If they are female, they deny their own needs to care for parents who offer them little autonomy. The only child character Woolson develops fully appears in "A Transplanted Boy" (*Harper's New Monthly Magazine,* February 1894), one of the last stories she published. For this story, which was collected in *Dorothy and Other Italian Stories,* she may have drawn on the same anecdote about a neglected American child in Europe that James used for his story "The Pupil" (1891), which was written at about the same time. In Woolson's version the child is left to fend for himself in Italy while his ill mother leaves the country to recuperate—and to have an affair. Woolson uses the boy to address issues of nationality and homelessness that her itinerant life had made so apparent to her. This American boy has lived in Europe so long that he does not even know the significance of the Fourth of July. Through the boy in this story, and in many of her other European stories, Woolson continued to look at place as an outsider and to observe issues surrounding outsiders to the insulated American communities in places such as Italy. These outsiders are no longer black or Minorcan or northern intruders as they were in her southern stories. Whether they are boys abandoned by the American community, or Swedish servants (in "A Waitress," *Harper's New Monthly Magazine,* June 1894) and poor Italian women (in "A Christmas Party," *Harper's New Monthly Magazine,* December 1892) who serve the American community, they are the dispossessed, who exist in Europe as much as in the United States.

Memorial to Woolson on Mackinac Island, Michigan, the setting for her novel Anne *(1882)*

In her European stories Woolson continued to examine ethnicity and class as well as art and the role of the artist. When she had been in Europe long enough to learn to see and appreciate her surroundings, she once again placed her characters in landscapes that are quite beautiful. She even pokes fun at characters who cannot appreciate landscape. They are people such as the New Englander in "The Front Yard" (*Harper's New Monthly Magazine,* December 1888) who marries into an Italian family she ends up having to support with her meager earnings. She dreams of tearing down a pigsty in order to plant a front yard like the one she left in New England. When some American tourists find her dying in poverty, they arrange to re-create her New England front yard, and she is comforted. Woolson, however, shows the reader how much more this woman is missing by opening up the now-unblocked view to reveal the ancient Italian landscape. Unlike this woman and other characters whose narrow view she satirized, Woolson had learned to see other landscapes. Moving away from the Great Lakes with its islands and rock formations, she had learned to see the Georgia coast, the Carolina hills, and the Florida swamps, as well as the constructed canals and labyrinthine streets, the walled heights, and the panoramic views of ancient Italy.

Woolson's themes remained constant throughout her career, but her treatment of them became increas-ingly realistic and social. While her Great Lakes stories emphasized imagined spaces, her southern stories emphasized social division. When she began to write in Europe, she developed the realistic, social texture of her fiction even more, particularly in terms of the marriage plot. Her friendship with James may have triggered a greater interest in marriage, and some critics continue to see this interest as a reflection of Woolson's attraction to James, though it could also stem from the marriage plots she saw in his fiction. Her letters indicate that she saw plenty of marriage intrigues around her, including that of the American Lizzie Boott, who lived with her father until the age of forty, when she married her art tutor—much as Woolson's character in "The Street of the Hya-cinth" lived with her mother and married the man she had sought to be her mentor.

Another reason that Woolson may have become more interested in the marriage plot is that in Europe she completed or wrote all her novels and her one novella. These longer forms allowed her greater range than did short fiction for exploring issues that had always inter-ested her. At the same time the longer form demanded that she satisfy her audience's expectations for characters to marry. Woolson often kept the characters of her short stories single, especially if they were artists, but only in her last novel, *Horace Chase,* does her most interesting female character remain single. Yet, Woolson does not allow the major women in her novels to marry easily. The title character in *Anne* marries only after the man she loves has married her best friend, been accused of murdering that friend, and been proven innocent by the detective work of Anne and her spinster companion. In *For the Major* (1883) the naive girl marries predictably, but her stepmother, the older woman in the novella, is not what she appears to be. Having been separated from her ne'er-do-well husband, she has married the major and masqueraded as the younger woman he wants her to be because she needs the security he provides her. Only at the end of *For the Major* does the woman discover that her husband is dead and legitimately marries the major, who has become senile and needs her support. Woolson portrays this woman sympathetically not because she accommodates herself to fulfill the wishes of others, but because she recognizes that accommodation is a weakness that she is not strong enough to resist.

East Angels (1886) and *Jupiter Lights* (1889) raise other issues about marriage. The young woman in *East Angels* easily marries–several times–and Woolson allows her a sexuality that is far less frightening than the female sexuality portrayed by writers such as Cooper and Hawthorne. The more mature character in *East Angels,* however, denies the sexual attraction she feels toward a man who is not her husband and remains married to someone who has betrayed her. Rather than killing off the husband, as many of Woolson's readers wished she had done, Woolson gave this woman power over her own destiny by giving her control of an orange grove that she runs. The naive woman in *Jupiter Lights* raises the most troubling issue relating to marriage in all of Woolson's fiction: that of alcohol and wife and child abuse. To save her from a drunken attack, the woman's more mature sister-in-law shoots the younger woman's husband, and the two women flee north, finding temporary shelter with the man's half brother. The more mature woman develops the same kind of passion for the half brother that the abused wife felt for her husband, but she refuses marriage because she recognizes the danger of this passion and because she believes herself a murderer. Only when she learns that the abusive male died not of gunshot wounds but of alcohol abuse does she feel free to reconsider marriage. Still, the novel ends with a note of violence in the air, when the lover bursts into the woman's conventlike retreat. Although Woolson suggests that this woman has found a way to feel passion without risking abuse, other women, she reminds the reader, may not be so strong.

All set in the regions of the United States that she loved, Woolson's novels address issues related to home and a sense of rootedness, issues she thought about often during the last years of her life, when she lived so much alone in places far from the familial home she had known. She also continued to explore issues of race, class, and art. Southern characters accuse northern ones of being uncomfortable around black people, while Woolson pillories anyone who thinks that whites should hold superior positions over blacks or who lumps all Indians into a racial stereotype. Women face poverty and dreary lives as schoolteachers if they do not marry, or they are mocked as finicky spinsters, but Woolson also allows them the freedom to move from place to place, occasionally offering adventures and wider experiences than they would have had as married women. Woolson's novels include some of her best comic portraits, and the artist figure is not exempt, as in the case of the feminist Maud Murial in *Horace Chase,* who smokes cigars and will use only ugly subjects for her art. Yet, her choice of subject, including her own naked back, also represents Woolson's belief that women should be able to employ areas of artistic expression denied them in the past.

When Woolson fell or jumped to her death on 24 January 1894, she had explored many avenues of artistic expression. The manner of her death eerily recalls a scene she had imagined in her short story "Dorothy" (*Harper's New Monthly Magazine,* March 1892). In that story the title character has been dying slowly under the overpowering influence of depression, and the narrator, seeing her at the edge of a precipice, imagines her throwing herself off and floating to the landscape below like a piece of thistle down. If Woolson acted on this romantic impulse and consciously decided to end her life, she also resisted this same impulse during the years that she lived. In a career that lasted less than a quarter of a century, she proved herself to be a complex realist who observed a far wider cultural milieu than most of her post–Civil War contemporaries. Even her rather conventional poems, as Caroline Gebhard has shown in an entry on Woolson for *The Garland Companion to Nineteenth-Century Verse* (1997), place characters in social situations and were complex enough to be used as stage-declamation pieces by popular actresses of her day. Her fiction and travel writing reflect the movement away from romance and the local into the highly textured social issues of a realism situated in the here and now of the late nineteenth century. Woolson's dislocation may have increased her sense of loneliness, but it also expanded her artistic range. Reading her work, the reader sees demographic changes in the industrializing North and reconstructing South, the loss of the wilderness and the belief in the wilderness experience, the insulation of the elite, the struggle of those on the fringes of society, and the tensions between races and ethnic groups. Woolson helps the reader to understand the particular problems of women in this changing century, whether they were wives, widows, or spinsters; mothers or daughters; painters or writers. Although her career was cut short, Constance Fenimore Woolson left a rich and potent legacy.

Letters:

Jay B. Hubbell, "Some New Letters of Constance Fenimore Woolson," *New England Quarterly,* 14 (1941): 715–735;

Alice Hall Petry, "'Always Your Attached Friend': The Unpublished Letters of Constance Fenimore Woolson to John and Clara Hay," *Books at Brown,* 29–30 (1982–1983): 11–107.

References:

Clare Benedict, *Appreciations* (Leatherhead, U.K.: F. B. Benger, 1941);

Benedict, *Five Generations,* 3 volumes (London: Ellis Press, 1930–1932; revised and enlarged, 1932);

Lynda S. Boren, "'Dear Constance,' 'Dear Henry': The Woolson/James Affair–Fact, Fiction, or Fine Art?" *American Studies,* 27 (1982): 457–466;

Sharon L. Dean, "Constance Fenimore Woolson and Henry James: The Literary Relationship," *Massachusetts Studies in English,* 7 (1980): 1–9;

Dean, *Constance Fenimore Woolson: Homeward Bound* (Knoxville: University of Tennessee Press, 1995);

Dean, "Constance Fenimore Woolson's Southern Sketches," *Southern Studies,* 25 (Fall 1986): 274–283;

Lyndall Gordon, *The Private Life of Henry James* (London: Norton, 1998; New York: Norton, 1999);

Linda Grasso, "'Thwarted Life, Mighty Hunger, Unfinished Work': The Legacy of Nineteenth-Century Women Writing in America," *American Transcendental Quarterly,* 8 (June 1994): 97–118;

Evelyn Thomas Helmick, "Constance Fenimore Woolson: First Novelist of Florida," in *Feminist Criticism: Essays on Theory, Poetry, and Prose,* edited by Cheryl L. Brown and Karen Olson (Metuchen, N.J.: Scarecrow Press, 1978);

Henry James, "Miss Woolson," *Harper's Weekly,* 31 (12 February 1887): 114–115;

John Dwight Kern, *Constance Fenimore Woolson: Literary Pioneer* (Philadelphia: University of Pennsylvania Press, 1934);

Harry Forrest Lupold, "Constance Fenimore Woolson and the Genre of Regional Fiction," *Ohioana Quarterly,* 29 (Winter 1986): 132–136;

Rayburn S. Moore, *Constance F. Woolson* (New York: Twayne, 1963);

Moore, "Constance Fenimore Woolson (1840–1894)," *American Literary Realism,* 3 (1963): 36–38;

L. Moody Simms Jr., "Constance Fenimore Woolson on Southern Literary Taste," *Mississippi Quarterly,* 22 (1969): 362–366;

Cheryl B. Torsney, "In Anticipation of the Fiftieth Anniversary of the Woolson House," *Legacy,* 2 (Fall 1985): 72–73;

Torsney, *Constance Fenimore Woolson: The Grief of Artistry* (Athens: University of Georgia Press, 1989);

Torsney, "The Strange Case of the Disappearing Woolson Memorabilia," *Legacy,* 11 (1994): 143–151;

Torsney, ed., *Critical Essays on Constance Fenimore Woolson* (New York: G. K. Hall, 1992);

Carolyn VanBergen (Rylander), "Constance Fenimore Woolson and the Next Country," *Western Reserve Studies,* 3 (1988): 86–92;

Joanne F. Vickers, "Woolson's Response to James: The Vindication of the American Heroine," *Women's Studies,* 18 (1990): 287–294;

Joan Myers Weimer, *Back Talk: Teaching Lost Selves to Speak* (New York: Random House, 1994);

Weimer, "Women Artists as Exiles in the Fiction of Constance Fenimore Woolson," *Legacy,* 3 (Fall 1986): 3–15.

Papers:

The major collections of Constance Fenimore Woolson's letters are at Brown University (John Hay Archives); Butler Library, Columbia University (E. C. Stedman Papers); Duke University (Paul Hamilton Hayne Papers); Houghton Library, Harvard University (Thomas Bailey Aldrich Papers, William Dean Howells Papers, and Henry James Papers); the Pierpont Morgan Library, New York City (Dr. W. W. Baldwin Papers); and Western Reserve Historical Society (Mather Family Papers). Other letters may be found at the Beverly Historical Society and Museum, Beverly, Massachusetts; Colby College; Fiske Free Library, Claremont, New Hampshire; Mackinac Island Historical Society, Mackinac Island, Michigan; New York Public Library; Ohio State University; and the University of Virginia. Clare Benedict gave some of Woolson's private library to the Claremont Historical Society and some to Rollins College in Florida. She gave other memorabilia to Rollins and donated money to the college to build a house in honor of her aunt. Benedict also withdrew many items from Rollins, however, and in the process all Woolson's manuscripts and notebooks, some of which had been examined by scholars at Rollins, disappeared.

Anzia Yezierska

(ca. 1880 – 21 November 1970)

Julie Prebel

University of Washington

See also the Yezierska entry in *DLB 28: Twentieth-Century American Jewish Fiction Writers.*

BOOKS: *Hungry Hearts* (Boston & New York: Houghton Mifflin, 1920; London: Unwin, 1922); enlarged as *Hungry Hearts and Other Stories* (New York: Persea, 1985);

Salome of the Tenements (New York: Boni & Liveright, 1923; London: Unwin, 1923);

Children of Loneliness (New York: Funk & Wagnalls, 1923; London: Cassell, 1923);

Bread Givers: A Struggle Between a Father of the Old World and a Daughter of the New (New York: Doubleday, Page, 1925; London: Heinemann, 1925);

Arrogant Beggar (New York: Doubleday, Page, 1927; London: Heinemann, 1927);

All I Could Never Be (New York: Brewer, Warren & Putnam, 1932);

Red Ribbon on a White Horse (New York: Scribners, 1950);

The Open Cage: An Anzia Yezierska Collection (New York: Persea, 1979).

Over a career of more than fifty years Anzia Yezierska was a prominent part of the vanguard in the literary treatment of the immigrant experience. As she stated in stories, essays, and interviews, Yezierska felt her mission as a writer was to "build a bridge of understanding between the American-born and myself," essentially to translate the experience of the Jewish ghetto for all America. Her work demonstrates not only her conviction that she could build this bridge, but also her belief in America as the promised land. Finding a common language through which to describe herself and her people was no easy task, however. While her tales express a belief in this land of opportunity, her female protagonists just as often articulate Yezierska's feeling of being "in" America but "not of them." The bridge between the Old World and New often seems like an illusion, with Yezierska and her characters caught between "worlds of difference that no words could bridge over."

When Yezierska emerged on the literary scene in the 1920s, the American public was generally interested in the immigrant experience. She was not the first voice to speak about the struggles of the Jewish immigrant. Writers such as Abraham Cahan and Israel Zangwill had already found success with stories that depict "real" life on the East Side of New York City. The positive reception of Yezierska's work was based on another historical factor as well. With the passing of the Nineteenth Amendment in 1920, women had gained the right to vote. In its attention to the experiences of the immigrant woman, Yezierska's work also addresses the specific concerns of women. The stereotype of the New Woman was extremely popular, and—while there is no evidence that Yezierska knew any of the "New Women" who dominated the New York scene in the 1920s—she certainly subscribed to similar individualistic, self-reliant ideals.

Much like the female characters she created, who exhibit an Emersonian sense of self-reliance, Yezierska persisted in her efforts to bring the Jewish immigrant experience to other Americans. The themes of her stories—immigrant anguish, poverty, and the cultural negotiation between the Old World and the New—are derived from her own experiences as an immigrant in America.

The daughter of Bernard and Pearl Yezierska, Anzia Yezierska was born around 1880 into a family of seven children in the Russian-Polish village of Plotsk. (Her exact date of birth is unknown.) The family came to America in 1890. At Ellis Island each member of the family was given a new name that was easier to pronounce and spell in America. Yezierska became Hattie Mayer. The family settled in a tenement on the Lower East Side of New York. Her sisters went to work in sweatshops, while young Anzia sold paper bags to pushcart peddlers when she was not in school. The Yezierska family quickly learned that America held opportunities for an individual with an education. All the brothers were given the opportunity for schooling, which enabled them to secure stable jobs and earn their own livings, while the sisters supported their rabbi father until they married and had children.

Anzia first worked as a servant in the home of immigrant relatives. Angry at not receiving any wages for her drudge work, she moved back to the tenement and went to work in sweatshops, where she carried on the tradition of her sisters. The exploitation of her labor, both as a servant and as a factory worker, caused Yezierska to rebel. She saw her brothers achieving success through education while her sisters were forced into unhappy marriages. She fought against this family tradition and decided to attend night school—a decision that was contested and criticized by her family.

To escape arguments at home, in 1899 Yezierska moved into a room of her own at the Clara de Hirsch Home for working girls. There she came to the attention of the wealthy patrons, who voted to pay her tuition at Columbia University. Once at Columbia, however, she found that she had been enrolled in the home-science program, and her dreams of becoming a scholar vanished. Although her tuition was paid, Yezierska continued to work in a laundry to earn money for her living expenses. She found her work at college no different from the drudge work in the tenement. In 1904 she received a degree in domestic science from the Teachers College of Columbia University, but with apparently little interest in cooking or teaching, she found only a few substitute teaching jobs.

In 1907 Yezierska won a scholarship to the American Academy of Dramatic Arts and began to pursue a career as an actress. Her study at the academy seems to have introduced her to socialist concerns, such as the problem of poor working conditions in the ghetto, and philosophical ideas, including Ralph Waldo Emerson's writings on self-reliance, that later became central themes in her work. She moved into a room at the socialist Rand School, perhaps to immerse herself further in the culture of young intellectuals. She had achieved her goal of becoming an independent woman, but she found life at the Rand School lonely. She frequently visited her sister Annie, who influenced her to become a writer.

After her studies at the Academy of Dramatic Arts ended, Yezierska decided to take her sister's advice and become a writer instead of an actress. Annie proved to be a source of inspiration. Although burdened with poverty and many children, she was not discouraged. Annie's self-reliant activities, such as organizing the women of the tenement for social change, and the vivid stories of her life provided the material for Yezierska's first short story, "The Free Vacation House," which focused on the problems of an immigrant wife and mother. The story was repeatedly rejected by publishers and revised by Yezierska.

During this time she met Arnold Levitas, her future husband and the father of her only child. In 1910 the two began a correspondence that seemed to ease Yezierska's loneliness. The correspondence quickly grew from letters between friends to love letters. Levitas visited Yezierska frequently at the Rand School, but later that year she rejected him and married his friend Jacob Gordon, a prominent New York attorney. The marriage was annulled six months later. Shortly thereafter, Levitas and Yezierska were married in a religious ceremony that was not legally binding. Yezierska apparently wanted to avoid the repetition of the legal complications that she had experienced in her separation from Gordon.

Her marriage to Levitas in 1911 proved a test for Yezierska's temperament. She found that she could not fulfill the obligations of a "traditional" wife—housework, cooking, and homemaking. Stifled by the conventions of married life and pregnant, Yezierska convinced Levitas that the West held promise for both of them. In 1912 she went to stay with her sister Fannie in California. Two months after the birth of her daughter, Louise, on 29 May 1912, Yezierska returned to Levitas in New York. Domestic bliss once again proved elusive. The couple frequently quarreled and grew further apart. The turmoil of her personal life, in addition to the marital troubles of her sisters, inspired Yezierska to write stories about enslavement of wives. Although stories such as "Rebellion of a Supported Wife" were never published and often never finished, they expressed Yezierska's growing dissatisfaction and anguish with Levitas, who insisted that a woman should be able to manage a household without complaint. To secure some freedom from her husband Yezierska took a job as a cooking teacher, but the additional income only brought about more disagreements with Levitas. In part to escape her marriage and also to help her sister, who was undergoing surgery, Yezierska made a sudden trip back to California in 1915, leaving Louise in the care of Levitas. Unable to reconcile with him Yezierska settled in California with her daughter later that year.

She continued to write during this time but had difficulty finding publishers for her stories. Unable to support herself and her daughter, Yezierska was forced to send her daughter back to New York to live with Levitas. Yezierska continued to teach in California. In December 1915 her story "The Free Vacation House" was published in *The Forum,* and nearly a year later another story, "Where Lovers Dream," appeared in *Metropolitan.*

In 1917 Yezierska moved back to New York, where she took a position as a managing housekeeper. She also found work as a substitute teacher, but again she became discouraged over the low wages. She encountered the same prejudices that she had experienced on graduation from Columbia. In her view she was turned down for full-time, higher-paying teaching positions because of her status as an immigrant.

Yezierska had apparently become aware of social scientist John Dewey and his writings on the place of the immigrant in America, and in 1917 she forced her way into his office at Columbia and demanded that he take up her fight for immigrants' rights. Dewey was apparently persuaded by her passion—and impressed with the two published stories she brought to their first meeting. He encouraged Yezierska to attend his graduate seminar in 1918 and to write about her experiences as an immigrant at Columbia. Thus began a relationship that might best

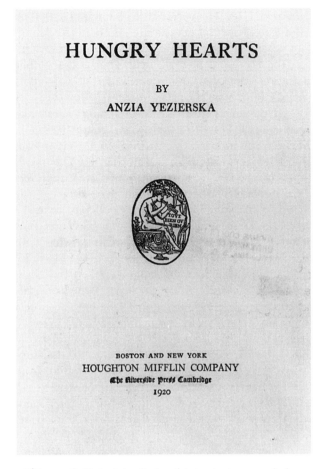

HUNGRY HEARTS

BY
ANZIA YEZIERSKA

BOSTON AND NEW YORK
HOUGHTON MIFFLIN COMPANY
The Riverside Press Cambridge
1920

Title page for Yezierska's collection of stories about women who have immigrated to the United States

be described as an inspirational bond between Yezierska and Dewey: she gave life and vitality to his philosophy, while he became the impetus for her writing career. Although their relationship ended later in 1918 when Dewey left for China, the theme of a passionate Jewish immigrant woman and an emotionally repressed Anglo-Saxon man appears in much of Yezierska's work.

The end of her relationship with Dewey also marked the beginning of the critical recognition of Yezierska's writings. Edward J. O'Brien named her short story "Fat of the Land" the best story of 1919 and included it in his *Best Short Stories of 1919.* In its attention to the rise of an immigrant family from the poverty of Hester Street to the affluence of Riverside Drive, "Fat of the Land" is one of the rags-to-riches stories collected in *Hungry Hearts* (1920). The first half of *Hungry Hearts* deals with the desire of immigrant women to make themselves "up for persons" either through marriage to Anglo-Saxon men or through their own self-reliant hard work. The second half of this collection is a critique of American values and myths from the perspective of immigrant women who experience the devastating effects of the American dream. Despite favorable reviews by literary critics, the book did not sell well. The lack of public attention seemed to be primarily a result of inadequate publicity on the part of the publisher.

Undaunted by this lack of support, Yezierska took it upon herself to find a market for her book. She demanded a meeting with Frank Crane, a leading newspaper columnist. Captivated by Yezierska's story of her struggles as an immigrant in the New World, Crane wrote a column that attracted the attention of Samuel Goldwyn, who offered Yezierska $10,000 for the movie rights to *Hungry Hearts,* plus another $10,000 a year for three years to work with Fox Studios on the movie version of her book. With interest in the immigrant experience and the Nineteenth Amendment at a high point, Yezierska's tale of her struggles as an immigrant woman to become a representative voice for her people had broad appeal. It was not only the stories in *Hungry Hearts* that captured the attention of Hollywood, but also the story of Anzia Yezierska, who had worked herself up from the sweatshops of the ghetto to become a writer.

Yezierska moved to California, where she became known as the "sweatshop Cinderella." Yet, this image, which Yezierska herself had promoted, created a dilemma for her. She enjoyed the wealth and fame that Hollywood offered, but she found herself becoming a part of American capitalist culture, which she saw as a betrayal of her own kind. She found it difficult to mediate between Hester Street and Hollywood, between poverty and success. In "This is what $10,000 did to me," first published in the 1985 edition of *Hungry Hearts,* Yezierska charted her economic rise and condemned herself for becoming one of the class that she criticized. She described her attempt to atone for her success by returning from a visit to Europe in steerage, but she realized that "you can't be an immigrant twice." In her fictionalized autobiography, *Red Ribbon on a White Horse* (1950), Yezierska described feeling as though she were caught between two worlds during this time in Hollywood, a feeling that stifled her ability to write.

The conflicting emotions she experienced in this period are apparent in *Children of Loneliness* and *Salome of the Tenements,* both published in 1923. *Children of Loneliness* is a collection of stories and essays about the children of immigrants who abandon their Old World parents only to discover that they cannot find emotional fulfillment as Americans.

Like *Children of Loneliness,* Yezierska's first novel, *Salome of the Tenements,* depicts the difficulties immigrants encounter in the process of becoming American. The rise of settlement houses in this period provides one of the main historical contexts for Yezierska's novel. In particular, the novel is a critique of settlement-house education projects aimed at Americanizing immigrants by assimilating them into the so-called American melting pot, a process that replaced the customs that immigrants had brought from the Old World with those of the dominant Anglo-Saxon culture. Yezierska's own experience with liberal reformers at the Clara de Hirsch Home provides a semi-autobiographical context for the novel. Much as Yezierska found loneliness and hypocrisy at the Clara de Hirsch Home, Sonya Vrunsky, the female protagonist in *Salome of the Tenements,* discovers fraudulent social mechanics at work in the seemingly liberal aims of the settlement house.

The real-life marriage of a poor, immigrant woman, Rose Pastor, to the millionaire philanthropist Graham Stokes, served as another historical context for *Salome of the Tenements.* Yezierska was particularly interested in her friend's "rags-to-riches" marriage because it also bridged the cultural gap between Jew and Gentile. While the relationship between Pastor and Stokes succeeded, Yezierska's novel dramatized the failure of a similar marriage. *Salome of the Tenements* also includes a fictionalized version of Yezierska's relationship with Dewey in its depiction of interethnic, interclass marriages. The romance between the immigrant Sonya Vrunsky and the Anglo-Saxon John Manning demonstrates the impossibility of philanthropic philosophies such as Manning's (or Dewey's), which maintain that any social chasms can be bridged with human love and understanding.

Although *Salome of the Tenements* sold well, critical disapproval of the novel far exceeded words of praise. Most reviewers did not focus on Yezierska's social critique. Instead, they called the book poorly written and criticized the characterization of Sonya, whom the reviewer for *The Nation* called a "devouring monster." Members of the Jewish community also accused Yezierska of using ethnic stereotypes. Throughout her work, Yezierska relied on and often seemed to reinforce racist stereotypes of the time. She attributed self-control, restraint, and silence to Anglo-Saxons and valued these qualities over the unbridled passion, greed, and noise of immigrants. At a time when the Ku Klux Klan flourished throughout the United States and immigration quotas favored Anglo Saxons, Yezierska's use of ethnic stereotypes seemed to reinforce the racist, conservative ideas of the period.

Yet, as recent feminist critics have pointed out, to describe Yezierska's use of stereotypes as uncritical fails to consider that her reliance on these stereotypes not only reinforced ethnic identity but also set in motion an examination of historically based ideas about race, class, and gender. Depicting the myth of America as the promised land from the perspective of an immigrant woman in *Salome of the Tenements,* Yezierska focused attention on the forces of race, class, and gender upon which the myth of America was constructed.

After the poor reception of *Salome of the Tenements* and *Children of Loneliness,* Yezierska seemed to fall into another period of desolation. Criticized by Anglo-Saxon and Jewish communities alike, she failed to receive the recognition she felt her work deserved.

Bread Givers (1925), however, earned Yezierska critical acclaim and respect as a mature artist. The subtitle—*A Struggle Between a Father of the Old World and a Daughter of the New*—indicates the conflicts between traditions, cultures, and genders that form the theme of the novel. In its attention to these tensions *Bread Givers* is perhaps Yezierska's most autobiographical work. The novel is based on events in her childhood, particularly the struggles she and her three sisters had with their patriarch father.

The story is told from the perspective of the youngest daughter, Sara Smolinsky, who, like Yezierska, sees the effects of the family tradition on her sisters and rebels against her father. Like Yezierska's sisters, the three older sisters in *Bread Givers* bear the burden of their father's tyranny. Like Yezierska's father, Reb Smolinsky, a Talmudic scholar, sends his daughters to work in sweatshops but refuses to work himself, claiming his right to be supported by them while he maintains the traditions of the Old World through his study and prayer. Reb Smolinsky eventually sells his three elder daughters into unhappy marriages, where they continue their drudge work as wives and mothers and suffer new forms of male tyranny. Young Sara, like young Anzia Yezierska, refuses to accept her father's Old World practices and decides to enroll in college so she can become an independent woman.

Sara's subsequent disillusionment resembles that Yezierska experienced at Columbia. Sara's rise to independence is fraught with obstacles that make her goal of becoming a "real American person" difficult to achieve. Although Sara succeeds at breaking from the oppression of the Old World, she finds the New World lonely. She finally finds a place for herself at college after she wins a prize for an essay in which she describes her experiences as an immigrant—an event that recalls O'Brien's selection of Yezierska's story as the best short story of 1919, after she had

Yezierska in 1952

taken Dewey's advice and written about her own experiences in America.

As elsewhere in Yezierska's works, an Anglo-Saxon male modeled on Dewey appears in this novel. Yet, Sara Smolinsky rejects the character type that Sonya Vrunsky in *Salome of the Tenements* viewed as a savior and went to great lengths to marry. Instead, Sara marries Hugo Seelig, a Jew who has been Americanized yet also retains a desire to learn the traditions of the Old World. Sara's choice at the end of the novel—marrying Hugo and taking her traditional father into her home—may seem problematic. This apparent reconciliation between Old and New Worlds resonates with Dewey's influence. Sara's marriage to Hugo is a marriage of past and present, and as such it may be read in the light of Dewey's philosophy of ethnic pluralism, which does not demand that immigrants conform to Anglo-Saxon models of culture but rather asserts that the two cultures can merge.

Women readers of the suffrage decade must certainly have been drawn to the self-reliant, proto-feminist Sara Smolinsky. Yet, the novel, although widely read and admired for several years after its publication in 1925, went out of print and into obscurity with the onset of the Great Depression in 1929. In 1975 *Bread Givers* was rediscovered by Alice Kessler Harris, who edited a new edition of the novel. This rediscovery came on the heels of the revival of the women's movement in the United States, and the novel has found a new audience of female readers.

The end of the 1920s marked a decline of interest in Yezierska's work. Previously praised for its realism, her style was criticized as sentimental and melodramatic. Her characters and plots were described as limited and overused. The Jewish community in particular resented her criticism of their beliefs, customs, and language. Public interest in the plight of immigrants had also declined. For many, a growing hatred for immigrants, as demonstrated by the restrictive immigration laws of 1924, culminated in the 1927 executions of Italian anarchists Nicola Sacco and Bartolomeo Vanzetti, who had been convicted of murder in a trial that revealed an undercurrent of anti-immigrant prejudice.

When Yezierska's next novel, *Arrogant Beggar,* was published in 1927, it was not well received. Its harsh critique of the scientization of social work must certainly have been lost on Americans, who generally approved of organized systems of charity during this time period. In *Arrogant Beggar* Yezierska returned to a theme she had treated in *Salome of the Tenements.* The novel opens with Adele Lindner's move from a tenement to the Hellman Home for Working Girls. Like Sonya, Adele initially sees the home as her only way out of the ghetto and considers the Anglo-Saxon Arthur Hellman (the son of her benefactress) a potential husband and savior. As with Sonya, there is an inevitable moment of disillusionment when Adele recognizes the shallowness of the wealthy patrons of the home. Yezierska's critique of the practices of settlement houses to teach girls to be patriotic and useful women is harsher in *Arrogant Beggar* than in *Salome of the Tenements.* Adele comes to realize that behind the illusion of charity, the Hellman Home stands for a way to systematize class distinctions and institutionalize racism. In contrasting the hypocritical charity of the rich with the genuine charity of the poor, *Arrogant Beggar* is a fictional version of Yezierska's experiences at the Clara de Hirsch Home and Columbia University.

The publication and poor reception of *Arrogant Beggar* coincided with a disappointing reunion with Dewey. According to Yezierska's daughter, Louise Levitas Henriksen, Yezierska found Dewey detached and impersonal, which made her feel like a failure not only as a writer but also as a woman. This sense of failure was compounded by the financial losses

Yezierska suffered as a result of the stock market crash of October 1929. In *Red Ribbon on a White Horse* Yezierska looks back on this period as a time in which she had stopped writing. The royalties on her books dwindled and finally ceased altogether. Bank failures wiped out all her savings, and her investments became worthless. She moved from Fifth Avenue to cheaper rooms on the crowded Lower West Side. She had to "learn all over again" how to manage poverty.

In 1929–1930 the Zona Gale fellowship at the University of Wisconsin offered financial relief and made few demands on Yezierska, who was able to write several stories and finish a novel. *All I Could Never Be* was published in 1932, after Yezierska had returned to New York City.

The novel was not a critical or commercial success. The central story of love and loss involving an immigrant woman, Fanya Ivanova, and Henry Scott, a famous professor who lectures on the rights of ethnic minorities, is Yezierska's most thorough examination of her relationship with Dewey. The first half of the book charts the relationship from beginning to end, when the professor dismisses Fanya with the argument that reason is more important than emotion. The second half of the novel focuses on Fanya's determination in the face of adversity and parallels Yezierska's own economic rise and decline.

Two elements introduced in the novel represent central influences in Yezierska's life: mysticism and quietism. During the mid 1920s many Americans became interested in mystical movements. Yezierska's attraction to mysticism is not surprising considering her earlier interest in Emerson and Transcendentalism. Carol B. Schoen, who has written a book-length study of Yezierska, argues that Yezierska's association with Zona Gale, whose writings demonstrate her mystic and spiritual values and beliefs, might also have contributed to the mystical strain in Yezierska's writing. Throughout her work, Yezierska hinted at her belief in a higher meaning of life. Her characters search for an existence beyond this world as a way to make sense of their unfulfilled yearnings for meaning in the reality of the everyday. This sense of yearning can be seen throughout *All I Could Never Be.* Yet, the novel ends in disheartened quietism. Fanya's passive acceptance of forces beyond herself in the face of adversity results in a quiescence that speaks to the sense of spiritual failure Yezierska experienced during the Depression.

The portrayal of a middle-aged heroine marks another innovation for Yezierska. Through Fanya, Yezierska introduces the problems of age for women who want to remain self-reliant. Her later stories, written mainly during her seventies and eighties, focus on older women and their struggles to maintain their individualism in the face of the constraints imposed by old age and an American culture that fails to recognize or appreciate the aging.

During the 1930s, however, there was little public interest in such themes. Yezierska returned to New York City in 1932, poor and in need of work. She found it difficult to find even domestic work. In the mid 1930s she went to work for the New York unit of the WPA Federal Writers Project, coming in contact with other artists and writers, including the then-unknown Richard Wright. She recorded her work with the Writers Project in vivid detail in *Red Ribbon on a White Horse*. She continued to write during this time but did not find a publisher for her work until 1950.

She broke her literary silence with the well-received *Red Ribbon on a White Horse*. Published when she was nearly seventy years old, it includes an introduction by W. H. Auden, who praised the book for its realistic and truthful account of the "pursuit of happiness" and desire for freedom.

Although she was nearly blind, Yezierska continued writing and having stories, articles, and book reviews published until her death in California on 21 November 1970. Auden's praise underscores the main theme of all Yezierska's work: what "real" liberation means for immigrants—particularly Jewish immigrant women—and at what cost this freedom is earned, if it comes at all.

Biographies:

Louise Levitas Henriksen, *Anzia Yezierska: A Writer's Life* (New Brunswick: Rutgers University Press, 1988);

Mary V. Dearborn, *Love in the Promised Land: The Story of Anzia Yezierska and John Dewey* (New York: Free Press, 1988).

References:

Thomas Ferraro, "'Working Ourselves Up' in America: Anzia Yezierska's *Bread Givers*," *South Atlantic Quarterly*, 89, no. 3 (1990): 547–581;

Alice Kessler Harris, Introduction to *Bread Givers* (New York: Braziller, 1975);

Mariolina Salvatori, "Women's Work in the Novels of Immigrant Life," *MELUS*, 9, no. 4 (1982): 39–58;

Carol B. Schoen, *Anzia Yezierska* (Boston: G. K. Hall, 1982);

Schoen, "Anzia Yezierska: New Light on the 'Sweatshop Cinderella,'" *MELUS*, 7, no. 3 (1980): 3–11;

Gay Wilentz, "Cultural Mediation and the Immigrant's Daughter: Anzia Yezierska's *Bread Givers*," *MELUS*, 17, no. 3 (1991–1992): 33–41.

Papers:

There is a small collection of Anzia Yezierska's manuscripts and letters at Boston University.

Books for Further Reading

Albertine, Susan, ed. *A Living of Words: American Women in Print Culture.* Knoxville: University of Tennessee Press, 1995.

Allen, Paula Gunn. *The Sacred Hoop: Recovering the Feminine in American Indian Traditions.* Boston: Beacon, 1986.

Allen, ed. *Spider Woman's Granddaughters: Traditional Tales and Contemporary Writing by Native American Women.* Boston: Beacon, 1989.

Ammons, Elizabeth. *Conflicting Stories: American Women Writers at the Turn into the Twentieth Century.* New York: Oxford University Press, 1991.

Ammons. *Short Fiction by Black Women, 1900–1920.* New York: Oxford University Press, 1991.

Ardis, Ann. *New Women, New Novels: Feminism and Early Modernism.* New Brunswick, N.J.: Rutgers University Press, 1990.

Bardes, Barbara, and Suzanne Gossett. *Declaration of Independence: Women and Political Power in Nineteenth-Century Fiction.* New Brunswick, N.J.: Rutgers University Press, 1990.

Bargainnier, Earl F., ed. *10 Women of Mystery.* Bowling Green, Ohio: Bowling Green University Popular Press, 1981.

Bataille, Gretchen M., and Laurie Lisa. *Native American Women: A Biographical Dictionary.* New York: Garland, 1993.

Baym, Nina. *American Women Writers and the Work of History, 1790–1860.* New Brunswick, N.J.: Rutgers University Press, 1995.

Baym, *Woman's Fiction: A Guide to Novels by and about Women in America, 1820–1870.* Ithaca, N.Y.: Cornell University Press, 1978.

Benstock, Shari. *Women of the Left Bank: Paris, 1900–1940.* Austin: University of Texas Press, 1986.

Brown, Gillian. *Domestic Individualism: Imagining Self in Nineteenth-Century America.* Berkeley: University of California Press, 1990.

Bruce, Dickson D., Jr. *Black American Writing from the Nadir: The Evolution of a Literary Tradition, 1877–1915.* Baton Rouge: Louisiana State University Press, 1989.

Carby, Hazel. *Reconstructing Womanhood: The Emergence of the Afro-American Woman Novelist.* New York: Oxford University Press, 1987.

Christian, Barbara. *Black Women Novelists: The Development of a Tradition, 1892–1976.* Westport, Conn.: Greenwood Press, 1980.

Clinton, Catherine. *The Plantation Mistress: Woman's World in the Old South.* New York: Pantheon, 1982.

389

Coultrap-McQuin, Susan M. *Doing Literary Business: American Women Writers in the Nineteenth Century.* Chapel Hill: University of North Carolina Press, 1990.

Dann, Martin E. *The Black Press, 1827–1890: The Quest for National Identity.* New York: Putnam, 1971.

DuCille, Anne. *The Coupling Convention: Sex, Text, and Tradition in Black Women's Fiction.* New York: Oxford University Press, 1993.

Fetterley, Judith, and Marjorie Pryse, eds. *American Women Regionalists, 1850–1910.* New York: Norton, 1992.

Foster, Frances Smith. *Written by Herself: Literary Production by African American Women, 1746–1892.* Bloomington: Indiana University Press, 1993.

Garvey, Ellen Gruber. *The Adman in the Parlor: Magazines and the Gendering of Consumer Culture, 1880s to 1910s.* New York: Oxford University Press, 1996.

Gates, Henry Louis, Jr., ed. *Reading Black, Reading Feminist.* New York: Meridian, 1990.

Giddings, Paula. *When and Where I Enter: The Impact of Black Women on Race and Sex in America.* New York: Morrow, 1996.

Green, Rayna. *Native American Women: A Contextual Bibliography.* Bloomington: Indiana University Press, 1983.

Harris, Sharon M. *Rebecca Harding Davis and American Realism.* Philadelphia: University of Pennsylvania Press, 1991.

Harris. *Redefining the Political Novel: American Women Writers, 1797–1901.* Knoxville: University of Tennessee Press, 1995.

Harris, Susan K. *Nineteenth-Century American Women's Novels: Interpretive Strategies.* Cambridge & New York: Cambridge University Press, 1990.

Higginbotham, Evelyn Brooks. *Righteous Discontent: The Women's Movement in the Black Baptist Church, 1880–1920.* Cambridge, Mass.: Harvard University Press, 1993.

Hine, Darlene Clark. *Hine Sight: Black Women and the Re-Construction of American History.* Brooklyn, N.Y.: Carlson, 1994.

A History of the Club Movement among the Colored Women of the United States of America. 1902. National Association of Colored Women's Clubs: Washington, D.C., 1978.

Honey, Maureen, ed. *Breaking the Ties that Bind: Popular Stories of the New Woman, 1915–1930.* Norman: University of Oklahoma Press, 1992.

Howe, Julia Ward, ed. *Sketches of Representative Women of New England.* Boston: New England Historical Publishing Company, 1904.

Howells, William Dean. *Literary Friends and Acquaintance: A Personal Retrospect of American Authorship.* New York & London: Harper, 1900.

Irons, Glenwood, ed. *Feminism in Women's Detective Fiction.* Toronto & Buffalo, N.Y.: University of Toronto Press, 1995.

Jones, Jacqueline. *Labor of Love, Labor of Sorrow: Black Women, Work and the Family, from Slavery to the Present.* New York: BasicBooks, 1985.

Kelley, Mary. *Private Woman, Public Stage: Literary Domesticity in Nineteenth-Century America*. New York: Oxford University Press, 1984.

Kerber, Linda K., Alice Kessler-Harris, and Kathryn Kish Sklar, eds. *U.S. History as Women's History: New Feminist Essays*. Chapel Hill: University of North Carolina Press, 1995.

Kessler, Carol Farley, ed. *Daring to Dream: Utopian Fiction by United States Women before 1950,* second edition. Syracuse, N.Y.: Syracuse University Press, 1995.

Kessler-Harris. *Out to Work: A History of Wage-Earning Women in the United States*. New York: Oxford University Press, 1982.

Krupat, Arnold, ed. *New Voices in Native American Literary Criticism*. Washington, D.C.: Smithsonian Institution Press, 1993.

Lauter, Paul. *Canons and Contexts*. New York: Oxford University Press, 1991.

Lichtenstein, Diane. *Writing Their Nations: The Tradition of Nineteenth-Century American Jewish Women Writers*. Bloomington: Indiana University Press, 1992.

Ling, Amy. *Between Worlds: Women Writers of Chinese Ancestry*. New York: Pergamon, 1990.

Lipow, Arthur. *Authoritarian Socialism in America: Edward Bellamy and the Nationalist Movement*. Berkeley: University of California Press, 1982.

Maida, Patricia D. *Mother of Detective Fiction: The Life and Works of Anna Katharine Green*. Bowling Green, Ohio: Bowling Green University Popular Press, 1989.

Marchalonis, Shirley, ed. *Patrons and Protegees: Gender, Friendship, and Writing in Nineteenth-Century America*. New Brunswick, N.J.: Rutgers University Press, 1988.

Okker, Patricia. *Our Sister Editors: Sarah J. Hale and the Tradition of Nineteenth-Century American Women Editors*. Athens: University of Georgia Press, 1995.

Our Famous Women: An Authorized Record of the Lives and Deeds of Distinguished American Women of Our Times. Hartford, Conn.: A. D. Worthington, 1884.

Penn, I. Garland. *The Afro-American Press and Its Editors*. New York: Arno, 1969.

Peterson, Carla. *Doers of the Word: African American Women Speakers and Writers in the North (1830–1880)*. New York: Oxford University Press, 1995.

Robinson, Harriet Hanson. *Loom and Spindle: or, Life Among the Early Mill Girls.* New York: Crowell, 1898.

Robinson, William H., Jr., *Early Black American Prose*. Dubuque, Iowa: W. C. Brown, 1971.

Ryan, Mary P. *Women in Public: Between Banners and Ballot, 1825–1880*. Baltimore: Johns Hopkins University Press, 1990.

Samuels, Shirley, ed. *The Culture of Sentiment: Race, Gender, and Sentimentality in Nineteenth-Century America*. New York: Oxford University Press, 1992.

Schriber, Mary Suzanne. *Telling Travels: Selected Writings by Nineteenth-Century American Women Abroad*. De Kalb: Northern Illinois University Press, 1995.

Scruggs, Lawson Andrew. *Women of Distinction: Remarkable in Works and Invincible in Character.* Raleigh, N.C.: L. A. Scruggs, 1893.

Shockley, Ann Allen. *Afro-American Women Writers, 1746–1933: An Anthology and Critical Guide.* Boston: G. K. Hall, 1988.

Shoemaker, Nancy, ed. *Negotiators of Change: Historical Perspectives on Native American Women.* New York: Routledge, 1995.

Solomon, Martha. *A Voice of Their Own: The Woman Suffrage Press, 1840–1910.* Tuscaloosa: University of Alabama Press, 1991.

Sterling, Dorothy. *We Are Your Sisters: Black Women in the Nineteenth Century.* New York: Norton, 1984.

Still, William. *The Underground Railroad.* Philadelphia: Porter & Coates, 1872; reprinted, Chicago: Johnson, 1970.

Tate, Claudia. *Domestic Allegories of Political Desire: The Black Heroine's Text at the Turn of the Century.* New York: Oxford University Press, 1992.

Tentler, Leslie Woodcock. *Wage-Earning Women: Industrial Work and Family Life in the United States, 1900–1930.* New York: Oxford University Press, 1979.

Walker, Cheryl. *Indian Nation: Native American Literature and Nineteenth-Century Nationalisms.* Durham, N.C.: Duke University Press, 1997.

Wall, Cheryl, ed. *Changing Our Own Words: Essays on Criticism, Theory, and Writing by Black Women.* New Brunswick, N.J.: Rutgers University Press, 1989.

Washington, Mary Helen, ed. *Invented Lives: Narratives of Black Women, 1860–1960.* Garden City, N.Y.: Anchor, 1987.

Contributors

José F. Aranda Jr. . . . . *Rice University*

Stephanie Athey . . . . *Stetson University*

Rosalind G. Benjet . . . . *University of Texas at Dallas*

Betty Bergland . . . . *University of Wisconsin–River Falls*

Susanne George Bloomfield . . . . *University of Nebraska at Kearney*

Kristin Boudreau . . . . *University of Georgia*

Alanna Kathleen Brown . . . . *Montana State University*

Karen Dandurand . . . . *Indiana University of Pennsylvania*

Sharon L. Dean . . . . *Rivier College*

Marylynne Diggs . . . . *Clark College*

Deborah M. Evans . . . . *Middlebury College*

Marie T. Farr . . . . *East Carolina University*

Grace Farrell . . . . *Butler University*

Katharine Gillespie . . . . *Sam Houston State University*

Paul Hansom . . . . *University of Southern California*

Maureen Honey . . . . *University of Nebraska at Lincoln*

Mary Hurd . . . . *East Tennessee State University*

Phoebe Jackson . . . . *Michigan State University*

Linda K. Karell . . . . *Montana State University*

Melanie Kisthardt . . . . *West Chester University*

Jennifer A. Kohout . . . . *University of Toledo*

Lydia Kualapai . . . . *University of Nebraska at Lincoln*

Victoria Lamont . . . . *University of Waterloo*

Shirley Wilson Logan . . . . *University of Maryland, College Park*

Shirley Marchalonis . . . . *Pennsylvania State University, Berks Campus*

Jean Carwile Masteller . . . . *Whitman College*

Susan Neal Mayberry . . . . *Alfred University*

Barbara McCaskill . . . . *University of Georgia*

Barbara J. McGuire . . . . *University of Washington*

Robin Miskolcze . . . . *University of Nebraska at Lincoln*

Joycelyn K. Moody . . . . *University of Washington*

Rose Norman . . . . *University of Alabama at Huntsville*

Venetria K. Patton . . . . *University of Nebraska at Lincoln*

Anne K. Phillips . . . . *Kansas State University*

Annmarie Pinarski . . . .

Julie Prebel . . . . *University of Washington*

Jennifer Putzi . . . . *University of Nebraska at Lincoln*

Mary Bortnyk Rigsby . . . . *Mary Washington College*

Kathy Ryder . . . . *University of South Florida*

Maggie Montesinos Sale . . . . *Columbia University*

E. Thomson Shields Jr. . . . . *East Carolina University*

Nicole Tonkovich . . . . *University of California, San Diego*

Annette Van Dyke . . . . *University of Illinois at Springfield*

Wendy Wagner . . . . *Pace University*

Priscilla Wald . . . . *Duke University*

Cumulative Index

Dictionary of Literary Biography, Volumes 1-221
Dictionary of Literary Biography Yearbook, 1980-1998
Dictionary of Literary Biography Documentary Series, Volumes 1-19

Cumulative Index

DLB before number: *Dictionary of Literary Biography,* Volumes 1-221
Y before number: *Dictionary of Literary Biography Yearbook,* 1980-1998
DS before number: *Dictionary of Literary Biography Documentary Series,* Volumes 1-19

A

Aakjær, Jeppe 1866-1930 . . . . .DLB-214

Abbey, Edwin Austin 1852-1911 . . . . . . .DLB-188

Abbey, Maj. J. R. 1894-1969 . . . . .DLB-201

Abbey Press DLB-49

The Abbey Theatre and Irish Drama,
1900-1945 .DLB-10

Abbot, Willis J. 1863-1934. . . . . .DLB-29

Abbott, Jacob 1803-1879 . . . . .DLB-1

Abbott, Lee K. 1947- DLB-130

Abbott, Lyman 1835-1922. . . . . .DLB-79

Abbott, Robert S. 1868-1940 . . . . . . .DLB-29, 91

Abe Kōbō 1924-1993 . . . . .DLB-182

Abelard, Peter circa 1079-1142? DLB-115, 208

Abelard-Schuman. .DLB-46

Abell, Arunah S. 1806-1888. . . . . .DLB-43

Abell, Kjeld 1901-1961. . . . . .DLB-214

Abercrombie, Lascelles 1881-1938. . . . . . .DLB-19

Aberdeen University Press Limited DLB-106

Abish, Walter 1931- DLB-130

Ablesimov, Aleksandr Onisimovich
1742-1783. .DLB-150

Abraham à Sancta Clara 1644-1709 . . . . . .DLB-168

Abrahams, Peter 1919- DLB-117

Abrams, M. H. 1912- DLB-67

Abrogans circa 790-800 . . . . .DLB-148

Abschatz, Hans Aßmann von
1646-1699 . . . . .DLB-168

Abse, Dannie 1923- DLB-27

Abutsu-ni 1221-1283 . . . . .DLB-203

Academy Chicago Publishers DLB-46

Accius circa 170 B.C.-circa 80 B.C. DLB-211

Accrocca, Elio Filippo 1923- DLB-128

Ace Books DLB-46

Achebe, Chinua 1930- DLB-117

Achtenberg, Herbert 1938- DLB-124

Ackerman, Diane 1948- DLB-120

Ackroyd, Peter 1949- DLB-155

Acorn, Milton 1923-1986. . . . . .DLB-53

Acosta, Oscar Zeta 1935?- DLB-82

Acosta Torres, José 1925- DLB-209

Actors Theatre of Louisville DLB-7

Adair, Gilbert 1944- DLB-194

Adair, James 1709?-1783?. DLB-30

Adam, Graeme Mercer 1839-1912 . . . . . . .DLB-99

Adam, Robert Borthwick II 1863-1940 . . .DLB-187

Adame, Leonard 1947- DLB-82

Adamic, Louis 1898-1951 . . . . .DLB-9

Adams, Abigail 1744-1818 . . . . .DLB-200

Adams, Alice 1926- Y-86

Adams, Brooks 1848-1927. . . . . .DLB-47

Adams, Charles Francis, Jr. 1835-1915 . . . .DLB-47

Adams, Douglas 1952-. Y-83

Adams, Franklin P. 1881-1960. . . . . .DLB-29

Adams, Hannah 1755-1832 . . . . .DLB-200

Adams, Henry 1838-1918 . . . . DLB-12, 47, 189

Adams, Herbert Baxter 1850-1901 . . . . . .DLB-47

Adams, J. S. and C. [publishing house] DLB-49

Adams, James Truslow
1878-1949 . . . . DLB-17; DS-17

Adams, John 1735-1826. . . . . .DLB-31, 183

Adams, John 1735-1826 and
Adams, Abigail 1744-1818. . . . . .DLB-183

Adams, John Quincy 1767-1848 . . . . .DLB-37

Adams, Léonie 1899-1988 . . . . .DLB-48

Adams, Levi 1802-1832 . . . . .DLB-99

Adams, Samuel 1722-1803 . . . . .DLB-31, 43

Adams, Sarah Fuller Flower
1805-1848 . . . . .DLB-199

Adams, Thomas 1582 or 1583-1652 . . . . .DLB-151

Adams, William Taylor 1822-1897 . . . . . . .DLB-42

Adamson, Sir John 1867-1950 . . . . .DLB-98

Adcock, Arthur St. John 1864-1930. . . . . .DLB-135

Adcock, Betty 1938- DLB-105

Adcock, Fleur 1934- DLB-40

Addison, Joseph 1672-1719 . . . . .DLB-101

Ade, George 1866-1944. . . . . .DLB-11, 25

Adeler, Max (see Clark, Charles Heber)

Adonias Filho 1915-1990 . . . . .DLB-145

Advance Publishing Company DLB-49

Ady, Endre 1877-1919 . . . . .DLB-215

AE 1867-1935. . . . . .DLB-19

Ælfric circa 955-circa 1010 . . . . .DLB-146

Aeschines circa 390 B.C.-circa 320 B.C.
. . . . .DLB-176

Aeschylus
525-524 B.C.-456-455 B.C. DLB-176

Aesthetic Poetry (1873), by Walter Pater. . .DLB-35

After Dinner Opera Company. Y-92

Afro-American Literary Critics:
An Introduction DLB-33

Agassiz, Elizabeth Cary 1822-1907 . . . . . .DLB-189

Agassiz, Jean Louis Rodolphe
1807-1873 . . . . .DLB-1

Agee, James 1909-1955 . . . . .DLB-2, 26, 152

The Agee Legacy: A Conference at the University
of Tennessee at Knoxville. Y-89

Aguilera Malta, Demetrio 1909-1981 . . . .DLB-145

Ai 1947- DLB-120

Aichinger, Ilse 1921- DLB-85

Aidoo, Ama Ata 1942- DLB-117

Aiken, Conrad 1889-1973 . . . . DLB-9, 45, 102

Aiken, Joan 1924- DLB-161

Aikin, Lucy 1781-1864. . . . . .DLB-144, 163

Ainsworth, William Harrison 1805-1882 . .DLB-21

Aistis, Jonas 1904-1973 . . . . .DLB-220

Aitken, George A. 1860-1917. . . . . .DLB-149

Aitken, Robert [publishing house] DLB-49

Akenside, Mark 1721-1770. . . . . .DLB-109

Akins, Zoë 1886-1958 . . . . .DLB-26

Aksahov, Sergei Timofeevich
1791-1859 . . . . .DLB-198

Akutagawa, Ryūnsuke 1892-1927 . . . . . . .DLB-180

Alabaster, William 1568-1640 . . . . .DLB-132

Alain de Lille circa 1116-1202/1203. . . . . .DLB-208

Alain-Fournier 1886-1914 . . . . .DLB-65

Alanus de Insulis (see Alain de Lille)

Alarcón, Francisco X. 1954- DLB-122

Alarcón, Justo S. 1930- DLB-209

Alba, Nanina 1915-1968 . . . . .DLB-41

Albee, Edward 1928- DLB-7

Albert the Great circa 1200-1280. . . . . . . .DLB-115

Albert, Octavia 1853-ca. 1889 . . . . .DLB-221

Alberti, Rafael 1902- DLB-108

Albertinus, Aegidius circa 1560-1620. . . . .DLB-164

Alcaeus born circa 620 B.C. DLB-176

Alcott, Amos Bronson 1799-1888 . . . . .DLB-1

Alcott, Louisa May
1832-1888 . . . . DLB-1, 42, 79; DS-14

Alcott, William Andrus 1798-1859 . . . . . . .DLB-1

Alcuin circa 732-804 . . . . .DLB-148

Alden, Beardsley and Company DLB-49

Alden, Henry Mills 1836-1919 . . . . .DLB-79

Alden, Isabella 1841-1930 . . . . DLB-42

Alden, John B. [publishing house] DLB-49

Aldington, Richard
1892-1962 . . . . DLB-20, 36, 100, 149

Aldis, Dorothy 1896-1966 . . . . DLB-22

Aldis, H. G. 1863-1919 . . . . DLB-184

Aldiss, Brian W. 1925- DLB-14

Aldrich, Thomas Bailey
1836-1907 . . . . DLB-42, 71, 74, 79

Alegría, Ciro 1909-1967 . . . . DLB-113

Alegría, Claribel 1924- DLB-145

Aleixandre, Vicente 1898-1984 . . . . DLB-108

Aleksandravičius, Jonas (see Aistis, Jonas)

Aleksandrov, Aleksandr Andreevich (see Durova,
Nadezhda Andreevna)

Aleramo, Sibilla 1876-1960 . . . . DLB-114

Alexander, Cecil Frances 1818-1895 . . . . . DLB-199

Alexander, Charles 1868-1923 . . . . DLB-91

Alexander, Charles Wesley
[publishing house] DLB-49

Alexander, James 1691-1756 . . . . DLB-24

Alexander, Lloyd 1924- DLB-52

Alexander, Sir William, Earl of Stirling
1577?-1640 . . . . DLB-121

Alexie, Sherman 1966- DLB-175, 206

Alexis, Willibald 1798-1871 . . . . DLB-133

Alfred, King 849-899 . . . . DLB-146

Alger, Horatio, Jr. 1832-1899 . . . . DLB-42

Algonquin Books of Chapel Hill DLB-46

Algren, Nelson 1909-1981 . . . . . DLB-9; Y-81, Y-82

Allan, Andrew 1907-1974 . . . . DLB-88

Allan, Ted 1916- DLB-68

Allbeury, Ted 1917- DLB-87

Alldritt, Keith 1935- DLB-14

Allen, Ethan 1738-1789 . . . . DLB-31

Allen, Frederick Lewis 1890-1954 . . . . . . DLB-137

Allen, Gay Wilson 1903-1995 . . . . . DLB-103; Y-95

Allen, George 1808-1876 . . . . DLB-59

Allen, George [publishing house] DLB-106

Allen, George, and Unwin Limited DLB-112

Allen, Grant 1848-1899 . . . . DLB-70, 92, 178

Allen, Henry W. 1912- Y-85

Allen, Hervey 1889-1949 . . . . DLB-9, 45

Allen, James 1739-1808 . . . . DLB-31

Allen, James Lane 1849-1925 . . . . DLB-71

Allen, Jay Presson 1922- DLB-26

Allen, John, and Company DLB-49

Allen, Paula Gunn 1939- DLB-175

Allen, Samuel W. 1917- DLB-41

Allen, Woody 1935- DLB-44

Allende, Isabel 1942- DLB-145

Alline, Henry 1748-1784 . . . . DLB-99

Allingham, Margery 1904-1966 . . . . DLB-77

Allingham, William 1824-1889 . . . . DLB-35

Allison, W. L. [publishing house] DLB-49

The *Alliterative Morte Arthure and the Stanzaic
Morte Arthur* circa 1350-1400 . . . . DLB-146

Allott, Kenneth 1912-1973 . . . . DLB-20

Allston, Washington 1779-1843 . . . . DLB-1

Almon, John [publishing house] DLB-154

Alonzo, Dámaso 1898-1990 . . . . DLB-108

Alsop, George 1636-post 1673 . . . . DLB-24

Alsop, Richard 1761-1815 . . . . DLB-37

Altemus, Henry, and Company DLB-49

Altenberg, Peter 1885-1919 . . . . DLB-81

Altolaguirre, Manuel 1905-1959 . . . . DLB-108

Aluko, T. M. 1918- DLB-117

Alurista 1947- DLB-82

Alvarez, A. 1929- DLB-14, 40

Alver, Betti 1906-1989 . . . . DLB-220

Amadi, Elechi 1934- DLB-117

Amado, Jorge 1912- DLB-113

Ambler, Eric 1909-1998 . . . . DLB-77

America: or, a Poem on the Settlement of the British Colonies
(1780?), by Timothy Dwight DLB-37

American Conservatory Theatre DLB-7

American Fiction and the 1930s DLB-9

American Humor: A Historical Survey
East and Northeast
South and Southwest
Midwest
West DLB-11

The American Library in Paris Y-93

American News Company DLB-49

The American Poets' Corner: The First
Three Years (1983-1986) Y-86

American Proletarian Culture: The 1930s . . .DS-11

American Publishing Company DLB-49

American Stationers' Company DLB-49

American Sunday-School Union DLB-49

American Temperance Union DLB-49

American Tract Society DLB-49

The American Trust for the
British Library Y-96

The American Writers Congress
(9-12 October 1981) Y-81

The American Writers Congress: A Report
on Continuing Business Y-81

Ames, Fisher 1758-1808 . . . . DLB-37

Ames, Mary Clemmer 1831-1884 . . . . DLB-23

Amiel, Henri-Frédéric 1821-1881 . . . . DLB-217

Amini, Johari M. 1935- DLB-41

Amis, Kingsley
1922-1995 . . . . . . DLB-15, 27, 100, 139, Y-96

Amis, Martin 1949- DLB-194

Ammianus Marcellinus
circa A.D. 330-A.D. 395 . . . . DLB-211

Ammons, A. R. 1926- DLB-5, 165

Amory, Thomas 1691?-1788 . . . . DLB-39

Anania, Michael 1939- DLB-193

Anaya, Rudolfo A. 1937- DLB-82, 206

Ancrene Riwle circa 1200-1225 . . . . DLB-146

Andersch, Alfred 1914-1980 . . . . DLB-69

Andersen, Benny 1929- DLB-214

Anderson, Alexander 1775-1870 . . . . DLB-188

Anderson, Frederick Irving 1877-1947 . . . DLB-202

Anderson, Margaret 1886-1973 . . . . DLB-4, 91

Anderson, Maxwell 1888-1959 . . . . DLB-7

Anderson, Patrick 1915-1979 . . . . DLB-68

Anderson, Paul Y. 1893-1938 . . . . DLB-29

Anderson, Poul 1926- DLB-8

Anderson, Robert 1750-1830 . . . . DLB-142

Anderson, Robert 1917- DLB-7

Anderson, Sherwood
1876-1941 . . . . DLB-4, 9, 86; DS-1

Andreae, Johann Valentin 1586-1654 . . . . DLB-164

Andreas Capellanus
flourished circa 1185 . . . . DLB-208

Andreas-Salomé, Lou 1861-1937 . . . . DLB-66

Andres, Stefan 1906-1970 . . . . DLB-69

Andreu, Blanca 1959- DLB-134

Andrewes, Lancelot 1555-1626 . . . . .DLB-151, 172

Andrews, Charles M. 1863-1943 . . . . .DLB-17

Andrews, Miles Peter ?-1814 . . . . DLB-89

Andrian, Leopold von 1875-1951 . . . . DLB-81

Andrić, Ivo 1892-1975 . . . . .DLB-147

Andrieux, Louis (see Aragon, Louis)

Andrus, Silas, and Son DLB-49

Andrzejewski, Jerzy 1909-1983 . . . . DLB-215

Angell, James Burrill 1829-1916 . . . . DLB-64

Angell, Roger 1920- DLB-171, 185

Angelou, Maya 1928- DLB-38

Anger, Jane flourished 1589 . . . . DLB-136

Angers, Félicité (see Conan, Laure)

Anglo-Norman Literature in the Development
of Middle English Literature DLB-146

The Anglo-Saxon Chronicle
circa 890-1154 . . . . DLB-146

The "Angry Young Men" DLB-15

Angus and Robertson (UK) Limited DLB-112

Anhalt, Edward 1914- DLB-26

Anners, Henry F. [publishing house] DLB-49

Annolied between 1077 and 1081 . . . . DLB-148

Annual Awards for *Dictionary of Literary Biography*
Editors and Contributors Y-98

Anselm of Canterbury 1033-1109 . . . . . . DLB-115

Anstey, F. 1856-1934 . . . . .DLB-141, 178

Anthony, Michael 1932- DLB-125

Anthony, Piers 1934- DLB-8

Anthony, Susanna 1726-1791 . . . . DLB-200

The Anthony Burgess Archive at the Harry Ransom
Humanities Research Center Y-98

Anthony Burgess's 99 Novels:
An Opinion Poll Y-84

Antin, David 1932- DLB-169

Antin, Mary 1881-1949 . . . . .DLB-221; Y-84

Anton Ulrich, Duke of Brunswick-Lüneburg
1633-1714 . . . . DLB-168

Antschel, Paul (see Celan, Paul)

Anyidoho, Kofi 1947- DLB-157

Anzaldúa, Gloria 1942- DLB-122

Anzengruber, Ludwig 1839-1889 . . . . . . .DLB-129

Apess, William 1798-1839 . . . . .DLB-175

Apodaca, Rudy S. 1939- DLB-82

Apollonius Rhodius third century B.C.
. . . . .DLB-176

Apple, Max 1941- DLB-130

Appleton, D., and Company DLB-49

Appleton-Century-Crofts. DLB-46

Applewhite, James 1935- DLB-105

Applewood Books DLB-46

Apuleius circa A.D. 125-post A.D. 164 . . .DLB-211

Aquin, Hubert 1929-1977 . . . . .DLB-53

Aquinas, Thomas 1224 or
1225-1274 . . . . .DLB-115

Aragon, Louis 1897-1982 . . . . .DLB-72

Aralica, Ivan 1930- DLB-181

Aratus of Soli circa 315 B.C.-circa 239 B.C.
. . . . .DLB-176

Arbasino, Alberto 1930- DLB-196

Arbor House Publishing Company DLB-46

Arbuthnot, John 1667-1735 . . . . .DLB-101

Arcadia House .DLB-46

Arce, Julio G. (see Ulica, Jorge)

Archer, William 1856-1924 . . . . .DLB-10

Archilochhus mid seventh century B.C.E.
. . . . .DLB-176

The Archpoet circa 1130?-? DLB-148

Archpriest Avvakum (Petrovich)
1620?-1682 . . . . .DLB-150

Arden, John 1930- DLB-13

Arden of Faversham DLB-62

Ardis Publishers Y-89

Ardizzone, Edward 1900-1979 . . . . .DLB-160

Arellano, Juan Estevan 1947- DLB-122

The Arena Publishing Company DLB-49

Arena Stage DLB-7

Arenas, Reinaldo 1943-1990 . . . . .DLB-145

Arensberg, Ann 1937- Y-82

Arghezi, Tudor 1880-1967 . . . . .DLB-220

Arguedas, José María 1911-1969 . . . . . . .DLB-113

Argueta, Manlio 1936- DLB-145

Arias, Ron 1941- DLB-82

Arishima, Takeo 1878-1923 . . . . .DLB-180

Aristophanes
circa 446 B.C.-circa 386 B.C. DLB-176

Aristotle 384 B.C.-322 B.C. DLB-176

Ariyoshi Sawako 1931-1984 . . . . .DLB-182

Arland, Marcel 1899-1986 . . . . .DLB-72

Arlen, Michael 1895-1956 . . . . DLB-36, 77, 162

Armah, Ayi Kwei 1939- DLB-117

Armantrout, Rae 1947- DLB-193

Der arme Hartmann ?-after 1150. . . . . . . .DLB-148

Armed Services Editions DLB-46

Armstrong, Martin Donisthorpe
1882-1974 . . . . .DLB-197

Armstrong, Richard 1903- DLB-160

Arndt, Ernst Moritz 1769-1860 . . . . .DLB-90

Arnim, Achim von 1781-1831 . . . . .DLB-90

Arnim, Bettina von 1785-1859 . . . . .DLB-90

Arnim, Elizabeth von (Countess Mary Annette
Beauchamp Russell) 1866-1941 . . . . .DLB-197

Arno Press DLB-46

Arnold, Edwin 1832-1904 . . . . .DLB-35

Arnold, Edwin L. 1857-1935 . . . . .DLB-178

Arnold, Matthew 1822-1888 . . . . DLB-32, 57

Arnold, Thomas 1795-1842 . . . . .DLB-55

Arnold, Edward [publishing house] DLB-112

Arnow, Harriette Simpson 1908-1986 . . . . . .DLB-6

Arp, Bill (see Smith, Charles Henry)

Arpino, Giovanni 1927-1987 . . . . .DLB-177

Arreola, Juan José 1918- DLB-113

Arrian circa 89-circa 155 . . . . .DLB-176

Arrowsmith, J. W. [publishing house] DLB-106

The Art and Mystery of Publishing:
Interviews Y-97

Arthur, Timothy Shay
1809-1885 . . . . DLB-3, 42, 79; DS-13

The Arthurian Tradition and Its European
Context DLB-138

Artmann, H. C. 1921- DLB-85

Arvin, Newton 1900-1963 . . . . .DLB-103

As I See It, by Carolyn Cassady DLB-16

Asch, Nathan 1902-1964 . . . . .DLB-4, 28

Ash, John 1948- DLB-40

Ashbery, John 1927- DLB-5, 165; Y-81

Ashbridge, Elizabeth 1713-1755 . . . . .DLB-200

Ashburnham, Bertram Lord
1797-1878 . . . . .DLB-184

Ashendene Press DLB-112

Asher, Sandy 1942- Y-83

Ashton, Winifred (see Dane, Clemence)

Asimov, Isaac 1920-1992 . . . . DLB-8; Y-92

Askew, Anne circa 1521-1546 . . . . .DLB-136

Aspazija 1865-1943 . . . . .DLB-220

Asselin, Olivar 1874-1937 . . . . .DLB-92

Asturias, Miguel Angel 1899-1974 . . . . . . .DLB-113

Atheneum Publishers DLB-46

Atherton, Gertrude 1857-1948 . . . . . DLB-9, 78, 186

Athlone Press DLB-112

Atkins, Josiah circa 1755-1781 . . . . .DLB-31

Atkins, Russell 1926- DLB-41

The Atlantic Monthly Press DLB-46

Attaway, William 1911-1986 . . . . .DLB-76

Atwood, Margaret 1939- DLB-53

Aubert, Alvin 1930- DLB-41

Aubert de Gaspé, Phillipe-Ignace-François
1814-1841 . . . . .DLB-99

Aubert de Gaspé, Phillipe-Joseph
1786-1871 . . . . .DLB-99

Aubin, Napoléon 1812-1890 . . . . .DLB-99

Aubin, Penelope 1685-circa 1731 . . . . .DLB-39

Aubrey-Fletcher, Henry Lancelot (see Wade, Henry)

Auchincloss, Louis 1917- DLB-2; Y-80

Auden, W. H. 1907-1973 . . . . .DLB-10, 20

Audio Art in America: A Personal Memoir . . . Y-85

Audubon, John Woodhouse
1812-1862 . . . . .DLB-183

Auerbach, Berthold 1812-1882 . . . . .DLB-133

Auernheimer, Raoul 1876-1948 . . . . .DLB-81

Augier, Emile 1820-1889 . . . . .DLB-192

Augustine 354-430 . . . . .DLB-115

Aulus Cellius
circa A.D. 125-circa A.D. 180? DLB-211

Austen, Jane 1775-1817 . . . . .DLB-116

Austin, Alfred 1835-1913 . . . . .DLB-35

Austin, Jane Goodwin 1831-1894 . . . . . . .DLB-202

Austin, Mary 1868-1934 . . . . . DLB-9, 78, 206, 221

Austin, William 1778-1841 . . . . .DLB-74

Author-Printers, 1476–1599 . . . . .DLB-167

Author Websites Y-97

The Author's Apology for His Book
(1684), by John Bunyan DLB-39

An Author's Response, by Ronald Sukenick . . Y-82

Authors and Newspapers Association DLB-46

Authors' Publishing Company DLB-49

Avalon Books DLB-46

Avancini, Nicolaus 1611-1686 . . . . .DLB-164

Avendaño, Fausto 1941- DLB-82

Averroëö 1126-1198 . . . . .DLB-115

Avery, Gillian 1926- DLB-161

Avicenna 980-1037 . . . . .DLB-115

Avison, Margaret 1918- DLB-53

Avon Books DLB-46

Awdry, Wilbert Vere 1911-1997 . . . . . . .DLB-160

Avyžius, Jonas 1922-1999 . . . . .DLB-220

Awoonor, Kofi 1935- DLB-117

Ayckbourn, Alan 1939- DLB-13

Aymé, Marcel 1902-1967 . . . . .DLB-72

Aytoun, Sir Robert 1570-1638 . . . . .DLB-121

Aytoun, William Edmondstoune
1813-1865 . . . . .DLB-32, 159

B

B. V. (see Thomson, James)

Babbitt, Irving 1865-1933 . . . . .DLB-63

Babbitt, Natalie 1932- DLB-52

Babcock, John [publishing house] DLB-49

Babits, Mihály 1883-1941 . . . . .DLB-215

Babrius circa 150-200. . . . . .DLB-176

Baca, Jimmy Santiago 1952- DLB-122

Bache, Benjamin Franklin 1769-1798 . . . . . .DLB-43

Bacheller, Irving 1859-1950 . . . . .DLB-202

Bachmann, Ingeborg 1926-1973 . . . . .DLB-85

Bačinskaitė-Bučienė, Salomėja (see Nėris, Salomėja)

Bacon, Delia 1811-1859 . . . . .DLB-1

Bacon, Francis 1561-1626 . . . . .DLB-151

Bacon, Roger circa 1214/1220-1292 . . . . . DLB-115

Bacon, Sir Nicholas circa 1510-1579 . . . . . DLB-132

Bacon, Thomas circa 1700-1768 . . . . DLB-31

Bacovia, George 1881-1957 . . . . DLB-220

Badger, Richard G., and Company DLB-49

Bage, Robert 1728-1801 . . . . DLB-39

Bagehot, Walter 1826-1877. . . . . DLB-55

Bagley, Desmond 1923-1983 . . . . DLB-87

Bagnold, Enid 1889-1981 . . . . . . DLB-13, 160, 191

Bagryana, Elisaveta 1893-1991 . . . . DLB-147

Bahr, Hermann 1863-1934. . . . . DLB-81, 118

Bailey, Abigail Abbot 1746-1815. . . . . . . DLB-200

Bailey, Alfred Goldsworthy 1905- DLB-68

Bailey, Francis [publishing house]. DLB-49

Bailey, H. C. 1878-1961 . . . . DLB-77

Bailey, Jacob 1731-1808 . . . . DLB-99

Bailey, Paul 1937- DLB-14

Bailey, Philip James 1816-1902. . . . . DLB-32

Baillargeon, Pierre 1916-1967. . . . . DLB-88

Baillie, Hugh 1890-1966. . . . . DLB-29

Baillie, Joanna 1762-1851 . . . . DLB-93

Bailyn, Bernard 1922- DLB-17

Bainbridge, Beryl 1933- DLB-14

Baird, Irene 1901-1981 . . . . DLB-68

Baker, Augustine 1575-1641 . . . . DLB-151

Baker, Carlos 1909-1987 . . . . DLB-103

Baker, David 1954- DLB-120

Baker, Herschel C. 1914-1990 . . . . DLB-111

Baker, Houston A., Jr. 1943- DLB-67

Baker, Samuel White 1821-1893 . . . . DLB-166

Baker, Thomas 1656-1740 . . . . DLB-213

Baker, Walter H., Company
("Baker's Plays") DLB-49

The Baker and Taylor Company. DLB-49

Balaban, John 1943- DLB-120

Bald, Wambly 1902- DLB-4

Balde, Jacob 1604-1668. . . . . DLB-164

Balderston, John 1889-1954 . . . . DLB-26

Baldwin, James 1924-1987 . . . . . DLB-2, 7, 33; Y-87

Baldwin, Joseph Glover 1815-1864. . . . . DLB-3, 11

Baldwin, Richard and Anne
[publishing house] DLB-170

Baldwin, William circa 1515-1563 . . . . . . DLB-132

Bale, John 1495-1563 . . . . DLB-132

Balestrini, Nanni 1935- DLB-128, 196

Balfour, Sir Andrew 1630-1694 . . . . DLB-213

Balfour, Arthur James 1848-1930. . . . . . . DLB-190

Balfour, Sir James 1600-1657 . . . . DLB-213

Ballantine Books. DLB-46

Ballantyne, R. M. 1825-1894 . . . . DLB-163

Ballard, J. G. 1930- DLB-14, 207

Ballard, Martha Moore 1735-1812 . . . . . . DLB-200

Ballerini, Luigi 1940- DLB-128

Ballou, Maturin Murray
1820-1895 . . . . DLB-79, 189

Ballou, Robert O. [publishing house] DLB-46

Balzac, Honoré de 1799-1855 . . . . DLB-119

Bambara, Toni Cade 1939- DLB-38, 218

Bamford, Samuel 1788-1872 . . . . DLB-190

Bancroft, A. L., and Company DLB-49

Bancroft, George 1800-1891. . . . . . DLB-1, 30, 59

Bancroft, Hubert Howe 1832-1918 . . .DLB-47, 140

Bandelier, Adolph F. 1840-1914 . . . . DLB-186

Bangs, John Kendrick 1862-1922 . . . . .DLB-11, 79

Banim, John 1798-1842. . . . . . .DLB-116, 158, 159

Banim, Michael 1796-1874 . . . . . DLB-158, 159

Banks, Iain 1954- DLB-194

Banks, John circa 1653-1706. . . . . DLB-80

Banks, Russell 1940- DLB-130

Bannerman, Helen 1862-1946 . . . . DLB-141

Bantam Books DLB-46

Banti, Anna 1895-1985. . . . . .DLB-177

Banville, John 1945- DLB-14

Banville, Théodore de 1823-1891. . . . . . . DLB-217

Baraka, Amiri 1934- DLB-5, 7, 16, 38; DS-8

Baratynsky, Evgenii Abramovich
1800-1844 . . . . DLB-205

Barbauld, Anna Laetitia
1743-1825. . . . . DLB-107, 109, 142, 158

Barbeau, Marius 1883-1969 . . . . DLB-92

Barber, John Warner 1798-1885. . . . . DLB-30

Bàrberi Squarotti, Giorgio 1929- DLB-128

Barbey d'Aurevilly, Jules-Amédée
1808-1889 . . . . DLB-119

Barbier, Auguste 1805-1882 . . . . DLB-217

Barbilian, Dan (see Barbu, Ion)

Barbour, John circa 1316-1395 . . . . DLB-146

Barbu, Ion 1895-1961 . . . . DLB-220

Barbour, Ralph Henry 1870-1944 . . . . DLB-22

Barbusse, Henri 1873-1935. . . . . DLB-65

Barclay, Alexander circa 1475-1552 . . . . . DLB-132

Barclay, E. E., and Company DLB-49

Bardeen, C. W. [publishing house]. DLB-49

Barham, Richard Harris 1788-1845 . . . . . DLB-159

Barich, Bill 1943- DLB-185

Baring, Maurice 1874-1945. . . . . DLB-34

Baring-Gould, Sabine
1834-1924 . . . . DLB-156, 190

Barker, A. L. 1918- DLB-14, 139

Barker, George 1913-1991 . . . . DLB-20

Barker, Harley Granville 1877-1946 . . . . . . DLB-10

Barker, Howard 1946- DLB-13

Barker, James Nelson 1784-1858 . . . . DLB-37

Barker, Jane 1652-1727 . . . . DLB-39, 131

Barker, Lady Mary Anne 1831-1911 . . . . DLB-166

Barker, William
circa 1520-after 1576 . . . . DLB-132

Barker, Arthur, Limited DLB-112

Barkov, Ivan Semenovich
1732-1768. . . . . DLB-150

Barks, Coleman 1937- DLB-5

Barlach, Ernst 1870-1938 . . . . DLB-56, 118

Barlow, Joel 1754-1812. . . . . DLB-37

Barnard, John 1681-1770 . . . . DLB-24

Barne, Kitty (Mary Catherine Barne)
1883-1957 . . . . DLB-160

Barnes, Barnabe 1571-1609 . . . . DLB-132

Barnes, Djuna 1892-1982 . . . . DLB-4, 9, 45

Barnes, Jim 1933- DLB-175

Barnes, Julian 1946- DLB-194; Y-93

Barnes, Margaret Ayer 1886-1967 . . . . DLB-9

Barnes, Peter 1931- DLB-13

Barnes, William 1801-1886 . . . . DLB-32

Barnes, A. S., and Company DLB-49

Barnes and Noble Books DLB-46

Barnet, Miguel 1940- DLB-145

Barney, Natalie 1876-1972 . . . . DLB-4

Barnfield, Richard 1574-1627 . . . . .DLB-172

Baron, Richard W.,
Publishing Company DLB-46

Barr, Amelia Edith Huddleston
1831-1919 . . . . DLB-202, 221

Barr, Robert 1850-1912 . . . . .DLB-70, 92

Barral, Carlos 1928-1989 . . . . DLB-134

Barrax, Gerald William 1933- DLB-41, 120

Barrès, Maurice 1862-1923. . . . . DLB-123

Barrett, Eaton Stannard 1786-1820. . . . . . DLB-116

Barrie, J. M. 1860-1937. . . . . . . .DLB-10, 141, 156

Barrie and Jenkins DLB-112

Barrio, Raymond 1921- DLB-82

Barrios, Gregg 1945- DLB-122

Barry, Philip 1896-1949 . . . . DLB-7

Barry, Robertine (see Françoise)

Barse and Hopkins DLB-46

Barstow, Stan 1928- DLB-14, 139

Barth, John 1930- DLB-2

Barthelme, Donald
1931-1989 . . . . .DLB-2; Y-80, Y-89

Barthelme, Frederick 1943- Y-85

Bartholomew, Frank 1898-1985. . . . . . . .DLB-127

Bartlett, John 1820-1905. . . . . DLB-1

Bartol, Cyrus Augustus 1813-1900. . . . . . . DLB-1

Barton, Bernard 1784-1849. . . . . DLB-96

Barton, Thomas Pennant 1803-1869 . . . . DLB-140

Bartram, John 1699-1777 . . . . DLB-31

Bartram, William 1739-1823 . . . . DLB-37

Basic Books DLB-46

Basille, Theodore (see Becon, Thomas)

Bass, Rick 1958- DLB-212

Bass, T. J. 1932- Y-81

Bassani, Giorgio 1916- DLB-128, 177

Basse, William circa 1583-1653 . . . . DLB-121

Bassett, John Spencer 1867-1928. . . . . . . .DLB-17

Bassler, Thomas Joseph (see Bass, T. J.)

Bate, Walter Jackson 1918- DLB-67, 103

Bateman, Christopher
[publishing house] DLB-170

Bateman, Stephen circa 1510-1584 . . . . . . DLB-136

Bates, H. E. 1905-1974. . . . . DLB-162, 191

Bates, Katharine Lee 1859-1929 . . . . DLB-71

Batiushkov, Konstantin Nikolaevich
1787-1855. . . . . DLB-205

Batsford, B. T. [publishing house] DLB-106

Battiscombe, Georgina 1905- DLB-155

The Battle of Maldon circa 1000 . . . . DLB-146

Baudelaire, Charles 1821-1867 . . . . DLB-217

Bauer, Bruno 1809-1882 . . . . DLB-133

Bauer, Wolfgang 1941- DLB-124

Baum, L. Frank 1856-1919 . . . . DLB-22

Baum, Vicki 1888-1960 . . . . DLB-85

Baumbach, Jonathan 1933- Y-80

Bausch, Richard 1945- DLB-130

Bausch, Robert 1945- DLB-218

Bawden, Nina 1925- DLB-14, 161, 207

Bax, Clifford 1886-1962 . . . . DLB-10, 100

Baxter, Charles 1947- DLB-130

Bayer, Eleanor (see Perry, Eleanor)

Bayer, Konrad 1932-1964 . . . . DLB-85

Baynes, Pauline 1922- DLB-160

Bazin, Hervé 1911-1996. . . . . DLB-83

Beach, Sylvia 1887-1962. . . . . DLB-4; DS-15

Beacon Press DLB-49

Beadle and Adams DLB-49

Beagle, Peter S. 1939- Y-80

Beal, M. F. 1937- Y-81

Beale, Howard K. 1899-1959. . . . . DLB-17

Beard, Charles A. 1874-1948 . . . . DLB-17

A Beat Chronology: The First Twenty-five
Years, 1944-1969. . . . . DLB-16

Beattie, Ann 1947- DLB-218; Y-82

Beattie, James 1735-1803 . . . . DLB-109

Beatty, Chester 1875-1968 . . . . DLB-201

Beauchemin, Nérée 1850-1931 . . . . DLB-92

Beauchemin, Yves 1941- DLB-60

Beaugrand, Honoré 1848-1906 . . . . DLB-99

Beaulieu, Victor-Lévy 1945- DLB-53

Beaumont, Francis circa 1584-1616
and Fletcher, John 1579-1625 . . . . DLB-58

Beaumont, Sir John 1583?-1627. . . . . DLB-121

Beaumont, Joseph 1616-1699. . . . . DLB-126

Beauvoir, Simone de 1908-1986 . . . . DLB-72; Y-86

Becher, Ulrich 1910- DLB-69

Becker, Carl 1873-1945 . . . . DLB-17

Becker, Jurek 1937-1997. . . . . DLB-75

Becker, Jurgen 1932- DLB-75

Beckett, Samuel 1906-1989 . . . . . DLB-13, 15; Y-90

Beckford, William 1760-1844. . . . . DLB-39

Beckham, Barry 1944- DLB-33

Becon, Thomas circa 1512-1567 . . . . DLB-136

Becque, Henry 1837-1899 . . . . DLB-192

Beùkoviù, Matija 1939- DLB-181

Beddoes, Thomas 1760-1808. . . . . DLB-158

Beddoes, Thomas Lovell 1803-1849 . . . . . DLB-96

Bede circa 673-735. . . . . DLB-146

Beecher, Catharine Esther 1800-1878 . . . . . DLB-1

Beecher, Henry Ward 1813-1887 . . . . . DLB-3, 43

Beer, George L. 1872-1920 . . . . DLB-47

Beer, Johann 1655-1700 . . . . DLB-168

Beer, Patricia 1919- DLB-40

Beerbohm, Max 1872-1956 . . . . DLB-34, 100

Beer-Hofmann, Richard 1866-1945. . . . . . DLB-81

Beers, Henry A. 1847-1926 . . . . DLB-71

Beeton, S. O. [publishing house] DLB-106

Bégon, Elisabeth 1696-1755 . . . . DLB-99

Behan, Brendan 1923-1964 . . . . DLB-13

Behn, Aphra 1640?-1689 . . . . DLB-39, 80, 131

Behn, Harry 1898-1973 . . . . DLB-61

Behrman, S. N. 1893-1973 . . . . DLB-7, 44

Belaney, Archibald Stansfeld (see Grey Owl)

Belasco, David 1853-1931 . . . . DLB-7

Belford, Clarke and Company. DLB-49

Belinksy, Vissarion Grigor'evich
1811-1848 . . . . DLB-198

Belitt, Ben 1911- DLB-5

Belknap, Jeremy 1744-1798 . . . . DLB-30, 37

Bell, Adrian 1901-1980 . . . . DLB-191

Bell, Clive 1881-1964. . . . . DS-10

Bell, George, and Sons. DLB-106

Bell, Gertrude Margaret Lowthian
1868-1926 . . . . DLB-174

Bell, James Madison 1826-1902. . . . . DLB-50

Bell, Madison Smartt 1957- DLB-218

Bell, Marvin 1937- DLB-5

Bell, Millicent 1919- DLB-111

Bell, Quentin 1910-1996 . . . . DLB-155

Bell, Robert [publishing house] DLB-49

Bell, Vanessa 1879-1961 . . . . DS-10

Bellamy, Edward 1850-1898 . . . . DLB-12

Bellamy, John [publishing house]. DLB-170

Bellamy, Joseph 1719-1790. . . . . DLB-31

Bellezza, Dario 1944-1996 . . . . DLB-128

La Belle Assemblée 1806-1837 . . . . DLB-110

Belloc, Hilaire 1870-1953 . . . . DLB-19, 100, 141, 174

Bellonci, Maria 1902-1986 . . . . DLB-196

Bellow, Saul 1915- DLB-2, 28; Y-82; DS-3

Belmont Productions DLB-46

Bemelmans, Ludwig 1898-1962. . . . . DLB-22

Bemis, Samuel Flagg 1891-1973. . . . . DLB-17

Bemrose, William [publishing house] DLB-106

Ben no Naishi 1228?-1271? DLB-203

Benchley, Robert 1889-1945 . . . . DLB-11

Bencúr, Matej (see Kukučin, Martin)

Benedetti, Mario 1920- DLB-113

Benedictus, David 1938- DLB-14

Benedikt, Michael 1935- DLB-5

Benediktov, Vladimir Grigor'evich
1807-1873. . . . . DLB-205

Benét, Stephen Vincent
1898-1943 . . . . DLB-4, 48, 102

Benét, William Rose 1886-1950 . . . . DLB-45

Benford, Gregory 1941- Y-82

Benjamin, Park 1809-1864. . . . . DLB-3, 59, 73

Benjamin, S. G. W. 1837-1914. . . . . DLB-189

Benlowes, Edward 1602-1676 . . . . DLB-126

Benn, Gottfried 1886-1956 . . . . DLB-56

Benn Brothers Limited DLB-106

Bennett, Arnold 1867-1931 . . . DLB-10, 34, 98, 135

Bennett, Charles 1899-1995. . . . . DLB-44

Bennett, Emerson 1822-1905. . . . . DLB-202

Bennett, Gwendolyn 1902- DLB-51

Bennett, Hal 1930- DLB-33

Bennett, James Gordon 1795-1872 . . . . DLB-43

Bennett, James Gordon, Jr. 1841-1918. . . . . DLB-23

Bennett, John 1865-1956 . . . . DLB-42

Bennett, Louise 1919- DLB-117

Benni, Stefano 1947- DLB-196

Benoit, Jacques 1941- DLB-60

Benson, A. C. 1862-1925. . . . . DLB-98

Benson, E. F. 1867-1940. . . . . DLB-135, 153

Benson, Jackson J. 1930- DLB-111

Benson, Robert Hugh 1871-1914. . . . . . . DLB-153

Benson, Stella 1892-1933. . . . . DLB-36, 162

Bent, James Theodore 1852-1897 . . . . DLB-174

Bent, Mabel Virginia Anna ?-? DLB-174

Bentham, Jeremy 1748-1832 . . . . DLB-107, 158

Bentley, E. C. 1875-1956 . . . . DLB-70

Bentley, Phyllis 1894-1977. . . . . DLB-191

Bentley, Richard [publishing house] DLB-106

Benton, Robert 1932- and Newman,
David 1937- DLB-44

Benziger Brothers DLB-49

Beowulf circa 900-1000 or 790-825 . . . . . . DLB-146

Berent, Wacław 1873-1940 . . . . DLB-215

Beresford, Anne 1929- DLB-40

Beresford, John Davys
1873-1947 . . . . DLB-162, 178, 197

Beresford-Howe, Constance 1922- DLB-88

Berford, R. G., Company DLB-49

Berg, Stephen 1934- DLB-5

Bergengruen, Werner 1892-1964 . . . . DLB-56

Berger, John 1926- DLB-14, 207

Berger, Meyer 1898-1959 . . . . DLB-29

Berger, Thomas 1924- DLB-2; Y-80

Berkeley, Anthony 1893-1971 . . . . DLB-77

Berkeley, George 1685-1753 . . . . DLB-31, 101

The Berkley Publishing Corporation. DLB-46

Berlin, Lucia 1936- DLB-130

Bernal, Vicente J. 1888-1915 . . . . DLB-82

Bernanos, Georges 1888-1948. . . . . DLB-72

Bernard, Harry 1898-1979 . . . . DLB-92

Bernard, John 1756-1828 . . . . DLB-37

Bernard of Chartres circa 1060-1124? DLB-115

Bernard of Clairvaux 1090-1153 . . . . DLB-208

Bernard Silvestris
 flourished circa 1130-1160 . . . . DLB-208

Bernari, Carlo 1909-1992 . . . . DLB-177

Bernhard, Thomas 1931-1989 . . . . . . DLB-85, 124

Bernstein, Charles 1950- DLB-169

Berriault, Gina 1926- DLB-130

Berrigan, Daniel 1921- DLB-5

Berrigan, Ted 1934-1983 . . . . DLB-5, 169

Berry, Wendell 1934- DLB-5, 6

Berryman, John 1914-1972 . . . . DLB-48

Bersianik, Louky 1930- DLB-60

Berthelet, Thomas [publishing house] DLB-170

Berto, Giuseppe 1914-1978 . . . . DLB-177

Bertolucci, Attilio 1911- DLB-128

Bertrand, Louis "Aloysius"
 1807-1841 . . . . DLB-217

Berton, Pierre 1920- DLB-68

Besant, Sir Walter 1836-1901 . . . . . . DLB-135, 190

Bessette, Gerard 1920- DLB-53

Bessie, Alvah 1904-1985 . . . . DLB-26

Bester, Alfred 1913-1987 . . . . DLB-8

Besterman, Theodore 1904-1976 . . . . DLB-201

The Bestseller Lists: An Assessment Y-84

Bestuzhev, Aleksandr Aleksandrovich (Marlinsky)
 1797-1837 . . . . DLB-198

Bestuzhev, Nikolai Aleksandrovich
 1791-1855 . . . . DLB-198

Betham-Edwards, Matilda Barbara (see Edwards,
 Matilda Barbara Betham-)

Betjeman, John 1906-1984 . . . . DLB-20; Y-84

Betocchi, Carlo 1899-1986 . . . . DLB-128

Bettarini, Mariella 1942- DLB-128

Betts, Doris 1932- DLB-218; Y-82

Beveridge, Albert J. 1862-1927 . . . . DLB-17

Beverley, Robert circa 1673-1722 . . . . . DLB-24, 30

Bevilacqua, Alberto 1934- DLB-196

Bevington, Louisa Sarah 1845-1895 . . . . . DLB-199

Beyle, Marie-Henri (see Stendhal)

Bianco, Margery Williams 1881-1944 . . . DLB-160

Bibaud, Adèle 1854-1941 . . . . DLB-92

Bibaud, Michel 1782-1857 . . . . DLB-99

Bibliographical and Textual Scholarship
 Since World War II Y-89

The Bicentennial of James Fenimore Cooper:
 An International Celebration Y-89

Bichsel, Peter 1935- DLB-75

Bickerstaff, Isaac John 1733-circa 1808 . . . . DLB-89

Biddle, Drexel [publishing house] DLB-49

Bidermann, Jacob
 1577 or 1578-1639 . . . . DLB-164

Bidwell, Walter Hilliard 1798-1881 . . . . . . DLB-79

Bienek, Horst 1930- DLB-75

Bierbaum, Otto Julius 1865-1910 . . . . DLB-66

Bierce, Ambrose
 1842-1914? DLB-11, 12, 23, 71, 74, 186

Bigelow, William F. 1879-1966 . . . . DLB-91

Biggle, Lloyd, Jr. 1923- DLB-8

Bigiaretti, Libero 1905-1993 . . . . DLB-177

Bigland, Eileen 1898-1970 . . . . DLB-195

Biglow, Hosea (see Lowell, James Russell)

Bigongiari, Piero 1914- DLB-128

Billinger, Richard 1890-1965 . . . . DLB-124

Billings, Hammatt 1818-1874 . . . . DLB-188

Billings, John Shaw 1898-1975 . . . . DLB-137

Billings, Josh (see Shaw, Henry Wheeler)

Binding, Rudolf G. 1867-1938 . . . . DLB-66

Bingham, Caleb 1757-1817 . . . . DLB-42

Bingham, George Barry 1906-1988 . . . . . DLB-127

Bingley, William [publishing house] DLB-154

Binyon, Laurence 1869-1943 . . . . DLB-19

Biographia Brittanica DLB-142

Biographical Documents I Y-84

Biographical Documents II Y-85

Bioren, John [publishing house] DLB-49

Bioy Casares, Adolfo 1914- DLB-113

Bird, Isabella Lucy 1831-1904 . . . . DLB-166

Bird, Robert Montgomery 1806-1854 . . . DLB-202

Bird, William 1888-1963 . . . . DLB-4; DS-15

Birken, Sigmund von 1626-1681 . . . . DLB-164

Birney, Earle 1904- DLB-88

Birrell, Augustine 1850-1933 . . . . DLB-98

Bisher, Furman 1918- DLB-171

Bishop, Elizabeth 1911-1979 . . . . DLB-5, 169

Bishop, John Peale 1892-1944 . . . . . DLB-4, 9, 45

Bismarck, Otto von 1815-1898 . . . . DLB-129

Bisset, Robert 1759-1805 . . . . DLB-142

Bissett, Bill 1939- DLB-53

Bitzius, Albert (see Gotthelf, Jeremias)

Bjørnvig, Thorkild 1918- DLB-214

Black, David (D. M.) 1941- DLB-40

Black, Winifred 1863-1936 . . . . DLB-25

Black, Walter J. [publishing house] DLB-46

The Black Aesthetic: Background DS-8

The Black Arts Movement, by
 Larry Neal DLB-38

Black Theaters and Theater Organizations in
 America, 1961-1982:
 A Research List DLB-38

Black Theatre: A Forum [excerpts] DLB-38

Blackamore, Arthur 1679-? DLB-24, 39

Blackburn, Alexander L. 1929- Y-85

Blackburn, Paul 1926-1971 . . . . DLB-16; Y-81

Blackburn, Thomas 1916-1977 . . . . DLB-27

Blackmore, R. D. 1825-1900 . . . . DLB-18

Blackmore, Sir Richard 1654-1729 . . . . . . DLB-131

Blackmur, R. P. 1904-1965 . . . . DLB-63

Blackwell, Basil, Publisher DLB-106

Blackwood, Algernon Henry
 1869-1951 . . . . DLB-153, 156, 178

Blackwood, Caroline 1931-1996 . . . . . DLB-14, 207

Blackwood, William, and Sons, Ltd. DLB-154

Blackwood's Edinburgh Magazine
 1817-1980 . . . . DLB-110

Blades, William 1824-1890 . . . . DLB-184

Blaga, Lucian 1895-1961 . . . . DLB-220

Blagden, Isabella 1817?-1873 . . . . DLB-199

Blair, Eric Arthur (see Orwell, George)

Blair, Francis Preston 1791-1876 . . . . DLB-43

Blair, James circa 1655-1743 . . . . DLB-24

Blair, John Durburrow 1759-1823 . . . . . . DLB-37

Blais, Marie-Claire 1939- DLB-53

Blaise, Clark 1940- DLB-53

Blake, George 1893-1961 . . . . DLB-191

Blake, Lillie Devereux 1833-1913 . . . DLB-202, 221

Blake, Nicholas 1904-1972 . . . . DLB-77
 (see Day Lewis, C.)

Blake, William 1757-1827 . . . . DLB-93, 154, 163

The Blakiston Company DLB-49

Blanchot, Maurice 1907- DLB-72

Blanckenburg, Christian Friedrich von
 1744-1796 . . . . DLB-94

Blaser, Robin 1925- DLB-165

Blaumanis, Rudolfs 1863-1908 . . . . DLB-220

Bledsoe, Albert Taylor 1809-1877 . . . . . . DLB-3, 79

Bleecker, Ann Eliza 1752-1783 . . . . DLB-200

Blelock and Company DLB-49

Blennerhassett, Margaret Agnew
 1773-1842 . . . . DLB-99

Bles, Geoffrey [publishing house] DLB-112

Blessington, Marguerite, Countess of
 1789-1849 . . . . DLB-166

The Blickling Homilies circa 971 . . . . DLB-146

Blind, Mathilde 1841-1896 . . . . DLB-199

Blish, James 1921-1975 . . . . DLB-8

Bliss, E., and E. White
 [publishing house] DLB-49

Bliven, Bruce 1889-1977 . . . . DLB-137

Blixen, Karen 1885-1962 . . . . DLB-214

Bloch, Robert 1917-1994 . . . . DLB-44

Block, Rudolph (see Lessing, Bruno)

Blondal, Patricia 1926-1959 . . . . DLB-88

Bloom, Harold 1930- DLB-67

Bloomer, Amelia 1818-1894 . . . . DLB-79

Bloomfield, Robert 1766-1823 . . . . DLB-93

Bloomsbury Group DS-10

Blotner, Joseph 1923- DLB-111

Bloy, Léon 1846-1917 . . . . DLB-123

Blume, Judy 1938- DLB-52

Blunck, Hans Friedrich 1888-1961 . . . . . . DLB-66

Blunden, Edmund 1896-1974 . . . . DLB-20, 100, 155

Blunt, Lady Anne Isabella Noel
 1837-1917 . . . . DLB-174

Blunt, Wilfrid Scawen 1840-1922 . . . . . DLB-19, 174

Bly, Nellie (see Cochrane, Elizabeth)

Bly, Robert 1926- DLB-5

Blyton, Enid 1897-1968 . . . . DLB-160

Boaden, James 1762-1839 . . . . DLB-89

Boas, Frederick S. 1862-1957 . . . . .DLB-149

The Bobbs-Merrill Archive at the
　Lilly Library, Indiana University Y-90

The Bobbs-Merrill Company. DLB-46

Bobrov, Semen Sergeevich
　1763?-1810. . . . . .DLB-150

Bobrowski, Johannes 1917-1965. . . . . .DLB-75

Bodenheim, Maxwell 1892-1954 . . . . . . .DLB-9, 45

Bodenstedt, Friedrich von 1819-1892 . . . .DLB-129

Bodini, Vittorio 1914-1970. . . . . .DLB-128

Bodkin, M. McDonnell 1850-1933 . . . . . . .DLB-70

Bodley, Sir Thomas 1545-1613 . . . . .DLB-213

Bodley Head DLB-112

Bodmer, Johann Jakob 1698-1783 . . . . . . .DLB-97

Bodmershof, Imma von 1895-1982 . . . . . . .DLB-85

Bodsworth, Fred 1918- DLB-68

Boehm, Sydney 1908- DLB-44

Boer, Charles 1939- DLB-5

Boethius circa 480-circa 524 . . . . .DLB-115

Boethius of Dacia circa 1240-?. DLB-115

Bogan, Louise 1897-1970 . . . . .DLB-45, 169

Bogarde, Dirk 1921- DLB-14

Bogdanovich, Ippolit Fedorovich
　circa 1743-1803 . . . . .DLB-150

Bogue, David [publishing house] DLB-106

Böhme, Jakob 1575-1624 . . . . .DLB-164

Bohn, H. G. [publishing house] DLB-106

Bohse, August 1661-1742. . . . . .DLB-168

Boie, Heinrich Christian 1744-1806. . . . . .DLB-94

Bok, Edward W. 1863-1930 . . . . . .DLB-91; DS-16

Boland, Eavan 1944- DLB-40

Bolingbroke, Henry St. John, Viscount
　1678-1751 . . . . .DLB-101

Böll, Heinrich 1917-1985 . . . . .DLB-69; Y-85

Bolling, Robert 1738-1775 . . . . .DLB-31

Bolotov, Andrei Timofeevich
　1738-1833 . . . . .DLB-150

Bolt, Carol 1941- DLB-60

Bolt, Robert 1924-1995 . . . . .DLB-13

Bolton, Herbert E. 1870-1953 . . . . .DLB-17

Bonaventura DLB-90

Bonaventure circa 1217-1274 . . . . .DLB-115

Bonaviri, Giuseppe 1924- DLB-177

Bond, Edward 1934- DLB-13

Bond, Michael 1926- DLB-161

Boni, Albert and Charles
　[publishing house] DLB-46

Boni and Liveright. DLB-46

Bonner, Paul Hyde 1893-1968. . . . . DS-17

Bonner, Sherwood 1849-1883 . . . . .DLB-202

Robert Bonner's Sons DLB-49

Bonnin, Gertrude Simmons (see Zitkala-Ša)

Bonsanti, Alessandro 1904-1984 . . . . . . .DLB-177

Bontemps, Arna 1902-1973 . . . . .DLB-48, 51

The Book Arts Press at the University
　of Virginia. Y-96

The Book League of America DLB-46

Book Publishing Accounting: Some Basic
　Concepts Y-98

Book Reviewing in America: I. Y-87

Book Reviewing in America: II. Y-88

Book Reviewing in America: III. Y-89

Book Reviewing in America: IV. Y-90

Book Reviewing in America: V. Y-91

Book Reviewing in America: VI. Y-92

Book Reviewing in America: VII. Y-93

Book Reviewing in America: VIII. Y-94

Book Reviewing in America and the
　Literary Scene Y-95

Book Reviewing and the
　Literary Scene Y-96, Y-97

Book Supply Company DLB-49

The Book Trade History Group Y-93

The Booker Prize. Y-96

The Booker Prize
　Address by Anthony Thwaite,
　Chairman of the Booker Prize Judges
　Comments from Former Booker
　Prize Winners Y-86

Boorde, Andrew circa 1490-1549 . . . . . . .DLB-136

Boorstin, Daniel J. 1914- DLB-17

Booth, Mary L. 1831-1889 . . . . .DLB-79

Booth, Franklin 1874-1948. . . . . .DLB-188

Booth, Philip 1925- Y-82

Booth, Wayne C. 1921- DLB-67

Booth, William 1829-1912. . . . . .DLB-190

Borchardt, Rudolf 1877-1945. . . . . .DLB-66

Borchert, Wolfgang 1921-1947 . . . . . .DLB-69, 124

Borel, Pétrus 1809-1859. . . . . .DLB-119

Borges, Jorge Luis 1899-1986 . . . . .DLB-113; Y-86

Börne, Ludwig 1786-1837 . . . . .DLB-90

Bornstein, Miriam 1950- DLB-209

Borowski, Tadeusz 1922-1951. . . . . .DLB-215

Borrow, George 1803-1881 . . . . . .DLB-21, 55, 166

Bosch, Juan 1909- DLB-145

Bosco, Henri 1888-1976. . . . . .DLB-72

Bosco, Monique 1927- DLB-53

Boston, Lucy M. 1892-1990 . . . . .DLB-161

Boswell, James 1740-1795. . . . . .DLB-104, 142

Botev, Khristo 1847-1876. . . . . .DLB-147

Bote, Hermann
　circa 1460-circa 1520. . . . . .DLB-179

Botta, Anne C. Lynch 1815-1891 . . . . .DLB-3

Botto, Ján (see Krasko, Ivan)

Bottome, Phyllis 1882-1963. . . . . .DLB-197

Bottomley, Gordon 1874-1948. . . . . .DLB-10

Bottoms, David 1949- DLB-120; Y-83

Bottrall, Ronald 1906- DLB-20

Bouchardy, Joseph 1810-1870 . . . . .DLB-192

Boucher, Anthony 1911-1968 . . . . .DLB-8

Boucher, Jonathan 1738-1804 . . . . .DLB-31

Boucher de Boucherville, George
　1814-1894 . . . . .DLB-99

Boudreau, Daniel (see Coste, Donat)

Bourassa, Napoléon 1827-1916 . . . . .DLB-99

Bourget, Paul 1852-1935 . . . . .DLB-123

Bourinot, John George 1837-1902 . . . . . . .DLB-99

Bourjaily, Vance 1922- DLB-2, 143

Bourne, Edward Gaylord
　1860-1908 . . . . .DLB-47

Bourne, Randolph 1886-1918 . . . . .DLB-63

Bousoño, Carlos 1923- DLB-108

Bousquet, Joë 1897-1950 . . . . .DLB-72

Bova, Ben 1932- Y-81

Bovard, Oliver K. 1872-1945. . . . . .DLB-25

Bove, Emmanuel 1898-1945 . . . . .DLB-72

Bowen, Elizabeth 1899-1973 . . . . . . .DLB-15, 162

Bowen, Francis 1811-1890. . . . . .DLB-1, 59

Bowen, John 1924- DLB-13

Bowen, Marjorie 1886-1952 . . . . .DLB-153

Bowen-Merrill Company. DLB-49

Bowering, George 1935- DLB-53

Bowers, Bathsheba 1671-1718 . . . . .DLB-200

Bowers, Claude G. 1878-1958 . . . . .DLB-17

Bowers, Edgar 1924- DLB-5

Bowers, Fredson Thayer
　1905-1991 . . . . .DLB-140; Y-91

Bowles, Paul 1910- DLB-5, 6, 218

Bowles, Samuel III 1826-1878 . . . . .DLB-43

Bowles, William Lisles 1762-1850 . . . . . . .DLB-93

Bowman, Louise Morey 1882-1944. . . . . . .DLB-68

Boyd, James 1888-1944 . . . . .DLB-9; DS-16

Boyd, John 1919- DLB-8

Boyd, Thomas 1898-1935 . . . . .DLB-9; DS-16

Boyesen, Hjalmar Hjorth
　1848-1895 . . . . .DLB-12, 71; DS-13

Boyle, Kay
　1902-1992 . . . . .DLB-4, 9, 48, 86; Y-93

Boyle, Roger, Earl of Orrery
　1621-1679 . . . . .DLB-80

Boyle, T. Coraghessan 1948- DLB-218; Y-86

Božić, Mirko 1919- DLB-181

Brackenbury, Alison 1953- DLB-40

Brackenridge, Hugh Henry
　1748-1816 . . . . .DLB-11, 37

Brackett, Charles 1892-1969 . . . . .DLB-26

Brackett, Leigh 1915-1978 . . . . .DLB-8, 26

Bradburn, John [publishing house] DLB-49

Bradbury, Malcolm 1932- DLB-14, 207

Bradbury, Ray 1920- DLB-2, 8

Bradbury and Evans DLB-106

Braddon, Mary Elizabeth
　1835-1915 . . . . .DLB-18, 70, 156

Bradford, Andrew 1686-1742 . . . . .DLB-43, 73

Bradford, Gamaliel 1863-1932. . . . . .DLB-17

Bradford, John 1749-1830 . . . . .DLB-43

Bradford, Roark 1896-1948. . . . . .DLB-86

Bradford, William 1590-1657 . . . . . . .DLB-24, 30

Bradford, William III 1719-1791 . . . . . .DLB-43, 73

Bradlaugh, Charles 1833-1891 . . . . DLB-57

Bradley, David 1950- DLB-33

Bradley, Marion Zimmer 1930- DLB-8

Bradley, William Aspenwall
1878-1939. . . . . DLB-4

Bradley, Ira, and Company DLB-49

Bradley, J. W., and Company DLB-49

Bradshaw, Henry 1831-1886 . . . . DLB-184

Bradstreet, Anne
1612 or 1613-1672 . . . . DLB-24

Bradūnas, Kazys 1917- DLB-220

Bradwardine, Thomas circa
1295-1349 . . . . DLB-115

Brady, Frank 1924-1986. . . . . DLB-111

Brady, Frederic A. [publishing house]. DLB-49

Bragg, Melvyn 1939- DLB-14

Brainard, Charles H. [publishing house]. . . DLB-49

Braine, John 1922-1986 . . . . .DLB-15; Y-86

Braithwait, Richard 1588-1673 . . . . DLB-151

Braithwaite, William Stanley
1878-1962. DLB-50, 54

Braker, Ulrich 1735-1798 . . . . DLB-94

Bramah, Ernest 1868-1942 . . . . DLB-70

Branagan, Thomas 1774-1843 . . . . DLB-37

Branch, William Blackwell 1927- DLB-76

Branden Press. DLB-46

Branner, H.C. 1903-1966. . . . . DLB-214

Brant, Sebastian 1457-1521 . . . . .DLB-179

Brassey, Lady Annie (Allnutt)
1839-1887. . . . . DLB-166

Brathwaite, Edward Kamau
1930- DLB-125

Brault, Jacques 1933- DLB-53

Braun, Matt 1932- DLB-212

Braun, Volker 1939- DLB-75

Brautigan, Richard
1935-1984 . . . . DLB-2, 5, 206; Y-80, Y-84

Braxton, Joanne M. 1950- DLB-41

Bray, Anne Eliza 1790-1883 . . . . DLB-116

Bray, Thomas 1656-1730 . . . . DLB-24

Brazdžionis, Bernardas 1907- DLB-220

Braziller, George [publishing house] DLB-46

The Bread Loaf Writers'
Conference 1983 . . . . .Y-84

The Break-Up of the Novel (1922),
by John Middleton Murry DLB-36

Breasted, James Henry 1865-1935 . . . . DLB-47

Brecht, Bertolt 1898-1956. . . . . DLB-56, 124

Bredel, Willi 1901-1964 . . . . DLB-56

Bregendahl, Marie 1867-1940. . . . . DLB-214

Breitinger, Johann Jakob 1701-1776 . . . . . . DLB-97

Bremser, Bonnie 1939- DLB-16

Bremser, Ray 1934- DLB-16

Brentano, Bernard von 1901-1964 . . . . DLB-56

Brentano, Clemens 1778-1842 . . . . DLB-90

Brentano's. DLB-49

Brenton, Howard 1942- DLB-13

Breslin, Jimmy 1929-1996. . . . . DLB-185

Breton, André 1896-1966 . . . . DLB-65

Breton, Nicholas
circa 1555-circa 1626 . . . . DLB-136

The Breton Lays
1300-early fifteenth century DLB-146

Brewer, Luther A. 1858-1933 . . . . DLB-187

Brewer, Warren and Putnam DLB-46

Brewster, Elizabeth 1922- DLB-60

Bridge, Ann (Lady Mary Dolling Sanders
O'Malley) 1889-1974 . . . . DLB-191

Bridge, Horatio 1806-1893 . . . . DLB-183

Bridgers, Sue Ellen 1942- DLB-52

Bridges, Robert 1844-1930 . . . . DLB-19, 98

The Bridgewater Library DLB-213

Bridie, James 1888-1951 . . . . DLB-10

Brieux, Eugene 1858-1932 . . . . DLB-192

Brigadere, Anna 1861-1933 . . . . DLB-220

Bright, Mary Chavelita Dunne (see Egerton, George)

Brimmer, B. J., Company. DLB-46

Brines, Francisco 1932- DLB-134

Brinley, George, Jr. 1817-1875 . . . . DLB-140

Brinnin, John Malcolm 1916-1998 . . . . DLB-48

Brisbane, Albert 1809-1890 . . . . DLB-3

Brisbane, Arthur 1864-1936 . . . . DLB-25

British Academy DLB-112

The British Critic 1793-1843 . . . . DLB-110

The British Library and the Regular
Readers' Group Y-91

British Literary Prizes. Y-98

*The British Review and London Critical
Journal 1811-1825* DLB-110

British Travel Writing, 1940-1997 . . . . . DLB-204

Brito, Aristeo 1942- DLB-122

Brittain, Vera 1893-1970. . . . . DLB-191

Brizeux, Auguste 1803-1858. . . . . DLB-217

Broadway Publishing Company. DLB-46

Broch, Hermann 1886-1951 . . . . DLB-85, 124

Brochu, André 1942- DLB-53

Brock, Edwin 1927- DLB-40

Brockes, Barthold Heinrich
1680-1747. . . . . DLB-168

Brod, Max 1884-1968. . . . . DLB-81

Brodber, Erna 1940- DLB-157

Brodhead, John R. 1814-1873. . . . . DLB-30

Brodkey, Harold 1930-1996 . . . . DLB-130

Brodsky, Joseph 1940-1996 . . . . .Y-87

Broeg, Bob 1918- DLB-171

Brøgger, Suzanne 1944- DLB-214

Brome, Richard circa 1590-1652 . . . . DLB-58

Brome, Vincent 1910- DLB-155

Bromfield, Louis 1896-1956 . . . . DLB-4, 9, 86

Bromige, David 1933- DLB-193

Broner, E. M. 1930- DLB-28

Bronk, William 1918- DLB-165

Bronnen, Arnolt 1895-1959 . . . . DLB-124

Brontë, Anne 1820-1849. . . . . DLB-21, 199

Brontë, Charlotte 1816-1855 . . . .DLB-21, 159, 199

Brontë, Emily 1818-1848 . . . . DLB-21, 32, 199

Brook, Stephen 1947- DLB-204

Brooke, Frances 1724-1789 . . . . DLB-39, 99

Brooke, Henry 1703?-1783 . . . . DLB-39

Brooke, L. Leslie 1862-1940. . . . . DLB-141

Brooke, Margaret, Ranee of Sarawak
1849-1936 . . . . .DLB-174

Brooke, Rupert 1887-1915 . . . . DLB-19, 216

Brooker, Bertram 1888-1955 . . . . DLB-88

Brooke-Rose, Christine 1926- DLB-14

Brookner, Anita 1928- DLB-194; Y-87

Brooks, Charles Timothy 1813-1883 . . . . . . DLB-1

Brooks, Cleanth 1906-1994 . . . . .DLB-63; Y-94

Brooks, Gwendolyn 1917- DLB-5, 76, 165

Brooks, Jeremy 1926- DLB-14

Brooks, Mel 1926- DLB-26

Brooks, Noah 1830-1903 . . . . DLB-42; DS-13

Brooks, Richard 1912-1992 . . . . DLB-44

Brooks, Van Wyck
1886-1963 . . . . .DLB-45, 63, 103

Brophy, Brigid 1929-1995 . . . . DLB-14

Brophy, John 1899-1965. . . . . DLB-191

Brossard, Chandler 1922-1993. . . . . DLB-16

Brossard, Nicole 1943- DLB-53

Broster, Dorothy Kathleen
1877-1950. . . . . DLB-160

Brother Antoninus (see Everson, William)

Brotherton, Lord 1856-1930. . . . . DLB-184

Brougham and Vaux, Henry Peter Brougham, Baron
1778-1868. . . . . .DLB-110, 158

Brougham, John 1810-1880 . . . . DLB-11

Broughton, James 1913- DLB-5

Broughton, Rhoda 1840-1920 . . . . DLB-18

Broun, Heywood 1888-1939 . . . . .DLB-29, 171

Brown, Alice 1856-1948. . . . . DLB-78

Brown, Bob 1886-1959. . . . . DLB-4, 45

Brown, Cecil 1943- DLB-33

Brown, Charles Brockden
1771-1810. . . . . .DLB-37, 59, 73

Brown, Christy 1932?-1981 . . . . DLB-14

Brown, Dee 1908- Y-80

Brown, Frank London 1927-1962. . . . . DLB-76

Brown, Fredric 1906-1972 . . . . DLB-8

Brown, George Mackay
1921-1996 . . . . .DLB-14, 27, 139

Brown, Harry 1917-1986 . . . . DLB-26

Brown, Marcia 1918- DLB-61

Brown, Margaret Wise 1910-1952 . . . . DLB-22

Brown, Morna Doris (see Ferrars, Elizabeth)

Brown, Oliver Madox 1855-1874. . . . . DLB-21

Brown, Sterling 1901-1989 . . . . DLB-48, 51, 63

Brown, T. E. 1830-1897. . . . . DLB-35

Brown, William Hill 1765-1793 . . . . DLB-37

Brown, William Wells
    1814-1884 . . . . .DLB-3, 50, 183

Browne, Charles Farrar 1834-1867 . . . . . . .DLB-11

Browne, Frances 1816-1879 . . . . .DLB-199

Browne, Francis Fisher 1843-1913 . . . . . . .DLB-79

Browne, J. Ross 1821-1875 . . . . .DLB-202

Browne, Michael Dennis 1940- DLB-40

Browne, Sir Thomas 1605-1682 . . . . . . .DLB-151

Browne, William, of Tavistock
    1590-1645 . . . . .DLB-121

Browne, Wynyard 1911-1964 . . . . .DLB-13

Browne and Nolan DLB-106

Brownell, W. C. 1851-1928 . . . . .DLB-71

Browning, Elizabeth Barrett
    1806-1861 . . . . .DLB-32, 199

Browning, Robert 1812-1889 . . . . .DLB-32, 163

Brownjohn, Allan 1931- DLB-40

Brownson, Orestes Augustus
    1803-1876 . . . . .DLB-1, 59, 73

Bruccoli, Matthew J. 1931- DLB-103

Bruce, Charles 1906-1971 . . . . .DLB-68

Bruce, Leo 1903-1979 . . . . .DLB-77

Bruce, Philip Alexander 1856-1933 . . . . . . .DLB-47

Bruce Humphries [publishing house] DLB-46

Bruce-Novoa, Juan 1944- DLB-82

Bruckman, Clyde 1894-1955 . . . . .DLB-26

Bruckner, Ferdinand 1891-1958 . . . . .DLB-118

Brundage, John Herbert (see Herbert, John)

Brutus, Dennis 1924- DLB-117

Bryan, C. D. B. 1936- DLB-185

Bryant, Arthur 1899-1985 . . . . .DLB-149

Bryant, William Cullen
    1794-1878. . . . . .DLB-3, 43, 59, 189

Bryce Echenique, Alfredo 1939- DLB-145

Bryce, James 1838-1922 . . . . .DLB-166, 190

Brydges, Sir Samuel Egerton
    1762-1837 . . . . .DLB-107

Bryskett, Lodowick 1546?-1612. . . . . .DLB-167

Buchan, John 1875-1940 . . . . .DLB-34, 70, 156

Buchanan, George 1506-1582 . . . . .DLB-132

Buchanan, Robert 1841-1901 . . . . . . .DLB-18, 35

Buchman, Sidney 1902-1975 . . . . .DLB-26

Buchner, Augustus 1591-1661 . . . . .DLB-164

Büchner, Georg 1813-1837 . . . . .DLB-133

Bucholtz, Andreas Heinrich
    1607-1671. . . . . .DLB-168

Buck, Pearl S. 1892-1973 . . . . .DLB-9, 102

Bucke, Charles 1781-1846 . . . . .DLB-110

Bucke, Richard Maurice
    1837-1902 .DLB-99

Buckingham, Joseph Tinker 1779-1861 and
    Buckingham, Edwin 1810-1833 . . . . . .DLB-73

Buckler, Ernest 1908-1984. . . . . .DLB-68

Buckley, William F., Jr. 1925- . . .DLB-137; Y-80

Buckminster, Joseph Stevens 1784-1812 . . .DLB-37

Buckner, Robert 1906- DLB-26

Budd, Thomas ?-1698 . . . . .DLB-24

Budrys, A. J. 1931- DLB-8

Buechner, Frederick 1926- Y-80

Buell, John 1927- DLB-53

Bufalino, Gesualdo 1920-1996. . . . . .DLB-196

Buffum, Job [publishing house] DLB-49

Bugnet, Georges 1879-1981 . . . . .DLB-92

Buies, Arthur 1840-1901 . . . . .DLB-99

Building the New British Library
    at St Pancras Y-94

Bukowski, Charles 1920-1994 . . . .DLB-5, 130, 169

Bulatović, Miodrag 1930-1991. . . . . .DLB-181

Bulgarin, Faddei Venediktovich
    1789-1859 . . . . .DLB-198

Bulger, Bozeman 1877-1932 . . . . .DLB-171

Bullein, William
    between 1520 and 1530-1576 . . . . . . .DLB-167

Bullins, Ed 1935- DLB-7, 38

Bulwer-Lytton, Edward (also Edward Bulwer)
    1803-1873 .DLB-21

Bumpus, Jerry 1937- Y-81

Bunce and Brother. DLB-49

Bunner, H. C. 1855-1896 . . . . .DLB-78, 79

Bunting, Basil 1900-1985 . . . . .DLB-20

Buntline, Ned (Edward Zane Carroll Judson)
    1821-1886 . . . . .DLB-186

Bunyan, John 1628-1688 . . . . .DLB-39

Burch, Robert 1925- DLB-52

Burciaga, José Antonio 1940- DLB-82

Bürger, Gottfried August 1747-1794 . . . . . .DLB-94

Burgess, Anthony 1917-1993 . . . . .DLB-14, 194

Burgess, Gelett 1866-1951 . . . . .DLB-11

Burgess, John W. 1844-1931 . . . . .DLB-47

Burgess, Thornton W. 1874-1965 . . . . . . .DLB-22

Burgess, Stringer and Company DLB-49

Burick, Si 1909-1986 . . . . .DLB-171

Burk, John Daly circa 1772-1808 . . . . .DLB-37

Burk, Ronnie 1955- DLB-209

Burke, Edmund 1729?-1797 . . . . .DLB-104

Burke, Kenneth 1897-1993. . . . . . . .DLB-45, 63

Burke, Thomas 1886-1945 . . . . .DLB-197

Burlingame, Edward Livermore
    1848-1922 .DLB-79

Burnet, Gilbert 1643-1715 . . . . .DLB-101

Burnett, Frances Hodgson
    1849-1924 . . . . .DLB-42, 141; DS-13, 14

Burnett, W. R. 1899-1982 . . . . .DLB-9

Burnett, Whit 1899-1973 and
    Martha Foley 1897-1977 . . . . .DLB-137

Burney, Fanny 1752-1840 . . . . .DLB-39

Burns, Alan 1929- DLB-14, 194

Burns, John Horne 1916-1953 . . . . Y-85

Burns, Robert 1759-1796 . . . . .DLB-109

Burns and Oates DLB-106

Burnshaw, Stanley 1906- DLB-48

Burr, C. Chauncey 1815?-1883 . . . . .DLB-79

Burr, Esther Edwards 1732-1758 . . . . .DLB-200

Burroughs, Edgar Rice 1875-1950 . . . . .DLB-8

Burroughs, John 1837-1921 . . . . .DLB-64

Burroughs, Margaret T. G. 1917- DLB-41

Burroughs, William S., Jr. 1947-1981. . . . .DLB-16

Burroughs, William Seward
    1914-1997 . . . . . .DLB-2, 8, 16, 152; Y-81, Y-97

Burroway, Janet 1936- DLB-6

Burt, Maxwell Struthers
    1882-1954 . . . . .DLB-86; DS-16

Burt, A. L., and Company. DLB-49

Burton, Hester 1913- DLB-161

Burton, Isabel Arundell 1831-1896 . . . . . .DLB-166

Burton, Miles (see Rhode, John)

Burton, Richard Francis
    1821-1890 . . . . .DLB-55, 166, 184

Burton, Robert 1577-1640 . . . . .DLB-151

Burton, Virginia Lee 1909-1968 . . . . .DLB-22

Burton, William Evans 1804-1860. . . . . . . .DLB-73

Burwell, Adam Hood 1790-1849 . . . . .DLB-99

Bury, Lady Charlotte 1775-1861 . . . . .DLB-116

Busch, Frederick 1941- DLB-6, 218

Busch, Niven 1903-1991 . . . . .DLB-44

Bushnell, Horace 1802-1876 . . . . DS-13

Bussieres, Arthur de 1877-1913 . . . . .DLB-92

Butler, Josephine Elizabeth 1828-1906. . . .DLB-190

Butler, Juan 1942-1981 . . . . .DLB-53

Butler, Octavia E. 1947- DLB-33

Butler, Pierce 1884-1953 . . . . .DLB-187

Butler, Robert Olen 1945- DLB-173

Butler, Samuel 1613-1680 . . . . .DLB-101, 126

Butler, Samuel 1835-1902 . . . . . . .DLB-18, 57, 174

Butler, William Francis 1838-1910 . . . . . .DLB-166

Butler, E. H., and Company DLB-49

Butor, Michel 1926- DLB-83

Butter, Nathaniel [publishing house] DLB-170

Butterworth, Hezekiah 1839-1905. . . . . . .DLB-42

Buttitta, Ignazio 1899- DLB-114

Buzzati, Dino 1906-1972 . . . . .DLB-177

Byars, Betsy 1928- DLB-52

Byatt, A. S. 1936- DLB-14, 194

Byles, Mather 1707-1788. . . . . .DLB-24

Bynneman, Henry [publishing house] DLB-170

Bynner, Witter 1881-1968. . . . . .DLB-54

Byrd, William circa 1543-1623 . . . . .DLB-172

Byrd, William II 1674-1744 . . . . .DLB-24, 140

Byrne, John Keyes (see Leonard, Hugh)

Byron, George Gordon, Lord
    1788-1824 . . . . .DLB-96, 110

Byron, Robert 1905-1941 . . . . .DLB-195

C

Caballero Bonald, José Manuel
    1926- DLB-108

Cabañero, Eladio 1930- DLB-134

Cabell, James Branch 1879-1958 . . . . . . .DLB-9, 78

Cabeza de Baca, Manuel 1853-1915 . . . . .DLB-122

Cabeza de Baca Gilbert, Fabiola
1898- DLB-122

Cable, George Washington
1844-1925 . . . . .DLB-12, 74; DS-13

Cable, Mildred 1878-1952 . . . . DLB-195

Cabrera, Lydia 1900-1991 . . . . DLB-145

Cabrera Infante, Guillermo 1929- DLB-113

Cadell [publishing house] DLB-154

Cady, Edwin H. 1917- DLB-103

Caedmon flourished 658-680 . . . . DLB-146

Caedmon School circa 660-899 . . . . DLB-146

Cafés, Brasseries, and Bistros DS-15

Cage, John 1912-1992. . . . . DLB-193

Cahan, Abraham 1860-1951. . . . . . DLB-9, 25, 28

Cain, George 1943- DLB-33

Caird, Mona 1854-1932 . . . . DLB-197

Čaks, Aleksandrs 1901-1950. . . . . DLB-220

Caldecott, Randolph 1846-1886. . . . . . . DLB-163

Calder, John (Publishers), Limited DLB-112

Calderón de la Barca, Fanny
1804-1882 . . . . DLB-183

Caldwell, Ben 1937- DLB-38

Caldwell, Erskine 1903-1987 . . . . DLB-9, 86

Caldwell, H. M., Company DLB-49

Caldwell, Taylor 1900-1985. . . . . .DS-17

Calhoun, John C. 1782-1850 . . . . DLB-3

Călinescu, George 1899-1965. . . . . DLB-220

Calisher, Hortense 1911- DLB-2, 218

A Call to Letters and an Invitation
to the Electric Chair,
by Siegfried Mandel. DLB-75

Callaghan, Mary Rose 1944- DLB-207

Callaghan, Morley 1903-1990 . . . . DLB-68

Callahan, S. Alice 1868-1894 . . . . .DLB-175, 221

Callaloo Y-87

Callimachus circa 305 B.C.-240 B.C.
 . . . . .DLB-176

Calmer, Edgar 1907- DLB-4

Calverley, C. S. 1831-1884. . . . . DLB-35

Calvert, George Henry 1803-1889 . . . . . DLB-1, 64

Calvino, Italo 1923-1985 . . . . DLB-196

Cambridge Press. DLB-49

Cambridge Songs (Carmina Cantabrigensia)
circa 1050. . . . . DLB-148

Cambridge University Press. DLB-170

Camden, William 1551-1623 . . . . .DLB-172

Camden House: An Interview with
James Hardin .Y-92

Cameron, Eleanor 1912- DLB-52

Cameron, George Frederick
1854-1885 . . . . DLB-99

Cameron, Lucy Lyttelton 1781-1858 . . . . DLB-163

Cameron, William Bleasdell
1862-1951 . . . . DLB-99

Camm, John 1718-1778. . . . . DLB-31

Camon, Ferdinando 1935- DLB-196

Campana, Dino 1885-1932. . . . . DLB-114

Campbell, Gabrielle Margaret Vere
(see Shearing, Joseph, and Bowen, Marjorie)

Campbell, James Dykes 1838-1895 . . . . . DLB-144

Campbell, James Edwin 1867-1896. . . . . . DLB-50

Campbell, John 1653-1728 . . . . DLB-43

Campbell, John W., Jr. 1910-1971 . . . . DLB-8

Campbell, Roy 1901-1957 . . . . DLB-20

Campbell, Thomas
1777-1844 . . . . DLB-93, 144

Campbell, William Wilfred
1858-1918 . . . . DLB-92

Campion, Edmund 1539-1581 . . . . DLB-167

Campion, Thomas
1567-1620. . . . . .DLB-58, 172

Camus, Albert 1913-1960. . . . . DLB-72

The Canadian Publishers' Records
Database. Y-96

Canby, Henry Seidel 1878-1961. . . . . DLB-91

Candelaria, Cordelia 1943- DLB-82

Candelaria, Nash 1928- DLB-82

Candour in English Fiction (1890),
by Thomas Hardy DLB-18

Canetti, Elias 1905-1994. . . . . DLB-85, 124

Canham, Erwin Dain 1904-1982 . . . . . . DLB-127

Canitz, Friedrich Rudolph Ludwig von
1654-1699 . . . . DLB-168

Cankar, Ivan 1876-1918 . . . . DLB-147

Cannan, Gilbert 1884-1955 . . . . .DLB-10, 197

Cannan, Joanna 1896-1961 . . . . DLB-191

Cannell, Kathleen 1891-1974 . . . . DLB-4

Cannell, Skipwith 1887-1957. . . . . DLB-45

Canning, George 1770-1827 . . . . DLB-158

Cannon, Jimmy 1910-1973 . . . . .DLB-171

Cano, Daniel 1947- DLB-209

Cantú, Norma Elia 1947- DLB-209

Cantwell, Robert 1908-1978. . . . . DLB-9

Cape, Jonathan, and Harrison Smith
[publishing house] DLB-46

Cape, Jonathan, Limited. DLB-112

Čapek, Karel 1890-1938. . . . . DLB-215

Capen, Joseph 1658-1725 . . . . DLB-24

Capes, Bernard 1854-1918 . . . . DLB-156

Capote, Truman
1924-1984 . . . . .DLB-2, 185; Y-80, Y-84

Caproni, Giorgio 1912-1990. . . . . DLB-128

Caragiale, Mateiu Ioan 1885-1936 . . . . . DLB-220

Cardarelli, Vincenzo 1887-1959 . . . . DLB-114

Cárdenas, Reyes 1948- DLB-122

Cardinal, Marie 1929- DLB-83

Carew, Jan 1920- DLB-157

Carew, Thomas 1594 or 1595-1640 . . . . DLB-126

Carey, Henry
circa 1687-1689-1743 . . . . DLB-84

Carey, Mathew 1760-1839 . . . . .DLB-37, 73

Carey and Hart DLB-49

Carey, M., and Company DLB-49

Carlell, Lodowick 1602-1675 . . . . DLB-58

Carleton, William 1794-1869 . . . . DLB-159

Carleton, G. W. [publishing house] DLB-49

Carlile, Richard 1790-1843. . . . . .DLB-110, 158

Carlyle, Jane Welsh 1801-1866 . . . . DLB-55

Carlyle, Thomas 1795-1881 . . . . DLB-55, 144

Carman, Bliss 1861-1929 . . . . DLB-92

Carmina Burana circa 1230. . . . . DLB-138

Carnero, Guillermo 1947- DLB-108

Carossa, Hans 1878-1956. . . . . DLB-66

Carpenter, Humphrey 1946- DLB-155

Carpenter, Stephen Cullen ?-1820? DLB-73

Carpentier, Alejo 1904-1980. . . . . DLB-113

Carrier, Roch 1937- DLB-53

Carrillo, Adolfo 1855-1926. . . . . DLB-122

Carroll, Gladys Hasty 1904- DLB-9

Carroll, John 1735-1815 . . . . DLB-37

Carroll, John 1809-1884 . . . . DLB-99

Carroll, Lewis 1832-1898. . . . . .DLB-18, 163, 178

Carroll, Paul 1927- DLB-16

Carroll, Paul Vincent 1900-1968 . . . . . . DLB-10

Carroll and Graf Publishers DLB-46

Carruth, Hayden 1921- DLB-5, 165

Carryl, Charles E. 1841-1920. . . . . DLB-42

Carson, Anne 1950- DLB-193

Carswell, Catherine 1879-1946. . . . . DLB-36

Carter, Angela 1940-1992 . . . . .DLB-14, 207

Carter, Elizabeth 1717-1806 . . . . DLB-109

Carter, Henry (see Leslie, Frank)

Carter, Hodding, Jr. 1907-1972. . . . . .DLB-127

Carter, John 1905-1975. . . . . DLB-201

Carter, Landon 1710-1778 . . . . DLB-31

Carter, Lin 1930- Y-81

Carter, Martin 1927-1997 . . . . .DLB-117

Carter and Hendee. DLB-49

Carter, Robert, and Brothers DLB-49

Cartwright, John 1740-1824 . . . . DLB-158

Cartwright, William circa 1611-1643 . . . . DLB-126

Caruthers, William Alexander
1802-1846 . . . . DLB-3

Carver, Jonathan 1710-1780 . . . . DLB-31

Carver, Raymond
1938-1988 . . . . .DLB-130; Y-84, Y-88

Cary, Alice 1820-1871 . . . . DLB-202

Cary, Joyce 1888-1957 . . . . .DLB-15, 100

Cary, Patrick 1623?-1657 . . . . DLB-131

Casey, Juanita 1925- DLB-14

Casey, Michael 1947- DLB-5

Cassady, Carolyn 1923- DLB-16

Cassady, Neal 1926-1968. . . . . DLB-16

Cassell and Company. DLB-106

Cassell Publishing Company DLB-49

Cassill, R. V. 1919- DLB-6, 218

Cassity, Turner 1929- DLB-105

Cassius Dio circa 155/164-post 229
 . . . . .DLB-176

Cassola, Carlo 1917-1987 . . . . .DLB-177

The Castle of Perseverance
circa 1400-1425 . . . . .DLB-146

Castellano, Olivia 1944- DLB-122

Castellanos, Rosario 1925-1974 . . . . .DLB-113

Castillo, Ana 1953- DLB-122

Castillo, Rafael C. 1950- DLB-209

Castlemon, Harry (see Fosdick, Charles Austin)

Čašule, Kole 1921- DLB-181

Caswall, Edward 1814-1878 . . . . .DLB-32

Catacalos, Rosemary 1944- DLB-122

Cather, Willa 1873-1947 . . . . .DLB-9, 54, 78; DS-1

Catherine II (Ekaterina Alekseevna), "The Great,"
Empress of Russia 1729-1796 . . . . . . .DLB-150

Catherwood, Mary Hartwell
1847-1902 . . . . .DLB-78

Catledge, Turner 1901-1983 . . . . .DLB-127

Catlin, George 1796-1872 . . . . . . .DLB-186, 189

Cato the Elder 234 B.C.-149 B.C. DLB-211

Cattafi, Bartolo 1922-1979 . . . . .DLB-128

Catton, Bruce 1899-1978 . . . . .DLB-17

Catullus circa 84 B.C.-54 B.C. DLB-211

Causley, Charles 1917- DLB-27

Caute, David 1936- DLB-14

Cavendish, Duchess of Newcastle,
Margaret Lucas 1623-1673 . . . . .DLB-131

Cawein, Madison 1865-1914 . . . . .DLB-54

The Caxton Printers, Limited DLB-46

Caxton, William [publishing house] DLB-170

Cayrol, Jean 1911- DLB-83

Cecil, Lord David 1902-1986 . . . . .DLB-155

Cela, Camilo José 1916- Y-89

Celan, Paul 1920-1970 . . . . .DLB-69

Celati, Gianni 1937- DLB-196

Celaya, Gabriel 1911-1991 . . . . .DLB-108

A Celebration of Literary Biography Y-98

Céline, Louis-Ferdinand 1894-1961 . . . . . . .DLB-72

The Celtic Background to Medieval English
Literature DLB-146

Celtis, Conrad 1459-1508 . . . . .DLB-179

Center for Bibliographical Studies and
Research at the University of
California, Riverside Y-91

The Center for the Book in the Library
of Congress Y-93

Center for the Book Research Y-84

Centlivre, Susanna 1669?-1723 . . . . .DLB-84

The Century Company DLB-49

Cernuda, Luis 1902-1963 . . . . .DLB-134

"Certain Gifts," by Betty Adcock DLB-105

Cervantes, Lorna Dee 1954- DLB-82

Chaadaev, Petr Iakovlevich
1794-1856 . . . . .DLB-198

Chacel, Rosa 1898- DLB-134

Chacón, Eusebio 1869-1948 . . . . .DLB-82

Chacón, Felipe Maximiliano 1873-? DLB-82

Chadwyck-Healey's Full-Text Literary Databases:
Editing Commercial Databases of
Primary Literary Texts Y-95

Challans, Eileen Mary (see Renault, Mary)

Chalmers, George 1742-1825 . . . . .DLB-30

Chaloner, Sir Thomas 1520-1565 . . . . . . .DLB-167

Chamberlain, Samuel S. 1851-1916 . . . . . . .DLB-25

Chamberland, Paul 1939- DLB-60

Chamberlin, William Henry
1897-1969 . . . . .DLB-29

Chambers, Charles Haddon
1860-1921 . . . . .DLB-10

Chambers, María Cristina (see Mena, María Cristina)

Chambers, Robert W. 1865-1933 . . . . . . .DLB-202

Chambers, W. and R.
[publishing house] DLB-106

Chamisso, Albert von 1781-1838 . . . . .DLB-90

Champfleury 1821-1889 . . . . .DLB-119

Chandler, Harry 1864-1944 . . . . .DLB-29

Chandler, Norman 1899-1973 . . . . .DLB-127

Chandler, Otis 1927- DLB-127

Chandler, Raymond 1888-1959 . . . . .DS-6

Channing, Edward 1856-1931 . . . . .DLB-17

Channing, Edward Tyrrell 1790-1856 . . .DLB-1, 59

Channing, William Ellery 1780-1842 . . . .DLB-1, 59

Channing, William Ellery, II
1817-1901 . . . . .DLB-1

Channing, William Henry
1810-1884 .DLB-1, 59

Chaplin, Charlie 1889-1977 . . . . .DLB-44

Chapman, George
1559 or 1560 - 1634 . . . . .DLB-62, 121

Chapman, John DLB-106

Chapman, Olive Murray 1892-1977 . . . . .DLB-195

Chapman, R. W. 1881-1960 . . . . .DLB-201

Chapman, William 1850-1917 . . . . .DLB-99

Chapman and Hall DLB-106

Chappell, Fred 1936- DLB-6, 105

Charbonneau, Jean 1875-1960 . . . . .DLB-92

Charbonneau, Robert 1911-1967 . . . . .DLB-68

Charles d'Orléans 1394-1465 . . . . .DLB-208

Charles, Gerda 1914- DLB-14

Charles, William [publishing house] DLB-49

The Charles Wood Affair:
A Playwright Revived Y-83

Charley (see Mann, Charles)

Charlotte Forten: Pages from her Diary . . .DLB-50

Charteris, Leslie 1907-1993 . . . . .DLB-77

Chartier, Alain circa 1385-1430 . . . . .DLB-208

Charyn, Jerome 1937- Y-83

Chase, Borden 1900-1971 . . . . .DLB-26

Chase, Edna Woolman 1877-1957 . . . . .DLB-91

Chase-Riboud, Barbara 1936- DLB-33

Chateaubriand, François-René de
1768-1848 . . . . .DLB-119

Chatterton, Thomas 1752-1770 . . . . .DLB-109

Chatto and Windus DLB-106

Chatwin, Bruce 1940-1989 . . . . . . .DLB-194, 204

Chaucer, Geoffrey 1340?-1400 . . . . .DLB-146

Chauncy, Charles 1705-1787 . . . . .DLB-24

Chauveau, Pierre-Joseph-Olivier
1820-1890 . . . . .DLB-99

Chávez, Denise 1948- DLB-122

Chávez, Fray Angélico 1910- DLB-82

Chayefsky, Paddy 1923-1981 . . . . DLB-7, 44; Y-81

Cheesman, Evelyn 1881-1969 . . . . .DLB-195

Cheever, Ezekiel 1615-1708 . . . . .DLB-24

Cheever, George Barrell 1807-1890 . . . . . . .DLB-59

Cheever, John
1912-1982 . . . . .DLB-2, 102; Y-80, Y-82

Cheever, Susan 1943- Y-82

Cheke, Sir John 1514-1557 . . . . .DLB-132

Chelsea House DLB-46

Chênedollé, Charles de 1769-1833 . . . . . . .DLB-217

Cheney, Ednah Dow (Littlehale)
1824-1904 . . . . .DLB-1

Cheney, Harriet Vaughn 1796-1889 . . . . . .DLB-99

Chénier, Marie-Joseph 1764-1811 . . . . . . .DLB-192

Cherry, Kelly 1940 . . . . .Y-83

Cherryh, C. J. 1942- Y-80

Chesebro', Caroline 1825-1873 . . . . .DLB-202

Chesnutt, Charles Waddell
1858-1932 . . . . .DLB-12, 50, 78

Chesney, Sir George Tomkyns
1830-1895 . . . . .DLB-190

Chester, Alfred 1928-1971 . . . . .DLB-130

Chester, George Randolph 1869-1924 . . . .DLB-78

The Chester Plays circa 1505-1532;
revisions until 1575 . . . . .DLB-146

Chesterfield, Philip Dormer Stanhope,
Fourth Earl of 1694-1773 . . . . .DLB-104

Chesterton, G. K. 1874-1936
. . . . .DLB-10, 19, 34, 70, 98, 149, 178

Chettle, Henry
circa 1560-circa 1607 . . . . .DLB-136

Chew, Ada Nield 1870-1945 . . . . .DLB-135

Cheyney, Edward P. 1861-1947 . . . . .DLB-47

Chiara, Piero 1913-1986 . . . . .DLB-177

Chicano History DLB-82

Chicano Language DLB-82

Child, Francis James 1825-1896 . . . . . . .DLB-1, 64

Child, Lydia Maria 1802-1880 . . . . .DLB-1, 74

Child, Philip 1898-1978 . . . . .DLB-68

Childers, Erskine 1870-1922 . . . . .DLB-70

Children's Book Awards and Prizes DLB-61

Children's Illustrators, 1800-1880 . . . . . . .DLB-163

Childress, Alice 1920-1994 . . . . .DLB-7, 38

Childs, George W. 1829-1894 . . . . .DLB-23

Chilton Book Company DLB-46

Chin, Frank 1940- DLB-206

Chinweizu 1943- DLB-157

Chitham, Edward 1932- DLB-155

Chittenden, Hiram Martin 1858-1917 . . . . .DLB-47

Chivers, Thomas Holley 1809-1858 . . . . . . .DLB-3

Cholmondeley, Mary 1859-1925 . . . . DLB-197

Chopin, Kate 1850-1904. . . . . DLB-12, 78

Chopin, Rene 1885-1953 . . . . DLB-92

Choquette, Adrienne 1915-1973 . . . . DLB-68

Choquette, Robert 1905- DLB-68

Chrétien de Troyes
circa 1140-circa 1190 . . . . DLB-208

Christensen, Inger 1935- DLB-214

The Christian Publishing Company. DLB-49

Christie, Agatha 1890-1976. . . . . DLB-13, 77

Christine de Pizan
circa 1365-circa 1431 . . . . DLB-208

Christus und die Samariterin circa 950 . . . . . . DLB-148

Christy, Howard Chandler
1873-1952. . . . . DLB-188

Chulkov, Mikhail Dmitrievich
1743?-1792 . . . . DLB-150

Church, Benjamin 1734-1778 . . . . DLB-31

Church, Francis Pharcellus 1839-1906 . . . . DLB-79

Church, Peggy Pond 1903-1986. . . . . . . DLB-212

Church, Richard 1893-1972 . . . . DLB-191

Church, William Conant 1836-1917 . . . . . DLB-79

Churchill, Caryl 1938- DLB-13

Churchill, Charles 1731-1764 . . . . DLB-109

Churchill, Winston 1871-1947 . . . . DLB-202

Churchill, Sir Winston
1874-1965. . . . . DLB-100; DS-16

Churchyard, Thomas 1520?-1604 . . . . . . DLB-132

Churton, E., and Company DLB-106

Chute, Marchette 1909-1994 . . . . DLB-103

Ciardi, John 1916-1986. . . . . DLB-5; Y-86

Cibber, Colley 1671-1757 . . . . DLB-84

Cicero 106 B.C.-43 B.C. DLB-211

Cima, Annalisa 1941- DLB-128

Čingo, Živko 1935-1987 . . . . DLB-181

Cioran, E. M. 1911-1995 . . . . DLB-220

Čipkus, Alfonsas (see Nyka-Niliūnas, Alfonsas)

Cirese, Eugenio 1884-1955. . . . . DLB-114

Cisneros, Sandra 1954- DLB-122, 152

City Lights Books. DLB-46

Cixous, Hélène 1937- DLB-83

Clampitt, Amy 1920-1994 . . . . DLB-105

Clapper, Raymond 1892-1944 . . . . DLB-29

Clare, John 1793-1864 . . . . DLB-55, 96

Clarendon, Edward Hyde, Earl of
1609-1674. . . . . DLB-101

Clark, Alfred Alexander Gordon (see Hare, Cyril)

Clark, Ann Nolan 1896- DLB-52

Clark, C. E. Frazer Jr. 1925- DLB-187

Clark, C. M., Publishing Company DLB-46

Clark, Catherine Anthony 1892-1977. . . . . DLB-68

Clark, Charles Heber 1841-1915 . . . . DLB-11

Clark, Davis Wasgatt 1812-1871 . . . . DLB-79

Clark, Eleanor 1913- DLB-6

Clark, J. P. 1935- DLB-117

Clark, Lewis Gaylord 1808-1873 . . . DLB-3, 64, 73

Clark, Walter Van Tilburg
1909-1971. . . . . DLB-9, 206

Clark, William (see Lewis, Meriwether)

Clark, William Andrews Jr.
1877-1934 . . . . DLB-187

Clarke, Austin 1896-1974 . . . . DLB-10, 20

Clarke, Austin C. 1934- DLB-53, 125

Clarke, Gillian 1937- DLB-40

Clarke, James Freeman 1810-1888 . . . . . DLB-1, 59

Clarke, Pauline 1921- DLB-161

Clarke, Rebecca Sophia 1833-1906 . . . . . . DLB-42

Clarke, Robert, and Company DLB-49

Clarkson, Thomas 1760-1846. . . . . DLB-158

Claudel, Paul 1868-1955 . . . . DLB-192

Claudius, Matthias 1740-1815 . . . . DLB-97

Clausen, Andy 1943- DLB-16

Clawson, John L. 1865-1933 . . . . DLB-187

Claxton, Remsen and Haffelfinger DLB-49

Clay, Cassius Marcellus 1810-1903 . . . . . DLB-43

Cleary, Beverly 1916- DLB-52

Cleary, Kate McPhelim 1863-1905. . . . . . DLB-221

Cleaver, Vera 1919-   and
Cleaver, Bill 1920-1981 . . . . DLB-52

Cleland, John 1710-1789 . . . . DLB-39

Clemens, Samuel Langhorne (Mark Twain)
1835-1910 . . . DLB-11, 12, 23, 64, 74, 186, 189

Clement, Hal 1922- DLB-8

Clemo, Jack 1916- DLB-27

Clephane, Elizabeth Cecilia
1830-1869 . . . . DLB-199

Cleveland, John 1613-1658. . . . . DLB-126

Cliff, Michelle 1946- DLB-157

Clifford, Lady Anne 1590-1676 . . . . DLB-151

Clifford, James L. 1901-1978 . . . . DLB-103

Clifford, Lucy 1853?-1929 . . . . . DLB-135, 141, 197

Clifton, Lucille 1936- DLB-5, 41

Clines, Francis X. 1938- DLB-185

Clive, Caroline (V) 1801-1873 . . . . DLB-199

Clode, Edward J. [publishing house] DLB-46

Clough, Arthur Hugh 1819-1861 . . . . DLB-32

Cloutier, Cécile 1930- DLB-60

Clutton-Brock, Arthur 1868-1924 . . . . . . DLB-98

Coates, Robert M. 1897-1973 . . . . . DLB-4, 9, 102

Coatsworth, Elizabeth 1893- DLB-22

Cobb, Charles E., Jr. 1943- DLB-41

Cobb, Frank I. 1869-1923 . . . . DLB-25

Cobb, Irvin S. 1876-1944 . . . . DLB-11, 25, 86

Cobbe, Frances Power 1822-1904 . . . . . . DLB-190

Cobbett, William 1763-1835. . . . . .DLB-43, 107

Cobbledick, Gordon 1898-1969 . . . . .DLB-171

Cochran, Thomas C. 1902- DLB-17

Cochrane, Elizabeth 1867-1922 . . . . . DLB-25, 189

Cockerell, Sir Sydney 1867-1962 . . . . . . DLB-201

Cockerill, John A. 1845-1896 . . . . DLB-23

Cocteau, Jean 1889-1963 . . . . DLB-65

Coderre, Emile (see Jean Narrache)

Coffee, Lenore J. 1900?-1984 . . . . DLB-44

Coffin, Robert P. Tristram 1892-1955 . . . . DLB-45

Cogswell, Fred 1917- DLB-60

Cogswell, Mason Fitch 1761-1830 . . . . . . DLB-37

Cohen, Arthur A. 1928-1986 . . . . DLB-28

Cohen, Leonard 1934- DLB-53

Cohen, Matt 1942- DLB-53

Colbeck, Norman 1903-1987 . . . . DLB-201

Colden, Cadwallader 1688-1776. . . . . . DLB-24, 30

Colden, Jane 1724-1766 . . . . DLB-200

Cole, Barry 1936- DLB-14

Cole, George Watson 1850-1939 . . . . DLB-140

Colegate, Isabel 1931- DLB-14

Coleman, Emily Holmes 1899-1974. . . . . . DLB-4

Coleman, Wanda 1946- DLB-130

Coleridge, Hartley 1796-1849. . . . . DLB-96

Coleridge, Mary 1861-1907 . . . . . . DLB-19, 98

Coleridge, Samuel Taylor
1772-1834. . . . . .DLB-93, 107

Coleridge, Sara 1802-1852 . . . . DLB-199

Colet, John 1467-1519 . . . . DLB-132

Colette 1873-1954. . . . . DLB-65

Colette, Sidonie Gabrielle (see Colette)

Colinas, Antonio 1946- DLB-134

Coll, Joseph Clement 1881-1921 . . . . DLB-188

Collier, John 1901-1980 . . . . DLB-77

Collier, John Payne 1789-1883 . . . . DLB-184

Collier, Mary 1690-1762. . . . . DLB-95

Collier, Robert J. 1876-1918 . . . . DLB-91

Collier, P. F. [publishing house] DLB-49

Collin and Small. DLB-49

Collingwood, W. G. 1854-1932 . . . . DLB-149

Collins, An floruit circa 1653 . . . . DLB-131

Collins, Merle 1950- DLB-157

Collins, Mortimer 1827-1876 . . . . DLB-21, 35

Collins, Wilkie 1824-1889 . . . . . . .DLB-18, 70, 159

Collins, William 1721-1759. . . . . DLB-109

Collins, William, Sons and Company . . . DLB-154

Collins, Isaac [publishing house]. DLB-49

Collis, Maurice 1889-1973 . . . . DLB-195

Collyer, Mary 1716?-1763?. DLB-39

Colman, Benjamin 1673-1747. . . . . DLB-24

Colman, George, the Elder 1732-1794 . . . . DLB-89

Colman, George, the Younger
1762-1836. . . . . DLB-89

Colman, S. [publishing house] DLB-49

Colombo, John Robert 1936- DLB-53

Colquhoun, Patrick 1745-1820. . . . . DLB-158

Colter, Cyrus 1910- DLB-33

Colum, Padraic 1881-1972 . . . . DLB-19

Columella fl. first century A.D. DLB-211

Colvin, Sir Sidney 1845-1927 . . . . DLB-149

Colwin, Laurie 1944-1992 . . . . . . .DLB-218; Y-80

Comden, Betty 1919- and Green,
Adolph 1918- DLB-44

Comi, Girolamo 1890-1968............DLB-114

The Comic Tradition Continued
[in the British Novel]...............DLB-15

Commager, Henry Steele 1902-1998......DLB-17

The Commercialization of the Image of
Revolt, by Kenneth Rexroth.........DLB-16

Community and Commentators: Black
Theatre and Its Critics.............DLB-38

Commynes, Philippe de
circa 1447-1511..................DLB-208

Compton-Burnett, Ivy 1884?-1969.......DLB-36

Conan, Laure 1845-1924...............DLB-99

Conde, Carmen 1901-..............DLB-108

Conference on Modern Biography.........Y-85

Congreve, William 1670-1729........DLB-39, 84

Conkey, W. B., Company..............DLB-49

Connell, Evan S., Jr. 1924-........DLB-2; Y-81

Connelly, Marc 1890-1980........DLB-7; Y-80

Connolly, Cyril 1903-1974.............DLB-98

Connolly, James B. 1868-1957..........DLB-78

Connor, Ralph 1860-1937.............DLB-92

Connor, Tony 1930-..............DLB-40

Conquest, Robert 1917-..............DLB-27

Conrad, Joseph 1857-1924....DLB-10, 34, 98, 156

Conrad, John, and Company..........DLB-49

Conroy, Jack 1899-1990..................Y-81

Conroy, Pat 1945-..................DLB-6

The Consolidation of Opinion: Critical
Responses to the Modernists.........DLB-36

Consolo, Vincenzo 1933-...........DLB-196

Constable, Henry 1562-1613...........DLB-136

Constable and Company Limited.......DLB-112

Constable, Archibald, and Company.....DLB-154

Constant, Benjamin 1767-1830.........DLB-119

Constant de Rebecque, Henri-Benjamin de
(see Constant, Benjamin)

Constantine, David 1944-...........DLB-40

Constantin-Weyer, Maurice
1881-1964.......................DLB-92

Contempo Caravan: Kites in a
Windstorm......................Y-85

A Contemporary Flourescence of Chicano
Literature........................Y-84

"Contemporary Verse Story-telling,"
by Jonathan Holden...............DLB-105

The Continental Publishing Company....DLB-49

A Conversation with Chaim Potok.........Y-84

Conversations with Editors...............Y-95

Conversations with Publishers I: An Interview
with Patrick O'Connor..............Y-84

Conversations with Publishers II: An Interview
with Charles Scribner III..............Y-94

Conversations with Publishers III: An Interview
with Donald Lamm.................Y-95

Conversations with Publishers IV: An Interview
with James Laughlin.................Y-96

Conversations with Rare Book Dealers I: An
Interview with Glenn Horowitz........Y-90

Conversations with Rare Book Dealers II: An
Interview with Ralph Sipper..........Y-94

Conversations with Rare Book Dealers
(Publishers) III: An Interview with
Otto Penzler.....................Y-96

The Conversion of an Unpolitical Man,
by W. H. Bruford.................DLB-66

Conway, Moncure Daniel 1832-1907......DLB-1

Cook, Ebenezer circa 1667-circa 1732.....DLB-24

Cook, Edward Tyas 1857-1919.........DLB-149

Cook, Eliza 1818-1889...............DLB-199

Cook, Michael 1933-..............DLB-53

Cook, David C., Publishing Company....DLB-49

Cooke, George Willis 1848-1923........DLB-71

Cooke, Increase, and Company.........DLB-49

Cooke, John Esten 1830-1886...........DLB-3

Cooke, Philip Pendleton 1816-1850....DLB-3, 59

Cooke, Rose Terry 1827-1892........DLB-12, 74

Cook-Lynn, Elizabeth 1930-....DLB-175

Coolbrith, Ina 1841-1928.........DLB-54, 186

Cooley, Peter 1940-..............DLB-105

Coolidge, Clark 1939-..............DLB-193

Coolidge, Susan (see Woolsey, Sarah Chauncy)

Coolidge, George [publishing house]......DLB-49

Cooper, Anna Julia 1858-1964.........DLB-221

Cooper, Giles 1918-1966...............DLB-13

Cooper, J. California 19??-..............DLB-212

Cooper, James Fenimore 1789-1851....DLB-3, 183

Cooper, Kent 1880-1965................DLB-29

Cooper, Susan 1935-..............DLB-161

Cooper, William [publishing house].....DLB-170

Coote, J. [publishing house]...........DLB-154

Coover, Robert 1932-...........DLB-2; Y-81

Copeland and Day...................DLB-49

Ćopić, Branko 1915-1984.............DLB-181

Copland, Robert 1470?-1548...........DLB-136

Coppard, A. E. 1878-1957...........DLB-162

Coppée, François 1842-1908...........DLB-217

Coppel, Alfred 1921-..............Y-83

Coppola, Francis Ford 1939-.........DLB-44

Copway, George (Kah-ge-ga-gah-bowh)
1818-1869.................DLB-175, 183

Corazzini, Sergio 1886-1907..........DLB-114

Corbett, Richard 1582-1635...........DLB-121

Corbière, Tristan 1845-1875..........DLB-217

Corcoran, Barbara 1911-..............DLB-52

Cordelli, Franco 1943-..............DLB-196

Corelli, Marie 1855-1924..........DLB-34, 156

Corle, Edwin 1906-1956...............Y-85

Corman, Cid 1924-..............DLB-5, 193

Cormier, Robert 1925-..............DLB-52

Corn, Alfred 1943-..........DLB-120; Y-80

Cornish, Sam 1935-..............DLB-41

Cornish, William
circa 1465-circa 1524..............DLB-132

Cornwall, Barry (see Procter, Bryan Waller)

Cornwallis, Sir William, the Younger
circa 1579-1614..................DLB-151

Cornwell, David John Moore (see le Carré, John)

Corpi, Lucha 1945-..............DLB-82

Corrington, John William 1932-........DLB-6

Corrothers, James D. 1869-1917.........DLB-50

Corso, Gregory 1930-..............DLB-5, 16

Cortázar, Julio 1914-1984.............DLB-113

Cortez, Carlos 1923-..............DLB-209

Cortez, Jayne 1936-..............DLB-41

Corvinus, Gottlieb Siegmund 1677-1746..DLB-168

Corvo, Baron (see Rolfe, Frederick William)

Cory, Annie Sophie (see Cross, Victoria)

Cory, William Johnson 1823-1892.......DLB-35

Coryate, Thomas 1577?-1617......DLB-151, 172

Ćosić, Dobrica 1921-..............DLB-181

Cosin, John 1595-1672...........DLB-151, 213

Cosmopolitan Book Corporation........DLB-46

Costain, Thomas B. 1885-1965..........DLB-9

Coste, Donat 1912-1957..............DLB-88

Costello, Louisa Stuart 1799-1870......DLB-166

Cota-Cárdenas, Margarita 1941-......DLB-122

Cotten, Bruce 1873-1954.............DLB-187

Cotter, Joseph Seamon, Sr. 1861-1949...DLB-50

Cotter, Joseph Seamon, Jr. 1895-1919....DLB-50

Cottle, Joseph [publishing house].......DLB-154

Cotton, Charles 1630-1687............DLB-131

Cotton, John 1584-1652..............DLB-24

Cotton, Sir Robert Bruce 1571-1631.....DLB-213

Coulter, John 1888-1980.............DLB-68

Cournos, John 1881-1966.............DLB-54

Courteline, Georges 1858-1929........DLB-192

Cousins, Margaret 1905-1996.........DLB-137

Cousins, Norman 1915-1990.........DLB-137

Coventry, Francis 1725-1754..........DLB-39

Coverdale, Miles 1487 or 1488-1569.....DLB-167

Coverly, N. [publishing house].........DLB-49

Covici-Friede.....................DLB-46

Coward, Noel 1899-1973..............DLB-10

Coward, McCann and Geoghegan.......DLB-46

Cowles, Gardner 1861-1946...........DLB-29

Cowles, Gardner ("Mike"), Jr.
1903-1985................DLB-127, 137

Cowley, Abraham 1618-1667......DLB-131, 151

Cowley, Hannah 1743-1809...........DLB-89

Cowley, Malcolm
1898-1989..........DLB-4, 48; Y-81, Y-89

Cowper, William 1731-1800.......DLB-104, 109

Cox, A. B. (see Berkeley, Anthony)

Cox, James McMahon 1903-1974.......DLB-127

Cox, James Middleton 1870-1957.......DLB-127

Cox, Palmer 1840-1924...............DLB-42

Coxe, Louis 1918-1993................DLB-5

Coxe, Tench 1755-1824...............DLB-37

Cozzens, Frederick S. 1818-1869........DLB-202

Cozzens, James Gould
1903-1978 . . . . DLB-9; Y-84; DS-2

Cozzens's *Michael Scarlett* Y-97

Crabbe, George 1754-1832 . . . . DLB-93

Crackanthorpe, Hubert 1870-1896 . . . . . . DLB-135

Craddock, Charles Egbert (see Murfree, Mary N.)

Cradock, Thomas 1718-1770 . . . . DLB-31

Craig, Daniel H. 1811-1895 . . . . DLB-43

Craik, Dinah Maria 1826-1887 . . . . . . DLB-35, 136

Cramer, Richard Ben 1950- DLB-185

Cranch, Christopher Pearse 1813-1892 . DLB-1, 42

Crane, Hart 1899-1932 . . . . DLB-4, 48

Crane, R. S. 1886-1967 . . . . DLB-63

Crane, Stephen 1871-1900 . . . . DLB-12, 54, 78

Crane, Walter 1845-1915 . . . . DLB-163

Cranmer, Thomas 1489-1556 . . . . . DLB-132, 213

Crapsey, Adelaide 1878-1914 . . . . DLB-54

Crashaw, Richard 1612 or 1613-1649 . . . DLB-126

Craven, Avery 1885-1980 . . . . DLB-17

Crawford, Charles 1752-circa 1815 . . . . . . DLB-31

Crawford, F. Marion 1854-1909 . . . . DLB-71

Crawford, Isabel Valancy 1850-1887 . . . . . DLB-92

Crawley, Alan 1887-1975 . . . . DLB-68

Crayon, Geoffrey (see Irving, Washington)

Creamer, Robert W. 1922- DLB-171

Creasey, John 1908-1973 . . . . DLB-77

Creative Age Press DLB-46

Creech, William [publishing house] DLB-154

Creede, Thomas [publishing house] DLB-170

Creel, George 1876-1953 . . . . DLB-25

Creeley, Robert 1926- . . . DLB-5, 16, 169; DS-17

Creelman, James 1859-1915 . . . . DLB-23

Cregan, David 1931- DLB-13

Creighton, Donald Grant 1902-1979 . . . . . DLB-88

Cremazie, Octave 1827-1879 . . . . DLB-99

Crémer, Victoriano 1909?- DLB-108

Crescas, Hasdai circa 1340-1412? DLB-115

Crespo, Angel 1926- DLB-134

Cresset Press DLB-112

Cresswell, Helen 1934- DLB-161

Crèvecoeur, Michel Guillaume Jean de
1735-1813 . . . . DLB-37

Crewe, Candida 1964- DLB-207

Crews, Harry 1935- DLB-6, 143, 185

Crichton, Michael 1942- Y-81

A Crisis of Culture: The Changing Role
of Religion in the New Republic
. . . . DLB-37

Crispin, Edmund 1921-1978 . . . . DLB-87

Cristofer, Michael 1946- DLB-7

"The Critic as Artist" (1891), by
Oscar Wilde DLB-57

"Criticism In Relation To Novels" (1863),
by G. H. Lewes DLB-21

Crnjanski, Miloš 1893-1977 . . . . DLB-147

Crocker, Hannah Mather 1752-1829 . . . . DLB-200

Crockett, David (Davy)
1786-1836 . . . . DLB-3, 11, 183

Croft-Cooke, Rupert (see Bruce, Leo)

Crofts, Freeman Wills 1879-1957 . . . . DLB-77

Croker, John Wilson 1780-1857 . . . . DLB-110

Croly, George 1780-1860 . . . . DLB-159

Croly, Herbert 1869-1930 . . . . DLB-91

Croly, Jane Cunningham 1829-1901 . . . . . DLB-23

Crompton, Richmal 1890-1969 . . . . DLB-160

Cronin, A. J. 1896-1981 . . . . DLB-191

Cros, Charles 1842-1888 . . . . DLB-217

Crosby, Caresse 1892-1970 . . . . DLB-48

Crosby, Caresse 1892-1970 and Crosby,
Harry 1898-1929 . . . . DLB-4; DS-15

Crosby, Harry 1898-1929 . . . . DLB-48

Cross, Gillian 1945- DLB-161

Cross, Victoria 1868-1952 . . . . DLB-135, 197

Crossley-Holland, Kevin 1941- DLB-40, 161

Crothers, Rachel 1878-1958 . . . . DLB-7

Crowell, Thomas Y., Company DLB-49

Crowley, John 1942- Y-82

Crowley, Mart 1935- DLB-7

Crown Publishers DLB-46

Crowne, John 1641-1712 . . . . DLB-80

Crowninshield, Edward Augustus
1817-1859 . . . . DLB-140

Crowninshield, Frank 1872-1947 . . . . DLB-91

Croy, Homer 1883-1965 . . . . DLB-4

Crumley, James 1939- Y-84

Cruz, Victor Hernández 1949- DLB-41

Csokor, Franz Theodor 1885-1969 . . . . . DLB-81

Cuala Press DLB-112

Cullen, Countee 1903-1946 . . . . DLB-4, 48, 51

Culler, Jonathan D. 1944- DLB-67

The Cult of Biography
Excerpts from the Second Folio Debate:
"Biographies are generally a disease of
English Literature" – Germaine Greer,
Victoria Glendinning, Auberon Waugh,
and Richard Holmes Y-86

Cumberland, Richard 1732-1811 . . . . DLB-89

Cummings, Constance Gordon
1837-1924 . . . . DLB-174

Cummings, E. E. 1894-1962 . . . . DLB-4, 48

Cummings, Ray 1887-1957 . . . . DLB-8

Cummings and Hilliard DLB-49

Cummins, Maria Susanna 1827-1866 . . . . . DLB-42

Cumpián, Carlos 1953- DLB-209

Cundall, Joseph [publishing house] DLB-106

Cuney, Waring 1906-1976 . . . . DLB-51

Cuney-Hare, Maude 1874-1936 . . . . DLB-52

Cunningham, Allan 1784-1842 . . . . . DLB-116, 144

Cunningham, J. V. 1911- DLB-5

Cunningham, Peter F. [publishing house] . . DLB-49

Cunquiero, Alvaro 1911-1981 . . . . DLB-134

Cuomo, George 1929- Y-80

Cupples and Leon DLB-46

Cupples, Upham and Company DLB-49

Cuppy, Will 1884-1949 . . . . DLB-11

Curiel, Barbara Brinson 1956- DLB-209

Curll, Edmund [publishing house] DLB-154

Currie, James 1756-1805 . . . . DLB-142

Currie, Mary Montgomerie Lamb Singleton,
Lady Currie (see Fane, Violet)

Cursor Mundi circa 1300 . . . . DLB-146

Curti, Merle E. 1897- DLB-17

Curtis, Anthony 1926- DLB-155

Curtis, Cyrus H. K. 1850-1933 . . . . DLB-91

Curtis, George William 1824-1892 . . . . DLB-1, 43

Quintus Curtius Rufus fl. A.D. 35 . . . . . . DLB-211

Curzon, Robert 1810-1873 . . . . DLB-166

Curzon, Sarah Anne 1833-1898 . . . . DLB-99

Cushing, Harvey 1869-1939 . . . . DLB-187

Cynewulf circa 770-840 . . . . DLB-146

Czepko, Daniel 1605-1660 . . . . DLB-164

D

D. M. Thomas: The Plagiarism
Controversy Y-82

Dabit, Eugène 1898-1936 . . . . DLB-65

Daborne, Robert circa 1580-1628 . . . . DLB-58

Dacey, Philip 1939- DLB-105

Dach, Simon 1605-1659 . . . . DLB-164

Daggett, Rollin M. 1831-1901 . . . . DLB-79

D'Aguiar, Fred 1960- DLB-157

Dahl, Roald 1916-1990 . . . . DLB-139

Dahlberg, Edward 1900-1977 . . . . DLB-48

Dahn, Felix 1834-1912 . . . . DLB-129

Dal', Vladimir Ivanovich (Kazak Vladimir
Lugansky) 1801-1872 . . . . DLB-198

Dale, Peter 1938- DLB-40

Daley, Arthur 1904-1974 . . . . DLB-171

Dall, Caroline Wells (Healey)
1822-1912 . . . . DLB-1

Dallas, E. S. 1828-1879 . . . . DLB-55

The Dallas Theater Center DLB-7

D'Alton, Louis 1900-1951 . . . . DLB-10

Daly, T. A. 1871-1948 . . . . DLB-11

Damon, S. Foster 1893-1971 . . . . DLB-45

Damrell, William S. [publishing house] . . . DLB-49

Dana, Charles A. 1819-1897 . . . . DLB-3, 23

Dana, Richard Henry, Jr.
1815-1882 . . . . DLB-1, 183

Dandridge, Ray Garfield DLB-51

Dane, Clemence 1887-1965 . . . . DLB-10, 197

Danforth, John 1660-1730 . . . . DLB-24

Danforth, Samuel, I 1626-1674 . . . . DLB-24

Danforth, Samuel, II 1666-1727 . . . . DLB-24

Dangerous Years: London Theater,
1939-1945 . . . . DLB-10

Daniel, John M. 1825-1865 . . . . DLB-43

Daniel, Samuel 1562 or 1563-1619 . . . . . . DLB-62

Daniel Press DLB-106

Daniells, Roy 1902-1979 . . . . DLB-68

Daniels, Jim 1956- DLB-120

Daniels, Jonathan 1902-1981 . . . . DLB-127

Daniels, Josephus 1862-1948 . . . . DLB-29

Danis Rose and the Rendering of *Ulysses* Y-97

Dannay, Frederic 1905-1982 and
　　Manfred B. Lee 1905-1971 . . . . DLB-137

Danner, Margaret Esse 1915- DLB-41

Danter, John [publishing house] DLB-170

Dantin, Louis 1865-1945 . . . . DLB-92

Danzig, Allison 1898-1987 . . . . DLB-171

D'Arcy, Ella circa 1857-1937 . . . . DLB-135

Darley, Felix Octavious Carr
　　1822-1888 . . . . DLB-188

Darley, George 1795-1846 . . . . DLB-96

Darwin, Charles 1809-1882 . . . . DLB-57, 166

Darwin, Erasmus 1731-1802 . . . . DLB-93

Daryush, Elizabeth 1887-1977 . . . . DLB-20

Dashkova, Ekaterina Romanovna
　　(née Vorontsova) 1743-1810 . . . . DLB-150

Dashwood, Edmée Elizabeth Monica
　　de la Pasture (see Delafield, E. M.)

Daudet, Alphonse 1840-1897 . . . . DLB-123

d'Aulaire, Edgar Parin 1898- and
　　d'Aulaire, Ingri 1904- DLB-22

Davenant, Sir William 1606-1668 . . . . DLB-58, 126

Davenport, Guy 1927- DLB-130

Davenport, Marcia 1903-1996 . . . . DS-17

Davenport, Robert ?-? DLB-58

Daves, Delmer 1904-1977 . . . . DLB-26

Davey, Frank 1940- DLB-53

Davidson, Avram 1923-1993 . . . . DLB-8

Davidson, Donald 1893-1968 . . . . DLB-45

Davidson, John 1857-1909 . . . . DLB-19

Davidson, Lionel 1922- DLB-14

Davidson, Robyn 1950- DLB-204

Davidson, Sara 1943- DLB-185

Davie, Donald 1922- DLB-27

Davie, Elspeth 1919- DLB-139

Davies, Sir John 1569-1626 . . . . DLB-172

Davies, John, of Hereford
　　1565?-1618 . . . . DLB-121

Davies, Rhys 1901-1978 . . . . DLB-139, 191

Davies, Robertson 1913- DLB-68

Davies, Samuel 1723-1761 . . . . DLB-31

Davies, Thomas 1712?-1785 . . . . DLB-142, 154

Davies, W. H. 1871-1940 . . . . DLB-19, 174

Davies, Peter, Limited DLB-112

Daviot, Gordon 1896?-1952 . . . . DLB-10
　　(see also Tey, Josephine)

Davis, Charles A. 1795-1867 . . . . DLB-11

Davis, Clyde Brion 1894-1962 . . . . DLB-9

Davis, Dick 1945- DLB-40

Davis, Frank Marshall 1905-? DLB-51

Davis, H. L. 1894-1960 . . . . DLB-9, 206

Davis, John 1774-1854 . . . . DLB-37

Davis, Lydia 1947- DLB-130

Davis, Margaret Thomson 1926- DLB-14

Davis, Ossie 1917- DLB-7, 38

Davis, Paxton 1925-1994 . . . . Y-94

Davis, Rebecca Harding 1831-1910 . . . . . . DLB-74

Davis, Richard Harding 1864-1916
　　. . . . . DLB-12, 23, 78, 79, 189; DS-13

Davis, Samuel Cole 1764-1809 . . . . DLB-37

Davis, Samuel Post 1850-1918 . . . . DLB-202

Davison, Peter 1928- DLB-5

Davydov, Denis Vasil'evich
　　1784-1839 . . . . DLB-205

Davys, Mary 1674-1732 . . . . DLB-39

DAW Books DLB-46

Dawn Powell, Where Have You Been All
　　Our lives? Y-97

Dawson, Ernest 1882-1947 . . . . DLB-140

Dawson, Fielding 1930- DLB-130

Dawson, William 1704-1752 . . . . DLB-31

Day, Angel flourished 1586 . . . . DLB-167

Day, Benjamin Henry 1810-1889 . . . . DLB-43

Day, Clarence 1874-1935 . . . . DLB-11

Day, Dorothy 1897-1980 . . . . DLB-29

Day, Frank Parker 1881-1950 . . . . DLB-92

Day, John circa 1574-circa 1640 . . . . DLB-62

Day, John [publishing house] DLB-170

Day Lewis, C. 1904-1972 . . . . DLB-15, 20
　　(see also Blake, Nicholas)

Day, Thomas 1748-1789 . . . . DLB-39

Day, The John, Company DLB-46

Day, Mahlon [publishing house] DLB-49

Dazai Osamu 1909-1948 . . . . DLB-182

Dąbrowska, Maria 1889-1965 . . . . DLB-215

Deacon, William Arthur 1890-1977 . . . . DLB-68

Deal, Borden 1922-1985 . . . . DLB-6

de Angeli, Marguerite 1889-1987 . . . . DLB-22

De Angelis, Milo 1951- DLB-128

De Bow, James Dunwoody Brownson
　　1820-1867 . . . . DLB-3, 79

de Bruyn, Günter 1926- DLB-75

de Camp, L. Sprague 1907- DLB-8

De Carlo, Andrea 1952- DLB-196

De Casas, Celso A. 1944- DLB-209

The Decay of Lying (1889),
　　by Oscar Wilde [excerpt] DLB-18

Dechert, Robert 1895-1975 . . . . DLB-187

Dedication, *Ferdinand Count Fathom* (1753),
　　by Tobias Smollett DLB-39

Dedication, *The History of Pompey the Little*
　　(1751), by Francis Coventry DLB-39

Dedication, *Lasselia* (1723), by Eliza
　　Haywood [excerpt] DLB-39

Dedication, *The Wanderer* (1814),
　　by Fanny Burney DLB-39

Dee, John 1527-1608 or 1609 . . . . . . DLB-136, 213

Deeping, George Warwick 1877-1950 . . . . DLB 153

Defense of *Amelia* (1752), by
　　Henry Fielding DLB-39

Defoe, Daniel 1660-1731 . . . . DLB-39, 95, 101

de Fontaine, Felix Gregory 1834-1896 . . . . . DLB-43

De Forest, John William
　　1826-1906 . . . . DLB-12, 189

DeFrees, Madeline 1919- DLB-105

DeGolyer, Everette Lee 1886-1956 . . . . . . DLB-187

de Graff, Robert 1895-1981 . . . . Y-81

de Graft, Joe 1924-1978 . . . . DLB-117

De Heinrico circa 980? DLB-148

Deighton, Len 1929- DLB-87

DeJong, Meindert 1906-1991 . . . . DLB-52

Dekker, Thomas circa 1572-1632 . . . . DLB-62, 172

Delacorte, Jr., George T. 1894-1991 . . . . . . DLB-91

Delafield, E. M. 1890-1943 . . . . DLB-34

Delahaye, Guy 1888-1969 . . . . DLB-92

de la Mare, Walter
　　1873-1956 . . . . DLB-19, 153, 162

Deland, Margaret 1857-1945 . . . . DLB-78

Delaney, Shelagh 1939- DLB-13

Delano, Amasa 1763-1823 . . . . DLB-183

Delany, Martin Robinson 1812-1885 . . . . . DLB-50

Delany, Samuel R. 1942- DLB-8, 33

de la Roche, Mazo 1879-1961 . . . . DLB-68

Delavigne, Jean François Casimir
　　1793-1843 . . . . DLB-192

Delbanco, Nicholas 1942- DLB-6

Del Castillo, Ramón 1949- DLB-209

De León, Nephtal 1945- DLB-82

Delgado, Abelardo Barrientos 1931- DLB-82

Del Giudice, Daniele 1949- DLB-196

De Libero, Libero 1906-1981 . . . . DLB-114

DeLillo, Don 1936- DLB-6, 173

de Lisser H. G. 1878-1944 . . . . DLB-117

Dell, Floyd 1887-1969 . . . . DLB-9

Dell Publishing Company DLB-46

delle Grazie, Marie Eugene 1864-1931 . . . . DLB-81

Deloney, Thomas died 1600 . . . . DLB-167

Deloria, Ella C. 1889-1971 . . . . DLB-175

Deloria, Vine, Jr. 1933- DLB-175

del Rey, Lester 1915-1993 . . . . DLB-8

Del Vecchio, John M. 1947- DS-9

Del'vig, Anton Antonovich
　　1798-1831 . . . . DLB-205

de Man, Paul 1919-1983 . . . . DLB-67

Demby, William 1922- DLB-33

DeMarinis, Rick 1934- DLB-218

Deming, Philander 1829-1915 . . . . DLB-74

Deml, Jakub 1878-1961 . . . . DLB-215

Demorest, William Jennings
　　1822-1895 . . . . DLB-79

De Morgan, William 1839-1917 . . . . DLB-153

Demosthenes 384 B.C.-322 B.C. DLB-176

Denham, Henry [publishing house] DLB-170

Denham, Sir John 1615-1669 . . . . DLB-58, 126

Denison, Merrill 1893-1975 . . . . DLB-92

Denison, T. S., and Company DLB-49

Dennery, Adolphe Philippe
1811-1899. DLB-192

Dennie, Joseph 1768-1812. . . . . DLB-37, 43, 59, 73

Dennis, John 1658-1734 . . . . DLB-101

Dennis, Nigel 1912-1989 . . . . DLB-13, 15

Denslow, W. W. 1856-1915. . . . . DLB-188

Dent, Tom 1932-1998 . . . . DLB-38

Dent, J. M., and Sons DLB-112

Denton, Daniel circa 1626-1703 . . . . DLB-24

DePaola, Tomie 1934- DLB-61

Department of Library, Archives, and Institutional
Research, American Bible Society Y-97

De Quille, Dan 1829-1898 . . . . DLB-186

De Quincey, Thomas 1785-1859 . . . DLB-110, 144

Derby, George Horatio 1823-1861. . . . . . . DLB-11

Derby, J. C., and Company DLB-49

Derby and Miller DLB-49

De Ricci, Seymour 1881-1942 . . . . DLB-201

Derleth, August 1909-1971 . . . . DLB-9; DS-17

The Derrydale Press. DLB-46

Derzhavin, Gavriil Romanovich
1743-1816. DLB-150

Desaulniers, Gonsalve 1863-1934. . . . . . . DLB-92

Desbordes-Valmore, Marceline
1786-1859. DLB-217

Deschamps, Emile 1791-1871 . . . . DLB-217

Deschamps, Eustache 1340?-1404 . . . . . DLB-208

Desbiens, Jean-Paul 1927- DLB-53

des Forêts, Louis-Rene 1918- DLB-83

Desiato, Luca 1941- DLB-196

Desnica, Vladan 1905-1967 . . . . DLB-181

DesRochers, Alfred 1901-1978 . . . . DLB-68

Desrosiers, Léo-Paul 1896-1967 . . . . DLB-68

Dessì, Giuseppe 1909-1977 . . . . .DLB-177

Destouches, Louis-Ferdinand
(see Céline, Louis-Ferdinand)

De Tabley, Lord 1835-1895 . . . . DLB-35

"A Detail in a Poem," by
Fred Chappell. DLB-105

Deutsch, Babette 1895-1982 . . . . DLB-45

Deutsch, Niklaus Manuel (see Manuel, Niklaus)

Deutsch, André, Limited DLB-112

Deveaux, Alexis 1948- DLB-38

The Development of the Author's Copyright
in Britain DLB-154

The Development of Lighting in the Staging
of Drama, 1900-1945 . . . . DLB-10

The Development of Meiji Japan DLB-180

De Vere, Aubrey 1814-1902. . . . . DLB-35

Devereux, second Earl of Essex, Robert
1565-1601 . . . . DLB-136

The Devin-Adair Company DLB-46

De Vinne, Theodore Low 1828-1914. . . . DLB-187

De Voto, Bernard 1897-1955 . . . . DLB-9

De Vries, Peter 1910-1993 . . . . DLB-6; Y-82

Dewdney, Christopher 1951- DLB-60

Dewdney, Selwyn 1909-1979 . . . . DLB-68

DeWitt, Robert M., Publisher DLB-49

DeWolfe, Fiske and Company DLB-49

Dexter, Colin 1930- DLB-87

de Young, M. H. 1849-1925. . . . . DLB-25

Dhlomo, H. I. E. 1903-1956. . . . . DLB-157

Dhuoda circa 803-after 843 . . . . DLB-148

The Dial Press DLB-46

Diamond, I. A. L. 1920-1988 . . . . DLB-26

Dibble, L. Grace 1902-1998 . . . . DLB-204

Dibdin, Thomas Frognall
1776-1847. DLB-184

Di Cicco, Pier Giorgio 1949- DLB-60

Dick, Philip K. 1928-1982 . . . . DLB-8

Dick and Fitzgerald. DLB-49

Dickens, Charles
1812-1870. . . . . DLB-21, 55, 70, 159, 166

Dickinson, Peter 1927- DLB-161

Dickey, James 1923-1997
. . . .DLB-5, 193; Y-82, Y-93, Y-96; DS-7, DS-19

Dickey, William 1928-1994 . . . . DLB-5

Dickinson, Emily 1830-1886 . . . . DLB-1

Dickinson, John 1732-1808. . . . . DLB-31

Dickinson, Jonathan 1688-1747 . . . . DLB-24

Dickinson, Patric 1914- DLB-27

Dickinson, Peter 1927- DLB-87

Dicks, John [publishing house] DLB-106

Dickson, Gordon R. 1923- DLB-8

Dictionary of Literary Biography
Yearbook Awards Y-92, Y-93, Y-97, Y-98

The Dictionary of National Biography
. . . . DLB-144

Didion, Joan 1934-
. . . . DLB-2, 173, 185; Y-81, Y-86

Di Donato, Pietro 1911- DLB-9

Die Fürstliche Bibliothek Corvey Y-96

Diego, Gerardo 1896-1987 . . . . DLB-134

Digges, Thomas circa 1546-1595 . . . . . . DLB-136

The Digital Millennium Copyright Act:
Expanding Copyright Protection in
Cyberspace and Beyond Y-98

Dillard, Annie 1945- Y-80

Dillard, R. H. W. 1937- DLB-5

Dillingham, Charles T., Company DLB-49

The Dillingham, G. W., Company DLB-49

Dilly, Edward and Charles
[publishing house] DLB-154

Dilthey, Wilhelm 1833-1911 . . . . DLB-129

Dimitrova, Blaga 1922- DLB-181

Dimov, Dimitr 1909-1966 . . . . DLB-181

Dimsdale, Thomas J. 1831?-1866. . . . . . . DLB-186

Dinesen, Isak (see Blixen, Karen)

Dingelstedt, Franz von 1814-1881 . . . . . . DLB-133

Dintenfass, Mark 1941- Y-84

Diogenes, Jr. (see Brougham, John)

Diogenes Laertius circa 200 . . . . .DLB-176

DiPrima, Diane 1934- DLB-5, 16

Disch, Thomas M. 1940- DLB-8

Disney, Walt 1901-1966. . . . . DLB-22

Disraeli, Benjamin 1804-1881. . . . . . . DLB-21, 55

D'Israeli, Isaac 1766-1848. . . . . .DLB-107

Ditlevsen, Tove 1917-1976 . . . . DLB-214

Ditzen, Rudolf (see Fallada, Hans)

Dix, Dorothea Lynde 1802-1887 . . . . DLB-1

Dix, Dorothy (see Gilmer, Elizabeth Meriwether)

Dix, Edwards and Company DLB-49

Dix, Gertrude circa 1874-? DLB-197

Dixie, Florence Douglas 1857-1905 . . . . . .DLB-174

Dixon, Ella Hepworth 1855 or
1857-1932. .DLB-197

Dixon, Paige (see Corcoran, Barbara)

Dixon, Richard Watson 1833-1900 . . . . . DLB-19

Dixon, Stephen 1936- DLB-130

Dmitriev, Ivan Ivanovich 1760-1837. . . . . DLB-150

Dobell, Bertram 1842-1914 . . . . DLB-184

Dobell, Sydney 1824-1874 . . . . DLB-32

Dobie, J. Frank 1888-1964 . . . . DLB-212

Döblin, Alfred 1878-1957 . . . . DLB-66

Dobson, Austin 1840-1921. . . . . DLB-35, 144

Doctorow, E. L. 1931- DLB-2, 28, 173; Y-80

Documents on Sixteenth-Century
Literature DLB-167, 172

Dodd, William E. 1869-1940 . . . . .DLB-17

Dodd, Anne [publishing house] DLB-154

Dodd, Mead and Company DLB-49

Doderer, Heimito von 1896-1968 . . . . DLB-85

Dodge, Mary Abigail 1833-1896 . . . . DLB-221

Dodge, Mary Mapes
1831?-1905. . . . . .DLB-42, 79; DS-13

Dodge, B. W., and Company. DLB-46

Dodge Publishing Company DLB-49

Dodgson, Charles Lutwidge (see Carroll, Lewis)

Dodsley, Robert 1703-1764. . . . . DLB-95

Dodsley, R. [publishing house]. DLB-154

Dodson, Owen 1914-1983 . . . . DLB-76

Dodwell, Christina 1951- DLB-204

Doesticks, Q. K. Philander, P. B. (see Thomson,
Mortimer)

Doheny, Carrie Estelle 1875-1958 . . . . . . DLB-140

Doherty, John 1798?-1854 . . . . DLB-190

Doig, Ivan 1939- DLB-206

Domínguez, Sylvia Maida 1935- DLB-122

Donahoe, Patrick [publishing house] DLB-49

Donald, David H. 1920- DLB-17

Donaldson, Scott 1928- DLB-111

Doni, Rodolfo 1919- DLB-177

Donleavy, J. P. 1926- DLB-6, 173

Donnadieu, Marguerite (see Duras, Marguerite)

Donne, John 1572-1631 . . . . DLB-121, 151

Donnelley, R. R., and Sons Company DLB-49

Donnelly, Ignatius 1831-1901. . . . . DLB-12

Donohue and Henneberry DLB-49

Donoso, José 1924-1996. . . . . DLB-113

Doolady, M. [publishing house]. DLB-49

Dooley, Ebon (see Ebon)

Doolittle, Hilda 1886-1961. . . . . .DLB-4, 45

Doplicher, Fabio 1938- DLB-128

Dor, Milo 1923- DLB-85

Doran, George H., Company DLB-46

Dorgelès, Roland 1886-1973 . . . . .DLB-65

Dorn, Edward 1929- DLB-5

Dorr, Rheta Childe 1866-1948 . . . . .DLB-25

Dorris, Michael 1945-1997. . . . . .DLB-175

Dorset and Middlesex, Charles Sackville,
    Lord Buckhurst, Earl of 1643-1706. . . .DLB-131

Dorst, Tankred 1925- DLB-75, 124

Dos Passos, John
    1896-1970 . . . . .DLB-4, 9; DS-1, DS-15

John Dos Passos: A Centennial
    Commemoration. Y-96

Doubleday and Company DLB-49

Dougall, Lily 1858-1923 . . . . .DLB-92

Doughty, Charles M.
    1843-1926. . . . . DLB-19, 57, 174

Douglas, Gavin 1476-1522. . . . . .DLB-132

Douglas, Keith 1920-1944 . . . . .DLB-27

Douglas, Norman 1868-1952. . . . . . . .DLB-34, 195

Douglass, Frederick 1817?-1895 . DLB-1, 43, 50, 79

Douglass, William circa 1691-1752 . . . . . .DLB-24

Dourado, Autran 1926- DLB-145

Dove, Arthur G. 1880-1946. . . . . .DLB-188

Dove, Rita 1952- DLB-120

Dover Publications. DLB-46

Doves Press DLB-112

Dowden, Edward 1843-1913 . . . . . . .DLB-35, 149

Dowell, Coleman 1925-1985 . . . . .DLB-130

Dowland, John 1563-1626 . . . . .DLB-172

Downes, Gwladys 1915- DLB-88

Downing, J., Major (see Davis, Charles A.)

Downing, Major Jack (see Smith, Seba)

Dowriche, Anne
    before 1560-after 1613. . . . . .DLB-172

Dowson, Ernest 1867-1900 . . . . .DLB-19, 135

Doxey, William [publishing house] DLB-49

Doyle, Sir Arthur Conan
    1859-1930 . . . . DLB-18, 70, 156, 178

Doyle, Kirby 1932- DLB-16

Doyle, Roddy 1958- DLB-194

Drabble, Margaret 1939- DLB-14, 155

Drach, Albert 1902- DLB-85

Dragojević, Danijel 1934- DLB-181

Drake, Samuel Gardner 1798-1875 . . . . . .DLB-187

The Dramatic Publishing Company DLB-49

Dramatists Play Service DLB-46

Drant, Thomas early 1540s?-1578. . . . . . .DLB-167

Draper, John W. 1811-1882. . . . . .DLB-30

Draper, Lyman C. 1815-1891 . . . . .DLB-30

Drayton, Michael 1563-1631 . . . . .DLB-121

Dreiser, Theodore
    1871-1945 . . . . DLB-9, 12, 102, 137; DS-1

Drewitz, Ingeborg 1923-1986 . . . . .DLB-75

Drieu La Rochelle, Pierre 1893-1945. . . . . .DLB-72

Drinker, Elizabeth 1735-1807. . . . . .DLB-200

Drinkwater, John 1882-1937
    . . . . .DLB-10, 19, 149

Droste-Hülshoff, Annette von
    1797-1848. .DLB-133

The Drue Heinz Literature Prize
    Excerpt from "Excerpts from a Report
    of the Commission," in David
    Bosworth's *The Death of Descartes*
    An Interview with David Bosworth . Y-82

Drummond, William Henry
    1854-1907 . . . . .DLB-92

Drummond, William, of Hawthornden
    1585-1649 . . . . .DLB-121, 213

Dryden, Charles 1860?-1931. . . . . .DLB-171

Dryden, John 1631-1700 . . . . . . DLB-80, 101, 131

Držić, Marin circa 1508-1567. . . . . .DLB-147

Duane, William 1760-1835 . . . . .DLB-43

Dubé, Marcel 1930- DLB-53

Dubé, Rodolphe (see Hertel, François)

Dubie, Norman 1945- DLB-120

Du Bois, W. E. B. 1868-1963 . . . . . DLB-47, 50, 91

Du Bois, William Pène 1916-1993. . . . . . .DLB-61

Dubus, Andre 1936- DLB-130

Ducange, Victor 1783-1833 . . . . .DLB-192

Du Chaillu, Paul Belloni 1831?-1903. . . . .DLB-189

Ducharme, Réjean 1941- DLB-60

Dučić, Jovan 1871-1943 . . . . .DLB-147

Duck, Stephen 1705?-1756 . . . . .DLB-95

Duckworth, Gerald, and Company
    Limited DLB-112

Dudek, Louis 1918- DLB-88

Duell, Sloan and Pearce. DLB-46

Duerer, Albrecht 1471-1528. . . . . .DLB-179

Dufief, Nicholas Gouin 1776-1834. . . . . . .DLB-187

Duff Gordon, Lucie 1821-1869 . . . . .DLB-166

Dufferin, Helen Lady, Countess of Gifford
    1807-1867 .DLB-199

Duffield and Green DLB-46

Duffy, Maureen 1933- DLB-14

Dugan, Alan 1923- DLB-5

Dugard, William [publishing house] DLB-170

Dugas, Marcel 1883-1947 . . . . .DLB-92

Dugdale, William [publishing house]. DLB-106

Duhamel, Georges 1884-1966 . . . . .DLB-65

Dujardin, Edouard 1861-1949. . . . . .DLB-123

Dukes, Ashley 1885-1959 . . . . .DLB-10

du Maurier, Daphne 1907-1989. . . . . . . .DLB-191

Du Maurier, George 1834-1896 . . . . DLB-153, 178

Dumas, Alexandre *fils* 1824-1895. . . . . . .DLB-192

Dumas, Alexandre *père* 1802-1870 . . . . .DLB-119, 192

Dumas, Henry 1934-1968 . . . . .DLB-41

Dunbar, Paul Laurence
    1872-1906 . . . . DLB-50, 54, 78

Dunbar, William circa 1460-circa 1522DLB-132, 146

Duncan, Norman 1871-1916 . . . . .DLB-92

Duncan, Quince 1940- DLB-145

Duncan, Robert 1919-1988 . . . . . . DLB-5, 16, 193

Duncan, Ronald 1914-1982. . . . . .DLB-13

Duncan, Sara Jeannette 1861-1922 . . . . . . .DLB-92

Dunigan, Edward, and Brother DLB-49

Dunlap, John 1747-1812. . . . . .DLB-43

Dunlap, William 1766-1839. . . . . . DLB-30, 37, 59

Dunn, Douglas 1942- DLB-40

Dunn, Harvey Thomas 1884-1952 . . . . . .DLB-188

Dunn, Stephen 1939- DLB-105

Dunne, Finley Peter 1867-1936 . . . . . . .DLB-11, 23

Dunne, John Gregory 1932- Y-80

Dunne, Philip 1908-1992. . . . . .DLB-26

Dunning, Ralph Cheever 1878-1930 . . . . . .DLB-4

Dunning, William A. 1857-1922 . . . . .DLB-17

Duns Scotus, John circa 1266-1308 . . . . . .DLB-115

Dunsany, Lord (Edward John Moreton
    Drax Plunkett, Baron Dunsany)
    1878-1957 . . . . DLB-10, 77, 153, 156

Dunton, John [publishing house] DLB-170

Dunton, W. Herbert 1878-1936. . . . . . . .DLB-188

Dupin, Amantine-Aurore-Lucile (see Sand, George)

Durand, Lucile (see Bersianik, Louky)

Duranti, Francesca 1935- DLB-196

Duranty, Walter 1884-1957. . . . . .DLB-29

Duras, Marguerite 1914-1996 . . . . .DLB-83

Durfey, Thomas 1653-1723 . . . . .DLB-80

Durova, Nadezhda Andreevna (Aleksandr
    Andreevich Aleksandrov) 1783-1866 .DLB-198

Durrell, Lawrence 1912-1990 DLB-15, 27, 204; Y-90

Durrell, William [publishing house]. DLB-49

Dürrenmatt, Friedrich 1921-1990 . . . .DLB-69, 124

Duston, Hannah 1657-1737 . . . . .DLB-200

Dutton, E. P., and Company. DLB-49

Duvoisin, Roger 1904-1980. . . . . .DLB-61

Duyckinck, Evert Augustus
    1816-1878 . . . . .DLB-3, 64

Duyckinck, George L. 1823-1863 . . . . . . .DLB-3

Duyckinck and Company DLB-49

Dwight, John Sullivan 1813-1893 . . . . .DLB-1

Dwight, Timothy 1752-1817 . . . . .DLB-37

Dybek, Stuart 1942- DLB-130

Dyer, Charles 1928- DLB-13

Dyer, George 1755-1841 . . . . .DLB-93

Dyer, John 1699-1757 . . . . .DLB-95

Dyer, Sir Edward 1543-1607 . . . . .DLB-136

Dyk, Viktor 1877-1931 . . . . .DLB-215

Dylan, Bob 1941- DLB-16

E

Eager, Edward 1911-1964 . . . . .DLB-22

Eames, Wilberforce 1855-1937 . . . . .DLB-140

Earle, Alice Morse 1853-1911 . . . . .DLB-221

Earle, James H., and Company DLB-49

Earle, John 1600 or 1601-1665........ DLB-151

Early American Book Illustration,
by Sinclair Hamilton DLB-49

Eastlake, William 1917-1997 .... DLB-6, 206

Eastman, Carol ?- DLB-44

Eastman, Charles A. (Ohiyesa)
1858-1939 ....DLB-175

Eastman, Max 1883-1969............. DLB-91

Eaton, Daniel Isaac 1753-1814 .... DLB-158

Eaton, Edith Maude 1865-1914 .... DLB-221

Eaton, Winnifred 1875-1954.......... DLB-221

Eberhart, Richard 1904- DLB-48

Ebner, Jeannie 1918- DLB-85

Ebner-Eschenbach, Marie von
1830-1916..................... DLB-81

Ebon 1942- DLB-41

E-Books Turn the Corner............. Y-98

Ecbasis Captivi circa 1045 .... DLB-148

Ecco Press........................ DLB-46

Eckhart, Meister
circa 1260-circa 1328 .... DLB-115

The Eclectic Review 1805-1868.......... DLB-110

Eco, Umberto 1932- DLB-196

Edel, Leon 1907-1997 .... DLB-103

Edes, Benjamin 1732-1803 .... DLB-43

Edgar, David 1948- DLB-13

Edgeworth, Maria
1768-1849..............DLB-116, 159, 163

The Edinburgh Review 1802-1929 .... DLB-110

Edinburgh University Press DLB-112

The Editor Publishing Company DLB-49

Editorial Statements DLB-137

Edmonds, Randolph 1900- DLB-51

Edmonds, Walter D. 1903-1998........ DLB-9

Edschmid, Kasimir 1890-1966 .... DLB-56

Edwards, Amelia Anne Blandford
1831-1892 ....DLB-174

Edwards, Edward 1812-1886 .... DLB-184

Edwards, James [publishing house]...... DLB-154

Edwards, Jonathan 1703-1758.......... DLB-24

Edwards, Jonathan, Jr. 1745-1801....... DLB-37

Edwards, Junius 1929- DLB-33

Edwards, Matilda Barbara Betham-
1836-1919.....................DLB-174

Edwards, Richard 1524-1566.......... DLB-62

Edwards, Sarah Pierpont 1710-1758 ..... DLB-200

Effinger, George Alec 1947- DLB-8

Egerton, George 1859-1945 .... DLB-135

Eggleston, Edward 1837-1902.......... DLB-12

Eggleston, Wilfred 1901-1986 .... DLB-92

Eglītis, Anšlavs 1906-1993 .... DLB-220

Ehrenstein, Albert 1886-1950.......... DLB-81

Ehrhart, W. D. 1948- DS-9

Ehrlich, Gretel 1946- DLB-212

Eich, Günter 1907-1972............ DLB-69, 124

Eichendorff, Joseph Freiherr von
1788-1857..................... DLB-90

Eifukumon'in 1271-1342............. DLB-203

1873 Publishers' Catalogues DLB-49

Eighteenth-Century Aesthetic Theories ... DLB-31

Eighteenth-Century Philosophical
Background DLB-31

Eigner, Larry 1926-1996 .... DLB-5, 193

Eikon Basilike 1649................. DLB-151

Eilhart von Oberge
circa 1140-circa 1195 .... DLB-148

Einhard circa 770-840............... DLB-148

Eiseley, Loren 1907-1977 ....DS-17

Eisenreich, Herbert 1925-1986........ DLB-85

Eisner, Kurt 1867-1919.............. DLB-66

Eklund, Gordon 1945- Y-83

Ekwensi, Cyprian 1921- DLB-117

Eld, George [publishing house]..........DLB-170

Elder, Lonne III 1931- DLB-7, 38, 44

Elder, Paul, and Company............ DLB-49

The Electronic Text Center and the Electronic
Archive of Early American Fiction at the University of Virginia Library Y-98

Elements of Rhetoric (1828; revised, 1846),
by Richard Whately [excerpt] DLB-57

Eliade, Mircea 1907-1986 .... DLB-220

Elie, Robert 1915-1973 .... DLB-88

Elin Pelin 1877-1949 .... DLB-147

Eliot, George 1819-1880........ DLB-21, 35, 55

Eliot, John 1604-1690................ DLB-24

Eliot, T. S. 1888-1965..........DLB-7, 10, 45, 63

Eliot's Court Press DLB-170

Elizabeth I 1533-1603 .... DLB-136

Elizabeth of Nassau-Saarbrücken
after 1393-1456 ....DLB-179

Elizondo, Salvador 1932- DLB-145

Elizondo, Sergio 1930- DLB-82

Elkin, Stanley 1930-1995 ....DLB-2, 28, 218; Y-80

Elles, Dora Amy (see Wentworth, Patricia)

Ellet, Elizabeth F. 1818?-1877 .... DLB-30

Elliot, Ebenezer 1781-1849 .... DLB-96, 190

Elliot, Frances Minto (Dickinson)
1820-1898 .... DLB-166

Elliott, Charlotte 1789-1871 .... DLB-199

Elliott, George 1923- DLB-68

Elliott, Janice 1931- DLB-14

Elliott, Sarah Barnwell 1848-1928 ..... DLB-221

Elliott, William 1788-1863 .... DLB-3

Elliott, Thomes and Talbot DLB-49

Ellis, Alice Thomas (Anna Margaret Haycraft)
1932- DLB-194

Ellis, Edward S. 1840-1916............ DLB-42

Ellis, Frederick Staridge
[publishing house] DLB-106

The George H. Ellis Company......... DLB-49

Ellis, Havelock 1859-1939 .... DLB-190

Ellison, Harlan 1934- DLB-8

Ellison, Ralph Waldo
1914-1994 ....DLB-2, 76; Y-94

Ellmann, Richard 1918-1987 ......DLB-103; Y-87

The Elmer Holmes Bobst Awards in Arts
and Letters....................... Y-87

Elyot, Thomas 1490?-1546 .... DLB-136

Emanuel, James Andrew 1921- DLB-41

Emecheta, Buchi 1944- DLB-117

The Emergence of Black Women Writers DS-8

Emerson, Ralph Waldo
1803-1882 ....DLB-1, 59, 73, 183

Emerson, William 1769-1811 .... DLB-37

Emerson, William 1923-1997............Y-97

Emin, Fedor Aleksandrovich
circa 1735-1770.................. DLB-150

Empedocles fifth century B.C. DLB-176

Empson, William 1906-1984 .... DLB-20

Enchi Fumiko 1905-1986 .... DLB-182

Encounter with the West DLB-180

The End of English Stage Censorship,
1945-1968 .... DLB-13

Ende, Michael 1929-1995.............. DLB-75

Endō Shūsaku 1923-1996............. DLB-182

Engel, Marian 1933-1985 .... DLB-53

Engels, Friedrich 1820-1895........... DLB-129

Engle, Paul 1908- DLB-48

English, Thomas Dunn 1819-1902...... DLB-202

English Composition and Rhetoric (1866),
by Alexander Bain [excerpt]........ DLB-57

The English Language: 410 to 1500..... DLB-146

The English Renaissance of Art (1908),
by Oscar Wilde DLB-35

Ennius 239 B.C.-169 B.C. DLB-211

Enright, D. J. 1920- DLB-27

Enright, Elizabeth 1909-1968 .... DLB-22

L'Envoi (1882), by Oscar Wilde DLB-35

Epic and Beast Epic DLB-208

Epictetus circa 55-circa 125-130 ....DLB-176

Epicurus 342/341 B.C.-271/270 B.C.
................................DLB-176

Epps, Bernard 1936- DLB-53

Epstein, Julius 1909- and
Epstein, Philip 1909-1952 .... DLB-26

Equiano, Olaudah circa 1745-1797 .....DLB-37, 50

Eragny Press....................... DLB-112

Erasmus, Desiderius 1467-1536 .... DLB-136

Erba, Luciano 1922- DLB-128

Erdrich, Louise 1954- DLB-152, 175, 206

Erichsen-Brown, Gwethalyn Graham
(see Graham, Gwethalyn)

Eriugena, John Scottus circa 810-877 .... DLB-115

Ernest Hemingway's Reaction to James Gould
Cozzens Y-98

Ernest Hemingway's Toronto Journalism
Revisited: With Three Previously
Unrecorded Stories Y-92

Ernst, Paul 1866-1933 .... DLB-66, 118

Ershov, Petr Pavlovich 1815-1869 ...... DLB-205

Erskine, Albert 1911-1993 . . . . Y-93

Erskine, John 1879-1951 . . . . DLB-9, 102

Erskine, Mrs. Steuart ?-1948 . . . . DLB-195

Ervine, St. John Greer 1883-1971 . . . . DLB-10

Eschenburg, Johann Joachim
    1743-1820 . . . . DLB-97

Escoto, Julio 1944- DLB-145

Esdaile, Arundell
    1880-1956 . . . . DLB-201

Eshleman, Clayton 1935- DLB-5

Espriu, Salvador 1913-1985 . . . . DLB-134

Ess Ess Publishing Company DLB-49

Essay on Chatterton (1842), by
    Robert Browning DLB-32

Essex House Press DLB-112

Estes, Eleanor 1906-1988 . . . . DLB-22

Eszterhas, Joe 1944- DLB-185

Estes and Lauriat DLB-49

Etherege, George 1636-circa 1692 . . . . DLB-80

Ethridge, Mark, Sr. 1896-1981 . . . . DLB-127

Ets, Marie Hall 1893- DLB-22

Etter, David 1928- DLB-105

Ettner, Johann Christoph 1654-1724 . . . . DLB-168

Eudora Welty: Eye of the Storyteller Y-87

Eugene O'Neill Memorial Theater
    Center DLB-7

Eugene O'Neill's Letters: A Review Y-88

Eupolemius flourished circa 1095 . . . . DLB-148

Euripides circa 484 B.C.-407/406 B.C.
    . . . . DLB-176

Evans, Caradoc 1878-1945 . . . . DLB-162

Evans, Charles 1850-1935 . . . . DLB-187

Evans, Donald 1884-1921 . . . . DLB-54

Evans, George Henry 1805-1856 . . . . DLB-43

Evans, Hubert 1892-1986 . . . . DLB-92

Evans, Mari 1923- DLB-41

Evans, Mary Ann (see Eliot, George)

Evans, Nathaniel 1742-1767 . . . . DLB-31

Evans, Sebastian 1830-1909 . . . . DLB-35

Evans, M., and Company DLB-46

Everett, Alexander Hill 1790-1847 . . . . DLB-59

Everett, Edward 1794-1865 . . . . DLB-1, 59

Everson, R. G. 1903- DLB-88

Everson, William 1912-1994 . . . . . DLB-5, 16, 212

Every Man His Own Poet; or, The
    Inspired Singer's Recipe Book (1877),
    by W. H. Mallock DLB-35

Ewart, Gavin 1916-1995 . . . . DLB-40

Ewing, Juliana Horatia 1841-1885 . . . . DLB-21, 163

The Examiner 1808-1881 . . . . DLB-110

Exley, Frederick 1929-1992 . . . . DLB-143; Y-81

Experiment in the Novel (1929),
    by John D. Beresford DLB-36

von Eyb, Albrecht 1420-1475 . . . . DLB-179

"Eyes Across Centuries: Contemporary
    Poetry and 'That Vision Thing,'"
    by Philip Dacey DLB-105

Eyre and Spottiswoode DLB-106

Ezzo ?-after 1065 . . . . DLB-148

F

"F. Scott Fitzgerald: St. Paul's Native Son
    and Distinguished American Writer":
    University of Minnesota Conference,
    29-31 October 1982 . . . . Y-82

Faber, Frederick William 1814-1863 . . . . . . DLB-32

Faber and Faber Limited DLB-112

Faccio, Rena (see Aleramo, Sibilla)

Fagundo, Ana María 1938- DLB-134

Fair, Ronald L. 1932- DLB-33

Fairfax, Beatrice (see Manning, Marie)

Fairlie, Gerard 1899-1983 . . . . DLB-77

Fallada, Hans 1893-1947 . . . . DLB-56

Falsifying Hemingway Y-96

Fancher, Betsy 1928- Y-83

Fane, Violet 1843-1905 . . . . DLB-35

Fanfrolico Press DLB-112

Fanning, Katherine 1927 . . . . DLB-127

Fanshawe, Sir Richard 1608-1666 . . . . DLB-126

Fantasy Press Publishers DLB-46

Fante, John 1909-1983 . . . . DLB-130; Y-83

Al-Farabi circa 870-950 . . . . DLB-115

Farah, Nuruddin 1945- DLB-125

Farber, Norma 1909-1984 . . . . DLB-61

Farigoule, Louis (see Romains, Jules)

Farjeon, Eleanor 1881-1965 . . . . DLB-160

Farley, Walter 1920-1989 . . . . DLB-22

Farmborough, Florence 1887-1978 . . . . DLB-204

Farmer, Penelope 1939- DLB-161

Farmer, Philip José 1918- DLB-8

Farquhar, George circa 1677-1707 . . . . DLB-84

Farquharson, Martha (see Finley, Martha)

Farrar, Frederic William 1831-1903 . . . . . . DLB-163

Farrar and Rinehart DLB-46

Farrar, Straus and Giroux DLB-46

Farrell, James T. 1904-1979 . . . . DLB-4, 9, 86; DS-2

Farrell, J. G. 1935-1979 . . . . DLB-14

Fast, Howard 1914- DLB-9

Faulks, Sebastian 1953- DLB-207

Faulkner and Yoknapatawpha Conference,
    Oxford, Mississippi Y-97

"Faulkner 100—Celebrating the Work," University of
    South Carolina, Columbia Y-97

Faulkner, William 1897-1962
    . . . . DLB-9, 11, 44, 102; DS-2; Y-86

Faulkner, George [publishing house] DLB-154

Fauset, Jessie Redmon 1882-1961 . . . . DLB-51

Faust, Irvin 1924- DLB-2, 28, 218; Y-80

Fawcett, Edgar 1847-1904 . . . . DLB-202

Fawcett, Millicent Garrett 1847-1929 . . . . . DLB-190

Fawcett Books DLB-46

Fay, Theodore Sedgwick 1807-1898 . . . . . DLB-202

Fearing, Kenneth 1902-1961 . . . . DLB-9

Federal Writers' Project DLB-46

Federman, Raymond 1928- Y-80

Feiffer, Jules 1929- DLB-7, 44

Feinberg, Charles E. 1899-1988 . . . . DLB-187; Y-88

Feind, Barthold 1678-1721 . . . . DLB-168

Feinstein, Elaine 1930- DLB-14, 40

Feiss, Paul Louis 1875-1952 . . . . DLB-187

Feldman, Irving 1928- DLB-169

Felipe, Léon 1884-1968 . . . . DLB-108

Fell, Frederick, Publishers DLB-46

Fellowship of Southern Writers Y-98

Felltham, Owen 1602?-1668 . . . . DLB-126, 151

Fels, Ludwig 1946- DLB-75

Felton, Cornelius Conway 1807-1862 . . . . . . DLB-1

Fenn, Harry 1837-1911 . . . . DLB-188

Fennario, David 1947- DLB-60

Fenno, Jenny 1765?-1803 . . . . DLB-200

Fenno, John 1751-1798 . . . . DLB-43

Fenno, R. F., and Company DLB-49

Fenoglio, Beppe 1922-1963 . . . . DLB-177

Fenton, Geoffrey 1539?-1608 . . . . DLB-136

Fenton, James 1949- DLB-40

Ferber, Edna 1885-1968 . . . . DLB-9, 28, 86

Ferdinand, Vallery III (see Salaam, Kalamu ya)

Ferguson, Sir Samuel 1810-1886 . . . . DLB-32

Ferguson, William Scott 1875-1954 . . . . . . DLB-47

Fergusson, Robert 1750-1774 . . . . DLB-109

Ferland, Albert 1872-1943 . . . . DLB-92

Ferlinghetti, Lawrence 1919- DLB-5, 16

Fermor, Patrick Leigh 1915- DLB-204

Fern, Fanny (see Parton, Sara Payson Willis)

Ferrars, Elizabeth 1907- DLB-87

Ferré, Rosario 1942- DLB-145

Ferret, E., and Company DLB-49

Ferrier, Susan 1782-1854 . . . . DLB-116

Ferril, Thomas Hornsby 1896-1988 . . . . . DLB-206

Ferrini, Vincent 1913- DLB-48

Ferron, Jacques 1921-1985 . . . . DLB-60

Ferron, Madeleine 1922- DLB-53

Ferrucci, Franco 1936- DLB-196

Fetridge and Company DLB-49

Feuchtersleben, Ernst Freiherr von
    1806-1849 . . . . DLB-133

Feuchtwanger, Lion 1884-1958 . . . . DLB-66

Feuerbach, Ludwig 1804-1872 . . . . DLB-133

Feuillet, Octave 1821-1890 . . . . DLB-192

Feydeau, Georges 1862-1921 . . . . DLB-192

Fichte, Johann Gottlieb 1762-1814 . . . . DLB-90

Ficke, Arthur Davison 1883-1945 . . . . DLB-54

Fiction Best-Sellers, 1910-1945 . . . . DLB-9

Fiction into Film, 1928-1975: A List of Movies
    Based on the Works of Authors in
    British Novelists, 1930-1959 . . . . DLB-15

Fiedler, Leslie A. 1917- DLB-28, 67

Field, Edward 1924- DLB-105

Field, Eugene
   1850-1895 . . . . DLB-23, 42, 140; DS-13

Field, John 1545?-1588 . . . . DLB-167

Field, Marshall, III 1893-1956 . . . . DLB-127

Field, Marshall, IV 1916-1965 . . . . DLB-127

Field, Marshall, V 1941- DLB-127

Field, Nathan 1587-1619 or 1620 . . . . DLB-58

Field, Rachel 1894-1942 . . . . DLB-9, 22

A Field Guide to Recent Schools of American
   Poetry. Y-86

Fielding, Henry 1707-1754. . . . . . DLB-39, 84, 101

Fielding, Sarah 1710-1768 . . . . DLB-39

Fields, Annie Adams 1834-1915 . . . . DLB-221

Fields, James Thomas 1817-1881 . . . . DLB-1

Fields, Julia 1938- DLB-41

Fields, W. C. 1880-1946. . . . . DLB-44

Fields, Osgood and Company DLB-49

Fifty Penguin Years. Y-85

Figes, Eva 1932- DLB-14

Figuera, Angela 1902-1984 . . . . DLB-108

Filmer, Sir Robert 1586-1653 . . . . DLB-151

Filson, John circa 1753-1788 . . . . DLB-37

Finch, Anne, Countess of Winchilsea
   1661-1720. . . . . DLB-95

Finch, Robert 1900- DLB-88

"Finding, Losing, Reclaiming: A Note on My
   Poems," by Robert Phillips DLB-105

Findley, Timothy 1930- DLB-53

Finlay, Ian Hamilton 1925- DLB-40

Finley, Martha 1828-1909. . . . . DLB-42

Finn, Elizabeth Anne (McCaul)
   1825-1921 . . . . DLB-166

Finney, Jack 1911-1995. . . . . DLB-8

Finney, Walter Braden (see Finney, Jack)

Firbank, Ronald 1886-1926 . . . . DLB-36

Fire at Thomas Wolfe Memorial Y-98

Firmin, Giles 1615-1697 . . . . DLB-24

Fischart, Johann
   1546 or 1547-1590 or 1591 . . . . .DLB-179

First Edition Library/Collectors'
   Reprints, Inc. Y-91

First International F. Scott Fitzgerald
   Conference. Y-92

First Strauss "Livings" Awarded to Cynthia
   Ozick and Raymond Carver
   An Interview with Cynthia Ozick
   An Interview with Raymond
   Carver Y-83

Fischer, Karoline Auguste Fernandine
   1764-1842. . . . . DLB-94

Fish, Stanley 1938- DLB-67

Fishacre, Richard 1205-1248 . . . . DLB-115

Fisher, Clay (see Allen, Henry W.)

Fisher, Dorothy Canfield
   1879-1958. . . . . DLB-9, 102

Fisher, Leonard Everett 1924- DLB-61

Fisher, Roy 1930- DLB-40

Fisher, Rudolph 1897-1934 . . . . DLB-51, 102

Fisher, Sydney George 1856-1927 . . . . DLB-47

Fisher, Vardis 1895-1968 . . . . DLB-9, 206

Fiske, John 1608-1677. . . . . DLB-24

Fiske, John 1842-1901 . . . . .DLB-47, 64

Fitch, Thomas circa 1700-1774 . . . . DLB-31

Fitch, William Clyde 1865-1909. . . . . DLB-7

FitzGerald, Edward 1809-1883 . . . . DLB-32

Fitzgerald, F. Scott 1896-1940
   . . . . DLB-4, 9, 86, 219; Y-81; DS-1, 15, 16

F. Scott Fitzgerald Centenary Celebrations. . . . Y-96

Fitzgerald, Penelope 1916- DLB-14, 194

Fitzgerald, Robert 1910-1985 . . . . Y-80

Fitzgerald, Thomas 1819-1891 . . . . DLB-23

Fitzgerald, Zelda Sayre 1900-1948 . . . . Y-84

Fitzhugh, Louise 1928-1974 . . . . DLB-52

Fitzhugh, William circa 1651-1701 . . . . . . DLB-24

Flagg, James Montgomery 1877-1960 . . . . DLB-188

Flanagan, Thomas 1923- Y-80

Flanner, Hildegarde 1899-1987. . . . . DLB-48

Flanner, Janet 1892-1978. . . . . DLB-4

Flaubert, Gustave 1821-1880 . . . . DLB-119

Flavin, Martin 1883-1967 . . . . DLB-9

Fleck, Konrad (flourished circa 1220)
   . . . . DLB-138

Flecker, James Elroy 1884-1915 . . . . . . DLB-10, 19

Fleeson, Doris 1901-1970 . . . . DLB-29

Fleißer, Marieluise 1901-1974. . . . . . DLB-56, 124

Fleming, Ian 1908-1964 . . . . .DLB-87, 201

Fleming, Paul 1609-1640 . . . . DLB-164

Fleming, Peter 1907-1971 . . . . DLB-195

The Fleshly School of Poetry and Other
   Phenomena of the Day (1872), by Robert
   Buchanan DLB-35

The Fleshly School of Poetry: Mr. D. G.
   Rossetti (1871), by Thomas Maitland
   (Robert Buchanan) DLB-35

Fletcher, Giles, the Elder 1546-1611 . . . . . DLB-136

Fletcher, Giles, the Younger
   1585 or 1586-1623 . . . . DLB-121

Fletcher, J. S. 1863-1935 . . . . DLB-70

Fletcher, John (see Beaumont, Francis)

Fletcher, John Gould 1886-1950 . . . . . . DLB-4, 45

Fletcher, Phineas 1582-1650 . . . . DLB-121

Flieg, Helmut (see Heym, Stefan)

Flint, F. S. 1885-1960 . . . . DLB-19

Flint, Timothy 1780-1840 . . . . DLB-73, 186

Flores-Williams, Jason 1969- DLB-209

Florio, John 1553?-1625 . . . . .DLB-172

Fo, Dario 1926- Y-97

Foix, J. V. 1893-1987 . . . . DLB-134

Foley, Martha (see Burnett, Whit, and
   Martha Foley)

Folger, Henry Clay 1857-1930 . . . . DLB-140

Folio Society DLB-112

Follen, Eliza Lee (Cabot) 1787-1860 . . . . . . DLB-1

Follett, Ken 1949- DLB-87; Y-81

Follett Publishing Company DLB-46

Folsom, John West [publishing house] DLB-49

Folz, Hans
   between 1435 and 1440-1513 . . . . . .DLB-179

Fontane, Theodor 1819-1898 . . . . DLB-129

Fontes, Montserrat 1940- DLB-209

Fonvisin, Denis Ivanovich
   1744 or 1745-1792 . . . . DLB-150

Foote, Horton 1916- DLB-26

Foote, Mary Hallock
   1847-1938. . . . . .DLB-186, 188, 202, 221

Foote, Samuel 1721-1777. . . . . DLB-89

Foote, Shelby 1916- DLB-2, 17

Forbes, Calvin 1945- DLB-41

Forbes, Ester 1891-1967 . . . . DLB-22

Forbes, Rosita 1893?-1967 . . . . DLB-195

Forbes and Company DLB-49

Force, Peter 1790-1868 . . . . DLB-30

Forché, Carolyn 1950- DLB-5, 193

Ford, Charles Henri 1913- DLB-4, 48

Ford, Corey 1902-1969 . . . . DLB-11

Ford, Ford Madox 1873-1939 . . . . DLB-34, 98, 162

Ford, Jesse Hill 1928-1996 . . . . DLB-6

Ford, John 1586-? DLB-58

Ford, R. A. D. 1915- DLB-88

Ford, Worthington C. 1858-1941. . . . . DLB-47

Ford, J. B., and Company DLB-49

Fords, Howard, and Hulbert DLB-49

Foreman, Carl 1914-1984 . . . . DLB-26

Forester, C. S. 1899-1966 . . . . DLB-191

Forester, Frank (see Herbert, Henry William)

"Foreword to Ludwig of Bavaria," by
   Robert Peters DLB-105

Forman, Harry Buxton 1842-1917 . . . . . . DLB-184

Fornés, María Irene 1930- DLB-7

Forrest, Leon 1937-1997 . . . . DLB-33

Forster, E. M. 1879-1970
   . . . . DLB-34, 98, 162, 178, 195; DS-10

Forster, Georg 1754-1794 . . . . DLB-94

Forster, John 1812-1876 . . . . DLB-144

Forster, Margaret 1938- DLB-155

Forsyth, Frederick 1938- DLB-87

Forten, Charlotte L. 1837-1914 . . . . DLB-50

Fortini, Franco 1917- DLB-128

Fortune, T. Thomas 1856-1928 . . . . DLB-23

Fosdick, Charles Austin 1842-1915 . . . . . . DLB-42

Foster, Genevieve 1893-1979 . . . . DLB-61

Foster, Hannah Webster
   1758-1840. . . . . .DLB-37, 200

Foster, John 1648-1681. . . . . DLB-24

Foster, Michael 1904-1956 . . . . DLB-9

Foster, Myles Birket 1825-1899 . . . . DLB-184

Foulis, Robert and Andrew / R. and A.
   [publishing house] DLB-154

Fouqué, Caroline de la Motte
   1774-1831. DLB-90

Fouqué, Friedrich de la Motte
   1777-1843 . . . . DLB-90

Four Essays on the Beat Generation,
    by John Clellon Holmes DLB-16

Four Seas Company. DLB-46

Four Winds Press. DLB-46

Fournier, Henri Alban (see Alain-Fournier)

Fowler and Wells Company DLB-49

Fowles, John 1926- DLB-14, 139, 207

Fox, John, Jr. 1862 or 1863-1919 . . . .DLB-9; DS-13

Fox, Paula 1923- DLB-52

Fox, Richard Kyle 1846-1922 . . . . .DLB-79

Fox, William Price 1926- DLB-2; Y-81

Fox, Richard K. [publishing house] DLB-49

Foxe, John 1517-1587 . . . . .DLB-132

Fraenkel, Michael 1896-1957 . . . . .DLB-4

France, Anatole 1844-1924 . . . . .DLB-123

France, Richard 1938- DLB-7

Francis, Convers 1795-1863. . . . . .DLB-1

Francis, Dick 1920- DLB-87

Francis, Sir Frank 1901-1988 . . . . .DLB-201

Francis, Jeffrey, Lord 1773-1850 . . . . .DLB-107

Francis, C. S. [publishing house] DLB-49

François 1863-1910 . . . . .DLB-92

François, Louise von 1817-1893. . . . . .DLB-129

Franck, Sebastian 1499-1542 . . . . .DLB-179

Francke, Kuno 1855-1930 . . . . .DLB-71

Frank, Bruno 1887-1945. . . . . .DLB-118

Frank, Leonhard 1882-1961 . . . . .DLB-56, 118

Frank, Melvin (see Panama, Norman)

Frank, Waldo 1889-1967 . . . . .DLB-9, 63

Franken, Rose 1895?-1988 . . . . .Y-84

Franklin, Benjamin
    1706-1790. . . . . .DLB-24, 43, 73, 183

Franklin, James 1697-1735 . . . . .DLB-43

Franklin Library. .DLB-46

Frantz, Ralph Jules 1902-1979 . . . . .DLB-4

Franzos, Karl Emil 1848-1904 . . . . .DLB-129

Fraser, G. S. 1915-1980 . . . . .DLB-27

Fraser, Kathleen 1935- DLB-169

Frattini, Alberto 1922- DLB-128

Frau Ava ?-1127 .DLB-148

Frayn, Michael 1933- DLB-13, 14, 194

Frederic, Harold
    1856-1898 . . . . .DLB-12, 23; DS-13

Freeling, Nicolas 1927- DLB-87

Freeman, Douglas Southall
    1886-1953 . . . . .DLB-17; DS-17

Freeman, Legh Richmond 1842-1915 . . . . .DLB-23

Freeman, Mary E. Wilkins
    1852-1930 . . . . .DLB-12, 78, 221

Freeman, R. Austin 1862-1943 . . . . .DLB-70

Freidank circa 1170-circa 1233. . . . . .DLB-138

Freiligrath, Ferdinand 1810-1876 . . . . .DLB-133

Frémont, John Charles 1813-1890 . . . . . . .DLB-186

Frémont, John Charles 1813-1890 and
    Frémont, Jessie Benton 1834-1902 . . .DLB-183

French, Alice 1850-1934 . . . . .DLB-74; DS-13

French Arthurian Literature DLB-208

French, David 1939- DLB-53

French, Evangeline 1869-1960. . . . . .DLB-195

French, Francesca 1871-1960 . . . . .DLB-195

French, James [publishing house] DLB-49

French, Samuel [publishing house]. DLB-49

Samuel French, Limited DLB-106

Freneau, Philip 1752-1832 . . . . .DLB-37, 43

Freni, Melo 1934- DLB-128

Freshfield, Douglas W. 1845-1934. . . . . . .DLB-174

Freytag, Gustav 1816-1895 . . . . .DLB-129

Fried, Erich 1921-1988 . . . . .DLB-85

Friedman, Bruce Jay 1930- DLB-2, 28

Friedrich von Hausen circa 1171-1190. . . .DLB-138

Friel, Brian 1929- DLB-13

Friend, Krebs 1895?-1967? DLB-4

Fries, Fritz Rudolf 1935- DLB-75

Fringe and Alternative Theater in
    Great Britain .DLB-13

Frisch, Max 1911-1991 . . . . .DLB-69, 124

Frischlin, Nicodemus 1547-1590 . . . . .DLB-179

Frischmuth, Barbara 1941- DLB-85

Fritz, Jean 1915- DLB-52

Froissart, Jean circa 1337-circa 1404. . . . .DLB-208

Fromentin, Eugene 1820-1876 . . . . .DLB-123

From *The Gay Science,* by E. S. Dallas DLB-21

Frontinus circa A.D. 35-A.D. 103/104 . . . .DLB-211

Frost, A. B. 1851-1928. . . . . .DLB-188; DS-13

Frost, Robert 1874-1963. . . . . .DLB-54; DS-7

Frothingham, Octavius Brooks
    1822-1895 . . . . .DLB-1

Froude, James Anthony
    1818-1894 . . . . .DLB-18, 57, 144

Fry, Christopher 1907- DLB-13

Fry, Roger 1866-1934 . . . . .DS-10

Fry, Stephen 1957- DLB-207

Frye, Northrop 1912-1991 . . . . .DLB-67, 68

Fuchs, Daniel 1909-1993 . . . . .DLB-9, 26, 28; Y-93

Fuentes, Carlos 1928- DLB-113

Fuertes, Gloria 1918- DLB-108

The Fugitives and the Agrarians:
    The First Exhibition Y-85

Fujiwara no Shunzei 1114-1204. . . . . . . .DLB-203

Fujiwara no Tameaki 1230s?-1290s?. DLB-203

Fujiwara no Tameie 1198-1275 . . . . .DLB-203

Fujiwara no Teika 1162-1241 . . . . .DLB-203

Fulbecke, William 1560-1603?. DLB-172

Fuller, Charles H., Jr. 1939- DLB-38

Fuller, Henry Blake 1857-1929 . . . . .DLB-12

Fuller, John 1937- DLB-40

Fuller, Margaret (see Fuller, Sarah Margaret,
    Marchesa D'Ossoli)

Fuller, Roy 1912-1991 . . . . .DLB-15, 20

Fuller, Samuel 1912- DLB-26

Fuller, Sarah Margaret, Marchesa
    D'Ossoli 1810-1850. . . . . . .DLB-1, 59, 73, 183

Fuller, Thomas 1608-1661. . . . . .DLB-151

Fullerton, Hugh 1873-1945 . . . . .DLB-171

Fulton, Alice 1952- DLB-193

Fulton, Len 1934- Y-86

Fulton, Robin 1937- DLB-40

Furbank, P. N. 1920- DLB-155

Furman, Laura 1945- Y-86

Furness, Horace Howard 1833-1912. . . . . .DLB-64

Furness, William Henry 1802-1896. . . . . . .DLB-1

Furnivall, Frederick James 1825-1910 . . . .DLB-184

Furthman, Jules 1888-1966 . . . . .DLB-26

Furui Yoshikichi 1937- DLB-182

Fushimi, Emperor 1265-1317. . . . . .DLB-203

Futabatei, Shimei (Hasegawa Tatsunosuke)
    1864-1909 . . . . .DLB-180

The Future of the Novel (1899), by
    Henry James .DLB-18

Fyleman, Rose 1877-1957 . . . . .DLB-160

G

The G. Ross Roy Scottish Poetry
    Collection at the University of
    South Carolina Y-89

Gadda, Carlo Emilio 1893-1973 . . . . .DLB-177

Gaddis, William 1922-1998. . . . . .DLB-2

Gág, Wanda 1893-1946. . . . . .DLB-22

Gagarin, Ivan Sergeevich 1814-1882 . . . . .DLB-198

Gagnon, Madeleine 1938- DLB-60

Gaine, Hugh 1726-1807 . . . . .DLB-43

Gaine, Hugh [publishing house] DLB-49

Gaines, Ernest J. 1933- DLB-2, 33, 152; Y-80

Gaiser, Gerd 1908-1976. . . . . .DLB-69

Galarza, Ernesto 1905-1984. . . . . .DLB-122

Galaxy Science Fiction Novels. DLB-46

Gale, Zona 1874-1938 . . . . .DLB-9, 78

Galen of Pergamon 129-after 210 . . . . . . .DLB-176

Gales, Winifred Marshall 1761-1839 . . . . .DLB-200

Gall, Louise von 1815-1855. . . . . .DLB-133

Gallagher, Tess 1943- DLB-120, 212

Gallagher, Wes 1911- DLB-127

Gallagher, William Davis 1808-1894. . . . . .DLB-73

Gallant, Mavis 1922- DLB-53

Gallegos, María Magdalena 1935- DLB-209

Gallico, Paul 1897-1976 . . . . .DLB-9, 171

Galloway, Grace Growden 1727-1782 . . . .DLB-200

Gallup, Donald 1913- DLB-187

Galsworthy, John
    1867-1933 . . . . . . .DLB-10, 34, 98, 162; DS-16

Galt, John 1779-1839 . . . . .DLB-99, 116

Galton, Sir Francis 1822-1911 . . . . .DLB-166

Galvin, Brendan 1938- DLB-5

Gambit. DLB-46

Gamboa, Reymundo 1948- DLB-122

Gammer Gurton's Needle DLB-62

Gan, Elena Andreevna (Zeneida R-va)
    1814-1842 . . . . .DLB-198

Gannett, Frank E. 1876-1957 . . . . DLB-29

Gaos, Vicente 1919-1980 . . . . DLB-134

García, Andrew 1854?-1943 . . . . DLB-209

García, Lionel G. 1935- DLB-82

García, Richard 1941- DLB-209

García-Camarillo, Cecilio 1943- DLB-209

García Lorca, Federico 1898-1936 . . . . . DLB-108

García Márquez, Gabriel 1928- . . .DLB-113; Y-82

Gardam, Jane 1928- DLB-14, 161

Garden, Alexander circa 1685-1756 . . . . . . DLB-31

Gardiner, Margaret Power Farmer (see
    Blessington, Marguerite, Countess of)

Gardner, John 1933-1982 . . . . DLB-2; Y-82

Garfield, Leon 1921-1996 . . . . DLB-161

Garis, Howard R. 1873-1962 . . . . DLB-22

Garland, Hamlin
    1860-1940 . . . . .DLB-12, 71, 78, 186

Garneau, Francis-Xavier 1809-1866 . . . . . . DLB-99

Garneau, Hector de Saint-Denys
    1912-1943 . . . . DLB-88

Garneau, Michel 1939- DLB-53

Garner, Alan 1934- DLB-161

Garner, Hugh 1913-1979 . . . . DLB-68

Garnett, David 1892-1981 . . . . DLB-34

Garnett, Eve 1900-1991 . . . . DLB-160

Garnett, Richard 1835-1906 . . . . DLB-184

Garrard, Lewis H. 1829-1887 . . . . DLB-186

Garraty, John A. 1920- DLB-17

Garrett, George
    1929- DLB-2, 5, 130, 152; Y-83

Garrett, John Work 1872-1942 . . . . DLB-187

Garrick, David 1717-1779 . . . . DLB-84, 213

Garrison, William Lloyd 1805-1879 . . . . DLB-1, 43

Garro, Elena 1920-1998 . . . . DLB-145

Garth, Samuel 1661-1719 . . . . DLB-95

Garve, Andrew 1908- DLB-87

Gary, Romain 1914-1980 . . . . DLB-83

Gascoigne, George 1539?-1577 . . . . DLB-136

Gascoyne, David 1916- DLB-20

Gaskell, Elizabeth Cleghorn
    1810-1865 . . . . DLB-21, 144, 159

Gaspey, Thomas 1788-1871 . . . . DLB-116

Gass, William Howard 1924- DLB-2

Gates, Doris 1901- DLB-22

Gates, Henry Louis, Jr. 1950- DLB-67

Gates, Lewis E. 1860-1924 . . . . DLB-71

Gatto, Alfonso 1909-1976 . . . . DLB-114

Gaunt, Mary 1861-1942 . . . . .DLB-174

Gautier, Théophile 1811-1872 . . . . DLB-119

Gauvreau, Claude 1925-1971 . . . . DLB-88

The *Gawain*-Poet
    flourished circa 1350-1400 . . . . DLB-146

Gay, Ebenezer 1696-1787 . . . . DLB-24

Gay, John 1685-1732 . . . . DLB-84, 95

The *Gay Science* (1866), by E. S. Dallas
    [excerpt] DLB-21

Gayarré, Charles E. A. 1805-1895 . . . . . . DLB-30

Gaylord, Edward King 1873-1974 . . . . . . DLB-127

Gaylord, Edward Lewis 1919- DLB-127

Gaylord, Charles [publishing house] DLB-49

Geddes, Gary 1940- DLB-60

Geddes, Virgil 1897- DLB-4

Gedeon (Georgii Andreevich Krinovsky)
    circa 1730-1763 . . . . DLB-150

Gee, Maggie 1948- DLB-207

Geibel, Emanuel 1815-1884 . . . . DLB-129

Geiogamah, Hanay 1945- DLB-175

Geis, Bernard, Associates DLB-46

Geisel, Theodor Seuss 1904-1991 . . . .DLB-61; Y-91

Gelb, Arthur 1924- DLB-103

Gelb, Barbara 1926- DLB-103

Gelber, Jack 1932- DLB-7

Gelinas, Gratien 1909- DLB-88

Gellert, Christian Füerchtegott
    1715-1769 . . . . DLB-97

Gellhorn, Martha 1908-1998 . . . . Y-82, Y-98

Gems, Pam 1925- DLB-13

A General Idea of the College of Mirania (1753),
    by William Smith [excerpts] DLB-31

Genet, Jean 1910-1986 . . . . .DLB-72; Y-86

Genevoix, Maurice 1890-1980 . . . . DLB-65

Genovese, Eugene D. 1930- DLB-17

Gent, Peter 1942- Y-82

Geoffrey of Monmouth
    circa 1100-1155 . . . . DLB-146

George, Henry 1839-1897 . . . . DLB-23

George, Jean Craighead 1919- DLB-52

George, W. L. 1882-1926 . . . . DLB-197

George III, King of Great Britain and Ireland
    1738-1820 . . . . DLB-213

Georgslied 896? DLB-148

Gerber, Merrill Joan 1938- DLB-218

Gerhardie, William 1895-1977 . . . . DLB-36

Gerhardt, Paul 1607-1676 . . . . DLB-164

Gérin, Winifred 1901-1981 . . . . DLB-155

Gérin-Lajoie, Antoine 1824-1882 . . . . . . DLB-99

German Drama 800-1280 . . . . DLB-138

German Drama from Naturalism
    to Fascism: 1889-1933 . . . . DLB-118

German Literature and Culture from
    Charlemagne to the Early Courtly
    Period DLB-148

German Radio Play, The DLB-124

German Transformation from the Baroque
    to the Enlightenment, The DLB-97

The Germanic Epic and Old English Heroic
    Poetry: *Widseth, Waldere, and The
    Fight at Finnsburg* DLB-146

Germanophilism, by Hans Kohn DLB-66

Gernsback, Hugo 1884-1967 . . . . .DLB-8, 137

Gerould, Katharine Fullerton
    1879-1944 . . . . DLB-78

Gerrish, Samuel [publishing house] DLB-49

Gerrold, David 1944- DLB-8

The Ira Gershwin Centenary Y-96

Gerson, Jean 1363-1429 . . . . DLB-208

Gersonides 1288-1344 . . . . DLB-115

Gerstäcker, Friedrich 1816-1872 . . . . DLB-129

Gerstenberg, Heinrich Wilhelm von
    1737-1823 . . . . DLB-97

Gervinus, Georg Gottfried
    1805-1871 . . . . DLB-133

Geßner, Salomon 1730-1788 . . . . DLB-97

Geston, Mark S. 1946- DLB-8

"Getting Started: Accepting the Regions You Own–
    or Which Own You," by
    Walter McDonald DLB-105

Al-Ghazali 1058-1111 . . . . DLB-115

Gibbings, Robert 1889-1958 . . . . DLB-195

Gibbon, Edward 1737-1794 . . . . DLB-104

Gibbon, John Murray 1875-1952 . . . . DLB-92

Gibbon, Lewis Grassic (see Mitchell, James Leslie)

Gibbons, Floyd 1887-1939 . . . . DLB-25

Gibbons, Reginald 1947- DLB-120

Gibbons, William ?-? DLB-73

Gibson, Charles Dana 1867-1944 . . . . .DS-13

Gibson, Charles Dana
    1867-1944 . . . . DLB-188; DS-13

Gibson, Graeme 1934- DLB-53

Gibson, Margaret 1944- DLB-120

Gibson, Margaret Dunlop 1843-1920 . . . . .DLB-174

Gibson, Wilfrid 1878-1962 . . . . DLB-19

Gibson, William 1914- DLB-7

Gide, André 1869-1951 . . . . DLB-65

Giguère, Diane 1937- DLB-53

Giguère, Roland 1929- DLB-60

Gil de Biedma, Jaime 1929-1990 . . . . DLB-108

Gil-Albert, Juan 1906- DLB-134

Gilbert, Anthony 1899-1973 . . . . DLB-77

Gilbert, Michael 1912- DLB-87

Gilbert, Sandra M. 1936- DLB-120

Gilbert, Sir Humphrey 1537-1583 . . . . . . DLB-136

Gilchrist, Alexander 1828-1861 . . . . DLB-144

Gilchrist, Ellen 1935- DLB-130

Gilder, Jeannette L. 1849-1916 . . . . DLB-79

Gilder, Richard Watson 1844-1909 . . . .DLB-64, 79

Gildersleeve, Basil 1831-1924 . . . . DLB-71

Giles, Henry 1809-1882 . . . . DLB-64

Giles of Rome circa 1243-1316 . . . . DLB-115

Gilfillan, George 1813-1878 . . . . DLB-144

Gill, Eric 1882-1940 . . . . DLB-98

Gill, Sarah Prince 1728-1771 . . . . DLB-200

Gill, William F., Company DLB-49

Gillespie, A. Lincoln, Jr. 1895-1950 . . . . . . DLB-4

Gilliam, Florence ?-? DLB-4

Gilliatt, Penelope 1932-1993 . . . . DLB-14

Gillott, Jacky 1939-1980 . . . . DLB-14

Gilman, Caroline H. 1794-1888 . . . . DLB-3, 73

Gilman, Charlotte Perkins 1860-1935 . . . DLB-221

Gilman, W. and J. [publishing house] DLB-49

Gilmer, Elizabeth Meriwether 1861-1951 .... DLB-29

Gilmer, Francis Walker 1790-1826 .... DLB-37

Gilroy, Frank D. 1925- DLB-7

Gimferrer, Pere (Pedro) 1945- DLB-134

Gingrich, Arnold 1903-1976 .... DLB-137

Ginsberg, Allen 1926-1997 .... DLB-5, 16, 169

Ginzburg, Natalia 1916-1991 .... DLB-177

Ginzkey, Franz Karl 1871-1963 .... DLB-81

Gioia, Dana 1950- DLB-120

Giono, Jean 1895-1970 .... DLB-72

Giotti, Virgilio 1885-1957 .... DLB-114

Giovanni, Nikki 1943- DLB-5, 41

Gipson, Lawrence Henry 1880-1971 ...... DLB-17

Girard, Rodolphe 1879-1956 .... DLB-92

Giraudoux, Jean 1882-1944 .... DLB-65

Gissing, George 1857-1903 ..... DLB-18, 135, 184

Giudici, Giovanni 1924- DLB-128

Giuliani, Alfredo 1924- DLB-128

Glackens, William J. 1870-1938 .... DLB-188

Gladstone, William Ewart 1809-1898 .... DLB-57, 184

Glaeser, Ernst 1902-1963 .... DLB-69

Glancy, Diane 1941- DLB-175

Glanville, Brian 1931- DLB-15, 139

Glapthorne, Henry 1610-1643? DLB-58

Glasgow, Ellen 1873-1945 .... DLB-9, 12

Glasier, Katharine Bruce 1867-1950 ..... DLB-190

Glaspell, Susan 1876-1948 .... DLB-7, 9, 78

Glass, Montague 1877-1934 .... DLB-11

The Glass Key and Other Dashiell Hammett Mysteries Y-96

Glassco, John 1909-1981 .... DLB-68

Glauser, Friedrich 1896-1938 .... DLB-56

F. Gleason's Publishing Hall DLB-49

Gleim, Johann Wilhelm Ludwig 1719-1803 .... DLB-97

Glendinning, Victoria 1937- DLB-155

Glinka, Fedor Nikolaevich 1786-1880 .... DLB-205

Glover, Richard 1712-1785 .... DLB-95

Glück, Louise 1943- DLB-5

Glyn, Elinor 1864-1943 .... DLB-153

Gnedich, Nikolai Ivanovich 1784-1833 .... DLB-205

Go-Toba 1180-1239 .... DLB-203

Gobineau, Joseph-Arthur de 1816-1882 .... DLB-123

Godbout, Jacques 1933- DLB-53

Goddard, Morrill 1865-1937 .... DLB-25

Goddard, William 1740-1817 .... DLB-43

Godden, Rumer 1907-1998 .... DLB-161

Godey, Louis A. 1804-1878 .... DLB-73

Godey and McMichael DLB-49

Godfrey, Dave 1938- DLB-60

Godfrey, Thomas 1736-1763 .... DLB-31

Godine, David R., Publisher DLB-46

Godkin, E. L. 1831-1902 .... DLB-79

Godolphin, Sidney 1610-1643 .... DLB-126

Godwin, Gail 1937- DLB-6

Godwin, Mary Jane Clairmont 1766-1841 .... DLB-163

Godwin, Parke 1816-1904 .... DLB-3, 64

Godwin, William 1756-1836 .... DLB-39, 104, 142, 158, 163

Godwin, M. J., and Company DLB-154

Goering, Reinhard 1887-1936 .... DLB-118

Goes, Albrecht 1908- DLB-69

Goethe, Johann Wolfgang von 1749-1832 .... DLB-94

Goetz, Curt 1888-1960 .... DLB-124

Goffe, Thomas circa 1592-1629 .... DLB-58

Goffstein, M. B. 1940- DLB-61

Gogarty, Oliver St. John 1878-1957 .... DLB-15, 19

Gogol, Nikolai Vasil'evich 1809-1852 .... DLB-198

Goines, Donald 1937-1974 .... DLB-33

Gold, Herbert 1924- DLB-2; Y-81

Gold, Michael 1893-1967 .... DLB-9, 28

Goldbarth, Albert 1948- DLB-120

Goldberg, Dick 1947- DLB-7

Golden Cockerel Press DLB-112

Golding, Arthur 1536-1606 .... DLB-136

Golding, Louis 1895-1958 .... DLB-195

Golding, William 1911-1993 ... DLB-15, 100; Y-83

Goldman, Emma 1869-1940 .... DLB-221

Goldman, William 1931- DLB-44

Goldring, Douglas 1887-1960 .... DLB-197

Goldsmith, Oliver 1730?-1774 .... DLB-39, 89, 104, 109, 142

Goldsmith, Oliver 1794-1861 .... DLB-99

Goldsmith Publishing Company DLB-46

Goldstein, Richard 1944- DLB-185

Gollancz, Sir Israel 1864-1930 .... DLB-201

Gollancz, Victor, Limited DLB-112

Gombrowicz, Witold 1904-1969 .... DLB-215

Gómez-Quiñones, Juan 1942- DLB-122

Gomme, Laurence James [publishing house] DLB-46

Goncourt, Edmond de 1822-1896 ...... DLB-123

Goncourt, Jules de 1830-1870 .... DLB-123

Gonzales, Rodolfo "Corky" 1928- DLB-122

Gonzales-Berry, Erlinda 1942- DLB-209

González, Angel 1925- DLB-108

Gonzalez, Genaro 1949- DLB-122

Gonzalez, Ray 1952- DLB-122

González de Mireles, Jovita 1899-1983 .... DLB-122

González-T., César A. 1931- DLB-82

"The Good, The Not So Good," by Stephen Dunn DLB-105

Goodbye, Gutenberg? A Lecture at the New York Public Library, 18 April 1995 .... Y-95

Goodison, Lorna 1947- DLB-157

Goodman, Paul 1911-1972 .... DLB-130

The Goodman Theatre DLB-7

Goodrich, Frances 1891-1984 and Hackett, Albert 1900-1995 .... DLB-26

Goodrich, Samuel Griswold 1793-1860 .... DLB-1, 42, 73

Goodrich, S. G. [publishing house] DLB-49

Goodspeed, C. E., and Company DLB-49

Goodwin, Stephen 1943- Y-82

Googe, Barnabe 1540-1594 .... DLB-132

Gookin, Daniel 1612-1687 .... DLB-24

Gordimer, Nadine 1923- Y-91

Gordon, Caroline 1895-1981 .... DLB-4, 9, 102; DS-17; Y-81

Gordon, Giles 1940- DLB-14, 139, 207

Gordon, Helen Cameron, Lady Russell 1867-1949 .... DLB-195

Gordon, Lyndall 1941- DLB-155

Gordon, Mary 1949- DLB-6; Y-81

Gordone, Charles 1925-1995 .... DLB-7

Gore, Catherine 1800-1861 .... DLB-116

Gorey, Edward 1925- DLB-61

Gorgias of Leontini circa 485 B.C.-376 B.C. DLB-176

Görres, Joseph 1776-1848 .... DLB-90

Gosse, Edmund 1849-1928 ..... DLB-57, 144, 184

Gosson, Stephen 1554-1624 .... DLB-172

Gotlieb, Phyllis 1926- DLB-88

Gottfried von Straßburg died before 1230 .... DLB-138

Gotthelf, Jeremias 1797-1854 .... DLB-133

Gottschalk circa 804/808-869 .... DLB-148

Gottsched, Johann Christoph 1700-1766 .... DLB-97

Götz, Johann Nikolaus 1721-1781 .... DLB-97

Goudge, Elizabeth 1900-1984 .... DLB-191

Gould, Wallace 1882-1940 .... DLB-54

Govoni, Corrado 1884-1965 .... DLB-114

Gower, John circa 1330-1408 .... DLB-146

Goyen, William 1915-1983 ..... DLB-2, 218; Y-83

Goytisolo, José Augustín 1928- DLB-134

Gozzano, Guido 1883-1916 .... DLB-114

Grabbe, Christian Dietrich 1801-1836 .... DLB-133

Gracq, Julien 1910- DLB-83

Grady, Henry W. 1850-1889 .... DLB-23

Graf, Oskar Maria 1894-1967 .... DLB-56

Graf Rudolf between circa 1170 and circa 1185 .... DLB-148

Grafton, Richard [publishing house] DLB-170

Graham, George Rex 1813-1894 .... DLB-73

Graham, Gwethalyn 1913-1965 .... DLB-88

Graham, Jorie 1951- DLB-120

Graham, Katharine 1917- DLB-127

Graham, Lorenz 1902-1989 .... DLB-76

Graham, Philip 1915-1963 .... DLB-127

Graham, R. B. Cunninghame
1852-1936 . . . . DLB-98, 135, 174

Graham, Shirley 1896-1977 . . . . DLB-76

Graham, Stephen 1884-1975 . . . . DLB-195

Graham, W. S. 1918- DLB-20

Graham, William H. [publishing house] . . . DLB-49

Graham, Winston 1910- DLB-77

Grahame, Kenneth
1859-1932 . . . . DLB-34, 141, 178

Grainger, Martin Allerdale 1874-1941 . . . . DLB-92

Gramatky, Hardie 1907-1979 . . . . DLB-22

Grand, Sarah 1854-1943 . . . . DLB-135, 197

Grandbois, Alain 1900-1975 . . . . DLB-92

Grandson, Oton de circa 1345-1397 . . . . . DLB-208

Grange, John circa 1556-? DLB-136

Granich, Irwin (see Gold, Michael)

Granovsky, Timofei Nikolaevich
1813-1855 . . . . DLB-198

Grant, Anne MacVicar 1755-1838 . . . . . . DLB-200

Grant, Duncan 1885-1978 . . . . DS-10

Grant, George 1918-1988 . . . . DLB-88

Grant, George Monro 1835-1902 . . . . DLB-99

Grant, Harry J. 1881-1963 . . . . DLB-29

Grant, James Edward 1905-1966 . . . . DLB-26

Grass, Günter 1927- DLB-75, 124

Grasty, Charles H. 1863-1924 . . . . DLB-25

Grau, Shirley Ann 1929- DLB-2, 218

Graves, John 1920- Y-83

Graves, Richard 1715-1804 . . . . DLB-39

Graves, Robert 1895-1985
. . . . DLB-20, 100, 191; DS-18; Y-85

Gray, Alasdair 1934- DLB-194

Gray, Asa 1810-1888 . . . . DLB-1

Gray, David 1838-1861 . . . . DLB-32

Gray, Simon 1936- DLB-13

Gray, Thomas 1716-1771 . . . . DLB-109

Grayson, William J. 1788-1863 . . . . DLB-3, 64

The Great Bibliographers Series Y-93

The Great Modern Library Scam Y-98

The Great War and the Theater, 1914-1918
[Great Britain] DLB-10

The Great War Exhibition and Symposium at the
University of South Carolina Y-97

Grech, Nikolai Ivanovich 1787-1867 . . . . . DLB-198

Greeley, Horace 1811-1872 . . . . . . DLB-3, 43, 189

Green, Adolph (see Comden, Betty)

Green, Anna Katharine
1846-1935 . . . . DLB-202, 221

Green, Duff 1791-1875 . . . . DLB-43

Green, Elizabeth Shippen 1871-1954 . . . . DLB-188

Green, Gerald 1922- DLB-28

Green, Henry 1905-1973 . . . . DLB-15

Green, Jonas 1712-1767 . . . . DLB-31

Green, Joseph 1706-1780 . . . . DLB-31

Green, Julien 1900-1998 . . . . DLB-4, 72

Green, Paul 1894-1981 . . . . DLB-7, 9; Y-81

Green, T. and S. [publishing house] DLB-49

Green, Thomas Hill 1836-1882 . . . . DLB-190

Green, Timothy [publishing house] DLB-49

Greenaway, Kate 1846-1901 . . . . DLB-141

Greenberg: Publisher DLB-46

Green Tiger Press DLB-46

Greene, Asa 1789-1838 . . . . DLB-11

Greene, Belle da Costa 1883-1950 . . . . . DLB-187

Greene, Benjamin H.
[publishing house] DLB-49

Greene, Graham 1904-1991 . . . .
DLB-13, 15, 77, 100, 162, 201, 204; Y-85, Y-91

Greene, Robert 1558-1592 . . . . DLB-62, 167

Greene Jr., Robert Bernard (Bob)
1947- DLB-185

Greenhow, Robert 1800-1854 . . . . DLB-30

Greenlee, William B. 1872-1953 . . . . DLB-187

Greenough, Horatio 1805-1852 . . . . DLB-1

Greenwell, Dora 1821-1882 . . . . DLB-35, 199

Greenwillow Books DLB-46

Greenwood, Grace (see Lippincott, Sara Jane Clarke)

Greenwood, Walter 1903-1974 . . . . . DLB-10, 191

Greer, Ben 1948- DLB-6

Greflinger, Georg 1620?-1677 . . . . DLB-164

Greg, W. R. 1809-1881 . . . . DLB-55

Greg, W. W. 1875-1959 . . . . DLB-201

Gregg, Josiah 1806-1850 . . . . DLB-183, 186

Gregg Press DLB-46

Gregory, Isabella Augusta
Persse, Lady 1852-1932 . . . . DLB-10

Gregory, Horace 1898-1982 . . . . DLB-48

Gregory of Rimini circa 1300-1358 . . . . . DLB-115

Gregynog Press DLB-112

Greiffenberg, Catharina Regina von
1633-1694 . . . . DLB-168

Grenfell, Wilfred Thomason
1865-1940 . . . . DLB-92

Gress, Elsa 1919-1988 . . . . DLB-214

Greve, Felix Paul (see Grove, Frederick Philip)

Greville, Fulke, First Lord Brooke
1554-1628 . . . . DLB-62, 172

Grey, Sir George, K.C.B. 1812-1898 . . . . DLB-184

Grey, Lady Jane 1537-1554 . . . . DLB-132

Grey Owl 1888-1938 . . . . DLB-92; DS-17

Grey, Zane 1872-1939 . . . . DLB-9, 212

Grey Walls Press DLB-112

Griboedov, Aleksandr Sergeevich
1795?-1829 . . . . DLB-205

Grier, Eldon 1917- DLB-88

Grieve, C. M. (see MacDiarmid, Hugh)

Griffin, Bartholomew flourished 1596 . . . .DLB-172

Griffin, Gerald 1803-1840 . . . . DLB-159

Griffith, Elizabeth 1727?-1793 . . . . DLB-39, 89

Griffith, George 1857-1906 . . . . .DLB-178

Griffiths, Trevor 1935- DLB-13

Griffiths, Ralph [publishing house] DLB-154

Griggs, S. C., and Company DLB-49

Griggs, Sutton Elbert 1872-1930 . . . . DLB-50

Grignon, Claude-Henri 1894-1976 . . . . DLB-68

Grigson, Geoffrey 1905- DLB-27

Grillparzer, Franz 1791-1872 . . . . DLB-133

Grimald, Nicholas
circa 1519-circa 1562 . . . . DLB-136

Grimké, Angelina Weld
1880-1958 . . . . DLB-50, 54

Grimm, Hans 1875-1959 . . . . DLB-66

Grimm, Jacob 1785-1863 . . . . DLB-90

Grimm, Wilhelm 1786-1859 . . . . DLB-90

Grimmelshausen, Johann Jacob Christoffel von
1621 or 1622-1676 . . . . DLB-168

Grimshaw, Beatrice Ethel 1871-1953 . . . . .DLB-174

Grindal, Edmund 1519 or 1520-1583 . . . DLB-132

Griswold, Rufus Wilmot 1815-1857 . . . . DLB-3, 59

Grosart, Alexander Balloch 1827-1899 . . . DLB-184

Gross, Milt 1895-1953 . . . . DLB-11

Grosset and Dunlap DLB-49

Grossman, Allen 1932- DLB-193

Grossman Publishers DLB-46

Grosseteste, Robert circa 1160-1253 . . . . . DLB-115

Grosvenor, Gilbert H. 1875-1966 . . . . DLB-91

Groth, Klaus 1819-1899 . . . . DLB-129

Groulx, Lionel 1878-1967 . . . . DLB-68

Grove, Frederick Philip 1879-1949 . . . . . . DLB-92

Grove Press DLB-46

Grubb, Davis 1919-1980 . . . . DLB-6

Gruelle, Johnny 1880-1938 . . . . DLB-22

von Grumbach, Argula
1492-after 1563? DLB-179

Grymeston, Elizabeth
before 1563-before 1604 . . . . DLB-136

Gryphius, Andreas 1616-1664 . . . . DLB-164

Gryphius, Christian 1649-1706 . . . . DLB-168

Guare, John 1938- DLB-7

Guerra, Tonino 1920- DLB-128

Guest, Barbara 1920- DLB-5, 193

Guèvremont, Germaine 1893-1968 . . . . . . DLB-68

Guidacci, Margherita 1921-1992 . . . . DLB-128

Guide to the Archives of Publishers, Journals,
and Literary Agents in North American
Libraries Y-93

Guillén, Jorge 1893-1984 . . . . DLB-108

Guilloux, Louis 1899-1980 . . . . DLB-72

Guilpin, Everard
circa 1572-after 1608? DLB-136

Guiney, Louise Imogen 1861-1920 . . . . . . DLB-54

Guiterman, Arthur 1871-1943 . . . . DLB-11

Günderrode, Caroline von
1780-1806 . . . . DLB-90

Gundulić, Ivan 1589-1638 . . . . .DLB-147

Gunn, Bill 1934-1989 . . . . DLB-38

Gunn, James E. 1923- DLB-8

Gunn, Neil M. 1891-1973 . . . . DLB-15

Gunn, Thom 1929- DLB-27

Gunnars, Kristjana 1948- DLB-60

Günther, Johann Christian
1695-1723 . . . . .DLB-168

Gurik, Robert 1932- DLB-60

Gustafson, Ralph 1909- DLB-88

Gütersloh, Albert Paris 1887-1973 . . . . . . .DLB-81

Guthrie, A. B., Jr. 1901-1991 . . . . .DLB-6, 212

Guthrie, Ramon 1896-1973 . . . . .DLB-4

The Guthrie Theater DLB-7

Guthrie, Thomas Anstey (see Anstey, FC)

Gutzkow, Karl 1811-1878 . . . . .DLB-133

Guy, Ray 1939- DLB-60

Guy, Rosa 1925- DLB-33

Guyot, Arnold 1807-1884 . . . . DS-13

Gwynne, Erskine 1898-1948 . . . . .DLB-4

Gyles, John 1680-1755 . . . . .DLB-99

Gysin, Brion 1916- DLB-16

H

H.D. (see Doolittle, Hilda)

Habington, William 1605-1654 . . . . .DLB-126

Hacker, Marilyn 1942- DLB-120

Hackett, Albert (see Goodrich, Frances)

Hacks, Peter 1928- DLB-124

Hadas, Rachel 1948- DLB-120

Hadden, Briton 1898-1929 . . . . .DLB-91

Hagedorn, Friedrich von 1708-1754 . . . . . .DLB-168

Hagelstange, Rudolf 1912-1984 . . . . .DLB-69

Haggard, H. Rider
1856-1925 . . . . .DLB-70, 156, 174, 178

Haggard, William 1907-1993 . . . . .Y-93

Hahn-Hahn, Ida Gräfin von
1805-1880 .DLB-133

Haig-Brown, Roderick 1908-1976 . . . . .DLB-88

Haight, Gordon S. 1901-1985 . . . . .DLB-103

Hailey, Arthur 1920- DLB-88; Y-82

Haines, John 1924- DLB-5, 212

Hake, Edward flourished 1566-1604 . . . . .DLB-136

Hake, Thomas Gordon 1809-1895 . . . . . . .DLB-32

Hakluyt, Richard 1552?-1616 . . . . .DLB-136

Halas, František 1901-1949 . . . . .DLB-215

Halbe, Max 1865-1944 . . . . .DLB-118

Haldone, Charlotte 1894-1969 . . . . .DLB-191

Haldane, J. B. S. 1892-1964 . . . . .DLB-160

Haldeman, Joe 1943- DLB-8

Haldeman-Julius Company DLB-46

Hale, E. J., and Son DLB-49

Hale, Edward Everett 1822-1909 . . . .DLB-1, 42, 74

Hale, Janet Campbell 1946- DLB-175

Hale, Kathleen 1898- DLB-160

Hale, Leo Thomas (see Ebon)

Hale, Lucretia Peabody 1820-1900 . . . . . . .DLB-42

Hale, Nancy
1908-1988 . . . . . . DLB-86; DS-17; Y-80, Y-88

Hale, Sarah Josepha (Buell)
1788-1879. . . . . .DLB-1, 42, 73

Hale, Susan 1833-1910. . . . . .DLB-221

Hales, John 1584-1656. . . . . .DLB-151

Halévy, Ludovic 1834-1908 . . . . .DLB-192

Haley, Alex 1921-1992 . . . . .DLB-38

Haliburton, Thomas Chandler
1796-1865 . . . . .DLB-11, 99

Hall, Anna Maria 1800-1881 . . . . .DLB-159

Hall, Donald 1928- DLB-5

Hall, Edward 1497-1547. . . . . .DLB-132

Hall, James 1793-1868 . . . . DLB-73, 74

Hall, Joseph 1574-1656 . . . . .DLB-121, 151

Hall, Radclyffe 1880-1943 . . . . .DLB-191

Hall, Sarah Ewing 1761-1830 . . . . .DLB-200

Hall, Samuel [publishing house]. DLB-49

Hallam, Arthur Henry 1811-1833 . . . . . . .DLB-32

Halleck, Fitz-Greene 1790-1867 . . . . .DLB-3

Haller, Albrecht von 1708-1777 . . . . .DLB-168

Halliwell-Phillipps, James Orchard
1820-1889 .DLB-184

Hallmann, Johann Christian
1640-1704 or 1716? DLB-168

Hallmark Editions DLB-46

Halper, Albert 1904-1984 . . . . .DLB-9

Halperin, John William 1941- DLB-111

Halstead, Murat 1829-1908 . . . . .DLB-23

Hamann, Johann Georg 1730-1788 . . . . . . .DLB-97

Hamburger, Michael 1924- DLB-27

Hamilton, Alexander 1712-1756 . . . . .DLB-31

Hamilton, Alexander 1755?-1804 . . . . .DLB-37

Hamilton, Cicely 1872-1952 . . . . DLB-10, 197

Hamilton, Edmond 1904-1977 . . . . .DLB-8

Hamilton, Elizabeth 1758-1816 . . . . .DLB-116, 158

Hamilton, Gail (see Corcoran, Barbara)

Hamilton, Gail (see Dodge, Mary Abigail)

Hamilton, Ian 1938- DLB-40, 155

Hamilton, Janet 1795-1873 . . . . .DLB-199

Hamilton, Mary Agnes 1884-1962 . . . . . .DLB-197

Hamilton, Patrick 1904-1962 . . . . DLB-10, 191

Hamilton, Virginia 1936- DLB-33, 52

Hamilton, Hamish, Limited DLB-112

Hammett, Dashiell 1894-1961 . . . . DS-6

Dashiell Hammett: An Appeal in *TAC* Y-91

Hammon, Jupiter 1711-died between
1790 and 1806. . . . . .DLB-31, 50

Hammond, John ?-1663. . . . . .DLB-24

Hamner, Earl 1923- DLB-6

Hampson, John 1901-1955 . . . . .DLB-191

Hampton, Christopher 1946- DLB-13

Handel-Mazzetti, Enrica von 1871-1955 . . .DLB-81

Handke, Peter 1942- DLB-85, 124

Handlin, Oscar 1915- DLB-17

Hankin, St. John 1869-1909. . . . . .DLB-10

Hanley, Clifford 1922- DLB-14

Hanley, James 1901-1985 . . . . .DLB-191

Hannah, Barry 1942- DLB-6

Hannay, James 1827-1873 . . . . .DLB-21

Hansberry, Lorraine 1930-1965 . . . . . . .DLB-7, 38

Hansen, Martin A. 1909-1955 . . . . .DLB-214

Hansen, Thorkild 1927-1989 . . . . .DLB-214

Hanson, Elizabeth 1684-1737 . . . . .DLB-200

Hapgood, Norman 1868-1937 . . . . .DLB-91

Happel, Eberhard Werner 1647-1690 . . . .DLB-168

Harcourt Brace Jovanovich DLB-46

Hardenberg, Friedrich von (see Novalis)

Harding, Walter 1917- DLB-111

Hardwick, Elizabeth 1916- DLB-6

Hardy, Thomas 1840-1928 . . . . . .DLB-18, 19, 135

Hare, Cyril 1900-1958. . . . . .DLB-77

Hare, David 1947- DLB-13

Hargrove, Marion 1919- DLB-11

Häring, Georg Wilhelm Heinrich (see Alexis,
Willibald)

Harington, Donald 1935- DLB-152

Harington, Sir John 1560-1612 . . . . .DLB-136

Harjo, Joy 1951- DLB-120, 175

Harkness, Margaret (John Law)
1854-1923 .DLB-197

Harley, Edward, second Earl of Oxford
1689-1741 .DLB-213

Harley, Robert, first Earl of Oxford
1661-1724 .DLB-213

Harlow, Robert 1923- DLB-60

Harman, Thomas
flourished 1566-1573 . . . . .DLB-136

Harness, Charles L. 1915- DLB-8

Harnett, Cynthia 1893-1981 . . . . .DLB-161

Harper, Fletcher 1806-1877 . . . . .DLB-79

Harper, Frances Ellen Watkins
1825-1911 . . . . .DLB-50, 221

Harper, Michael S. 1938- DLB-41

Harper and Brothers DLB-49

Harraden, Beatrice 1864-1943 . . . . .DLB-153

Harrap, George G., and Company
Limited DLB-112

Harriot, Thomas 1560-1621 . . . . .DLB-136

Harris, Benjamin ?-circa 1720 . . . . DLB-42, 43

Harris, Christie 1907- DLB-88

Harris, Frank 1856-1931 . . . . DLB-156, 197

Harris, George Washington
1814-1869 .DLB-3, 11

Harris, Joel Chandler
1848-1908 . . . . DLB-11, 23, 42, 78, 91

Harris, Mark 1922- DLB-2; Y-80

Harris, Wilson 1921- DLB-117

Harrison, Mrs. Burton
(see Harrison, Constance Cary)

Harrison, Charles Yale 1898-1954. . . . . . .DLB-68

Harrison, Constance Cary 1843-1920 . . . .DLB-221

Harrison, Frederic 1831-1923 . . . . DLB-57, 190

Harrison, Harry 1925- DLB-8

Harrison, Jim 1937- Y-82

Harrison, Mary St. Leger Kingsley
(see Malet, Lucas)

Harrison, Paul Carter 1936- DLB-38

Harrison, Susan Frances 1859-1935 . . . . . . DLB-99

Harrison, Tony 1937- DLB-40

Harrison, William 1535-1593 . . . . DLB-136

Harrison, James P., Company DLB-49

Harrisse, Henry 1829-1910. . . . . DLB-47

Harryman, Carla 1952- DLB-193

Harsdörffer, Georg Philipp 1607-1658 . . . DLB-164

Harsent, David 1942- DLB-40

Hart, Albert Bushnell 1854-1943 . . . . DLB-17

Hart, Anne 1768-1834 . . . . DLB-200

Hart, Elizabeth 1771-1833. . . . . DLB-200

Hart, Julia Catherine 1796-1867 . . . . DLB-99

The Lorenz Hart Centenary. Y-95

Hart, Moss 1904-1961 . . . . DLB-7

Hart, Oliver 1723-1795 . . . . DLB-31

Hart-Davis, Rupert, Limited. DLB-112

Harte, Bret 1836-1902 . . . .DLB-12, 64, 74, 79, 186

Harte, Edward Holmead 1922- DLB-127

Harte, Houston Harriman 1927- DLB-127

Hartlaub, Felix 1913-1945 . . . . DLB-56

Hartlebon, Otto Erich 1864-1905. . . . . . . DLB-118

Hartley, L. P. 1895-1972. . . . . DLB-15, 139

Hartley, Marsden 1877-1943. . . . . DLB-54

Hartling, Peter 1933- DLB-75

Hartman, Geoffrey H. 1929- DLB-67

Hartmann, Sadakichi 1867-1944. . . . . DLB-54

Hartmann von Aue
circa 1160-circa 1205 . . . . DLB-138

Harvey, Gabriel 1550?-1631. . . . . . .DLB-167, 213

Harvey, Jean-Charles 1891-1967 . . . . DLB-88

Harvill Press Limited DLB-112

Harwood, Lee 1939- DLB-40

Harwood, Ronald 1934- DLB-13

Hašek, Jaroslav 1883-1923 . . . . DLB-215

Haskins, Charles Homer 1870-1937 . . . . . DLB-47

Haslam, Gerald 1937- DLB-212

Hass, Robert 1941- DLB-105, 206

Hatar, Győző 1914- DLB-215

The Hatch-Billops Collection DLB-76

Hathaway, William 1944- DLB-120

Hauff, Wilhelm 1802-1827 . . . . DLB-90

A Haughty and Proud Generation (1922),
by Ford Madox Hueffer. DLB-36

Haugwitz, August Adolph von
1647-1706 . . . . DLB-168

Hauptmann, Carl 1858-1921 . . . . . . DLB-66, 118

Hauptmann, Gerhart 1862-1946 . . . . DLB-66, 118

Hauser, Marianne 1910- Y-83

Havergal, Frances Ridley 1836-1879 . . . . DLB-199

Hawes, Stephen 1475?-before 1529 . . . . . DLB-132

Hawker, Robert Stephen 1803-1875. . . . . . DLB-32

Hawkes, John 1925-1998 . . . .DLB-2, 7; Y-80, Y-98

Hawkesworth, John 1720-1773 . . . . DLB-142

Hawkins, Sir Anthony Hope (see Hope, Anthony)

Hawkins, Sir John 1719-1789 . . . . . . DLB-104, 142

Hawkins, Walter Everette 1883-? DLB-50

Hawthorne, Nathaniel
1804-1864 . . . . .DLB-1, 74, 183

Hawthorne, Nathaniel 1804-1864 and
Hawthorne, Sophia Peabody
1809-1871 . . . . DLB-183

Hay, John 1835-1905 . . . . .DLB-12, 47, 189

Hayashi, Fumiko 1903-1951. . . . . DLB-180

Haycox, Ernest 1899-1950 . . . . DLB-206

Haycraft, Anna Margaret (see Ellis, Alice Thomas)

Hayden, Robert 1913-1980 . . . . DLB-5, 76

Haydon, Benjamin Robert
1786-1846. . . . . DLB-110

Hayes, John Michael 1919- DLB-26

Hayley, William 1745-1820 . . . . . . DLB-93, 142

Haym, Rudolf 1821-1901. . . . . DLB-129

Hayman, Robert 1575-1629 . . . . DLB-99

Hayman, Ronald 1932- DLB-155

Hayne, Paul Hamilton 1830-1886 . . .DLB-3, 64, 79

Hays, Mary 1760-1843 . . . . DLB-142, 158

Hayward, John 1905-1965 . . . . DLB-201

Haywood, Eliza 1693?-1756 . . . . DLB-39

Hazard, Willis P. [publishing house] DLB-49

Hazlitt, William 1778-1830 . . . . .DLB-110, 158

Hazzard, Shirley 1931- Y-82

Head, Bessie 1937-1986 . . . . .DLB-117

Headley, Joel T. 1813-1897 . . DLB-30, 183; DS-13

Heaney, Seamus 1939- DLB-40; Y-95

Heard, Nathan C. 1936- DLB-33

Hearn, Lafcadio 1850-1904 . . . . . .DLB-12, 78, 189

Hearne, John 1926- DLB-117

Hearne, Samuel 1745-1792 . . . . DLB-99

Hearne, Thomas 1678?-1735 . . . . DLB-213

Hearst, William Randolph 1863-1951 . . . . DLB-25

Hearst, William Randolph, Jr.
1908-1993 . . . . DLB-127

Heartman, Charles Frederick
1883-1953 . . . . DLB-187

Heath, Catherine 1924- DLB-14

Heath, Roy A. K. 1926- DLB-117

Heath-Stubbs, John 1918- DLB-27

Heavysege, Charles 1816-1876. . . . . DLB-99

Hebbel, Friedrich 1813-1863 . . . . DLB-129

Hebel, Johann Peter 1760-1826. . . . . DLB-90

Heber, Richard 1774-1833 . . . . DLB-184

Hébert, Anne 1916- DLB-68

Hébert, Jacques 1923- DLB-53

Hecht, Anthony 1923- DLB-5, 169

Hecht, Ben 1894-1964
. . . . .DLB-7, 9, 25, 26, 28, 86

Hecker, Isaac Thomas 1819-1888 . . . . DLB-1

Hedge, Frederic Henry 1805-1890 . . . . . DLB-1, 59

Hefner, Hugh M. 1926- DLB-137

Hegel, Georg Wilhelm Friedrich
1770-1831. . . . . DLB-90

Heidish, Marcy 1947- Y-82

Heike monogatari DLB-203

Hein, Christoph 1944- DLB-124

Hein, Piet 1905-1996 . . . . DLB-214

Heine, Heinrich 1797-1856 . . . . DLB-90

Heinemann, Larry 1944- DS-9

Heinemann, William, Limited DLB-112

Heinesen, William 1900-1991 . . . . DLB-214

Heinlein, Robert A. 1907-1988 . . . . DLB-8

Heinrich Julius of Brunswick
1564-1613 . . . . DLB-164

Heinrich von dem Türlîn
flourished circa 1230 . . . . DLB-138

Heinrich von Melk
flourished after 1160 . . . . DLB-148

Heinrich von Veldeke
circa 1145-circa 1190 . . . . DLB-138

Heinrich, Willi 1920- DLB-75

Heinse, Wilhelm 1746-1803 . . . . DLB-94

Heinz, W. C. 1915- DLB-171

Heiskell, John 1872-1972 . . . . .DLB-127

Heißenbüttel, Helmut 1921-1996 . . . . DLB-75

Hejinian, Lyn 1941- DLB-165

Heliand circa 850 . . . . DLB-148

Heller, Joseph 1923- DLB-2, 28; Y-80

Heller, Michael 1937- DLB-165

Hellman, Lillian 1906-1984 . . . . .DLB-7; Y-84

Hellwig, Johann 1609-1674. . . . . DLB-164

Helprin, Mark 1947- Y-85

Helwig, David 1938- DLB-60

Hemans, Felicia 1793-1835 . . . . DLB-96

Hemingway, Ernest
1899-1961 . . . . .DLB-4, 9, 102, 210;
Y-81, Y-87; DS-1, DS-15, DS-16

Hemingway: Twenty-Five Years Later. Y-85

Hémon, Louis 1880-1913. . . . . DLB-92

Hempel, Amy 1951- DLB-218

Hemphill, Paul 1936- Y-87

Hénault, Gilles 1920- DLB-88

Henchman, Daniel 1689-1761 . . . . DLB-24

Henderson, Alice Corbin 1881-1949 . . . . . DLB-54

Henderson, Archibald 1877-1963 . . . . DLB-103

Henderson, David 1942- DLB-41

Henderson, George Wylie 1904- DLB-51

Henderson, Zenna 1917-1983. . . . . DLB-8

Henisch, Peter 1943- DLB-85

Henley, Beth 1952- Y-86

Henley, William Ernest 1849-1903 . . . . . . DLB-19

Henningsen, Agnes 1868-1962. . . . . DLB-214

Henniker, Florence 1855-1923 . . . . DLB-135

Henry, Alexander 1739-1824 . . . . DLB-99

Henry, Buck 1930- DLB-26

Henry VIII of England 1491-1547. . . . . . DLB-132

Henry, Marguerite 1902-1997 . . . . DLB-22

Henry, O. (see Porter, William Sydney)

Henry of Ghent
circa 1217-1229 - 1293 . . . . DLB-115

Henry, Robert Selph 1889-1970 . . . . .DLB-17

Henry, Will (see Allen, Henry W.)

Henryson, Robert
1420s or 1430s-circa 1505 . . . . DLB-146

Henschke, Alfred (see Klabund)

Hensley, Sophie Almon 1866-1946 . . . . . . DLB-99

Henson, Lance 1944- DLB-175

Henty, G. A. 1832?-1902 . . . . DLB-18, 141

Hentz, Caroline Lee 1800-1856 . . . . DLB-3

Heraclitus flourished circa 500 B.C.
. . . . DLB-176

Herbert, Agnes circa 1880-1960 . . . . DLB-174

Herbert, Alan Patrick 1890-1971 . . . . . DLB-10, 191

Herbert, Edward, Lord, of Cherbury
1582-1648 . . . . DLB-121, 151

Herbert, Frank 1920-1986 . . . . DLB-8

Herbert, George 1593-1633 . . . . DLB-126

Herbert, Henry William 1807-1858 . . . . . DLB-3, 73

Herbert, John 1926- DLB-53

Herbert, Mary Sidney, Countess of Pembroke
(see Sidney, Mary)

Herbst, Josephine 1892-1969 . . . . DLB-9

Herburger, Gunter 1932- DLB-75, 124

Hercules, Frank E. M. 1917-1996 . . . . DLB-33

Herder, Johann Gottfried 1744-1803 . . . . . . DLB-97

Herder, B., Book Company DLB-49

Heredia, José-María de 1842-1905 . . . . DLB-217

Herford, Charles Harold 1853-1931 . . . . . DLB-149

Hergesheimer, Joseph 1880-1954 . . . . . . DLB-9, 102

Heritage Press DLB-46

Hermann the Lame 1013-1054 . . . . DLB-148

Hermes, Johann Timotheus
1738-1821 . . . . DLB-97

Hermlin, Stephan 1915-1997 . . . . DLB-69

Hernández, Alfonso C. 1938- DLB-122

Hernández, Inés 1947- DLB-122

Hernández, Miguel 1910-1942 . . . . DLB-134

Hernton, Calvin C. 1932- DLB-38

"The Hero as Man of Letters: Johnson,
Rousseau, Burns" (1841), by Thomas
Carlyle [excerpt] DLB-57

The Hero as Poet. Dante; Shakspeare (1841),
by Thomas Carlyle DLB-32

Herodotus circa 484 B.C.-circa 420 B.C.
. . . . DLB-176

Heron, Robert 1764-1807 . . . . DLB-142

Herr, Michael 1940- DLB-185

Herrera, Juan Felipe 1948- DLB-122

Herrick, Robert 1591-1674 . . . . DLB-126

Herrick, Robert 1868-1938 . . . . DLB-9, 12, 78

Herrick, William 1915- Y-83

Herrick, E. R., and Company DLB-49

Herrmann, John 1900-1959 . . . . DLB-4

Hersey, John 1914-1993 . . . . DLB-6, 185

Hertel, François 1905-1985 . . . . DLB-68

Hervé-Bazin, Jean Pierre Marie (see Bazin, Hervé)

Hervey, John, Lord 1696-1743 . . . . DLB-101

Herwig, Georg 1817-1875 . . . . DLB-133

Herzog, Emile Salomon Wilhelm (see
Maurois, André)

Hesiod eighth century B.C. DLB-176

Hesse, Hermann 1877-1962 . . . . DLB-66

Hessus, Helius Eobanus 1488-1540 . . . . . DLB-179

Hewat, Alexander circa 1743-circa 1824 . . . DLB-30

Hewitt, John 1907- DLB-27

Hewlett, Maurice 1861-1923 . . . . DLB-34, 156

Heyen, William 1940- DLB-5

Heyer, Georgette 1902-1974 . . . . DLB-77, 191

Heym, Stefan 1913- DLB-69

Heyse, Paul 1830-1914 . . . . DLB-129

Heytesbury, William
circa 1310-1372 or 1373 . . . . DLB-115

Heyward, Dorothy 1890-1961 . . . . DLB-7

Heyward, DuBose 1885-1940 . . . . . . DLB-7, 9, 45

Heywood, John 1497?-1580? DLB-136

Heywood, Thomas
1573 or 1574-1641 . . . . DLB-62

Hibbs, Ben 1901-1975 . . . . DLB-137

Hichens, Robert S. 1864-1950 . . . . DLB-153

Hickey, Emily 1845-1924 . . . . DLB-199

Hickman, William Albert 1877-1957 . . . . . DLB-92

Hidalgo, José Luis 1919-1947 . . . . DLB-108

Hiebert, Paul 1892-1987 . . . . DLB-68

Hieng, Andrej 1925- DLB-181

Hierro, José 1922- DLB-108

Higgins, Aidan 1927- DLB-14

Higgins, Colin 1941-1988 . . . . DLB-26

Higgins, George V. 1939- . . . DLB-2; Y-81, Y-98

Higginson, Thomas Wentworth
1823-1911 . . . . DLB-1, 64

Highwater, Jamake 1942?- DLB-52; Y-85

Hijuelos, Oscar 1951- DLB-145

Hildegard von Bingen 1098-1179 . . . . DLB-148

Das Hildesbrandslied circa 820 . . . . DLB-148

Hildesheimer, Wolfgang
1916-1991 . . . . DLB-69, 124

Hildreth, Richard 1807-1865 . . . . DLB-1, 30, 59

Hill, Aaron 1685-1750 . . . . DLB-84

Hill, Geoffrey 1932- DLB-40

Hill, "Sir" John 1714?-1775 . . . . DLB-39

Hill, Leslie 1880-1960 . . . . DLB-51

Hill, Susan 1942- DLB-14, 139

Hill, Walter 1942- DLB-44

Hill and Wang DLB-46

Hill, George M., Company DLB-49

Hill, Lawrence, and Company,
Publishers DLB-46

Hillberry, Conrad 1928- DLB-120

Hillerman, Tony 1925- DLB-206

Hilliard, Gray and Company DLB-49

Hills, Lee 1906- DLB-127

Hillyer, Robert 1895-1961 . . . . DLB-54

Hilton, James 1900-1954 . . . . DLB-34, 77

Hilton, Walter died 1396 . . . . DLB-146

Hilton and Company DLB-49

Himes, Chester 1909-1984 . . . . DLB-2, 76, 143

Hindmarsh, Joseph [publishing house] . . . DLB-170

Hine, Daryl 1936- DLB-60

Hingley, Ronald 1920- DLB-155

Hinojosa-Smith, Rolando 1929- DLB-82

Hippel, Theodor Gottlieb von
1741-1796 . . . . DLB-97

Hippocrates of Cos flourished circa 425 B.C.
. . . . DLB-176

Hirabayashi, Taiko 1905-1972 . . . . DLB-180

Hirsch, E. D., Jr. 1928- DLB-67

Hirsch, Edward 1950- DLB-120

The History of the Adventures of Joseph Andrews
(1742), by Henry Fielding [excerpt] DLB-39

Hoagland, Edward 1932- DLB-6

Hoagland, Everett H., III 1942- DLB-41

Hoban, Russell 1925- DLB-52

Hobbes, Thomas 1588-1679 . . . . DLB-151

Hobby, Oveta 1905- DLB-127

Hobby, William 1878-1964 . . . . DLB-127

Hobsbaum, Philip 1932- DLB-40

Hobson, Laura Z. 1900- DLB-28

Hobson, Sarah 1947- DLB-204

Hoby, Thomas 1530-1566 . . . . DLB-132

Hoccleve, Thomas
circa 1368-circa 1437 . . . . DLB-146

Hochhuth, Rolf 1931- DLB-124

Hochman, Sandra 1936- DLB-5

Hocken, Thomas Morland
1836-1910 . . . . DLB-184

Hodder and Stoughton, Limited DLB-106

Hodgins, Jack 1938- DLB-60

Hodgman, Helen 1945- DLB-14

Hodgskin, Thomas 1787-1869 . . . . DLB-158

Hodgson, Ralph 1871-1962 . . . . DLB-19

Hodgson, William Hope
1877-1918 . . . . DLB-70, 153, 156, 178

Hoe, Robert III 1839-1909 . . . . DLB-187

Hoeg, Peter 1957- DLB-214

Højholt, Per 1928- DLB-214

Hoffenstein, Samuel 1890-1947 . . . . DLB-11

Hoffman, Charles Fenno 1806-1884 . . . . DLB-3

Hoffman, Daniel 1923- DLB-5

Hoffmann, E. T. A. 1776-1822 . . . . DLB-90

Hoffman, Frank B. 1888-1958 . . . . DLB-188

Hoffmanswaldau, Christian Hoffman von
1616-1679 . . . . DLB-168

Hofmann, Michael 1957- DLB-40

Hofmannsthal, Hugo von
1874-1929 . . . . DLB-81, 118

Hofstadter, Richard 1916-1970 . . . . DLB-17

Hogan, Desmond 1950- DLB-14

Hogan, Linda 1947- DLB-175

Hogan and Thompson DLB-49

Hogarth Press DLB-112

Hogg, James 1770-1835 . . . . DLB-93, 116, 159

Hohberg, Wolfgang Helmhard Freiherr von 1612-1688. . . . . DLB-168

von Hohenheim, Philippus Aureolus Theophrastus Bombastus (see Paracelsus)

Hohl, Ludwig 1904-1980 . . . . DLB-56

Holbrook, David 1923- DLB-14, 40

Holcroft, Thomas 1745-1809 . . . . DLB-39, 89, 158

Holden, Jonathan 1941- DLB-105

Holden, Molly 1927-1981 . . . . DLB-40

Hölderlin, Friedrich 1770-1843 . . . . DLB-90

Holiday House DLB-46

Holinshed, Raphael died 1580 . . . . DLB-167

Holland, J. G. 1819-1881 . . . . DS-13

Holland, Norman N. 1927- DLB-67

Hollander, John 1929- DLB-5

Holley, Marietta 1836-1926 . . . . DLB-11

Hollinghurst, Alan 1954- DLB-207

Hollingsworth, Margaret 1940- DLB-60

Hollo, Anselm 1934- DLB-40

Holloway, Emory 1885-1977 . . . . DLB-103

Holloway, John 1920- DLB-27

Holloway House Publishing Company . . . DLB-46

Holme, Constance 1880-1955 . . . . DLB-34

Holmes, Abraham S. 1821?-1908 . . . . DLB-99

Holmes, John Clellon 1926-1988 . . . . DLB-16

Holmes, Mary Jane 1825-1907 . . . . . DLB-202, 221

Holmes, Oliver Wendell 1809-1894 . . . DLB-1, 189

Holmes, Richard 1945- DLB-155

Holmes, Thomas James 1874-1959 . . . . . . DLB-187

Holroyd, Michael 1935- DLB-155

Holst, Hermann E. von 1841-1904 . . . . . . DLB-47

Holt, John 1721-1784 . . . . DLB-43

Holt, Henry, and Company DLB-49

Holt, Rinehart and Winston DLB-46

Holtby, Winifred 1898-1935 . . . . DLB-191

Holthusen, Hans Egon 1913- DLB-69

Hölty, Ludwig Christoph Heinrich 1748-1776 . . . . DLB-94

Holz, Arno 1863-1929 . . . . DLB-118

Home, Henry, Lord Kames (see Kames, Henry Home, Lord)

Home, John 1722-1808 . . . . DLB-84

Home, William Douglas 1912- DLB-13

Home Publishing Company DLB-49

Homer circa eighth-seventh centuries B.C. DLB-176

Homer, Winslow 1836-1910 . . . . DLB-188

Homes, Geoffrey (see Mainwaring, Daniel)

Honan, Park 1928- DLB-111

Hone, William 1780-1842 . . . . DLB-110, 158

Hongo, Garrett Kaoru 1951- DLB-120

Honig, Edwin 1919- DLB-5

Hood, Hugh 1928- DLB-53

Hood, Thomas 1799-1845 . . . . DLB-96

Hook, Theodore 1788-1841 . . . . DLB-116

Hooker, Jeremy 1941- DLB-40

Hooker, Richard 1554-1600 . . . . DLB-132

Hooker, Thomas 1586-1647 . . . . DLB-24

Hooper, Johnson Jones 1815-1862 . . . . . DLB-3, 11

Hope, Anthony 1863-1933 . . . . DLB-153, 156

Hopkins, Ellice 1836-1904 . . . . DLB-190

Hopkins, Gerard Manley 1844-1889 . . . . DLB-35, 57

Hopkins, John (see Sternhold, Thomas)

Hopkins, Lemuel 1750-1801 . . . . DLB-37

Hopkins, Pauline Elizabeth 1859-1930 . . . . DLB-50

Hopkins, Samuel 1721-1803 . . . . DLB-31

Hopkins, John H., and Son DLB-46

Hopkinson, Francis 1737-1791 . . . . DLB-31

Hoppin, Augustus 1828-1896 . . . . DLB-188

Hora, Josef 1891-1945 . . . . DLB-215

Horace 65 B.C.-8 B.C. DLB-211

Horgan, Paul 1903-1995 . . . . . . DLB-102, 212; Y-85

Horizon Press DLB-46

Hornby, C. H. St. John 1867-1946 . . . . . DLB-201

Hornby, Nick 1957- DLB-207

Horne, Frank 1899-1974 . . . . DLB-51

Horne, Richard Henry (Hengist) 1802 or 1803-1884 . . . . DLB-32

Hornung, E. W. 1866-1921 . . . . DLB-70

Horovitz, Israel 1939- DLB-7

Horton, George Moses 1797?-1883? DLB-50

Horváth, Ödön von 1901-1938 . . . . . DLB-85, 124

Horwood, Harold 1923- DLB-60

Hosford, E. and E. [publishing house] DLB-49

Hoskens, Jane Fenn 1693-1770? DLB-200

Hoskyns, John 1566-1638 . . . . DLB-121

Hosokawa Yūsai 1535-1610 . . . . DLB-203

Hostovský, Egon 1908-1973 . . . . DLB-215

Hotchkiss and Company DLB-49

Hough, Emerson 1857-1923 . . . . DLB-9, 212

Houghton Mifflin Company DLB-49

Houghton, Stanley 1881-1913 . . . . DLB-10

Household, Geoffrey 1900-1988 . . . . DLB-87

Housman, A. E. 1859-1936 . . . . DLB-19

Housman, Laurence 1865-1959 . . . . DLB-10

Houwald, Ernst von 1778-1845 . . . . DLB-90

Hovey, Richard 1864-1900 . . . . DLB-54

Howard, Donald R. 1927-1987 . . . . DLB-111

Howard, Maureen 1930- Y-83

Howard, Richard 1929- DLB-5

Howard, Roy W. 1883-1964 . . . . DLB-29

Howard, Sidney 1891-1939 . . . . DLB-7, 26

Howard, Thomas, second Earl of Arundel 1585-1646 . . . . DLB-213

Howe, E. W. 1853-1937 . . . . DLB-12, 25

Howe, Henry 1816-1893 . . . . DLB-30

Howe, Irving 1920-1993 . . . . DLB-67

Howe, Joseph 1804-1873 . . . . DLB-99

Howe, Julia Ward 1819-1910 . . . . DLB-1, 189

Howe, Percival Presland 1886-1944 . . . . . DLB-149

Howe, Susan 1937- DLB-120

Howell, Clark, Sr. 1863-1936 . . . . DLB-25

Howell, Evan P. 1839-1905 . . . . DLB-23

Howell, James 1594?-1666 . . . . DLB-151

Howell, Warren Richardson 1912-1984 . . . . DLB-140

Howell, Soskin and Company DLB-46

Howells, William Dean 1837-1920 . . . . DLB-12, 64, 74, 79, 189

Howitt, Mary 1799-1888 . . . . DLB-110, 199

Howitt, William 1792-1879 and Howitt, Mary 1799-1888 . . . . DLB-110

Hoyem, Andrew 1935- DLB-5

Hoyers, Anna Ovena 1584-1655 . . . . DLB-164

Hoyos, Angela de 1940- DLB-82

Hoyt, Palmer 1897-1979 . . . . DLB-127

Hoyt, Henry [publishing house] DLB-49

Hrabanus Maurus 776?-856 . . . . DLB-148

Hronský, Josef Cíger 1896-1960 . . . . DLB-215

Hrotsvit of Gandersheim circa 935-circa 1000 . . . . DLB-148

Hubbard, Elbert 1856-1915 . . . . DLB-91

Hubbard, Kin 1868-1930 . . . . DLB-11

Hubbard, William circa 1621-1704 . . . . . . DLB-24

Huber, Therese 1764-1829 . . . . DLB-90

Huch, Friedrich 1873-1913 . . . . DLB-66

Huch, Ricarda 1864-1947 . . . . DLB-66

Huck at 100: How Old Is Huckleberry Finn? Y-85

Huddle, David 1942- DLB-130

Hudgins, Andrew 1951- DLB-120

Hudson, Henry Norman 1814-1886 . . . . . DLB-64

Hudson, Stephen 1868?-1944 . . . . DLB-197

Hudson, W. H. 1841-1922 . . . . . DLB-98, 153, 174

Hudson and Goodwin DLB-49

Huebsch, B. W. [publishing house] DLB-46

Hueffer, Oliver Madox 1876-1931 . . . . . . DLB-197

Hugh of St. Victor circa 1096-1141 . . . . . DLB-208

Hughes, David 1930- DLB-14

Hughes, John 1677-1720 . . . . DLB-84

Hughes, Langston 1902-1967 . . . . DLB-4, 7, 48, 51, 86

Hughes, Richard 1900-1976 . . . . DLB-15, 161

Hughes, Ted 1930-1998 . . . . DLB-40, 161

Hughes, Thomas 1822-1896 . . . . DLB-18, 163

Hugo, Richard 1923-1982 . . . . DLB-5, 206

Hugo, Victor 1802-1885 . . . . . . DLB-119, 192, 217

Hugo Awards and Nebula Awards DLB-8

Hull, Richard 1896-1973 . . . . DLB-77

Hulme, T. E. 1883-1917 . . . . DLB-19

Hulton, Anne ?-1779? DLB-200

Humboldt, Alexander von 1769-1859 . . . . DLB-90

Humboldt, Wilhelm von 1767-1835 . . . . . DLB-90

Hume, David 1711-1776 . . . . DLB-104

Hume, Fergus 1859-1932 . . . . DLB-70

Hume, Sophia 1702-1774 . . . . DLB-200

Humishuma (see Mourning Dove)

Hummer, T. R. 1950- DLB-120

Humorous Book Illustration DLB-11

Humphrey, Duke of Gloucester
1391-1447 . . . . .DLB-213

Humphrey, William
1924-1997 . . . . .DLB-6, 212

Humphreys, David 1752-1818 . . . . .DLB-37

Humphreys, Emyr 1919- DLB-15

Huncke, Herbert 1915-1996 . . . . .DLB-16

Huneker, James Gibbons 1857-1921 . . . . . .DLB-71

Hunold, Christian Friedrich
1681-1721 .DLB-168

Hunt, Irene 1907- DLB-52

Hunt, Leigh 1784-1859 . . . . .DLB-96, 110, 144

Hunt, Violet 1862-1942 . . . . .DLB-162, 197

Hunt, William Gibbes 1791-1833 . . . . . . .DLB-73

Hunter, Evan 1926- Y-82

Hunter, Jim 1939- DLB-14

Hunter, Kristin 1931- DLB-33

Hunter, Mollie 1922- DLB-161

Hunter, N. C. 1908-1971 . . . . .DLB-10

Hunter-Duvar, John 1821-1899 . . . . .DLB-99

Huntington, Henry E. 1850-1927 . . . . . . .DLB-140

Huntington, Susan Mansfield
1791-1823 .DLB-200

Hurd and Houghton DLB-49

Hurst, Fannie 1889-1968 . . . . .DLB-86

Hurst and Blackett DLB-106

Hurst and Company DLB-49

Hurston, Zora Neale
1901?-1960 . . . . .DLB-51, 86

Husson, Jules-François-Félix (see Champfleury)

Huston, John 1906-1987 . . . . .DLB-26

Hutcheson, Francis 1694-1746 . . . . .DLB-31

Hutchinson, R. C. 1907-1975 . . . . .DLB-191

Hutchinson, Thomas 1711-1780 . . . . . .DLB-30, 31

Hutchinson and Company
(Publishers) Limited DLB-112

von Hutton, Ulrich 1488-1523 . . . . .DLB-179

Hutton, Richard Holt 1826-1897 . . . . .DLB-57

Huxley, Aldous
1894-1963 . . . . DLB-36, 100, 162, 195

Huxley, Elspeth Josceline
1907-1997 . . . . .DLB-77, 204

Huxley, T. H. 1825-1895 . . . . .DLB-57

Huyghue, Douglas Smith 1816-1891 . . . . . .DLB-99

Huysmans, Joris-Karl 1848-1907 . . . . . . .DLB-123

Hwang, David Henry 1957- DLB-212

Hyde, Donald 1909-1966 and
Hyde, Mary 1912- DLB-187

Hyman, Trina Schart 1939- DLB-61

I

Iavorsky, Stefan 1658-1722 . . . . .DLB-150

Iazykov, Nikolai Mikhailovich
1803-1846 .DLB-205

Ibáñez, Armando P. 1949- DLB-209

Ibn Bajja circa 1077-1138 . . . . .DLB-115

Ibn Gabirol, Solomon
circa 1021-circa 1058 . . . . .DLB-115

Ibuse, Masuji 1898-1993 . . . . .DLB-180

Ichijō Kanera (see Ichijō Kaneyoshi)

Ichijō Kaneyoshi (Ichijō Kanera)
1402-1481 .DLB-203

The Iconography of Science-Fiction Art DLB-8

Iffland, August Wilhelm 1759-1814 . . . . . .DLB-94

Ignatow, David 1914-1997 . . . . .DLB-5

Ike, Chukwuemeka 1931- DLB-157

Ikkyū Sōjun 1394-1481 . . . . .DLB-203

Iles, Francis (see Berkeley, Anthony)

The Illustration of Early German
Literary Manuscripts,
circa 1150-circa 1300 . . . . .DLB-148

Illyés, Gyula 1902-1983 . . . . .DLB-215

"Images and 'Images,'" by
Charles Simic DLB-105

Imbs, Bravig 1904-1946 . . . . .DLB-4

Imbuga, Francis D. 1947- DLB-157

Immermann, Karl 1796-1840 . . . . .DLB-133

Impressions of William Faulkner Y-97

Inchbald, Elizabeth 1753-1821 . . . . . . .DLB-39, 89

Inge, William 1913-1973 . . . . .DLB-7

Ingelow, Jean 1820-1897 . . . . .DLB-35, 163

Ingersoll, Ralph 1900-1985 . . . . .DLB-127

The Ingersoll Prizes Y-84

Ingoldsby, Thomas (see Barham, Richard Harris)

Ingraham, Joseph Holt 1809-1860 . . . . .DLB-3

Inman, John 1805-1850 . . . . .DLB-73

Innerhofer, Franz 1944- DLB-85

Innis, Harold Adams 1894-1952 . . . . .DLB-88

Innis, Mary Quayle 1899-1972 . . . . .DLB-88

Inō Sōgi 1421-1502 . . . . .DLB-203

Inoue Yasushi 1907-1991 . . . . .DLB-181

International Publishers Company DLB-46

Interview with Benjamin Anastas Y-98

An Interview with David Rabe Y-91

An Interview with George Greenfield,
Literary Agent Y-91

Interview with George V. Higgins Y-98

An Interview with James Ellroy Y-91

Interview with Melissa Bank Y-98

Interview with Norman Mailer Y-97

An Interview with Peter S. Prescott Y-86

An Interview with Russell Hoban Y-90

Interview with Stanley Burnshaw Y-97

Interview with Thomas McCormack Y-98

An Interview with Tom Jenks Y-86

"Into the Mirror," by Peter Cooley DLB-105

Introduction to Paul Laurence Dunbar,
Lyrics of Lowly Life (1896),
by William Dean Howells DLB-50

Introductory Essay: Letters of Percy Bysshe
Shelley (1852), by Robert Browning DLB-32

Introductory Letters from the Second Edition
of Pamela (1741), by Samuel
Richardson DLB-39

Irving, John 1942- DLB-6; Y-82

Irving, Washington 1783-1859
. . . . DLB-3, 11, 30, 59, 73, 74, 183, 186

Irwin, Grace 1907- DLB-68

Irwin, Will 1873-1948 . . . . .DLB-25

Isherwood, Christopher
1904-1986 . . . . DLB-15, 195; Y-86

Ishiguro, Kazuo 1954- DLB-194

Ishikawa Jun 1899-1987 . . . . .DLB-182

The Island Trees Case: A Symposium on
School Library Censorship
An Interview with Judith Krug
An Interview with Phyllis Schlafly
An Interview with Edward B. Jenkinson
An Interview with Lamarr Mooneyham
An Interview with Harriet Bernstein Y-82

Islas, Arturo 1938-1991 . . . . .DLB-122

Ivanišević, Drago 1907-1981 . . . . .DLB-181

Ivers, M. J., and Company DLB-49

Iwaniuk, Wacław 1915- DLB-215

Iwano, Hōmei 1873-1920 . . . . .DLB-180

Iwaszkiewicz, Jarosław 1894-1980 . . . . . . .DLB-215

Iyayi, Festus 1947- DLB-157

Izumi, Kyōka 1873-1939 . . . . .DLB-180

J

Jackmon, Marvin E. (see Marvin X)

Jacks, L. P. 1860-1955 . . . . .DLB-135

Jackson, Angela 1951- DLB-41

Jackson, Helen Hunt
1830-1885 . . . . DLB-42, 47, 186, 189

Jackson, Holbrook 1874-1948 . . . . .DLB-98

Jackson, Laura Riding 1901-1991 . . . . .DLB-48

Jackson, Shirley 1919-1965 . . . . .DLB-6

Jacob, Naomi 1884?-1964 . . . . .DLB-191

Jacob, Piers Anthony Dillingham
(see Anthony, Piers)

Jacobi, Friedrich Heinrich 1743-1819 . . . . . .DLB-94

Jacobi, Johann Georg 1740-1841 . . . . .DLB-97

Jacobs, Joseph 1854-1916 . . . . .DLB-141

Jacobs, W. W. 1863-1943 . . . . .DLB-135

Jacobs, George W., and Company DLB-49

Jacobsen, Jørgen-Frantz 1900-1938 . . . . . .DLB-214

Jacobson, Dan 1929- DLB-14, 207

Jacobson, Howard 1942- DLB-207

Jacques de Vitry
circa 1160/1170-1240 . . . . .DLB-208

Jæger, Frank 1926-1977 . . . . .DLB-214

Jaggard, William [publishing house] DLB-170

Jahier, Piero 1884-1966 . . . . .DLB-114

Jahnn, Hans Henny 1894-1959 . . . . . .DLB-56, 124

Jakes, John 1932- Y-83

James, Alice 1848-1892 . . . . .DLB-221

James, C. L. R. 1901-1989 . . . . .DLB-125

James Dickey Tributes Y-97

James, George P. R. 1801-1860 . . . . DLB-116

James Gould Cozzens–A View from Afar Y-97

James Gould Cozzens Case Re-opened Y-97

James Gould Cozzens: How to Read Him Y-97

James, Henry
 1843-1916. . . . . . .DLB-12, 71, 74, 189; DS-13

James, John circa 1633-1729 . . . . DLB-24

James Jones Papers in the Handy Writers' Colony
 Collection at the University of Illinois at
 Springfield Y-98

The James Jones Society Y-92

James Laughlin Tributes. Y-97

James, M. R. 1862-1936 . . . . DLB-156, 201

James, Naomi 1949- DLB-204

James, P. D. 1920- DLB-87; DS-17

James, Thomas 1572?-1629 . . . . DLB-213

James, Will 1892-1942 . . . . .DS-16

James Joyce Centenary: Dublin, 1982 . . . . . . .Y-82

James Joyce Conference Y-85

James VI of Scotland, I of England
 1566-1625 . . . . .DLB-151, 172

James, U. P. [publishing house] DLB-49

Jameson, Anna 1794-1860. . . . . DLB-99, 166

Jameson, Fredric 1934- DLB-67

Jameson, J. Franklin 1859-1937 . . . . DLB-17

Jameson, Storm 1891-1986 . . . . DLB-36

Jančar, Drago 1948- DLB-181

Janés, Clara 1940- DLB-134

Janevski, Slavko 1920- DLB-181

Janvier, Thomas 1849-1913 . . . . DLB-202

Jaramillo, Cleofas M. 1878-1956. . . . . . . DLB-122

Jarman, Mark 1952- DLB-120

Jarrell, Randall 1914-1965 . . . . DLB-48, 52

Jarrold and Sons DLB-106

Jarry, Alfred 1873-1907. . . . . DLB-192

Jarves, James Jackson 1818-1888 . . . . DLB-189

Jasmin, Claude 1930- DLB-60

Jaunsudrabiņš, Jānis 1877-1962 . . . . DLB-220

Jay, John 1745-1829 . . . . DLB-31

Jean de Garlande (see John of Garland)

Jefferies, Richard 1848-1887 . . . . DLB-98, 141

Jeffers, Lance 1919-1985. . . . . DLB-41

Jeffers, Robinson 1887-1962 . . . . DLB-45, 212

Jefferson, Thomas 1743-1826 . . . . DLB-31, 183

Jégé 1866-1940 . . . . DLB-215

Jelinek, Elfriede 1946- DLB-85

Jellicoe, Ann 1927- DLB-13

Jenkins, Elizabeth 1905- DLB-155

Jenkins, Robin 1912- DLB-14

Jenkins, William Fitzgerald (see Leinster, Murray)

Jenkins, Herbert, Limited DLB-112

Jennings, Elizabeth 1926- DLB-27

Jens, Walter 1923- DLB-69

Jensen, Johannes V. 1873-1950. . . . . DLB-214

Jensen, Merrill 1905-1980. . . . . DLB-17

Jensen, Thit 1876-1957 . . . . DLB-214

Jephson, Robert 1736-1803. . . . . DLB-89

Jerome, Jerome K. 1859-1927 . . . . .DLB-10, 34, 135

Jerome, Judson 1927-1991. . . . . DLB-105

Jerrold, Douglas 1803-1857 . . . . DLB-158, 159

Jesse, F. Tennyson 1888-1958 . . . . DLB-77

Jewett, Sarah Orne 1849-1909 . . . .DLB-12, 74, 221

Jewett, John P., and Company DLB-49

The Jewish Publication Society. DLB-49

Jewitt, John Rodgers 1783-1821 . . . . DLB-99

Jewsbury, Geraldine 1812-1880 . . . . DLB-21

Jewsbury, Maria Jane 1800-1833 . . . . DLB-199

Jhabvala, Ruth Prawer 1927- DLB-139, 194

Jiménez, Juan Ramón 1881-1958 . . . . DLB-134

Joans, Ted 1928- DLB-16, 41

Jōha 1525-1602. DLB-203

Johannis de Garlandia (see John of Garland)

John, Eugenie (see Marlitt, E.)

John of Dumbleton
 circa 1310-circa 1349 . . . . DLB-115

John of Garland (Jean de Garlande, Johannis de
 Garlandia) circa 1195-circa 1272 . . . . DLB-208

John Edward Bruce: Three Documents . . . DLB-50

John Hawkes: A Tribute Y-98

John O'Hara's Pottsville Journalism. Y-88

John Steinbeck Research Center. Y-85

John Updike on the Internet. Y-97

John Webster: The Melbourne
 Manuscript. Y-86

Johns, Captain W. E. 1893-1968 . . . . DLB-160

Johnson, Mrs. A. E. ca. 1858-1922. . . . . . DLB-221

Johnson, Amelia (see Johnson, Mrs. A. E.)

Johnson, B. S. 1933-1973 . . . . DLB-14, 40

Johnson, Charles 1679-1748 . . . . DLB-84

Johnson, Charles R. 1948- DLB-33

Johnson, Charles S. 1893-1956. . . . . . DLB-51, 91

Johnson, Denis 1949- DLB-120

Jephson, Diane 1934- Y-80

Johnson, Dorothy M. 1905–1984. . . . . . DLB-206

Johnson, Edgar 1901-1995 . . . . DLB-103

Johnson, Edward 1598-1672. . . . . DLB-24

Johnson E. Pauline (Tekahionwake)
 1861-1913 .DLB-175

Johnson, Fenton 1888-1958 . . . . DLB-45, 50

Johnson, Georgia Douglas 1886-1966 . . . . DLB-51

Johnson, Gerald W. 1890-1980 . . . . DLB-29

Johnson, Helene 1907-1995 . . . . DLB-51

Johnson, James Weldon 1871-1938 . . . . . . DLB-51

Johnson, John H. 1918- DLB-137

Johnson, Linton Kwesi 1952- DLB-157

Johnson, Lionel 1867-1902 . . . . DLB-19

Johnson, Nunnally 1897-1977 . . . . DLB-26

Johnson, Owen 1878-1952 . . . . Y-87

Johnson, Pamela Hansford 1912- DLB-15

Johnson, Pauline 1861-1913 . . . . DLB-92

Johnson, Ronald 1935-1998 . . . . DLB-169

Johnson, Samuel 1696-1772 . . . . DLB-24

Johnson, Samuel
 1709-1784 . . . . .DLB-39, 95, 104, 142, 213

Johnson, Samuel 1822-1882 . . . . DLB-1

Johnson, Susanna 1730-1810 . . . . DLB-200

Johnson, Uwe 1934-1984 . . . . DLB-75

Johnson, Benjamin [publishing house] DLB-49

Johnson, Benjamin, Jacob, and
 Robert [publishing house] DLB-49

Johnson, Jacob, and Company DLB-49

Johnson, Joseph [publishing house] DLB-154

Johnston, Annie Fellows 1863-1931 . . . . . . DLB-42

Johnston, David Claypole 1798?-1865 . . . DLB-188

Johnston, Basil H. 1929- DLB-60

Johnston, Denis 1901-1984. . . . . DLB-10

Johnston, Ellen 1835-1873 . . . . DLB-199

Johnston, George 1913- DLB-88

Johnston, Sir Harry 1858-1927 . . . . .DLB-174

Johnston, Jennifer 1930- DLB-14

Johnston, Mary 1870-1936 . . . . DLB-9

Johnston, Richard Malcolm 1822-1898 . . . DLB-74

Johnstone, Charles 1719?-1800? DLB-39

Johst, Hanns 1890-1978 . . . . DLB-124

Jolas, Eugene 1894-1952. . . . . DLB-4, 45

Jones, Alice C. 1853-1933. . . . . DLB-92

Jones, Charles C., Jr. 1831-1893. . . . . DLB-30

Jones, D. G. 1929- DLB-53

Jones, David 1895-1974 . . . . .DLB-20, 100

Jones, Diana Wynne 1934- DLB-161

Jones, Ebenezer 1820-1860. . . . . DLB-32

Jones, Ernest 1819-1868 . . . . DLB-32

Jones, Gayl 1949- DLB-33

Jones, George 1800-1870 . . . . DLB-183

Jones, Glyn 1905- DLB-15

Jones, Gwyn 1907- DLB-15, 139

Jones, Henry Arthur 1851-1929 . . . . DLB-10

Jones, Hugh circa 1692-1760 . . . . DLB-24

Jones, James 1921-1977. . . . . . .DLB-2, 143; DS-17

Jones, Jenkin Lloyd 1911- DLB-127

Jones, John Beauchamp 1810-1866. . . . . . DLB-202

Jones, LeRoi (see Baraka, Amiri)

Jones, Lewis 1897-1939. . . . . DLB-15

Jones, Madison 1925- DLB-152

Jones, Major Joseph (see Thompson, William
 Tappan)

Jones, Preston 1936-1979 . . . . DLB-7

Jones, Rodney 1950- DLB-120

Jones, Sir William 1746-1794 . . . . DLB-109

Jones, William Alfred 1817-1900 . . . . DLB-59

Jones's Publishing House DLB-49

Jong, Erica 1942- DLB-2, 5, 28, 152

Jonke, Gert F. 1946- DLB-85

Jonson, Ben 1572?-1637 . . . . DLB-62, 121

Jordan, June 1936- DLB-38

Joseph, Jenny 1932- DLB-40

Joseph, Michael, Limited DLB-112

Josephson, Matthew 1899-1978 . . . . .DLB-4

Josephus, Flavius 37-100. . . . . .DLB-176

Josiah Allen's Wife (see Holley, Marietta)

Josipovici, Gabriel 1940- DLB-14

Josselyn, John ?-1675 . . . . .DLB-24

Joudry, Patricia 1921- DLB-88

Jovine, Giuseppe 1922- DLB-128

Joyaux, Philippe (see Sollers, Philippe)

Joyce, Adrien (see Eastman, Carol)

A Joyce (Con)Text: Danis Rose and the Remaking of
Ulysses. Y-97

Joyce, James 1882-1941 . . . . . . DLB-10, 19, 36, 162

Jozsef, Attila 1905-1937 . . . . .DLB-215

Judd, Sylvester 1813-1853 . . . . .DLB-1

Judd, Orange, Publishing Company DLB-49

Judith circa 930 . . . . .DLB-146

Julian of Norwich 1342-circa 1420. . . . . .DLB-1146

Julian Symons at Eighty. Y-92

Julius Caesar 100 B.C.-44 B.C. DLB-211

June, Jennie (see Croly, Jane Cunningham)

Jung, Franz 1888-1963 . . . . .DLB-118

Jünger, Ernst 1895- DLB-56

Der jüngere Titurel circa 1275 . . . . .DLB-138

Jung-Stilling, Johann Heinrich
1740-1817 . . . . .DLB-94

Justice, Donald 1925- Y-83

Juvenal circa A.D. 60-circa A.D. 130 . . . . .DLB-211

The Juvenile Library (see Godwin, M. J., and
Company)

K

Kacew, Romain (see Gary, Romain)

Kafka, Franz 1883-1924. . . . . .DLB-81

Kahn, Roger 1927- DLB-171

Kaikō Takeshi 1939-1989 . . . . .DLB-182

Kaiser, Georg 1878-1945 . . . . .DLB-124

Kaiserchronik circca 1147 . . . . .DLB-148

Kaleb, Vjekoslav 1905- DLB-181

Kalechofsky, Roberta 1931- DLB-28

Kaler, James Otis 1848-1912 . . . . .DLB-12

Kames, Henry Home, Lord
1696-1782 . . . . .DLB-31, 104

Kamo no Chōmei (Kamo no Nagaakira)
1153 or 1155-1216 . . . . .DLB-203

Kamo no Nagaakira (see Kamo no Chōmei)

Kampmann, Christian 1939-1988 . . . . . . .DLB-214

Kandel, Lenore 1932- DLB-16

Kanin, Garson 1912- DLB-7

Kant, Hermann 1926- DLB-75

Kant, Immanuel 1724-1804 . . . . .DLB-94

Kantemir, Antiokh Dmitrievich
1708-1744. . . . . .DLB-150

Kantor, MacKinlay 1904-1977 . . . . .DLB-9, 102

Kanze Kōjirō Nobumitsu 1435-1516 . . . . .DLB-203

Kanze Motokiyo (see Zeimi)

Kaplan, Fred 1937- DLB-111

Kaplan, Johanna 1942- DLB-28

Kaplan, Justin 1925- DLB-111

Kapnist, Vasilii Vasilevich 1758?-1823 . . .DLB-150

Karadžić,Vuk Stefanović 1787-1864 . . . . . .DLB-147

Karamzin, Nikolai Mikhailovich
1766-1826 .DLB-150

Karinthy, Frigyes 1887-1938 . . . . .DLB-215

Karsch, Anna Louisa 1722-1791. . . . . .DLB-97

Kasack, Hermann 1896-1966. . . . . .DLB-69

Kasai, Zenzō 1887-1927 . . . . .DLB-180

Kaschnitz, Marie Luise 1901-1974 . . . . . . .DLB-69

Kassák, Lajos 1887-1967 . . . . .DLB-215

Kaštelan, Jure 1919-1990 . . . . .DLB-147

Kästner, Erich 1899-1974. . . . . .DLB-56

Katenin, Pavel Aleksandrovich
1792-1853 .DLB-205

Kattan, Naim 1928- DLB-53

Katz, Steve 1935- Y-83

Kauffman, Janet 1945- DLB-218; Y-86

Kauffmann, Samuel 1898-1971 . . . . .DLB-127

Kaufman, Bob 1925- DLB-16, 41

Kaufman, George S. 1889-1961. . . . . .DLB-7

Kavanagh, P. J. 1931- DLB-40

Kavanagh, Patrick 1904-1967 . . . . . . .DLB-15, 20

Kawabata, Yasunari 1899-1972 . . . . .DLB-180

Kaye-Smith, Sheila 1887-1956 . . . . .DLB-36

Kazin, Alfred 1915-1998 . . . . .DLB-67

Keane, John B. 1928- DLB-13

Keary, Annie 1825-1879 . . . . .DLB-163

Keating, H. R. F. 1926- DLB-87

Keats, Ezra Jack 1916-1983 . . . . .DLB-61

Keats, John 1795-1821 . . . . .DLB-96, 110

Keble, John 1792-1866. . . . . .DLB-32, 55

Keeble, John 1944- Y-83

Keeffe, Barrie 1945- DLB-13

Keeley, James 1867-1934 . . . . .DLB-25

W. B. Keen, Cooke and Company DLB-49

Keillor, Garrison 1942- Y-87

Keith, Marian 1874?-1961 . . . . .DLB-92

Keller, Gary D. 1943- DLB-82

Keller, Gottfried 1819-1890 . . . . .DLB-129

Kelley, Edith Summers 1884-1956. . . . . . . .DLB-9

Kelley, Emma Dunham ?-? DLB-221

Kelley, William Melvin 1937- DLB-33

Kellogg, Ansel Nash 1832-1886. . . . . .DLB-23

Kellogg, Steven 1941- DLB-61

Kelly, George 1887-1974 . . . . .DLB-7

Kelly, Hugh 1739-1777. . . . . .DLB-89

Kelly, Robert 1935- DLB-5, 130, 165

Kelly, Piet and Company. DLB-49

Kelman, James 1946- DLB-194

Kelmscott Press DLB-112

Kemble, E. W. 1861-1933 . . . . .DLB-188

Kemble, Fanny 1809-1893 . . . . .DLB-32

Kemelman, Harry 1908- DLB-28

Kempe, Margery circa 1373-1438 . . . . . . .DLB-146

Kempner, Friederike 1836-1904 . . . . .DLB-129

Kempowski, Walter 1929- DLB-75

Kendall, Claude [publishing company] DLB-46

Kendell, George 1809-1867 . . . . .DLB-43

Kenedy, P. J., and Sons DLB-49

Kenkō circa 1283-circa 1352 . . . . .DLB-203

Kennan, George 1845-1924. . . . . .DLB-189

Kennedy, Adrienne 1931- DLB-38

Kennedy, John Pendleton 1795-1870 . . . . . .DLB-3

Kennedy, Leo 1907- DLB-88

Kennedy, Margaret 1896-1967 . . . . .DLB-36

Kennedy, Patrick 1801-1873 . . . . .DLB-159

Kennedy, Richard S. 1920- DLB-111

Kennedy, William 1928- DLB-143; Y-85

Kennedy, X. J. 1929- DLB-5

Kennelly, Brendan 1936- DLB-40

Kenner, Hugh 1923- DLB-67

Kennerley, Mitchell [publishing house] DLB-46

Kenneth Dale McCormick Tributes Y-97

Kenny, Maurice 1929- DLB-175

Kent, Frank R. 1877-1958 . . . . .DLB-29

Kenyon, Jane 1947-1995 . . . . .DLB-120

Keough, Hugh Edmund 1864-1912. . . . . .DLB-171

Keppler and Schwartzmann. DLB-49

Ker, John, third Duke of Roxburghe
1740-1804 .DLB-213

Ker, N. R. 1908-1982 . . . . .DLB-201

Kerlan, Irvin 1912-1963. . . . . .DLB-187

Kern, Jerome 1885-1945 . . . . .DLB-187

Kerner, Justinus 1776-1862 . . . . .DLB-90

Kerouac, Jack 1922-1969 . . . . . . .DLB-2, 16; DS-3

The Jack Kerouac Revival. Y-95

Kerouac, Jan 1952-1996. . . . . .DLB-16

Kerr, Orpheus C. (see Newell, Robert Henry)

Kerr, Charles H., and Company DLB-49

Kesey, Ken 1935- DLB-2, 16, 206

Kessel, Joseph 1898-1979 . . . . .DLB-72

Kessel, Martin 1901- DLB-56

Kesten, Hermann 1900- DLB-56

Keun, Irmgard 1905-1982 . . . . .DLB-69

Key and Biddle DLB-49

Keynes, Sir Geoffrey 1887-1982. . . . . . . .DLB-201

Keynes, John Maynard 1883-1946 . . . . DS-10

Keyserling, Eduard von 1855-1918 . . . . . .DLB-66

Khan, Ismith 1925- DLB-125

Khaytov, Nikolay 1919- DLB-181

Khemnitser, Ivan Ivanovich
1745-1784 .DLB-150

Kheraskov, Mikhail Matveevich
1733-1807 .DLB-150

Khomiakov, Aleksei Stepanovich
1804-1860 .DLB-205

Khristov, Boris 1945- DLB-181

Khvostov, Dmitrii Ivanovich
1757-1835 . . . . DLB-150

Kidd, Adam 1802?-1831. . . . . DLB-99

Kidd, William [publishing house] DLB-106

Kidder, Tracy 1945- DLB-185

Kiely, Benedict 1919- DLB-15

Kieran, John 1892-1981 . . . . .DLB-171

Kiggins and Kellogg DLB-49

Kiley, Jed 1889-1962. . . . . DLB-4

Kilgore, Bernard 1908-1967 . . . . DLB-127

Killens, John Oliver 1916- DLB-33

Killigrew, Anne 1660-1685. . . . . DLB-131

Killigrew, Thomas 1612-1683 . . . . DLB-58

Kilmer, Joyce 1886-1918. . . . . DLB-45

Kilwardby, Robert circa 1215-1279 . . . . . DLB-115

Kimball, Richard Burleigh 1816-1892 . . . DLB-202

Kincaid, Jamaica 1949- DLB-157

King, Charles 1844-1933 . . . . DLB-186

King, Clarence 1842-1901 . . . . DLB-12

King, Florence 1936 . . . . .Y-85

King, Francis 1923- DLB-15, 139

King, Grace 1852-1932. . . . . DLB-12, 78

King, Harriet Hamilton 1840-1920. . . . . . DLB-199

King, Henry 1592-1669 . . . . DLB-126

King, Stephen 1947- DLB-143; Y-80

King, Thomas 1943- DLB-175

King, Woodie, Jr. 1937- DLB-38

King, Solomon [publishing house] DLB-49

Kinglake, Alexander William
1809-1891 . . . . DLB-55, 166

Kingsley, Charles
1819-1875. . . . . .DLB-21, 32, 163, 178, 190

Kingsley, Mary Henrietta 1862-1900 . . . .DLB-174

Kingsley, Henry 1830-1876 . . . . DLB-21

Kingsley, Sidney 1906- DLB-7

Kingsmill, Hugh 1889-1949 . . . . DLB-149

Kingsolver, Barbara 1955- DLB-206

Kingston, Maxine Hong
1940- DLB-173, 212; Y-80

Kingston, William Henry Giles
1814-1880. . . . . DLB-163

Kinnan, Mary Lewis 1763-1848 . . . . DLB-200

Kinnell, Galway 1927- DLB-5; Y-87

Kinsella, Thomas 1928- DLB-27

Kipling, Rudyard
1865-1936 . . . . .DLB-19, 34, 141, 156

Kipphardt, Heinar 1922-1982. . . . . DLB-124

Kirby, William 1817-1906. . . . . DLB-99

Kircher, Athanasius 1602-1680. . . . . DLB-164

Kireevsky, Ivan Vasil'evich
1806-1856 . . . . DLB-198

Kireevsky, Petr Vasil'evich
1808-1856 . . . . DLB-205

Kirk, Hans 1898-1962 . . . . DLB-214

Kirk, John Foster 1824-1904. . . . . DLB-79

Kirkconnell, Watson 1895-1977 . . . . DLB-68

Kirkland, Caroline M.
1801-1864 . . . . .DLB-3, 73, 74; DS-13

Kirkland, Joseph 1830-1893 . . . . DLB-12

Kirkman, Francis [publishing house] DLB-170

Kirkpatrick, Clayton 1915- DLB-127

Kirkup, James 1918- DLB-27

Kirouac, Conrad (see Marie-Victorin, Frère)

Kirsch, Sarah 1935- DLB-75

Kirst, Hans Hellmut 1914-1989 . . . . DLB-69

Kiš, Danilo 1935-1989 . . . . DLB-181

Kita Morio 1927- DLB-182

Kitcat, Mabel Greenhow 1859-1922. . . . . DLB-135

Kitchin, C. H. B. 1895-1967 . . . . DLB-77

Kittredge, William 1932- DLB-212

Kiukhel'beker, Vil'gel'm Karlovich
1797-1846 . . . . DLB-205

Kizer, Carolyn 1925- DLB-5, 169

Klabund 1890-1928 . . . . DLB-66

Klaj, Johann 1616-1656 . . . . DLB-164

Klappert, Peter 1942- DLB-5

Klass, Philip (see Tenn, William)

Klein, A. M. 1909-1972. . . . . DLB-68

Kleist, Ewald von 1715-1759 . . . . DLB-97

Kleist, Heinrich von 1777-1811 . . . . DLB-90

Klinger, Friedrich Maximilian
1752-1831. . . . . DLB-94

Klopstock, Friedrich Gottlieb
1724-1803. . . . . DLB-97

Klopstock, Meta 1728-1758. . . . . DLB-97

Kluge, Alexander 1932- DLB-75

Knapp, Joseph Palmer 1864-1951. . . . . . . DLB-91

Knapp, Samuel Lorenzo 1783-1838 . . . . . DLB-59

Knapton, J. J. and P.
[publishing house] DLB-154

Kniazhnin, Iakov Borisovich
1740-1791 . . . . DLB-150

Knickerbocker, Diedrich (see Irving, Washington)

Knigge, Adolph Franz Friedrich Ludwig,
Freiherr von 1752-1796 . . . . DLB-94

Knight, Damon 1922- DLB-8

Knight, Etheridge 1931-1992 . . . . DLB-41

Knight, John S. 1894-1981 . . . . DLB-29

Knight, Sarah Kemble 1666-1727 . . . . DLB-24, 200

Knight, Charles, and Company DLB-106

Knight-Bruce, G. W. H. 1852-1896 . . . . . .DLB-174

Knister, Raymond 1899-1932. . . . . DLB-68

Knoblock, Edward 1874-1945 . . . . DLB-10

Knopf, Alfred A. 1892-1984 . . . . .Y-84

Knopf, Alfred A. [publishing house] DLB-46

Knorr von Rosenroth, Christian
1636-1689 . . . . DLB-168

"Knots into Webs: Some Autobiographical
Sources," by Dabney Stuart. DLB-105

Knowles, John 1926- DLB-6

Knox, Frank 1874-1944 . . . . DLB-29

Knox, John circa 1514-1572 . . . . DLB-132

Knox, John Armoy 1850-1906 . . . . DLB-23

Knox, Ronald Arbuthnott 1888-1957. . . . . DLB-77

Knox, Thomas Wallace 1835-1896 . . . . . DLB-189

Kobayashi, Takiji 1903-1933 . . . . DLB-180

Kober, Arthur 1900-1975 . . . . DLB-11

Kocbek, Edvard 1904-1981 . . . . .DLB-147

Koch, Howard 1902- DLB-26

Koch, Kenneth 1925- DLB-5

Kōda, Rohan 1867-1947 . . . . DLB-180

Koenigsberg, Moses 1879-1945 . . . . DLB-25

Koeppen, Wolfgang 1906-1996 . . . . DLB-69

Koertge, Ronald 1940- DLB-105

Koestler, Arthur 1905-1983 . . . . .Y-83

Kohn, John S. Van E. 1906-1976 and
Papantonio, Michael 1907-1978 . . . . .DLB-187

Kokoschka, Oskar 1886-1980 . . . . DLB-124

Kolb, Annette 1870-1967 . . . . DLB-66

Kolbenheyer, Erwin Guido
1878-1962. . . . . DLB-66, 124

Kolleritsch, Alfred 1931- DLB-85

Kolodny, Annette 1941- DLB-67

Kol'tsov, Aleksei Vasil'evich
1809-1842 . . . . DLB-205

Komarov, Matvei circa 1730-1812 . . . . . . DLB-150

Komroff, Manuel 1890-1974. . . . . DLB-4

Komunyakaa, Yusef 1947- DLB-120

Koneski, Blaže 1921-1993. . . . . DLB-181

Konigsburg, E. L. 1930- DLB-52

Konparu Zenchiku 1405-1468? DLB-203

Konrad von Würzburg
circa 1230-1287 . . . . DLB-138

Konstantinov, Aleko 1863-1897 . . . . .DLB-147

Kooser, Ted 1939- DLB-105

Kopit, Arthur 1937- DLB-7

Kops, Bernard 1926?- DLB-13

Kornbluth, C. M. 1923-1958 . . . . DLB-8

Körner, Theodor 1791-1813. . . . . DLB-90

Kornfeld, Paul 1889-1942. . . . . DLB-118

Kosinski, Jerzy 1933-1991 . . . . .DLB-2; Y-82

Kosmač, Ciril 1910-1980 . . . . DLB-181

Kosovel, Srečko 1904-1926 . . . . .DLB-147

Kostrov, Ermil Ivanovich 1755-1796 . . . . DLB-150

Kotzebue, August von 1761-1819. . . . . . . DLB-94

Kotzwinkle, William 1938- DLB-173

Kovačić, Ante 1854-1889 . . . . .DLB-147

Kovič, Kajetan 1931- DLB-181

Kozlov, Ivan Ivanovich 1779-1840 . . . . . . DLB-205

Kraf, Elaine 1946- Y-81

Kramer, Jane 1938- DLB-185

Kramer, Mark 1944- DLB-185

Kranjčević, Silvije Strahimir
1865-1908 . . . . .DLB-147

Krasko, Ivan 1876-1958 . . . . DLB-215

Krasna, Norman 1909-1984. . . . . DLB-26

Kraus, Hans Peter 1907-1988 . . . . .DLB-187

Kraus, Karl 1874-1936 . . . . DLB-118

Krauss, Ruth 1911-1993 . . . . DLB-52

Kreisel, Henry 1922- DLB-88

Kreuder, Ernst 1903-1972 . . . . .DLB-69

Krève-Mickevičius, Vincas 1882-1954. . . .DLB-220

Kreymborg, Alfred 1883-1966. . . . . . . .DLB-4, 54

Krieger, Murray 1923- DLB-67

Krim, Seymour 1922-1989. . . . . .DLB-16

Kristensen, Tom 1893-1974. . . . . .DLB-214

Krleža, Miroslav 1893-1981. . . . . .DLB-147

Krock, Arthur 1886-1974. . . . . .DLB-29

Kroetsch, Robert 1927- DLB-53

Krúdy, Gyula 1878-1933 . . . . .DLB-215

Krutch, Joseph Wood 1893-1970. . . . .DLB-63, 206

Krylov, Ivan Andreevich 1769-1844 . . . . .DLB-150

Kubin, Alfred 1877-1959 . . . . .DLB-81

Kubrick, Stanley 1928-1999. . . . . .DLB-26

Kudrun circa 1230-1240 . . . . .DLB-138

Kuffstein, Hans Ludwig von
    1582-1656 . . . . .DLB-164

Kuhlmann, Quirinus 1651-1689 . . . . .DLB-168

Kuhnau, Johann 1660-1722 . . . . .DLB-168

Kukol'nik, Nestor Vasil'evich
    1809-1868 . . . . .DLB-205

Kukučín, Martin 1860-1928 . . . . .DLB-215

Kumin, Maxine 1925- DLB-5

Kuncewicz, Maria 1895-1989. . . . . .DLB-215

Kunene, Mazisi 1930- DLB-117

Kunikida, Doppo 1869-1908 . . . . .DLB-180

Kunitz, Stanley 1905- DLB-48

Kunjufu, Johari M. (see Amini, Johari M.)

Kunnert, Gunter 1929- DLB-75

Kunze, Reiner 1933- DLB-75

Kupferberg, Tuli 1923- DLB-16

Kurahashi Yumiko 1935- DLB-182

Kureishi, Hanif 1954- DLB-194

Kürnberger, Ferdinand 1821-1879 . . . . . . .DLB-129

Kurz, Isolde 1853-1944 . . . . .DLB-66

Kusenberg, Kurt 1904-1983. . . . . .DLB-69

Kuttner, Henry 1915-1958. . . . . .DLB-8

Kyd, Thomas 1558-1594. . . . . .DLB-62

Kyffin, Maurice circa 1560?-1598 . . . . . . .DLB-136

Kyger, Joanne 1934- DLB-16

Kyne, Peter B. 1880-1957 . . . . .DLB-78

Kyōgoku Tamekane 1254-1332. . . . . . . .DLB-203

L

L. E. L. (see Landon, Letitia Elizabeth)

Laberge, Albert 1871-1960. . . . . .DLB-68

Laberge, Marie 1950- DLB-60

Labiche, Eugène 1815-1888. . . . . .DLB-192

Labrunie, Gerard (see Nerval, Gerard de)

La Capria, Raffaele 1922- DLB-196

Lacombe, Patrice (see Trullier-Lacombe,
    Joseph Patrice)

Lacretelle, Jacques de 1888-1985 . . . . .DLB-65

Lacy, Sam 1903- DLB-171

Ladd, Joseph Brown 1764-1786 . . . . .DLB-37

La Farge, Oliver 1901-1963. . . . . .DLB-9

Lafferty, R. A. 1914- DLB-8

La Flesche, Francis 1857-1932 . . . . .DLB-175

Laforge, Jules 1860-1887 . . . . .DLB-217

Lagorio, Gina 1922- DLB-196

La Guma, Alex 1925-1985. . . . . .DLB-117

Lahaise, Guillaume (see Delahaye, Guy)

Lahontan, Louis-Armand de Lom d'Arce,
    Baron de 1666-1715?. DLB-99

Laing, Kojo 1946- DLB-157

Laird, Carobeth 1895- Y-82

Laird and Lee DLB-49

Lalić, Ivan V. 1931-1996. . . . . .DLB-181

Lalić, Mihailo 1914-1992. . . . . .DLB-181

Lalonde, Michèle 1937- DLB-60

Lamantia, Philip 1927- DLB-16

Lamartine, Alphonse de 1790-1869 . . . . . .DLB-217

Lamb, Charles 1775-1834 . . . . . . DLB-93, 107, 163

Lamb, Lady Caroline 1785-1828. . . . . . . .DLB-116

Lamb, Mary 1764-1874 . . . . .DLB-163

Lambert, Betty 1933-1983 . . . . .DLB-60

Lamming, George 1927- DLB-125

L'Amour, Louis 1908-1988 . . . . . . DLB-206; Y-80

Lampman, Archibald 1861-1899. . . . . . . .DLB-92

Lamson, Wolffe and Company DLB-49

Lancer Books. DLB-46

Landesman, Jay 1919- and
    Landesman, Fran 1927- DLB-16

Landolfi, Tommaso 1908-1979 . . . . .DLB-177

Landon, Letitia Elizabeth 1802-1838. . . . .DLB-96

Landor, Walter Savage 1775-1864. . . .DLB-93, 107

Landry, Napoléon-P. 1884-1956. . . . . . . .DLB-92

Lane, Charles 1800-1870 . . . . .DLB-1

Lane, Laurence W. 1890-1967. . . . . .DLB-91

Lane, M. Travis 1934- DLB-60

Lane, Patrick 1939- DLB-53

Lane, Pinkie Gordon 1923- DLB-41

Lane, John, Company DLB-49

Laney, Al 1896-1988 . . . . DLB-4, 171

Lang, Andrew 1844-1912 . . . . . . DLB-98, 141, 184

Langevin, André 1927- DLB-60

Langgässer, Elisabeth 1899-1950. . . . . . . .DLB-69

Langhorne, John 1735-1779 . . . . .DLB-109

Langland, William
    circa 1330-circa 1400. . . . . .DLB-146

Langton, Anna 1804-1893. . . . . .DLB-99

Lanham, Edwin 1904-1979. . . . . .DLB-4

Lanier, Sidney 1842-1881 . . . . . . .DLB-64; DS-13

Lanyer, Aemilia 1569-1645 . . . . .DLB-121

Lapointe, Gatien 1931-1983. . . . . .DLB-88

Lapointe, Paul-Marie 1929- DLB-88

Lardner, John 1912-1960. . . . . .DLB-171

Lardner, Ring
    1885-1933 . . . . . . DLB-11, 25, 86, 171; DS-16

Lardner, Ring, Jr. 1915- DLB-26

Lardner 100: Ring Lardner
    Centennial Symposium. Y-85

Larkin, Philip 1922-1985. . . . . .DLB-27

La Roche, Sophie von 1730-1807. . . . . . . .DLB-94

La Rocque, Gilbert 1943-1984. . . . . .DLB-60

Larcom, Lucy 1824-1893. . . . . .DLB-221

Laroque de Roquebrune, Robert (see Roquebrune,
    Robert de)

Larrick, Nancy 1910- DLB-61

Larsen, Nella 1893-1964 . . . . .DLB-51

La Sale, Antoine de
    circa 1386-1460/1467 . . . . .DLB-208

Lasker-Schüler, Else 1869-1945. . . . . .DLB-66, 124

Lasnier, Rina 1915- DLB-88

Lassalle, Ferdinand 1825-1864. . . . . .DLB-129

Latham, Robert 1912-1995. . . . . .DLB-201

Lathrop, Dorothy P. 1891-1980 . . . . .DLB-22

Lathrop, George Parsons 1851-1898. . . . . .DLB-71

Lathrop, John, Jr. 1772-1820 . . . . .DLB-37

Latimer, Hugh 1492?-1555 . . . . .DLB-136

Latimore, Jewel Christine McLawler (see Amini,
    Johari M.)

Latymer, William 1498-1583. . . . . .DLB-132

Laube, Heinrich 1806-1884. . . . . .DLB-133

Laud, William 1573-1645 . . . . .DLB-213

Laughlin, James 1914-1997 . . . . .DLB-48

Laumer, Keith 1925- DLB-8

Lauremberg, Johann 1590-1658 . . . . .DLB-164

Laurence, Margaret 1926-1987 . . . . .DLB-53

Laurentius von Schnüffis 1633-1702 . . . . .DLB-168

Laurents, Arthur 1918- DLB-26

Laurie, Annie (see Black, Winifred)

Laut, Agnes Christiana 1871-1936. . . . . . .DLB-92

Lauterbach, Ann 1942- DLB-193

Lautreamont, Isidore Lucien Ducasse, Comte de
    1846-1870 . . . . .DLB-217

Lavater, Johann Kaspar 1741-1801 . . . . . .DLB-97

Lavin, Mary 1912-1996. . . . . .DLB-15

Law, John (see Harkness, Margaret)

Lawes, Henry 1596-1662. . . . . .DLB-126

Lawless, Anthony (see MacDonald, Philip)

Lawrence, D. H.
    1885-1930 . . . . . DLB-10, 19, 36, 98, 162, 195

Lawrence, David 1888-1973 . . . . .DLB-29

Lawrence, Seymour 1926-1994. . . . . Y-94

Lawrence, T. E. 1888-1935 . . . . .DLB-195

Lawson, George 1598-1678 . . . . .DLB-213

Lawson, John ?-1711 . . . . .DLB-24

Lawson, Robert 1892-1957 . . . . .DLB-22

Lawson, Victor F. 1850-1925. . . . . .DLB-25

Layard, Sir Austen Henry
    1817-1894 . . . . .DLB-166

Layton, Irving 1912- DLB-88

LaZamon flourished circa 1200. . . . . . . .DLB-146

Lazarević, Laza K. 1851-1890 . . . . .DLB-147

Lazarus, George 1904-1997 . . . . DLB-201

Lazhechnikov, Ivan Ivanovich
1792-1869 . . . . DLB-198

Lea, Henry Charles 1825-1909 . . . . DLB-47

Lea, Sydney 1942- DLB-120

Lea, Tom 1907- DLB-6

Leacock, John 1729-1802 . . . . DLB-31

Leacock, Stephen 1869-1944 . . . . DLB-92

Lead, Jane Ward 1623-1704 . . . . DLB-131

Leadenhall Press DLB-106

Leapor, Mary 1722-1746 . . . . DLB-109

Lear, Edward 1812-1888 . . . . . . DLB-32, 163, 166

Leary, Timothy 1920-1996 . . . . DLB-16

Leary, W. A., and Company DLB-49

Léautaud, Paul 1872-1956 . . . . DLB-65

Leavitt, David 1961- DLB-130

Leavitt and Allen DLB-49

Le Blond, Mrs. Aubrey 1861-1934 . . . . . . .DLB-174

le Carré, John 1931- DLB-87

Lécavelé, Roland (see Dorgeles, Roland)

Lechlitner, Ruth 1901- DLB-48

Leclerc, Félix 1914- DLB-60

Le Clézio, J. M. G. 1940- DLB-83

Lectures on Rhetoric and Belles Lettres (1783),
by Hugh Blair [excerpts] DLB-31

Leder, Rudolf (see Hermlin, Stephan)

Lederer, Charles 1910-1976 . . . . DLB-26

Ledwidge, Francis 1887-1917 . . . . DLB-20

Lee, Dennis 1939- DLB-53

Lee, Don L. (see Madhubuti, Haki R.)

Lee, George W. 1894-1976 . . . . DLB-51

Lee, Harper 1926- DLB-6

Lee, Harriet (1757-1851) and
Lee, Sophia (1750-1824) DLB-39

Lee, Laurie 1914-1997 . . . . DLB-27

Lee, Li-Young 1957- DLB-165

Lee, Manfred B. (see Dannay, Frederic, and
Manfred B. Lee)

Lee, Nathaniel circa 1645 - 1692 . . . . DLB-80

Lee, Sir Sidney 1859-1926 . . . . DLB-149, 184

Lee, Sir Sidney, "Principles of Biography," in
Elizabethan and Other Essays DLB-149

Lee, Vernon
1856-1935 . . . . DLB-57, 153, 156, 174, 178

Lee and Shepard DLB-49

Le Fanu, Joseph Sheridan
1814-1873 . . . . DLB-21, 70, 159, 178

Leffland, Ella 1931- Y-84

le Fort, Gertrud von 1876-1971 . . . . DLB-66

Le Gallienne, Richard 1866-1947 . . . . DLB-4

Legaré, Hugh Swinton 1797-1843 . . . DLB-3, 59, 73

Legaré, James M. 1823-1859 . . . . DLB-3

The Legends of the Saints and a Medieval
Christian Worldview DLB-148

Léger, Antoine-J. 1880-1950 . . . . DLB-88

Le Guin, Ursula K. 1929- DLB-8, 52

Lehman, Ernest 1920- DLB-44

Lehmann, John 1907- DLB-27, 100

Lehmann, Rosamond 1901-1990 . . . . DLB-15

Lehmann, Wilhelm 1882-1968 . . . . DLB-56

Lehmann, John, Limited DLB-112

Leiber, Fritz 1910-1992 . . . . DLB-8

Leibniz, Gottfried Wilhelm 1646-1716 . . . DLB-168

Leicester University Press DLB-112

Leigh, W. R. 1866-1955 . . . . DLB-188

Leinster, Murray 1896-1975 . . . . DLB-8

Leisewitz, Johann Anton 1752-1806 . . . . . . DLB-94

Leitch, Maurice 1933- DLB-14

Leithauser, Brad 1943- DLB-120

Leland, Charles G. 1824-1903 . . . . DLB-11

Leland, John 1503?-1552 . . . . DLB-136

Lemay, Pamphile 1837-1918 . . . . DLB-99

Lemelin, Roger 1919- DLB-88

Lemercier, Louis-Jean-Népomucène
1771-1840 . . . . DLB-192

Lemon, Mark 1809-1870 . . . . DLB-163

Le Moine, James MacPherson
1825-1912 . . . . DLB-99

Le Moyne, Jean 1913- DLB-88

Lemperly, Paul 1858-1939 . . . . DLB-187

L'Engle, Madeleine 1918- DLB-52

Lennart, Isobel 1915-1971 . . . . DLB-44

Lennox, Charlotte
1729 or 1730-1804 . . . . DLB-39

Lenox, James 1800-1880 . . . . DLB-140

Lenski, Lois 1893-1974 . . . . DLB-22

Lenz, Hermann 1913-1998 . . . . DLB-69

Lenz, J. M. R. 1751-1792 . . . . DLB-94

Lenz, Siegfried 1926- DLB-75

Leonard, Elmore 1925- DLB-173

Leonard, Hugh 1926- DLB-13

Leonard, William Ellery 1876-1944 . . . . . . DLB-54

Leonowens, Anna 1834-1914 . . . . . . DLB-99, 166

LePan, Douglas 1914- DLB-88

Leprohon, Rosanna Eleanor 1829-1879 . . . DLB-99

Le Queux, William 1864-1927 . . . . DLB-70

Lermontov, Mikhail Iur'evich
1814-1841 . . . . DLB-205

Lerner, Max 1902-1992 . . . . DLB-29

Lernet-Holenia, Alexander 1897-1976 . . . . . DLB-85

Le Rossignol, James 1866-1969 . . . . DLB-92

Lescarbot, Marc circa 1570-1642 . . . . DLB-99

LeSeur, William Dawson 1840-1917 . . . . . DLB-92

LeSieg, Theo. (see Geisel, Theodor Seuss)

Leslie, Doris before 1902-1982 . . . . DLB-191

Leslie, Eliza 1787-1858 . . . . DLB-202

Leslie, Frank 1821-1880 . . . . DLB-43, 79

Leslie, Frank, Publishing House DLB-49

Leśmian, Bolesław 1878-1937 . . . . DLB-215

Lesperance, John 1835?-1891 . . . . DLB-99

Lessing, Bruno 1870-1940 . . . . DLB-28

Lessing, Doris 1919- DLB-15, 139; Y-85

Lessing, Gotthold Ephraim
1729-1781 . . . . DLB-97

Lettau, Reinhard 1929- DLB-75

Letter from Japan Y-94, Y-98

Letter from London Y-96

Letter to [Samuel] Richardson on *Clarissa*
(1748), by Henry Fielding DLB-39

A Letter to the Editor of *The Irish Times* Y-97

Lever, Charles 1806-1872 . . . . DLB-21

Leverson, Ada 1862-1933 . . . . DLB-153

Levertov, Denise 1923-1997 . . . . DLB-5, 165

Levi, Peter 1931- DLB-40

Levi, Primo 1919-1987 . . . . .DLB-177

Levien, Sonya 1888-1960 . . . . DLB-44

Levin, Meyer 1905-1981 . . . . . . .DLB-9, 28; Y-81

Levine, Norman 1923- DLB-88

Levine, Philip 1928- DLB-5

Levis, Larry 1946- DLB-120

Levy, Amy 1861-1889 . . . . DLB-156

Levy, Benn Wolfe 1900-1973 . . . . . . .DLB-13; Y-81

Lewald, Fanny 1811-1889 . . . . DLB-129

Lewes, George Henry 1817-1878 . . . . DLB-55, 144

Lewis, Agnes Smith 1843-1926 . . . . .DLB-174

Lewis, Alfred H. 1857-1914 . . . . DLB-25, 186

Lewis, Alun 1915-1944 . . . . DLB-20, 162

The Lewis Carroll Centenary Y-98

Lewis, C. Day (see Day Lewis, C.)

Lewis, C. S. 1898-1963 . . . . .DLB-15, 100, 160

Lewis, Charles B. 1842-1924 . . . . DLB-11

Lewis, Henry Clay 1825-1850 . . . . DLB-3

Lewis, Janet 1899-1998 . . . . .Y-87

Lewis, Matthew Gregory
1775-1818 . . . . .DLB-39, 158, 178

Lewis, Meriwether 1774-1809 and
Clark, William 1770-1838 . . . . . DLB-183, 186

Lewis, Norman 1908- DLB-204

Lewis, R. W. B. 1917- DLB-111

Lewis, Richard circa 1700-1734 . . . . DLB-24

Lewis, Sinclair 1885-1951 . . . . . . DLB-9, 102; DS-1

Lewis, Wilmarth Sheldon 1895-1979 . . . . DLB-140

Lewis, Wyndham 1882-1957 . . . . DLB-15

Lewisohn, Ludwig 1882-1955 . . DLB-4, 9, 28, 102

Leyendecker, J. C. 1874-1951 . . . . DLB-188

Lezama Lima, José 1910-1976 . . . . DLB-113

The Library of America DLB-46

Libbey, Laura Jean 1862-1924 . . . . DLB-221

The Licensing Act of 1737 . . . . DLB-84

Lichfield, Leonard I [publishing house] . . .DLB-170

Lichtenberg, Georg Christoph
1742-1799 . . . . DLB-94

The Liddle Collection Y-97

Lieb, Fred 1888-1980 . . . . .DLB-171

Liebling, A. J. 1904-1963 . . . . .DLB-4, 171

Lieutenant Murray (see Ballou, Maturin Murray)

The Life of James Dickey: A Lecture to the Friends
of the Emory Libraries, by Henry Hart . . . Y-98

Lighthall, William Douw 1857-1954 . . . . . .DLB-92

Lilar, Françoise (see Mallet-Joris, Françoise)

Lili'uokalani, Queen 1838-1917 . . . . .DLB-221

Lillo, George 1691-1739 . . . . .DLB-84

Lilly, J. K., Jr. 1893-1966 . . . . .DLB-140

Lilly, Wait and Company DLB-49

Lily, William circa 1468-1522 . . . . .DLB-132

Limited Editions Club DLB-46

Limón, Graciela 1938- DLB-209

Lincoln and Edmands DLB-49

Lindesay, Ethel Forence (see Richardson, Henry Handel)

Lindsay, Alexander William, Twenty-fifth Earl of Crawford 1812-1880 . . . . .DLB-184

Lindsay, Sir David circa 1485-1555 . . . . .DLB-132

Lindsay, Jack 1900- Y-84

Lindsay, Lady (Caroline Blanche Elizabeth Fitzroy Lindsay) 1844-1912 . . . . .DLB-199

Lindsay, Vachel 1879-1931 . . . . .DLB-54

Linebarger, Paul Myron Anthony (see Smith, Cordwainer)

Link, Arthur S. 1920-1998 . . . . .DLB-17

Linn, John Blair 1777-1804 . . . . .DLB-37

Lins, Osman 1¹24-1978 . . . . .DLB-145

Linton, Eliza Lynn 1822-1898 . . . . .DLB-18

Linton, William James 1812-1897 . . . . . . .DLB-32

Lintot, Barnaby Bernard [publishing house] DLB-170

Lion Books. DLB-46

Lionni, Leo 1910- DLB-61

Lippard, George 1822-1854 . . . . .DLB-202

Lippincott, Sara Jane Clarke 1823-1904 . . . . .DLB-43

Lippincott, J. B., Company DLB-49

Lippmann, Walter 1889-1974 . . . . .DLB-29

Lipton, Lawrence 1898-1975 . . . . .DLB-16

Liscow, Christian Ludwig 1701-1760 . . . . .DLB-97

Lish, Gordon 1934- DLB-130

Lisle, Charles-Marie-René Leconte de 1818-1894 . . . . .DLB-217

Lispector, Clarice 1925-1977 . . . . .DLB-113

The Literary Chronicle and Weekly Review 1819-1828 . . . . .DLB-110

Literary Documents: William Faulkner and the People-to-People Program Y-86

Literary Documents II: *Library Journal* Statements and Questionnaires from First Novelists Y-87

Literary Effects of World War II [British novel] DLB-15

Literary Prizes [British] DLB-15

Literary Research Archives: The Humanities Research Center, University of Texas. Y-82

Literary Research Archives II: Berg Collection of English and American Literature of the New York Public Library Y-83

Literary Research Archives III: The Lilly Library Y-84

Literary Research Archives IV: The John Carter Brown Library Y-85

Literary Research Archives V: Kent State Special Collections Y-86

Literary Research Archives VI: The Modern Literary Manuscripts Collection in the Special Collections of the Washington University Libraries Y-87

Literary Research Archives VII: The University of Virginia Libraries Y-91

Literary Research Archives VIII: The Henry E. Huntington Library Y-92

Literary Societies Y-98

"Literary Style" (1857), by William Forsyth [excerpt] DLB-57

Literatura Chicanesca: The View From Without. DLB-82

Literature at Nurse, or Circulating Morals (1885), by George Moore DLB-18

Littell, Eliakim 1797-1870 . . . . .DLB-79

Littell, Robert S. 1831-1896 . . . . .DLB-79

Little, Brown and Company DLB-49

Little Magazines and Newspapers DS-15

The Little Review 1914-1929 . . . . DS-15

Littlewood, Joan 1914- DLB-13

Lively, Penelope 1933- DLB-14, 161, 207

Liverpool University Press DLB-112

The Lives of the Poets. DLB-142

Livesay, Dorothy 1909- DLB-68

Livesay, Florence Randal 1874-1953 . . . . . .DLB-92

"Living in Ruin," by Gerald Stern DLB-105

Livings, Henry 1929-1998 . . . . .DLB-13

Livingston, Anne Howe 1763-1841 . . . DLB-37, 200

Livingston, Myra Cohn 1926-1996 . . . . . . .DLB-61

Livingston, William 1723-1790 . . . . .DLB-31

Livingstone, David 1813-1873 . . . . .DLB-166

Livy 59 B.C.-A.D. 17 . . . . .DLB-211

Liyong, Taban lo (see Taban lo Liyong)

Lizárraga, Sylvia S. 1925- DLB-82

Llewellyn, Richard 1906-1983 . . . . .DLB-15

Lloyd, Edward [publishing house] DLB-106

Lobel, Arnold 1933- DLB-61

Lochridge, Betsy Hopkins (see Fancher, Betsy)

Locke, David Ross 1833-1888 . . . . . . .DLB-11, 23

Locke, John 1632-1704. . . . . DLB-31, 101, 213

Locke, Richard Adams 1800-1871 . . . . . . .DLB-43

Locker-Lampson, Frederick 1821-1895 . . . . .DLB-35, 184

Lockhart, John Gibson 1794-1854 . . . . .DLB-110, 116 144

Lockridge, Ross, Jr. 1914-1948 . . . . DLB-143; Y-80

Locrine and Selimus. DLB-62

Lodge, David 1935- DLB-14, 194

Lodge, George Cabot 1873-1909 . . . . .DLB-54

Lodge, Henry Cabot 1850-1924 . . . . .DLB-47

Lodge, Thomas 1558-1625 . . . . .DLB-172

Loeb, Harold 1891-1974 . . . . .DLB-4

Loeb, William 1905-1981 . . . . .DLB-127

Lofting, Hugh 1886-1947. . . . . .DLB-160

Logan, Deborah Norris 1761-1839 . . . . . .DLB-200

Logan, James 1674-1751. . . . . .DLB-24, 140

Logan, John 1923- DLB-5

Logan, Martha Daniell 1704?-1779 . . . . . .DLB-200

Logan, William 1950- DLB-120

Logau, Friedrich von 1605-1655 . . . . .DLB-164

Logue, Christopher 1926- DLB-27

Lohenstein, Daniel Casper von 1635-1683 . . . . .DLB-168

Lomonosov, Mikhail Vasil'evich 1711-1765 . . . . .DLB-150

London, Jack 1876-1916 . . . . . . DLB-8, 12, 78, 212

The London Magazine 1820-1829 . . . . .DLB-110

Long, Haniel 1888-1956 . . . . .DLB-45

Long, Ray 1878-1935. . . . . .DLB-137

Long, H., and Brother DLB-49

Longfellow, Henry Wadsworth 1807-1882 . . . . .DLB-1, 59

Longfellow, Samuel 1819-1892 . . . . .DLB-1

Longford, Elizabeth 1906- DLB-155

Longinus circa first century DLB-176

Longley, Michael 1939- DLB-40

Longman, T. [publishing house] DLB-154

Longmans, Green and Company DLB-49

Longmore, George 1793?-1867 . . . . .DLB-99

Longstreet, Augustus Baldwin 1790-1870 . . . . DLB-3, 11, 74

Longworth, D. [publishing house] DLB-49

Lonsdale, Frederick 1881-1954 . . . . .DLB-10

A Look at the Contemporary Black Theatre Movement. DLB-38

Loos, Anita 1893-1981. . . . . DLB-11, 26; Y-81

Lopate, Phillip 1943- Y-80

López, Diana (see Isabella, Ríos)

López, Josefina 1969- DLB-209

Loranger, Jean-Aubert 1896-1942 . . . . . . .DLB-92

Lorca, Federico García 1898-1936 . . . . . . .DLB-108

Lord, John Keast 1818-1872 . . . . .DLB-99

The Lord Chamberlain's Office and Stage Censorship in England DLB-10

Lorde, Audre 1934-1992 . . . . .DLB-41

Lorimer, George Horace 1867-1939 . . . . . .DLB-91

Loring, A. K. [publishing house] DLB-49

Loring and Mussey DLB-46

Lorris, Guillaume de (see *Roman de la Rose*)

Lossing, Benson J. 1813-1891 . . . . .DLB-30

Lothar, Ernst 1890-1974 . . . . .DLB-81

Lothrop, Harriet M. 1844-1924 . . . . .DLB-42

Lothrop, D., and Company DLB-49

Loti, Pierre 1850-1923 . . . . .DLB-123

Lotichius Secundus, Petrus 1528-1560 . . . DLB-179

Lott, Emeline ?-? DLB-166

The Lounger, no. 20 (1785), by Henry
  Mackenzie DLB-39

Louisiana State University Press Y-97

Lounsbury, Thomas R. 1838-1915. . . . . . DLB-71

Louÿs, Pierre 1870-1925 . . . . DLB-123

Lovelace, Earl 1935- DLB-125

Lovelace, Richard 1618-1657 . . . . DLB-131

Lovell, Coryell and Company DLB-49

Lovell, John W., Company DLB-49

Lover, Samuel 1797-1868 . . . . DLB-159, 190

Lovesey, Peter 1936- DLB-87

Lovinescu, Eugen 1881-1943 . . . . DLB-220

Lovingood, Sut (see Harris, George Washington)

Low, Samuel 1765-? DLB-37

Lowell, Amy 1874-1925 . . . . DLB-54, 140

Lowell, James Russell
  1819-1891. . . . . .DLB-1, 11, 64, 79, 189

Lowell, Robert 1917-1977 . . . . DLB-5, 169

Lowenfels, Walter 1897-1976 . . . . DLB-4

Lowndes, Marie Belloc 1868-1947 . . . . . . DLB-70

Lowndes, William Thomas 1798-1843 . . . DLB-184

Lownes, Humphrey [publishing house] . . .DLB-170

Lowry, Lois 1937- DLB-52

Lowry, Malcolm 1909-1957 . . . . DLB-15

Lowther, Pat 1935-1975 . . . . DLB-53

Loy, Mina 1882-1966 . . . . DLB-4, 54

Lozeau, Albert 1878-1924 . . . . DLB-92

Lubbock, Percy 1879-1965 . . . . DLB-149

Lucan A.D. 39-A.D. 65. . . . . DLB-211

Lucas, E. V. 1868-1938 . . . . DLB-98, 149, 153

Lucas, Fielding, Jr. [publishing house] DLB-49

Luce, Henry R. 1898-1967 . . . . DLB-91

Luce, John W., and Company DLB-46

Lucian circa 120-180. . . . . .DLB-176

Lucie-Smith, Edward 1933- DLB-40

Lucilius circa 180 B.C.-102/101 B.C. DLB-211

Lucini, Gian Pietro 1867-1914 . . . . DLB-114

Lucretius circa 94 B.C.-circa 49 B.C. DLB-211

Luder, Peter circa 1415-1472 . . . . .DLB-179

Ludlum, Robert 1927- Y-82

Ludus de Antichristo circa 1160 . . . . DLB-148

Ludvigson, Susan 1942- DLB-120

Ludwig, Jack 1922- DLB-60

Ludwig, Otto 1813-1865. . . . . DLB-129

Ludwigslied 881 or 882. . . . . DLB-148

Luera, Yolanda 1953- DLB-122

Luft, Lya 1938- DLB-145

Lugansky, Kazak Vladimir (see
  Dal', Vladimir Ivanovich)

Lukács, György 1885-1971 . . . . DLB-215

Luke, Peter 1919- DLB-13

Lummis, Charles F. 1859-1928 . . . . DLB-186

Lupton, F. M., Company DLB-49

Lupus of Ferrières circa 805-circa 862 . . . DLB-148

Lurie, Alison 1926- DLB-2

Luther, Martin 1483-1546 . . . . .DLB-179

Luzi, Mario 1914- DLB-128

L'vov, Nikolai Aleksandrovich
  1751-1803. DLB-150

Lyall, Gavin 1932- DLB-87

Lydgate, John circa 1370-1450 . . . . DLB-146

Lyly, John circa 1554-1606. . . . . DLB-62, 167

Lynch, Patricia 1898-1972 . . . . DLB-160

Lynch, Richard flourished 1596-1601 . . . .DLB-172

Lynd, Robert 1879-1949. . . . . DLB-98

Lyon, Matthew 1749-1822 . . . . DLB-43

Lysias circa 459 B.C.-circa 380 B.C. DLB-176

Lytle, Andrew 1902-1995. . . . . .DLB-6; Y-95

Lytton, Edward (see Bulwer-Lytton, Edward)

Lytton, Edward Robert Bulwer
  1831-1891 . . . . DLB-32

M

Maass, Joachim 1901-1972 . . . . DLB-69

Mabie, Hamilton Wright 1845-1916 . . . . . DLB-71

Mac A'Ghobhainn, Iain (see Smith, Iain Crichton)

MacArthur, Charles 1895-1956 . . . . .DLB-7, 25, 44

Macaulay, Catherine 1731-1791 . . . . DLB-104

Macaulay, David 1945- DLB-61

Macaulay, Rose 1881-1958. . . . . DLB-36

Macaulay, Thomas Babington
  1800-1859 . . . . DLB-32, 55

Macaulay Company DLB-46

MacBeth, George 1932- DLB-40

Macbeth, Madge 1880-1965 . . . . DLB-92

MacCaig, Norman 1910-1996 . . . . DLB-27

MacDiarmid, Hugh 1892-1978 . . . . DLB-20

MacDonald, Cynthia 1928- DLB-105

MacDonald, George
  1824-1905 . . . . .DLB-18, 163, 178

MacDonald, John D.
  1916-1986 . . . . .DLB-8; Y-86

MacDonald, Philip 1899?-1980 . . . . DLB-77

Macdonald, Ross (see Millar, Kenneth)

MacDonald, Wilson 1880-1967 . . . . DLB-92

Macdonald and Company (Publishers) . . DLB-112

MacEwen, Gwendolyn 1941- DLB-53

Macfadden, Bernarr 1868-1955 . . . . . . DLB-25, 91

MacGregor, John 1825-1892 . . . . DLB-166

MacGregor, Mary Esther (see Keith, Marian)

Machado, Antonio 1875-1939. . . . . DLB-108

Machado, Manuel 1874-1947 . . . . DLB-108

Machar, Agnes Maule 1837-1927 . . . . DLB-92

Machaut, Guillaume de
  circa 1300-1377 . . . . DLB-208

Machen, Arthur Llewelyn Jones
  1863-1947. . . . . .DLB-36, 156, 178

MacInnes, Colin 1914-1976 . . . . DLB-14

MacInnes, Helen 1907-1985 . . . . DLB-87

Mačiulis, Jonas (see Maironis, Jonas)

Mack, Maynard 1909- DLB-111

Mackall, Leonard L. 1879-1937 . . . . DLB-140

MacKaye, Percy 1875-1956 . . . . DLB-54

Macken, Walter 1915-1967 . . . . DLB-13

Mackenzie, Alexander 1763-1820 . . . . DLB-99

Mackenzie, Alexander Slidell
  1803-1848 . . . . DLB-183

Mackenzie, Compton 1883-1972 . . . . .DLB-34, 100

Mackenzie, Henry 1745-1831 . . . . DLB-39

Mackenzie, William 1758-1828. . . . . .DLB-187

Mackey, Nathaniel 1947- DLB-169

Mackey, William Wellington 1937- DLB-38

Mackintosh, Elizabeth (see Tey, Josephine)

Mackintosh, Sir James 1765-1832. . . . . . . DLB-158

Maclaren, Ian (see Watson, John)

Macklin, Charles 1699-1797 . . . . DLB-89

MacLean, Katherine Anne 1925- DLB-8

Maclean, Norman 1902-1990. . . . . DLB-206

MacLeish, Archibald
  1892-1982 . . . . .DLB-4, 7, 45; Y-82

MacLennan, Hugh 1907-1990 . . . . DLB-68

Macleod, Fiona (see Sharp, William)

MacLeod, Alistair 1936- DLB-60

Macleod, Norman 1906-1985. . . . . DLB-4

Mac Low, Jackson 1922- DLB-193

Macmillan and Company. DLB-106

The Macmillan Company DLB-49

Macmillan's English Men of Letters,
  First Series (1878-1892) DLB-144

MacNamara, Brinsley 1890-1963 . . . . DLB-10

MacNeice, Louis 1907-1963 . . . . DLB-10, 20

MacPhail, Andrew 1864-1938 . . . . DLB-92

Macpherson, James 1736-1796 . . . . DLB-109

Macpherson, Jay 1931- DLB-53

Macpherson, Jeanie 1884-1946. . . . . DLB-44

Macrae Smith Company. DLB-46

Macrone, John [publishing house] DLB-106

MacShane, Frank 1927- DLB-111

Macy-Masius DLB-46

Madden, David 1933- DLB-6

Madden, Sir Frederic 1801-1873. . . . . . . DLB-184

Maddow, Ben 1909-1992 . . . . DLB-44

Maddux, Rachel 1912-1983 . . . . .Y-93

Madgett, Naomi Long 1923- DLB-76

Madhubuti, Haki R. 1942- DLB-5, 41; DS-8

Madison, James 1751-1836 . . . . DLB-37

Madsen, Svend Åge 1939- DLB-214

Maeterlinck, Maurice 1862-1949 . . . . DLB-192

Magee, David 1905-1977 . . . . .DLB-187

Maginn, William 1794-1842 . . . . .DLB-110, 159

Mahan, Alfred Thayer 1840-1914 . . . . . . DLB-47

Maheux-Forcier, Louise 1929- DLB-60

Mafūz, Najīb 1911- Y-88

Mahin, John Lee 1902-1984 . . . . DLB-44

Mahon, Derek 1941- DLB-40

Maikov, Vasilii Ivanovich
 1728-1778. . . . . .DLB-150

Mailer, Norman 1923-
 . . . . DLB-2, 16, 28, 185; Y-80, Y-83; DS-3

Maillart, Ella 1903-1997. . . . . .DLB-195

Maillet, Adrienne 1885-1963 . . . . .DLB-68

Maillet, Antonine 1929- DLB-60

Maillu, David G. 1939- DLB-157

Maimonides, Moses 1138-1204 . . . . .DLB-115

Main Selections of the Book-of-the-Month
 Club, 1926-1945 . . . . .DLB-9

Main Trends in Twentieth-Century Book
 Clubs. DLB-46

Mainwaring, Daniel 1902-1977 . . . . .DLB-44

Mair, Charles 1838-1927 . . . . .DLB-99

Maironis, Jonas 1862-1932 . . . . .DLB-220

Mais, Roger 1905-1955 . . . . .DLB-125

Major, Andre 1942- DLB-60

Major, Charles 1856-1913 . . . . .DLB-202

Major, Clarence 1936- DLB-33

Major, Kevin 1949- DLB-60

Major Books DLB-46

Makemie, Francis circa 1658-1708 . . . . . . .DLB-24

The Making of Americans Contract Y-98

The Making of a People, by
 J. M. Ritchie DLB-66

Maksimović, Desanka 1898-1993 . . . . . . .DLB-147

Malamud, Bernard
 1914-1986 . . . . DLB-2, 28, 152; Y-80, Y-86

Malerba, Luigi 1927- DLB-196

Malet, Lucas 1852-1931. . . . . .DLB-153

Mallarmé, Stéphane 1842-1898 . . . . .DLB-217

Malleson, Lucy Beatrice (see Gilbert, Anthony)

Mallet-Joris, Françoise 1930- DLB-83

Mallock, W. H. 1849-1923 . . . . DLB-18, 57

Malone, Dumas 1892-1986 . . . . .DLB-17

Malone, Edmond 1741-1812 . . . . .DLB-142

Malory, Sir Thomas
 circa 1400-1410 - 1471. . . . . .DLB-146

Malraux, André 1901-1976 . . . . .DLB-72

Malthus, Thomas Robert
 1766-1834 . . . . DLB-107, 158

Maltz, Albert 1908-1985 . . . . .DLB-102

Malzberg, Barry N. 1939- DLB-8

Mamet, David 1947- DLB-7

Manaka, Matsemela 1956- DLB-157

Manchester University Press DLB-112

Mandel, Eli 1922- DLB-53

Mandeville, Bernard 1670-1733 . . . . .DLB-101

Mandeville, Sir John
 mid fourteenth century DLB-146

Mandiargues, André Pieyre de 1909- DLB-83

Manfred, Frederick 1912-1994. . . . . . .DLB-6, 212

Manfredi, Gianfranco 1948- DLB-196

Mangan, Sherry 1904-1961 . . . . .DLB-4

Manganelli, Giorgio 1922-1990 . . . . .DLB-196

Manilius fl. first century A.D. DLB-211

Mankiewicz, Herman 1897-1953 . . . . .DLB-26

Mankiewicz, Joseph L. 1909-1993 . . . . . . .DLB-44

Mankowitz, Wolf 1924-1998 . . . . .DLB-15

Manley, Delarivière 1672?-1724. . . . . . .DLB-39, 80

Mann, Abby 1927- DLB-44

Mann, Charles 1929-1998 . . . . Y-98

Mann, Heinrich 1871-1950 . . . . .DLB-66, 118

Mann, Horace 1796-1859 . . . . .DLB-1

Mann, Klaus 1906-1949. . . . . .DLB-56

Mann, Thomas 1875-1955. . . . . .DLB-66

Mann, William D'Alton 1839-1920 . . . . . .DLB-137

Mannin, Ethel 1900-1984 . . . . .DLB-191, 195

Manning, Marie 1873?-1945 . . . . .DLB-29

Manning and Loring DLB-49

Mannyng, Robert
 flourished 1303-1338. . . . . .DLB-146

Mano, D. Keith 1942- DLB-6

Manor Books. DLB-46

Mansfield, Katherine 1888-1923 . . . . . . .DLB-162

Manuel, Niklaus circa 1484-1530 . . . . . . .DLB-179

Manzini, Gianna 1896-1974. . . . . .DLB-177

Mapanje, Jack 1944- DLB-157

Maraini, Dacia 1936- DLB-196

March, William 1893-1954 . . . . .DLB-9, 86

Marchand, Leslie A. 1900- DLB-103

Marchant, Bessie 1862-1941 . . . . .DLB-160

Marchessault, Jovette 1938- DLB-60

Marcus, Frank 1928- DLB-13

Marden, Orison Swett 1850-1924 . . . . . . .DLB-137

Marechera, Dambudzo 1952-1987 . . . . . . .DLB-157

Marek, Richard, Books DLB-46

Mares, E. A. 1938- DLB-122

Mariani, Paul 1940- DLB-111

Marie de France flourished 1160-1178. . . .DLB-208

Marie-Victorin, Frère 1885-1944 . . . . .DLB-92

Marin, Biagio 1891-1985 . . . . .DLB-128

Marincovič, Ranko 1913- DLB-147

Marinetti, Filippo Tommaso
 1876-1944 . . . . .DLB-114

Marion, Frances 1886-1973 . . . . .DLB-44

Marius, Richard C. 1933- Y-85

The Mark Taper Forum DLB-7

Mark Twain on Perpetual Copyright Y-92

Markfield, Wallace 1926- DLB-2, 28

Markham, Edwin 1852-1940. . . . . . .DLB-54, 186

Markle, Fletcher 1921-1991 . . . . . . .DLB-68; Y-91

Marlatt, Daphne 1942- DLB-60

Marlitt, E. 1825-1887. . . . . .DLB-129

Marlowe, Christopher 1564-1593 . . . . .DLB-62

Marlyn, John 1912- DLB-88

Marmion, Shakerley 1603-1639. . . . . .DLB-58

Der Marner before 1230-circa 1287 . . . . . .DLB-138

Marnham, Patrick 1943- DLB-204

The *Marprelate Tracts* 1588-1589 . . . . .DLB-132

Marquand, John P. 1893-1960. . . . . . .DLB-9, 102

Marqués, René 1919-1979 . . . . .DLB-113

Marquis, Don 1878-1937 . . . . .DLB-11, 25

Marriott, Anne 1913- DLB-68

Marryat, Frederick 1792-1848 . . . . . . .DLB-21, 163

Marsh, George Perkins 1801-1882 . . . . .DLB-1, 64

Marsh, James 1794-1842 . . . . .DLB-1, 59

Marsh, Capen, Lyon and Webb DLB-49

Marsh, Narcissus 1638-1713 . . . . .DLB-213

Marsh, Ngaio 1899-1982 . . . . .DLB-77

Marshall, Edison 1894-1967 . . . . .DLB-102

Marshall, Edward 1932- DLB-16

Marshall, Emma 1828-1899. . . . . .DLB-163

Marshall, James 1942-1992 . . . . .DLB-61

Marshall, Joyce 1913- DLB-88

Marshall, Paule 1929- DLB-33, 157

Marshall, Tom 1938- DLB-60

Marsilius of Padua
 circa 1275-circa 1342. . . . . .DLB-115

Mars-Jones, Adam 1954- DLB-207

Marson, Una 1905-1965 . . . . .DLB-157

Marston, John 1576-1634. . . . . DLB-58, 172

Marston, Philip Bourke 1850-1887 . . . . . . .DLB-35

Martens, Kurt 1870-1945. . . . . .DLB-66

Martial circa A.D. 40-circa A.D. 103 . . . . .DLB-211

Martien, William S. [publishing house] DLB-49

Martin, Abe (see Hubbard, Kin)

Martin, Charles 1942- DLB-120

Martin, Claire 1914- DLB-60

Martin, Jay 1935- DLB-111

Martin, Johann (see Laurentius von Schnüffis)

Martin, Thomas 1696-1771 . . . . .DLB-213

Martin, Violet Florence (see Ross, Martin)

Martin du Gard, Roger 1881-1958 . . . . . . .DLB-65

Martineau, Harriet 1802-1876
 . . . . DLB-21, 55, 159, 163, 166, 190

Martínez, Demetria 1960- DLB-209

Martínez, Eliud 1935- DLB-122

Martínez, Max 1943- DLB-82

Martínez, Rubén 1962- DLB-209

Martyn, Edward 1859-1923 . . . . .DLB-10

Martone, Michael 1955- DLB-218

Marvell, Andrew 1621-1678 . . . . .DLB-131

Marvin X 1944- DLB-38

Marx, Karl 1818-1883 . . . . .DLB-129

Marzials, Theo 1850-1920. . . . . .DLB-35

Masefield, John
 1878-1967 . . . . DLB-10, 19, 153, 160

Mason, A. E. W. 1865-1948 . . . . .DLB-70

Mason, Bobbie Ann 1940- DLB-173; Y-87

Mason, William 1725-1797 . . . . .DLB-142

Mason Brothers. DLB-49

Massey, Gerald 1828-1907 . . . . .DLB-32

Massey, Linton R. 1900-1974 . . . . .DLB-187

Massinger, Philip 1583-1640 . . . . .DLB-58

Masson, David 1822-1907 . . . . .DLB-144

Masters, Edgar Lee 1868-1950 . . . . DLB-54

Mastronardi, Lucio 1930-1979 . . . . .DLB-177

Matevski, Mateja 1929- DLB-181

Mather, Cotton 1663-1728 . . . . . . DLB-24, 30, 140

Mather, Increase 1639-1723 . . . . DLB-24

Mather, Richard 1596-1669 . . . . DLB-24

Matheson, Richard 1926- DLB-8, 44

Matheus, John F. 1887- DLB-51

Matthew of Vendôme
    circa 1130-circa 1200 . . . . DLB-208

Mathews, Cornelius 1817?-1889 . . . . . . DLB-3, 64

Mathews, John Joseph 1894-1979 . . . . . . .DLB-175

Mathews, Elkin [publishing house] DLB-112

Mathias, Roland 1915- DLB-27

Mathis, June 1892-1927 . . . . DLB-44

Mathis, Sharon Bell 1937- DLB-33

Matković, Marijan 1915-1985 . . . . DLB-181

Matoš, Antun Gustav 1873-1914 . . . . DLB-147

Matsumoto Seichō 1909-1992 . . . . DLB-182

The Matter of England 1240-1400 . . . . . . DLB-146

The Matter of Rome early twelfth to late
    fifteenth century DLB-146

Matthews, Brander
    1852-1929 . . . . .DLB-71, 78; DS-13

Matthews, Jack 1925- DLB-6

Matthews, Victoria Earle 1861-1907 . . . . . DLB-221

Matthews, William 1942-1997 . . . . DLB-5

Matthiessen, F. O. 1902-1950 . . . . DLB-63

Maturin, Charles Robert 1780-1824 . . . . .DLB-178

Matthiessen, Peter 1927- DLB-6, 173

Maugham, W. Somerset
    1874-1965 . . . . . . DLB-10, 36, 77, 100, 162, 195

Maupassant, Guy de 1850-1893 . . . . DLB-123

Mauriac, Claude 1914-1996 . . . . DLB-83

Mauriac, François 1885-1970 . . . . DLB-65

Maurice, Frederick Denison
    1805-1872 . . . . DLB-55

Maurois, André 1885-1967 . . . . DLB-65

Maury, James 1718-1769 . . . . DLB-31

Mavor, Elizabeth 1927- DLB-14

Mavor, Osborne Henry (see Bridie, James)

Maxwell, Gavin 1914-1969 . . . . DLB-204

Maxwell, William 1908- DLB-218; Y-80

Maxwell, H. [publishing house] DLB-49

Maxwell, John [publishing house] DLB-106

May, Elaine 1932- DLB-44

May, Karl 1842-1912 . . . . DLB-129

May, Thomas 1595 or 1596-1650 . . . . DLB-58

Mayer, Bernadette 1945- DLB-165

Mayer, Mercer 1943- DLB-61

Mayer, O. B. 1818-1891 . . . . DLB-3

Mayes, Herbert R. 1900-1987 . . . . DLB-137

Mayes, Wendell 1919-1992 . . . . DLB-26

Mayfield, Julian 1928-1984 . . . . DLB-33; Y-84

Mayhew, Henry 1812-1887 . . . . DLB-18, 55, 190

Mayhew, Jonathan 1720-1766 . . . . DLB-31

Mayne, Ethel Colburn 1865-1941 . . . . . . DLB-197

Mayne, Jasper 1604-1672 . . . . DLB-126

Mayne, Seymour 1944- DLB-60

Mayor, Flora Macdonald 1872-1932 . . . . . DLB-36

Mayrocker, Friederike 1924- DLB-85

Mazrui, Ali A. 1933- DLB-125

Mažuranić, Ivan 1814-1890 . . . . DLB-147

Mazursky, Paul 1930- DLB-44

McAlmon, Robert
    1896-1956 . . . . DLB-4, 45; DS-15

McArthur, Peter 1866-1924 . . . . DLB-92

McBride, Robert M., and Company DLB-46

McCabe, Patrick 1955- DLB-194

McCaffrey, Anne 1926- DLB-8

McCarthy, Cormac 1933- DLB-6, 143

McCarthy, Mary 1912-1989 . . . . .DLB-2; Y-81

McCay, Winsor 1871-1934 . . . . DLB-22

McClane, Albert Jules 1922-1991 . . . . . . .DLB-171

McClatchy, C. K. 1858-1936 . . . . DLB-25

McClellan, George Marion 1860-1934 . . . . DLB-50

McCloskey, Robert 1914- DLB-22

McClung, Nellie Letitia 1873-1951 . . . . . . DLB-92

McClure, Joanna 1930- DLB-16

McClure, Michael 1932- DLB-16

McClure, Phillips and Company DLB-46

McClure, S. S. 1857-1949 . . . . DLB-91

McClurg, A. C., and Company DLB-49

McCluskey, John A., Jr. 1944- DLB-33

McCollum, Michael A. 1946 . . . . Y-87

McConnell, William C. 1917- DLB-88

McCord, David 1897-1997 . . . . DLB-61

McCorkle, Jill 1958- Y-87

McCorkle, Samuel Eusebius
    1746-1811 . . . . DLB-37

McCormick, Anne O'Hare 1880-1954 . . . . DLB-29

McCormick, Robert R. 1880-1955 . . . . . . DLB-29

McCourt, Edward 1907-1972 . . . . DLB-88

McCoy, Horace 1897-1955 . . . . DLB-9

McCrae, John 1872-1918 . . . . DLB-92

McCullagh, Joseph B. 1842-1896 . . . . DLB-23

McCullers, Carson 1917-1967 . . . . . .DLB-2, 7, 173

McCulloch, Thomas 1776-1843 . . . . DLB-99

McDonald, Forrest 1927- DLB-17

McDonald, Walter 1934- DLB-105, DS-9

McDougall, Colin 1917-1984 . . . . DLB-68

McDowell, Obolensky DLB-46

McEwan, Ian 1948- DLB-14, 194

McFadden, David 1940- DLB-60

McFall, Frances Elizabeth Clarke
    (see Grand, Sarah)

McFarlane, Leslie 1902-1977 . . . . DLB-88

McFee, William 1881-1966 . . . . DLB-153

McGahern, John 1934- DLB-14

McGee, Thomas D'Arcy 1825-1868 . . . . . DLB-99

McGeehan, W. O. 1879-1933 . . . . .DLB-25, 171

McGill, Ralph 1898-1969 . . . . DLB-29

McGinley, Phyllis 1905-1978 . . . . DLB-11, 48

McGinniss, Joe 1942- DLB-185

McGirt, James E. 1874-1930 . . . . DLB-50

McGlashan and Gill DLB-106

McGough, Roger 1937- DLB-40

McGraw-Hill DLB-46

McGuane, Thomas 1939- . . .DLB-2, 212; Y-80

McGuckian, Medbh 1950- DLB-40

McGuffey, William Holmes 1800-1873 . . . DLB-42

McHenry, James 1785-1845 . . . . DLB-202

McIlvanney, William 1936- DLB-14, 207

McIlwraith, Jean Newton 1859-1938 . . . . . DLB-92

McIntyre, James 1827-1906 . . . . DLB-99

McIntyre, O. O. 1884-1938 . . . . DLB-25

McKay, Claude 1889-1948 . . . . .DLB-4, 45, 51, 117

The David McKay Company DLB-49

McKean, William V. 1820-1903 . . . . DLB-23

McKenna, Stephen 1888-1967 . . . . .DLB-197

The McKenzie Trust Y-96

McKerrow, R. B. 1872-1940 . . . . DLB-201

McKinley, Robin 1952- DLB-52

McLachlan, Alexander 1818-1896 . . . . DLB-99

McLaren, Floris Clark 1904-1978 . . . . DLB-68

McLaverty, Michael 1907- DLB-15

McLean, John R. 1848-1916 . . . . DLB-23

McLean, William L. 1852-1931 . . . . DLB-25

McLennan, William 1856-1904 . . . . DLB-92

McLoughlin Brothers DLB-49

McLuhan, Marshall 1911-1980 . . . . DLB-88

McMaster, John Bach 1852-1932 . . . . DLB-47

McMurtry, Larry
    1936- DLB-2, 143; Y-80, Y-87

McNally, Terrence 1939- DLB-7

McNeil, Florence 1937- DLB-60

McNeile, Herman Cyril 1888-1937 . . . . . . DLB-77

McNickle, D'Arcy 1904-1977 . . . . . .DLB-175, 212

McPhee, John 1931- DLB-185

McPherson, James Alan 1943- DLB-38

McPherson, Sandra 1943- Y-86

McWhirter, George 1939- DLB-60

McWilliams, Carey 1905-1980 . . . . .DLB-137

Mead, L. T. 1844-1914 . . . . DLB-141

Mead, Matthew 1924- DLB-40

Mead, Taylor ?- DLB-16

Meany, Tom 1903-1964 . . . . .DLB-171

Mechthild von Magdeburg
    circa 1207-circa 1282 . . . . DLB-138

Medieval French Drama DLB-208

Medieval Travel Diaries DLB-203

Medill, Joseph 1823-1899 . . . . DLB-43

Medoff, Mark 1940- DLB-7

Meek, Alexander Beaufort 1814-1865 . . . . . DLB-3

Meeke, Mary ?-1816? DLB-116

Meinke, Peter 1932- DLB-5

Mejia Vallejo, Manuel 1923- DLB-113

Melanchthon, Philipp 1497-1560 ....DLB-179

Melançon, Robert 1947- DLB-60

Mell, Max 1882-1971.............DLB-81, 124

Mellow, James R. 1926-1997 ....DLB-111

Meltzer, David 1937- DLB-16

Meltzer, Milton 1915- DLB-61

Melville, Elizabeth, Lady Culross
circa 1585-1640.................DLB-172

Melville, Herman 1819-1891 ....DLB-3, 74

Memoirs of Life and Literature (1920),
by W. H. Mallock [excerpt] DLB-57

Mena, María Cristina 1893-1965....DLB-209, 221

Menander 342-341 B.C.-circa 292-291 B.C.
...........................DLB-176

Menantes (see Hunold, Christian Friedrich)

Mencke, Johann Burckhard
1674-1732 ....DLB-168

Mencken, H. L.
1880-1956 ....DLB-11, 29, 63, 137

Mencken and Nietzsche: An Unpublished
Excerpt from H. L. Mencken's *My Life
as Author and Editor*..................Y-93

Mendelssohn, Moses 1729-1786.........DLB-97

Mendes, Catulle 1841-1909...........DLB-217

Méndez M., Miguel 1930- DLB-82

Mens Rea (or Something) Y-97

The Mercantile Library of New York Y-96

Mercer, Cecil William (see Yates, Dornford)

Mercer, David 1928-1980 ....DLB-13

Mercer, John 1704-1768..............DLB-31

Meredith, George
1828-1909 .... DLB-18, 35, 57, 159

Meredith, Louisa Anne 1812-1895 ......DLB-166

Meredith, Owen (see Lytton, Edward Robert
Bulwer)

Meredith, William 1919- DLB-5

Mergerle, Johann Ulrich
(see Abraham ä Sancta Clara)

Mérimée, Prosper 1803-1870 ....DLB-119, 192

Merivale, John Herman 1779-1844 ....DLB-96

Meriwether, Louise 1923- DLB-33

Merlin Press.....................DLB-112

Merriam, Eve 1916-1992 ....DLB-61

The Merriam Company DLB-49

Merrill, James 1926-1995.....DLB-5, 165; Y-85

Merrill and Baker...................DLB-49

The Mershon Company DLB-49

Merton, Thomas 1915-1968 ....DLB-48; Y-81

Merwin, W. S. 1927- DLB-5, 169

Messner, Julian [publishing house].......DLB-46

Metcalf, J. [publishing house]..........DLB-49

Metcalf, John 1938- DLB-60

The Methodist Book Concern..........DLB-49

Methuen and Company..............DLB-112

Meun, Jean de (see *Roman de la Rose*)

Mew, Charlotte 1869-1928 ....DLB-19, 135

Mewshaw, Michael 1943- Y-80

Meyer, Conrad Ferdinand 1825-1898 ....DLB-129

Meyer, E. Y. 1946- DLB-75

Meyer, Eugene 1875-1959 ....DLB-29

Meyer, Michael 1921- DLB-155

Meyers, Jeffrey 1939- DLB-111

Meynell, Alice 1847-1922...........DLB-19, 98

Meynell, Viola 1885-1956 ....DLB-153

Meyrink, Gustav 1868-1932 ....DLB-81

Mézières, Philipe de circa 1327-1405 .....DLB-208

Michael, Ib 1945- DLB-214

Michael M. Rea and the Rea Award for the
Short Story Y-97

Michaëlis, Karen 1872-1950...........DLB-214

Michaels, Leonard 1933- DLB-130

Micheaux, Oscar 1884-1951 ....DLB-50

Michel of Northgate, Dan
circa 1265-circa 1340..............DLB-146

Micheline, Jack 1929-1998...........DLB-16

Michener, James A. 1907?-1997..........DLB-6

Micklejohn, George
circa 1717-1818 ....DLB-31

Middle English Literature:
An Introduction DLB-146

The Middle English Lyric DLB-146

Middle Hill Press...................DLB-106

Middleton, Christopher 1926- DLB-40

Middleton, Richard 1882-1911 ....DLB-156

Middleton, Stanley 1919- DLB-14

Middleton, Thomas 1580-1627 ....DLB-58

Miegel, Agnes 1879-1964..............DLB-56

Mieželaitis, Eduardas 1919-1997 ....DLB-220

Mihailović, Dragoslav 1930- DLB-181

Mihalić, Slavko 1928- DLB-181

Miles, Josephine 1911-1985 ....DLB-48

Miliković, Branko 1934-1961 ....DLB-181

Milius, John 1944- DLB-44

Mill, James 1773-1836 .... DLB-107, 158

Mill, John Stuart 1806-1873........DLB-55, 190

Millar, Kenneth 1915-1983 ....DLB-2; Y-83; DS-6

Millar, Andrew [publishing house] DLB-154

Millay, Edna St. Vincent 1892-1950 .....DLB-45

Miller, Arthur 1915- DLB-7

Miller, Caroline 1903-1992 ....DLB-9

Miller, Eugene Ethelbert 1950- DLB-41

Miller, Heather Ross 1939- DLB-120

Miller, Henry 1891-1980 .... DLB-4, 9; Y-80

Miller, Hugh 1802-1856 ....DLB-190

Miller, J. Hillis 1928- DLB-67

Miller, James [publishing house] DLB-49

Miller, Jason 1939- DLB-7

Miller, Joaquin 1839-1913 ....DLB-186

Miller, May 1899- DLB-41

Miller, Paul 1906-1991 ....DLB-127

Miller, Perry 1905-1963............. DLB-17, 63

Miller, Sue 1943- DLB-143

Miller, Vassar 1924-1998.............DLB-105

Miller, Walter M., Jr. 1923- DLB-8

Miller, Webb 1892-1940 ....DLB-29

Millhauser, Steven 1943- DLB-2

Millican, Arthenia J. Bates 1920- DLB-38

Mills and Boon DLB-112

Milman, Henry Hart 1796-1868 ....DLB-96

Milne, A. A. 1882-1956.....DLB-10, 77, 100, 160

Milner, Ron 1938- DLB-38

Milner, William [publishing house] DLB-106

Milnes, Richard Monckton (Lord Houghton)
1809-1885 ....DLB-32, 184

Milton, John 1608-1674 ....DLB-131, 151

Miłosz, Czesław 1911- DLB-215

Minakami Tsutomu 1919- DLB-182

Minamoto no Sanetomo 1192-1219......DLB-203

The Minerva Press DLB-154

Minnesang circa 1150-1280 ....DLB-138

Minns, Susan 1839-1938 ....DLB-140

Minor Illustrators, 1880-1914 ....DLB-141

Minor Poets of the Earlier Seventeenth
Century.......................DLB-121

Minton, Balch and Company DLB-46

Mirbeau, Octave 1848-1917........ DLB-123, 192

Mirk, John died after 1414?............DLB-146

Miron, Gaston 1928- DLB-60

A Mirror for Magistrates DLB-167

Mishima Yukio 1925-1970.............DLB-182

Mitchel, Jonathan 1624-1668...........DLB-24

Mitchell, Adrian 1932- DLB-40

Mitchell, Donald Grant
1822-1908...................DLB-1; DS-13

Mitchell, Gladys 1901-1983.............DLB-77

Mitchell, James Leslie 1901-1935.........DLB-15

Mitchell, John (see Slater, Patrick)

Mitchell, John Ames 1845-1918..........DLB-79

Mitchell, Joseph 1908-1996 .... DLB-185; Y-96

Mitchell, Julian 1935- DLB-14

Mitchell, Ken 1940- DLB-60

Mitchell, Langdon 1862-1935 ....DLB-7

Mitchell, Loften 1919- DLB-38

Mitchell, Margaret 1900-1949 ....DLB-9

Mitchell, S. Weir 1829-1914 ....DLB-202

Mitchell, W. O. 1914- DLB-88

Mitchison, Naomi Margaret (Haldane)
1897- DLB-160, 191

Mitford, Mary Russell 1787-1855.... DLB-110, 116

Mitford, Nancy 1904-1973............DLB-191

Mittelholzer, Edgar 1909-1965 ....DLB-117

Mitterer, Erika 1906- DLB-85

Mitterer, Felix 1948- DLB-124

Mitternacht, Johann Sebastian
1613-1679 ....DLB-168

Miyamoto, Yuriko 1899-1951 ....DLB-180

Mizener, Arthur 1907-1988 ....DLB-103

Mo, Timothy 1950- DLB-194

Modern Age Books. DLB-46

"Modern English Prose" (1876),
by George Saintsbury. DLB-57

The Modern Language Association of America
Celebrates Its Centennial Y-84

The Modern Library DLB-46

"Modern Novelists – Great and Small" (1855), by
Margaret Oliphant DLB-21

"Modern Style" (1857), by Cockburn
Thomson [excerpt]. DLB-57

The Modernists (1932),
by Joseph Warren Beach DLB-36

Modiano, Patrick 1945- DLB-83

Moffat, Yard and Company DLB-46

Moffet, Thomas 1553-1604 . . . . DLB-136

Mohr, Nicholasa 1938- DLB-145

Moix, Ana María 1947- DLB-134

Molesworth, Louisa 1839-1921 . . . . DLB-135

Möllhausen, Balduin 1825-1905 . . . . DLB-129

Molnár, Ferenc 1878-1952 . . . . DLB-215

Momaday, N. Scott 1934- DLB-143, 175

Monkhouse, Allan 1858-1936. . . . . DLB-10

Monro, Harold 1879-1932 . . . . DLB-19

Monroe, Harriet 1860-1936 . . . . DLB-54, 91

Monsarrat, Nicholas 1910-1979 . . . . DLB-15

Montagu, Lady Mary Wortley
1689-1762. . . . . DLB-95, 101

Montague, C. E. 1867-1928 . . . . DLB-197

Montague, John 1929- DLB-40

Montale, Eugenio 1896-1981 . . . . DLB-114

Montalvo, José 1946-1994 . . . . DLB-209

Monterroso, Augusto 1921- DLB-145

Montesquiou, Robert de 1855-1921 . . . . . DLB-217

Montgomerie, Alexander
circa 1550?-1598 . . . . DLB-167

Montgomery, James 1771-1854. . . . . . DLB-93, 158

Montgomery, John 1919- DLB-16

Montgomery, Lucy Maud
1874-1942. . . . . DLB-92; DS-14

Montgomery, Marion 1925- DLB-6

Montgomery, Robert Bruce (see Crispin, Edmund)

Montherlant, Henry de 1896-1972 . . . . DLB-72

The Monthly Review 1749-1844 . . . . DLB-110

Montigny, Louvigny de 1876-1955. . . . . . . DLB-92

Montoya, José 1932- DLB-122

Moodie, John Wedderburn Dunbar
1797-1869 . . . . DLB-99

Moodie, Susanna 1803-1885. . . . . DLB-99

Moody, Joshua circa 1633-1697 . . . . DLB-24

Moody, William Vaughn 1869-1910 . . . .DLB-7, 54

Moorcock, Michael 1939- DLB-14

Moore, Catherine L. 1911- DLB-8

Moore, Clement Clarke 1779-1863. . . . . . . DLB-42

Moore, Dora Mavor 1888-1979 . . . . DLB-92

Moore, George 1852-1933 . . . .DLB-10, 18, 57, 135

Moore, Marianne 1887-1972. . . . . . . DLB-45; DS-7

Moore, Mavor 1919- DLB-88

Moore, Richard 1927- DLB-105

Moore, T. Sturge 1870-1944 . . . . DLB-19

Moore, Thomas 1779-1852. . . . . DLB-96, 144

Moore, Ward 1903-1978 . . . . DLB-8

Moore, Wilstach, Keys and Company. . . . DLB-49

Moorehead, Alan 1901-1983 . . . . DLB-204

Moorhouse, Geoffrey 1931- DLB-204

The Moorland-Spingarn Research
Center DLB-76

Moorman, Mary C. 1905-1994 . . . . DLB-155

Mora, Pat 1942- DLB-209

Moraga, Cherríe 1952- DLB-82

Morales, Alejandro 1944- DLB-82

Morales, Mario Roberto 1947- DLB-145

Morales, Rafael 1919- DLB-108

Morality Plays: *Mankind* circa 1450-1500 and
Everyman circa 1500 . . . . DLB-146

Morante, Elsa 1912-1985 . . . . .DLB-177

Morata, Olympia Fulvia 1526-1555 . . . . . .DLB-179

Moravia, Alberto 1907-1990 . . . . .DLB-177

Mordaunt, Elinor 1872-1942 . . . . .DLB-174

More, Hannah
1745-1833. . . . . DLB-107, 109, 116, 158

More, Henry 1614-1687 . . . . DLB-126

More, Sir Thomas
1477 or 1478-1535 . . . . DLB-136

Moreno, Dorinda 1939- DLB-122

Morency, Pierre 1942- DLB-60

Moretti, Marino 1885-1979. . . . . DLB-114

Morgan, Berry 1919- DLB-6

Morgan, Charles 1894-1958. . . . . . . DLB-34, 100

Morgan, Edmund S. 1916- DLB-17

Morgan, Edwin 1920- DLB-27

Morgan, John Pierpont 1837-1913 . . . . . . DLB-140

Morgan, John Pierpont, Jr. 1867-1943 . . . DLB-140

Morgan, Robert 1944- DLB-120

Morgan, Sydney Owenson, Lady
1776?-1859 . . . . DLB-116, 158

Morgner, Irmtraud 1933- DLB-75

Morhof, Daniel Georg 1639-1691 . . . . . . DLB-164

Mori, Ōgai 1862-1922 . . . . DLB-180

Morier, James Justinian
1782 or 1783?-1849 . . . . DLB-116

Mörike, Eduard 1804-1875. . . . . DLB-133

Morin, Paul 1889-1963. . . . . DLB-92

Morison, Richard 1514?-1556 . . . . DLB-136

Morison, Samuel Eliot 1887-1976 . . . . DLB-17

Morison, Stanley 1889-1967 . . . . DLB-201

Moritz, Karl Philipp 1756-1793 . . . . DLB-94

Moriz von Craûn circa 1220-1230 . . . . DLB-138

Morley, Christopher 1890-1957 . . . . DLB-9

Morley, John 1838-1923. . . . . . . DLB-57, 144, 190

Morris, George Pope 1802-1864 . . . . DLB-73

Morris, James Humphrey (see Morris, Jan)

Morris, Jan 1926- DLB-204

Morris, Lewis 1833-1907 . . . . DLB-35

Morris, Margaret 1737-1816 . . . . DLB-200

Morris, Richard B. 1904-1989 . . . . .DLB-17

Morris, William
1834-1896 . . . . . DLB-18, 35, 57, 156, 178, 184

Morris, Willie 1934- Y-80

Morris, Wright
1910-1998 . . . . .DLB-2, 206, 218; Y-81

Morrison, Arthur 1863-1945 . . . .DLB-70, 135, 197

Morrison, Charles Clayton 1874-1966 . . . . DLB-91

Morrison, Toni
1931- DLB-6, 33, 143; Y-81, Y-93

Morrow, William, and Company. DLB-46

Morse, James Herbert 1841-1923 . . . . DLB-71

Morse, Jedidiah 1761-1826 . . . . DLB-37

Morse, John T., Jr. 1840-1937 . . . . DLB-47

Morselli, Guido 1912-1973 . . . . .DLB-177

Mortimer, Favell Lee 1802-1878. . . . . DLB-163

Mortimer, John 1923- DLB-13

Morton, Carlos 1942- DLB-122

Morton, H. V. 1892-1979. . . . . DLB-195

Morton, John P., and Company. DLB-49

Morton, Nathaniel 1613-1685 . . . . DLB-24

Morton, Sarah Wentworth 1759-1846 . . . . DLB-37

Morton, Thomas circa 1579-circa 1647 . . . DLB-24

Moscherosch, Johann Michael
1601-1669 . . . . DLB-164

Moseley, Humphrey
[publishing house] DLB-170

Möser, Justus 1720-1794 . . . . DLB-97

Mosley, Nicholas 1923- DLB-14, 207

Moss, Arthur 1889-1969 . . . . DLB-4

Moss, Howard 1922-1987 . . . . DLB-5

Moss, Thylias 1954- DLB-120

The Most Powerful Book Review in America
[*New York Times Book Review*] Y-82

Motion, Andrew 1952- DLB-40

Motley, John Lothrop 1814-1877 . . . DLB-1, 30, 59

Motley, Willard 1909-1965 . . . . .DLB-76, 143

Motte, Benjamin Jr. [publishing house]. . . DLB-154

Motteux, Peter Anthony 1663-1718 . . . . . . DLB-80

Mottram, R. H. 1883-1971 . . . . DLB-36

Mouré, Erin 1955- DLB-60

Mourning Dove (Humishuma) between
1882 and 1888?-1936. . . . . .DLB-175, 221

Movies from Books, 1920-1974 . . . . DLB-9

Mowat, Farley 1921- DLB-68

Mowbray, A. R., and Company,
Limited. DLB-106

Mowrer, Edgar Ansel 1892-1977 . . . . DLB-29

Mowrer, Paul Scott 1887-1971 . . . . DLB-29

Moxon, Edward [publishing house] DLB-106

Moxon, Joseph [publishing house] DLB-170

Móricz, Zsigmond 1879-1942 . . . . DLB-215

Mphahlele, Es'kia (Ezekiel) 1919- DLB-125

Mtshali, Oswald Mbuyiseni 1940- DLB-125

Mucedorus DLB-62

Mudford, William 1782-1848 ....DLB-159

Mueller, Lisel 1924- DLB-105

Muhajir, El (see Marvin X)

Muhajir, Nazzam Al Fitnah (see Marvin X)

Mühlbach, Luise 1814-1873............DLB-133

Muir, Edwin 1887-1959 .... DLB-20, 100, 191

Muir, Helen 1937- DLB-14

Muir, John 1838-1914 ....DLB-186

Muir, Percy 1894-1979................DLB-201

Mujū Ichien 1226-1312 ....DLB-203

Mukherjee, Bharati 1940- DLB-60, 218

Mulcaster, Richard
    1531 or 1532-1611 ....DLB-167

Muldoon, Paul 1951- DLB-40

Müller, Friedrich (see Müller, Maler)

Müller, Heiner 1929-1995 ....DLB-124

Müller, Maler 1749-1825 ....DLB-94

Müller, Wilhelm 1794-1827 ....DLB-90

Mumford, Lewis 1895-1990 ....DLB-63

Munby, A. N. L. 1913-1974............DLB-201

Munby, Arthur Joseph 1828-1910 ....DLB-35

Munday, Anthony 1560-1633 .... DLB-62, 172

Mundt, Clara (see Mühlbach, Luise)

Mundt, Theodore 1808-1861 ....DLB-133

Munford, Robert circa 1737-1783........DLB-31

Mungoshi, Charles 1947- DLB-157

Munk, Kaj 1898-1944 ....DLB-214

Munonye, John 1929- DLB-117

Munro, Alice 1931- DLB-53

Munro, H. H. 1870-1916 .... DLB-34, 162

Munro, Neil 1864-1930 ....DLB-156

Munro, George [publishing house] DLB-49

Munro, Norman L. [publishing house] DLB-49

Munroe, James, and Company DLB-49

Munroe, Kirk 1850-1930 ....DLB-42

Munroe and Francis...................DLB-49

Munsell, Joel [publishing house] DLB-49

Munsey, Frank A. 1854-1925 ....DLB-25, 91

Munsey, Frank A., and Company.......DLB-49

Murakami Haruki 1949- DLB-182

Murav'ev, Mikhail Nikitich
    1757-1807......................DLB-150

Murdoch, Iris 1919- DLB-14, 194

Murdoch, Rupert 1931- DLB-127

Murfree, Mary N. 1850-1922 .... DLB-12, 74

Murger, Henry 1822-1861............DLB-119

Murger, Louis-Henri (see Murger, Henry)

Murner, Thomas 1475-1537 ....DLB-179

Muro, Amado 1915-1971...............DLB-82

Murphy, Arthur 1727-1805 ....DLB-89, 142

Murphy, Beatrice M. 1908- DLB-76

Murphy, Dervla 1931- DLB-204

Murphy, Emily 1868-1933............DLB-99

Murphy, John H., III 1916- DLB-127

Murphy, John, and Company DLB-49

Murphy, Richard 1927-1993 ....DLB-40

Murray, Albert L. 1916- DLB-38

Murray, Gilbert 1866-1957 ....DLB-10

Murray, Judith Sargent 1751-1820.... DLB-37, 200

Murray, Pauli 1910-1985.............DLB-41

Murray, John [publishing house].......DLB-154

Murry, John Middleton 1889-1957 .....DLB-149

Musäus, Johann Karl August 1735-1787 ...DLB-97

Muschg, Adolf 1934- DLB-75

The Music of *Minnesang*.............DLB-138

Musil, Robert 1880-1942...........DLB-81, 124

Muspilli circa 790-circa 850 ....DLB-148

Musset, Alfred de 1810-1857 ...... DLB-192, 217

Mussey, Benjamin B., and Company DLB-49

Mutafchieva, Vera 1929- DLB-181

Mwangi, Meja 1948- DLB-125

Myers, Frederic W. H. 1843-1901......DLB-190

Myers, Gustavus 1872-1942 ....DLB-47

Myers, L. H. 1881-1944 ....DLB-15

Myers, Walter Dean 1937- DLB-33

Mykolaitis-Putinas, Vincas 1893-1967....DLB-220

Myles, Eileen 1949- DLB-193

N

Na Prous Boneta circa 1296-1328 ....DLB-208

Nabl, Franz 1883-1974................DLB-81

Nabokov, Vladimir
    1899-1977 .... DLB-2; Y-80, Y-91; DS-3

Nabokov Festival at Cornell Y-83

The Vladimir Nabokov Archive
    in the Berg Collection Y-91

Nádaši, Ladislav (see Jégé)

Naden, Constance 1858-1889 ....DLB-199

Nadezhdin, Nikolai Ivanovich
    1804-1856......................DLB-198

Naevius circa 265 B.C.-201 B.C........DLB-211

Nafis and Cornish DLB-49

Nagai, Kafū 1879-1959................DLB-180

Naipaul, Shiva 1945-1985 .... DLB-157; Y-85

Naipaul, V. S. 1932- ... DLB-125, 204, 207; Y-85

Nakagami Kenji 1946-1992 ....DLB-182

Nakano-in Masatada no Musume (see Nijō, Lady)

Nałkowska, Zofia 1884-1954...........DLB-215

Nancrede, Joseph [publishing house]......DLB-49

Naranjo, Carmen 1930- DLB-145

Narezhny, Vasilii Trofimovich
    1780-1825 ....DLB-198

Narrache, Jean 1893-1970 ....DLB-92

Nasby, Petroleum Vesuvius (see Locke, David Ross)

Nash, Ogden 1902-1971................DLB-11

Nash, Eveleigh [publishing house].......DLB-112

Nashe, Thomas 1567-1601?............DLB-167

Nast, Conde 1873-1942 ....DLB-91

Nast, Thomas 1840-1902..............DLB-188

Nastasijević, Momčilo 1894-1938 ....DLB-147

Nathan, George Jean 1882-1958 ....DLB-137

Nathan, Robert 1894-1985 ....DLB-9

The National Jewish Book Awards Y-85

The National Theatre and the Royal
    Shakespeare Company: The
    National Companies DLB-13

Natsume, Sōseki 1867-1916 ....DLB-180

Naughton, Bill 1910- DLB-13

Navarro, Joe 1953- DLB-209

Naylor, Gloria 1950- DLB-173

Nazor, Vladimir 1876-1949 ....DLB-147

Ndebele, Njabulo 1948- DLB-157

Neagoe, Peter 1881-1960................DLB-4

Neal, John 1793-1876................DLB-1, 59

Neal, Joseph C. 1807-1847 ....DLB-11

Neal, Larry 1937-1981 ....DLB-38

The Neale Publishing Company DLB-49

Neely, F. Tennyson [publishing house] DLB-49

Negoiţescu, Ion 1921-1993 ....DLB-220

Negri, Ada 1870-1945 ....DLB-114

"The Negro as a Writer," by
    G. M. McClellan..................DLB-50

"Negro Poets and Their Poetry," by
    Wallace Thurman..................DLB-50

Neidhart von Reuental
    circa 1185-circa 1240..............DLB-138

Neihardt, John G. 1881-1973..........DLB-9, 54

Neledinsky-Meletsky, Iurii Aleksandrovich
    1752-1828......................DLB-150

Nelligan, Emile 1879-1941.............DLB-92

Nelson, Alice Moore Dunbar 1875-1935 ...DLB-50

Nelson, Thomas, and Sons [U.S.] DLB-49

Nelson, Thomas, and Sons [U.K.] DLB-106

Nelson, William 1908-1978 ....DLB-103

Nelson, William Rockhill 1841-1915......DLB-23

Nemerov, Howard 1920-1991..... DLB-5, 6; Y-83

Nepos circa 100 B.C.-post 27 B.C........DLB-211

Nèris, Salomèja 1904-1945 ....DLB-220

Nerval, Gerard de 1808-1855 ....DLB-217

Nesbit, E. 1858-1924 .... DLB-141, 153, 178

Ness, Evaline 1911-1986 ....DLB-61

Nestroy, Johann 1801-1862............DLB-133

Neukirch, Benjamin 1655-1729 ....DLB-168

Neugeboren, Jay 1938- DLB-28

Neumann, Alfred 1895-1952 ....DLB-56

Neumann, Ferenc (see Molnár, Ferenc)

Neumark, Georg 1621-1681 ....DLB-164

Neumeister, Erdmann 1671-1756........DLB-168

Nevins, Allan 1890-1971 .... DLB-17; DS-17

Nevinson, Henry Woodd 1856-1941 ....DLB-135

The New American Library DLB-46

New Approaches to Biography: Challenges
    from Critical Theory, USC Conference
    on Literary Studies, 1990 .... Y-90

New Directions Publishing
    Corporation DLB-46

A New Edition of *Huck Finn*.............. Y-85

New Forces at Work in the American Theatre:
   1915-1925. . . . . DLB-7

New Literary Periodicals:
   A Report for 1987 . . . . Y-87

New Literary Periodicals:
   A Report for 1988 . . . . Y-88

New Literary Periodicals:
   A Report for 1989 . . . . Y-89

New Literary Periodicals:
   A Report for 1990 . . . . Y-90

New Literary Periodicals:
   A Report for 1991 . . . . Y-91

New Literary Periodicals:
   A Report for 1992 . . . . Y-92

New Literary Periodicals:
   A Report for 1993 . . . . Y-93

The New Monthly Magazine
   1814-1884. DLB-110

The New Ulysses Y-84

The New Variorum Shakespeare Y-85

A New Voice: The Center for the Book's First
   Five Years. Y-83

The New Wave [Science Fiction] DLB-8

New York City Bookshops in the 1930s and 1940s:
   The Recollections of Walter Goldwater. . . Y-93

Newbery, John [publishing house] DLB-154

Newbolt, Henry 1862-1938 . . . . DLB-19

Newbound, Bernard Slade (see Slade, Bernard)

Newby, Eric 1919- DLB-204

Newby, P. H. 1918- DLB-15

Newby, Thomas Cautley
   [publishing house] DLB-106

Newcomb, Charles King 1820-1894. . . . . . . DLB-1

Newell, Peter 1862-1924. . . . . DLB-42

Newell, Robert Henry 1836-1901. . . . . DLB-11

Newhouse, Samuel I. 1895-1979. . . . . . . DLB-127

Newman, Cecil Earl 1903-1976 . . . . DLB-127

Newman, David (see Benton, Robert)

Newman, Frances 1883-1928 . . . . Y-80

Newman, Francis William 1805-1897. . . . DLB-190

Newman, John Henry
   1801-1890 . . . . DLB-18, 32, 55

Newman, Mark [publishing house]. DLB-49

Newnes, George, Limited. DLB-112

Newsome, Effie Lee 1885-1979. . . . . DLB-76

Newspaper Syndication of American
   Humor. DLB-11

Newton, A. Edward 1864-1940 . . . . DLB-140

Nexø, Martin Andersen 1869-1954 . . . . . DLB-214

Nezval, Vítěslav 1900-1958 . . . . DLB-215

Németh, László 1901-1975 . . . . DLB-215

Ngugi wa Thiong'o 1938- DLB-125

Niatum, Duane 1938- DLB-175

The Nibelungenlied and the Klage
   circa 1200. DLB-138

Nichol, B. P. 1944- DLB-53

Nicholas of Cusa 1401-1464. . . . . DLB-115

Nichols, Beverly 1898-1983 . . . . DLB-191

Nichols, Dudley 1895-1960 . . . . DLB-26

Nichols, Grace 1950- DLB-157

Nichols, John 1940- Y-82

Nichols, Mary Sargeant (Neal) Gove
   1810-1884 . . . . DLB-1

Nichols, Peter 1927- DLB-13

Nichols, Roy F. 1896-1973 . . . . DLB-17

Nichols, Ruth 1948- DLB-60

Nicholson, Edward Williams Byron
   1849-1912 . . . . DLB-184

Nicholson, Norman 1914- DLB-27

Nicholson, William 1872-1949 . . . . DLB-141

Ní Chuilleanáin, Eiléan 1942- DLB-40

Nicol, Eric 1919- DLB-68

Nicolai, Friedrich 1733-1811 . . . . DLB-97

Nicolas de Clamanges circa 1363-1437. . . DLB-208

Nicolay, John G. 1832-1901 and
   Hay, John 1838-1905. . . . . DLB-47

Nicolson, Harold 1886-1968. . . . . . .DLB-100, 149

Nicolson, Nigel 1917- DLB-155

Niebuhr, Reinhold 1892-1971. . . . . .DLB-17; DS-17

Niedecker, Lorine 1903-1970 . . . . DLB-48

Nieman, Lucius W. 1857-1935 . . . . DLB-25

Nietzsche, Friedrich 1844-1900. . . . . . . DLB-129

Nievo, Stanislao 1928- DLB-196

Niggli, Josefina 1910- Y-80

Nightingale, Florence 1820-1910 . . . . . . DLB-166

Nijō, Lady (Nakano-in Masatada no Musume)
   1258-after 1306 . . . . DLB-203

Nijō, Yoshimoto 1320-1388 . . . . DLB-203

Nikolev, Nikolai Petrovich
   1758-1815. . . . . DLB-150

Niles, Hezekiah 1777-1839 . . . . DLB-43

Nims, John Frederick 1913- DLB-5

Nin, Anaïs 1903-1977 . . . . DLB-2, 4, 152

1985: The Year of the Mystery:
   A Symposium. Y-85

The 1997 Booker Prize. Y-97

The 1998 Booker Prize. Y-98

Niño, Raúl 1961- DLB-209

Nissenson, Hugh 1933- DLB-28

Niven, Frederick John 1878-1944 . . . . DLB-92

Niven, Larry 1938- DLB-8

Nixon, Howard M. 1909-1983. . . . . DLB-201

Nizan, Paul 1905-1940 . . . . DLB-72

Njegoš, Petar II Petrović 1813-1851. . . . DLB-147

Nkosi, Lewis 1936- DLB-157

"The No Self, the Little Self, and the Poets,"
   by Richard Moore DLB-105

Nobel Peace Prize

The 1986 Nobel Peace Prize: Elie Wiesel. Y-86

The Nobel Prize and Literary Politics Y-86

Nobel Prize in Literature

The 1982 Nobel Prize in Literature:
   Gabriel García Márquez. Y-82

The 1983 Nobel Prize in Literature:
   William Golding Y-83

The 1984 Nobel Prize in Literature:
   Jaroslav Seifert Y-84

The 1985 Nobel Prize in Literature:
   Claude Simon Y-85

The 1986 Nobel Prize in Literature:
   Wole Soyinka Y-86

The 1987 Nobel Prize in Literature:
   Joseph Brodsky Y-87

The 1988 Nobel Prize in Literature:
   Najīb Mahfūz. Y-88

The 1989 Nobel Prize in Literature:
   Camilo José Cela Y-89

The 1990 Nobel Prize in Literature:
   Octavio Paz Y-90

The 1991 Nobel Prize in Literature:
   Nadine Gordimer. Y-91

The 1992 Nobel Prize in Literature:
   Derek Walcott Y-92

The 1993 Nobel Prize in Literature:
   Toni Morrison. Y-93

The 1994 Nobel Prize in Literature:
   Kenzaburō Ōe Y-94

The 1995 Nobel Prize in Literature:
   Seamus Heaney Y-95

The 1996 Nobel Prize in Literature:
   Wisława Szymborsha. Y-96

The 1997 Nobel Prize in Literature:
   Dario Fo. Y-97

The 1998 Nobel Prize in Literature
   José Saramago Y-98

Nodier, Charles 1780-1844. . . . . DLB-119

Noel, Roden 1834-1894 . . . . DLB-35

Nogami, Yaeko 1885-1985 . . . . DLB-180

Nogo, Rajko Petrov 1945- DLB-181

Nolan, William F. 1928- DLB-8

Noland, C. F. M. 1810?-1858 . . . . DLB-11

Noma Hiroshi 1915-1991. . . . . DLB-182

Nonesuch Press DLB-112

Noonan, Robert Phillipe (see Tressell, Robert)

Noonday Press DLB-46

Noone, John 1936- DLB-14

Nora, Eugenio de 1923- DLB-134

Nordbrandt, Henrik 1945- DLB-214

Nordhoff, Charles 1887-1947 . . . . DLB-9

Norman, Charles 1904-1996 . . . . DLB-111

Norman, Marsha 1947- Y-84

Norris, Charles G. 1881-1945 . . . . DLB-9

Norris, Frank 1870-1902. . . . . . . .DLB-12, 71, 186

Norris, Leslie 1921- DLB-27

Norse, Harold 1916- DLB-16

Norte, Marisela 1955- DLB-209

North, Marianne 1830-1890. . . . . .DLB-174

North Point Press. DLB-46

Nortje, Arthur 1942-1970 . . . . DLB-125

Norton, Alice Mary (see Norton, Andre)

Norton, Andre 1912- DLB-8, 52

Norton, Andrews 1786-1853 . . . . DLB-1

Norton, Caroline 1808-1877 . . . .DLB-21, 159, 199

Norton, Charles Eliot 1827-1908 . . . . . . DLB-1, 64

Norton, John 1606-1663 . . . . .DLB-24

Norton, Mary 1903-1992. . . . . .DLB-160

Norton, Thomas (see Sackville, Thomas)

Norton, W. W., and Company DLB-46

Norwood, Robert 1874-1932 . . . . .DLB-92

Nosaka Akiyuki 1930- DLB-182

Nossack, Hans Erich 1901-1977. . . . . .DLB-69

A Note on Technique (1926), by
    Elizabeth A. Drew [excerpts]. DLB-36

Notker Balbulus circa 840-912. . . . . .DLB-148

Notker III of Saint Gall
    circa 950-1022 . . . . .DLB-148

Notker von Zweifalten ?-1095 . . . . .DLB-148

Nourse, Alan E. 1928- DLB-8

Novak, Slobodan 1924- DLB-181

Novak, Vjenceslav 1859-1905 . . . . .DLB-147

Novalis 1772-1801 . . . . .DLB-90

Novaro, Mario 1868-1944 . . . . .DLB-114

Novás Calvo, Lino 1903-1983 . . . . .DLB-145

"The Novel in [Robert Browning's] 'The Ring
    and the Book' " (1912), by
    Henry James DLB-32

The Novel of Impressionism,
    by Jethro Bithell DLB-66

Novel-Reading: *The Works of Charles Dickens,
The Works of W. Makepeace Thackeray*
(1879), by Anthony Trollope DLB-21

Novels for Grown-Ups Y-97

The Novels of Dorothy Richardson (1918),
    by May Sinclair DLB-36

Novels with a Purpose (1864), by
    Justin M'Carthy DLB-21

Noventa, Giacomo 1898-1960 . . . . .DLB-114

Novikov, Nikolai Ivanovich
    1744-1818 .DLB-150

Novomeský, Laco 1904-1976. . . . . .DLB-215

Nowlan, Alden 1933-1983 . . . . .DLB-53

Noyes, Alfred 1880-1958 . . . . .DLB-20

Noyes, Crosby S. 1825-1908 . . . . .DLB-23

Noyes, Nicholas 1647-1717. . . . . .DLB-24

Noyes, Theodore W. 1858-1946 . . . . .DLB-29

N-Town Plays circa 1468 to early
    sixteenth century DLB-146

Nugent, Frank 1908-1965 . . . . .DLB-44

Nugent, Richard Bruce 1906- DLB-151

Nušić, Branislav 1864-1938 . . . . .DLB-147

Nutt, David [publishing house] DLB-106

Nwapa, Flora 1931-1993 . . . . .DLB-125

Nye, Bill 1850-1896 . . . . .DLB-186

Nye, Edgar Wilson (Bill) 1850-1896 . . .DLB-11, 23

Nye, Naomi Shihab 1952- DLB-120

Nye, Robert 1939- DLB-14

Nyka-Niliūnas, Alfonsas 1919- DLB-220

O

Oakes, Urian circa 1631-1681 . . . . .DLB-24

Oakley, Violet 1874-1961 . . . . .DLB-188

Oates, Joyce Carol 1938- . . . DLB-2, 5, 130; Y-81

Ōba Minako 1930- DLB-182

Ober, Frederick Albion 1849-1913 . . . . . .DLB-189

Ober, William 1920-1993 . . . . Y-93

Oberholtzer, Ellis Paxson 1868-1936. . . . . .DLB-47

Obradović, Dositej 1740?-1811 . . . . .DLB-147

O'Brien, Edna 1932- DLB-14

O'Brien, Fitz-James 1828-1862. . . . . .DLB-74

O'Brien, Kate 1897-1974 . . . . .DLB-15

O'Brien, Tim 1946- DLB-152; Y-80; DS-9

O'Casey, Sean 1880-1964 . . . . .DLB-10

Occom, Samson 1723-1792 . . . . .DLB-175

Ochs, Adolph S. 1858-1935 . . . . .DLB-25

Ochs-Oakes, George Washington
    1861-1931 .DLB-137

O'Connor, Flannery
    1925-1964 . . . . DLB-2, 152; Y-80; DS-12

O'Connor, Frank 1903-1966 . . . . .DLB-162

Octopus Publishing Group DLB-112

Oda Sakunosuke 1913-1947 . . . . .DLB-182

Odell, Jonathan 1737-1818 . . . . .DLB-31, 99

O'Dell, Scott 1903-1989. . . . . .DLB-52

Odets, Clifford 1906-1963 . . . . DLB-7, 26

Odhams Press Limited. DLB-112

Odoevsky, Aleksandr Ivanovich
    1802-1839 .DLB-205

Odoevsky, Vladimir Fedorovich
    1804 or 1803-1869 . . . . .DLB-198

O'Donnell, Peter 1920- DLB-87

O'Donovan, Michael (see O'Connor, Frank)

Ōe Kenzaburō 1935- DLB-182; Y-94

O'Faolain, Julia 1932- DLB-14

O'Faolain, Sean 1900- DLB-15, 162

Off Broadway and Off-Off Broadway DLB-7

Off-Loop Theatres. DLB-7

Offord, Carl Ruthven 1910- DLB-76

O'Flaherty, Liam 1896-1984 . . . DLB-36, 162; Y-84

Ogilvie, J. S., and Company DLB-49

Ogilvy, Eliza 1822-1912. . . . . .DLB-199

Ogot, Grace 1930- DLB-125

O'Grady, Desmond 1935- DLB-40

Ogunyemi, Wale 1939- DLB-157

O'Hagan, Howard 1902-1982 . . . . .DLB-68

O'Hara, Frank 1926-1966 . . . . .DLB-5, 16, 193

O'Hara, John 1905-1970 . . . . .DLB-9, 86; DS-2

O'Hegarty, P. S. 1879-1955 . . . . .DLB-201

Okara, Gabriel 1921- DLB-125

O'Keeffe, John 1747-1833. . . . . .DLB-89

Okes, Nicholas [publishing house]. DLB-170

Okigbo, Christopher 1930-1967 . . . . .DLB-125

Okot p'Bitek 1931-1982. . . . . .DLB-125

Okpewho, Isidore 1941- DLB-157

Okri, Ben 1959- DLB-157

Olaudah Equiano and Unfinished Journeys:
    The Slave-Narrative Tradition and
    Twentieth-Century Continuities, by
    Paul Edwards and Pauline T.
    Wangman .DLB-117

Old English Literature:
    An Introduction DLB-146

Old English Riddles
    eighth to tenth centuries DLB-146

Old Franklin Publishing House DLB-49

Old German Genesis and *Old German Exodus*
    circa 1050-circa 1130. . . . . .DLB-148

Old High German Charms and
    Blessings DLB-148

The *Old High German Isidor*
    circa 790-800 . . . . .DLB-148

Older, Fremont 1856-1935 . . . . .DLB-25

Oldham, John 1653-1683. . . . . .DLB-131

Oldman, C. B. 1894-1969 . . . . .DLB-201

Olds, Sharon 1942- DLB-120

Olearius, Adam 1599-1671 . . . . .DLB-164

Oliphant, Laurence 1829?-1888. . . . . . .DLB-18, 166

Oliphant, Margaret 1828-1897. . . . . . .DLB-18, 190

Oliver, Chad 1928- DLB-8

Oliver, Mary 1935- DLB-5, 193

Ollier, Claude 1922- DLB-83

Olsen, Tillie
    1912 or 1913- DLB-28, 206; Y-80

Olson, Charles 1910-1970 . . . . .DLB-5, 16, 193

Olson, Elder 1909- DLB-48, 63

Omotoso, Kole 1943- DLB-125

"On Art in Fiction " (1838),
    by Edward Bulwer DLB-21

On Learning to Write Y-88

On Some of the Characteristics of Modern
    Poetry and On the Lyrical Poems of
    Alfred Tennyson (1831), by Arthur
    Henry Hallam. DLB-32

"On Style in English Prose" (1898), by
    Frederic Harrison DLB-57

"On Style in Literature: Its Technical
    Elements" (1885), by Robert Louis
    Stevenson DLB-57

"On the Writing of Essays" (1862),
    by Alexander Smith DLB-57

Ondaatje, Michael 1943- DLB-60

O'Neill, Eugene 1888-1953 . . . . .DLB-7

Onetti, Juan Carlos 1909-1994 . . . . .DLB-113

Onions, George Oliver 1872-1961 . . . . . . .DLB-153

Onofri, Arturo 1885-1928 . . . . .DLB-114

Opie, Amelia 1769-1853. . . . . .DLB-116, 159

Opitz, Martin 1597-1639 . . . . .DLB-164

Oppen, George 1908-1984. . . . . .DLB-5, 165

Oppenheim, E. Phillips 1866-1946 . . . . . .DLB-70

Oppenheim, James 1882-1932. . . . . .DLB-28

Oppenheimer, Joel 1930-1988 . . . . . . .DLB-5, 193

Optic, Oliver (see Adams, William Taylor)

Oral History Interview with Donald S.
    Klopfer Y-97

Orczy, Emma, Baroness 1865-1947. . . . . .DLB-70

Origo, Iris 1902-1988. . . . . .DLB-155

Orlovitz, Gil 1918-1973 . . . . .DLB-2, 5

Orlovsky, Peter 1933- DLB-16

Ormond, John 1923- DLB-27

Ornitz, Samuel 1890-1957 . . . . DLB-28, 44

O'Rourke, P. J. 1947- DLB-185

Orten, Jiří 1919-1941 . . . . DLB-215

Ortese, Anna Maria 1914- DLB-177

Ortiz, Simon J. 1941- DLB-120, 175

Ortnit and *Wolfdietrich* circa 1225-1250. . . . DLB-138

Orton, Joe 1933-1967 . . . . DLB-13

Orwell, George 1903-1950 . . . . . . DLB-15, 98, 195

The Orwell Year. Y-84

Ory, Carlos Edmundo de 1923- DLB-134

Osbey, Brenda Marie 1957- DLB-120

Osbon, B. S. 1827-1912. . . . . DLB-43

Osborn, Sarah 1714-1796 . . . . DLB-200

Osborne, John 1929-1994. . . . . DLB-13

Osgood, Herbert L. 1855-1918. . . . . DLB-47

Osgood, James R., and Company DLB-49

Osgood, McIlvaine and Company DLB-112

O'Shaughnessy, Arthur 1844-1881. . . . . . DLB-35

O'Shea, Patrick [publishing house] DLB-49

Osipov, Nikolai Petrovich 1751-1799 . . . . DLB-150

Oskison, John Milton 1879-1947. . . . . . . .DLB-175

Osler, Sir William 1849-1919 . . . . DLB-184

Osofisan, Femi 1946- DLB-125

Ostenso, Martha 1900-1963 . . . . DLB-92

Ostriker, Alicia 1937- DLB-120

Osundare, Niyi 1947- DLB-157

Oswald, Eleazer 1755-1795 . . . . DLB-43

Oswald von Wolkenstein
 1376 or 1377-1445 . . . . .DLB-179

Otero, Blas de 1916-1979 . . . . DLB-134

Otero, Miguel Antonio 1859-1944 . . . . . . DLB-82

Otero, Nina 1881-1965. . . . . DLB-209

Otero Silva, Miguel 1908-1985. . . . . DLB-145

Otfried von Weißenburg
 circa 800-circa 875? DLB-148

Otis, James (see Kaler, James Otis)

Otis, James, Jr. 1725-1783 . . . . DLB-31

Otis, Broaders and Company. DLB-49

Ottaway, James 1911- DLB-127

Ottendorfer, Oswald 1826-1900. . . . . DLB-23

Ottieri, Ottiero 1924- DLB-177

Otto-Peters, Louise 1819-1895 . . . . DLB-129

Otway, Thomas 1652-1685 . . . . DLB-80

Ouellette, Fernand 1930- DLB-60

Ouida 1839-1908 . . . . DLB-18, 156

Outing Publishing Company DLB-46

Outlaw Days, by Joyce Johnson DLB-16

Overbury, Sir Thomas
 circa 1581-1613 . . . . DLB-151

The Overlook Press DLB-46

Overview of U.S. Book Publishing,
 1910-1945. . . . . DLB-9

Ovid 43 B.C.-A.D. 17 . . . . DLB-211

Owen, Guy 1925- DLB-5

Owen, John 1564-1622 . . . . DLB-121

Owen, John [publishing house]. DLB-49

Owen, Robert 1771-1858 . . . . .DLB-107, 158

Owen, Wilfred 1893-1918 . . . . DLB-20; DS-18

Owen, Peter, Limited DLB-112

The Owl and the Nightingale
 circa 1189-1199 . . . . DLB-146

Owsley, Frank L. 1890-1956 . . . . DLB-17

Oxford, Seventeenth Earl of, Edward de Vere
 1550-1604 .DLB-172

Ozerov, Vladislav Aleksandrovich
 1769-1816. DLB-150

Ozick, Cynthia 1928- DLB-28, 152; Y-82

P

Pace, Richard 1482?-1536 . . . . DLB-167

Pacey, Desmond 1917-1975 . . . . DLB-88

Pack, Robert 1929- DLB-5

Packaging Papa: *The Garden of Eden* Y-86

Padell Publishing Company DLB-46

Padgett, Ron 1942- DLB-5

Padilla, Ernesto Chávez 1944- DLB-122

Page, L. C., and Company. DLB-49

Page, P. K. 1916- DLB-68

Page, Thomas Nelson
 1853-1922 . . . . .DLB-12, 78; DS-13

Page, Walter Hines 1855-1918. . . . . . DLB-71, 91

Paget, Francis Edward 1806-1882 . . . . . . DLB-163

Paget, Violet (see Lee, Vernon)

Pagliarani, Elio 1927- DLB-128

Pain, Barry 1864-1928 . . . . .DLB-135, 197

Pain, Philip ?-circa 1666 . . . . DLB-24

Paine, Robert Treat, Jr. 1773-1811 . . . . . . DLB-37

Paine, Thomas 1737-1809 . . . . .DLB-31, 43, 73, 158

Painter, George D. 1914- DLB-155

Painter, William 1540?-1594 . . . . DLB-136

Palazzeschi, Aldo 1885-1974 . . . . DLB-114

Paley, Grace 1922- DLB-28, 218

Palfrey, John Gorham 1796-1881 . . . . . . DLB-1, 30

Palgrave, Francis Turner 1824-1897. . . . . DLB-35

Palmer, Joe H. 1904-1952. . . . . .DLB-171

Palmer, Michael 1943- DLB-169

Paltock, Robert 1697-1767. . . . . DLB-39

Paludan, Jacob 1896-1975. . . . . DLB-214

Pan Books Limited DLB-112

Panama, Norman 1914-   and
 Frank, Melvin 1913-1988. . . . . DLB-26

Panaev, Ivan Ivanovich 1812-1862. . . . . . DLB-198

Pancake, Breece D'J 1952-1979. . . . . DLB-130

Panduro, Leif 1923-1977. . . . . DLB-214

Panero, Leopoldo 1909-1962 . . . . DLB-108

Pangborn, Edgar 1909-1976 . . . . DLB-8

''Panic Among the Philistines'': A Postscript,
 An Interview with Bryan Griffin Y-81

Panizzi, Sir Anthony 1797-1879 . . . . DLB-184

Panneton, Philippe (see Ringuet)

Panshin, Alexei 1940- DLB-8

Pansy (see Alden, Isabella)

Pantheon Books DLB-46

Papadat-Bengescu, Hortensia
 1876-1955. DLB-220

Papantonio, Michael (see Kohn, John S. Van E.)

Paperback Library DLB-46

Paperback Science Fiction. DLB-8

Paquet, Alfons 1881-1944. . . . . DLB-66

Paracelsus 1493-1541 . . . . .DLB-179

Paradis, Suzanne 1936- DLB-53

Pardoe, Julia 1804-1862 . . . . DLB-166

Paredes, Américo 1915- DLB-209

Pareja Diezcanseco, Alfredo
 1908-1993 . . . . DLB-145

Parents' Magazine Press DLB-46

Parise, Goffredo 1929-1986 . . . . .DLB-177

Parisian Theater, Fall 1984: Toward
 A New Baroque Y-85

Parizeau, Alice 1930- DLB-60

Parke, John 1754-1789 . . . . DLB-31

Parker, Dorothy 1893-1967 . . . . . . DLB-11, 45, 86

Parker, Gilbert 1860-1932 . . . . DLB-99

Parker, James 1714-1770 . . . . DLB-43

Parker, Matthew 1504-1575 . . . . DLB-213

Parker, Theodore 1810-1860 . . . . DLB-1

Parker, William Riley 1906-1968. . . . . . . DLB-103

Parker, J. H. [publishing house] DLB-106

Parker, John [publishing house] DLB-106

Parkman, Francis, Jr.
 1823-1893 . . . . .DLB-1, 30, 183, 186

Parks, Gordon 1912- DLB-33

Parks, William 1698-1750. . . . . DLB-43

Parks, William [publishing house] DLB-49

Parley, Peter (see Goodrich, Samuel Griswold)

Parmenides late sixth-fifth century B.C.
 . . . . .DLB-176

Parnell, Thomas 1679-1718 . . . . DLB-95

Parnicki, Teodor 1908-1988. . . . . DLB-215

Parr, Catherine 1513?-1548 . . . . DLB-136

Parrington, Vernon L. 1871-1929. . . . . .DLB-17, 63

Parrish, Maxfield 1870-1966. . . . . DLB-188

Parronchi, Alessandro 1914- DLB-128

Partridge, S. W., and Company DLB-106

Parton, James 1822-1891 . . . . DLB-30

Parton, Sara Payson Willis
 1811-1872. . . . . .DLB-43, 74

Parun, Vesna 1922- DLB-181

Pasinetti, Pier Maria 1913- DLB-177

Pasolini, Pier Paolo 1922- DLB-128, 177

Pastan, Linda 1932- DLB-5

Paston, George (Emily Morse Symonds)
 1860-1936 . . . . .DLB-149, 197

The Paston Letters 1422-1509 . . . . DLB-146

Pastorius, Francis Daniel
 1651-circa 1720 . . . . DLB-24

Patchen, Kenneth 1911-1972 . . . . DLB-16, 48

Pater, Walter 1839-1894. . . . . .DLB-57, 156

Paterson, Katherine 1932- DLB-52

Patmore, Coventry 1823-1896.......DLB-35, 98

Paton, Alan 1903-1988.................DS-17

Paton, Joseph Noel 1821-1901..........DLB-35

Paton Walsh, Jill 1937- DLB-161

Patrick, Edwin Hill ("Ted") 1901-1964 ...DLB-137

Patrick, John 1906-1995.................DLB-7

Pattee, Fred Lewis 1863-1950 ....DLB-71

Pattern and Paradigm: History as
　　Design, by Judith Ryan............DLB-75

Patterson, Alicia 1906-1963 ....DLB-127

Patterson, Eleanor Medill 1881-1948......DLB-29

Patterson, Eugene 1923- DLB-127

Patterson, Joseph Medill 1879-1946.......DLB-29

Pattillo, Henry 1726-1801 ....DLB-37

Paul, Elliot 1891-1958 ....DLB-4

Paul, Jean (see Richter, Johann Paul Friedrich)

Paul, Kegan, Trench, Trubner and Company
　　Limited DLB-106

Paul, Peter, Book Company DLB-49

Paul, Stanley, and Company Limited DLB-112

Paulding, James Kirke 1778-1860....DLB-3, 59, 74

Paulin, Tom 1949- DLB-40

Pauper, Peter, Press DLB-46

Pavese, Cesare 1908-1950 ....DLB-128, 177

Pavlova, Karolina Karlovna
　　1807-1893 ....DLB-205

Pavić, Milorad 1929- DLB-181

Pavlov, Konstantin 1933- DLB-181

Pavlov, Nikolai Filippovich 1803-1864.....DLB-198

Pavlova, Karolina Karlovna 1807-1893 ....DLB-205

Pavlović, Miodrag 1928- DLB-181

Paxton, John 1911-1985.................DLB-44

Payn, James 1830-1898 ....DLB-18

Payne, John 1842-1916 ....DLB-35

Payne, John Howard 1791-1852 ....DLB-37

Payson and Clarke...................DLB-46

Paz, Octavio 1914-1998.............Y-90, Y-98

Pazzi, Roberto 1946- DLB-196

Peabody, Elizabeth Palmer 1804-1894.....DLB-1

Peabody, Elizabeth Palmer
　　[publishing house] DLB-49

Peabody, Oliver William Bourn
　　1799-1848 ....DLB-59

Peace, Roger 1899-1968..............DLB-127

Peacham, Henry 1578-1644? DLB-151

Peacham, Henry, the Elder 1547-1634....DLB-172

Peachtree Publishers, Limited DLB-46

Peacock, Molly 1947- DLB-120

Peacock, Thomas Love 1785-1866 ...DLB-96, 116

Pead, Deuel ?-1727....................DLB-24

Peake, Mervyn 1911-1968..........DLB-15, 160

Peale, Rembrandt 1778-1860 ....DLB-183

Pear Tree Press DLB-112

Pearce, Philippa 1920- DLB-161

Pearson, H. B. [publishing house] DLB-49

Pearson, Hesketh 1887-1964 ....DLB-149

Peck, George W. 1840-1916 ....DLB-23, 42

Peck, H. C., and Theo. Bliss
　　[publishing house] DLB-49

Peck, Harry Thurston 1856-1914 .....DLB-71, 91

Peele, George 1556-1596 ....DLB-62, 167

Pegler, Westbrook 1894-1969 ....DLB-171

Pekić, Borislav 1930-1992 ....DLB-181

Pellegrini and Cudahy.................DLB-46

Pelletier, Aimé (see Vac, Bertrand)

Pemberton, Sir Max 1863-1950..........DLB-70

de la Peña, Terri 1947- DLB-209

Penfield, Edward 1866-1925 ....DLB-188

Penguin Books [U.S.]..................DLB-46

Penguin Books [U.K.] DLB-112

Penn Publishing Company DLB-49

Penn, William 1644-1718...............DLB-24

Penna, Sandro 1906-1977 ....DLB-114

Pennell, Joseph 1857-1926 ....DLB-188

Penner, Jonathan 1940- Y-83

Pennington, Lee 1939- Y-82

Pepys, Samuel 1633-1703.........DLB-101, 213

Percy, Thomas 1729-1811 ....DLB-104

Percy, Walker 1916-1990 .....DLB-2; Y-80, Y-90

Percy, William 1575-1648 ....DLB-172

Perec, Georges 1936-1982 ....DLB-83

Perelman, Bob 1947- DLB-193

Perelman, S. J. 1904-1979............DLB-11, 44

Perez, Raymundo "Tigre" 1946- DLB-122

Peri Rossi, Cristina 1941- DLB-145

Periodicals of the Beat Generation........DLB-16

Perkins, Eugene 1932- DLB-41

Perkoff, Stuart Z. 1930-1974 ....DLB-16

Perley, Moses Henry 1804-1862 ....DLB-99

Permabooks......................DLB-46

Perovsky, Aleksei Alekseevich (Antonii Pogorel'sky)
　　1787-1836......................DLB-198

Perrin, Alice 1867-1934 ....DLB-156

Perry, Bliss 1860-1954................DLB-71

Perry, Eleanor 1915-1981 ....DLB-44

Perry, Matthew 1794-1858............DLB-183

Perry, Sampson 1747-1823 ....DLB-158

Persius A.D. 34-A.D. 62 ....DLB-211

"Personal Style" (1890), by John Addington
　　Symonds DLB-57

Perutz, Leo 1882-1957................DLB-81

Pesetsky, Bette 1932- DLB-130

Pestalozzi, Johann Heinrich 1746-1827 ....DLB-94

Peter, Laurence J. 1919-1990...........DLB-53

Peter of Spain circa 1205-1277 ....DLB-115

Peterkin, Julia 1880-1961................DLB-9

Peters, Lenrie 1932- DLB-117

Peters, Robert 1924- DLB-105

Petersham, Maud 1889-1971 and
　　Petersham, Miska 1888-1960 ....DLB-22

Peterson, Charles Jacobs 1819-1887 ......DLB-79

Peterson, Len 1917- DLB-88

Peterson, Levi S. 1933- DLB-206

Peterson, Louis 1922-1998 ....DLB-76

Peterson, T. B., and Brothers DLB-49

Petitclair, Pierre 1813-1860 ....DLB-99

Petrescu, Camil 1894-1957 ....DLB-220

Petronius circa A.D. 20-A.D. 66 ....DLB-211

Petrov, Aleksandar 1938- DLB-181

Petrov, Gavriil 1730-1801 ....DLB-150

Petrov, Vasilii Petrovich 1736-1799......DLB-150

Petrov, Valeri 1920- DLB-181

Petrović, Rastko 1898-1949............DLB-147

Petruslied circa 854? DLB-148

Petry, Ann 1908-1997 ....DLB-76

Pettie, George circa 1548-1589 ....DLB-136

Peyton, K. M. 1929- DLB-161

Pfaffe Konrad flourished circa 1172......DLB-148

Pfaffe Lamprecht flourished circa 1150 ...DLB-148

Pfeiffer, Emily 1827-1890..............DLB-199

Pforzheimer, Carl H. 1879-1957 ....DLB-140

Phaedrus circa 18 B.C.-circa A.D. 50 ....DLB-211

Phaer, Thomas 1510?-1560...........DLB-167

Phaidon Press Limited................DLB-112

Pharr, Robert Deane 1916-1992 ....DLB-33

Phelps, Elizabeth Stuart 1815-1852 ......DLB-202

Phelps, Elizabeth Stuart 1844-1911 ...DLB-74, 221

Philander von der Linde
　　(see Mencke, Johann Burckhard)

Philby, H. St. John B. 1885-1960........DLB-195

Philip, Marlene Nourbese 1947- DLB-157

Philippe, Charles-Louis 1874-1909........DLB-65

Philips, John 1676-1708 ....DLB-95

Philips, Katherine 1632-1664...........DLB-131

Phillipps, Sir Thomas 1792-1872 ....DLB-184

Phillips, Caryl 1958- DLB-157

Phillips, David Graham 1867-1911 .....DLB-9, 12

Phillips, Jayne Anne 1952- Y-80

Phillips, Robert 1938- DLB-105

Phillips, Stephen 1864-1915.............DLB-10

Phillips, Ulrich B. 1877-1934 ....DLB-17

Phillips, Willard 1784-1873 ....DLB-59

Phillips, William 1907- DLB-137

Phillips, Sampson and Company........DLB-49

Phillpotts, Adelaide Eden (Adelaide Ross)
　　1896-1993 ....DLB-191

Phillpotts, Eden
　　1862-1960...........DLB-10, 70, 135, 153

Philo circa 20-15 B.C.-circa A.D. 50
　　..............................DLB-176

Philosophical Library..................DLB-46

"The Philosophy of Style" (1852), by
　　Herbert Spencer DLB-57

Phinney, Elihu [publishing house].......DLB-49

Phoenix, John (see Derby, George Horatio)

PHYLON (Fourth Quarter, 1950),
The Negro in Literature:
The Current Scene............... DLB-76

Physiologus circa 1070-circa 1150 .... DLB-148

Piccolo, Lucio 1903-1969 .... DLB-114

Pickard, Tom 1946- DLB-40

Pickering, William [publishing house] ... DLB-106

Pickthall, Marjorie 1883-1922.......... DLB-92

Pictorial Printing Company DLB-49

Piercy, Marge 1936- DLB-120

Pierro, Albino 1916- DLB-128

Pignotti, Lamberto 1926- DLB-128

Pike, Albert 1809-1891 .... DLB-74

Pike, Zebulon Montgomery
1779-1813.................... DLB-183

Pillat, Ion 1891-1945............... DLB-220

Pilon, Jean-Guy 1930- DLB-60

Pinckney, Eliza Lucas 1722-1793 .... DLB-200

Pinckney, Josephine 1895-1957 .... DLB-6

Pindar circa 518 B.C.-circa 438 B.C.
..................................DLB-176

Pindar, Peter (see Wolcot, John)

Pineda, Cecile 1942- DLB-209

Pinero, Arthur Wing 1855-1934........ DLB-10

Pinget, Robert 1919-1997 .... DLB-83

Pinnacle Books DLB-46

Piñon, Nélida 1935- DLB-145

Pinsky, Robert 1940- Y-82

Pinter, Harold 1930- DLB-13

Piontek, Heinz 1925- DLB-75

Piozzi, Hester Lynch [Thrale]
1741-1821.................. DLB-104, 142

Piper, H. Beam 1904-1964 .... DLB-8

Piper, Watty........................ DLB-22

Pirckheimer, Caritas 1467-1532 ....DLB-179

Pirckheimer, Willibald 1470-1530.......DLB-179

Pisar, Samuel 1929- Y-83

Pitkin, Timothy 1766-1847 .... DLB-30

The Pitt Poetry Series: Poetry Publishing
Today Y-85

Pitter, Ruth 1897- DLB-20

Pix, Mary 1666-1709 .... DLB-80

Pixerécourt, René Charles Guilbert de
1773-1844.................... DLB-192

Plaatje, Sol T. 1876-1932 .... DLB-125

The Place of Realism in Fiction (1895), by
George Gissing................. DLB-18

Plante, David 1940- Y-83

Platen, August von 1796-1835 .... DLB-90

Plath, Sylvia 1932-1963 .... DLB-5, 6, 152

Plato circa 428 B.C.-348-347 B.C.
..................................DLB-176

Platon 1737-1812 .... DLB-150

Platt and Munk Company DLB-46

Plautus circa 254 B.C.-184 B.C........ DLB-211

Playboy Press...................... DLB-46

Playford, John [publishing house].......DLB-170

Plays, Playwrights, and Playgoers DLB-84

Playwrights and Professors, by
Tom Stoppard DLB-13

Playwrights on the Theater DLB-80

Der Pleier flourished circa 1250 .... DLB-138

Plenzdorf, Ulrich 1934- DLB-75

Plessen, Elizabeth 1944- DLB-75

Pletnev, Petr Aleksandrovich
1792-1865.................... DLB-205

Pliekšāne, Elza Rozenberga (see Aspazija)

Pliekšāns, Jānis (see Rainis, Jānis)

Plievier, Theodor 1892-1955 .... DLB-69

Plimpton, George 1927- DLB-185

Pliny the Elder A.D. 23/24-A.D. 79 ..... DLB-211

Pliny the Younger
circa A.D. 61-A.D. 112............ DLB-211

Plomer, William 1903-1973 .... DLB-20, 162, 191

Plotinus 204-270 ....DLB-176

Plume, Thomas 1630-1704............ DLB-213

Plumly, Stanley 1939- DLB-5, 193

Plumpp, Sterling D. 1940- DLB-41

Plunkett, James 1920- DLB-14

Plutarch circa 46-circa 120 ....DLB-176

Plymell, Charles 1935- DLB-16

Pocket Books DLB-46

Poe, Edgar Allan 1809-1849.....DLB-3, 59, 73, 74

Poe, James 1921-1980................ DLB-44

The Poet Laureate of the United States
Statements from Former Consultants
in Poetry Y-86

"The Poet's Kaleidoscope: The Element of
Surprise in the Making of the Poem," by
Madeline DeFrees DLB-105

"The Poetry File," by Edward Field DLB-105

Pogodin, Mikhail Petrovich
1800-1875.................... DLB-198

Pogorel'sky, Antonii (see Perovsky, Aleksei
Alekseevich)

Pohl, Frederik 1919- DLB-8

Poirier, Louis (see Gracq, Julien)

Polanyi, Michael 1891-1976 .... DLB-100

Poláček, Karel 1892-1945............. DLB-215

Pole, Reginald 1500-1558............. DLB-132

Polevoi, Nikolai Alekseevich
1796-1846.................... DLB-198

Polezhaev, Aleksandr Ivanovich
1804-1838.................... DLB-205

Poliakoff, Stephen 1952- DLB-13

Polidori, John William 1795-1821....... DLB-116

Polite, Carlene Hatcher 1932- DLB-33

Pollard, Alfred W. 1859-1944 .... DLB-201

Pollard, Edward A. 1832-1872 .... DLB-30

Pollard, Graham 1903-1976 .... DLB-201

Pollard, Percival 1869-1911 .... DLB-71

Pollard and Moss DLB-49

Pollock, Sharon 1936- DLB-60

Polonsky, Abraham 1910- DLB-26

Polotsky, Simeon 1629-1680 .... DLB-150

Polybius circa 200 B.C.-118 B.C........DLB-176

Pomilio, Mario 1921-1990 ....DLB-177

Ponce, Mary Helen 1938- DLB-122

Ponce-Montoya, Juanita 1949- DLB-122

Ponet, John 1516?-1556 .... DLB-132

Poniatowski, Elena 1933- DLB-113

Ponsard, François 1814-1867 .... DLB-192

Ponsonby, William [publishing house]....DLB-170

Pontiggia, Giuseppe 1934- DLB-196

Pony Stories DLB-160

Poole, Ernest 1880-1950............... DLB-9

Poole, Sophia 1804-1891 .... DLB-166

Poore, Benjamin Perley 1820-1887....... DLB-23

Popa, Vasko 1922-1991 .... DLB-181

Pope, Abbie Hanscom 1858-1894 ..... DLB-140

Pope, Alexander 1688-1744 .....DLB-95, 101, 213

Popov, Mikhail Ivanovich
1742-circa 1790.................. DLB-150

Popović, Aleksandar 1929-1996........ DLB-181

Popular Library DLB-46

Porete, Marguerite ?-1310 .... DLB-208

Porlock, Martin (see MacDonald, Philip)

Porpoise Press DLB-112

Porta, Antonio 1935-1989 .... DLB-128

Porter, Anna Maria 1780-1832......DLB-116, 159

Porter, David 1780-1843............. DLB-183

Porter, Eleanor H. 1868-1920 .... DLB-9

Porter, Gene Stratton (see Stratton-Porter, Gene)

Porter, Henry ?-? DLB-62

Porter, Jane 1776-1850 ....DLB-116, 159

Porter, Katherine Anne
1890-1980 ....DLB-4, 9, 102; Y-80; DS-12

Porter, Peter 1929- DLB-40

Porter, William Sydney
1862-1910 ....DLB-12, 78, 79

Porter, William T. 1809-1858 .... DLB-3, 43

Porter and Coates................. DLB-49

Portillo Trambley, Estela 1927-1998..... DLB-209

Portis, Charles 1933- DLB-6

Posey, Alexander 1873-1908...........DLB-175

Postans, Marianne circa 1810-1865 ..... DLB-166

Postl, Carl (see Sealsfield, Carl)

Poston, Ted 1906-1974................ DLB-51

Postscript to [the Third Edition of] *Clarissa*
(1751), by Samuel Richardson DLB-39

Potok, Chaim 1929- DLB-28, 152; Y-84

Potter, Beatrix 1866-1943............. DLB-141

Potter, David M. 1910-1971 ....DLB-17

Potter, John E., and Company DLB-49

Pottle, Frederick A. 1897-1987 .....DLB-103; Y-87

Poulin, Jacques 1937- DLB-60

Pound, Ezra 1885-1972..... DLB-4, 45, 63; DS-15

Povich, Shirley 1905- DLB-171

Powell, Anthony 1905- DLB-15

Powell, John Wesley 1834-1902........ DLB-186

Powers, J. F. 1917- DLB-130

Pownall, David 1938- DLB-14

Powys, John Cowper 1872-1963 . . . . .DLB-15

Powys, Llewelyn 1884-1939 . . . . .DLB-98

Powys, T. F. 1875-1953 . . . . .DLB-36, 162

Poynter, Nelson 1903-1978 . . . . .DLB-127

The Practice of Biography: An Interview
     with Stanley Weintraub Y-82

The Practice of Biography II: An Interview
     with B. L. Reid Y-83

The Practice of Biography III: An Interview
     with Humphrey Carpenter Y-84

The Practice of Biography IV: An Interview with
     William Manchester Y-85

The Practice of Biography V: An Interview
     with Justin Kaplan Y-86

The Practice of Biography VI: An Interview with
     David Herbert Donald Y-87

The Practice of Biography VII: An Interview with
     John Caldwell Guilds Y-92

The Practice of Biography VIII: An Interview
     with Joan Mellen Y-94

The Practice of Biography IX: An Interview
     with Michael Reynolds Y-95

Prados, Emilio 1899-1962 . . . . .DLB-134

Praed, Winthrop Mackworth
     1802-1839 . . . . .DLB-96

Praeger Publishers DLB-46

Praetorius, Johannes 1630-1680. . . . . . . .DLB-168

Pratolini, Vasco 1913-1991 . . . . .DLB-177

Pratt, E. J. 1882-1964. . . . . .DLB-92

Pratt, Samuel Jackson 1749-1814 . . . . . . .DLB-39

Preciado Martin, Patricia 1939- DLB-209

Preface to *Alwyn* (1780), by
     Thomas Holcroft. DLB-39

Preface to *Colonel Jack* (1722), by
     Daniel Defoe DLB-39

Preface to *Evelina* (1778), by
     Fanny Burney .DLB-39

Preface to *Ferdinand Count Fathom* (1753), by
     Tobias Smollett DLB-39

Preface to *Incognita* (1692), by
     William Congreve. DLB-39

Preface to *Joseph Andrews* (1742), by
     Henry Fielding DLB-39

Preface to *Moll Flanders* (1722), by
     Daniel Defoe DLB-39

Preface to *Poems* (1853), by
     Matthew Arnold DLB-32

Preface to *Robinson Crusoe* (1719), by
     Daniel Defoe DLB-39

Preface to *Roderick Random* (1748), by
     Tobias Smollett DLB-39

Preface to *Roxana* (1724), by
     Daniel Defoe DLB-39

Preface to *St. Leon* (1799), by
     William Godwin DLB-39

Preface to Sarah Fielding's *Familiar Letters*
     (1747), by Henry Fielding [excerpt] DLB-39

Preface to Sarah Fielding's *The Adventures of
     David Simple* (1744), by
     Henry Fielding DLB-39

Preface to *The Cry* (1754), by
     Sarah Fielding DLB-39

Preface to *The Delicate Distress* (1769), by
     Elizabeth Griffin DLB-39

Preface to *The Disguis'd Prince* (1733), by
     Eliza Haywood [excerpt] DLB-39

Preface to *The Farther Adventures of Robinson
     Crusoe* (1719), by Daniel Defoe DLB-39

Preface to the First Edition of *Pamela* (1740), by
     Samuel Richardson DLB-39

Preface to the First Edition of *The Castle of
     Otranto* (1764), by Horace Walpole DLB-39

Preface to *The History of Romances* (1715), by
     Pierre Daniel Huet [excerpts] DLB-39

Preface to *The Life of Charlotta du Pont* (1723),
     by Penelope Aubin DLB-39

Preface to *The Old English Baron* (1778), by
     Clara Reeve. DLB-39

Preface to the Second Edition of *The Castle of
     Otranto* (1765), by Horace Walpole DLB-39

Preface to *The Secret History, of Queen Zarah,
     and the Zarazians* (1705), by Delariviere
     Manley DLB-39

Preface to the Third Edition of *Clarissa* (1751),
     by Samuel Richardson [excerpt] DLB-39

Preface to *The Works of Mrs. Davys* (1725), by
     Mary Davys DLB-39

Preface to Volume 1 of *Clarissa* (1747), by
     Samuel Richardson DLB-39

Preface to Volume 3 of *Clarissa* (1748), by
     Samuel Richardson DLB-39

Préfontaine, Yves 1937- DLB-53

Prelutsky, Jack 1940- DLB-61

Premisses, by Michael Hamburger DLB-66

Prentice, George D. 1802-1870 . . . . .DLB-43

Prentice-Hall DLB-46

Prescott, Orville 1906-1996 . . . . Y-96

Prescott, William Hickling
     1796-1859 . . . . .DLB-1, 30, 59

The Present State of the English Novel (1892),
     by George Saintsbury DLB-18

Prešeren, Francn 1800-1849. . . . . .DLB-147

Preston, May Wilson 1873-1949 . . . . . . .DLB-188

Preston, Thomas 1537-1598. . . . . .DLB-62

Price, Reynolds 1933- DLB-2, 218

Price, Richard 1723-1791 . . . . .DLB-158

Price, Richard 1949- Y-81

Priest, Christopher 1943- DLB-14, 207

Priestley, J. B. 1894-1984
     . . . . .DLB-10, 34, 77, 100, 139; Y-84

Primary Bibliography: A Retrospective Y-95

Prime, Benjamin Young 1733-1791 . . . . . .DLB-31

Primrose, Diana floruit circa 1630. . . . . . .DLB-126

Prince, F. T. 1912- DLB-20

Prince, Thomas 1687-1758 . . . . .DLB-24, 140

The Principles of Success in Literature (1865), by
     George Henry Lewes [excerpt] DLB-57

Printz, Wolfgang Casper 1641-1717. . . . . .DLB-168

Prior, Matthew 1664-1721 . . . . .DLB-95

Prisco, Michele 1920- DLB-177

Pritchard, William H. 1932- DLB-111

Pritchett, V. S. 1900-1997 . . . . .DLB-15, 139

Probyn, May 1856 or 1857-1909 . . . . . . .DLB-199

Procter, Adelaide Anne 1825-1864 . . .DLB-32, 199

Procter, Bryan Waller 1787-1874 . . . . .DLB-96, 144

Proctor, Robert 1868-1903 . . . . .DLB-184

*Producing Dear Bunny, Dear Volodya: The Friendship
     and the Feud* Y-97

The Profession of Authorship:
     Scribblers for Bread. Y-89

The Progress of Romance (1785), by Clara Reeve
     [excerpt] DLB-39

Prokopovich, Feofan 1681?-1736. . . . . . . .DLB-150

Prokosch, Frederic 1906-1989 . . . . .DLB-48

The Proletarian Novel. DLB-9

Propertius circa 50 B.C.-post 16 B.C. DLB-211

Propper, Dan 1937- DLB-16

The Prospect of Peace (1778),
     by Joel Barlow. DLB-37

Protagoras circa 490 B.C.-420 B.C.
     . . . . .DLB-176

Proud, Robert 1728-1813. . . . . .DLB-30

Proust, Marcel 1871-1922 . . . . .DLB-65

Prynne, J. H. 1936- DLB-40

Przybyszewski, Stanisław 1868-1927 . . . . .DLB-66

Pseudo-Dionysius the Areopagite floruit
     circa 500 . . . . .DLB-115

Public Domain and the Violation of Texts Y-97

The Public Lending Right in America
     Statement by Sen. Charles McC.
     Mathias, Jr. PLR and the Meaning
     of Literary Property Statements on
     PLR by American Writers Y-83

The Public Lending Right in the United Kingdom
     Public Lending Right: The First Year in the
     United Kingdom Y-83

The Publication of English
     Renaissance Plays DLB-62

Publications and Social Movements
     [Transcendentalism] DLB-1

Publishers and Agents: The Columbia
     Connection Y-87

A Publisher's Archives: G. P. Putnam Y-92

Publishing Fiction at LSU Press. Y-87

The Publishing Industry in 1998:
     Sturm-und-drang.com Y-98

Pückler-Muskau, Hermann von
     1785-1871 . . . . DLB-133

Pufendorf, Samuel von 1632-1694. . . . . . .DLB-168

Pugh, Edwin William 1874-1930 . . . . . . .DLB-135

Pugin, A. Welby 1812-1852 . . . . .DLB-55

Puig, Manuel 1932-1990 . . . . .DLB-113

Pulitzer, Joseph 1847-1911 . . . . .DLB-23

Pulitzer, Joseph, Jr. 1885-1955. . . . . .DLB-29

Pulitzer Prizes for the Novel, 1917-1945 . . . .DLB-9

Pulliam, Eugene 1889-1975 . . . . .DLB-127

Purchas, Samuel 1577?-1626 . . . . .DLB-151

Purdy, Al 1918- DLB-88

Purdy, James 1923- DLB-2, 218

Purdy, Ken W. 1913-1972 . . . . .DLB-137

Pusey, Edward Bouverie
1800-1882 . . . . DLB-55

Pushkin, Aleksandr Sergeevich
1799-1837 . . . . DLB-205

Pushkin, Vasilii L'vovich
1766-1830 . . . . DLB-205

Putnam, George Palmer 1814-1872 . . . . DLB-3, 79

Putnam, Samuel 1892-1950 . . . . DLB-4

G. P. Putnam's Sons [U.S.] DLB-49

G. P. Putnam's Sons [U.K.] DLB-106

Puzo, Mario 1920- DLB-6

Pyle, Ernie 1900-1945 . . . . DLB-29

Pyle, Howard 1853-1911 . . . . DLB-42, 188; DS-13

Pym, Barbara 1913-1980 . . . . . DLB-14, 207; Y-87

Pynchon, Thomas 1937- DLB-2, 173

Pyramid Books DLB-46

Pyrnelle, Louise-Clarke 1850-1907 . . . . . . DLB-42

Pythagoras circa 570 B.C.-? DLB-176

Q

Quad, M. (see Lewis, Charles B.)

Quaritch, Bernard 1819-1899 . . . . DLB-184

Quarles, Francis 1592-1644 . . . . DLB-126

The Quarterly Review 1809-1967 . . . . . . DLB-110

Quasimodo, Salvatore 1901-1968 . . . . . . DLB-114

Queen, Ellery (see Dannay, Frederic, and
Manfred B. Lee)

The Queen City Publishing House DLB-49

Queneau, Raymond 1903-1976 . . . . DLB-72

Quennell, Sir Peter 1905-1993 . . . . . DLB-155, 195

Quesnel, Joseph 1746-1809 . . . . DLB-99

The Question of American Copyright
in the Nineteenth Century Headnote
Preface, by George Haven Putnam
The Evolution of Copyright, by
Brander Matthews
Summary of Copyright Legislation in
the United States, by R. R. Bowker
Analysis oæ the Provisions of the
Copyright Law of 1891, by
George Haven Putnam
The Contest for International Copyright,
by George Haven Putnam
Cheap Books and Good Books,
by Brander Matthews DLB-49

Quiller-Couch, Sir Arthur Thomas
1863-1944 . . . . DLB-135, 153, 190

Quin, Ann 1936-1973 . . . . DLB-14

Quincy, Samuel, of Georgia ?-? DLB-31

Quincy, Samuel, of Massachusetts
1734-1789 . . . . DLB-31

Quinn, Anthony 1915- DLB-122

Quinn, John 1870-1924 . . . . DLB-187

Quiñónez, Naomi 1951- DLB-209

Quintana, Leroy V. 1944- DLB-82

Quintana, Miguel de 1671-1748
A Forerunner of Chicano
Literature DLB-122

Quintillian circa A.D. 40-circa A.D. 96 . . . DLB-211

Quist, Harlin, Books DLB-46

Quoirez, Françoise (see Sagan, Françoise)

R

R-va, Zeneida (see Gan, Elena Andreevna)

Raabe, Wilhelm 1831-1910 . . . . DLB-129

Raban, Jonathan 1942- DLB-204

Rabe, David 1940- DLB-7

Raboni, Giovanni 1932- DLB-128

Rachilde 1860-1953 . . . . DLB-123, 192

Racin, Kočo 1908-1943 . . . . DLB-147

Rackham, Arthur 1867-1939 . . . . DLB-141

Radauskas, Henrikas 1910-1970 . . . . DLB-220

Radcliffe, Ann 1764-1823 . . . . DLB-39, 178

Raddall, Thomas 1903- DLB-68

Radichkov, Yordan 1929- DLB-181

Radiguet, Raymond 1903-1923 . . . . DLB-65

Radishchev, Aleksandr Nikolaevich
1749-1802 . . . . DLB-150

Radnóti, Miklós 1909-1944 . . . . DLB-215

Radványi, Netty Reiling (see Seghers, Anna)

Rahv, Philip 1908-1973 . . . . DLB-137

Raich, Semen Egorovich 1792-1855 . . . . . DLB-205

Raičković, Stevan 1928- DLB-181

Raimund, Ferdinand Jakob 1790-1836 . . . . DLB-90

Raine, Craig 1944- DLB-40

Raine, Kathleen 1908- DLB-20

Rainis, Jānis 1865-1929 . . . . DLB-220

Rainolde, Richard
circa 1530-1606 . . . . DLB-136

Rakić, Milan 1876-1938 . . . . DLB-147

Rakosi, Carl 1903- DLB-193

Ralegh, Sir Walter 1554?-1618 . . . . DLB-172

Ralin, Radoy 1923- DLB-181

Ralph, Julian 1853-1903 . . . . DLB-23

Ralph Waldo Emerson in 1982 . . . . Y-82

Ramat, Silvio 1939- DLB-128

Rambler, no. 4 (1750), by Samuel Johnson
[excerpt] DLB-39

Ramée, Marie Louise de la (see Ouida)

Ramírez, Sergío 1942- DLB-145

Ramke, Bin 1947- DLB-120

Ramler, Karl Wilhelm 1725-1798 . . . . DLB-97

Ramon Ribeyro, Julio 1929- DLB-145

Ramos, Manuel 1948- DLB-209

Ramous, Mario 1924- DLB-128

Rampersad, Arnold 1941- DLB-111

Ramsay, Allan 1684 or 1685-1758 . . . . . . DLB-95

Ramsay, David 1749-1815 . . . . DLB-30

Ramsay, Martha Laurens 1759-1811 . . . . DLB-200

Ranck, Katherine Quintana 1942- DLB-122

Rand, Avery and Company DLB-49

Rand McNally and Company DLB-49

Randall, David Anton 1905-1975 . . . . DLB-140

Randall, Dudley 1914- DLB-41

Randall, Henry S. 1811-1876 . . . . DLB-30

Randall, James G. 1881-1953 . . . . DLB-17

The Randall Jarrell Symposium: A Small
Collection of Randall Jarrells
Excerpts From Papers Delivered at
the Randall Jarrel Symposium Y-86

Randolph, A. Philip 1889-1979 . . . . DLB-91

Randolph, Anson D. F.
[publishing house] DLB-49

Randolph, Thomas 1605-1635 . . . . . . DLB-58, 126

Random House DLB-46

Ranlet, Henry [publishing house] DLB-49

Ransom, Harry 1908-1976 . . . . DLB-187

Ransom, John Crowe 1888-1974 . . . . . DLB-45, 63

Ransome, Arthur 1884-1967 . . . . DLB-160

Raphael, Frederic 1931- DLB-14

Raphaelson, Samson 1896-1983 . . . . DLB-44

Rashi circa 1040-1105 . . . . DLB-208

Raskin, Ellen 1928-1984 . . . . DLB-52

Rastell, John 1475?-1536 . . . . DLB-136, 170

Rattigan, Terence 1911-1977 . . . . DLB-13

Rawlings, Marjorie Kinnan
1896-1953 . . . . DLB-9, 22, 102; DS-17

Rawlinson, Richard 1690-1755 . . . . DLB-213

Rawlinson, Thomas 1681-1725 . . . . DLB-213

Raworth, Tom 1938- DLB-40

Ray, David 1932- DLB-5

Ray, Gordon Norton 1915-1986 . . . . DLB-103, 140

Ray, Henrietta Cordelia 1849-1916 . . . . . DLB-50

Raymond, Ernest 1888-1974 . . . . DLB-191

Raymond, Henry J. 1820-1869 . . . . DLB-43, 79

Raymond Chandler Centenary Tributes
from Michael Avallone, James Elroy, Joe Gores,
and William F. Nolan Y-88

Reach, Angus 1821-1856 . . . . DLB-70

Read, Herbert 1893-1968 . . . . DLB-20, 149

Read, Herbert, "The Practice of Biography," in The
English Sense of Humour and Other
Essays DLB-149

Read, Martha Meredith DLB-200

Read, Opie 1852-1939 . . . . DLB-23

Read, Piers Paul 1941- DLB-14

Reade, Charles 1814-1884 . . . . DLB-21

Reader's Digest Condensed Books DLB-46

Readers Ulysses Symposium Y-97

Reading, Peter 1946- DLB-40

Reading Series in New York City Y-96

Reaney, James 1926- DLB-68

Rebhun, Paul 1500?-1546 . . . . DLB-179

Rèbora, Clemente 1885-1957 . . . . DLB-114

Rebreanu, Liviu 1885-1944 . . . . DLB-220

Rechy, John 1934- DLB-122; Y-82

The Recovery of Literature: Criticism in the 1990s:
A Symposium Y-91

Redding, J. Saunders 1906-1988 . . . . DLB-63, 76

Redfield, J. S. [publishing house] DLB-49

Redgrove, Peter 1932- DLB-40

Redmon, Anne 1943- Y-86

Redmond, Eugene B. 1937- DLB-41

Redpath, James [publishing house] DLB-49

Reed, Henry 1808-1854. . . . . .DLB-59

Reed, Henry 1914- DLB-27

Reed, Ishmael 1938- DLB-2, 5, 33, 169; DS-8

Reed, Rex 1938- DLB-185

Reed, Sampson 1800-1880. . . . . .DLB-1

Reed, Talbot Baines 1852-1893 . . . . .DLB-141

Reedy, William Marion 1862-1920 . . . . . .DLB-91

Reese, Lizette Woodworth 1856-1935. . . . .DLB-54

Reese, Thomas 1742-1796 . . . . .DLB-37

Reeve, Clara 1729-1807 . . . . .DLB-39

Reeves, James 1909-1978 . . . . .DLB-161

Reeves, John 1926- DLB-88

"Reflections: After a Tornado,"
by Judson Jerome DLB-105

Regnery, Henry, Company DLB-46

Rehberg, Hans 1901-1963 . . . . .DLB-124

Rehfisch, Hans José 1891-1960 . . . . .DLB-124

Reich, Ebbe Kløvedal 1940- DLB-214

Reid, Alastair 1926- DLB-27

Reid, B. L. 1918-1990 . . . . .DLB-111

Reid, Christopher 1949- DLB-40

Reid, Forrest 1875-1947 . . . . .DLB-153

Reid, Helen Rogers 1882-1970. . . . . .DLB-29

Reid, James ?-? DLB-31

Reid, Mayne 1818-1883. . . . . .DLB-21, 163

Reid, Thomas 1710-1796 . . . . .DLB-31

Reid, V. S. (Vic) 1913-1987 . . . . .DLB-125

Reid, Whitelaw 1837-1912 . . . . .DLB-23

Reilly and Lee Publishing Company DLB-46

Reimann, Brigitte 1933-1973 . . . . .DLB-75

Reinmar der Alte
circa 1165-circa 1205 . . . . .DLB-138

Reinmar von Zweter
circa 1200-circa 1250 . . . . .DLB-138

Reisch, Walter 1903-1983 . . . . .DLB-44

Reizei Family .DLB-203

Remarks at the Opening of "The Biographical
Part of Literature" Exhibition, by
William R. Cagle. Y-98

Remarque, Erich Maria 1898-1970 . . . . . .DLB-56

"Re-meeting of Old Friends": The Jack
Kerouac Conference Y-82

Reminiscences, by Charles Scribner Jr. DS-17

Remington, Frederic
1861-1909 . . . . .DLB-12, 186, 188

Renaud, Jacques 1943- DLB-60

Renault, Mary 1905-1983 . . . . Y-83

Rendell, Ruth 1930- DLB-87

Rensselaer, Maria van Cortlandt van
1645-1689 .DLB-200

Repplier, Agnes 1855-1950 . . . . .DLB-221

Representative Men and Women: A Historical
Perspective on the British Novel,
1930-1960 .DLB-15

(Re-)Publishing Orwell Y-86

Research in the American Antiquarian Book
Trade Y-97

Responses to Ken Auletta Y-97

Rettenbacher, Simon 1634-1706. . . . . . . .DLB-168

Reuchlin, Johannes 1455-1522. . . . . .DLB-179

Reuter, Christian 1665-after 1712 . . . . . .DLB-168

Reuter, Fritz 1810-1874 . . . . .DLB-129

Reuter, Gabriele 1859-1941 . . . . .DLB-66

Revell, Fleming H., Company DLB-49

Reventlow, Franziska Gräfin zu
1871-1918 .DLB-66

Review of Reviews Office DLB-112

Review of [Samuel Richardson's] *Clarissa* (1748), by
Henry Fielding DLB-39

The Revolt (1937), by Mary Colum
[excerpts] DLB-36

Rexroth, Kenneth
1905-1982 . . . . DLB-16, 48, 165, 212; Y-82

Rey, H. A. 1898-1977 . . . . .DLB-22

Reynal and Hitchcock DLB-46

Reynolds, G. W. M. 1814-1879 . . . . .DLB-21

Reynolds, John Hamilton 1794-1852 . . . . .DLB-96

Reynolds, Mack 1917- DLB-8

Reynolds, Sir Joshua 1723-1792 . . . . .DLB-104

Reznikoff, Charles 1894-1976 . . . . . . .DLB-28, 45

"Rhetoric" (1828; revised, 1859), by
Thomas de Quincey [excerpt] DLB-57

Rhett, Robert Barnwell 1800-1876. . . . . . .DLB-43

Rhode, John 1884-1964 . . . . .DLB-77

Rhodes, James Ford 1848-1927 . . . . .DLB-47

Rhodes, Richard 1937- DLB-185

Rhys, Jean 1890-1979 . . . . DLB-36, 117, 162

Ricardo, David 1772-1823 . . . . DLB-107, 158

Ricardou, Jean 1932- DLB-83

Rice, Elmer 1892-1967 . . . . .DLB-4, 7

Rice, Grantland 1880-1954 . . . . DLB-29, 171

Rich, Adrienne 1929- DLB-5, 67

Richard de Fournival
1201-1259 or 1260 . . . . .DLB-208

Richards, David Adams 1950- DLB-53

Richards, George circa 1760-1814 . . . . . . .DLB-37

Richards, I. A. 1893-1979. . . . . .DLB-27

Richards, Laura E. 1850-1943 . . . . .DLB-42

Richards, William Carey 1818-1892 . . . . . .DLB-73

Richards, Grant [publishing house] DLB-112

Richardson, Charles F. 1851-1913. . . . . . .DLB-71

Richardson, Dorothy M. 1873-1957 . . . . . .DLB-36

Richardson, Henry Handel (Ethel Florence
Lindesay) 1870-1946 . . . . .DLB-197

Richardson, Jack 1935- DLB-7

Richardson, John 1796-1852 . . . . .DLB-99

Richardson, Samuel 1689-1761 . . . . . .DLB-39, 154

Richardson, Willis 1889-1977 . . . . .DLB-51

Riche, Barnabe 1542-1617 . . . . .DLB-136

Richepin, Jean 1849-1926 . . . . .DLB-192

Richler, Mordecai 1931- DLB-53

Richter, Conrad 1890-1968 . . . . .DLB-9, 212

Richter, Hans Werner 1908- DLB-69

Richter, Johann Paul Friedrich
1763-1825 .DLB-94

Rickerby, Joseph [publishing house] DLB-106

Rickword, Edgell 1898-1982 . . . . .DLB-20

Riddell, Charlotte 1832-1906. . . . . .DLB-156

Riddell, John (see Ford, Corey)

Ridge, John Rollin 1827-1867 . . . . .DLB-175

Ridge, Lola 1873-1941 . . . . .DLB-54

Ridge, William Pett 1859-1930 . . . . .DLB-135

Riding, Laura (see Jackson, Laura Riding)

Ridler, Anne 1912- DLB-27

Ridruego, Dionisio 1912-1975 . . . . .DLB-108

Riel, Louis 1844-1885 . . . . .DLB-99

Riemer, Johannes 1648-1714 . . . . .DLB-168

Rifbjerg, Klaus 1931- DLB-214

Riffaterre, Michael 1924- DLB-67

Riggs, Lynn 1899-1954 . . . . .DLB-175

Riis, Jacob 1849-1914 . . . . .DLB-23

Riker, John C. [publishing house] DLB-49

Riley, James 1777-1840. . . . . .DLB-183

Riley, John 1938-1978 . . . . .DLB-40

Rilke, Rainer Maria 1875-1926 . . . . .DLB-81

Rimanelli, Giose 1926- DLB-177

Rimbaud, Jean-Nicolas-Arthur
1854-1891 .DLB-217

Rinehart and Company DLB-46

Ringuet 1895-1960. . . . . .DLB-68

Ringwood, Gwen Pharis 1910-1984 . . . . . .DLB-88

Rinser, Luise 1911- DLB-69

Ríos, Alberto 1952- DLB-122

Ríos, Isabella 1948- DLB-82

Ripley, Arthur 1895-1961 . . . . .DLB-44

Ripley, George 1802-1880 . . . . DLB-1, 64, 73

The Rising Glory of America:
Three Poems. DLB-37

The Rising Glory of America: Written in 1771
(1786), by Hugh Henry Brackenridge and
Philip Freneau DLB-37

Riskin, Robert 1897-1955. . . . . .DLB-26

Risse, Heinz 1898- DLB-69

Rist, Johann 1607-1667 . . . . .DLB-164

Ristikivi, Karl 1912-1977 . . . . .DLB-220

Ritchie, Anna Mowatt 1819-1870 . . . . .DLB-3

Ritchie, Anne Thackeray 1837-1919 . . . . . .DLB-18

Ritchie, Thomas 1778-1854 . . . . .DLB-43

Rites of Passage [on William Saroyan] Y-83

The Ritz Paris Hemingway Award Y-85

Rivard, Adjutor 1868-1945 . . . . .DLB-92

Rive, Richard 1931-1989 . . . . .DLB-125

Rivera, Marina 1942- DLB-122

Rivera, Tomás 1935-1984 . . . . .DLB-82

Rivers, Conrad Kent 1933-1968 . . . . .DLB-41

Riverside Press .DLB-49

Rivington, James circa 1724-1802 . . . . . . .DLB-43

Rivington, Charles [publishing house] DLB-154

Rivkin, Allen 1903-1990 . . . . .DLB-26

Roa Bastos, Augusto 1917- DLB-113

Robbe-Grillet, Alain 1922- DLB-83

Robbins, Tom 1936- Y-80

Robert Pinsky Reappointed Poet Laureate. . . . Y-98

Roberts, Charles G. D. 1860-1943 . . . . . . DLB-92

Roberts, Dorothy 1906-1993 . . . . DLB-88

Roberts, Elizabeth Madox
1881-1941 . . . . DLB-9, 54, 102

Roberts, Kenneth 1885-1957 . . . . DLB-9

Roberts, William 1767-1849 . . . . DLB-142

Roberts Brothers. DLB-49

Roberts, James [publishing house] DLB-154

Robertson, A. M., and Company DLB-49

Robertson, William 1721-1793 . . . . DLB-104

Robins, Elizabeth 1862-1952 . . . . DLB-197

Robinson, Casey 1903-1979 . . . . DLB-44

Robinson, Edwin Arlington 1869-1935 . . . DLB-54

Robinson, Henry Crabb 1775-1867 . . . . . DLB-107

Robinson, James Harvey 1863-1936 . . . . . DLB-47

Robinson, Lennox 1886-1958 . . . . DLB-10

Robinson, Mabel Louise 1874-1962 . . . . . . DLB-22

Robinson, Marilynne 1943- DLB-206

Robinson, Mary 1758-1800 . . . . DLB-158

Robinson, Richard circa 1545-1607 . . . . . DLB-167

Robinson, Therese 1797-1870 . . . . DLB-59, 133

Robison, Mary 1949- DLB-130

Roblès, Emmanuel 1914-1995 . . . . DLB-83

Roccatagliata Ceccardi, Ceccardo
1871-1919 . . . . DLB-114

Rochester, John Wilmot, Earl of
1647-1680 . . . . DLB-131

Rock, Howard 1911-1976 . . . . DLB-127

Rockwell, Norman Perceval
1894-1978 . . . . DLB-188

Rodgers, Carolyn M. 1945- DLB-41

Rodgers, W. R. 1909-1969 . . . . DLB-20

Rodríguez, Claudio 1934- DLB-134

Rodríguez, Joe D. 1943- DLB-209

Rodríguez, Luis J. 1954- DLB-209

Rodriguez, Richard 1944- DLB-82

Rodríguez Julia, Edgardo 1946- DLB-145

Roe, E. P. 1838-1888 . . . . DLB-202

Roethke, Theodore 1908-1963 . . . . . . DLB-5, 206

Rogers, Jane 1952- DLB-194

Rogers, Pattiann 1940- DLB-105

Rogers, Samuel 1763-1855 . . . . DLB-93

Rogers, Will 1879-1935 . . . . DLB-11

Rohmer, Sax 1883-1959 . . . . DLB-70

Roiphe, Anne 1935- Y-80

Rojas, Arnold R. 1896-1988 . . . . DLB-82

Rolfe, Frederick William
1860-1913. . . . . DLB-34, 156

Rolland, Romain 1866-1944. . . . . DLB-65

Rolle, Richard circa 1290-1300 - 1340 . . . DLB-146

Rölvaag, O. E. 1876-1931 . . . . DLB-9, 212

Romains, Jules 1885-1972 . . . . DLB-65

Roman, A., and Company DLB-49

Roman de la Rose: Guillaume de Lorris
1200 to 1205-circa 1230, Jean de Meun
1235-1240-circa 1305 . . . . DLB-208

Romano, Lalla 1906- DLB-177

Romano, Octavio 1923- DLB-122

Romero, Leo 1950- DLB-122

Romero, Lin 1947- DLB-122

Romero, Orlando 1945- DLB-82

Rook, Clarence 1863-1915 . . . . DLB-135

Roosevelt, Theodore 1858-1919 . . . . . .DLB-47, 186

Root, Waverley 1903-1982 . . . . DLB-4

Root, William Pitt 1941- DLB-120

Roquebrune, Robert de 1889-1978 . . . . . . DLB-68

Rosa, João Guimarāres 1908-1967 . . . . . DLB-113

Rosales, Luis 1910-1992 . . . . DLB-134

Roscoe, William 1753-1831 . . . . DLB-163

Rose, Reginald 1920- DLB-26

Rose, Wendy 1948- DLB-175

Rosegger, Peter 1843-1918 . . . . DLB-129

Rosei, Peter 1946- DLB-85

Rosen, Norma 1925- DLB-28

Rosenbach, A. S. W. 1876-1952 . . . . DLB-140

Rosenbaum, Ron 1946- DLB-185

Rosenberg, Isaac 1890-1918 . . . . DLB-20, 216

Rosenfeld, Isaac 1918-1956 . . . . DLB-28

Rosenthal, M. L. 1917-1996 . . . . DLB-5

Rosenwald, Lessing J. 1891-1979 . . . . . . DLB-187

Ross, Alexander 1591-1654 . . . . DLB-151

Ross, Harold 1892-1951 . . . . DLB-137

Ross, Leonard Q. (see Rosten, Leo)

Ross, Lillian 1927- DLB-185

Ross, Martin 1862-1915 . . . . DLB-135

Ross, Sinclair 1908- DLB-88

Ross, W. W. E. 1894-1966 . . . . DLB-88

Rosselli, Amelia 1930-1996 . . . . DLB-128

Rossen, Robert 1908-1966 . . . . DLB-26

Rossetti, Christina Georgina
1830-1894 . . . . DLB-35, 163

Rossetti, Dante Gabriel 1828-1882 . . . . . . DLB-35

Rossner, Judith 1935- DLB-6

Rostand, Edmond 1868-1918 . . . . DLB-192

Rosten, Leo 1908-1997 . . . . DLB-11

Rostenberg, Leona 1908- DLB-140

Rostopchina, Evdokiia Petrovna
1811-1858 . . . . DLB-205

Rostovsky, Dimitrii 1651-1709 . . . . DLB-150

Rota, Bertram 1903-1966 . . . . DLB-201

Bertram Rota and His Bookshop Y-91

Roth, Gerhard 1942- DLB-85, 124

Roth, Henry 1906?-1995 . . . . DLB-28

Roth, Joseph 1894-1939 . . . . DLB-85

Roth, Philip 1933- DLB-2, 28, 173; Y-82

Rothenberg, Jerome 1931- DLB-5, 193

Rothschild Family DLB-184

Rotimi, Ola 1938- DLB-125

Routhier, Adolphe-Basile 1839-1920 . . . . . DLB-99

Routier, Simone 1901-1987 . . . . DLB-88

Routledge, George, and Sons DLB-106

Roversi, Roberto 1923- DLB-128

Rowe, Elizabeth Singer 1674-1737 . . . . DLB-39, 95

Rowe, Nicholas 1674-1718 . . . . DLB-84

Rowlands, Samuel circa 1570-1630 . . . . . . DLB-121

Rowlandson, Mary
circa 1637-circa 1711 . . . . DLB-24, 200

Rowley, William circa 1585-1626 . . . . DLB-58

Rowse, A. L. 1903-1997 . . . . DLB-155

Rowson, Susanna Haswell
circa 1762-1824 . . . . .DLB-37, 200

Roy, Camille 1870-1943 . . . . DLB-92

Roy, Gabrielle 1909-1983 . . . . DLB-68

Roy, Jules 1907- DLB-83

The Royal Court Theatre and the English
Stage Company DLB-13

The Royal Court Theatre and the New
Drama DLB-10

The Royal Shakespeare Company
at the Swan Y-88

Royall, Anne 1769-1854 . . . . DLB-43

The Roycroft Printing Shop DLB-49

Royde-Smith, Naomi 1875-1964 . . . . DLB-191

Royster, Vermont 1914- DLB-127

Royston, Richard [publishing house] DLB-170

Ruark, Gibbons 1941- DLB-120

Ruban, Vasilii Grigorevich 1742-1795 . . . DLB-150

Rubens, Bernice 1928- DLB-14, 207

Rudd and Carleton. DLB-49

Rudkin, David 1936- DLB-13

Rudolf von Ems
circa 1200-circa 1254 . . . . DLB-138

Ruffin, Josephine St. Pierre
1842-1924 . . . . DLB-79

Ruganda, John 1941- DLB-157

Ruggles, Henry Joseph 1813-1906 . . . . DLB-64

Ruiz de Burton, María Amparo
1832-1895 . . . . DLB-209, 221

Rukeyser, Muriel 1913-1980 . . . . DLB-48

Rule, Jane 1931- DLB-60

Rulfo, Juan 1918-1986 . . . . DLB-113

Rumaker, Michael 1932- DLB-16

Rumens, Carol 1944- DLB-40

Runyon, Damon 1880-1946 . . . . . .DLB-11, 86, 171

Ruodlieb circa 1050-1075 . . . . DLB-148

Rush, Benjamin 1746-1813 . . . . DLB-37

Rush, Rebecca 1779-?. DLB-200

Rushdie, Salman 1947- DLB-194

Rusk, Ralph L. 1888-1962 . . . . DLB-103

Ruskin, John 1819-1900 . . . . . . .DLB-55, 163, 190

Russ, Joanna 1937- DLB-8

Russell, B. B., and Company DLB-49

Russell, Benjamin 1761-1845 . . . . DLB-43

Russell, Bertrand 1872-1970 . . . . DLB-100

Russell, Charles Edward 1860-1941 . . . . . . DLB-25

Russell, Charles M. 1864-1926 . . . . DLB-188

Russell, Countess Mary Annette Beauchamp
(see Arnim, Elizabeth von)

Russell, George William (see AE)

Russell, R. H., and Son DLB-49

Rutebeuf flourished 1249-1277 . . . . DLB-208

Rutherford, Mark 1831-1913. . . . . DLB-18

Ruxton, George Frederick 1821-1848 . . . . DLB-186

Ryan, Michael 1946- Y-82

Ryan, Oscar 1904- DLB-68

Ryga, George 1932- DLB-60

Rylands, Enriqueta Augustina Tennant
1843-1908 . . . . DLB-184

Rylands, John 1801-1888. . . . . DLB-184

Ryleev, Kondratii Fedorovich
1795-1826 . . . . DLB-205

Rymer, Thomas 1643?-1713 . . . . DLB-101

Ryskind, Morrie 1895-1985. . . . . DLB-26

Rzhevsky, Aleksei Andreevich
1737-1804. . . . . DLB-150

S

The Saalfield Publishing Company DLB-46

Saba, Umberto 1883-1957 . . . . DLB-114

Sábato, Ernesto 1911- DLB-145

Saberhagen, Fred 1930- DLB-8

Sabin, Joseph 1821-1881 . . . . DLB-187

Sacer, Gottfried Wilhelm 1635-1699 . . . . . DLB-168

Sachs, Hans 1494-1576 . . . . DLB-179

Sack, John 1930- DLB-185

Sackler, Howard 1929-1982. . . . . DLB-7

Sackville, Thomas 1536-1608 . . . . DLB-132

Sackville, Thomas 1536-1608
and Norton, Thomas
1532-1584 . . . . DLB-62

Sackville-West, Edward 1901-1965 . . . . . . DLB-191

Sackville-West, V. 1892-1962 . . . . DLB-34, 195

Sadlier, D. and J., and Company DLB-49

Sadlier, Mary Anne 1820-1903 . . . . DLB-99

Sadoff, Ira 1945- DLB-120

Sadoveanu, Mihail 1880-1961 . . . . DLB-220

Sáenz, Benjamin Alire 1954- DLB-209

Saenz, Jaime 1921-1986 . . . . DLB-145

Saffin, John circa 1626-1710 . . . . DLB-24

Sagan, Françoise 1935- DLB-83

Sage, Robert 1899-1962 . . . . DLB-4

Sagel, Jim 1947- DLB-82

Sagendorph, Robb Hansell 1900-1970 . . . . DLB-137

Sahagún, Carlos 1938- DLB-108

Sahkomaapii, Piitai (see Highwater, Jamake)

Sahl, Hans 1902- DLB-69

Said, Edward W. 1935- DLB-67

Saigyō 1118-1190. . . . . DLB-203

Saiko, George 1892-1962. . . . . DLB-85

St. Dominic's Press DLB-112

Saint-Exupéry, Antoine de 1900-1944 . . . . . DLB-72

St. John, J. Allen 1872-1957 . . . . DLB-188

St. Johns, Adela Rogers 1894-1988 . . . . DLB-29

The St. John's College Robert Graves Trust . . Y-96

St. Martin's Press DLB-46

St. Omer, Garth 1931- DLB-117

Saint Pierre, Michel de 1916-1987 . . . . DLB-83

Sainte-Beuve, Charles-Augustin
1804-1869 . . . . DLB-217

Saints' Lives DLB-208

Saintsbury, George 1845-1933. . . . . . . DLB-57, 149

Saiokuken Sōchō 1448-1532 . . . . DLB-203

Saki (see Munro, H. H.)

Salaam, Kalamu ya 1947- DLB-38

Šalamun, Tomaž 1941- DLB-181

Salas, Floyd 1931- DLB-82

Sálaz-Marquez, Rubén 1935- DLB-122

Salemson, Harold J. 1910-1988 . . . . DLB-4

Salinas, Luis Omar 1937- DLB-82

Salinas, Pedro 1891-1951. . . . . DLB-134

Salinger, J. D. 1919- DLB-2, 102, 173

Salkey, Andrew 1928- DLB-125

Sallust circa 86 B.C.-35 B.C. DLB-211

Salt, Waldo 1914- DLB-44

Salter, James 1925- DLB-130

Salter, Mary Jo 1954- DLB-120

Saltus, Edgar 1855-1921 . . . . DLB-202

Salustri, Carlo Alberto (see Trilussa)

Salverson, Laura Goodman 1890-1970 . . . . DLB-92

Samain, Albert 1858-1900 . . . . DLB-217

Sampson, Richard Henry (see Hull, Richard)

Samuels, Ernest 1903-1996 . . . . DLB-111

Sanborn, Franklin Benjamin 1831-1917. . . . . DLB-1

Sánchez, Luis Rafael 1936- DLB-145

Sánchez, Philomeno "Phil" 1917- DLB-122

Sánchez, Ricardo 1941-1995 . . . . DLB-82

Sánchez, Saúl 1943- DLB-209

Sanchez, Sonia 1934- DLB-41; DS-8

Sand, George 1804-1876 . . . . DLB-119, 192

Sandburg, Carl 1878-1967 . . . . DLB-17, 54

Sanders, Ed 1939- DLB-16

Sandoz, Mari 1896-1966 . . . . DLB-9, 212

Sandwell, B. K. 1876-1954 . . . . DLB-92

Sandy, Stephen 1934- DLB-165

Sandys, George 1578-1644 . . . . DLB-24, 121

Sangster, Charles 1822-1893 . . . . DLB-99

Sanguineti, Edoardo 1930- DLB-128

Sanjōnishi Sanetaka 1455-1537 . . . . DLB-203

Sansay, Leonora ?-after 1823 . . . . DLB-200

Sansom, William 1912-1976. . . . . DLB-139

Santayana, George
1863-1952 . . . . DLB-54, 71; DS-13

Santiago, Danny 1911-1988. . . . . DLB-122

Santmyer, Helen Hooven 1895-1986. . . . . . . Y-84

Sanvitale, Francesca 1928- DLB-196

Sapidus, Joannes 1490-1561. . . . . DLB-179

Sapir, Edward 1884-1939 . . . . DLB-92

Sapper (see McNeile, Herman Cyril)

Sappho circa 620 B.C.-circa 550 B.C.
. . . . DLB-176

Saramago, José 1922- Y-98

Sardou, Victorien 1831-1908. . . . . DLB-192

Sarduy, Severo 1937- DLB-113

Sargent, Pamela 1948- DLB-8

Saro-Wiwa, Ken 1941- DLB-157

Saroyan, William 1908-1981 . . DLB-7, 9, 86; Y-81

Sarraute, Nathalie 1900- DLB-83

Sarrazin, Albertine 1937-1967 . . . . DLB-83

Sarris, Greg 1952- DLB-175

Sarton, May 1912-1995 . . . . DLB-48; Y-81

Sartre, Jean-Paul 1905-1980 . . . . DLB-72

Sassoon, Siegfried
1886-1967 . . . . DLB-20, 191; DS-18

Sata, Ineko 1904- DLB-180

Saturday Review Press DLB-46

Saunders, James 1925- DLB-13

Saunders, John Monk 1897-1940 . . . . DLB-26

Saunders, Margaret Marshall
1861-1947 . . . . DLB-92

Saunders and Otley DLB-106

Savage, James 1784-1873 . . . . DLB-30

Savage, Marmion W. 1803?-1872 . . . . DLB-21

Savage, Richard 1697?-1743 . . . . DLB-95

Savard, Félix-Antoine 1896-1982. . . . . DLB-68

Saville, (Leonard) Malcolm 1901-1982 . . . DLB-160

Sawyer, Ruth 1880-1970 . . . . DLB-22

Sayers, Dorothy L.
1893-1957 . . . . DLB-10, 36, 77, 100

Sayle, Charles Edward 1864-1924 . . . . DLB-184

Sayles, John Thomas 1950- DLB-44

Sbarbaro, Camillo 1888-1967 . . . . DLB-114

Scalapino, Leslie 1947- DLB-193

Scannell, Vernon 1922- DLB-27

Scarry, Richard 1919-1994 . . . . DLB-61

Schaefer, Jack 1907-1991 . . . . DLB-212

Schaeffer, Albrecht 1885-1950 . . . . DLB-66

Schaeffer, Susan Fromberg 1941- DLB-28

Schaff, Philip 1819-1893 . . . . DS-13

Schaper, Edzard 1908-1984 . . . . DLB-69

Scharf, J. Thomas 1843-1898. . . . . DLB-47

Schede, Paul Melissus 1539-1602 . . . . DLB-179

Scheffel, Joseph Viktor von 1826-1886 . . . DLB-129

Scheffler, Johann 1624-1677. . . . . DLB-164

Schelling, Friedrich Wilhelm Joseph von
1775-1854 . . . . DLB-90

Scherer, Wilhelm 1841-1886 . . . . DLB-129

Scherfig, Hans 1905-1979 . . . . DLB-214

Schickele, René 1883-1940 . . . . DLB-66

Schiff, Dorothy 1903-1989. . . . . DLB-127

Schiller, Friedrich 1759-1805 . . . . DLB-94

Schirmer, David 1623-1687 . . . . DLB-164

Cumulative Index

Schlaf, Johannes 1862-1941 . . . . DLB-118

Schlegel, August Wilhelm 1767-1845 . . . . . DLB-94

Schlegel, Dorothea 1763-1839. . . . . DLB-90

Schlegel, Friedrich 1772-1829 . . . . DLB-90

Schleiermacher, Friedrich 1768-1834 . . . . . DLB-90

Schlesinger, Arthur M., Jr. 1917- DLB-17

Schlumberger, Jean 1877-1968 . . . . DLB-65

Schmid, Eduard Hermann Wilhelm (see
   Edschmid, Kasimir)

Schmidt, Arno 1914-1979 . . . . DLB-69

Schmidt, Johann Kaspar (see Stirner, Max)

Schmidt, Michael 1947- DLB-40

Schmidtbonn, Wilhelm August
   1876-1952. . . . . DLB-118

Schmitz, James H. 1911- DLB-8

Schnabel, Johann Gottfried
   1692-1760. . . . . DLB-168

Schnackenberg, Gjertrud 1953- DLB-120

Schnitzler, Arthur 1862-1931 . . . . DLB-81, 118

Schnurre, Wolfdietrich 1920-1989 . . . . DLB-69

Schocken Books DLB-46

Scholartis Press. DLB-112

Scholderer, Victor 1880-1971 . . . . DLB-201

The Schomburg Center for Research
   in Black Culture. DLB-76

Schönbeck, Virgilio (see Giotti, Virgilio)

Schönherr, Karl 1867-1943 . . . . DLB-118

Schoolcraft, Jane Johnston 1800-1841. . . . .DLB-175

School Stories, 1914-1960. . . . . DLB-160

Schopenhauer, Arthur 1788-1860 . . . . DLB-90

Schopenhauer, Johanna 1766-1838 . . . . . . DLB-90

Schorer, Mark 1908-1977 . . . . DLB-103

Schottelius, Justus Georg 1612-1676 . . . . . DLB-164

Schouler, James 1839-1920. . . . . DLB-47

Schrader, Paul 1946- DLB-44

Schreiner, Olive 1855-1920 . . . . DLB-18, 156, 190

Schroeder, Andreas 1946- DLB-53

Schubart, Christian Friedrich Daniel
   1739-1791 . . . . DLB-97

Schubert, Gotthilf Heinrich 1780-1860 . . . . DLB-90

Schücking, Levin 1814-1883. . . . . DLB-133

Schulberg, Budd 1914- DLB-6, 26, 28; Y-81

Schulte, F. J., and Company DLB-49

Schulz, Bruno 1892-1942 . . . . DLB-215

Schulze, Hans (see Praetorius, Johannes)

Schupp, Johann Balthasar 1610-1661 . . . . DLB-164

Schurz, Carl 1829-1906 . . . . DLB-23

Schuyler, George S. 1895-1977 . . . . . . DLB-29, 51

Schuyler, James 1923-1991. . . . . DLB-5, 169

Schwartz, Delmore 1913-1966 . . . . . . DLB-28, 48

Schwartz, Jonathan 1938- Y-82

Schwartz, Lynne Sharon 1939- DLB-218

Schwarz, Sibylle 1621-1638 . . . . DLB-164

Schwerner, Armand 1927- DLB-165

Schwob, Marcel 1867-1905. . . . . DLB-123

Sciascia, Leonardo 1921-1989. . . . . .DLB-177

Science Fantasy. DLB-8

Science-Fiction Fandom and Conventions . . DLB-8

Science-Fiction Fanzines: The Time
   Binders. DLB-8

Science-Fiction Films. DLB-8

Science Fiction Writers of America and the
   Nebula Awards. DLB-8

Scot, Reginald circa 1538-1599. . . . . DLB-136

Scotellaro, Rocco 1923-1953. . . . . DLB-128

Scott, Dennis 1939-1991. . . . . DLB-125

Scott, Dixon 1881-1915 . . . . DLB-98

Scott, Duncan Campbell 1862-1947 . . . . . . DLB-92

Scott, Evelyn 1893-1963 . . . . DLB-9, 48

Scott, F. R. 1899-1985. . . . . DLB-88

Scott, Frederick George 1861-1944. . . . . . . DLB-92

Scott, Geoffrey 1884-1929 . . . . DLB-149

Scott, Harvey W. 1838-1910 . . . . DLB-23

Scott, Paul 1920-1978 . . . . .DLB-14, 207

Scott, Sarah 1723-1795 . . . . DLB-39

Scott, Tom 1918- DLB-27

Scott, Sir Walter
   1771-1832. . . . . DLB-93, 107, 116, 144, 159

Scott, William Bell 1811-1890 . . . . DLB-32

Scott, Walter, Publishing
   Company Limited DLB-112

Scott, William R. [publishing house] DLB-46

Scott-Heron, Gil 1949- DLB-41

Scribe, Eugene 1791-1861. . . . . DLB-192

Scribner, Arthur Hawley 1859-1932. . . . . DS-13, 16

Scribner, Charles 1854-1930. . . . . DS-13, 16

Scribner, Charles, Jr. 1921-1995 . . . . .Y-95

Charles Scribner's Sons DLB-49; DS-13, 16, 17

Scripps, E. W. 1854-1926. . . . . DLB-25

Scudder, Horace Elisha 1838-1902. . . . DLB-42, 71

Scudder, Vida Dutton 1861-1954. . . . . . . DLB-71

Scupham, Peter 1933- DLB-40

Seabrook, William 1886-1945 . . . . DLB-4

Seabury, Samuel 1729-1796 . . . . DLB-31

Seacole, Mary Jane Grant 1805-1881 . . . . DLB-166

The Seafarer circa 970. . . . . DLB-146

Sealsfield, Charles (Carl Postl)
   1793-1864. . . . . DLB-133, 186

Sears, Edward I. 1819?-1876. . . . . DLB-79

Sears Publishing Company. DLB-46

Seaton, George 1911-1979 . . . . DLB-44

Seaton, William Winston 1785-1866 . . . . . DLB-43

Secker, Martin, and Warburg Limited . . . DLB-112

Secker, Martin [publishing house] DLB-112

Second-Generation Minor Poets of the
   Seventeenth Century. DLB-126

Second International Hemingway Colloquium:
   Cuba Y-98

Sedgwick, Arthur George 1844-1915 . . . . . DLB-64

Sedgwick, Catharine Maria
   1789-1867. . . . . .DLB-1, 74, 183

Sedgwick, Ellery 1872-1930 . . . . DLB-91

Sedley, Sir Charles 1639-1701 . . . . DLB-131

Seeberg, Peter 1925-1999 . . . . DLB-214

Seeger, Alan 1888-1916 . . . . DLB-45

Seers, Eugene (see Dantin, Louis)

Segal, Erich 1937- Y-86

Šegedin, Petar 1909- DLB-181

Seghers, Anna 1900-1983 . . . . DLB-69

Seid, Ruth (see Sinclair, Jo)

Seidel, Frederick Lewis 1936- Y-84

Seidel, Ina 1885-1974 . . . . DLB-56

Seifert, Jaroslav 1901-1986. . . . . . . .DLB-215; Y-84

Seigenthaler, John 1927- DLB-127

Seizin Press. DLB-112

Séjour, Victor 1817-1874. . . . . DLB-50

Séjour Marcou et Ferrand, Juan Victor
   (see Séjour, Victor)

Sekowski, Józef-Julian, Baron Brambeus
   (see Senkovsky, Osip Ivanovich)

Selby, Bettina 1934- DLB-204

Selby, Hubert, Jr. 1928- DLB-2

Selden, George 1929-1989 . . . . DLB-52

Selden, John 1584-1654 . . . . DLB-213

Selected English-Language Little Magazines
   and Newspapers [France, 1920-1939] . . DLB-4

Selected Humorous Magazines
   (1820-1950) DLB-11

Selected Science-Fiction Magazines and
   Anthologies DLB-8

Selenić, Slobodan 1933-1995 . . . . DLB-181

Self, Edwin F. 1920- DLB-137

Self, Will 1961- DLB-207

Seligman, Edwin R. A. 1861-1939 . . . . . . DLB-47

Selimović, Meša 1910-1982 . . . . DLB-181

Selous, Frederick Courteney
   1851-1917. . . . . .DLB-174

Seltzer, Chester E. (see Muro, Amado)

Seltzer, Thomas [publishing house] DLB-46

Selvon, Sam 1923-1994 . . . . DLB-125

Semmes, Raphael 1809-1877 . . . . DLB-189

Senancour, Etienne de 1770-1846. . . . . . DLB-119

Sendak, Maurice 1928- DLB-61

Seneca the Elder
   circa 54 B.C.-circa A.D. 40 . . . . DLB-211

Seneca the Younger
   circa 1 B.C.-A.D. 65. . . . . DLB-211

Senécal, Eva 1905- DLB-92

Sengstacke, John 1912- DLB-127

Senior, Olive 1941- DLB-157

Senkovsky, Osip Ivanovich (Józef-Julian Sekowski,
   Baron Brambeus) 1800-1858 . . . . DLB-198

Šenoa, August 1838-1881 . . . . .DLB-147

"Sensation Novels" (1863), by
   H. L. Manse. DLB-21

Sepamla, Sipho 1932- DLB-157

Seredy, Kate 1899-1975 . . . . DLB-22

Sereni, Vittorio 1913-1983 . . . . DLB-128

Seres, William [publishing house]. DLB-170

Serling, Rod 1924-1975. . . . . DLB-26

Serote, Mongane Wally 1944- DLB-125

Serraillier, Ian 1912-1994. . . . . .DLB-161

Serrano, Nina 1934- DLB-122

Service, Robert 1874-1958 . . . . .DLB-92

Sessler, Charles 1854-1935 . . . . .DLB-187

Seth, Vikram 1952- DLB-120

Seton, Elizabeth Ann 1774-1821. . . . . . . .DLB-200

Seton, Ernest Thompson
    1860-1942 . . . . .DLB-92; DS-13

Setouchi Harumi 1922- DLB-182

Settle, Mary Lee 1918- DLB-6

Seume, Johann Gottfried 1763-1810. . . . . .DLB-94

Seuse, Heinrich 1295?-1366. . . . . .DLB-179

Seuss, Dr. (see Geisel, Theodor Seuss)

The Seventy-fifth Anniversary of the Armistice: The
    Wilfred Owen Centenary and the Great War
    Exhibit at the University of Virginia. Y-93

Severin, Timothy 1940- DLB-204

Sewall, Joseph 1688-1769 . . . . .DLB-24

Sewall, Richard B. 1908- DLB-111

Sewell, Anna 1820-1878. . . . . .DLB-163

Sewell, Samuel 1652-1730 . . . . .DLB-24

Sex, Class, Politics, and Religion [in the
    British Novel, 1930-1959] DLB-15

Sexton, Anne 1928-1974 . . . . .DLB-5, 169

Seymour-Smith, Martin 1928-1998 . . . . . .DLB-155

Sgorlon, Carlo 1930- DLB-196

Shaara, Michael 1929-1988 . . . . Y-83

Shadwell, Thomas 1641?-1692 . . . . .DLB-80

Shaffer, Anthony 1926- DLB-13

Shaffer, Peter 1926- DLB-13

Shaftesbury, Anthony Ashley Cooper,
    Third Earl of 1671-1713 . . . . .DLB-101

Shairp, Mordaunt 1887-1939 . . . . .DLB-10

Shakespeare, William 1564-1616. . . . . DLB-62, 172

The Shakespeare Globe Trust Y-93

Shakespeare Head Press DLB-112

Shakhovskoi, Aleksandr Aleksandrovich
    1777-1846. .DLB-150

Shange, Ntozake 1948- DLB-38

Shapiro, Karl 1913- DLB-48

Sharon Publications DLB-46

Sharp, Margery 1905-1991 . . . . .DLB-161

Sharp, William 1855-1905 . . . . .DLB-156

Sharpe, Tom 1928- DLB-14

Shaw, Albert 1857-1947 . . . . .DLB-91

Shaw, George Bernard
    1856-1950 . . . . DLB-10, 57, 190

Shaw, Henry Wheeler 1818-1885 . . . . . . .DLB-11

Shaw, Joseph T. 1874-1952 . . . . .DLB-137

Shaw, Irwin 1913-1984 . . . . DLB-6, 102; Y-84

Shaw, Robert 1927-1978. . . . . .DLB-13, 14

Shaw, Robert B. 1947- DLB-120

Shawn, William 1907-1992 . . . . .DLB-137

Shay, Frank [publishing house] DLB-46

Shea, John Gilmary 1824-1892 . . . . .DLB-30

Sheaffer, Louis 1912-1993 . . . . .DLB-103

Shearing, Joseph 1886-1952. . . . . .DLB-70

Shebbeare, John 1709-1788 . . . . .DLB-39

Sheckley, Robert 1928- DLB-8

Shedd, William G. T. 1820-1894. . . . . . .DLB-64

Sheed, Wilfred 1930- DLB-6

Sheed and Ward [U.S.] DLB-46

Sheed and Ward Limited [U.K.] DLB-112

Sheldon, Alice B. (see Tiptree, James, Jr.)

Sheldon, Edward 1886-1946 . . . . .DLB-7

Sheldon and Company DLB-49

Shelley, Mary Wollstonecraft
    1797-1851. . . . . DLB-110, 116, 159, 178

Shelley, Percy Bysshe
    1792-1822 . . . . DLB-96, 110, 158

Shelnutt, Eve 1941- DLB-130

Shenstone, William 1714-1763 . . . . .DLB-95

Shepard, Ernest Howard 1879-1976. . . . . .DLB-160

Shepard, Sam 1943- DLB-7, 212

Shepard, Thomas I, 1604 or 1605-1649 . . .DLB-24

Shepard, Thomas II, 1635-1677. . . . . .DLB-24

Shepard, Clark and Brown DLB-49

Shepherd, Luke
    flourished 1547-1554 . . . . .DLB-136

Sherburne, Edward 1616-1702. . . . . .DLB-131

Sheridan, Frances 1724-1766 . . . . .DLB-39, 84

Sheridan, Richard Brinsley 1751-1816. . . . .DLB-89

Sherman, Francis 1871-1926 . . . . .DLB-92

Sherriff, R. C. 1896-1975 . . . . .DLB-10, 191

Sherry, Norman 1935- DLB-155

Sherwood, Mary Martha 1775-1851 . . . . .DLB-163

Sherwood, Robert 1896-1955 . . . . DLB-7, 26

Shevyrev, Stepan Petrovich
    1806-1864 . . . . .DLB-205

Shiel, M. P. 1865-1947. . . . . .DLB-153

Shiels, George 1886-1949 . . . . .DLB-10

Shiga, Naoya 1883-1971. . . . . .DLB-180

Shiina Rinzō 1911-1973 . . . . .DLB-182

Shikishi Naishinnō 1153?-1201 . . . . .DLB-203

Shillaber, B.[enjamin] P.[enhallow]
    1814-1890 .DLB-1, 11

Shimao Toshio 1917-1986 . . . . .DLB-182

Shimazaki, Tōson 1872-1943 . . . . .DLB-180

Shine, Ted 1931- DLB-38

Shinkei 1406-1475 . . . . .DLB-203

Ship, Reuben 1915-1975 . . . . .DLB-88

Shirer, William L. 1904-1993 . . . . .DLB-4

Shirinsky-Shikhmatov, Sergii Aleksandrovich
    1783-1837 . . . . .DLB-150

Shirley, James 1596-1666. . . . . .DLB-58

Shishkov, Aleksandr Semenovich
    1753-1841 . . . . .DLB-150

Shockley, Ann Allen 1927- DLB-33

Shōno Junzō 1921- DLB-182

Shore, Arabella 1820?-1901 and
    Shore, Louisa 1824-1895. . . . . .DLB-199

Short, Peter [publishing house] DLB-170

Shorthouse, Joseph Henry 1834-1903 . . . . .DLB-18

Shōtetsu 1381-1459 . . . . .DLB-203

Showalter, Elaine 1941- DLB-67

Shulevitz, Uri 1935- DLB-61

Shulman, Max 1919-1988 . . . . .DLB-11

Shute, Henry A. 1856-1943. . . . . .DLB-9

Shuttle, Penelope 1947- DLB-14, 40

Sibbes, Richard 1577-1635 . . . . .DLB-151

Siddal, Elizabeth Eleanor 1829-1862 . . . . .DLB-199

Sidgwick, Ethel 1877-1970 . . . . .DLB-197

Sidgwick and Jackson Limited DLB-112

Sidney, Margaret (see Lothrop, Harriet M.)

Sidney, Mary 1561-1621 . . . . .DLB-167

Sidney, Sir Philip 1554-1586 . . . . .DLB-167

Sidney's Press DLB-49

Siegfried Loraine Sassoon: A Centenary Essay
    Tributes from Vivien F. Clarke and
    Michael Thorpe Y-86

Sierra, Rubén 1946- DLB-122

Sierra Club Books DLB-49

Siger of Brabant
    circa 1240-circa 1284. . . . . .DLB-115

Sigourney, Lydia Howard (Huntley)
    1791-1865 . . . . DLB-1, 42, 73, 183

Silkin, Jon 1930- DLB-27

Silko, Leslie Marmon 1948- DLB-143, 175

Silliman, Benjamin 1779-1864 . . . . .DLB-183

Silliman, Ron 1946- DLB-169

Silliphant, Stirling 1918- DLB-26

Sillitoe, Alan 1928- DLB-14, 139

Silman, Roberta 1934- DLB-28

Silva, Beverly 1930- DLB-122

Silverberg, Robert 1935- DLB-8

Silverman, Kenneth 1936- DLB-111

Simak, Clifford D. 1904-1988 . . . . .DLB-8

Simcoe, Elizabeth 1762-1850 . . . . .DLB-99

Simcox, Edith Jemima 1844-1901 . . . . . . .DLB-190

Simcox, George Augustus 1841-1905 . . . . .DLB-35

Sime, Jessie Georgina 1868-1958 . . . . .DLB-92

Simenon, Georges 1903-1989 . . . . . . DLB-72; Y-89

Simic, Charles 1938- DLB-105

Simmel, Johannes Mario 1924- DLB-69

Simmes, Valentine [publishing house] DLB-170

Simmons, Ernest J. 1903-1972 . . . . .DLB-103

Simmons, Herbert Alfred 1930- DLB-33

Simmons, James 1933- DLB-40

Simms, William Gilmore
    1806-1870 . . . . DLB-3, 30, 59, 73

Simms and M'Intyre DLB-106

Simon, Claude 1913- DLB-83; Y-85

Simon, Neil 1927- DLB-7

Simon and Schuster DLB-46

Simons, Katherine Drayton Mayrant
    1890-1969 . . . . Y-83

Simović, Ljubomir 1935- DLB-181

Simpkin and Marshall
[publishing house] DLB-154

Simpson, Helen 1897-1940 . . . . DLB-77

Simpson, Louis 1923- DLB-5

Simpson, N. F. 1919- DLB-13

Sims, George 1923- DLB-87

Sims, George Robert
1847-1922 . . . . DLB-35, 70, 135

Sinán, Rogelio 1904- DLB-145

Sinclair, Andrew 1935- DLB-14

Sinclair, Bertrand William 1881-1972 . . . . . DLB-92

Sinclair, Catherine 1800-1864 . . . . DLB-163

Sinclair, Jo 1913-1995 . . . . DLB-28

Sinclair Lewis Centennial Conference Y-85

Sinclair, Lister 1921- DLB-88

Sinclair, May 1863-1946 . . . . DLB-36, 135

Sinclair, Upton 1878-1968 . . . . DLB-9

Sinclair, Upton [publishing house] DLB-46

Singer, Isaac Bashevis
1904-1991 . . . . DLB-6, 28, 52; Y-91

Singer, Mark 1950- DLB-185

Singmaster, Elsie 1879-1958 . . . . DLB-9

Sinisgalli, Leonardo 1908-1981 . . . . DLB-114

Siodmak, Curt 1902- DLB-44

Siringo, Charles A. 1855-1928 . . . . DLB-186

Sissman, L. E. 1928-1976 . . . . DLB-5

Sisson, C. H. 1914- DLB-27

Sitwell, Edith 1887-1964 . . . . DLB-20

Sitwell, Osbert 1892-1969 . . . . DLB-100, 195

Skalbe, Kārlis 1879-1945 . . . . DLB-220

Skármeta, Antonio 1940- DLB-145

Skeat, Walter W. 1835-1912 . . . . DLB-184

Skeffington, William
[publishing house] DLB-106

Skelton, John 1463-1529 . . . . DLB-136

Skelton, Robin 1925- DLB-27, 53

Škėma, Antanas 1910-1961 . . . . DLB-220

Skinner, Constance Lindsay
1877-1939 . . . . DLB-92

Skinner, John Stuart 1788-1851 . . . . DLB-73

Skipsey, Joseph 1832-1903 . . . . DLB-35

Skou-Hansen, Tage 1925- DLB-214

Slade, Bernard 1930- DLB-53

Slamnig, Ivan 1930- DLB-181

Slančeková, Božena (see Timrava)

Slater, Patrick 1880-1951 . . . . DLB-68

Slaveykov, Pencho 1866-1912 . . . . DLB-147

Slaviček, Milivoj 1929- DLB-181

Slavitt, David 1935- DLB-5, 6

Sleigh, Burrows Willcocks Arthur
1821-1869 . . . . DLB-99

A Slender Thread of Hope: The Kennedy
Center Black Theatre Project DLB-38

Slesinger, Tess 1905-1945 . . . . DLB-102

Slick, Sam (see Haliburton, Thomas Chandler)

Sloan, John 1871-1951 . . . . DLB-188

Sloane, William, Associates DLB-46

Small, Maynard and Company DLB-49

Small Presses in Great Britain and Ireland,
1960-1985 . . . . DLB-40

Small Presses I: Jargon Society Y-84

Small Presses II: The Spirit That Moves
Us Press Y-85

Small Presses III: Pushcart Press Y-87

Smart, Christopher 1722-1771 . . . . DLB-109

Smart, David A. 1892-1957 . . . . DLB-137

Smart, Elizabeth 1913-1986 . . . . DLB-88

Smedley, Menella Bute 1820?-1877 . . . . . DLB-199

Smellie, William [publishing house] DLB-154

Smiles, Samuel 1812-1904 . . . . DLB-55

Smith, A. J. M. 1902-1980 . . . . DLB-88

Smith, Adam 1723-1790 . . . . DLB-104

Smith, Adam (George Jerome Waldo Goodman)
1930- DLB-185

Smith, Alexander 1829-1867 . . . . DLB-32, 55

Smith, Amanda 1837-1915 . . . . DLB-221

Smith, Betty 1896-1972 . . . . Y-82

Smith, Carol Sturm 1938- Y-81

Smith, Charles Henry 1826-1903 . . . . DLB-11

Smith, Charlotte 1749-1806 . . . . DLB-39, 109

Smith, Chet 1899-1973 . . . . DLB-171

Smith, Cordwainer 1913-1966 . . . . DLB-8

Smith, Dave 1942- DLB-5

Smith, Dodie 1896- DLB-10

Smith, Doris Buchanan 1934- DLB-52

Smith, E. E. 1890-1965 . . . . DLB-8

Smith, Elihu Hubbard 1771-1798 . . . . DLB-37

Smith, Elizabeth Oakes (Prince)
1806-1893 . . . . DLB-1

Smith, Eunice 1757-1823 . . . . DLB-200

Smith, F. Hopkinson 1838-1915 . . . . DS-13

Smith, George D. 1870-1920 . . . . DLB-140

Smith, George O. 1911-1981 . . . . DLB-8

Smith, Goldwin 1823-1910 . . . . DLB-99

Smith, H. Allen 1907-1976 . . . . DLB-11, 29

Smith, Harry B. 1860-1936 . . . . DLB-187

Smith, Hazel Brannon 1914- DLB-127

Smith, Henry circa 1560-circa 1591 . . . . . DLB-136

Smith, Horatio (Horace) 1779-1849 . . . . . DLB-116

Smith, Horatio (Horace) 1779-1849 and
James Smith 1775-1839 . . . . DLB-96

Smith, Iain Crichton 1928- DLB-40, 139

Smith, J. Allen 1860-1924 . . . . DLB-47

Smith, Jessie Willcox 1863-1935 . . . . DLB-188

Smith, John 1580-1631 . . . . DLB-24, 30

Smith, Josiah 1704-1781 . . . . DLB-24

Smith, Ken 1938- DLB-40

Smith, Lee 1944- DLB-143; Y-83

Smith, Logan Pearsall 1865-1946 . . . . DLB-98

Smith, Mark 1935- Y-82

Smith, Michael 1698-circa 1771 . . . . DLB-31

Smith, Red 1905-1982 . . . . DLB-29, 171

Smith, Roswell 1829-1892 . . . . DLB-79

Smith, Samuel Harrison 1772-1845 . . . . . . DLB-43

Smith, Samuel Stanhope 1751-1819 . . . . . . DLB-37

Smith, Sarah (see Stretton, Hesba)

Smith, Sarah Pogson 1774-1870 . . . . DLB-200

Smith, Seba 1792-1868 . . . . DLB-1, 11

Smith, Sir Thomas 1513-1577 . . . . DLB-132

Smith, Stevie 1902-1971 . . . . DLB-20

Smith, Sydney 1771-1845 . . . . DLB-107

Smith, Sydney Goodsir 1915-1975 . . . . . . DLB-27

Smith, Wendell 1914-1972 . . . . DLB-171

Smith, William flourished 1595-1597 . . . . DLB-136

Smith, William 1727-1803 . . . . DLB-31

Smith, William 1728-1793 . . . . DLB-30

Smith, William Gardner 1927-1974 . . . . . . DLB-76

Smith, William Henry 1808-1872 . . . . . . DLB-159

Smith, William Jay 1918- DLB-5

Smith, Elder and Company DLB-154

Smith, Harrison, and Robert Haas
[publishing house] DLB-46

Smith, J. Stilman, and Company DLB-49

Smith, W. B., and Company DLB-49

Smith, W. H., and Son DLB-106

Smithers, Leonard [publishing house] . . . DLB-112

Smollett, Tobias 1721-1771 . . . . DLB-39, 104

Smythe, Francis Sydney 1900-1949 . . . . . DLB-195

Snelling, William Joseph 1804-1848 . . . . . DLB-202

Snellings, Rolland (see Touré, Askia Muhammad)

Snodgrass, W. D. 1926- DLB-5

Snow, C. P. 1905-1980 . . . . DLB-15, 77; DS-17

Snyder, Gary 1930- DLB-5, 16, 165, 212

Sobiloff, Hy 1912-1970 . . . . DLB-48

The Society for Textual Scholarship and
TEXT Y-87

The Society for the History of Authorship, Reading
and Publishing Y-92

Sønderby, Knud 1909-1966 . . . . DLB-214

Sørensen, Villy 1929- DLB-214

Soffici, Ardengo 1879-1964 . . . . DLB-114

Sofola, 'Zulu 1938- DLB-157

Solano, Solita 1888-1975 . . . . DLB-4

Soldati, Mario 1906- DLB-177

Šoljan, Antun 1932-1993 . . . . DLB-181

Sollers, Philippe 1936- DLB-83

Sollogub, Vladimir Aleksandrovich
1813-1882 . . . . DLB-198

Solmi, Sergio 1899-1981 . . . . DLB-114

Solomon, Carl 1928- DLB-16

Solway, David 1941- DLB-53

Solzhenitsyn and America Y-85

Somerville, Edith Œnone 1858-1949 . . . . DLB-135

Somov, Orest Mikhailovich
1793-1833 . . . . DLB-198

Song, Cathy 1955- DLB-169

Sono Ayako 1931- DLB-182

Sontag, Susan 1933- DLB-2, 67

Sophocles 497/496 B.C.-406/405 B.C.
.................................DLB-176

Šopov, Aco 1923-1982................DLB-181

Sorensen, Virginia 1912-1991 ....DLB-206

Sorge, Reinhard Johannes 1892-1916 ....DLB-118

Sorrentino, Gilbert 1929- DLB-5, 173; Y-80

Sotheby, James 1682-1742 ....DLB-213

Sotheby, John 1740-1807 ....DLB-213

Sotheby, Samuel 1771-1842 ....DLB-213

Sotheby, Samuel Leigh 1805-1861.......DLB-213

Sotheby, William 1757-1833.........DLB-93, 213

Soto, Gary 1952- DLB-82

Sources for the Study of Tudor and Stuart
    Drama.........................DLB-62

Souster, Raymond 1921- DLB-88

The *South English Legendary circa thirteenth-fifteenth
centuries*.........................DLB-146

Southerland, Ellease 1943- DLB-33

Southern Illinois University Press Y-95

Southern, Terry 1924-1995 ....DLB-2

Southern Writers Between the Wars DLB-9

Southerne, Thomas 1659-1746 ....DLB-80

Southey, Caroline Anne Bowles
    1786-1854 ....DLB-116

Southey, Robert 1774-1843 ..... DLB-93, 107, 142

Southwell, Robert 1561?-1595.........DLB-167

Sowande, Bode 1948- DLB-157

Sowle, Tace [publishing house] DLB-170

Soyfer, Jura 1912-1939................DLB-124

Soyinka, Wole 1934- DLB-125; Y-86, Y-87

Spacks, Barry 1931- DLB-105

Spalding, Frances 1950- DLB-155

Spark, Muriel 1918- DLB-15, 139

Sparke, Michael [publishing house] DLB-170

Sparks, Jared 1789-1866..............DLB-1, 30

Sparshott, Francis 1926- DLB-60

Späth, Gerold 1939- DLB-75

Spatola, Adriano 1941-1988............DLB-128

Spaziani, Maria Luisa 1924- DLB-128

Special Collections at the University of Colorado
    at Boulder Y-98

The Spectator 1828- DLB-110

Spedding, James 1808-1881 ....DLB-144

Spee von Langenfeld, Friedrich
    1591-1635 ....DLB-164

Speght, Rachel 1597-after 1630 ....DLB-126

Speke, John Hanning 1827-1864 ....DLB-166

Spellman, A. B. 1935- DLB-41

Spence, Thomas 1750-1814 ....DLB-158

Spencer, Anne 1882-1975............DLB-51, 54

Spencer, Charles, third Earl of Sunderland
    1674-1722 ....DLB-213

Spencer, Elizabeth 1921- DLB-6, 218

Spencer, George John, Second Earl Spencer
    1758-1834 ....DLB-184

Spencer, Herbert 1820-1903 ....DLB-57

Spencer, Scott 1945- Y-86

Spender, J. A. 1862-1942 ....DLB-98

Spender, Stephen 1909-1995 ....DLB-20

Spener, Philipp Jakob 1635-1705 ....DLB-164

Spenser, Edmund circa 1552-1599.......DLB-167

Sperr, Martin 1944- DLB-124

Spicer, Jack 1925-1965..........DLB-5, 16, 193

Spielberg, Peter 1929- Y-81

Spielhagen, Friedrich 1829-1911 ....DLB-129

"Spielmannsepen"
    (circa 1152-circa 1500) DLB-148

Spier, Peter 1927- DLB-61

Spinrad, Norman 1940- DLB-8

Spires, Elizabeth 1952- DLB-120

Spitteler, Carl 1845-1924 ....DLB-129

Spivak, Lawrence E. 1900- DLB-137

Spofford, Harriet Prescott
    1835-1921 ....DLB-74, 221

Spring, Howard 1889-1965 ....DLB-191

Squier, E. G. 1821-1888...............DLB-189

Squibob (see Derby, George Horatio)

Stacpoole, H. de Vere 1863-1951 ....DLB-153

Staël, Germaine de 1766-1817 ......DLB-119, 192

Staël-Holstein, Anne-Louise Germaine de
    (see Staël, Germaine de)

Stafford, Jean 1915-1979 ....DLB-2, 173

Stafford, William 1914-1993 ....DLB-5, 206

Stage Censorship: "The Rejected Statement"
    (1911), by Bernard Shaw [excerpts] ...DLB-10

Stallings, Laurence 1894-1968 ....DLB-7, 44

Stallworthy, Jon 1935- DLB-40

Stampp, Kenneth M. 1912- DLB-17

Stanev, Emiliyan 1907-1979 ....DLB-181

Stanford, Ann 1916- DLB-5

Stangerup, Henrik 1937-1998..........DLB-214

Stankevich, Nikolai Vladimirovich
    1813-1840 ....DLB-198

Stanković, Borisav ("Bora")
    1876-1927 ....DLB-147

Stanley, Henry M. 1841-1904 ....DLB-189; DS-13

Stanley, Thomas 1625-1678...........DLB-131

Stannard, Martin 1947- DLB-155

Stansby, William [publishing house] DLB-170

Stanton, Elizabeth Cady 1815-1902.......DLB-79

Stanton, Frank L. 1857-1927 ....DLB-25

Stanton, Maura 1946- DLB-120

Stapledon, Olaf 1886-1950.............DLB-15

Star Spangled Banner Office DLB-49

Stark, Freya 1893-1993 ....DLB-195

Starkey, Thomas circa 1499-1538 ....DLB-132

Starkie, Walter 1894-1976 ....DLB-195

Starkweather, David 1935- DLB-7

Starrett, Vincent 1886-1974 ....DLB-187

Statements on the Art of Poetry.........DLB-54

The State of Publishing Y-97

Stationers' Company of London, The.... DLB-170

Statius circa A.D. 45-A.D. 96.........DLB-211

Stead, Robert J. C. 1880-1959 ....DLB-92

Steadman, Mark 1930- DLB-6

The Stealthy School of Criticism (1871), by
    Dante Gabriel Rossetti DLB-35

Stearns, Harold E. 1891-1943 ....DLB-4

Stedman, Edmund Clarence 1833-1908 ...DLB-64

Steegmuller, Francis 1906-1994........DLB-111

Steel, Flora Annie 1847-1929 .....DLB-153, 156

Steele, Max 1922- Y-80

Steele, Richard 1672-1729 ....DLB-84, 101

Steele, Timothy 1948- DLB-120

Steele, Wilbur Daniel 1886-1970 ....DLB-86

Steere, Richard circa 1643-1721..........DLB-24

Stefanovski, Goran 1952- DLB-181

Stegner, Wallace 1909-1993 ....DLB-9, 206; Y-93

Stehr, Hermann 1864-1940 ....DLB-66

Steig, William 1907- DLB-61

Stein, Gertrude
    1874-1946 ....DLB-4, 54, 86; DS-15

Stein, Leo 1872-1947 ....DLB-4

Stein and Day Publishers...............DLB-46

Steinbeck, John 1902-1968.... DLB-7, 9, 212; DS-2

Steiner, George 1929- DLB-67

Steinhoewel, Heinrich 1411/1412-1479 ...DLB-179

Steloff, Ida Frances 1887-1989 ....DLB-187

Stendhal 1783-1842 ....DLB-119

Stephen Crane: A Revaluation Virginia
    Tech Conference, 1989.............. Y-89

Stephen, Leslie 1832-1904 ...... DLB-57, 144, 190

Stephen Vincent Benét Centenary..........Y-97

Stephens, Alexander H. 1812-1883 ....DLB-47

Stephens, Alice Barber 1858-1932 ....DLB-188

Stephens, Ann 1810-1886 ....DLB-3, 73

Stephens, Charles Asbury 1844?-1931 ....DLB-42

Stephens, James 1882?-1950 ....DLB-19, 153, 162

Stephens, John Lloyd 1805-1852........DLB-183

Sterling, George 1869-1926 ....DLB-54

Sterling, James 1701-1763...............DLB-24

Sterling, John 1806-1844 ....DLB-116

Stern, Gerald 1925- DLB-105

Stern, Gladys B. 1890-1973 ....DLB-197

Stern, Madeleine B. 1912- DLB-111, 140

Stern, Richard 1928- DLB-218; Y-87

Stern, Stewart 1922- DLB-26

Sterne, Laurence 1713-1768 ....DLB-39

Sternheim, Carl 1878-1942 ....DLB-56, 118

Sternhold, Thomas ?-1549 and
    John Hopkins ?-1570.............DLB-132

Steuart, David 1747-1824 ....DLB-213

Stevens, Henry 1819-1886..............DLB-140

Stevens, Wallace 1879-1955.............DLB-54

Stevenson, Anne 1933- DLB-40

Stevenson, D. E. 1892-1973............DLB-191

Stevenson, Lionel 1902-1973 ....DLB-155

Stevenson, Robert Louis 1850-1894
    ....DLB-18, 57, 141, 156, 174; DS-13

Stewart, Donald Ogden
  1894-1980 .... DLB-4, 11, 26

Stewart, Dugald 1753-1828............. DLB-31

Stewart, George, Jr. 1848-1906......... DLB-99

Stewart, George R. 1895-1980 .... DLB-8

Stewart and Kidd Company........... DLB-46

Stewart, Randall 1896-1964 .... DLB-103

Stickney, Trumbull 1874-1904 .... DLB-54

Stieler, Caspar 1632-1707 .... DLB-164

Stifter, Adalbert 1805-1868........... DLB-133

Stiles, Ezra 1727-1795 .... DLB-31

Still, James 1906- DLB-9

Stirner, Max 1806-1856 .... DLB-129

Stith, William 1707-1755 .... DLB-31

Stock, Elliot [publishing house]........ DLB-106

Stockton, Frank R.
  1834-1902 .... DLB-42, 74; DS-13

Stoddard, Ashbel [publishing house] DLB-49

Stoddard, Charles Warren
  1843-1909 .... DLB-186

Stoddard, Elizabeth 1823-1902........ DLB-202

Stoddard, Richard Henry
  1825-1903 .... DLB-3, 64; DS-13

Stoddard, Solomon 1643-1729 .... DLB-24

Stoker, Bram 1847-1912 ....DLB-36, 70, 178

Stokes, Frederick A., Company DLB-49

Stokes, Thomas L. 1898-1958 .... DLB-29

Stokesbury, Leon 1945- DLB-120

Stolberg, Christian Graf zu 1748-1821 .... DLB-94

Stolberg, Friedrich Leopold Graf zu
  1750-1819..................... DLB-94

Stone, Herbert S., and Company DLB-49

Stone, Lucy 1818-1893............... DLB-79

Stone, Melville 1848-1929 .... DLB-25

Stone, Robert 1937- DLB-152

Stone, Ruth 1915- DLB-105

Stone, Samuel 1602-1663 .... DLB-24

Stone, William Leete 1792-1844 .... DLB-202

Stone and Kimball DLB-49

Stoppard, Tom 1937- DLB-13; Y-85

Storey, Anthony 1928- DLB-14

Storey, David 1933- DLB-13, 14, 207

Storm, Theodor 1817-1888........... DLB-129

Story, Thomas circa 1670-1742........ DLB-31

Story, William Wetmore 1819-1895...... DLB-1

Storytelling: A Contemporary Renaissance ... Y-84

Stoughton, William 1631-1701 .... DLB-24

Stow, John 1525-1605................ DLB-132

Stowe, Harriet Beecher
  1811-1896...........DLB-1, 12, 42, 74, 189

Stowe, Leland 1899- DLB-29

Stoyanov, Dimitr Ivanov (see Elin Pelin)

Strabo 64 or 63 B.C.-circa A.D. 25
  ....DLB-176

Strachey, Lytton
  1880-1932 .... DLB-149; DS-10

Strachey, Lytton, Preface to Eminent
  Victorians..................... DLB-149

Strahan and Company DLB-106

Strahan, William [publishing house]..... DLB-154

Strand, Mark 1934- DLB-5

The Strasbourg Oaths 842 .... DLB-148

Stratemeyer, Edward 1862-1930 .... DLB-42

Strati, Saverio 1924- DLB-177

Stratton and Barnard DLB-49

Stratton-Porter, Gene
  1863-1924 .... DLB-221; DS-14

Straub, Peter 1943- Y-84

Strauß, Botho 1944- DLB-124

Strauß, David Friedrich 1808-1874...... DLB-133

The Strawberry Hill Press DLB-154

Streatfeild, Noel 1895-1986 .... DLB-160

Street, Cecil John Charles (see Rhode, John)

Street, G. S. 1867-1936 .... DLB-135

Street and Smith DLB-49

Streeter, Edward 1891-1976 .... DLB-11

Streeter, Thomas Winthrop
  1883-1965 .... DLB-140

Stretton, Hesba 1832-1911 .... DLB-163, 190

Stribling, T. S. 1881-1965.............. DLB-9

Der Stricker circa 1190-circa 1250 ..... DLB-138

Strickland, Samuel 1804-1867.......... DLB-99

Stringer and Townsend DLB-49

Stringer, Arthur 1874-1950............ DLB-92

Strittmatter, Erwin 1912- DLB-69

Strniša, Gregor 1930-1987 .... DLB-181

Strode, William 1630-1645........... DLB-126

Strong, L. A. G. 1896-1958 .... DLB-191

Strother, David Hunter 1816-1888....... DLB-3

Strouse, Jean 1945- DLB-111

Stuart, Dabney 1937- DLB-105

Stuart, Jesse 1906-1984......DLB-9, 48, 102; Y-84

Stuart, Ruth McEnery 1849?-1917 ...... DLB-202

Stuart, Lyle [publishing house] DLB-46

Stubbs, Harry Clement (see Clement, Hal)

Stubenberg, Johann Wilhelm von
  1619-1663 .... DLB-164

Studio DLB-112

The Study of Poetry (1880), by
  Matthew Arnold.................. DLB-35

Sturgeon, Theodore 1918-1985 .....DLB-8; Y-85

Sturges, Preston 1898-1959 .... DLB-26

"Style" (1840; revised, 1859), by
  Thomas de Quincey [excerpt] DLB-57

"Style" (1888), by Walter Pater DLB-57

Style (1897), by Walter Raleigh
  [excerpt]...................... DLB-57

"Style" (1877), by T. H. Wright
  [excerpt]..................... DLB-57

"Le Style c'est l'homme" (1892), by
  W. H. Mallock.................. DLB-57

Styron, William 1925- DLB-2, 143; Y-80

Suárez, Mario 1925- DLB-82

Such, Peter 1939- DLB-60

Suckling, Sir John 1609-1641? DLB-58, 126

Suckow, Ruth 1892-1960.......... DLB-9, 102

Sudermann, Hermann 1857-1928....... DLB-118

Sue, Eugène 1804-1857.............. DLB-119

Sue, Marie-Joseph (see Sue, Eugène)

Suetonius circa A.D. 69-post A.D. 122... DLB-211

Suggs, Simon (see Hooper, Johnson Jones)

Sui Sin Far (see Eaton, Edith Maude)

Suits, Gustav 1883-1956.............. DLB-220

Sukenick, Ronald 1932- DLB-173; Y-81

Suknaski, Andrew 1942- DLB-53

Sullivan, Alan 1868-1947 .... DLB-92

Sullivan, C. Gardner 1886-1965........ DLB-26

Sullivan, Frank 1892-1976 .... DLB-11

Sulte, Benjamin 1841-1923............ DLB-99

Sulzberger, Arthur Hays 1891-1968 .....DLB-127

Sulzberger, Arthur Ochs 1926- DLB-127

Sulzer, Johann Georg 1720-1779........ DLB-97

Sumarokov, Aleksandr Petrovich
  1717-1777 .... DLB-150

Summers, Hollis 1916- DLB-6

Sumner, Henry A. [publishing house] DLB-49

Surtees, Robert Smith 1803-1864....... DLB-21

Surveys: Japanese Literature,
  1987-1995..................... DLB-182

A Survey of Poetry Anthologies,
  1879-1960..................... DLB-54

Surveys of the Year's Biographies

A Transit of Poets and Others: American
  Biography in 1982 .... Y-82

The Year in Literary Biography....... Y-83–Y-98

Survey of the Year's Book Publishing

The Year in Book Publishing............. Y-86

Survey of the Year's Book Reviewing

The Year in Book Reviewing and the Literary
  Situation........................ Y-98

Survey of the Year's Children's Books

The Year in Children's Books Y-92–Y-96, Y-98

The Year in Children's Literature Y-97

Surveys of the Year's Drama

The Year in Drama Y-82–Y-85, Y-87–Y-96

The Year in London Theatre............. Y-92

Surveys of the Year's Fiction

The Year's Work in Fiction: A Survey....... Y-82

The Year in Fiction: A Biased View........ Y-83

The Year in Fiction... Y-84–Y-86, Y-89, Y-94–Y-98

The Year in the Novel Y-87, Y-88, Y-90–Y-93

The Year in Short Stories................ Y-87

The Year in the Short Story Y-88, Y-90–Y-93

Surveys of the Year's Literary Theory

The Year in Literary Theory Y-92–Y-93

Survey of the Year's Literature

The Year in Texas Literature............. Y-98

Surveys of the Year's Poetry

The Year's Work in American Poetry Y-82

The Year in Poetry Y-83–Y-92, Y-94–Y-98

Sutherland, Efua Theodora
1924-1996 . . . . .DLB-117

Sutherland, John 1919-1956. . . . . .DLB-68

Sutro, Alfred 1863-1933. . . . . .DLB-10

Svendsen, Hanne Marie 1933- DLB-214

Swados, Harvey 1920-1972 . . . . .DLB-2

Swain, Charles 1801-1874 . . . . .DLB-32

Swallow Press DLB-46

Swan Sonnenschein Limited DLB-106

Swanberg, W. A. 1907- DLB-103

Swenson, May 1919-1989 . . . . .DLB-5

Swerling, Jo 1897- DLB-44

Swift, Graham 1949- DLB-194

Swift, Jonathan 1667-1745 . . . . . . .DLB-39, 95, 101

Swinburne, A. C. 1837-1909 . . . . .DLB-35, 57

Swineshead, Richard
floruit circa 1350 . . . . .DLB-115

Swinnerton, Frank 1884-1982 . . . . .DLB-34

Swisshelm, Jane Grey 1815-1884. . . . . . . .DLB-43

Swope, Herbert Bayard 1882-1958 . . . . . . .DLB-25

Swords, T. and J., and Company DLB-49

Swords, Thomas 1763-1843 and
Swords, James ?-1844 . . . . .DLB-73

Sykes, Ella C. ?-1939 . . . . .DLB-174

Sylvester, Josuah
1562 or 1563 - 1618 . . . . .DLB-121

Symonds, Emily Morse (see Paston, George)

Symonds, John Addington
1840-1893 . . . . DLB-57, 144

Symons, A. J. A. 1900-1941. . . . . .DLB-149

Symons, Arthur 1865-1945 . . . . . DLB-19, 57, 149

Symons, Julian 1912-1994 . . . . . DLB-87, 155; Y-92

Symons, Scott 1933- DLB-53

A Symposium on *The Columbia History of*
the Novel Y-92

Synge, John Millington 1871-1909 . . . . .DLB-10, 19

Synge Summer School: J. M. Synge and the
Irish Theater, Rathdrum, County Wiclow,
Ireland Y-93

Syrett, Netta 1865-1943 . . . . .DLB-135, 197

Szabó, Lőrinc 1900-1957 . . . . .DLB-215

Szabó, Magda 1917- DLB-215

Szymborska, Wisława 1923- Y-96

T

Taban lo Liyong 1939?- DLB-125

Tabucchi, Antonio 1943- DLB-196

Taché, Joseph-Charles 1820-1894 . . . . . . .DLB-99

Tachihara Masaaki 1926-1980. . . . . .DLB-182

Tacitus circa A.D. 55-circa A.D. 117 . . . . .DLB-211

Tadijanović, Dragutin 1905- DLB-181

Tafdrup, Pia 1952- DLB-214

Tafolla, Carmen 1951- DLB-82

Taggard, Genevieve 1894-1948. . . . . .DLB-45

Taggart, John 1942- DLB-193

Tagger, Theodor (see Bruckner, Ferdinand)

Taiheiki late fourteenth century. DLB-203

Tait, J. Selwin, and Sons DLB-49

Tait's Edinburgh Magazine 1832-1861 . . . . . .DLB-110

The Takarazaka Revue Company. Y-91

Talander (see Bohse, August)

Talese, Gay 1932- DLB-185

Talev, Dimitr 1898-1966 . . . . .DLB-181

Taliaferro, H. E. 1811-1875 . . . . .DLB-202

Tallent, Elizabeth 1954- DLB-130

TallMountain, Mary 1918-1994 . . . . . . .DLB-193

Talvj 1797-1870 . . . . .DLB-59, 133

Tamási, Áron 1897-1966 . . . . .DLB-215

Tammsaare, A. H.
1878-1940 . . . . .DLB-220

Tan, Amy 1952- DLB-173

Tanner, Thomas
1673/1674-1735 . . . . .DLB-213

Tanizaki, Jun'ichirō 1886-1965 . . . . .DLB-180

Tapahonso, Luci 1953- DLB-175

Taradash, Daniel 1913- DLB-44

Tarbell, Ida M. 1857-1944 . . . . .DLB-47

Tardivel, Jules-Paul 1851-1905 . . . . .DLB-99

Targan, Barry 1932- DLB-130

Tarkington, Booth 1869-1946 . . . . . . .DLB-9, 102

Tashlin, Frank 1913-1972 . . . . .DLB-44

Tate, Allen 1899-1979 . . . . . . DLB-4, 45, 63; DS-17

Tate, James 1943- DLB-5, 169

Tate, Nahum circa 1652-1715 . . . . .DLB-80

Tatian circa 830 . . . . .DLB-148

Taufer, Veno 1933- DLB-181

Tauler, Johannes circa 1300-1361 . . . . . . .DLB-179

Tavčar, Ivan 1851-1923. . . . . .DLB-147

Taylor, Ann 1782-1866 . . . . .DLB-163

Taylor, Bayard 1825-1878 . . . . .DLB-3, 189

Taylor, Bert Leston 1866-1921 . . . . .DLB-25

Taylor, Charles H. 1846-1921. . . . . .DLB-25

Taylor, Edward circa 1642-1729 . . . . .DLB-24

Taylor, Elizabeth 1912-1975 . . . . .DLB-139

Taylor, Henry 1942- DLB-5

Taylor, Sir Henry 1800-1886. . . . . .DLB-32

Taylor, Jane 1783-1824 . . . . .DLB-163

Taylor, Jeremy circa 1613-1667. . . . . . . .DLB-151

Taylor, John 1577 or 1578 - 1653 . . . . . . .DLB-121

Taylor, Mildred D. ?- DLB-52

Taylor, Peter 1917-1994. . . . . DLB-218; Y-81, Y-94

Taylor, Susie King 1848-1912 . . . . .DLB-221

Taylor, William, and Company DLB-49

Taylor-Made Shakespeare? Or Is "Shall I Die?" the
Long-Lost Text of Bottom's Dream? Y-85

Teasdale, Sara 1884-1933 . . . . .DLB-45

The Tea-Table (1725), by Eliza Haywood
[excerpt]. DLB-39

Telles, Lygia Fagundes 1924- DLB-113

Temple, Sir William 1628-1699. . . . . . . .DLB-101

Tenn, William 1919- DLB-8

Tennant, Emma 1937- DLB-14

Tenney, Tabitha Gilman
1762-1837 . . . . DLB-37, 200

Tennyson, Alfred 1809-1892. . . . . .DLB-32

Tennyson, Frederick 1807-1898. . . . . .DLB-32

Tenorio, Arthur 1924- DLB-209

Tepliakov, Viktor Grigor'evich
1804-1842 . . . . .DLB-205

Terence
circa 184 B.C.-159 B.C. or after DLB-211

Terhune, Albert Payson 1872-1942. . . . . . .DLB-9

Terhune, Mary Virginia
1830-1922 . . . . DS-13, DS-16

Terry, Megan 1932- DLB-7

Terson, Peter 1932- DLB-13

Tesich, Steve 1943-1996 . . . . Y-83

Tessa, Delio 1886-1939 . . . . .DLB-114

Testori, Giovanni 1923-1993. . . . . . DLB-128, 177

Tey, Josephine 1896?-1952 . . . . .DLB-77

Thacher, James 1754-1844. . . . . .DLB-37

Thackeray, William Makepeace
1811-1863 . . . . DLB-21, 55, 159, 163

Thames and Hudson Limited DLB-112

Thanet, Octave (see French, Alice)

Thatcher, John Boyd 1847-1909 . . . . . . .DLB-187

Thayer, Caroline Matilda Warren
1785-1844 . . . . .DLB-200

The Theater in Shakespeare's Time DLB-62

The Theatre Guild DLB-7

Thegan and the Astronomer
flourished circa 850. . . . . .DLB-148

Thelwall, John 1764-1834 . . . . .DLB-93, 158

Theocritus circa 300 B.C.-260 B.C.
. . . . .DLB-176

Theodorescu, Ion N. (see Arghezi, Tudor)

Theodulf circa 760-circa 821 . . . . .DLB-148

Theophrastus circa 371 B.C.-287 B.C.
. . . . .DLB-176

Theriault, Yves 1915-1983. . . . . .DLB-88

Thério, Adrien 1925- DLB-53

Theroux, Paul 1941- DLB-2, 218

Thesiger, Wilfred 1910- DLB-204

They All Came to Paris. DS-16

Thibaudeau, Colleen 1925- DLB-88

Thielen, Benedict 1903-1965 . . . . .DLB-102

Thiong'o Ngugi wa (see Ngugi wa Thiong'o)

Third-Generation Minor Poets of the
Seventeenth Century. DLB-131

This Quarter 1925-1927, 1929-1932 . . . . DS-15

Thoma, Ludwig 1867-1921 . . . . .DLB-66

Thoma, Richard 1902- DLB-4

Thomas, Audrey 1935- DLB-60

Thomas, D. M. 1935- DLB-40, 207

Thomas, Dylan 1914-1953 . . . . . .DLB-13, 20, 139

Thomas, Edward
1878-1917 . . . . .DLB-19, 98, 156, 216

Thomas, Frederick William
1806-1866 . . . . .DLB-202

Thomas, Gwyn 1913-1981 . . . . DLB-15

Thomas, Isaiah 1750-1831 . . . . . . .DLB-43, 73, 187

Thomas, Isaiah [publishing house] DLB-49

Thomas, Johann 1624-1679 . . . . DLB-168

Thomas, John 1900-1932 . . . . DLB-4

Thomas, Joyce Carol 1938- DLB-33

Thomas, Lorenzo 1944- DLB-41

Thomas, R. S. 1915- DLB-27

The Thomas Wolfe Collection at the University of North Carolina at Chapel Hill Y-97

The Thomas Wolfe Society Y-97

Thomasîn von Zerclære circa 1186-circa 1259 . . . . DLB-138

Thomasius, Christian 1655-1728 . . . . DLB-168

Thompson, David 1770-1857 . . . . DLB-99

Thompson, Daniel Pierce 1795-1868 . . . . DLB-202

Thompson, Dorothy 1893-1961 . . . . DLB-29

Thompson, Francis 1859-1907 . . . . DLB-19

Thompson, George Selden (see Selden, George)

Thompson, Henry Yates 1838-1928 . . . . . DLB-184

Thompson, Hunter S. 1939- DLB-185

Thompson, John 1938-1976 . . . . DLB-60

Thompson, John R. 1823-1873 . . . . DLB-3, 73

Thompson, Lawrance 1906-1973 . . . . DLB-103

Thompson, Maurice 1844-1901 . . . . . .DLB-71, 74

Thompson, Ruth Plumly 1891-1976. . . . . . DLB-22

Thompson, Thomas Phillips 1843-1933. . . DLB-99

Thompson, William 1775-1833 . . . . DLB-158

Thompson, William Tappan 1812-1882. . . . . DLB-3, 11

Thomson, Edward William 1849-1924 . . . DLB-92

Thomson, James 1700-1748 . . . . DLB-95

Thomson, James 1834-1882 . . . . DLB-35

Thomson, Joseph 1858-1895 . . . . .DLB-174

Thomson, Mortimer 1831-1875 . . . . DLB-11

Thoreau, Henry David 1817-1862 . . . . DLB-1, 183

Thornton Wilder Centenary at Yale Y-97

Thorpe, Thomas Bangs 1815-1878. . . . . DLB-3, 11

Thorup, Kirsten 1942- DLB-214

Thoughts on Poetry and Its Varieties (1833), by John Stuart Mill. DLB-32

Thrale, Hester Lynch (see Piozzi, Hester Lynch [Thrale])

Thubron, Colin 1939- DLB-204

Thucydides circa 455 B.C.-circa 395 B.C. DLB-176

Thulstrup, Thure de 1848-1930 . . . . DLB-188

Thümmel, Moritz August von 1738-1817 . . . . DLB-97

Thurber, James 1894-1961 . . . . .DLB-4, 11, 22, 102

Thurman, Wallace 1902-1934 . . . . DLB-51

Thwaite, Anthony 1930- DLB-40

Thwaites, Reuben Gold 1853-1913 . . . . . DLB-47

Tibullus circa 54 B.C.-circa 19 B.C. DLB-211

Ticknor, George 1791-1871 . . . . . . DLB-1, 59, 140

Ticknor and Fields DLB-49

Ticknor and Fields (revived) DLB-46

Tieck, Ludwig 1773-1853 . . . . DLB-90

Tietjens, Eunice 1884-1944 . . . . DLB-54

Tilney, Edmund circa 1536-1610 . . . . . . DLB-136

Tilt, Charles [publishing house] DLB-106

Tilton, J. E., and Company DLB-49

Time and Western Man (1927), by Wyndham Lewis [excerpts] DLB-36

Time-Life Books. DLB-46

Times Books. DLB-46

Timothy, Peter circa 1725-1782 . . . . DLB-43

Timrava 1867-1951. . . . . DLB-215

Timrod, Henry 1828-1867 . . . . DLB-3

Tindal, Henrietta 1818?-1879 . . . . DLB-199

Tinker, Chauncey Brewster 1876-1963. DLB-140

Tinsley Brothers. DLB-106

Tiptree, James, Jr. 1915-1987 . . . . DLB-8

Tišma, Aleksandar 1924- DLB-181

Titus, Edward William 1870-1952. . . . . DLB-4; DS-15

Tiutchev, Fedor Ivanovich 1803-1873. . . . . DLB-205

Tlali, Miriam 1933- DLB-157

Todd, Barbara Euphan 1890-1976 . . . . . DLB-160

Tofte, Robert 1561 or 1562-1619 or 1620 . . . . .DLB-172

Toklas, Alice B. 1877-1967 . . . . DLB-4

Tokuda, Shūsei 1872-1943 . . . . DLB-180

Tolkien, J. R. R. 1892-1973 . . . . DLB-15, 160

Toller, Ernst 1893-1939 . . . . DLB-124

Tollet, Elizabeth 1694-1754 . . . . DLB-95

Tolson, Melvin B. 1898-1966. . . . . . . DLB-48, 76

Tom Jones (1749), by Henry Fielding [excerpt] DLB-39

Tomalin, Claire 1933- DLB-155

Tomasi di Lampedusa, Giuseppe 1896-1957. . . . . .DLB-177

Tomlinson, Charles 1927- DLB-40

Tomlinson, H. M. 1873-1958 . . . . .DLB-36, 100, 195

Tompkins, Abel [publishing house] DLB-49

Tompson, Benjamin 1642-1714 . . . . DLB-24

Ton'a 1289-1372. . . . . DLB-203

Tondelli, Pier Vittorio 1955-1991 . . . . . . DLB-196

Tonks, Rosemary 1932- DLB-14, 207

Tonna, Charlotte Elizabeth 1790-1846. . . . . DLB-163

Tonson, Jacob the Elder [publishing house] DLB-170

Toole, John Kennedy 1937-1969 . . . . Y-81

Toomer, Jean 1894-1967 . . . . DLB-45, 51

Tor Books DLB-46

Torberg, Friedrich 1908-1979. . . . . DLB-85

Torrence, Ridgely 1874-1950 . . . . DLB-54

Torres-Metzger, Joseph V. 1933- DLB-122

Toth, Susan Allen 1940- Y-86

Tottell, Richard [publishing house] DLB-170

Tough-Guy Literature DLB-9

Touré, Askia Muhammad 1938- DLB-41

Tourgée, Albion W. 1838-1905 . . . . DLB-79

Tourneur, Cyril circa 1580-1626 . . . . DLB-58

Tournier, Michel 1924- DLB-83

Tousey, Frank [publishing house] DLB-49

Tower Publications. DLB-46

Towne, Benjamin circa 1740-1793 . . . . DLB-43

Towne, Robert 1936- DLB-44

The Townely Plays fifteenth and sixteenth centuries. DLB-146

Townshend, Aurelian by 1583 - circa 1651. . . . . DLB-121

Toy, Barbara 1908- DLB-204

Tracy, Honor 1913- DLB-15

Traherne, Thomas 1637?-1674. . . . . DLB-131

Traill, Catharine Parr 1802-1899 . . . . DLB-99

Train, Arthur 1875-1945 . . . . DLB-86; DS-16

The Transatlantic Publishing Company . . DLB-49

The Transatlantic Review 1924-1925 . . . . .DS-15

Transcendentalists, American. DS-5

transition 1927-1938 . . . . .DS-15

Translators of the Twelfth Century: Literary Issues Raised and Impact Created DLB-115

Travel Writing, 1837-1875 . . . . DLB-166

Travel Writing, 1876-1909 . . . . .DLB-174

Traven, B. 1882? or 1890?-1969? DLB-9, 56

Travers, Ben 1886-1980 . . . . DLB-10

Travers, P. L. (Pamela Lyndon) 1899-1996 . . . . DLB-160

Trediakovsky, Vasilii Kirillovich 1703-1769. DLB-150

Treece, Henry 1911-1966. . . . . DLB-160

Trejo, Ernesto 1950- DLB-122

Trelawny, Edward John 1792-1881. . . . . .DLB-110, 116, 144

Tremain, Rose 1943- DLB-14

Tremblay, Michel 1942- DLB-60

Trends in Twentieth-Century Mass Market Publishing DLB-46

Trent, William P. 1862-1939 . . . . DLB-47

Trescot, William Henry 1822-1898 . . . . . . DLB-30

Tressell, Robert (Robert Phillipe Noonan) 1870-1911. .DLB-197

Trevelyan, Sir George Otto 1838-1928 . . . . DLB-144

Trevisa, John circa 1342-circa 1402 . . . . . DLB-146

Trevor, William 1928- DLB-14, 139

Trierer Floyris circa 1170-1180 . . . . DLB-138

Trillin, Calvin 1935- DLB-185

Trilling, Lionel 1905-1975 . . . . DLB-28, 63

Trilussa 1871-1950 . . . . DLB-114

Trimmer, Sarah 1741-1810 . . . . DLB-158

Triolet, Elsa 1896-1970. . . . . DLB-72

Tripp, John 1927- DLB-40

Trocchi, Alexander 1925- DLB-15

Troisi, Dante 1920-1989 ....DLB-196

Trollope, Anthony 1815-1882 .... DLB-21, 57, 159

Trollope, Frances 1779-1863 ....DLB-21, 166

Trollope, Joanna 1943- DLB-207

Troop, Elizabeth 1931- DLB-14

Trotter, Catharine 1679-1749...........DLB-84

Trotti, Lamar 1898-1952 ....DLB-44

Trottier, Pierre 1925- DLB-60

Troubadours, *Trobaíritz,* and
  Trouvères DLB-208

Troupe, Quincy Thomas, Jr. 1943- DLB-41

Trow, John F., and Company DLB-49

Trowbridge, John Townsend
  1827-1916 ....DLB-202

Truillier-Lacombe, Joseph-Patrice
  1807-1863 ....DLB-99

Trumbo, Dalton 1905-1976.............DLB-26

Trumbull, Benjamin 1735-1820.........DLB-30

Trumbull, John 1750-1831.............DLB-31

Trumbull, John 1756-1843.............DLB-183

Tscherning, Andreas 1611-1659 ....DLB-164

T. S. Eliot Centennial Y-88

Tsubouchi, Shōyō 1859-1935 ....DLB-180

Tucholsky, Kurt 1890-1935.............DLB-56

Tucker, Charlotte Maria
  1821-1893 ....DLB-163, 190

Tucker, George 1775-1861...........DLB-3, 30

Tucker, Nathaniel Beverley 1784-1851 .....DLB-3

Tucker, St. George 1752-1827 ....DLB-37

Tuckerman, Henry Theodore
  1813-1871 ....DLB-64

Tumas, Juozas (see Vaižgantas)

Tunis, John R. 1889-1975 ....DLB-22, 171

Tunstall, Cuthbert 1474-1559 ....DLB-132

Tuohy, Frank 1925- DLB-14, 139

Tupper, Martin F. 1810-1889..........DLB-32

Turbyfill, Mark 1896- DLB-45

Turco, Lewis 1934- Y-84

Turgenev, Aleksandr Ivanovich
  1784-1845 ....DLB-198

Turnball, Alexander H.
  1868-1918 ....DLB-184

Turnbull, Andrew 1921-1970 ....DLB-103

Turnbull, Gael 1928- DLB-40

Turner, Arlin 1909-1980 ....DLB-103

Turner, Charles (Tennyson)
  1808-1879 ....DLB-32

Turner, Frederick 1943- DLB-40

Turner, Frederick Jackson 1861-1932 . DLB-17, 186

Turner, Joseph Addison 1826-1868......DLB-79

Turpin, Waters Edward 1910-1968......DLB-51

Turrini, Peter 1944- DLB-124

Tutuola, Amos 1920-1997 ....DLB-125

Twain, Mark (see Clemens, Samuel Langhorne)

Tweedie, Ethel Brilliana
  circa 1860-1940.................DLB-174

The 'Twenties and Berlin,
  by Alex Natan....................DLB-66

Twysden, Sir Roger 1597-1672 ....DLB-213

Tyler, Anne 1941- DLB-6, 143; Y-82

Tyler, Mary Palmer 1775-1866 ....DLB-200

Tyler, Moses Coit 1835-1900 .... DLB-47, 64

Tyler, Royall 1757-1826...............DLB-37

Tylor, Edward Burnett 1832-1917......DLB-57

Tynan, Katharine 1861-1931...........DLB-153

Tyndale, William circa
  1494-1536 ....DLB-132

U

Udall, Nicholas 1504-1556 ....DLB-62

Ugrêsić, Dubravka 1949- DLB-181

Uhland, Ludwig 1787-1862 ....DLB-90

Uhse, Bodo 1904-1963 ....DLB-69

Ujević, Augustin ("Tin") 1891-1955 .....DLB-147

Ulenhart, Niclas flourished circa 1600....DLB-164

Ulibarrí, Sabine R. 1919- DLB-82

Ulica, Jorge 1870-1926.................DLB-82

Ulivi, Ferruccio 1912- DLB-196

Ulizio, B. George 1889-1969 ....DLB-140

Ulrich von Liechtenstein
  circa 1200-circa 1275 ....DLB-138

Ulrich von Zatzikhoven
  before 1194-after 1214..............DLB-138

Ulysses, Reader's Edition Y-97

Unamuno, Miguel de 1864-1936.......DLB-108

Under, Marie 1883-1980 ....DLB-220

Under the Microscope (1872), by
  A. C. Swinburne DLB-35

Unger, Friederike Helene 1741-1813 .....DLB-94

Ungaretti, Giuseppe 1888-1970 ....DLB-114

United States Book Company DLB-49

Universal Publishing and Distributing
  Corporation DLB-46

The University of Iowa Writers' Workshop
  Golden Jubilee..................Y-86

The University of South Carolina Press Y-94

University of Wales Press DLB-112

University Press of Kansas Y-98

"The Unknown Public" (1858), by
  Wilkie Collins [excerpt]............DLB-57

Uno, Chiyo 1897-1996.................DLB-180

Unruh, Fritz von 1885-1970........DLB-56, 118

Unspeakable Practices II: The Festival of
  Vanguard Narrative at BrownUniversity . Y-93

Unsworth, Barry 1930- DLB-194

The Unterberg Poetry Center of the
  92nd Street Y Y-98

Unwin, T. Fisher [publishing house] DLB-106

Upchurch, Boyd B. (see Boyd, John)

Updike, John 1932-
  .... DLB-2, 5, 143, 218; Y-80, Y-82; DS-3

Upīts, Andrejs 1877-1970 ....DLB-220

Upton, Bertha 1849-1912 ....DLB-141

Upton, Charles 1948- DLB-16

Upton, Florence K. 1873-1922.........DLB-141

Upward, Allen 1863-1926 ....DLB-36

Urban, Milo 1904-1982...............DLB-215

Urista, Alberto Baltazar (see Alurista)

Urrea, Luis Alberto 1955- DLB-209

Urzidil, Johannes 1896-1976 ....DLB-85

Urquhart, Fred 1912- DLB-139

The Uses of Facsimile Y-90

Usk, Thomas died 1388 ....DLB-146

Uslar Pietri, Arturo 1906- DLB-113

Ussher, James 1581-1656..............DLB-213

Ustinov, Peter 1921- DLB-13

Uttley, Alison 1884-1976 ....DLB-160

Uz, Johann Peter 1720-1796............DLB-97

V

Vac, Bertrand 1914- DLB-88

Vaičiulaitis, Antanas 1906-1992 ....DLB-220

Vail, Laurence 1891-1968 ....DLB-4

Vailland, Roger 1907-1965 ....DLB-83

Vajda, Ernest 1887-1954 ....DLB-44

Vaižgantas 1869-1933 ....DLB-220

Valdés, Gina 1943- DLB-122

Valdez, Luis Miguel 1940- DLB-122

Valduga, Patrizia 1953- DLB-128

Valente, José Angel 1929- DLB-108

Valenzuela, Luisa 1938- DLB-113

Valeri, Diego 1887-1976 ....DLB-128

Valerius Flaccus fl. circa A.D. 92........DLB-211

Valerius Maximus fl. circa A.D. 31......DLB-211

Valesio, Paolo 1939- DLB-196

Valgardson, W. D. 1939- DLB-60

Valle, Víctor Manuel 1950- DLB-122

Valle-Inclán, Ramón del 1866-1936......DLB-134

Vallejo, Armando 1949- DLB-122

Vallès, Jules 1832-1885 ....DLB-123

Vallette, Marguerite Eymery (see Rachilde)

Valverde, José María 1926-1996 ....DLB-108

Van Allsburg, Chris 1949- DLB-61

Van Anda, Carr 1864-1945 ....DLB-25

van der Post, Laurens 1906-1996 ....DLB-204

Van Dine, S. S. (see Wright, Williard Huntington)

Van Doren, Mark 1894-1972...........DLB-45

van Druten, John 1901-1957 ....DLB-10

Van Duyn, Mona 1921- DLB-5

Van Dyke, Henry 1852-1933 ..... DLB-71; DS-13

Van Dyke, John C. 1856-1932 ....DLB-186

Van Dyke, Henry 1928- DLB-33

van Gulik, Robert Hans 1910-1967........DS-17

van Itallie, Jean-Claude 1936- DLB-7

Van Loan, Charles E. 1876-1919........DLB-171

Van Rensselaer, Mariana Griswold
  1851-1934......................DLB-47

Van Rensselaer, Mrs. Schuyler (see Van
  Rensselaer, Mariana Griswold)

Van Vechten, Carl 1880-1964 . . . . DLB-4, 9

van Vogt, A. E. 1912- DLB-8

Vanbrugh, Sir John 1664-1726 . . . . DLB-80

Vance, Jack 1916?- DLB-8

Vančura, Vladislav 1891-1942 . . . . DLB-215

Vane, Sutton 1888-1963 . . . . DLB-10

Vanguard Press DLB-46

Vann, Robert L. 1879-1940 . . . . DLB-29

Vargas, Llosa, Mario 1936- DLB-145

Varley, John 1947- Y-81

Varnhagen von Ense, Karl August
        1785-1858 . . . . DLB-90

Varro 116 B.C.-27 B.C. DLB-211

Vasiliu, George (see Bacovia, George)

Vásquez, Richard 1928- DLB-209

Varnhagen von Ense, Rahel
        1771-1833 . . . . DLB-90

Vásquez Montalbán, Manuel
        1939- DLB-134

Vassa, Gustavus (see Equiano, Olaudah)

Vassalli, Sebastiano 1941- DLB-128, 196

Vaughan, Henry 1621-1695 . . . . DLB-131

Vaughn, Robert 1592?-1667 . . . . DLB-213

Vaughan, Thomas 1621-1666 . . . . DLB-131

Vaux, Thomas, Lord 1509-1556 . . . . DLB-132

Vazov, Ivan 1850-1921 . . . . DLB-147

Véa Jr., Alfredo 1950- DLB-209

Vega, Janine Pommy 1942- DLB-16

Veiller, Anthony 1903-1965 . . . . DLB-44

Velásquez-Trevino, Gloria 1949- DLB-122

Veley, Margaret 1843-1887 . . . . DLB-199

Velleius Paterculus
        circa 20 B.C.-circa A.D. 30 . . . . DLB-211

Veloz Maggiolo, Marcio 1936- DLB-145

Vel'tman Aleksandr Fomich
        1800-1870 . . . . DLB-198

Venegas, Daniel ?-? DLB-82

Venevitinov, Dmitrii Vladimirovich
        1805-1827 . . . . DLB-205

Vergil, Polydore circa 1470-1555 . . . . DLB-132

Veríssimo, Erico 1905-1975 . . . . DLB-145

Verlaine, Paul 1844-1896 . . . . DLB-217

Verne, Jules 1828-1905 . . . . DLB-123

Verplanck, Gulian C. 1786-1870 . . . . DLB-59

Very, Jones 1813-1880 . . . . DLB-1

Vian, Boris 1920-1959 . . . . DLB-72

Viazemsky, Petr Andreevich 1792-1878 . . DLB-205

Vickers, Roy 1888?-1965 . . . . DLB-77

Vickery, Sukey 1779-1821 . . . . DLB-200

Victoria 1819-1901 . . . . DLB-55

Victoria Press DLB-106

Vidal, Gore 1925- DLB-6, 152

Viebig, Clara 1860-1952 . . . . DLB-66

Viereck, George Sylvester 1884-1962 . . . . DLB-54

Viereck, Peter 1916- DLB-5

Viets, Roger 1738-1811 . . . . DLB-99

Viewpoint: Politics and Performance, by
        David Edgar DLB-13

Vigil-Piñon, Evangelina 1949- DLB-122

Vigneault, Gilles 1928- DLB-60

Vigny, Alfred de 1797-1863 . . . . DLB-119, 192, 217

Vigolo, Giorgio 1894-1983 . . . . DLB-114

The Viking Press DLB-46

Vilde, Eduard 1865-1933 . . . . DLB-220

Villanueva, Alma Luz 1944- DLB-122

Villanueva, Tino 1941- DLB-82

Villard, Henry 1835-1900 . . . . DLB-23

Villard, Oswald Garrison 1872-1949 . . DLB-25, 91

Villarreal, Edit 1944- DLB-209

Villarreal, José Antonio 1924- DLB-82

Villaseñor, Victor 1940- DLB-209

Villegas de Magnón, Leonor
        1876-1955 . . . . DLB-122

Villehardouin, Geoffroi de
        circa 1150-1215 . . . . DLB-208

Villemaire, Yolande 1949- DLB-60

Villena, Luis Antonio de 1951- DLB-134

Villiers de l'Isle-Adam, Jean-Marie
        Mathias Philippe-Auguste, Comte de
        1838-1889 . . . . DLB-123, 192

Villiers, George, Second Duke
        of Buckingham 1628-1687 . . . . DLB-80

Villon, François 1431-circa 1463? DLB-208

Vine Press DLB-112

Viorst, Judith ?- DLB-52

Vipont, Elfrida (Elfrida Vipont Foulds,
        Charles Vipont) 1902-1992 . . . . DLB-160

Viramontes, Helena María 1954- DLB-122

Virgil 70 B.C.-19 B.C. DLB-211

Vischer, Friedrich Theodor
        1807-1887 . . . . DLB-133

Vitruvius circa 85 B.C.-circa 15 B.C. DLB-211

Vitry, Philippe de 1291-1361 . . . . DLB-208

Vivanco, Luis Felipe 1907-1975 . . . . DLB-108

Viviani, Cesare 1947- DLB-128

Vivien, Renée 1877-1909 . . . . DLB-217

Vizenor, Gerald 1934- DLB-175

Vizetelly and Company DLB-106

Voaden, Herman 1903- DLB-88

Voigt, Ellen Bryant 1943- DLB-120

Vojnović, Ivo 1857-1929 . . . . DLB-147

Volkoff, Vladimir 1932- DLB-83

Volland, P. F., Company DLB-46

Vollbehr, Otto H. F. 1872?-
        1945 or 1946 . . . . DLB-187

Volponi, Paolo 1924- DLB-177

von der Grün, Max 1926- DLB-75

Vonnegut, Kurt
        1922- DLB-2, 8, 152; Y-80; DS-3

Voranc, Prežihov 1893-1950 . . . . DLB-147

Voß, Johann Heinrich 1751-1826 . . . . DLB-90

Voynich, E. L. 1864-1960 . . . . DLB-197

Vroman, Mary Elizabeth
        circa 1924-1967 . . . . DLB-33

W

Wace, Robert ("Maistre")
        circa 1100-circa 1175 . . . . DLB-146

Wackenroder, Wilhelm Heinrich
        1773-1798 . . . . DLB-90

Wackernagel, Wilhelm 1806-1869 . . . . . . DLB-133

Waddington, Miriam 1917- DLB-68

Wade, Henry 1887-1969 . . . . DLB-77

Wagenknecht, Edward 1900- DLB-103

Wagner, Heinrich Leopold 1747-1779 . . . . DLB-94

Wagner, Henry R. 1862-1957 . . . . DLB-140

Wagner, Richard 1813-1883 . . . . DLB-129

Wagoner, David 1926- DLB-5

Wah, Fred 1939- DLB-60

Waiblinger, Wilhelm 1804-1830 . . . . DLB-90

Wain, John 1925-1994 . . . . . DLB-15, 27, 139, 155

Wainwright, Jeffrey 1944- DLB-40

Waite, Peirce and Company DLB-49

Wakeman, Stephen H. 1859-1924 . . . . . . DLB-187

Wakoski, Diane 1937- DLB-5

Walahfrid Strabo circa 808-849 . . . . DLB-148

Walck, Henry Z. DLB-46

Walcott, Derek 1930- DLB-117; Y-81, Y-92

Waldegrave, Robert [publishing house] . . . DLB-170

Waldman, Anne 1945- DLB-16

Waldrop, Rosmarie 1935- DLB-169

Walker, Alice 1900-1982 . . . . DLB-201

Walker, Alice 1944- DLB-6, 33, 143

Walker, George F. 1947- DLB-60

Walker, Joseph A. 1935- DLB-38

Walker, Margaret 1915- DLB-76, 152

Walker, Ted 1934- DLB-40

Walker and Company DLB-49

Walker, Evans and Cogswell
        Company DLB-49

Walker, John Brisben 1847-1931 . . . . DLB-79

Wallace, Alfred Russel 1823-1913 . . . . . . DLB-190

Wallace, Dewitt 1889-1981 and
        Lila Acheson Wallace
        1889-1984 . . . . DLB-137

Wallace, Edgar 1875-1932 . . . . DLB-70

Wallace, Lew 1827-1905 . . . . DLB-202

Wallace, Lila Acheson (see Wallace, Dewitt,
        and Lila Acheson Wallace)

Wallant, Edward Lewis
        1926-1962 . . . . DLB-2, 28, 143

Waller, Edmund 1606-1687 . . . . DLB-126

Walpole, Horace 1717-1797 . . . . . DLB-39, 104, 213

Walpole, Hugh 1884-1941 . . . . DLB-34

Walrond, Eric 1898-1966 . . . . DLB-51

Walser, Martin 1927- DLB-75, 124

Walser, Robert 1878-1956 . . . . DLB-66

Walsh, Ernest 1895-1926 . . . . DLB-4, 45

Walsh, Robert 1784-1859 . . . . DLB-59

Waltharius circa 825 . . . . DLB-148

Walters, Henry 1848-1931 . . . . .DLB-140

Walther von der Vogelweide
circa 1170-circa 1230 . . . . .DLB-138

Walton, Izaak 1593-1683. . . . . .DLB-151, 213

Wambaugh, Joseph 1937- DLB-6; Y-83

Waniek, Marilyn Nelson 1946- DLB-120

Wanley, Humphrey 1672-1726 . . . . .DLB-213

Warburton, William 1698-1779 . . . . .DLB-104

Ward, Aileen 1919- DLB-111

Ward, Artemus (see Browne, Charles Farrar)

Ward, Arthur Henry Sarsfield
(see Rohmer, Sax)

Ward, Douglas Turner 1930- DLB-7, 38

Ward, Lynd 1905-1985 . . . . .DLB-22

Ward, Lock and Company DLB-106

Ward, Mrs. Humphry 1851-1920 . . . . . . .DLB-18

Ward, Nathaniel circa 1578-1652. . . . . . . .DLB-24

Ward, Theodore 1902-1983 . . . . .DLB-76

Wardle, Ralph 1909-1988 . . . . .DLB-103

Ware, William 1797-1852. . . . . .DLB-1

Warne, Frederick, and Company [U.S.] . . .DLB-49

Warne, Frederick, and
Company [U.K.] DLB-106

Warner, Anne 1869-1913 . . . . .DLB-202

Warner, Charles Dudley 1829-1900 . . . . . .DLB-64

Warner, Marina 1946- DLB-194

Warner, Rex 1905- DLB-15

Warner, Susan Bogert 1819-1885 . . . . .DLB-3, 42

Warner, Sylvia Townsend
1893-1978 . . . . .DLB-34, 139

Warner, William 1558-1609 . . . . .DLB-172

Warner Books .DLB-46

Warr, Bertram 1917-1943 . . . . .DLB-88

Warren, John Byrne Leicester
(see De Tabley, Lord)

Warren, Lella 1899-1982 . . . . Y-83

Warren, Mercy Otis 1728-1814 . . . . . .DLB-31, 200

Warren, Robert Penn
1905-1989 . . . . DLB-2, 48, 152; Y-80, Y-89

Warren, Samuel 1807-1877 . . . . .DLB-190

Die Wartburgkrieg
circa 1230-circa 1280. . . . . .DLB-138

Warton, Joseph 1722-1800. . . . . . . .DLB-104, 109

Warton, Thomas 1728-1790 . . . . . . .DLB-104, 109

Washington, George 1732-1799 . . . . .DLB-31

Wassermann, Jakob 1873-1934 . . . . .DLB-66

Wasson, David Atwood 1823-1887 . . . . . . .DLB-1

Watanna, Onoto (see Eaton, Winnifred)

Waterhouse, Keith 1929- DLB-13, 15

Waterman, Andrew 1940- DLB-40

Waters, Frank 1902-1995 . . . . . . .DLB-212; Y-86

Waters, Michael 1949- DLB-120

Watkins, Tobias 1780-1855 . . . . .DLB-73

Watkins, Vernon 1906-1967 . . . . .DLB-20

Watmough, David 1926- DLB-53

Watson, James Wreford (see Wreford, James)

Watson, John 1850-1907 . . . . .DLB-156

Watson, Sheila 1909- DLB-60

Watson, Thomas 1545?-1592 . . . . .DLB-132

Watson, Wilfred 1911- DLB-60

Watt, W. J., and Company DLB-46

Watten, Barrett 1948- DLB-193

Watterson, Henry 1840-1921 . . . . .DLB-25

Watts, Alan 1915-1973. . . . . .DLB-16

Watts, Franklin [publishing house] DLB-46

Watts, Isaac 1674-1748. . . . . .DLB-95

Wand, Alfred Rudolph 1828-1891 . . . . . .DLB-188

Waugh, Alec 1898-1981 . . . . .DLB-191

Waugh, Auberon 1939- DLB-14, 194

Waugh, Evelyn 1903-1966 . . . . .DLB-15, 162, 195

Way and Williams. DLB-49

Wayman, Tom 1945- DLB-53

Weatherly, Tom 1942- DLB-41

Weaver, Gordon 1937- DLB-130

Weaver, Robert 1921- DLB-88

Webb, Beatrice 1858-1943 and
Webb, Sidney 1859-1947 . . . . .DLB-190

Webb, Frank J. ?-? DLB-50

Webb, James Watson 1802-1884. . . . . . . .DLB-43

Webb, Mary 1881-1927. . . . . .DLB-34

Webb, Phyllis 1927- DLB-53

Webb, Walter Prescott 1888-1963. . . . . . . .DLB-17

Webbe, William ?-1591 . . . . .DLB-132

Webber, Charles Wilkins 1819-1856?. . . .DLB-202

Webster, Augusta 1837-1894 . . . . .DLB-35

Webster, Charles L., and Company DLB-49

Webster, John
1579 or 1580-1634?. DLB-58

Webster, Noah 1758-1843 . . . DLB-1, 37, 42, 43, 73

Weckherlin, Georg Rodolf 1584-1653. . . .DLB-164

Wedekind, Frank 1864-1918 . . . . .DLB-118

Weeks, Edward Augustus, Jr.
1898-1989 . . . . .DLB-137

Weeks, Stephen B. 1865-1918 . . . . .DLB-187

Weems, Mason Locke
1759-1825 . . . . DLB-30, 37, 42

Weerth, Georg 1822-1856. . . . . .DLB-129

Weidenfeld and Nicolson DLB-112

Weidman, Jerome 1913-1998 . . . . .DLB-28

Weigl, Bruce 1949- DLB-120

Weinbaum, Stanley Grauman
1902-1935 . . . . .DLB-8

Weintraub, Stanley 1929- DLB-111

Weise, Christian 1642-1708. . . . . .DLB-168

Weisenborn, Gunther 1902-1969 . . . .DLB-69, 124

Weiß, Ernst 1882-1940 . . . . .DLB-81

Weiss, John 1818-1879. . . . . .DLB-1

Weiss, Peter 1916-1982 . . . . .DLB-69, 124

Weiss, Theodore 1916- DLB-5

Weisse, Christian Felix 1726-1804. . . . . . .DLB-97

Weitling, Wilhelm 1808-1871 . . . . .DLB-129

Welch, James 1940- DLB-175

Welch, Lew 1926-1971?. DLB-16

Weldon, Fay 1931- DLB-14, 194

Wellek, René 1903-1995 . . . . .DLB-63

Wells, Carolyn 1862-1942. . . . . .DLB-11

Wells, Charles Jeremiah
circa 1800-1879 . . . . .DLB-32

Wells, Gabriel 1862-1946 . . . . .DLB-140

Wells, H. G. 1866-1946. . . . . DLB-34, 70, 156, 178

Wells, Helena 1758?-1824 . . . . .DLB-200

Wells, Robert 1947- DLB-40

Wells-Barnett, Ida B. 1862-1931 . . . . .DLB-23, 221

Welty, Eudora
1909- DLB-2, 102, 143; Y-87; DS-12

Wendell, Barrett 1855-1921. . . . . .DLB-71

Wentworth, Patricia 1878-1961 . . . . .DLB-77

Werder, Diederich von dem
1584-1657 . . . . .DLB-164

Werfel, Franz 1890-1945 . . . . .DLB-81, 124

The Werner Company DLB-49

Werner, Zacharias 1768-1823 . . . . .DLB-94

Wersba, Barbara 1932- DLB-52

Wescott, Glenway 1901- DLB-4, 9, 102

We See the Editor at Work. Y-97

Wesker, Arnold 1932- DLB-13

Wesley, Charles 1707-1788. . . . . .DLB-95

Wesley, John 1703-1791. . . . . .DLB-104

Wesley, Richard 1945- DLB-38

Wessels, A., and Company DLB-46

Wessobrunner Gebet circa 787-815 . . . . .DLB-148

West, Anthony 1914-1988. . . . . .DLB-15

West, Dorothy 1907-1998 . . . . .DLB-76

West, Jessamyn 1902-1984 . . . . .DLB-6; Y-84

West, Mae 1892-1980 . . . . .DLB-44

West, Nathanael 1903-1940. . . . . . . .DLB-4, 9, 28

West, Paul 1930- DLB-14

West, Rebecca 1892-1983 . . . . .DLB-36; Y-83

West, Richard 1941- DLB-185

Westcott, Edward Noyes 1846-1898. . . . .DLB-202

West and Johnson DLB-49

Western Publishing Company. DLB-46

The Westminster Review 1824-1914. . . . . . . .DLB-110

Weston, Elizabeth Jane
circa 1582-1612 . . . . .DLB-172

Wetherald, Agnes Ethelwyn 1857-1940. . . .DLB-99

Wetherell, Elizabeth (see Warner, Susan Bogert)

Wetzel, Friedrich Gottlob 1779-1819 . . . . .DLB-90

Weyman, Stanley J. 1855-1928 . . . . .DLB-141, 156

Wezel, Johann Karl 1747-1819 . . . . .DLB-94

Whalen, Philip 1923- DLB-16

Whalley, George 1915-1983 . . . . .DLB-88

Wharton, Edith
1862-1937 . . . . . . DLB-4, 9, 12, 78, 189; DS-13

Wharton, William 1920s?- Y-80

Whately, Mary Louisa 1824-1889. . . . . . .DLB-166

Whately, Richard 1787-1863 . . . . .DLB-190

What's Really Wrong With Bestseller Lists . . .Y-84

Wheatley, Dennis Yates 1897-1977 . . . . . . DLB-77

Wheatley, Phillis circa 1754-1784 . . . . . DLB-31, 50

Wheeler, Anna Doyle 1785-1848? . . . DLB-158

Wheeler, Charles Stearns 1816-1843 . . . . . . DLB-1

Wheeler, Monroe 1900-1988 . . . . DLB-4

Wheelock, John Hall 1886-1978 . . . . DLB-45

Wheelwright, John circa 1592-1679 . . . . . . DLB-24

Wheelwright, J. B. 1897-1940 . . . . DLB-45

Whetstone, Colonel Pete (see Noland, C. F. M.)

Whetstone, George 1550-1587 . . . . DLB-136

Whicher, Stephen E. 1915-1961 . . . . DLB-111

Whipple, Edwin Percy 1819-1886 . . . . . DLB-1, 64

Whitaker, Alexander 1585-1617 . . . . DLB-24

Whitaker, Daniel K. 1801-1881 . . . . DLB-73

Whitcher, Frances Miriam
    1812-1852. . . . . DLB-11, 202

White, Andrew 1579-1656 . . . . DLB-24

White, Andrew Dickson 1832-1918 . . . . . . DLB-47

White, E. B. 1899-1985 . . . . DLB-11, 22

White, Edgar B. 1947- DLB-38

White, Ethel Lina 1887-1944 . . . . DLB-77

White, Henry Kirke 1785-1806 . . . . DLB-96

White, Horace 1834-1916. . . . . DLB-23

White, Phyllis Dorothy James (see James, P. D.)

White, Richard Grant 1821-1885 . . . . DLB-64

White, T. H. 1906-1964 . . . . DLB-160

White, Walter 1893-1955 . . . . DLB-51

White, William, and Company DLB-49

White, William Allen 1868-1944 . . . . . DLB-9, 25

White, William Anthony Parker
    (see Boucher, Anthony)

White, William Hale (see Rutherford, Mark)

Whitechurch, Victor L. 1868-1933. . . . . . . DLB-70

Whitehead, Alfred North 1861-1947 . . . . DLB-100

Whitehead, James 1936- Y-81

Whitehead, William 1715-1785. . . . . . DLB-84, 109

Whitfield, James Monroe 1822-1871 . . . . . DLB-50

Whitgift, John circa 1533-1604. . . . . DLB-132

Whiting, John 1917-1963 . . . . DLB-13

Whiting, Samuel 1597-1679 . . . . DLB-24

Whitlock, Brand 1869-1934 . . . . DLB-12

Whitman, Albert, and Company DLB-46

Whitman, Albery Allson 1851-1901 . . . . . . DLB-50

Whitman, Alden 1913-1990 . . . . Y-91

Whitman, Sarah Helen (Power)
    1803-1878. . . . . DLB-1

Whitman, Walt 1819-1892 . . . . DLB-3, 64

Whitman Publishing Company DLB-46

Whitney, Geoffrey
    1548 or 1552?-1601 . . . . DLB-136

Whitney, Isabella
    flourished 1566-1573 . . . . DLB-136

Whitney, John Hay 1904-1982. . . . . DLB-127

Whittemore, Reed 1919-1995. . . . . DLB-5

Whittier, John Greenleaf 1807-1892 . . . . . . DLB-1

Whittlesey House DLB-46

Who Runs American Literature? Y-94

Whose *Ulysses?* The Function of
    Editing Y-97

Wideman, John Edgar 1941- DLB-33, 143

Widener, Harry Elkins 1885-1912 . . . . . DLB-140

Wiebe, Rudy 1934- DLB-60

Wiechert, Ernst 1887-1950 . . . . DLB-56

Wied, Martina 1882-1957. . . . . DLB-85

Wiehe, Evelyn May Clowes (see Mordaunt,
    Elinor)

Wieland, Christoph Martin
    1733-1813. DLB-97

Wienbarg, Ludolf 1802-1872 . . . . DLB-133

Wieners, John 1934- DLB-16

Wier, Ester 1910- DLB-52

Wiesel, Elie 1928- DLB-83; Y-86, Y-87

Wiggin, Kate Douglas 1856-1923. . . . . . . DLB-42

Wigglesworth, Michael 1631-1705 . . . . . . DLB-24

Wilberforce, William 1759-1833. . . . . . . DLB-158

Wilbrandt, Adolf 1837-1911 . . . . DLB-129

Wilbur, Richard 1921- DLB-5, 169

Wild, Peter 1940- DLB-5

Wilde, Lady Jane Francesca Elgee
    1821?-1896. . . . . DLB-199

Wilde, Oscar 1854-1900
    . . . . DLB-10, 19, 34, 57, 141, 156, 190

Wilde, Richard Henry 1789-1847 . . . . . . DLB-3, 59

Wilde, W. A., Company DLB-49

Wilder, Billy 1906- DLB-26

Wilder, Laura Ingalls 1867-1957 . . . . DLB-22

Wilder, Thornton 1897-1975 . . . . DLB-4, 7, 9

Wildgans, Anton 1881-1932. . . . . DLB-118

Wiley, Bell Irvin 1906-1980 . . . . DLB-17

Wiley, John, and Sons DLB-49

Wilhelm, Kate 1928- DLB-8

Wilkes, Charles 1798-1877 . . . . DLB-183

Wilkes, George 1817-1885 . . . . DLB-79

Wilkinson, Anne 1910-1961 . . . . DLB-88

Wilkinson, Eliza Yonge
    1757-circa 1813 . . . . DLB-200

Wilkinson, Sylvia 1940- Y-86

Wilkinson, William Cleaver
    1833-1920 . . . . DLB-71

Willard, Barbara 1909-1994 . . . . DLB-161

Willard, Frances E. 1839-1898 . . . . DLB-221

Willard, L. [publishing house] DLB-49

Willard, Nancy 1936- DLB-5, 52

Willard, Samuel 1640-1707 . . . . DLB-24

William of Auvergne 1190-1249 . . . . DLB-115

William of Conches
    circa 1090-circa 1154 . . . . DLB-115

William of Ockham
    circa 1285-1347 . . . . DLB-115

William of Sherwood
    1200/1205 - 1266/1271 . . . . DLB-115

The William Chavrat American Fiction
    Collection at the Ohio State University
    Libraries. Y-92

William Faulkner Centenary Y-97

Williams, A., and Company DLB-49

Williams, Ben Ames 1889-1953 . . . . DLB-102

Williams, C. K. 1936- DLB-5

Williams, Chancellor 1905- DLB-76

Williams, Charles 1886-1945 . . . . . . DLB-100, 153

Williams, Denis 1923-1998 . . . . DLB-117

Williams, Emlyn 1905- DLB-10, 77

Williams, Garth 1912-1996 . . . . DLB-22

Williams, George Washington
    1849-1891 . . . . DLB-47

Williams, Heathcote 1941- DLB-13

Williams, Helen Maria 1761-1827 . . . . . . DLB-158

Williams, Hugo 1942- DLB-40

Williams, Isaac 1802-1865 . . . . DLB-32

Williams, Joan 1928- DLB-6

Williams, John A. 1925- DLB-2, 33

Williams, John E. 1922-1994 . . . . DLB-6

Williams, Jonathan 1929- DLB-5

Williams, Miller 1930- DLB-105

Williams, Raymond 1921- DLB-14

Williams, Roger circa 1603-1683 . . . . DLB-24

Williams, Rowland 1817-1870 . . . . DLB-184

Williams, Samm-Art 1946- DLB-38

Williams, Sherley Anne 1944- DLB-41

Williams, T. Harry 1909-1979 . . . . DLB-17

Williams, Tennessee
    1911-1983 . . . . DLB-7; Y-83; DS-4

Williams, Terry Tempest 1955- DLB-206

Williams, Ursula Moray 1911- DLB-160

Williams, Valentine 1883-1946 . . . . DLB-77

Williams, William Appleman 1921- DLB-17

Williams, William Carlos
    1883-1963 . . . . DLB-4, 16, 54, 86

Williams, Wirt 1921- DLB-6

Williams Brothers. DLB-49

Williamson, Henry 1895-1977 . . . . DLB-191

Williamson, Jack 1908- DLB-8

Willingham, Calder Baynard, Jr.
    1922-1995 . . . . DLB-2, 44

Williram of Ebersberg
    circa 1020-1085 . . . . DLB-148

Willis, Nathaniel Parker
    1806-1867 . . . . . DLB-3, 59, 73, 74, 183; DS-13

Willkomm, Ernst 1810-1886 . . . . DLB-133

Willumsen, Dorrit 1940- DLB-214

Wilmer, Clive 1945- DLB-40

Wilson, A. N. 1950- DLB-14, 155, 194

Wilson, Angus 1913-1991 . . . . . . DLB-15, 139, 155

Wilson, Arthur 1595-1652 . . . . DLB-58

Wilson, Augusta Jane Evans
    1835-1909 . . . . DLB-42

Wilson, Colin 1931- DLB-14, 194

Wilson, Edmund 1895-1972. . . . . DLB-63

Wilson, Ethel 1888-1980 . . . . DLB-68

Wilson, F. P. 1889-1963 . . . . DLB-201

Wilson, Harriet E. Adams
1828?-1863? DLB-50

Wilson, Harry Leon 1867-1939 . . . . .DLB-9

Wilson, John 1588-1667 . . . . .DLB-24

Wilson, John 1785-1854. . . . . .DLB-110

Wilson, John Dover 1881-1969 . . . . .DLB-201

Wilson, Lanford 1937- DLB-7

Wilson, Margaret 1882-1973 . . . . .DLB-9

Wilson, Michael 1914-1978 . . . . .DLB-44

Wilson, Mona 1872-1954. . . . . .DLB-149

Wilson, Robley 1930- DLB-218

Wilson, Romer 1891-1930. . . . . .DLB-191

Wilson, Thomas 1523 or
1524-1581 . . . . .DLB-132

Wilson, Woodrow 1856-1924 . . . . .DLB-47

Wilson, Effingham [publishing house] DLB-154

Wimsatt, William K., Jr. 1907-1975 . . . . . . .DLB-63

Winchell, Walter 1897-1972. . . . . .DLB-29

Winchester, J. [publishing house]. DLB-49

Winckelmann, Johann Joachim
1717-1768 . . . . .DLB-97

Winckler, Paul 1630-1686 . . . . .DLB-164

Wind, Herbert Warren 1916- DLB-171

Windet, John [publishing house] DLB-170

Windham, Donald 1920- DLB-6

Wing, Donald Goddard 1904-1972 . . . . . .DLB-187

Wing, John M. 1844-1917 . . . . .DLB-187

Wingate, Allan [publishing house] DLB-112

Winnemucca, Sarah 1844-1921 . . . . .DLB-175

Winnifrith, Tom 1938- DLB-155

Winning an Edgar Y-98

Winsloe, Christa 1888-1944 . . . . .DLB-124

Winslow, Anna Green 1759-1780 . . . . . . .DLB-200

Winsor, Justin 1831-1897. . . . . .DLB-47

John C. Winston Company. DLB-49

Winters, Yvor 1900-1968 . . . . .DLB-48

Winterson, Jeanette 1959- DLB-207

Winthrop, John 1588-1649 . . . . .DLB-24, 30

Winthrop, John, Jr. 1606-1676. . . . . .DLB-24

Winthrop, Margaret Tyndal
1591-1647 . . . . .DLB-200

Winthrop, Theodore 1828-1861 . . . . .DLB-202

Wirt, William 1772-1834 . . . . .DLB-37

Wise, John 1652-1725 . . . . .DLB-24

Wise, Thomas James 1859-1937 . . . . .DLB-184

Wiseman, Adele 1928- DLB-88

Wishart and Company DLB-112

Wisner, George 1812-1849 . . . . .DLB-43

Wister, Owen 1860-1938. . . . . .DLB-9, 78, 186

Wister, Sarah 1761-1804 . . . . .DLB-200

Wither, George 1588-1667 . . . . .DLB-121

Witherspoon, John 1723-1794 . . . . .DLB-31

Withrow, William Henry
1839-1908 . . . . .DLB-99

Witkacy (see Witkiewicz, Stanisław Ignacy)

Witkiewicz, Stanisław Ignacy
1885-1939 . . . . .DLB-215

Wittig, Monique 1935- DLB-83

Wodehouse, P. G. 1881-1975 . . . . . . .DLB-34, 162

Wohmann, Gabriele 1932- DLB-75

Woiwode, Larry 1941- DLB-6

Wolcot, John 1738-1819 . . . . .DLB-109

Wolcott, Roger 1679-1767 . . . . .DLB-24

Wolf, Christa 1929- DLB-75

Wolf, Friedrich 1888-1953. . . . . .DLB-124

Wolfe, Gene 1931- DLB-8

Wolfe, John [publishing house] DLB-170

Wolfe, Reyner (Reginald)
[publishing house] DLB-170

Wolfe, Thomas
1900-1938 . . . .DLB-9, 102; Y-85; DS-2, DS-16

Wolfe, Tom 1931- DLB-152, 185

Wolfenstein, Martha 1869-1906 . . . . .DLB-221

Wolff, Helen 1906-1994 . . . . Y-94

Wolff, Tobias 1945- DLB-130

Wolfram von Eschenbach
circa 1170-after 1220 . . . . .DLB-138

Wolfram von Eschenbach's *Parzival*:
Prologue and Book 3. . . . . .DLB-138

Wollstonecraft, Mary
1759-1797. . . . . .DLB-39, 104, 158

Wolker, Jiří 1900-1924 . . . . .DLB-215

Wondratschek, Wolf 1943- DLB-75

Wood, Anthony à 1632-1695 . . . . .DLB-213

Wood, Benjamin 1820-1900 . . . . .DLB-23

Wood, Charles 1932- DLB-13

Wood, Mrs. Henry 1814-1887 . . . . .DLB-18

Wood, Joanna E. 1867-1927 . . . . .DLB-92

Wood, Sally Sayward Barrell Keating
1759-1855 . . . . .DLB-200

Wood, Samuel [publishing house] DLB-49

Wood, William ?-? DLB-24

Woodberry, George Edward
1855-1930 . . . . .DLB-71, 103

Woodbridge, Benjamin 1622-1684 . . . . . .DLB-24

Woodcock, George 1912-1995 . . . . .DLB-88

Woodhull, Victoria C. 1838-1927 . . . . . . .DLB-79

Woodmason, Charles circa 1720-? DLB-31

Woodress, Jr., James Leslie 1916- DLB-111

Woodson, Carter G. 1875-1950. . . . . .DLB-17

Woodward, C. Vann 1908- DLB-17

Woodward, Stanley 1895-1965 . . . . .DLB-171

Wooler, Thomas 1785 or 1786-1853 . . . . .DLB-158

Woolf, David (see Maddow, Ben)

Woolf, Leonard 1880-1969 . . . . . .DLB-100; DS-10

Woolf, Virginia
1882-1941 . . . . .DLB-36, 100, 162; DS-10

Woolf, Virginia, "The New Biography,"
New York Herald Tribune, 30 October 1927
. . . . .DLB-149

Woollcott, Alexander 1887-1943 . . . . .DLB-29

Woolman, John 1720-1772. . . . . .DLB-31

Woolner, Thomas 1825-1892 . . . . .DLB-35

Woolsey, Sarah Chauncy 1835-1905 . . . . .DLB-42

Woolson, Constance Fenimore
1840-1894 . . . . .DLB-12, 74, 189, 221

Worcester, Joseph Emerson 1784-1865 . . . . .DLB-1

Worde, Wynkyn de [publishing house]. . .DLB-170

Wordsworth, Christopher 1807-1885 . . . .DLB-166

Wordsworth, Dorothy 1771-1855 . . . . . . .DLB-107

Wordsworth, Elizabeth 1840-1932 . . . . . . .DLB-98

Wordsworth, William 1770-1850 . . . .DLB-93, 107

Workman, Fanny Bullock 1859-1925 . . . .DLB-189

The Works of the Rev. John Witherspoon
(1800-1801) [excerpts] DLB-31

A World Chronology of Important Science
Fiction Works (1818-1979) DLB-8

World Publishing Company DLB-46

World War II Writers Symposium at the University
of South Carolina, 12–14 April 1995 . . . . Y-95

Worthington, R., and Company DLB-49

Wotton, Sir Henry 1568-1639. . . . . .DLB-121

Wouk, Herman 1915- Y-82

Wreford, James 1915- DLB-88

Wren, Sir Christopher 1632-1723 . . . . . . .DLB-213

Wren, Percival Christopher
1885-1941 . . . . .DLB-153

Wrenn, John Henry 1841-1911. . . . . .DLB-140

Wright, C. D. 1949- DLB-120

Wright, Charles 1935- DLB-165; Y-82

Wright, Charles Stevenson 1932- DLB-33

Wright, Frances 1795-1852 . . . . .DLB-73

Wright, Harold Bell 1872-1944 . . . . .DLB-9

Wright, James 1927-1980. . . . . .DLB-5, 169

Wright, Jay 1935- DLB-41

Wright, Louis B. 1899-1984 . . . . .DLB-17

Wright, Richard 1908-1960 . . .DLB-76, 102; DS-2

Wright, Richard B. 1937- DLB-53

Wright, Sarah Elizabeth 1928- DLB-33

Wright, Willard Huntington ("S. S. Van Dine")
1888-1939 . . . . DS-16

Writers and Politics: 1871-1918,
by Ronald Gray DLB-66

Writers and their Copyright Holders:
the WATCH Project. Y-94

Writers' Forum Y-85

Writing for the Theatre,
by Harold Pinter DLB-13

Wroth, Lady Mary 1587-1653. . . . . .DLB-121

Wroth, Lawrence C. 1884-1970 . . . . .DLB-187

Wurlitzer, Rudolph 1937- DLB-173

Wyatt, Sir Thomas
circa 1503-1542 . . . . .DLB-132

Wycherley, William 1641-1715 . . . . .DLB-80

Wyclif, John
circa 1335-31 December 1384 . . . . . . .DLB-146

Wyeth, N. C. 1882-1945 . . . . .DLB-188; DS-16

Wylie, Elinor 1885-1928 . . . . .DLB-9, 45

Wylie, Philip 1902-1971. . . . . .DLB-9

Wyllie, John Cook 1908-1968 . . . . .DLB-140

Wyman, Lillie Buffum Chace
1847-1929 . . . . DLB-202

Wynne-Tyson, Esmé 1898-1972 . . . . DLB-191

X

Xenophon circa 430 B.C.-circa 356 B.C. . . .DLB-176

Y

Yasuoka Shōtarō 1920- DLB-182

Yates, Dornford 1885-1960 . . . . .DLB-77, 153

Yates, J. Michael 1938- DLB-60

Yates, Richard 1926-1992 . . . . . .DLB-2; Y-81, Y-92

Yavorov, Peyo 1878-1914 . . . . DLB-147

Yearsley, Ann 1753-1806 . . . . DLB-109

Yeats, William Butler
1865-1939 . . . . .DLB-10, 19, 98, 156

Yep, Laurence 1948- DLB-52

Yerby, Frank 1916-1991 . . . . DLB-76

Yezierska, Anzia 1880-1970 . . . . DLB-28, 221

Yolen, Jane 1939- DLB-52

Yonge, Charlotte Mary 1823-1901 . . . DLB-18, 163

The York Cycle circa 1376-circa 1569 . . . DLB-146

A Yorkshire Tragedy DLB-58

Yoseloff, Thomas [publishing house] DLB-46

Young, Al 1939- DLB-33

Young, Arthur 1741-1820 . . . . DLB-158

Young, Dick 1917 or 1918 - 1987 . . . . . . .DLB-171

Young, Edward 1683-1765 . . . . DLB-95

Young, Francis Brett 1884-1954 . . . . DLB-191

Young, Gavin 1928- DLB-204

Young, Stark 1881-1963 . . . . . . DLB-9, 102; DS-16

Young, Waldeman 1880-1938 . . . . DLB-26

Young, William [publishing house] DLB-49

Young Bear, Ray A. 1950- DLB-175

Yourcenar, Marguerite 1903-1987 . . .DLB-72; Y-88

"You've Never Had It So Good," Gusted by
"Winds of Change": British Fiction in the
1950s, 1960s, and After DLB-14

Yovkov, Yordan 1880-1937 . . . . DLB-147

Z

Zachariä, Friedrich Wilhelm 1726-1777 . . . DLB-97

Zagoskin, Mikhail Nikolaevich
1789-1852 . . . . DLB-198

Zajc, Dane 1929- DLB-181

Zamora, Bernice 1938- DLB-82

Zand, Herbert 1923-1970 . . . . DLB-85

Zangwill, Israel 1864-1926 . . . . . .DLB-10, 135, 197

Zanzotto, Andrea 1921- DLB-128

Zapata Olivella, Manuel 1920- DLB-113

Zebra Books DLB-46

Zebrowski, George 1945- DLB-8

Zech, Paul 1881-1946 . . . . DLB-56

Zeimi (Kanze Motokiyo) 1363-1443 . . . . . DLB-203

Zepheria DLB-172

Zeidner, Lisa 1955- DLB-120

Zelazny, Roger 1937-1995 . . . . DLB-8

Zenger, John Peter 1697-1746 . . . . DLB-24, 43

Zesen, Philipp von 1619-1689 . . . . DLB-164

Zhukovsky, Vasilii Andreevich
1783-1852 . . . . DLB-205

Zieber, G. B., and Company DLB-49

Zieroth, Dale 1946- DLB-60

Zigler und Kliphausen, Heinrich Anshelm von
1663-1697 . . . . DLB-168

Zimmer, Paul 1934- DLB-5

Zingref, Julius Wilhelm 1591-1635 . . . . . . DLB-164

Zindel, Paul 1936- DLB-7, 52

Zinnes, Harriet 1919- DLB-193

Zinzendorf, Nikolaus Ludwig von
1700-1760 . . . . DLB-168

Zitkala-Ša 1876-1938 . . . . .DLB-175

Zīverts, Mārtiņš 1903-1990 . . . . DLB-220

Zola, Emile 1840-1902 . . . . DLB-123

Zolla, Elémire 1926- DLB-196

Zolotow, Charlotte 1915- DLB-52

Zschokke, Heinrich 1771-1848 . . . . DLB-94

Zubly, John Joachim 1724-1781 . . . . DLB-31

Zu-Bolton II, Ahmos 1936- DLB-41

Zuckmayer, Carl 1896-1977 . . . . DLB-56, 124

Zukofsky, Louis 1904-1978 . . . . DLB-5, 165

Zupan, Vitomil 1914-1987 . . . . DLB-181

Župančič, Oton 1878-1949 . . . . .DLB-147

zur Mühlen, Hermynia 1883-1951 . . . . DLB-56

Zweig, Arnold 1887-1968 . . . . DLB-66

Zweig, Stefan 1881-1942 . . . . DLB-81, 118

ISBN 0-7876-3130-2

90000

9 780787 631307